Table of Contents

Dedication

This lap-squishing tome is dedicated to my librarian parents, Mary Mac and Robert Franklin, in whose basement I have been writing for many years; to my Grand Mamma, Willie Lee Burton; to my brother, Robbie, and his family; and to Melba Hamlet, a memorable Colorado cook. The lighter parts are courtesy of the pleasure brought me by friends — Andrea, Terry, Frank, Judy, Rose, Bill and Linda — who put up with my whining and punning on the phone; my beagle Darwin, the best flea market find I ever made, and my other clown-psychologists, Nicky Copernicus, DuMonticello, and Emitte.

Acknowledgments

Special thanks go to the publisher of the three previous incarnations of this book, Dan Alexander, whose faith in me never wavered, even when I presented him with a 1200-page book to tackle. Thanks also for the appreciation of my work by Krause Publications, and editors Elizabeth Noll and Don Gulbrandsen who probably didn't fully know that they were taking on an *encyclopaedia kitchenica* when they acquired Books Americana from Dan.

I am lucky to have had the assistance, encouragement, cooperation and patience of many collectors, dealers, auctioneers, librarians and curators. Many of them first agreed to help with the third edition. Since then I've met many more generous and enthusiastic collectors who have undertaken to help me make many corrections, additions, rearrangements, and value assessments in areas of their particular interest, so that this fourth edition might truly live up to its reputation. Several of these people, at my urging, have allowed me to insert "squibs" alerting readers to their specialist subjects. This is an important source for feeding new data to me, and I look forward to serving new information to you all in the next edition of this book — a few years from now.

My heartfelt thanks go to Joel Schiff, Georgiana Sanders, Bunny Upchurch & Kyle Goad, Pat Guthman, David G. Smith, Don & Diana Thornton, all the Holroyds of Oregon, the Moffets, Joe Young, Bill Griffiths, Wayne Smith, Teri & Joe Dziadul, Lillian & Roger Cole, Carol & Jim Bohn, Sheri & John Ficken, Donna & Bob Gaither, Lois & Clark Lewis, Steve Stephens, Oveda Maurer, Ron Barlow, Clifford Boram, Terry & Rufus Ackerman, Meryle Evans, John & Mary Ann Lambert, Anne Serio, Rodris Roth, Ann Golovin, Joe & Jill MacMillan, Vernon Ward, the late Ray Townsend, Kate Urquhart, Evelyn Welch, Tom Wiggins, Peggy Wainscott, Pat Gross, Dolores Thomas, Robert Carr, Karol Atkinson, the late Marion Levy, James Trice, Bob Cahn, Georgia Levett, Litchfield Auction Gallery, Clayton Bailey, James D. Julia, Jeannine Dobbs, A. H. T. Robb-Smith, Gail Lettick, Barbara Bowditch, Betty Landis, the late Phyllis Wetherall, all the people whose names I should have included, and the hundreds of readers who've written to share information.

Photographs include those taken by Paul Persoff of the Keillor Family Collection and other collections; those by David Arky, who did most of the photographs in the second edition; those bought from various sources or lent for free by others; those contributed by readers; and those taken by the author.

Fourth Edition

❧ 300 YEARS OF ❧
Kitchen
Collectibles

Linda Campbell Franklin

Published by

krause
publications

700 E. State Street • Iola, WI 54990-0001
Telephone: 715/445-2214

www.krause.com

BOOKS AMERICANA
INC.

ISBN: 0-89689-112-7

Printed in the United States of America

INTRODUCTION

The objects we collect are the tickets to everyday life of the past. With them, we are able to move along that "shadow line, that faint demarcation between a world that is vanishing and another that is inexorably taking its place," as described by novelist Joseph Conrad.

To keep that "shadow line" from being smeared and erased, we need to protect its integrity. Collectors need to get noisy and agitated about fakes and reproductions. I'm sick to death of greedy importers and sellers who knowingly take advantage of collectors by passing off "aged," "antique-looking," bleached, stained, nicked, rubbed, and distressed wrought iron and wooden items. Sellers who know that a man in the next town is making certain "old-looking" spice chests in his garage, but write on their price tags "possibly early American" or "true folk art," break the law. A seller who knows an old hearth tool was recently made in Asia, but writes "Fine Colonial hearth tool" breaks the law, even if that Asian country could have been described at some time as a "colony." Ad nauseum, to the tune of hundreds of thousands of dollars. This fraud is largely possible because of the absence or failure of legal requirements for permanent marks showing country of origin and date and a disclaimer such as "This is a replica made in 199-." Because the profit margin is so much greater for imported items made by dime-a-day third world workers, this is especially important for imports. The Customs Service, which is a division of the U.S. Treasury Department, certainly has a mandate to protect us from fraud. Write the Office of Cargo Enforcement & Facilitation, Room 3112, 1301 Constitution Avenue, N.W., Washington, DC 20229 and protest. While you're at it, write your Congressperson.

The long-ago things we collect have only our voices to speak up for them, and we should demand that their integrity be preserved and protected against domestic and foreign imitators. And you may want to subscribe to the monthly *Antique & Collectors Reproduction News,* which exposes fakes and repros. (See the bibliography, or call 1-800-227-5531.)

Price Guides – What Good Are They?

Think of a price guide as a topographical field map. You can use it to develop unexplored ares and markets, and to expand frontiers of age, price and form — forward, backward, and off to the sides! Price guides aren't mail order catalogs. As everyone knows, the true market value of any particular object is what a particular buyer is willing to pay at a particular time. The particular seller can ask anything, but a willing buyer is the only thing that'll make it a sale. All the value ranges in this book have been vetted by specialist collectors from different parts of the country. I will never ever do a price guide that has "all new listings." What good would that do the new kitchen collector? He or she would never know about the classic pieces, nor would any collector be able to track fundamental elements over a long period, from edition to edition. Price guide authors get picked on because their books' immediate effect on prices seems to be to raise them. In time, prices always find a natural market level. And, many things are actually rescued because price guides help people to notice overlooked things. One more word on prices: I force myself to set an intuitive "feels-right" price limit I'll pay for an item — before I ask the price or look at the tag. This technique factors in my personal reaction to the item and the state of my finances. I'm often pleasantly surprised, and also, I often revise my limit upwards — after careful consideration.

Using This Book

Just a few notes. The book is divided into seven broad categories with 18 separate chapters having to do with processes and tasks in the kitchen, patents and patent researching. A huge bibliography helps you too. Each chapter's introductory paragraphs have some trend information, plus clubs and newsletters where applicable. Two generalist organizations that you all may want to join are EAIA (Early American Industries Association, where I got my start in this subject), and KOOKS (Kollectors of Old Kitchen Stuff). There's also a newsletter (*Kitchen Antiques & Collectibles News*). All three are in the bibliography at the end of this book. Caveat: In a book of any size, let alone one like this, mistakes are inevitable. I hope that mistakes are few and trivial, and that you won't base all your buying and selling decisions on the information and values given in this book. We cannot take responsibility for either loss or fortune — you must write your own recipe for collecting.

Other Resources for Study

Ephemera & Trade Catalogs — Vital information is found in old manufacturer's or store catalogs and other papers like bills of sale and ads. It's called Ephemera — here today, gone tomorrow! It was meant to be discarded, but lucky collectors have rescued lots of fragile paper documentation, and it can still be bought. • Join (and get publications from) Ephemera Society of America, POB 95, Cazenovia, NY 13055, 1-315-655-1078; Ephemera Society of Canada, 5863 Leslie St., Ste 909, North York, Ontario, CAN M2H1J8; and P.A.C. (Paper & Advertising Collectors), POB 500, Columbia, PA 17552. • Subscribe also to Paper Pile Quarterly, Box 337, San Anselmo, CA 94960. • Three specialty trade catalog dealers are Hillcrest Books, Miles Clark, 961 Deep Draw Rd., Crossville, TN 38555; Harold R. Nestler, 13 Pennington Ave., Walwick, NJ 07463; Kenneth E. Schneringer, 271 Sabrina Ct. Woodstock, GA 30188.

Cookbooks — Four centuries of cookery books reveal forgotten tools & techniques. Find middle-aged cookbooks at thrift & used book stores, library book sales & yard sales. • I have two tried 'n' true recipes for hard-to-find old cookbooks: Mail order from **Bonnie Slotnick Cook Books**, Box G-27, 332 Bleeker St., NYC, NY 10014, (1-212-989-8962), open by chance or appointment. Bonnie's phenomenal memory has recovered books for me after *I've* forgotten the titles! Another dealer/scholar is **Jan Longone, Wine & Food Library**, 1207 W. Madison St., Ann Arbor, MI 48103. • For new & older books, join Cookbook Collectors' Exchange. Sue Erwin, ed., POB 32369, San Jose, CA, 95152-2369, bimonthly news & ads; and Cook Book Collectors Club. Col. Bob Allen, ed., POB 56, St. James, MO 65559, monthly news.

PREPARING

I. CORE, CUT, CHOP, PARE & PIT

The two fundamental processes that underlie the selection of most of the implements and gadgets in this chapter are: (1) removal of inedible or undesirable portions of the food (viz. pits, stones, stems, rinds, and skins in the case of fruit and vegetables; bones, gristle, skin, and offal, in the case of animals, fish or fowl); and (2) division of the edible portions into smaller pieces for various purposes.

Some of the most popular and varied kitchen collectibles fall into this preparation category, including apple parers, cherry pitters, chopping knives and nutmeg graters. The most ancient of cooking tools (as separate from utensils or vessels) would be put here — anything with a cutting edge or a smashing surface. In fact, you will find a surprise three-quarters of the way through: a "kitchen collectible" that is ten million years old!

The **apple parer** is the device with the greatest number of organized collectors. Any one of the members of **International Society for Apple Parer Enthusiasts** knows a great deal more than I do about apple parers, and I urge you to join them, share their camaraderie (they try to have a conference every year), and learn from the newsletter. Send an SASE for information to founder and first president, John Lambert, 117 E. High St., Mt. Vernon, OH 43050; or James Ennenga, 1621 N. 85th St., Omaha, NE 68114.

The fastest growing field of those covered in this chapter is still mechanical **nutmeg graters**. But while there are several hundreds of apple parers, including improved versions, there are probably under two hundred mechanical nutmeg graters, few of which (besides the popular "Edgar") have gone through several variations. In fact, mechanical parers are still being made, but mechanical nutmeg graters enjoyed a very short period of production, mainly in the 1860s and 1870s. Almost everyone today uses tinned ground nutmeg or has one of the "coffin" types with a curved grating surface and the little hinged compartment for a nutmeg. These are still being made, but I know of no mechanical one being made today. At the time of this writing there is still no book on mechanical nutmeg graters, but Don Thornton is planning one for 1998 or 1999. Prices have risen amazingly high, reflecting scarcity of supply and very avid demand. There are probably graters as yet undis-covered — perhaps because they were manufactured in very small quantities.

Implements for grinding, crushing and mashing are among the most basic and ancient. They're a crude form of a knife, in a way: it would take a delicate, fine-edged "micro-knife" to cut seeds and grains for eating whereas a mortar and pestle are macro-mashers. Somehow Lucy or another very ancient ancestor had to reduce cereals (or extremely tough roots or animal parts) into something that could be eaten. So two rocks, or a rock and a hard piece of wood, were the first mortars and pestles. Cooking wasn't even necessary — at least not at first. Eventually it was discovered that food became a bit more durable and portable by mixing the mashed grains with liquid (water, milk and blood being the choices) before cooking, and a giant step forward was taken. Viewed from the end of the twentieth century, surrounded by toaster waffles, hotdog buns, and evocative "hunters' grain" sliced breads, it seems an amazing feat of imagination for *homo sapiens* (perhaps even *homo erectus*) to have thought up the mortar and pestle.

For many collectors, **nutcrackers** are the most appealing subgroup of kitchen collectibles in the hit or mash category. They can be viewed as refined mortars or miniature precision clubs. Fortunately a book on nutcracker patents now exists — see James Rollband's *American Nutcrackers* in my bibliography.

All values have been carefully reviewed by experts in the individual "fancies" of the kitchen field. **Remember that values are different from prices.** Values are harder to track over a vast geographical expanse than are prices. In order for a price to be agreed upon you've got to have a willing seller and a willing buyer who are both in the right place (physically and fiscally) at the same time. Even so, it's possible that the seller places a higher or lower value on a particular item than does the buyer, which means either the buyer buys happily or walks away from the purchase.

Here and throughout the book, the common or preferred name for an item is given first. If there are alternative terms (sometimes because of alternative functions), I have written either "also called a ___" or "or" followed by the term. "Or" does not mean that I am unsure what an item is called. For more information see page 71.

Apple cider or wine press, cast iron heavy-legged round base, vertical screw & horizontal handle, wooden staved body, embossed "M. Amendola & Co.," NYC, NY, last quarter 19th C. **$150-$175**

Apple cider press, cast iron, red, green & black paint, "Americus," pat'd 1872. **$450-$500**

Apple corer, hand held, tin, with T handle, marked "H" on each end of handle, about 6" L, American, late 19th C. **$15-$25**

Apple corer, tin tubular corer, wooden knob handle; piece inside keeps corer from going all the way through the apple — for making baked apples, "The Gem Apple Corer," pat'd by James Fallows, Philadelphia, pat'd Jan. 2, 1877 & sold for many years. **$15-$35**

Apple corer, tin, wood handle, "Boye Needle Co.," Chicago, offices in NYC & San Francisco, pat'd 1916. (Boye also made a nutmeg grater, can opener and still makes crochet hooks.) **$12-$18**

Apple corer & parer combined, heavy sheet steel, nickel or tin plated. "Real-A-Peel," mfd by Tarrson Co., Chicago, IL, (another marked "Grayline Housewares, Inc," Elgin, IL), 5" L, pat'd 1937. **$15-$35**

Apple corer & parer combined, tin & wood, hand held, non-mechanical, 2 parts — the corer fits into handle of a broad blade parer, "Dandy," American, pat'd 1913. **$12-$20**

Apple corer & quarterer, best to use with already sliced apples as it is rather flimsy, very narrow outer ring of tin to hold 4 tin segmenting blades that spoke out from a circular corer, 2 vertical shanks for crosswise turned-wood handle, American, 5-3/4" H x 4-1/2" diameter, last quarter 19th C. **$50-$75**

Apple corer & segmenter, tin, with 2 handles, smallest of this class of tools, used by pressing firmly down on handle, called "The Vantage," marked "S. Joseph Co." (probably the importer), and "Made in Germany," late 19th C. **$25-$45**

Apple parer, also potato & turnip parer, cast iron mounted to wood, rather skeletal with several gears, simple rod crank with dogleg bend, "Sargent & Foster's Patent," Shelburne Falls, MA, pat'd Oct. 4, 1853. **$120-$150**

I-1. Apple scoops or corers. *Carved sheep's metacarpal bones. Decoration style dates back at least to 1200s; these are prob. 18th-19th C. Fancy one with hearts & "M. C." is 5" L. Courtesy Bob Cahn.* **$35-$100**

I-3. Apple cutter or slicer. *Cast iron, steel, wood. Marked only "PATENTED" on quadrant wheel, but probably pat'd by Daniel Davis, 2nd, March 13, 1834. 7" x 13", 19th C. Ex-Keillor Collection.* **$150-$300**

I-2. Apple corers & dividers, or quarterers. *Pieced tin, 19th C. (L) 4-3/4" H, for up to 5" apple. Collection of Meryle Evans. (R) Wood handle. 5-1/2" H x 4" diam. Ex-Keillor Collection.* **$50-$75**

I-4. Apple corer. *"Alcott's," pat'd by A. N. Alcott, Gowanda, NY, 2/22/1859. Converts to parer by slipping prongs (arrow) over coring shaft. Note quartering accessory.* **$200+**

German Imports.— We can never estimate the vast quantities of kitchen & housewares imported from Germany at the end of the 19th C. One wholesaler in NYC, G. M. Thurnauer, made regular buying trips for about 20 years to Germany & Austria, buying wood, aluminum, tin & china wares that were sold to retailers all over the country.

• • • •

First Mechanical Parer.— According to Thomas Wiggins, the Sargent & Foster of 1853 was the first mass-produced iron parer "readily available" to people at mid-century who wanted to buy a mechanical parer with replaceable parts. The **first** widely-known apple parer, which was wood with a small blade and prong of iron or steel, was patented by Moses Coates, Chester County, PA, Feb. 14, 1803, and presented in a drawing in Anthony Willich's *Domestic Encyclopedia*, (1803-04 Philadelphia). Willich's purpose was to present the latest knowledge about raw materials, methods, machinery, and inventions that might be applicable to "rural and domestic economy." People have reported finding obviously one-of-a-kind handmade parers very like Coates', so it is obvious that the rural readers of Willich built their own from the drawing and specifications. Dr. Willich himself wrote about the parer that "on account of its simplicity, and the expedition with which it works, will no doubt come into general use. ... The Editor has tried the experi-

ment with the machine, and found it to pare apples with great rapidity." The **second** parer patented was Bostonian W. Badger's "Machine for paring, quartering, and coring apples," on Feb. 10, 1809. *The Journal of the Franklin Institute*, April 1838, noticed Robert W. Mitchell's "Machine for Paring, Coring, & Dividing Apples," patented April 13. Mitchell lived in Martin's Mill (Springfield), Richland County, OH. The editor wrote "This, we believe, is the **fourth** [patent #686] obtained for the purpose; ... the apple is to be placed on a fork at the end of a shaft, or mandrel, turned by a crank, whilst the paring knife, furnished with a guard, is held in the right hand, and passed from end to end over the apple; this is then pushed towards the shaft which is furnished with knives that cut it into quarters; a centre, tubular knife removing the core." Obtained earlier, and unnumbered, but counted by the same editor as the **sixth** was a "Machine for Peeling Apples and Peaches" patented Feb. 3, 1836, by J. W. Hatcher [Hatch in *Gazette Index*] of Bedford County, VA. The editor said "This ... is the sixth peeling machine that has been patented, and we do not think it any improvement upon the first, which was that of Moses Coates, obtained in 1803. The [Hatcher] has a spindle, with a fork to receive the apple, a second spindle with an endless screw, a cog wheel, pinion, whirl & band, & other appendages for moving the knife; the apparatus for moving the knife the only part claimed." (*Ibid.*).

Bench Parers. — One of the oldest apple parers in the country is a bench type — the bench being a rather elegant plank with 3 legs, and a large 11" D wooden belt-drive wheel built into the bench. It belongs to The Bennington Museum, VT. Their records say it was made in West Woodstock, VT, in 1785 by Daniel Cox and his sons.

• • • •

"Apple Butter — Being at the house of a good old German friend in Pennsylvania, in September last, we noticed upon the table what was called apple butter; and finding it an agreeable article, we inquired into the *modus operandi* in making it. To make the article according to German law, the host should in the autumn invite his neighbors, particularly the young men and maidens, to make up an apple butter party. Being assembled, let three bushels of fair sweet apples be pared, quartered, and the cores removed. Meanwhile let two barrels of new cider be boiled down to one-half. When this is done, commit the prepared apples to the cider, and henceforth let the boiling go on briskly and systematically. But to accomplish the main design, the party must take turns at stirring the contents without cessation, that they do not become attached to the side of the kettle and be burned. Let this stirring go on till the liquid becomes concrete — in other words, till the amalgamated cider and apples become as thick as hasty pudding — then throw in seasoning of pulverized allspice, when it may be considered as finished, and committed to pots for future use. This is apple butter — and it will keep sweet for very many years. And depend upon it, it is a capital article for the table — very much superior to any thing that comes under the name of apple sauce." Reprinted from *Gospel Banner*, in *The Farmers' Cabinet; Devoted to Agriculture, Horticulture and Rural Economy* . Phil.: Vol. III, Aug.1838-July 1839.

Apple parer, all wood except for forged iron fork & handle, pale bird's-eye maple, clamps to table with its own clamp, 19th C. **$175-$250**

Apple parer, bench type, wood with forged iron fork, no attached parer on this type, American; bench is 17" H x 25" L, c.1830s-40s. **$300-$400**

Apple parer, cast iron, "Turntable," mfd by Lockey & Howland, after Keyes himself mfd it, Leominster, MA, pat'd by Horatio Keyes, June 17 & Dec. 16, 1856. Very rare. **$400 and up**

Apple parer, cast iron, Reading Hardware Co., Reading, PA, pat'd May 5, 1868; May 3, 1875; Oct. 19, 1875; Nov. 14, 1875; May 22,1877. **$55-$75**

Apple parer, cast iron, "Triumph," mfd by Boutell, American, pat'd 1899. **$225-$275**

Apple parer, cast iron, 4 gear, C. E. Hudson Parer Co., Leominster, MA, Jan. 24, 1882. **$50-$65**

Apple parer, cast iron, clamps to table, "Keyes' Patent," pat'd by Horatio Keyes, Leominster, MA, marked June 17, 1856 & Dec. 16, 1856. An earlier version, showing only June date, was mounted to wooden board. The patent for it states that "as the prominences and cavities of the apple pass [a part that Keyes called "the lip"] ... the cutter will be moved in a corresponding inverse manner ... and consequently the apple will be pared in a perfect manner." **$50-$65**

Apple parer, cast iron, commercial size, "Rival #296," American, pat'd 1889. **$140-$195**

Apple parer, cast iron, cutout on gear slightly different from other Turntable, screw clamp nut also slightly different, "Goodell Turntable '98, No. 41," Goodell Co., pat'd May 24, 1898. **$50-$60**

Apple parer, cast iron, has big ax head or keystone-like logo on gear wheel, "Keen Kutter," mfd by E. C. Simmons Hardware Co., St. Louis, MO, pat'd May 24, 1898. **$80-$95**

Apple & peach parer, cast iron, heart design gear wheel, 8 gears, rotary knife, Sinclair Scott Co., Baltimore, MD, late 19th C. **$45-$65**

Apple parer, cast iron, heart motif wheel, very like 1858 Monroe Brothers' parer, "The Waverly," mfd by L. A. Sayre, Newark, NJ, frame is 5-1/2" H, gear wheel is 4-3/4" diameter, pat'd Jan. 29, 1884. **$90-$125**

Apple parer, cast iron, heavy multiple gears, screw clamps to table, "The Union," marked pat'd Nov. 11, 1866 (date incorrect because in 1866, Nov. 11 wasn't a Tuesday. See chart of "patent Tuesdays" in Chapter XX.) Parer sold since 1864. This is the same as the "Union Apple Paring Machine" mfd by the Whittemore Brothers, Worcester, MA, advertised in Aug. 1865 as "patent pending." It too has several large gears, the most interesting one with cutouts in curved "rays" from center of gear. An 1868 ad in *American Agriculturist* stated "The knife pares going both ways, thus saving time without increasing the speed of the apple. It throws the parings from the machine. It contains a less number of parts than any other machine in the market." **$90-$125**

Apple parer, cast iron lathe type, angled screw clamp, large gear wheel has teeth on inside that move a small gear, which turns the apple, almost round wooden knob to crank. Very clean & modern looking. "Family Bay State," D. H. Goodell Co., based on Whittemore's patent, Antrim, NH, (Whittemore's patent Aug. 10, 1869) this one late 19th & early 20th C. An Improved

I-5. Apple corers & dividers. (T-L) *Steel, 1-1/2" H x 4-1/2" diam. 14 or 18 segments. For potatoes too. c.1905.* **(L)** *Rollman Mfg. Co., Mt. Joy, PA, for 8ths or 12ths. Tinned cast iron. c.1901.* **(R)** *"Westerman's," with coring attachment. c.1908.* **$15-$30; $200+**

I-6. Apple corer & slicer — or segmenter. *"Climax," D. H. Goodell Mfr. 10" H x 7". Pat'd 2/16/1869, by C. D. Read, Lowell, MA. 1870 ad.* **$200 and up**

I-7. Apple corers of pieced tin.
"T" handles or wood knobs. (1) c.1906. (2) 7", Geuder, Paeschke & Frey, 1925. (3) c.1904. (4) "Spengler Corer," German silver or heavy tin, perforated "saw-edged" blade, 1910. (5) 1905 Breck catalog. (6) (7) 1920 Central Stamping, 6-1/2" L, one has parer. (8) Pat'd by S. Jennie Renner, Petersburg, PA, 3/27/1877. (9) "Gem," Matthai-Ingram, c.1890. **$10-$25**

Bay State was made in late 1890s & early 1900s by Goodell. It has 2 of the angled screw clamps to hold the apple out over space instead of the working parts. The "Family" one was supposed to have been a "remodeled, strengthened and otherwise improved" version of the Whittemore Bay State, suitable for "hotels, restaurants and boarding houses or any place where any considerable quantity of apples are to be prepared." The "Improved Bay State" was "adapted for packers and evaporators of fruit or in families where an extra strong parer is needed. It is practically the same as the Family ..., except in the matter of durability. The machine is larger and stronger in every way. It has a steel screw and is fastened to the table at both ends, making it very firm. ... This machine has an automatic push off for removing the cores." (Joseph Breck & Sons 1902 catalog copy.) The gear wheel is also proportionally much larger to the small gear, and the crank is more curved, and the handle is longer. Value range for "Family" version: **$55-$65**

Apple parer, cast iron, mechanical type mounted to board, gear wheel cast with heart design used by the Monroes, in fact almost duplicates the Monroe Brothers' apple parer only it's slightly larger, marked "Gold Medal," American, dates on parer from 1850s, but not actually made until late 1870s. **$85-$100**

"The pies made of the **Tomatus** are excellent. As this is a new desert [sic], those who wish to make them will slice the fruit, and pursue the same process as with a common pie made of apples." *Lancaster Journal*, PA, Sept. 6, 1822.

Apple parer, cast iron, mounted to wood, skeletal simple frame, crank mounted at right angles; one set of gears turns skinny, surgical tool-looking parer, another gear directly turns the apple stuck on the prongs, simple bent rod crank, no knob, pat'd by J. D. Seagrave, mfd by Larned & Seagrave, Worcester, MA (?), base is 10" L x 4" W (at its longest, parer is about 8" L), pat'd June 17, 1856. Seagrave received another patent for a "Machine for paring apples" on April 18, 1854. **$100-$150**

Apple parer, cast iron, openwork wheel has heart motif, apparently a real favorite of the Monroe Brothers, (James & Edwin), Fitchburg, MA. Frame is 5-3/4" H, wheel is 3-3/4" diameter, frame pat'd May 6, 1856, Sept 9, 1858, Aug. 21, 1866; wheel: Sept. 9, 1858. **$90-$125**

Apple parer, cast iron, quarter circle gear rack, pares, cores & segments, "The Thompson," mfd by New England Butt Co., pat'd Aug. 14, 1877, by G. Thompson. **$300-$500**

Apple parer, cast iron, red wooden plank base is original, paper label on plank, "Automatic Apple Parer," mfd by C. A. Foster, Shelburne Falls, MA, says pat'd 1853. **$65-$90**

Apple parer, cast iron, "S" curve heavy wire or thin rod crank with wooden handle, lathe type parer, screw-clamps to table, bar below threaded shaft is straight — almost resembles a plumber's wrench, "Little Star," mfd by C. E. Hudson Co., Leominster, MA, pat'd June 9, 1885. A slightly later model of "Little Star" — the #125 — has a completely differently shaped bar beneath screw that curves & dips down near apple's end. About this "Little Star" was written: "The only parer in which the paring knife always faces the fruit when brought against it." (Joseph Breck & Sons catalog, 1902.) **$35-$50**

Apple parer, cast iron, screw clamps to table, "White Mountain Turntable '98," mfd by Goodell Co., Antrim, NH, pat'd May 24, 1898. Another Goodell parer from 1898 was the "Winesap." **$45-$65**

Apple parer, cast iron, screw clamps to table, "Reading '78," mfd by Reading Hardware Co., PA, 11" x 6" W, pat'd 1878. **$45-$60**

Apple parer, cast iron, screw clamps, spiral eccentric cam gear underneath, 2 cutters (this is the second model, according to an expert), S. N. Maxam, Shelburne Falls, MA, pat'd April 10, 1855. Bob Cahn, The Primitive Man, showed this to me at Renninger's Extravaganza, June 1989. It was earmarked for an advanced collector. I didn't ask the price, nor would he have told me, because it was sold. I'm guessing price range from the rarity. If I'm way off, I know I'll hear from you. If I'm low, it'll be "Where can I get one for that?" **$400-$600+**

Apple parer, cast iron, screw clamps to table, unusual starfish-like spokes to gear wheel, "Hudson's Improved," mfd by F. W. Hudson Parer Co., Leominster, MA, 7" to bottom of clamp frame, pat'd Dec. 2, 1862. Yet another "Improved" was granted a patent on March 5, 1872, to F. W. Hudson. **$115-$140**

Apple parer, cast iron, screw clamps to table, very large toothed gear with six 3-lobe heart cutouts, 2 small gears, claimed to pare the whole apple with one & a half turns of the crank, at which point you took one apple off & put another on, then turned again one & a half times, pat'd by S. S. Hersey (his name should be cast on frame below date), Farmington, ME, pat'd June 18, 1861. (Another patent, Aug. 30, 1864.) This was sold by Dover Stamping Co., Boston, MA, in their 1869 catalog. **$125-$165**

Apple parer, cast iron, turntable, screw clamps, "The Centennial," Reading Hardware Co., pat'd by W. A. C. Oakes, Reading, PA, pat'd Dec. 10, 1872, July 22, 1873. **$100-$125**

Apple parer, cast iron, turntable type, nice round knob to crank, gear wheel very open casting with 4 contiguous circles, screw clamps to table, "The Domestic," Landers, Frary & Clark, pat'd by A. Turnbull & R. L. Webb, New Britain, CT, pat'd June 10, 1873. **$100-$125**

Apple parer, cast iron, vertical turntable, screw clamps, round wood crank knob, "Transit," Hunt Mfg. Co., Antrim, NH, 19th C. **$125-150**

Apple parer, cast iron, very high legs, Tippecanoe Apple Paring Machine Co., NYC, NY, c.1870s. **$145-$165**

Apple parer, cast iron, with 4 spoke gear wheel, one of which is elongated past rim to form handle, screw clamps to table — fancy thumbscrew, intriguing spring steel wire that curls around & has knife on end, "Non Pareil," mfd by J. L. Haven & Co., Cincinnati, OH, pat'd May 6, 1856. (Puzzle: In Loris Russell's *Handy Things To Have About the House*, he said that this parer was patented by J. D. Browne, of Cincinnati, OH, on Sept. 9, 1856, and mfd by Scott Mfg. Co. of Baltimore.) **$250-$300**

I-8. Apple parers from the Marion Levy Collection. *The late great Marion Levy let me reprint his lengthy 1979 article, "There's Fascination in Apple Parers" (The Antique Trader), in the 2nd edition. With so little room here, I can only hint at why all apple parer collectors pay him tribute. These 7 pictures (and more) illustrated his historical & mechanical overview of home-made and manufactured types. "The first thing I did," he wrote, "was classify the parers into homemade or manufactured. If I had been interested in variety rather than evolution I most certainly would have concentrated on the former, as each one was distinctive, showing the ingenuity and craftsmanship of its maker. The designs were often taken from a farmer's magazine article, or copied, with embellishment, from one a neighbor had built. But for evolution one has to examine the manufactured product." Most homemade were simple lathe types with a horizontal shaft, and frequently no gear or pulley. Levy wrote, "In the 1850s, ideas of apple parers began to proliferate and they were developed along several rather definitive avenues of approach: <u>turntable</u>, <u>quick return</u>, <u>geared segment</u>, and <u>lathe</u> classes (each with many versions & sub-divisions)." **Turntables**: knife arm travels 360° per cycle. **Quick return**: knife pares 180°, lifts off & returns to starting point. **Geared segment**: Generally a stationary curved gear rack & a geared fork that is moved in semi-circle by a handle (supplanting a crank). **Lathe**: spiral-threaded horizontal shaft with crank at one end, fork on other. In some models the apple stays stationary & parer/slicer move toward apple; vice versa for others. Levy said, "Because of their simplicity & low cost, they [lathe types] ultimately outsold all" other types of parers. (A) First pat'd parer, simple lathe with cranked axle with the fork on one end, and a paring blade attached to a "sweep." Moses Coates, Downings Field, PA, 2/14/1803. (B) Homemade iron & wood parer of the Coates type. c.1810. (C) Gears or pulleys speeded up rotation. This pulley type, nearly all wood, cored & quartered. Early 1820s, type seen in Indiana & Ohio. Pat'd 7/24/1847, by Jesse Bullock, Jr., and Sewall Benson, of NYC. (This one $500+.) (D) Sargent & Foster, pat'd 10/4/1853, by E. L. Pratt, Worcester, MA. Prob. first "practical parer with blade mechanically guided over the apple." Apple turned once per crank cycle. Notable is the spiral on the shaft, which meshes with a large gear, hence another gear which is partially toothed. (E) Fork is geared for faster action per cycle; blade arm swivels. Pat'd 1856 by J. D. Seagraves; mfd. Larned & Seagraves, Worcester, MA. (F) First of a Lockey & Howland turntable series, pat'd 6/17 & 12/16/1856 by J. Keyes, Leominster, MA. (G) Quick return type of turntable, with the gears covered to protect from apple juice, Harbster Bros. Co. Foundry, Reading Hardware or Penn Hardware, pat'd 1868. SEE Fig. I-15 for a geared segment type. All photos this page by Marion Levy.*

I-9. SOME RARE APPLE PARERS:
Historical Notes by John Lambert.

Perhaps no other kitchen collectible has such a wide and fascinating application of mechanical principles as does the apple parer. With the advent of cast iron gears c.1850, inventors waged a furious battle to perfect the paring machine. By 1890, after well over 100 patents, home-use parers faded in popularity; most new designs were for larger commercial models. What had occupied talented inventors for over 40 years died a quiet death. The parers — arranged by age to show evolution — on these three pages are rare; most are patented. **(A)** *Others of this gallows-like parer exist, suggesting commercial production. The 12" H post is threaded into base; cross-piece holding blade arm lifts off easily for cleaning. "J. S." stamped on base front. c.1830. Pieces at left are the screw clamp.* **(B)** *A steel spiral track activates a sliding bar under 13-1/2" wood wheel. As it turns, bar slides 2" and pulls blade across apple. At end of 1 turn, crank handle contacts lever that transfers movement through 3 different rods to push off apple. Blade snaps back as roller falls off end of track. Very early (1840s) try for full automatism.* **(C)** *Early cast iron parer — blade still hand-held, 9" H, gear teeth are round pegs. "J. L. Havens Cin. Oh." c.1850.* **(D)** *"E.L. Pratt Patent" stamped in base. First mass-produced metal parer, Sargent & Foster. Commoner model has 4 round openings in gear instead of 5 spokes. 10" x 4-1/2" base. Pat'd 10/4/1853.* **(E)** *"Yankee Apple Paring & Slicing Machine," D. F. Randall, Chicopee, MA. Pat'd 12/1855. Some (without decoratively stenciled box) marked "M.S. Ault New Ha-*

ven, Conn." Pared with hand-guided knife. When a latch is flipped, apple pivots 90° for slicing by whirling blades, as user turned apple with crank on small gear. Slivers drop through box into pail. **(F)** *"Maxam's Patent Automatic Scroll Wheel Apple Parer. Maxam & Smith Shelburne Falls, Mass. Apr. 10, 1855." Blade is advanced across apple as follower runs on inclined spiral ridge. Blade snaps back after 3 full cranks. Intact paper label with directions. Base 4-1/2" x 9".* **(G-1 & 2)** *Pat'd by Charles P. Carter, Ware, MA, 8/26/1856. Some have paper labels. Circular corer/ slicer design eliminates need for threading on shaft to advance apple forward. Use of flat spring for tension & curved blade unique. Carter held other parer patents.* **$250 and up**

I-10. MORE RARE APPLE PARERS:
Historical Notes by John Lambert.

(H) *"Nonpareil Parer J. L. Havens & Co. Cin., Oh. Pat'd by J. D. Browne, May 6, 1856." First all-metal clamp-on parer. Paring head on end of large coiled spring. 4 crank turns, then blade snaps back to starting position. Only 8-1/4" H, this small parer with clocklike movement pares flawlessly. Rare & choice.* (H) **$500 and up.** (I) *"Whittemore, Harrington & Co's Patent. Pat. Nov. 11, 1856 and Jan. 13, 1857." Worcester, MA. First with threaded shaft to advance apple. Coring ring atop blade missing here.* (J) *Marked "S.N. Maxam Shelburne Falls, Mass. Pat. Apr. 1855," but really pat'd 1/27/1857, by Clarissa Hubbard for her husband, who was killed by fall from his horse before he could submit design. 11-1/2" H parer hinged at base. Leaning right, it's cranked to right to pare. Leaning left, crank is reversed while hinged slicing knife is hand-guided toward user to slice thin rings for drying, leaving core on fork. Brittle iron, often found with broken pieces.* (J) **$400+.** (K) *"J. J. Parker Patent Apr. 7, 1857." 5-1/2" gear with 4 horseshoes. Unique in that it pares apple with 1 turn of crank which hits frame*

& must be cranked in reverse to start over. Parker from Marietta, OH. (K) **$400-$500.** (L) *Pat'd 6/3/1862, by Jonathan White, Antrim, NH. 9" W. Move handle across ornate crescent arc to pare apple in 1 second. Forerunner of the "Lightning," also a half-moon type but smaller.* (M) *"Selick's Pat. Aug. 21, 1866." Cast iron frame, poss. early commercial model. Other Selick's are wood. After paring with hand-guided blade, user shoves lever handle forward to core & segment. 8-3/4" H x 15".* (N) *8-3/4" L. Not uncommon parer with rare breaker attachment. During paring, spiral slices kept from rotating, causing them to break off in 1/4" thick semicircles. "D. H. Whittemore." Pat'd 8/10/1869; ext'd 1/13/ & 2/17/1871.* (O) *"Turntable," mfd by Lockey & Howland, Leominster, MA. Pat'd by Horatio Keyes 6/17 & 12/16/1856 & 11/22/1870. 6-1/2" H. Unique push-off: has split frame, so after apple pared, 1/2 frame tilts back (as shown here) to bump apple against other half, loosening it. Before crank reaches 12 o'clock position, small gear moves bak in line to avoid crank. Rarest version, with turntable slanted 45° to keep juice & paring off gears.* (O) **$400 and up.** *Those not specifically priced:* **$250 and up**

I-11. EVEN MORE RARE APPLE PARERS:
Historical Notes by John Lambert.

(P-1 & P-2) *Top: "Missouri Apple Parer & Cutter. Mfd by G. Bergner. Washington, Mo. Pat. Jan. 9, 1872." 18" L in position shown. After paring, the long shaft was pushed forward with palm of user's hand to core & segment apple. George Bergner was a gunmaker & as far as we know, his parer was the only model made west of the Mississippi. Truly unusual, and prized by collectors. Bottom: The shorter 12" L version is marked "Missouri Peach and Apple Parer. Mfd by G. Bergner. Wachington, Mo. Pat. Jan. 9, 1872." On most of these "Washington" is clearly misspelled with a "c." It had the added feature that pushes fruit from forks, but doesn't have a corer/segmenter.* **(Q)** *What collectors call "the Ultimate Union" parer. Marked "Pat. Nov. 11, 1866 Pat. Apr. 6, '80," but it's really a Whittemore, pat'd 11/20/1866. Highly refined device pares apple on forward movement of blade; then on reverse movement, 2nd blade (far right) slices, cores, & breaks ap-*

ple into pieces for pies or drying. Q: **$300 and up. (R)** *Marked "R. & Mc.C Speed," & known to collectors as "Speedboy." 10-3/4" H. Poss. Canadian, it closely resembles common Reading '78 model (see I-14). Real rarity is gear lid, cast with figural resembling Gothic man with crossed arms.* **(S-1).** *"Oriole," pat'd by Robt. P. Scott, Cadiz, OH, 5/16/1871. "Scott Mfg. Co. Balt. Pat. Pnd." is mark. 12" L. Instead of rack that leans over, spiral lip has permanent gap allowing crank to be pulled back when alligned with teeth. 2-pronged fork splits old core as new apple forced on.* **(S-2).** *Quite rare "Oriole" pat'd 8/14/1883. Gate has been added to open & close gap in lip. 3-prong fork.* **(T)** *Some models marked "Jersey," prob. because they were sold by L. A. Sayre, Newark, NJ. 12" L. Pat'd 6/2/1885. Spiral lip around main gear 'worms' through teeth in rack to advance apple. Rack falls to side, so crank can be pulled back to start position. Longer-lasting than similar lathe types with threaded shafts. Others this page:* **$250 and up.**

Photos I-9, I-10, I-11 are courtesy of John Lambert.

Apple parer, cast iron, concave gear wheel with very abstract casting pattern, screw clamps to table, activated by small gear, has push-off, "Rocking Table," C. E. Hudson Parer Co., Leominster, MA, c.7-1/2" H x 8" W, pat'd Jan. 24, 1882. **$40-$50**

Apple parer, cast iron with wooden handle, fixed arc, semicircular gear rack, "The New Lightning," mfd by D. H. Goodell Co., Antrim, 7" D of half-circle gear, pat'd Oct. 6, 1863 & Aug. 23, 1864 by E. L. Pratt of Boston. Great looking but not all that uncommon once you start focusing on the gear. An *American Agriculturalist* ad from August 1875 states: "This machine drops parings clear of machinery, does better work than any other machine, does double the amount ..., loosens the apple on the fork by the neatest arrangement ever yet invented." **$75-$100**

Apple parer, iron, lathe type, the same "machine for paring apples" on which he received a patent a little over a month earlier, pat'd by David H. Whittemore, pat'd Feb. 17, 1857, extended Feb. 16, 1871. **$75-$100**

Whittemore's Patent. — Excerpts from the "Decisions of the Commissioner of Patents" in 1871, shed some interesting light on Whittemore's application to extend his Feb. 17, 1857 apple parer patent. The examiners-in-chief reported that "No question is made of the novelty and utility of the invention." But, they add, although the application papers were incompetently and carelessly filled out, by his attorney, his application was granted. Part of his affidavit charged $1,000 as his "share of loss of Whittemore, H. & Co." The examiners say that "... all we can learn of this company is that the applicant put his patents into it as his share of the stock, and the company failed after having expended $15,000. His patents were sold with the rest of their assets, and were bought back by him, and he charges the purchase money. It does not appear that he ever disbursed a dollar of his own money on account of the company in any other way. . . . The sworn statement narrates several transactions, however, from which it may be fairly and safely inferred that the invention was really worth a large sum, perhaps $50,000 or more. On one of those transactions the applicant endeavors, in fact, to form some estimate for the purpose. The right of the patent before us, and a previous patent on the same machine, were once sold for the State of New York for $1,500 per year. Both patents had then over eleven years to run, and at that rate were worth $16,500. The applicant estimates that the use of the patent for New York was worth one-tenth as much as that for all the other States, and that the whole was therefore worth at least $150,000, and this patent worth half that sum. The former patent has been already extended, and on that occasion the applicant placed the same comparative estimate on the two patents. His estimate may therefore be considered a fair one on that point.")See Chapters XIX - XXI for more on patents.)

I-12. Apple parers. (L) *Handmade, wood, iron crank, 2-prong fork. Clamps like bench-vise to table; pulley fitted with leather or cording belt. 18" H x 3-1/2" x 10", early 19th C. Ex-Keillor Collection.* Top **(R)** *Handmade, light-colored wood, perhaps maple, possibly made by experienced cabinet-maker, 2-prong forged iron fork. 6" H x 9-1/4" L. Meryle Evans Collection.* **(B)** *Straddle type, meant to be sat upon. PA German, wood painted pumpkin & dark green, cast iron gears. Needs hand-held blade. 29-1/2" L x 8" W, mid 19th C.* **$175+**

I-13. Apple parer. *Seems homemade, but many examples are known, with some variations in the knife arm. Three sizes, with 6" (like this one), 7" or 8" large gear wheel, red painted wood base — some have 'breadboard' ends. Maine, mid 19th C.* **$175-$225**

I-14. Apple parer. *"Turntable '78," Reading Hardware Co., Reading, PA, pat'd 1878. Marion Levy said, "The gears are protected by an artistically-decorated bronzed cover. Mechanism canted at angle to improve visibility and insure that parings fall into a bucket. Besides a "push-off" and "blossom cutter," it features an anti-reverse pawl to keep it from being cranked backwards."* **$50-$60**

I-15. Apple parer. *Cast iron, geared or ribbed quadrant with lever action. 23-3/4" L. Pat'd 11/2/1880 by George R. Thompson, Quincy, IL, as improvement on his 8/14/1877 patent. Pares, cores, divides & discharges core in a "single sweep of lever." Mfd. by New England Butt Co., Providence, RI, known mostly for making butt hinges. Rare & desirable.* **$300-$500**

I-16. Apple parer. *"Machine á peler les fruits," by French inventor Faucherre. He also invented an almond-grating machine. Screw clamps to table. Illustration from Urbain Dubois' La Patisserie d'Aujourd'hui, c.1860s. Dubois said of the picture that it was drawn too large; "in fact, it is a tiny apparatus, occupying little space."* **$125+**

Other parers granted in 1857, which may or may not represent actual production parers, are: • Machine for paring apples, J. O. M. Ingersoll, Ithaca, NY, Jan. 20, 1857; • Apple paring & slicing machine, G. H. Hubbard, Shelburne Falls, MA, Jan. 27, 1857; • Machine for paring apples, D. H. Whittemore, Worcester, MA, Feb. 17, 1857; • Machine for paring apples, B. F. Joslyn, Worcester, MA, Mar. 17, 1857; • Machine for paring, coring & quartering apples, C. F. Bosworth, Petersham, MA, June 9, 1857; • Machine for paring apples, J. J. Parker, Marietta, OH, Apr. 7, 1857; • Apple paring & slicing machine, R. W. Thickins, Brasher Iron Works, NY, July 28, 1857.

Apple parer, mostly wood, painted red, oblong wood base meant to be clamped (with a separate clamp) to a table edge, simple cast iron wheel, steel prong fork, steel cutting blade on parer. Looks homemade, but mass-produced in Maine, 7" H x 13" L x 6-3/4" W, mid 19th C, maybe a bit earlier. I've been told they came with 3 sizes of wheels: 6" D, 7" D and 8" D. This one has 6" D wheel. Perhaps company who made them had a pile of assorted wheels they'd needed before to make something else, so they just fit whatever one came to hand. **$175-$225**

Apple parer, strap-to-leg type, hand carved wood, forged iron fork, remnants of leather strap, American, 1820s-1840s. **$85-$120**

> Oh! those were joyous times,
> The times of which we've read,
> Of good old fashioned pandowdy,
> Of rye-and-Indian bread.
> *Knickerbocker* magazine June 1847

Apple parer, straddle type (put it on a bench, then sit on its long board base while operating it), mostly wood, painted black, white & old orangey red in geometric design, 2 thick chunky iron gears, wood crank, American, prob. PA-European heritage, 29" L, early to mid 19th C. I bought this treasure at the Keillor Family Collection auction in the mid-1970s. Much, but by no means all, of that fabulous collection formed the nucleus of my first book. **$200-$275**

Regional Price Variations. — Prices of Bonanzas in the Midwest have been reported over $200. I'm in a quandary about reporting prices; I can't do a regional price guide, but some pieces, particularly patented iron gadgets, go much higher in certain areas than in others. I suspect the upward $$ trend will spread throughout the country. Overinflated prices will tend, however, to crash the whole kitchen antiques market.

Apple parer & corer, cast iron, looks like an oil drilling rig, for bakeries, hotels & dried apple industry. Can be made to pare only, without coring. "Bonanza," mfd by Goodell Co., Antrim, NH, 15" H x 16" L, pat'd March 13, 1888, but introduced June 1890. A Bonanza owned by my father and one I saw in ad have old weld-repairs to the top "beam" of the frame — perhaps a weak spot, or metal fatigue? Is everyone finding the "Bonanza" in repaired condition? **$125-$175**

Apple parer, corer & slicer, cast iron frame, screw clamps to table, lathe action, rather like the "Little Star" except that instead of having a separate short foot above the screw clamp, this one uses a cross bar of main frame, "Daisy," mfd by Hudson Parer Co., Leominster, MA, prob. based on July 11, 1882 patent for a lathe-type parer. This was made & sold well into the 20th C. Advertisements I have for the Daisy, from various 1931 *American Cookery* magazines, state: "Cores and Slices at the same time. Three cuts and it's ready for pies, apple sauce or canning." The 3 cuts are a separate step done with a paring knife. Other ad says "... will pare, core and slice an apple in one operation — quickly." **$25-$35**

Apple parer, corer & slicer, extremely simple cast & malleable iron lathe type, screw clamps to table, single gear without teeth follows horizontal toothed ratchet along bottom of frame. "Oriole," Scott Mfg. Co., Baltimore, MD, c.1883. **$250 and up**

Apple parer, corer & slicer, skeletal cast iron, meant to be hooked up to power source, but could be cranked by hand, 3 spindles with prongs, 4 stanchions to be bolted to surface, between them & beyond is elaborate system of gears & snapping flipping levers & push offs. "Every part of the 'Eureka' is made with an eye to simplicity, durability and strength. All its parts are adjustable, and in case of breakage can be easily and cheaply duplicated. It has a record of 80 bushels a day by hand, and 100 bushels by power. All the operator has to do is to put the apples on the fork and the machine does the rest." (Joseph Breck & Sons catalog, 1902.) You could load 3 apples at a time, but was there ever one made that would pare 3 at a time? "88 Eureka," Goodell Co., Antrim, NH, 18-1/2" H, pat'd Aug. 4, 1874, April 27 & Nov. 6, 1886. I don't know how this differs from the "86 Eureka," touted as an improvement on the "85 Eureka." I don't know why it's the "88," if the last patent was 1886. **$200-$300**

Apple parer, corer, & slicer, skeletal cast iron & steel commercial model, to be bolted to tabletop, 4 high oil rig stanchions or legs at one end, large toothed gear & 5 other small gears (within the legs) turned by crank, horizontal intricate spindle works unsupported at other end, "Dandy," mfd by Goodell Co., Antrim, NH, 18-1/4" x 19-1/2" x 9-5/8", pat'd Nov. 16, 1886, Mar. 13 & May 8, 1888. It seems almost identical to the "Eureka," mfd by Goodell Co., Antrim, NH, although that was sold prior to the patent on the Dandy. **$175-$250**

I-17. Apple parer, corer, quarterer or slicer. *"Tippecanoe," mfd. by Tippecanoe Apple Paring Machine Co., NYC. Operator stood to use it; apple held upright on 3-prong fork. Looks as if it combines treadle & cranked action. Ad from* Hearth & Home, *10/28/1871.* **$145-$165**

I-18. Apple parers. (A) *"Turntable '98" parer, Goodell & Co., Antrim, NH. Shown with throw-off or push-off attachment.* **(B)** *"Lightning" apple parer, very similar to the Lightning peach parer. A Goodell parer, this one embossed "patented" on one spoke. Others have dates of Oct. 6, 1863 & Aug. 23, 1864.* **(C)** *C. E. Hudson, Leominster, MA. Advertised as a "throw-off" parer.* **(D)** *"Rocking Table" parer, C. E. Hudson, pat'd 1/24/1882 & 2/9/1892.* **(E)** *Family size "Bay State," mfd. by Goodell Co., based on Whittemore patent of 1869. Ad from 1906.* **(F)** *"White Mountain," made for 90+ years by Goodell.* **(G)** *"Daisy," Hudson Parer Co., 1931 ad.* **(H)** *"Little Star" parer, slicer, corer, C. E. Hudson, redesign of 6/7/1885 patent.* *(A)* **$45-$65***; (B)* **$75-$100***; (C)* **$50-$60***; (D)* **$40-$50***; (E)* **$55-$65***; (F)* **$35-$50***; (G)* **$25-$35***; (H)* **$35-$50**

I-19. Apple parer patents. (A) *Pat'd 8/26/1856, by Marvin Smith, New Haven, CT. Oscillating fork. Probably never made, and might not have worked — although it's the same principle as the "Yankee," shown in group I-9 of rarities.* **(B)** *Pat'd 7/24/1847, by Jesse Bullock, Jr., & Sewall Benson, NYC. (See I-8-C, on Marion Levy's page.)* **(C)** *Parer, corer & quarterer, pat'd 6/9/1857, by C. F. Bosworth, Petersham, MA. Probably never made.* **(D)** *Parer & slicer, pat'd 1/27/1857 (but says "1855" on it), by G. H. Hubbard, Shelburne Falls, MA.* (B) **$500 and up***; (D)* **$400 and up**.

Apple parer, corer & spiral slicer, cast iron, nice wooden knobby handle on crank, lathe type, originally D. H. Whittemore patent, the "White Mountain," mfd by Goodell Co., Antrim, 6-1/2" H x 11" L, pat'd April 6, 1880, May 3, 1881. This parer, green enameled cast iron with steel shaft & wood handle, continues to be made. It is sold by Cumberland General Store, Crossville, TN. A letter printed in a 1984 Cumberland catalog, from a 93-year-old woman, said that her father, Henry H. Hebbard, "patented this type parer in 1868." Anyone know about it? **$45-$55**

Apple scoop or corer, carved sheep bone, prob. English; poss. American examples around somewhere, 5" to 6-1/2" L, 19th C. **$28-$45**

Apple scoops or corers, carved sheep bone, with knuckle as handle grip, mostly plain but for one carved with hearts & initials "M. C.," English or American, about 5" L, early 19th C. **$28-$45**

Apple segmenter, tin with wooden handles, hand held, quarters & cores apple with one push, American, c.1880s. **$22-$30**

Apple segmenter & corer, cast iron frame, screw clamps, plunger presses apple down on sharp tin wheel-like plate with 8 "spokes" radiating from a small round hole, to make 8 segments and core in one step. The frame of this "Climax" segmenter looks almost identical to a Goodell gadget for making Saratoga potato chips, patented just a few months later, but no maker's mark — probably the one pat'd by C. D. Read, Lowell, MA, 10" H x 7" W, pat'd Feb. 16, 1869. **$200-$250**

Apple segmenter & corer, cast iron round frame has 2 rectangular handles, Mt. Joy, PA, 5-1/2" diameter exclusive of frame, c.1880. **$22-$30**

Apple slicer, 9 steel blades, black painted cast iron frame, apple pushed across the blades, looks like a strange xylophone & probably could be played, for those of you with a kitchenware orchestra, "Sun," C. M. Heffron, Rochester, NY, pat'd June 10, 1890. **$150-$175**

Apple slicer, wood & iron, 6 slicing blades. Apple is fitted onto prong mounted to a sliding piece of wood, & is pushed through the gauntlet of slicing blades. "Primitive" style, but mass-produced. American, 42" L, 19th C. **$175-$225**

Asparagus buncher & cutter, wood, steel, "Ward's Keen Edge," English, late 1800s. See asparagus bunchers in Chapter V (Measuring). **$100-$125**

Baby food grinder, fine puréer, cast iron clamp-on frame, once painted turquoise, tin grinding drum, American or European, late 19th or early 20th C. **$35-$55**

Bean cutter, cast iron, screw clamps to table, for making French style green beans, feed one bean at a time into a sort of diagonal chute & turn crank, has 3 steel blades, removable so you can sharpen, turned wood handle, cast design of hand at bottom, "Harras No. 37," "Germany 374," 10-1/2" H, early 20th C. **$55-$65**

Bean slicer, 2 beans at a time, cast iron painted pale avocado green, "Rose," Belgian, 8-5/8" L, 20th C. **$60-$75**

Bean slicer, cast iron, very ornate, japanned dark brown & bronze, beans fed into hopper & pass between 2 rollers to be sliced. Screw clamps to table, American, 6-1/2" H, late 19th C (?). **$55-$65**

Bean slicer, cast iron painted blue, leaf design cast in it, screw clamp, 2 skinny bean-insertion places in back, turn crank & it turns 2 beans against cutting blade, tin cover holds beans in place & keeps them from flying out, no mark, 9" H, early 20th or late 19th C. **$60-$85**

Bean slicer, oak case, iron and tin, tin slots where you feed beans in, 4 cutting blades on cutting disc, which is removable for sharpening, lid of case slides off, flywheel is perfectly balanced & it almost hums as you turn crank, no mark, 14-1/4" W, 19th C. **$90-$125**

Bean slicer & pea sheller, cast iron, screw clamps to table, green wood handle (sometimes seen in black), "Vaughn's," Chicago, IL, 12" H, early 20th C. **$35-$50**

Bean slicer & pea sheller combo, cast iron, interchangeable rollers of iron & rubber, screw clamp, American, 12" H, early 20th C. **$35-$50**

I-20. Commercial-size apple parers for hotels, etc. *All Goodell Co., Antrim, NH.* **(A)** *"Bonanza Parer & Corer." Called a "successful three-turn machine" by maker. Cast iron, mounted to board or worktable. 15" H x 17-1/2" L. Pat'd 11/16/1886 & 3/13/1888 but not, I believe, introduced until 1890. A drawing used for the "Improved '98" in c.1906-1930s catalogs shows dates 11/24/1886 & March 1881, but these are engraving mistakes. The '98 is described as being 21" H x 17" L.* **(B)** *"Eureka," hand or power. Pat'd 8/4/1874 & 4/27 & 11/16/1886, sharing a patent with "Bonanza." "It has a record of 80 bushels a day by hand." Has 3 forks, so user can continuously load.* **(C)** *"Dandy," pat'd 11/16/1886 & 3/13 & 5/8/1888. Crank 3 times to pare, core & slice one apple.* **$125-$250**

I-21. Bean slicers or stringers. *Photo at* **(L)** *is a "Harras No.37" bean cutter, made in Germany, cast iron, screw-clamps to table. Feed one bean at a time into chute, turn crank, and make French-style string beans. Removable steel blades. Trademark of a hand embossed on lower casting. 10-1/2" H. Courtesy Dennis Robida, Scotland, CT.* **(M)** *6-1/2" H "German bean cutter," yet prob. mfd by Spong, an English firm. Exact same "slicer" in Brigitte ten Kate-von Eicken's German book on kitchenwares (see Bibliography); she writes that it's marked "gesetzltoh geschutzt" (which means patented, or registered). It has no maker's mark, but looks just like one in a Spong trade catalog.* **(R)** *"German Bean Stringer." Both in c.1906 NYC houseware importer's catalog.* **$35-$75**

I-22. Beetles, potato pounders or mashers. *Two at right common forms, turned wood, late 19th or early 20th C. Double-headed one much less commonly found. I have found them as large as 24" L, for use in restaurants or boarding houses. Same date range. Fancy turned handle has a white ceramic "porcelain" (probably ironstone) head. It's from 1860s, and looks like a pestle for an ironstone mortar.* **$10-$55**

Bean stringer & slicer, little blued steel blade, springs, "Bean-X," Orange, NJ, 6-1/2" L, "pat. pend.," turn of century (?). **$15-$22**

Beetle, also called a <u>meat fret</u> or <u>steak pounder</u>, turned wood, all one piece, this one dual-purpose, having a small mushroom-shaped pestle at handle's end, American, 10" L, late 19th C. **$25-$40**

Beetle, or potato masher, handmade, one piece of maple, very dried out so it feels lighter than it should, 10-1/2" H, late 19th C. **$25-$40**

Beetle, turned wood, 2 piece, with handle (sometimes painted black or dark green) that screws into large head with large age or dryness check, American or imported, 9" L, c.1900. **$15-$22**

Beetle, turned wood, handle has nice patina, head has a few chips on business end, probably for a hotel, maybe American, unusually long at 23", turn of century. **$45-$55**

Added value. — As a rule, the beetles turned of one piece of wood bring more money than the two-piece type because they are usually somewhat older. An exceptionally nice turning or paint on handle of a two-piece one, however, would add money too. **$25-$50**

I-23. Betel nut cutter. *Often mistaken for a kitchen tool. Rooster, with iron or steel blade & silver handle, 7-5/8" L, from India. Engraved steel around eyes & chiseled design. Most are brass. The nut was cut in half, then the meat picked out with end of handle. From stock of Mona Sawyer, Stamford, CT.* **$100-$150**

Beetle, walnut, turned of one piece of wood, nice patina, American, 12" L, late 19th C.

Beetle or cracker roller, turned wood, 2 pieces (head & screw-in handle), narrow rows of ridges on face of head. Perhaps meat tenderer too? German (?), head is 8" L, handle another 5-1/2" L, turn of century. **$40-$55**

Beetle — See also potato masher and herb masher

Berry or fruit press, wood platform like for an oil drilling rig, tinned iron saucepan-shape berry holder is perforated on bottom, short handle. Levered presser pivots in 2 places, no mark, American, 11-3/4" H x 26-1/2" L, pan about 7-1/4" D, mid 19th C. Possibly patented rather than a one-off piece. **$175-$225**

Betel nut cutter, scissor action, iron blade & silver handle, in form of rooster, engraved steel around eyes & design is chiseled in, the betel nut was cut in half then the meat picked out with end of handle, made in India, 7-5/8" L, 19th C. **$125-$150**

Most **betel nut cutters** are cast brass. They look Indian, most of them, but you can be thrown off guard by some simpler ones. Betel nuts are the seeds of a type of pepper plant, and the leaves, nut "and a little lime from burnt sea shells" is chewed by people from India and Malay.

● ● ● ●

Bread Board Mottoes include "Give Us This Day Our Daily Bread," "Waste Not Want Not" and "Staff of Life." There are also nineteenth- and early twentieth-century bread boards from Germany, with similar mottoes in German. A few are appearing at American shows.

● ● ● ●

Fake alert.— For some years, the carved words or mottoes, on knives and plates have been faked on old uncarved knives having plain wooden handles, or on newly-made but distressed turned wooden plates.

● ● ● ●

Reproduction alerts. — Bread boards have turned up in such great quantities, all worn as if they'd been run over by a belt sander, bleached out too (wouldn't surprise me if a police pathologist wouldn't find household bleach in the woodgrain), that I personally wouldn't advise making a big collection of these. • A company called Bread Boards, in Landisville, PA, has advertised "hand carved" and "beautifully crafted" 12" diameter bread boards for sale to dealers. The Country Cottage Collection, in Elkins Park, PA, sells 12" diameter "handcrafted Breadboards from Sheffield, England. These hand-carved and turned Breadboards are part of an English country tradition dating back to 1840. Carved from durable sycamore wood, known for its rich grain and hue which mellows with age. Because each is hand-carved, no two are exactly alike." (Brochure, 1987.) Some of Sheffield boards are carved on the outer rim, one has word "Bread," and the 5th is carved on the center of the board.

● ● ● ●

Knife Rip-offs. — I thought the knives were not being reproduced, but saw a few obviously reproduced at fleas as early as 1988. (Also smaller sets for "Butter.") For example, I saw a nineteenth-century English bread knife, "Sheffield" steel blade, with a recently well-carved handle done in old style. The dealer's label read "Old knife, new carving." I hummed a few bars of "Your Cheatin' Heart" to calm down. You know what happened to the dealer's conscience-salving delineation of age as soon as it was sold. Although the blade was marked "Sheffield," and it was a nineteenth-century knife, the 1980s carving turns it into at best a new secondhand knife worth $9-$12. This kind of irresponsible thing drives me crazy. What right did the modern carver have to take an old knife and do new old-style carving on it? The intention is only to fool everyone. **"Oh, what a tangled web we weave, When first we practise to deceive!"** — *Sir Walter Scott*

• • • •

Blanks for Home Carvers. — One dealer I talked to said that knife and board blanks were sold in the old days for people to carve themselves. This seems a reasonable assumption, when you see the variations in the carving. The carving technique for the raised block letters is basic, but results are often strikingly different, especially in spacing and size. Mottoes relating to bread abound the world over — ranging from jokes to blessings — so it is possible that this kind of carving is a tradition, at least in some countries. I have never found a document to back up this dealer's assertion, but would appreciate hearing from anyone who knows of a catalog or such, or who knows firsthand, perhaps through a family member, of this practice.

• • • •

Bread knives — See also cake knife. Some can be used for both, but the basic rule is that the more widely spaced serrations or scallops are on cake knives, the more narrowly spaced ones are on bread knives.

Boat mill — See herb crusher and spice grinder

Bread board, carved wood, motto "Speed the Plough" around border, American or English, about 9-1/2" diameter, early 1900s. **$35-$65**

Bread board, carved wood, motto "Welcome" around border, American or English, 20th C. **$35-$65**

Bread board & matching knife, carved wood, carbon steel blade for knife, both say "Bread" — around border & on handle, English (?), early 20th C. **$60-$80**

Bread fork, carved wood handle with wheat sheaf on one side & motto "Manners Makyth Man" on other, English (?), 12" L, late 19th C. Bread forks, if that's really what they are, are unusual. **$35-$45**

Bread fork, carved wooden handle says "Bread," 3-tine broad silver-plated fork, American ?, 19th C. **$75-$85**

Bread grater, heavy tinned sheet iron, slightly curved grating surface with coarse punctured holes fairly close set, wood handle, American, 12" L, early 19th C. These are still useful, and you can really work up an appetite for scraped toast. A hundred years ago, invalids were treated to **toast water**, made by soaking a burnt piece of toast in water, and straining off the colored water. **$75-$120**

Bread grater, punctured tin cylinder, fixed & braced handle, coarse grating surface, American, 10" L, late 19th C. **$65-$100**

Bread grater, punctured tin cylinder, the proportions of large tomato juice can, with 2 appended cylindrical graters, much smaller, fixed midway up on 2 sides, bracket strap handle across top. The large grater has coarsest holes; the other 2 provide medium & fine grating surfaces. Called a "bread grater" in the 1891 *Scammell's Treasure House* , but probably useful for grating other things too. American, 10" H, late 19th C. **$65-$100**

Bread knife, black wooden handle, carbon steel blade, "Ontario Knife Co.," 13" L, turn of century. **$12-$18**

Look for thickness of tin (thicker is older) and irregular (rather than absolutely regular) machine punctures. By the mid 1800s punctured tin blanks were available in tinsmiths' supply catalogs, for use in making graters and probably for pie safe door panels. Dover Stamping Co., for example, in their 1869 catalog, offered what they called "grater blanks," rather coarse, with the puncture holes exactly 1/4" apart, center to center in either direction. These could be ordered in full sheets (not given, but I believe probably 16" x 16"), half sheets and quarter sheets. A quarter sheet, presuming the above measurement, would thus be big enough to make a grater, though square, and thus unusual.

• • • •

"Spinach Fritters. — Boil the spinach until quite tender; drain, press and mince it fine; add half the quantity of grated stale bread, one grate of nutmeg, and a small teaspoon of sugar; add a gill of cream and as many eggs as will make a thick batter, beating the whites separately; pepper and salt to taste. Drop a little at a time in boiling lard. If it does not form fritters, add a little more bread crumbs. Drain and serve immediately or they will fall." *Ladies Home Journal* , April 1890. • A **gill** in the U.S. is equal to 1/4 liquid pint; in Britain it's a 1/4 Imperial pint (based on metric system), but in British dialect, a half-pint. It is possible that in early nineteenth-century American recipes a half pint was meant. Later recipes which call for a gill require a half cup or 4 ounces.

Bread knife, carbon steel, iron loop handle, "Comet," mfd by Christy, Fremont, OH, 12" L, pat'd Nov. 12, 1890. **Other brand names** of the period include "Universal" and "Aetna" made by Landers, Frary & Clark, also "Always Sharp," the Samson "Never Crumb," and the Clyde. What intrigues me is that there are no bread knife (or cake knife) patents at all in the *Subject Index to Patents, 1790 to 1873* , and just 10 or 15 years after that they seemed to be a hot item. **$12-$18**

Bread knife, carved wooden handle, says "Bread," carbon steel blade, American, 12-1/2" L, 19th C. **$25-$35**

Bread knife, plain wooden handle, carbon steel blade with truncated tip, "Climax," American, 13-1/4" L, late 19th C. **$15-$20**

Bread knife, primitive leaf carved on handle, 19th C. **$35-$40**

Bread knife, steel blade, carved wood handle, blade marked "G. Gill & Sons," Sheffield, England, 11" L, 19th C. **$30-$40**

Bread knife, steel blade, carved wood handle says "Bread," blade has trademark silhouetted twins & "J. A. Henckels Twin Works," Sölingen, Germany, sold by importers in NYC, c.1910. **$12-$18**

Bread knife, "Want Not" on wood handle, 12" L, 19th C. **$35-$50**

Bread knife, wheat sheaf carved on handle, blade marked "Alexander E. Foulis," English, 19th C (?). **$45-$65**

Bread knife, wheat sheaf carved on handle, carbon steel blade, all very worn, unusually short, only 8" L, 19th C. **$35-$40**

Bread knife, wheat sheaf carved on wooden handle, carbon blade, American (?), 11-1/2" L, 19th C. **$35-$45**

Bread knife, wood & steel, advertises "The Pride of Brooklyn, McGarvey's Home Made Bread," no place, turn of century. **$15-$20**

Bread knife, wooden handle, carbon steel blade, "Victor," American Cutlery Co., late 19th or early 20th C. **$12-$18**

Bread knife, wooden handle, pointed carbon steel blade, "Tip-Top Boy," trademark of boy's head, American, 15" L, late 19th C. **$15-$22**

Bread knife, wood handle, truncated tip to carbon steel blade, "Victoria," American Cutlery Co., 14 3/4"L, late 19th C. **$12-$18**

Bread knife & matching board, wheat carved on knife handle & around board, with words "Bread Knife" engraved on steel blade, English or American, 9-1/2" D board or plate, 19th C. **$85-$110**

Bread or cake knife, long scalloped carbon tool steel blade, metal handle cast with encircling bands like screw threads, marked "Lightning" & "Prussia," American, 15" L, early 20th C. **$18-$25**

Bread rasp, heavy forged iron, rough chiseled teeth, wood handle. Shaped like mason's concrete trowel; standard bakery equipment, used like bread grater to remove burned crust, American, 9" L, late 18th, early 19th C. **$85-$125**

Bread slicing box, heavily varnished wood, the 2 sides have 12 slots & are attached to cutting board base. Works sort of like a mitre box — the slots guide the bread knife. Simple but efficient. American or English, 5-3/4" H x 13-1/2" L, 19th C. **$75-$125**

Butcher knife, homemade, walnut handle with brass rivets, large heavy steel blade, American, 14" L, turn of century. **$15-$20**

Butcher knife, handmade brass & wood handle, brass rivets, carbon steel blade, quite heavy, American, 12" L, turn of century. **$15-$22**

Butcher's steel, for sharpening knives, a long slightly tapered steel rod with faintly roughened surface, barely discernable when you run your fingernail along it, turned wooden handle, "Keen Kutter," Simmons Hardware, 20th C. **$6-$10**

Butter cutter, painted & nickeled cast iron, screw clamps to table edge, horizontal platform for large 1-lb block of butter, which moves at preset calibrations through the levered wire cutter. It comes through 2 crossed wires which quarters it just a millisecond before it is cut into 4 pats of any thickness. Early ad shows pats falling into basin of ice water, sold by V. Clad & Sons, Phila., early 20th C. **$65-$90**

Added value. — Homemade cabbage cutters cost more than commercial ones. Look for interesting cutouts for hanging, or interesting treatment of wood, or nice joining of sides of box, or old wrought wingnuts for adjusting blade, etc. If it has too much going for it, caveat emptor. Homemade, and big, it might be $125 to $225, but a nineteenth-century commercial one is worth less.

• • • •

"Bubble and Squeak. — Slice of cold boiled beef; chopped potatoes; chopped up cabbage; both previously boiled; pepper, salt and a little butter; set it aside to keep hot; lightly fry some slices of cold boiled beef; put them in a hot dish with alternate layers of the vegetables, piling high in the middle." *Scammel's Treasure House*, 1891.

Cabbage cutter, also called a kraut or slaw cutter, a box grater, worn & silky wood frame with steel blade, prob. American, 26" L, 19th C. **$45-$90**

Cabbage cutter, a wood box grater, with steel blade, box well-made, probably by hand, American, 22" L, 19th C. **$100-$150**

Cabbage cutter, wood with 2 steel blades, "The Indianapolis Kraut Kutter," Tucker & Dorsey Mfg. Co., Indianapolis, IN, made in different sizes, pat'd 1905. **$45-$55**

Cabbage cutter, also slaw board, walnut with large heart cutout hanging hole at one end, steel blades, one replaced side molding, all the wood unfortunately refinished at some point with dull, dead, no-color undersurface, finish typical of poorly applied Minwax™ & combination of stains & waxes. If you can't imagine the color, think of thickly spreading brown makeup all over your face, then heavily powdering it with gray or white powder. Pennsylvania German, 20-5/8" L x 7-1/4" W, 19th C. This slaw board was from the **Earl F. & Ada F. Robacker**

Collection. (**NOTE:** As in all the Robacker pieces described in this book, the measurements & sometimes other attributed information are adapted from author's notes & Clarence Spohn's catalog for T. Glenn Horst Auctions.) In this case, the Minwax™ description is the author's, and has nothing to do with Mr. Spohn, Mr. Horst or the Robackers. $140 at May 1989 auction would have been double or more with original finish.

Cabbage cutter, gray graniteware, steel blade, "Ideal," turn of century. **$200-$250**

Cabbage cutter, or cabbage plane, handmade box style, wood with peg construction, one very worn (much sharpened) carbon steel blade, American, 30" L, 19th C. **$50-$75**

Cabbage cutter, simple wood board with steel blade, very worn, but nice patina, American (?), 34-1/2" L x 12-1/4" W, to fit over large kraut barrel, 19th C. **$45-$65**

"Sour-Krout. — Take a large, strong wooden vessel, or cask resembling a salt beef cask, and capable of holding as much as is sufficient for the winter's consumption of a family; gradually break down or chop the cabbages in very small pieces; begin with one or two cabbages at the bottom of the cask; add others at intervals; press them by means of a wooden spade against the side of the cask, until it is full; then place a heavy weight upon the top of it, and allow it to stand near a warm place for from 4 to 5 days; then place the cask in a cool situation; keep it always covered up; strew anise seeds among the layers of the cabbages during its preparation." Henry Scammel, compiler, *Treasure House*, 1891.

Cabbage cutter, thick carved wood, heart shaped at top, bench end or straddle type used by putting on a bench or chair & sat upon, all wood with wooden screws to adjust steel blade, cabbage pusher missing. Stood on end it resembles a simple bust sculpture, American, prob. PA, 46-3/8" L, mid 19th C. **$225-$350**

Cabbage cutter, interesting swinging box that passes over blade, describing about 15 degrees of a full circle, wood, cast iron hinge, steel cutting blade, porcelain handle on heavily sprung lid to box, which acts to hold cabbage firmly, like a foller in a press, American or German, 13" H w/ 17" sweep to box, 19th C. **$150-$200**

Cabbage cutter, walnut, 1 adjustable steel blade, cast iron handle, "Brady," Lancaster, PA, 25" L x 7-3/4" W, pat'd March 9, 1880. **$125-$150**

Cabbage cutter, walnut, 3 steel blades, "Disston & Morss" (Morse? Morris?), Philadelphia, PA, 24" L x 9" W, 19th C. This must have a connection with saw makers Henry Disston & Son, but at this time I can't find anything about Morss, Morse, Morris. **$45-$75**

Cabbage cutters, walnut, iron & steel, with cutout hanging holes at ends of boards (one a sort of bird's head heart, the other a tulip), one with a cutout for fitting against hip or waist while using, American, most likely Pennsylvania German, one 18-1/2" L, one 19" L, heart one dated 1883, other about same age. These are in the collection of the National Museum of American History, Smithsonian Institution. If I had to give a value to them, I'd say this range: **$250-$350**

Cake knife, cast iron handle, carbon steel blade, "Christy," Fremont, OH, 14-1/4" L, pat'd 1889, 1891. **$12-$18**

Cake knife, corrugated cast iron handle, carbon steel blade, "Comet," mfd by Christy, Fremont, OH, 14-1/4" L, 1890s to turn of century. See also Breadknife listings. **$12-$18**

Cake knife, clear glass, in original box, "Vitex," American, c.1940s. Glass cake & fruit knives were made in cooperation with the war effort metal drives and war materials conservation efforts. **$12-$18**

I-24. Bread & cake knives. *Scalloped & beveled cutting edges to carbon steel blades. Scallops closer-set for bread knives. Wood handles. All c.1890s to early 20th C. From top:* **(1)** *"Climax," 13-1/4" L.* **(2)** *"Tip-Top," with trademark of boy's head — the "Tip-Top Boy." 15" L.* **(3)** *"Victoria," American Cutlery Co., 14-3/4" L.* **(4)** *"Aetna" tradename, "Universal" trademark, Landers, Frary & Clark, New Britain, CT. 14-1/4" L. Collection of Paul Persoff.* **$12-$20**

Replaced leg. — I bought a cherry pitter specifically because one leg was replaced with a wooden leg. What I didn't realize, blush, until I actually took its picture and studied that, was that the little mouth or spout-trough was missing. It pays to look at everything and do a run-through in your mind, especially if you are highly attracted to one element to the exclusion of others. Hope this helps you someday ... remember: "Learn from other people's mistakes. You won't have time to make them all yourself."

Cake knife, clear glass, rather chunky handle, slightly serrated cutting edge, "Cryst-O-Lite," 8-1/2" L, 1930s-1940s. Clear glass is not as desirable, by a long shot, as colored. And cobalt blue would be the most valuable of all. **$12-$22**

Cake knife, green glass, with flower & leaf design on handle, in its original box, "DUR-X," 9" L, 1938 (design patent #112059). Also used for fruit, as it could not be stained by acids. **$20-$25**

Carving fork, for meat, steel with bone handle, 2 tined, American (?), mid to late 19th C. Low value for lone pieces, without matching carving knife & steel. If handle is well-worked, carved as a one-of-a-kind piece, it has definite value on its own. This one does not. **$3-$6**

Carving set, carbon steel, knife, fork & sharpening steel, "Keen Kutter," by Simmons Hardware. **$60-$75**

Cheese grater, 2 turned wood parts, with punctured tin grating surface in between. The shorter knobby part has short prongs on which to fix the piece of hard cheese (this wouldn't work for soft cheese). After putting the 2 parts together you grate by working your wrists back & forth, like wringing out clothes. Attractive pale wood. American or European, 6-1/2" L, 19th C. or early 20th. **$65-$100**

Cheese scoop, hand machined & cut steel, ivory handle, steel shaft decorated with 4 facets surrounded by zigzags & a sort of rope or scallop design, spade-shaped concave spoon-blade has very sharp cutting edge, thumb screw holds the pusher or follower on its track inside the scoop, can be turned to lift up pusher for cleaning, English, 10-1/16" L, scoop is 1-5/8" L x 1-1/4" W, c.1840s. Not all that rare, I've seen several of them, but the work is individually done. Cast iron, necessarily thicker & less refined looking, obviated all the handwork needed to make such tools as this scoop. **$75-$100**

Cheese slicer, aluminum, very musical if you pluck the wires, "Cut-Rite, No. 300," mfd by Wagner Ware, Sidney, OH, 7" L x 3-1/8" W, "patent pending," 20th C. **$30-$38**

Cheese slicer, plated wire bent in sort of hacksaw shape, including loop handle, thin steel wire stretched between frame is what slices the cheese, American, 6-5/8" L, c.1920 to 1949. **$3-$10**

Cherry pitter or stoner, almost all wood, iron hinges. Stones 20 cherries at a time. After you load the separate hinged cherry carrier tray, you insert it into the box, fit the foller or levered press (which has 20 longish pegs) into the top so the holes line up & push out 20 pits. Pits fall out underneath, & the pitted cherries are dumped from the carrier into a bowl. Most ingenious. American, box part is 6-1/4" H x 6-1/4" L x 5-3/4" W, 19th C. **$150-$225**

This boxy 20-hole stoner, owned by Meryle Evans, was described in my 2nd edition as "homemade." Instead, I think it was a hand-made production piece, albeit made in small quantities. A picture of a similar one, possibly the original from which the 20-cherry one was copied, was recently found by me in a B. K. Bliss & Son's Seed Catalog, dated 1876. It is for "Fisher's Cherry Stoner," which will with "Five strokes stone one hundred Cherries. The rapidity and certainty with which it performs its work will make this machine a necessity in every household. Under or over ripe fruit equally well stoned, and can be done five times as rapidly as by the old way by hand, and much neater, as it leaves the fruit round and in perfect shape." The Fisher, a wooden box-like hinged device with a levered top "press" with 100 pegs, and a bottom part with 100 small holes (on which to place the cherries like Chinese Checkers), was pat'd "1870." The only 2 cherry stoners pat'd that year were one by J. Marchant, Farmington, IL, April 19; and one by J. N. Webster, Peoria, IL, on May 31.

I-25. Cherry stoner. *Although this looks skillfully "homemade," it is mass-produced. It's a "Fisher's Patent Cherry Stoner," pat'd by C. A. Fisher, Philadelphia, 5/24/1870. "Five strokes stone 100 cherries" claims early catalog. Wood box with cherry-holder of wood, iron hinges, lever action. Does 20 at a time. Fit holder with cherries (like Chinese Checkers), insert into box, fit the levered follower into box, push out pits, which fall below. 6-1/4" H x 6-1/4" L x 5-3/4" W. Collection of Meryle Evans.* **$150-$225**

Cherry pitter, cast iron, 3 legs, mounted to board, hopper & crank, lightweight casting, sort of cabriole legs nicely shaped with "spurs" like a dog's dew claws, Scott Mfg. Co., Baltimore, MD, 6-3/4" H x 12" L, turn of century. **$45-$60**

Cherry pitter, cast iron, brightly nickel plated, screw clamps to table, has interesting works: a platform with 4 little holed cups holds 4 cherries at a time; when pitter is cranked, plunger goes up & down & punches pits out, one by one, New Standard Corp., Mount Joy, PA, 10-1/4" H, "patents pending," prob. turn of century. **$75-$100**

Cherry pitter, cast iron, even crank knob is cast iron, 4 legs, mounted to board that has a rectangular cutout for cherries (or their stones?) to fall through, Scott Manufacturing Co., Baltimore, MD, stem to stern 7" H x 10-7/8" L, "patent pending" 19th C. **$45-$65**

Cherry pitter, cast iron finished in blue enamel, screw clamps to table edge, punches out 2 at a time, "Home Cherry Stoner," mfd by Schroeter Bros. Hardware Co., St. Louis, MO, 10-1/2" H x 9-1/2" L x 3" W, pat'd Aug. 17, 1917. According to *House Furnishing Review* in 1918, "It is fast and very convenient; is self-feeding, due to the rocking hopper which agitates the cherries, causing them to roll into pitting sockets. Hopper large enough to hold 12 or more cherries at a time." **$40-$55**

Cherry pitter, cast iron, hopper has cranked rub plate, clamps on, deep spout, handle is missing turned wood knob, replacement is old wooden spool, "The New Brighton," Logan & Strobridge, turn of century. **$18-$25**

Cherry pitter, cast iron, long hopper, swiveling hinge above the clamp that fastens it to the table, is a sort of shock absorber while plunger-punch is in action. Hopper can be filled with about 8 cherries, which roll down one at a time for pitting, "Duke," mfd by Reading Hardware Co., Reading, PA, 11" L, not including wooden handle on crank, "patent pending," 19th C. **$200-$250**

Cherry pitter, cast iron painted turquoise, 2 plungers, screw clamp, Rollman Mfg. Co., Mt. Joy, PA, 14" H, turn of century or later. **$30-$40**

Cherry pitter, cast iron, pits 2 at a time with 2 curved rods that have ragged sharp ends. Punches pits through holes in double trough, & when pair of pitters is pulled back through a pry-off sheet of metal, the pitted cherries are knocked into a slanted wooden trough & roll into a bowl, "The Family Cherry Stoner," Goodell Co., Antrim, NH, 8" H, pat'd 1886. According to Loris Russell, this was based on the patent of George Geer, Galesburg, IL, of April 9, 1867. **$35-$50**

Cherry pitter, cast iron, screw clamp, "Cherry Stoner No. 17," & on bottom of clamp "2884," "Enterprise" not cast on piece, 12" H exclusive of screw, pat'd Mar. 31 1903. **$30-$45**

Cherry pitter, cast iron, screw clamps to table, simple figure 8 heavy wire thumbscrew, the #17 (japanned) & #18 (tinned) can be regulated or adjusted for different size cherries, which are fed into the hopper, whereupon a crank rubs them against a ridge plate which splits them & removes pits, "Enterprise #17," Enterprise Mfg. Co., Philadelphia, PA, pat'd March 31, 1903. **$30-$50**

Cherry pitter, cast iron, tinned finish, hopper & crank, adjusted by thumb screws to adapt to different size cherries, Enterprise #2, mfd by Enterprise Mfg. Co., Philadelphia, PA, 12" H x 9" W, pat'd March 31, 1903. The #1 was japanned and sold for half to three-quarters the price of the tinned one originally. **$30-$45**

Lookalike alarm. — A brand new cherry pitter, styled exactly like the old Enterprise, is being manufactured (not to fool collectors). Cast into the body is "CHOP-RITE Pottstown U.S.A. Approximate new price about same as for old: **$30-$45**

Cherry pitter, cast iron, tinned (later, c.1913, offered also in bronze japan finish), screw clamped to table, ridged wheel in center of hopper is cranked to rub stones out of the cherries, this one in its original cardboard box, "Brighton #2," mfd by Logan & Strobridge Iron Co., sold by future mfrs, Wrightsville Hardware Co., L&S from New Brighton, PA; WHCo. in Wrightsville, PA, pat'd May 15, 1866, by William Weaver, Phoenixville, PA. Made for many years after 1866, and advertised as being made by Wrightsville Hardware in 1913. In an ad from *House Furnishing Review*, March 1913, this cherry seeder is described as being "adjustable" — like the Enterprise ones, finished in "Bronze Japan or Tinned," & "furnished either with clamp for attaching to table or with four legs." Old ones get the most money: **$50-$65**

Cherry pitter, hand held, nickeled spring steel wire, loop-de-looped so that it fits over thumb & middle finger, fed cherries one by one with other hand, & squeezed to make sharp-ended plunger push pit out, John Houck, Chicago, IL, 7-1/4" L, pat'd Dec. 28, 1909. **$25-$35**

I-26. Cherry stoners. *Two versions of cast iron 4-legged pitter, based on original patent (SEE I-30) of H. Buckwalter, Kimberton, PA, 11/17/1863, as improved by William Weaver, Phoenixville, PA, 5/15/1866. Handle on crank is also cast iron. Note one at top has wingnuts holding legs on; it's newer than other. Some marked "Scott Man'fg Co. Pat. Pending, Baltimore, MD." 7" H x 10-7/8" L.* **$55-$85**

I-27. Cherry stoner. *Cast iron, 3 legs. Henry Buckwalter's patent, 11/17/1863. Missing wooden handle to crank. Picture courtesy of The Smithsonian Institution, Museum of History and Technology. A real classic, but not rare.* **$55-$85**

Cherry pitter, hand held, small metal device with finger holes at each side & a plunger worked with the thumb in center, has to be hand fed, "Perfection" is name given it by a distributer, F.W. Seastrand, American, about 4" L, marked only "PAT." Seastrand catalog is c.1910, so it's earlier than that. **$25-$35**

Cherry pitter, or cherry stoner, cast iron, mounted to wood board cut out to match footprint of pitter; has tin-lined hole so whole thing could be set up over large receptacle; hopper has fabulous, almost Art Nouveau, sorrel leaf with waving tip cast in it, turned wheel inside hopper, which rubs cherries off their stones, ribbed on both sides; this is the improvement on the original patent — pat'd by William Weaver on H. Buckwalter's patent. Weaver from Phoenixville, PA, Buckwalter from Kimberton, PA, 6" H, board 8-7/8" x 4-1/2", pat'd Nov. 17, 1863 & May 15, 1866. **$140-$165**

Cherry pitter, cast iron, square-cut letters & numbers, square hopper, 4 straight legs, comes apart for cleaning, mounted to board, name not marked, but pat'd by H. Buckwalter as a "cherry-stoner," Kimberton, PA, 5" H exclusive of board, pat'd Nov. 17, 1863. **$125-$165**

I-28. Cherry stoner. *Lightweight cast iron, 3 legs attached with wingnut bolts, mounted on plank through holes in feet. Marked "Scott Mfg. Co., Baltimore." 6-3/4" H x 12" L.* **$55-$85**

I-29. Cherry stoner "make-do" *or repaired piece. The Weaver patent, showing both dates, with sorrel-leaf decoration cast into hopper. Legs missing or removed purposely; body mounted to shaped wood base, 8-7/8" x 4-1/2", carved to match sinuous curves of cast iron. Iron part only 2-7/8" H; overall 6" H. Note piece at one end for mounting to tabletop. Strict kitchenware dealers devalue this kind of thing; folk art and make-do collectors would snap it up.* **$65-$125**

"Cherry Bounce. — Take a peck of morella cherries, and a peck of black hearts. Stone the morellas and crack the stones. Put all the cherries and the cracked stones into a demi-john, with three pounds of loaf-sugar slightly pounded or beaten. Pour in two gallons of double-rectified whisky. Cork the demi-john, and in six months the cherry-bounce will be fit to pour off and bottle for use; but the older it is, the better." Miss Leslie, of Philadelphia, *Seventy-Five Receipts for Pastry, Cakes, and Sweetmeats . Appended to The Cook's Own Book and Housekeeper's Register ....*, by a Boston Housekeeper. Boston: Munroe & Francis, 1833.

Cherry pitter, skeletal cast iron frame, with 3 spraddly, insectually grasshopper graceful heavy-gauge rod legs. Hopper feeds cherries against one side of the spiral-ridged wheel that is turned with a crank that has (or is supposed to have) a slim wooden handle, marked only with patent date, but pat'd by Henry Buckwalter, Kimberton, PA, pat'd Nov. 17, 1863. The William Weaver patent of three years later (May 15, 1866) is an improvement in that both sides of the wheel are ridged, doing twice as many cherries. **$125-$165**

Cherry pitter, tinned cast iron, cranked action that pulls down vertical pit puncher, leather insert at point of impact on hopper, screw clamps to table, wooden handle (older ones natural or varnished), "New Standard #50," New Standard Hardware Works, Mt. Joy, PA, 10" H x 5-1/2" W, pat'd in the 1870s. Also came in a 12" H size, the "New Standard #75." **$25-$40**

Lookalike alarm. — A similar one-cherry pitter, also of tinned cast iron, is now being made by the White Mountain Freezer Inc., Winchendon, MA 01475. It seems to be a variation of the John H. Webster, May 31, 1870, patent for a straight-plunger style pitter. These were made over a very, very long time; I believe the ones seen with red wooden handles are as late as the 1940s. Another 1940s variation, the "50A Dandy," is made of cast iron and heavy stamped sheet metal, heavily tinned (or nickeled?), with a piston that drives pitter up and down when you turn crank. The pitter is marked New Standard Corp., Mt. Joy, but sold by White Mountain Freezer Co., Nashua, NH. (Value of 1940s one is under $25).

I-31. Cherry pitter or stoner. *Skeletal wire & stamped sheet metal, spring-activated plungers. 8" H, no mark. Seems to pit cherry on one side, and split it on other. Courtesy Arden L. Fisher.* **$85-$135**

I-30. Cherry stoners. *All cast iron; all screw clamp to table edge.* **(A)** *"Enterprise No. 2," pat'd 1903. No.s 1 & 2 not adjustable for different cherry sizes, as were Enterprise 17 & 18. 12" L.* **(B)** *"Duke," Reading Hardware Co., "pat. pend." Very unusual. Swiveling hinge just above clamp functions as a shock absorber while pitter in operation. 11" L, exclusive of handle. Late 19th C.* **(C)** *"The Family Cherry Stoner," Goodell Co., c.1895. 8" H. Wonderful lever action plunges double pitters through cherries.* **(D)** *"New Standard No. 50," Mt. Joy, PA, 10" H, c.1900.* **(E)** *Another by New Standard Corporation, Mt. Joy. "patents pending." Nickeled iron. All parts numbered, therefore replaceable with stock parts — the touted advantage of all uniformly cast iron appliances. Feed cherries with left hand, and as you crank, platform holding 4 cherries revolves to lie briefly under punch. 10-1/4" H.* **(F)** *Another New Standard pitter, with eccentric wheel, horizontal action. Courtesy Bob Cahn. (A), (C) & (D) Collection of Robert D. Franklin. (B) & (E) Collection of Meryle Evans. (A)* **$30-$35***; (C)* **$35-$50***; others* **$55-$125**

Cherry pitter, tinned cast iron, screw clamps, crank is not on a wheel, but at right angles & behind hopper. This one "is intended to stone cherries with the least possible cutting or disfiguring. Every good housewife will appreciate this for preserving purposes. The most satisfactory results are obtained by dropping the cherries one at a time into the Hopper immediately after Sweeper has passed the hole. With practice one can become very expert." "The New Cherry Stoner," Enterprise #12, c.1890s to c.1905 at least. **$40-$60**

Cherry pitter, tinned metal & wire, hand held, "The 'HAND'-Y," American, 3" H, c.1920s (?). **$10-$20**

Cherry pitter, skeletal heavy gauge wire & metal, 2 spring plungers worked with 2 hands, put cherries on platform below to be pitted & split, no mark, 8" H, turn of century to 1910s. **$85-$135**

Cherry stoner, red painted cast iron screw clamp frame, tall vertical shaft has large knob at top, to be pushed down for spring action, one cherry at a time, oval concave white porcelainized cast iron receiver, "Excelsior 85," pat'd 1885 (?). **$75-$100**

Chocolate grater, tin & cast iron, a mechanical gadget with a rectangular spring-loaded holder for a chunk or block of chocolate, has 3 rods going length of cylindrical punctured tin grating surface, 2 of which are the track for the chocolate holder, rubbed back & forth across grater in same way as this company's Edgar nutmeg grater, "The Edgar," mfd by William J. Bride Co., Reading, MA, cylinder 7-1/4" L x 2-1/8" diameter, with handle 8-1/2" L, chocolate holder is 2-7/8" H x 2" x 1-7/8", pat'd 1891, and again Nov. 10, 1896. **$175-$250**

"Caramel Potato Cake. — 1/2 cup butter, 1 cup sugar, 2 eggs, 1/2 cup milk, 1/2 cup hot riced potatoes, 1 cup flour, 2 teaspoons baking powder, 1/2 teaspoon cinnamon, 1/2 teaspoon [ground] clove, 1/2 teaspoon [grated] nutmeg, 1/2 cup grated chocolate, 1/2 cup chopped nut meats. — Cream butter and add gradually, while beating constantly, sugar; then add eggs, well beaten, milk and potatoes. Beat thoroughly and add flour, mixed and sifted with baking powder, and spices, chocolate and nut meats. Turn into a buttered and floured cake pan and bake in a moderate oven fifty-five minutes. Remove from pan and cover with Fudge Frosting.

Fudge Frosting. — 2 tablespoons butter, 1 cup sugar, 1/4 cup milk, 1 square unsweetened sugar, 1/2 teaspoon vanilla. — Put butter in saucepan and when melted, add sugar and milk. Bring to the boiling point and let boil ten minutes. Add chocolate and let boil five minutes, taking care that chocolate does not adhere to bottom or sides of pan. Remove from range, add vanilla and beat until the right consistency to spread." Fannie Merritt Farmer, *A New Book of Cookery* . Boston: Little, Brown, 1915 edition of 1912 book.

Chopping bowl, carved wood, a few minor age checks, 16-5/8" L x 9-1/2" W, mid 19th C. **$225-$300**

Chopping bowl, crudely hewn thick wood, American, rectangle 5" x 11" x 4" D, very early 19th C, poss. 18th C. **$135-$175**

Chopping bowl, hand carved wood, nice patina, American, 25" L x 10-1/2" W x 4" D, early to mid 19th C. This proportion is most common — over twice as long as wide & not very deep. Old chopping bowls should show signs of vigorous cutting. The wonder is that they look so good on the inside; maybe really badly scarred ones were burned in the fireplace generations ago. I've seen many repaired ones, where bottom has been chopped through, bad section cut out & hole fitted with another piece of wood, flush as possible, or metal patch has been added. Added value. — Often imaginatively repaired ones bring more than those with good condition but less personality. **$75-$150**

Chopping bowl, hand carved wood, oblong, old red paint on outside, American, 22-1/2" L x 8-1/2" W, 19th C. **$200-$300**

Paint & Patina: Old paint, red, ochre, blue, green or even gray, adds to collector appeal. If not painted, a scrubbed, old patina is what you should look for. These were cut from split logs, then hollowed out with a special curved cutting scraping tool called a scorp; somewhere twin bowls, made from the two halves of a log, may exist.

Chopping bowl, wood with old red paint on outside, oblong, American, quite extraordinarily large at 25" L x 17" W, early or mid 19th C. Sold at a 1982 auction for $300. Now would depend on where it was sold, if it would go much higher. **$275-$500**

Chopping knife, 2 nickeled steel rocker blades set at right angles & forming almost round shape, big wooden ball knob handle, "Androck," Rockford, IL, 1930s-1940s. **$8-$15**

Chopping knife, 2 plated steel sausage-shaped blades, 2 tangs welded at one end, fit over a rod going through turned wooden handle at other end. By use of wingnut to loosen tangs, the distance between blades can be adjusted. "James F. Foster," Buffalo, NY, 6" H x 5-3/4" W, pat'd Dec. 27, 1887. **$18-$25**

Chopping knife, 2 tang straight bottom steel blade, turned wooden handle, "Brades Co.," American or English, 6" W, 19th C. **$40-$50**

Chopping knife, 3 slightly bowed hotdog-shaped steel blades, iron frame & wooden handle, called a tension chopper. "In this knife the blades are ... kept firm by the tension of the frame in which they are set. It does very rapid work, and is an excellent knife for family use. Most people consider hash a very delicious breakfast dish, in spite of all the hits newspaper paragraphers have made on it, and a good implement for making it is indispensible." *Practical Housekeeper*, 1884. American, about 6" W, pat'd 1867. **$20-$30**

"The Knife-Life of the Kitchen. — [A] late product of steel ... is ... fast coming to the markets of the world. It is stainless steel. A steel (with an admixture of chromium) which resists rust, does not corrode or scale, and is impervious to food acids (with the exception of mustard, plus vinegar and salt which equal muriatic acid). ... The steel we now use is carbon steel. ... Think of not having to scour or polish your knives. Think of the knife having an indefinite life and always looking highly polished. Soon, too, even the handle will be made of this steel and the knife will be made of this steel and the knife will look like a highly polished silver utensil. No cleaning powders must be used to clean this steel; only warm water and soap. Its advent reminds one of the early days of aluminum utensils, doesn't it? Manufacturers are planning to make kettles, pots and pans of it, as they will wear well, and will not scale and wear as do iron ones." *House & Garden* , March 1921.

•　　•　　•　　•

Think English as soon as you see **fancy cutouts** on the blade, or very deep blades with profiles of roosters or animals along top non-cutting edge, or combinations of brass & iron; most such pieces are not American.

Chopping knife, 4 stainless steel blades set at right angles to form bell-like shape, painted wooden handle, "A & J," Binghamton, NY, 6" H x 3" W, c.1925. Knobs were painted green, yellow or red. Blue is not mentioned in the catalog. **$12-$18**

Chopping knife, also called a **chopper** or **mincer**, fancily shaped cast steel blade, brass inset decoration, smooth mahogany colored handle, 2 tangs, English, c.1820s or 1830s. **$75-$150**

Chopping knife, brass & steel, handmade (at least it looks one-of-a-kind & not commercial), tubular brass handle with long slit into which was slid, then soldered, the well-shaped steel blade with fancy shoulder, American (?), 4-1/2" H x 6-1/2" W, 19th C. **$120-$150**

Chopping knife, cast iron handle with cutout in top, usually painted, stainless steel rocker blade with distinct swellings at each end. This looks exactly like the "Double Action" knife, except for cutout in horizontal part of handle. I don't know if they were made by same company, 20 years apart, or if Voos got license to make them & altered handle for some purpose. Marked "Voos," American, 5" H x 6-1/8" W, c.1920s. **$12-$20**

Chopping knife, cast iron handle with no cutout, cast steel blade shaped like baby's bottom, hence its name "Double Action." American, pat'd Oct. 20, 1892. **$12-$20**

Chopping knife, cast iron stirrup-shaped handle, 2 bell-shaped steel blades, rocker action, "N. R. S. & Co. No. 20," (Nelson R. Streeter & Co.), Groton, NY, 5-1/2" H, pat'd May 2, 1893. **$20-$30**

Chopping knife, cast steel blade, 2 tangs, forged iron handle, marked only "Cast Steel," American, 5-1/2" L blade, c.1870s. **$35-$45**

Chopping knife, cast steel blade, cast iron shank & turned wood T-handle, blade is lightly rocked & has very high rounded shoulders, "S. H. F.," "Bingham" (may be last name of maker or town — there were a number of Binghams in America, including three Michigan towns), prob. American, 7" H x 5-1/2" W, 19th C. **$35-$45**

Chopping knife, cast steel blade, wooden handle, "Universal," mfd by Landers, Frary & Clark, 19th C. **$15-$20**

Chopping knife, cast steel, quadrant handle screws to 6 "flying buttress" blades that form bell shape, taken apart for sharpening or cleaning, J. B. Foote Foundry, pat'd 1906. **$10-$15**

Chopping knife, cast steel, wood, "L. D. Wheeler," n.p. (American ? might be Wheeler Can Opener Co., St. Louis), 19th C. **$35-$50**

Carpet Cutters. — In the nineteenth century a type of rocking chair with relatively thin wooden rocker blades rounded on the ends was called by some wags a "carpet cutter."

Chopping knife, curved steel blade, wood handle, "Henry Disston & Sons," the famous saw makers, Phila., 6-1/2" L, 19th C. I've never seen one, but Henry Disston did get a potato parer patent on Nov. 29, 1859. **$18-$25**

Chopping knife, steel blade, 2 tangs, turned wooden handle, "Henry Disston," Philadelphia, late 19th C. **$18-$25**

Chopping knife, cutlery steel blade, long tang, turned wood handle, "Mason & Parker." English, 13-1/2" L, late 19th C. **$40-$55**

Chopping knife, deep half-ovoid blade, one tang, wood handle, marked "PERK" on blade, American, 5" W, mid to late 19th C. **$50-$60**

Chopping knife, double blade, steel with wood handle, heart-shaped rivet head, American, 7" L, c.1870s. **$165-$180**

Chopping knife, double bladed rocker type, black turned wood handle, loosen wing nut to take blade off for sharpening or cleaning, distance between 2 parallel blades is NOT adjustable — it locks in only one position. Ad from Dec. 27, 1890, *Metal Worker* has imaginary dialogue between housewife & hardware clerk: " 'I do not want one of those double bladed chopping knives. You cannot wash, scour or sharpen them without cutting the fingers.' 'But,' said the clerk, 'This is one of the new Buffalo ... mincing knives which opens for cleaning and sharpening.' 'Why, that's splendid. I'll take that!' said she." Called a "Buffalo Adjustable," mfd by Sidney Shepard & Co., Buffalo, NY, 6" H x 5-7/8" W blade, pat'd Dec. 27, 1887. **$30-$40**

Chopping knife, forged crescent blade, bentwood handle, American (?), 6" W, early 19th C. **$65-$75**

Chopping knife, forged iron blade 2 long tangs, thick, slightly carved wood handle, American, 6-1/2" H x 5" W, early 19th C. **$55-$70**

Chopping knife, forged iron, curved blade with unusually shaped shoulders leading to single shank & turned wooden T handle, American, mid 19th C. **$35-$45**

Chopping knife, forged steel, anchor-shaped, wood handle, thin crescent moon blade, prob. American, 6" W, mid 19th C. **$50-$60**

Chopping knife, forged steel straight-bottom blade, with turned wood handle, nicely shaped cutout for hand is almost like the top of a Valentine, American (?), 19th C. **$35-$50**

Chopping knife, iron blade curves like sleeping dog, 3 tangs become one shank T handle, American (?), 6-1/4" H, 19th C. **$45-$60**

Chopping knife, iron blade, very fat & curved, unusual brass tang, fat cigar-shaped T handle grip, American, 19th C. **$50-$65**

Chopping knife, iron & tin, pat'd May 2, 1893. **$15-$20**

Chopping knife, iron with wood tiller handle off one end (just imagine the tiller of a small sailboat to get idea of shape & angle), blade's other end is fat & rounded, American, 3" H x 10" L, 19th C. **$25-$35**

Chopping knife, ornate steel & wood, 4 brass rivets fasten handle to blade, cutout & scrolly carved wooden handle (with "horns" to cradle hand), almost a mirror image of fat scrolls of rocker blade, which also has a heart near the haft, birds perched on scrolled tips, European, poss. English, although some hints at German origin, 12-1/2" H, 18th or 19th C (?).I think 1830s. Somehow the handle does not look as old as I think it should for blade. This chopper has been for sale at least twice — once for $2800 — in the late 1980s, possibly in 1987. **$400-$500**

Ornately UnAmerican. — In the late 1980s very ornate choppers began to appear regularly on the market. The blades look old; sometimes you look for more wear on the handles than is there. They are so "Good" you have to wonder where did they come from. I've heard from some dealers that this ornate type is being skillfully reproduced in England for export to America.

● ● ● ●

Parloa's Advice. — "A chopping knife with only one blade is much better than one with two blades. The blade should be almost straight across. When it is rounded a good deal, much time and strength are wasted in chopping." Maria Parloa, *Kitchen Companion* , Boston: Estes & Lauriat, 1887. It is instructive to read period literature about utensils and gadgets. While "artistically" we may admire the curved double blades, Parloa, who came with the highest credentials (founder of the original Boston Cooking School, and author of several cookbooks), obviously didn't like them.

Chopping knife, rocker blade is thin long crescent, tang at each end of single straight wood handle, American (?), 7" W, mid 19th C. **$60-$75**

Chopping knife, rocker blade, handles at each end, steel with turned wood knobby handles, French, 11-1/2" L, dated 1878. **$55-$70**

Chopping knife, stainless steel, triple blades have spring action to make center blade look (& sound) like it's doing extra work. "Foley Chopper," 7-1/2" H x 33-3/4" W, pat'd 1938. **$10-$15**

Chopping knife, steel 2 tang rocker blade, cast iron handle, illegible mark, American, c.1890. **$10-$15**

Chopping knife, 2 steel blades, curved hotdog shape, high arching bentwood handle, not marked, but probably a mfd piece, American, 6" L blades, c.1880. Odd handle accounts for value. **$35-$45**

Chopping knife, steel blade has nicely shaped shoulder & truncated ends, 1 tang, wood handle, American, 5-7/8" W, 19th C. **$40-$50**

Chopping knife, steel blade with tang split at top so the **Y** gives extra strength to handle, like an inverted wishbone tang, prob. American, 5" W blade, mid 19th C. **$40-$50**

Chopping knife, steel with upside-down **Y** or wishbone tang, wooden handle, deep double rocker blades have truncated ends, American, 6" H x 5-3/4" W, early 20th C. **$25-$32**

Chopping knife, steel crescent blade, single tang with wooden handle set crooked on it, angle makes it more comfortable to use, prob. American, 5-3/4" W, mid 19th C. **$50-$60**

Chopping knife, steel, ovoid blade pivots for dual purpose: one edge makes scalloped cuts, other minces; wood handle, filed or chiseled tooling on shaft, American, 6-1/2" H x 6-1/4" W, 19th C. **$35-$45**

Chopping knife, steel rocker blade, 2 hander has fat wood crosswise knob at each end, marked "9," American, 9-1/2" W, 1870s. Similar one has been made, with stainless steel blades,

I-32. Chopping knives with crescent blades. *Big beauty at* (**L**) *hand-forged iron, single tang branched to 2 before inserting in wood handle. 8" H x 9-1/4" L blade, early 19th C. Top* (**R**) *Commercially made, 6-3/8" H x 7-1/2" W, prob. last third 19th C. Lower* (**R**) *Hand-forged, unusual curved wood handle fits hand comfortably. Collection of Meryle Evans.* $100-$200; $25 or so; $55-$70

since c.1950s by Hoan Products in NJ — in Italy these are called a *mezzaluna* or half-moon. **$30-$40**

Chopping knife, steel rocker blade in fat sausage or pickle shape, top side has small section of saw teeth, rosette rivet points on blade, basketwork-looking cast iron handle, like a heat-dissipating stove lid lifter handle, American, 6-1/2" W, 19th C. **$20-$25**

Chopping knife, steel rocker blade with truncated ends, single tang, bullet-ended turned cylindrical handle assembled from discs of varying widths & different materials — including ivory, ebony & other wood, English (?), 7" H, prob. craftsman-made, mid 20th C. **$145-$160**

Chopping knife, steel sausage-shape blade riveted to wooden handle 3 times the height of the blade, cutout hand hold in wood, American, 7" H x 8" W overall, early 19th C. **$60-$85**

Chopping knife, steel & wood, 2 blades, "Hercules," early 20th C. **$20-$25**

Chopping knife, turned wood **T** handle, single wide tang, deep nearly rectangular blade with rounded corners, marked "W. Butcher," well known iron plane maker, mid to 3rd quarter 19th C. **$50-$65**

Chopping knife, cast steel & wood, rocker blade, large fat handle fits comfortably in hand, American, late 19th C. **$15-$20**

Chopping knife, forged blade, beautiful arrow-tipped tang, turned wooden handle, American (?), 19th C. **$50-$75**

Chopping knife, forged iron, single tang, wide crescent blade, crude wood handle, American (?), 7-1/2" W, early 19th C. **$55-$70**

Chopping knife, half circle forged iron blade, the top, non-cutting edge, fancifully scalloped like waves, riveted to fancy carved wooden handle rather like a saw handle, American (?), 8-1/2" H x 6-1/2" W, early to mid 19th C. **$85-$100**

Chopping knife, nickeled steel, tubular handle, deep rocker blade with flat tangs going up to handle, very modern looking, American, 4-5/8" H x 5-1/4" W, c.1910. **$15-$20**

Chopping knife, wrought iron in elongated bell shape, wood crosswise handle crammed down on short tang, American (?), 5-1/4" L, 18th C. The iron is badly pitted, the form is beautiful. I bought it at auction of Keillor Family Collection, once probably the largest, finest household tool collection (now dispersed) ever assembled in the U.S. **$25-$50**

Chopping knife, wrought iron, crescent blade has 2 wide tangs riveted to wooden handle, pat'd by "B. Denton," Auburn, NY, about 6" W blade, 1850s-1860s(?). **$55-$80**

Chopping knife, wrought iron, half moon blade with longish tang, wooden T-handle, "T. Collins," about 5-1/2" W blade x 5-1/2" H, 19th C. **$55-$65**

I-33. Chopping knife, *with fancy cutout blade of wrought steel, and machined cast brass handle typical of English choppers of 19th C. 5" H x 7" W. I think these are usually overpriced, and should be worth half or less of great indigenous iron choppers as in I-32. Value range what's being asked:* **$150-$185**

I-34. Chopping knives, double-bladed rockers. (**L**) *Two heavy steel blades, ground & polished, riveted to steel shanks that encircle handle. Green enameled handle or plain wood. Kidney-bean-shaped blades 6" W, late 19th or early 20th C.* (**R**) *Cast steel blades, truncated ends, wishbone shank. Probably c.1870s.* **$20-$45**

"To Make a Cold Hash, or Salmagundy. — Take a turkey, and two chickens that have been roasted; cut the flesh from their breasts into thin slices, and mince the legs of the chickens; then wash and bone 10 large anchovies, add eight large pickled oysters, 10 or 12 fine green pickled cucumbers, and one whole lemon. Chop all these very small, and mix it with the minced-meat; lay it in the middle of a dish and the slices of the white part around it, with halved anchovies, whole pickled oysters, quartered cucumbers, sliced lemon, whole pickled mushrooms, capers or any pickle you like; cut also some fine lettuce, and lay round among the garnish; but put not oil and vinegar to the minced-meat till it comes to table." Eliza F. Haywood, *A New Present for a Servant-Maid; Necessary Cautions and Precepts to Servant-Maids for Gaining Good-Will and Esteem* , Dublin, Ireland: 1771.

● ● ● ●

Pickles of nuts, fruits, vegetables and meats were given a lot of space in eighteenth-century cookbooks. The corresponding ingredients in the late twentieth century would be conveniently canned (therefore preserved) pineapple or peaches, peas or corn, ham or chicken. You would find canned nuts, in liquid, in Oriental groceries, but most Western recipes requiring nuts could be made with freshly shelled, dry roasted, or packaged nutmeats.

Chopping knife, wrought iron, oak handle which is ovoid in section, tang inserted through simple handle then hammered over, neat little prickery shoulder point spurs just above half-moon blade, American (?), 3-3/4" W blade, late 18th C. **$125-$135**

Chopping knife, wrought iron or tool steel half moon blade, single tang, simple turned wood cigar-shaped handle, "Isaac Greaves," Basking Ridge, NY, 6-1/8" L x 5-3/4" W, mid 19th C. **$65-$75**

Chopping knife, wrought iron, proportionately small blade, 2 projections at top of each end of blade bent around & forged together to form handle loop, almost look as if they were originally intended to be tangs for a wooden handle before maker changed his mind, American, 5-11/16" W, early 19th C. **$28-$40**

Chopping knife, wrought steel with wooden T-handle, half moon shaped blade, marked "Coldwell," American or English, blade is 6" W, height including blade, tang & handle is 7-3/4", 19th C. **$50-$65**

Chopping knife & chopping board, forged iron & wood, the very thick wood cutting board cut in fancy outline, blade cut at top in shape of a trotting horse, with fat turned wooden handle "tail," prob. English, 7" H x 14-1/4" L, 19th C. **$500-$600**

Chopping knife & cutting board, knife hinged & mounted to simple wooden board, knife is not figural, American or English, about 16" L x 11" W, 19th C. Price depends on details, anything unusual or special about hinge or pivot part; gracefulness or length or interesting angle of handle; thickness of cutting board (a full inch or inch and a quarter plank is older than the 3/4" or 7/8" thickness of today's so-called 1-inch board); or shape of board. <u>Most desirable are figural knifes</u> (often in the shape of a horse, the tail being the handle), or at least ones with little extra forged details or decoration. Value range for this type: **$150-$750**

Chopping knife & cutting board, type that looks like food chopper but is often called a tobacco cutter, pivoting steel blade, remounted to thick chestnut block, other side of block deeply hollowed, showing where blade was mounted before, English, block 2" thick, 10-5/8" L x 6-1/8" W, 19th C. **$40-$50**

Chopping knife — See also pastry knife.

I-36. Chopping knives, *as depicted in two early cookbooks.* **(L)** *Very substantially made "meat chopper, for chopping and disjointing bones," in* Warne's Model Cookery, *London: 1868.* **(R)** *"Chop knife. Iron handle, steel blade." American Home Cook Book, 1854.* **$35-$65**

I-35. Chopping knives. (L) *Steel rocker blade, riveted cast iron handle with cutout, 5-1/2" H x 5-3/4" W, c.1890s.* **Top:** *Carved wooden handle, crescent carbon steel blade, 5-5/8" H x 8" W. Probably mass-produced, but on small scale, and individually finished.* **(R)** *A "Hachinette," from France. Carbon steel, wood, 6-3/4" x 5-1/4". Angel mark. Used by centering grip over blade's center, chopping down into smallish wooden bowl, which you continuously turned with your other hand. Think of this turning/chopping motion when you see I-58.* **(B)**: *Solid steel, with all-in-one tubular steel handle, c.1890s-1920s.* **$20-$50**

I-37. Chopping knife & board. *Forged iron & wood. Blade topped by cutout trotting horse, turned wood handle. 7" H x 14-1/4" L overall. Often referred to as tobacco cutters, I believe the boards would smell if this were true of all. Ex-Seymour Collection; sold in 1982 at Christie's. Picture courtesy of Christie, Manson & Woods International, Inc.* **$400-$650**

Figural knives, pinned to and pivoting around a chopping board, are often described as tobacco leaf cutters, although none of the ones I've smelled have any odor of tars or nicotine. Some have been remounted to the reverse side of the board, after enough chopping has made the first surface concave. I saw a horse one at a Connecticut show in about 1984 for only $95. I don't know what kept me from buying it, but I guess the price was *too* low; it was very appealing, but somehow it didn't grab me right. At the prices today, I guess I've lived to regret it ... a little. If it had been a serpent or a different animal, I might have leapt at the chance to buy it.

Chopping tool, iron fingers ride in a long slot & function, possibly as a blade cleaner (?) or push-offs, turned wooden handles, American (?), 14-3/4" L, there is a patent #1666. I don't know what kind of patent so can't date. If it's a design patent it is 1862, if a reissue patent 1864, and if a regular patent is the more doubtful 1840. And as I can't find this tool under Beef-steak chopper, Food chopper, Meat chopper or Vegetable chopper, it's possible it isn't a kitchen tool, but rather a saddlery tool for cutting leather. **$75-$90**

Citrus juicer — See juicers and lemon squeezers, this chapter.

Cleaver, figural blade of carbon steel, bird head forms hook at top front of blade, flat lead handle is a replacement, probably old, of missing wooden handle. The figure probably denoted kind of meat, by kosher dietary law, to be chopped with it. Russian or Polish kosher butcher's cleaver, 4-1/8" H x 13-1/2" L, turn of century. This one and its mate have a known family history, shared with me by owner Marvin Tanner. There are probably non-Jewish figural cleavers, although I've never seen any identified as such. **$300-$400**

Cleaver, magnetic tool steel, turned wood handle, "I. F. W. & S. Co.," American, 3-7/8" H x 12" L, blade 6" L, late 19th C. **$15-$20**

Cleaver, steel blade, wood handle, marked with a steer & "Wm. Beatty & Sons," Chester, PA, only 6" L, 19th C. **$15-$20**

Cleaver, tool steel blade with big hanging hole in top front, wooden handle, "Samuel Lee, L. F. & C." (Landers, Frary & Clark), 4" W x 13" L, pat'd May 1886. **$20-$30**

Cleaver, carbon steel blade, iron handle has cutout for fingers, simple, even crude in design, American, 13" L, late 19th C. **$15-$20**

Cleaver, forged iron blade ending in upturned "genie shoe" curl, wooden handle, American or English, prob. late 18th C. **$45-$60**

Cleaver & can opener combined, also meat tenderizer, bottle opener, bone saw, hammer. Steel cleaver blade, shaped wooden handle, other tools screwed to large front end of blade, adding desirable weight. American, 14-1/4" L, 19th C. **$45-$65**

Cleaver & tenderizer combined, steel, cast iron handle, "Tenda-Cleve," American, early 20th C. **$12-$20**

Coconut grater, handcrafted from variety of parts made of cast iron, brass, steel, sheet metal. Upright shaft is turned iron, serrated blades act like reamer when you push half a coconut against the turning blades. Brass & wood handle. English (?), for colonial use in Jamaica or the West Indies, 7" H, mid 19th C. **$150-$200**

Coffee mills — See Chapter XIV (Coffee, Tea & Chocolate).

Cook's knife, elongated carbon steel triangular blade, wooden handle, "Guelon," with trademark on blade of boy with ladder, French, 12" L, c.1920s. Worth more to a person needing a really good kitchen knife than to a collector. **$5-$10**

Cookie cutters — See the Chapter IV (Form, Mold, Shape and Decorate).

Corer, nickeled steel tube, half of which is perforated "to reduce resistance," has effect of toothed edge around top, fitted with stop inside so core could be pushed out, turned wood knob handle, sold by Spengler Specialties, NYC, NY, early 20th C. **$10-$15**

Corer & doughnut cutter combined, tin, doughnut cutter has strap handle, corer attachment fits into "hole-making" inner ring, American, 3" diameter x 3-7/8" H when corer in place, turn of century. **$12-$18**

Corer & slicer combined, metal, wood handled corer fits into handle of slicer, American, 8-3/8" L, pat'd Oct. 12, 1915. **$15-$22**

Corer, slicer, scraper combo, metal, 9-3/4" L, 20th C. **$15-$22**

Corn cutter, a half cylinder of heavy tin about hand sized, strap handle from top to bottom, across inside at heel end is narrow row of sharp teeth, the same distance apart as most full grown corn; above is a heavy wire which braces the cylinder & "presses out" the contents of each kernel after it is slit by cutter. As to why this would be desirable for fresh corn, the *American Agriculturist* says that the undigested whole kernel is "just as much a foreign body as a gravel-stone," therefore "careful parents and those not blessed with teeth that can crush and grind every grain, slit the kernels by drawing a sharp knife along each row, so the digestible and nutritious contents slip out." "Yankee Corn-Cutter," maker unknown, possibly patent of V. Baker for "Green corn cutter," poss., then, Otisfield, ME, maybe the one pat'd May 31, 1870, advertised c.1872. **$30-$50**

Corn grater, a little wooden bench-like contrivance on 4 turned wood legs, iron grater teeth & blade, American, 4-1/2" H x 11-3/4" L, c.1870s-1880s. **$55-$65**

Corn grater, arched steel blade with prickers, mounted over an oval hole in board, American, 12" L, late 19th C. **$15-$25**

I-39. Coconut grater. *Apparently hand-crafted from variety of parts, although manufactured ones exist. Cast iron bolt probably went through hole in table top. Brass handle with steel handle; heavy sheet metal serrated or sawtooth blades to shred an opened coconut from the inside. Quite possibly English for colonial use, perhaps in Jamaica. 7" H, mid 19th C. Located by Primitive Man, Bob Cahn, Carmel, NY.* **$150-$200**

I-38. Cleaver. *Steel blade with zoomorphic bird head. Flat lead handle replaces original wood handle. 13-1/2" x 4-1/8", Russian or Polish, 19th C. This cleaver, one of a pair used in preparing kosher food, was brought to this country in 1903; the handle was repaired about that time. Collection of Marvin Tanner. Priceless as family heirloom; very valuable for form of blade. Figural cleavers, generally speaking:* **$125-$200**

I-40. Corn graters, *or* **corn gritters** *in the vernacular.* **(L)** *Meant to slit kernels and release innards. Pieced, soldered tin, 3" H, strap handle, marked "F. A. Walker, Boston," so either mfd or imported by them. Rare to find Walker mark on anything. Picture courtesy National Museum of American History, Smithsonian Institution.* **(R)** *Nicely made, wood, iron slitting teeth & scraping blade. 4-1/2" H x 11-3/4" L, 3rd to 4th quarter 19th C. Collection of Meryle Evans.* **$45-$65; $55-$75**

Corn grater, crude, homemade, half cylinder of punctured tin stuck on a wooden board, dealer's tag said "Corn Gritter," which may be local usage or phonetic spelling, anyway it makes sense if you think of grits; maybe this was used for dry corn, not fresh? American, 18" L x 7" W, late 19th C.   **$55-$75**

Corn grater, wood & metal, signed "C. Frankenfield," Pennsylvania German (?), 12-7/8" L x 3-7/8" W, 19th C.   **$60-$100**

Corn husker, or **corn shucker** or **corn pick**, hand carved wood peg, leather strap, American, 4" L, 19th C, early 20th C.   **$12-$15**

"A Grater For Potatoes, Etc. — A reader has written in to show how a grater to prepare the potatoes for yeast may be made very easily. Place an oyster or fruit can upon the stove or near a fire, until the solder is melted; this will allow the top and bottom to be removed, and the seam to be opened. Open the large piece of tin, and with a nail punch numerous holes from the inside. A nail, which will make a ragged hole, is better than a regular punch; after punching lay the tin upon a block of rather hard wood; turn the edges, to give a place for tacks, and fasten to a board. A hole may be made in the board to hang it by. We have used such a grater for horseradish and other purposes, and it works admirably." "Household Notes & Queries," *American Agriculturist*, NYC, April 1879.

Corn husker, or **husking pin**, forged steel blade, homemade leather strap to fit around hand has extra loop for forefinger, mended with WWI (?) shoe lace. Pin used with the pick part to the inside of your hand, point up, so that you could guide the slightly hooked point with your forefinger & thumb, and rip down through the shucks while corn was still on stalk, to check the ripeness, or after picking before shelling. I have seen a few photos of them being held point down, as if you would stab & rip, which would be very dangerous, no mark, American, about 5" L, 19th C. Dozens of corn huskers were patented in the 1860s & 1870s, most of steel & leather, and there's a book on them — see Jim Moffet in my bibliography. Thousands, maybe hundreds of thousands, were made by hand of wood or steel and leather. A few fancy ones that were patented are corn husking gloves or mitts, to protect the hand, and quite a number of the others have some kind of protection at least for the forefinger. Some husking pins are for right or left hand, others specifically for one or the other. General value range: **$5-$20**

Corn husking hook, fixed to leather mitt, wrist strap, nickeled steel plate & hook in center of palm, pat'd & mfd by Clark (Edwin or Richard F.), Chicago, IL, 1910s-1920s.   **$7-$10**

Corn husking hook, with leather mitt, steel hook in center of palm, 3 straps to mitt, looks like Skinhead apparel, name stamped on palm plate "Common Sense Husker No. 6," pat'd & mfd by Robert N. Thomas, Shenandoah, IA, early 20th C.   **$7-$10**

Corn sheller, cast iron arms with turned wooden **T** handle; tool is threaded onto the cob held in one hand, brass springs keep grooved curved-end arms around dried cob, while other hand turns sheller round & round. When half done, you switch hands, then thread another cob on. By intention, kernels go in every direction — to feed chickens. American, arms 5-1/2" L, handle 7-1/2" L, early 20th C.   **$45-$60**

Corn sheller, cast iron, compact, geared mechanical with 2 large gears, hopper on top has smallish mouth but slants out to serve also as gear housing, screwed to shelf, or bench, "The Home," Livingston & Co., Pittsburgh, PA, mid 1870s.   **$30-$45**

Corn sheller, cast iron, cranked, adjusts for use as walnut huller, marked "Fulton," early 20th or poss. late 19th C.   **$35-$40**

Corn sheller, cast iron non-mechanical tool in shape of numeral 8; inside of each round half (one smaller than other) has 8 rather widely spaced teeth, fits various sizes of cobs, or for both ends of large cobs, American, 4" L, pat'd July 10, 1883.   **$75-$125**

Anyone collecting corn-related items would be interested in this club. In 1980, the **International Corn Husking Hooks & Pegs Collectors Association** formed to "collect & share information and tools that farmers used to plant, till, and harvest corn." For info: SASE to Millie Byrne, 1 Esti Court, Madison, NJ 07940.

Corn sheller, cast iron, screw clamp, "Little Iowa," early 1900s.   **$18-$25**

Corn sheller, cast iron with lots of openwork, crank handle, screw clamps, "Black Hawk," mfd by A. H. Patch, Clarksville, TN, turn of century.   **$18-$30**

Corn sheller, floor standing model for lotsa cobs, very graceful 4 legged A frame, top chamber houses toothed disc & is shaped like point-down bellows. Large cranked wheel turns disc, cob is dropped into mouth & is forced around inside by cranking before coming out another hole, picked clean. Kernels fall out funnel bottom of body into container, pat'd & mfd by T. D. Burrall, Geneva, NY, pat'd Dec. 6, 1845. He pat'd a sheller (this one improved?) Mar. 24, 1863. A write-up in *American Agriculturist* says, "We strongly recommend this machine to farmers, notwithstanding its cost, as an improvement in every respect over the common mode of shelling corn with a frying-pan or fire-shovel, by hand. Price $10 to $12." Nov. 1846.   **$175-$225**

Corn sheller, for dried corn cobs, cast iron body & turned wooden handle, cob slipped into sheller & crank turned, kernels to shoot out in all directions, made specifically for chicken feeding, F. & F. Co. (possibly related to Foos Mfg. Co., who later made corn shellers), Springfield, OH, pat'd 1869.   **$45-$60**

Corn sheller, for dry corn, cast iron frame with 5 stepped steel blades curved to fit ear, 4 wingnuts hold top half & bottom of frame together so blades can be removed & sharpened, worked by pulling ear across it, because of stepped blades you barely have to pull cob at all, longish handle could be clamped to table or work surface, supposedly Shaker, American, about 13" L, 19th C.   **$130-$150**

Corn sheller, hand held, scoop-like tin piece with cutter & strap handle, American, 2-1/4" x 3" x 2-1/4", late 19th C.   **$75-$95**

Corn sheller, hand held, toothed iron & leather strap, Carver, NY, dated July 30, 1873. A search of the *Subject Index to Patents* turned up nothing for this date, at least under "corn sheller," and it isn't a corn husker, so it is possible it was never patented, or that it is really something else. The hard part of of searching patent indices is that what inventors called something & what you think (or even know) it is, may differ. **$35-$45**

Corn sheller, hand held, turned wooden handle (like small dumbbell) has 4 spring steel wires attached to center to form large coil within which is a sort of metal scraper. Corn is manually worked through center. Dollar Corn-Sheller Co., Lima, NY, adv'd 1872. **$15-$20**

Corn sheller, painted cast iron, mechanical, with 2 cranks, mounted to a straddle board, one hand to feed the corn, "Family," Harrisburg, PA, pat'd Sept. 2, & Dec. 6, 1870. **$75-$85**

Crooked knife, chip carved wood, heart & diamonds on handle, blade has string-wrapped "bolster," American, prob. not Amerindian, 9" L, 19th C. **$95-$125**

Crooked knife, tool steel blade, crooked wooden handle carved with hound dog's head, much carved detail, small roundhead brass pin or tack eyes, New England, in style borrowed from Indians in lower Canada or Maine, 10-3/8" L, dog's head only 2" L, 19th C. **$175-$225**

Cucumber slicer, cast iron, screw clamps to table, completely vertical round hopper or chute is cuke-sized, blades cranked, "The Patent Slicer," mfd by Spong, London, England, 9-5/8" H, c.1920s or 1930s (?) poss. earlier. Another type is very like a cabbage plane, made of wood with a steel blade, but much smaller. **$65-$95**

Cucumber slicer, silver & ivory, oblong, like tiny kraut cutter, silversmith was Hester Bateman, English, 1775. **$1500-$1800**

Cutting board, elephant form, wood, 14-3/4" L, turn of century. **$70-$90**

Cutting board, fish shape, wood with burn rings like many cutting boards have (from being used as hot pads), American, 12" L x 7-1/4" W, prob. early 20th C. **$45-$55**

Cutting board, pig shape, burl figured wood with very nice patina, pig has rather more detail around face than usual, PA-German (?), 13-1/8" L x 7-5/8" W, prob. late 19th C. Robacker $300 May 1989 price is a bit over the money. Many pig-shaped boards have been made in the last 40 years or so. **$125-$150**

Dough scraper — See Chapter IV (Form, Mold, Shape and Decorate)

Egg opener, or egg topper, scissors style, nickeled steel (also available in silver plated steel), 2 round loop handles for thumb & little finger, curved "blades" with a number of longish sharp teeth on inside to pierce shell of cooked egg. According to 1890s ads, this was an "improvement" on their earlier model which had straight handles without finger loops, first made by Champion Egg Opener Co., by 1909 made by W. R. Hartigan, Hartford, CT, then Collinsville, CT, approx. 3-1/2" L, pat'd Jan. 4, 1887 & Dec. 22, 1903, sold at least to 1910s. **$6-$15**

Egg slicer, nickeled metal, wires, marked in shield outline "D. R. P.," German, 8-3/4", early 20th C. **$35-$45**

I-41. Cucumber slicer (underside shown). *Ivory with silver blade. 8-1/4" L x 2-1/2" W. Beautiful tiny thumb screws adjust blade. Supposedly Asian ivory stays very white; African ivory ages to mellow golden tones.* **$350 and up**

Egg slicer, plated cast iron, wire, lever action, mounted on a round pedestal base screwed to a countertop, sold by V. Clad & Sons, Philadelphia, early 20th C. **$45-$55**

Egg slicer, sheet aluminum, hinged top with 10 wires, very cheap construction, but nifty, American, 5" L x 2-3/4" W, 1930s. Extremely similar to this was one marked along the edge "D.R.G.M. Aust. Pat." and imported from Austria c.1910. I wouldn't be surprised if after the war an American manufacturer simply started making them. **$8-$15**

Egg slicer, well-made cast aluminum, cupped base holds egg, hinged slicer top is strung with 10 wires; by rotating sliced egg 90 degrees you can dice it, "Bloomfield Industries," Chicago, 4" x 4", c.1935. **$12-$15**

Egg slicer, wood & wire, heavy green painted frame, 10 slicing wires, no maker's name but ink stamped on bottom gives original price, 15¢, 4-1/8" L x 2-3/4" W, 20th C. **$18-$25**

Egg wedge cutter, cast aluminum, steel wire & spring, put boiled egg in cup, push wire blades down to cut 6 wedges, German, 5-3/4" L, early 20th C. **$12-$20**

Egg wedge cutter, cast aluminum, steel wire & spring, tripetal footed base, from which rises a 6 petal "flower" cup to hold egg. Push down spring-resisting circle strung with 6 crisscross wires, German, 5" H, 20th C. **$15-$20**

Egg wedge cutter, japanned & decorated cast iron, heavy stepped plinth base, cylindrical egg holder, the blades are set in a frame that slides down 2 "columns" on either side of the egg to cut it into 6 wedges. Sold to restauranteurs, but useful for families too, sold by V. Clad & Sons, Philadelphia, about 8" H, early 20th C. **$40-$60**

Fish cleaner, carved wood with small steel or iron blade, handle is carved & colored portrait of woman with garters, from Belle Isle, ME, 6-5/8" L, c.1880s to 1890s. **$250-$300**

Fish scaler, cast iron, "Champion," American, 20th C. **$10-$15**

Fish scaler, cast iron, "C. D. Kenny," American, 9" L, 19th C. **$20-$30**

I-42. Egg slicers & opener. (L) *Japanned & decorated cast iron, sliding cutter with 5 blades, to use in salad-making. c.1870s-80s, V. Clad, Philadelphia.* **Top (R):** *Slicer, for sandwiches. Lever pulls wires through. Also V. Clad.* **(R)** *Scissor-action device, an egg topper, "to remove a portion of the shell without crushing either the removed or remaining portion of shell." Imported by G. M. Thurnauer, NYC, 1904.* **(B):** *an imported aluminum & wire slicer, of type frequently seen, made in metal or wood. c.1927 catalog. (L) & (T-R)* **$35-$50;** *Others* **$5-$12**

Fish scaler, homemade using narrow wooden paddle carved from a piece of wood, 5 bottle caps nailed rough edge up, one cap reads "Reading Brewery Co.," others from Shenandoah Beer, Old Reading, etc., Pennsylvania, 8-3/4" L, early (?) 20th C. This is the kind of thing beginning to show up at folk art shows, with values maybe twice the "kitchen" market. **$12-$20**

Fish scaler, japanned cast iron, business end is slightly curved & narrow with 34 projections, handle is long loop of cast iron, American, 9" L overall, half handle, late 19th C. **$15-$22**

Fish scaler & knife, chromium plated steel with stainless steel blade, in shape of fish, bottom has perforated steel scaling blade, knife handle is whole back half of body & pulls out of front half sheath, "Fish-Master," "Made in U. S. A.," c.1961. **$10-$15**

Flour grinder or mill, painted heavy sheet metal, decal decoration, Arcade, Freeport, IL, c.1920. **$75-$100**

Fodder & feed grinder, cast iron, several steel cutter blades, "O. V. B. Hibbard, Spencer & Bartlett," ("Our Very Best"), early 20th C. **$20-$30**

Fodder & root cutter, or chopper, sometimes called a **silage** or **ensilage cutter** — an agricultural device used in barns to chop up culinary treats (root vegetables, hay, cornstalks, etc.) for livestock. Two types, both on high wooden frames or trestles: A semi-mechanical type with a levered blade that works like a bread slicer — you push the long stuff through & chop it into whatever lengths you like. Other type has hopper & crank & the stalks, turnips, etc., are put in & cut into small pieces or slices. This type's wheel could be fitted with a pulley to attach to a power source. Back in the 1870s, I presume the power was steam or a treadmill operated by livestock earning a meal. Various makers, some of whom also made corn shellers & other small tools. C. Pierpont (New Haven); New York Plow (NYC); Silver & Deming (Salem, OH); and Belcher & Taylor (Chicopee Falls, MA) are a few makers from 1870s on. I don't know if anyone collects these, but they are worth collecting. **$25-$125**

Food chopper, meat or **root vegetable chopper** or **hasher**, but called a **meat cutter** by the inventor, painted cast iron, tin canister hopper with wooden bottom, mounted to green painted wooden base with a cast iron ratchet gear. Crank and the hopper revolves, while the chopping blade goes up and down like a pile driver or oil rig, Athol Machine Co., Leroy Starrett, Athol Depot, MA, pat'd May 23, 1865 by Starrett. Various sizes: No. 1, 8" cylinder; No. 2, 10" cyl.; No. 3, 12" cyl., weighs 37 lbs; No. A, 12" cyl., weighs 43 lbs; No. 4, 15" cyl., weighs 120 lbs; and two even larger commercial ones with 18" and 20" cylinders. (**NOTE:** In German Glossary Chapter XXIII, you'll see translations reflecting various uses.) **$125-$350**

I-43. Fish scalers & combo scaler & corn grater. (T) *Nickeled steel, turned wood handle. A "unique culinary device . . . patented 1906. . . . Practically the best corn grater ever invented. For taking scales off of fish or scraping vegetables it can not be excelled. It is the first and only pineapple shredder ever." Montgomery Ward catalog, c.1910.* **(B)** *Japanned cast iron fish scaler. S. B. Sexton, 1930s.* **$65-$85; $10-$20**

Recycled. — A most amusing example of ingenious adaptation appeared in an ad in 1989. Long ago someone converted a Starrett chopper into a churn by removing the round pan part and building a wooden framework 18" H mounted to the 18" L base, with a plunger attached to the iron where the chopping blade was once attached. A small churn replaced the tin hopper: with each crank, the plunger moved up and down. Who knows now if it really worked all that well? For sale in April 1989 for $195.

• • • •

Previously invented. — Mr. V. Price, of Wardour Street, Soho, London, exhibited, at the Great Exhibition, London, 1851, "a chopping-knife for the reduction of suet, &c., into small particles. It consists of three blades fixed side by side, to the lower surface of a flat metal frame, which is hinged at one end to a fixed metal pillar or support, and at the other is provided with a handle, whereby the blades are alternately lifted and brought down upon the suet or other substance to be chopped, which is laid upon a circular wooden dish or chopping-block. Each time that the knife-frame is raised, a hooked rod, suspended therefrom, catches into the teeth of a ratchet wheel, and turns it partly round; on the axis of this ratchet wheel is a small cog-wheel, which takes into the teeth of a circular rack or wheel, fixed to the underside of the chopping-block; and thus, at each ascent of the knife-frame, the block will be moved partly round, and made to present fresh portions of suet to the action of the descending knives." Quoted from *Newton's Journal*, XXXIX. 132. in Andrew Ure's *A Dictionary of Arts, Manufactures, and Mines*, 2nd Vol., American ed., 1854. Mr. Price also showed a clothes washer.

Food chopper, mostly wood, probably homemade copy or repair (much less likely to be a prototype) of Starrett or Athol chopper, made up with decorative cast iron apple parer gear, also heavy simple cast 4 spoked wheel with very thick & rounded rim that looks like a sewing machine wheel but is the same as the Starrett wheel; the frame is cut out of quarter-inch wood, handpainted rather crudely in brown & gold (like Starrett meat & cheese press); tin tub nailed to wooden bottom, but no gear

I-44. Food chopper for meat & vegetables. *Also called a "steamboat meat chopper." Also referred to as the "American," the "Starrett," or the "Athol" chopper. Cast iron, tin, painted wood. Pat'd 5/23/1865, by Leroy Starrett, mfd. by Athol Machine Co., Athol Depot, MA. Two outlined shapes represent cutouts in frame of choppers. Upper one on post-1877 "improved" ones. 3 sizes — 8", 10" & 12" diameter cylinder, which rotated on ratchet underneath as chopping blade rose & fell. Three larger ones (15", 18" & 20") have intermittent gears instead of ratchet & pawl. This chopper was sold in Europe too, and shows up in books on English and German kitchen antiques.* **$125-$250**

to turn the tub, you have to turn it by hand as you crank, gear reads "Reading Hardware Works," "Reading, PA," 19th C (the Athol chopper was pat'd 1865). **$200-$250**

Food chopper, plated metal, screw clamps to table, works with crank, 3 discs for grating, slicing, shredding, "Kitchmaster," mfd by Chicago Flexible Shaft Co. (which Sunbeam was part of), Chicago, IL, c.1934. Chicago Flexible Shaft started out in 1890 as a manufacturer of sheep-shearing machines! **$20-$30**

Food chopper, tinned cast iron, screw clamps, available with 5 cutting or grinding blades & a wooden pestle, "The American," mfd by American Cutlery Co., Chicago, IL; four sizes, viz. #10, 8-1/2" H; #20, 9-1/4" H; #30, 10" H; and #40, 12" H, c.1920. **$18-$25**

Food chopper or grinder, nickeled cast iron, wood handle, "Universal No. 00," mfd by Landers, Frary & Clark, New Britain, CT, pat'd 1897 & 1900. According to a trade catalog, this came in four sizes: #00 for small families, #1 for regular family, #2 for large family, and #3 for hotel or market. All are about the same price, though maybe add $5 to $10 for the largest. **$20-$30**

Food chopper, grinder or mill, tinned cast iron, screw clamps, short shaft, rather large hopper, 4 "knife" discs (fine has 15 teeth, medium has 9, coarse has 3, and the nut butter cutter has close-set sharp diagonal grooves instead of teeth). "Enterprise No. 501," turn of century. **$20-$30**

Food grinder, cast iron plated with brass, unusual sheet iron trough or chute, screw clamps, large hopper, side crank, retains its fine perforated metal tapered cutter insert (probably came with several, for fine, medium & coarse), "No. 1 Fruit Strainer," "Vitantonic Co.," Cleveland, OH, 9-1/4" H, pat'd Feb. 15, 1888 (?). **$75-$90**

Food grinder, cast iron, strong & handsome, wedges to table edge or shelf, no screw clamp. Top plate that rests on top of table is 2-lobed like baby bottom or heart top, central PA, 9-1/2" H, mid 19th C. This is truly the first food grinder I've ever coveted. The late, much-missed dealer Darryl Dudash exhibited it at Hillsville, VA, late 1988. **$225-$275**

Food grinder, plated iron, hopper hinged to remove cutters for cleaning, "Russwin #2," Russell & Erwin Mfg. Co., New Britain, CT, 1902 patent. **$22-$30**

Food grinders, enameled cast iron, screw clamps to table, wooden crank handles, some mottled emerald green like malachite, others slightly lighter plain green enameling, one plain green one has red painted wooden handle, the other plain varnished wood, part of paper label on one reads "HARPER No. 40"; one of plain ones is still in original cardboard box, "National Mincer, V. Enameled, Spong & Co., Ltd.," Harper; Spong, London, England, 9" L and 6-7/8" L mottled ones; 7-1/2" L plain green ones, c.1920s or 1930s. Collected by Wanda Hegedus, whose daughter, dealer Nancy Conklin, Silver Creek, NY, had them wholesale priced at $35 and $45, which is way under the money. **$75-$115**

Food mill, and meat grinder, tabletop, zinc plated (ie. galvanized) cast iron frame, hopper & crank, a piece at bottom of shaft slides into cutout in base — a shaped & "molded" cast iron platform. Painted white, with white rubber feet, complete with various cutters & blades, in original cotton bags, "Rayflex Foodmaster," Rayflex Mfg. Co., Bridgeport, CT, about 7" H, c.1930s, but "patent pending." **$25-$35**

Food mill, cast iron, "Dana Mfg. Co.," (their ice cream freezers were more famous), Cincinnati, OH, turn of century. **$15-$20**

Food mill, cast iron, graniteware hopper, wooden pusher, American or German, c.1880s. **$50-$65**

Food mill, cast iron, screw clamps, "Keen Kutter #11," mfd by E. C. Simmons, 9-1/2" H, pat'd May 29, 1906. **$25-$40**

Food mill, cast iron, screw clamps, "Keen Kutter #10," Simmons Hardware, pat'd May 15, 1904. **$20-$28**

Food mill, cast iron, screw clamps, "Eveready #55," 8" H, 20th C. **$18-$25**

I-46. Cast iron working parts *of chopper in I-47. Has 3 patent dates: "6/5/1865" (probably mistake for 1866, the date for C. A. Foster's patent, Winchendon, MA); 7/11/1865; and "Jan. 31" with no year, but is 1865. Last 2 dates for A. F. Spaulding & S. M. Scott's patents, also Winchendon, MA). 8" H x 10" L. Cast iron but for steel blade & bucket scraper. From stock of David Antinore, at Brimfield, MA.* **$50+**

I-45. Food & meat chopper, *butchers' size No. 5, elevated on cast iron frame. 20" diameter chopping block inside the cylindrical can. From 1906 catalog.* **$225-$350**

I-47. Food & meat chopper similar to the Starrett. *Picture from Henry Scammell's* Treasure-House of Knowledge, *1890. "Indispensable where sausage & mince pies are favorites. Men who buy mowing machines and hay forks cannot afford to let their wives work away in the kitchen with old-fashioned implements when better ones are to be had for little money. If any husband refuses to buy it, let the wife cut off his supply of hash and sausages on trial, and then take severer means afterward if necessary."* **$150-$200**

I-48. Food grinders & meat cutters. (1) *"Enterprise No.2" meat chopper for 1 lb. a minute. Not the most collectible Enterprise, but it shows the interior part which grinds & moves meat from hopper forward. 1905 catalog shows sizes 2, 4, 6, 8, 5, 10, 12, 20, 22, 32 & 42.* **(2)** *Tinned cast iron "Universal No.344," Landers, Frary & Clark. Hopper 5" x 6" diameter, 9-3/4" H, "geared down to get greater ease in operation," does 4 lbs. meat a minute.* **(3)** *"Ellrich" meat cutter, Ellrich Hardware Mfg. Co., Plantsville, CT, drawing marked pat'd 5/15/189- (has to be 1888 for "patent Tuesday"). 1892, The Metal Worker ad.* **(4)** *"Universal No.3", 4" x 5" hopper, 3 lbs. per minute.* **(5)** *"Russwin," originally Russell & Erwin. Pat'd Aug. 21, 1901.* **(6)** *Small "Gem No. 20" food chopper, Sargent & Co. 2 lbs.pm. For meat, vegetables, fruit, crackers, bread, boiled eggs, cheese, nuts, raisins, figs, etc.* **(7)** *"The Little Giant No. 410"*

cutter. Peck, Stow & Wilcox Co., Southington, CT. Stuffer attachment. 1892 ad. **(8)** *"Great American Meat Cutter No. 112," Hibbard, Spencer, Bartlett & Co. 1870s catalog. Case/barrel 5-1/8" L x 2-1/4" diameter plate. 2 lbs.pm.* **(9)** *"Diamond Edge No. 61," with DE pierced by arrow mark. Shapleigh Hardware Co., St. Louis. 7-1/2" H, hopper is 3-3/8" x 2-5/8", 2 lbs.pm. c.1914.* **(10)** *"Keen Kutter No. 22 1/2," E. C. Simmons. 10" H, hopper 3-1/2" x 4-1/2", 3 lbs. pm. Four cutter plates; holed ones for chopping from coarse to fine. Reversible one does fine one side, extra fine other. c.1920 catalog. The more attachments, the more value. Form counts for something too: (2), (3), (7), and (8) have the most unusual forms. Keen Kutter items have specialist collectors whose value ranges may differ.* **$20+**

Food mill, cast iron, screw clamps, "Winchester," turn of century. **$30-$40**

Food mill, cast iron, screw clamps, "Rollman Food Chopper #12," Rollman Mfg. Co., turn of century. **$12-$18**

Food mill, cast iron, screw clamps, "Chipaway Food Grinder," 20th C. **$8-$12**

Galvanized Iron and Zinc Plating. — Zinc-plating — also called "galvanizing" — is a rust-preventing coating used for some of the same applications as tinning, but it works in a different way. When "zinc" is used in a description of a houseware, it almost invariably means galvanized iron or steel, which is iron or steel with a zinc coating. You will see the word "zinc" used sometimes in a way that makes you think an object is made of pure zinc. In the nineteenth century (possibly even now) sculpture was sometimes cast in pure zinc, then bronze plated to suit the aesthetic standards of the period. I doubt if any kitchen tools are pure cast zinc. And the only zinc sheet metals are zinc alloys. Brass is an alloy of copper and zinc (sometimes tin is also added; sometimes up to 1% aluminum, which means more zinc can be added to make a pale-colored brass). Bronze is an alloy of copper and tin. "The process of galvanizing," states the unnamed author of *The First Hundred Years of The New Jersey Zinc Company* (NY: 1948), "or the coating of iron or steel with zinc to prevent it from rusting, is older than the zinc industry in the United States. As far back as 1778, in France, zinc was applied as a coating to iron utensils. In 1805, in England, a patent was taken out which recommended the use of 'nails coated with zinc' and, in 1837, also in England, the first patent on hot dip galvanizing was issued. The galvanizing industry in the United States started in 1864. ... Zinc is the most effective coating for preventing [rust] because zinc protects iron electrolytically. As a result, corroding agents in air, water and the soil attack zinc in preference to iron. ... This action is ... important when ... a small area of the base metal is exposed. ... The base [is] protected from corrosion as long as sufficient zinc remains." Zinc is sometimes called a "**sacrificial metal**" when used in this way, as it is sacrificed so that the iron is protected from oxidizing, hence rusting. "**Hot dip galvanizing** and **electrogalvanizing** are very different methods of applying zinc coatings, each ... suitable for certain applications." The writer adds that hot dip galvanizing is used "when the product is to be bent and formed after coating, ... wire is a familiar example of such an application." By the 1930s, at least, some zinc-plating was done by spraying on molten zinc (sometimes in conjunction with aluminum) to a thickness of at least 1/500 of an inch. I suspect that most "zinc" or "galvanized" products known to housewares collectors — food mills, lemon squeezers, meat grinders, vegetable slicers, washboards, pails, corrugated waste cans, and so-called "linings" of dry sinks or refrigerators — are formed *before* galvanizing, and therefore were electrogalvanized. Zinc alloy castings are found inside washing machines, refrigerators and some electrical appliances. Glass canning jars patented by metalworker John L. Mason in 1858 had the first threaded necks, and the screw-on lids for them were made of the relatively soft metal zinc, which imparted a metallic taste, but which created a good seal. In 1869 Lewis Boyd patented a glass liner (clear at first, then opalescent glass) for zinc screw-caps. **Zinked or Tinned?** — Visual and tactile comparisons must be made with tinned, nickeled or chromed objects. Worn galvanized metal tends to look dark and somewhat mottled, and feel almost like soapstone — very smooth, yet with just a hint of drag or grab to the touch. Really corroded zinc gets a rather unpleasant white powdery film on the surface. Sort of like mealybugs on the aspidistra.

Food mill, cast iron, screw clamps, "#7, O. V. B." Hibbard, Spencer, Bartlett & Co., (Our Very Best), 8" H, pat'd May 17, 1904. **$15-$25**

Food mill, cast iron, screw clamps, should have several blades, "Universal #2," Landers, Frary & Clark, pat'd Oct. 12, 1897; April 18, 1899; & in 1900. **$15-$25**

Food mill, cast & plated iron, red Bakelite™ or other molded phenolic resin handle, original box, "Acme Rotary Mincer," American, 1935. **$15-$20**

Food mill, cream painted cast iron, varnished round wood pusher, marked "P. C.," 9-3/4" H, early 20th C. **$15-$22**

Food mill, metal, saucepan-shaped, hook opposite handle, mark is old good luck symbol (backwards swastika) & "DILVER," Dilver Mfg. Co., —?—burger, PA, 8" diameter, pat'd Nov. 3, 1903 & Mar. 17, 1906. **$30-$40**

Food mill, saucepan body of plated metal, graduated or stepped ridges down into bottom, which comes off with bayonet fastening, cranked blades, choice of grating or straining surfaces, this one has only the insert for fine grating, looks like a Mouli but isn't marked, French (?) or American, early 20th C. **$20-$30**

Food mill, sheet iron & wood, handmade, with wrought iron handle, mounted to board, with various adjustments, no mark, American, hopper 4" D, board 16-1/2" L, early 1800s. **$250-$300**

Food mill, tin, 2 front teeth, green stained wooden handle, wire forms feet & handle, only 1 blade, "Moulinette," "Made in England," but a French device originally, "pat'd in all countries," 20th C. **$30-$35**

I-49. Food mills. *Two small cast iron screw-clamp mills.* **(T-R)**: *"Schroeter's Improved Grater No. 100." Pat'd 11/1903;* **Foreground**: *Small painted & decorated cast iron mill, an "Improved Schroeter" almond & vegetable grater, I think a No. 10. Schroeter Bros. Hardware, St. Louis. Other types to look for are the colorful, decorative, cast iron German-made mills bearing women's names — Anna, Inge, Victoria, Carmen, Amanda & Kitty — make a great collection.* **$25-$65**

Food mill, cast iron, tin hopper with wood pusher, screw clamps, "Edith," German, small, early 20th C. Many German mills had rather ornate, or at least very decorative, cast frames (even though the screw clamps were very simple), and many had women's names embossed on the frame above the crank: "Anna," "Kitty," "Lücilie," "Victoria," "Amanda," etc.   **$20-$25**

Food mill, cast iron, 2 cutters (one of which reverses coarse to fine, other is marked "Universal Bread Crumber"), "Universal," Landers, Frary & Clark, pat'd 1897 & 1899.   **$25-$30**

Food or meat grinder, cast metal, steel, Winchester #W33, 20th C. Winchester made several sizes, including #W11 ($40-$50), #W12 (about $60-$70), #W13, a very large one ($75-$90), and #W32 ($50-$65). #W33 is valued between   **$50-$60.**

Food or meat grinder, plated cast iron, screw clamps, opens to clean, Rollman Mfg Co., Mt. Joy, PA, advertised in 1902.   **$20-$25**

Food or meat grinder, tinned cast iron, screw clamps, in original box with different blades, "Universal #1," Landers, Frary & Clark, New Britain, CT, turn of century.   **$30-$40**

Early Hamburgers. — We tend to think of hamburgers as twentieth-century fast-food, but as far back as 1853 the term "dodger," meaning a soft, flat, pancake sort of patty (usually made with cornmeal), was applied to a minced beef patty called a beef-dodger.

Food press, cast iron frame & sheet iron rectangular press box, decoratively painted & japanned in dark red & gold, vertical screw press action with heavy iron presser foot, perforated insert for bottom, "Starrett's Patent Food Press #1," mfd by Athol Machine Co., Athol, MA, 9-1/2" L x 6-1/4" W, pat'd Apr. 15, 1873.   **$75-$100**

Food press, potato ricer, etc., heavy tin, 4 parts, viz. straight-sided kettle with side handles, bottom & first inch up side of seeding pan is perforated; it sets down into top of kettle; another insert pan has fine wire mesh in bottom; the "plunger," as it was called by the maker, is a thick wooden disc with a sadiron-type wood handle, that was 'skated' around to mash food through the insert pan into the kettle. Ads state that this would "revitalize cold potatoes" as well as seed strawberries, raspberries, etc., and could be used to strain soup or gravy, etc., "Stocking's Simplex Straining and Seeding-Press," mfd by The 4-S-Food-Press Co., NYC, NY, pat'd Feb. 10, 1903. **$20-$25**

Food press, white porcelainized iron & tin, iron juice catcher, lion's paw feet, lion's head design, marked only "No. 00," French, 8-3/4" H, 19th C.   **$100-$150**

Fruit baller, 2 red wooden turned handles, nickeled steel lever handles terminate in hinged perforated cutting ring, used by pulling handles apart to cause hinged blade to scoop out ball of melon, American, 5-1/4" L, with open ring blade 1-1/2" diameter, pat'd Mar. 29, 192-? [would be 1921 or 1927].   **$4-$8**

Fruit baller, cigar-shaped red wooden handle with a stainless steel shaft out each end, one with a small bowled scoop, other with an even smaller scoop; both bowls have a small air release hole, probably Androck or A & J or the like, American, 7-3/4" L, 1940s.   **$3-$5**

Fruit & vegetable press, also called a potato ricer, japanned iron, cast iron levered handles, hopper looks like steam shovel, "Henis," mfd by Charles F. Henis Co., Philadelphia, PA, pat'd Nov. 1, 1881. The patent design for this, which Henis called a "Disintegrator and Strainer," had a perforated tin hopper like the steam shovel mentioned above, but the opposing presser handles were wooden paddles. We don't know if Henis maybe manufactured them at first with wood.   **$15-$20**

Fruit, wine & jelly press, plated cast iron, cranked auger-like bit fits into openwork tapered part connected to large bowl-

shaped hopper, 2 legged screw clamp frame. Ad copy from **1889** reads: "For seeding and extracting Juice from all Fruits & Berries. Every housekeeper should have one. With this press, can be extracted the juices from Strawberries, Raspberries, Cranberries, Huckleberries, Gooseberries, Elderberries, Black-berries, Cherries, Currants, Peaches, Plums, Tomatoes, Pineapples, Pears, Quinces, Grapes, Apples, etc. The seeds and skins are discharged perfectly dry. Nothing is wasted." Enterprise Mfg. Co., Phila., 12" H x 11" L (the #46 is 19" H x 18" L and has added value), pat'd Sept. 30, 1879, still for sale early 20th C.   **$50-$65**

Garlic press, cast aluminum, many 1940s designs, made in U.S.A., Italy, Taiwan, etc. Should be collected, but value very low.   **$1-$5**

Garlic press, wood, 2 hinged parts like a lemon squeezer but much smaller, American (?), 19th C.   **$35-$40**

Grape press, tinned sheet iron reservoir in black painted cast iron frame; downcurved tapered lever; lift lever to push wood pusher or foller down; 4 wide spraddled leg rests so press fits on various sized bowls or pots; includes 3 perforated tin inserts with fine to coarse openings, "Littlefield's," (or Little Field's),

I-50. Fruit, lard or meat presses. (M) *"Starrett's Domestic Press," "for corned beef, boiled mutton, tongue, boned turkey, head cheese . . . and for extracting juice from fruit & berries; also for pressing lard, cottage cheese, squash, turnip, &c." Cast & sheet iron, japanned & decorated. 3 sizes: 4" deep x 6" x 9"; 5" deep x 8" x 12"; and 6" x 10" x 14". 1870s.* (L) *"Enterprise," 2, 4 or 8 qts. Turn of century.* (R) *English-made "enameled iron fruit presser." 1895 catalog.* **$90-$150**

I-51. Fruit, wine & jelly press. *Enterprise Mfg. Co., Philadelphia. Cast iron, double screw clamp. Fruit put into hopper; when cranked through, skins & seeds came out tip; juice poured out of the long slots whole length of horizontal nozzle-like barrel. 12" H overall x 11" L. Pat'd 9/30/1879; sold for years. Collection of Meryle Evans.* **$50-$65**

I-52. Grapefruit corer. *It is, it is. For all you doubters — see c.1927 catalog drawings at right. Turner & Seymour, Torrington, CT, pat'd 5/26/1923, & poss. again in 1925. 7" H with 1-3/4" diameter corer. The "real" one, with wire handles, is the "hotel size." One shown in drawings is the household size, sheet metal.* **$4-$10**

English (?), 7" diameter, 7-1/2" H, with 14" L lever handle, pat'd June 16, 1868. **$75-$125**

Grape scissors, forged iron, stubby blades, long handles, American (?), 5" L, 19th C. **$45-$65**

Grape scissors, forged steel, engraved, brass spring, European?, 7" L, late 18th or early 19th C. **$30-$45**

Grape scissors, tool steel & black painted iron, longish handles with same size loop ends, stubby blades with broad flat jaws, one edge of one has cutting blade, flat spring steel insert holds stem until it can be dropped into basket, pat'd & mfd by S. W. Valentine, Bristol, CT, 8" L, early 1870s. **$50-$65**

Grapefruit corer, nickel plated steel, sharp edged cylinder with moving cutter blades inside, worked by 2 handles that stick up. Turner & Seymour Mfg. Co., Torrington, CT, 7" L, coring part 1-3/4" diameter, pat'd May 28, 1923, & Aug. 18, 1925 (?). Overkill for grapefruit, no? Collector Robert Rollman wrote "Have you ever heard of a grapefruit corer? What core? The size itself would preclude such activity for it would destroy half the fruit. The most common designation given in antique shops where I have seen these is a 'fruit baller.' Yet, when I tried ours on melon it did not make a very nice ball." Hear hear. In my first book I identified this as a baller, but I have seen actual ads for this from the 1920s, calling it a grapefruit corer. **$6-$8**

Grater, 2 parts, cylindrical tin hopper for food, steel cutting blade is marked, turned wooden pusher, "Spong & Co.," London, 3" H cylinder, tin part 8" L, wooden pusher 9-3/4" L, 1920s or 1930s. **$50-$65**

Grater, blue enamelware, demi-round with hoop handle opposite end with 2 steadying feet, 9" L, late 19th C. **$65-$75**

Grater, blue painted cast iron & blue enameled sheet metal, clamps to table edge, Art Deco-ish geometric pattern cast into iron, wood pusher, "Helvetia," 20th C. **$55-$65**

Grater, cast iron frame, screw clamp, cranked tin cylindrical grater for carrots, etc., pat'd & mfd in Montpelier, VT, by Enos Stimson, c. 10-1/2" H x 11-1/2" L, pat'd Aug. 14, 1866. **$60-$85**

Grater, enamelware, wide rectangle cut out at one end for handgrip, circular rayed pattern of punctured holes, bottom embossed "IDEAL," Czechoslovakian import to U.S.A., late 19th C. **$45-$55**

Grater, fixed handle is not reversible for left- & right-handed users, wooden handle, box says "For Nuts, Cheese, Farfal & Nutmeg." (Farfal is small formed bits of pasta.) "Mouli," mfd by Moulinex, French, 8" L, "patent applied for," c.1945. **$18-$22**

Grater, half cylinder of pierced copper mounted to board, unusual in copper, American (?), 22" L x 5" x 3-1/2", 19th C. **$135-$150**

Grater, handmade, half cylinder of punctured tin tacked to long narrow wooden paddle with lollipop handle, prob. American, 15-1/2" L x 3-3/4" W, mid 19th C. **$160-$180**

Grater, homemade mechanical grater in wooden frame, crank turns 2 flat cutout cast iron gears, which cause cone-shaped punctured tin drum to revolve, sheet metal trough under grater was put on with brads, American, frame 7" H x 11" square, early 20th C. **$25-$45**

Grater, pierced tin cylinder with wide strap handle bridging the top, this one has only 2 grating surfaces, fine & medium, but others have 3, including coarse, American (?), 7-1/2" H, pat'd 1901. This type comes in many sizes, from just a few inches high to 16" H, maybe even bigger. Sometimes the handles are of heavy wire. **$15-$35**

Grater, pierced tin half-cylinder on wooden paddle back, American (?), 10" H x 3-1/2" W, late 19th C. Age can generally be determined by thickness of wooden back, the craft or shaping of it, patina on the tin, and hand- or machine-punctured grating teeth. **$50-$65**

Grater, fairly thin sheet brass, punctured grating holes, plain steel handle & frame, marked "DRGM & DRP" in a diamond lozenge, the DRP possibly ORP or GRP, as it was poorly struck, German, 14-1/4" L, 19th C. **DRGM** stands for <u>Deutsches Reichs-Gebrauchsmuster</u>, the pre-1918 mark meaning registered trademark of Germany; **DRP** stands for <u>Deutsches Reichspatent</u>, after the division of Germany after WWII. This grater looks 19th C, so the "DRP" is confusing. **$85-$120**

Grater, punctured sheet brass, strap brass frame, a pronounced trapezoidal shape, reeded border (narrow ridge, size of slender reed or stalk) to grating surface done with a punch & mallet, moving it along bit by bit so rather uneven, English or German, 11" L, early 19th C to early 20th C (?). See previous listing. **$85-$125**

Grater, punctured tin, rounded rectangle, wide tin strap, held like curry comb, American (?), 4-1/4" L, prob. early 20th C. **$7-$15**

Grater, punctured tin with heart motif, carved wood hoop, American, 7-7/8" L x 4" W, c.1870s. **$200-$225**

Grater, punctured tin with wide tin strap handle, oval grating surface, held like a curry comb, paper label says "Easy to use. Grates rapidly. Safe and Sanitary for all grating purposes," "Bromwell's Greater-Grater," Saranac, MI, 20th C. Hard to find with original paper label. Such documentation is worth extra $$ to collectors. **$10-$20**

Grater, rectangular, aluminum, large center field is fine punctured surface, top has a few rows of large pierced holes for coarse grating, bottom has pivoting potato peeler of tinned steel, going width of grater, "Triple Helper," with profile Indian head, mfd by Chief Products, Los Angeles, CA, pat'd but no date, c.1940s (?). **$12-$18**

Grater, revolving, cast iron screw clamp frame, double gears, punctured tin rotating grater drum, very similar, except for shorter drum, to Enos Stimson's "Grater for carrots, etc.," American, poss. mfd 15+ years before appearance in 1881 cookbook. **$60-$90**

Grater, revolving, rectangular wooden box with lid, tin grating drum inside, 2 drawers below, American, 9-1/2" H x 9-1/4" L, poss. late 18th C, more likely early 19th C. Sold at 1982 auction: estimated between $150 & $175, rare & interesting, especially with the two drawers, but it made only $50. I vote it back up. **$125-$150**

Grater, revolving, tin, cast iron screw clamp frame, wood foller or pusher, "B M E No. 620," 13" H, c.1930s. **$15-$25**

Grater, revolving, tin & cast iron, very heavy duty large size, clamps to table, American (?), c.1880s. **$20-$45**

Grater, revolving, tin, wood & nickeled metal, 3 grating drums, screw clamps to table, American (?), c. 1925. **$20-$35**

Grater, revolving, tin & wood with very simple stamped sheet metal frame, knobless crank & 3 grating drums, prob. American, poss. German though not marked, 6-1/2" H, early 20th C. **$20-$35**

Grater, semi-cylindrical brass, with iron handle, English, 14" L, early 19th C. These have become a popular "smalls" item brought in by container loads. They are usually highly polished and quite handsome (and expensive). There is no evidence that they were ever plated. Decorative value placed on polished brass accounts for often very high prices. **$55-$125**

Grater, stamped & punctured tin, slightly curved, nice oval opening for hand, no mark, American (?), 9-1/2" L, c.1910. **$10-$15**

Grater, punctured tin, "Gilmore," pat'd 1897. **$10-$15**

Grater, tin cylinder with 3 surface grades, strap handle, American, 9-1/4" H x 3-3/4" D, early 20th C. **$12-$20**

Grater, tin, mechanical, with 3 grating discs that insert in frame & slide back & forth to fine or coarse grate or to slice, "Safety Veg-E-Grater," Knapp-Monarch Mfg. Co., Webster City, IA, or St. Louis, MO, 12-1/2" L, 20th C. **$18-$25**

Really Dopey Inventions.— I don't know where else to put this, but it's funny. From *Journal of the Franklin Institute*, Philadelphia, 1836, comes this description of Ebenezer B. Story's, Buffalo, NY, **grater patent**: "This grater consists of a sheet of tin perforated with holes, and placed in a box in a sloping direction, so as to make an angle of fourteen degrees with the horizon. 'The length of the box on the top is to be two feet one and one fourth inch. The length of the bottom is one foot eight and one fourth inch; the width ten inches, the height thereof nine inches. The size of the grater may be varied to suit the wishes of the person for whose use it is made. I claim therefore the invention of such grater, and such improvements as herein set forth and described.'" To which the editor adds, "A more trifling patent than this does not often find its way to the office." Yet it did happen. Amazingly uninventive inventions were granted patents in the early days. For more on patents see Chapters XIX to XXI.

I-53. Tin hand graters c.1905-1920. *Most of these are done in time-honored styles dating back 200 years.* (**T**) **row**: *all curved, almost half-rounds, with metal or wood handles, different feet, some reinforced.* (**B**) **row**: *two 4-sided combination graters with strap handles, 7-1/2" H. Next a cylindrical one, the "Midget," with coarse & fine perforations. 6-1/4" H. Last a 10" x 5" (also 13" x 6") half-round.* **$10-$45**

I-54. Box graters. (**T**) *Most likely homemade. Wood & punctured tin, porcelain knob on drawer. Could be hung from wall. 15" L, mid 19th C. Picture courtesy of the National Museum of American History, Smithsonian Institution.* (**M**) *All tin, with white porcelain knob on drawer. Mid to late 19th C. Picture & collection of Phyllis & Jim Moffet.* (**B**) *Linecut of one that's all tin, 13" L x 7", from c.1904-1910 Duparquet, Huot & Moneuse restauranteur catalog.* **$150 and up**

I-55. Mechanical graters. *Wood & punctured tin.* (**L**) **Carrot grater**: *"For carrots, &c." Cast iron ribbed gears, counterweighted cast iron balance wheel. Revolving wooden drum has square nails driven into it. Only place to feed in food is a carrot-sized 'mouse-hole' in front. No signs of use, no marks. 8" H x 7-1/2" L x 5-1/2" W. Mfd & pat'd by Enos Stimson, Montpelier, VT, 8/14/1866. Ex-Keillor Collection. There is in the Patent Index only one carrot grater listing: Stimson's.* (**R**) *"H. P. Arthur's Vegetable Grater," pat'd 10/8/1867, Martinsburgh, NY. Stenciled on top. Wood frame, metal grater drum, wood hoop & foller & crank. 13-3/4" H to top of hopper; 19" H to fulcrum of lever. Frame 13" L x 6" W. Both Collection of Meryle Evans.* **$175-$300**

Grater, tin & wire, 2 grating surfaces, a slicer & a Saratoga (French fry) slicer, "Ekco," American, 10-1/2" L, 20th C. **$8-$15**

Grater, tin & wire, 3 grating surfaces plus a slicer, "All-in-One," American, 10-5/8" L x 4-1/4" W, c. 1940. **$5-$10**

Grater, tin & wire, half is a woven wire mesh, other half is machine-punched tin, "Kitchen Novelty Co." (Atlantic City, NJ), mfd in Germany, 12-1/2" L, c.1890s to 1910. **$10-$15**

Grater, tin with wire handle, "A Gadget Master Product #8," "Made in U.S.A.," 10" L x 7" W, 20th C. **$8-$12**

Grater, tin with wood handle, circular grating area, American, 7" L, late 19th C. **$15-$22**

Grater, box style, wood frame fitted with drawer with porcelain knob, hand-punched tin grating surface set into frame, American, 15" L, prob.1830s-1850s. **$150-$200**

Grater, revolving, green painted cast iron, screw clamps, wooden handle, "Lorraine Metal Mfg.," 8-1/2" H, 20th C. **$22-$35**

Grater, white enamel, countertop, American, 19th C. **$30-$40**

Grater, wood & tin, "Favorite," 12-1/2" L x 3" W, c.1910. **$18-$25**

Grater & slicer, double action, wood, steel, one blade makes thin julienne strips, other makes 1/4" thick slices, American, 16" L, late 19th C. **$25-$40**

Grating machine, all wood bench-style frame & hopper, levered pusher, punctured tin drum, "H. P. Arthur's Vegetable Grater," Martinsburgh, NY, 13-3/4" H x 13" L x 6" W, pat'd Oct. 8, 1867. **$150-$200**

Reproduction alert. — A new tinned screw clamp cast iron mill for cereal or flour is sold by White Mountain Freezer Co. Large hopper, natural pale wood handle; it could be mistaken for an old one, although it doesn't look as old-fashioned as other White Mountain mills. Price of a new one is half again as much as antique.

Grist mill, for corn, cast iron, screw clamps, Arcade, turn of century. **$35-$45**

I-56. Herb boats, or herb crushers. *Cast iron with wood handles, c.1800-1820s.* **(T)** *18" L. Photo courtesy Litchfield Auction Gallery, Litchfield CT. Ex-Harold Corbin Collection, auctioned 1/1/1989 for $750.* **(B)** *Wood handles stained or stove-blacked. 17" L; 7" diameter wheel. Collection of Meryle Evans. Most likely Asian. See long value listings for more information.* **$175-$350+**

Grist mill, cast iron, clamps to work surface, great big wheel with curved spokes, mill & hopper are small & behind wheel, chute below, "Apache," mfd by A. H. Patch, Clarksville, TN, wheel is approx. 16" diameter, late 19th or early 20th C. **$65-$75**

Hasher — See food chopper, Athol or Starrett

Herb boat or grinder, also called a herb crusher, cast iron boat, bootjack legs, interesting because wheel is wooden & its narrow edge is ribbed, & has straight wooden handles; wheel possibly replaced original iron one. Prob. Oriental, early 19th or late 18th C. This one is shown in and credited to the kitchen of the Whim Greathouse in Time-Life's *Cooking of the Caribbean Islands*, and is probably an import from the Orient. The value below is not just for this particular one, but for one with an iron boat & handmade wooden wheel. **$135-$185**

Herb boat or grinder, cast iron footed boat-shaped mortar, rolling pestle wheel has 2 long wooden handles, wheel was operated by the feet in Asian countries, primarily China, where they originated (?). Another name for it is ship grinder. No marks, prob. Asian, 26" L boat, exceptionally large, 19th C. (A very small one with 10" L boat, 3" diameter wheel, was in a Nov. 1989 Garth auction. Smallest I ever heard of.) **$170-$250**

Herb boat or grinder, cast iron boat on bootjack legs at each end, rolling wheel-like mill or pestle, with long wooden handles stained black, sometimes called a **go-devil**, American, European, Chinese, one is 17" L with 7" D wheel, early 19th C. Another that does not have same bootjack legs measures 18" L x 4-1/2" W with 7" D wheel; a third, without bootjack legs, is 13-1/4" L with 7" diameter wheel. A fourth, advertised by Stephen-Douglas just as this book was going to press, has bootjack feet or legs, with a simple wooden "dowel-like" rod through the roller, and in their words "a most unusual embossed foliated end." This is a sort of shield-shaped tip to one end of the boat or trough, and perhaps had to do with how the grinder was operated — with the feet (?) as above? I do not believe any are American-made. **$175-$350+**

Ballast? — You rarely see herb boats; when you do they are always given an American provenance, c.1800. But clues pointing to a Chinese origin are impossible to ignore, and it is possible to suppose them ballast on early Chinese trade ships to America, beginning in 1784 with the "Empress of China" and continuing into the 1840s. Canton blue & white china was packed into the holds as ballast on tea, spices, lacquers, and silk & cotton cloth. So why not the even heavier herb mills?

• • • •

Philadelphia collector Ellen Blaw wrote me in 1986 saying "I have a friend who recently moved here from China ... who showed me her 'crusher' that had been her mother's, and her mother's grandmother. It is one of the 'old things' they brought with them from China; they use it for rice not spices. The feet on my friends' mill are shorter, the cut out arch is not so deep. I hope this can shed some light on this somewhat mysterious item!" The Keillor Family Collection had one about which Archibald Keillor said only that he thought it was American. He had traveled in China in the 1920s and 1930s. Carl W. Drepperd, in his *Primer of American Antiques*, wrote that these are "Chinese in origin but much used in America in the early 19th century." He goes on to say that the "operator [of the mill], barefooted, sat on a chair and rolled the wheel with [his/her] feet." Other names, according to Drepperd, are sow & pig mill, and ship mill.

Herb boat or grinder, wooden brick-shape mortar has boat-shape depression cut in it, rolling hardwood crushing wheel with long side handles. Like the all cast iron mill above, the Keillors believed this one was either European or Asian in origin, box 5" H x 12-1/2" L with approx. 7" D wheel, early 19th C. The late Archie & Myra Keillor, early stalwarts in the Early American Industries Association and discerning as well as omnivorous collectors of kitchenwares, tools, dairy implements, etc., died in the 1970s. Photographs of many pieces in their family kitchen collection first appeared in my first book. It was a great privilege to know them, and to meet their children, and grandchildren, who have collections of their own. **$225-$280**

Herb masher or beetle, turned maple with small head carved with concentric circles, American (?), 7" H, 19th C. **$45-$60**

Herb mill, japanned tin, sheet iron hopper, wood drawer below, small wooden handle on crank, American (?), 7" H, 19th C. **$75-$100**

Horseradish grater, homemade, wooden box, punctured tin drum, sheet iron cover with simple latches (appropriated from something else), American, 14-1/8" L x 7-5/8" W, 19th C. **$125-$145**

"Melon Mangoes. — Cut a small square out of each melon; take out the seed; shred some garlic small, and mix it with mustard seed; fill the melon full; then replace the square piece; bind it up with small twine; boil a quantity of vinegar; in which, put white and long pepper, salt, ginger, and mustard seed; pour it boiling hot on the mangoes every day for four days; put a little horse radish, and flour of mustard, in the vinegar the last day; when the vinegar boils, take great care that the mangoes are well covered; you may pickle large cucumbers in the same way, they are much esteemed as a pickle." Joseph Bell, *A Treatise on Confectionary*, Newcastle, England, 1817.

Horseradish grater, mechanical, screw clamp cast iron skeletal frame, cranked large tinned sheet steel disc with sharp projections, small iron shelf on left side supports radish or potato or root vegetable against vertical revolving blade. A "bike fender" shield covers half of disc nearest to user. Replaceable blade. "Distelhorst's," Chicago Nickel Works, Chicago, IL, c.1890. **$35-$45**

Huller or pin feather picker — See strawberry huller.

Juice extractor, yellow china pitcher, modernistic sharp-edged molded diagonal swags across old-fashioned round-bellied pitcher-shape body; reamer sets into top & is activated to turn by pressure of pushing half a grapefruit (orange, lemon) down on it. Also came in blue or green. Ade-O-Matic Co., Los Angeles, CA, 1930. **$9-$15**

Juicer, bright tin, bright green painted cast iron, mixer & juicer part lift off, "Made for the Deluxe Sales Co., Inc.," NYC, 9-3/4" H, 20th C. **$85-$100**

Juicer, cast aluminum, chromed & red painted cast iron, rack & pinion lever action type in stand, reamer cone has fine concentric ridges & small holes around base for juice, the Tilt-Top™ presser has teeth all around edge, "Juice-O-Mat," Rival Mfg. Co., Kansas City, MO, 7-7/8" H x 6-1/2" x 5-3/4", pat'd 1937. Improved models with colored bases, etc., selling in 1948. An ad placed by Bloomingdale's in 1938 calls this the "Streamline Juice King." It was available in ivory with red, blue, green or chrome; also red & chrome. Was Bloomingdale's licensed to use a name they made up? **$12-$20**

Juicer, cast aluminum, screw clamps, crank turns one of 3 different-sized bladed reamers around in horizontal position over large funnel, below which is put a tumbler or bowl, "California Fruit Juice Extractor, Sr.," Strite-Anderson Mfg. Co., Minne-apolis, MN, c.1929-30. (They also made a smaller Junior model in bright colors.) **$40-$50**

Juicer, cast aluminum, simple lever action, mounted to board, cup & reamer set at angle, Rival Mfg. Co., Kansas City, MO, c.1935. **$35-$45**

Lookalike alarm. — A 1976 Hammacher Schlemmer ad had a cast aluminum juice extractor very like the Rival, with pedestal base. It could be used, like the earlier one, for citrus fruits, berries, pineapple, grapes, etc.

Juicer, cast iron screw clamp frame, cranked ball-bearing gear under reamer turns the clear glass bowl & its reamer cone. Bowl has side opening to funnel juice into waiting tumbler; bowl & reamer lift off for cleaning, American, c.1929-30. **$30-$50**

Juicer, cast metal frame & base, rack & pinion lever action raises ridged conical reamer up to squash half a citrus fruit against conical upper cup, "National Juice King," National Die Casting Co., Chicago, IL, late 1930s. **$25-$40**

Juicer, electric, footed metal cylinder, pump-like spout near top, white glass (maker called "alabaster") bowl & reamer. 1929 ad copy makes us giggle now: "To meet Fresh Fruit Juice speed requirements comes along the perfected and proved Orange and Lemon go-getter known far & near as Sunkist Junior Electric Extractor. ... Not only a handsome donation [?], but much wanted because it snaps out a glass or a gallon of juice for breakfast — or other purposes — with alacrity equaled by no other method. ... [The] whizzing cone gets all the Orange or Lemon Juice without the usual work — and mess. Two instantly removable parts to wash under faucet." "Sunkist Jr," mfd by California Fruit Growers' Exchange, Chicago, 10" H, late 1920s. **$20-$35**

Juicer, for fruit, meat & onions, a horizontal press like small bench lathe, cast aluminum frame, the retainer cup & convex plunger or press, should have shallow aluminum holder underneath to catch juice. First the retainer pivots upright to place half lemon or piece of raw meat, then put back down into horizontal position to face plunger, which is moved toward the cup by turning the wheel. "20th Century Power Juice Extractor," mfd by the Album Mfg. Co., Freeport, IL, late 1890s, though it looks much more recent. **$50-$75**

Juicer, for lemons or limes, cast aluminum-like alloy, plier action, "Ebaloy Inc., 12-1-4," Rockford, IL, 8" L, c.1930s. **$15-$18**

I-57. Juicers. (L) *"Streamline Juice King," " rack & pinion action with lever. Red baked enamel with chrome. 9" H x 8" x 5-3/4". 1942 catalog.* **(R)** *"California/Florida" fruit juice extractor, for all citrus fruit. Entirely of aluminum — stamped or cast — the funnel bowl, removable aluminum strainer, reamer & frame. 13" H x 6" diameter. c.1909.* **$20-$35**

Juicer, for oranges, aluminum with reamer inside, crank at top, hand held, Knapps, 1930 patent #1743661. **$9-$12**

Juicer, green painted heavy stamped iron & aluminum, 4 widely splayed legs, hopper & reamer at top, side crank turns small geared wheel, very unusual & handsome, "Universal," Landers, Frary & Clark, 10" H x 5-3/4", turn of century. **$20-$35**

Juicer, painted red cast iron, black handle, chrome top, aluminum reamer & cup, "The Juice-King," National Diecasting Co., Inc., Chicago, IL, 9" H, 1938 patent #2131440 & 1944 design patent #138983. **$7-$15**

Juicer, reamer in sort of space station stand, cranked to work, stamped aluminum & painted tin, flimsy but as cute as R2-D2, came with red or green painted base, "Handy Andy," mfd by H. A. Specialty Co., Inc., American, 10-1/2" H x 6-7/8" diameter, pat'd July 23, 1935, although on the market since about 1930. **$15-$35**

I-58. Juicer & reamers. *All aluminum. Big one is the funny "Handy Andy," this one with red painted base. Others found green. 10-1/2" H x 6-7/8" diameter. Two-part one is accessory for juicer.* **$15-$25;** *small ones* **$2-$5**

I-59. Julienne cutter *and four steel dies for it, of 16 offered. Note eagle pattern of one. To use: cut raw vegetable in thin slices; lay a slice on the disc and press handle down. Then lay a second slice on disc & press, which forces first slice through. Meant for cutting carrots & turnips, etc., in shapes for soups, garnishing, etc. Probably French. See more in Chapter IV.* **$75-$150**

Juicer, red painted cast iron horseshoe base fits around tumbler, upright part has cast aluminum cup fixed at top, rack & pinion lever raises ridged reamer, with half an orange on it, up into cup to express juice, American, 8" H, c.1940s. A company advertised the "Mighty OJ" squeezer in 1982, a new version of old one. **$35-$45**

Juicer, sheet metal with green finished wooden knob, screw clamps, a triple extractor with 3 reamers, for grapefruit, oranges, lemons, even tomatoes! American, c.1931. **$10-$15**

Juicer, steel & aluminum, hand held, cup has simple wire reamer, domed lid with crank, hinged handles to be clasped firmly to increase pressure on orange inside, very small lip on side of cup for pouring juice without opening, Kwikway Products, Inc. St. Louis, MO, 6-1/2" x 4" diameter cup, 1929 patent. **$15-$20**

Juicer, wall bracket type, heavy cast aluminum with thinner spun aluminum reamer insert, crank with wooden knob, "The Speedo Super Juicer," mfd by Central States Mfg. Co., 5 x 4-3/4", c. 1930. The wall bracket is almost always missing, alas, but sometimes you can find the whole thing at a yard sale. The value is somewhat higher than the price usually asked. Value is **$8-$20.**

Juicer or reamer, aluminum, brass gears inside with stainless steel pin for reamer, wooden knob, 3 rubber feet, lift-off reamer with gear in it, "The Gem Squeezer," mfd by Quam-Nichols Co., Chicago, IL, 6" H, 1-1/2 cup capacity, "patents pending," c.1930s. **$15-$20**

Juicer & reamer, mottled garnet color Catalin™ plastic (like the more familiar Bakelite™ or other molded phenolic resin), reamer part screws on & holds in place a heavy duty screen seed-catcher, marked on handle "Ex-Squeeze-It" BCM, and stamped under handle "Catalan Company," Made in England, various patent numbers for different countries, c. 1930s or 1940s. Art plastic crossover collector interest here. **$22-$35**

Juicer — See also reamer and lemon squeezer, this chapter.

Julien cutter, or **julienne cutter,** for cutting sliced vegetables into decorative little flowerettes or snowflake-like patterns to float prettily in clear soups, cast iron with 20 different cutting dies to be inserted. 4 legs (including 2 long hind legs) all with holes to screw securely to work surface, lever action with turned wooden handle on lever, imported by F. A. Walker, French (?), prob. about 7" L x 4" H, with 1" cutting discs or dies, late 19th C. An American raisin seeder, pat'd 1895, is very similar to this, with long "hind" legs & lever action, so this cutter could have been made in the U.S.A. **$50-$150**

Kitchen saw, adjustable carbon steel saw blade in cast aluminum frame, very attractive modernistic form, in general outline ob-

I-60. Decorating & paring knives. *A very small selection. Scalloped ones, some German, some French, for slicing Saratoga potatoes, and raw veggies & fruits into fancy garnishes or for preserving. Also for butter — even "pudding" says one ad. Middle ones have guards. Bottom one is a "razor edge paring knife." All early 20th C.* **$10-$25**

viously a kitchen knife, in concept like a hacksaw, "Always Sharp," mfd by Charles Wohr, Lancaster, PA, 15-3/4" L, early 20th C. **$12-$18**

Kitchen saw, carbon steel, turned wooden handle, "Keen Kutter," Simmons Hardware, 13-1/2" L, 20th C. **$10-$15**

Kitchen saw & cake knife combined, carbon steel with wooden handle, top edge is saw, the along bottom edge is scalloped cake knife, "Victor," mfd by American Cutlery Co., 14-3/4" L, turn of century. **$8-$15**

Knife, wide steel blade, rounded end, cut out & painted wood handle is Black Americana figural black chef, American (?), 12-1/2" L, c.1930s-1940s. **$8-$12**

Knife & fork combined, tool steel, cut & filed, brass snake winds around blade & fork, handmade from crosscut saw, artisan Jim Webb, Hillsville, VA, 8-1/4" L, 1980s. **$15-$22**

Knife, parer & corer combined, tinned steel, in original box, "Castello's Sixteen Tools in One,"American, 8-7/8" L, 1913. **$10-$15**

Kraut cutters — See cabbage cutters

Lard & fruit press, cast iron, Griswold #2, early 20th C. **$40-$65**

Fork Feeding. — *The Young Lady's Friend* (Boston, 1836) advised: "If you wish to imitate the French or English, you will put every mouthful into your mouth with your fork; but if you think as I do that Americans have as good a right to their fashions as the inhabitants of any other country, you may choose the convenience of feeding yourself with your right hand armed with a steel blade; and providing you do it neatly and do not put in large mouthfuls, or close your lips tight over the blade, you ought not to be considered as eating ungenteely."

• • • •

Naughty Forks. — "Forks were not generally used at table until the reign of James I, in England [r.1567-1625]. They were, however, known in Europe long before this. The first fork mentioned in history belonged to a Byzantine lady, who, on coming to Venice as a bride in the middle of the 11th century, brought with her a golden 'prong' as it is called in the pamphlet describing it. This fork, which probably had only two prongs, evidently caused a great sensation, for St. Peter Damian, afterwards Bishop of Ostia, mentioned it in a sermon, wherein he severely rebuked the lady for her luxury and extravagence in actually taking up her food with a golden prong, when God had given her fingers for that very purpose.

"The preponderance of patties in these [Medieval] menus is probably due to the fact that fingers then supplied, to a great extent, the place of knives and forks. Spoons were used, but knives were not general till about 1563, and forks were not commonly used in England until 1611." Excerpt of "Medieval Cookery," reprinted from *Gentleman's Magazine*, in *House & Garden*, Oct. 1906.

• • • •

"Green Tomato Pickle. — One peck of green tomatoes sliced; one dozen onions sliced; sprinkle with salt, and let them stand until the next day; then drain them. Use the following as spices: one box of mustard [ground], half an ounce of black pepper [ground?], one ounce of whole cloves, and one ounce of white mustard seed. Alternate layers of tomatoes, onions, and spices. Cover with vinegar. Wet the mustard before putting it in. Boil the whole twenty minutes." Mrs. A. P. Hill, *Mrs. Hill's New Family Receipt Book,* NY: 1870.

Lard press, heavy varnished wood, nickeled iron hinge, corrugated inside 2 long paddle handles, American, 12" L, late 19th C. **$35-$50**

Lemon & lime squeezer, cast metal, hand held, "Quick & Easy," Erie Specialty Co., Erie, PA, 6" L, 20th C. **$5-$8**

Lemon & lime squeezer, zinc-coated cast iron, scissor action, compartment with holes to capture seeds, "Vaughn Co.,"Chicago, IL, 6" L, 20th C. For an explanation of **zinc and galvanizing**, see the long paragraph p 35. **$10-$12**

Lemon or lime squeezer, heavy cast aluminum, works like pliers, marked "Acid & Rust Free," American, 6" to 7-1/4" L, turn of century. **$20-$30**

Lemon reamer, turned hard wood, grooved end, nice patina, American, 9" L, turn of century. **$18-$30**

Reproduction alert. — A very well-carved wooden hand-held reamer, deeply grooved, with a small, delicately rounded point & well-shaped handle, 7" L, was mfd during the 1970s, and probably still is, to sell for about $7. It was so well made and attractive that it could easily be mistaken for an earlier reamer. Advice on buying antique treen (turned wooden wares, etymologically related to a tree) is very difficult, especially for simple pieces that are essentially variations on the theme of a stick! Hollowed out pieces are more likely to show signs of true age, with checks, warping, more variation in patina. Lehman's Hardware, 4779 Kidron Rd., Kidron, OH 44636, offer a similar, cheap one with a hole through the end of the handle in recent "Non-Electric Good Neighbor Amish Country" catalog. **$18-$30**

Lemon sqeezer, japanned cast iron, with separate, heavily-tinned cup which can be used separately as a reamer, "American Queen," c.1906. **$20-$30**

Lemon squeezer, wood, 4-legged bench, hinged top with pressing cup, long turned wooden lever, 2 inserts of heavily tinned sheet iron, possibly Shaker, 19th C. **$150-$200**

Lemon squeezer, all maple, 2 hinged arms, with holes in the concave "bowl" or cup of one part, American, 10-3/4" L, late 19th C. **$45-$75**

Lemons Well-Rolled. — "An old-time Philadelphia Housewife said yesterday: 'None of your new-fangled lemon squeezers for me. Anything, especially acid — squeezed through metal, such as many of the improved ones are, is very bad. The wooden ones do not have this fault; neither do those made of glass or porcelain. But they all have one fault that there is no getting rid of, and that is that the skin of the lemon is squeezed so that its flavor mixes with that of the juice. This is all wrong. There is but one way to squeeze a lemon, and that is the simple, old-fashioned way, between your fingers. Plenty of power can be brought to bear, particularly if the lemon is well-rolled first.'" *Ladies Home Journal,* Sept. 1889.

Lemon squeezer, wood on wooden base, hinged press, marked "The F. F. Adams Co., Erie, PA, for the Atlantic Wringer Co.," Erie, PA, 9" H x 14" L x 4" W, late 19th C. **$125-$150**

Lemon squeezer, dense, well patinated hardwood, oblong board base with decorative notches at both ends, 3 fat dowel rod legs holding 2 part squeezer above base. Lower part holds perforated female cup, upper hinged part has handle at one end with same notched decoration & male presser, PA (?), mid 19th C. **$135-$200**

Lemon squeezer, levered hand-held type, turned wood "drum" set in nickel plated iron frame & handles (also came japanned for less), white glazed porcelain inset, small pouring channel in wood rim, "Drum," Manning-Bowman, Meriden, CT, 10" L, late 19th C. **$45-$55**

Lemon squeezer, maple, hinged male & female halves, American (?), 10-3/4" L, c.1870s to 1880s. **$30-$40**

Lemon squeezer, maple, hinged, with porcelain insert, 8-1/2" L, late 19th C. **$30-$40**

Lemon squeezer, wood, hinged, 2 part broad maple paddles, 2 pottery inserts, hanging holes in both handles, German (?), turn of century. **$45-$50**

Lemon squeezer, wood, footed tabletop model, lever action, possibly Shaker — at least priced as such, 19th C. **$150-$200**

Lemon squeezer, wood (maple?), with extremely hard *lignum vitae* wood insert, American, 19th C. (*Lignum vitae* means <u>living rock</u> in Latin.) **$45-$55**

Lemon squeezer, wood with white porcelain insert, mark is eagle with "S" in beak, "UPW" underneath, for Union Porcelain Works, American, 19th C. **$125-$150**

Lemon squeezer & slicer, hinged 2-part wooden squeezer, iron stand with 2 cutting blades, American, 15" x 7", c.1900. **$95-$150**

Lemon squeezer, black painted cast iron, hinged, 2 glazed white china or ironstone reamer inserts, a loose cup with 4 holes, presser is screwed to the iron, not so marked, but pat'd by T. C. Smith, NYC, NY, 8-15/16" L, marked "pat'd Apr. 7, 1868." **$65-$75**

Lemon squeezer, black porcelainized cast iron, aluminum cup, levered hinged device, marked "LIDON," mfd by Gilchrist Co., Newark, NJ, c.1906. **$15-$20**

Lemon squeezer, cast iron, "X-Ray," mfr unknown, perhaps same (also unknown) company who made the "X-Ray Raisin Seeder," American, late 19th or early 20th C. **$35-$50**

Lemon squeezer, cast iron, 2 parts hinged, one corrugated "male," one fluted "female," not marked but from Matthai-Ingram Co., American, two sizes: 8-1/2" L & 10-1/2" L, c.1890s. **$25-$45**

Lemon squeezer, cast iron frame with fancy little legs, stands on countertop, slotted concave cup, long lever handle with enameled convex presser, <u>sold also as a nutcracker & food press</u>, ad claimed it was useful for 12 different kitchen processes, "All-In-One," Ford Mfg. Co., Inc., Newark, NJ, about 11" L, late 19th C. **$135-$160**

Lemon squeezer, cast iron, hinged, 8-1/2" L with 2-1/2" D bowl, late 19th C. **$15-$20**

Lemon squeezer, cast iron with glass insert, "King's," English, 1882. **$25-$35**

Lemon squeezer, cast iron with pottery reamer insert, hand held, "The Arcade," Freeport, IL, late 19th C. **$35-$45**

Lemon squeezer, cast iron with unusual glass cup insert, "Williams," late 19th C. **$35-$50**

Lemon squeezer, hinged 2-part cast iron with milk glass reamer insert, instead of more commonly found pottery or ironstone insert, American (?), late 19th C. **$50-$75**

Lemon squeezer, cast iron, hinged, "Pearl," American, 19th C. **$25-$35**

Lemon squeezer, iron, hinged 2 part, "Diamond Point," American, pat'd July 10, 1888. **$40-$55**

Lemon squeezer, cast iron with porcelain liner, hinged, American, patent applied for in 1888. **$40-$55**

Lemon squeezer, nickeled cast iron, tin plunger & cup, horizontal reamer action activated by long lever (what maker called a "positive spiral pressure"), screw clamp, small adjustable-height platform for tumbler is attached to a thin rod, "The Leader," mfd by Rocky Hill Hardware Co., Rocky Hill, CT, about 10" L, c.1908. **$60-$80**

Lemon squeezer, plated cast iron, hinged hand-held press: one half is cup with holes, & other half is fluted reamer, no mark, American, 7-1/4" L, 19th C. **$30-$45**

Lemon squeezer, sheet metal frame clamps to table, iron lever, cast aluminum perforated cup, concave glass "receiver," lever rotated to press juice, arm with ring holds glass tumbler, "Walker's Quick & Easy No. 42," Erie Specialty Co., Erie, PA, c.1906. **$50-$75**

Lookalike alarm. — In 1982, a kitchen supply shop in NYC advertised a hand-held cast iron lemon or lime squeezer, with lustrous black enameled finish inside & out, hinged two-part. It does not seem to have the little foot for steadying on counter. Visible in the photograph of it is a mark inside one handle, but I cannot read it. The mark almost looks like July *and* June patent dates, and this could be an exactly cast copy of one pat'd in the 1880s.

I-61. Lemon squeezer. *Wood with heavily tinned male & female inserts, small 4-legged bench with hinged male lid and lever action. Closely resembles early 20th C. hotel lemon squeezer; this one probably mass-produced on small scale, mid 19th C. Picture courtesy of the National Museum of American History, Smithsonian Institution.* **$100-$175**

I-62. Lemon squeezers. *Just 3 of many varieties.* **(T)** <u>*Lignum vitae*</u> *(very hard wood — in Latin the words mean living rock) cup & bowl in hinged paddle form, 10-1/2" x 3" (also came 13" L x 3-1/2" for lemons & 15-1/2" x 4-1/2" for oranges). Late 19th C.* **(M)** *A so-called "drum" squeezer that looks like small saucepan with lid. The "Janes," nickeled malleable iron frame, wooden presser, zinc-lined maple bowl. Pat'd 5/20/1885 & sold for decades.* **(B)** *Cast iron with porcelain-lined cup. Berger Bros., Philadelphia. 1895 ad.* **$25-$55**

Lemon squeezer, tinned malleable cast iron frame clamps to underside of shelf or bar, with lever in upright position so the lemon half can be put in place against reamer, which is also upright. When lever is depressed to right, both cup & lever move into horizontal position, cone & cup remove for cleaning, adjustable holder for tumbler, "Perfect," Arcade Mfg Co., Freeport, IL, c.1903. **$65-$100**

Lemon squeezer, white enameled cast iron, hinged 2 part, both cups have ribbed rims. Female cup has small ring base & its handle has a projecting foot, so it can be set down on work surface & hold the juice until needed, German, about 8-1/4" L, 4th quarter 19th C. **$55-$85**

Lemon squeezer or press, cast iron, a press with a screw to be tightened from above, juice collects in reservoir underneath, handle at side to resist torque of turning screw — for doing those really old, petrified lemons from the back of the fridge, marked "Landers, Frary & Clark, New Britain, CT," 7" x 8" x 4", late 19th C. **$75-$100**

Lemon squeezer & slicer combined, cast iron mounted to wooden board with "bite" taken out of edge at halfway point, long legged body with high tail lever, rack & pinion mechanism, had glass or china cup insert (this one missing), probably for restaurant or bar or soda fountain use, no marks on squeezer itself, mark is stamped into wood board: "Acme, The F. F. Adams Co.," Erie, PA, 12" H, pat'd Dec. 20, 1887. **$95-$125**

Lemon squeezer — See also juicer, reamer

Lemon wedge squeezer, silver-plated springy metal, in shape of abstract bird; lemon wedge fits between the "wings," which were then pressed together. Not marked. 4-1/2" L, 20th C. **$30-$40**

Marmalade cutter, cast iron, steel, wood, nice big one, probably for hotel or restaurant kitchen, "New Universal," Follows & Bates Ltd., Manchester, England, about 16" H, turn of century. **$125-$175**

Marmalade cutter, cast iron with japanning & gold striping, raised letters picked out in gold, a sort of cone with a wood pusher to move orange peel across blade, mfd by Follows & Bate Ltd., Manchester, England, late 19th C. **$125-$150**

Marmalade cutter, japanned cast iron, crank handle, clamps to table, "Magic," English, about 11" H, late 19th C. **$125-$150**

Marmalade cutter, cast iron & steel, screw clamp, cheap but serviceable, "The Rapid," Follows & Bates Ltd., Manchester, England, c.12-13" H, provisional patent #25866/32, turn of century(?). **$75-$125**

Meat & cheese press, brown painted cast iron in rectangular shape, yellow stenciling, tin hopper, Starrett's (Leroy Starrett), prob. pat'd by J. I. Danforth but mfd by Starrett, Newburyport, MA (?), 7-1/2" H x 9" L, poss. another size too, pat'd 1873, prob. Nov. 4, 1873. **$80-$125**

Meat chopper, cast iron frame, turned wood crank handle, wooden tub, cranked gear wheels move blade & scraper inside tub, pat'd by A. F. Spaulding & S. M. Scott, of Massachusetts. (Addresses in 2 *Patent Index* listings are: Winchester, MA, & Winchendon, MA.) 8" H x 10" L, pat'd June 5, 1865 (not in *Index*); July 11, 1865; & Jan. 31, 1865. **$125-$175**

Meat chopper, galvanized metal, screw clamp, "The Home #1," 1890s. See paragraph on zinc & galvanizing up in food mill listings. **$15-$25**

Meat cutter, japanned cast iron, tabletop style with horizontal cylinder, hinged top lifts off to remove blade drum & crank, bolts to table, one of O. D. Woodruff's two patents, mfd by Peck, Stow & Wilcox, came in "family" or relatively small size, & "medium" size, Woodruff's patents date to Jan. 10, 1860, and Mar. 9, 1869. Still being sold in 1890s, possibly into 20th C. **$100-$150**

Meat chopper or grinder, tinned cast iron, height of hopper & grinder adjust with side screw & telescoping vertical frame, screw clamps to table, very similar choppers had feet for tabletop use, "The Little Giant #205," mfd by The Peck, Stow & Wilcox Co., Southington, CT, brought out in 1890. **$50-$65**

Old Peck, Stow & Wilcox brochures I own have several choppers like this, but no 205, only a 305, as well as a 310 and a 320. An ad in a Dec. 1890 *Metal Worker* shows the No. 222. A June 25, 1892, notice (op. cit) shows the Little Giant No. 410, tinned cast iron, with <u>sausage stuffer attachment</u>. We learn that: "The patterns have been changed this season so as to permit the application of a meat stuffer attachment, which can be quickly adjusted to the machine. The shape of the knife has been altered somewhat, and is referred to as stronger and less liable to break. The regular series will be known as Nos. 305, 310, 312, 320 and 322, and will be prepared for the attachments, which are not furnished with them, but which can be ordered and put on at any time. The meat cutters when furnished with attachments will be designated as Nos. 405, 410, 412, 420 and 422. Another feature of the Little Giant is that two perforated plates, with holes of different diameters, are packed with each machine. All cutters made this season will be tinned instead of galvanized, which [adds] materially to their appearance. The company claim that the smallest cutter, No. 305, will easily cut 3 pounds of meat a minute." The notice didn't mention a 205; it was probably introduced later in the 1890s.

Meat cutter's glove, brass wire woven mesh glove, wrist strap, protection for left hand while cutting with right, American, early 20th C. Another crossover folk art collectible. **$15-$45**

Meat & food chopper or grinder, galvanized cast iron, screw clamp, "Saxon," Steinfeld Brothers, NYC, NY, pat'd 1904. **$15-$20**

Meat & food grinder, tinned cast iron, little hopper, screw clamps to table, relatively long crank behind, small family size, "Enterprise #5," Enterprise Mfg. Co., turn of century. **$18-$25**

Meat & food slicer, cast iron, painted frame & decals, handsome & big for stores, "Enterprise," Enterprise Mfg. Co., "1881." **$65-$85**

Meat & food slicer, cast metal, cranks, "General," 20th C. **$15-$30**

Meat & food slicer, screw clamp, "Eagle," 20th C. **$15-$30**

Meat & food slicer, tin, wooden handle, "Dandy," 20th C. **$10-$15**

Meat & fruit juice press, plated malleable cast iron, frame has side handle for grasping with one hand, fitted into this is cup with handle, presser fits into cup & is screwed up & down with a sort of cotter pin handle above, "Walker's Quick & Easy," mfd by Erie Specialty Co., Erie, PA, c.1905. **$125-$175**

Meat & fruit press, nickeled brass with wood foller, "Wilder's," pat'd 1906. (In 1984 I predicted some brass & flash dealer would take this piece down to the brass & buff it near to death, & price it at $100, it happened.) **$25-$45**

Meat grinder, cast iron, double barrel horizontal body hinged so top half lifts up, short crank, flared hopper, not marked except date, but this is an original J. G. Perry "meat-cutter," Kingston, RI, body 7" L, pat'd March 15, 1859. **$125-$150**

Meat grinder, japanned cast iron, mounts to tabletop, long 2-part horizontal cylinder, hinged top half opens to lift out cutter drum with crank handle, "Perry's Patent No. 1," Peck, Stow & Wilcox Co., small size for families, 1890s. J. G. Perry, of Kingston, then South Kingston, RI, had 12 "meat-cutter" patents between 1859 & 1869, as well as a "meat-cutting machine" patented Feb. 26, 1850. Look for ones made in the 1860s or 1870s by Perry himself, before he sold rights to P.S. & W. as well as Ames Plow Co. **$90-$135**

Meat grinder, cast iron, to be mounted to table, horizontal body, 4 feet, large mouth flared hopper, large "S" crank with long turned wood grip, "Perry's Patent No. 3," Ames Plow Co., 9-1/2" L, patent ext. Feb. 28, 1864, poss. made much later. **$100-$135**

Meat grinder, cast iron painted red, white enameled hopper interior, wood crank handle, only one blade (for medium to coarse), "Aalwerke #5, R AALEN," German or Dutch, 9" H, late 19th C. **$20-$30**

Meat grinder, cast iron, screw clamps to table, "Gem Chopper," Sargent & Co., NYC, NY, large size, pat'd March 8, 1892. **$30-$42**

Meat grinder, cast metal, white porcelainized hopper, "Harras #52," German, turn of century or early 20th C. **$35-$45**

Meat grinder, cast & sheet iron, cranked, screw clamp, oblong hopper, short tapered perforated tubular blade, worm screw action pushes meat against & through holes, "Perfection" American Machine Co., Philadelphia, 3 sizes: #1, 2 & 3, pat'd May 7, 1889. **$25-$50**

Meat grinder, homemade, oblong wooden box with lift-off top, forged iron cutting blades on long wooden axle inside, forged iron crank, described by dealer Ron Motter, Erma's Attic, Athens, OH, as having a "bone bushing." Marked "A. F.," American (?), about 16" L, dated 1842. **$200-$250**

"Bermuda Onions, Stuffed. — Make a round hole in the upper end of each, dig out at least half of the contents; set in a dish covered with warm, slightly salted water, and bring to a simmer. Throw away the water; carefully fill the onions with minced poultry or veal, put a bit of butter in the dish to prevent burning, scatter fine crumbs thickly over the onions, and bake, covered, a half hour." Marion Harland, *House & Home, a Complete Housewife's Guide*, Phila., 1889.

Meat grinder, large size for butchers, cast iron horizontal cylinder, flared hopper opening in top, 4 bolting legs, flywheel at end has turned wood knob, "New Triumph #634," Peck, Stow & Wilcox, Southington, CT, pat'd Apr. 19, 1892 & Sept. 3, 1895. **$100-$135**

Meat grinder, nickeled cast iron, screw clamps to table, thumb screw is heavy wire or small rod bent in rounded triangle (a sign of late date), different face plates for fine to coarse grinding, Chop-Rite #0, Choprite Mfg. Co., Pottstown, PA, this one late 20thC, but in production since 1870 (as "Enterprise"). The plating, the material of the knob on the crank, & the material and form of the thumb screw are all clues to age. Oldest would be marked "Enterprise," and would have by now dull plating, worn in many places, turned wood knob, and probably a cast iron rather openwork fancy screw. Latest have shiny plating, plastic knob, and the above-described simple screw. **$20-$30**

Meat grinder, plated cast iron, very simple long barrel, widely flared hopper, spraddled 2 leg screw clamp, worm screw cutter with crank, 2 interchangeable plates with fine or medium perforations to clamp on front, barrel & hopper pull up out of clamp base when thumbscrew loosened, "Family No. 1," Ellrich Hardware Mfg. Co., Plantsville, CT, pat'd May 15, 1888. **$30-$45**

Meat grinder & juicer, cast iron, marked only "No. 1," Canadian, 1901. **$15-$20**

Meat grinder wingnut wrench, cast iron, loop handle with elongated teardrop opening, business end almost half the length, & has a long cutout with rounded ends, & a larger round cutout midway that fits over wingnut, American, 4-1/2" L, turn of century. **$10-$15**

Meat juice extractor, also for fruit, tinned cast iron, large hopper, frame & hopper one piece, long tapered cylinder into which the grinding or pressing part inserts & turns; holes in bottom only to allow juice to drip into waiting bowl. Pulp or fibrin exits front into waiting receptacle, "Enterprise #21," Enterprise Mfg. Co., 12" H x 9" L, c.1880s, still selling early 20th C. Catalog of c.1905 states, "The use of meat juice for medicinal purposes is a growing one, and is recommended for the aged, delicate infants and invalids, in all cases where complete nourishment is required in a concentrated form." **$30-$50**

Lookalike alarm. — A sausage stuffer & lard & fruit press marked "CHOPRITE" [CHOP-RITE?] is still being sold. It bolts to a table top or board. Lehman's Hardware & Appliances, 4779 Kidron Rd., Kidron, OH, 44636, offer one of these in their "Non-Electric Good Neighbor Amish Country" catalog. Lehman's say "The original all-cast iron press you've seen in antique stores — built to last for generations." Lehman's also has the "Chop-Rite" small grinders, one screw clamped, one with horizontal barrel and 4 legs to be bolted down, in Nos. 5, 10, 12, 22, and 32. They also sell parts and say that "All Chop-Rite parts will interchange with Enterprise parts IF you have the same model number."

Meat mincer, cast iron, double barrel body with large mouth, widely flared hopper at crank end, tube out other end fits onto sausage skin, or feeds ground meat to platter, latched hinged top, "Hale," pat'd by A. W. Hale, New Britain, CT, pat'd Mar. 15, 1859. In the early 20th C. this same meat cutter was sold (and the rights probably owned) by V. Clad & Sons of Philadelphia. **$90-$150**

Meat press, cast iron, 3 parts: cup, reamer & screw-action press, "Columbia #2," Landers, Frary & Clark, 19th C. **$85-$115**

Meat press, cast iron frame screw clamps to table, T-bar screw at top attached to press plate, removable cup is shaped like spade & set at 45 degree angle within frame, it has pointed front end with long slot to let out juice, "cannot clog up as in perforated pans, or soak back as is often the case. As a result more juice is obtained." "Quick & Easy," Erie Specialty Co., Erie, PA, c.1905. **$55-$80**

Meat press, enameled cast iron, cobalt outside, white inside, 2 hinged parts, corrugated inside, hollow cast longish handles, hand-held plier action, no marks, 8" L, turn of century. **$85-$125**

Meat slicer, cast iron, painted & decorated with gilt scrolls, mounted on small piece of wood, adjustable steel blades, cast iron handle looks like turned wood — the foundry casting pattern for it undoubtedly was. American (?), 17-1/2" L, pat'd May 15, 1894. **$85-$100**

Meat slicer, white enameled metal, wood handle, "General #208," American , 20th C. **$35-$45**

Meat tenderizer, all wood with 6 sharp points carved on business end, American (?), 9" L, late 19th or early 20th C. **$15-$20**

Meat tenderizer, (also called: bovinizer, meat fret, pounder, or tenderer), hand-held tool with round head fitted with 52 steel knife points; upright handle, spring-activated plate with holes through which the points pass with each downward jabbing pound, the spring pushes the plate back down, clearing the meat from the points, "Henis Bovinizer" mfd by William G. Henis' Sons & Co., Philadelphia, PA, pat'd Aug. 20, 1907. **$35-$55**

Henis also made a restaurant version with a long levered action, a stationary holey plate, and below it on a platform of the frame a wooden cutting board. Another device that looks something like a chopping knife with a double row of 9 very sharp steel blades, set in cast iron, with turned wood handle, was offered as a subscription premium in the May 1883 *American Agriculturist*. The maker isn't given, but it is called the "new and novel **Steakgreith**" in the ad. "Greith" is an ancient Anglo-Saxon word meaning "to make ready," a word that might have survived in some isolated American community. Perhaps the inventor used the word all his life.

Meat tenderizer, Blue Onion pottery, wooden handle, European, 19th C. **$125-$135**

Meat tenderizer, cast iron hammer with multi-toothed head, American, 7" L, 19th C. **$20-$30**

Meat tenderizer, cast iron hammer-like instrument with grid of tiny pyramids, American, 7-1/2" L, late 19th C. **$20-$30**

Meat tenderizer, cast iron head with 4 concentric rings of ripples, turned wood handle, hard to read name, possibly "Jachutti Co., No. 2," Philadelphia, PA, 8-1/2" L, 19th C. **$30-$50**

Meat tenderizer, cast iron round-cornered oblong frame, wooden axle rod stuck with many sharp steel blades, "Yale Meat Scorer," 8-1/4" L, patent applied for 1892. **$45-$60**

Meat tenderizer, galvanized tin with wooden handle, 4 rows of deep teeth zigzags, no mark, American, 4-1/2" L, 19th C. **$25-$30**

Meat tenderizer, iron hammer with waffled grid, wooden handle, American, pat'd 1892. **$20-$30**

Meat tenderizer, turned wooden handle, white glazed stoneware pottery with delicate blue floral decoration, round head has a waffled pattern of little pointed pyramids, European, 12" L x 3-1/3" diameter, c.1890s. **$75-$100**

Meat tenderizer, rolling type, cast iron drum with sharp prickers or spikes, turned wood handles at both ends, with brass ferrules, stamped "Charles E. Miller," also some illegible numbers, probably the patent date, 12" L, turn of century. See similar bun divider in Chapter IV (Form, Mold, Shape and Decorate): probably made by same company. **$50-$65**

Meat tenderizer, rolling type, wood roller deeply carved with pyramidal points, heavy wire handle, American, roller 9-1/2" W, whole thing 12" L including handle, 19th C. **$20-$35**

Meat tenderizer, rolling type, small roller has steel blades set in it, long turned wood handle, American, 9" L, 19th C. **$20-$35**

I-63. Meat tenderizers, *also called* **tenderers.** *Clockwise from top:* **(1)** *Cast iron, rolling, marked only "pat appl for."* **(2)** *"Varty Mfg. Co., Chicago, pat'd 1/27/1885. Has 2 leaf springs to push meat off prongs. From the John Lambert Collection.* **(3)** *Galvanized tin, wood handle, 4-1/2" L, 19th C. Collection of Meryle Evans.* **(4)** *"Yale Meat Scorer," patent applied for 1892. Cast iron frame, wooden rod axle, set with very sharp steel blades. 8-1/4" L. Located by the Primitive Man, Bob Cahn, Carmel, NY.* **(5)** *Small rolling one has iron blades, wood handle.* **(6)** *Lawn roller type with toothed wood roller, wire handle, 12" L x 9-1/2" W. 19th C. Both collection of Meryle Evans.* **$35-$75;** *"Yale,"* **$150+**

Meat tenderizer, head is thick cast iron "hockey puck," one side has wide-spaced blunt projections, other has many sharper, closer-set ridges, wood handle, American, head 3-1/2" diameter, late 19th C. **$40-$50**

Meat tenderizer, cast iron, rocker action, has 20 pointed lethal teeth set 5 x 4, arched iron rod forms handle, American, 4" x 2-3/4", pat'd Sept. 20, 1892. **$25-$45**

Meat tenderizer, ironstone head with turned wooden handle, 14" L, mid to late 19th C. **$135-$160**

Meat tenderizer, saltglazed stoneware drum head has sharp modeled points in waffled pattern, thick turned wood handle painted black, 6" L, head 3" diameter, American, pat'd Dec. 25, 1877. **$75-$85**

Meat tenderizer, stoneware head with waffled pattern, saltglazed with brown Albany slip underneath salt glaze, prob. NY state, 9" L, pat'd Dec. 25, 1877. **$75-$100**

Meat tenderizer, vertical turned wooden handle, head set with 14 steel chisel point blades (used in same position as hand stamp), "Pettes' Beefsteak Tenderer," pat'd by M. M. Pettes, Worcester, MA, pat'd March 5, 1872. **$35-$45**

Meat tenderizer, white glazed ironstone with a waffled surface, turned wooden handle, 1890. **$50-$75**

Meat tenderizer & ax, cast iron or cast steel(?), meant for a wooden handle, head has waffled meat pounder on one end, sharp ax on other, American, head only: 5-3/4" L, 19th C. I hate stuff like this, being a vegetarian, so may be pricing low. **$10-$15**

Meat tenderizer & ax, nickeled steel ax or hatchet head with curved blade, opposite a tenderizing device with 3 rows of 5 thick teeth, wooden handle, comes apart for cleaning — wingnut holds head to handle, Tyler Mfg. Co., Muncie, IN, 10" L x 4-1/4", pat'd Dec. 5, 1922. **$15-$22**

Meat tenderizer, cap lifter, ice shaver & mincer combined, cast steel (?), heavy wooden handle, ice shaver part can be locked in at least 2 positions, very well-made but odd combination of functions. Bridge Cutlery Co., St. Louis, MO, 11" L, pat'd Aug. 15, 1916. **$25-$35**

Meat tenderizer & chopper, iron, homemade from old rasp, coarse rasp teeth on one side, finer on the other, has head & handle, late 19th C or early 20th. **$15-$20**

Mincing knives — See chopping knives, this chapter

Mortar, ash burl, nicely shaped with small pedestal base, American, 7" H x 6" D, early 19th or late 18th C. **$200-$250**

Mortar, hollowed log, bottom repaired with iron bands to hold age checks together, some kind of whitish composition (probably a clay cement) in crank on inside, rather thick walls & very beat up around edges, many insect holes & some dry rot, thoroughly "picturesque" & "country." American, 22" H, 19th C. **$95-$150**

"**Beating Hommony**. — Soak the hommony corn ten minutes in boiling water; then take the corn up and put it into the hommony mortar, and beat it until the husks are all separated from the corn. Once or twice while beating it, take it out of the mortar and fan it; that is, throw up on a tray or bowl so as to allow the husks to fly off. When sufficiently beaten, fan it until all the husks are out." *The Farmers' Cabinet, Devoted to Agriculture, Horticulture and Rural Economy.* Phila.: Vol. II, No. 1, Aug. 1, 1837.

● ● ● ●

In October 1850, the *American Agriculturist* published a letter from *M* on how "**To Make Hommony**" [sic]. The *M* stood for Maryland, where the correspondent was from. "I have so often been asked for our Maryland receipt for making hommony, that I send it to your journal, as the surest method of making it public.

Some gristmills have a way of preparing it beautifully, by making a trifling addition to the machinery of the mill, which beats the hommony while the meal is being ground; but many people still prefer the old Negro way, and many mills have not the new machinery. I wish I could tell the quantity of water it takes for any given quantity...but the negroes do everything by guess; and when I asked the man who makes it best for me, the only answer I could get was, 'jest 'xactly 'nuff... only don't let 'em make de corn too wet, dat spiles all.'

"Take a gum-tree or oak block, and burn or dig it out to the depth of twenty inches or two feet; rub the hollow clean and smooth, and you have the mortar. A wooden pestle, equally rude, is formed, into the flat end of which drive gently, (for fear of splitting it,) the sharp end of a large-sized wood cutter's wedge; the broad end being thus ready for breaking and hulling the corn. The best corn must be carefully selected and shelled; moisten it well by pouring boiling water over it; when part is broken up and hulled, it should be taken out of the mortar, and fanned, again moistened with boiling water, and put in again; this fanning and moistening,...and beating to be continued until it is free from husks. Spread it out to dry, and then sift it, first through a coarse seive, which will retain only the hommony, then through a fine one, which will retain the grits. The coarse meal that remains is excellent for cakes and puddings." (**NOTE:** now skins of the corn kernels are removed with lye.)

Mortar & pestle, carved gray marble, simple thick-walled bowl mortar with hexagonal sides, fat simple pestle, European (?), mortar 5" H, pestle 7-1/2" L, 19th C.   **$50-$75**

Mortar & pestle, cast bell metal or bronze, nearly straight sided mortar, with widely flared lip, bold square ear handles, turned with bands, long-handled pestle, mortar engraved "N.A.D.S. + K.B.D." with date, European, 3-3/4" H, dated 1770.   **$150-$200**

Mortar & pestle, cast bell metal or bronze. There were a number of founders who cast bells & mortars. In fact, the type of flared rim this one has is called a <u>bell mouth</u>. English or American (?), 4-3/4" H x 3" D, 19th C.   **$80-$100**

I-64. Mortars (L) *Rev. Larry Pearson of Snellville, GA, found this marble mortar about 30 miles south of New Orleans, on the Mississippi's east bank "lying in the mud off shore near an old fort below Shell Beach. This area was settled in early days by the Spanish." In the water or mud for maybe 150 years or more, it's surprising only one oyster attached itself (atop projection on rim's far side). 4-1/2" H x 8-1/2" across at widest points. Info & photo courtesy Larry Pearson, & Cheryl & David Hitchcock.* **(R)** *Lathe-turned mortar, with interestingly shaped carved pestle. Red buttermilk paint. 7" H x 4-1/2" diam.; pestle 9" L. Early 19th C. Collection of Meryle Evans.* **$30-$50; $140-$180**

Mortar & pestle, cast brass, straight sides with flared rim, probably for pharmacist, no mark, 6" H, 19th C.   **$50-$75**

Mortar & pestle, cast iron, footed, 7" H x 6-3/4" D, American or English or German, prob. 1840s to 1860s.   **$50-$65**

Mortar & pestle, cast iron, nice size: wider than high, 8" H x 9" D, 19th C.   **$65-$80**

Mortar & pestle, cast iron, mortar has flared sides & rim, American (?), 6-3/4" H x 6-3/4" D, 19th C.   **$45-$65**

"Wedgwood mortar — Mortars made for druggists of marble or ironstone are expensive, but one made of Wedgwood earthenware will answer all household needs." Todd S. Goodholme, *Domestic Cyclopedia of Practical Information*, NY: Henry Holt, 1877. Harrod's Stores, Ltd., of London, showed a similar mortar & pestle in their 1895 retail catalog. They called its material "composition." The mortar appears to be slightly off round, but perhaps that is just the drawing, which shows a rather big pouring lip. The bowl has a very small ring foot, and the pestle is the wood and ironstone ("composition"?) common to the type. This was offered in several diameters: 7", 8", 9", 10", 11" and 12". The bigger they are the thicker they are. (I saw one about 14" diameter that was well over an inch thick. Heavy as an anvil almost, and $350 in 1989.)

I-65. Mortar & pestle patent. *Called a "grinding & triturating apparatus" by inventor. Pat'd 3/20/1877, by Joseph J. Lancaster, London, Ontario, Canada. Pestle has rotary motion. If it exists:* **$400+**

I-66. Mortars & pestles of various classic types. *Most of upper ones are cast — bell metal, bronze, brass or iron (footed one at* **(R)** *is cast iron & called "goblet shaped" by seller). Stoneware & marble ones often have a small depression or pouring lip. Knobby projections aid steadying. Sizes from 4" to 15". 18th to late 19th C. classic forms. Most mortars & pestles are* **$35-$65**; *very large or unusual ones would bring* **$125+**

47

Lookalike Alarm.— Brand new white ceramic mortar & pestle sets are being made now. If you can put an old & new one side by side, you'll see differences. Generally, new ones aren't quite as heavy, often they are highly glazed on the outside of the mortar, and the wooden pestle handles aren't as nicely turned, have little patina but lotsa varnish, and don't fit as neatly and snugly to the ceramic business end of the pestle.

Mortar & pestle, cut marble, with 4 ears or nubs around flat top, for lifting, poss. English, or a French import, different sizes, 1860s-1870s. Harrod's Stores, Ltd., of London, England, advertised these in several sizes in their 1895 retail catalog. They came in eight diameters: 8", 9", 10", 11", 12", 13", 14" and 16". With them you could order a simple turned lignum vitae pestle with cylindrical handle part ending in larger head, which came in five sizes to suit the mortar. **$85-$125**

Mortar & pestle, heavy turned tiger maple, both pieces attractively figured, small or large end of pestle can be used, American, mortar: 7" H x 6" diameter, pestle: 9" L, early to mid 19th C. **$165-$200**

Mortar & pestle, heavy white earthenware, bowl-like with small pouring lip, glazed outside, inside unglazed, pestle with wild-onion-shaped earthenware head, with turned wooden handle screwed to it, sometimes marked on bottom, made by several potteries, notably Wedgwood. English, various sizes, 19th C. **$45-$250**

Mortar & pestle, heavy white ironstone, with wood-handled ironstone pestle, English (?), 6" diameter, 19th C. Added value: really big ones bring most. **$45-$80**

Mortar & pestle, ironstone & wood, mortar has pouring lip, American (?), 6" x 9-1/2", 19th C. **$85-$100**

Mortar & pestle, lignum vitae, the hardest densest wood available, beautiful graining — or figure, as it's called — & patina, American, 7" H, early 19th C. **$125-$160**

Mortar & pestle, lignum vitae, turned, with a great pedestal base, American, 7-3/4" H x 4" D, early 19th C. **$145-$180**

Mortar & pestle, lignum vitae, with slightly checked pestle, American, 7" H x 5-3/8" D, 19th C. "A lignum-vitae mortar and pestle will last for generations, and there should be one in every kitchen." Maria Parloa, *Kitchen Companion*, Boston: Estes & Lauriat, 1887. **$125-$160**

Mortar & pestle, polished cast iron, flared sides with big foot, decorative swag design around side, long-handled pestle, for candy makers, mfd by Thomas Burkhard, 1/2-pint capacity (came in 1 pt., 1, 2, 4 & 8 qt. sizes too), c.1870s. **$65-$90**

Mortar & pestle, tiger maple with a nice figure, 7" H, American, early 19th C. **$100-$135**

Mortar & pestle, turned painted wood, with pedestal base, well worn pestle with idiosyncratic worn places on handle, American, 7" H x 4-1/2" D, early to mid 19th C. **$65-$150**

Mortar & pestle, turned wood, dark patina, chunky, footed mortar probably turned from a burl, worn on one edge from long rugged use, mortar is fitted with a 1/2-inch thick dowel "leg," splayed downward from near the top, actually a handle to be grasped with one hand while pounding. The worn area on rim is to the left of this handle, so the tool was probably used by a left-handed person. Pestle has thick handle with beetle-like heavy duty head & small rounded mushroom cap on other end, American, 7" H x 6" diameter, pestle 7" L. Ex-Keillor Collection. **$175-$250**

Mortar & pestle, turned wood, with base, notable for height, American (?), 13-1/2" H, 19th C. **$75-$100**

Mortar & pestle, very large hollowed-out log with tall wooden pestle, top of log is waist high, hands must be raised above shoulders to use pestle or pounder, American, 19th C. **$350-$500**

Mortar & pestle, turned maple with footed mortar, some dry checks in mortar, 7" H, 19th C. **$60-$75**

Mortar & pestle, white stoneware mortar with slightly flared sides, rounded rim & pouring lip, wood-handled stoneware pestle, Maddock's Sons, with anchor trademark, Trenton, NJ, mortar 2-3/4" H x 4-1/2" diameter, pestle 6-3/4" L, late 19th C or early 20th. **$35-$50**

Noodle cutter — See Chapter IV (Form, Mold, Shape and Decorate)

Nutcrackers or Nutcracks.— Although for some people even today a molar or a wisdom tooth is adequate for the job, probably a rock and a hard place comprised the first or earliest nutcracking contrivance. Thus we find many variations on the anvil and hammer theme. The nutcrackers we are most familiar with are mechanical — based on one of two systems: the screwed press, or the levered jaw (which can be as simple as a plier). The latter is particularly well-suited to wild and whimsical designs on the theme of animal or human mouths. The two main types for collectors are figural and mechanical (although, of course, both are mechanical because they have moving parts.) Both types are devised to break the nut with a screwed or levered pressure. There are many crossover collectors interested in figural and zoomorphic examples, plus some interest by folk art collectors — especially in subjects folk art collectors have staked out, such as alligators and the Black Americana pieces. In the mechanicals, old and odd patents bring the most money. If you're serious about the **figurals**, you must get the **Rollband patent book** to see some mid-20th C shockers: a levered dog cracker patented in 1960; an alligator head plier type pat'd 1954; a squirrel with levered tail pat'd in 1953; a Cro-Magnon man's head, pat'd 1950; a fabulous squirrel & "log" tray, pat'd 1948; another dog with fancy cast iron base, pat'd 1947; yet another dog with levered handle and backplate so it could also be a bookend, pat'd 1947; a terrific alligator (a nutcrocker, heh heh), pat'd 1934; modern alligator, pat'd 1929; squirrel on log, pat'd 1923; a squirrel in a bowl, pat'd 1922; an ugly pointy-muzzled dog head, pat'd 1920; squirrel-head pliers, pat'd 1920; a fat friendly dog with levered tail, pat'd 1912; two different squirrels from 1902 — one the wonderful folky one on a long log, and one sitting up high in tray; the best squirrel of all, levered so it cracks nuts between paws and chin, pat'd 1902; another full-bodied dog, levered tail, pat'd 1900; the first figural squirrel on plinth, pat'd by F. A. Humphrey, May 28,1878; and the first dog, with geared ratchet inside for high-lifted levered tail, pat'd as a "Tobacco Cutter & Nut Cracker," by H. Tilden, May 29, 1866. What I don't get at all (am I just too hard-headed?) is how all the similar dogs and squirrels got patents.

● ● ● ●

The Nut Museum: 303 Ferry Road, Old Lyme, CT. Open by appointment only, this museum has quite a collection of world nuts, art made from nuts, and a large collection of nutcrackers. Call ahead for further information.

Nut chopper, iron & tin on wooden board base. The 8" cylinder Leroy Starrett food & meat chopper, in smallest size, was sold to confectioners and bakers as a nut chopper. **$95-$125**

Nutcracker, alligator, cast iron, large detailed 'gator in 2 parts: bottom includes marshy cattails & is mounted to 3-3/4" x 10-1/2" board. Upper body has looped tail; head & jaws are angled to the left. "Blake" patent, probably later than 1853 patent. **NOTE:** P.E.W. and J.A. Blake (Blake Brothers & Co., New Haven, CT) patented a plain, platform, iron, levered nutcracker on Sept. 6, 1853. It was mounted on an oblong board, and had angled jaws and worked with a lever. At some point their patent was used as the mechanical basis for a zoomorphic alligator nutcracker, probably in the 1870s or 1880s. This two-way type of "gussied up" strictly mechanical kitchen gadget is very rare, and collectors should try to find one of each of these. **$150-$250**

Nutcracker, alligator, cast brass in 2 parts, mounted to base, American, 7-1/2" L, late 19th C to early 20th C. **$90-$125**

Nutcracker, alligator, cast iron, detailed casting, American, late 19th C. **$100-$150**

Nutcracker, alligator, cast iron with old silver radiator paint, cast in 2 parts: (1) upper jaw and "naked underbody" with legs & lower part of curving tail, (2) lower jaw & scaled top of body & tail, pretty good detail, no marks, 13-3/4" L, poss. early 20th C. **$65-$80**

Reproduction alert. — John Wright, Inc., made a black painted cast aluminum alligator, only 1-3/4" W x 6-1/4" L, in the 1960s.

Nutcracker, alligator, rather delicate & small, lever action, dark satiny cast iron, 2 parts: slender upper jaw, patterned back, slightly wavery tail, separate lower body unusual because it has shortish pointed "tail," marked "Nestor," 9" L, 20th C (?). **$125-$150**

Nutcracker, antelope head, lever type, carved wood with set in glass eyes, long horns, very detailed carving, Tyrolean (?), 8-7/8" H x 3-1/2" W nose to ear tips, 19th C. Try to get a look at the dozens of fabulous carved wood lever crackers in Pinto's book on treen (see bibliography). Most in his collection are human — grotesques or comic characters with gaping jaws, some dating to 16th C. Very elaborate carving of all parts. Many others are dogs or other animals. **$125-$145**

Nutcracker, bawdy legs, cast iron shapely woman's legs, large concavity in inner thighs, very unusual because painted flesh color, original because decal put on over paint: "Souvenir of New York City," 6" L, c.1940s-1950s. **$30-$45**

Nutcracker, bawdy woman's legs, carved wood, 19th C. **$45-$55**

Nutcracker, bawdy woman's legs with high heels, cast aluminum, no mark, 6-7/8" L, c.1940s (?). **$100-$150**

Nutcracker, bawdy woman's legs, cast brass, various between 4" L and 5-1/2" L, turn of century into early 20th C. **$45-$90**

Nutcracker, bawdy women's legs, feet well-defined, pale-colored cast brass, two almost alike — one 4-1/2" L, other 4-3/8" L, late 19th C. **$55-$90**

Nutcracker, bearded man with skull cap, lever type, carved wood, Tyrolean or Swiss(?), 19th C. **$125-$175**

Nutcracker, Black Americana man in overcoat, hands in pockets over knees, painted cast iron, modeled with ring of white hair & white eyebrows like popular illustrations of "Uncle Tom," lever works lower jaw or chin, American, prob. 3rd quarter 19th C. **$600-$750**

Nutcracker, Black Americana man's head, cast iron, more portrait than caricature, hair, brow, eyes, nose & upper lip have good detail, lower jaw worked by slightly curved short lever in back, head mounted to widely flared footed base, American, about 6" H, mid 19th C. **$400-$550**

Nutcracker, black man's head, caricatured Black Americana, painted cast iron in 4 parts: 2 flat halves of the head, riveted together, a lever (which comes out back of head) that works the jaw, & a diamond-shape base to which all is screwed, very exaggerated eyes, lips & ears, partly painted red & white, no mark at all, American, 6-1/8" H, looks maybe c.1880s, poss. much earlier. **$600-$800**

Nutcracker, black painted cast iron, small anvil & blacksmith's hammer, probably not a repro. of an old one, but a "new" idea, John Wright, Inc., Wrightsville, PA, hammer 4" L, 1960s. **$15-$20**

Nutcracker, blue-decorated Meissen porcelain platform frame fitted with iron screw mechanism with big porcelain knobs at each end (it looks like small decorative book press for miniature books). Meissen, German, about 6" H, 19th C. **$200-$300**

Nutcracker, brass, "Big Ben," English, 20th C. souvenir(?). **$55-$75**

Nutcracker, carved boxwood lever type, one tapered handle is L-shaped, the other has pivot part fitting through bottom of L, rounded on outside with small carved double-crossed squares as decoration, ball finials, carved on one lever or handle is the name, on other is a very, very early date — surprising because the name sounds like a patent or trade name, on flat surface inside L lever is "Broughtons Cracknut," the inscribed date is "October 5, 1667," English, 5-3/8" L, 1667 (?). Dealers Michael & Jane Dunn, Claverack, NY, had this at a show in 1984. I did not get to examine it, and am taking description from picture appearing in *Maine Antique Digest*, April 1984. (My value range.) **$600-$850**

Futile Research on the "**Broughton Cracknuts.**" — I spent several hours trying to do intuitive research on the date, the name "Broughton," and the term "Cracknut." Leads I investigated included a British regiment, originally "The Third Foot," later the "Buffs," which had the nickname the "Nutcrackers." This regiment was definitely in existence in 1667. And it fought in the Second Dutch War — one of several Restoration wars between England and Holland — which ended in 1667. With my resources, the name Broughton led nowhere, nor did I have time to really delve into the date. I did look at a very early nineteenth-century "every day" almanac, which details events important to England on every day of the year, but found nothing significant for October 5. One of that set of books, William Hone's *The Every-Day Book* (the one I quote here, London: 1826), yields several squibs on nuts or nut-cracking. Sept. 14, or Holy Rood, was for nutting, signifying the "fruitfulness of autumn, and the deadly cold of the coming winter." On October 31, Hallowe'en, the Vigil night for November 1, All Saints Day, it was traditional "in many parts of England" to bob for apples and crack nuts. It is possible that the elusive "Nutcrack Night" of which I have seen only passing mention, refers to the e'en of October 31.

I-67. Zoömorphic nutcrackers. (T) *Dinosaur/dragon or griffin. Cast iron painted gold, 2-part body bolted together, sawtooth spine ridges & tail, 13" L. Pat.#206454 (?). Stock of Richard Ferry, Mystic Fine Arts, Mystic, CT.* **(B)** *Alligators (not crocodiles) with blunt tips. Author's large one silver-painted cast iron, 2 parts come apart. Scaled back, tail & lower jaw lift out revealing naked underbody & legs. 13-3/4" L. Small one cast brass in reddish hue, 2-part, riveted pivot, no marks, 7-7/8" L. Collection of Peg & Ralph Latham. All c.1920+. See text for information on 20th C. patented figurals.* **$200-$300; $30-$60**

Nutcracker, carved & painted wood, wrinkled man with red & green cap, like a liberty cap, Tyrolean, either Swiss or German, 6-1/4" L, new, but in style of 19th C ones. **$95-$125**

Nutcracker, carved & turned oak, doughnut shape pierced on one side by wooden screw used to press against opposite side nut placed within "hole" of doughnut, English, only 2" diameter, late 19th C. I've also seen modern ones, especially in woods & finishes favored by Danish furniture makers. **$15-$20**

Nutcracker, cast iron, anvil-like contrivance, small, square, with curved undersurface to fit a seated person's knee, small short column in center has concavity for nut, used with mallet or small hammer, "Lawrence," American, about 4" square, c. 1840s. **$65-$100**

Nutcracker, cast iron, anvil-like nutcracking block, fits kneecap, shield-shaped with raised nut holder, fits over knee & used sitting down with small mallet or hammer, American, 3-1/2" L, 1840s-1860s. **$65-$100**

Nutcracker, cast iron, 2-part, walled oblong green painted base with sort of mortar with long-handled flattish plate that fits inside base, paper label reads: "DIRECTIONS: Place cracker on a solid foundation. Place all nuts on end and hit blow with hammer or mallet. Empty the base after cracking each nut. Use 36 ounce mallet if possible until after the war." "Potter Walnut Cracker Co.," pat'd by C. E. Potter, Sapulpa, OK, pestle about 3" L, June 5, 1945, patent #2377369. A collector/dealer sent me a photo of a completely different C. E. Potter cracker, which has the same 1945 patent. His is cast aluminum, a large squarish open frame to be wall-mounted, with big lever that ratchets along outer vertical member of the frame. A totally different piece and a mystery. **$35-$50**

Nutcracker, cast iron exactly like screw-clamp model, but this one screwed to a "countersunk plate" in bottom of a shallow turned wood bowl with very rounded sides & narrow foot, "all the shells & other litter fall into the bowl & are not scattered about," The Perfection Nut Cracker Co., Waco, TX, pat'd Nov. 17, 1914, advertised in early 1917 as a "new item." This is the scarcest of the Perfection crackers. **$50-$65**

Nutcracker, cast iron, nickeled or tinned, clamps to table, looks like small bench vise, horizontal screw pushes nut against end plate, big cast T handle has swelled knobs on ends like leg bone, "Perfection," Malleable Iron Fittings Co., Branford, CT, pat'd 1889. **$50-$65**

Nutcracker, cast iron, nickeled, screw clamps to table top & looks like small bench vise, vertical "lathe" type action, large T handle, slightly finer casting than earlier one, ornate letters in curve to fit frame, The Perfection Nut Cracker Co., Waco, TX, 4-1/2" H x 3-3/4" W, pat'd Nov. 17, 1914. Another one, a little leaner, and made of nickeled cast steel, is very plain. It is marked "Perfection Nut Cracker Pat." Pecans, which are supposed to be hard to crack (perhaps to crack & get perfect nutmeats out), were Texas' biggest cash crop at the time the "Perfection" was patented. **$40-$60**

Nutcracker, cast iron, lever action, Arcade Mfg. Co., Freeport, IL, early 20th C. **$50-$65**

Nutcracker, cast iron, levered jaws stick out slightly over end, mounted to oblong wooden board, lower corrugated jaw stationary, upper one opens & depresses when curved lever is raised, pat'd by Russel Frisbie, Middletown, CT, pat'd May 17, 1859. Similar to the P. E. W. and J. A. Blake patents of six years earlier, which was the first pat'd nutcracker, and extremely modern looking. (**NOTE:** Back in the 1830s, before patents were numbered in the U.S., Eli W. Blake, Johan A. Blake, and Philos Blake got a number of patents for door escutcheons, locks and mortises.) **$65-$80**

Nutcracker, cast iron, mounted to oblong wooden board, long corrugated jaws stick out over side near one end, lever moves endmost jaw while other remains stationary. Similar to Frisbie patent; a letter by Ernest J. Rolland to *Spinning Wheel* in 1977 reported that both these nutcrackers are "often mistaken for a cork press," pat'd by P. E. W. & J. A. Blake, New Haven, CT, base 10-1/2" L x 3" W, pat'd Sept. 6, 1853. (See more on the Blake Brothers under a corkscrew entry in Chapter VIII (Open & Close).) **Later edition.** — One of these was seen with black painted finish & marked "P. & S. & W. Co.," Peck, Stow & Wilcox, Southington, CT. **$65-$80**

Reproduction alert. — An extremely similar nutcracker with slight differences, including a board with a turned molded edge & a spring between lever & lower part. Called the "Herkimer Jr., No. 602," & being made by White Mountain Freezer Co. of Winchendon, MA. They make one mounted to larger board with a nut "firkin" attached at one end, and this one, which is supposed to be "modeled after the original Herkimer cracker." I couldn't find any patent by a Herkimer.

Nutcracker, cast iron, screw clamps to table, lever action, long slightly arched lever pulled down over small nut-holding jaw, "Enterprise," Enterprise Mfg. Co., Phila., c.1914. **$30-$45**

Nutcracker, cast iron, screw clamps to table, long lever, "Home," American, 19th C. **$28-$40**

Nutcracker, cast iron, tabletop vise type, "The Hamilton," early 20th C. **$30-$45**

Nutcracker, cast & turned brass, with engraved decoration, handles shaped like a sort of whoop-tee-do dancing master's leg, squared cracking face plate tooled with little teeth for grabbing the nut, English, range from about 3-1/2" L to 4-1/4" L, late 18th or very, very early 19th C. The same people who made fire tools, andirons, bells, etc., made these heavy little crackers, which are all variations on a theme. Some have more exaggerated "legs" or handles than others. **$75-$125**

Nutcracker, cherub, cast brass, English (?), looks 19th C, but could be 20th C. **$75-$95**

Nutcracker, chromed metal, hand held lever action that was advertised as working "like a car jack" but looks like a vise grip, English, about 8" L, c.1963. **$7-$15**

I-68. Figural nutcrackers. (L) *Full figure of town-crier-like figure, carved & painted wood on plinth. 8-1/2" H, collection of Priors Bank, Fulham, London, from early 19th C. book.* **(M)** *Jockey's head, in Thornhill's ad in the* Illustrated Sporting & Dramatic News, *12/1882. English.* **(R)** *Carved hardwood toothy man in moon, iron hinge in back. 5" H. Mid 19th C. Has been reproduced by Boston Museum of Art in cast polymer resin & in brass, about 6" H with small base. This one courtesy Robert & Mary Lou Sutter, East Chatham, NY.* **(L & R) $225-$350 ;** *(M)* **$150-$225**

Nutcracker, cast iron, nickel plated, held cupped in hand, T handle to screw, adv'g "Cook Muffler Co.," American, approx. 4-1/2" L when screwed fully in. Frank B. Cook pat'd this Aug. 6, 1918. **$8-$15**

Nutcracker, concave part of cast iron fits in palm, T handle with slightly knobby ends, screw action, this one is chrome with enameled green body, others are nickeled or even just highly polished iron, some have narrower bodies & T bar has no knobbed ends, or have a simple looped handle, actually pat'd Aug. 6, 1918, patentee & mfr Frank B. Cook advertised "The Ideal"; later, without knobbed ends, "Ideal" was mfd by Cook Electric Co., Chicago, IL, 3-1/4" W x about 5" L, sold prior to patent in 1917 ad, then 1923 ad. **$5-$12**

Nutcracker, dog, bronzed cast iron, on oblong stepped base, L.A. Althoff & Co., Chicago, IL, early 20th C. I think I'd like a kennel full of the dog crackers — so many variations! **$85-$125**

Nutcracker, dog on base, cast iron, well-defined hair, advertising "L. A. Althoff," Makers of Headlights, Stoves & Ranges, Laporte, IN, (or La Port?), 11" L, 20th C. This nutcracker might appeal to some stove collectors, although for most of them home is nowhere but on the range. It also came in nickeled finish. It is not uncommon, but prices (like with anything else) really depend on who's buying & who's selling. One with "worn nickel finish with light rust" brought only $40 at the 1989 Garth Auction, Delaware, OH. **$85-$125**

Nutcracker, dog, cast brass, on brass base, lots of hair detail, no marks, 4-3/4" H without base, 5-3/8" H with it, x 11-1/4" L, c.1870s to 1890s or is this 20th C? **$70-$100**

Nutcracker, dog cast in 2 halves, plus tail lever. Cast brass, rather crude & lumpy, filed roughly & bolted. Looks like St. Bernard (according to contemporaneous reports, they & Newfoundlands were most popular breeds at the end of the 19th C), no marks, 4-3/4" H x 11-1/2" L, looks c.1870s or 1880s, but with so many 20th C patents that look old-fashioned going up to 1960 I just don't know. **$75-$100**

Nutcracker, dog, cast iron with copper finish, smaller than most you see, "Made in England," 8-1/4" L, marked on inside of tail "Patent No. 273480," which is 1863 in England. **$75-$100**

Nutcracker, dog, nickel plated iron, English, 8-3/4" L, 1863 patent #273480. By the way, nickeled dog and squirrel nutcrackers in old designs were advertised as new products for sale in 1924 in the United States. **$75-$90**

Nutcracker, dog with levered tail, crudely formed cast iron, English, 11-1/2" L, patent No. 273480 marked on tail. **$55-$70**

Nutcracker, dog, on flat base with openwork that makes it look like sidewalk grating, marvelous jowls, cast iron, "Dog Tray Nut Cracker" (for Stephen C. Foster's song, "Old Dog Tray"?), mfd by Harper Supply Co., North Chicago, IL, 13" L, "patent applied for," late 19th or early 20th C. A fairly simple plier-type nutcracker was pat'd in 1915 by J. M. Harper, so this may be his too. **$95-$125**

Dog Reproduction Alerts.— John Wright, Inc., in PA, made (at least in the 1960s) a very small black-painted cast iron dog, levered tail, only 5-1/2" L, which was cast in two parts, bolted through middle of body. Emig Products, Inc., of Reading, PA, reproduced (at least in the 1960s) a dog-on-platform nutcracker; the platform on theirs has much more openwork & simpler pattern than old one. (Emig's was 5" H x 10" L, sold for about $5.) Plus — why reproduce, when so many were pat'd in the first six decades of the twentieth century?

Nutcracker, dog with belled collar, cast brass, European, 5-1/2" L, looks early 19th C. **$90-$125**

Nutcracker, dog with levered tail, cast iron porcelainized in black & white, American, late 19th C. Dogs also exist in a cobalt blue porcelainized finish & they'd bring more. **$250-$350**

Nutcracker, dog's or wolf's head, cast iron, levered jaw, this looks very European — English or German, but it shows up in Rollband's patent book as a June 15, 1920, design patent, granted to A. W. & J. J. Geigand. Marked also with what's probably a pattern number "1820." **$75-$100**

Nutcracker, dragon, griffin or even possibly dinosaur, unusual, gold painted cast iron, body's 2 parts bolt together, sawtooth ridges on back & tail, American, 13" L, "#206454," which would be an 1878 patent if American or if it's a design patent and American, it wasn't made until 1966 or 1967. It sure looked and felt older. **$200-$300**

I-70. Mechanical nutcrackers. (A) *"Enterprise," Philadelphia. c.1910.* **(B)** *"Home," Schroeter Bros. Hardware Co., St. Louis, MO. Nickeled cast malleable iron, 6" H x 4" W with 7-1/2" lever. Pat'd c.1915.* **(C)** *Handheld "Ideal" with old-style knobbed handle. Nickeled cast iron, c.1915.* **(D)** *"Perfect" pecan cracker, Thomas Mills & Bros., Philadelphia, c.1930.* **(E)** *"Perfection," Waco, TX. Screw clamps to table. 1917 ad.* **(F)** *Levered cracker, cast iron, F. A. Walker catalog, 1870s.* **(G)** *"Harper," nickeled cast steel, c.1910.* **$20-$75**

I-69. "Kneewarmer" nutcrackers — *cast iron anvil part only. To be put over thigh near knee and used to break nuts with a small hammer. Size approx. 3-1/2" x 6". 2nd & 3rd quarter 19th C. Collection of Phyllis & Jim Moffet.* **$60-$110**

Nutcracker, eagle head, cast iron, on primitive 4-legged base, which is quite different from flat base of new lookalike nutcracker, American, 7" L, 19th C(?). Could this be 1920s and made as a design variation of the point-faced dog or wolf, pat'd 1920? **$75-$85**

Lookalike alarm. — Nutcracker, eagle head, cast iron, upraised head on flat iron base, lever moves lower beak up & down, American? 6" H, 1980s. Cumberland General Store, Crossville TN, sells this one as "just like those available in the 19th century." I've never seen an old one. New/used: $12-$15. Old (?): **$125-$175**

Nutcracker, elephant, cast iron, painted red & black, with a little white, the red has aged to a salmon color, trunk is lever, American, 5" H x 10" L, early 20th C. **$125-$165**

Nutcracker, elephant form, modernistic cast iron painted orange, high arched back, lever action, 20th C. **$100-$150**

Nutcracker, gold fish or koi with teeth in mouth, gold painted cast iron (also found nickel plated), glued-on glass eyes (poss. not original), upper fin is spring-loaded lever, English, 8" L, Regist'd #751619. Prob. c.1920s. **$90-$125**

Nutcracker, grotesque man's head on small round collar-base, wearing liberty cap, extremely long sausage nose curves down, forked beard, carved walnut, American (?), 6-1/2" L from nose tip to back of head, 3rd quarter 19th C. **$200-$300**

Nutcracker, hand held crossover plier type, handles flip around axis to accommodate another size nut, cast iron, English, European or American, about 6" L, 19th C. There's quite a variety available. I like the cast iron ones best; others have nickeled or silver-plated finishes. **$12-$20**

Nutcracker, hand held crossover plier type, handmade (?) cast iron, maybe cast in multiples then finished by hand?, hinged levers, inside face of one are tiny V gouges, the other has O gouges, English (?), 6-1/2" L, c.1850s to 1900. **$20-$25**

Nutcracker, hand held crossover pliers, pointy handles, engraved steel, English, 5-1/2" L, 19th C. **$12-$20**

Nutcracker, hand held crossover pliers, silver-plated iron, bulbous knobs on handles, English (?), 5-1/4" L, turn of century. **$10-$20**

It's In the Picture. — One very similar to this, a crossover type with little rough projections on jaw parts, tapered turned handles, silver-plated, appears in "Still Life with Apples, Walnuts and Holly," painted by American artist Eloise H. Stannard in 1899. You should always examine still life and genre scene pictures for objects in our collecting fields. At least you get an "as early as" date.

• • • •

It's In the Catalog. — Harrod's Stores, Ltd., London, England, carried 10 different styles of this type in the late 19th C. The turnings of the handles (or lack thereof) as well as overall decoration, and style of jaw, vary considerably. The cheapest has nicely shaped handles narrow near the jaws, swelling out, then coming to a dull pointed end. The jaws, on both sides, have flat faces with a pattern of small nicks or gouges. The piece between the hinged jaws that determines the minimum space between the jaws while in use is crown-shaped rather than teardrop or ovoid. Slightly more expensive is one with pointed handles, two sets of turned bands, ovoid spacer, and oval grooved or fluted concavities for nuts. Another has decorated hinge pins, but wide spoon-handle levers. Another, again with oval concavity, has bamboo-like cast iron handles; another has baluster turnings with round knobs at ends; another has the crown spacer, very decorative "rattlesnake rattle" turnings, and a zigzag line of small gouges or nicks on all faces of jaws. Another is not the 2-hinge flip-over type and can be used only one way (though, like the rest, as pliers are used), but the longish jaws are corrugated inside, with an area for larger nuts near the handles. This "nut crack" came with allover fancy Renaissance chased decoration, or with chased head and plain handles. The handles of this one are the shapely ones of first type listed above. Harrod's nutcrackers came plated and plain, and were ordered through the jewellery, watch, electro plate & cutlery department of the huge store.

Nutcracker, hand held plier type, cast iron, knobbed ends to handles, corrugated parts for 2 sizes of nuts — small (like almonds) & large (like walnuts), American?, 5-1/8" L, 19th C. **$12-$18**

Nutcracker, horse, modern stylized form, 2 halves screwed together, tail lever, bronzed or coppered cast iron, English, 4-1/4" H x 7-1/4" L, marked with same pat. # as dog crackers, #273480. Crossover collectors from Art Moderne. **$200-$300**

Nutcracker, jester & knight, cast brass, plier type, English or poss. American, late 19th or early 20th C. **$35-$55**

Nutcracker, lions' heads, one to each jaw, cast iron, plier type, pronounced concavity inside mouths, no marks, English (?), 6-1/2" L, 19th C. **$60-$100**

Nutcracker, man in moon in crescent shape, mouth is pivot point, carved wood, very smooth patination, lots of expression in face, European — prob. Swiss or German, about 5" to 7" L, early to mid 19th C. **$175-$225**

Reproduction alert. — The Boston Museum of Art has reproduced a **Moon Man** from their collection and mounted it to a small rectangular base. A late 1980s museum shop catalog shows one of cast polymer resin that is 5-1/2" H including base, and one of cast brass, which is 6" H with base.

Nutcracker, man in moon, with neat little teeth, levered mechanical, carved hardwood, crescent moon, iron hinge, English or American, moon if full would form 5" circle, mid 19th C. **$325-$365**

Nutcracker, man who looks like Mr. Magoo, cast iron & wood, lever action, homemade wooden box painted yellow, 3-D cast iron front of man stands squint-eyed with hands in overcoat pockets, his feet inside box, mounted to a wooden back cut to fit his outline, lever works lower jaw, not marked, American, man is 7-1/2" H, 19th C. Folk art crossover interest. **$300-$350**

Nutcracker, man's head, perhaps a comic caricature of a peasant, wearing a Phrygian liberty cap of the type worn in France before & during their revolution, large jaw with indication of teeth, forged iron, very long lever handles, French, dated 1761. This piece was for sale in early 1989 by Pat Guthman Antiques, Southport, CT. It is an example of the very best kind of iron work that you could hope to find. It is so extraordinary that it matters little if it be American, French, German or whatever, because it is art. Value range mine. **$550-$800**

Nutcracker, nickel-plated metal rachet mechanism & lever, black enameled metal tray, in original orange & black cardboard box, "Krag's Whole Kernel Nut Cracker," American, 7" L, pat'd Mar. 23, 1937, by G. M. Krag. **$60-$75**

Nutcracker, nickeled malleable cast iron, screw clamps to table, pushing down lever operates worm causing longish cupped jaws to close in, jaws stepped & with opposing concavities for small, medium & large nuts, device especially meant for pecans, "Home," Schroeter Brothers Hardware Co., St. Louis, MO, 6" H x 4" W with 7-1/2" L lever, "patent pending" in 1915. **$40-$60**

Nutcracker, parrot, cast brass, 5-1/2" H.   **$30-$50**

Nutcracker, pheasant, bronze, French, 19th C.   **$90-$120**

Nutcracker, rocket-shaped, cast iron on wooden base, adjusts for different nuts, "Reed's Rocket," American, 20th C (?).   **$45-$60**

Nutcracker, rooster, cast brass, 20th C.   **$25-$35**

Nutcracker, rooster, cast iron, turn of century.   **$65-$80**

Nutcracker, sailor & girlfriend, they kiss (the nut) when handles squeezed, cast brass, 6-1/4" L, 20th C.   **$30-$40**

Nutcracker, sailor's head with liberty cap, concave roof of mouth accommodates nut, 4-part carved base, carved wood, European, prob. Tyrolean, 7" H, c.1860s.   **$140-$175**

Nutcracker, skull & bones, nut goes between face & back of skull, bones are levered handles, cast iron has some remaining copper plating, very lean & hungry, English, 6" L, register #740410, prob. c.1920s. Crossover skull collectors vie for this. **$125-$175**

Nutcracker, squirrel, carved wood, probably walnut, threaded screw action presses against nut, Tyrolean or English ?, 19th C. Not as large a variety of the screw-type wooden nutcrackers as the levered ones, but others to look for include various barrels or cylinders with simple or fancy knobs to the screws — from a simple bird to a knob faceted like a golfball to a standing woman. The most commonly found wood is boxwood.   **$150-$165**

I-71. Dog nutcrackers. *Just 3 examples of the many versions of a St. Bernard or Mastiff type dog, most popular dog breed in 1860s-1880s — although access to a new patent book makes me revise dating of many (not all) dog nutcrackers to mid-20th C.* **(T)** *Nickeled iron, 8-3/4" L, pat. # appears to be #375460 (not same as modern-style horse #273480; nor the dinosaur). This one English.* **(M)** *Dog on fancy base, with sheep-like hair, is nickeled iron, marked "L. A. Althoff Mfg. Co. Makers of Headlights, Stoves & Ranges, La Port, IN."* **(B)** *Cast brass, 5-3/8" H with base x 11-1/4" L. Prob. English.* **$85-$150**

Nutcracker, squirrel, cast brass of very reddish hue, 2 parts with riveted pivot in jaw, no marks, lots of detail, 7-7/8" L, late 19th C or early 20th.   **$90-$125**

Nutcracker, squirrel, cast iron, "Squirrel Cracker," Tyler, TX, pat'd 1913.   **$75-$125**

Nutcracker, squirrel on leaf, cast iron, American, 19th C. (Evidently this was also made in a nickeled finish at least until 1924.) I've seen only three in all my wanderings. A picture of five squirrel nutcrackers, from the booth of dealer Clifton Anderson, Lexington, KY, who was set up at "Atlantique City" in March 1989, makes it clear that the variations are not subtle. One squirrel, in the foreground, has the most Alert Squirrel head ... wary, tail tucked along curved back, holding a leaf on his paws, which is where the nut went. Another I recognize as the reproduction I bought through the mail from someone else, smallish and very poorly cast, very furry tail, with gap between front paws. Looking at these and at the racing, chasing busybodies in our yard, I find it impossible to call them rodents. Anderson wanted $1500 for the five, which seems high.   **$95-$125**

Nutcracker, squirrel on rustic branch, cast bronze or bell metal, extremely finely detailed, squirrel has funny long skinny arms & very pointed nose, lever is uplifted plumy tail widely separated from curve of back, English? or poss. American, 6" L, 19th C. This is one of the best-looking squirrels. The abstracting is very refined: angular slender legs and funny little ears. It sometimes seems to be a bronzed cast iron; possibly different periods? I have also seen this one with no leaf but mounted to a turned wooden tray or plate.   **$175-$225**

Nutcracker, squirrel sitting on hind legs on huge grape leaf, cast aluminum painted black, rather crudely cast but nice idea. The tail lifts up to lever the jaw, no mark, American?, 7-1/2" H overall, leaf 11-1/2" L, 20th C. <u>Flat or dull black painted aluminum is almost a sure sign of rather recent origin</u> (or recent painting). I think it's intended to fool the unknowing into thinking they've found a cast iron piece. There are c.1900 cast aluminum pieces of many kinds, however, but the novel metal, considered an attractive silvery pewter lookalike, was rarely painted, and usually in gold.   **$30-$45**

Nutcracker, squirrel, standing high, tail curled, cast iron, good detail, American, only 5" H, late 19th or early 20th C.   **$75-$125**

Nutcracker, squirrel with paws held palms up, on log, levered tail, silver-gray painted lightweight cast aluminum, brown log, green eyes, the squirrel & base case in 2 pieces down through center of squirrel & length of log, bolted together, dealer's tag says "signed H. E. Cox, Norfolk, VA," but I couldn't find any mark at all, 5-1/2" H, log 5-3/4" L, looks 1980s, and pretty awful.   **$15-$20**

Nutcracker, tabletop screw type, cast brass machined to look like ship's wheel, on wooden base, American, 4-1/2" H, 20th C.   **$40-$55**

Nutcracker, with its own bowl, simple footed, rimmed bowl of "imitation rosewood, zebra ash or genuine mahogany," with nickeled metal high-rise frame like a guillotine screwed to bottom, adjustable for 4 different size nuts, lever used to move top part down to pop nut open, "New Champion," c.1915.   **$20-$28**

Nutcracker bowl, turned wood, with cast iron round central "anvil" & iron hammer, American, 7" L hammer & 10" diameter bowl, 20th C.   **$25-$35**

Nutcracker & picks, nickel-plated, heavily knurled, 6 picks in original box, American, c.1910.   **$12-$15**

Nutcracker & lemon sqeezer combination, "All-in-One," Ford Mfg. Co., Newark, NJ, 11" L, top, slotted concave cup, long lever handle with enameled convex presser, late 19th C.   **$100-$125**

Nutcracking block, kneecap — See nutcracker, cast iron, anvil type

Nutcracking maul or mallet, for walnuts, probably made of chestnut, but very stained, American, 11-3/4" L, block is 3-7/8" x 4-3/4" x 2-3/8" thick, turn of century. **$25-$30**

Nutgrinder, cast iron & tin, "Climax." Nutgrinder, glass jar, screw-on tin hopper filled with "fingers" that rotate when cranked, American, 1940s. **$12-$15**

Nutgrinder, green painted metal, "Lorraine Metal Mfg. Co.," NY, turn of century. **$22-$30**

Nutgrinder, painted metal screw-on top, usually with small decal on hopper, cranked finger-like teeth, glass jar, 1940s & 1950s, American. **$4-$8**

Nutmeg & ginger mill, tin with little crank, looks like music box, brown asphaltum japanning, marked "Portable Ginger & Nutmeg Mill," English, 3-3/16" x 2-7/16", reg'd Nov. 11, 1857. **$475-$495**

Nutmeg grater, asphaltum japanned tin, looks like miniature bug bomb gun, label reads "simple, economical, rapid and durable. Every particle of the nut used. Satisfaction Guaranteed. None wasted, easy to handle, a pleasure to use," "The Rapid Nutmeg Grater," 5-1/4" L, late 19th C. **$350-$395**

Nutmeg grater, big, round, robust black-glazed ceramic knob (instead of the usual wood), triangular tin chute where grated meg comes out, storage in back, "British made," disk is 3-3/4" diameter, British patent applied for, #32492/32. **$160-$180**

Nutmeg grater, cast iron crank, wire handle, ingeniously bent so as to hold nutmeg against small grating disc, handle looks like a spark striker handle, American, 7" L, 1880s. **$575-$675**

Nutmeg grater, cast iron housing for nutmeg & other cast iron parts, wire handle, tin grating disc, no marks, 7" L, c.1870s. **$195-$250**

Nutmeg grater, cast iron with tin grater, shaped like small bellows, crank handle, unpin & unhinge it & it reveals brass spring-loaded catch for cartridge holder of single nutmeg, directional arrow cast in side to show which way to turn handle, 2 holes for screwing to shelf edge or cupboard side (another model marked the same way had a screw clamp frame), not marked with name, but invented by J. M. Smith, Seymour, CT, 3-7/8" L, pat'd June 7, 1870. **$275-$350**

I-72. Nutcrackers of pliers type. *Also called* **nutcracks.** *A confusable, because it could be used with large nuts, is the lobster cracker at far left. Next are two cast iron late 19th C.* <u>nutcracks</u>, *one made for 2 sizes; one for big nuts only. Then 5 of the* "**cross over**" *types, which reversed for small or large nuts. All but one shown in small nut position. Nickeled or plain cast iron or steel, more or less decorative. Many are English, c.1880-1930s.* **$12-$28**

Nutmeg grater, coffin style, tin, has lidded storage at top near hanging hole or loop, biggest variety seen in the back of these — the ingenious ways tin was poked out to create the platform inside to hold the nutmeg, mostly American, 5-1/8" L to 5-3/4" L, 19th to 20th C. Slightly fancier ones (usually with embossed designs on little lidded compartment, or with sliding lids) are English. **$40-$45**

Nutmeg grater, coffin type but very big, tin, with compartment, 2 grating surfaces on the curved front & flat back, "Acme Nut Grater," English, Register #11467. **$35-$45**

Nutmeg grater, coffin type modified, stamped tin, has sliding lid to nutmeg compartment, back unusual in that it's stamped with an 8-rayed star, English, 6-3/8" L x 2-9/16" W, c.1900. **$40-$45**

Nutmeg grater, coffin type, very large, stamped & punctured tin, with storage box with sliding lid with embossed design, no marks, English, 6-1/2" L x 2-1/2" W, 19th C. **$40-$45**

Nutmeg grater, ebonized wood, or bog oak, carved to look like small champagne bottle, no marks, remnants of paper label that is illegible, European, 3-3/4" H, 19th C. **$200-$350**

Nutmeg grater, fancy little box grater, japanned or lacquered tin, 4" L, late 19th C. **$50-$60**

Nutmeg grater, fancy turned wood body & handle, cube of wood has working part inside, plus barrel for storing the megs, tin grater, brass side plates & cap, Champion Grater Co., invented by C. L. Gilpatric, of South Dedham, MA, but mfd in Boston, MA, 7-1/2" L, pat'd Oct. 9, 1866; brass cap at end of handle marked April 2, 1867. **$450-$500**

Nutmeg grater, heavy cast iron with brass & wood, pinned hinges or hooks hold back on, pat'd Jan. 30, 1877. **$110-$130**

Nutmeg grater, interesting long skinny tin mechanical grater, flat piece pulls down to protect grating surface, nutmeg holder is small cylinder mounted to track along folded edges, "William Bradley," Lynn, MA, 6" L in closed-up position, "patent applied for" on one; pat'd July 26, 1854 on another. Very similar to this one are the "Monitor" from 1863, which does resemble an ironclad submarine, and an ingenious one pat'd Aug. 17, 1897. The latter has a "smokestack" cylinder for the nutmeg, and tracks the long skinny grating surface that's like an angular tunnel. A hole in the top at one end permits insertion of nutmeg into the cylinder when it's positioned over the hole. **$350-$450**

Nutmeg grater, long tin barrel, hinged lid at end for inserting nutmeg, hinge wire is also hanging ring, grating drum made up of assembled battery of 12 toothed rings with deep & jagged teeth like harrow discs, slightly jaywhoppered, seems like overkill, stamped "The —s Davidson Automatic Nutmeg Grater," Boston, MA, 6-3/4" W, pat'd June 2, 1908. (I've seen this given as June 9, also a Tuesday). One seen at 1994/95 show was $1200. **$700-$900**

Nutmeg grater, long tin tube, screw caps at each end plus one 1/3 of the way up, like odd pocket periscope crossed with a cigar tube. Crank comes out one end, meg goes in hole in side, other end stores more. See also the "Standard." American, 6-1/2" L, late 19th C. **$195-$200**

Nutmeg grater, nickel-plated cast iron, hinged nutmeg holder, punctured tin disc, small crank with wood knob, black holding handle in center of disc, American, 3-3/4" L x 2-3/4" D, c. 1870s to 1880s. **$95-$125**

I-73. Nutmeg graters — some rare, some not. (A) *Simple coffin-box type, backs show 2 of many ways platform created for lidded nutmeg box atop grating surface. 5-1/4" L. Early 20th C., type still sold. 3¢ in 1905! Author's.* **(B)** *M. H. Sexton, Utica NY, pat'd 5/1896. Tin, nickeled spring metal hold nutmeg. 4-3/4" L x 3" W. (Larger size known).* **(C)** *Two names: "Unique" & "Monitor", pat'd 3/19/1889 by T. L. Holt. "Unique" mfd by Steel Edge Stamping & Retinning Co., Boston; "Monitor" mfd by New England Novelty Mfg. Co., Boston (poss. same company.) Marked "Press down lightly." 4-3/8" L x 2" W; pinkish-stained wood frame with diagonal tracks over tin grater. Photo'd as sled. In England, a close-to-identical grater was patented Apr. 1, 1889 by A. J. Boult & assigned (?) to C. O. Blood. (not the same Bloods who patented a flour sifter).* **(D)** *2 versions "Edgar." Older one at left. Edgar Mfg. Co., Reading, MA, pat'd 8/18/1891. 5-7/8" L. Green-painted wood; varnished wood.* **(E)** *Richard H. Chinn, Washington, DC, pat'd 7/16/1867. No marks. All tin, sliding, spring-loaded hopper, 6-1/4" L.* **(F)** *Nathan Ames, Saugus, MA, assignor 1/2 to Edmund Brown, Lynn, MA, pat'd 10/13/1857. Tin with orig. blue paint; wood spring-return pusher inside cylindrical holder. About 5-3/8" L diagonally. Patent drawing shows small loop handle; 1871 picture shows large "cup handle" of strap tin.* **(G)** *"H. Carsley, Lynn, Mass. Patent applied for" stamped on cylindrical holder. Pat'd 11/20/1855. 3-7/8" L. Bob Cahn.* **(H)** *Skeletal form, no mark, 7-1/2" L. Screwed pressure foot; pierced drum with holes at slight angle.* **(I) & (J)** *Two versions of same grater. Cast iron, tin, wire. 5-1/4" L (Another is 7" L). Pat'd 3/9/1886. Ex-Keillor Collection.* **(K)** *"Gem," rotary motion, nickeled cast iron. Caldwell Mfg. Co., Rochester, NY. 4" x 2-3/4". 1908 ad. All not attributed are courtesy Joe & Teri Dziadul, dealers in Enfield, CT. Over $2000 if you had one of each!*
(A) $7-$12; (B) $850-$950; (C) $165-$200; (D) $65-$85; (E) $850-$950; (F) $120-$150; (G) $750-$850; (H) $300-$400; (I) & (J) $150-$200; (K) $75-$125

I-74. More rare & desirable nutmeg graters. (L) *Tin & wood. Small knob in slot pulls back, spring-load pressure foot holds nutmeg against grating drum. 6-1/8" L, pat'd 12/25/1877. In 1890, this design was changed — tin box part elongated to form handle & nutmeg storage, with lid on end. Spring, knob, wire crank & grating drum remained same. Mfd. under old patent by The Standard Co., Boston, called "new" by them.* **(M)** *"Champion Grater Co., Boston, Mass." Two patent dates: 10/9/1866, & on end of brass cap "April 2, 1867." 7-1/2" L.* **(N)** *Tin, spring-loaded, rather crude wheel. No mark. 4-1/4" L.* **(O)** *Long tin 4-sided barrel holder with hinged lid at end. Grating drum encircled by battery of discs with deep, jagged teeth, like harrow discs. Stamped "The —S (?) Davidson Automatic Nutmeg Grater. Boston, Mass. Pat'd June 2, 1908." 6-3/4" L.* **(P)** *Two slightly different "The Handy," screw-cap ends for nutmeg storage chamber & spring-loaded hatch for 'meg being grated. Wood knobs, threads on caps, and lengths differ. 4-3/4" L and 5-3/8" L and 6-1/2" L. Late 19th C.* **(Q)** *"Rapid," japanned tin cylinder, tapered nozzle. 5-1/4" L. Another measures 6-1/4" L. By 1906, an almost identical, much stubbier grater, called "Ever-Ready," of nickeled brass, was only 4-1/4" L.* **(R)** *Tin, hollow tin storage handle with tiny ovoid hinged lid at end, underside, for putting 'megs in. 7-1/2" L, only mark "press lightly."* **(S)** *Skillin & Reed grater, Portland, ME, pat'd 9/3/1867. Albion S. Skillin & George W. Reed; assignors of 1/2 to Henry Hanson & J. Butler. Turned wood, tin disc, springy wood pressure foot underneath to hold nutmeg in. 6-7/8" L.* **(T)** *"Brown & Hasler, Lynn, Mass. Pat. applied for." Wood handle & presser, tin body, black paper label, gold lettering. 7" L.* **(U)** *Stamped "Portable Ginger & Nutmeg Mill. Reg. Nov. 11, 1857." English. Japanned tin, 3-3/16" x 2-7/16".* **(V)** *Wood & tin "Common Sense," pat'd 7/23/1867, by R. W. Whitney & Joseph P. Davis, South Berwick, ME. 5-1/8" L.* **(W)** *Pat'd 6/7/1870, by J. M. Smith, Seymour, CT. Cast iron, hinged bellow-shaped body, spring-loaded cartridge for 1 'meg. Directional arrow cast in for crank. Could be screwed to cupboard. 3-7/8" L.* **(X)** *Tin, wood, spring "The Champion" (see (M)), pat'd 2/27/1877, 3-1/2" diag. All graters courtesy Joe & Teri Dziadul.* **$6000+ if you had one of each! (L) $200+; (M) $450-$500; (N) $500-$650; (O) $700-$900; (P) $500-$600; (Q) $350-$395; (R) $850-$950; (S) $400-$500; (T) $850-$950; (U) $475-$500; (V) $400-$475; (W) $275-$350; (X) $425-$475**

Nutmeg grater, nickel-plated metal, horizontal cylinder with squared funnel below & cylindrical "chimney" or hopper above, crank in end of grater barrel, marked inside a diamond "MTE & Co.," American, 3-1/2" L, 19th C, sometimes called "The Ever Ready." **$75-$100**

Nutmeg grater, non-mechanical, homemade, tin & wood, paddle shape with semicylindrical punctured tin arched grating surface, American, 4" L, 19th C. **$50-$85**

Nutmeg grater, oddly modern & efficiently mechanical, screwed pressure foot, pierced drum with grater punch holes at slight angle, no-nonsense action, 7-1/2" L, late 19th or early 20th C. **$300-$400**

Nutmeg grater, plated metal, in cylinder shape with lift-out grater that forms top, nutmegs are stored inside cylinder, no marks, American (?), 4-1/2" L, 19th C. **$125-$150**

Nutmeg grater, pocket, carved coquilla nut with ivory trim, shaped like a barrel. Unscrew bottom for tin grater & nutmeg storage, prob. English, though poss. American scrimshander work, only 2-1/2" L, very early 19th C. **$300+**

Coquilla nuts, from piassaba palm of Brazil, washed up on beaches, were found by sailors, who used the richly colored, hard dense material to make intricate small carvings. These carvings and turnings, snuff boxes, patch boxes, nutmeg graters, "pretties" & tokens of love, were often trimmed with carved ivory.

Nutmeg grater, pocket grater, silver, bright cut engraving, English, 3" L, c.1830s. **$300-$400**

Nutmeg grater, pocket grater, silver, tall column with tiny modeled pixie at top, English, 3-1/2" H, c.1850s (?). **$300-$400**

Nutmeg grater, pocket style for a gent to carry, silver & tin, bottom hinged to hold megs, "Phipps & Robinson," English (?), dated 1811. **$1900-$2250**

Nutmeg grater, pocket style, ivory with tin grater inside, caps unscrew for grater at one end, nutmeg at other, English (?), 3-1/2" L, early 19th C, or poss. late 18th. **$350-$450**

Nutmeg grater, pocket type, carved wood & ivory, nutmeg-holding lid screws onto grater part, English(?), early 19th C. **$325-$375**

Nutmeg grater, pocket type, silver, heart-like overall shape, impressed flower designs, opens at both sides, like a 2-sided compact or something, English, only 1-7/8" W x 1" H, 19th C examples: $300-$400; 18th C ones approx. **$650-$750**

Nutmeg grater, pocket, silver, fancy cast handle like flatware knife handle, marked with 2 eagle wings with an "S" in middle, also #69, 7" L, pat'd June 29, 1897. **$1200-$1400**

Nutmeg grater, rotary action, large turned handle to hold in one hand, round tin grating surface screwed through center & screw also secures nutmeg holder. Metal crank, screwed to edge of disc, has a wooden knob & a small round presser foot to hold nutmeg while the crank is turned, "Gem," Caldwell Mfg. Co., Rochester, NY, c.1907. **$75-$125**

Nutmeg grater, slide & pivot action, wire frame, punctured tin, works like trombone, wooden holding handle & small wooden knob on foller that holds nutmeg against grating surface; made over a long time period with various knobs & handles, some stained green. Nutmeg could be moved "forward and back, and from side to side, preventing the grated Nutmeg adhering to the surface of the Grater and bringing every part of its surface into use," said 1892 ad. "The Edgar," mfd by Edgar Mfg. Co., Reading, MA, 5-7/8" L, pat'd Aug. 18, 1891. These were pat'd (as a variation of 1891 nutmeg grater of George H. Thomas, Chicopee Falls, MA) by Charles E. Damon, of Edgar & Damon. **$65-$85**

Classic. — These are a gotta-have, but as I reported last time, they've about reached their limit, and price seems to have stabilized or plateaued. Most are at lower level of this range.

Nutmeg grater, spring-loaded tin cylinder for nutmeg set at right angles to cranked grating disc, skinny tin tubular handle, attached with even narrower tubes, "The E. Carsley," pat'd by H. Carsley, Lynn, MA, 3-1/2" L, disk nearly 3" diameter (one without date is 4" L), pat'd Nov. 20, 1855, but made while "patent applied for." **$750-$850**

Nutmeg grater, nickeled steel, squeeze action, 2 halves consisting of tube with spring-held presser for nutmeg, & a curved backplate that has a curved rasping surface fixed at the bottom at right angles. This backplate is held against the palm, the fingers squeeze the cylinder with the nutmeg — causing it to move back & forth along rasp. A spring is also in the pivot & assists "the grasping and relaxation of the fingers." German (?), called "The Automatic" in ads, 4-1/2" x 2-1/2", pat'd c.1902. **$120-$150**

An anonymous **tip on grating nutmegs** appears in Aug. 1851 *American Agriculturist* , viz. "If a person begin to grate a nutmeg at the stalk end, it will prove hollow throughout; whereas the same nutmeg, grated on the other end, would have proved sound and solid to the last. This circumstance may thus be accounted for: The centre of a nutmeg consists of a number of fibres issuing from the stalk and its continuation through the centre of the fruit, the other ends of which fibres, though closely surrounded and pressed by the fruit, do not adhere to it. When the stalk is grated away, those fibres, having lost their hold, gradually drop out, and the nutmeg appears hollow; as more of the stalk is grated away, others drop out in succession, and the hollow continues through the whole nut by beginning at the contrary end, the fibres above mentioned are grated off at their core end, with the surround fruit, and do not drop out and cause a hole."

•   •   •   •

Several companies made nutmeg graters in Lynn, Massachussetts, but Lynn's largest industry by far was comprised of 150 ladies' shoe factories, which in 1870 employed 20,000 people. It certainly makes me wonder if there doesn't exist a good-luck shoe-shaped nutmeg grater made in Lynn to celebrate the town's main industry!

•   •   •   •

"General Directions for Making Cake. — When cake or pastry is to be made, take care not to make trouble for others by scattering materials, and soiling the table or floor, or by needless use of many dishes. Put on a large and clean apron, roll your sleeves above the elbows, tie something over your head lest hair may fall, take care that your hands are clean, and have a basin of water and a clean towel on hand. Place everything you will need on the table, butter your pans, grate your nutmegs and squeeze your lemons. Then break your eggs, each in a cup by itself, lest adding a bad one should spoil the whole. Make your cake in wood or earthen, and not in tin." Mrs. Mary Hooker Cornelius, *The Young Housekeeper's Friend* , Boston, 1846. Twenty years after this — even longer — people were dying after being operated on by medical doctors who didn't know enough about the causes of sepsis and infection to wear clean coveralls, cover their hair, or wash their hands and instruments. It's too bad doctors didn't learn from cookbooks.

Nutmeg grater, tall tin pocket grater, side unfolds & reveals grating surface, American (?), 2-3/4" H, 3rd quarter of the 19th C. **$175-$275**

Nutmeg grater, tin body, round grating disc, wood handle & presser that holds meg against grater, black paper label with gold lettering, "Brown & Hasler," Lynn, MA, 7" L, "patent applied for" c. 1870s to 1890s. **$850-$950**

It is always possible with "**pat apple**" (as Bob Cahn says) pieces, that a patent was never granted. Examiners in the patent office were always complaining how silly some submitted ideas were, and how they exhibited no new (and therefore patentable) mechanisms or design, and in fact, how many of them didn't work. By putting "patent applied for" on your goods, however, you put a mantle of respectability on your item, and perhaps a tiny measure of protection, though the notion that someone else might copy your unpatentable invention is wishful thinking. Mystery writer Margery Allingham had her detective Albert Campion muse in *Flowers For the Judge* (a highly recommended mystery), while looking at a strange old key, that it "was squat and heavy and had that curious unsatisfactory appearance which is peculiar to old-fashioned patent devices which have never been really successful."

Nutmeg grater, tin, "cigar" cylinder with "chimney" nutmeg holder, wood knob, 4-3/4" L, marked "Edw. Snyder, Massilon Ohio," late 19th or early 20th C. **$500-$575**

Nutmeg grater, tin, cigar cylinder with "chimney" nutmeg holder, wood knob slightly fancier than other shorter one, grating surface differs too, American, 5-3/8" L, late 19th or early 20th C. **$500-$600**

Nutmeg grater, stamped, pieced & punctured tin, combination grater, pie crimper & can opener, probably "Morgan," English, late 19th C. **$250-$300**

Nutmeg grater, tin, looks like Mississippi steam boat, round tin bottom, sliding, spring-loaded hopper for nutmeg, little hanging wire loop, no mark, 6-1/4" L, pat'd 7/16/1867 by R. H. Chinn. **$850-$950**

Nutmeg grater, tin, loopy wire handle, cast iron with cast iron crank, big grating disc, American, 7" L, pat'd March 9, 1886. **$75-$100**

Nutmeg grater, tin, mechanical type like small Boye, but has wood knob on nutmeg housing, marked "The Del," American, 19th C. **$150-$200**

Nutmeg grater, tin & nickel-plated spring metal holds nutmeg in place, swings back & forth, mark stamped on back in the tin, "M. H. Sexton," Utica, NY, 4-3/4" L x 3" W, pat'd May 1896. This is a very desirable grater. **$850-$950**

Nutmeg grater, tin, oblong shallow piece with diagonal grating surface and with turned wooden end. Turned wooden nutmeg "barrel" has small wooden presser tamp that must be held against the nutmeg. The barrel slides on diagonal or transverse tracks (actually kittycorner) over grater, gratings fall out front. See also the "Monitor" grater. "Unique," Steel Edge Stamping & Retinning Co., Boston, MA, advertised in 1892 (maybe. before); poss. rip-off of 1889 "Monitor"; or poss. is the 1889 A. J. Boult's English patent. This grater used to be (back in the 1970s & early 1980s) the desirable rarity that occasionally showed up at antique shows priced above $150. It's been passed in the long stretch by all the oddities that have surfaced in last decade. **$125-$200**

Nutmeg grater, tin, simple crank mechanism, odd bridge effect of small pencil-thin tin tubes and struts (see first group picture of nutmeg graters), marked "H. Carsley," Lynn, MA, 3-7/8" L, marked "patent applied for," but pat'd 11/20/1855. **$575-$675**

Nutmeg grater, tin, small box grater, oblong shape with flat side almost completely covered with grating surface, large hanging hole, pat'd by W. Bradley, Lynn, MA, pat'd Jan. 29, 1867. **$110-$135**

1867, a Grate Year — The Bradley almost starts the year off for nutmeg graters. But **(1)** patent was granted Jan. 8, 1867, to L.V. Badger, Chicago, IL.; **(2)** granted Bradley; **(3)** granted March 5, to J. A. Hooper, South Berwick, ME; **(4)** & **(5)** granted July 16, to R. H. Chinn, Washington, DC, and to C. A. Durgin, NYC, NY; **(6)** granted July 23, to R. W. Whitney & J. P. Davis, South Berwick, ME; **(7)** granted Aug. 6, to L. Von Froben, Washington, DC; **(8)** granted Sept. 3, to A. S. Skillin and G. W. Reed, Portland, ME; **(9)** granted Sept. 24, to C. Worden, Binghamton, NY; and **(10)** Dec. 17, to W. W. Owen and D. Kelly. <u>I have not been able to find out what was the impetus in that year.</u> Of 27 nutmeg patents granted up through 1873, 10 were 1867 (plus the cap on another), 2 were 1866, and 4 were 1868, leaving only 11 from 1854 (the earliest specific nutmeg grater) through 1873. I tried to check tariffs, cookbooks, periodicals, but nothing popped out as significant. Any ideas?

Nutmeg grater, tin, spring-loaded boxed housing for nutmeg tracks along edges of oblong grating surface, "The Boye," Boye Needle Co., Chicago, NYC & San Francisco, about 6" L, pat'd Sept. 22, 1914. **$75-$125**

Nutmeg grater, tin & varnished turned wood (also found with wood part stained a sort of pinky-red color), rectangular grating plate, set in braced tin frame with turned wooden end. A little straight-sided nutmeg holder with wooden screw-top, is slid back & forth over grater along diagonal edge track. Printed with direction "Press Down Lightly." See also the "Unique" grater identified in old ads as "The Monitor," Boston, MA, 4-1/2" L x 1-15/16" W, pat'd March 18, 1889, in circle on lid of meg holder. The name Monitor may appear on a paper label, if

I-75. Nutmeg graters. *Clockwise from one with hand:* **(1)** *The "Automatic," squeeze-action, grating on inside of curved surface. 4-1/4" x 2-1/2", nickeled steel, c.1903. "Nutmeg is placed in the hollow tube, the tube is grasped by the hand, and 'there you are.'" A bar-suppliers' catalog said "It is the only automatic nutmeg grater where you can hold the glass in one hand and manipulate the grater with the other."* **(2)** *1924 subscription premium from* American Cookery *magazine. Maker not identified, but style is 19th C.* **(3)** *Patent drawing. Albert L. Platt, 10/3/1893. May not have been made — not known.* **(4)** *"Boye Sanitary" grater, Boye Needle Co., pat'd 9/29/1914. Box holding nutmegs opens when slid out of side tracking.* **(5)** *"Little Rhody," wood & tin, red & black paper label, 1880s.* *(1)* **$120-$175;** *(2)* **$400 and up;** *(4)* **$75-$125;** *(5)* **$200-$275**

any such remain, distributed or possibly even mfd by New England Novelty Manufacturing Co., which in 1890 was apparently the only manufacturer of nutmeg graters. I suppose by that time powdered nutmeg in tins had pretty much obviated the need for the graters. **$165-$200**

Nutmeg grater, tin & wire, "New Rapid," mfd by Hamlin & Russell Mfg. Co., Worcester, MA, came in 2 sizes, small and large, pat'd Dec. 26, 1877. **$45-$65**

Nutmeg grater, tin & wire, curved quadrant grating surface, spring-loaded nutmeg holder with blue painted wooden foller or plunger moves in arc over grater, looks like rocket launcher, American, about 5" (hard to measure this shape), 19th C. **$550-$650**

Nutmeg grater, tin & wire, strap handle, launching cylinder with spring-loaded wooden foller, wire crank with small wood knob, about 6-1/4" L diagonally, pat'd 10/13/1857 by Nathan Ames. **$120-$150**

Nutmeg grater, tin & wire, "Will grate four times faster than any other yet made," "Yankee No. 1," mfd by Hamlin & Russell Mfg. Co., Worcester, MA, c.1884. **$45-$55**

Nutmeg grater, tin, with musical-note-shaped hollow tin handle with ovoid hinged lid covering nutmeg storage & grating chamber. Only marking: "Press lightly." 7-1/2" L, late 19th C. One of most asked-for graters but very scarce. **$850-$950**

Nutmeg grater, tin & wood, oblong wooden body with works at one end, nutmeg storage at other end has tin cap & little wooden knob on top to pull back spring-loaded pressure foot, wire crank on side turns grating cylinder against nutmeg, "Standard," Standard Co, Boston, 6-1/8" L, marked pat'd Dec. 25, 1877; re-introduced to trade in July 1890, now with elongated box body & handle, unlike original of 1877, which had a turned wood handle. See "L" in second group photo. Although a date is stamped on this grater, a patent search fails to turn one up. <u>The so-called patent date sometimes turns out to be the date the application was filed for consideration</u>, but no nutmeg grater was patented in 1878 (or 1877 either). (The 25th was on a Tuesday in 1877.) Original "Standard" was called the "Rajah" grater in c.1880 catalog of novelties for traveling salesmen, and when advertised in Simmons Hardware Co.'s 1885 catalog. **$200 and up**

Nutmeg grater, turned wood, 3-part, little cup with knobbed lid that is fitted with punctured tin grating surface; lower part is fitted with the same (the nutmeg is rubbed between the 2 graters by twisting the top back & forth), & the grated nutmeg goes into bottom, poss. American, prob. English, 6" H, mid 19th C. **$175-$200**

Nutmeg grater, turned wood with punctured tin disc, very nice screwed-on springy wood pressure foot, pat'd by A. S. Skillin and G. W. Reed, Portland, ME, 6-7/8" L, pat'd Sept. 3, 1867. **$400-$500**

Nutmeg grater, wood knob & tin body, black & red paper label still attached, "The Little Rhody," American, late 19th C. **$200-$275**

Nutmeg grater, wood, tin & wire, long wooden piece with wire & wood piece to hold nutmeg against rather big grating disc, crank comes out of center of disc, paper label on long wood piece, "Common Sense" grater, invented by R. W. Whitney & J. P. Davis, not necessarily made by the inventors, who lived in South Berwick, ME, 5-1/4" L, pat'd July 23, 1867. **$400-$475**

Nutmeg grater & cookie cutter combined — See Chapter IV (Form, Mold, Shape and Decorate), picture IV-255.

Orange juicer, mechanical, cast iron, oak base painted a dark brown, lever action, definitely for oranges not lemons, no maker, 9-1/2" H, pat'd Jan. 31, 1886. **$150-$200**

Orange peeler, small, curved steel blade with painted turned wooden handle. Held in the right hand, the blade is slipped under the peel & is drawn toward the thumb while the orange is turned with the other hand. (Works same way as successful 1980s orange peeler made by a man in the Midwest, featured on *60 Minutes* & sold through mail.) Mfd by Robert S. West, Cleveland, OH, c.1890. **$5-$8**

Oyster knife, fish-shaped metal, poss. CT, 19th C. **$20-$25**

Oyster knife, one piece of cast tool steel, square handle so it wouldn't slip easily, sword-like blade, prying edges are thin but not sharp, "Stortz & Son," Philadelphia, PA, early 20th C. **$25-$30**

Paring knife, steel blade, wooden handle & brass bolster (a bolster on a knife is like a ferrule on a tool), handle marked "POTATO," American (?), 6" L, 20th C. **$45-$65**

Pastry knife, a form of dough scraper & cutter, sometimes called a chopping knife & probably used as such, this type for dividing dough for loaves of bread, for example, or for scraping pastry board. This one is made of a single wide piece of steel, rolled top edge forms cylindrical handle, no finger cutout, American, 4-1/2" H x 5" W, turn of century. **$12-$18**

Pea sheller, cast iron, screw clamps, 2-sided to split the pod, goes through rollers to pop peas out, marked only with date, but pat'd by S. Ustick, Philadelphia, PA, May 5, 1868. See knife sharpener entry in Chapter IX (Wash, Repair and Sharpen). **$55-$85**

Pea sheller, galvanized cast iron, screw clamp, downturned spout releases shelled peas, angled hopper on top, hook at bottom of frame holds small pail to catch (we wonder how well) the shells as they are expelled from rear of cranked machine, "Acme," Acme Pea Sheller Co., NYC, 7" H, patent applied for c.1880s-1890s. **$80-$110**

Puree of Peas. — Wash a pint of green peas in cold water; then put them in a saucepan with boiling water and cook 20 minutes. Have them dry when done. Press through a colander. Boil one half pint milk, add a small onion, three or four cloves and a small sprig of parsley. Rub a tablespoon each of flour and butter together. Strain the milk over the peas, put back in saucepan, stir in the flour and butter, and let boil, stirring to prevent sticking. Season with salt and pepper and serve." *Ladies Home Journal,* April 1890.

• • • •

"Pea Fritters. — Boil a pint of green peas until tender. Mash them while hot and rub through a colander. Season with pepper, salt and a tablespoon of butter. Let cool, add the yolks of two well-beaten eggs, a cup of cream, one teacupful and a half of flour, and a half teaspoon of soda and one of cream of tartar, sifted several times with the flour. Stir and beat well. When ready to use, beat in the white of the eggs and fry, a spoonful at a time, in boiling lard." (*Ibid .*)

I-76. Pea sheller. *"Acme," Acme Pea Sheller Co., NYC. Galvanized cast iron, screw clamps. Pods fell out back into pail hung on frame's hook; peas fell into dish.* **$45-$60**

Pea sheller, sheet metal painted green, rubber feet, crank with yellow wooden knob, you roll pea pods between 2 black hard rubber rollers; presumably pods pop & peas patooie out the chute, decal label, "Holmes Pea-Sheller," Holmes Mfg. Co., Los Angeles, CA, 5-1/4" L, patent pending, c.1910s to 1930s. **$40-$60**

Peach parer, cast iron on long wooden board base, has 2 forks opposing each other; the "large fork turns the peach, the small one turns upon the rod like a swivel when the peach is turned, and serves to hold up the outer end of the peach. The stone in each peach prevents the peach from being pushed on to one fork and held by that alone," mfd by David H. Whittemore, successor to Whittemore Brothers, Worcester, MA, 1860s. "The above machine," continues an 1868 ad, "is also superior for paring potatoes, and even when the potato is long and wilted, it works complete, the small or outer fork serving to hold up the outer end of the potato while it is being pared. It is also a good apple paring machine — the use of the small or sliding fork being dispensed with." Whittemore, earlier of Chicopee Falls, MA, also was issued apple parer & slicer patents. **$125-$150**

Peach parer, cast iron, screw clamps, "Lightning," D. H. Goodell Co., Antrim, NH, a county fair winner in fall 1869, but pat'd May 10, 1870. **$60-$75**

Peach parer — See also apple parer and peach parer

Peanut shucker, wood, 2-part mill, turned on an axle by means of fancy turned handlebar-like handle. American, 19" D grinding surfaces, mid 19th C. **$250-$325**

Pepper mill, cast iron, wall-mounted side mill like small coffee mill, c.1900. **$16-$22**

Pepper mill, turned maple, in shape of wine bottle, with "laser engraved" label depicting a vineyard, works in guise of corkscrew with T-handle, grounds come out bottom, sold through Bloomingdales in 1983 catalog, 1980s. **$35-$45**

Pepper mill, turned wood cylinder with glass liner forming effect of windows, metal crank, "Peugot" (yes, it's the bicycle manufacturer), French, 20th C. **$25-$40**

Pepper mill, turned hardwood (prob. oak) base topped by complicated steel geared mechanism, including cranked bevel gears, 7-3/4" H, American, 1944 to present (new ones offered in mail order catalogs). **$8-$20**

I-77. Peach stoners & parers. (L) *Cast iron stoner, screw clamps, plunges and apparently cuts peach in half with blade. From F. A. Walker catalog, Boston, 1870s.* **(M)** *"Lightning" parer, mfd. by Goodell Co., Antrim, NH. Sargent & Co., agents (their name may appear on some gadgets like this, I don't know). Exhibited at 1869 NY, St. Louis and other agricultural fairs & won prizes. Pat'd 8/17/1869.* **(R)** *"Rollman No.6", Rollman Mfg. Co., Mt. Joy, PA. "Patent applied for" in c.1901-05 catalog.* **$125-$150; $60-$70; $110-$135**

Pepper mill, turned hardwood, nickeled mountings, 3-1/2" to 4" H, American, late 19th C. In the 1880s Americans, used to using pepper shakers at table, seemed to find the French use of pepper mills a novel good idea, for flavor & to avoid adulterated packaged ground pepper. This was about 1880. Many styles of carved or turned hardwood mills were offered in the 1920s. **$10-$15**

Pineapple eye snips, cast iron painted black, scissor action with attached steel blades, one a sort of scoop beak with sharp tapered end, other an open oval, with sharp top edge nearest scoop part, W. H. Collins, NYC, 5-5/8" L, 1930 ad, prob. made before that. **$8-$12**

Peter Piper Peeled a Peck of Peaches. — I have at hand the Sept. 15, 1866 issue of the weekly *Alexandria Price Current Letter-Sheet*, a flimsy-paper report on market prices of goods from Agricultural Implements to Wamsutta cotton prints, from Ale to Shingles, published by Knox & Wattles, Forwarding & Commission Merchants, of Alexandria, VA. A run of them for a year would be more interesting, but still, there are some tidbits. For example, "DRIED FRUIT — Demand dull. Tendency downwards. We quote: PEACHES peeled ....17@20¢ per lb. [17 lbs at 20¢ each] PEACHES not peeled ....11@12 APPLES ....10@11." It was worth peeling peaches, in other words. As a comparative, 50 lbs of new potatoes cost 60¢ whereas sweet potatoes were $8 a bushel, and New Orleans molasses was $1.30 a gallon!

• • • •

Finding patent dates is sometimes hard, but it's fun. This one eluded me at first, but then I found, under "Parer, Fork for peach," in the *Subject Index to Patents*, two patents with the right dates, which were for the 4-pronged fork that slips into the end of the peach and sort of cradles the pit or stone. They were awarded to C. D. House, Lake Village, NH, on Aug. 17, 1869, and to D. H. Goodell, Antrim, NH, May 10, 1870. Otherwise, the machine itself is like the Lightning apple parer. In the *American Agriculturist*, June 1872, there is this about a peach parer: "<u>A continuous and urgent inquiry for a machine for Paring Peaches, has been ringing in our ears from all Peach-growing sections, for the past five years,</u> and in response to this universal appeal, the manufacturers of the Lightning & Turn-Table Apple Parers have at last succeeded in obtaining and securing a device for Holding and Paring Peaches, which is as practical and economical as the Apple Parer, and cannot fail to come into immediate and general use." An ad in the same magazine, a year earlier, shows a detailed linecut of the Lightning Peach Parer, with the half round horizontal gear, clearly shown with patent date of Aug. 17, 1869. I reread a letter from collector Evelyn Welch, from Sept. 1983, exactly six years later, and found something I must have missed before. She writes about a non-mechanical hand-held peach pitter, "Sometime take a peach pitter, cut a ring around a clingstone peach with a knife, beginning at the stem hole, following the line across the peach. Take the proper sized pitter for that sized peach, slip it into the peach around the pit with the line on the peach on your left, turn pitter to side, then back around under pit, and the top will slip off. Then scoop the pit out of other half. Seems the pit has a ledge on the side and this is the professional way I was taught to cut clings at the Pacific Pea Co. Cannery (now Hunt Wesson) in Oakdale, California, when I was 16 years old (1930) and proudly earned $6 per day. We wore white cotton gloves in case the pitter slipped. We would "ring" a lugbox of clings with the knife, then pit them by the box. What I'm getting at is the story behind the need for a tool to remove pits. Pear pitting is different altogether." For more on patents see chapters XIX-XXI.

It's so Easy **PATTERSON'S Pineapple Eye Clip**

I-78. Pineapple Eye Clip. *"Patterson's," M. E. Mosher, Mfr., Rochester, NY. Trigger action, nickeled steel. Introduced in 1905.* **$15-$25**

Pineapple eye snips, looks like small pair of scissors; one hardened steel blade terminates in small spoon, other has a hollow cutter that fits into spoon bowl — as the inventor put it — "adapted to engagement with each other accurately, somewhat like the beak of parrot or an eagle," pat'd by John F. Pack, on Aug. 27, 1901. **$12-$18**

Pineapple eye snips, or eye clips, nickeled steel curved cylinder, sort of with a pistol grip, with trigger near front that you pull to make top part of little cutter clip out the eye, "Patterson's," mfd by M. E. Mosher, Rochester, NY, c.1905. **$15-$25**

Pineapple eye snips, or pineapple eyer, simple turned wood handle, triggered snip with spring to return to starting position, one fixed piece like tiny cone, open along top side, which would be stabbed under the pineapple eye before pulling trigger to cause cutter blade to come forward & slip into top of eye, completing the small conical excision, "Dixie," mfd by W. H. Glenny & Co., Rochester, NY, 5-1/2" L, patent applied for c.1904. **$15-$25**

Poppyseed mill, green painted iron, screw clamps, "Kosmos," 20th C. **$30-$50**

Poppyseed mill, turquoise green painted cast iron, spun brass hopper, screw clamps to table, "Standard," prob. PA, by the cherry pitter company, in Mt. Joy, 9-1/4" H, c.1890s. Thin hopper usually bent, even split. **$28-$40**

Reproduction alert: Cumberland General Store offers a new $35+ poppyseed mill with white enameled screw clamp frame, "hand ground steel milling cone."

Potato chip machine, "machined steel with spring steel knife and lasts indefinitely," "unexcelled for slicing potatoes, carrots, beets, onions or any vegetable or fruit," black enameled handle, mfd by Mebhut & Platts, Ilion, NY, 8-3/8" L, "patent pending" c. 1920s (?). $2 was original cost! **$15-$20**

Potato cutter, stamped tin, counter top, for making french fries, "Maid of Honor," American, 1930s (?). See the whatzit cutter at end of Chapter IV (Form, Mold, Shape and Decorate). **$7-$10**

Potato french fry cutter or Saratoga chipper, tin cylinder with a cutting frame (like a tic-tac-toe game) to do 25 french fries or Saratogas at a time, "Silver's Sure-Cut," 4" H, turn of century. **$40-$60**

Potato & fruit press, what other makers called a **ricer**, japanned malleable cast iron frame, handle & lever handle, heavily tinned plunger & perforated cup removable for cleaning, marked on top handle or lever is "Silver & Co., NY"; "Genuine Silver Press" on lower handle, Brooklyn, NY, one size only, claimed to be "the largest and most powerful," c.1880-1910. In an early 20th C catalog Silver & Co. claimed to be "originators of the hand press and have for 30 years maintained its quality and steadily decreased its price." **$25-$40**

Potato masher, heavy twisted wire, wooden handle, American, 22-1/2" L, large hotel or restaurant size, 20th C. **$22-$30**

Potato masher, long turned handle with little round mushroom or button end, heavy round steel head, flat disc with perforated holes in small & medium size, "Hercules," mfd by Handy Things Co., Ludington, MI, c.1904. **$15-$25**

Potato masher, turned upright wooden handle, flat mashing head of nickeled iron wire woven into intricate openwork "snowflake," "web," or "gear wheel" head of heavy wire, American, 9" L, c.1880s to 1900. This masher is particularly referred to by Parloa, as follows: "Many housekeepers prefer the kind of potato masher shown below to the wooden one. In unskilled hands it gives a lighter dish of potatoes than the wooden masher, but the wooden one will be needed for other things which the wire one would not answer." Maria Parloa, *Kitchen Companion*, Boston, 1887. **$10-$20**

Potato masher, turned wooden handle, heavy wire, double action: push on handle & upper set of wires goes down, A & J, Binghamton, NY, 11-1/4" H down to 9-1/2" H, pat'd 1912. In 1984 there was a UPI story about an artist named Byron Randall who ran a bed & breakfast in Tomales, CA, & decorated the B & B with his collection of 384 potato mashers. Now there's a goal for you, collectors! **$30-$40**

Potato masher, turned wooden handle, mashing head is 2 heavy wire flat spirals, American, 10" L, c.1920s-30s. **$15-$18**

Reproduction alert. — The Androck masher/ricer, next listing, was update of an older one. But the strange story concerns Virginia Nicoll of Meridith, NH, and her MMPM Company (My Mother's Potato Masher). She started in 1984 making a "reproduction" of the tool, which she says her grandmother "purchased from an itinerant peddler in rural Pennsylvania back in the 1800s." In my opinion, the earliest model of this masher dates back to the 1890s at the earliest, although (MMPM ads say "patent circa 1882"). The Nicolls had a tool and die company make the mashing plate of carbon steel with turned birch wood handle, and they have received a lot of publicity and enjoyed great sales. I have no idea how many of the original 10,000 ordered from the die-maker have been sold, or if they are now into the hundreds of thousands.

I-79. Metal potato mashers. *Along back row are just 4 of the scores of cleverly bent, woven, twisted, coiled & braided wire mashers, with vertical turned wood handles. Made by many makers. About 7" H to 14" H for household ones; even longer for hotel or restaurant versions. Two in front, galvanized or tinned cast iron, are called potato muddlers, and date at least to 1870.* **$10-$25**

Potato masher, turned wooden handle with round palm-fitting knob at end, with nickeled iron L-shape masher blade with 2 rows of long slots cut lengthwise, bent at right angles to the handle, Androck "potato ricer," mfd by Washburn Co., Worcester, MA, 9-1/2" L, c.1936. **$10-$20**

Potato masher, turned wooden handle, twisted wire arch with 2 rows of 4 curvy zigzags, Kilbourne Mfg. Co., Troy, NY, c.1908. **$22-$30**

Potato masher, wires bent in shape of fingers, looks like glove dryer, 2 tiers of fingers set 20 degrees or so on horizontal plane, white-painted turned wood handle, A & J, Binghamton, NY, 11" L, 20th C. **$15-$18**

Potato masher, zigzag wire with long turned wooden handle, commercial size one, 22" L, 20th C. **$25-$30**

Potato masher — See also eggbeater & potato masher, in Chapter II (Mix, Beat, Stir, Churn and Blend).

I-80. Plunger potato mashers, *like big versions of potato ricers. Perforated tin cylinders, wood plungers, wrought iron stands. Sizes from 6" diameter to 9" diameter. Early 20th C.* **$20-$45**

"Imitation Spaghetti. — Boil and mash potatoes, adding salt and butter, but only a tablespoonful of milk, as you want a stiff paste. Rub this through a colander into a buttered pie or pudding dish. It will fall in small, pipe-like shapes. Leave them as they lie, and, when all the potato has passed through, set the dish on the upper grating of the oven to brown delicately." Marion Harland, *House & Home, a Complete Housewife's Guide*, Philadelphia, 1889.

Potato mashers, wire & wood, various designs from a flat spiraled head, or a wire grid, to a slightly rocking set of 8 fingers stamped of steel or a criss-cross of loosely strung wires, most with wooden handles, some few have nickeled iron loop handles, American or German, most about 8" to 10" H, late 19th or early 20th C. **$10-$25**

Potato peeler, also for sweet potatoes, parsnips, carrots, turnips or beets, large cylindrical chamber sets down into base that screw clamps to table, chamber is lined with perforated steel or carborundum to scrape off paring, reservoir of water at top of cylinder, cast iron gear in bottom, side crank, long hose-like tube that leads from base carries off ground-away peelings by the water stream coming from chamber above, American, about 16" H x 8" diameter, c.1910s. **$40-$55**

Potato peeler, looks like lathe-style apple parer, tiny paring blade, cast iron frame, turn the handle, stick potato on spade like prong that rotates, "Nu-Way Automatic," mfd by Guaranty Products Co., St. Louis, MO, early 20th C. **$65-$80**

Potato peeler, tin with gritty composition that literally sands off the peeling. Looks like a shallow oval tart pan with crimped edges, filled with the grit compo cement, with a bracket strap handle across back, "Hamlinite Peeler," maker not known, 4-1/2" L x 2-1/4" W, pat'd July 20, 1920; prob. made for fewer than 10 years. **$10-$15**

I-81. Potato parers. (T) *"Saratoga Chips. 75 Cents" embossed on horizontal framework. "Sold by Agents" on screw clamp. Taylor Mfg. Co., New Britain, CT. Pat'd 6/18/1878. Photo courtesy John Lambert.* **(B)** *"White Mountain" parer, Goodell Co. "This machine will also pare Quinces and Pears" say ads. Late 19th C. on — sold for many years.* **$75+**

I-82. Potato ricers, *or hand presses. Showing 2 basic styles — the round cylinder "drum" style, and the "V"-shaped one like the famous Henis press.* **(L)** *"Genuine Silver Press," Silver & Co., Brooklyn, removable cups. Strong & durable, "the castings are made of a peculiar composition of iron which absolutely guarantees their unbreakability." c.1910.* **(R)** *4-1/4" x 4-1/4" cup. Tinned malleable cast iron. c.1905.* **$10-$25**

I-83. Potato slicers. (L) *"Marguerita Macaroni" — the "only practical machine for preparing the potatoes in continuous curling strips, for boiling, stewing, or potato ribbon." Nickeled iron. Could also be used for cutting "beets, carrots, turnips, &c." for garnishing. 1914 catalog.* **(R)** *Potato slicer, pat'd 1870, and 1871 (?) or 1877 (?). A witch in a diamond-patterned dress, stirring her brew. F. A. Walker catalog, 1870s.* **$75-$150**

Potato peeler, tin with wooden handle, "Morton Salt Potato Peeler," 20th C. **$10-$15**

Potato ricer, red paint enameled malleable iron lever handles, tinned perforated cup, tinned metal presser, mfd by Handy Things, Ludington, MI, about 12" L, c.1940s. **$6-$12**

Potato slicer, cast iron, tabletop, 3 knee-bent legs attached to large round slicer housing, with potato-size hopper & tall vertical shaft with crank to turn blade inside, a plate could be set underneath to catch the slices of potato (or other raw root vegetables), mfd by W. L. & T. M'Clinton (?) or W. L. & T. M. Clinton (sold in early 20th C by V. Clad & Sons), Ithaca, NY, about 15" diameter, pat'd Oct. 1-?, 187-?. (Looks like Oct. 10, 1876.) **$95-$125**

Potato slicer, clamp on, high cast iron frame with diamond cutouts, stanchion divides into 2 arms to take shaft for crank, the other end of which is stuck into the potato, the blade is fixed at table level, supposed to slice a potato into one long continuous spiral (although it would fall apart before it could ever get as long as the old advertising picture), advertised for making Saratoga chips or cucumber garnishes, "Saratoga Potato Peeler & Slicer," Goodell Co., Antrim, NH, pat'd 1870, 1871. **$100-$150**

Potato slicer, iron mounted on wood, potato stuck on "piston" is drawn toward revolving cranked slicing blade by long spring, sold by F. A. Walker, Boston, pat'd by S. Walker, NYC, June 6, 1865. **$50-$75**

"Silver Pie. — Peel and grate one large white potato into a deep plate; add the juice and grated rind of one lemon, the beaten white of one egg, one teacup of white sugar, and one teacup of cold water. Pour this into a nice undercrust and bake. When done, have ready the whites of three eggs well beaten, half a cup of powdered sugar, a few drops of rose-water, all thoroughly beaten. Put this mixture on the top of the pie evenly and return to the oven, to stiffen a few moments. When sent to the table just cold lay a spoonful of currant jelly on the center of each piece to ornament if you wish." Mrs. M. L. Scott, *Home Cook Book*, 1876.

I-84. Potato & vegetable slicers. (1) *Also called a "citron slicer" in confectioners' catalogs. "Lightning," japanned cast iron, screw clamps. 4 cutting blades to disc. 10-1/2" L, late 19th C. & sold for decades.* **(2)** *"Clinton Patent," M. L. & C. M. Clinton, Ithaca, NY, Pat'd Oct. 10, 1874. Japanned cast iron. For making Saratoga potato chips up to 1/4" thick, & for apples, cucumbers & cabbage.* **(3)** *"Rapid Tomato Slicer." In Valentine Clad, Philadelphia, catalog, c.1870s-1890s.* **(4)** *"Enterprise No. 49" vegetable slicer. 16" H x 11" diameter cylinder revolves. Sometimes called the "Boss." Late 19th, early 20th C.* (1) **$55-$65;** *others:* **$125-$200**

Onion peelers are valuable but not collectible. "The earliest onion peeler I know about wore a gingham apron and sat on a chair while she peeled the onions and cried." Henry Landis, Landis Valley (PA) Museum, in response to a query in the Early American Industries "*Chronicle,*" April 1951.

• • • •

Dr. Samuel Johnson defined it thus: "The quern consists of two stones, about a foot and a half in diameter; the lower is a little convex, to which the concavity of the upper must be fitted. In the middle of the upper stone is a round hole, and on one side is a long handle. The grinder [person operating the quern] sheds the corn gradually into the hole with one hand, and works the handle round with the other. The corn slides down the convexity of the lower stone, and, by the motion of the upper, is ground in its passage." As quoted in Webster & Parkes, *An Encyclopædia of Domestic Economy*, 1848 NY edition of English book of 1845.

Querne, primitive grinding mill for seeds, grains, etc., used for the same purposes as a mortar & pestle. Small section of half a log, fitted with wooden peg feet, round hollowed out "mortar" portion with a millstone to fit, high bracket or "goalpost" frame above has rod or handle to turn the upper small millstone against the lower one, prob. Scottish though found in 18th C American kitchens, about 12" to 14" L x 15" to 18" H overall, 18th or very early 19th C. **$175-$300**

Raisin seeder, 7 wires set into wood block, upright mushroom knob handle, "The Everett," Boston, 3-1/8" H x 2" W, 1880s to 1890s. **$50-$75**

Raisin seeder, also for grapes, tinned cast iron, screw clamps to table, giraffe-neck arched frame, side crank moved a "saw disc" inside that rubbed against the raisins, small hopper with regulating device in side, rubber rollers, "will seed a pound in 5 minutes," embossed "Wet the raisins" cast in side. "Enterprise #36" family size, Enterprise Mfg. Co., 11" H, hopper 2-1/2" x 2-1/8", pat'd April 2 & Aug. 20, 1895; still being sold into 20th C. The No. 38, twice as expensive and somewhat larger, was for hotels, bakeries, restaurants, etc. **$30-$60**

Raisin seeder, black knobby turned wood handle, tinned ferrule, 7 close-set tinned wire needles enclosed in a ring with wire, American, 3-1/2" L, business part is 1-1/4" L, late 19th C. Date stamped on end of handle is clearly May 2, followed by a date that appears

I-85. Querne. *A fairly primitive grinding mill for seeds, spices & grains. 2 round mill stones, from 6" to 10" diameter (these are 6"), the upper one turned by a handle or knob. Wood frame, 17-1/2" H x 13" L x 7" W. Swedish or Danish, 18th or early 19th C. Ex-Keillor Collection.* **$200-$300**

either to be 1888 or 1883 (perhaps it is 1893?). A raisin seeder *was* pat'd May 2, 1871, by W. Curtiss, Jr., of Wolcottville, CT: this may be his. Perhaps an extension or an improvement (such as the adding of 5 more wires) of the patent was granted and a new name "Columbian" given as a deliberate tie-in with the World's Columbian Exposition of 1893. (May 2 came on a Tuesday in 1882 and 1893, but no raisin seeders were patented then.) Very similar is the "Columbian Raisin Seeder," with knobbed & turned wooden handle, tin ferrule & 12 wires, made in the 1890s. **$50-$75**

"Indian Chutney. — For this boil 1 1/2 dozen sour apples, peeled, cored and chopped, in 3 pints of cider vinegar, adding a pound of stoned and chopped raisins, 1 pound light brown sugar, 1 tablespoon salt, 1/4 pound finely chopped ginger root, 1/4 pound chopped onions, chopped garlic clove, 1/2 pound mustard seed that has been heated in oven, and either a small fiery pepper chopped, or a shake or two of cayenne. Cook until apple is soft, stirring constantly." *The Housewife* , Nov. 1909.

Raisin seeder, cast iron, 4 legs, levered press has 8 wires, no maker mark, American, approx. 6" L, pat'd May 7, 1895. **$350-$400**

Raisin seeder, cast iron, clamps to table, "EZY Raisin Seeder," with message to "Scald the Raisins," cast into frame, 5" H exclusive of wingnut, pat'd May 21, 1899. All I can say is, thank heaven for seedless grapes. **$325-$375**

Raisin seeder, cast iron, ornate, 3 legs, beautifully cast with grapes & leaves, cranked wheel, sits on table. (What is probably a later casting of this seeder was nickel-plated. Price now about the same.) This was in F. A. Walker dealer catalog, American (?) or maybe French — see quote below. Only 6-1/2" H x 4" W, c.1870. **$450 and up**

"A few days ago," wrote an editor in *American Agriculturist* , Nov. 1871, "we saw in a store a little machine which <u>looks like a bit of European workmanship.</u> It had a crank, and when that was turned there were all sorts of motions, evidently intended to accomplish

something, but what that was we could not guess. Here was a pretty position for an editor of a household department, not to know at sight what a household implement was for. But we had our compensation. We took possession of the little machine and submitted it to one after another at the offices. At last came Mr. Judd [publisher], who has the quickest eye for 'crinkums' and the sharpest mechanical talent of any one within our knowledge. He turned the machine, looked at it in all ways, then gave up. This ingenious machine is for removing the seeds from raisins, and we have had it figured as an illustration of the wonderful mechanical ingenuity that is at work to facilitate the simple operations of the household. Every housekeeper knows that raisins are all the better for being stoned, and she also knows how tedious is the operation when performed in the ordinary manner. With this machine, the stoning is performed with comparative rapidity. It has so many parts and so many movements, that it is not easy to represent it in a drawing. The machine being fastened to the table by a clamp, the raisins are pushed one by one upon the grating. The crank being turned, the plate above comes down and holds it in place; then another plate, which contains numerous blunt needles which pass through holes in the second plate is pressed down. These needles punch out the seeds of the raisins through the grating, and to make sure that they will be removed, there works underneath this grating a blunt knife, moved by a notch on the moving wheel as it is cranked. As the driving wheel revolves, an arm comes over and pushes the seeded raisin away to make room for another. We are aware that this may seem to be complicated when shown in an engraving, but if one sees the machine in operation it appears simple enough." Thanks, I think I'll pit prunes instead.

Raisin seeder, cast iron, painted black, screw clamps to table, spring tension lever action, levered part has 5 rows of prickers, then there's a moving plate with 5 slots through which prickers fit, then a plate with oval opening with one divider across short axis, finally a fixed flat plate against which prickers hit, no mark, American, about 5" H x 6-3/4" L handle, "patent applied for" late 19th C. **$150+**

Raisin seeder, cast iron, wire & rubber, screw clamps to table, not so elegant as the Enterprise, "Lightning," American, 7-1/4" H, pat'd 1895 & March 28, 1898. **$20-$35**

Raisin seeder, iron, "The Gem," Auburn, ME, 1895 patent. (Another one, slightly lower in value, is marked "Improved Gem.") **$50-$60**

I-87. Raisin seeders. *Cast iron, nickeled or galvanized, screw clamps.* **(L)** *"Enterprise No.36," Philadelphia. Embossed "Wet the raisins" along upright frame. Rubber roller inside. Pat'd 4/2/1895. A later patent seen on them is 8/20/1895. 11" H. The No.38 was for bakers & hotels; this for family use.* **(R)** *"X-Ray" seeder, composed of 38 different parts put together "as true and perfect as a watch." 1890s.* **$30-$60**

I-86. Raisin seeders. *Clockwise from top:* **(1)** *Nickeled cast iron, very decorative casting. (Not always plated.) 6-1/2" H x 4" W, 1870s.* **(2)** *"EZY" seeder, pat'd 5/21/1899. "Scald the raisins" cast into other side. 5" H, clamps to table edge.* **(3)** *"Everett," from 1890s, marked "patent applied for." Wire & wood, 3-1/8" L.* **(4)** *Cast iron with 8-wire seeder attached to lever. 4 legs. Pat'd 5/7/1895. (2) & (4) Located by the Primitive Man, Bob Cahn, Carmel, NY. (1) & (3) Collection of Meryle Evans. (1)* **$450+;** *(2)* **$325-$375;** *(3)* **$50-$75;** *(4)* **$350-$400**

Raisin seeder, cast iron with "38 different parts," screw clamps to & arches over table, for a tray & a tumbler to fit underneath, long crank handle, X-Ray Raisin Seeder Co., American, 1880s. **$30-$60**

A flyer for the X-Ray model states "The Seeder That Seeds! Finds Every Seed and Removes It! This is a model machine, composed of 38 different parts put together as true and perfect as a watch, not a single part can possibly get out of order. It will seed raisins as fast as you can drop them into the hopper and turn the crank. When we say seed, we mean it will remove every single seed! It will simply perforate the raisin and not cut it into shreds or mutilate it, every seed will come out dry and without the slightest waste. Talk about perfection — this machine is the very acme of it. . . We will replace any defective part free of charge any time within five years!" The original price was a dollar.

Reamer, cast aluminum, pours out either side, "Wearever E-12-1," mfd by Ebaloy Inc., Rockford, IL, 6" H, 20th C. **$5-$8**

Reamer, for citrus fruit, clear molded glass, saucer bowl & ribbed reamer cone, "Ideal," American, pat'd Jan. 31, 1888. **$20-$30**

Reamer, for oranges, lemons, limes, heavy molded glass, wide-lipped saucer with flat tab handle, very pointed conical reamer in center with 3 edges or "blades" full length, & 3 short ones, Easley No. 4, William F. Easley Mfg. Co., NYC, NY, 1909. **$30-$45**

Reamer, molded glass, conical reamer has blades or sharp edges & pointed projections in waffled pattern, base has holes, edge fits over tumbler, juice goes through holes, "Easley No. 2A," Easley Mfg. Co., early 20th C, they discontinued this non-saucer style by 1910. **$35-$45**

Reamer, for oranges, lemons, limes, 1-piece molded glass saucer & rounded conical reamer with 4 long "blades" or sharp edges from top to bottom, plus 7 little pyramidal points in each of 4 sections, no handle, basket pattern & rope border, Easley Mfg. Co., c.1902. **$30-$45**

Reamer, green plastic, "Ex-Squeeze-It," mfd by B C M, marked "D. R. G. M.," German, 5-1/4" diameter, patent #362187, c.1930s. **$10-$25**

Reamer, & lipped pouring bowl which it fits into, clear glass, painted flowers, "Baby's Orange" on bowl, American, turn of century. **$25-$35**

Reamer, sheet metal, painted white, stainless steel reamer & cup, long lever action, American, 9" H, 20th C. **$12-$15**

Reamer, spun aluminum with small ear handle, 20th C. **$3-$8**

Reamer, wall mounted, cast aluminum, usually missing wall bracket, "Mason's Sealed Sweet Juicer," c.1930s. **$8-$15**

Reamer & lemon slicer, die-molded red plastic, figural little chef, c.1940s to 1950s. **$5-$7**

Reamer or orange juicer, stamped aluminum, little pan with reamer cone inside, worked by rotating handle back & forth, "rotates on pivot base. Hold orange still ... swing handle!," doesn't work very well, "Kwicky," Quam-Nichols Co., Chicago, late 1940s. **$5-$9**

Reamer — See also juicer; lemon squeezer

Rutabaga slicer, or root vegetable & potato slicer, iron & brass on round wooden base, a sort of brace bit tool, blade makes "French fry" slices, or Saratoga clices, no mark, American (?), 18-1/2" H, base is 9" diameter and 5/8" thick, c.1870s (?). **$250-$275**

Sausage filler, japanned cast iron, like a curved elbow pipe with hopper & very long down-curved lever & presser at top, has long leg in back to bolt to table, short crosspiece for bolting in front, filling funnel fitted on lower end, one of three first pat'd by J. G. Perry, Kingston, RI, in 1859, 1860 and 1863, mfd by Peck, Stow & Wilcox, Southington, CT, 1890s. **$100-$145**

Sausage filler — See also meat grinders

Sausage grinder, cast iron, "O. V. B." or "Our Very Best," Hibbard, Spencer, Bartlett & Co., #8, turn of century. **$15-$20**

Sausage grinder, cast iron, "Keen Kutter #112," Simmons Hardware, 20th C. **$20-$30**

Sausage grinder, cast iron double cylinder type, cranked, mfd by Russell & Erwin, New Britain, CT, mid to late 19th C. **$24-$38**

Sausage grinder, cast iron, long body & long lever, American, late 19th C. **$25-$35**

Sausage grinder, homemade & primitive, very powerful looking, wooden box with hand forged hook latch, hinges unfortunately replaced by someone (who may have been using it right up into the 1980s) with cheapo 1950s kitchen cabinet hinges in "Colonial" hammered surface. Lift-out wooden drum inside has iron pins set in it, sort of spiralling around it, on pencil marked intersections carefully drawn by maker, American, 16-1/2" L x 8" diameter, early 19th C. **$135-$175**

Sausage grinder, iron, hangs on wall, 27" L, pat'd 1885. **$25-$55**

Sausage grinder, all wood, except for iron nails or spikes on revolving cranked drum inside, American, mid 19th C. **$120-$165**

Sausage grinder & stuffer, cast iron, 2 hinged parts, catch on side holds top on, 2 cutting blades & crank handle, bolts to table surface, needs funnel or gun fitted to end, no mark except "12," American, 7-5/8" L exclusive of crank handle, c. 3rd quarter 19th C. **$75-$95**

Sausage grinder & stuffer, screw clamp, tinned iron, Enterprise #38, pat'd 1888. **$40-$50**

Sausage grinder & stuffer, wood & wrought iron, tin gun, on platform meant to bridge 2 chairs, sawhorses or tables; water pump-like lever works up & down to stuff casings fitted onto gun, American, 19th C. **$90-$135**

Sausage gun, mostly wood with tin gun & iron bolts holding gun together, wooden frame pegged, on bench frame, long lever makes it look like a sculpture of an elephant. According to dealer Lenny Kislin it was made on the Yantz Farm, Red Hook, NY, 26-1/2" H x 37-1/2" L, 19th C. With this one you pay for sculpture. **$350-$400**

I-88. Mechanical sausage stuffers. Top: *"Stow's Patent," Russell & Erwin Mfg. Lever action in 2 sizes, for butchers or families. Pat'd 7/6/1858 by O. W. Stow, Plantsville, CT.* **Lower (L)** *"Hale Meat Cutter" and stuffer, also R & E and in their 1865 catalog, and later in a c.1900 catalog! Grinding drums lift out. Three sizes: 5", 6" & 7-1/2" cylinders. Couldn't find Hale in Patent Index.* **(R)** *"Sausage meat cutter," from* American Home Cook Book, *1854. There were several patents previous to 1854.* **$75-$250**

Sausage gun, tin cylinder with strap handle & small strap loop near gun end, long snout, perforations in flat end around where snout or spout is soldered, turned wooden foller or pusher, American, about 15" L exclusive of foller, c.1850s to 1860s. A Jan. 1850 article in *American Agriculturist* told how to make an almost identical "sausage cutter," and said the meat "is made finer or coarser according to the rapidity with which it is fed" into the hopper. **$65-$80**

Sausage stuffer, "Hubbard," 6 qt. capacity. **$35-$50**

Sausage stuffer, cast iron, mounted to plank, cranked, "Wagner Stuffer No. 3," Salem Tool Co., Salem, OR, mfd c.1900 from 1859 patent. Salem also mfd meat presses, ham pumps & brine guns. **$35-$45**

Sausage stuffer, commercial size, cast iron, hand cranked, hinged top, "Wagner Stuffer" cast in body, brass plate reads "Silver Mfg. Co.," "Salem, ORE," 36" L, prob. the J. Wagner (Pittsburgh, PA) patent of March 29, 1859. **$275-$375**

Sausage stuffer, handmade, all wood, including long box & turned screw which is cranked & slowly pushes ground sausage out end, sliding lid entire length of box for cleaning, prob. PA, 25" L x 5-3/4" square, c.1840s to 1850s. **$125-$160**

Sausage stuffer, tin & cast iron, spring-loaded lever action, mounts to tabletop, shaped sort of like an urn, "Angers Perfect No. 1 Filler," Sargent & Co., late 19th C. **$40-$60**

Sausage stuffer, tin cone with cast iron base, wooden plunger, American (?), c.1880s. **$25-$40**

Sausage stuffer, tin, hard maple plunger. Different size casing funnels attached by bayonet mount at end, needed 2 people or worked plunger against belly, American, each part 18" L, 19th C. **$55-$90**

Sausage stuffer, tin & wood, hand cranked, screw clamps to table, "P. S. & W. Co., No. 112," mfd by Peck, Stow & Wilcox Co., Southington, CT, 19th C. An 1890s brochure from P, S & W gives only one No. 112 "meat cutter and stuffer," that pat'd by A. W. Hale, New Britain, CT, on March 15, 1859. It's japanned cast iron, works horizontally, has detachable tin stuffing tube, feeds into top & has lift-out cast iron grinding drum with swirled "blades." Dover Stamping Co. offered Hale's machine in a 1869 catalog. Maybe tin version is a bit later. **$45-$55**

Sausage stuffer, handmade wooden box, sliding cover, wooden works inside too, no metal, 30" L, 19th C. **$75-$100**

Sausage stuffer, pieced tin cylinder, wood foller, casings fit over "gun" end, American, 21" L, late 19th C. **$50-$100**

Sausage stuffer, fruit & lard press, japanned & decoratively stenciled heavy tin (one design being a basket of flowers), with lid, cast iron legs and vertical center threaded rod — with beveled gears & screw, came with removable corrugated "spout" or nozzle, perforated disc, interior perforated canister, # 25, Enterprise Mfg. Co., Phila., table top, canisters depicted as 4 qt. capacity, c. 16" to 18" H, pat'd July 11, 1876, still selling early 20th C. <u>Sizes of japanned presses</u>: #5 = 2 qt. rack; #15 = 2 qt. screw; #25 = 4 qt. screw; #31 = 6 qt. screw; #35 = 8 qt. screw. <u>Sizes of tinned presses</u>: #10 = 2 qt. rack; #20 = 2 qt. screw; #30 = 4 qt. screw; #40 = 8 qt. screw. "Rack" refers to cranked rack mechanism, also on central threaded shaft. **$75-$100**

Shark's tooth, petrified, dark slatey brown, roughly triangular in shape, with tiny sawtooth ridge of teeth, works perfectly to cut things up, quite easily recognizable as a naturally occuring, ad hoc saw, which works on root vegetables (and probably meat, but I don't eat it, so don't know). About 3"-5" L, 14,000,000 years old. **$12-$45**

Shredder, metal with green wooden handle, "Lightning 3-in-1," 8" L, c.1930s or 1940s. **$9-$18**

Slaw cutters — See cabbage cutters

Slicer for root vegetables or potatoes, japanned cast iron, horizontal action, cranked, screw clamps, choice of 4 cutting blades to fit on end, no mark, American, 10-1/2" L, c.1870s to 1890s. **$65-$90**

Spice boat — See herb boat or grinder

Spice mill, cast iron, like rowboat with troughed opening at bow & wider at stern, with the effect of a seat & raised gunwhale (sides), high bootjack legs, large wheel pestle with rough wooden handles. (See also herb boat.) Prob. American, poss. PA, early 19th C. **$250-$300**

"To make Tomato Ketchup. — For half a gallon take a gallon of skinned tomatoes, four table spoonfuls of salt, four of black pepper, half a spoonful of alspice, eight pods of red pepper, three table spoonfuls of mustard; grind them finely, and simmer them slowly in sharp vinegar, in a pewter basin, three or four hours, strain through a wire sieve, and bottle it closely. Those who like the article may add, after the ingredients are somewhat cool, two table spoonfuls of the juice of garlic." *The Farmers' Cabinet*, Phila., Oct. 15, 1836.

I-89. Sausage guns or stuffers. *Pieced tin, wood plungers. Sausage casings (scraped intestines, yuck) fit over nozzle ends. Top* (**L**) *29-1/2" L; takes different casing-funnel sizes. Lower* (**R**) *is 19-1/2" L. 1870s-1880s. Collection of Meryle Evans.* **$40-$100**

I-90. Spice mills. *"Enterprise," No. OO (at left) & No. O. Decoratively painted cast iron; one is for wall, one screw clamps. c.1898.* **$30-$60; $50-$85**

Spice mill, japanned & stenciled cast iron, wall-mounted side mill with one flat side, cup-like hopper above, iron cup catches grounds below, crank in middle. No. 00, Enterprise Mfg. Co., c.1890s. **$30-$60**

Spice mill, sheet iron, curvy hourglass shape with pronounced waist, flat top, large-knobbed crank, screw clamps to table, English (?) or American, 11" H, late 18th, early 19th C. **$1000-$1300**

Spice, salt & pepper containers — See Chapter VII (Storage and Containers)

Strawberry huller, brass (maybe once nickeled), 1890s. **$15-$20**

Strawberry huller, like tweezers, made from a fold of spring steel, narrows toward tips then opens into concave round discs with centers cut out, mfd by A. S. Bunker, Lawrence, MA, c.1877. **$7-$10**

Strawberry huller, or pin feather picker, tinned spring steel pincher, "Nip-It," American, 1-1/4" L x 7/8" W, pat'd Dec. 18, 1906. **$5-$10**

Strawberry huller, & pin feather puller, inch-wide flat piece of nickel-plated spring steel, bent to "hairpin" curve, uses pinching action, mounted on color printed cardboard with strawberry design, "Spee-Dee," mfd by Kenberry, American, turn of century. **$5-$10**

Strawberry huller, spring steel, stamped with strawberry design, marked "Berry Huller," American, about 2" L, turn of century. **$5-$10**

In the Good Old Summertime. — "A housekeeper's work lies in the house. If she has a large family, the customary three meals take about all of her time, and her daily and weekly round of work takes her full time and strength, so that she has as little inclination as opportunity to go roaming abroad for exercise. Last summer, for the second time in eight years, I had my cook-stove in a shanty, or rough 'lean-to' shed, adjoining the house. How can I ever again be contented to spend a summer with the family cook-stove in a walled-up kitchen, being myself the family cook?

"No house is worth the name of home which has nowhere about it a shady porch or airy shed where a housekeeper or a hired girl can sit down in cool comfort, to shell the peas, hull the strawberries, or peel the potatoes, where she can set her ironing table, and wash her dishes without foregoing fresh breezes, and near neighborhood to grass and vines. Thoreau, who had a contempt for such treasures as most mortals love to lay up here below, observed that when a man had compassed his desire and got him a house, it seemed after all to be the house that had got him. So it is with many women — their houses keep them quite as much as they keep the houses." Faith Rochester, "Home Topics," *American Agriculturist*, June 1876.

I-91. Strawberry huller & pinfeather picker. *"Nip-It," Windsor Stephens & Co., Waltham, MA, pat'd 12/18/1906. Nickeled spring steel. "By its use one avoids stained fingers, seeds under finger-nails, crushed fruit."* **$7-$10**

Sugar cutter, cast iron, clamps to table edge, has 2 legs, levered action, marked "Bartlett & Son," Bristol, England, about 9" L, late 19th C. **$55-$85**

Sugar nippers, beautifully tooled steel, floriate design, turned knuckle guard, 9-3/4" L, early 19th or poss. late 18th C. **$225-$250**

Sugar nippers, cast steel, concentric rings around pin, leaf spring good, ball ends on handles, English, early 19th C. **$150-$175**

Sugar nippers, hand held, lathe-turned steel, leaf spring intact, English (?), 7-1/2" L, late 18th or early 19th C. **$100-$150**

"Case-hardening of Iron, is a superficial conversion of that metal into steel, by a cementation of it with vegetable or animal coals. This operation is usually performed on small pieces of iron, worked into tools and instruments, by putting them together with the cement, into an iron box, which is closely shut, and exposed to a red heat for several hours. Thus, the surface of the iron, to a certain depth, is converted into steel, to which a proper degree of hardness may be given, by a sudden immersion of the heated pieces into a cold liquid." Anthony Florian Madinzer Willich, *The Domestic Encyclopedia; or A Dictionary of Facts & Useful Knowledge*, 1st American edition, Philadelphia: W. Y. Birch & A. Small, 1803-04.

• • • •

Cutting Up Sugar. — Sugar nippers were necessary because sugar came in hard molded cones, with a heavy string or cord up through the long axis like a wick, but there so that the sugar could be conveniently hung up, always wrapped in blue paper. The cones were hard and after chunks were cut or hacked off for the table, the nippers were needed to reduce the size of the pieces. I've never understood why they didn't just grate the sugar. Conical sugar molds of pottery or wood were used by pouring hot sugar syrup into them and cooling until solid. They range from about 8" H to 16" H. These molds are very rare, especially those with some intaglio decoration inside to make a pattern on the cone. The blue paper, by the way, was recycled by soaking to get the indigo color as a dye for cloth. And for laundry blueing? **Soda for Washing**. — We have been requested by a correspondent, to publish the recipe for washing with Sub-carbonate of Soda. To five gallons of water add a pint and a half of soft soap and two ounces soda. Put the clothes (after soaking over night) into the mixture when at boiling heat, rubbing the parts most soiled with soap. Boil them one hour — drain — rub, and rinse them in warm water, after being put into indigo water, they are fit for drying. Half the soap and more than half the labor is saved by washing in this manner." *Silk Culturist*, as quoted in *The Farmers' Cabinet*, Philadelphia, Oct. 15, 1836.

• • • •

Loaf or Broken Sugar. — A bill of sale from Daniel E. Bailey, a grocer of Lynchburg, VA, dated 1839, lists two types of sugar sold to John G. Merme (?): "Loaf sugar" and "Broken sugar." The latter cost half as much. (The units of each are illegible, but probably pounds.) Loaf was 20¢ a pound and broken was only 11¢ a pound. For cooking, the broken would have been more convenient by far; in fact, you wonder why anyone bought a whole loaf if it wasn't necessary and was so much harder to use. Perhaps the fear of adulteration (intentional or insect-ional) made people want the loaf. Other things on that interesting bill included 20 yards of "counterpane checks" for $5, 7 yards of "Blue Jeans" for $1.40, a pair of "Side Combs" for 6¢, and 6 pounds of coffee for 90¢.

Sugar nippers, or cutters, for store counter, grain painted wood box base, double arched iron frame or blade guard & wrought steel blade with decorative finial, turned knob for drawer underneath, turned handle for cutter's lever. Punctured tin plate to "sift" sugar before it fell into drawer, no mark, American, 4-1/2" H x 11-5/8" L x 11-1/8" W, mid 19th C. **$325-$400**

Sugar nippers, steel, marked "P R," with tiny long-handled posnet punch mark between the initials, English or American, 8-1/4" L, 18th or early 19th C. Offered for sale by Clara Jean Davis, and as she says, "This is the first pair I've had that were signed, and I think that's rare." Very rare, and accounts for value I have put on them. **$175-$200**

Sugar nippers, steel, mounted on wooden base, American or English, 10" L, early 19th C. **$70-$120**

Sugar nippers, steel, not finely polished, very stylized cut design at pivot, not the usual flat leaf spring but instead a pronounced S-curved spring inside, American (?), 8-13/16" L, early 19th C. **$175-$200**

Sugar nippers, steel, very nice lathe turning around pin pivot & handles, finger guard pin stuck at right angles to one handle, catch or keeper as well as leaf spring intact, English (?), 8-1/2" L, late 18th C. **$120-$150**

Sugar nippers, tooled steel, ivory handle with brass ferrule, screwed to shaped wooden base, English (?), early 19th C. **$300-$425**

Sugar nippers, heavy wrought iron, mounted on wood, brass ferrule and unusual wooden handle, English (?), early 19th C. **$125-$160**

Sugar nippers, wrought iron, finely finished, steel leaf spring, finger guard peg, catch intact, nice curve to little gingko-leaf-shaped blades, American (?), 8 3/4"L, late 18th or early 19th C. **$100-$135**

Sugar nippers, wrought iron, hand held, extremely simple, leaf spring still seems fine but I wouldn't try it out, American, 9-1/2" L, 19th C. **$75-$100**

Sugar nippers, wrought iron, large, turned brass stanchion, base & handle of fruitwood or chestnut, English, early 19th C. **$250-$325**

Sugar nippers, wrought iron, not steel, very slender & sculptural, almost insect-like in appearance, American, 11" L, 18th C. **$150-$175**

Toffee ax or hatchet & hammer, cast iron, "For Toffee" cast into surface, English, 7-3/8" L, 19th C. **$35-$50**

Tomato knife, for slicing, steel blade rather like most vegetable knives, but with tip round & wider than blade, turned wood handle, small brass bolster, marked "I*X*L Geo. Wolstenholm & Son" on blade, & chef's cap trademark containing words "Firth Stainless," "Sheffield, England," 7-1/2" L, Reg. # 747488, July 18, 1929. **$15-$20**

Tomato knife, or tomato slicer, sort of a small cleaver like tool, with turned wooden handle, stainless steel blade much shorter than other one but with even bigger round end, marked "E -B Stainless," Sheffield, England, Reg. # 809290. **$8-$15**

"**Tomato Jam**. — Remove all the seeds, pull off the skins, and boil the fruit with a pound of sugar for every pound. To every pound of tomato allow two lemons, rind and pulp, well boiled."

•   •   •   •

"**Apple Jam**. — Weigh equal quantities of brown sugar and good sour apples. Pare and core them, and chop them fine. Make a syrup of the sugar, and clarify it very thoroughly; then add the apples, the grated peel of two or three lemons, and a few pieces of white ginger. Boil it until the apple looks clear and yellow. This resembles foreign sweetmeats. The ginger is essential to its peculiar excellence." Mrs. Cornelius, *The Young Housekeepers Friend, or, A Guide to Domestic Economy & Comfort* , Boston & NY: 1846.

•   •   •   •

Reduced value. — The leaf spring is sometimes broken off, and often the <u>keeper</u> is missing. (The keeper is a catch like those found on small pruning clippers we use in the garden).

•   •   •   •

Be Careful of Old Iron.— This has the leaf spring between the handles, but I'd never dare to try it. PLEASE PLEASE PLEASE when you examine old wrought iron pieces, don't "try them out" because all tensile strength and springiness may have been lost. And while you're at it, be very careful of cast iron, as it is easily broken under certain conditions.

I-92. Sugar cone & sugar nippers. (L) *Conical molded cake of granulated sugar, wrapped in blue paper & tied, as customary for maybe centuries in Europe, & in US in 18th & early 19th C. This one is from Belgium, but form is the same. About 10" H x 4-3/4" diameter. Photo courtesy National Museum of American History, Smithsonian Institution.* **(R)** *Prettiest nippers I ever saw. Steel, cut design at pivot, leaf spring, very stylized form. 8-13/16" L. Stock of Lauri & Bill Sweetman, Laubill Antiques, Golfstown, NH.* **$30-$40; $125-$175**

I-93. Sugar cone cutter. *For country store. Grain-painted wood box, iron arched frame or blade guard & blade. Turned wood knob & handle. Hand-punched tin plate for sifting sugar before going in drawer. Identified & located by The Primitive Man, Bob Cahn, Carmel, NY. Courtesy Mike & Sunny Kolba Collection.* **$250+**

Tomato peeler, wood handle, scoop-like steel blade, "Ontario" stamped on handle, 20th C. **$7-$10**

Tomato slicer, cast iron, round base screws to tabletop, vertical shaft with crank on top. Tomato is put into cylindrical holder with 3/8" horizontal slots, into which fit the 6 steel blades that you crank through the holder. Cuts 7 slices. "Rapid," sold by V. Clad & Sons, Philadelphia, about 9" H, early 20th C. **$55-$75**

Vegetable chopper, long 1/4" plywood box base, midway is bent basswood arch with slot the full length of it into which fits a carbon steel knife, looks very European, marked only "MARTA" which sounds Scandinavian, but Pinto's book on treen claims this is English, 12-3/4" L, 20th C. **$45-$75**

Vegetable cutters — See also julienne cutter, this chapter

Vegetable cutter, hammered sheet iron, fish-shaped footed base with hinged iron cutter blade in abstract form of animal's head, from India, 10-3/4" L, 19th C. type, but almost certainly mid 20th C. I bought this, hesitant a bit because of feeling it wasn't "right," as a 19th C. homemade American cutting tool. Found picture of one in Pease Binder's *Magic Symbols of the World* on page 97, enabling identification. **$20-$35**

"Tomato Figs. — Use thoroughly ripe tomatoes; pour boiling water over them to remove the skin; weigh them; place them in a stone jar, with an equal quantity of good sugar. Let them stand two days; then pour off the syrup; boil and skim it until no scum rises. Pour it over the tomatoes; let it stand two days; boil, and skim again. After repeating this process for the third time, they are fit to dry, if the weather suits; if not, keep them in the syrup. They will dry in a week. Pack in boxes lined with white paper, putting powdered sugar between the layers of fruit. Should any syrup remain, it may be used for making common marmalade, or for sweetening pies." Mrs. A. P. Hill, *Mrs. Hill's New Family Receipt Book*, NY: 1870.

Vegetable cutter, tin, wood paddle-shaped frame, slides back & forth, corrugated blade to cut fluted chips of root vegetables, American, 12" L, early 20th C. **$25-$35**

Vegetable cutter, corrugated tin strip with hourglass wire handle, used to make fancy slices in root vegetables or potatoes, for soups, etc., American, small size, turn of century or early 20th C. **$5-$10**

Vegetable cutters, graduated set of tapered cylindrical conical cutters, in hinged tin box with conical lid, used for making decorative shapes of sliced root vegetables, there should be about 15 cutters in the box, the smallest possibly small enough to stone olives (as an early ad stated), though I'd hate to try. Seen in F. A. Walker catalog, Boston, also Harrod's Stores catalog, London — they're either American, or European imports from 1870s. About 8" H, last quarter 19th C, poss. more recently than that. **$30-$55**

Vegetable cutters, pieced tin, sort of like cookie cutters, in such designs as a shamrock, snowflake, etc., deep cutting edge, came in 20 styles, in F. A Walker catalog, French (?), only about 3/4" to c. 1-1/2" across, so you are unlikely to think they're cookie cutters, c.1880s to 1890s. **$15-$25**

Vegetable & fruit parer, smooth cast iron, horizontal lathe type, with wheel with interior gear teeth at one end, longish sharp knitting-needle-like adjustable "spear" held & pushed fruit or veggie against revolving paring fork (Tom Wiggins says that when doing potatoes, it's just the opposite). According to contempory ads does apples, pears, quinces, potatoes, even carrots, "The Victor," mfd by Goodell Co., Antrim, NH, pat'd Jan. 5, 1885. **$75-$100**

Vegetable & fruit press, also colander, tinned steel "saucepan" with round bottom, perforated 3/4 of way up, to be set into

heavy bent-rod screw-clamp frame, blade inside turned by center crank, mashing food against holes, "McCoy's Improved," mfd by Dilver Mfg. Co., St. Paul, MN, c.1911. A very similar one made by Utility Sales Co., Davenport, IA, was advertised in 1911; it differed because only the bottom of pan is perforated & flatter. **$18-$25**

Vegetable garnish cutter, metal, with original instructions & envelope, "Acme," American, 20th C. **$7-$15**

Vegetable grater & slicer, oblong tin grating surface with alternating perforations & sharp slits, wire frame with large handle hoop at top, curled to 2 feet at bottom, stamped with mark of 2 fish, European (?), 11" H x 4-1/4" W, early 20th C. **$7-$15**

Vegetable knife, almost like regular carbon steel knife with turned wooden handle, except the blade is not pointed but has an attached very small concave round blade to scoop out potato eyes & "defective places from all vegetables designed for the table" (as opposed to livestock), Gilbert & Durand's Patent, F. Durand, Derby, CT, pat'd Aug. 16, 1870 by F. Durand & W. E. Gilbert. **$8-$12**

Vegetable & nut chopper, glass jar with paneled sides, tin lid fitted with spring-action plunger above, which gave the 4 blades an extra bounce, inch-thick wooden disc inside jar, marked The Ernestreich Co. (possibly meant to be Ernest Reich), Chicago, IL, 10-1/2" H x 4-1/4" diameter, c.1910 to 1920. **$12-$20**

Vegetable or slaw slicer, white porcelain (china) table that slides in wooden frame, 2 steel blades, beautiful handle tips protrude from side, gorgeous elegant piece, prob. European, 14-1/2" L x 5-1/4" W, early 20th C., poss. late 19th C. **$55-$65**

Vegetable parer, aluminum frame with steel blade, "De Vault Peeler," mfd by W. R. Feemster Co., Inc., Los Angeles - Chicago, 3" W, 1935 patent #1990127. **$5-$10**

Vegetable parer, white plastic, comes apart, one steel blade cores apples & tomatoes, other blade pares, "Item No. 990," "Made in U. S. A.," 7" L, "U.S. and World Pat's Pend." 1940s or 1950s. **$5-$7**

Vegetable parer, corer & slicer combined, nickeled steel, wood handle set at a 45-degree angle to bullet-shaped blade, "Universal," Landers, Frary & Clark, c.1900. **$7-$12**

"**A set of vegetable cutters will add much to the beauty of many a dish.** Should be made of best tin. Boxes of graded cutters may be had. Use for stamping out vegetables, forced meat, jellies and also are valuable for coring apples and other fruit and stoning olives." Maria Parloa, *Kitchen Companion* , Boston: Estes & Lauriat, 1887. An 1895 Harrod's catalog shows a set with fancy cutters, tin crimped to form crested medallions or heraldic scrolly shapes. They could be ordered plain or fancy: the plain came 9, 12 & 15 cutters to the case and the fancy 4, 6 or 9 to the case.

• • • •

"**Garnishing**. — The art of garnishing dishes is the art of ornamenting them, and making them look elegant, and thus satisfying the eye as well as the palate. Various materials are used for this purpose. Among the most popular are cocks' combs, plovers, and hens' eggs boiled hard, prawns and small crayfish, button mushrooms glazed, stamped pieces of vegetables such as carrot, turnip, parsnip, beet root, and truffles, stoned olives, gherkins, fried croutons of bread, aspic jelly, horse radish, cut lemon and parsley. Everything depends on the artistic arrangement of the ornamentation, determined by the taste of the garnisher. Where the taste has been cultivated, or where there is a natural faculty for decoration, the task of garnishing effectively is an easy one." Henry Scammel, *Treasure House*, 1891.

Vegetable scraper, corn grater & fish scaler combined, nickel-plated iron, turned wood handle, looks like small gardening or mason's tool, with 4 different edges: sharp beveled blade, sharp corrugated edge, comb-like edge with 6 long fork tine teeth, & curved sharp edge, sold by Montgomery Ward, pat'd 1906, c.1910 catalog. **$10-$18**

Vegetable slicer, japanned cast iron & tin, freestanding tabletop, with encased horizontal revolving cylinder, side crank, does all kinds of vegetables, "Enterprise #49," Enterprise Mfg. Co., 16" H, cylinder is 11" diameter, late 19th C. **$75-$115**

"Walnut Ketchup. — Boil or simmer a gallon of the expressed juice of walnuts when they are tender, and skim it well; add 2 pounds of anchovies, 2 pounds shalots, 1 ounce cloves, 1 ounce mace, 1 ounce pepper, 1 clove garlic. Let all simmer until the shalots sink. Put the liquor in a pan till cold, bottle and divide the spices to each." Anthony Florian Willich, *The Domestic Encyclopedia*, Philadelphia: A. Small, 1821.

Vegetable slicer, steel, with large wood handle & press bar, American, pat'd 1900. **$45-$65**

Vegetable slicer, tin, counter top, "Morris," 1890s-1910s. **$7-$12**

Vegetable slicer, turned wood handle, twisted wire, works like kraut slicer, "A & J Pat'd," Binghamton, NY, 16" L, c.1930s. **$15-$20**

Vegetable slicer, deep fluted tinned blade with wire handle, hand operated, not mechanical, American, c. 1900-1920. **$5-$10**

Vegetable slicer, long wooden slide frame, steel blades, feed block of wood, hanging hole at end, "The Home Vegetable Slicer," Catawissa Specialty Mfg. Co., pat'd 1898. Collector Dorcas Luecke copied out original paper label, reading in part: "For slicing potatoes and similar vegetables place same in front of feed block, grip handle firmly and shove through without stopping. For cabbage head pieces place the slicer over a receptacle with the end abutting against the wall or other support and [hold] cabbage in place with the hand. Avoid hot water, rinse thoroughly and wipe knives dry. In case of accident to knives we furnish new ones at 5 cents. ... The slices being corrugated cook more evenly and in less time than if they were plain. Also

slices apples for canning. Is indispensible for slicing onions, cucumbers, radishes and the toothsome raw fry and Saratoga chips. A great many dishes can be prepared with it. We claim that this is the most efficient and satisfactory vegetable slicer on the market. It is neat and convenient to handle, it is easily and quickly cleaned and ... always ready for use." **$35-$65**

Vegetable slicer, wood frame, box for veggies slides, 6 blades with teeth, "Home Vegetable Slicer," Catawissa Specialty Mfg., Catawissa, PA, 20-1/2" L x 3-1/2" W, pat'd Feb. 22, 1896. **$65-$75**

Vegetable slicer, zinc-plated iron with wooden handle, screw clamps to table, comes apart by unscrewing halves, "Universal Vegetable Slicer," mfd by Landers, Frary & Clark, New Britain, CT, approx. 12" H exclusive of screw, turn of century. **$40-$60**

Watermelon plugger, iron gouging tool, 19th C (?). This tool was used to cut out a sample plug to see if the inside was red and sweet. If not, you just stuck the plug back in. My father used one when we lived on a farm in Toledo. (Along the same line was our practice of testing corn for ripeness by pulling down a bit of husk. If it needed more time, you crumbled some pollen-bearing silk from a nearby stalk and dusted it over the silk of the husk you opened and closed it back up.) **$12-$15**

Whatzit, tool steel blades, cast iron handle, slightly tapered blades, hinged with pin, comes apart at hinge like poultry scissors, stamped "Disston," Phila., 11" L, blades 2-7/16" W, pat'd Oct. 16, 1877. **$35-$55**

Whatzit cutting wheel, interesting hand-forged iron piece like a pizza cutter, which it may be; rattail handle attaches to wheel at right angle, point of axle has star shape outlined in dots punched into iron, around rim are what may be maker's name or name of place [pizza parlor?], looks like "ALBERTOS A CASIANO" or "CASIMO" or "CASA DO CASIMO," American, wheel 4-3/8" diameter, dated 1975. **$15-$25**

Wheat berry mill, green enameled steel box with drawer, partly nickel-plated, wheat berries fed into hopper, fine to coarse settings, crank black wood knob, bracket on back but wall half of bracket usually missing. "Wheat Krinkler," mfd by The Wheat Krinkler Corp., Columbus, OH, 8-1/4" H x 6-1/4" W x 2-3/4" D, c.1930s. **$40-$50**

Whatzit grater, or . . . ? When we first saw them at flea markets in Pennsylvania and Virginia, we thought they were graters made of rough punctured tin. The third one solved the mystery. It too was a cylinder with torpedo-pointed ends, rectangular strap or bracket handle in middle, punched from inside before soldering to create a pattern of closely spaced bumps on outside but no holes. Dealer Ed Wilson, at the Brimfield flea market in the fall of 1987, had a third one plus a little wire & tin Y-shaped tool. Theirs was partly made of a Diet Pepsi can. They found out what the "grater" was at a Boston Pops concert when they saw it being played like a washboard during a reggae piece: underline it's a musical instrument! Jamaican, Bermudan or West Indian, 18-1/2" L x 2-1/2" diameter, mid 20th C. **$12-$15**

I-94. Vegetable & fruit slicer, *for creating "various beautiful and attractive designs . . . to make them tempting and attractive. Lattice Potatoes are exquisite garnishes; bananas sliced in these charming patterns make a most excellent dessert." Grasgreen & Ritzinger catalog, c.1906-1907.* **$7-$12**

For More Information:

APPLE PARER INFORMATION

You may write for more information concerning particular parers, as well as the collector club, many of whose members also collect other crank and gear kitchen gadgets. Please always enclose an SASE (self-addressed stamped envelope, preferably a #10 or business size).

John Lambert
117 E. High St.
Mt. Vernon, OH 43050

James Ennenga
1621 N. 85th St.
Omaha, NE 68114

APPLE PARER CUTTER BLADES

Replacement cutter blades for a wide variety of old apple parers are available. Please send SASE for information on ordering to:

Thomas E. Wiggins
89 Concord Rd.
Billerica, MA 01821

NUTMEG GRATER INFORMATION

Teri Dziadul, an antique dealer and collector since the 1960s, specializes in early kitchen accessories and hearth cooking tools. She wants to help the novice & advanced collector, and dealer. Please enclose an SASE (self-addressed stamped envelope, preferably a #10). To receive an annual list (in time for holiday gift-buying) send name & address and $1.25 to:

Teri Dziadul
6 South George Washington Rd.
Enfield, CT 06082
(203) 749-6274

PREPARING

II. MIX, BEAT, STIR, CHURN, & BLEND

"Eat and run" and "grab a bite" were the only ways to eat in mankind's earliest days. The concept of having a meal, let alone fixing a meal, had to wait for tools and techniques of preparation. The most basic of those techniques involve cutting or mashing (dealt with in Chapter I.)

Implements and gadgets in this chapter accomplish the next level of preparation: they change texture, taste or other attributes, mainly by creating mixtures. You might argue that eggbeaters belong in the first chapter, because the "blades" cut the yolks and whites. But eggbeaters are here because their purpose and their effect is to blend two separate or disparate parts into one.

Eggbeaters are by far the most popular mechanical device in this chapter; we are beguiled by the poetry of their motion. They look like ballet dancers, twirling and spinning. (Well, some of them are more like four-year-olds at a recital — not so graceful as primas, but just as spirited.) At rest, their curved blades, small waists and waiting arms promise the dance to come, and those with "aprons" are wearing big tutus! Five years ago, when the third edition of this book came out, there was only one small book devoted to eggbeaters. Now there's good news: Don Thornton, the author of the little beater book, has whipped up a beater tome to beat all. See the boxed notice, page 86, in with the eggbeater listings on how to order *Beat This* from the author.

Prices for eggbeaters have skyrocketed. Rarities for which only a few collectors competed a few years ago have gone from $100 or $150 to often well over $350. A result of high prices is that some previously unknown beaters have been discovered, flushed out by eager collectors. When a lot of collectors pursue one category of collectible, unknown examples begin to surface, even after months or years of being hunted. There has also been a slight downtrend for beaters that we may have thought were rarer than they really were, or which seemed more distinctive or odder than they now seem with all the many examples that have been discovered.

If you are just beginning, don't despair. You can still collect for form, and many beaters that are classics, the basic beaters of any collection, can still be bought quite cheaply.

Unfortunately, collectors have gotten in the habit in the last decade of emphasizing rarity and awarding it top billing, all but ignoring design or form in the price structure. Maybe that's the only way the collectibles market can work, but as individuals you can collect using any criteria you want. The bottom line must be that you like something and get pleasure from having it in your collection. And you might as well, if your moolah is limited, put something besides great rarity at the top of your list.

In addition, when a single-focus book is written, the role-model collections on display in that book invite emulation. The demand part of the equation grows and the supply increases briefly when publicity brings the stuff out, then drops because desirable beaters are socked away in collections. Each new surge of publicity brings out a few more (for a first or serial appearance on the market). At some point, unfulfilled demand — and the high prices it brings — encourages the manufacture of fakes, forgeries and reproductions. We are not aware of any repro eggbeaters, probably because the cost of casting and/or tooling would be too expensive for the return expected from slowly releasing a dozen or so examples of a "newly discovered" beater. But several beaters are ripe for rip-offs: some because they would be relatively simple to manufacture, like the "propeller" mixing spoon.

Patent records convince me that many eggbeaters still await discovery. Although a large percentage of patented gadgets were never manufactured, numerous patented manufactured oddities have been found in the last ten or fifteen years, and the possibility that they were made in commercial quantities gives hope.

Some collectors have enough energy and room to collect **churns**, even floor-standing models, but most people have to treat large churns more like pieces of furniture than accessories, and consider them adjuncts to other collections. It's too bad, because so much variety exists in their form, function and finish.

The **mixing bowls** in this chapter were originally part of a larger group of bowls in the Storage and Containers chapter. I moved them here because mixing bowls and beater jars are half of the whole, just as a churn body forms a whole tool with a dasher. I find it difficult to assess clay kitchen collectibles, because ceramics have been collected for so long and standards, rules and lingo are well-established. When I commandeer ceramics to put into a book on kitchen collectibles, to a certain extent I have to reevaluate bowls, cookie jars, salt boxes, etc., that have already been categorized, classified, rated and priced within another collecting context. If we are going to compete with ceramics collectors at flea markets and antique shows, we're the newcomers who have to abide by their rules, so I suggest loading up on authoritative books on ceramic objects. You can never read too much.

Apple butter stirrer, long wood handle set at right angles to heavy oak pear-shaped blade, with curvy "X" cutout, good patina on handle, American, handle about 6 feet long, blade about 6" W and 13" L, 1840s to 1860s. **$60-$100**

"**Apple butter**. — Stir apples and cider all the time; you should have for the purpose a stick made of hickory wood, somewhat like a common hoe, with holes in it." Elizabeth E. Lea, *Useful Receipts and Hints to Young Housekeepers,* 10th ed., Baltimore, 1859 (1st ed. 1851).

Apple butter stirring paddle, long wood handle with paddle with largish cutout holes, used with handle horizontal & paddle in a vertical position, dragged back & forth across rim of the huge kettle, so that the paddle would stir the viscous liquid, American, 43" L, 19th or early 20th C. These looked the same for at least 150 years. New ones were advertised into the 1920s, often using 1860s-1880s illustrations. Best choice are those that show use, with real good dark patina, handles polished with the wear of hands, worn paddles, repairs or interesting wooden or metal bracing, even a bit of warping gives character. **$60-$100**

Batter bowl, yellowware, big pouring lip, acanthus leaves decoration, badly cracked, alas, mark is big deep diamond, can't read name, 13-5/8" diameter, 19th C. By the way, if the crack had an old repair — staples, or some kind of metal filler, for example — the value would at least quadruple. **$12-$18**

Batter jug, also called a **batter pot**, brown "Albany" glaze, with tin lid and wire bail handle, from Havana, NY, 19th C. **$75-$125**

Batter jug, bulbous saltglazed gray stoneware, with funny stick-out ear handles, wire bail with wooden grip, tin cap on spout, tin lid (probably replacement, as it fits inside the opening, rather than capping the entire top opening) with strap handle, "Evan B. Jones," Pittston, PA, about 12" H, c.1870s to 1890s. **$700-$900**

Batter jug, dark brown saltglazed stoneware, with odd clay clamshells applied on sides, as "ears" for square-wire bail handle, knotty carved wood grip, tin covers on spout and top, no mark, from Bryant Pond, ME (last place in America with crank telephones), 8-1/2" H, 19th C. **$150-$225**

Batter jug, dark brown stoneware, having what's called "Albany" slip glaze, tin cover on top, missing spout cover, wire bail, Bennington, VT, 19th C. **$175-$225**

Batter jug, saltglazed stoneware, ovoid shape, rather wide applied tilting handle at base opposite the side of the pouring spout, pretty lugs on either side fitted with wire handle with wooden grip, a very desirable form. Unusual cobalt decoration of a leafy wreath encircling a humorous big-nosed-man's profile, called by the collectors "Man in the Moon" (called by Donald Blake Webster "Punch"), has stoneware lid rather than fitted tin one, spout lid missing, also stamped with a desirable maker's mark, "Cowden & Wilcox," Harrisburg, PA, made c.1850s or early 1860s. The Robacker May 1989 auction price for this entry is a record for batter jugs, but the price breaks down to much more for decoration than form: **$10,000**

II-1. Apple butter stirrer. *This sketch appeared in the "Ladies' Department" of* American Agriculturist, *9/1847. "Any handy lad of fourteen years can easily make one for his mother. The handle should be about six feet long, in order that the cook may keep from the heat and danger of fire. The other part should be of heavy oakboard, six inches broad, with two transverse slits in the lower part, and long enough to reach the bottom of the kettle, so that while it moves, the handle has need only of a steady horizontal motion." The "kettle" referred to, by the way, was used outdoors, and was suspended or supported above a fire; it held from a half barrel to nearly a barrel of cider. I once made apple butter from a gallon of cider; on the electric stove, it took 15 hours!* **$45-$90+**

II-2. Batter jugs & pail. *Three stoneware batter jugs; note bails and tipping handles near bottom. Far* (**L**) *decorated in cobalt;* (**2**) *has original fitted tin spout cap and lid;* (**3**) *missing lid. American, mid 19th C. Generally speaking, for non-remarkable ones, the value range of plain as well as simply decorated gray stoneware is high. Brown Albany-glazed jugs probably a quarter to a half the value for gray stoneware. Far* (**R**) *pieced tin, came in 3 sizes: 4, 6 and 8 qts. Late 19th C. form, but in c.1904-1910 catalog.* **$300-$900; $125-$300**

Batter jug, squat saltglazed stoneware, ear handles, wire bail, blue decoration (viz. a sort of wreath surrounding folky man's profile with big nose & ear way up the side of the head instead of halfway like most ears), tin lid, wire bail handle with wooden grip, "Cowden & Wilcox," c.1850s to early 1860s. In Donald Blake Webster's book on decorated stoneware is a picture of a somewhat ovoid crock owned by him with another version of the decoration. Webster's man has a huge chin. The batter jug in this entry is similar to the Robacker one in previous entry but surfaced on the market in the early 1980s. The price range brackets what would be expected prior to the $10,000 Robacker sale. When an auction price jolts the market, it's impossible right away to predict long term effect on the market. **$4500-$6500**

Added value — For nice, but fairly common decoration, values up to $2500 or more. For terrific human or animal subjects, with excellent drawing, good detail, verve, spontaneity, over $15,000. Repros and fakes with newly painted decoration on old jugs, abound. It pays to study.

Batter pitcher, bulbous shape, 2 spouts, spongeware with brown, green & yellow glaze, American, 19th C. **$200-$250**

Batter pitcher, Rockingham flintware, yellow & brown glaze, American, 19th C. **$200-$250**

Batter pitcher, stoneware with yellow glaze, wire bail with wooden grip, American, 19th C. **$150-$200**

Beaten biscuit machine, also called a **biscuit brake**, cast iron frame screw-clamps to table, 2 nickel-plated rollers with iron crank, cast iron base rather like a sewing machine base, with marble top. These machines took some of the work out of cooking this Southern treat, which was once made by beating the dough with the side of a cook's axe or hatchet, wooden mallet, or heavy rolling pin until dough made cracking sounds. The dough is fed through the rollers, which are reset closer & closer, to really work dough until it starts to form bubbles ("blisters") that make cracking snapping sounds when they break. (For the sound, think of a mouthful of really old bubble gum.) The biscuits keep very well, even frozen, and aren't tough or crusty but dense & chewy. They are baked to the faintest tinge of tan. "The DeMuth Improved Dough Kneader & Beaten Biscuit Machine," mfd by J. A. DeMuth, St. Joseph, MO, approx. 36" H overall, table is 30-1/2" H x 36" L x 16" W; rollers are 2-1/4" diameter x 14" L, c.1890. Uncommon. **$250-$500**

"Miss Fort's Beaten Biscuit. — 1 1/2 lb. flour, 5 oz. lard, 1 1/2 tsp. salt, 2 tsp. sugar , dissolved in 1 cup water. Blend flour, lard and salt. Mix into a stiff dough with water in which sugar has been dissolved. Work well. Beat or roll until dough blisters. Bake in moderate oven until light brown.

Beaten Biscuit No. 2. — 1 qt. flour, 1/2 tsp. baking powder, 1 level tsp. salt, lard size of goose egg, 2/3 cup of milk and water, half of each with 1 tsp. of sugar dissolved in milk; have dough very stiff. Beat or roll until it blisters." Mrs. W. H. Wilson, *Mrs. Wilson's Cook Book*, 1914.

"To Make Little Cracknels. — Take three pounds of flour finely dried, three ounces of lemon and orange-peel dried, and beaten to a powder, an ounce of coriander-seeds beaten and searced [sieved], and three pounds of double refined sugar beaten fine and searced; mix these together with fifteen eggs, half of the whites taken out, a quarter of a pint of rose-water, as much [quarter pint] orange-flower water; beat the eggs and water well together, then put in your or-ange-peel & coriander-seeds, and beat it again very well with two spoons, one in each hand; then beat your sugar in by little and little, then your flour by a little at a time, so beat with both spoons an hour longer; then strew sugar on papers, and drop then the bigness of a walnut, and set them in the oven; the oven must be hotter than when pies are drawn; do not touch them with your finger before they are bak'd; let the oven be ready for them against [before] they are done [and] be careful the oven does not colour them." Elizabeth Smith, *The Compleat Housewife*, 1753.

• • • •

Beater jars have grown in popularity in last 15 years or so, along with the increased interest in the beaters. The jars are mainly twen-tieth century saltglazed stoneware, or earthenware, usually in blue or brown, sometimes with stripes, having straight sides like crocks, approx. 6" H x 4-1/2" D. Taller than wide, they're ideal for insert-ing an eggbeater. The most popular ones were made by various Red Wing (MN) potteries, starting c. 1900. Red Wing's jars have vari-ous finishes: "Blue Band," "Gray Line" (grayish white with blue & red bands), "Saffron," yellowware, etc. **Advertising** — Many jars were printed with a legend, message or motto on the side, advertis-ing (or used for promotion of) a variety of retail or service business-es, mostly in the Midwest. Examples include: Cairo Mercantile Co., Cairo, NE; E. C. Reed, North English, IA; Swanson's, West Union, IA,; Semons, Athens, WI; Stewart Olson & Sons; Farmer's Elevator, Peterson, IA; Babers Mercantile, Hansel, IA; and Ard-more Lumber, Ardmore, SD. (See also rolling pins, in Chapter IV (Form, Mold, Shape and Decorate) for other advertising stone-ware.) **Red Wing** is one of the most sought-after ceramic lines in this field. There are hundreds, perhaps thousands, of pieces from — flowerpots to milkjugs — available from this Minnesota city's pot-teries, and there is a definitive book by Gary & Bonnie Tefft (see bibliography). Organized in 1977, the Red Wing Collectors Soci-ety's 1989 address is Helen Bell, 1718 W. 6th St., Red Wing, MN 55066. **Some other potters** who made beater jars are A. S. Laurit-son, Tyler, MN; Gross Mercantile Co., Bridgewater, SD; and Frank

J. Martin, Ackley, IA. Most fall within same value range, but those advertising a special crossover business may bring even more than the high end of the range. **$50-$150**

Beaten biscuit machine, tabletop model, mainly wood, cranked rollers, American, c.1860s. **$165-$200**

Beater jar, green glazed crockery, "D. B. Wich Beater," American, 20th C. **$25-$50**

Beater jar, saltglazed stoneware, "Red Wing Beater Jar, Eggs, Cream Salad Dressing," 20th C. **$60-$85**

Beater jar, saltglazed stoneware, blue stripe, for eggs, cream, salad dressings, made by Red Wing, advertising "You Beat Eggs, We Beat Prices, Star Grocery, Parkersburg, Iowa," 20th C. **$65-$100**

Beater jar, saltglazed stoneware, blue striped, adv'g "Wesson Oil For Making Good Things to Eat," 20th C. **$35-$55**

Beater jar, saltglazed stoneware, blue stripes, with adv'g motto, "Mix with Us, Save Dough, Rockwell City, IA," 20th C. **$65-$80**

Beater jar, saltglazed stoneware, marked "Holiday Greeting," Red Wing, dated 1924. **$60-$85**

Beater jar, yellowware, marked "Foremost Dairies," American, 20th C. **$45-$55**

Bowls — See mixing bowls; see also bowls in Chapter VII (Stor-age and Containers)

Bread machine, also called a **mixing machine**, also a **dough mixer**, **dough kneader**, or **dough machine**. Frame of cast iron, 4 arched legs, tinned horizontal body, various gears, side crank, horizontal bar to hang on to with user's non-cranking hand, top lifts off the "basin," the lower part is where the kneaded dough rested or rose. Cyrus Chambers, Jr., Scientific Bread Machine Co., Phila., about 16" H, turn of century to 1910s. **$85-$110**

Bread machine, relatively shallow, broad tin bowl, with slanted sides, cast iron 3-legged frame arches up to support the handle, gear & crank, & suspend the 2 kneading blades. American, prob-ably about 11" to 13" H, c. 1860s to 1880s. Illustrated in 1881 cookbook (but style is at least 20 years earlier). **$85-$135**

Bread maker, screw clamps to table, tin with cast iron gears, "White House Bread Maker," American, 1902. **$85-$125**

Bread maker, heavy charcoal tin plate, steel, cast iron. Slope-sided, shallow tin pail & lid, screw clamp iron frame, iron crank. Heavy gauge wire snaky kneader assembled as part of lid.

II-3. Beaten biscuit machine, *or* **dough kneader**. *Cast iron base, marble table top, nickeled iron rollers adjusted closer together with each successive pass-through so dough gets increasingly harder to roll through as gluten builds up & makes snap-crack sounds. 30-1/2" H x 36" L x 16" W; rollers 2-1/4" diameter x 14" L. Medallion on base reads: "The DeMuth Improved Dough Kneader & Beaten Biscuit Machine, Manf'd. by J. A. DeMuth, St. Joseph, MO." Courtesy Margaret Minich.* **$250-$500**

II-4. Dough brake, *or beater. Wood, including corrugated "ramp" and roller, iron crank. Probably either homemade or limited produc-tion piece. American, mid- to late-19th C. Courtesy Mrs. A. J. Min-ichiello. (The name coincidence has not escaped me!)* **$150-$175**

Stamped on lid are the directions: "Put in all liquids first — then flour — turn 3 minutes — raise in pail — after raising turn until dough forms a ball — take off cross piece — lift out dough with kneader." Advertising copy of the period read "The process of kneading with this machine is thoroughly scientific and sanitary. It makes no difference what kind of bread flour is used. Results are always the same — better bread. Directly opposite to hand kneading is the work of the Universal. ... In hand kneading the particles of flour are necessarily pressed together, and the liquid does not thoroughly moisten each particle of the starch granules, while with the bread maker these particles are lightly held apart until thoroughly wetted ... and kneaded." "Universal No. 8," mfd by Landers, Frary & Clark, New Britain, CT, 11-7/8" H. (Other numbers — such as No. 2, 4, No. 44 — are different heights & capacities.) Some are marked "Awarded Gold Medal St. Louis Exposition" which was in 1904. These were made for quite a long time from the 1890s on. Add $6-$10 for original paper label on pail. **$75-$115**

Bread maker, tin pail, never had a lid, screw clamp, "Universal No. 2," Landers, Frary & Clark. **$30-$45**

Bread mixer, heavy tin pail, side handles, side crank turns U-shaped wire blade inside, domed crimped tin lid with wooden knob, screw clamp, labeled "Chauvauquat Bread Mixer," Polar Star, mfd by Smith & Hemenway Co. (S. & H. Co.), NYC, NY, four sizes from 2- to 16-loaf capacity, c.1909. **$35-$55**

Reproduction alert. — In a 1973 *House Beautiful*, a "Home Accessories" company in Massachusetts advertised an $18 "Old Fashioned Bread Mixer" that consists of a wooden bucket with a cranked apparatus fitted to its rim. The ad reads "Remember the unforgettable aroma of good old yeast breads while they're baking. And, that wonderful taste sensation of a loaf still warm from the oven. Here is an 8 quart walnut finished wooden bucket with inside surfaces clear sealed. A stainless steel mixing rod & hammered aluminum diecast hardware. Free 'Old Time' bread recipes included."

II-5. Bread maker. *Heavy tin, cast iron crank & gears. "Sifts the flour and mixes 10 lbs. of best bread in 3 minutes." Scientific Bread Machine Co., Philadelphia. Pat'd by Mrs. Lydia C. Sharpless, Philadelphia, c.1902. Ad in* Table Talk, *4/1903.* **$85-$135**

II-6. Batter or dough-mixing machines. *Clockwise from top right:* **(1)** *"Mixing machine" from 1881 cookbook, copied from c.1860s or even earlier cookbook.* **(2)** *c.1881 "Stantan" bread mixer, heavy tin. As liquid gets mixed into flour, cranking motion causes pan to turn by itself.* **(3)** *"Universal No.4," for 4 loaves. (#8 made 8.) Landers, Frary & Clark, New Britain, CT. Tinned pieced metal, with kneading rod, lid, crank, & clamp put on under the lid to provide holder for rod. Stamped on lid is: "Put in all liquids first - then flour - turn 3 minutes - raise in pail - after raising turn until dough forms a ball - take off cross-piece — lift out dough with kneader." 11-7/8" H, 1904, but sold for many years.* **(4)** *"Universal mixer for beating eggs, whipping cream or mixing soft batters . . . also for cake." A curved rod kneaded heavy batter or bread dough.* **(5)** *"Centrifugal Mixer," The Sparrow Kneader & Mixer Co., Boston, MA. Tin & Cast iron; "stirrers" have horizontal cross pieces. Four sizes; 2 pans (5 or 10 qts.), 2 tanks (10 or 75 gallons). Flyer on flimsy paper, c.1860: "Although but a few months old, hundreds of them are in use by druggists all over, who find them invaluable for compounding emulsions and ointments heretofore made with a mortar; also, for blending powders mixed by the slow, dusty and wasteful use of the sieve. . . Each stirrer in its revolution sweeps entirely outside of its centre, and the other follows in."* **$75-$200**

II-7. Dough mixer. *Double bentwood, nailed construction. Cast iron crank with large wood knob, iron blade, iron side handle. This fits in crook of arm, held against body, and you apply plenty of body English to make it do its thing. 5" H x 10" diameter. Mid 19th C. Collection of Meryle Evans.* **$175-$250**

Bread or dough mixer, sometimes called a dough brake, double layer of bent wood for body, nailed construction, cast iron crank, wooden knob, iron mixing blade, iron handle. Fits in crook of arm, held against body, may be American, but crank looks European, 5" H x 10" D, 19th C.   **$175-$225**

Bread rising tray, for bakers, wood, for 6 loaves, American, about 39" L x 6-5/6" W, late 19th C.   **$125-$200**

Butter churn — See churn

Butter fork, painted wood, 5 thick tines, looks like an Afro comb, handle is like a paintbrush's, "Mrs. Bragg's Butter Fork," not marked, American, about 6" L, late 19th C.   **$12-$25**

Butter hands — See Chapter IV (Form, Mold, Shape and Decorate)

What Does He Need? A joke from the period, reported as appearing in a North Dakota newspaper: "It is reported that one of our fastidious, newly married ladies kneads bread with her gloves on. The incident may be somewhat peculiar, but there are others. For instance, the editor of this paper needs bread with his shoes on; he needs bread with his shirt on; he needs bread with his pants on, and unless some delinquent subscribers pay up, he will need bread without anything on — and North Dakota is no Garden of Eden in the winter time." *House Furnishing Review*, June 1905.

•　•　•　•

"Bread: What Ought It to Be? It should be light, sweet, tender. This matter of lightness is the distinctive line between civilized and savage bread. The savage mixes simple flour and water into balls of paste, which he throws into boiling water, and which come out, solid, glutinous masses, of which his common saying is, 'Man eat dis, he no die,' which a facetious traveller interpreted to mean, 'Dis no kill you, nothing will.'" Catherine Beacher & Harriet Beecher Stowe, *American Woman's Home*, 1869. Hmmm, they sound like bagels. Speaking of beagles — some people say that stale bagels are the best teeth-cleaners for dogs!

Butter paddle, also called **butter spade** or **butter ladle**, carved wood with very shallow bowl & short crook-necked or hooked handle, beautiful mellow patina, 8" L, 19th C. Added value — Really good patina, signs of hand-carving, exceptional figure in the grain, even knots: all add value, because they are signs of age or uniqueness.   **$35-$45**

11-8. Butter worker. *Table-top model, bentwood, in simple wood frame (note well-finished post finials), wood gears, iron handle. 13-1/2" H x 9" x 8", c.1850s-1870s. It looks more substantial than Lilly's Patent in II-9-R, but quite possibly is that. Linecuts used in ads and furnished to editors, often idealized, simplified, or otherwise made image more "readable." Collection of Meryle Evans.* **$250-$400**

Butter paddle, carved tiger maple, all one piece of wood, standard shape, hooked handle has wonderful small man wearing top hat seated atop handle, incised heart midway down flat shank of handle, age crack in bowl, from PA & NY border, 10-1/2" L, prob. early to mid 19th C. More evidence of the folk art tradition in kitchenwares. This marvelous piece was discovered & for sale by Doris Axtell, Deposit, NY, in 1985. Price range is mine.   **$300-$500**

Butter or curd paddle, carved from burl, beautiful patina, old iron repair to handle, found in NJ, 13" L, poss. 18th C.   **$100-$200**

Butter paddle, carved wood, shaped like a thick, slightly scooped ping-pong paddle, 9" L x 5-1/4" W, late 19th C. Really good patina might add to value, but otherwise it's pretty dull.   **$20-$30**

What's a Butter Paddle For? — "For working butter, keep a wooden bowl and ladle. This last article is seldom found in New England, but always in the state of New York." Mrs. Mary Hooker Cornelius, *The Young Housekeeper's Friend* 1859. All of the familiar types (the nearly round slightly bowled one with short crook-necked handle; the flat, straight-sided, slightly rounded front edge one with angled rounded handles; and the one most resembling a spade, with flat longish blade with straight edges, handle raised slightly) were shown in Montgomery Ward's 1895 catalog. I'm sure they were sold well into twentieth century (& perhaps today through dairy suppliers).

Butter paddle, carved wood with shallow convex bowl, hooked handle in exaggerated angle where it joins bowl, American (?), 4-1/4" D with 5" L handle, 19th C. I never even used to look at these, but have noticed lately how much variation there is in this form, particularly in handle detail & imaginative use of grain and knots. That's one of the secrets of collecting, as you know: looking for & finding variations on a theme. Bach & Bartok did it for music!   **$40-$75**

Butter paddle, maple handle, wire blade, 8-3/4" L, turn of century.   **$15-$18**

Butter paddle, maple, with hanging hole in handle, rather long at 14" L, late 19th C.   **$18-$25**

Butter scoop or paddle, carved lightweight pale wood, curved, slightly irregular neck, American, 8-1/2" L, late 19th C.   **$18-$25**

Butter worker, for use in dairy barn or buttery, wood with remains of old blue paint on outside, a trough & 2 corrugated rollers, on skeletal frame, American, trough is 30" L, late 19th C.   **$180-$225**

II-9. Butter workers. (L) *"California," used in a large dairy — the Point Reyes' Ranch, CA. Three-legged base screwed to floor, top revolves. Wooden "knife" fits into socket. Butter is put on top, cut and squeezed or squushed against table to remove all liquid, over & over, then patted into molds. American Agriculturist, 3/1870.* **(R)** *"Lilly's Patent," for working butter, and for adding optional salt. C. H. R. Triebels, Philadelphia, 1879 American Agriculturist ad. Probably same as sturdier looking one in other photo.* **$250-$400**

Butter worker, tabletop for home use, wood with corrugated swinging arm, very worn, with good patina, American, turn of century. The market value of all wood wares, especially dairy implements, is enhanced by a satiny patina that results from the butterfat. **$75-$110**

Butter worker, tabletop, stool-like wooden frame, bentwood holder for butter & mechanism, wooden gears, iron crank handle, American, 13-1/2" H x 9" x 8", 19th C. **$175-$225**

Cake mixer, tin & cast iron, screw clamps to table like bread mixer, "Universal," Landers, Frary & Clark, turn of century. **$35-$50**

Cake mixer, tin dough pail, with cast iron gears, crank & frame, screw clamps to table, "American Machine Co.," pat'd 1873. **$45-$65**

Cake mixer & cream whip, tin, "Rumford," pat'd 1908. **$15-$18**

Cake spoon — See mixing spoon

Cheese curd knives were dairy tools with multiple blades to break up the curd in the process of cheese-making. American, 22" L, late 19th C. Two types were advertised in turn-of-the-century Montgomery Ward catalogs. (1) The first version had an oblong metal frame, open at one end with a short, turned wood handle at other, many blades set across the short axis. For cutting the curds up into fine pieces. Came in one length, 20", but five widths: 4", 6", 8", 10" and 12". (2) The other style is a version of a curd whip, and had 20" L blades, set 6", 8", 10", 12", 14", 15" and 20" W. These thin narrow blades, set about 3 or 4 to the inch, would swish through the curds. Version 1: **$20-$35**. Version 2: **$30-$45**

Cheese curd whip or whipper, 4 or 5 spring steel blades, 18" L x 1" W, set into a turned wooden handle or grip. Overall length: 24-1/2". It dates to the 1870s-1890s. **$30-$45**

Churn, barrel on A-frame stand, side crank, top loading, O. R. Flyers, Grafton, VT, about 46" H, 19th C. This type of barrel churn was called an "end over end" churn in England. The dealer advertised this as being from 1826 (probably typo for 1876). I read listings for every churn, every washing machine & every combination patent listing in *Subject Index to Patents, 1790-1873*, as well as an unnumbered patents index from 1790 to 1836. No "Flyers," and no Grafton, VT. But two churns had patentees from towns called Grafton: H. D. Smith, Grafton, OH, May 5, 1868, and T. Conely, Grafton, IL, June 25, 1872. Possibly this Flyers' churn was never actually patented. **$150-$200**

Churn, cast iron wheel & handle, nickeled blades, speckled blue saltglazed stoneware body, thin wooden lid with knob, no maker's name, American, 14-3/4" overall height, crock 8" H, pat'd May 15, 1906 & Feb. 26, 1907. **$160-$200**

II-10. Three Dutch churn mechanisms. (1) *large fly-wheel churns.* **(2)** *"At Almenaar, a churn made to go by the feet, the weight of the body being moved alternately from one side to the other, on a platform" attached by series of pivots to dasher.* **(3)** *a Gouda, Holland churn made "to work from the ceiling in a very easy way; a piece of wood, in the shape of an obtuse angle, was attached at the elbow to a pivot in one of the beams of the ceiling; the churn-stick attached to the one end" and worked by moving lever at left up & down. Article sharing mechanical motives and marvels with Americans adds that "in North Holland they churn using dogs in wheels, in a similar way to the turn-spits."* Mechanics' Magazine, and Register of Inventions and Improvements*, NYC, March 1834.*

Churn, crank type with wooden paddles, glass jar with metal gears & screw-on lid, no mark, American, 4 qt. size, turn of century. **$65-$85**

Churn, cranked, cream-color painted wood, has large crank wheel & smaller iron gear wheel above, natural finish lid, "Dazey," 18" H body, plus 12" H wheel & frame, pat'd Dec. 18, 1877. **$130-$150**

Churn, cylinder type on 4 shoe feet, wood with iron side crank, "R.W.," label shows initials over an anchor, sold through Montgomery Ward, American, various sizes, 1890s-1910. **$45-$75**

Wooden Churn Makers. — Unless stenciled or burned-in branded names remain, few wooden churns can be identified by maker. Around 1900, many U.S. companies were making churns, including Moseley & Pritchard Mfg. in Clinton, IA; Aspinwall Mfg. Co., in Jackson, MI; Frank L. Jones in Utica, NY; Anderson & Carothers, Sidney, OH; Standard Churn Co., Wapakonetta, OH; A. H. Reid, Philadelphia, PA; Stoddard Mfg. Co., Rutland, VT; Cornish, Curtis & Greene Mfg. Co., Fort Atkinson, WI; and Menasha Woodenware Co., Menasha, WI.

Churn, cylinder type, on rather delicate shoe-footed stand, wood painted yellow, 15-3/4" x 18" x 21", 19th C. **$175-$225**

Churn, cylinder type, sometimes called a **bowler churn**, tin in cast iron frame, square body, flywheel, mechanical movement, dated 1907. **$100-$125**

Churn, cylinder type, Tennessee "white wood" (as it was described in early catalog) box with iron hoops, iron crank, "Diamond Balance Churn Co.," named for shape of its box body, various sizes from 1 to 60 gal. (the biggest were dog-,

II-11. Two-footed dasher churn. *This unusual butter churn was found in Alabama. Heavy tin container is 19-1/2" H; all wood stomping dasher is 45" L. Operates on a rope-pulley system; handles sticking out on each side are tied to a rope and pulley inside the tall housing shaft, and when handles are turned the rope operates the two feet, making them stomp the butter. Very unusual. Could be a patented piece, but could have been constructed from the kinds of how-to articles that explained the Dutch churns to readers 170+ years ago. Collection of Kyle Goad & Margaret Upchurch.* **$400+**

sheep- or horse-powered), pat'd May 28, 1889; Oct. 27, 1891; & Nov. 17, 1891. Just for a price perspective, this is for the 10-gal. size: **$125-$175**

Churn, cylinder type with side crank, ochre painted wood, rectangular hopper & wooden lid, 4 sturdy shoe feet, American (?), 21" H x 15-1/2" x 19", turn of century. **$225-$300**

Churn, cylinder type, wood barrel & wood frame, crank on side, lock-on lid, "Fairy Churn," mfd by N. H. (or H. H. ?) Palmer Co., Rockford, IL, turn of century. **$110-$135**

Churning. — "The process of churning is necessary to force out the serous fluid from the cream in order to produce butter. This is done by agitation and in a churn. There are various kinds of churns, but the best churn is the one that will preserve the proper temperature, or the same temperature that is in the churn and cream when put into it. In warm weather cold water for some time is to be put into the churn, and in cold weather scalding water, and also putting hot or cold water in the cream according to the season. As it is important to preserve the same temperature while churning — the best churns are those which are used in an horizontal position — such as the stationary barrel with dashers to move in the inside. A small churn is in use on this principle, and answers a good purpose, as a hole of sufficient size from one half an inch to an inch, may be made on the top, to let out the warm air produced by the agitation of the cream, and to admit the cool air. A barrel churn of this kind has been used, when 36 to 38 lb. of butter was made twice a week." *The Farmers' Cabinet*, Philadelphia, July 1, 1836, some 60 years before the Fairy Churn (listed above) was advertised, though it would answer the purpose very well.

Churn, cylinder type, wood with (original?) greenish gray paint, supposedly Shaker, 19th C. If it were absolute that this was (1) Shaker, and (2) had the old, original paint, the churn might go for upwards of $1000. "Paint is all" say all Shaker experts. **$250-$450**

Churn, cylinder type, wood with beautiful patina, Canterbury Community of Shakers, Londonderry, NH, 19th C. **$500-$650**

Churn, cylinder type, wooden drum with red stenciling & cow design, American, 13" H, early 20th C. **$100-$135**

Churn, cylinder type, wooden, on frame, "White Cedar, No. 1," possibly by Richmond Cedar Works, American, 8-gal. size, turn of century. **$85-$100**

Churn, cylinder floor model, painted cast iron frame, 4 short splayed feet support 2 wheels & crank, vertical shaft with 4 large wooden paddles, heavily tinned square-based sheet metal receptacle or body, Dazey Churn, St. Louis, MO, 2 sizes: a 2-wheel 6-gal. with 3 bars on sides of frame; or 1-wheel 3-gal. with 1 bar on each side; on sale by 1910 — the date Dec. 18, 1917 found on it is prob. for an improvement or extension. **$110-$150**

Churn, cylinder floor model, rectangular wooden box, side crank at one end, fancy parlor-furniture-like turned & carved legs set slightly splayed, inside is oddly shaped container with foldout lids, Julien Churn Co., Dubuque, IA (?), 1870s. **$125-$160**

Churn, dasher type, barrel construction with tapered sides, one stave elongated to become handle, original old red paint, has lid & dasher, New England, 18-1/2" H, early to mid 19th C. **$350-$450**

Churn, dasher type, barrel with old blue buttermilk paint, wide lapped band at top, 4 iron bands, has lid & dasher. American (?), 25" H x 11" D at top, 1870s-1880s. Many painted churns have been imported in container loads of "country" smalls — from other countries. **$275-$350**

Churn, dasher type, bentwood, decoration in Norwegian rosemaling paint, from "Wapa Koneta," OH (town was spelled

II-12. Dasher, dash or broomstick churns. (L) *Gray stoneware, wood lid & dasher; 7 sizes (2-10 gals.). Old style, but in 1909 catalog. Cost from 40¢ to $1.50; lids extra!* **(R)** *Oak staved churn, with metal rim. Painted blue. Sizes holding 7, 9, 11, 13 1/2, 16, 20, 24 and 28 gallons, from $6 to $14.40, in catalog of D. J. Barry, 1924 — a lot later than you'd think. The blue paint must fool a lot of people. Similar churns were also made in cedar.* **$50-$200**

Wapakonetta, so that may have been a brand or a style name), 4-gal. size, dated 1882. It seems improbable that the decoration is contemporaneous to the churn. It was probably added in the 1950s during the rage for tole and rosemaling paint decoration. **$200-$250**

Churn, dasher type, brown "Albany glaze" stoneware, lacks wooden lid & dasher, American, 6-gal. capacity. **$55-$75**

Churn, dasher type, cooper's barrel-like product, wooden staves heavy tin bands, hand-forged nails, has lid & dasher, American (?), 1850s. **$250-$350**

Churn, dasher type, one elongated stave for handle, has 4 fingered wooden hoops, American (?), 12" H, early 19th C. **$400-$500**

Churn, dasher type, pieced tin, flared sides, 2 strap handles, lid with funnel, American (?), 18-1/4" H, 19th C. **$225-$275**

Churn, dasher type, pottery, lacking lid & dasher, Catawba, NC, 19th C. **$250-$300**

No butter, thanks. — "My greatest objection, after all, to the use of butter and cheese both, grows out of the consideration that their manufacture involves a great amount of female labor, while no permanent or substantial benefit is obtained." William A. Alcott, *The Young Housekeeper, or Thoughts on Food and Cookery*, Boston, 1838, 1842.

● ● ● ●

"Cream. — The peculiarly rich cream of Devonshire, England, called clouted cream, is obtained by using zinc pans of a peculiar construction, consisting of an upper and lower apartment. The milk is put into the upper apartment; and after it has stood 12 hours, an equal quantity of boiling water is introduced into the lower one. At the end of another 12 hours, the cream is taken off much more easily and perfectly than in the common way, and is also more abundant and richer. ... The same principles may be applied in the use of common pans. It would be very easy, for instance, to prepare some kind of trough, of tin, perhaps, or even wood, into which the pans could be set, and hot water afterwards introduced. As a close trough would be much better than an open one, you may have a cover with holes in which to set the pans. An ingenious yankee tinman would soon make a range in this way, sufficient for a common dairy, at no very great expense. It would last indefinitely. If it is true, that you would thus get some two pounds more butter a week from each cow, the apparatus and the trouble would soon be paid for, — to say nothing of the time saved in churning. We do not see why zinc pans — which are said to be decidedly preferable to any other for the dairy — with the tin range as above, would not be quite as good as the complicated and expensive Devonshire pans. And it would be easy for a dairy woman to satisfy herself respecting the principle, without either. By using cold water instead of hot, the range would serve to keep milk sweet in warm weather." *Vermont Farmer*, as quoted in *The Farmers' Cabinet*, Phila., July 1, 1836.

• • • •

Hey, Linnaeus! Use Biology to Improve Collecting Skills — You can practice by lining up 4 or 5 different examples of a type of collectible, similar enough to be the same species, different enough to allow (or invite) comparison. Look at each thing, make a gut or snap judgment about which you like best, which least. Turn away. Look again, and see if your eye is drawn to the same one. Now try to figure out why. (You may have to start by figuring out why you don't like the others.) The more alike the examples are, the closer they become to being a subspecies and the harder this exercise is. The less alike they are, the easier. For example: choosing between various types of churns is easier than choosing the best dasher churn, which in turn is easier than selecting the best painted wood dasher churn. To apply the whole **biology classification system** to collecting churns:

Kingdom — Material Object
Phylum — Collectible
Subphylum — Household Implement
Class — Dairy Implement
Order — Butter Making Implement
Family — Hollow Container
Genus — Churn
Species — Dasher Churn
Subspecies — Painted Wood Dasher Churn

(P.S. Prejudice or bigotry can be better understood, though never excused, if you examine it as a manifestation of the strong, natural biological imperative to select & classify — the tendency toward discrimination is also a force behind collecting.)

• • • •

Another repro alert — "An authentic reproduction from America's past. This beautiful churn is handcrafted completely of rich, fragrant cedar with brass-colored metal bands. It makes a handsome decorative item in the kitchen or by the hearth, calling to mind the simpler life of days gone by." Maybe the fragrant cedar does something to the butter, but why then were many old churns made from cedar? Maybe they aged it longer? This 34" H churn, with slightly tapered staves, round wooden top, and "brass-colored metal bands" (probably that thin yellow-lacquered metal you find hanging treacherously off old packing crates at the dump) was advertised by Abbey Gifts of Meinrad, IN, in the October 1975 issue of *Early American Life*.

• • • •

Churn lid value. — If present, the original lid (usually wood, whether a stoneware or wooden churn) & dasher should be considered as contributing a lot to value. No lid or dasher at all subtracts value. But it is next to impossible to know beyond a shadow of a doubt if they are really original. Look for warping & patina that seem to match age. Lid should fit, after taking warpage into account.

• • • •

The Milk-House of Col. M'Allister, Fort Hunter, on the Susquehanna, in 1828. "A household convenience worthy of imitation," reported visitor Judge Buel. "The Milk-house was built in the north-east side of a slope near the well, and not far from the mansion. It was composed of stout stone walls, and the roof, which rose six or eight feet above the surface of the ground, appeared to be covered with earth or tile, and was deeply shrouded with the scarlet trumpet creeper (*Bignonia radicans*), then in splendid bloom. The interior of the house, principally under ground, was fitted up with cisterns, in which water stood nearly to the tops of the pans of milk, which were arranged in them. The house was entered by a flight of steps on the south, and there was a window on the north, which could be opened or darkened at pleasure, to give ventilation. For want of a natural spring, which many Pennsylvanians consider almost indispensable in a milk-house, the water was conducted in a pipe from the well-pump, and after filling the cisterns to a certain height, passed off at the opposite side. The object was to obtain a cool temperature, in the heat of summer, which greatly facilitates the separation of the cream from the milk; this object was amply effected, with the labor of working occasionally at the well-pump." *The Farmers' Cabinet*, Vol. I, No. 1, Philadelphia, July 1, 1836.

Churn, dasher type, pottery, no lid or dasher, poss. "Hewell," Gillesville, GA, 19th C. Added value — Southern origin is the big plus here. Partly this is fashion. Other origins are pluses too: for example, Texas, California and the Southwest. **$250-$300**

Churn, dasher type, red cedar staves with white oak bands, has lid & cover, 19" H with 33" L dasher, 1980s. **$20-$30**

Reproduction alert — The old-fashioned churn above is being produced today and advertised "For Decorative Use Only!" and is sold through the Cumberland General Store, Rte 3, Crossville TN 38555. Their catalogue, which costs about $5, is a must for reference on variety of "country" kitchen items, still being made exactly like long ago. Dashers sold separately, and they have other churns. Lehman's Hardware & Appliances, 4779 Kidron Rd., Kidron, OH 44636 offer this churn in their 1989 "Non-Electric Good Neighbor" catalog (about $2).

II-13. Side crank churn. *"Blanchard," mfd. by Porter Blanchard's Sons, Concord, NH. Came in 7 sizes, for from 2 to 150 gallons. With pulleys could be empowered by animals or windmills. 1875-76 flyer states that it can be operated whilst sitting down. "Women have not been as much benefited as men by the invention of labor-saving machines for the farm," said flyer, comparing sit-down Blanchard with tiresome "old upright dash churn . . . which tasks the whole upper portion of the body." (Aerobically speaking, the dash provided a much superior exercise, as the Blanchard worked only "the muscles of the arms.")* **$50-$175**

Churn, dasher type, stripped cedar with 4 brass hoops, wooden lid, dasher, sold by Montgomery Ward, American, 3-, 4-, 5- & 6-gal. capacity, 1890s. Very much like new Cumberland or Lehman's churns (above entry), except for the brass hoops instead of white oak bands. Dasher is virtually identical. **$55-$85**

Churn, dasher type, redware with dark olive-green glaze, turned wood dasher, simply beautiful, NC, 19th C. **$400-$500**

Churn, dasher type, saltglazed stoneware, bail handle, Red Wing #5. **$165-$175**

Churn, dasher type, saltglazed stoneware crock with ear handles, wooden lid & dasher, American, 4-gal. size, 19th C. **$75-$100**

Churn, dasher type, saltglazed stoneware, white & blue, 2 ear handles, wood lid, American, 3-gal. size, 19th C. **$125-$170**

Churn, dasher type, saltglazed stoneware, wood lid & dasher, "Love & Fields Pottery," Dallas, TX, 20th C. **$120-$175**

Churn, dasher type, saltglazed stoneware, wooden lid, Red Wing, capacity mark #2, 1915. **$85-$100**

Churn, dasher type, stoneware, no lid or dasher, Red Wing, 5 gal., 20th C. **$85-$100**

Churn, dasher type, stoneware with brown glaze, NY state, 3-gal. size, 19th or early 20th C. **$75-$85**

"Good" or "Nice" — I've excised most instances of these two adjectives because they are basically meaningless, being relative to physical and cultural contexts and the viewpoint of the observer. Many catalog writers wear out the adjectives "very fine," "important," "exceedingly good," "good" and "nice." When you are selling something, those words add nothing to the description and are self-serving. When you're a writer, you need a new vocabulary. I have tried to use both sparingly, when I needed to imply some degree of added desirability, without being able to go into all nuances of what makes a patina good or a shape nice. Israel Sack rates furniture with "good" being the lowest level acceptable to him. He has a mental checklist of attributes against which everything is measured; as a collector, you have to develop one too.

Churn, dasher type, tin body, tin lid, wooden dasher. These & other dasher churns are sometimes called broomstick churns because of the dasher handle, which I assume was replaceable with a screw-on type broomstick handle, American, 19th C. **$125-$200**

Churn, dasher type, tin with flared out lip, slightly conical body, 2 handles, all with original mustard paint, American, 25" H, 3rd or 4th quarter 19th C. **$250-$325**

Matching Toy — This is exactly the type of churn with flared lip found on the Ives "Churning Woman" (or "Lady Churner") clockwork mechanical toy (pat'd 1874), right down to the mustard color! If you had that rare toy (which might cost you thousands to buy), you might even pay twice as much as the suggested price for this churn to use it as a pedestal base for the toy.

Churn, dasher type, white saltglazed stoneware with blue bands, wood lid & dasher, capacity mark "No. 3," early 20th C. **$125-$170**

Churn, dasher type, with original (or at least old) wood lid with turned knob, staved straight-sided wooden body painted light ochre, bentwood hoop at top, also iron bands, good patina & color, American (?), or poss. Canadian, 19-3/4" H x 9" D, c. 1830s-1850s. **$275-$320**

Churn, dasher type, wooden staves in old faded red paint, American (?), 18-1/2" H, 19th C. **$195-$225**

Churn, dog-powered, 2-part, wood with painted churn body, requires treadmill & big, strong dog, maybe a Newfoundland. (I'm sure the family pet, in the sense we think of it today, was much different a century ago. Sentiment was OK for lap dogs, but a bigger dog earned its keep.) American, late 19th C. **$250-$400**

Churn, electric, glass barrel has embossed cow on front & back, wire bail handle, screw-on lid, long aluminum shaft & simple triangular cutout dasher blade adjustable on shaft to suit height of vessel used, "Duraglas" & "Use with Gem Dandy Electric Churn" embossed on barrel, mfd by Alabama Mfg. Co., Birmingham, AL, 21-3/4" H with cover & motor, 2-gal. capacity, c.1947. A 1947 ad says "Can be used with crock or jar, but we recommend Gem Dandy Duraglas jar — sold separately. 3 gal. and 5 gal. about $1.95 and $2.45." They also advertised, without delineating differences, a "Deluxe Model" motor without jar, and a "Standard Model" motor also without jar. These were $19.95 and $16.95 fifty years ago. **$80-$100**

Churn, electric, jar & screw-on metal lid to be mounted with motor (none here), glass barrel has embossed cows, wire bail, "Gem Dandy Deluxe Electric Churn," mfd by Alabama Mfg. Co., Birmingham, 18" H jar, mid 20th C. **$40-$50**

II-14. Dasher churn. *Gray saltglazed stoneware with cobalt partridge decoration. Note beautiful spotted chest, and number "5". Impressed near one handle with mark: "T. Harrington." 18" H. Photo courtesy Litchfield Auction Gallery, Litchfield CT. Ex-Harold Corbin Collection, auctioned 1/1/1990, for $4200.* **$3500+**

II-15. Dog power churns. *Both are homemade versions of more "expensive" tread-power churns. American Agriculturist, 4/1876.*

Churn, glass, aluminum lid with dome, "Hazel Atlas, 10K 4249" mark on jar, 13" H, 20th C. **$65-$85**

Churn, glass, cast iron gears, wooden blades, Hazel Atlas, 20th C. **$65-$85**

Churn, glass jar, egg-shaped gear housing, wood blades, "Dazey Churn #80," Dazey Churn Mfg. Co., St. Louis, MO, about 17" H, glass jar about 8" square, pat'd Feb. 14, 1922. **$75-$85**

Churn, gray stoneware with blue bands, wooden lid & dasher, "Davis Brothers" stamped into clay, 14" H, 20th C. **$75-$100**

Churn, "piggy" type, suspended & worked like a rocker churn, without the cradle. Pieced tin with torpedo ends, 4 little legs, rectangular built-up lid in top, with handle, American, 19th C. **$300-$400**

Churn, powered by washing machine, aluminum, Maytag, 15" H x 13-1/2" D, early 20th C. **$75-$90**

Churn, rocker style, all wood including crank & paddles, 4 legs, original blue milk paint, American, 30" H, 19th C. **$185-$225**

II-16. "Piggy" style swinging churn. *"The Pendulum Churn," mfd. by Dairy Supply Co., NYC. Pieced tin, with "no dasher, paddles, or inside work of any kind to injure the grain of the butter — surpasses all dash and crank churns. ... Takes up no floor room and is hung up out of the way when not in use." 1879 ad.* **$175-$300**

II-17. Butter merger. *"Holt's Jar Cream Whip" used for adding milk to butter to extend it. "Put 1 pint unskimmed sweet milk in the 1 quart jar; add 1 lb. of butter. Pour luke warm water between jar and can. Let it stand between 5 and 7 minutes. Turn crank two minutes and you will have 2 lbs. of sweet butter." Here dasher beater is shown screwed onto inner glass jar down inside a metal can. Holt-Lyon Co., Tarrytown, NY. Pat'd Apr. 3, 1900. House Furnishing Review ad, 3/1911.* **$60-$100**

Churn, rocker type, in 4-legged wooden cradle, old red milk paint, supposedly Shaker, 19th C. (another color found is gray). **$225-$300**

Shaker is "hot" in the same way "early American" used to be, and the attribution is often given when unwarranted and unsupported by documents or documented examples. It is hard to say if the Shakers' works will ever be sufficiently documented. Furthermore, pieces made for sale to the world at large were mass-produced, and have much less value than pieces made for community use. Study books and visit Shaker museums.

Churn, saltglazed stoneware, applied ear handles, overheated (or underheated?) & sagged in kiln, rugged but tired (or dashed-but-no-dasher), marked only with capacity "No. 6," American, 18" H, approx. diameter 7-1/2", 19th C. It is very hard to price things like this. I like the crazy look of it, the personality, but the maker must have been disappointed. (You may ask, if the artist didn't like it, is it art?) **$200-$300**

Carl W. Drepperd wrote in *A Dictionary of American Antiques* that reject ceramic wares like the above were called **reffus wares**, and were sold cheap from what was called the reffus box. Modern collectors, always on the outlook for personality and distinctiveness (as separate from, even sometimes opposite to, *distinguished*) often rummage through that box of refuse with great success. The pieces have tales to tell in their sagged lips, misshapen bellies and discolored glazes. I was at a country auction in late 1988 where a much smaller saggy churn sold for $100, so I assume there's a growing market for such things. See **Wabi-sabi** in the index, to read more on the Japanese aesthetic of imperfection.

Churn, tabletop, glass 4-sided jar, wooden beaters, screw-on tin lid, gear housed in red metal cone with handle grip on one side, & nice arching crank (with red wood knob) on other side. Embossed on jar is circle with smiling lion's head. "Monarch Finer Foods Churn," American (?), 9-3/4" H, c.1940s. **$80-$100**

II-18. Butter machine. *The "Premier" Two Minute Butter Machine, Culinary Mfg. Co., c.1910. Square glass jar with original label, wooden paddle inside, cast iron frame & compound gears. Probably made in 1, 2, 3 and 4 qt sizes. This one, with its shapely hand grip, was also marketed as the "Crest" churn.* **$50-$75**

Churn, tabletop, glass with metal lid with bulbous crank housing painted red, wood paddles, "Dazey #4," 20th C. **$65-$95**

Churn, tabletop, glass body, iron crank & screw-on lid, & wood beater blades, embossed "Dazey Churn & Manufacturing Co.," (Sometimes people advertise these as "Daisy" churns — same thing, wrong spelling.) St. Louis, MO, various sizes found: 1, 2, 4, 6 & 8 qts, numbered by adding "0" to quart size, pat'd Feb. 14, 1922. **$80-$100**

Churn, tabletop, glass jar with cast iron frame & gears, metal blades. "Mak-Mor Butter Machine," NYC, NY, "Makes two pounds from one pound of butter." Pat'd May 30, 1911. This isn't really a churn, but a way of stretching butter: you add one pint of milk to one pound of butter & end up with two pounds of butter! **$80-$100**

Dazey Prices Are a Doozie. — I have not yet been able to sort out all sizes & numbers, having not found a catalog. The price range has been pretty stable for years, inching up just a bit all the time until recently. A #10 goes for $750 to $1000; a #20 is zooming up, now about $100 to $200. Surprising numbers of these have survived, possibly because people still enjoy using them. (Cumberland General Store sells what they call "a copy of the old Dazey" that is "imported from Far East.") **Dazey Sizes:** the one quart is #10, the two quart is #20, etc. Often the paper label is incomplete. An ad from January 1911 gives the sizes as 3, 5, 7 1/2 and 9 pints, and — due out by March — 2 and 3 gallon sizes. Whooo boy. I hesitate printing the new prices, as everybody will think they're sitting on a gold mine, and then the bubble will burst. Believe me, it surely will: perhaps by the time this is published. Some can still be found in the $50-$100 range, but it looks like the sky is the limit, up over $1000 for a 1-quart. In March 1989 an auctioneer in Springfield, MO, headlined the fact that he had two 1-quart Dazey churns coming up. A person at a greater remove than I from the subject should write a long thoughtful essay on values vs. prices. I can't imagine myself ever paying that kind of money for an item produced in quantity barely 60 years ago.

Churn, tabletop, glass, metal & wood, gear housing is domed metal top painted white, red wood crank handle, much simpler than earlier Dazeys, "Dandy Deluxe Churn," designed by J. P. Dazey, Jr., mfd by Taylor Brothers Churn & Mfg. Co., St. Louis, MO, 1 qt. size, 1940s? **$80-$100**

Churn, tabletop, glass with wooden paddles, "Elgin," original paper label, 2-qt. size, 20th C. **$80-$100**

Churn, tabletop, glass square jar, iron gears & lid, wood dasher-beaters, The "Premier" Two Minute Butter Machine, Culinary Mfg. Co., Orange, NJ, 13" H x 4-3/4" square, c. 1910. The "Premier's" paper labels are usually intact & mostly readable. Amazing in something washed so often. **$75-$110**

Churn, tabletop, tin container with wooden top, 4 short legs, "Dazey Churn Co.," St. Louis, MO, 14" H x 12" square, 20th C. **$150-$200**

II-20. Tabletop churn. *All metal, painted blue, cream or other colors. Natural wood top, wood dashers, cast iron gears & crank, 18" H. "Dazey," mfd. by Dazey Churn Mfg. Co., St. Louis, MO. pat'd 12/18/1877, but sold for many years, at least 20 years into 20th C. (Later ones with large flywheel at crank were pat'd by Nathan Dazey, 12/18/1917.) #s 100 to 1600, holding from 1 to 16 gallons. Photographed stock of Country Basket, West Dennis, MA.* **$95-$125**

II-19. Tabletop cylinder churns. *Wood, in two popular styles.* **(L)** *Cedar, on shoe feet, marked "R.W." with an anchor; sold through Montgomery Ward, 1890s-1910 or so.* **(R)** *"The Lightning," mfd. by Porter Blanchard's Sons, Rutland, VT, late 19th to early 20th C. Both in several sizes.* **$45-$125**

II-21. Tabletop churn & butter worker. *"Julien — The standard churn of our country," Julien Churn Co., probably Dubuque, IA. Three sizes: holds 8 gallons (churns 5), holds 10 (churns 7), holds 13 (churns 10). Wood & metal. American Agriculturist, 1/1869.* **$100-$150**

Churn, tabletop, turned wood, beautiful patina, American, 13-1/8" H, 19th C. **$300-$400**

Churn, tabletop type, glass jar, iron gears, wood paddles, "Perfection MixMaster," American, 1-gal. size. **$75-$100**

Churn, tabletop type, top cranked, japanned tin cylinder, American, 19th C. **$125-$175**

Churn, tabletop, vivid grain painted wood, brown & ochre, American, 19th C. **$225-$275**

Churn, tabletop, wood barrel, wood blades, cranked handle, red stenciled cow decoration, J. B. Varick Co., 14-1/4" H x 13" diameter, early 20th C. **$175-$200**

Churn, tin with wood paddle, "Connfaut Can Co.," American, 21-1/2" H, 40-qt. capacity, 20th C. **$135-$160**

Churn, wood, tin, iron, 2 handles, "Buffums Little Wonder," American, 34" H. **$130-$150**

Churn, wooden tub on high turned legs, cranked paddles, American, 19th C. **$225-$250**

Churn, yellow painted wood, floor-standing with 3 legs, lid with wooden knob, stenciled "Union Churn," mfd by Grand Detour Wagon Co., Dixon, IL, pat'd Dec. 20, 1864. Pat'd by C. H. Warren & A. C. Baldwin, Tiffin, OH. **$200-$250**

Churn & butter maker, tabletop, glass with wood, has original instructions. "Home Butter Maker," American, 1-gal. size. **$80-$110**

Churn & butter worker, wooden frame, triangular A-shape supports like a swing set, and indeed, the churn can swing "when desired, but while being worked it is retained in an upright position by a board and catch," which are midway up the frame. Over the churn body, which is octagonal with slightly flared-out sides, is an arched cast iron frame with a beveled gear in the center worked by a small crank. The short, slightly curved dashers are stuck at angles up and down and around the central fat wooden dasher shaft, working like a turbine. Has 2-part wooden cover. In an 1858 *Scientific American* write-up, it is claimed, "This churn renders the operation of churning and preparing butter for the market very simple and easy." Pat'd by & for sale by Justin M. Smith, Lyme, CT, pat'd Jan. 12, 1858. **$200-$300**

Churn or butter maker, hexagonal glass vessel used in horizontal position, screw-on zinc caps at each end, "Churn your butter while riding across country," 7-1/2" L, "pat. appl. for," but early 20th C. **$50-$75**

Churn or butter separator, cranked, wood body with iron hoops, spout on side has wood plug, wood handle, "Fayway," American, 16" H, 19th C. • How does King Kong make butter? With a Fayway. Hee hee. **$200-$225**

Cocktail shaker, bowling pin shape, top of turned maple, unscrews from lower chromed part, American, 56-oz. capacity, same size as regulation bowling pin, late 1930s. This is the kind of thing that in the right booth at the right "moderne" show is just kitschy enough to get good money! **$45-$75**

Cocktail shaker, chrome coffee boiler shape with odd phallic spout, yellow Catalin™ (or other molded phenolic resin) plastic handle & knobs, black incised bands on handle, "Krome Kraft," Farber Brothers, NYC, NY, 12" H, c.1930s, after 1933 (when Prohibition ended). **$30-$45**

Cocktail shaker, schoolmarm's bell shape, stainless steel, turned wooden handle screws off bell body to add ingredients; small shaker spout on side with screw cap, American, 11" H, 20th C. A full set has 4 bell-shaped glasses, each with a clapper in the bottom that rings when the glass is lifted, and an 18" tray, and might bring up to $300. Just the shaker: **$35-$55**

Cocktail shaker, World's Fair souvenir, aluminum with black letters & depiction of buildings around top border. American, 1933 — same year Prohibition ended. Crossover competition here from Expo & World's Fairs collectors might add to price. **$85-$110**

II-22. Cocktail shaker. *Realistic bell-shape. Nickeled brass, screw on cap, turned wood handle. 11" H, 20th C. Alas, although real ringing schoolbells would be brass (or bell metal), this one should have it's nickeled finish. I wouldn't be surprised to see them showing up stripped, at high prices. Some crossover interest from bell collectors.* **$45-$90**

II-23. Cocktail shaker set, *in rocket ship shape. For more information, see value listings under Cocktail shaker. 12" H, German, c.1930s (?)* **$650-$950**

Cocktail shaker set, rocket ship, chromed brass, the shaker body stores 4 cups, 1 small footed jigger cup, a lemon reamer, 4 spoons. Rocket has 4 fins at small bottom end. Top is larger-diameter dome. Only mark is "Made in Germany," 12" H, prob. 1930s, after 1933 (?). A bit scary this — what does it really represent? Not only does it look like a space rocket, it could also be a torpedo, and given the time, who knows? However, the fact that it's marked "Made in Germany" means that at least some were intended for import to the U.S.A., which required country of origin after March 1, 1891. **$650-$1000**

Cream separator, cast iron base, parts bolted on, heavy gauge tin top, crank, all painted in farm machinery orange, with yellow & black pinstriping, adjustable belt drive, bent wire lever regulates hole in top hopper, "Egret" in gold script, and shield-shaped brass ID plate reading "Entrahmen Reinigen ZU," which is prob. Zurich, Switzerland, 15" H x 12-1/2" L, late 19th C. **$165-$185**

Cream separator, sheep-powered, wood & iron treadmill on wooden frame; iron base for cream separator tank, Vermont Farm Machine Co., Bellows Falls, VT, sold by Montgomery Ward, late 19th C. Could be powered by other animals such as dogs, if they were large enough to move the treadmill by walking. **$250-$300**

Cream separator, table top, "Royal Blue Jr," American, turn of century. **$80-$100**

Cream separator, tin with wooden legs, uses gravity, "Marvel," 20th C. **$35-$45**

Cream whip, drink mixer, eggbeater, mixer or syllabub churn??? Smallish devices used for these purposes are often interchangeable, but I've tried to list them with the subject heading under which they are most noted or were most commonly advertised.

II-24. Cream whips, _egg beaters,_ or _batter mixers._ **(L)** _not marked; probably same as one on_ **(R)**_, which is a "Fries". _ **(R)** _8" H x 6" x 4-1/2". Ex-Keillor Collection. Note differences in lids, and the wood grip on crank. One ad I have calls it the "Economy" cream and topping beater, and gives 3 sizes: 10" H x 6" x 5-1/2"; 10-1/2" H x 6-1/2" x 6-1/4"; and 12-7/8" H x 7-1/2" x 8-1/8", holding from 6 to 16 pts. Other sizes appear in other ads. An electric one, the "Dumore," looks like these, but has crankshaft hooked up to a pulley with a small electric motor. Late 19th to early 20th C, made many years._ **$90-$110**

Cream whip, footed tin container, "Hodges," c.1900. **$50-$65**

Cream whip, squared tin blade beater-whipper, tinned cast metal gear marked "WHIPPO Super-Whip," tin lid slips over lip of glass jar marked on bottom with an "I" in an elongated diamond, 10-1/2" H, mfd. by Dover Stamping & Mfg. Co. and based on a turbine beater pat'd Nov. 25, 1924 by Wells G. Ruggles. **$125-$150**

Cream whip, metal & stained wooden handle, Archimedean drill action, advertising legend on handle reads, "We have competition beaten to a froth and whipped to a cream paste. Henry Brooks, General Merchandise. James Store, Virginia," mfd by A & J, mfd in Binghamton, NY, 12-1/2" L, pat'd Oct. 15, 1907. **$30-$45**

Cream whip, nickeled sheet metal, long vertical shaft with wooden knob, rectangular perforated blade curves up to fit into sides of its glass mixing bowl, "New Dream Cream Whip," Kohler Die & Specialty, De Kalb, IL, about 12" L, c.1926. Added value — Costs the most with original shouldered glass "Utility" mixing bowl. **$30-$40**

The Census & Collecting (or: Don't Get Discouraged) — If you think all the good stuff is probably gone, think again. Just look at the population figures for any given decade, and think how many probable owners of a corkscrew, frying pan, nutcracker, grater or cream whip those numbers imply. The rounded-off population of the U.S. in 1890 was 65,000,000 people. Even if we divide that by 6, to represent households of two adults and four children, that leaves almost 11 million homes. Of those, maybe one in 50 or 100 had a cream whip, but that's still encouraging — say 110,000 cream whips in use during the last decades of the 19th C. Even if only one in 10 survived rust, moving, war drives, and the unblushing blandishments of advertisers of "newer" things, there may be 11,000 of them still around. Even if there's but one in every village in the U.S., there is probably one for you. I've never bought one — one of you can have the one I didn't buy! And this hypothesis is only for something that was probably uncommonly owned to begin with. There were millions of Dover and A & J eggbeaters sold over the years; millions of frying pans; hundreds of millions of forks and spoons. Still not convinced? **Advertising Claims & Collecting** — In many old ads you will see manufacturers' claims about the quantity sold. For example, an 1890 ad for the "Morgan Broiler," made by The Sun Stamping Co., it was said that "50,000 Housewives" bear out the claim that the broiler is a demonstrated success." Even if they stopped making them that day, that still means an awful lot of those collectible broilers are possible finds!

Cream whip, tin body, 4 little strap tin legs, cast iron crank & beaters inside, "Fries," American, 8" H x 6" L x 4-1/2" W, c.1890s. **$90-$100**

Cream whip, turbine type, steel with nickel silver curved rectangular blade. Looks like NASA skywatch dish, with cutout gear wheel & angled wood handle. Small depression or dimple in bottom of bowl fits pivot on bottom of beater so it won't slip during use, "Dunlap's Sanitary Silver Blade Cream & Egg Whip, No Splash or Waste," J. S. Dunlap; dist. by Casey-Hudson Co, Chicago, 11" L, pat'd 1906-1916. **$25-$35**

Cream whip & eggbeater, glass & stainless steel, lid, beaters & crank all in one, Androck, Rockford, IL, 1930s. **$22-$30**

Cream whip & eggbeater, tin cylinder with wire dasher handle, "Lightning," marked "pat'd 1868" on the one I saw at a flea. Authority Don Thornton finds no evidence to support the name-and-date combo that I'm 999% sure I once saw. **$45-$50**

Cream whips — See also eggbeaters, syllabub churns

Crock, for mixing bread, saltglazed gray stoneware, "White Hall," 18" diameter, early 20th or late 19th C. **$85-$100**

Dough bowl, trough-shaped, carved wood, very smooth patina, indicating long use, American (?), 24" L x 10" W, 19th C. In Sept. 1988, at the big flea market in Hillsville, VA, I saw a large number of skillfully produced but primitive-looking carved dough troughs priced $35, which wouldn't take long to age. (I didn't see them in 1989.) **$100-$200**

Dough bowl, trough-shaped, primitively carved oak, American, 18" L x 9-1/2" W, early 19th C. Value depends on patina, size, wood, & supposed age. "American" on a price tag often equals a lot of moolah on your receipt. **$100-$200**

Dough box, also bread or **dough brake,** oblong pine box with slanting sides, cover has "inchworm" carved handles, American, 8-1/2" H x 23" L, 19th C. **$300-$400**

Dough box, slanted sides, 4 simply turned legs, on outside wood has original dark brown paint under flaking white, American, 26-1/2" H x 41-5/8" L x 22-1/2" W, c.1870s. **$225-$400**

Hey, Archimedes! Whaddyuh call it? — I used to call this mechanism (as in the next listing, and many eggbeaters) an "Archimedean screw," but this is inaccurate. It is an **Archimedean drill mechanism**. The screw mechanism lifted water. Here is the definition from *Hawkins' Mechanical Dictionary*, Audel's, 1909: "A hand drill for light work, whose stock is formed into a multiple spiral of quick pitch over which a nut or spool slides easily. The act of sliding the nut up and down the stock makes the latter and consequently the drill, rotate first one way and then the other, pressure being applied by a knob or ball at the opposite end of the stock." The Archimedian drill was also called a "Persian drill" in turn-of-century inventors' books on mechanical movements.

Drink mixer, Archimedean drill action, domed snap-on metal lid with simple twisted or spiraled flat strip of metal, 4 upturned turbine blades at bottom, wooden knob at top, tall glass tumbler, "Roberts Lightning," mfd by Dorsey Mfg. Co., Boston, MA, 12" H, c.1910s well into 1920s, perhaps later. **$60-$75**

Drink mixer, Archimedean drill action, glass jar with tin lid, spiral tin whipper, 16" H, pat'd Mar. 30, 1915. This one is marked simply with a monogram of an A & D (not A & J). Maker not yet identified. Another one, same patent date, has wire finger-like beater, like a glove-drying form, worked by the Archimedean drill, and is valued approximately the same as the spiral, perhaps a bit more. **$45-$55**

Drink mixer, Archimedean drill, wire with turned wooden handle, steel blades in small balloon, small pivoting "foot" on bottom seats it steady in bowl or jar, A & J, 12-1/2" L, Oct. 15, 1907. **$22-$35**

Drink mixer, from a drugstore or soda fountain, nickeled cast metal, complete protective gear housing, golden oak base, "Quik Mix, A-1," base 8-1/4" H, mixing mechanism 9" H, c.1920s. **$150-$170**

Drink mixer, metal shaker & lid, "Ovaltine," early 1900s. Ovaltine, by the way, is a malt drink mix that originated in Great Britain.

II-25. Drink mixer for soda fountain. *Gibson "Twin-Mixer," H. B. Gibson Co., NYC, hooked up to a Hamilton-Beach motor, Racine, WI. Could be had quadruple silver-plated, or nickel-plated. 6/1919 ad in* The Soda Fountain. **$100-$400**

II-26. Soda fountain drink mixers. *Cranked hand-power, not electric.* **(L)** *"Quick and Easy" shaker, possibly Conant Co. Nickeled & painted cast iron, 22" H, for all beverages. c.1905 catalog.* **(R)** *"Philadelphia" milk shake machine, 24" H, 7-1/2" x 12" base. "Each turn of the crank-wheel gives ten distinct shocks to the liquid." T. Mills, 1915. Maker not known.* **$250-$600**

II-27. Drink mixer — electric. *Electric "Arnold Sanitary Mixer No. 12," nickeled. In suppliers' catalog of 1921.* **$45-$85**

The American version was formulated with more and more sugar as the 20th C progressed, but now the original version, as sold nowadays in Europe, is obtainable through the Vermont Country Store, Weston, VT. They also have other old-time foods & chewing gum. **$18-$25**

Drink mixer or shaker, for children, plastic with decals, Captain Midnight character, "Ovaltine" mixer, 20th C. **$30-$45**

Drink mixer & measure, aluminum, graduated cup shows 1/3, 2/3, and "1 cup to top"; other side marked 1/4, 1/2 and 3/4 cup, screw-on lid, marked "Smoothie Mixer & Measure" on top, 3-7/8" H x 2-3/4" diameter, 20th C. **$7-$12**

Drink or malted milk mixer, aluminum container with lid, "Thompson's Double Malted," 7" H, 20th C. **$8-$15**

II-28. Eggbeater trade card. *"Surprise," Cragin Mfg. Co., Cragin, IL. "An Egg Beater that beats the Whites of Eggs better than any other. Cranks will not be tolerated in Egg Beaters any more. Five Dollars offered for a better Egg Beater for the Whites of Eggs. All first-class Cooks recommend them. Take one home and TRY IT, and if not convinced it is the best bring it back." c.1870s card; beater sold at least 30 years. In separate cut below, note difference in braced handle from similar ones shown in next two pictures. The card:* **$6-$15**

II-29. Egg whips or egg whisks. *Tinned wire, various gauges. One has spring wire coiled around rim, inner network of thin wire. Two variations of the "Surprise" are in what the trade called "diamond pattern" wire-weaving. Other one is "checker" pattern. About 8-1/2" to 10" L. Late 19th - early 20th C. SEE also Whisk pictures and listings at end of this chapter.* **$8-$20**

Drink or malted milk mixer, all wire frame, small sheet metal thumb piece to work Archimedean drill, for making a "Horlick's" drink. 9-1/2" L, American. Horlick's also had a malted milk plant in England, and the Horlick's "Aero Beater," similar to this one, was patented in England. **$20-$30**

Drink mixer or stirrer, battery-powered, chrome, in original box, 1940s. **$10-$15**

Drink mixer or stirrer, cast metal golf club, from a club car on the "B & O" railroad, 20th C. Two-way crossover: golf and trains! **$25-$40**

Drink mixer, jigger & swizzle sticks, chromium top hat & 4 golf clubs, very jazzy, Chase Brass & Copper, Waterbury, CT, 1-1/2-oz. capacity jigger, mid 1930s. $1 was the original price. **$20-$40**

II-30. Egg whips or egg whisks. *The "chicken-wire" type is called "diamond" (at bottom); closer-woven wires are "checker." Such standard names helped retailers order from different mfrs. Four are "coiled spring" pattern, two have wire lacing holding springs in place around rim. Criss-cross smaller springs is the "cross cut" pattern. Other named ones are marked with letters: "F" for "Flexible"; "E" for "Electric" (earlier known as the "Electra"); "G" for "Gem" — all Washburn Androck catalog, 1927. Wire Goods Co., Worcester, MA, apparently had earliest patents on these; later Washburn made same or similar designs.* **$8-$20**

Drink mixer or stirrer, silver-plated coil with handle, "Holmes, Edwards," dated 1889. **$12-$15**

Drink mixer or stirrer, stainless steel, telescoping, "Spoonomat," 11-3/4" L, pat'd 3/15/1938. **$15-$20**

Drink mixer — See also syllabub churn

Egg whip, sheet metal, on wire frame, with large flat spoon with 4 large cutouts, also used as a pastry blender, stamped at end of handle "The Vandeusen Egg Whip, C. A. Chapman, Geneva, NY," 11" L, pat'd Mar.13, 1894. **$15-$20**

Wire Drawing.— It seems impossible that something as logical as wire isn't older than it is. The useful art of wire-drawing (pulling malleable or soft metal through a small hole in a hard metal die plate) was known in the 1300s in Europe, and was introduced into England after 1650.

Egg whips or whisks, sauce whips, etc., tinned wire, usually bound-wire handles, sometimes turned wooden handles with ferrules, some have wire slip ring to adjust "ballooning" of the wire loops for beating in different size bowls, or for different needs. A sauce whip, for example, has wires bound in a longer, tighter conformation, while the egg whip has a rounder ballooning shape. American, French, etc., various lengths — about 5-1/2" L to 12" L, 1890s to the present. Some have been made almost identically for a century or more. Unless really unusual, the price is quite low. **$6-$15**

The following eggbeater listings are divided into mechanical types: mainly Archimedean drill and different types of rotary beaters.

EGGBEATERS, Archimedean:

Eggbeater, all metal, a thin tin tube is handle grip that you move up & down the twisted wire shaft to activate Archimedean drill, no maker's name, French (?), 12-3/4" L, late 19th or early 20th C. I used to call this mechanism an Archimedean screw, but it is an Archimedean drill mechanism (see explanation above, preceding first "Cream whip" price entry). **$135-$150**

Eggbeater, skeletal steel wire coiled in flat, vertical spiral, Archimedean drill action, 12" L. Called the "Dudley-Bryant Patent," but actually pat'd by George Dudley, July 17, 1888, and assigned to, and mfd by Woods, Sherwood & Co., Lowell, MA, at first. Later mfd by Paine, Diehl & Co., Philadelphia. Bryant had another patent that same day, an Archimedean drill action skeletal beater with a spiral-effect stationary wire blade and a turning one within it. The Dudley-Bryant: **$175-$195**

Eggbeater, tin, wire, & turned black wooden vertical handle, Archimedean drill, 2 wings with 4 curved ribs joined to outer circle bow of the blade. "Bryant's Patent," 13-3/4" L, 1885. **$125-$150**

Eggbeater & cream whip, glass jar, metal lid, Archimedean drill, turned wooden knob on twisted wire shaft, oblong pattern of close vertical wires — described by the inventor Maurice Roberts as having a "plurality of beater members." (That's what an octopus with a rug beater has.) "Simplex," mfd by Jeannette Glass Co., Jeannette, PA, 12" H, "patent pending" — pat'd Dec. 31, 1918. **$85-$100**

Eggbeater, simple wire frame & blades, 2-part shaft (one adds rigidity, one is twisted for Archimedean drill action & threaded through turned wood knob),12-7/8" L, turn of century. **$18-$25**

Eggbeater, plated wire, Archimedean drill, "Skyline," English, 10-1/2" L, 20th C. **$12-$18**

Eggbeater, iron & steel, 4 "wing" metal blades form a pear shape around central rod shaft, turned & painted upright wooden handle, Archimedean drill mechanism, this particular one has 4 little balancing feet on circular base to settle it firmly in bottom of beater jar, "Johnson's," pat'd Dec. 18, 1917 by Edward H. Johnson. This beater was made with several different stabilizing devices on the bottom — or none. **$55-$75**

Counting Eggbeater Wings — Each half of a blade, as counted from top to bottom (where they are joined or are part of a continuous bent blade) counts as a wing in the old eggbeater-manufacturing lingo. A 4-wing beater means 2 blade circles — blades that come down from the top, then bell out or balloon out at the business end, then continue on back to the top. An 8-wing means 4 blade circles. Blade wings were also called members (and also dashers), so that a 2-blade, 4-wing beater could also be described as having 4 members or 4 dashers. The term "dashers" was borrowed from churn-making, and in fact a few eggbeaters have a dasher churn-like motion (up and down) but not many.

Eggbeater, metal, turned wood handle, side action Archimedean drill, "Batteur [de?] Bolero," French, 12-1/4" L, late 19th C. or early 20th C. Similar in action to the George Paine patent of 6/ 28/1887 (See Fig. 7-14 in Thornton's book of eggbeaters). **$170-$200**

Eggbeater, nickel-plated, like an Archimedean drill vegetable whip, no maker's mark, 12" L, early 20th C. **$45-$60**

Eggbeater & cream whip, wire with square frame at bottom filled in with rotating fork-like vertical tines, Archimedean drill, marked on thumbpiece "The Up To Date Egg & Cream Whip," 11-1/2" L, pat'd Apr. 10, 1906 by George Flowers of Philadelphia. **$135-$160**

Eggbeater & cream whip, glass jar, short wire dasher moved up & down as Archimedean drill with white china knob, "Roberts' Lightning Mixer," Dorsey Mfg. Co., Boston. 8" H, based on various 1912/1913 patents of Henry P. Roberts'. At least 3 sizes — the 12" one worth twice as much. **$35-$45**

Eggbeater or drink mixer, nickeled wire, metal, wood, Archimedean drill action, "Boun-C Beater," American, 13" L, 20th C. **$55-$70**

Eggbeater or liquid mixer, tall Archimedean drill action, long shaft with only about 9 twists, wooden spool to run up and down the drill, large loop of wire for other hand, 2 small ballooned blades with 2 little curved reinforcements that, by adding more cutting edges, make blades more effective. This "Clipper" was advertised as having a "double action" because the inner vertical blades ballooned out when the spool was at its lowest point on the drill. The round blade with curved ribs or reinforcements is the same kind of blade that's part of the much older rotary "Earle's Patent." 13" H, pat'd by Thomas Brown Aug. 30, 1887. (For more Archimedean — See also the many Archimedean cream whips and drink mixers.) **$165-$180**

EGGBEATERS, rotary (those with a drive gear rotated by hand):

Eggbeater, all metal, including heavy gauge wire handle, sheet metal gear wheel & coiled wire knob, small diameter 4-wing "balloon," "Big Bingo #70," 11" L, A & J, Binghamton, NY, pat'd 1923, made into 1940s. **$15-$20**

Eggbeater, black-finished cast iron gear & crank with black wooden knob; very unusual because gear wheel doesn't stick up vertically but is built horizontally into black screw-on lid, long, thin wire beaters that reach almost to bottom of straight-sided embossed glass jar, "Jewel 'Beater Mixer Whipper Freezer'," mfd by Juergens Brothers, Minneapolis, MN, about 7" H, pat'd 6/20/1893. Though not spectacular like some, it's extremely rare and a very desirable addition to any collection. **$55-$70**

Eggbeater, cast iron, gear wheel like Dover, grip handle, very strange beater blades — 2 heavy gauge outer wire wings (blades) with 3 fat vertical scallops, one central vertical rod with 3 horizontal wire crosspieces that rotate within the scallops, ball bottom to fit in bowl dimple, 11" L. I'm sure this unmarked beater was another "Aerate the Egg" conceptual piece, sold through F.A. Walker (importers & wholesalers), as the "Three-Minute Egg Beater," Boston, MA, c.1880s. **$350-$450**

Eggbeater, cast iron handle, wheel, gear, sheet metal 4-wing (2 blades) plus central vertical rod, blades somewhat flattened at bottom to enable it to do its touted job: "Beats to the bottom of the bowl." Pat'd by Clarence A. Taplin, Apr 14, 1903. Taplin Mfg. Co., New Britain, CT. **$30-$40**

Cast Iron — It has been said that cast iron is really the art of woodcarving, because by the 1840s or so, carved wooden patterns were used by founders to create matrices or molds into which the molten metal could be poured. Gear wheel **foundry patterns** are most common, but all other cast parts had patterns too. In the mid-nineteenth century the economical concept of uniformly sized parts, which could be bolted or screwed together, meant that only the broken parts need be replaced rather than the whole tool or machine. Wooden patterns were made with lathes, drills & table saws, or were handcarved, or both, often not from a solid piece of wood, but from laminated (glued together) layered blocks, with grain running in two directions to make the laminate stronger and much less liable to warp. Patterns were used sometimes for many years. Small parts that stick out from the main part of the pattern were usually carved or turned separately, then glued or pegged into the main part. Patterns were varnished or painted — also to protect from warping. Painted ones are fun to collect because different parts of the pattern might be painted different colors — usually red, green, yellow & black. Each pattern was marked, usually stamped with a several-digit number and one or more letters, but sometimes stenciled or painted with a number. I have never seen a foundry pattern for a kitchen utensil or gadget, at least not to recognize it, but they probably exist (or did exist) somewhere. Occasionally a dealer at a flea market will show up with a box or pile of foundry patterns, priced from $3 up to $60 or more, having rescued discarded patterns from a foundry no longer requiring them or even defunct.

• • • •

I use the adjectives "**cutout**" or "**openwork**" throughout this book to describe castings with large "negative spaces" giving the appearance of cutouts, although the cast gear wheels are not machined and cut out after casting; only the casting model is.

II-31. Egg whips or batter beaters. (T) *Five-fingered one is tinned iron wire "Whipster," green wood handle. "Especially good for Angel Food Cakes." Washburn, 1936.* **(B)** *Other is a "batter whip," for eggs, batter or cream; choice of Blutip, green, blue or yellow wood handle. 11-1/4" L. A & J Mfg. Co., Binghamton, NY, 1930.* **$4-$12**

Eggbeater, cast iron or nickel-plated iron, 4 perforated tin wings (2 blades) plus heavy gauge wire with loop at bottom to capture the blades and hold in place. Name "Cyclone" is connotative of a wild "stirring" of air, pat'd by William G. Browne, Kingston NY, 11-1/2" L or 11-3/4" L, pat'd June 25, 1901 & July 16, 1901. Browne's patent drawing for the *Official Gazette* shows beater

II-32. Swizzle stick & egg whips, *some also called spoon egg beaters. From top:* **(T)** *is small branched twig, peeled of bark, and used by rolling shaft between hands.* **(2)** *is a "Flat egg-whip, the best shape and easily cleaned." American Home Cook Book, 1854.* **(3)** *Next spoon one, 10-1/2" L, has long maroon wood handle; Wire Goods Co., 1915.* **(4)** *Another, by Lalance & Grosjean, came with tin or wood handle, 1890.* **(5)** & **(6)** *Two like garden tools with thick handles, are homemade ones "greatly superior to the common fork or table spoon." 10" L overall. American Agriculturist, 6/1876. An* American Agriculturist *Nov. 1871 article on beaters said "several wire beaters are only forks in a modified form." A pear-shaped wire whisk was called "a refinement on bundles of twigs long used by confectioners and bakers." (Such twig bundles, in a very small size, have long been used in Japan in the tea ceremony.)* **$8-$35**

II-33. Cake whip & mixing spoons. *Also called vegetable servers.* **(L)** *Slotted & perforated steel spoon with shellacked wood "antique oak" finish handles, 11" L, Wire Goods Co., 1915.* **(R)** *Earlier version of perforated one was called the "Perfection Cake Spoon," and sold c.1900. (M) cake whip, stainless steel, handles in ivory with blue band or green with ivory band, 12-1/2" L. A & J Mfg., 1930. Many variations exist. SEE also mixing & cake spoons at end of this chapter.* **$4-$15**

very like one manufactured, except that handle is part of heavy gauge metal strip forming shaft, twisted so that it was parallel, not at right angles, to gear wheel. Manufactured one has modified vertical loop handle as seen in a 1903 patent. **$70-$80**

Eggbeater, cast iron handle & gear, 6-wing (2 tinned blades, plus one bowed wire blade), "Dover Stamping Co.," Boston, MA, several sizes: 9-1/2" L, 10-1/2" L, 11-3/8" L, etc. This "Standard" Mfg. Co. beater with improvements pat'd July 14, 1885, by Thomas Brown, was prob. made for close to 35 to 40 years. This particular one, like others found not infrequently, has a mix of elements that confuse the collector. The 1885 patent was supposed to refer to a

II-34. Eggbeaters & drink mixers. *All Archimedean drill. Far left* **(1)** *is Horlick's drink mixer in glass tumbler, 9-1/4" L, c.1910.* **(2)** *Tin, green-painted wood, wire, 12-1/4" L, German, c.1900.* **(3)** *A. & J. Mfg. Co., wire & wood, 12-1/2" L, October 1907. Note little brass swiveling cap to be centered in bottom of bowl to help keep beater in place. A smaller size was for nursery & sick room use.* **(4)** *Tin, wood, wire, 11" L, English, no maker's mark.* **(5)** *The "Up To Date Egg & Cream Whip," 11-3/4" L, marked "April 10, 1906."* *(1) & (3)* **$28-$32;** *(2)* **$32-$38;** *(4)* **$12-$15;** *(5)* **$135-$160**

II-35. Eggbeaters & patents — Archimedean drill. (1) *Pat'd 6/2/1885, by Charles A. Bryant, Wakefield, MA.* **(2)** *Pat'd 5/27/1890, by Alvin Judd Austin, Shelby, NE. Entirely "wire, whereby a very cheap, simple, and durable egg-beater is produced."* **(3)** *"Dudley-Bryant" patent beater, pat'd 7/17/1888 by George Dudley;* **(4)** *"Lightning Chain" eggbeater, mfd. by B.P. Forbes, successor to Tarbox & Bogart, Cleveland, OH. 1903 ad.* **(5)** *"Bryant's Patent," with much tighter twisting of vertical rod that forms beater screw. They claimed 3200 revolutions a minute, by pushing 4 times up & down per second. 1888 ad.* **$100-$150** *except (3)* **$175**

steel-handled beater based on the Dover original, but it appears sometimes on those with cast iron handle & frame. It should be marked "Standard" but instead is marked "Dover." **$60-$80**

Eggbeaters & Treasure Island.— According to his classic travel book *Travels with a Donkey in the Cévannes,* Robert Louis Stevenson (of *Treasure Island* fame) in 1878 packed a little donkey named Modestine with a sleeping bag and a number of supplies for a 12-day hike in the mountains of France. He took a lamp and candles, clothing, books, a milk jug, chocolate blocks, wine, black bread, and — ta da! — an eggbeater! Wonder what kind.

Eggbeater, cast iron (sometimes tinned) handle, gears & frame, 6-wing (2 tinned sheet metal blades & 1 wire blade), "Taplin's Dover Pattern Improved," Taplin Mfg. Co., New Britain, CT. There are several sizes, from 8-3/4" L to about 12" L, pat'd Apr. 14, 1903. Most fit in this range: **$35-$75**

Eggbeater, cast iron & tinned sheet metal & wire, 6-wing, clamps to shelf above bowl, "Dover Stamping Co.," Boston, MA, 17" L, the #4 hotel size called "Mammoth" (an even larger one was advertised as the "Leviathan"), c. 1891. Later the "Dover Mammoth #300" was made by Taplin Mfg. Co. **$135-$165**

The original Dover was patented May 31, 1870 by Turner Williams, and it was called then the "Williams Egg Beater."

• An ad for The Dover Egg Beater, in *Ladies Home Journal,* March 1887, reads: "Pat. May 31, 1870; May 6, 1878. The one thing always needful in the kitchen. Always satisfactory. Popular, 4,000,000 in use. Stand first in all countries, has never had a rival. Used by all practical Housekeepers, endorsed by all teachers of cooking. Four sizes. Send for circular. Regular size sent by mail upon receipt of 50¢."

• At first glance many of the **Dovers** look the same, but look more closely — at slight variations in the casting of gear wheel "petals," at blade diameter, size and bowing or "ballooning" of wings. Handle grips are different too. The Dover became so popular, indeed omnipresent, that many cookbook authors made "dover" the generic term for rotary eggbeaters. One of the neatest (if not the most valuable, say $75-$80) to find is one that has a teensy blade balloon, about one inch across, to fit down into a tall tumbler. It has a patent date of May 6, 1973 on it. You just can't get to the bottom of the Dover story without reading Don Thornton's book.

• • • •

"Rice Fritters — Boil 1 teaspoonful of rice until it is tender; strain upon it 1 quart of milk; let it boil ten minutes; cool it; add flour enough to make a batter as thick as will fry easily on the griddle; 2 tablespoonfuls of yeast; let it rise 3 hours; add 2 well-beaten eggs, and cook on a heated griddle." Henry Scammel, *Treasure House of Useful Knowledge,* 1891.

• • • •

Earle's Classic — I have no idea why the gap between patent and production. As far as I know, this first appeared in Dover's 1869 catalog, which says: "This, while it is the simplest, is the most effective Egg Beater made. Held in the hand with an immovable rest, it stands firmly wherever placed and will beat eggs with greater rapidity than any other; while the price places it within reach of all. It is cleaned by a moment's rapid turning in hot water."

II-36. Eggbeater patent — rotary. *Pat'd 4/24/1866, by Timothy Earle. If this one was made, the value would be sky high what with hearts and elegant compact styling.*

II-38. Eggbeaters — rotary. (L) *"Cyclone," Browne Mfg. Co., Kingston, NY, perforated flanges, cast iron (some are nickel-plated), 11-3/4" L (some are 11-1/2"). 6/25/1901 and 7/16/1901.* **(R)** *Taplin "Light Running" center drive, 12-1/4" L, Taplin Mfg. Co., New Britain, CT, pat'd 1908. Note handle style. This one came in a 10-1/2" L size also.* **$70-$80; $50-$55**

II-37. Dover — the Classic rotary! *Dover Stamping Co., Boston. "Dover" was, for a long while, a generic term for eggbeater. Patent dates are 5/31/1870; 5/6/1873; 4/3/1888; and 11/24/1891. Three handle styles are shown here; a fourth is rectangular. Sizes in picture not proportional. The names are prosaic and describe size one way or the other.* **(1)** *"Extra Family Size," 9-3/4" L, Dover Cookbook, 1899.* **(2)** *"Mammoth." 1899, with screw-clamp shelf mount.* **(3)** *"Tumbler," 10-3/4" L, marked "Taplin Co., Wire Goods Co. 1915 catalog. This was to be used in a tumbler — a non-footed drinking glass, that hundreds of years ago actually tumbled because it had a rounded bottom. Imbibers couldn't set it down between sips.* **(4)** *"Hotel," 12-1/2" L, handle & wheel "chestnut bronzed" or tinned. 1915.* **(5)** *"Taplin Light Running," with center drive, wide flared dashers, 10-1/2" L, bronzed finish. 1927 catalog.* **(6)** *10-3/4" L, 1927 version. Note handle of these later ones.* **(7)** *"Small," 8-1/2" L, described as having "chestnut bronzed" wheel & handle. 1915.* **(8)** *Another "Tumbler," 10-3/4", 1899.* **(9)** *"Family," 9" L, 1899. Blades from 1890 one start higher and describe bigger circle.* **(10)** *"Family," from c.1904-1910 catalog. Note wheel knob & change in handle grip.* **$45-$200**

II-39. Eggbeaters — rotary. (T) *"Holt's Egg Beater," pat'd 8/22/1899, iron & tin, 12-1/2" L. Has the so-called "flare dashers."* **(B-L)** *is a side-handled "Holt's Pat'd Flare Dasher," 8-3/4" L, iron & tin. One on* **(R)** *has the same name, but much less flair! and not so well made. Collection of Meryle Evans.* **$45-$55; $200; $185**

II-40. Eggbeaters — rotary. *Left to right:* **(1)** *Nickeled steel, wood, 7-1/4" L, "Beats anything in a cup or bowl." A & J, mfd. by Edward Katzinger Co. (which took over the original A & J).* **(2)** *An 8-wing, nickeled steel beater with "extra large drive wheel." Red or green angular handles. This and next 3 from Washburn Androck catalog, 1936. Note differences in handles and frames.* **(3)** *Also 8 wings, with green, yellow or red handle.* **(4)** *Four wings, nickeled steel, coiled wire knob, wooden handle in green.* **(5)** *another, with longer straight part to wings.* **$7-$35**

Cut Me In — In specifications for an egg-beater, granted patent #39,134, Timothy Earle wrote: "Various devices have been employed for the purpose of beating eggs more expeditiously than by the familiar hand-process. One of these devices consists of two wire frames, one within the other, and made to revolve in opposite directions; another consists of a propeller blade which is made to rotate while a pair of beaters have at the same time a reciprocating motion. All these machines, and all others with which I am acquainted, possess the common fault that the beaters, whether of wire or of the form of propeller-blades, do not cut the yolks and whites of the egg, but literally beat them. Now, as the albumen of an egg consists of a peculiar thick, glazy substance, it can be worked more effectually with a cutting instrument than with one which has a blunt edge. In fact, so well is this understood that housewives universally make use of the blade of a knife for the purpose." Another was patented by Earle at the same time, with a ratchet-action mechanism to turn the blades. Earle patented several eggbeaters over a long period.

Eggbeater, cast iron & tin, gear wheel with the familiar 6 petals, turned by a wooden knob, but the business end is an interesting geometric pattern of 2 curved metal wings, pat'd by Timothy Earle, mfd by Dover Stamping Co., as "Earl's [sic] Patent Egg Beater," "The Standard #1," or "Patent Standard Egg Beater," Earle from Smithfield, RI; Dover in Boston. Pat'd July 7, 1863. (I believe that decades later this "Standard" was made by Standard Mfg. Co.) **$165-$200**

Eggbeater, cast iron gear, two wire "rabbit ear" vertically alert handles, & tin angled bladewings somewhat like the "Three Minute" and the "Loll" beaters, name spelled out as the spokes of cast iron gear wheel. "The Hill" in serif letters, American, pat'd by John E. Hill Nov. 5, 1901 and Jan. 15, 1907. 11-1/2" L. Mfd by J. E. Hill Co., Boston. Because Hill designed his beater so that the blades could be removed for washing, it's possible that this contributed, in the long run, to this beater's extreme rarity. **$350-$400**

II-41. Eggbeaters — rotary. **(L)** *"Ram Beater" with wiggly fingerhold grip that looks like crown. Chromed, 12" L.* **(M)** *A Dover, 11-3/8" L, iron & tin, with teensiest bow to its wings ever — the narrowest tumbler, or perhaps you mixed something down inside a bottle.* **(R)** *"Whip Well," yellow wood handle, no knob on crank handle, 11" L, pat'd 3/23/1920 and 5/2/1921. Handle is different from ones marked only with 1920 patent, blade profile differs, and there's no knob on crank. The 1921 patent, not in Thornton's book, must relate to something beside mechanism.* **$150; $75; $20**

II-42. Eggbeater — rotary. *The incomparable "Aluminum Beauty." Sometimes marked "Aluminum Beauty Beater VIKO Instant Whip." Ullman Aluminum, Division, NY. 10-3/8" L, cast & sheet aluminum. Pat'd 4/20/1920. In reality, to a collector the value would be lower than the price you might expect to buy the best eggbeater for everyday use that there is!* **$15-$20**

Eggbeater, cast & stamped aluminum, solid gear wheel, 8-wing, 4-blade, plus wire, marked either "Aluminum Beauty," or "Aluminum Beauty Beater VIKO Instant Whip," Ullman Aluminum Co., Division, NY, 10-3/8" L, pat'd April 20, 1920. **$15-$25**

Eggbeater, chromed steel with wooden T-handle, "Ladd Ball Bearing No. 3," Ladd Bros.; mfd by Traut & Hine Mfg. Co. and Humphrey Mfg. Co., both of New Britain, CT, 11" L, pat'd Oct. 18, 1921 by Lavern Bordwell, marked "Other patents pending." (**NOTE:** The close vertical wings of the #5, meant for use in a tumbler, make that one worth twice the #3.) **$12-$15**

Eggbeater, green painted T-handle, sheet steel, stamped gear with teeth, "High Speed Super Center Drive Beater," "Pat Apld for," pat'd Oct. 27, 1931, mfd by A & J, 12" L. **$8-$12**

Eggbeater, metal with off-white egg-shaped knob handle, #72, A & J Mfg. Co., Binghamton, NY, 11" L, pat'd Oct. 9, 1923. **$10-$15**

Eggbeater, heavy stamped metal, 3 narrow fold-flat upside-down heart-shaped beater blades, one fitted within the next, 11-1/2"

II-43. Eggbeater — rotary. *The "Biltrite," mfd. by Stuber & Kuck Co., Peoria, IL. Tinned steel, center drive wheel, nameplate is a "locking device holding blades permanently in place," waved beater blades "result in 50% quicker results," and the blades are "so close to plate that one egg is drawn up from a flat plate ... impossible with other makes." 1919 ad in* House Furnishing Review. **$25-$30**

II-44. Eggbeaters — rotary. (L) *Another waved-blade type with center drive — the "Flint Mixer 'Rhythm Beater,'" mfd. by Ekco Products Co., 1958.* **(M)** *Unnamed eggbeater mfd. by F. W. Loll Mfg. Co., Meriden, CT. 1/1909* House Furnishing Review. *Pat'd Oct. 9, 1906.* **(R)** *"Three-Minute Egg Beater," cast iron, Dover-like gear wheel, grip handle, 2 heavy wire blades with scallops, crosswires and vertical rod, 11" L. Sold through F. A. Walker, Boston, c.1880s, and named by them.* **$6-$15; $300-$375; $350-$450**

L, "Minute Maid," mfd by Henderson Corp., Seattle, WA, pat'd May 13, 1930 by F. W. Henderson. **$115-$130**

Eggbeater, iron gear wheel, wire, tin, white porcelain crank knob, double blade fold-flat with central vertical wire shaft, "Peerless #2," 10-1/4" L, American but place & mfg. unknown. **$125-$150**

Price Agreements — Dealers hope to spot upcoming attractions in time to lay in a good cheap supply. Collectors do too. But after a while, both need publicity so that more stuff will surface (and be saved from landfill or raw material recycling), even though it means competition. Then, dealers want to move merchandise, so they are glad when something happens to create a large demand that they can help supply. This should happen fast for cash flow purposes for dealers and somewhat slower for collectors, so that they can accumulate broadly and enjoy leisurely before selling or trading up.

• • • •

How are prices arrived at in that early stage when the field goes public? A couple of decades ago, it took several years to establish market values (the second tier of prices, not the lucky, serendipitous bargain one-off prices). Prices hovered at plateaus for years. After a couple of articles in magazines, prices would rise again. A book could cause prices to take a big jump, and at the same time bring out hidden treasures. In the 1980s these processes happened

II-45. Eggbeater patent — rotary. *Pat'd 1/13/1931, by Henry J. Edlund, Burlington, VT, #1,789,224. Mfd. by Edlund Co., Inc., Burlington.* **$10-$15**

II-46. Eggbeater — rotary. *"No. 75 Super Center Drive," nickeled steel, wood handles in Blutip, green, blue or yellow. A & J Mfg. Co./EKCO, Edward Katzinger Co., Chicago, 1930.* **$10-$15**

II-47. Eggbeaters & patent drawing — rotary. (L) *The reality — with cast iron gear wheel spells out mfr's initials: "P. D. & Co." (Paine, Diehl & Co.), Philadelphia. Note flying saucer-like wire dasher: "a double or compound dasher, having its two parts vibrating in opposition to each other upon the egg between them, and also reciprocating up and down against the egg in the bottom of the dish. ... It automatically fits itself to and gathers up the egg from any shaped dish whether spherical or flat bottomed inside. It whips one egg in a teacup in 15 seconds, 6 eggs in a bowl in 70 seconds." Pat'd 12/1/1885.* **(M)** *The 12/1/1885 patent, by George H. Thomas, Chicopee Falls, MA., followed by one in 1886 were the basis for the PD & Co. one at left, although neither patent shows the name spelled out.* **(R)** *The reciprocating motion, cast iron & wire "Easy," was sold through Montgomery Ward, c.1895 ad. Name spelled out in gear wheel spokes. The "Easy" was also based on George Thomas' 9/28/1886 patent. Don Thornton has seen some "Easy" beaters marked with Mar. 6, 1886 patent* application *date. Many Easy's were sold — why aren't there more out there for collectors! • Note angled rods that connect dasher parts with gear wheels on all three.* **$500-$550**

II-48. Eggbeaters — rotary wire blades. (L) *Stamped metal gear wheel with holes around perimeter, wire dashers. "Mayonnaise Toujours - Creme Chantilly - Reussis Le Roides Batteurs - CBM - Brevete SGDG." French, 12" L.* **(M)** *Spade handle, double circle "soap bubble blower" dashers. Clarence E. Elliott's "Kansas City" beater, or, as marked: "K. C. USA." Marked "Pat. # 1,992,564", but actually should be 1,992,654, 1934.* **(R)** *Zig Zag, "Le Tourbillon," French, early 20th C. Pictures courtesy Bob Cahn.* **$65-$100**

faster and faster. I have started (and had to call completed) at least 10 collections having nothing to do with kitchen utensils, since 1979. The ones I started in the mid 1980s had to be finished within two years because the speed with which something caught on, making prices escalate like Reagan's national deficit, swept collectible after collectible out of my reach. Most influential now in creating a national market value are collector conventions & specialist newsletters, although neither is a new idea. Everything is collected. Scan *Antique Trader Weekly* for a while, notably "Wanted Miscellaneous" ads, to uncover discrete specialties developing, which — you can bet your crocheted doilies, handpainted neckties, tea strainers, or preserved gingerbread men — will have their own conventions before 2001. Conventions expose glamorous or rare items, and generally they boost prices, but still the market tends to settle out. Most collectors will continue to decide for themselves what attracts them and how much it's worth. It is paramount to remember that **trash is treasure is trash**. We still find bargains because some sellers don't know a field, or don't care for the particular type of thing, or they use a delightful old-fashioned markup system based on the seller's cost, not what the market might bear. **Whoa!** It is necessary and wise to put a drag on runaway prices in order to build broad strength at beginning levels. **Future resale markets depend on widespread interest.**

Eggbeater, iron & tin, 2 blades (4 wings) with finger-like projections — the so-called "flare dasher." "Holt's Egg Beater," Holt Lyon, Tarrytown, NY, 12-1/2" L (there is also an 11-1/2" L one, maybe others), pat'd Aug. 22, 1899. **$50-$60**

Eggbeater, iron & tin, somewhat conical 2-bar wire frame, supporting a long central crankshaft with the handle at top, the scrolly blades horizontal at the bottom. The gear, instead of being at the top, is close to the bottom, and the curvy wings turn or revolve on the teeth of that horizontal circular gear. 11" L. "Dodge Race Course Egg Beater" is name given by collectors (only one is known to exist ... so far!), probably American, probably 1880s. **$1000 and up**

II-49. Wallmount eggbeater — rotary with wire whisk bows. *"Silver Wall Style No.6," mfd. by Silver & Co., Brooklyn, c.1910. Black japanned cast iron, tinned spring steel wire bows. "For hotels and restaurants. very quick in operation, and very easily cleaned." Has a "suspended arm to which is cast a socket which fits into a corresponding pocket socket ... which may remain permanently affixed to the wall and the beater portion be removed. In use large bowls or large glasses or pails or deep dishes or any other similar article may be used as a receptacle." This Silver piece has a confusing history tied in with (or rivalling) the Edwin Baltzley 12/15/1885 patent assigned to North Bros.* **$200-$300**

II-50. Eggbeaters — all fold flat rotaries, *a particular love of these collectors. (L) to (R).* **(1)** *"Standard" egg beater, 10-1/4" L, pat'd 6/29/ & 9/21/1880, and 3/8/1881.* **(2)** *"Dover," pat'd Mar. 8, 1881, Jul. 14, 1885, 10-1/4" L.* **(3)** *"Family," 10-1/4" L, pat'd 9/26/1876.* **(4)** *"The Hill," over 12" L. Note that name is spelled out in the cast iron gear wheel, below the rabbit ear handle. Pat'd Jan/15/1907.* **(5)** *Marked "USA." 9-1/4" L. Some of these have slotted dashers.* **(6)** *10-1/2" L, pat'd 6/29/1880.* **(7)** *"Centripetal," pat'd 6/13/1887. Collection of Phyllis & Jim Moffet.* **$180; $75; $300; $350; $75; $175; $400**

II-51. Eggbeater — rotary with container. *"Silver Hotel Egg Beater No.5," Silver & Co., c.1910. "Framework ... is heavy cast iron retinned with pure tin which ... makes it sanitary. The beater portion is constructed of heavy steel piano wire and will stand a great deal of hard usage. Shown ready to attach to table. Excellent for large cake mixtures, or where a large quantity of doughy mixture, eggs or mixing of any liquids or light dough is desired. It is splendid for hotels, bakers, boarding houses, and other similar places. For convenience, it disjoints at the upper portion of the arms, and is adjustable for height." Note wheel's quatrefoil cutouts.* **$400-$500**

II-52. Eggbeater or drink mixer. *My first prize — now in another collection. "Standard Specialty Co., Milwaukee, WI," with Root Mason fruit jar. The beater is fixed to the lid, but obviously other jars could replace this one. Cast iron, tin, green glass, 12" H x 3-7/8" diameter. Pat'd 6/11/1907.* **$350-$400**

II-53. Eggbeater or drink mixer. *Cast iron horizontal gear in lid, wire handle & beaters. 7-1/2" H. Glass embossed "JEWEL BEATER, MIXER, WHIPPER & FREEZER. MANF BY GRAVITY TWINE BOX CO. CLEVELAND, OHIO." Called the "Household Jewel" in period ads, pat'd 6/20/1893 by Henry Juergens. Some are marked "Jewel Beater Mixer Whipper & Freezer Made by Juergens Bros. Minneapolis." Photo courtesy Phyllis & Jim Moffet.* **$450-$475**

Eggbeater, iron & tin, cast iron 6-petal gear wheel, with "fingered" blades (so-called "flare dashers"), but the fingers are slightly stubbier than on the bigger, vertical-handle kind. This has looped iron handle at right angles to blade shaft. "Holt's Pat'd Flare Dasher Egg Beater," Tarrytown, NY, 8-3/4" L, dated with pat'd Aug. 22, 1899, like other one, and Apr 3, 1900, but seems to be based on Ulysses Grant Teetsell's patent of Valentine's Day, 1922. The flare dashers seem to have grown, like mutants, out of the crimped-edge blades of "Holt's Improved Dover" beater, although they

II-54. Eggbeaters & original vessels. (L) *Rotary "A & J" with its original beating bowl. Pat'd Oct. 9, 1923.* **(R)** *a Liquid mixer marked with an intermingled monogram of "AD," pat'd Mar. 30, 1915 and assigned to the canned milk people, Bordens Milk. Archimedean drill for one-handed, 3 wire finger-mixing.* **$25-$55**

II-55. Eggbeater. *"Silver Egg Beater No. 4," with a "receptacle made of heavy lime glass graduated for dry or liquid measuring. The dashers or beaters are made of extra heavy bessemer steel, retinned bright, the air tube is made of XXXX tin. The valve adjustment at the base of the tube is made of german silver. The tinplate cover is heavily nickelplated and polished. The handle of enameled wood." One quart capacity only. 11-1/2" H x 4-1/2" diameter. Silver & Co., Brooklyn, c.1910. A few years later, the style of the wooden handle was slightly changed to be more angular, and with more turnings.* **$75-$100**

have same & later patent dates. Another with same name, same side handle, has no fingers at all, just the ripply edges, and its gear wheel has six curved spokes. **$200-$225**

Eggbeater, iron & tin, with green wood T-handle & knob (also came with red handles), 8 wings (4 blade circles, each half counting as a wing), A & J "High Speed Super Center Drive Beater," Binghamton, NY, 11-1/2" L, patent #2,049,727 (1936). **$25-$35**

Eggbeater, ivory colored plastic handle & knob, chromed metal blades, handle set at angle to make it very easy & comfortable to grip, particularly when beating a cake for 30+ minutes. "Whirlbeater," Los Angeles, CA, 10" L, marked "patent pending," 20th C. **$15-$30**

The above item is probably is one of the great 1930s Maynard Mfg. Co. beaters & mixers: the company used the phrase "whirl-whip design" in advertising. Probably meant to capitalize on earlier Whirl beaters such as the "Blue Whirl," and the "Merry Whirl," pat'd in 1916 and 1921. The styling of all the Maynard beaters is so sleek and modern that these beaters will undoubtedly gain in popularity with crossover collectors coming in from nifty Fifties field.

• • • •

Visualize Whirled Peas — In the 1920s, Turner & Seymour, Torrington, CT, made Blue Whirl "Dainty Whirl" beaters, Blue Whirl "Kitchen Whirl" beaters, and "Merry Whirl" beaters — with various handle styles, pat'd Nov. 28, 1916, and also Aug. 2, 1921. And in the late 1920s, Androck [Washburn] made a "Whirlwind" turbine beater, nickel-plated and 10-1/2" L. It was all metal except for the "ivory"-painted wooden crank knob. It was also very like their same-size regular turbine beater, except that instead of heavy nickeled iron wire it was made of flat metal. At the same time, Androck offered a set for the "Whirlwind," with a small (5" diameter) "French gray" glazed mixing bowl, with white stripes. Very *moderne*. These whirls are valued between $15 and $20.

Eggbeater, nickel-plated sheet metal, 4 wings, metal tubular T-handle is angled 45 degrees off the gear wheel; design of everything but handle is same as Oct. 9, 1923 patent, not marked, but A & J — same gear wheel, same coiled wire knob for crank, same blades. Binghamton, NY, 10" H, 1923+. **$15-$20**

Eggbeater, nickeled sheet metal, long hexagonal yellow painted wooden vertical handle, tin, wire, "Whipwell," 11" L, pat'd March 23, 1920 & May 2, 1921. Winsted Hardware Mfg. Co., Winsted, CT. Whip through that egg in the 1920s & 1930s with the familiar Whipwell, Quik-Whip, & Whippit; also Whiprite Egg Beater, Champion Machinery Co., Joliet, IL (I've not found one of theirs.) **$18-$25**

Eggbeater, sheet metal, spade handle with wooden grip, ball-bearing gear, spectacular 3 beaters (12 wings) worked from only one geared wheel, each set of blades with vertical rod through center. Aurelius Brothers, Braham, MN, 11-1/2" L. Says only "Patent applied for," but pat'd Aug. 28, 1923. They must have big eggs out there! (Which is odd, considering the mosquito is Minnesota's state bird!) **$275-$300**

Eggbeater, stamped metal & wire, nickel-plated, bottle-shaped frame for the wire beater "wings," designed with back & forth hairpin curves. Extremely elegant & modern looking: crank the simple round sheet metal wheel with 3 large holes and its border of small holes mesh with small teeth of small gear to turn blades. Handle has coiled wire with effect of a crown. "Ram Beater," 12" H, marked "patented" but no date. Pat'd by Robert Moore, Aug. 18, 1915; mfd by Ram Metal Products Co., NYC. Moore also patented a turbine "Ram" beater in 1925. **$45-$55**

EGGBEATERS, rotary (containers):

Eggbeater, horizontal wire balloon blades like whisk, 2 gears, cranked on side, cast iron frame set into painted wood box or stand, with porcelain (ceramic) pan, mfd by J. L. Newcomer, Baltimore, MD, pat'd May 26, 1885. **$200-$400**

Eggbeater, nickeled, with close-fitting jar lid, long 4 blades that do not balloon out at bottom, green painted wooden crank knob & T-handle (this handle is cigar-shaped, not banded in the middle), Depression glass green beater jar with slightly flared sides, Ladd, New Britain, CT, 11-1/4" H, prob. late 1920s. **$45-$55**

"**Nondescripts** — Yolks of four eggs beaten light, one teaspoonful of salt, flour enough to form a stiff dough; beat the dough well, and roll as thin as tissue paper; cut out by a saucer, and fold twice. Cut with a knife into narrow strips, leaving them united at the extreme point. Fry in plenty of boiling lard. When taken up, sprinkle loaf sugar thickly over them. Instead of shaping as above, the dough may be cut in strips about an inch wide and four inches long, and fried as directed. The former, however, is prettier." Mrs. A. P. Hill, *Mrs. Hill's New Family Receipt Book*, NY: 1870.

Eggbeater, stamped metal, detachable skirt or apron bowl cover, green glass bowl has 4 squat stubby feet, bowl embossed "Patent Applied for," mfd by A & J, 12" H, pat'd Oct. 9, 1923. Common beater, but hard to find with original bowl. **$45-$55**

Eggbeater, with all-metal beater bowl, cast iron & tin beater with vertical stumpy red-painted wooden handle, interesting coiled or spiraled wire around edge of gear wheel forms the teeth of the gear, openwork frame clips over edge of bowl & supports beater. Openness provides "full vision" of name. "Ingredients can be added while beating operation is in progress," as the original ad copy reads, "Full Vision Egg Beater Set," A & J, bowl: 3-3/4" H x 4-3/4" diameter; 1-1/2-pint capacity; 9-1/2"

II-56. Eggbeaters or drink mixers. (L) *Originally mfd. as the "Silver No.3," Silver & Co., c.1910, with japanned cast iron top, nickeled gears, tinned steel piano wire bows, glass, enameled wood handle. Used also for mayonnaise or butter-merging. This one is actually "The New Keystone Beater," "Culinary Utilities Co." (Others may bear North Bros. name.) Scalloped iron top same as the Silver. Measures embossed on sides of glass — 1 qt. liquid (worked 3 cups); "coffee cups full" on another; Flour and sifted flour; liquids in ounces. Collection Meryle Evans.* **(R)** *"E-Z Mixer," National Mfg. & Supply Co., Pittsburg, PA. Pat'd 6/30/1903. 32 oz., 13" H. Cast iron top with flat padlike knob for pressing against heel of hand while mixing. No marks in metal. Lid has oil funnel hole for making mayo. Courtesy Bob Cahn.* **$300-$450**

overall height with beater, based on Oct. 9, 1923 patent; prob. made in 1930s. **$30-$40**

Eggbeater & batter mixer, white ironstone beater jar, with one side of rim raised up with a small stepped notch on either side to support cast iron beater. Gear wheel cast with 6 hearts, short handle has white porcelain knob. Extended arms off each side of shaft supports beater in its jar. Beater has wide-skirted beater blade profile, made up of interestingly twisted heavy gauge wires & heavy central shaft that turns within a tiny cup at bottom. Beater wheel is marked & also the ironstone jar has an underglaze design of a floral wreath & the words "Kents Improved Monroes Patent Egg Beater & Batter Mixer," (no apostrophes), plus a paper label (with instructions) which could be washed off, "Kents Patent" on beater, "Kents Improved Monroes [James & Edwin] Patent ...," address given as High Holborn. London, England, about 13" H, late 19th C. The English manufacturing firm of Kent also put out a set with a beautiful footed beater jar, with same markings. This is an extraordinary outfit — either style is highly desirable. (The "Monroe" referred to American inventor brothers — James F. Monroe, of Fitchburg, MA, and Edwin P. Monroe, of NYC — whose eggbeater got US patent in 1859. Their beater was mfd by Dover, Boston, but looks nothing like Kent one described in this entry.) **$250-$350**

Eggbeater & cream whip, tall tin cylinder with wire-rolled top and bottom, used with a heavy wire dasher that has ring loop at one end & 2 metal discs cut rather like flower petals at other, divided by washer at bottom, paper label "The Ideal Egg Beater," Ideal Coffee Pot Co., Philadelphia, PA, c.1880. **$100-$110**

Eggbeater/cream whips — For more that resemble this, although they are activated by shaking, see eggbeaters, shaker.

Eggbeater or liquid mixer, green glass jar, with tin screw-on lid, to which is attached the cast iron handle, gears & the wire beater blades, "Root Mason" jar, Standard Specialty Co. works, Milwaukee, WI, 12" H x 3-7/8" D, pat'd June 11, 1907. The top of the beater itself looks like a 1873 Dover. I've never seen another one like this. In early 1960s, I found this in a central Ohio antique shop, and felt sinful spending $16 on it ... the most I'd ever spent for anything! **$350-$400**

Eggbeater or mixer, for eggs or mayonnaise, footed glass "egg-shaped bottom" vessel with flat metal lid fitted with upright iron beater frame, gear, side crank & 2 sets of wire blades inside bent to form 6 rectangular side wings that fit within slope of vessel, "E-Z Mixer," National Mfg. & Supply Co., Pittsburg, PA, pat'd June 30, 1903. **$400-$450**

II-57. Eggbeater & liquid mixer. *"New Keystone Beater 'Even Full,'" Culinary Utilities, c.1929. Note the simple top, and perforations instead of gear teeth.* **$110-$160**

II-58. Eggbeater with passive beater wings & pitcher. *Pat'd glass pitcher with interior (see bird's-eye view inset) that's supposed to "do half the work" of making the liquid move around. It's "marked by a series of vertical ridges gaining in depth as they go downward and forming, on the inside bottom, a serrated cup. These vertical ridges act as passive beater wings and help to break up and beat the contents." Green or clear glass, and to fit the Senior or Junior beaters, which had Blutip or green wood handles. 12-1/2" H overall. A & J, 1930.* **$40-$50**

II-59. Eggbeater & pitcher sets. *Also A & J, in pint size glass pitchers. Edward Katzinger catalog, 1940.* **$25-$40**

II-60. Eggbeater patents for containers. *All bowl-fitting.* **(T)** *Pat'd 6/19/1877, by Eustache R. Dulje, Newark, NJ. Lower* **(L)** *Pat'd 5/26/1885, by Jacob L. Newcomer, Baltimore, MD. See next picture for finished piece.* **(R)** *Pat'd 5/8/1877, by James H. Scofield. With side handle and compact design. Small arrow points to break in drawing — original drawing had some unspecified length cut from it at that point.*

II-61. Eggbeater. *With pan and frame, this is almost a mixing machine. "Newcomer's Improved," with a chain-drive "rotary egg whip consisting of a shaft, having skeleton heads, and wires which are so curved as to make the exterior of the whip conform very nearly in shape with the hemispherical bottom of the pan. By coming very near the surface of the pan, small quantities of eggs can be whipped." Iron frame secured to wooden stand, obviously decorated. The small continuous chain goes from the small wheel seen fully in drawing down to a small sprocket wheel which turns the beater. Pat'd 5/26/1885 and mfd. by inventor, J. L. Newcomer, Baltimore, MD. 1885 article in* Scientific American. **$200-$400**

II-62. French eggbeater & container. *A "petite batteuse," depicted in Urbain Dubois' La Patisserie d'Aujourd'hui, c.1860s.* **$100-$200**

II-63. Eggbeater, rotary paddle or sweep action. *"Express," called by collectors the "fly swatter" beater, malleable cast iron, tinned wire, 11-1/2" L, 3" gear wheel, picture from c. 1915 A. E. Rayment Supply Co. but beater shows up as early as a 1904 catalog. Actual beater marked with patent date 10/25/1887 (David T. Winter, Peabody, MA, patentee). Beater however looks very much like the 1906 patent of Nicholas Stromer.* **$450-$650**

II-64. Eggbeater — rotary paddler/sweep type. *Machine shop prototype or patent model? Handmade, machined brass and iron wire, wooden handle, screw clamps to table or shelf edge, modest little back-and-forth or wigway movement of the dasher to "enable a person to perfectly beat an egg in 35 seconds." 9-1/4" L. 19th C. Everyone thought this was a homemade one-off contrivance until dealer Bob Cahn, who sold it to me, found its patent, granted 4/22/1873, to Nathaniel C. Miller, Stroudsburg, PA. On 2/1/1870, Miller had patented a horizontally geared eggbeater resembling this one only in its wigwag "vibratory instead of rotary motion." Ex-Franklin Collection; now Thornton Collection.* **$450-$550**

II-65. Eggbeater patent: rotary fork-beater. *Pat'd 6/16/1891, by David A. Wilkinson, St. Louis, MO. A mechanical double fork with a horizontal gear. What a percussion instrument this would make! Probably never made.*

Eggbeater or mixer, glass vessel with slightly flared sides, fitted tin lid with attached mixer which has tall wire handle with small wood knob at top, spiraled coil "blades" inside motivated by up & down action, marked Lorraine Metal Mfg., Inc., NYC, 11-1/2" H, c. 1930s. **$20-$30**

Eggbeater or mixer, "Silver's" and also "Keystone." Cast iron gear wheel with iron crank & wooden knob, set onto cast iron "mansard" roof-like lid with scalloped edge, over tall square-sided glass container, marked on all 4 sides with various measures, ballooning whisking wires inside flare out more in later versions. "New Keystone Beater," was made by North Brothers Mfg. of Philadelphia, who claimed they had "secured control of the machine manufactured by Keystone Beater Co., and are now [1892] the only manufacturers of it." That's from an ad in *The Metal Worker* in late 1892. Some Keystones still have the original, small chromolith paper label on cast iron top, showing a little girl looking at a mixing bowl and the beater, plus the words: "The New Keystone Beater. Reduces Work. Improves the Food. Detachable Whip. Easy to Clean. Culinary Utilities Dept., Bloomfield, NJ." Later versions of "The New Keystone Beater" had sheet metal wheel, modernized tops or lids of sheet metal, with straight edges (not scalloped). However they kept the same glass container. Culinary Utilities was listed in directories as being in NJ and NYC. The original cast iron "New Keystone" is very similar, and possibly related, to the "Silver Egg Beater." However, the "Silver" has snake-like spokes in its cast iron gear wheel — compared to the straight ones of the "New Keystone." The cast iron "Silvers" are marked "Silver Egg Beater" by Silver & Co., Brooklyn, NY; "Silver New Egg Beater" with the image of the Brooklyn Bridge and words "Silvers Brooklyn" embossed on the jar's bottom — possibly contemporary with the beautiful, technically advanced bridge's 1883 opening. Both Keystone and Silver also made wall-mount mixers, some with their own jars. Silver also made plunger-type beaters with round jars, but marked the same as their square ones. These had tubes through the plungers to allow finger control to introduce more air to the aerated mixture. All very scientific! A real rarity, belonging to Reid Cooper and shown in Thornton's book, p. 109, is a Silver beater with scalloped edge to its cast iron top, embossed/cast on it "Horlick's." **$250-$400**

"Silvers" Chronology — The chronology of the Silvers/Keystone defies exactitude. The marks, names & dates in the above price listing was a collaboration by Don Thornton and Linda Campbell Franklin. I'm so mixed up now I could liquify. Thornton is not convinced that the maker-name confusion relates to successive manufacturers; he thinks it is highly likely that Silver and North were contemporaneous rivals. I'll just throw in a few more notes: I found a "Keystone" in Gene Florence's book *Kitchen Glassware of the Depression Era*, 3rd ed., with what appears to be a <u>nickel-plated lid,</u> patent date given by Florence as Dec. 1885, and the mfr as North Brothers. The April 30, 1878 patent date found on the glass jar was actually Silver's patent for the cylindrical jar for another plunger-style beater. Some examples are known that say only "patent pending," which implies a pre-1878 beginning. Silver & Co., etc., had at least two marks, viz: "Silver Egg Beater," "Silver New Egg Beater," with the Brooklyn Bridge and words "Silvers Brooklyn" around the bridge. The first time I saw a Silver/Keystone depicted, it was in the United Profit Sharing Co.'s 1914 premium catalog. The linecut shows the old iron gear, with "Silver & Co.'s New Beater" on lid.

EGGBEATERS, rotary paddle:

Eggbeater, cast iron frame & gear wheel, with odd, sweeping, back & forth motion to its oblong wire mesh paddle, "Express Egg Beater," pat'd Oct. 25, 1887 but made into 1910s at least, because it appears in a catalog of A. E. Rayment Supply Co., Rockford, IL, of that date. 11-1/2" L. Called by collectors the "fly swatter beater." My friend, the late Ray Townsend, known to thousands of tool & kitchenware collectors, wrote about his Express beater that, "It's always reminded me of a paddle on a steamboat; and, my daughter says, when she was a kid, she used to work it so her mother would think the snow plow was going by outside and she would not have to go to school." **$450-$650**

Eggbeater, handmade machined brass & wire, with modestly flirtateous & charming little back & forth movement of slender gauge wire blades when crank is turned, not marked, but pat'd by Nathaniel Miller, Stroudsburg, PA, 9-1/4" L, pat'd April 22, 1873. I bought this from Bob "Primitive Man" Cahn in early 1983, liking its homemade quality. Bob — who often does info followups for his customers — discovered a patent awarded Nathaniel C. Miller, of Stroudsburg PA, #138094, April 22, 1873 for this beater. (Miller's first eggbeater patent was award-ed Feb.1, 1870, #99337.) This eggbeater is now owned by Mr. Eggbeater — Don Thornton. The questions remain: Was this Miller's shop model, or a copy made by a craftsman who thought it nifty, and were there ever any more? **$450-$550**

EGGBEATERS, scissor & squeeze, one-hand actions:

Eggbeater, chromed metal, spring, & red plastic little knob or nut in top of levered grip. Name: "One Hand WIP," by Eagle Precision Mfg. Co., (also seen as Precision Tool & Die Corp.), NYC, NY, (or Long Island City, NY), 12-1/2" to 12-3/4" L. Probably based on Dec. 18, 1923 patent of William Crocker, although one-hand devices had been patented since the Civil War (when many veterans lost a hand or arm). If you didn't have to squeeze it too long, this handsome beater was very efficient: you could pour in ingredients with one hand while beating with the other. **$25-$32**

Eggbeater, scissor action for one-hand use, iron & wire, balloon wire blades like a whisk, cast around pivot is "PAT NO 1" prob. meaning pat'd, & that this one was the #1 model. 7-3/8" L. Smallest of the four Harry Jaquette (Jacquette Bros., Philadelphia), beaters, pat'd Nov. 28, 1893. Smallest (7-3/8") and largest (20") most valuable. **$375-$500**

Eggbeater & cream whip, nickel-plated sheet metal, with unusual action: fit top knob in palm, use forefinger to pull up on spring-tension hook, then release. Over & over. Good for arm-wrasslers in training, or pianists or aggie champeens. "Quik-Whip," American, 11" L, "patent pending" & pat'd by Ray Sowers, Nov. 10, 1931. (See also the eggbeater & potato masher below.) **$75-$90**

II-66.Eggbeaters for one hand use. *Left to right:* (**1**) *Squeeze action "One Hand 'WIP',"* by Eagle Precision Mfg. Co., chrome & red plastic, 12-1/2" L, 20th C. *Archimedean drill action:* (**2**) *beater with black wooden handle, 13-3/4" L, early 20th C. Note swiveling button for holding it in center of bowl.* (**3**) *Fold-flat "Bryant's Patent," from 1886, 12-7/8" L Collection of Meryle Evans.* **$25-$30; $35-$40; $140-$160**

EGGBEATERS, rotary turbine:

(Turbine beaters churn liquid up from the bottom, by means of either curved, upturned blades, or slots or perforations in a single disc blade, or with a stacked series of blades.)

Eggbeater, cast iron, sheet metal & wire, 2-tier turbine, upturned propeller blades, "Lyon Egg Beater & Cream Whip, No. 2," Al-

II-68. Eggbeaters & cream whips, rotary turbine. *The inventive debate over the best eggbeating motion included strong arguments for turbine beaters. Turbines, which circulate fluids, including gas, and impart a circular motion to them (providing power in some instances), have been known at least since Hero of Alexander built a small steam-driven turbine in 120 B.C. For eggbeaters & cream whips, turbines are used to cause liquids on bottom to continually circulate upwards where they can be whipped.* (**L**) *Tinned steel, 10" L x 2-1/4" diameter of slotted turbine. Wire Goods Co., 1915.* (**M**) *Nickeled steel, wood handle is green. Washburn Co., 1936.* (**R**) *Note handle on this "Whirlwind." Ivory white knob. 10-1/2" L. Washburn Co., 1927.* **$20-$45**

II-67. Eggbeater & potato masher: one-hand, spring-powered. *"Lebanon Beater," Seltzer Specialty Co., Lebanon, PA. Two interchangeable perforated cylinders (coarse or fine holes), with cast iron plunger that fits within the cylinder, and is attached to lower end of handle rod. Black wood handle. Looped wire adds spring action. 13" L x 2-3/4" diameter. Tinned or nickel plated. Pat'd 11/29/1892 by Uriah D. Seltzer. 1892 ad. Trade cards for this tool are fairly common and sell for about $10.* **$225-$250**

bany, NY, 10" L, pat'd Sept. 7, 1897 by Edward John Scopes, assigned to Nelson Lyon. **$115-$130**

Eggbeater, sheet metal, wire & wood, with propeller-like perforated turbine blade at bottom, "The NECO," mfd by M.A. Hougen, Minneapolis, MN, 11" L, patent pending, c. 1910 to 1920. **$25-$35**

Eggbeater, stamped metal & wire, turbine blade at bottom, "Turbine," Cassady-Fairbanks, Chicago, 12-1/4" L, c.1910-20. **$25-$35**

Eggbeater, tin & wood, Androck's "Turbine," Washburn Co., also marked "Lutz File Company," Rockford, IL (Androck); Worcester, MA (Washburn); Cincinnati, OH (Lutz), 13-1/2" L, 1920s. **$18-$25**

Eggbeater & cream whip, sheet metal, double-slotted turbine blade, fluted disc above another that has a sort of funneling projection that would channel liquid out to edge and back over top, long central shaft, vertical wood handle is marbleized green, white & teal blue (came in red & white too), "WHIPPIT" Cream & Egg Beater, mfd by Duro Metal Products Co., Chicago, IL, 13-1/4" or 13-1/2" L or 14" L, based on Ernest Fahlberg's March

II-69. Eggbeaters or cream whips - rotary turbine. (L) *"Lyon No.2," two-tiered turbine blades. Iron & tin, note outer frame & 6-holed gear wheel. 10" L, mfd. in Albany, NY, pat'd 9/7/1897. (Very similar is the "Perfection," with double blades, a 4-holed gear wheel and no frame; it was pat'd 2/22/1898.)* **(R)** *Tin, wire, Cassady-Fairbank Mfg. Co., Chicago, IL, marked "patent allowed," pat'd actually granted Nov. 13, 1917, to a Thomas Jones. Note simplicity of the gear wheel, with round perforated holes meshing with the teeth of the small horizontal gear not visible here. Great collecting pleasure is found in ingenious gear wheels. Collection of Meryle Evans.* **$115-$130; $22-$30**

II-71. Eggbeaters & cream whips - rotary turbine. (L) *"The NECO," M. P. Hougen, Minneapolis, patent pending.* **(2)** *"WHIPPIT" Cream & Egg Beater, Duro Metal Products Co., Chicago. Pat. #1,705,639, white & teal blue marbled wood handle, 2 slotted dished blades & upright scraper, 13-1/2" L. 1929.* **(3)** *"Dunlap's Sanitary Silver Blade Cream Whip," Casey Hudson Co., Chicago, 3 patents — 1906, 1907, 1916. Curved perforated blade fits dimple in bottom of "Non-slip" brown-outside, white-inside glazed earthenware mixing bowl which came with the beater.* **(R)** *"Quik-Whip," patent pending, nickel plated, 11" L. Unusual one-hand action: you fitted your palm to top, then used forefinger to pull up spring-tension hook, which, when released, caused perforated turbine blade to spin.* **$50-$60; $20-$25; $30-$35; $75-$85**

II-70. Eggbeater patent — rotary turbine. *Pat'd 11/14/1882, by James T. Carley, Greenport, NY. I don't know if this eggbeater & cream whip was made, but it seems — except for short shaft & overlarge gear wheel — to be an ideal combination of turbine with revolving blades. It is so perfect, in fact, that I wager it'll be discovered in next few years. And if it does exist, it'll bring:* **$500+**

II-72. Bow drill eggbeater. *Earliest type of mechanical beater, bow drill or* **fiddle drill** *beater, works when bow is sawed back & forth. A cord passing through two small holes in support frame turns beater first one way, then the other, as it winds & unwinds on central shaft. Devices like this were used in very ancient times for starting fires, or for drilling holes. American, probably very early 19th C. Picture courtesy of the National Museum of American History, Smithsonian Institution.* **$115-$175+**

19, 1929 patent, although it was made at least four years before then. Jane Celehar, who did some company history research, says Duro Metal Products Co. sold Whippits in 1927 for $1, and that White & Hallock, Inc, Muskegon, MI, registered the Whippit™ trademark on Sep.18, 1928 though it was "used by their predecessor" since July 15, 1925. She explains that EKCO acquired the patent in 1945 and was selling it from then on. It's possible the patent number on my eggbeater, indicating a late-1940s patent, is a patent re-registration number. Various companies marketed the Whippit. **$20-$25**

Eggbeater & cream whip, simple metal frame & handle, sort of doll-shaped, with openwork or cutout gear wheel, turbine blade at bottom is in horizontal position relative to shaft, "Turbine," The Cassady-Fairbanks Mfg. Co., Chicago, 10" L, patent applied for c.1910. **$25-$35**

EGGBEATERS, rotary, whisk blades:

Eggbeater, cast iron, gear wheel with hearts, has screw clamp for shelf edge, & wire whisk beaters, fairly flat on bottom, the wires broadly spread at the bottom, narrowing to the gear "waist." Advertised in 1869 catalog as coming in 2 sizes: "Extra Family" & "Mammoth, for Hotels & Bakeries." Invented by James & Edwin Monroe. (Catalog misspells name with a "u," ie. *Munroe.*) Monroes Patent, mfd by Dover Stamping Co., Boston, MA, pat'd April 19, 1859. The patent drawing has a much simpler gear wheel and longer frame for clamp. The beater was manufactured like patent drawing at first & "improved" with a more conventional gear and clamp by time of 1869 catalog. **$600-$700**

Eggbeater, spiral-coiled wire beaters, long shaft, cast iron gear wheel, odd bracebit-type handle. Cast into wheel on each of 4 spokes are letters spelling name: "E A S Y." Sold by Montgomery Ward, American, 1890s. MW's ad reads, "It consists of a spirally coiled wire, which in use opens and closes with exceeding rapidity, and instead of cutting the egg, as most beaters do, thoroughly aerates it." **$45-$55**

II-73. Mechanized bow drill or fiddle drill eggbeater patents. (T) & (R) *are two views of Howard M. Brittain's (Martin's Creek, PA) egg beater, pat'd 4/12/1892. Action is same idea as aboriginal bow drill fire-starting tool: beater is set firmly in bowl, gripped and held in place by vertical handle, while horizontal wire bow and its spooled cord is moved back & forth to turn beaters this way then that.* **(L)** *pat'd 7/7/1863, by Timothy Earle, then of Smithfield, RI. He invented a number of eggbeaters (and fruit jar closures) over a long period. The curved ribs seen on the bow are found in several collectible eggbeaters.*

EGGBEATER, shaker:

Eggbeater, syllabub churn or cream mixer, tapered cylindrical tin body, used by shaking up & down to made the blades spin inside, sort of like a one-underpants clothes washer, only it's for one syllabub at a time. Removable turbine blades halfway down, snug-fitting lid marked "Tilden's Patent Aug. 1, 1865," 8" L x 1-3/4" diameter, another is 9-1/2" x 2-1/2". Found in patent index not as syllabub churn but as an egg-beater. **$155-$180**

EGGBEATER, waterpowered:

Eggbeater, aluminum, brass, rubber, glass. Water actually circulates through the U-shaped mechanism built into the lid. Body is glass quart-size canning jar fitted with lid that's not round but sort of pear-shaped (narrow extended neck in back), and inside jar are simple flared blades that revolve as the water circulates through the lid via a metal device that connects faucet & lid. The water exits out a long tube that comes out under the back "neck" of the lid. Round stick-on label on lid is missing, but trade name is "World Beater." Pat'd by H. L. Thompson, Apr. 29, 1924, but mfd prior to that by World Novelty Co., Elgin, IL. **$95-$115**

Eggbeater & potato masher, 2 interchangeable cylindrical perforated steel receptacles (called a "hopper" by the manufacturer), medium & fine holes, for cooked potato or stewed apples or eggs, nickeled cast iron vertical shaft, round-topped turned wood handle; the spring steel wire that connects ferrule of shaft & top of the "hopper" provides the tension & return power as handle is pumped up & down, "Lebanon Beater," mfd by Seltzer Specialty Co., Lebanon, PA, 13" L x 2-3/4" diameter hopper, pat'd 11/29/1892 by Uriah D. Seltzer. Added value for both hoppers. **$225-$250**

Electric eggbeaters and electric mixers — See Chapter XVIII (Gadgets and Appliances), but pictures on p. 102.

Food preparer, electric, enameled metal base and bowl, lid has large central opening, blades inside, "mixes batter, juices fruits, whips, shreds, slices, chops, grinds. Eliminates the uncertainty & fatigue of food preparation." "Culinaire," mfd by P. A. Geier Co. & affiliate Continental Electric Co., Ltd., Cleveland, OH, and Toronto, Canada, c.1934. Two years later Geier had a new "Royal Culinaire," with chromium-plated bowl, and a juicer attachment. **$50-$65**

Larding needles in case, steel in brass cylinder (or steel in japanned tin); a set of long needles in cylindrical case, used to lard in, or

II-74. Eggbeater patents. (L) *Pat'd 12/15/1857, by John B. Heich, Cincinnati, OH. The "net work" beater is activated by a ratcheted bowing action. Central gear disk is described by inventor as made of India rubber, "or other elastic material, attached to the top of the rod. ... The beater is operated by the pressure produced upon the elastic disk by the motion backwards and forwards of the grooved bar" bow. From Patent Commissioner's Annual Report, 1857.* **(R)** *Pat'd 5/21/1867, by Marvin T. Williams, Milwaukee, WI. Note little coils on bottom horizontals of beater wings to help aerate the egg.*

in effect insert or mix fat (especially strips of bacon) into lean cuts of meat before roasting, available through F.A. Walker wholesale catalog, French (?), c.1870s-1880s. **$25-$45**

Malted milk mixers — See drink mixers

II-75. Water power eggbeaters. *Can be attached by a hose or directly to faucet.* **(L)** *Painted metal housing on glass jar. 8-1/2" H. Turbine action of water coursing through pear-shaped lid causes beaters to turn. Discharged water apparently came out tube below the lid. Fit a quart canning jar with a screw top. Not marked, although it once had a round paper label identifying it as "The World Beater, Mfd. by the World Novelty Co., Elgin, IL." It was pat'd 4/29/1924.* **(R)** *highly polished brass lid & metal dashers. I wonder if a company that made lawn sprinklers didn't make this beater. This one not marked except for "patent pending." It was not made to screw onto a beater jar but after attaching to faucet it could be used with any container. Pictures courtesy Glenda Clark and Phyllis & Jim Moffet.* **$100; $50**

Mayonnaise mixer, blue painted cast iron, openwork heart gear, glass jar, hole for funnel, original blue paper label on jar, "FUPA" is maker (although it sounds like an acronym for 4 words beginning in F U P A or P A F U), "Made in France," turn of century. **$75-$125**

Mayonnaise mixer & eggbeater, cast iron frame, hearts cast in gear wheel like so many geared objects of the late 19th C., funnel for mayonnaise oil, screw-on jar, red painted wooden crank handle, marked only "Made in France" on bottom, 10" H, early 20th C. **$75-$125**

Mayonnaise mixer, cast iron, clamps to table, cast iron frame supports oil drip funnel behind vertical 6-petal cast iron gear wheel; lower part is a hinged cast iron basket frame to hold a bowl (glass? ceramic? metal?), wire balloon whip blades, with two X-shaped supports to hold wires, 11" H. Only mark "PAT APLD. FOR" — patent was granted 10/10/1893 to Jennie De Witt Harvey, and is called by collectors "The Jennie." This belongs to the Moffets in IL, and they want to know what sort of bowl it had; any information would be appreciated. Very rare. **$400-$450**

Mayonnaise mixer, footed glass bowl, glass lid has built-in oil "funnel" with large well & small drip hole, iron frame fastened to lid, fancy iron gear wheel & short crank knob fixed on wheel, tin blades, "S & S, Hutchinson," sometimes "J. Hutchinson," Long Island, NY, 9-3/4" H x c.7" diameter bowl, marked "patent appl for" — patent granted later: 9/2/1913. **$300-$350**

Mayonnaise mixer, called a "mixer churn" by maker, footed glass bowl, with close-fitting lid, eggbeater can be disengaged from lid, "Ladd Beater #1," "United Royalties Corp.," American, 13" H, the beater bears patent dates July 7, 1908, Feb. 2, 1915. While the glass container and fitted measuring lid or apron was patented by Lavern Bordwell, Feb. 15, 1916. **$150-$200**

II-77. Electric food mixer. *"Dormeyer," mfd. by A. F. Dormeyer Mfg. Co., Chicago.* American Cookery *magazine, 1930. For more electric things see Chapter XVIII.* **$20-$45**

II-76. Electric eggbeaters & mixers. **(L)** *Electric "Challenge," mfd. by CEM Co., "Tyre Avub" (?). Simple single dasher blade, works perfectly, even hums. 3-cup capacity, 8-1/2" H, 110-120 volts.* **(R)** *"Ladd Beater #1," as in II-74. Pat'd 7/7/1908, 2/2/1915. Beater can be dismantled from lid. 13" H. Collection of Meryle Evans.* **$20-$35; $175-$200**

II-78. Larding needles — or "Beef à la Mode" needles. **(T)** *Brass & steel needles in tin fitted case. F.A. Walker catalog, 1870s, but sold for at least another 30 years.* **(B)** *Other is a mechanized larding needle with wooden hand, sort of like a latchhook for making rugs. c.1906-07 catalog.* **$20-$35**

II-79. Mayonnaise mixer & eggbeater. *Clamps to table, nickeled cast iron, tin, 10" H, removable beater blades, supposed to have a funnel. No mark, no date on this one, but they are sometimes marked "Christy Knife Patented Fremont," Ohio. Some are found with flat rudder-like blade at bottom. Collection of Meryle Evans. SEE also the container-type rotary eggbeaters earlier in this chapter. As shown:* **$200-$250**

II-82. Mayonnaise mixer. *Blue painted cast iron with heart cutout gear, large handle, glass jar, oil funnel hole. Original blue paper label reads "VITESSE-MAYONNAISE." Trademark is a diamond with "FUPA" inside. French, c.1900.* **$75-$125**

II-80. "Mixing churn," *or* mayonnaise maker *or* eggbeater. *"Ladd #1" in quart size footed paneled bowl, showing oil funnel in 2-part, fold-back lid or apron. 12-1/2" H. The #2 is substantially larger and more impressive. This linecut is from a 1914 ad, but pat'd 2 years later on Feb. 15, 1916, and sold for at least another 15 years.* **$195-$225**

II-81. Mayonnaise mixer & bowl. *"The Silver" mixer came in one size only — 2 pts. Note oil-funnel with drop stopper for making mayonnaise. "Imported bone china" bowl, chestnut wood cover, nickelplated brass beater. Blade is sort of half-moon shape with a few bent-up fingers. Silver & Co., Brooklyn, c.1910.* **$150-$200**

II-83. Mayonnaise mixers. (L) *"Universal Mayonnaise Mixer & Cream Whipper," Landers, Frary & Clark, patent applied for. Nickeled iron top, nickeled dashers with long fingers, lid has swivel cover for oil hole. 2-1/2 to 3 cup capacity, approx. 9-3/8" H, late 19th C.* **(R)** *"S & S No. 1," or "Scientific & Sanitary." A very beautiful piece. The "S & S" forms casting design of gear wheel. Glass lid with oil funnel built in. Regular eggbeater blades. 9-3/4" H overall. This one marked "patent pending." It was patented 9/2/1913, and was used for omelets, salad dressings, desserts, & beverages also. Collection of Meryle Evans.* **$500; $350**

Mayonnaise mixer, metal with original heavy glass jar that has 6 little feet & is embossed, "The Holt-Lyon Jar Cream Whip and Mayonnaise Maker," cast iron "Dover" beater has elongated blades with slight crimping at curves, and 48 rather than 60 or 63 cogs in the large gear, long conical oil dripper funnel with little rod to regulate drip, Holt-Lyon Co., Tarrytown, NY, 15" H, 1910s to 1920. A somewhat older one is 5/8" shorter & has 63 cogs to the gear; the conical oil dripper has a snap-strap that slips over grip of beater part. With original jar: **$250-$275**

Mayonnaise mixer, nickeled iron top, straight-sided glass handleless cup, iron gear wheel & long crank handle, wooden knob, nickeled dasher has long horizontal fingers & a set of odd vertical fingers at bottom. Lid has oil hole with its own tiny swivel cover. "Universal Mayonnaise Mixer & Cream Whip Whipper," Landers, Frary & Clark, New Britain, CT, 9-3/8" H, 2-1/2- to 3-cup capacity, pat'd 4/17/1915. **$400-$500**

Mayonnaise mixer, tall marked glass tumbler, metal screw-on lid has mixer blade shaft, convex perforated metal dasher is horizontal, small convexity in jar's bottom fits dimple on dasher blade bottom. "Wesson Oil Mayonnaise Maker," 11" H jar, 20th C. **$20-$30**

Mayonnaise mixer & cream whip, white porcelain footed bowl, tin lid (edge or rim only) with interior crosspiece that supports cranked beater blade of tin, funnel hole in wide rim of lid for adding oil, imported — prob. from Germany. 4" H bowl, late 19th C. **$50-$65**

Mixer, cast iron, screw clamps to shelf, green wood handle, reamer clips onto the top, "Cake Drink Mixer, Egg Cream Mixer," mfd by New Standard Corp., Mt. Joy, PA, patent pending, c.1900. Dealer Elissa Weitz of Lahaska, PA, said that there "supposedly is a Mount Joy bowl to use with this," and that the bowls came in a lot of sizes. However, New Standard itself advertised that practically any kitchen bowl could be used with the mixer. **$90-$100**

II-84. Mayonnaise mixer, eggbeater, drink mixer, *and cream whipper. Two views of "Air-O-Mixer," patent pending, mfd. by Bentley-Jones Inc., Montgomery, AL. Collector Glenda Clark owns one marked with manufacturer "Bentley-Beale, Inc." Glass embossed with directions. Perforated conical beater is of type used by makers of mixer churns & syllabub churns for at least 75 years before. This beater appeared in Wesson Oil "make your own mayonnaise" ads from late 1933 through 1934.* **$25-$40**

Mixer, chromed white metal gears, red plastic, "Maynard Mixer," Los Angeles, CA, 11-1/8" L, 1933 patent #1,910,303. The sleek mod look will attract new collectors. **$15-$20**

Mixer, nickeled metal device mounted to board, with vertical cranked wheel, metal band holds container, "Kwikmix," Schenker Mfg. Co., NYC, NY, about 8" H, pat'd 1922. **$80-$100**

Mixer, tall glass container, tin lid with snap fitting, iron shaft & nickel-plated perforated dasher, there's a spring in lid so when you pump the handle up & down it really goes to town. "Jones Wonder Mixer," American, c.1920. **$50-$75**

Mixer, wind-up, clear glass container, metal top, on-off switch, American. Pat'd 7/9/1935 by Samuel Berger. **$25-$35**

Mixer & sifter, tightly coiled springy wire, 2 handles, squeeze action makes wires go in & out, rather like a cross between a Slinky toy & an accordian. "___sse Carlson Co.," "Nifty Sifter," Rockford, IL (Andrews Wire Goods Co. was here about the same time), 8-1/2" L, pat'd Feb. 25, 1930 by Bror N. Carlson. Thanks readers! • Vivian Robertson sent photocopy of battered advertising card — in part reading, "A 100 uses in cooking; prevents lumping of flour, sugar and . . . similar ingredients... Hotel chefs have found it indispensible in preparing gravies, sauces, cake batters . . . dip into flour, sugar or other ingredients; release spring and sift into gravy skillet, stew pan, or batter bowl . . . The Nifty Sifter . . . used in preparing scores of dishes where lumping will spoil the efforts of the chef." • Tiffin, OH, dealer Ralph Frankart wrote me in 1984 about a woman who purchased one in 1929 in Detroit and called it a "Sprinkler." "She uses it in her baking, opens it and dips it into the sugar bowl, lets it close and by slightly opening it, sprinkles sugar on her cookies, pies, etc. Also dips it into her flour and fills it then sprinkles it on her rolling pin, rolling board, pie pans, etc. She loves it and was quite disturbed that I would not sell her mine as she wanted it as a gift for her sister." **$15-$20**

Mixing bowl, blue & gray saltglazed stoneware, adv'g message for "Dentel's, Ackley Iowa," 20th C. **$60-$75**

Mixing bowl, blue & gray saltglazed stoneware, with cherry motif, 9-1/2" diameter, 20th C. **$35-$45**

Mixing bowl, blue & red sponged "Saffron" yellowware, wide shoulder band, narrow panelling below band, Red Wing pottery, Red Wing, MN, 7" diameter (these bowls were made in 1" increments from 5" to 10" diameter, 1930s. Value varies widely with size, presence of advertising or name, and condition, (apt to be poor for relatively porous Saffron pieces.) **$50-$75**

Mixing bowl, blue & red stripes, Red Wing, advertising "Rock Dell," 8-1/2" diameter, 20th C. **$40-$65**

Mixing bowl, blue, rust & gray spongeware, shouldered, with 6 panels, American, 8" diameter, 20th C. **$50-$60**

Mixing bowl, blue & rust spatter decoration, "Boyne's Grocery," West Union, IA, 8" diameter, 20th C. **$55-$65**

Mixing bowl, blue & rust sponged stoneware, for "Waddington's," Geneva, IA, by Red Wing, early 20th C. **$110-$130**

Mixing bowl, ceramic, green with pink & blue stripes, "Watt's Oven Ware," 14" diameter, early 20th C. **$45-$65**

Mixing bowl, creamware, white inside, English, 9" diameter, turn of century. **$25-$35**

Mixing bowl, dark brown saltglazed stoneware, shouldered, marked "Weller," Fultonham, OH, 8" D, late 19th C. Small dimple indent inside bottom, perfect for use with some egg beaters. **$25-$35**

Mixing bowl, decorated china, cottage scene, girl & flowers, 9" diameter, 20th C. **$25-$35**

Mixing bowl, graniteware, yellow & white marbleized, American, 9-1/2" diameter, early 20th C. **$28-$40**

Mixing bowl, green glaze, ribbed, square base goes up into round bowl, mark is shield with "9" inside circle, American, 9-1/2" diameter, early 20th C. **$20-$28**

II-85. Mixing bowls. (T-L) *is wood, ranging from 12" to 37" diameter. Jaburg Brothers, who sold supplies to confectioners, advertised that they would "strap Bowls and repair same." Meaning to fix cracked ones with iron bands, etc. That was in 1908, much later that we previously thought wooden bowls were being artfully repaired rather than discarded & replaced.* **(B-R)** *footed bowl is heavy tin, made in sizes from about 7" to 15" diameter. Sold by German company, c.1904. Not shown: Jaburg also sold seamless steel mixing bowls, from 25" to 34" diameter, finished black or galvanized. High amount reflects prices asked for handsomely repaired wooden bowls.* **$10-$200**

Mixing bowl, green glazed pottery, "Kitchen Kraft," Homer Laughlin China Co., 8" diameter, c.1940s. **$25-$30**

Mixing bowl, green-glazed yellowware, square base goes up to circle, molded geometric designs, no mark, American, 10" diameter, early 20th C. If I had the '80s to do over again, I'd buy a few green-glazed yellowware bowls. What gorgeous lively color. **$45-$55**

Mixing bowl, large & relatively low, yellow glaze with green sponge decoration, gold rim, tiny crack not affecting careful use, American, 3-1/2" H x 10-3/4" diameter, 19th C. **$95-$125**

Mixing bowl, pumpkin colored ceramic, "Watt's Oven Ware," 7" diameter, 20th C. **$15-$20**

Mixing bowl, red & cream spongeware, American, 8" diameter, turn of century. **$45-$55**

Mixing bowl, redware with cream colored glaze inside, American, 16" diameter, 19th C. **$65-$85**

Mixing bowl, ribbed spongeware, mottled brown & green glaze over yellow background glaze, 8-1/2" diameter, 20th C. **$160-$200**

Mixing bowl, Saffron spatterware, with shoulder, Red Wing, with "Christmas Greetings, 1938, Protovin, Iowa," 20th C. **$50-$75**

Mixing bowl, saltglazed stoneware, adv'g "It pays to mix with Thoren Brothers, Rock City & Rock Grove, Illinois" on the inside, American, 6" H x 8" diameter, early 20th C. Punning advertising messages are the most fun — on mixing bowls, beater jars & rolling pins. **$65-$85**

Mixing bowl, saltglazed stoneware, Western Stoneware Co., Monmouth, IL, 10" diameter, late 19th C to early 20th. **$50-$65**

Mixing bowl, saltglazed stoneware with adv'g message: "Farmer's Complete Department Store," late 19th or early 20th C. **$45-$55**

Mixing bowl, saltglazed stoneware, apple motif, "Watt's Oven Ware #8," "Farmer's Co-Op Elevator Co.," 8" diameter, 20th C. **$50-$65**

Mixing bowl, saltglazed stoneware, apple motif, Watt's "Oven Ware #7," advertises "Leistikow's," 7" diameter, 20th C. **$50-$60**

Mixing bowl, saltglazed stoneware with white & brown glaze, 10" diameter, early 20th C. **$20-$30**

Mixing bowl, sponged blue, rust & cream stoneware, Red Wing, 6" diameter, 20th C. **$50-$60**

Lead Glazes: Caution to the Public — Mr. Editor — Sir: Will you permit me to acquaint the public . . . that there is a kind of Crockery Ware, manufactured in almost every city in the Union, which is dangerous to use — and which the public will understand by the term Common Red Pottery. This ware is made of common clays from the brick yards, and when formed, is coated with a liquid called Glaze, which is nothing less than a coat of lead. The clays being of the commonest kind, cannot be subjected to any heat in the burning that will make them safe for family use — being porous — and it is very unsafe to deposit any articles of family use in them, such as milk, butter, or in fact water, as a portion of the Lead Glazing will be extracted, and the article will, in consequence, become dangerous to use. I have noticed no fewer than ten instances within the last twelve months, of families sustaining injury by the use of such ware.

"In selecting the article of crockery that is suitable for family use, it is only necessary to ascertain that the body of the ware — the clay — has been hard burnt, which any person can understand by the sound of it — if well burnt, it will have a clear sound. The poorest kind will not ring at all, and therefore can be easily detected. An article of this kind will, in the course of a month's use, become very foul. Let any one who doubts this break the vessel, and they will ascertain the fact. There is a kind of ware, however, that is manufactured in almost every city in the Union, called stone ware, which is perfectly good for family use. This ware is formed of strong and superior clays, and undergoes a great heat in the burning, — and moreover, the glazing is not a thick coat of lead, but is accomplished by throwing salt into the kiln. All kinds of Liverpool [Ohio?] ware are adapted to all purposes of family use, being made of sound clays and well burnt. As a preventive is better than a cure, if I should be the means of preventing any person suffering from the use of the poisonous article — lead — this advertisement will answer the ends I design. [signed] C. S." [Who adds] "Glass may be used in all cases, and is the most beautiful and safe article extant in manufactures." *The Farmers' Cabinet* (reprinted from *The Pittsburger*), Philadelphia, Vol I, No. 7, Oct. 15, 1836.

Mixing bowl, sponged blue & red, Red Wing, 7" diameter, advertisement reads, "It pays to Mix With Weisensels, Sun Prairie, Wis." 20th C. **$135-$150**

Mixing bowl, sponged, no marks, 5-1/2" diameter, nice small size, 20th C. **$40-$50**

Mixing bowl, spongeware, slight hairline crack, advertising message, "It Pays to Mix with Andrew Westin, Newberry, Michigan," 5" H x 8-1/2" diameter, early 20th C. **$80-$100**

II-86. Mixing bowls. *Called* schneekessel. *German nickel plated, copper* **(A) (B),** *tin* **(C),** *and glass* **(D)** *bowls. Generally between 8" to 15" diameter.* **$10-$100**

Mixing bowl, very worn inside bottom down to the clay body, yellowware, brown mocha decoration on cream band, cream slip banded decoration, small foot, NJ, 11-3/8" diameter, 19th C. **$175-$250**

Mixing bowl or biscuit pan, white glazed earthenware, thick sloping walls, removable & set into much deeper heavily tinned vessel with inward slanting sides, 2 strap handles with handgrip braces, little filling spout poking out on side under handle, with cap, English, 19th C. Price for 2 parts: **$110-$150**

"Biscuit Pan — Hitherto consisted only of a single vessel . . . Used for beating up or whisking batters. The improved pan is formed either of metal or earthenware, inclosed within an exterior vessel, furnished with a plugged aperture, for the introduction of hot water." Thomas Masters, *A Short Treatise Concerning Some Patent Inventions...Also the Newly Improved Culinary Utensils,* London, 1850. ("Biscuit" here is in the English sense, of crackers.)

Mixing bowl, yellow glazed ceramic, "Kitchen Kraft," Homer Laughlin China Co., Newell, WV, 10" diameter, c.1940s. **$30-$40**

Mixing bowl, yellow Fiesta Ware #7, mid 20th C. **$50-$65**

Mixing bowl, yellow & green spongeware, gilt scalloped edge, 8-3/4" diameter, American, 19th C. **$90-$110**

Mixing bowl, yellow & green spongeware, gilt scalloped edge, 13" diameter x 5" deep, American, 19th C. **$115-$140**

Mixing bowls, yellow glazed earthenware with green sponge design, some have gold-glazed rim, American, range from quite small — 5-1/2" to 14" diameter & larger. The bowls tend to be relatively shallow in relation to their diameter. Turn of century. **$45-$200**

Mixing bowl, yellowish green glaze, molded pattern of little "pillows" rather than concentric bands, mark is a shield with 8 in a circle inside it, also #4 (or possibly #14), American, 8-1/2" diameter, early 20th C. **$40-$55**

Mixing bowl, yellowware, all over foliated swag design, 12" diameter, late 19th C. **$125-$150**

Mixing bowl, yellowware, deep cobalt mocha decoration on band, rolled rim, very small foot, 13-1/4" diameter, mid 19th C. **$300-$400**

Rolled rims — A rim or edge that is described as "rolled" may actually be rolled, such as a piece of tinware, or steel — even that which has later been enameled. The term is also used to describe the look of a rounded rim that couldn't possibly have been actually rolled — such as a turned wooden bowl or a ceramic piece.

Mixing bowl, yellowware, deep lip, scalloped rim , ribbed melon sides, American, late 19th C. "Mixing bowls come in deep yellow and light buff earthenware. Also in white stone china. Deep yellow is made of a rather soft material and breaks easily." Maria Parloa, *Kitchen Companion,* Boston: Estes & Lauriat, 1887. **$75-$90**

Mixing bowl, yellowware, simple zigzag design around side, American or English, 5-3/8" diameter, late 19th or early 20th C. **$30-$40**

Mixing bowl, yellowware, triple brown band, one wide, 2 narrow, marked "20" & "Made in U. S. A.," 8" diameter, early 20th C. **$25-$30**

Mixing bowl, yellowware with white glaze, stepped bands, American, 8" diameter, 20th C. **$18-$25**

Mixing bowl set, 3 nested bowls, yellowware, yellow with cream bands, turned setback bases, Watt, 6-1/2" H x 10" diameter, and 5" H x 8" diameter, and 4" H x 6" diameter, 20th C. **$125-$150**

Mixing bowl set, Delphite glass, 3 nesting bowls in "Teardrop" pattern, Fire King, 20th C. **$80-$100**

Mixing bowl nest of 3, sponged red & blue on stoneware, a Red Wing pottery, 5", 6", and 7" diameter (not complete set, as they were made on up to 10" diameter), 20th C. **$225-$250**

Mixing bowls, opaque green — "Jadite," Depression glass, nesting set of 4, actually "Skokie Green" in catalog of manufacturer, McKee Glass Co., Jeannette, PA, 6", 7", 8" & 9" diameter, all relatively tall bowls, 1930s. "Jadite" is the trade name for an opaque green that Jeannette Glass Co. (also Jeannette, PA) made; "Jad-ite" was used by Hocking, but it's such a perfect descriptive name — anyone familiar with green jade thinks translucent. Collectors use it for wide range of very pale to rather richly green opaque glass. Price for set: **$50-$65**

Mixing machines — See bread machines & makers; also mayonnaise mixers; also mixers

Mixing spoon, commercial or manufactured wooden spoon, of common type, but with head carved on end of handle, very African in style, high forehead, pronounced eyes & hair, American, 13" L, prob. 20th-C carving, but it looks awfully good and not fakey folk. I paid $3.50, surprise surprise, but believe this is a more realistic price range: **$25-$35**

Mixing spoon, stamped & slotted metal, nickeled, green wood handle, stamped "Rumford Baking Powder," 10-3/4" L, 20th C. **$15-$20**

Mixing spoon, stamped tin & iron, "Rumford Cake Mixer & Cream Whip," Saltsmans, 10-1/4" L, 20th C., unclear patent date on it is Oct. 6, 1908, a Tuesday. Aaron Saltsman held a patent for a slotted mixing spoon dated 4/27/1897. Another "Rumford" mixing spoon has sheet metal bowl, with slots, and wire handle, stamped in one place to read "Rumford Baking Powder." **$15-$20**

Mixing spoon, eggbeater, tinned steel, deep bowl with 16 paired slots or transverse ribs, deep division down center, looks like abstract skeletal rib cage, turned wooden handle with blunt end, "Ideal," manufacturer only partly legible on mine: "Mfd by ___ater" (or possibly ___ster"). American, 10" L x 3" W, mine says "pat'd March 30, 1908" but really it was pat'd Mar 31, 1903 by Carrie Bentley. Bentley called it an "Egg Beater" but I've always thought of it as a spoon, so it's here. Her patent shows a continuous piece of stamped & slotted sheet metal with no wooden handle. Classic — I still give this pride of place in my pantheon of kitchen collectibles, for sheer design and looks and heft. See "Eclipse" mixing spoon & beater, next listing. **$18-$28**

II-87. Mixing bowls. (T) *White semi-porcelain with wide blue band and blue pin stripes. "Heavily glazed." 4" to 13" diameter, holding from 6 oz. to 7 qts. c.1895 ad.* **(B-L)** *is "heavy yellow stoneware, rolled edge, neat blue band decoration. Used all over the country." 4-1/2" to 15-1/2" diameter, c.1895 ad.* **(B-R)** *"Yellow bowl," earthenware, holding from 1/4 to 12 qts. Duparquet wholesaler catalog, c.1904-1910. Size, condition, and glaze color determine values.* **$20-$200**

"Another Way to mix Cakes. — Take six pieces of cane about 18 inches long; tie them fast together at one end; but, to make them open, put in the middle where you tie them one or two pieces half the length: this is called a mixing rod. Provide a tall water pot as upright as can be procured, which make hot; work your butter on a marble slab, then put it in the pan, and work it well round with the rod until it is nicely creamed; put in the sugar, and incorporate both together; add one or two eggs at a time, and go on in this progressive way until they are all used; work away with the rod with all speed; and as soon as it is properly light, (which you may know by its smoothness, and rising in the pan) take it out, and mix in the flour, spices, currants, &c. &c. with a spatter [spurtle]. This is esteemed the very best mode of mixing cakes." Joseph Bell, *A Treatise on Confectionary*. Newcastle, England, 1817. Spare the rod and spoil the cake, eh?

• • • •

The word spurtle is Scottish, and refers to a cooking implement primarily used for stirring, with an edge to fit different kinds of pots, pans and kettles. They have been a longtime favorite shop project, and are so useful that one made in the 1930s of good hardwood might looks about the same as one made in the 1850s. In the early 1970s, Time-Life Books, in their *Family Creative Workshop* series, had a chapter on making your own spurtle. In 1973, Graham Kerr, the "Galloping Gourmet," introduced a set of five spurtles with their own hanging rack, made of hardwood. They ranged in length from about 8" to 13". The flat spoon-shaped one had a pair of holes, and a shorter butter-knife-shaped one had one large hole near end of the blade. The others were without holes in the blade, but all five had hanging holes. An 1817 English confectionery cookbook, by Joseph Bell, calls frequently for a spatte, the same tool.

Mixing spoon or beater, stamped tinned sheet metal, ridged handle shank, large bowl slotted like skeleton rib cage, small diamond cutout at top of bowl. Although handle is different, bowl is like the beautiful "Ideal." "The Eclipse Beater," mfd by Stuber & Kuck, Peoria, IL, 11" L, stamped "Pat. Mar. 30, 1903." Wrong date — the 30th was a Monday, not a Tuesday. Oddly, the "Ideal," which is so close to this in appearance, is marked with the wrong date too. Mine says "Mar. 30, 1908," and that was a Monday also. The year numerals are clear — I am not mistaking 1903 for 1908. **$18-$28**

II-88. Mixing spoons or cake spoons. (T) *Skeletal, rib-cage-like "Ideal" is tinned steel, with a simple turned wood handle. 10" L. Spoon is a deep bowled shape, and is for "beating eggs, cream pan cakes, and all other kinds of cakes and batters. For mashed potatoes it can't be beat. Can also be used for lifting vegetables from the pot or eggs from the pan. Unsurpassed for mixing or stirring of fruits." Pat'd 3/31/1903 by Carrie Bentley, marked "Mfd. by —-ster" (or —-ater). Others (earlier? later?) mfd by Stuber & Kuck, Peoria, IL.* **(B)** *Wire handle, 10-1/4" L, has "Rumford. The Wholesome Baking Powder" stamped into flattened part of handle.* **$18-$28; $5-$25**

Mixing spoon beater, tinned stamped iron with black painted turned wood handle, smallish spoon bowl is cut out leaving narrow crosspiece to which a 4 blade propeller is riveted, 10" L to 11" L, no mark but date, pat'd Aug. 3, 1909, by James H. Collins. **$200-$250**

II-89. Cake or mixing spoons. *Slotted spoons of 3 types.* **(M)** *Rumford advertising one, 12" L, is worth most. It's stamped "Saltsmans Improved Royal Pat'd Oct 6 08 RUMFORD Cake Mixer & Cream Whip."* **(T)** *Dark one is stamped tin, possibly German.* **(B)** *Slotted & perforated one probably A & J, c.1930s-1940s.* **$5-$22**

II-90. Pastry blenders. *Wire, steel & wood, 5-3/4" x 4". Both Androck, pat'd 1/12/1929. Note the 6 wires; in catalogs & ads, there are always 7 wires. One lying down is oldest, other is newer. In a 1936 catalog, the handle of green or red is made of Catalin plastic rather than painted wood.* **$5-$12**

II-91. Spurtles. *Idiosyncratically shaped carved wooden stirring paddles, adapted to various uses (like the rubber spatulas we use today) — from turning griddle cakes to stirring porridge. The verb "spurtle" means "to cover with spatterings," which is what usually happens when I make pancakes or stir oatmeal. The word is Scottish; the tool is universal. A few years ago, Galloping Gourmet™ Graham Kerr hawked carved bamboo spurtles.* **$4-$12**

Mixing spoon & fork combined, tinned iron with black painted turned wood handle, strange mechanical combination of fairly normal mixing spoon with small bowl & sliding fork mounted to shank, marked L & J Novelty Co., with trademark of "L & J" inside hexagon, Brooklyn, NY, 12-15/16" L, pat'd 1925. **$40-$50**

Mixing spoons, slotted, tinned metal, look exactly like catbox litter scoops, in fact, such are sold for that purpose now at my local pet store, some with stamped advertising. One I have is marked "CHIEF. Lifts, whips, mixes, mashes, crushes, strains," between 10-1/4" and 11" L x 3-1/2" to 3-3/4" W, turn of century to 1970s. Most may be 1930s or 1940s. Good variety in slot patterns, just as in cake turners. **$2.50-$6**

Mixing spoons, tinned sheet iron, or nickeled iron, with various wood handles, differences in turning, finish (natural, varnished, painted, stained), & in pattern of holes & slots in the spoon bowls, various makers, including A & J, Androck, Ekco, Samson, PM, etc., American & European, all about 10" L, 1890s to 1940s. Cast & stamped aluminum ones (mainly German) are a sub-specialty. Advertising ones with wire handles, and those with plastic handles adds even more variety to the field. **$5-$20**

Paddles — See butter paddle

Pastry blender, 6 springy wire half-circles, crimped into stainless steel tips mounted to wooden handle. Several styles of wooden handle — a simple rod with turned grooves, or a thicker, tapered one — the rest is basically the same. The grooved rod is probably newer one. Androck, Rockford, IL (but poss. Worcester, MA), 5-3/4" L x 4" W, pat'd Jan. 12, 1929. Androck is a combination of Andrews Wire Mfg. Co., and the location; it's unclear how and when Washburn of Worcester, MA, took on or absorbed or merged with Andrews. **$5-$20**

Pastry blender, also pie crust mixer & flaker, wire chopper (as described in the *Official Gazette* of the Patent Office), 6 wires in perfectly round hoop, threaded through 2 slots in the top (1 in each side) of sheet metal handle, "Lambert," pat'd by Clara Burchard Lambert, Pasadena, CA, 4-1/4" W, #1,486,255, pat'd March 11, 1924. **$15-$20**

Pastry blender, like a fork, heavy nickeled iron, wooden handle, American, 9-1/4" L, patent probably either Cram's of Feb. 19, 1907 or Hayward's of Dec. 19, 1922. **$8-$12**

Slotted spoon — See mixing spoons

Spurtle, oddly shaped wooden stirring or scraping tool with hole in blade part, worn, some staining to end of blade, looks old but may not be, unknown origin, 13" L, looks like 19th C. **$3-$10**

Stirrer, carved wood, turned handle with small ball knob at end, wide blade is 1/3 of full length, overall it looks like a finely made canoe paddle, American, 13-1/2" L, poss. 2nd to 3rd quarter 19th C. **$40-$60**

KAN-U-KATCH

II-93. Whisk-like game of "Kan-U-Katch." *I found this picture in a c.1916 St. Nicholas children's magazine, and include it as a confusable, seen at least once marked "old whisk."* **$10-$15**

II-94. Whisks for the baker, chef, and candyman. *Clockwise from coiled wire:* **(1)** *"Egg beater wire," for replacing whisk wires, c.1906.* **(2)** *Candy makers' "sugar spinner," 15" L, 1927.* **(3)** *c1870s, with chained ring to adjust ballooning of bows to suit the job.* **(4)** *Long flat one ("snowshoe" or "fan"-shaped) with bound handle is called the "Sensible Egg Whip," and made in sizes from 9" to 15" L, over a long period. Note central wire, which is soldered to others and stabilizes them.* **(- - -)** *These unnumbered 3 are cream whips from Germany, c.1904.* **(5)** *"W.H.T. Patent Egg Beater," sold through candy makers' suppliers, c.1908.* **(6)** *is16"L, big ballooned bows. c.1927.* **(7)** *Wood handle steel (or brass) whip, c.1908.* **(8)** *For restaurants — "Mayonnaise Whip," 5-1/2" diameter x 13-1/2" L with "four foot pole attached."* c.1927. **$5-$40**

II-92. Syllabub churns & eggbeaters. *Very old type, called a whip churn. All have a perforated dasher. Similar-looking ones might use another kind of dasher.* **(L)** *was for making whipped cream or syllabub, and is from* American Home Cook Book, *1854.* **(2)** *and* **(3)** *are parts of the Matthai-Ingram syllabub churn, 8" L x 1-3/4" diameter. c.1890.* **(4)** *and* **(5)** *is the dasher & body of the "Lightning Egg Beater," also mfd. by Matthai-Ingram. "The white of an egg can be beaten in one minute to a froth stiff enough to cut with a knife." Pat'd 1888 (?), ad c.1890.* **$45-$70**

Syllabub churns — See also cream whips, eggbeaters

Syllabub churn, Tilden's — See eggbeater, shaker

Syllabub churn, tin, with a tin rack (shaped like a doll stand) that adjusts in height, simple wooden knob handle, deeply conical bottom to churn, inside has a conical dasher, 9" H, marked "pat'd Sept. 14, 1875." Others found that are 12" L x 4" D, and 11" L x 3-1/2" D. Pat'd by Friedrich E. Schonmeyer, Cleveland, OH. Don Thornton has one marked "Bon Ton." **$50-$95**

Toddy mixer, glass & metal, "Toddy Man," c.1930s. **$10-$15**

Whip or whisk, for baking, wire, "Omar Wonder Flour," 20th C. **$6-$10**

Whip or whisk, large flat metal with stenciled wooden handle, not for food, but for mixing wallpaper paste, "TIK Wheat Paste, Clark Stek-O Corp.," Rochester, NY, 14-5/8" L, 20th C. Other marked paste company whisks are known. **$10-$15**

Whip or whisk, wire in flat snowshoe shape (Thornton calls this a fan shape), wire-wrapped handle, 9" L, 20th C. **$8-$10**

Whisk, wood, tin & string, long handle you rub between palms to make it turn back & forth, small balloon blades, probably a drink mixer, American, 16" L, mid 19th C. **$15-$20**

Whisks or egg whips, twisted wire, spoonlike in outline, with criss-cross wires, springs & wires wrapped around "bowl," or a sort of chicken wire effect of wire stretched across bowl, various, some found in catalogs, like that of Androck, mostly American, about 12" to 13" L, mainly 20th C. Many variations are pictured. **$8-$20**

Whisks, new types include: tinned steel wire with wire-wrapped handles for sauces, & a more ballooning stainless steel whisk with wooden handle, adjusting ring on wires to regulate size of balloon, American or imports (mainly France & Germany), first type: 6", 8" & 10" L; second type: 12" L, new, sold in all kinds of kitchen specialty shops & departments. Approx. new value: **$4-$20**

PREPARING

III. SEPARATE, STRAIN, DRAIN, SIFT, & DREDGE

In the last chapter we mixed things; here we separate them. This preparation category includes implements that assist the cook by allowing wanted solid foodstuff to be retained (in a sieve, colander, skimmer, etc.); wanted liquids or solids to be cleared of unwanted particles too large to slip through the holes; or lumpy food to be pushed through a perforated (or screened) surface in order to render the lumps smaller, make them uniform in size or aerate them. When used with a pestle, a strainer is a form of mortar, so see potato ricers in Chapter I (as well as the one described here).

Colanders are among the most popular utensils in this category, collected today for the material from which they are made (especially enameled iron), for their shape and for the variety of perforated patterns. A single colander can be a thing of great and simple beauty because its form tells the whole story of its function, but a *collection* of different colanders, each with its particular tattoo of holes, is spectacular. The colander's lineage is ancient: bronze ones were uncovered in the archaeological digs in Pompeii (which had been buried by a volcano in A.D. 79). Perfect for collectors who seek something interesting but not expensive, colanders — partly because there are no gears and cranks — are not pricey collectibles, and the value has remained stable for years.

Cheese drainers are in the next chapter (with molds) because although they look like colanders, and the method is to strain the whey from the curds, their ultimate function is to mold a cheese once the whey has dripped out. Funnels with built-in sieves (mostly vintners' or brewers' types) are here; other funnels are in Chapter V (Weight, Amount, Size, Time and Temperature).

Flour sifters form the most popular category in this chapter. They satisfy mechanically because of cranks, squeeze handles, shakers. The classic is the Hunter, described fully in its entry.

Kitchen Glossary: Foot or Base? I have tried to consistently use the term "foot" (or sometimes "footed base") in the singular, when I'm writing about a sort of fixed or attached flared or convex ring or narrow band that serves as the base of a vessel, utensil or other object. The term foot has long been used in describing the bases of glass, ceramic, metal, stone and wooden containers. A glass tumbler, for example, had to be drained in one quaff, it couldn't stand up. A drinking glass with stem and foot could be sipped from all evening. Two major types of colanders are either foot loose or foot fast. (Simple colanders are foot loose *and* fancy free!) Foot loose means that there's a ring separate from the colander used on any surface so that a bowl-bottom colander can be set down. In China, metal rings are used with woks; in Africa, cloth rings are used for balancing baskets or clay vessels on a woman's head. Foot fast means the ring is stuck fast — soldered or riveted in place in the case of metal colanders. Some writers and antiques cataloguers call this type of fixed ring foot a "gallery foot." More exact terms include spreading foot, for the widely flaring incurved foot; molded foot, for one with beading, reeding or ogee curves or other moldings familiar in wood carving and cabinetry; and round foot, for a simple convex or outcurved foot. Descriptive terms haven't been codified or standardized to a high degree concerning kitchen wares, so some applicable terms must be borrowed from fields of collecting such as silver, pewter, porcelain, and furniture, as well as wood- and metal-working tools.

• • • •

Metal Drives for Munitions & Material — Affecting Today's Supply of Antique Iron, Pewter, Copper & Brass Wares — There is probably plenty of documentary evidence, so far unexplored, touching on the necessity for metal or scrap drives during (and perhaps preceding each of) the first four wars of the U. S., viz. the War for Independence, 1775-1781; the War of 1812, 1812-1815; the War Between the States, 1861-1865; and the Spanish-American War, 1898. Such documents presumably would be found in the National Archives, the Library of Congress, and in privately or publicly-held collections of family papers, letters, newspapers, broadsides, perhaps even court-ordered seizure records. The wars swallowed an incalculable number of sound household wares and tools, as well as scraps of same, pooled to recast or forge as cannon and musket balls, soldiers' canteens & eating kits, uniform buttons, army horseshoes, ironclad vessels, guns, pistols and bullets. Basically we are talking about iron, lead and pewter, with some brass and copper. I can't now search primary or secondary sources, but will quote from Ledlie Irwin Laughlin's *Pewter in America*, 1940, to hint at the scope of the loss. Anything said about pewter is true in spades about iron. Laughlin writes, Vol. I, p. 109, "During the [Revolutionary] war the country was combed for everything containing lead to supply munitions for the Continental troops. Little beyond the absolutely essential, and probably new, pewter would have escaped the melting-pot." In Laughlin, Vol. II, p. 69, we read that, "It has been said that the dearth of Southern pewter may be chargeable to confiscation by agents of the Confederate Government of all available metal that could be used in the manufacture of munitions during the Civil War." Inexplicable to me so far is the vast supply of seventeenth-, eighteenth- and nineteenth-century iron, pewter, brass and copper wares found today all over Europe, which has been ravaged by wars for centuries.

• • • •

Meltdowns in the Pursuit of Commerce — Easily reviewed old newspapers, or "gleanings" of ads done by Dow and Gottesman, give ample proof that most if not all metal artisans in the U.S. solicited and bought "old iron, pewter, brass, copper, lead & tin" for melting down or reworking into new objects in more fashionable or necessary forms. These war and peace metal drives have left us with only sketchy written descriptions and incidental depictions of countless old pieces gone forever.

Bean sizing sieve, also called a **sorting frame**, or **bean sizer**, square wood frame moveable at corners, crisscrossed with wood slats not tightly affixed to the frame. Adjust the sieve from coarse to finer by pulling two opposite sides out from a square shape into a parallelogram out to an elongated diamond shape — this changes the size of the interstices, or spaces, between the slats, from an inch or so down to a quarter of that. American, approx. 18" x 18", 19th C. Either handmade or limited production pieces, patina and condition are important. **$100-$135**

Colander, also spelled in old inventory records <u>cullender</u>, <u>cullinder</u>, <u>callender</u>, <u>collander</u> and <u>colender</u>. This one is pewter, wide flared sides and fairly shallow — in what would have been advertised in the 1750s as a "dish cullender" (rather than the deeper, more narrowly-rimmed "basin cullender"), foot fast, ring handles, scalloped pattern of small perforations. American (?), no discernable touchmark, 11" diameter, late 18th or very early 19th C. **$300-$600**

Colander, aqua enamelware, 11" D, mid 20th C. and quite possibly European. **$35-$45**

Colander, brown & white swirled enamel, prob. "Onyx," Columbian Enameling & Stamping, American, 10" D, late 19th, early 20th C. (A sort of spotty rich brown & white enamelware line, including many flat-bottomed colanders seend in last decade, probably are European, and are valued at less than half that for American.) **$85-$115**

Colander, dark cobalt blue enamelware, black rim & handles, elegant bowl shape, high fixed foot, prob. European, 7" H x 7-1/2" diameter, late 19th C. **$60-$80**

Colander, dark cobalt enamelware flecked with white, wire handles, footed, American (?), 8" diameter, turn of century. **$75-$100**

Colander, dark cobalt & white graniteware, riveted strap handles, rounded ring fixed foot, American (?), 12" diameter, turn of century. **$60-$90**

Colander, gray graniteware, American or German, 9-1/2" D, late 19th or early 20th C. **$55-$85**

Colander, gray graniteware, ear handles, short feet & attached drip tray, 19th C. **$125-$150**

III-1. Ash sifter & coal sieve. (T) *"Hustler," mfd. by Hill Dryer Col, Worcester, MA. Galvanized sheet metal, horizontal cylinder with hopper at one end with crank, and perforated end that lets ashes through into bucket. Turn of century ad with infant imps.* **(B)** *"The Convex Coal Sieve," mfd. by Lock Haven Sifter Co., Lock Haven, PA. Heavy double-seamed sheet metal, cast iron ears riveted on for handle. The convex bottom prevents ashes accumulating in the center (most ash sifters had flat bottoms). Pat'd Apr. 16, 1889; put on market in late fall of 1890. The Metal Worker, 5/1890.* **$10-$20**

III-2. Colanders — *foot-loose and foot-fast (soldered on). Four sizes, from 9-7/8" to 13" diameter. Matthai-Ingram, c.1890.* **$15-$25**

III-3. Colanders. *All tin, with old-fashioned styling, and possibly the cuts were already 40 years old when used in Harrod's Stores, Ltd., catalog of 1895. Clockwise from* **top (L)**: *deep bowl type, 9", 10" and 12"; (2) is stamped, with riveted handles; (3) is pieced, with riveted strap handles, 8" to 10-1/4" diameter. c.1895.* **$15-$35**

III-4. Round bottom colanders or cullenders. *All foot-fast, as most colanders are. (L) (R) (L) (R) from top.* **(1)** *"Greystone" graniteware, from 9-7/8" to 13" diameter. Matthai-Ingram.* **(2)** *3-1/2" to 4-1/2" deep x 9-3/8" to 12" diameter. D. J. Barry, 1924.* **(3)** *White "Sterling" enameled, 4-7/8" H x 9-1/2" to 6" H x 12" diameter, Central Stamping Co., 1920.* **(4)** *Stamped tin, of large size for hotels mostly — 4-3/4" H x 13" diameter up to 7-5/8" H x 19" diameter. Lalance & Grosjean, 1890, and same cut used in catalogs of 30 years later.* **(5)** *Tin version of #3.* **(6)** *Hotel colander in 3 big sturdy sizes. "Puritan," Central Stamping, 1920.* **(7)** *Tin, in 4 sizes from 3" H x 9-1/2" to 4-1/2" H x 13-1/4".* *Lalance & Grosjean, 1890.* **$15-$55**

III-7. Colander. *Flared sides, brightly tinned, dished, foot fast. Note on this one that the sides have 2 seams — a pattern that saved tin. 4-1/2" H x 12" diameter. Late 19th to early 20th C. Collection Mary Mac Franklin.* **$15-$30**

III-5. Slant-sided, mostly flat bottom colanders. (1) *"Greystone" graniteware, 9-3/4" and 10-7/8", Matthai-Ingram, c.1890.* **(2)** *Called the "Eastern Pattern" for the body shape and flat bottom (?), probably not for star-point perforations, wrought iron (though not handmade) handles, 10" to 12". Pattern offered by many companies, this one from Geuder, Paeschke & Frey, 1925.* **(3)** *Heavy pieced tin, soldered strap handles, 11-1/2" and 13-1/2", Shapleigh Hardware, 1914.* **(4)** *Flat-bottom & footless, strap handle, in 14", 16", 18" and 20", and four hole size choices: 1/8", 1/4", 3/16" and 5/16". Jaburg, 1908.* **(5)** *Tinned steel, from 5-3/4" H x 13-3/4" to 7-5/8" x 19-1/2". Pick-Barth, 1929.* **(6)** *Planished tin, 9-1/2" to 15" diameter, Albert Pick, 1909.* **(7)** *9-3/4" and 11", Matthai-Ingram, c.1890.* **(8)** *Widely flared, another "Eastern" style, 12", GP & F, 1925. It's interesting to me how much variety, including hole sizes, was available to people even 70 years ago, from ordinary hardware stores. Things have certainly changed.* **$15-$55**

III-8. Copper colanders. *Bowl-shaped colanders made of copper;* **(L)** *sold in sizes from 10" to 18", would be set down in a pot or large mixing bowl to drain, Duparquet, Huot & Moneuse, c.1902-1910.* **(R)** *One with small ball feet is tinned in and out, in 5 sizes from 10" to 14". Henry Rogers, Wolverhampton, England, 1914.* **$35-$55**

III-9. Colander. *Copper, with large handles making it usable with many size bowls or other vessels, on whose rim the handles would rest. 9" diameter, bottom is flat and joined to sides with strong dovetail seam. Ex-Wiggins Tavern Collection of Northampton, MA. Photograph courtesy of Luella McCloud Antiques, Shelburn Falls, MA. NOTE: An exhibit in 1986 of Shaker artifacts included a beautiful simple tin strainer, much like this, with two very large strap handles on the sides.* **$100-$150**

III-6. Colander. *Perforated tin, ring foot is soldered on — foot-fast, 3-3/4" H x 9-3/4" diameter. Late 19th to early 20th C. Note the seam where the collar-shaped tin pattern was soldered together before the bottom and foot were soldered on. Collection Mary Mac Franklin.* **$15-$30**

III-10. Confusable — *not a colander but a <u>dip basket</u>. Pressed fiber dip basket for brass foundries, nickel-plating works, etc., mfd. by United Indurated Fiber Co., whose agents were Cordley & Hayes. The Metal Worker, 11/8/1890.* **$20-$30**

Colander, green speckled enamelware with cobalt blue rim & ear handles, foot fast, lovely color, 10-7/8" diameter, 19th C. **$145-$170**

Colander, mottled green graniteware, strap handles, foot fast, American (?), 10" D, late 19th or early 20th C. **$85-$110**

Colander, perforated sheet iron, foot fast, commercial but looks handmade, good condition, 10" D, late 19th or early 20th C. **$15-$25**

Colander, perforated tin, flat bottom has radiating holes lining up with every 3rd row of holes in sides, deeply flared, strap handles, foot fast, American, 4-1/4" H x 12" D, late 19th or early 20th C. **$18-$30**

Colander, pierced tin, flat bottom, foot fast, tinned iron loop handles, in F. A. Walker catalog, 3-3/4" H x 9-3/4" D, 1870s-1880s. **$18-$30**

Colander, rounded bowl body, pierced tin, iron loop handles, nice rolled edge foot ring, separate or loose, Matthai-Ingram, 13" D, 1890s. This is a hypothetical or what-if entry: although the catalogs offered foot loose as well as foot fast colanders, the chances of an old foot ring surviving with its separate colander bowl are slim. **$18-$25**

Colander, sheet iron, very large with good size holes, crudely soldered foot ring, primitive & imposing, American, 14" D, mid to end of 19th C. This is a good example of the kind of object segueing out of the cheaper kitchen collectibles field into the expensive and vol-

III-11. Colander-strainers *of saucepan style.* **(T)** *"Mirro" aluminum, with steel hollow handle, 6-1/4" to 8-1/2" diameter. Aluminum Goods Mfg. Co., Manitowoc, WI, 1927.* **(B)** *Pieced tin, large holes in slightly dished bottom only. Tubular handle, c.1870s-1900. Courtesy Lar Hothem.* **$3-5; $15-$30**

III-12. Colander-strainers. **(L)** *Tin, in 9 sizes, from 2-1/2" H x 5" diameter to 5" H x 11" diameter. Saucepan style, with strap support for resting within a pan. Matthai-Ingram, c.1890. Identical pictures appeared in Lalance & Grosjean 1890 catalog, and Duparquet catalog, c.1904-1910.* **Lower** **(R)** *Stamped metal (quite possibly tinned copper) colander depicted in Urbain Dubois' La Patisserie D'Aujourd'hui, Paris, c.1860s-80s. The colander is being used as a support for glazed orange segments stuck on skewers to air dry.* **$10-$35**

atile folk art market, where — presented out of context — such a piece as this qualifies as sculpture. **$30-$50**

Colander, tinned pieced sheet metal, hollow ear handles, small flat bottom has many holes, lower part of sides not perforated, then band of several rows of holes partway up sides, American, 14" diameter, late 19th C. **$25-$35**

Colander, white enamelware, blue rim, strap handles & foot, turn of century. **$25-$35**

"Cauliflower Fritters — Boil the cauliflower until perfectly tender, drain and cool; break carefully into flowerettes, season with salt and pepper, dip into fritter batter and fry in deep fat. (If cauliflower has been served with a white sauce at dinner, cut into small pieces and dip in batter, and fry.) Serve very hot or put in a shallow baking dish, sprinkle freely with parmesan cheese or other cheese and bake in hot oven." *Woman's Home Companion*, June 1899.

Colander, wire mesh in tin & wire frame, wooden ear handles, also used as a purée sieve, Androck, Rockford, IL, 1936. **$12-$18**

Colander, yellowware, footed, rather thick walls with pierced bottom, American, 10" diameter, 19th C. **$175-$200+**

Colander, yellowware, small foot, nice pattern of holes, 2 eyeholes near rim for a hanging cord, English, 10-3/4" diameter, mid 19th C. Broken: very small hairline crack may lower value by 25% or so. Repaired: conversely, if the crack has been repaired with a tin band or an intricate weaving of wire, or the use of metal staples, the value might even double! (See Chapter IX for tools used to wash, sharpen & repair housewares.) **$120-$150**

Colander or strainer, dark brown glazed stoneware, smallish, roundish body with rim & base the same diameter, thick arched handle like a basket, rather large holes piercing sides & bottom, PA German, 8" H including handle x 6-1/4" diameter, mid 19th C (?). **$275-$350**

Colander scoop, pieced & perforated tin, missing wood handle, 6" L, 19th C. **$7-$10**

Drainer or strainer, a sort of perforated metal half-lid that fit into cooking vessel & held back the beans while pouring off liquid, "Drain-a-Way," 20th C. **$6-$10**

Draining pan, or sink drainer, aluminum in triangular shape, for corner of sink, "Wearever Aluminum," 1920s-30s. **$12-$18**

Dredger, or muffineer, tin cup with pierced convex top, mug-type handle, 2-tier base, used for flour, or sugar, for dredging or coating meat with flour to make gravy, or cutlets to bake, or dusting pastry boards before rolling, for sprinkling cookies or muffins before baking (the word dredge relates to a Latin word for confection). American (?), 7" H, mid-19th C. **$45-$55**

Dredger, for flour, tin cup with handle & snug snap-on domed lid with perforations; also called a dredge, dredge box, dredging box, or drudger. American (?) — probably impossible to tell origin unless marked, c.1880s-1900. This is true because simple linecut illustrations of many kinds of kitchen tools were used for decades, sometimes by several manufacturers who would order linecuts from an engraving house, much like we can buy clip art books today. **$15-$22**

Lookalike — A tin cup that appears to be identical is called a Pepper Box (made also in Britannia metal), with very small, closely spaced holes. It was advertised in the retail catalog of Harrod's Stores, Ltd., in 1895.

Dredger, tin, double lid — the inside one is pierced, "Steele's Dredge Box," New Haven, CT, 3-1/4" H x 2" D, pat'd Dec. 27, 1870. **$45-$65**

Dredger, tin, double lid — the inside one is pierced, "Steele's Dredge Box," New Haven, CT, 3-1/4" H x 2" D, pat'd Dec. 27, 1870. **$45-$65**

Dredger, heavy old dark tin, footed like a goblet, domed pierced lid, big strap handle on side, American, 6" H, early to mid 19th C. **$18-$25**

Dredger, japanned tin cup with mug handle & slightly flared base, domed pierced lid, American or imported, in F. A. Walker catalog of 1870s or 1880s. **$18-$22**

Reproduction alert — Possibly this has been made continuously since the 1870s or 1860s, or whenever the style of dredger with the wide flared concave foot (I've seen this called a "gallery base") was first made. But we know it was being reproduced at least by 1974. An ad placed by Williams & Sons Country Store, Stockbridge, MA, in the Aug. 1974 *Early American Life*, pictures a well-made, somewhat shiny tin dredger, with a 5-point star perforation pattern on the lid and a dark tin foot. The copy reads "Grandmother never baked a pie, cake or loaf of bread without her old tinware flour dreger [sic] at her side." The repro is 5" H x 4-1/2" diameter at widest part of foot, and cost only $5.25 ppd. 20 years ago.

Dredger, japanned (asphaltum) tin, small handle, domed lid, American, 4" H, late 19th C. **$20-$30**

Dredger, grater, pastry jagger combination tool — See the picture IV-255, in Chapter IV, with the pastry jagger listings.

Dredger, so-called milk glass, metal screw-on lid, word "Flour" painted on side, American, 4-1/2" H x 2-1/2" D, early 20th C. **$12-$15**

Dredger, or flour shaker, green custard glass, "McKee," Pittsburg, 1930s. **$20-$30**

Dredger, probably for cinnamon sugar, shapely pigeon-breasted glass container that looks something like a fire hydrant in profile, one flat side to fit against back of stove shelf, screw-on tin lid, American, 6" H, prob. late 19th C. **$20-$32**

III-13. Dredgers or shakers. (1) *Sugar dredger or caster, polished brass or nickel-plated brass. Jaburg Brothers, 1908.* (2) *Unidentified, probably English, mug-handled dredger, c.1870s.* (3) *Lightweight "Mirro" aluminum salt or flour shaker in paneled "Colonial" pattern (which they used for coffee pots and some other wares). 2-5/8" H x 2-3/8" diameter. 1927.* (4) *"Dredge box," available with or without handle. Tin, or nickeled tin, or nickeled stamped brass. Jaburg, 1908.* (5) *Flat-top (others had convex top) salt or flour shaker, "Mirro," 4" H x 3", 1927.* (6) *Stamped and polished tin, high domed top, two sizes. In very old style, at least back to 1850s, this picture from 1908 Jaburg catalog of supplies for candy-makers.* **$3-$45**

The **1914 advertising** in the V. Clad catalog says "You," meaning mostly restauranteurs, "no doubt, in breaking eggs have many times come in contact with and broken a bad or musty egg, and in most cases have spoiled quite a number of good ones, by letting the bad one fall among them. With this Detector the chances of losing eggs by this cause will be avoided, as it contains but one egg, therefore you can only spoil one, and not from one to six or ten dozen, as the case may be, by breaking them the old way. By this machine you cut your shell; you do not smash it and get your batch full of small pieces. You get all out of the egg in your vessel, as there is no chance for part of each egg to run on the outside, as in the old way. You do not make a mess on your table or bench; besides, you can break eggs much faster than in the old way, thereby saving valuable time."

Egg detector, for bad eggs, heavily tinned stamped & pieced metal, very shallow but wide-mouthed funnel-like contrivance with a curved sharp shell-breaker ridge from the rim down to opening of the narrow neck, which forms a sort of crook-necked double elbow "S" curve, the whole raised high on 3 tall legs, sold by, possibly mfd. by V. Clad & Sons, Philadelphia, early 20th C. **$35-$45**

III-14. Drink strainers. (T) *Shaker strainer, nickel silver. Cherry-Bassett, 1921.* **(R)** *A Julep strainer, with shell-shaped perforated bowl, with star cutout in handle. Duparquet, Huot & Moneuse, c.1904-1910.* Lower **(L)** *Coiled spring wire strainer, "fits all sizes of mixing glasses. Made of 18% nickel silver heavily silver plated."* *D. J. Barry, 1924.* **$3-$15**

III-15. Egg separators. (T-R) *"Degerdon's Improved Egg Separator & Saver. No loss of albumen. No waste in yolk or white." Tin, Jaburg, 1908.* **(B-R)** *"Perfect" separator. Albert Pick, 1909.* **(B-L)** *"The 1892" spun aluminum, 4-1/2" x 3-1/2", with four slots around center part. (Other companies made them with two slots ringing the center.) American Aluminum Mfg. Co., Lemont, IL, 1911.* **$65-$85; $15-$20; $10-$15**

Egg separator, 2 parts, enameled cast iron, cup is blue, slotted shallow yolk catcher that sets into it is enameled white, 4" diameter, T. S. Ceeton, pat'd Oct. 8, 1891. **NOTE:** Look for a book on egg separators from Don "Eggbeater" Thornton's Off Beat Publishing Co. **$95-$135**

Egg separator, aluminum, 2 large ear handles with hanging holes, 2 slots in shallow cup, 3-3/4" diameter, 6-3/8" L overall, c.1915. **$5-$8**

Egg separator, stamped, slotted tin, advertising "Nathan Fletcher's Soda," American, 20th C. **$8-$12**

Egg separator, stamped tin, thumb handle, 3-1/4" D, advertising message "Do You Know Kemo?" on rim, early 20th or late 19th C. Egg separators advertising dairies or egg farms, stamped of tin or aluminum, are an under-appreciated collectible. **$7-$12**

Egg separators, stamped tin, advertising "Excelsior Stove Works," another "Cinderella Stoves," early 20th C. Added value because of stove. **$10-$18**

Egg separator, stamped tin, prettily shaped thumb handle, "Jewel Stoves & Ranges," 3-3/8" D, turn of century. **$10-$18**

Egg separator, white enamelware, single thumb grip tab handle, hanging hole, early 20th C. **$10-$20**

Fish drainer, (or some kind of combined grater-strainer), <u>whitesmithed</u> (hammered, filed & highly polished) wrought iron, large slightly concave bowl in elongated trowel shape, many holes punctured rough side down, relatively short twisted iron handle, American, 15-5/8" L, late 18th C. or early 19th. **$150-$200**

Fish slice, perforated tin with wooden handle, called a *slice* but not for slicing, it's for lifting cooked fish from a fish cooker and is perforated so juices drain out. The word "slice" relates to the elongated but broad shape (on which a typical fish would fit), American, 12-1/2" L, 19th C. **$65-$95**

Flour Bolts — When searching patent indexes and records for flour sifters, don't forget that a <u>bolt</u> was a sifter, and some patents may be hidden to us modern folk behind old-fashioned words.

Flour sifters and bins:

Flour bin & sieve, tall tin cylinder, paint enameled finish, ornamented with wheat sheaf design & name, tight-fitting lid with knob on top, wire & wood crank 2/3 way down, pull-out curved-front drawer near bottom, "Perfection," mfd. by Sherman, Tangenberg & Co., Chicago, IL, 25-lb capacity (also made for 50 lbs and 100 lbs), 1890s. "Does away with barrels,

sacks, pans, scoops & sieves. A few turns of the handle and you have enough for baking." Ad, March 1890. **$55-$80**

Flour bin & sifter, metal, probably for store, "Superior," 3' H, 20th C. **$150-$200**

Flour bin & sifter, tall tin cylinder, painted white at some date, has tin divider halfway down into which is set a sifter, cranked from outside front. The lower compartment has hinged door that swings out to reveal handled pan that catches sifted flour, possibly Geuder, Paeschke & Frey Co., Milwaukee, WI, 14" H x 11-1/4" diameter, early 20th C to c.1930. <u>Added value</u> — If this were in its original baked-on enamel finish, with stenciled decoration and word "FLOUR," it would be worth at least four times as much. It's possible that you could refinish by gently removing the mid-20th C paint, but it would be chancy. **$35-$50**

Flour sifters, wood tabletop:

III-17. Flour or sugar sifter. *"Blood's" patent, patented as a flour sifter by A. E. and J. B. Blood, Lynn, MA. Two patents, I don't know which one this is — 9/17/1861 or 1/9/1866. Wood with bootjack ends, 2 wooden roller blades and wire screen bottom. Comes apart so you can clean. Body stands 8-3/4" H, with space for tray pan beneath about 9" x 10-1/2". Rocker action, pivoting at center. Collection of Meryle Evans.* **$175-$300**

III-16. Flour sifter. *"Tilden's Universal." Wood slant-sided box on little legs, woven iron screen sifter, leather sifter blades. 11-3/4" H x 9-1/2" L x 7-3/4" W. Pat'd 3/28/1865. Collection of Meryle Evans.* **$175-$300**

III-18. Flour sifter. *Tin and cast iron, woven wire mesh in bottom, 2 paddles on inside. 10" H x 7-1/2" diameter. Late 19th C. Collection of Meryle Evans.* **$150 and up**

Flour or sugar sifter, tabletop, wooden box frame with pointy boot-jack legs (and sides), open top, wooden rocker crossbar handle moves the 2 connected wooden roller blades across wire screen bottom, to sift flour or sugar. It comes apart for cleaning, a pan to catch the sifted sugar (or flour) was slid on table underneath, paper label reads, "Blood's Patent," A. E. & J. B. Blood, Lynn, MA, 8-3/4" H, with approx. 10-1/2" x 9" space underneath for a pan to catch siftings, pat'd Sept. 17, 1861. They patented an improvement on Jan. 9, 1866. **$175-$300**

In the 1869 catalog of the Dover Stamping Co. (which was beautifully reprinted by the Pyne Press, Princeton, NJ, 1971, in their historical catalog series), two pages are devoted to the <u>Blood's Patent Sifter</u>, about which it was said, "... its greatest superiority is not as a flour sifter. In preparing Squash, Apple or Pumpkin for Pies, or other Fruits for Jams or Jellies, its value is increased a hundred fold. ... [also] stewed tomatoes, currants, grapes. ... Molasses is seldom clean enough for use, — Blood's Sifter Cleanses It Thoroughly. In the West it is used to strain Sorghum as it comes from the Mill. Those who do much with CREAM TARTAR find it invaluable. Druggists find it indispensable in sifting and straining their various Medicines. So with Glaziers, in sifting Whiting. ..." The catalog copy goes on to say that because imitators don't dare to use Blood's patent "vibrating rollers," they have "substituted various contrivances in hope to answer the purpose. Among these are Cranks, India Rubber, Bristles, Leather, Stationary Wood, &c., &c." They add that these things impart odors, wear out, get sour & filthy, and even "crumble and become incorporated with the bread or pies, constituting a violent poison."

Flour sifter, commercial size one for bakery or hotel, wood with brushes & screen, mfd. by J. H. Day & Co., #100, 20th C. **$100-$150**

Flour sifter, wood bin with bootjack legs at each end, screen bottom, rubber-tipped paddles, crank action, American, 10" H x 9" L, 1860s. This is very like the Tilden's. **$150-$275**

Flour sifter, wooden with metal crank, bin shape, crank in side, 11-3/4" H x 9-1/2" L x 7-3/4" W. "Tilden's Patent," pat'd by H. Tilden, who first lived in Philadelphia, then in Boston, pat'd Mar. 28, 1865; Tilden's 3 other patents are: May 16 & June 13, 1865, with a reissue Nov. 14; and Jan 2, 1866. (Tilden — like Hunter — was another sifter inventor who also patented a toy, although his 1867 patent was a toy bow-gun.) (**NOTE:** This sifter and a few others have a wide value range, which reflects two things: location of dealer, and the relatively new interest in such things (not yet reflected in some markets). **$175-$300**

III-20. Flour scoop & sifter. *"Earnshaw's." Tinned sheet iron, iron cran, woven wire mesh, strap handle. 8-1/2" H. Pat'd 7/25/1865 by J. Earnshaw, Lowell, MA. Picture courtesy of the National Museum of American History, Smithsonian Institution.* **$75-$85**

Flour sifters, scoop rim cylinders:

Flour sifter, dark tin cylinder with "scoop" rim, fat tubular handle from which wooden knobbed crank sticks out, wire mesh sifting screen, "Hunter's Sifter, Standard of the World," mfd. by The Fred J. Meyers Mfg. Co., at that time in Hamilton, OH (made earlier in Covington, KY). 6-1/2" H x 4-3/4" D x 11-1/2" L (including handle and tip of knobbed crank), pat'd Aug. 5, 1879 by Jacob M. Hunter. Sold for decades. **$20-$40**

Flour sifter, scoop top rim, tin cylinder, wire mesh at bottom, side handle with squeeze action, "Sift-Chine" ("Sift-ing Ma-chine"), mfd. by Meets a Need Mfg. Co., Seattle, WA, c.1931. **$8-$15**

Flour sifter, scoop top rim, tin cylinder, wire mesh, wooden side handle, knobbed side crank, "Savory Sift-Chine," about 6-1/2" H x 4-3/4" D, c.1910-20s. (See other type of scoop sifters at end of these sifter listings.) **$8-$12**

Multipurpose Classic — The Hunter is a must-have for a kitchen collection. It was advertised over 100 years ago as combining "... 12 kitchen utensils in one. It is a Mixer, Scoop, Measure, Weigher, Dredger, Rice Washer, Starch, Tomato, Wine, and Fruit Strainer. It is the most useful kitchen utensil made." A *Ladies Home Journal* ad in Sept. 1889 reads: "Tomato-sauce, tomato soup and tomato catsup are favorite compounds . . . In no other way can they be so easily and quickly strained as with the Hunter Sifter. Owing to its construction, it can be placed in the tureen and the soup strained while boiling hot, losing little or none of its heat in the process. Bean, pea, potato, and mixed vegetable soups are strained with equal ease and rapidity." (So much for truth in advertising.) An ad in the Jan. 1879 *American Agriculturist* said that this "Hunter's Perfection Rotary Flour & Meal Sifter" is the "only sifter in the world that can be taken in four parts to clean. 75,000 sold in 180 days. 200,000 now in use. Send 65¢ for small or $1 for large sample, or stamp for catalog." (The "small" is possibly the miniature one, though it doesn't say that.) If 1/5 of a million full-size Hunters were sold in 2 years; and they were still selling 10 years later, it's a wonder we don't all have at least 10 in our collections! After all, there are only an estimated 175,000 collectors of kitchen collectibles.

III-19. Flour scoop & sifter. *Cranked, handheld "Earnshaw's Patent." This picture from F. A. Walker catalog, 1870s. See how closely the catalog cut resembles the real thing in the next picture.* **$75-$85**

Miniature Hunter Sifter — The toy/sample version came first. It is only 2-1/4" H, made exactly like the bigger one of tinned sheet iron, with a tubular handle with crank. It's stamped in relief on one side, "HUNTER'S-TOY-SIFTER (pat. May 16 71 - Apr. 7 74) BUY A BIG ONE." It was patented eight years before the date given on the big one, and was made in Covington, KY. In the January 1889 issue of *Ladies Home Journal* was an ad for the Hunter outlining its multiple uses. The ad went on, " . . . A toy sifter which shows how the large sifter works, and which will afford amusement to any little girl, will be sent free to anyone who will mention where this advertisement was seen, and enclose 2 cents for postage to the Fred J. Meyers Mfg. Co." Can you imagine that? Only 2¢! **$125-$175**

Flour sifters, scoop-shaped:

Flour sifter & scoop, tin, "Pillsbury's Flour," "UNIVERSAL SCOOP WITH SIFTER ATTACHMENT." 20th C. **$35-$45**

Flour sifter, grater & holder combined, metal & wood scoop shape, on remnant of paper label: "Improved Combination Sifter, F. Bucknam," Portland, ME, pat'd May 15, 1866, #54,679. **$85-$100**

Flour sifter & scoop combined, tin, boxy shape like a square-cornered scoop, strap handle at back, with paddles inside cranked with wire crank on right side, "Earnshaw's Patent," J. Earnshaw, Lowell, MA, 8-1/2" L, pat'd July 25, 1865. **$65-$85**

Flour sifter & scoop, fine wire mesh with rim, scoop lip & strap handle all of tin. This is an oval basket elongated into pronounced scoop shape at one end, opposite which is a strap handle, "Handy," Handy Mfg. Co., Chicago, IL, about 7" L, c.1880. **$10-$15**

Flour sifters, one-hand use:

Flour sifter, shaker action, top rim scoop-shaped, tin cylinder with flat bottom, on side is vertical turned wooden handle with wire that goes through handle & down inside to bottom of sifter to make the wire grid that rubs the flour through mesh. An 1892 ad stated, "You have heard of flour sifters that require two hands to operate! That have a round bottom which cannot be repaired! That grind through the sieve any impurities which may be in the flour! That give a handle which interferes with the use of the sifter as a scoop! But have you heard of the new . . . sifter which is free from these objections? Shaking the sifter gently with one hand works the internal mechanism." Shaker Sifter, "Best In the World," mfd. by Sidney Shepard & Co. & C. Sidney Shepard & Co., Buffalo, NY & Chicago, IL, pat'd July 14, 1885. **$20-$25**

Flour sifter, tin, has tubular handle enclosing a squeeze action mechanism like a strength test machine (which it may have become after a few minutes), that pulls the slotted sifter grid across the screen in bottom, 2-cup size, "The Foster," 7" H, pat'd Dec. 1, 1914. **$20-$25**

Flour sifter, tin, lithographed advertising, wooden handle, shaking one-hand action, "Arenzville Bank ... able to do for its customers everything that a good bank ought to do." Mfd. by Erickson, Des Moines, IA, 2-cup capacity, early 20th C. **$15-$18**

Flour sifter, tin canister, screw clamps to shelf edge, perforated mesh bottom, spring tension dasher, 6" H, early 20th or poss. late 19th C. **$20-$35**

Flour sifter, tin, squeeze-handle type like old strength testers, "Foley," 20th C. **$10-$12**

Flour sifters, multiple siftings:

Flour sifter, double-ended, 2 snug lids, funny-looking sifter, white painted tin with name stenciled in blue, almost size of oatmeal carton, screen ball inside, from center of cylindrical body comes tube with wood plug through which is inserted a wire crank, "The Swan's Down Sifter" in blue on body, both lids embossed "R. E. P.," mfd. by Repath-Carver Co., Los Angeles, CA, 9-1/2" H x 4-1/2" diameter, 20th C. **$40-$50**

Flour sifter, tin, 3 layers of screen, "Three screens for triple sifting," squeeze action, but the best part of this sifter is the kitchen scene depicted on side: mother & daughter with doll, & son with baseball mitt. She's serving pie (obviously just made with this squeeze sifter), utensils hang above, we see canisters, checkered floor, venetian blinds on the window, fruit in a bowl on top of the refrigerator, all in red, yellow & white, with a little green, "Androck Handi-Sift," late 1940s patent #2607491. **$12-$15**

Flour sifter, double-ended tin, yellow wood handle, "KWIK," holds 5 cups, 20th C. **$15-$20**

Flour sifter, tin, with green side handle, lids at each end, work it by shaking it back & forth with one hand, "Bromwell's Multiple," Saranac, MI, 7" H, 20th C. **$15-$20**

Flour sifter, tin, double lid (top & bottom) so you can sift twice without removing flour, simply by turning the sifter bottom side up, turned wood handle painted turquoise, "Duplex Sifter," mfd. by Uneek Utilities Co., 6-3/4" H, pat'd 1922. **$15-$20**

Flour sifters, miscellaneous:

Flour sifter, tin, "Hook Aston Milling Co., Flour & Feed, Mills & Elevators," Zanesville, OH, 2-cup size, early 20th C. **$20-$30**

Flour sifter, tin body, cast iron legs, body painted green, 3 feet painted black with gold pinstriping, paper label, 3 cranked blades, screening on bottom of body, label reads, "To use this sifter press down upon the crank; while putting articles in the sifter to be sifted always let the wheel rest upon the bottom." No maker's name, American, 9-3/4" H exclusive of crank, 19th C. **$150-$250**

Flour sifter, tin bucket with 3 long cast iron legs painted black, crank in open top, 3 iron paddles go around against iron screening in bottom, "The GEM Flour & Sauce Sifter," Wells' Patent, Brooklyn, NY (where J. Wells lived, not necessarily where sifter was made), bucket about 6" H x 8" diameter, legs about 5" H, pat'd Dec. 26, 1865. **$150-$250+**

Flour sifter, tin-pail-shaped body, brace inside & crank, 2 paddles inside, 3 cast iron legs, no mark, American, 10" H x 7-1/2" D, 1870s or 1880s. **$100-$170**

Flour sifter, tin, crank in side, "Brite Pride Visible Measure," 20th C. **$7-$10**

Flour sifter, tin, mug style with side crank, green wooden knob on crank, "H. & Hodges," 6-1/2" H x 6" diameter, with 4-1/2" L handle, late 19th or early 20th C. **$10-$15**

Flour sifter, tin & wire mesh in saucepan shape, tubular tin handle & wire crank, "Banner Sifter #15," Saranac, MI, early 20th C. **$18-$22**

Flour sifter, tin saucepan style, woven mesh in bottom, rather nifty spiraling wire in bottom is cranked with knob on open top, American, 9-1/4" D, very early 20th C. My personal favorite. **$7-$12**

Flour sifter, tin, wood crank knob, Bromwell, 3-cup size, 20th C. **$5-$10**

Flour sifter, tin, braced tin strap handle, reinforced rim, side crank with wooden knob, 6" H x 6" D, highly collectible manufacturer "Fries," c. 1910. **$15-$25**

Flour sifter, tin with side crank, "New Standard," 7" H, pat'd Oct. 15, 1918. **$10-$15**

Flour sifter, tin, bracket to attach inside Hoosier-style kitchen cabinet, maker not marked, American, turn of century or early 20th C. **$45-$55**

III-21. Flour sifter bin. *Japanned and decorated tin, in assorted background colors. "Cream City" line of wares by Geuder, Paeschke & Frey, Milwaukee, 1925.* **$135-$175**

III-24. Flour sifter - fruit strainer. *"The Standard," mfd. by Washington Stamping Co., Washington, OH. Detachable bottom and agitator. Pat'd 3/12/1878. 1882 ad in* The Metal Worker. **$75-$100**

III-22. Flour sifters *of the basket type.* **(T)** *The "Handy" scoop, sifter and measure. "The Ladies are Delighted with its Convenience." Handy Mfg. Co., Chicago, 1882 ad. Lower* **(L)** *"Mystic Sifter," with crossbars and wire agitator. "Press the Sifter lightly into the flour, at the same time twist it and it will fill." 6-1/2" diameter. Wire Goods Co., Worcester, MA, 1915.* **(R)** *Called the "Magic" in turn of century catalog. Same maker. No agitator, only crossbar support.* **$15-$25**

III-25. Scoop-rim flour sifters. *All showing innards.* **(1)** *"Victor," tin strap handle, shows crank and the tripart agitator. Joseph Breck catalog, 1905.* **(2)** *and* **(3)** *are same sifters, 6-1/4" H x 5" diameter, shows choice of wood and strap handle.* **(4)** *Copycat of Hunter sifter (see photo) by Savory.* **(5)** *"Shaker Sifter Best In The World," Sidney Shepard & Co., Buffalo, NY. Ripply wires on bottom move back and forth over sieve wire when you shake the sifter from side to side. 1892 ad.* **(6)** *Another shaker sifter — also called a* <u>one-hand sifter</u>. *(2), (4) and (6) all from Savory, Inc., Newark, NJ, c.1925-28 catalog.* **$10-$35**

III-23. Flour sifter patents. **(L)** *Flour & meal sifter, pat'd by C. O. Peck, Pittsfield, MA, 2/13/1877. "A combined scoop and sifter, with crank, reciprocating bowl and sieve, suspended from rods" (the parallel ones going across top). Note the small crank knob partway along handle — it was turned to agitate the sieve;* **(T-R)** *Top crank with tubular side handle, pat'd by Willoughby F. Kistler, Cleveland, OH, 12/9/1884.* **(B-R)** *Basket with T-handle agitator, pat'd by C. F. Wickwire, Cortland, NY, 1/30/1877. This one was almost undoubtedly made because Wickwire was name of a wire-goods company, and would bring* **$65-$95**

III-26. Flour sifters with tubular handles, *and all with scoop rims.* **(T-L)** *"Reliance," with back handle, side crank. 5-1/2" x 6-1/2" x 5". Excelsior Stove & Mfg. Co., Quincy, IL, c.1916.* **(R)** *Very similar one, from Geuder, Paeschke & Frey catalog, 1925.* **(B)** *"Nesco," with crank in handle like the Hunter (see next picture). Also Excelsior Stove Co.* **$10-$25**

III-29. Flour sifters for extra sifting. (L) *"Triple" sifter, 4-cup capacity, 3 stacked screens, top crank.* **(R)** *"Twin-Sift," with double screen to "sift flour two times in one operation." 2-cup capacity. Both are tin, decorated with black bands & handle; ads touted "attractive yellow & black label." Trade name "Androck," mfd. by Washburn, 1936.* **$6-$15**

III-27. Flour sifter classics. *Scoop rims.* **(L)** *Savory "Sift-Chine," tin body, wood handle & knob, side cranked, 1910s-20s.* **(R)** *Famous and classic "Hunter's Sifter," pat'd by Jacob Hunter, Cincinnati, OH, 8/5/1879. Mfd. by The Fred J. Meyers Mfg. Co. after a while, but first by J. M. Hunter, Cincinnati. The inventor described it as a "Perfection Rotary Flour & Meal Sifter, Mixer, Measure, Scoop, Weigher, Rice Washer, Egg Beater, Tomato, Wine, Starch, and Fruit Strainer." 11-in-one combination tool beloved of salesmen and manufacturers, but possibly not used as such by housewives. Inventor claimed shortly after patenting that in six months 200,000 were in use. See price listings for info on the miniature.* **$10-$15; $20-$40**

III-30. Flour sifters. (L) *Cheap tin saucepan style, woven mesh, spiraled wire agitator with crank. 9-1/4" L overall, turn-of-century. Author's.* **(R)** *Tin with mesh bottom, spring tension to crank so that it presses flour through the mesh, screw clamps to shelf. 6" H, early 20th C. Collection of Meryle Evans.* **$5-15; $15-$35**

III-28. Multiple sifters. *Both double-ended, for doing double sifting for lighter cakes. (Triple and even more multiple sifters were available in professional styles of sifters).* **(L)** *"Bromwell's Multiple," patent pending. Medium green wood handle. This one works by shaking back and forth in one hand. 7" H. Author's collection.* **(R)** *"Duplex," light turquoise wood handle, 5-5/8" H x 5-7/8" diam., holds 5 cups. Some marked "Duplex: Ullrich Tinware co., Chicago," some "Uneek Utilities." Collection of Meryle Evans.* **$15-$35**

III-31. Flour sifter & scoop. *"Universal" Scoop with sifter attachment, large letters say "PILLSBURY'S FLOUR," with "UNIVERSAL SCOOP WITH SIFTER ATTACHMENT" in small caps above and below. Sheet iron, wire mesh, wood, in perfect condition. Photograph courtesy of Phyllis & Jim Moffet. Only one known, so rarity as well as the "Pillsbury" name adds value.* **$65-$100**

III-32. Gravy & soup strainers. *Enormous variety of handled strainers, some with perforated bottoms, some with wire mesh of different grades.* **(1)** *Gravy (L) and Soup (R) strainers, from* American Home Cook Book, *1854.* **(2)** *Gravy, from* Warne's Model Cookery & Housekeeping Book, *1868.* **(3)** *Copper, for gravy, high sides, flat bottom, 7 sizes from 5-1/2" to 8" diameter. Henry Rogers, England, 1914.* **(4)** *For soup, tin, 3-1/2" H x 8", tubular handle, Geuder, Paeschke & Frey, 1925.* **(5)**, **(6)** & **(7)** *are "Sterling" enamelware, for gravy, "Handy," and "Soup or culinary," 4-1/4", 4" and 7-3/8" diameter, Central Stamping, 1920.* **(8)**, **(10)** *and* **(12)** *are similar gravy strainers, about 4-1/2", with wood handles, from Matthai-Ingram, Central Stamping and Buhl, c.1890-1912.* **(9)** *"Large soup strainer," tin, perforated bottom, wire handle is 4-1/2" L. Butler Brothers, 1899.* **(11)** *Soup or culinary, 7-3/8", graniteware by Central Stamping.* **(13)** *Copper gravy strainer, conical, 5-1/2" to 8" diameter. Henry Rogers, 1914.* **(14)** *Deep-footed gravy, 4-1/8" or 5-1/4", looks like strainer part has own handle and lifts out. Matthai-Ingram, c.1890.* **(15)** *Tubular, bent handle, tinned wire, 4-3/4" to 8" diameter, note hook. Sexton Stove & Mfg., c.1930s.* **(16)** *Soup, pieced tin, 6" and 10", Matthai-Ingram.* **(17)** *Gravy, tin handle, 4-1/4", Buhl.* **(18)** *Another deep-footed one, with perforated tin bottom — fine, medium or coarse, in 4 sizes from 4-1/4" to 7". D. J. Barry, 1924.* **(19)** *Soup, tin, braced tubular handle, 5" to 10", 12" & 14" diameter, Duparquet, c.1904-1910. Enamelware ones in perfect condition might bring a lot more than high figure here.* **$10-$50**

III-33. Soup strainer or sieve. *Note resemblance to the Mr. Blood's sifter in Fig. III-17. "Kent's Patent," which "will be found most useful for procuring the transparency so much required by fashion in modern soups." Note pouring spout on corner, and the tipping handle at left. Kent manufactured many kitchen tools, including knife sharpeners, for the British market. Many were subsequently im-*

Kent's Patent Soup Strainer.

Kent's Patent Strainer will be found most useful for procuring the transparency so much required by fashion in modern soups.

ported. This one, for example, was sold around 1905 by Duparquet, Huot & Moneuse in NYC as an "English Purée Sieve for passing soups, sauces, etc." **$150-$250**

Wringing Sauces through the Tammy.

Rubbing Sauces through the Tammy.

III-34. Tammy cloths. *Both pictures from* Mrs. A. B. Marshall's Cookery Book, *London, c.1900 edition. Captions are from the book — a book you should look for in antiquarian cookbook dealers for about $100. Tammy is the anglicized French word tamis, a kind of wool or wool and cotton cloth, often glazed, and used, among other things, for these strainers.*

III-37. Jelly bag & stand. *More elegant, with wooden stand having turned knobs at top for easier fitting of the loops of the cloth bag. Called for to make calves foot jelly and other dishes. Urbain Dubois, La Patisserie D'Aujourd'hui, Paris, c.1860s-70s.* **$40-$55**

III-35. Tammy cloth or jelly bag, *with wooden handles. Unseamed strip of heavy coarse crash cloth, probably linen or linen & cotton. Two metal rings hold it to 2 wooden "jump rope" like handles. Put very liquid jelly, sauce or other food in cloth, hold handles and twist to squeeze out excess liquid (if making jelly), or the usable liquid (for sauces needing straining). Fully extended it's 24" L. Beautiful, warm, rusty stained color like a darling Carolina wren. 3rd quarter to late 19th C. Collection of Meryle Evans.* **$65-$100**

III-38. Jelly bag strainers. *Modern types. Wire with cloth.* **(L)** *Two sizes, 6" and 8" diameter, with 3 or 4 legs, removable rim holds cloth. "Androck" by Washburn, 1936.* **(R)** *Two sizes — 12" H or 7" H, both 5-1/4" diameter. Wire Goods Co., 1915.* **$8-$15**

III-39. Jelly strainer. *Pieced tin, with inner conical strainer frame for bag, and lid. Spigot at bottom. It "is made double and filled in with hot water, this heat keeps the mass limpid and a much greater amount of jelly is made from the same materials." American Home Cook Book, 1854. The identical linecut was used in the Duparquet, Huot & Moneuse hoteliers' supply catalog, c.1904-1910.* **$50-$85**

III-36. Jelly bags *plus one filtration bag.* **(1)** *and* **(2)** *are drawings from French scientist Antoine Lavoisier's book on chemistry, late 18th C. The drawings were done by his wife, Marie-Anne Paulze Lavoisier. Monsieur Lavoisier described the conical bag as made of "very close and finely woven woollen." The "point" of the conical bag was to concentrate the draining liquid so that it could easily be caught as it dripped.* **(3)** *A "felt" jelly bag, that's "seamless and strains jelly handsomely." Note ties to attach it to a stand like that seen bottom right. Picture of bag from* American Home Cook Book, *1854.* **(4)** *Very similar, from* Warne's Model Cookery, London, *1868.* **(5)** *Jelly bag & stand, from catalog of William S. Adams & Son, London, c.1860-61. Bags are worth very little without a wooden stand with good patina.*

III-40. Lard strainer. *Two-part, tin, with cup with spout and perforated tin strainer that catches the cracklins. V. Clad & Sons, Philadelphia, c.1890-1900.* **$15-$25**

III-41. Cream skimmer. *Perforated tin, turned wood handle. Nine sizes, from 6-1/2" to 10-1/2" diameter in half-inch increments. Henry Rogers, Wolverhampton, England, 1914.* **$15-$45**

Flour sifter, electric, metal, "The Miracle Electric Flour Sifter. Do not immerse in water." Mfd. by Miracle Mfg. Co., Chicago, IL, 20th C, patent pending. **$30-$40**

Fruit press — See Chapter I (Core, Cut, Chop, Pare and Pit)

Funnel, copper, with filter & brass thumb piece, American, 7" L x 4" D, late 19th C. See funnels and pie birds, Chapter V (Weight, Amount, Size, Time and Temperature). **$28-$35**

Funnel, tin, with brass screen strainer, 7" H, 19th or 20th C. **$10-$12**

III-42. Milk skimmers. (T-R) *with extended-rim thumb handle is pierced with diapered or diamond pattern. Although surely other patterns exist, I found only this one in old catalogs of several makers. 5-3/8" x 5". Both of the other two companies here made this skimmer pattern. The two skimmers* **(L)** *with perforated and unperforated bowls, both with curvy iron handles are 4-1/2" diameter. Geuder, Paeschke & Frey, 1925. Lower plain skimmer is described as having a "deep bowl," but that's relative — to other skimmers not ladles, for instance. 4-5/8" diameter. Matthai-Ingram.* **$7-$15**

III-43. Milk strainer. *Tin bowl, foot fast, with brass wirecloth bottom. 8-1/4", 9" or 10" diameter, also plain one with iron wire, 10-5/8". Central Stamping co., 1920.* **$7-$15**

III-44. Milk strainer buckets or pails. (L) *"The Gem Combination," mfd. by Gem Bucket Co., St. Louis, MO. Steel, with "fine brass cloth strainer which fits into a swag just below the wire in the spout, and is also held in place by the wire clasp at the back of the strainer." It has a "dairy pail bottom," which I take to mean a recessed bottom that protects the bottom from being punctured or dented or dirtied when set on barn floor. 1892 ad. Similar to many such strainer-pourer buckets.* **(R)** *"The Perfect," which "preserves milk from specks and lumps of dirt and dung, and from the atmosphere of the stable, which give the so-called animal odors. It's a seat for the milker; holds 14 quarts; cannot be stepped in nor kicked over by the cow." Dairy Supply Co., NYC. American Agriculturist, 7/1879.* **$15-$40**

Funnel, with attached strainer, which hinges & folds into bowl of funnel, the strainer being fine wire mesh in tin frame like the funnel, used with or without the strainer in place, unmarked, American, 9" L x 3-5/8" D, pat'd Aug. 24, 1875. **$15-$25**

Funnel for vintner, copper, dovetail seam, brass hanging ring, fine gauze to strain out cork debris or whatever might appear in the bottle, stamped "G. E. R.," 9-3/4" L, 19th C. The 3 initials are made with individual letter stamps, which I understand indicates it is probably an owner's initials since a maker would have a stamp in one piece with his own 2 or 3 initials. **$100-$125**

Gravy & soup strainer, tin & wire mesh, tubular handle with ring hanger, American, 6-7/8" diameter, c.1890s. These are ideal for collecting because they are found in so many variations. **$10-$15**

Gravy & soup strainer, cobalt enamelware, elongated oval bowl, turn of century. **$35-$45**

Gravy strainer or sieve, tin with brass screen, prob. American, tapers from 9-1/2" diameter down to 2-1/2", turn of century. **$10-$15**

Jelly bag, unseamed strip of <u>crash</u> (a heavy, coarse linen cloth used for towels), attached by metal rings at each end to the 2 turned wooden "jump rope" handles. Put very liquid jelly in cloth, hold handles & twist to squeeze out excess liquid. Possibly Shaker manufacture, American, 24" L fully extended, mid 19th C. **$75-$125**

Kettle strainer, pierced tin & wire, used to strain contents of preserve kettle when pouring from it, American, 16" L x 10" W, pat'd 1898. **$15-$18**

Maple sugar skimmer, galvanized pierced tin cup has long wooden handle, needed because these were used to skim large pots of boiling maple sugar, American, 55" L, 19th C. Most of these were homemade and modeled after images in mid-19th C. agriculture magazines; I know of only one patented one, but don't know if it went into production. **$65-$90**

Meat press — See Chapter I (Core, Cut, Chop, Pare and Pit)

Milk skimmer, stamped tin, perforations form diamond pattern, rim is crimped & turned & a sort of tab handle formed where rim is widened, American, 6-1/8" L x 5-5/8" W, 19th or early 20th C. **$10-$15**

III-45. Molasses or sorghum skimmer. *Homemade, 29-7/8" L overall, with 5" x 5" aluminum bowl made from oil can. Campbell County, VA, near Lynchburg, c.1920s-30s.* **$15-$25**

III-46. Syrup skimmer. *"For sugar planters." Perforated stamped tin, tubular socket handle meant to be fitted with long wood handle. 11-1/2" diameter. Matthai-Ingram, c.1890.* **$15-$22**

Milk skimmer, tin, for milk or cream, stamped & pierced with perforations in a diamond pattern, hanging hole in thumb handle, Geuder, Paeschke & Frey, Milwaukee, WI, 6" x 6", 19th C. A much older implement for the same purpose was a <u>fleeting dish</u> or <u>flit</u>, a shallow dish with a ring handle. **$6-$8**

Milk strainer, stamped tin, shallow perforated dish, adv'g "Forbes Quality Coffee" in raised letters around rim, 3-1/4" diameter, 4-3/8" L overall with tab, early 20th C. **$7-$12**

Milk strainer, stamped tin, small perforated shallow dish, tab handle, embossed legend "Keep Coming to Fuller's Less Expensive Store," 3-1/4" diameter, 4-3/8" L overall, early 20th C. **$7-$12**

Molasses skimmer, homemade, aluminum sheeting formed & folded to scoop shape, then nailed to wood heel, nail puncture holes filed smooth, long wooden handle whittled to fit into hole of wooden heel of scoop-like skimmer. Dealer had 3, all from same place; one was made from an oil can, partly cut off & nailed to a wooden handle, the other was a large rusted tin can. From old farm home in Campbell County, VA, near Lynchburg, 29-7/8" L, skimmer bowl 5" x 5", c.1920s or 1930s. When I bought this in about 1985, I bought it as a part of my kitchen collection, and because of Campbell connection. Now, with a houseful of folk art and found art, I'm glad I have it for *those* collections. It may not appeal to you, but I really appreciate having items which move along with me as I dance from collection to collection! **$25-$65**

"**Molasses**, or melasses, the gross fluid matter, which remains after refining sugar; and which cannot by simple boiling be reduced to a more solid consistence than that of common syrup, vulgarly called treacle." Anthony Florian Madinzer Willich, *The Domestic Encyclopedia; or A Dictionary of Facts & Useful Knowledge . . .*, 1st American edition, Philadelphia: W. Y. Birch & A. Small, 1803-04. The sugar referred to was at the time one of several cane sugars, beet root sugar or grape sugar. We are familiar with the term **sorghum molasses** because the cereal grain *Sorghum saccharatum,* known for centuries in India, China and Africa, has been cultivated in the U.S. for about 150 years, and a sweet syrup is made from it. Sometimes a molasses skimmer will be termed a <u>sorghum skimmer</u>.

Molasses faucet — Another molasses-related item is a suction faucet used to draw off amounts of molasses. It is geared and made of metal, and when the crank was turned it would in effect pump the gooey mess, "winter and summer, directly into a jug or bottle, without the use of a funnel. ... Free from flies and dirt." Enterprise Mfg. Co., Philadelphia, c.1885. **$20-$35**

Molasses can — This container of japanned tin was a half cylinder with a flat back to fit against wall, and came in 10- and 20-gallon sizes. It has a spigot close to the bottom for measuring out smaller quantities. Matthai-Ingram made these in the late 19th C. Both articles probably more for grocers than housewives. **$15-$20**

Muffineer — See dredger, also sugar shaker

Pea skimmers or vegetable lifters, fanciful wire twistings, some with wood handles, American, vary from about 13" L to 14-3/4" L, c.1870s to 1900. **$16-$25**

> I eat my peas with honey,
> I have did it all my life.
> Not because I like it,
> But it keeps 'em on my knife!
>
> *A child-tickling ditty recited by my grandmother, Grace Campbell Franklin, Memphis, TN every time we had peas*

Potato ricer, or food press, zinc-coated (galvanized) cast iron frame & levered handles, heavy tin perforated cup, "Genuine Kreamer Press," 4" H x 3-3/8" diameter x 11" L including handles, c.1930s. **$10-$15**

Potato ricers — See Chapter I (Core, Cut, Chop, Pare and Pit)

Puréer, nickeled iron, no maker's name, marked "MIL. WISC." & "Pat. Appl." **$15-$20**

Zinc coatings have a peculiar dark gray silvery look quite different from tin coating (which when new is very shiny and silvery), or from nickel plating or chroming. When corroded (by salts in a liquid or air) a powdery white deposit will occur on the surface. See page 35 for essay on galvanizing.

III-47. Wirewares. **(T-L)** *is a combination whisk or vegetable skimmer and "grapple" for a dishcloth to clean lamp chimneys or bottles.* **(R)** *Curved across is a vegetable skimmer or server, also called a pea skimmer. Several sizes, from 4" to 5-1/2" diameter bowl.* **(B)** *is a folding 6-egg rack, for boiling & serving. All late 19th or early 20th C.* **$15-$25**

III-48. Vegetable skimmers. **(1)** *Wire, enameled wood handle, 4-1/2" bowl. Matthai-Ingram, c.1890.* **(2)** *This one 9-1/4" L, "Sherwood," Wire Goods Co., 1915. Other companies made nearly identical ones.* **(3)** *Red wood handle or maroon handle, 9-1/4" L, also Sherwood.* **(4)** *Wire handle 10" L, wire mesh bowl. Sherwood.* **(5)** *Stubby wood handle & spiraled wire, 13-3/4" L, c.1920s-30s.* **(6)** *Wire handle, two sizes — 12" or 18" L, wire mesh bowl. Sherwood.* **(7)** *With bound-wire handle. Called by some dealers a "scroll wire skimmer" for oysters, croquettes & potatoes, in five sizes, from 5" diameter x 16" L to a 14" diameter "pretzel lifter." S. Joseph, c.1927, also Sexton, c.1930s.* **$15-$25**

Salad washer, or **lettuce basket,** wire globe in 2 halves, hinged & with 2 twisted wire grips to hold while swinging around head (is this apocryphal?) or shaking over sink, American, 9-1/2" diameter (but they came smaller and larger), late 19th to early 20th C. **$18-$25**

Other Wire Baskets — Some wire baskets were for gathering eggs; many of those are shaped like barnyard fowl. Another type of wire basket, often mistaken for a salad washer especially now that we have so many foreign antiques imported every year (usually poorly documented), is a snail basket for gathering snails for cooking. They are the same size or slightly larger than lettuce baskets, have a bulging body with narrowed neck and sometimes have a lid. I believe that in today's antique market a high percentage of wire wares are either antique European wares or contemporary reproductions from the U.S., France or Thailand.

Sieve, 2-part tin, like a ricer, perforated concave cup, the presser is convex, has tubular tin handle with a hanging loop, odd & attractive, American (?), about 7" D, 19th C. **$35-$45**

Sieve, woven horsehair, all white, in 2-fingered bentwood frame, possibly Shaker, 9" diameter x 4" deep, 19th C. **$150-$200**

Sieve, woven horsehair & bentwood, fastened with copper nails, pale ivory hair, probably Shaker, 6" diameter, 19th C. **$150-$200**

III-49. Salad washers. *Clockwise from* **(L)***: a "salad shaker" for lettuce, 8", 9", 10", 11" and 12" diameter. Duparquet, Huot & Moneuse, c.1904-1910.* **(2)** *is "French Salad Washing Basket," in 7 sizes from 6" to 12". S. Joseph, c.1927.* **(3)** & **(4)** *Next two are a very popular long-lived ball style, in 7", 8", 9" and 10" sizes. First made by Wire Goods Co., c.1915. Advertised in a 1924 catalog, and in a 1930 magazine subscription premium ad. The ball kind is worth the least, but wire goods are very popular now with collectors. SEE also III-61.* **$20-$100**

III-50. Sieve-makers. *Unidentified early 19th C. illustrations for a book of trades. Man on left is making the bentwood hoops; man at right is sewing and weaving the hair or wire. Print valued at:* **$10.**

Sieve, woven horsehair in black & white plaid, heavily (recently?) varnished wooden frame, unfortunately the varnish even dripped on the horsehair, Shaker-style, 7" diameter, 19th C. though varnish more recent. **$250-$350**

Sieve, woven horsehair sifter, plaid black & ivory hairs, in bentwood frame with original old dark green paint, Shaker-style, 6"

III-51. Purée sieve & syrup strainer. **(T)** *Linecut shows how to "rub the purée through the sieve." To make a "Farce or Purée of Chestnuts.— Cut off the tops of one and a half pounds of nuts and roast them for fifteen minutes, then take off the outer and inner skins and put them to cook in a pan with sufficient light stock to cover them and cook for 45 minutes with buttered paper over, when they whould be quite dry. Pass them through a wire sieve, then mix with a little cream or milk, a pat of butter, a little pinch of salt and sugar, a good tablespoonful of anisette, and colour with liquid carmine to a pale salmon shade, add a dust of coralline pepper, warm and use to garnish entrées. It may also be used cold." Mrs. A. B. Marshall's Cookery Book, c.1900.* **(B)** *Sugar syrup strainer propped on wooden spoons. Urbain Dubois, La Patisserie D'Aujourd'hui, 7th ed., Paris: c.1890. (Illustration 20-30 years older.)* **$30-$45**

III-52. Sieves. **(1)** *Flour sieve, tinned wire mesh bottom, 11" or 12" diameter. D. J. Barry, 1924.* **(2)** *Sugar sieve, brass or iron mesh, 14" diameter.* **(3)** *Footed "hotel purrie sieve," brass mesh bottom, tin frame, 16" or 20" diameter. D. J. Barry, 1924.* **(4)** *Stack of flour and fruit sieves, with cross wires to support the iron or brass mesh, 18" and 20" diameter.* **(5)** *Stamped tin, perforated bottom, 2-3/4" H x 12-5/8" diameter. Excelsior c.1916.* **(6)** *Copper sieve "for Purée" with tin frame, 12" to 16" diameter. Duparquet, Huot & Moneuse, c.1904-1910, hoteliers' supply catalog.* **(7)** *Wood rim flour sieve, wire mesh, 11" or 12" diameter. Butler Brothers, 1899.* **(8)** *Wood frame, iron mesh, 20", Jaburg, 1908.* **$15-$40**

diameter, 19th C. <u>Most valuable are those with the plaid effect</u> achieved by weaving dark & light or white horse hairs. Checkered patterns valued about the same. This one was from the collection of Greg & Linette Salisbury, sold at a James D. Julia auction, Aug. 23, 1989, for $500. The catalog description of condition states that it "*appears* to be excellent throughout, even horsehair webbing is all intact and original." I have seen them with broken or missing strands (they do look as sad as old guitars or violin bows with broken springy strings). As has been proven over and over in 1988 and 1989, original old paint on a supposedly Shaker piece adds a so-far incalculable amount to value. Value determined by plaid and paint. A very large one would bring high range. **$350-$600**

"Purées are fashionable nowadays. A coarse and a fine sieve are needed for purée. The frame may be of wood or strong tin; the strainer of strong wires — coarse netting — being strengthened by two crosspieces of coarse wire. Substance placed in sieve and rubbed through with wooden vegetable masher." Maria Parloa, *Kitchen Companion*, Boston: Estes & Lauriat, 1887. The sieve depicted in her book is quite large, perhaps 24" in diameter, and is set up on wooden frame with short legs. The "catching" pan was slid underneath.

• • • •

Gold Dust Pans — Recently I saw in an 1849 business directory a sieve company advertisement for gold miner's pans. I guess you might find one: look for heavy tin and details in the edging and construction that relate to mid-nineteenth-century construction of other tinwares.

Sieve or riddle, iron wire screening in bentwood frame, fairly crude in construction, possibly used like winnower for separating out chaff, or for mincing cooked root vegetables or potatoes, 12" D, late 19th C. **$18-$20**

III-53. Sink strainers. *Clockwise from center* **top (1)** *"Mrs. Vrooman's," blue enamel ware, wire stand, 8" x 9". It came in 2 sizes and three enamel colors: turquoise exterior with white in; stone gray with mottled white inside, and plain white. It was not depicted well in catalog picture, but it has a press that pivots at bottom and pushes water out of the gooky garbage and scrapings left inside. Emeline B. Vrooman was the patentee in 1896, and she and her husband manufactured them at least through 1904, in Chicago. In 1908 it was made by Andrews Wire & Iron Works, Rockford, IL. Later by Washburn.* **(2-R)** *Next is a simple Mrs. Vrooman's with wire hangers. Best to find with the labels! Washburn Co., Worcester, MA, 1927.* **(3)** *Dark picture but really white enamel of another Washburn.* **(4)** *White enamelware with petal-like perforations, 2-3/4" H x 9-3/4" L or 3-1/4" H x 11" L, Reed Mfg. Co., 1927.* **(5)** *Top left is a wire mesh one from style that came in various combos of galvanized wire and tin, or white or blue enameled, from 2-3/4" H x 9-1/4" L to 2-1/2" H x 10-1/2" L. Wire Goods Co., 1915.* **$10-$45**

Sieves, perforated tin, shallow with slightly sloped sides, look like gold miners' pans, various perforations from coarse to fine, American, various diameters, from about 8" to 12", late 19th C. **$12-$20**

Sifters — See a mixer & sifter in Chapter II; also flour sifters, this chapter. The reason I don't just say "sifters" is that a long time ago ash sifters and starch sifters were commonly known.

Sink strainer, green enamelware with attached brass plate, "Sanitary Under-the-Sink Strainer," by Kitchen Katch-All Corp., Greenwhich, OH, 1930s. **$20-$25**

Skimmer, cast aluminum, flat bowl with many small perforations in concentric rings, long tapered handle with center rib, hanging hole, marked "WSuCL." My computer can't find this in my database of metalware American companies, prob. German, 14" L x 4-3/8" diameter bowl, c.1920s. **$15-$22**

Skimmer, brass bowl, copper rivets to iron handle, American, 11" L handle, 4" D bowl, 19th C. **$50-$65**

Skimmer, brass bowl with iron handle, very nice-looking as are most bimetal implements, American or English, 28" L, 19th C. **$90-$125**

Skimmer, brass & forged iron, handle has heart cutout, copper rivets, American (?), 17-1/4" L, early 19th C.(?) **$400+**

Watch out: If you're paying top dollar for a bimetal skimmer, particularly with a cutout favored by collectors and decorators, you have to be very sure you're not buying a skillful repro or a hearted-up, tarted-up plain old piece. This goes for all bimetal implements. A well-known, reputable, knowledgeable dealer is your second best protection; your own confident knowledge is the first.

Skimmer, brass & iron with only one copper rivet holding handle on, no mark, English (?), 24-1/2" L, early 19th C. **$65-$80**

Skimmer, brass with wrought-iron handle, 12-1/2" L, early or mid 19th C. Actually, brass and iron skimmers & other utensils were made well into the 1880s, probably the 1890s, so you have to judge workmanship, details, wear, style, thickness of brass, etc. **$165-$200**

Skimmer, finely worked forged iron, somewhat deep beautiful bowl with pierced pattern of holes, shaped handle with hook, signed "W. Werntz," Lancaster County, PA, bowl is 5-3/8" diameter, with 13-1/2" L handle, 2nd to 3rd quarter 19th C. **$400+**

III-54. Reproductions of ancient skimmers. *Bronze, in ancient designs found in Pompeian ruins during 19th C. archaeological digs. These repros were made by Fonderie Artistiche Riunite, J. Chiurazzi & Fils — S. De Angelis & Fils, Naples, Italy, 1910-11. That foundry made thousands of reproductions of ancient household items, from firedogs to scales. Skimmer at* **(L)** *is about 15-3/4" L; one at* **(R)** *is about 12-1/2" L. Very easy to get fooled by such things if they're sold as genuine antiquities — or, more likely, as very "fine antiques."*

Skimmers, for sorghum, perforated tin with long wooden handle, American, about 45" to 49" L, 19th or early 20th C. These are often homemade, and those I like best. Look for interesting details or idiosyncracies in the tin scoop part, or carving on the wood, or nifty ways of attaching skimmer to handle; also for skimmers made from old cans such as coffee cans or oil cans. See also molasses skimmer. **$25-$65**

Skimmer, large, very shallow brass bowl with simple large pierced design of tripartite tulip, tapered & polished forged iron handle with hook at end, the hook on same plane as handle, rather than turned under on back of handle, Pennsylvania, bowl 6-3/8" diameter, with 13-7/8" L handle, early 19th C. **$400+**

Skimmer, pierced brass, marked on iron handle, "W. R. Boston," probably maker's initials plus place name, Boston, MA, 22" L, 19th C. **$150-$225**

Skimmer, pierced & engraved brass pan, iron handle, 22" L, 19th C. **$160-$200**

Skimmer, pierced iron with brass trim, long narrow coffin-shaped handle, spoon is quite pear-shaped, handle attached to fat pear bottom end, American, 12" L, early 19th C. **$95-$125**

Skimmer, shallow brass bowl with holes pierced in concentric rings, simple forged iron handle with punched stipple decoration, Adams County, PA, 17" L, 2nd to 3rd quarter 19th C. **$120-$155**

Skimmer, shallow perforated brass bowl, riveted to forged iron handle that widens at end & finishes off with rattail hanging loop, American, 16-1/2" L with 5-1/2" diameter bowl, 19th C. **$135-$160**

Skimmer, slightly ovoid shallow brass bowl, pierced decoration of 6-point star against background of tight concentric rings of round holes, simple forged iron handle riveted to bowl, prob. PA, 23" L, 2nd to 3rd quarter 19th C. **$225-$300**

Skimmer, oak handle, imperfectly cut galvanized sheet metal disc, American, 22" L, mid to late 19th C. **$130-$145**

Skimmer, pieced tin, long tapered tubular tin handle, American, 15" L, 19th C. This kind of utensil, with the well-made, tapered tubular handle, is usually advertised as "Shaker," although that may or may not turn out to be accurate. Many Shaker pieces with this kind of handle also had a fitted brace (called a boss) at the junction of handle and whatever kind of utensil it was, from dustpan to scoop. The term **pieced** is not a typo for **pierced**. "Pieced" means composed of joined-together pieces — in this case pieces of tin. **$55-$95**

III-55. Reproduction skimmers, *in antique styles. Lengths from top: 23", 19", 19", 22", 19" and the sun face is 22" L. These were also sold as chestnut roasters. Mfd. by Pearson-Page, Birmingham, England, 1925. This English company made reproductions of wares from the 15th, 16th and 17th centuries. Their items are even more confusing to collectors now, especially as they are now nearly a century old.*

III-57. Skimmer. *Extremely simple, even crude. Sheet brass, truncated flat handle, simple 8-ray perforated pattern, marked with stamp at end of handle above hanging hole, "B. S. Porter." Although it looks like work of unskilled tinsmith, the person did have a stamp — a sign of someone in business. 13-1/2" L x 5-1/8" W. 19th C. Picture courtesy of the National Museum of American History, Smithsonian Institution. Because of name not beauty, value roughly* **$100.**

III-56. Perforated skimmers & egg poachers. *Three dark ones at* **(T-L)** *are all flat, with different handles. Ridged one at top is a "threaded" handle made strong with the stamped "beading;" next is a hooked "flat" handle; next is enameled wood on "long malleable shank." All in four sizes, from 4" to 5-1/8" diameter bowls. Matthai-Ingram, c.1890.* **(R)** *with curved handle is a "threaded handle egg poacher," 4-1/4" diameter, Lalance & Grosjean, 1890. 2nd from* **bottom:** *One with perforated oval bowl is a "croquette spoon," and at* **(B),** *with coarsely woven wires in metal frame, is a "fried oyster skimmer." Last two from V. Clad catalog, c.1890-1900.* **$10-$35**

III-58. Perforated ladle & spoon. *One with apparently bigger, oval bowl, is a "peculiar dipper, made of a round shallow tin pan, with a long handle, the tin being perforated to drain off the liquid." It is for putting eggs down gently into bath of pickling brine to keep for months. American Agriculturist, 10/1878. Lower one is a perforated ladle with long malleable shank and delicately turned wood handle, in 4 sizes, from 3-7/8" to 4-7/8" diameter. Matthai-Ingram, c.1890.* **$15-$40**

Skimmer, tin bowl with iron handle, 18" L, late 19th C. **$30-$40**

Skimmer, tin bowl with long turned wood handle, 21" L, late 19th C. **$55-$60**

Skimmer, wrought iron, big bowl, with relatively short handle looped at end for hanging, 9-1/2" L, late 18th or early 19th C. **$65-$80**

Skimmer, yellow spatter enamelware with brown handle, American (?) or eastern European, prob. 20th C as color doesn't belong to late 19th C. **$25-$40**

Skimmer & dipper, matched pair, brass bowls, brass shafts, delicate tapered turned wooden handles, American, 15-1/8" L, early 19th C. **$250-$300**

Skimmer & dipper, matched pair, wrought iron, marked "W. Werntz," Lancaster County, PA, 19" L, 19th C. **$250-$350**

Skimmer & fork combined, metal, long handle, for stew or soup, you flipped up the skimmer to reveal the meat fork, good for poking out potatoes & meaty chunks, American, 19th C. **$45-$65**

Skimmer or butter paddle, hand-carved, figured chestnut wood, graining perfectly placed for great visual appeal, deep bowl, American, 5" across, mid 19th C. **$200-$225**

Skimmers, blue enamelware or gray graniteware, in good condition, about 18" to 20" L, turn of century. **$30-$60**

Skimmers & dippers, 5 pieces, all signed, brass bowls with narrow wrought-iron handles tapered at hook or hanging hole ends, some pitted or split, "J. Schmidt" or "John S. Schmidt," Pennsylvania, 19" to 20" L, all are dated: 1844, 1849, 1853, 1854 & 1854. Assembled set: **$900-$1100**

III-59. Strainer spoon & ladle. *Perforated bowls, with choice of handles. 11-1/2" L spoon has "Blutip" (cream with blue tip), green, blue or yellow handle. 11" L ladle (called that in the catalog, though we'd probably assume a ladle shouldn't have holes) in the same handle choices. Both A & J Mfg. Co., 1930.* **$5-$15**

Skimmers for Oil Spills — What's the point of spending thousands upon thousands of hours working on a book if the author can't "file" information in it that she wants to retrieve later!?! The "Magic Mop," mfd. by Pro Diet Mop, Inc., of Belle Chasse, LA, is made of a special plastic that "attracts grease from food like a magnet." It was developed to use in ocean oil spills. Later it was made into mops used to stir hot soup and other food from which grease has to be skimmed or removed. Patent No. 3,748,682.

Soup strainer — See gravy & soup strainers

Spout strainer, tin & wire, for teapot or coffeepot. Perfectly made deep-bowl fine mesh strainer hanging from a sort of springy long hairpin that sticks into end of spout. See also Chapter XIV (Coffee,Tea and Chocolate). 2" diameter, c.1890s. **$12-$15**

Strainer, also called a **pea ladle,** wire with crude wooden handle, bowl made up of concentric spiralling rings of wire, not crisscrossed, American, 13" L x 4-3/8" W, early 20th C. This type of strainer or skimmer with the long handle was used for serving vegetables out of pot likker. They were made from about

III-60. "Chinese" strainers, *in conical shape. (Another is shown in group of gravy & soup strainers.) Many companies had these, all with tin rims, iron handles, and in fine mesh. Sizes from 5" to 9" diameter. (L) has wire braces, from D. J. Barry, 1924 catalog. (R) is older one from V. Clad, c.1890-1900.* **$15-$22**

III-61. Combination salad washer & bowl strainers, *showing how two special bowl strainers with triple hooks opposite handle can be, in effect, hinged together to make a salad washer. Two sizes — 2-3/4" deep x 5-1/4" diameter or 3-1/4" deep x 6". One shown made up as washer has wire-reinforced bowl. Wire Goods Co., 1915. Most likely found singly, but a matched pair:* **$10-$15**

III-62. Strainers. *Three types by Wire Goods Co., Worcester, MA. (T) Round bottom, rigid rest, 1-3/4", 2-1/8", 2-1/2", 3-1/8" and 3-7/8" diameter, fine mesh. (M) Flat bottom, rigid and reinforced, 2-1/2", 3-1/8" or 3-7/8" diameter. (B) "Quality Dripless Strainer," Fine mesh fitted with a nickel-plated brass "drip cup," maroon wood handle. Only 1-3/4" diam., about 5" L overall.* **$5-$10; $5-$10; $15-$22**

the 1870s well into the 20th C. Some had interwoven wires done in various basketweaves, many had beautiful turned wooden handles, others had simple wire handles that were an integral part of the strainer's outer rim. Really nice ones might bring $10 more than price of this crude one. **$12-$22**

Strainer, blue graniteware with white enameling inside, 2 handles, American, late 19th C. **$40-$60**

Strainer, brown marbled enamelware, 8" diameter, late 19th C. **$45-$65**

Strainer, dark blue & white speckled graniteware, with hook on rim for hanging, American, 7-3/4" diameter, late 19th C. **$65-$90**

Strainer, extremely unusual, large perforated shallow bowl, long, "bird beak" or snipe spout off side & 40 degrees further around circumference, turned wood handle, American (?), 13-1/4" L, 19th C. **$175-$225**

Strainer, for milk, tin with brass mesh, meant to fit into milk can top before pouring in contents of milking pail, American, 10-3/4" diameter, late 19th or early 20th C. **$15-$20**

Strainer, gray graniteware, tab feet, 7-1/2" diameter, 19th C. **$55-$65**

Strainer, pierced tin, conical bowl, tubular tin handle with ring hanging loop, could be used with pointed wooden pestle to push pulp of cooked tomatoes (for example) through, leaving seeds & skin inside strainer, American, 17" L x 8-1/2" diameter, late 19th C. **$25-$38**

Strainer, pierced tin, handmade, 11" diameter, 19th or early 20th C. Country, handyman pieces such as this are extremely difficult to date. Only when something like a dateable coffee can, with the lithographed label left on, has been used for the sheet metal, can a confident dating be given. **$20-$40**

Strainer, probably used in dairy, white glazed Delftware, figural bird of type seen in PA German folk decoration, Holland, 6" L, early 19th C. Figurals are extremely rare. Other forms include fish & hearts. **$1200-$1500**

Strainer, tin with wooden handle, "Wheat -?- for Breakfast," American, 13" L with handle, 20th C. **$20-$28**

Strainer, tin with wooden handle, "Ajax," made in at least two sizes, 5" L and 8" L, early 20th C. **$6-$10**

Strainer, turquoise green & white swirl enamelware, poss. "Chrysolite," late 19th or early 20th C. **$65-$90**

Strainer or skimmer, called a **pea skimmer** at the time, spiralled wire with wooden handle, sold by, but not necessarily made by Dover Stamping Co., c.1870s. See also Pea skimmer. **$25-$40**

Sugar shaker or caster, copper container with pierced brass screw-on lid, interesting slanted sides almost look like Arts & Crafts Movement, American (?), 9" H, 19th C. See also dredgers. **$35-$55**

Sugar shaker, decorated figural ceramic, "Cleminson's Girl," The California Cleminsons, CA, mid 20th C. **$40-$55**

Sugar shaker, or muffineer, tin cup with slightly domed perforated lid, strap handle on side, marked "Fries" on bottom, 4" H x 2-1/2" diameter, late 19th C or early 20th. **$22-$30**

Sugar sifter — See dredger, also flour sifter

Tea strainer — See Chapter XIV (Coffee, Tea and Chocolate)

Vegetable strainer, called a **cabbage strainer** by manufacturer, a sort of combination colander & press: a handled pan with perforated bottom, and a pressure plate with lever handle that is pressed against watery vegetables to press out pot likker, then pivoted to other side while dumping food into serving dish, heavily tinned, "New Process," Silver & Co., Brooklyn, NY, c.1890. **$25-$35**

Whatzit sifter, some sort of sifter, possibly an ash sifter, cast metal with odd finish, almost as if it were a baked-on brownish gray paint, 3 short peg feet with cork tips, looks like an old-style something or other made of modern materials, a sort of dustpan pan with 3 walls, scoop-like handle, 15" L, 20th C. **$15-$25**

III-63. "Demountable Bowl Strainers," *with handles and wire frames, shown here with plain and reinforced bowls, maroon wood handles. 5-1/4" diameter for all bowls, which you could also buy separately. Wire Goods Co., Worcester, MA, 1915.* **$10-$20**

III-64. Bowl strainers. (T) *Wire frame fits over "pan rim." In 4 sizes, from 3-7/8" to 6" diameter. Wire Goods Co., 1915.* **(M)** *7" and 8", in simple 4-legged wire frame. Washburn, 1936.* **(B)** *Extension strainer with sliding wire frame, in 5", 6" or 8" diameter. Also Washburn.* **$10-$22**

III-65. Vegetable or cabbage strainer. *"New Process," mfd. by Silver & Co., Brooklyn, NY. This is like a ricer for cooked potatoes. When the press was inverted, and the press part folded back over, the food fell out onto serving dish in a sort of vegetable cake layer or huge steaming hockey puck.* **$30-$45**

PREPARING

IV. FORM, MOLD, SHAPE, & DECORATE

Not only am I late in coming to an appreciation of molds, so were molds late in coming to kitchens. I can't think of a single mold that is necessary in the way a knife, pot, fireplace or stirring stick are. They are for pretty *fer schay*: they gussy up food.

But although I'm late, others have been collecting all kinds of molds for many years. The Renaissance had decorated foods, although I don't believe the fancy copper molds typical of the late eighteenth and early nineteenth centuries were yet in existence. By 1800 or so, households of French, Italian, English, German, Russian (and probably Austrio-Hungarian and Swedish) nobility could count hundreds of copper molds (or "shapes" as the English called them) in their *batteries de cuisine*. When there was a surplus of money, food and servants, and hours spent at the banquet table were considered hours well-spent, no decoration was considered excessive, no frou-frou frivolous. So what if guests only nibbled? The servants or the pigs could eat the leftovers. Confined to noble households until the early nineteenth century, thereafter highly decorated food became fashionable among wealthy merchant and professional classes.

By the last quarter of the nineteenth century, molds were considered necessary in every middle-class kitchen. Chromolithography's advent in the early 1880s meant that cookbooks could have sumptuous, scrumptious full-page pictures showing towering molded and decorated main courses and side dishes. While we might find it intimidating to face a foot-high molded aspic, quivering on its crystal stand, pictures would lead you to believe that the Victorians loved it. It's my feeling that labor-intensive manipulated food was inevitable . . . philosophically related to a fervent Christian belief in the beauty of an ordered universe, within which humans were only doing God's leftover work by forcing everything (animals, furniture, children, clothing, buildings, landscapes . . . and food) to take on shapes, appearances and functions that were unnatural, though "inspired."

In any case, I didn't used to notice molds because they were in with the finer things that I never looked at (furniture, crystal, porcelain), and besides, the more active mechanical things were what attracted me. It's as if molds (including copper molds, ice cream molds, chocolate molds, etc.) had to wait until my attention wandered! If you are a generalist collector, like me, you probably will have experienced this delayed reaction in one area of kitchen collecting or another. The unanswerable but nagging question that's raised is, of course, "How many (fill in the blank) did I miss?!"

Perhaps the major appeal of molds is that **motifs** and **figures** are so common amongst them. There are probably hundreds of thousands of people who collect by motif — squirrels, elephants, cats, frogs, etc. I have tried throughout this book to give background information on motifs, especially information that assists further research. Many paragraphs have a bold motif heading — from stars or birds to palm trees or Kewpies.

Alternatively, the mold category may have such lasting intrigue and appeal because some of the tools used to shape food are also clever **mechanical** inventions that make you admire the inventors. Ice cream dishers are a good example. Some tools are next to useless without the inventiveness and artistry of the cook (such as jaggers for cutting out pastry shapes to decorate pies), but molds give a boost to mundane food without much effort or imagination by the cook — kind of in the way some people wear (or are worn by?) designer clothes.

It would be hard to say what is the most popular subsection in this chapter. Fancy **jelly molds** of copper have been seriously accumulated, if not "collected" as they are today, for at least 75 years, partly because of their house-decoration potential. (All that family of molds are listed under Molds.) **Cookie cutters** have been collected for at least 70 years. You could say 100 or more years, because the women who used them to make fancy holiday cookies also collected them, often on a length of twine hung up on a nail in the pantry. Cutters have recently gained widely publicized attention because of the interest folk art collectors now have in them. Of all specialties, probably only cookie cutters have more women collectors than men, but that is changing.

Butter molds & stamps got a real boost from a book a few years ago by Paul Kindig, who took the subject to a very serious level. Carved wooden **cake boards & springerle molds** have gotten serious attention from high-end folk art collectors. Figural **chocolate & ice cream molds** are widely collected; here in the U.S., this is one of the few kitchen fields where a majority of pieces are European, and are known to have been imports from the start. **Ice cream dishers** or scoops have a dedicated following: astounding prices are paid for rarities, but these aren't one-of-a-kind rarities like handmade cookie cutters because dishers or scoops have been mass-produced since the turn of the century. Their heyday was in the 1920s and 1930s when ice cream parlors were really popular. **Waffle irons** are yet another upcoming field, mainly because of strong interest in all cast iron goods — cookwares as well as decorative pieces such as hitching posts, doorstops, garden decorations, and architectural elements.

Cast iron **muffin pans** and **cake molds** have become part of an established market with strong resale potential and probably even daily price fluctuations, as more and more collectors actively deal amongst themselves. This trend — known throughout all fields of collecting — will increase as more collectors and dealers go online and create international websites. As experienced iron collector Joel Schiff told me, "Iron prices were low and slow for at least 15 years, but have never gone down. Now with the rise in value, the stock of available pieces is 'drying up,' and what might be termed the 'Griswold Feeding Frenzy' has spread to the wares of other companies (Wagner, Sidney, Filley, Wapak, etc.). Prices are rising precipitously."

NOTE: You may want to check the long set of listings under Molds if your mold is fairly deep or big, or if it's made of copper or tin.

PENNSYLVANIA GERMAN/DUTCH BACKGROUND INFORMATION

References to Pennsylvania German motifs, origins, recipes and molds are clarified in the following paragraphs. Incidental information appears with the appropriate listing.

"Pennsylvania German" or "Pennsylvania Dutch." Ruth Hutchison writes an interesting explanation of the "Pennsylvania Dutch" [from Deutsch or German] which I have not read before. "The first of the Plain Sects to sail for Philadelphia in 1683 [from the Low Countries] were the Mennonites . . . followed by the Amish, Seventh-Day Baptists, Dunkards, Schwenkfelders, and Moravians. Later came the Lutherans and Reformed, so that by the time of the Revolutionary War there were so many Germanic people in Pennsylvania it was feared they outnumbered the English. Strictly speaking, there was no Germany in that day, but emigrants from the Low Countries were loosely called Germans, most of them spoke Low German, and the first of their American settlements was called Germantown." p. xi, *The New Pennsylvania Dutch Cook Book,* 1958.

Is it more accurate to use the term Pennsylvania Dutch, or to assume that that is a corruption of Pennsylvania *Deutsch,* therefore that it should be Pennsylvania German? Get Carl W. Drepperd's *A Dictionary of American Antiques,* and look up "Pennsylvania Dutch." In part, Drepperd says, "More misinformation, erroneous claims, and wrong beliefs are current [book was published in 1952 after 10 years' compilation] in respect to the meaning of this term than any other phrase pertaining to American social history and objects that survive. What is now Pennsylvania was colonized by the Swedes and the Dutch half a century before William Penn [c.1680] . . . With Swedes, Dutch, and some Finns in residence on his arrival, Penn offered haven . . . to French Huguenots, Swiss Mennonites, Amish from Flanders, Rhinish Palatinates, Swabians, Danes, Dutch, Walloons, Swedes, and Flemings [who] arrived in the colony from 1630s to 1760s."

Drepperd says that "Pennsylvania Dutch" is more accurate and accuses numerous societies of fostering the falsehood that Pennsylvania folk arts and crafts are purely Germanic. But a *Farmers' Cabinet* of 1836 relates that 54 ships' loads of German emigrants arrived in Philadelphia in just one summer, and tells of a 1750 law prohibiting "importing too many Germans in one vessel," ostensibly to limit overall emigration. In 1677, Penn offered refuge to Quakers in the Netherlands and Germany in what was then western New Jersey, already settled by Swedes and Dutch for decades. Before he had ever seen "Pennsylvania," he invited Quakers from England and Wales to emigrate too.

The 11th edition of the *Encyclopaedia Britannica* states that, "In no other colony were so many different races and religions represented . . . Dutch, Swedes, English, Germans, Welsh, Irish and Scotch-Irish; Quakers, Presbyterians, Episcopalians, Catholics, Reformed Lutherans, Mennonites, Dunkers, Schwenkfelders, and Moravians . . . most now merged in the general type." The *Encyclopaedia Britannica* says that [the language] "Pennsylvania Dutch" is a "corrupt German dialect, largely Rheno-Franconian in origin."

And More. In *The Magazine ANTIQUES,* March 1944, a cover story explained with a note from Gregor Norman-Wilcox that in Pennsylvania of the eighteenth century "German" meant a "composite racial group whose homelands included Germany. Especially, our Pennsylvania-German colonists came from the west-German (Bavarian) Palatinate, lying along the Rhine and neighbor to the Dutch on the north." Norman-Wilcox's use of Pennsylvania-

dutch with a small *d* shows that he means just *deutsch,* not really Dutch nor yet really German.

Early Pennsylvania German Motifs. Frances Lichten, writing in *Folk Art Motifs of Pennsylvania,* NY: Hastings House, 1954, wrote that the early motifs, not just for cookie cutters but for all the decorated arts, included tulips or lilies, hearts, several birds (especially finches, often called distelfink, or thistle finch; song birds; doves; cocks; parrots; peacocks; and eagles), stars, geometric shapes, stags, unicorns, urns, mermaids, cherubs and angels. She explains that the Pennsylvania Dutch only began to make decorated utilitarian wares after several generations spent establishing their farms. "A rough guess, judging by the objects which bear dates, would place this revival of the more decorative aspects of folk life somewhere around 1765." At first traditional motifs were taken from remembered and remaining objects and furniture brought to America from Germany, Switzerland, Moravia and other countries. Lichten explains, "In the first decades of the 19th century [the Pennsylvania German craftsman's] work began to show traces of the period decoration fashionable during the previous quarter century. Although quite out of keeping with the boldness of his traditional motifs, he adopted these ideas, [and] used them as he saw fit . . . ." These adopted motifs included "certain ornamental details high in favor during the Empire period . . . great looped draperies [used] as a frame . . . rococo scrolls," and later, "the symbols of the Romantic period — the classic column, bow-knot, rose, forget-me-not, and wreath." Fraternal orders, such as the Odd Fellows and Freemasons, used the column motif, so lodge decorations may have influenced, over a long period of limited exposure, non-member artisans among the Pennsylvania Germans. See a lot more on this below in "Fraternal Orders: Their Symbols & Motifs," under a butter stamp listing, page 45. **Parrots** are often depicted by the Pennsylvania Germans. The Carolina parakeet, grass green with a bright red head, was once native to Pennsylvania. Unlike some other birds, the parrot was probably not symbolic. **Symbolic Birds**. The cock or rooster was a Christian symbol of vigilance, and an emblem of Christ's Passion; the swan symbolized the Virgin Mary; the peacock represented immortality and resurrection; and the dove was a symbol for innocence, conjugal affection or the Holy Ghost. The symbolisms were not necessarily known or referred to by PA German artisans, but were copied from much older European traditional work. **Other early motifs** include flowers, pomegranates, fish, humans, horsemen, crowns and heraldic animals. All these motifs are found in American eighteenth-century decorative arts, fraktur, taufschien (cut paper documents), etc., and for centuries before that in Europe and Great Britain.

Ableskiver, or Aebelskiver pan — See Ebelskiver pan

Angelfood cake pans — See molds in enamelware and tin sections, in the spouted or tubed listings

Bake molds. Also called baking molds, baking pans, bake pans or baking tins, as well as cake molds or cake pans, muffin pans and roll pans. See also molds, muffin pans and roll pans.

Bake mold, 2 parts, tin, a sort of pie pan, plus a very shallow "pork-pie hat" inset; pan says "sponge mixture." You can put inset pan in 2 positions. "This way up for flans," with inset all the way down & the rim part placed crown up. The second way, crown down, is marked, "This way up for sandwiches." "Green's Two-Way Tin," English, 8-1/4" diameter, registered design #77660, early 20th C. See also the cake pan for making "Mary Ann base." **$30-$40**

Bake mold for gems (a small, shaped muffin), cast iron, 8 shallow cups: leaf, house, rooster, spade, 6-point star, petalled flower, crescent moon & club, plus 3 small diamonds between the rows, newly made but not a reproduction of an old design, sold through Cumberland General Store, possibly marked, 14" L x 6" W, shipping weight with package is 6 lbs, 1980s. **$7-$10**

Similar Bake Molds & Repros. There's an 8-cup cast iron ornamental mold for gems or muffins with a pear, beet, two leaves, an apricot (?), cherries, pomegranate, and a turk's head (whorled, and resembling a turkish turban). Originally made by Schofield Mfg. Co., NYC, c. 1890-1900, the mold cost 75¢. The mold was also made in a 6-cup size, and the flat top frame into which the cups were cast has a scalloped edge that conforms to the cups' outline. A **repro**, with oblong body with a ridge on the edge and fancy handles, was offered by *McCall's* magazine in about 1984 for $16.95. It is 15" L x 7-1/2" W x 1-3/4" deep. In the 1990s, other fancy molds in cast iron were offered mail order from catalogs and include an oblong saguaro cactus pan (15-1/2" x 5-3/4" x 1"); a 6-cup "Tex-Mex" motif pan with star, wolf, cactus, armadillo, pea-pod-like crescent moon, and sun (11" x 7-1/4"); a 7-cup Christmas pan with Santa, bell, tree, star, bow, cherub, and holly sprig (12" x 7-1/2"); and another Christmas one with four reindeer, snowman, tree and sleigh (12-1/2" x 8"). New fancy molds may become collectors' items, so you may want to sock them away.

Bake mold, cast iron, fat fish with overshot under-jaw, especially fat in tail, appears from picture to have hanging hole in tail-end tab, maker not known, found in catalog of Cumberland General Store, 8-1/2" W, shipping weight (with pkg) 8-1/2 lbs, 1980s. **$8-$12. New or Old?** This fish mold may, in a very short time, if well made, look old; they're becoming collectible, but values are still as for "secondhand" wares.

Bake mold, for cookies or little cakes, 12 heart-shaped cups made of rolled-edged strips of tin, each cup separate & riveted to blued steel flat sheet iron, no handle, prob. American, 13-1/2" L x 6-1/4" W, each heart is 2-1/2" L, late 19th C. **$45-$65**

"Royal Hearts. 1 lb. Valentia almonds, 1 lb. 8 oz. beat sugar, 8 oz. flour, 10 eggs and 6 yolks. Beat the almonds fine with yolk of egg; then add the sugar; mix it well with a spatter; keep adding one egg at a time; when beat well up, mix in your flour gently; set tin rims in the shape of hearts, neatly buttered, on paper placed on an iron sheet; fill the rims three parts full, and bake them in a slow oven." Joseph Bell, *A Treatise on Confectionary*, Newcastle, England, 1817. A **spatter** is a stirring implement described by Bell as "made of ash or elm, resembling a large wood spoon, only flat on each side." *Ibid* . Undoubtedly the same wooden tool is the Scottish spurtle. See Chapter II (Mix, Beat, Stir, Churn and Blend).

● ● ● ●

"Queen or Heart Cakes. One pound of sifted Sugar, one pound of Butter, eight Eggs, one pound and a quarter of Flour, two ounces of Currants, and half a Nutmeg grated.

"Cream the butter as in 'Twelfth Cake' [Put the Butter into a stewpan, in a warm place, and work it into a smooth cream with the hand"], and mix it well with the sugar and spice, then put in half the eggs, and beat it ten minutes -- add the remainder of the eggs, and work it ten minutes longer, -- stir in the flour lightly, and the currants afterwards, -- then take small tin pans of any shape (hearts the most usual,) rub the inside of each with butter, fill and bake them a few minutes in a hot oven, on a sheet of matted wire, or on a baking plate, -- when done, remove them as early as possible from the pans." William Kitchiner, *The Cook's Oracle*, London, 1827. By the way, "Queen or Heart Cakes" is correct, although a cardplayer might suspect the "or" should be "of."

Bake mold, professional bakery size, heavy blackened tin, 24 heart-shaped shallow cups in flat tin frame, American, 29" L x 17" W, 20th C. **$55-$80**

Baking pan, tin, rectangular, stamped "Free 49 cent pan with your initial purchase of new Py-O-My Pastry Mix," 20th C. **$15-$20**

Baking pan, tin, small square, "Py-O-My," 1" deep x 7" x 7", 20th C. **$15-$20**

Bake molds & pans — See also bread stick pan, molds, muffin pans

Barley sugar mold, clipper ship design, pewter, 4-1/2" x 5", 19th or early 20th C. **$40-$50**

IV-1. Baking mold, *or backform. Leering man's head — mythological. Copper, 10-5/8" diameter, German, mid to late 19th C. Picture courtesy Waltraud Boltz Auctionhouse, Bayreuth, Germany.* **$300-$500**

IV-2. Baking molds, *of small size, 3" to 4" — for patties or tart cases. Stamped tin. See others farther on in chapter. From A. Bertuch catalog, Berlin, Germany, c.1904.* **$10-$20**

IV-3. Bird's nest fryers. *For molding cooked noodles or shredded raw potatoes into shape of bird's nest, and then deep frying them. Tinned iron wire, 2 nesting baskets with long handles.* **(T)** *Four sizes, 3-1/2" to 6-1/2" diameter. S. Joseph Co., suppliers in NY, c.1927 catalog.* **(B)** *Two sizes — outer bowl 3-1/4" or 4" diameter. Washburn Co., Androck line, 1936 catalog.* **$20-$40**

Barley sugar mold, eagles, 3, cast iron, 19th C. **$40-$60**

Bird nest fryer, tin & wire mesh, 2 nesting bowls, with long wire handles, used by immersing in boiling fat after making a bird's nest of either cooked noodles, julienned or riced potatoes, Androck, from this maker, there was a choice of 2 diameters: 3-1/4" or 4". 1930s. Added value: With its original cookbooklet, add about $5. **$20-$40**

Biscuit cutter, gray graniteware with strap handle, 2-1/2" diameter, 19th C. **$50-$75**

"Cheese Biscuit. 2 oz. of butter; 2 of flour; 2 of grated cheese; a little cayenne pepper, and salt; make into paste, and roll out very thin; cut into shape desired; bake a very light brown, and serve as hot as possible." *Treasure House of Useful Knowledge*, compiled by Henry Scammel, 1891.

Biscuit cutter, rotary or rolling style, tin with wire handle, "Chicago Rotary Cutters," pat'd May 1892. **$40-$50**

Biscuit or cookie cutter, rolling kind that cuts multiples, stamped aluminum with turned wire handle, adv'g "Louella -- The Finest Butter in America," as well as "Gold Seal Flour -- For Best Results," American, 6-1/2" L x 2-7/8" W, c.1920s or 1930s. **$25-$35**

Biscuit cutter, stamped tin, strap handle in hoop shape, marked "Old Gristmill," probably a brand of milled flour, 2" diameter, early 20th C. **$10-$13**

Biscuit cutter, stamped tin with fixed loop handle, Matthai-Ingram, c.1890s. **$6-$10**

IV-5. Biscuit cutter & roll cutter. (L) *Tin, rolls out 4 biscuits with each full revolution of wheel, wire handle, 8-3/4" L, early 20th C. Author's collection.* **(R)** *Tin roll cutter with wooden handles, to cut rolled dough into long rolls. Makes 14 rolls each revolution. Roller is 11" L overall and makes rolls 5" L. From Mennonite boarding house, Olley Valley, PA, 19th C. Collection of Meryle Evans.* **$18-$45**

IV-4. Biscuit cutters. *All stamped or pieced tin except 2nd row left, which is "Mirro" aluminum. All are between 1-1/2" and 3" diameter. (L) to (R), row by row from top, #1 to #10.* **(1 & 2),** *1-1/2" to 2-3/4" diameter, S. Joseph, c.1927.* **(3)** *Savory Tinware, Newark, NJ, c.1926-28.* **(4)** *Aluminum Goods Mfg. Co., Manitowoc, WI, 1927.* **(5)** *Geuder, Paeschke & Frey, Milwaukee, WI, 1925.* **(6)** *Sexton Stove & Mfg. co., Baltimore, c.1930s.* **(7)** *and* **(9)** *Fluted edges & plain circle, Matthai-Ingram, Baltimore, c.1890 catalog, pat'd 10/15/1889.* **(8)** *Pick-Barth jobbers' catalog, 1929.* **(10)** *Deep, commercial one, 2" or 2-1/2" diameter. Pick-Barth.* **$10-$20**

IV-6. Biscuit cutters. *From top:* **(1)** *Scalloped pieced tin, heavy duty strap handle, 2" diameter, late 19th or early 20th C.* **(2)** *Rolling aluminum & wire one, advertises "Loella - the Finest Butter in America" and "Gold Seal Flour — For Best Results." Words embossed. 6-1/2" L x 2-7/8" W, c.1915.* **(3)** *Embossed stamped tin, wire handle. "White Lily Flour Has No Equal." 2-1/4" diameter, mfd. by Metal Specialty Mfg. Co., Chicago, c.1910.* **$8-$20**

Biscuit cutter, tin, long fat tubular handle, closed on top & stamped: "Rumford Yeast Powder," 4" H x 2" diameter, (others measure 4-1/2" H), turn of century. A very similar one was offered by Horsford's Baking Powder. It had a removable small cylinder inside for cutting "crullers" (doughnuts). **$22-$30**

Biscuit cutter, tin & wire, "Cottolene" (a cottonseed oil shortening), Chicago, IL, early 20th C. **$10-$15**

Biscuit cutter, tin with scalloped or fluted edge, strap handle. Older ones are composed of 3 separate pieces: cutter body, its soldered-on corrugated cutting edge, & a strap handle. Newer ones have stamped one-piece body & soldered-on strap handle, various makers of these in 19th C, including most big tin houses, but most aren't marked, American, between 2" and 3" diameter, came in various sizes, c.1870s to 1910s. **$12-$20**

Biscuit cutter, turned wood, knob handle, very thin cutting edge, traces of original white paint, American (?), 2-1/2" diameter x 5-1/2" L, could cut 3" thick dough, 4th quarter 19th C. **$22-$30**

Biscuit cutter, tin with wire finger loop, stamped with advertising message, "White Lily Flour Has No Equal," Metal Specialty Mfg. Co., (the flour from Conrad Becker Milling Co.), Chicago, (mill in Red Bud, IL), 2-3/4" diameter, early 20th C. **$10-$15**

Biscuit cutter & pricker, tinned iron, quite sharp edged, tall, turned wood handle painted black, 3 wires come out of ferrule on handle, American, 6-7/8" H, makes biscuit 2-7/8" diameter, 19th C. **$30-$40**

Biscuit cutters, nested set of 3, stamped aluminum, they snap together thanks to the 2 nifty little half-round tabs punched up on top of each one as handle, "Calumet Pastry Cutter," mfd. by Wearever, 1-1/2", 2-1/4" and 3-1/4" diameter, 1931 patent #1797859. Watch out for a snapped-off tab. **$18-$22**

Biscuit cutters, nested set of 9, crinkle-edged cutters, in tin box stenciled in blue, "Veritas. Made in Italy for G. M. Thurnauer Co., Inc.," a big wholesale house, in NYC, that sold mostly imported European kitchenwares, from 1" to 3" diameter, turn of century. These are often sold as "toy" cutters, and as such are priced high. New sets in round tin boxes are still sold in kitchen supply houses. **$25-$35**

"Common Gingerbread. -- A pint of molasses. One pound of fresh butter. Two pounds and a half of flour, sifted. A pint of milk. A small tea-spoonful of pearl-ash, or if it is strong. [Sic. No indication what is the choice if "it" be strong .] A tea-cup full of ginger. -- Cut the butter into the flour. Add the ginger. -- Having dissolved the pearl-ash [an early baking soda, with which the molasses would react] in a little vinegar, stir it with the milk and molasses alternately into the other ingredients. Stir it very hard for a long time, till it is quite light.

"Put some flour on your paste-board, take out small portions of the dough, and make it with your hand into long rolls. Then curl up the rolls into round cakes, or twist two rolls together, or lay them in straight lengths or sticks side by side, and touching each other. Put them carefully in buttered pans, and bake them in a moderate oven, not hot enough to burn them. If they should get scorched, scrape off with a knife, or grater, all the burnt parts, before you put the cakes away.

"You can, if you choose, cut out the dough with tins, in the shape of hearts, circles, ovals, &c. or you may bake it all in one, and cut it in squares when cold. If the mixture appears to be too thin, add, gradually, a little more sifted flour." Miss Leslie, of Philadelphia, *Seventy-Five Receipts for Pastry, Cakes, and Sweetmeats* . Appended to *The Cook's Own Book and Housekeeper's Register . . . ,* by a Boston Housekeeper. Boston: Munroe & Francis, 1833.

Biscuit or cake cutter, pieced tin, outer cylinder has inner cylinder with screw-on cap, spring wire coiled loosely around that, pusher plate on bottom, high arched strap handle. The pusher plate retreats up inside depending on the thickness of dough, but spring serves to push dough out. Cap screws off to fill inner cylinder with flour so that it continually dusts cutter as you spring your way through a sheet of rolled dough. (Nice home for insects if you didn't clean it often.), marked "D. S. Co.," Dover Stamping Co., Boston, MA, 2-7/8" diameter & almost that deep, pat'd, poss. May 19, 1868. **$50-$65**

Biscuit or cookie cutter, round, metal, adv'g "Malleable Range," Engman-Matthews Range Co., South Bend, IN, 1-1/2" D, turn of century. **$6-$10**

Biscuit or cookie cutter, stamped, pieced tin, round deep cutter with great 3-D egg-shaped knob handle that's as long as cutter's diameter, 3 air holes, embossed "Egg Baking Powder" on the egg, Chicago, IL, 2-3/4" H overall x 1-15/16" diameter, cutter itself is 1-1/4" deep (also found 2" H x 2" diameter, 1" deep), c.1902-1905. **$65-$100**

Biscuit or cracker cutter & pricker, heavy tin with nail-like prickers inside, slightly convex cap to fit comfortably in palm, one mfd. by Fries, other tin houses made them too, American, 1-1/2" deep x 2" diameter, late 19th or early 20th C. **$55-$100**

Biscuits. A notice in the 1837 *Journal of the American Institute* (NY: T. B. Wakeman) about Pierce's patent kitchen range, manufactured by Lockwood & Andrews, NYC, and awarded a premium at the 9th annual Fair (Oct. 1836) of the American Institute, includes a biscuit treat: "This article [the range] attracted a great attention at the Fair, and was kept in constant operation. On the sixth day of the Fair, Mr. Pierce [S. Pierce of Troy, NY] provided a dinner, and cooked in it for between fifty and a hundred gentlemen, at Niblo's. Among the articles presented at this repast, were several fine biscuits, made and stamped in twelve minutes from the sheaf! That is, the wheat in sheaf was threshed, winnowed, ground, kneaded, baked, rolled, stamped, and pricked, in the incredibly short space of twelve minutes!"

IV-7. Biscuit or cracker stamp. *Mechanical, cast iron, spring steel with wooden block fixed with little 2-pronged prickers. Spring-load action, this knocks out pricked biscuits or crackers just short of 2" square. Stamp is 3-3/4" H. Pat'd December 13, no year marked, but patent Tuesday the 13th came in 1870, 1881, 1887, 1892 and 1898. I think probably 1880s. Collection of Meryle Evans.* **$70-$100**

133

Biscuit or cracker pricker, wooden knob handle with sturdy metal teeth in pattern, American, 4" x 3-1/2", 19th C. **$65-$100**

Biscuit pan, & matching cutter, rectangular brown & creamy white enamelware tray with raised edge & 12 round slight depressions, also enameled biscuit cutter with strap handle, "Onyx," Columbian Enameling & Stamping Co., Terre Haute, IN, 10" L, c.1915. **$100-$150**

Blancmange molds — See molds, especially the copper and tin ones

Border molds — See molds, especially tin

Bouche iron, also what was later called a **patty** or **timbale iron**, cast iron with iron shaft ending with wood handle, at right angles to shaft is screw-on bouche iron, shaped like a small cupcake (fluted, corrugated or plain). The iron was used by dipping it in bouche batter to coat the bottom and sides of the iron, then quickly dipping it in deep hot fat to make a little fluted shell or case for stuffing with crab meat salad or other ladies' delicacies. Skilled users could dip the forms of an entire mold to just the right depth in the batter, and so make 4 cups at a time.

American, or French import, about 8" to 10" L, c.1870s-1890s. Much more recent ones were made at least into 1950s. New ones: $8-$12; Old: **$35-$50**

Old & New. The older bouche irons have nicely turned wooden shafts, decorative ferrules and nice turned wooden handles: everything seems carefully machined and decoratively designed. Newer ones, including some from the 1920s and later, have the simplest forms. Most conspicuous is the iron rod shaft with a right angle bend and machine screw threading on the end. These are often seen at fleas, but the old ones are the real prizes. **From Thailand** comes a similar device, with longish wood handle & 2 brass heads (one a small fluted cup, one a corrugated cup) which are dipped in hot oil, then in batter, then back in boiling oil. The 2 little pastry cups "float away" from the mold, according to *The International Cooks' Catalog*, NY: Random House, 1977.

• • • •

Bouche or Dariole Batter. "Take two tablespoons of flour, drop two eggs into it, and mix with enough milk to make a batter, similar to fritter batter. Heat iron in boiling lard; then dip Iron into batter, take out and leave on Iron till batter drops off." Recipe accompanying the linecut of a tool that appears twice in an 1886 F. A. Walker catalog, under the names <u>Bouche Iron</u> as well as <u>Dariole Iron</u>.

IV-8. Border molds, *also called* **ring molds.** *For forming rings of one kind of food (such as rice or a salmon mousse) around another kind or color. These are all pieced tin. "Plain" came in rounds from 5-1/2" to 9-3/4" diameter, and in ovals from 6-1/4" to 10-1/4" L. "Concave" in similar but slightly smaller dimensions. "Savarin" came in rounds, from 1-1/2" to 11-3/4" diameter, and in ovals, 6-1/4" to 11-3/4" L. It was used for making a Savarin cake, soaked in spirits while still warm, but served cold with a cold sauce. Hexagonal "Corenflot" came 3-1/2" to 10" diameter . Duparquet, Huot & Moneuse jobbers' catalog, c.1904-1910.* **$15-$35**

IV-9. "Breton" border mold. *Six lobes, offered in two sizes (not given, but probably about 7" and 10" diameter). One page of "moulds for entrées, sweets, savouries, &c." Mrs. A. B. Marshall's Larger Cookery Book of Extra Recipes, London, c.1902. Mrs. Marshall, in addition to writing cookbooks, had a cooking school, and a large shop for culinary tools. Her books all have advertising pages in the back, all identified as coming from her "Book of Moulds"— a catalog of 68 pages. One mold dealer in NYC has seen a large book of moulds; cookbook dealers here and in England have turned up only one much smaller one. The search continues. For the mold:* **$25-$45**

IV-10. Border molds. *All "imported tin." Clockwise from top (**L**):* **(1)** *Came in rounds, 8" or 8-3/4" diameter, or ovals, 10-1/4" or 11" L.* **(2)** *Rounds in 7", 8" or 8-3/4" diameter, or ovals, 7", 8" or 22" L.* **(3)** *Oval only, 5-1/2", 6-1/4" or 7" L.* **(4)** *Round only, 7", 8" or 8-3/4" diameter. Note in last one, especially, how one color of food could be pressed into the knurled knobs on top. All from Duparquet, Huot & Moneuse catalog, c.1904-1910.* **$35-$75**

IV-11. Covered border molds. *Metal not mentioned — could be stamped tin or stamped copper that's tinned inside; probably tin.* **(L)** *2-quart.* **(R)** *3-1/2 quarts, fruit wreath design, lid not shown. S. Joseph Co., c.1927. The copper mold value would be two or three times as much as tin:* **$35-$45**

Bread baking mold, deliberately blackened tin, small isinglass window, hinged double loaf pan looks like 2 bombs or blimps lying side by side, or some kind of odd bivalve mollusk, "Ideal", mfd. by Matthai-Ingram Co., Baltimore, MD, 3-1/4" H x 12-1/2" L x 5" W (twice that for the double ones), stamped with patent date near little catch: Aug. 3, 1897. This item also came in single-loaf size. Original advertising claimed, "Makes a crisp, moist and wholesome loaf a certainty . . . The bread is more nutritious, more tasty, and more digestible. Professor Morse, of Westfield, NJ, says bread baked in the Ideal . . . is a remedy for dyspepsia and of the highest nutritive value." **$35-$50**

Bread baking mold or pan, blackened tin, 4 trough compartments for French bread loaves, early 20th C. **$15-$25**

Bread loaf pan, cast iron, single loaf, Griswold #961. **$1000**

Bread loaf pan, cast iron, double loaf, Griswold #960. **$500**

Bread pan, cast iron, hinged 2-part pans, dated 1879. **$30-$40**

Bread pan, oblong blackened sheet iron, called <u>Russia iron</u>, folded corners, rolled rim, slanted sides, very substantial, ring handle at both ends, one kind was "Beaman's Patent," mfd. by Matthai-Ingram Co., 4" deep x 18" L x 12" W at top, late 19th C., into early 20th. **$15-$25**

Russian iron, **Russia iron** or russia iron is a form of planished wrought iron used for roasting, baking and dripping pans. According to Elsie Hutchinson, in a book to instruct department store employees titled *The House Furnishings Department*, 1918, it is a "special grade of sheet iron with a glossy black, slightly mottled appearance due to oxide adhering to the surface; it is produced by passing a pack of heated sheets back and forth under a steam hammer, the bit and anvil of which have indentations on their surfaces." It originated in Russia and had an almost purple appearance, according to nineteenth-century books.

IV-12. Bread dockers. *Used to mark bread before baking.* **(L)** *Tin & wood, in 6 sizes, from 2-1/2" to 5" diameter.* **(R)** *"We make our bread dockers of a very heavy grade of tin, so that the letters will positively stay in place. We make these dockers in any shape and of any number of letters. They cost according to the number of letters." Both from Jaburg Brothers catalog, NYC, 1908.* **$15-$50**

IV-13. Bread pan or baking mold. *"No. 140," in corrugated spiral shape "which gives the finished baked loaf a peculiar but appetizing appearance, the bread or cake may be sliced through the indentations." XX imported tin plate, 12-1/2" x 3-1/2" diameter. Silver & Co., Brooklyn, c.1900 - 1910. A similar one, "The Ideal," which came in single or double loaf size, was blackened tin, without the corrugations. They're almost same value.* **$45-$65**

Bread stick pan, riveted tin, 12 compartments, "Kreamer," August Kreamer & Co., Brooklyn, NY, early 20th C. **$15-$22**

Bread stick pan, cast iron, makes 22 bread sticks, 11" x 11" side by side, design based on old pan, sold through Cumberland General Store, but may not be marked, American, 12-1/2" L x 7" W, 1980s. **$8.50-$10**

Bride & groom cake dolls, crpie doll figures, dressed in white & black crepe paper outfits glued to them, standing on flat hockey-puck disc or or pillbox base, with heart-shaped trellis over them made of cloth lily-of-the-valley flowers, no maker, American or German (?), dolls 3" H, 6" overall height x 3" diameter, c.1930s (?). **The kewt Kewpies** (take-off on "cute cupids") were created by artist Rose O'Neill about 1915 and became ex-

IV-14. Bread stick pan & confusable molds. (T) *Wagner Ware Style E, cast iron, for 11 bread sticks. From 1915 Wagner catalog, Sidney, OH.* **(M)** *and* **(B)** *Both of these are solder molds for plumbers to use. Made of cast iron, and while size is not given, they are about 7" to 14" L, and were used to make sticks of lead solder. Both apparently cast by C. S. Osborne & Co., Newark & Harrison, NJ. That foundry also made can openers, meat choppers, tools, oyster knives, kitchen furnishings, nutcrackers, nutpicks, sardine scissors, and cheese scoops, from about 1890 to c.1920. Pictures in Alfred Revill's* American Plumbing, *NY: 1894.* **$25-$45**

IV-15. Bride & groom figures. *One of many fancy designs shown in a confectionery tools & supplies catalog. Materials not given, but probably silk flowers, molded & painted plaster or bisque figures & base. Dressed in cloth & paper clothing. 9" H x 4" W. From Joseph Middleby Jr., Inc., Boston, catalog, 1927. They also had designs with the couple in autos or blimps, also birds, bells, bowers, and clasped hands.* **$45-$85**

tremely popular. O'Neill licensed German doll manufacturers to make Kewpies plus hundreds of thousands of hankies, jewelry, banks, post cards, etc. O'Neill did Kewpie art for Jell-O and for smaller local dairies such as Hendler's in Baltimore, and there's lots of crossover interest today. Condition very important with easily breakable celluloid figures. **$30-$50**

Bride & groom cake dolls, bisque, painted & dressed in real cloth clothes, American (?), 4" H, 1940s.

Futurewatch. This is an undervalued collector field, offering a huge variety over a period of at least 100 years. A nice addition to a collection of them would include the arches and altars, as well as photographs of decorated wedding cakes in bakery windows. In the Jan. 25, 1989 *Antique Trader*, there was an appealing ad for 50+ sets from the 1920s on. They were from Japan, Occupied Japan & the U.S., and the dealer, Shirley Rice, had them priced $15 to $35 per set, or $650 for all. **Black Americana**. I have not seen African American bride & groom dolls that appear to date before the 1970s. This would be a good specialty area — especially dolls with "Afro" styled hair from the groovy '70s. I'm sure that older ones must exist but must be rare. I'd say their value would generally be higher than "white" dolls. I assume there may be Oriental versions from after WWII: have you seen any? **Get 'em while they're hot**. Many bakeries and pastry shops seem to have the same tired old brides and grooms year after year. Keep an eye on them; you might be able to buy old pieces or trade for some brand new ones **$35-$55**

Bride & groom cake dolls, cast & painted plaster of Paris, lacy filigree base, flower arch, glass & plaster bell above heads, American, c.1910 to 1920. **$35-$50**

Bride & groom cake dolls, molded plaster of Paris, painted with black, white, pink, also pearlized white paint on bride's headdress & bodice, American (?), 5" H, dated 1948. **$10-$15**

Bun cutter, rolling pin cutter, tin, turned wooden handle, 18 iron blades set in large diameter cast metal roller, cuts 18 buns with each revolution of the sectioned drum, "Millers Bun Divider," (possibly mfd. by Charles E. Miller Co. See the meat tenderizer in Chapter I), Milwaukee, WI, roller 7" diameter, blades 6" W, pat'd Feb. 1907. **$65-$100**

A **Revolving Chip Cutter** is a similar implement, on a smaller scale, with 2 turned wooden handles and a 3" W tin revolving cutter divided into eight sections, 3" x 2". Rolled back & forth & crosswise ir would make chocolate chips from blocks. This tool found in Dec. 1925 *Sethness Candy Maker,* Chicago.

IV-16. Kewpie groom & bride. *Pink celluloid or other plastic, paper & real cloth clothing. From Middleby catalog, 1927. Condition is all.* **$30-$50**

Bundt cake mold or bundt pan, cast iron, cobalt blue enamel, American or German, 10" diameter, early 20th C. or late 19th. **$200-$400**

Bundt cake mold, cast iron, large scallops alternating with sharply-defined zigs (zags?), conical spout, American, 12" diameter, 19th C. **$100-$200**

Bundt: The German word relates to the word for band or bundle, and refers to the banded effect of the flutes (such as would be found in a wheat sheaf or straw wreath, tied at intervals with twine). It probably originated as a harvest celebration cake.

● ● ● ●

Bundt Pan Progenitor. The well-known cast aluminum bundt pan, alternating 8 large scallops with 8 small pointed flutes, first made in 1949 by Northland Aluminum Products of Minneapolis, MN, was a reproduction of a nineteenth-century European cast iron bundt pan, reportedly brought over by a European immigrant to Minnesota. Northland has now registered "Bundt" for their own use. It is not known how long ago the first bundt pan was made, probably in ceramic.

● ● ● ●

Lookalike alarm. Lehman's Hardware & Appliances, Kidron, OH, offer a spouted bundt pan, 10" diameter, with 2 handles, in their "Non-Electric Good Neighbor Amish Country" catalog. They say that all their cast iron is "produced in a family foundry — Lodge, in South Pittsburgh, TN — dating back to 1896," and that all are sand cast and "finished by hand."

Bundt cake mold, spouted, redware with green & orangey red glaze, American, 7" D, 19th C. **$150-$200**

Bundt cake mold, earthenware with brown glaze, spouted, fluted sides, crack mended with twisted wire, wire all around rim too, German or Austrian, late 19th C. From the looks of the wire around the rim you might almost assume that these pans were sold with wire bindings to hold them together in case of bustin' in the oven. What a mess! **$200-$400**

Bundt cake mold, finely cast iron with wire bail, open spouted, Griswold Mfg. Co., #965, 4-1/2" H x 9-1/2" dia., 1st third 20th C. **$900-$1100**

Bundt cake mold, cast iron, bail handle of type called a <u>stop bail</u>, a sort of ear that would would allow the bail to fall only on one side and on the other side to be held rigid for tipping. This would make it much easier & safer to tip pan over to release cake. A stop bail of one form or another was used on many kinds of heavy cast hollowwares. Frank W. Hay & Sons, Johnstown, PA, pat'd Mar. 10, 1891. Except for marks, this looks just like the Griswold bundt pan. **$300-$400**

IV-17. Bundt cake mold. *Called by them a "Style B" mold. Cast iron, spouted, 10" diameter, Wagner Ware #310, c.1915 - 1940. All bundt pans are similar; the earliest were imported from Europe in the 19th C. Value depends on size and quality of casting — and sometimes on the "name brand." Overall value range for such molds is $45 to over a thousand dollars for a 9-1/2" bail handle Griswold bundt pan. This Wagner:* **$125-$200**

Bundt cake mold, cast iron, scalloped, solid tapered cone in center (where otherwise a closed spout or open tube would be), German or other European origin, 10-1/2" D, 19th C. **$200-$300**

Bundt cake mold, cast iron, tubed, very exaggerated flutes & scallops, very deep, signs of real wear, not marked, American (?), about 11" to 13" diameter, 19th C. **$100-$200**

Bundt cake mold, gray & white mottled graniteware, American (?), 13" D, 19th C. **$115-$155**

Man- & Machine-Made Butter Hands. Factory-made butter hands are relatively cheap: they look machine-made, with fairly crudely finished off beveled edges and perfectly regularly spaced corrugations. They also are flat-backed. Handmade ones have the appearance of being lovingly made, carefully smoothed and finished, and often with somewhat convex backs. Pairs don't tend to match exactly. They bring three to four times as much money as factory made ones.

Butter curler, steel & wood, curved "J" corrugated blade set in wood handle, 8" L. Used by dragging across cold butter block, to make a shallow "peel" that naturally curled. **$12-$18**

Butter hands, also called **Scotch hands,** corrugated wood, usually maple, well-made & usually satiny from use, American, between 8" and 9" L and 2-1/2" and 3" W, even 4" W, 19th C. I used to think these were pretty much all the same but now I can report differences. Although most are within small size range, there are things the connoisseur of Scotch hands can look for. Instead of a lighter weight, dull wood, wide grooves, seek out

IV-18. Butter curler. *Nickel-plated, wooden handle, 8" L. From Ritzinger & Grasgreen catalog for traveling salesmen, c.1906-07.* **$5-$15**

IV-19. Butter hands, *also called* **Scotch hands***. Corrugated French boxwood, or rock maple, commercially made, and this is not a matched pair. 9-1/2" L x 2-1/2" W. Late 19th C. or early 20th C.* **$20-$30**

heavier wood, pale golden satiny patina; instead of machine carved regular corrugations, look for carefully hand-carved grooves; instead of pattern-cut simple paddle handles, look for more artistically formed ones, especially those that are flat on corrugated side where they must fit together, but are curved on their backs. I even like slightly mismatched pairs, perhaps perversely. Nice wooden butter hands are still being manufactured. Price for pair of hand-carved ones: **$50-$100**

"A **pair of creased wooden hands**, for making butter balls, should be included in the outfit of the kitchen. With a little practice, butter may be shaped in many pretty forms, so that the dish will look very nice on the table. Be particular to select hands with fine grooves -- much better results than coarse." Maria Parloa, *Kitchen Companion*, Boston: Estes & Lauriat, 1887. "**How To Use Butter Hands**. -- Let stand in boiling water for five minutes. Next put in cold water for five minutes or longer. Must be cold when used. Have large bowl half full of cold water. Cut some firm butter into pieces about the size of a hickory nut. Roll these pieces between the butter-hands into any shape you please -- grooved balls, little pineapples, scrolls, etc. Dip the hands frequently in ice water." *Ibid.*

Butter hands, finely corrugated sycamore, backs of paddles convex in section, good patina, handmade, American (?), 8-9/16" L, mid 19th C. **$50-$100**

Butter hands, machine-made corrugated wood paddles, for rolling butter balls, American, 9" L, late 19th or early 20th C. **$20-$35**

Butter mold, acorn & oak leaves, plunger type, factory-made, lathe-turned case & plunger, American, 1-7/8" D, late 19th C. **$75-$95**

Butter mold, bee, large carving on round stamp, fits into turned wood mold, plunger type, turned & carved wood, marked "Germany," 3-1/2" x 1-1/2", 20th C. **$35-$45**

Butter mold, box & plunger type, wood with nickeled brass hardware, imprints "JERSEY," early 20th C. **$85-$100**

Butter mold, cow, incised carving, cylinder with pewter bands, hexagonal shape, American, 4-1/2" H x 3" diameter, 19th C. **$200-$300**

IV-20. Wooden butter tools. (T) *"Mrs. Bragg's" butter fork, maple, 12" x 5". Montgomery Ward catalog, 1895.* **(M)** *Butter spades, plain & grooved. The grooved one is the same as a butter hand. Joseph Breck agricultural supply catalog, 1905.* **(B)** *Butter ladle with hooked handle. Duparquet, Huot & Moneuse, c.1904-1910. Patina of wood determines value.* **$20-$50**

Butter mold & stamp collecting tips. Do you call them "molds" or "stamps"? Technically, a butter mold is a form for butter (quarter or half pound, pound or two pound) and may in addition decorate the top surface. Box molds and plunger molds are the two basic types. Most collectors call the decorated plunger part of the mold a butter mold, but it could also be called a butter stamp. In the listing of makers, no distinction was made between molds, printers and stamps. **Butter Mold Manufacturers.** In the1905-06 Buyers' Guide of *Thomas' Register of American Manufacturers*, I found a few butter mold makers listed under molds. And though not broken down that way, there are probably others to be found in Thomas' section on woodenware too. The makers are: Robert E. Turner, Lebanon, CT; Creamery Package Mfg. Co., Chicago, IL; Freeman Mfg. Co., Kalkaska, MI; Ludington Woodenware Co., Ludington, MA; A. H. Reid, Pittsburg, PA; Vermont Farm Machine Co., Bellows Falls, VT; Moseley & Stoddard Mfg. Co., Rutland, VT; and Cornish, Curtis & Green Mfg. Co., Fort Atkinson, WI.

Machine made? You can see the concentric rings, especially inside the case, that are the mark of the tools used with the lathe.

Craftsmen in shops making butter molds were highly skilled, and bridged the world of the one-of-a-kind completely hand-carved or whittled butter stamp (much less likely to be a mold, as the cases were hard to do by hand), and the dime-a-dozen (though still attractive to us as collectors today) completely factory-made stamps, with templates and jigs guiding the cutting.

• • • •

Reproduction alerts. So far at least, nowhere near all the designs of machine-made butter molds or stamps have been reproduced. **Alert I.** A company (mfr? dlr?) in Atkins, VA, began (?) advertising in early 1989, "wooden butter molds: 1/2 lb. round reproductions. Starburst design." They were priced at six for $34.50 ppd. **Alert II.** Another company, with "Antique" in their name, advertised in May 1989 (possibly before too) *Southern Antiques* a wholesale deal: "Wooden Butter Molds, 1/2 lb. size Two Piece, Round Shell or cup Type Stamp. Cow, Wheat, Pineapple, Starburst, Swan. Great Repro. Sample $16 each, per dozen $145 ppd." Sounds like the same repro molds. **Alert III.** Nettle Creek Industries advertised in early 1976 that they had "superb quality reproductions of authentic ships figureheads, scrimshaw, buttermolds and dozens of other interesting items for the collector." They seem to have missed the point: collectors don't collect reproductions. **Alert IV.** New cow molds are sold through catalogs of "country" wares; the new glass has no faint tint of green and tends to be lighter than it looks. Look for signs of wear along bottom edge of glass and on wooden handle.

Butter mold, cow, 2 parts: round glass (very pale greenish blue) case, molded disc or plunger prints simple standing cow, the disc is molded on top with threaded hole for screwed-in turned wooden handle, "Bomer," American, round, 4-1/2" diameter, 8-1/4" L overall including handle, marked "Pat Apld for," very late 19th C. A presumably much <u>rarer glass cow plunger mold</u>, depicted in Kindig's book, and belonging to him, has four cows molded on the case as decoration. His does not have the name "Bomer." See also butter stamps: glass & ceramic. **$150-$200**

Butter mold, cow, pleasantly abstracted lathe-turned case & plunger in one-pound size, a craftsman-shop production of pointy-leg cow resembling what Paul Kindig calls the "Vigilant Cow,"

written about extensively in *Butter Prints and Molds* (see bibliography). American, 2nd half 19th C. **$200-$275**

Butter mold, fern pattern, cylinder, turn of century. **$40-$50**

Butter mold, flowers, 4 with four petals & 4 eight-pointed stars, box type, wood, marked "Porter Blanchards Son's Co.," Nashua, NH, 19th C. **$100-$140**

Butter mold, flowers & fruit, box in 2-lb size, makes 8 mini prints, turn of century. **$70-$100**

Butter mold, fruit (probably pomegranate) design, plunger type, 3 pieces, very small size, American (?), 19th C. **$55-$75**

Butter mold, goose, deep carved, plunger type, American, 1/2-lb. size, 3-3/4" diameter, late 19th C. **$135-$150**

Butter mold, melon carving, very finely done, case & plunger, 19th C. **$65-$95**

Butter mold box , no pattern, wood box with iron fittings including frame & handle, 1-lb. press, American, 5-3/4" L x 3-5/8" W, 19th C. This is a nice mold, and there is one in the collection of the Smithsonian. However, it is not worth $300 because it is "in a museum," as a dealer I know told a collector. **$45-$85**

"In a museum" and **"in the book"** are explanatory phrases used when raising prices, but it's pretty much meaningless, especially when the museum (Smithsonian) and book (mine in particular, and some others) are known for including a wide range of things for study.

IV-21. Butter mold or stamp. *Relatively unusual paddle shape. Cow in elongated oval, rope border. Note pine tree, flower and the cow's bell. 11" L x 4-1/4" W. According to the auction catalog, this was one of Harold Corbin's "most highly regarded" carved molds. Photo courtesy Litchfield Auction Gallery, Litchfield, CT. Ex-Harold Corbin Collection, auctioned 1/1/1990. Today's value probably more than price realized:* **$750**

IV-22. Butter stamps. *Both quite small.* **(L)** *Miniature with swan. 1-1/4" diameter.* **(R)** *Rooster with 2 bees or stars. 2" diameter. Photo courtesy Litchfield Auction Gallery. Ex-Harold Corbin Collection, auctioned 1/1/1990, $275 and $250.* **$250-$300; $275-$400**

IV-23. Butter stamps, (L) *Pennsylvania style heart-shaped tulip with leaves. 2-3/4" diameter.* **(M)** *Cow under tree branch, piecrust border. Note cow has deer-like 2-point antlers. 3-3/4" diameter.* **(R)** *Civil War soldier's bust in profile, with beard & cap. Concentric ring border. 3-1/2" diameter. Photo courtesy Litchfield Auction Gallery. Ex-Harold Corbin Collection, each auctioned 1/1/1990 for $355 or less.* **$350-$450; $350-$450; $800-$1000**

IV-24. Butter stamp. *Deeply carved ram with tree branch. Piecrust edge. 4-1/4" diameter. Photo courtesy of Robert W. Skinner Inc., Auctioneers, Bolton, MA.* **$400-$500**

IV-25. Butter stamp. *Cow with tree branch and tall grass. Piecrust border. Courtesy Joe & Teri Dziadul, Enfield, CT.* **$275 -$375**

IV-26. Butter stamp. *Demilune stamp, cow & tree, cross-hatched border with wear. Collection & photograph of James E. Trice, author of Butter Molds, Collector Books, 1980.* **$450-$700**

IV-27. Butter stamps. (L) *Finely detailed carved wood anchor with line. Long handle. 3-1/4" diameter. For more anchors see IV-47 & 48.* **(M)** *The sheep or ram here (see IV-24) appears on a* <u>brass</u> *rather than a wooden mold rather than wood. 4-1/4" diameter.* **(R)** *Cow under tree, facing right and with* <u>raised or repoussé</u> *design rather than intaglio design of a carved wooden mold. 3-1/2" diameter.* <u>Redware</u>; *probably made by impressing damp clay with a carved wooden mold. Butter printed with this one would have intaglio design. Photo courtesy Litchfield Auction Gallery. Ex-Harold Corbin Collection, auctioned 1/1/1990.* **$325, $775, $750**

IV-28. Butter stamp. *Leaping hare or rabbit, with log & grass. Very unusual. 19th C. Collection & photograph James E. Trice.* **$350-$500**

IV-29. Butter stamp. *Elongated oval with heart & flowers, thickly carved wood. 6" L. Ephrata Cloister provenance, Pennsylvania. While the appearance is somewhat crude, and the design not so pleasing as certain eccentric animals, the provenance and obvious PA-Dutch design add value. Photo courtesy Litchfield Auction Gallery. Ex-Harold Corbin Collection, auctioned 1/1/1990, $700.* **$700-$800**

IV-30. Butter stamp. *Sitting squirrel, with nut in paw. Unusual zig-zag or sawtooth border. Squirrels are a popular motif for nutcrackers, but are unusual in butter stamps. Courtesy Joe & Teri Dziadul.* **$750-$850**

IV-31. Butter stamp. *Very unusual big-footed baby armadillo or tortoise on demilune stamp. Notched border. A fancy carved handle seems out of sync with mold. 6-1/4" L, age hard to judge because style is old, but subject is perhaps unique. Courtesy Bonnie Myers, B & J's Unclaimed Treasures, Dillsburg, PA.* **$300 and up**

IV-32. Butter stamp. *Spotted deer with corn plant curved over head — which he may have been eating! Piecrust border, 4" diameter. American, 19th C. Picture courtesy of Robert W. Skinner Inc., Auctioneers, Bolton, MA.* **$500-$600**

IV-33. Butter stamp. *Demilune, carved wood with pineapple & leaves. Rope border on curve only, meaning it could be used to create a round print, without a line across the center, which would mark off the half-pound division. 7" W. American, 19th C.* **$450 and up**

IV-34. Butter stamp. *Demilune, with abstract tulip and curved leaves. 4" H x 7-1/4" W. Picture courtesy of Robert W. Skinner Inc., Auctioneers. Bolton, MA.* **$350-$450**

IV-35. Butter stamp. *Carved eagle clutching budding branch, within border reading dairyman's name "A. F. Thompson * New York." Star above eagle's head matches star in border words, 4-1/2" diameter, American, 19th C. This was cracked, and has old repair. Picture courtesy of Robert W. Skinner Inc., Auctioneers, Bolton, MA.* **$650-$750**

IV-36. Butter stamp. *Eagle stamps are among the most sought-after designs. This eagle, with odd baby-bird liplike beak, resembles carvings by Schimmel. It is unclear if there is a clutch of arrows. And it's possible there are a couple of stars — or are those marks claws? Collection and photograph of James E. Trice.* **$600-$750**

IV-37. Butter stamps. *All eagle motif, finely carved. One, 3-5/8" diameter, is mounted on old paddle board — not necessarily a new mount. One with shield body is 4-3/4" diameter; other is 3-3/4". 19th C. Picture courtesy of Christie, Manson & Woods International Inc., NYC, from 1980 Brooke sale.* **$300-$600**

IV-38. Butter molds. *All eagle designs, with handles. (L) Tulip-like eagle with graceful leaf-like wings, crosshatched body, narrow piecrust border, a single star. 4-1/4" diameter. (M) Eagle facing left, with shield body, long neck, flanked by laurel [?] leaves. Not an uncommon carving, but very appealing. Concentric 5-ring border, 5" diameter. (R) Eagle & large 8-pt star, leaves. 3-3/4" diameter. Photo courtesy Litchfield Auction Gallery. Ex-Harold Corbin Collection, auctioned 1/1/1990.* **$450-$550; $200-$250; $450-$550**

Butter mold box , no pattern, wood, very small, marked "Munsing," American. Munsing not in *Thomas' Register*. **$15-$25**

Butter mold, rose & other flowers in center design, hand-carved wood, square with fluted sides (unusual), Pennsylvania (?), 5-1/4" x 5-1/2", mid to 3rd quarter 19th C. **$200-$300**

Butter mold, rosette, plunger type, machine-carved maple, 4" square, late 19th or early 20th C. **$35-$50**

Butter mold, swan with rope border, cylinder & plunger, English or possibly American, 3-1/2" diameter, late 19th C. or early 20th C. **$35-$55**

Butter mold, wheat ear, 2 parts, very small rectangular box, motif carved inside, string holds halves together, paper label reads, "Wheat-Ear Moulds. Directions for Use**.** First, thoroughly soak the mould in water and then with a table knife fill in both halves of Butter Mould. Then lay a clean straw in the centre of one half, then press the two halves evenly together. Take away the top half and lift out wheat-ear on the straw." No manufacturer's name, English, overall size is 1-1/4" H x 4" L x 1-5/8" W, with 3-3/4" L wheat-ear carving, c.1900 from the looks of label. **$50-$75**

Butter mold, sheaf of wheat with leaves in the border on stamp, plunger type, American, 3-1/2" diameter, 19th C. **$45-$55**

Butter mold, star design, cast aluminum,. R. Hall, Burlington, NC, 1/2-lb size, about 3-1/2" diameter, prob. c. 1930s to 1950s. **$15-$25**

Butter molds, fruit, nut or geometric designs, plunger or barrel type, maple or walnut with pewter bands, 19th C. **$85-$125**

Butter press — See also pastry tube, cookie press

Butter printer, flower designs, rolling type, carved wood, English (?), 5-1/2" L, 19th C. Rolling butter printers were used to make border prints at a dairy store. The large tray of butter, an inch thick or whatever, was divided off into sections, square-by-square of designs, so that so many squares could be cut off for so much poundage. **$100-$150**

"Stamp" or "Print"? Carl W. Drepperd, in *A Dictionary of American Antiques*, makes this common sense distinction between the oft-used terms stamp and print: the tool used to mark the butter is the stamp; the marked butter is the print. In an 1890 cookbook, *On the Chafing Dish, Compliments of the Meriden Britannia Co.*, by Harriet P. Bailey (NY: G. W. Dillingham), there is a recipe for "Eggs With Macaroni" to which Mrs. Bailey adds this genteel note: "Note: -- For cooking on the chafing dish, I advise always using print butter. It may seem a little extravagant. But surely when one in evening attire prepares a dish which proves to be above reproach, one may say with the March Hare, 'It is the best butter,' without losing the reputation of being an economical as well as a good housekeeper." Neither Bailey nor Drepperd, unfortunately, commented on rolling "stamps," so I have opted to call them printers.

Butter printer, rolling type, carved wood (ash?), roller prints a thistle & 2 star-like flowers & a leaf, English (?), 4-1/2" L x 1-7/8" diameter, 19th C. **$200-$225**

Butter slicer, nickel-plated iron, 11 thin cutting wires, porcelainized cast iron base, cuts a pound block of butter into quarters, then slices them into pats, probably for hotel or restaurant use, worked by pushing wire-strung frame down using thumb tab, "Elgin #48", mfd. by Cleveland Faucet Co., 8-1/2" H x 8-1/2" L, pat'd Dec. 31, 1901 in Canada, Sept. 1911 in U.S.A. **$45-$55**

Butter stamp, 4-petaled rosette, hearts on one side; stars on other, carved wood, PA (?), 19th C. Ex-Robacker, $140. **$140-$175**

Butter stamp, acorn & oak leaf, lathe-turned, factory-made, American, late 19th C. **$45-$55**

IV-39. Butter stamps. *Acorn motifs. Very beautiful carving & designs, but acorns are not accorded the high value placed on them by squirrels. Courtesy James E. Trice.* **$125-$175**

IV-40. Butter stamp. *Flower with curious curved vertebraeic stem, rope border. Courtesy James E. Trice.* **$150-$200**

Butter stamp, acorn & oak leaves, simple factory-made, American, small round, 20th C. **$25-$40**

Butter stamp, armadillo or strange turtle, carved wood, crescent shape with knobby handle, looks old except for new-looking handle, subject matter makes me wary of age, 6-1/4" W, 20th C (?). (**NOTE:** the only other armadillo motif in this book is found on a white earthenware mold from England, c.1922.) **$60-$75**

Butter stamp, bird in the grass design, carved wood, corrugated border, very detailed, American, 3" diameter, 19th C. **$240-$300**

Butter stamp, bird with plant, carved from one block of wood, 4-7/8" diameter, mid 19th C. **$400-$550**

IV-41. Butter stamps, molds & cases. *All machine-carved wood.* (**A & B**) *Two views of what seller called individual "butter prints," in "Hollywood" pattern. Three sizes, for 1/2 oz., 3/4 oz. and 1 oz pats.* (**C**) *Two molds "by which butter may be put up in pound or half-pound cakes for the market. They are made of soft wood, as white-ash or soft maple, and are generally kept for sale at all country stores where willow-ware is sold.* **The manner of using them** *is as follows: when the butter is ready for making up, it is weighed out into the proper quantities, and each piece is worked in the butter-dish with the ladle into flat round cakes. These cakes are either pressed with the mold shown in the upper picture, or are made to go into the cup of the lower mold. Inside the cup is a mold with a handle which works through a hole in the upper part of the cup. The cup is inverted on to the table, and when this handle is pressed down it forces the mold on to the butter, which is squeezed into a very neat ornamental cake. By pushing down on the handle and lifting the cup, the cake is pushed out of the mold. This makes a very favorite mode of putting up fine butter for market, and is also well adapted for preparing butter for the table in houses where neatness of appearance is studied. The molds when in use should be kept wetted in cold water to prevent the butter from sticking." American Agriculturist, 5/1872.* (**D**) *Flower pattern in four sizes: 1 oz., 3 oz., 1/2 lb. and 1 lb. From Duparquet, Huot & Moneuse catalog, c.1904-1910.* (**E**) *Wheat sheaf in square design, Valentine Clad & Sons, Philadelphia, c.1890-1900.* (**F**) *3" to 4" stamps, Joseph Breck catalog, 1905.* (**G**) *"Butter pat in Case. — This gives the butter a handsome form and print at the same time." American Home Cook Book, 1854.* (**H**) *Same as (D).* (**I**) *Swan in case, 1 oz. and 2 oz. Jaburg Brothers, 1908.* (**J**) *Swan in 1/2 oz., 3/4 oz., 1 oz., 2 oz. sizes. Ritzinger, Grasgreen, c. 1906-07.* **$40-$150**

Butter stamp, cow at barnyard gate, hand-carved, piecrust border, American, 19th C. **$225-$275**

Butter stamp, cow, detailed hand-carving of unusual rearing bovine surrounded by more typical combination of gate, overhanging branch & long grass, cable border, long handle, American, 19th C. Teri Dziadul, who has probably had more beautiful butter molds and stamps pass through her hands than anybody except Paul Kindig (who wrote THE book), offered this for $195 in 1984. Price range is mine, not hers. **$250-$350**

Butter stamp, cow with fence behind her, eager expectant horns, nice little tail, pointed udders, well-defined hooves, hair on flanks, body of mold worn, but well-carved figure is perfect, American, 4-1/2" overall x 2-1/2" deep, stamp itself 3-5/8" diameter, 19th C. **$245-$300**

Butter stamp, cow with pointy legs, ears and horns, in Kindig's "Vigilant Cow" style, well-cut, knob handle, American, 2nd half 19th C. **$225-$300**

Butter stamp, deer, with bent corn stalk (which he may have been eating!) overhanging him and long grass, piecrust border, American, 4" diameter, 19th C. **$400-$500**

Butter stamp, donkey, with wonderfully bent front legs, slogging along on a sort of rayed ground, probably a plowed field, and with bursts of something, like leaves or flowers, filling the sky, deeply carved wooden disc, chip out of one side, age cracking, very unusual motif, American, 3-3/4" diameter, 19th C. Sold for $625 at a 1984 James D. Julia auction, in Fairfield, ME. **$700-$900**

Butter stamp, dove on one side, a vase of flowers on other, 3-1/4" diameter, 19th C. **$150-$200**

Butter stamp, eagle, carved wood, American, 4-1/2" x 4-1/4", 19th C. **$325-$360**

Butter stamp, eagle, deep carved abstract figure with corrugated border, lathe-turned one-piece blank, lathe marks evident, American, 4-1/2" diameter, 19th C. **$450-$500**

Butter stamp, eagle, hand-carved wood in half moon shape, very beautiful carving of benign but spread-winged eagle, wide-eyed & looking over his right wing (left wing in the printed butter), the details of breast and wing feathers done with ge-

IV-42. Butter stamp. *Rayed flower with dandelion-like leaves. Courtesy James E. Trice.* **$150-$200**

nius, little chips perfectly spaced for visual appeal, and long parallel curving lines to follow sweep of ruff, back of head, tail and ends of wings, two spaces filled in with rayed suns (one a moon?), initials, and a few 4-point stars between letters just inside the piecrust border. Clarence Spohn, in catalog, quotes Robacker as stating in his 1965 *Touch of the Dutchland*, that, "The eagle pictured here has been called the most important piece of its kind in primitive woodcarving." Border has initials "S. M.", PA German, 3-3/4" H x 7-5/8" L, 19th C. Ex-Robacker, $6000. **$5000-$7000**

Butter stamp, eagle on shield, very abstract, 3 concentric rings around outside, English, 4-1/2" diameter, 19th C. **$160-$200**

Butter stamp, eagle with an 8-point "star," American, 2-3/4" diameter, 19th C. **Still a star?** After eight points, I'm not sure the pointed motif is necessarily a star, but maybe it is meant to represent or allude to a star, so instead of thinking up some new word like octopunctus let's just continue calling it a star. You'll encounter this shape, sometimes reminiscent of a compass rose, on quilts too. **NOTE:** Even with 12 points, some writers still call this a star design. **$250-$350**

Butter stamp, eagle with shield body, deeply carved, the words "JAMES HOFMAN - SHIP BUILDER" around the border, American, 19th C. Sold in early 1982 for $800, most likely because of relationship to ship building. Would probably bring at least that much today. Also ship- or marine-related, is a whale ivory butter stamp, with a very large knob handle, that was part of the Jeffrey Cohen Collection auctioned by Richard Bourne on July 31, 1989 for $2750. [It appears in Flayderman's *Scrimshaw and Scrimshanders: Whales and Whalemen*, 1972.] Lita Solis Cohen, writing in the Oct. 1989 *Maine Antique Digest,* said that the auctioneer said it was the only example known of a whale ivory butter stamp, but Lita's unnamed seatmate told her that wasn't so because she had one too. More may surface. Costa Rican imports still appear in the market at very high prices; even vetted dealers have presented them as old at shows, so watch out. **$700-$1000**

Butter stamp, eagle & shield, deeply hand-carved on machined blank, rather naturalistic, American, 3-1/2" diameter, 19th C. **$225-$250**

Butter stamp, elliptical design with central 6-point pinwheel (or flower), flanked by a heart at each end, intricate border deeply chip-carved maple, 9-1/4" L. Several are known that are virtually identical with three small pinwheels or floriate forms between every other ray. This one may be from Nova Scotia, 2nd quarter 19th C. **$700-$900**

Butter stamp, fish, 3 large ones facing same way & 2 smaller, piecrust border, handle on back, poss. New England, 3-1/2" W, mid 19th C. **$350-$450**

Butter stamp, fish, very fat (croppie? sunfish?) with several regularly patterned lines of waves, dentil border, 2 part, very finely carved, with separate carved and inserted knob handle (partly chewed -- by piranha?), American, found in barn in Dresden, ME, 3-3/4" diameter, mid 19th C. The detailed, well-ordered, and patterned appearance reminds you of classical Greco-Roman tiles or wall murals, especially the compact puddle-sized water body hovering just behind the lower fin. Perhaps the carver's inspiration was in some recently published account of an archaeological dig in the 1840s or 1850s. This stamp (or "butter print," as it is called in the catalog), from the collection of Greg & Linette Salisbury, was sold at a James D. Julia auction, Aug. 23, 1989, for $950 plus 10% premium. The presale estimate was $400-$700. It was by far the most outstanding mold among the ones offered. **$700-$1200**

Butter stamp, flower with beaded border, carved wood, 2-2/3" diameter, late 19th C. **$45-$65**

Butter stamp, flowers, 3 of them with fat petals, primitive rope border design, carved wood, American, 19th C. **$65-$70**

Butter stamp, fox, running, big tail brush, overhead branch, pointy enough to be a "vigilant fox" as Kindig might term it, dense, faintly yellow wood with wormholes, American, 2nd half 19th C. **$750-$850**

Butter stamp, half-moon shape, heart & leaf design, attached handle on back, good patina on carved wood, which means a lot with butter stamps & molds, PA (?), 6-3/4" L x 3-1/4" diameter, mid 19th C. **$800-$900**

Butter stamp, lollipop type & also double-sided, carved wood, has unusually long handle; designs are a double heart on one side, a pinwheel or fylfot design on other, PA German, 11" L overall with handle, stamp only 4-3/4" diameter, mid 19th C. **$1000-$1300**

Butter stamp, lollipop type, carved from one piece of wood, double-ended with 2 prints: a square print with chip-carved eagle & 4 stars separated by shank a hand's breadth long from a round print carved with 8-point snowflake-like design, American, prob. 2nd to 3rd quarter 19th C. **$600-$900**

Butter stamp, lollipop type, carved with 6-petal flower, serrated border, elongated shield-shaped handle ending in heart, American, 10" L, 19th C. **$400-$700**

Butter stamp, lollipop type, double carving of an abstract hex-type flower, & a fern leaf, American, 8-1/2" L, 19th C. **$400-$500**

Butter stamp, lollipop type, large size, with stylized flowers & geometric border, American, 9" L, 19th C. **$200-$300**

Butter stamp, lollipop type, one piece carved wood, unusual because handle is angled somewhat to side instead of joining disc at right angles, simple 6-petal star flower (with small ellipses between each point) carved on both sides, simple bead border, American, 8-1/2" L, approx. 3-3/4" diameter stamp, prob. 3rd quarter 19th C. **$325-$550**

Butter stamp, lollipop type, separate turned wooden handle, nice carving of bulky cow standing on groundline that looks like cable, the words being TRADE MARK, above & below cow, maybe mid 19th C. **$750-$1000**

Butter stamp, Masonic building trade symbols, carved wood, carved handle, American, 4-7/8" diameter, 3/4" thick, late 19th C. Value here is tied to the Masonic symbols, assuming they are Freemason symbols. **$1200-$1300**

FRATERNAL ORDERS: THEIR SYMBOLS & MOTIFS

The three orders expounded on here all make use of Christian symbols and sometimes secular symbols manipulated to hint at Christian beliefs. Because all these orders are supposedly secret and have well-guarded rites and rituals, it is not so easy to discover the meaning of their symbols. Depending on the era, it has sometimes been considered a great advantage in business and politics to be a member of an order.

The Freemasons are generally thought to date back to the seventeenth century in England, and to 1733 in North America (Boston). The 1804 *English Encyclopaedia* traces the Freemasons back to the sixth century in England, but this may be romanticizing loose guilds or fraternal orders of masons and stone- and brickworkers. Basically, Freemasons use masonry tools, viz. a trowel, crossed squares, a level, a plumb rule or bob, a mallet, a pick-axe, or an iron rod. To that short list is added the "All-Seeing Eye"; a radiant sun, stars, comets and moon; three steps; a triangle; three triangles forming a 9-point star; three columns of various architectural orders representing wisdom, strength and beauty; a checkerboard floor; the Bible as an open book; Moses' two stone tablets in round-top gravestone shape; a beehive; a balance scale; a ladder; an incense pot; an anchor and the Ark; an hourglass with wings; a scythe, crossed hammer and spade; Aaron's budding rod; a coffin; a cord; a shoe; crossed keys; crossed quill pens; crossed swords;

and probably other subjects. Masonic motifs include at least one design used by non-Masons too — a square and compass arranged to make a frame. Another motif sometimes used by both Mason and non-Mason is a flexed arm and mason's hammer. These are definitely Freemason symbols when accompanied by a sun or crescent moon and the letters "G" (for geometry or "The Great Architect of the Universe," i.e., God) or "A" (for architect), but often are Masonic symbols even when not so accompanied.

The Odd Fellows (I.O.O.F. — International Order of Odd Fellows) don't seem to be as old an order, so objects decorated with their symbols have values that are slightly, shall we say, younger. The Odd Fellows were around by 1745 in "isolated lodges" in England and found countrywide by 1812, according to one expert. In America the two dates given are 1806 and 1819, the latter — for a lodge in Baltimore — generally being the accepted date. Then in 1850-51 the Odd Fellows-related Degree of Rebekah was established for women. Odd Fellows seem to have the most symbols — some of them the same as Masonic symbols. The list includes the three-link chain that often has the initials "F," "L," and "T" within the links (for friendship, love and truth); an All-Seeing Eye; skull and crossbones; scythe; bow, arrows and quiver; bundle of rods; a serpent; scales and a sword; crossed swords; the Bible; an hourglass (sometimes with wings); a coffin; a hatchet; fireman's pike; what looks like roman numeral III but is really a symbol for

three columns or pillars, representing faith, hope and charity (sometimes faith, love and truth or F.L.T.) as well as wisdom, strength and beauty of religion; an open tent; an altar of sacrifice; tablets of stone (Moses' Ten Commandments); a pilgrim's sandals, staff and scrip (a satchel or bag); a shepherd's crook; a sun; an owl; a huge sheep-like lamb with a cross; half-moon; crossed gavels; baton; 5-point star; crossed quill pens; crossed wands; burning torch; and — perhaps most familiar, and most beloved by even non-Odd Fellows — a hand with heart in palm. The women's **Rebekah** degree of Odd Fellows uses a beehive, a dove, the moon and seven stars, a lily and an image of Rebecca at the well.

Knights Templar belongs to an order of knights founded during the Second Crusade (about 1118), but are thought by some to date back even further. In the United States, the members of some Masonic orders are called Knights Templar. The Knights use a paschal (Passover or Easter) lamb with a banner; a Maltese cross (with four equal arms that look like stylized arrowheads pointing to the center); another cross with long vertical member; triangles; coffins; tents; etc.

Other fraternal and "benevolent" orders include Shriners, Woodmen of America, Improved Order of Red Men, Knights of Pythias, Knights of Maccabees, Knights of the Orient, Knights of Malta and Knights of the Red Cross.

BUTTER STAMPS, glass & ceramic:

Butter stamp, wheat sheaf, rayed or piecrust border, pressed glass disc, knob handle, M'Kee & Brothers, Pittsburgh, 1868. **$400-$500**

Butter stamp, fleur-de-lis pattern, round glass, screw-in wooden knob, French Canadian (?), 3-1/2" diameter, 20th C. **$75-$85**

Butter stamp, geometric curved-ray design, saltglazed stoneware with large knobby handle, 23 rays around small indented circle, deeply molded, poss. OH, mid 19th C. **$1200-$1700**

BUTTER STAMPS, wood:

Butter stamp, name in very nice serif lettering around border, oval sunburst design in center, carved wood, reads "G. Haughton" and "A. Southington," New England (?), oval 5" L x 3-1/2" W, 19th C, prob. 2nd to 3rd quarter. Brought $325 at Garth Auction, May 5/6, 1989, Delaware, OH. Good old patina, but hard to explain price when it's hand-carved but not figural, unless the buyer had a Haughton or Southington connection. **$200-$325**

Butter stamp, name & legend around edge, geometric design in center, carved wood with knob handle, "J. CARRINGTON PAVE CASTEL," 5-1/8" diameter, early 19th C (?). This was offered by collector & dealer Teri Dziadul of Enfield, CT, in early 1980s. Anything with a name I try to include, even if I've not seen it, because by having this all on computer I can cross-reference, or at least look things up. The only other J. Carrington in my records is James Carrington, of Wallingford, CT, who patented a coffee mill in 1829. Possibly the same man, this being about the right age. Teri was asking $225 in her catalog. The price range here is mine, not hers. **$225-$250**

Butter stamp, palm tree with stars & little amoebic odds & ends floating in sky, hand-carved wood, large slightly concave (warped?) disc with short all-in-one knob on back, very unusual stylized design, dark patina, American, prob. PA, 5" diameter, mid 19th C. **$225-$300**

IV-43. Butter stamp "hand stamp." 'Fancy Butter' *packages are, of course, of many forms, as each maker wishes his butter to be both attractive and unique. All* **'print-butter,'** *or butter in small packages marked with the name of the maker, is properly regarded as ;fancy, whether it bring a higher price than other good butter or not. Still, it ought to be good enough to sell higher than good* **tub or firkin butter.** *Philadelphia has long been famous for its excellent print-butter. This is generally put up upon the common hand stamps in pound '* **pats,** *' which may have either of the two forms represented by the dotted lines. Simple devices, such as a sheaf of wheat, roses, pineapples, acorns, and oak leaves and nondescript leaves are common. Monograms or single letters are not rare, with occasionally a more elaborate device. These 'pats,' for they are patted into form upon the stamps [with a butter spade or paddle], are marketed in what are known as* **Philadelphia tubs,** *which are oval tubs of cedar, lined with tin, and having ice chambers in each end, having a nearly rectangular space in the center, in which the butter is packed upon shelves 2-1/4" to 3" apart. A good deal of butter is now made in rectangular, square or brick-shaped prints, and shipped in these Philadelphia tubs, or in square packages, with provision for ice in hot weather." The article goes on to extol* **round butter boxes** *that are made by an "ingenious application of the new kind of veneering, cut in a continuous ribbon round and round the log" and then sewing the ribbons of wood at a seam. American Agriculturist, 1/1880. Ultimately, price depends on appeal and quality of carving — even for these mass-produced dairy pieces.* **$125-$175**

Palms and Xmas Trees. There are two sacred trees in the Christian religion: the palm and the evergreen. The palm generally symbolizes the birthplace of Christ; more specifically, His entry into Jerusalem on Palm Sunday. If you, like I, always thought that "Xmas" was a slangy and incorrect way to write "Christmas," you'll be as relieved as I was to find out that it is many hundreds of years old, the X standing for "criss-cross" or Christ's cross. I wonder if the common early decorative use of an **X** (often between straight lines above and below like a Roman numeral), wasn't used (especially by blacksmiths with their chisels and files) <u>to signify a criss-cross</u>, a sort of secularly-awarded religious blessing on the object. Taking this idea further, the lines may represent heaven and earth. The mark is found, sometimes in multiples, on many seventeenth-, eighteenth- and early nineteenth-century forged iron and carved wood utilitarian objects. On the other hand, because decorating hot iron with a chisel or file was not the easiest thing to do, it is possible that an X and some straight lines was just the easiest form of decoration.

Butter stamp, pineapple motif, deeply carved, with cross-hatching. Probably hand-carved on machine blank, American (?), 4-1/2" diameter, 19th C. **$100-$125**

Butter stamp, pineapple on a demilune stamp, turned knob handle on back, American, 7" W, mid 19th C. **$200-$225**

Butter stamp, pineapple with geometric border design, fairly crudely carved thick pine (a nice soft wood for amateurs to attack!), with no handle, American, 19th C. According to Mary Earle Gould's woodenware book, these handleless stamps were actually <u>cookie stamps</u>, while the ones with handles were for butter. Is this true, you expert collectors out there? **$100-$120**

Butter stamp, pineapple with leaves, short knob handle, abstract simple carving, American, 3-1/2" diameter, pre-1850. **$95-$125**

Butter stamp, rooster, probably carved shop piece on machine-turned blank, American, 3-1/2" diameter, latish 19th C. **$275-$375**

Butter stamp, rooster with leaves on branch, in mid crow, lathe-turned blank, screw-in handle, craftsman-shop production, nicely & competently carved wood, with simple corrugated border design, American, 3-1/2" diameter, 19th C. **$275-$375**

Butter stamp, rose, craftsman-shop production, lathe-turned blank with hand carving, very late 19th C or early 20th C. **$55-$85**

Butter stamp, fullblown rose, with rosebud & leaves, craftsman-shop carving but very nice, on machined blank, American, 2" diameter, late 19th C. **$55-$85**

Butter stamp, rose & leaves design, for single pat, carved wood, American or imported from Europe, 1-7/8" diameter, late 19th or early 20th C. **$45-$65**

Butter stamp, rose, thistle, & 3-leaf clover, single pat size, 3 finely carved designs, only 1-3/4" diameter, 19th C. **$90-$110**

Butter stamp, rosette with 4 radial petals, craftsman-carved, common abstract design, American, 2" diameter, 19th C. **$45-$55**

Butter stamp, snowflake design, for single pat, carved wood, 1-7/8" diameter, late 19th or early 20th C. **$45-$65**

Butter stamp, star, 7 points, hole in the middle, carved birch, American, 4-3/8" L x 1-1/16" diameter, 3rd quarter 19th C. **$30-$45**

Butter stamp, strawberries, 2 wild ones with viney leaves, deeply carved wood, American, 1-1/2" diameter, 19th C. **$85-$95**

Butter stamp, swan, dense wood, longish handle, simple but well-carved, English, 3-1/8" H, mold is 2-5/8" diameter, 19th C. **$75-$100**

Butter stamp, tulips, 3 of them with stars, hand-carved wood, marked on handle "C. I.," with date, PA (?), 3-1/4" diameter, dated 1827. **$300-$400**

Butter stamp, wheat sheaf, ear of corn, grapes & leaves, a rose & leaf, 4 carvings for 4 separate prints, factory-made, with box case, American, 4-1/2" x 4-1/8", early 20th C. **$250-$300**

IV-44. Butter stamps, *so-called* **lollipop style.** *Simple geometric carvings from single pieces of wood. Probably Pennsylvania German, early 19th C. Photograph & collection of James E. Trice.* **$375-$550**

147

IV-45. Butter stamp. *Hand carved from one piece, with unusual handle. Zinnia-like flower with leaves. 5-1/4" H x 4-3/8" diameter. 19th C. Courtesy Joe & Teri Dziadul.* **$400-$600**

IV-47. Butter stamp. *Anchor & line with some odd berry-like motifs. Minor cracks and handle missing, 3-3/8" diameter. American, 19th C. Estimated to sell from $350 to $450 at a 1980 auction, it realized only $75, despite very good carving & subject. Picture courtesy of Robert W. Skinner Inc., Auctioneers, Bolton, MA. We don't know what the glitch was, but value is much higher.* **$300-$450**

IV-46. Butter stamp or mold-making at home! *"In reply to readers who say they can not procure the butter molds which we described in a former issue, we give directions for making them at home. The difficulty lies in getting the stamp made. Any one who can work a foot lathe, can turn the mold and the plain stamp with the handle, but the device which ornaments the stamp troubles them. To make this, take a piece of wood free from grain — a piece of soft maple or birch-root is very good — and have it turned or dressed the proper size, and a smooth face made on it. Then either draw on the face, the wrong way, or cut out letters from a printed bill or newspaper, and paste them on to the face of the mold, the wrong way, and make a border to suit the fancy, in the same manner. Then take a small, sharp gouge, like the one shown, not larger than a quarter of an inch in diameter, and smoothly cut away the wood beneath the letters, making them deep enough to show well when printed on the butter. About a quarter of an inch would be right. The depression should be neatly smoothed out, so as to make a neat, smooth print. A pretty border for the mold is a quantity of clover leaves; they may be pasted on, and the wood then cut out as before, or any other leaves would answer."* American Agriculturist, 12/1872.

IV-48. Butter stamp. *This was described by the auction house as being a "highly stylized eagle." The resemblance to an anchor is much greater. 3-1/2" diameter, American, mid 19th C. Picture courtesy Robert W. Skinner Inc., Auctioneers, Bolton, MA.* **$250-$400**

IV-49. Rolling butter printer. *Simple botanical motif & border. 5-1/2" L. Courtesy R. C. Bowen. SEE also IV-340 for a cookie roller which is quite similar — perhaps interchangeable functions.* **$95-$150**

IV-50. Butter stamp. *Carved wood in five parts, with holding pegs. Simple star motif. Maker's (?) mark are initials "H.Y." Block of butter would be 3-3/8" x 2" x 2-3/4". Collection of Meryle Evans.* **$125-$200**

IV-51. Box mold butter stamp — How To Use. *"There is rivalry amongst fancy butter makers to excel, not only in quality, but also to offer their product in the most acceptable form, and in attractive, convenient packages. The favorite method of putting up butter for immediate sale, is that of pound cakes, ornamented with a stamp, and marked in the center, so that each can be divided into half pounds for use on the table. For this, moulds and stamps are used. This illustration shows a stamp bearing the maker's initial. Being square, the prints may be packed upon the shelves in any butter-carrier without loss of space."* American Agriculturist, 9/1878.

IV-52. Butter molds. *Box molds of more mechanical type than the one in IV-50. Note how closely the carving and styles resemble springerle boards (further on in this chapter). Perhaps they were interchangeable.* **(T)** *Carved wood "Blanchard" butter mold, by maker of churns. Brass latches. Came in three sizes: 1/2 lb., marked to make two 1/4 lb. prints; 1 lb., for four prints; and 2 lb., for eight prints. This company also sold a cheaper version, which they claimed was the "same pattern as Blanchard."* **(B)** *This box did not come apart. It came in 11 sizes, making 3, 4, 6, 8, 12, 16 and 24 "cakes," from 1-1/4" x 1-1/3" (one ounce cakes) up to 3-1/2" x 3-1/3" (8 oz. cakes). From Breck catalog, 1905.* **$100-$400**

IV-53. Butter mold & butter stamps. *A hinged box mold, that comes apart completely. Makes a 4 or 5 lb brick, marked off by grooves made by stamps (lying in right foreground). The* **technique for use** *differs from others, and is as follows: "A pound of butter is weighed and packed into the end of the mold by means of the stamps, one of which presses the side, and the other the top, the latter having the packer's initials or trade-mark. Then another pound is weighed and packed in the same manner, and so on. In the packing, grooves are left in the butter, marking the divisions between the pounds, by which the retailer may cut it up into pieces of exact weight, each piece having been weighed previously." The finished cake with marks & divisions shown at center.* American Agriculturist, 5/1876.

IV-54. Butter mold for butter rolls. *After the butter is worked to removed excess moisture, it is packed into a mold. The one shown here is "made of lignum vitae [an extremely hard wood], in the manner of a pair of bullet-molds. Each half being filled with the finished butter, the handles are forcibly squeezed together, and the butter is compressed firmly into a solid roll [note curved interior], which drops from the mold when it is opened. The mold is kept wetted with cold water during the operation." These rolls, which were then wrapped individually in muslin, were made to fit vertically into a large trunk-like butter box which held 30 rolls.* American Agriculturist, 3/1876. **$55-$75**

Butter stamp, zinnia-like multiple-petaled flower, with leaves, carved from one-piece handle & all, American, 5-1/4" H x 4-3/8" diameter, mid 19th C. **$200-$225**

Butter stamp & butter paddle combined, cow & 2 acorns on the stamp, one piece of wood, hand-carved, American, paddle is 14" L overall, stamp is 4" diameter, 19th C. Estimated to go at auction in 1982 for between $600 and $800 because of rarity and interest, but sold for only $500. In today's market, a decade or so later, with vastly improved scholarship and heightened interest, as well as increasing difficulty in finding spectacular pieces considered folk art, it would bring a lot more. **$600-$900**

Butter stamp & paddle combined, star with 6 points on stamp, carved of one piece of wood, with a small shaped shovel scoop or paddle at one end, and the other end of the "handle" widening out to a large disc, about the size of a child's sand shovel, PA German (?), 9-1/2" L overall, with stamp 2-7/8" diameter, mid to 4th quarter 19th C. **$600-$800**

IV-55. Butter molds. *All are of "close-grained hardwood," and all have a "handcarved sheaf of wheat" printing block. Upper (T-L) "Eureka," with a self-gauging attachment. Prints pounds or half-pounds, by adjusting a collar on the upright standard, which is kept in place by a clamp and screw. Nickel-plated brass. (T-R) "Philadelphia," made of cherry, screwed together with brass screws. Block has wooden stem, and mold's top is fitted with hardwood moveable cap. Pound size: 5-3/4" L x 3-5/8" W. Also came in 1/2-pound size. (B) "Economy" self-adjuster. Brass screws. "Cut the butter from the churn batch on the table, press the hopper full, cut surplus off smoothly with hand paddle, press block from printer by pressure on the wood stem of block, extending through the printer head block." Cherry-Bassett Co., Baltimore dairy supplier, 1921.* **$55-$85**

IV-56. Butter press or "French butter forcer." *Tin with insert disc with heart cutout, wooden plunger. Virtually identical to those in IV-124. "There are 12 different forms to each, that give an infinite variety to this decorative manner of serving butter."* American Home Cook Book, *1854. See also the jumble machines, listed with cake & cookies, and the "Kiss Machine" with the candy listings.* **$35-$65**

IV-57. Whatsit butter worker? cracker crumber? pastry roller? *It seems much too large for a coggling tool used by a potter to make a corrugated design onto damp clay. Hand-carved wood with roller, 17-3/4" L; roller 3-1/2" diameter; paddle-handle is 1-3/4" thick. Courtesy Alice Solomon, Schnectady, NY.* **$150-$200**

Butter stamp & pastry jagger combined, cow, with wheel of jagger making leaf design, very unusual, PA German (?), 5-1/8" L overall, stamp is only 1-5/8" diameter, mid to 4th quarter 19th C. **$300-$400**

"**Mushroom Biscuits**. 8 oz. of butter, and 3 lb. 8 oz. of fine flour. Rub the butter and flour together, and mix them into a stiff paste with water; it must be made very smooth and fine; then make it into biscuits, about two ounces each; to be made round, and stamped in the middle with a butter print; prick them in the hollow with a fork to prevent blistering; bake them on iron plates in a good oven." Joseph Bell, *A Treatise on Confectionary*. Newcastle, England, 1817.

● ● ● ●

Thanks to Teri & Joe Dziadul, 6 So. George Washington Rd, Enfield, CT 06082, for their generous help on nutmeg graters, biscuit stamps, and butter molds and stamps, as well as hearth tools. From the very first edition of this book I have relied on the Dziaduls for pictures and information. Any errors are mine, not theirs. If you wish to write them, please enclose an SASE.

CAKE BOARDS, MARZIPAN BOARDS & SPRINGERLE MOLDS

In this edition, cake board listings and cake and marzipan board listings are together, and springerle mold listings are separate. Undoubtedly all these, as well as some butter stamps and intaglio cast iron or pewter molds, could be used for thin, fine-textured cookies with lots of super-fine sugar (such as "New Year's Cakes," speculas and gingerbread figures), as well as the fine-textured marzipan. Molds were used by applying the mold to the rolled-out, slightly dried paste or dough, or by rolling the dough into the molds (if they were small) and carefully peeling it off.

Strong collector market for cake or marzipan boards. Those carved of wood in European style (even if some motifs were specifically American, such as George Washington, Columbia, and Indians) are among the most expensive kitchen antiques and are a fairly new field of specialty. Folk art collectors have joined in since the identification of one nineteenth-century master carver who practiced his craft in New York City: John Conger. Dealers of old American "folk art" and furniture have embraced the beautiful carved boards of Conger and others and featured them in full page ads in collector publications. According to food historian William Woys Weaver, Conger laid "out his design with a compass and trace[d] off patterns from his set repertoire," which to my mind means they are craft, not art; but then, I don't call pattern quilts or pattern molded weathervanes folk art either. Be that as it may, it's in the interest of dealers and investment collectors to claim all well-carved boards as Conger's, but also to be wary of offering too many of them. Many unmarked carved boards have been attributed to Conger, especially after prices went above three or four thousand dollars! Many sellers take the imprinted housewares dealer's name, J. Y. Watkins, as proof that Conger actually carved that mold, but it is believed that Watkins not only kept on selling Conger's old stock but that new molds were made with Conger's patterns at least until 1900. I have listed the signed and attributed and related cake boards first, then the others, no matter how old.

James Y. Watkins. Watkins was in business as a tin-smith in NYC, and listed in city directories beginning in 1830. His son, James Y. Jr., joined the firm in 1852 (or at least "& Son" was added to the firm's name in the 1852-53 *Rode's Directory*). James Y. Watkins & Son, Inc. were listed variously as house furnishings or tinware dealers, who by 1866 were listed as dealing in "house furnishings and bakers' utensils." According to one note I've seen recently, Watkins also "made" ice cream molds; but I suspect they imported ice cream molds. The cake or marzipan boards marked with the Watkins' stamp are carved with early traditional motifs and in an early style, but we don't know now how many could have been made by John Conger or by an American or European imitator of his work.

Fakes & Frauds Bulletin. As of the early 1990s, William Woys Weaver says the Conger "touchmark," a stamped intaglio mark, "is now being counterfeited."

New Cake Boards. With container load imports, particularly from cookie countries in Scandinavia, and with the continuing appeal of *emmerlinguistication* (or recountrification) in America, you will see many many carved cake or cookie boards around, many with equestrian figures, flowers in baskets, roosters, cats, pigs, etc. Dark brown Min-Wax[a] coloration, unsubtle gouges to "age" the board, and a thickness conforming to modern mill practices (often 7/8"), and the use of pine are strong clues to modern work.

Lookalike alarm. The most commonly found images on carved wood cookie molds are single figures in peasant or old military costume. Many are reproductions, but in the strictest sense, most are just lookalikes "in the style of." A 1967 ad in *McCall's Needlework & Crafts* magazine has photos of two long skinny boards, one carved with a man and woman, arms akimbo, both standing on little tufts of ground; the other with five images including a basket, bird & branch, windmill, and two that can't be identified. The ad reads: "Dutch Cookie Molds sent directly from Holland with foreign stamps. All the charm of old Holland is captured in these charming hand-carved cookie molds. It's a double Dutch treat for not only are they the most enchanting decorations for anywhere in the house, but they make the most delightful cookies, including farmer and wife, windmills, baskets, etc. (Recipe and history of boards included.) They will make a cherished and unique gift for every woman on your Christmas list. Antique brown elm wood, 15-1/2" x 2-1/4". $3 ea. 2 for $5.50. 4 for $10." *Brochure of Cookie Mold Collection* 10¢. I have no idea if they are still in business, but this company (probably but one of several that made these molds for export and for sale in Holland to tourists and housewives) was Holland Handicrafts, P.B. 74 Ridderkerk, Holland. This is a 1967 ad, so don't try to order from it!

CONFECTIONS MADE IN THESE CAKE BOARDS

Marzipan, Marchpane, Massepain, or **Matzabaum:** the words are, respectively, German, English, French and Pennsylvania German. Marzipan is sort of a cross between a cookie and a candy, is always very sweet, and always has two main ingredients: confectioner's (or finely pounded) sugar and almond paste, made from ground (or pounded in a mortar) blanched almonds. A typical recipe would call for one pound of confectioner's sugar, one pound almond paste, and a little rosewater (which I assume you can buy in some specialty shop, rather than distilling it in an alembic yourself) to make the sugar and almonds into a paste which can be molded. New recipes sometimes call for a teaspoon of almond extract. The almond paste was originally made by pounding the almonds into a paste in a mortar with lots of sugar and some rosewater to sort of emulsify it to keep if from "oiling ," but it's now made much more easily in a food processor or even bought already made in specialty shops. Today, we think of marzipan as a highly colored figural sweet in folky designs, wrapped in paper or foil. The coloring was mixed into the paste or painted on after the confection was formed. Marzipan was worked with fingers or small shaping tools like sculptors' tools, stamped with a carved mold, rolled with a rolling pin or pressed into intaglio carved molds such as cake boards, springerle molds and butter stamps. Afterward it was air dried or very lightly browned in a very slow oven. Leaving them in the oven a little bit longer results in a really wonderful toasted marchpane. In Eliza Leslie's *Directions for Cookery,* the 1848 edition, is a recipe for Almond Maccaroons, sounding very like a marzipan recipe. The recipe is reproduced in the cake pan listings a little further on in this chapter.

Water marzipan. According to William Woys Weaver, the marzipan molds were for New Year's Cake (a tradition borrowed from Germany) and were used to make a so-called "water marzipan," which was a less expensive non-almond version of the real thing (p.116, *America Eats*). However, sugar wasn't so cheap that the mere omission of almonds could make New Year's Cake affordable for the masses.

Marzipan for Christmas, Springerle for Easter. Jean Lipman, in *American Folk Art in Wood, Metal & Stone* (NY: Pantheon, 1948), wrote briefly about "carved marzipan and springerle cake molds [that] made it possible for thin Christmas and Easter cakes to be stamped in low-relief designs. The hardwood springerle boards were carved intaglio, most often in composite groups of two to twelve patterns enclosed in separate squares, to mark the cutting lines for small individual cakes; while the marzipan boards were often designed for a single large cake. ... The finished cakes could be kept for months and, though they were so hard that it has been said it was as easy to eat the board as the cake, they were evidently a popular delicacy." (p.144)

"**New-Year's Cake.** Seven pounds of flour, sifted. Half a pound of butter. Half a pound of lard. Two pounds and a half of white Havanna sugar. Having sifted the flour, spread the sugar on the paste-board, a little at a time, and crush it to powder by rolling it with the rolling-pin. Then mix it with the flour. Cut up in the flour the butter and lard, and mix it well by rubbing it in with your hands. Add by degrees enough of cold water to make a stiff dough. Then knead the dough very hard, till it no longer sticks to your hands. Cover it, set it away for an hour or two, and then knead it again in the same manner. You may repeat the kneading several times. Then cut it into pieces, roll out each piece into a sheet half an inch thick. Cut it into large flat cakes with a tin cutter. You may stamp each cake with a wooden print, by way of ornamenting the surface.

"Sprinkle with flour some large flat tin or iron pans, lay the cakes in them, and bake them of a pale brown, in an oven of equal heat throughout. These cakes require more and harder kneading than any others, therefore it is best to have them kneaded by a man, or a very strong woman. They are greatly improved by the addition of some carraway seeds worked into the dough." Miss Leslie, of Philadelphia, *Seventy-Five Receipts for Pastry, Cakes, and*

Sweetmeats. Appended to *The Cook's Own Book and Housekeeper's Register*. By a Boston Housekeeper. Boston: Munroe & Francis, 1833. Eliza Leslie, in the 31st edition of her *Directions for Cookery*, published 1848, gives a recipe for "New York Cookies," which she says are similar to New Year's Cakes. She describes the finishing and decorating process thusly: "...Take the lump of dough out of the pan, and knead it on the paste-board till it becomes quite light. Then roll it out rather more than half an inch thick, and cut it into square cakes with a jagging iron or with a sharp knife. Stamp the surface of each with a cake print. Lay them in buttered pans, and bake them of a light brown in a brisk oven."

CATCHING JOHN CONGER

I hated for the third edition of this book to go to press in 1991 without finding out more about carver John Conger (probably pronounced kon´-ger, with a hard "g," like the eel), who had been so elusive, and about whom I could find nothing in standard books on folk art carvers. Most dealers advertising a signed Conger cake board, or an attributed board, said "New York State." An occasional rebel would say "Probably Pennsylvania." For all the information I was able to get, I can thank my computer (with its cross-referencing capabilities), and the wonderful microfiche collection of New York City directories at the New York Public Library, long a favorite and fruitful haunt of mine.

The first lead came in an ad for a mold that was marked both "J. Conger" and "James Y. Watkins, NYC." At least this placed Conger in New York. After a few useless references to Conger in a couple of books on folk art sculpture, I found my second lead in *Folk Artists Biographical Index,* edited by George H. Meyer. He cited mentions of Conger in Pauline A. Pinckney's *American Figureheads and Their Carvers* (NYC: W. W. Norton, 1940), and in Kenneth L. Ames' excellent *Beyond Necessity. Art in the Folk Tradition* (Exhibition catalog, pub. by Winterthur Museum, Winterthur, DE, distributed by W. W. Norton, 1977). Pinckney's book, on a subject I had already superficially researched in hopes of finding Conger, has a lengthy list of shipcarvers and possible shipcarvers, a list on which John Conger appears with a "flourished" date of 1830. The directories I later consulted all included both "carvers" and "shipcarvers" and from that I concluded that Conger did not describe himself as a shipcarver and probably was not one. On the other hand, *Beyond Necessity* confirmed the lead to Watkins given by an advertiser some years ago of an attributed Conger board that was marked only with Watkins' name.

Catalog item 143 in the Winterthur exhibition was a cake board stamped "J. Conger" as well as "J. Y. Watkins, N.Y." It is in the Winterthur collection, acquisition #55.48.60, but I did not get a picture of it for reprint here. Watkins is described as a "tinsmith and owner of a kitchen furnishing warehouse," and Conger as a "carver and baker." The most recent work on Conger was done by Louise C. Belden, a research associate at the Henry Francis du Pont Winterthur Museum, Winterthur, DE. Her excellent article, "Cake Boards," in *The Magazine ANTIQUES,* December 1990, depicts many Conger boards and related cake boards. Earlier, food historian William Woys Weaver wrote an article in *The Clarion,* the magazine of the Museum of American Folk Art, in New York City. It is "The New Year's Cake Print. A distinctively American Art Form," (Fall 1989). He also researched Conger for an exhibition and an accompanying cookbook and history, entitled *America Eats: Forms of Edible Folk Art* (Harper & Row, 1989). Weaver wrote that Conger used "stock motifs" (which would include cornucopias, low baskets or urns of flowers or produce, Indians, Revolutionary War soldiers, garlands of flowers or fruit, militia men on horseback, ladies and gentlemen in faux rusticant garb (àla Marie Antoinette playing dairymaid), eagles, roses, thistles, Scottish folk, and other romantic, even then old-fashioned, designs.

In 1995, a descendant of John Conger sent me a letter accompanied by a photocopied page from the Conger Family geneology. From it we learn that John Conger was born October 8, 1803

in Norwich, Connecticut, where he was married in 1837 to Caroline B. Mingus. Their first child was Walter Mingus Conger, born in August 1838. From the directories I used to research the chronology that follows, it is not absolutely clear, but it seems probable that John traveled the relatively short distance to Manhattan's lower east side at about age 23 or 24 and became a carver (or perhaps an apprentice?). Then, from 1833 to 1836, it is possible that he returned to Norwich, where he met and wed Caroline Mingus, his junior by 15 years, and then the pair went back to New York City. They had four children (two survived), none named John. John Conger, master carver, died January 27, 1869.

In constructing the following dramatization of Conger's New York City in the late 1820s and 1830s, one of the most readable, useful and absorbing books that I consulted was Sean Wilentz's *Chants Democratic: New York City & the Rise of the American Working Class, 1788-1850.* It was published by Oxford University Press, 1984, and in paperback, with corrections, in 1986. Wilentz's book provided some of the wage figures relating to carters, and the characterization of many reverends of the period.

Thanksgiving week, 1989, I spent mostly in the lofty embrace of reading room 315 North in the New York Public Library (NYPL), a room whose virtues I have extolled in previous books. I huddled over a microfiche machine, peering at a bright screen, to skim-read hundreds of thousands of names in New York City directories from 1815-16 through 1873-74. This collection of directories, which could be the primary source book behind a hundred books on the social history of New York City, on early trades, on the plight of widow women in the nineteenth century and a host of other subjects, includes the first published New York City directory, from 1799.

I not only tracked Conger through the years, but also James Y. Watkins, and a few makers of andirons, grates, stoves, and other things of interest, information about which may appear later in a separate book, working title *American Metal Makers & Manufacturers.* Time constraints forced me to stop when the object of my main search — John Conger — had been gone from the directory for three years. Watkins and one or more of his sons were still listed, and that is a subject I invite anyone to pursue. William Woys Weaver, in the two publications cited above, was apparently a year ahead of me in his research into Conger and Watkins and confectionery in America. I read in *America Eats* that Conger was not only a carver but also a baker (making his own New Year's cakes in his own molds) and that the Watkins firm "remained in business into this century" (*op cit,* p.116), and until "at least 1900" "was responsible for the continued manufacture of Conger designs." Weaver also states that Conger worked in Philadelphia "for a time as a furniture carver." (*op cit,* p.115).

Below, with a few side trips, is my skeletal charted chronology of John Conger, based solely on the city and business directories available through a microfiche collection. This information is not from any census records, jury lists, or other valuable, supplementary primary sources also on microfiche and available at NYPL, and it is not drawn from the research of William Woys Weaver, who came to the conclusion that Conger worked (or flourished) only between 1827 and 1835, the restrictive dates cited in an earlier reference. This tantalizingly vast microfiche collection is also at the Library of Congress and a number of large metropolitan libraries throughout the country. If you've got about $5000 you can buy a set of directory microfiches yourself.

The name John Conger appeared first in the 1818-19 *Longworth's Directory,* but this John Conger was an edge tool manufacturer who stayed in the directory for the next 32 years and was then replaced by his son or son-in-law, who was called either John Conger Berry or John Congerberry. In the 1819-20 book, a John Conger, carpenter at 5 Provost Street, appeared, but he disappeared the next year. Using the directories only, it is impossible to determine if perhaps these two wood-related artisans were related — to each other and/or to our Conger. After one appearance, the carpenter's alphabetical place was "taken" by the long-lived John S. Conger, physician, who stayed in the directory for many decades. The edge tool maker and the doctor appeared year after year as the only John Congers until suddenly, in *Longworth's* 1827-28 book, we find our man.

John Conger, carver, 121 Hester St., New York City. 121 Hester Street, at the corner of Forsythe, was six long blocks below Houston St. and only two short blocks east of the Bowery (where even today there are wholesale restaurant supply houses). It wasn't that far from some of the prettiest parts of lower Manhattan, a city then of about 175,000 people. Conger lived — probably as a boarder, or at least a space-sharer — at the corner of Forsythe and Hester, according to a "Runners' Vade Mecum": an address finder or guide that appeared every year in the directories. This guide was to help people locate addresses on streets that were not infrequently renumbered or even renamed as the city grew and the centers of population expanded northward. According to "The Fireman's Guide" of 1834, which was a map of the city from the Battery up to 22nd Street, and from the piers and slips of thae East River across to those of the North River, there was a firehouse a couple of blocks away, and plenty of hydrants within two or three. A terrible fire raged through the area in 1832, stopping just two blocks away from 121 Hester. Conger had moved from Hester in 1828.

Having become somewhat obsessed with the directories and the glimpse of life in the city where I lived for a quarter of a century myself, and knowing Hester Street just a little from the 1975 movie *Hester Street* (set at the turn of the century), I made my first side trip: a short list of other occupants of the street, within a block or so of Conger. Next door at 123 Hester, for example, lived the Reverand John W. Gibbs, a man who may or may not have had a congregation in a church. His calling was not common at that time and in that area of New York, where self-styled preachers and irreligious laborers were much more easily found. Across the street at 120 Hester lived Jacob Bolmore — no occupation given in the 1827-28 directory. In the next year's directory, Benedict Bolmore, printer, was listed at 120, with Jacob as a clerk at the same address. Also next year, although John Conger had moved on to 1 Hamersley and carried on his business on Sullivan Street, J. D. P. Champlin & Co., business unknown, stayed on at 121 Hester, where, under some arrangement, they had shared a roof with Conger.

It is tempting to docu-dramatize the city life of the time, but there is no evidence, beyond the baldest, on which to base speculations. Drama requires a protagonist (here we have Conger), and people, places, things, or social forces against which there is some kind of struggle. If a movie were made of his life, we'd have to know more about his family life, who his clients were, his friends, and exactly what characterized what we assume was his struggle to leave Hester Street. We don't know if the man ever had more than a few minutes a day to leave his work, or if he frequented one or more of the numerous porter houses or taverns, or if it took him four anxious days or a week to finish a cake board, or what else he might have spent most of his time carving. But just to indicate who his "neighbors" were, we will imagine that Conger might have stepped out the doorway of 121 to turn right, cross Forsythe, and go a few doors to see John G. Hughes, a carpenter at 113, about some mahogany or walnut wood scraps. If he went on a few more doors, maybe he encountered the whitesmith, Peter C. Cortelyou, at 110; he may have bought an apple from John Lyon, the grocer at 93; or stopped to talk to Clarissa Adams, the widow who ran a boarding house at 87, about a room; or perhaps he needed to ask David Coit, shoemaker, at 73 Hester, about fixing the only boots he had.

If he turned left when he left his abode (which was also his workplace that first year in the directory, and which may have housed several home-work artisans, or other workers), maybe he saw Thomas Gedney, the combmaker who lived and worked at 132 Hester. Or Stephen Lockwood, whose occupation was not listed, also at 132. (Next year, the clock-manufacturer and brass founder Engell Friend also lived at 132.) Margaret Wilcox, a carpet weaver at 140, was possibly working in the cellar, trying to make the $2 or $3 a week she needed for the most frugal living. Because she was not listed as a widow, it is likely she was pretty much on her own.

Did John Conger, in fact, know any of these people the year he lived on Hester? We know he carved fancy cakeboards with formal, traditional European images of militia men and bounteous flowers; but was he doing them this early? Where would he have got his inspiration? Did he, in fact, come to New York City after a short time in Pennsylvania, where a European folk tradition was beginning to flourish and where many carvings and graphics comprised similar motifs? The prosaic, not to say squalid, images surrounding him in everyday life seem not to have influenced his work at all, except perhaps to make him work harder to get out. Not that there were many "good" neighborhoods at the time in New York City; only wealthy merchants and bankers lived somewhat within their own enclaves, down around Wall Street, where there were fancy retail shops as well as banking and insurance institutions.

In the area way below what is now called the "Lower East Side" — where Conger (and later his wife Caroline) lived throughout his approximately four decades in the city — also lived most of the day laborers, jobless, and desperately poor people of New York. Pigs wandered the streets in the daytime, actually performing a sort of service by eating garbage, but creating a nuisance of more than one kind on the pavement. Hundreds of cartmen clogged the streets, pushing wooden wheelbarrows or hand barrows, or pulling hand carts, laden with whatever had to be transferred, hoping to pick up a job that would bring them from 12-1/2¢ to 25¢ a half mile. The noise — from the squealing of pigs; the crying of children; the rattle of looms; the shouts of people selling services or food; the clang and crash of hammers beating on gold (to make foil), steel (to make tools), brass (to make vessels or trims or decorations), nails or pegs (to make shoes), iron nails and wooden boards (to make houses, coffins, more carts, barrels, ships), or chisels (to make carvings); to the clatter of horseshoes and cartwheels on cobblestones — must have been close to deafening.

By the next year, 1828, probably on May 1 (traditional moving day in New York City for 100 years or more, because all annual leases, as well as the quarter spring leases, were up that day) Conger had moved and was doing well enough, we suppose, to have a workplace separate from his home. It would still be nine years before he married.

There was a lot of competion in the carving trade. Although the directories do not make much differentiation between the types of carvers, a computer study of addresses of all carvers, as well as the carver-gilders, along with the addresses of cabinet makers, chair makers, and frame and furniture makers, would probably tie together some of the unknown craftsmen. Men with the dual trade of carving and gilding often worked on picture or looking-glass frames; a very few probably carved trade-signs (some of which may have been freestanding figures such as cigar store Indians). In the 1827-28 *Longworth's Directory*, simple carvers were apparently slightly in the majority; shipcarvers were the rarest of all the carvers.

One interesting entry I found was William Alcock, calico-print cutter, 8 Watts. Later I was glad to have found him and his job description, when, after three years missing from the directory [see below], John Conger (I believe the same one as our man) reappears as a printcutter. Cake boards, for printing New Year's Cakes, were widely known as cake prints. The job description "printcutter" may have referred specifically to cake prints, or it may mean than John Conger made carved wooden printing blocks either for a cloth-printer or a publisher — of books, broadsides, or perhaps even wallpaper.

The main publishers of the directories I used were Thomas Longworth (*Longworth's Annual Almanac, New-York Register & City Directory*); John Doggett, later John Doggett, Jr., later Doggett & Rode, still later Rode alone (*Doggett's The New York Directory* or *Doggett's New York Business Directory*; later *Rode's Directory of New York City*); and John F. Trow, compiler H. Wilson (*Wilson's Business Directory of New York City*, later *Trow's New York City Directory*). All addresses are streets except where noted. An occasional "skipped" date indicates a break in the city directories, not the absence of a listing.

DATE	NAME	OCCUPATION	WORK -- ADDRESSES -- HOME	
1827-28	John Conger	carver	121 Hester	121 Hester
1828-29	John Conger	carver	65 Sullivan	1 Hamersley
1829-30	John Conger	carver	15 Stanton	29 Stanton
1830-31	John Conger	carver	15 Stanton	23 Stanton
1831-32	John Conger	carver	222 Greene	222 Greene
1832-33	John Conger	carver	242 Greene	117 Fourth Av.
1833-34	not listed	-0-	-0-	-0-
1834-35	not listed	-0-	-0-	-0-

For 1834-35 only, a John Conger, baker, appears.

1835-36	not listed	-0-	-0-	-0-
1836-37	John Conger	printcutter	211 Orange	211 Orange
1837-38	John Conger	printcutter	211 Orange	211 Orange
1838-39	John Conger	printcutter	211 Orange	211 Orange
1839-40	not listed	-0-	-0-	-0-
1840-41	John Conger	printcutter	25 Marion	25 Marion
1841-42	John Conger	printcutter	25 Marion	25 Marion
1842-43	John Conger	printcutter	25 Marion	25 Marion
1843-44	John Conger	printcutter	23 Marion	23 Marion
1844-45	John Conger	printcutter	23 Marion	23 Marion
1845-46	John Conger	printcutter	23 Marion	23 Marion
1846-47	John Conger	printcutter	23 Marion	23 Marion
1847-48	John Conger	printcutter	23 Marion	23 Marion
1848-49	John Conger	printcutter	foot of Bank St.	foot of Bank
1850-51	John Conger	printcutter	Bank	Bank
1851-52	John Conger	printcutter	Bank	Bank
1852-53	not listed	-0-	-0-	-0-
1854-55	John Conger	printcutter	181 Bank	101 Bank
ditto	a John Conger	carver	138 Bank	101 Bank

At this point, 1854-55, the new (or renewed) listing <u>John Conger carver</u> suddenly appears with <u>John Conger printcutter</u>, both listings with same home address but different work addresses. The only way to find out more information would be to turn to census records or other more detailed records that are probably available in New York or Washington, D.C., on microfilm or fiche. Because this is the only year when two listings with the same name and related occupations are given, it is quite possible that the names are evidence of an error in information-gathering by the compiler of the directory (Trow's at this point), or that one is father, one son, and that one or the other (probably the printcutter, who I assume was the elder) died that year. The listing resumes in 1856-57, when John Conger was 53 years old.

1856-57	John Conger	cutter	138 Bank	101 Bank
1857-58	John Conger	cutter	138 Bank	101 Bank
1858-59	John Conger	cutter	138 Bank	101 Bank
1859-60	John Conger	carver	138 Bank	-?-
1860-61	John Conger	carver	138 Bank	131 Bank
1861-62	John Conger	cutter	138 Bank	131 Bank
1862-63	John Conger	carver	525 Hudson	131 Bank
1863-64	John Conger	carver	525 Hudson	131 Bank
1864-65	John Conger	carver	-?-	131 Bank
1865-66	John Conger	carver	525 Hudson	131 Bank

In 1865, for one year only, a firm appears called Conger, Smith & Heath, Tin Ware & House Furnishing Goods, at 580 Hudson as well as 400, 402, and 404 W. 15th St. The Conger in question is Walter M. Conger, of unknown relationship to John Conger. It is interesting in more than one way because John Conger's carvings have been tied, by marks, to the house furnishing establishment of James Y. Watkins. For years James Y. Watkins & Son have at least two business establishments, including the one at 16 Catharine Street where James Y. Watkins started his business life in New York City as a tinsmith in 1830. By 1865 the Watkins firm is back to only one address — the place at 16 Catharine (or Catherine) Street, three or four long blocks south of Hester, where we believe the young Conger began his career.

1866-67	John Conger	carver	214 W. Houston	

In the 1866-67 edition, Walter Conger shows up as a maker of trays.

1868-69	John Conger	carver	at the rear of 94 Charlton	
1870-71	not listed	-0-	-0-	-0-

Because John Conger was not listed in the next three directories I assumed, although I lacked the time to check another five years or more of listings, that he was now gone for good. (Whichever Conger he was.) It was a rather strange moment when I found him missing for four years. I had avidly followed his progress (and apparent decline) and made somewhat romantic assumptions about the rise and fall in fortune as his skill — his artistry — seemed to have fallen out of favor (his last address was in the rear of a building not far from where he began 41 years earlier). Conger's disappearance from the directories was accompanied by a sense of real personal loss for me. It wasn't until a descendent wrote me in 1995 that I learned that John Conger, master carver, died in early 1869. James Y. Watkins and his son, who had been joined, for one year only, by another son, were still working out of 16 Catharine, but the elder was living at 450 Lexington, which was up between 44th and 45th Streets, and his son was making the daily commute down to Catherine from the increasingly fashionable if rather bucolic West 128th Street near Fifth Avenue.

There really is nothing like these directories to give you a sort of Wellesian time trip. It is ironic that the current market price of one really outstanding board carved by Conger could be worth more than his total life income: this situation is often encountered when you consider the income of an artisan and the market value of his or her work 50 or 100 or 200 years later. It is also possible that the date chart given here will cause a re-evaluation and a certain amount of backpedaling on prices. **NOTE:** If it is correct, as William Woys Weaver writes, that Watkins bought Conger's old stock and continued to sell either Conger or Conger-like prints until 1900, then surely the market value will drop somewhat.

CAKE BOARDS, Conger-signed, -attributed or -related:

Cake board, basket, round carving centered on rectangular walnut board, neat sawtooth edge frames low basket, ribbed flared sides, a lively flower arrangement of roses, tulip and leaves, composition filled in with leaves under the basket, signed "J. Conger," catalog writer speculates "possibly PA," but provenance is actually NYC, NY. 15-1/4" L x 9-1/2" W, diameter of circle is about 6-3/4", 19th C. Sold at the Richard A. Bourne Co. (Hyannis, MA) auction of the Cushman Estate of Duxbury, MA, November 25-26, 1988. Price realized $1500. **$2500-$3500**

Cake board, boy & girl, carved walnut (?), square with round medallion depicting a boy & girl and tulips, rather Dutch in feeling, not the subject treatment expected from carver John Conger to whom the unsigned board was attributed by the dealer. 11-1/2" H x 11" W, medallion about 7" diameter, NYC (?), probably 1st two-thirds 19th C. **$3200-$4000**

Cake board, Columbia, carved mahogany board, elliptical overall carving barely fits within oblong bounds, no separate medallions, gracefully draped Columbia figure, surrounded by laurel (olive?) wreath, holds striped shield with legend "America" at top; spread-winged eagle holds arrows in foot & scales of justice (left pan has trade symbols & barrels, right has plow, rake, pitchfork) in beak over backs of 2 horses; other figure is American Indian in plumed headdress and cape, holding staff with Old Glory flag with 16 stars, topped by the Phrygian cap or liberty cap (originated in French Revolution), further decorated with cornucopia full of fruit, many flowers, grapes, 10 large stars, sunflower, acorns, wheel, wheat, etc. An extraordinary unsigned board as fine as the "J. Conger" boards, American, 27-1/4" L x 15-1/2" W, motifs circa 1800, carving possibly mid 19th C. **Astronomical Ellipses:** This double-pointed shape is often called "elliptical" in ads and descriptions. Technically, only an elliptical orbit, in astronomical terms, would have the apparently pointed ends; in geometry, an ellipse is what most of us call an oval. However, in these cake board descriptions I am using the astronomical meaning. **16 Stars**: Although there was never a flag with 16 stars, the 16th state was Tennessee from 1786 to 1803. This extraordinary mold was sold by John Zan, Washington, NJ, in 1979, and again at auction, by Sotheby's, June 23, 1988. A good photograph appears in the catalog (Lot 307). Price range reflects the value of American patriotic motifs to collectors. **$7000-$10,000**

Cake board, cornucopia & star, carved walnut, square with chamfered & truncated corners (probably to make room for a finger to tuck under to lift the mold off the dough), round carving. Design of 5-point star in center (unusual because only 5 points), flanked by cornucopia with flowers & fruit. Above is small shield flanked by busts of 2 Revolutionary War-period military men, one has "H" next to him, other has [backwards of course] "P." This may be a centennial or 50-year commemorative for the Battle of Bunker Hill of June 5, 1775, in which case the "P" may be for Colonel William Prescott, said to have commanded, "Don't shoot until you see the whites of their eyes," and the "H" may represent the British commander, Major General William Howe. Also in the design is a sort of barge-like ship with a flag (possibly lying off in Boston harbor). A lacy finely scalloped border surrounds a cartouche reading "M. Hall" below the ship. This could be the name of the baker Michael Hall, who appeared at least as early as 1820 and as late as 1827-28 in NY directories. Board is American, probably NY, 12" x 12", c.1820s-1830s. This politico-military cake board was in the Schorsch collection sale at Sotheby's, May 1-2, 1981. **$2500-$4000**

IV-58. Cake mold or cake board, *Square, two-sided. One side has three men in hats, two in a sort of pugilist pose, or perhaps they're fighting to gain control of a handgun, while a third looks on. Lots of stars in a circle. Verso has a bird and a dog. 8-1/2" square. Photograph courtesy Litchfield Auction Gallery. Ex-Harold Corbin Collection, auctioned 1/1/1990. Price realized, only $850. Very unusual, valuable subject.* **$950-$1500**

Cake board, dog, carved wood, rectangular, with elliptical carving, nice but simple, depicting a large St. Bernard dog being ridden by small bonneted child carrying whip stick, the prognathious dog panting, and with tail awkwardly curved upwards, a single tulip growing up from teardrop chip-carved border nearly to dog's belly; figures surrounded by stems with many leaves & with 15 stars, somewhat haphazardly placed, the whole resembling Conger's work only in that there is a carved ellipse. Dealer's ad states "attributed" to Conger; his name does help sell cake boards. NYC, NY provenance, probably, if Conger, but there's a Germanic (Pennsylvania German?) look to it. It's obvious that Conger used popular prints and graphics for design sources. 6-1/4" H x 11-3/4" L, 19th C. Pictured in *Maine Antique Digest*, Feb. 1982. Price range is my estimate, not Spring Valley Antique's asking or selling price. It would be higher if signed.   **$2200-$3800**

Cake board, eagle, square board with round carving, beaded edge, features eagle standing on shield with 4 flags, grapes and leaves in woven border, decorated in background with 45 stars, signed "J. Conger," NYC, NY, 13" H x 12" W, 19th C.   **$4000-$6,000**

Cake board, fire truck, carved walnut or mahogany, has three Conger-like elliptical carvings lined up vertically on oblong board. Top is an elaborate eagle; middle has a fire truck similar to "The Superior" described below, but with no number and a row of XXX; bottom carving depicts a horse race, showing crowds in the stands, two horses and jockeys, and in the foreground, the words "ECLIPS SUB HENBY." This extraordinary mold, probably a Conger, was advertised in the April 1973 *Magazine ANTIQUES* by dealers John Bihler & Henry Coger, who dated it c.1825. Price then and present location unknown. The current value would probably be in the range of   **$9000-$15,000**

Fire Engine Motif Detection Story. A carved "mahogany" cake board, very like the work of "Conger," is shown in Figure 159 of Jean Lipman's *American Folk Art in Wood, Metal & Stone*, 1948. It's owned by the New York Historical Society, NYC. The oblong board, 14-3/8" L x 7/8" thick, has an elliptical wheat-ear bordered cartouche with a depiction of a fire engine being pulled by three long-coated firemen with boots & hats, the first one blowing a horn. The engine has "17" on its cistern & boiler. I thought that research into early nineteenth-century fire companies might reveal a specific engine & engine company. I proposed to investigate three lines of enquiry: identification of the (**1**) style of engine; (**2**) style of firemen's coats; and (**3**) style of firemen's hats, all very detailed and distinctive. But after contacting several historical societies and fire engine museums, the only conclusive information is that it is a "goose neck" side stroke engine, with an air chamber in the back, the main body being a water cistern. It is of a type dating probably to the 1820s, possibly the 1830s. In addition, in a cartouche above the engine is the word "SUPERIOR." Charles Radzinsky, the former curator of the American Museum of Fire Fighting, in Middletown, NY, wrote me that, " 'SUPERIOR' could be a pet or nickname given to the company and/or engine, such as 'Water Witch,' 'Good Intent,' 'Excelsior,' etc. The rather high number, 17, would indicate that the company was in an urban rather than a rural community." I conclude from the best book on fire fighting equipment, *Enjine! Enjine! A Story of Fire Protection,* by Kenneth Holcomb Dunshee (NYC: Home Insurance Co., 1939), that the pieced hats with brim worn by the three firemen carved on the board are of the four comb type, c.1812 to 1830. Finally, the long-skirted, belted coats appear to be from the 1820s. A long fire ladder is shown below the

IV-59. Cake board. *Elliptical lozenge shape on oblong board, side-saddle equestrienne wearing a plaid or tartan fringed skirt, fitted jacket, and small riding hat, in center floral circle, flanked by small ellipses with Colonial man (**L**) and American Indian (**R**). Cornucopias below.* **John Conger's mark**. *Auctioned by Litchfield Auction Gallery. 3/25/1990. American, mid (?)19th C. (Read the Conger article in this chapter for a range of dates.)* **$6000-$10,000**

corrugated road where the engine is being pulled over; in the sky surrounding the engine are six 9-point blazing stars. I conclude that the motifs of the board date between 1820 to 1830. The provenance given in Lipman (and probably the *Index of American Design*, from which the picture was taken), is "Pennsylvania." Boards marked or attributed to Conger are from New York State, but I believe this may be a Conger. There was an engine company 17 in Manhattan, that in 1832 was about 15 blocks from Conger on Hester. After 1865, Engine company 17 was close to Sullivan St. and Ludlow Place (later Houston) and a year later, Conger moved to within a few blocks of the company. Therefore, it is my conclusion that this is a Conger cake board, and that he carved it probably in 1866, making it one of his last boards. Value is difficult to assign to the fire engine board: the subject matter is highly collectible, with many thousands of dollars customarily paid for early chief's horns, ceremonial helmets, decorated fire buckets, etc. **NOTE:** As this book went to press, a signed J. Conger cake board was found with an elliptical design on both sides: one was a very official-looking eagle bearing a banner in its beak reading "HAPPY NEW YEAR," and the reverse was a fire truck design showing the barrel-like water tank or reservoir, the two- or four-man pumping lever (something like a seesaw), laurel leaves, and a ladder lying alongside. Price unavailable.

Cake board, George Washington patriotic design, ellipse on large 14-1/2" H x 24" L mahogany board, round design within ellipse has GW in breeches & plumed tricorn hat, with his last name in banner below him, flanked by Columbia & Justice and further out by 2 cornucopias, each with one star next to it, with huge eagle & shield above GW's head (with banner reading "E. PLURIBUS UNUM"), grape cluster border. In two ends of the ellipse are a sailor and an Amerindian, with boughs of corn and tulips. Outer border of 39 stars and swagged ribbon. This board, "attributed to John Conger" and dated "c.1830" by dealer David A. Schorsch, was advertised in *Maine Antique Digest*, April 1996, for an undisclosed amount. Of course, we know that Conger worked for some 35 years more, and there's no reason for assuming this is as early as 1830, although that may make it more desirable to some collectors. This is not a bargain dealer either, and because of "Father of Our Country" motif, it probably has a price range around **$12,000-$15,000**

Cake board, horseman, carved rectangular piece of wood, elliptical (a double-pointed shape, sometimes called a <u>lozenge shape</u>, an <u>ellipse</u> or a <u>boat</u>) carving with round center medallion with horseman, flanked by vertical ellipses with figural carvings within, marked only "Old Rough and Ready," American, 18" H x 24" L, c.1815 motif, possibly, even probably, much later for actual carving. The name "Old Rough and Ready" refers to Za-

IV-60. Cake board. *Mahogany, elliptical carving typical of Conger's boards. Central round medallion has footed urn or fountain with 2 doves and many flowers. The fountain/urn is obviously drawn from the elaborate cast iron urns & fountains from the 2nd and 3rd quarters of the 19th century, such as those made by another New Yorker, Jordan L. Mott. Flanking figures are a Colonial man (**L**) and a milkmaid-type woman in knee-length dress and apron (**R**). Typical cornucopias below, roses above. 15" H x 26" L. Used for making "New Year's Cakes." Signed "**J. Congers**" twice. New York City, 19th C. Photo courtesy Litchfield Auction Gallery. Ex-Harold Corbin Collection, 1/1/1990. Price realized then was $2950.* **$5000-$9,000 NOTE:** *It's hard to guess value, partly because these don't change hands or come on the market often, and there aren't enough known, yet, to find duplicates or deduce rarity. Subject matter, size, collector provenance, and the dealer who's selling determine price. In the early 1990s a Conger-attributed tiger maple board with an American eagle, Lafayette, the NY state coat of arms, an American Indian, 35 stars in the border and 14 stars within the ellipse, as well as an extremely rare figure of Uncle John (precursor to Sam) was for sale for $25,000.*

chary Taylor, who fought in the War of 1812, and who was U.S. president in 1849-50. **NOTE:** In *The Magazine ANTIQUES*, Aug. 1953, appeared a picture of a carved mahogany board, slightly rectangular, large round medallion nearly filling surface, with frontal standing figure of man with deer behind him, a memorial of Andrew Jackson, inscribed "New Orleans Jany 8," the 1815 battle, in the War of 1812, won by Jackson. This pastry mold was from the collection of Mrs. Edward R. Ferriss, St. Charles, IL, formerly in the collection of George Horace Lorimer. I don't know where it is now. "Rough & Ready" was offered for sale in 1985, by unnamed seller, who was asking $2500 or best offer. **$3500-$5000**

Cake board, horseman, carved wood, with one side depicting large man with beard & hat riding on a high-stepping horse, other side depicts a rooster and a soldier or militia man on horseback (a very common archetypal image, found also in American pieces), edge marked "I. W.," which might be James Watkins or possibly the initials (an "I" frequently was used for "J" in America and Europe) of a European, 13-1/2" H x 10-3/4", 19th C. **$1000-$2000**

Cake board, horseman, oblong with rounded corners, horseman with lance & plumed helmet, banner behind him reads "New York Lancers," flanked by cornucopias and floral sprays, piecrust border, of the "Conger" type, American, in style early 19th C., but could be mid 19th C. or later. **$2800-$3500**

Cake board, horseman, carved mahogany (according to dealer, although some other similar boards are American black walnut), large oblong plank with elliptical carving filling most of width & length, central round medallion with horse and rider, flanked by 2 vertical ellipses with flowers, rest of space filled in with

IV-62. Cake board. *"New Year Cake Board," of carved wood, with round medallion filled with horse & rider, flowers, stars and deep decorative border. The naiveté of catalog drawing may surpass that of the actual carving, at least to some extent. Mold came in two sizes, "large" for a one-pound print cake, and "small" for a half-pound print. Also offered, though not depicted, were one-pound size metal cake boards probably for springerle (?). Design & style is early to mid-19th C., but this picture is from Jaburg Brothers catalog of 1908 which brings probable date of many existing boards forward. Selling price of such a board might be in thousands. I can't imagine a way to know for sure the age, unless the owner inscribed the date of purchase.* **$300-$500**

Photo © 1989 Sotheby's, Inc.

IV-61. Cake board. *Mahogany oblong board, design within ellipse. Many symbolic and patriotic motifs, including American Indian, holding a staff with the American flag, topped with the Phrygian "liberty" cap, borne in cornucopia-shaped chariot, drawn by horse toward the figure of Columbia, wearing flowing dress and holding a shield and laurel wreath aloft. The shield, with stars & stripes, is inscribed "America." Above is the American eagle with an olive branch in one talon and with a pair of balance scales in its beak, the left one bearing small kegs or barrels, and the right one with a plow, rake and pitchfork. Large cornucopia at left, many grapes, leaves, stars fill background. 15-1/2" H x 27-1/2" L. Typical in motif, though more fussily elaborate in execution than others known of John Conger's work. There's an almost art nouveau quality in the scrolling forms — from stems, flowers, the horse's trappings to the woman's drapery, and the busy decorativeness leads me to believe this postdates the 1870s.* **Unsigned but Conger attributed.** *Photo courtesy of Sotheby's, NYC. Auctioned 6/23/1988.* **$6,000-$10,000**

leaves & fruits of the vine, very Eastern European-looking, Slavik or Czech, but possibly carved by J. Conger or made from his pattern. Marked "J. Y. Watkins," NYC, NY, 25-1/2" L x 13-1/2" W. This closely resembles the J. Conger cookie or so-called marzipan boards, all of which I have seen only in pictures. They all look very European. This one was advertised in *Maine Antique Digest,* February 1989, by Byron & Craig White, of Sterling, PA. The Whites cite Bishop's *American Folk Sculpture* and Lipman's *American Folk Art in Wood, Metal, and Stone* for mentions of Conger, but mentions are all they are — no real information. **$2500-$3000**

Cake board, man & woman, carved walnut, nearly square board with round carving with central figures of man & woman in round-brimmed hats, flowers & reeded border around outside, fully carved, dealer says "attributed to John Conger," NYC, NY, size not given in ad, date estimated as "c.1810," which is probably at least 14 years too early (Conger was born in 1803) and possibly as many as 40 or 50 years too early — if indeed it's a Conger. **$2800-$3200**

Cake board, man & woman, rectangular walnut board with elliptical carving composed of 3 parts. In a round medallion in center is a basket of fruit, background heavily carved with flowers, flanking this are 2 vertical elliptical cartouches, within one is man with shepherd's crook & hat, other has woman with sheaf of wheat, signed "J. Conger" in two places, for John Conger,

NYC, NY. 25-1/2" L x 15-1/2" W, 1st quarter19th C. to 1860s (?). This was auctioned by the Hesse Galleries, Otego, NY, in Sept. 1986. Since that time, a few other similarly carved boards have come up for sale or auction and are usually described in ads as "attributed to J. Conger." **$3000-$4000**

Cake boards, Conger — See also springerle roller

CAKE BOARDS, probably not Conger-related:

Cake board, basket of flowers on one side is typical of late 18th or early 19th style, tulips on other side, deep carved cherry wood, thick board, beautiful patina, 7" L x 6" W, poss. early 19th C. c.1810-1830, but could be later in early style, as so many Conger molds probably are. **$175-$235**

Cake board, bird & cherry with leaves, carved cherry or other fruitwood, American, 2" x 3", 19th C. **$65-$90**

Cake board, cat wearing collar, tabby striped & sitting, carved board, 10" H x 6-1/2" W, poss. English, early to mid 19th C. **$450-$550**

Cake board, corrugated very finely, with a center line so that you could break cookie in half, for sugar cookies, lightweight wood, American (?), 13-1/8" L, makes a 3-5/8" W cookie, late (?)19th C. **$60-$75**

Cake board, fish on one side, on the other a stylized flower, American (?), 10-3/8" L x 3-3/4" W, mid to late 19th C. (?) Not a very distinguished carving. **$150-$200**

IV-63. Cake board, maple sugar mold, and confection mold. *Carved wood. (L) In vertical ellipse is American Indian bearing bow in one hand and chief's feathered staff in other, 8" H x 5-1/4", American, probably prior to but near 1876 Centennial; (M) Maple sugar mold, for two cakes, each bearing banded large heart and 2 stars. 10-1/2" H x 4" W. American or Canadian, probably mid 19th C. (R) Two-sided board, with pistol on one side, tobacco pipe on other. 8-1/2" x 4". American, late 19th C. Photograph courtesy Litchfield Auction Gallery. Harold Corbin Collection, auctioned 1/1/1990, $375, $350, $300.* **$600-$1000; $350.00-$500; $300-$450**

Cake board, geometric, carved maple, elliptical, deeply carved geometric border in what might be called, by cut glass collectors, "strawberry diamonds," center design is a 6-point star, with other tiny chip-carved designs between the petals or points, flanked by 2 hearts, chamfered back, Pennsylvania or Canadian, 9-1/2" L x 4-1/4" W x 1" thick, early 19th C, c.1820-1840. Occasionally these molds are labeled "*butter prints*." One auctioned in 1983, exactly the same, was said to be from Nova Scotia. **$275-$500**

Pattern Glass Motifs. When trying to describe the border design, I got out my *American Glass*, by George & Helen McKearin, which depicts hundreds of pattern glass pieces. I was struck, while looking at cup plates, how similar some patterns are to butter prints; it is to be expected, as the art of woodcarving is of primary importance in making the molds for pressed glass. The period is the same too. I believe careful study would reveal many close relationships in motif and style, perhaps even traceable to a region. The McKearins say, for example, that pinwheels are typical of Midwestern (pattern-glass) designs; we think of them as Pennsylvanian when we see them on butter prints. Study! Study!

Cake board, harlequin figure or possibly Pero, carved wood, Dutch (?), 9" H, prob. early 19th C. **$150-$200**

Cake board, horse & sleigh, lion, flower pot, courting couple, 3 carvings per side, European, 22-1/2" L x 4-1/2" W, early to mid 19th C. **$135-$165**

Cake board, horseman on one side, deer on other, mellow, smooth, even "greasy" feel to wood, European, 13-1/2" L, board is 1-5/8" thick, c.1800 to 1820. **$250-$350**

Cake board, horseman, a dandy dressed up, perhaps a Yankee Doodle, with flowers, high boots, knee britches, roll brim hat with feather, carved wood, slightly warped plank with 2 small age or dryness checks and a drilled hole in each corner, nice dark patina, American (?), 1-1/8" thick x 10-5/8" H x 8-3/8" W, 2nd quarter 19th C. **$500-$650**

Cake board, man & woman, carved wood, man on one side, woman with tiered gathered skirt on other, European probably, hard to be certain without documentation, 17-1/4" L, board is 1-3/8" thick, looks c.1830s to 1850, but could be later. **$400-$600**

Reproduction alert. Cake board, man in kneepants & fancy hat, Dutch, 18" L, mid to 3rd quarter 20th C. Wood is stained dark brown to resemble a harder wood but is carved from pine. Edges of this only 1-1/4" thick board show saw marks, and the back shows no evidence of hand-planing. Finally, there are no signs of wear, and the design is not as intricate as the really old ones (texture of fabric, etc.): in fact it couldn't be, because it's carved of softish pine, not hard dense walnut, bass, mahogany, or fruitwood. **$75-$100**

Cake board, mason's tools (square, hammer, mallet, pointing tool, compass), round shape, deeply carved, beaded border, possibly a Masonic piece, carved with initials "I. D.," which are probably not the maker's initials; if they are, "I" could be old style "J," American, 7/8" thick wood, 5-1/2" diameter, 19th C. The dealer said this was advertised to be for "butter cookies" but in my experience butter cookies spread so much during baking that any form or molded design would be lost. All cookies have some shortening in them. **$1200-$1800**

Cake board, old woman, a cat & a little dog on one side (prominent in her costumes is a big bonnet, and a pocket tied to the waist of her dress, hung from her belt, with slit opening), a plant & pot with big berries on obverse, European, 1" thick x 4" x 7", early 19th C. **$400-$500**

IV-65. Cake board. *Carved wood with wormholes, two-sided (see other side under springerle molds, IV-378.) Large heart with flowers growing from small heart. Pennsylvania German or European. 9-1/4" H x 6-1/4" W. Signed "F. G." Ex-Keillor Collection.* **$700-$1200**

IV-64. Cake board. *Square with round medallion decorated with an American eagle, shield body with stripes & stars, clutching arrows, surrounded by wreaths of leaves. 10-1/4" H x 11". Photograph courtesy Litchfield Auction Gallery, Litchfield CT. Ex-Harold Corbin Collection, auctioned 1/1/1990, for $525.* **$700-$900**

Cake board, owl & rabbit on one side, parrot & songbird on other, carved wood, signed "T B. W. W. 20" along one side edge, prob. European, number "20" may be pattern number. 11-1/2" L x 3-1/4" W, 19th C. **$140-$165**

Cake board, pears & leaves on one side, flowers on other, deep carved cherry wood, prob. American, 7" x 5", early to mid 19th C. **$180-$220**

Cake board, pickup truck from 1920s, spare tire, possibly depicts a common sight in the Great Depression, of a family moving all belongings in an old car or truck, carved wood, definitely unusual, American (?), 23-1/2" L x 9-1/2" W, 1920s or 1930s. **Unusual image**: the fact of the truck image existence, with fairly good & detailed carving, forces you to look warily at many other cookie boards with undateable images such as flowers and animals. Auctioned by Garth's in 1986 for only $150. Estimated price range a few years later is higher because of image, which now has crossover appeal. **$165-$225**

Cake board, woman sitting in chair spinning thread or fine yarn, carved wood, English (?), 1" thick x 2-5/8" x 3-1/8", early 19th C. (There are lots of chair collectors who'd love this!) **$250-$400**

Cake board, wreath of leaves, deep carved maple (?), American (?), 4-1/2" D, mid to late 19th C. **$125-$175**

Cake boards, **new**, carved bass wood with hanging hole in back that doesn't show on front, offered in at least 6 designs: large round with wheat sheaf; heart with tulip and daisies on large square board; pineapple and laurel wreath on small round; seated cat on small oblong; and woman & man in "native" (i.e. European) costumes, where woman has basket, man has sword, each on oblong boards. These were made "using authentic European cookie molds and incorporating Pennsylvania Dutch designs," but they are rather hokey/cutesy, especially the man & woman, who are called "George and Martha" in the catalog I saw. They are carved by Don Dillon and possibly signed on back by him, Camp Hill, PA, 12" diameter; 6-1/2" H x 6" W; 8" diameter; 6" H x 4" W; and the two figures are 10-1/2" H x 3-1/4" W, c.1983-1984. New retail prices were between $12 (for cat) and $38 (for wheat sheaf). You know from the retail price (assuming the wholesale is half that) that these were created on a machine, not hand-carved. Value now might be same as 1984 retail, or less. They won't appreciate in real value for a very long time, although there's no estimating sentimental value. **$12-$38**

Cake boards — See also cookie mold; gingerbread man mold; pie top-crust mold; springerle mold

Cake decorations, bride & grooms — See bride & groom

IV-67. Twelfth-Day scene outside a Confectioner. *Probably similar to the scene outside pastry shops in America for New Year's Cakes (see the cake boards by Conger et al). This one in London. "From the taking down of the shutters in the morning, the pastry-cook and his men, with additional assistants, male and female, are fully occupied by attending to the dressing out of the window, executing orders of the day before, receiving fresh ones, or supplying the wants of chance customers. Before dusk the important arrangement of the window is completed. Then the gas is turned on, with supernumerary argand-lamps and manifold wax-lights, to illuminate countless cakes of all prices and dimensions, that stand in rows and piles on the counters and sideboards, and in the windows. The richest in flavour and heaviest in weight and price are placed on large and massy salvers; one, enormously superior to the rest in size, is the chief object of curiosity; and all are decorated with all imaginable images of things animate and inanimate. Stars, castles, kings, cottages, dragons, trees, fish, palaces, cats, dogs, churches, lions, milkmaids, knights, serpents, and innumerable other forms in snow-white confectionary, painted with variegated colours, glitter by 'excess of light' from mirrors against the walls. This 'paradise' of dainty devices is crowded by successive desirers of the seasonable delicacies." William Hone, Every-Day Book, Vol. I. London: [1825-26]. The scene above with disconcerted customers pinned together in the front, illustrates the typical London boys' Twelfth-night tricks of nailing gentleman's coats to the door frame, or pinning stranger ladies and gents together.*

IV-66. Cake board. *"Ancient Carving ... on an ancient oak board, two feet in diameter. It represents the letters A, H, C [backwards] in the centre, surrounded by this legend, viz. 'An harte that is wyse wyll obstine from sinnes and increas in the workes of God.' As this legend reads backward, and all the carving is incuse, it was evidently intended to give impression to something; I imagine pastry." William Hone's* The Every-day Book, *Vol. II, n.d. [1827 or 1828]. Hone also reproduces part of a 1778 letter from the Lord Chancellor Thurlow, from Bath, England, which says that he had received the mold from a farmer from Norfolk, England, prior to 1778.*

Cake decorations, candleholders, 10 pieces (probably a full set), stamped tin, each "petaled" holder for small birthday candles has thin, long tapered point for sticking in cake, somewhat rusted overall. Very like Christmas tree candleholders but with spikes not clips, and probably made by same people. American (?), each about 1-1/4" L overall, turn of century. **$15-$25**

Cake decorations, candleholders, painted iron flowers on spikes, American, late 19th or early 20th C. Set of four: **$25-$45**

Cake decorations, set of four Beatles figures, plastic, in original package, 1965. Crossover collectors might pay even more. **$15-$30**

Cake decorator set, or frosting tubes, plunger or syringe type, 12 different inserts or nozzle tubes to make frosting come out in stars, rosettes, pointed pixie caps, etc., with instruction book, in original box, "Ateco," mfd. by The Thomsen Co., NYC, NY, pat'd 1925, but sold in that form for many years. A full page 1931 ad, in the *Boston Cooking School* magazine, showed an Ateco set as a premium for getting a new subscriber signed up; it included a three-tube boxed set, called "Special Set No. 700. — Aluminum syringe with three assorted Standard Brass Ornamenting Tubes . . . in its attractive display box. The satin-finished barrel with its highly polished caps and brass tubes produce a fine contrast in metals which harmonize with the color combination of the box." The ad also depicted the 99 other tubes you could get, "any eight as a premium" or $1 a dozen — "each [tube is] worked out to produce a certain line, scalloped border or rosette, etc., when icing is forced through them." This is still being sold, though in different package. I think the metal may be discernably different too. Price for 12-tube boxed set: **$15-$20**

Cake fortune-telling charms, cast unID heavy metal (some kind of slush metal alloy), 15 very detailed pieces, viz. owl, purse, top hat, thimble, man's wedding ring, woman's ring, sadiron, heart, baby shoe, boat, button, automobile, and 3 unID forms, in original box that has orange, black & white label depicting a fortune teller lighting cake candles, "Made in U.S.A.," between 3/4" and 1-1/2" H, c.1930s-1940s. **$15-$30**

These relatively late **fortune-telling charms** carry on an old tradition used at bride's parties, baby showers, birthdays, New Year's ft in the cake, with a charm in what would become each slice. Depending on its aptness, or complete absence thereof, the chance receipt of a particular charm in a guest's slice was occasion for oohs, ahs, or guffaws. Another set, described in Carl W. Drepperd's *A Dictionary of American Antiques* as pudding-cake charms, all had a tiny hanging ring. The set consisted of a pig, spoon, beaver, wishbone, nut, duck, mug, wedding band, fortune wheel, bachelor button, money bag, bell, horseshoe, donkey, and seated old maid — a set less exclusively marriage-related, & suitable for general fortune telling.

IV-68. Cake board, *or cookie mold. Carved wood, great detail of sporty gent in plaid or checkered suit, bearing a pig on his head — cushioned by a tam o'shanter. In some ways he resembles a Scotsman. 19-1/2" H x 7-7/8" W, late 19th C. Collection of Mary Mac Franklin.* **$350-$450**

IV-69. Cake ornamenting stamp, *and a design that could be made using it. "These little stamps (probably nickeled brass, with wooden handles) enables any person to make the most difficult designs such as scrolls, console, valutes, etc. They are stamped direct on the cake" and were then traced over using an icing bag or ornamenting tube. At bottom, the clasped hands, lyre, and scrolls all done with simple star or plain tubes. "A few flowers and leaves will finish the cake, however the designs will look considerably better when other tubes are used such as the star ruffler, crimper, rope, etc., especially when the shoving, swinging or pushing motion is used." Hueg's* The Little Confectioner, *1921. For the stamp:* **$35-$50**

IV-70. Cake decorating stencils. *Unidentified metal (probably brass, like most other stencils), 10" diameter, but others made to order. 12 designs, with which "a boy can ornament six layer cakes in one minute. **DIRECTIONS**: Place the Stencil on top of a layer cake iced with either chocolate or water icing, then sift a little xxxx sugar on top of the stencil and remove stencil carefully." Child labor! Hueg, Book of Designs for Bakers & Confectioners, 1896.* **$15-$30**

CAKE MOLDS:

In general, all figural animal or Santa cake molds are here. Spouted or tubed cake molds or pans, especially those of ceramic or enamelware, are found further on in the molds listings under their respective materials. This is because many of those molds were used for a variety of purposes, not just cake.

Cake mold, 12 parts, tin, the 12 parts put together form a heart, from F. A. Walker catalog, they are mostly imported wares, in the 1870s and 1880s. Cakes, with each part apparently equal in crumb count, could be made in other multipart molds: floral crosses (for christenings, Easter and Christmas), a horn of plenty (for Thanksgiving), rounds and diamonds. **$30-$40**

"Corn Starch Cake. One pound of sugar, half a pound of butter; six eggs, beaten separately; three-quarters of a pound of corn starch; three tablespoonfuls of flour. Flavor to taste. Bake in small shapes or cups." Mrs. A. P. Hill, *Receipt Book,* NYC, 1870.

IV-71. Cake decorating stencils *or* <u>schablonen</u>. *Unidentified metal. These were used very like the full cake-top stencil in IV-70, but with more freedom. The biggest one, at bottom, was for making palm leaves; the fancy big one for making grape leaves. Bertuch, Berlin, c.1904.* **$10-$20**

IV-73. Baker decorating cake. *Statue of Liberty cake, on revolving stand. Note how baker supports his right hand to steady it as he makes a fancy border with the icing tube. From Hueg's 1896 how-to book.*

IV-72. Paper decorations, *on sticks. For use with confections, and for roasts and joints of meat. Sailboat, buck, swan, flowers, and various towers. Bertuch, c.1904.* **$5-$15**

IV-74. Decorating bulb & ornamenting tubes. (L) *Rubber bulb with threaded mouth. Various tubes and extension tubes could be used with it; it was supposed to make it easier to squeeze out the icing.* **(R)** *The "Boss" ornamenting bag and tubes (bag not shown, but it was a rubber). Cloth bags also used. Before the turn of the century, the tubes, and threaded bag screw were silverplated brass; later they were nickeled. Hueg, 1896.* **$8-$20**

Cake mold, heart, cast iron, "Griswold #2," Erie, PA, 3" deep, 20th C. **$20-$30**

Cake mold, heart-shaped with slightly slanted sides, ring hanger, bright tin, American, 7" x 7", c.1920s. **$15-$22**

Cake mold, hearts, 3 on long oblong tray, tin, Ekco #52, American, 29" L overall, each pan 9" H x 8" W, 20th C. **$45-$60**

Cake mold, lamb, cast iron enameled green outside, white inside, very unusual, about 9" L, turn of century. **$200-$250**

Cake mold, lamb, couchant (lying down with head up), cast aluminum, along bottom of base reads "Bakers Coconut," 20th C. **$65-$85**

Cake mold, lamb, couchant, cast iron, 2 parts, Wagner but not marked, 7-3/4" H x 11-3/4" L, late 1920s on. **$130-$140**

Cake mold, lamb, couchant, cast iron, 2 parts, American, 7" H x 13" L x 4" W, late 19th or early 20th C. **$180-$200**

Cake mold, lamb, couchant, cast iron, large ring ear handles at neck and tail, 2 parts, protrusions as steadying "feet," backside flatter than front, has 3 small holes (for escaping steam or overflowing batter?), no mark, 17" L, 19th or early 20th C. **$275-$325**

Cake mold, lamb, couchant, head turned to left, ears stuck straight out at sides, cast iron, looped handle at each end, Griswold #866 (I've seen these advertised as Wagner #866 also, possibly just after G bought W), Erie, PA, 9" L, c.1940s-1950s. **$250-$300**

Cake mold, lamb, couchant, heavy stamped aluminum, 2-piece (like the Wagner mold), about 8" H, c.1960. **$4-$12**

Cake mold, lamb, couchant, cast iron, 2-part, marked Schaab Stove & Furnace Co., no place except 2024 S. Broadway, which is not a NYC, NY address, turn of century. **$150-$175**

Cake mold, lamb, couchant, polished cast "lustre" aluminum, 2 parts, Maid of Scandinavia Co., Minneapolis, MN, 8" H x 13" L, late 1940s on. **$30-$40**

IV-75. Decorated cakes. *Clockwise from top left the names of the cakes are:* **(1)** *Gâteau aux fleurs;* **(2)** *Gâteau Vénitien au sucre;* **(3)** *Gâteau Jeanne-d'Arc;* **(4)** *Gâteau Palestine;* **(5)** *Gäteau Moucey;* *and* **(6)** *Gâteau moscovite à l'ananas. From Urbain Dubois' La Patisserie, c.1860s-70s.*

IV-77. Angel cake pan. *Loose bottom with spout that projects an inch above sides of pan, which is 4-1/8" H x 10-1/2" diameter; 3 legs assist when you turn the mold upside down to get cake out. Savory Inc., Newark, NJ, c.1925-28 catalog.* **$5-$15**

IV-76. Ancient molds reproductions. *Cast bronze cake molds, the originals of which were found buried under the volcanic debris at Herculaneum* **(L)**, *and at Pompei* **(R)**, *almost 1800 years after the eruption of Vesuvius destroyed the towns in minutes.* **(L)** *Scallop shell-shape. Original 2" deep x 8-1/4" diameter.* **(R)** *Scalloped with more detail. 2-7/8" deep x 8-3/4" diameter. They both have simple round bottoms, and the reproductions were only made with a polished finish. From catalog of the Fonderie Artistiche Riunite, of J. Chiurazzi & Fils and S. De Angelis & Fils, Naples, Italy, c.1910-11.*

IV-78. Spouted cake molds, *all called* **turban molds,** *or* **turk's head** *molds, despite differences in the fluting.* **(T-L)** *Stamped tin, made in six sizes, from 3-3/4" H x 7-1/4" diameter to 4-1/4" H x 11" diameter. Matthai-Ingram, c.1890.* **(T-R)** *Similar one with less-angled flutes, to be had with or without the spout. Stamped tin, 4 sizes, all somewhat smaller than the previous one. Savory, Inc., c.1925-28.* **(B)** *Unusual ovoid flutes, stamped & pieced tin, made in 3 sizes, from 7-7/8" to 10" diameter, holding 2, 4, 5 and 6 quarts. Lalance & Grosjean, 1890.* **$30-$45**

IV-79. Kugelhopf or gugelhupf cake mold. *Two views. Stamped copper, tinned inside, 4" deep x 10" diameter. Probably German, late 19th C. A* **gugelhupf** *cake has a yeast dough mixed with seedless raisins, grated lemon peel, chopped almonds. The mold is first greased with butter, coated with chopped almonds & bread crumbs, filled about half full, put in a warm spot to raise the dough, then baked. Served sprinkled with powdered sugar. Collection of Mary Mac Franklin.* **$100-$135**

IV-80. Baba cake, *shown in the* Ryzon Baking Book, *1916. Advertising cookbooklet for baking powder maker.*

IV-81. Baba cake mold. *Stamped & pieced copper, heavily tinned. Another name for this, from the German, is "Old German pound cake mold." Came in 8 sizes, in 3/4" increments, from 6-1/4" to 11-3/4" diameter. Bertuch, c.1904.* **$125-$180**

IV-82. Fluted mold, *with spout. Stamped tin, with spout soldered on separately. 7-1/2" diameter. Late 19th or early 20th C.* **$35-$45**

IV-83. Dessert made in "biscuit mold," *which you might think could mean an unglazed ceramic mold, or one in which biscuits or cookies (or cake) were made. But, many copper molds are called "biscuit molds." In French catalogs, similar-looking molds were described as being "pour biscuit ou pour glaces." A particular type of frozen dessert was called an "iced biscuit," made of different colors and flavors of a frozen meringue, puréed fruit & whipped cream, put into the various nooks or compartments of the biscuit molds. I believe from my reading of the catalogs that indeed some biscuit molds were meant for a cake-like dessert. This picture from Urbain Dubois,* La Patisserie, *c.1870s.*

Reproductions. According to Joel Schiff of New York, "There are reproductions of the lamb, rabbit and Santa, and they tend to be better castings than the usual reproductions, though not as good as the originals. The good Santa should be smooth, have a tongue in its mouth, and frequently a mold flaw 'line' down the side of his bag of goodies! The rabbit is harder to distinguish because of all his fur. The good rabbit should be smooth and have a capital I in the 'GRISWOLD' mark. In both, the Griswold company markings should be centered and not extend beyond the handle 'ears' inside."

Cake molds, rabbits, etc. The French mold and pastry-making equipment company, Letang Fils, show several rabbit molds made of *fer blanc*, which translates as "white iron": a type of cast iron very low in carbon and high in iron. (Another series in their catalog is made of *étain* (tin).) Letang Fils made four rabbits: • #3499, a crouching or couchant rabbit, ears tucked along the back, in three sizes: 18 cm (about 7" L), 20 cm (about 7-3/4" L), and 22 cm (about 8-1/2" L); • #3501, a trotting (!) rabbit with grass clumps, in one size only: 24 cm (about 9-1/3"L); • #3510, a sitting rabbit, ears cocked in an alert "V," in two sizes: 28 cm (almost 11" H), and 30 cm (about 11-3/4" H); • and #3517, a rabbit sitting high on haunches, front feet tucked up to chest, ears straight up, in three sizes: 27 cm (about 10" H); 29 cm (about 11-1/4" H); and 31 cm (about 12" H). Along with the rabbits and several other animals, is one **lamb**, couchant, #3497, in three sizes: 19 cm (7-1/2" L); 20 cm (about 7-3/4" L); and 22 cm (about 8-1/2" L). **NOTE:** a centimeter (cm) is .39 of an inch.

Cake mold, rabbit, cast iron, Griswold #862, Erie, PA, c.1920s on. **$275-$350**

Cake mold, rabbit, couchant, 2-piece redware mold, American, mid 19th C. **$250-$350**

Cake mold, rabbit, vertical sitting, heavy cast aluminum, 10" H, 20th C. **$40-$55**

Cake mold, Santa Claus, cast iron, marked "Hello Kiddies" on base at Santa's foot, mfd. by Griswold, Erie, PA, 12" H, mid 20th C. Best thing about this one, to my mind, is the original instruction to bake him on his face for 25 minutes, then on his back, as if he were at the beach. I think the asking price range is ridiculously high, but let's face it, the Griswold frenzy continues. **$500-$700**

Cake mold, Santa Claus from waist up, climbing out of brick chimney, heavy stamped aluminum, 2-piece, about 9" H, c.1960. **$7-$12**

Cake mold, Santa Claus head with floppy liberty cap on Santa, tin, slightly slanted sides, 6" H Santa head within 9" diameter pan, 20th C. I never thought about it before, but the Santa Claus we know and feed cookies to often wears a Phrygian cap very like a liberty cap, and because the jolly fellow's appearance is derived from a combination of Thomas Nast's late nineteenth-century cartoons and Haddon Sundblom's Coca-Cola Santa in ads, and therefore American, it is possible that his cap may have been deliberately designed by Nast as a patriotic symbol. Harrumph. Of course, it could be that the typical cap worn by skaters and skiers was the inspiration for Claus's headgear. **$45-$55**

Cake mold, Santa's sleigh, cast iron, 7" H x 14-3/4" L, modern fake, wholesales at about **$6**

Cake or gelatin molds — See also molds

Cake or gelatin molds, graphic detail of body parts, stamped copper, for "adult cake," chocolate, ice cream cakes, ice sculpture, & "punch bowl frozen centerpiece" (guaranteed to thaw out party?), "Erotiᵃ", mfd. by Delectable Fantasies, Inc., Ft. Lauderdale, FL, 12-1/2" L x 2-1/2" W; 10-1/8"L; 11" H; 10" x 7-1/2", 1983. **$6-$12**

Cake or marzipan boards — See cake boards; cookie boards; springerle molds

Cake molds — See also cake pans and molds, especially tubed or spouted molds that could be used for food other than cakes

IV-84. Sandtorten molds. *These have similar tops (or bottoms) for almonds, but one has high plain sides, one has low "fancy" sides. Both from 8" to 13" diameter, pieced tin. S. Joseph Co., c.1927.* **$55-$85**

IV-85. Spouted mold. *Redware, glazed inside & out. Handle on one side. 3-1/8" deep x 9-1/2" diameter. American, mid 19th C. Ex-Keillor Collection.* **$200-$300**

IV-86. Cake mold. *Cast iron rabbit, 2 halves #862, #863, 11" H (when I measured I got 12"), Griswold Mfg. Co., Erie, PA. Also comes in chrome finish for slightly less.* **$250-$380**

Cake pan, angel food cake, with sliding door in side for loosening cake, tin, spouted, advertising "Swan's Down Cake Flour," American, small, only 6-1/2" D, c.1920s. **Slots & Slides**: this pan, like the Van Deusen described a few listings down, has a slide in the side. The VD has two, and the slide ends extend way up above rim, whereas the SD has but one, the slot is bigger, and it does not extend up beyond the rim. The SD slot and slide looks rather like little slot on front of file cabinet drawers where you slide in a card with name of what's in the file. **$13-$18**

Cake pan, angel food or regular layer cake, stamped tin, 4 parts to make either spouted or plain, mfd. by Perfection, about 9" diameter, late 19th C. **$15-$20**

Cake pan, gray graniteware, with cast iron handles, 13" x 9", 19th C. **$35-$50**

Cake pan, blue & white swirl enamelware, 13" L x 8" W, early 20th C. **$60-$80**

"Twelfth Night Cake. For Twelfth Night — January 6 — bake a round loaf of pound cake (put a pea and a bean in the batter) and ice with a plain icing. When firm, arrange alternately small red and white candles on the top so as to form a five-pointed star, piping a rose of icing round each candle, and garnishing with a wreath of holly." *Table Talk,* Philadelphia, January 1903.

• • • •

"Almond Maccaroons. Take a pound of shelled sweet almonds, and a quarter of a pound of shelled bitter almonds. Blanch them in scalding water, mix them together, and pound them, one or two at a time, in a mortar to a very smooth paste; adding frequently a little rose water to prevent them from oiling and becoming heavy. Prepare a pound of powdered loaf-sugar. Beat the whites of seven eggs to a stiff froth, and then beat into it gradually the powdered sugar, adding a table-spoonful of mixed spice, (nutmeg, mace, and cinnamon.) Then mix in the pounded almonds, (which it is best to prepare the day before,) and stir the whole very hard. Form the mixture with a spoon into little round or oval cakes, upon sheets of buttered white paper, and grate white sugar over each. Lay the paper in square shallow pans, or on iron sheets, and bake the maccaroons a few minutes in a brisk oven, till of a pale brown. When cold, take them off the papers.

"It will be well to try two or three first, and if you find them likely to lose their shape and run into each other, you may omit the papers and make the mixture up into little balls with your hands well floured; baking them in shallow tin pans slightly buttered." Eliza Leslie, *Directions for Cookery,* 31st edition, Philadelphia, 1848. (See also marzipan in the introduction to cake boards.)

Cake pan, round spouted mold, highish sides, 2 wide slides like sliding doors, opposite each other in sides, which you would pull up & insert palette knife or spatula into revealed slot to loosen cake from mold, "being made solid, they will not get out of order & leak batter, as the loose bottom pans do," heavy tin, "Van Deusen Cake Molds," mfd. by C. A. Chapman, Geneva, NY, 3 sizes, up to 12" diameter, 1910s. **They stood under their pans**. Chapman also made the "Van Deusen" molds, with slides in the sides, in oblong, square and round layer cake sizes. The original ads said, "The slides are made long to act as rests to turn the mould on while the cake cools, allowing the air to circulate under the cake to keep it from sweating. The cake, being stuck to the mould, will hang in it until loosened." **$10-$15**

Cake pan, round, stamped tin, embossed "Free 49 cent Pan with Py-O-My Pastry Mix," 9-1/2" diameter. Another is embossed " 'Py-O-My' Puddin' Cake." Both about same value. **$12-$18**

Cake pan, round, stamped tin, advertising "Calumet Baking Powder," American, 20th C. Others embossed "Up & Up Flour," Buffalo, NY & "George Urban Milling Co." Buffalo, NY. **$12-$18**

A Clean Sweet. "The broom splint has occupied a prominent position among aids to cooking for an indefinite time, and housekeepers who are immaculate in other matters . . . often take a splint from a broom with which they have, perhaps, swept the kitchen . . . A much better way is to buy a cheap little brush-broom, and keep it for this and no other purpose; one will last a lifetime." Emma Babcock, *Household Hints,* 1881.

A 1903 ad reads, "**SOME FACTS ABOUT CAKE MAKING**. The old way was to grease the cake tin to keep the cake from sticking, then add flour until the cake would not settle, until it was stiff enough to stand alone, like bread. The new way is to discard the grease, and at least 1/4 of the flour, make a delicate batter and let it stick to the mold, which will support the cake while baking; and when baked invert the mold and allow the cake to hang in it to cool, which is the only way known to keep a delicate cake from settling; and when cold, loosen the cake . . . with a knife."

Whose Crud Is This Anyway? Collectors sometimes ask if it's safe to use old cake pans for baking, even if they have a bit of rust. It's safe to the user, not quite as safe for the pan, but only if you don't carefully wash and dry thoroughly after use. The solder used in such late pieced pieces is not dangerous, and rust only adds a bit of extra minerals to your cake. If you use such pieced tin pans (cake pans or muffin pans, etc.) don't scour vigorously with steel wool or a brass pot brush. Try to use a stiff dry fiber brush and then very very hot soapy water, then dry thoroughly. Hot water won't melt the solder. My rule is: if I buy an old pan with some rust and the baked-on crud that happens when fat and flour and sugar are baked, especially over a gas flame, and if I keep this pan a month before using, not only the pan but the crud too becomes mine, and harmless! It's all a matter of rationalization.

Cake pan, spring cake pan — called this because it springs open when the clamp is released, round, heavy tinned steel, with ring side, open in one place, with little clamp, and with 3 different bottoms: (1) plain flat disc, (2) bottom with large spout, (3) what was called a "Mary Ann" base, which looks like a wide-lipped pie pan but inserted upside down, so that when a cake was baked it would have a big depression in top for putting in fillings, like strawberries and whipped cream. "Cream City Ware," mfd. by Geuder, Paeschke & Frey Co., Milwaukee, WI, about 9" across, c.1930. Other companies made spring cake pans. One I saw, made of heavy tin, has the same kind of wire pin going through sort of hinge knuckle & barrel joints, that some ice cream and chocolate molds have. **$15-$22**

IV-87. Cake pan, *for small cakes. Six-point star, pieced tin, spouted. Three sizes, plus the smallest one, probably about 5" across, came 12 fixed on a frame. Jaburg, 1908. The sizes of many of these cake and candy molds were described in the early catalogs by the retail price of the cake or candy baked within. For example, this one came in penny, 5¢ and 10¢ sizes, referring to the little cake's price. Crossover interest from folk art collectors, who might pay more.* **$20-$35**

Cake pan, spring form cake pan, heart-shaped, 3-part heavy tinned steel, ring opens at point, heart-shaped flat bottom fits inside ring, plus clip or clamp to hold sides. "When the baking is finished and cake has cooled, all you have to do is remove the simple little clamp and the sides spring off the cake." "Cream City Ware," mfd. by Geuder, Paeschke & Frey, Milwaukee, WI, about 9" across, c.1930. **$12-$18**

Cake pan, spring form heart, tin, spout also heart-shaped, American, 3" deep x 9" diameter, 20th C. **$35-$40**

"The London Way of mixing Cakes, used by Pastry Cooks. — Weigh down the flour and sugar on a clean smooth table; make a hole in it; and bank it well up; in this hole put your eggs; cream the butter in an earthen pan; then put to the flour and sugar, the eggs and butter; mix all together, and beat it up well with both your hands; you may work it up this way as light as a feather; then add the currants, spices, &c. Put it up in pound or two pound hoops, neatly papered at the bottom and sides; to be baked on iron sheets, in a slow oven." Joseph Bell, *A Treatise on Confectionary.* Newcastle, England, 1817.

Cake pan, square, stamped tin, wire loop handle, marked "Fries," 12" x 12", 20th C. **$10-$15**

Cake pan, round, tin with spout, side handle, "Vanity Co.," American, 10" diameter, 20th C. **$15-$20**

Cake pan, round, stamped tin, Turk's head, spouted, 9" diameter, 20th C. **$15-$18**

Cake pans, a pair, tin in colorful cardboard box, with recipes too, "Kate Smith's Bake-A-Cake Kit," 9" diameter, 20th C. **$18-$22**

Cake pans — See also pie pans. Cake pans have straight sides, pie pans have flared or slanted sides.

Canape or <u>truffle cutters</u>, at least that's the fancy name. I think I've seen the same thing in a 1950s box labeled "cookie cutters," corrugated tin circles, 9 nested cutters, in tin box, lid stamped "242" and also either "9" or "6," probably 9 for the 9 cutters inside, "Made in Germany," box 4-15/16" diameter, 20th C. Dealer had this for $55, priced too high because they aren't old and are still made. **$18-$25**

Candle mold, crimped tin, strap handle, square base & top, makes 4 candles, PA, 5" H x 6-1/8" W, 19th C. **$350-$450**

Candle mold, japanned tin, 3 tubed, strap handle, American, 6-1/2" H x 3" W x 5" L, 19th C. **$175-$200**

IV-88. Cake pans. (L) *"Perfect," with removable bottom, available with or without spout. Stamped tin, two sizes, 3" deep x 9-5/8" diameter, or 3-1/8" deep x 10-1/2" diameter. Also made square with upside down legs called lugs. Central Stamping Co., 1920.* **(R)** *"Perfection," removable bottom, 1-5/8" H x 8-3/4" square or 2-5/8" H x 9-1/8" square. Savory, c.1925-28.* **$10-$20**

Candle mold, redware & fruitwood, bench type with bootjack ends, 24 redware tubes (actually 1 missing), American, 14" H x 24" L, c.1830s to 1850s. **$1300-$1500**

Candle mold, tin, 2 rows of 6 tubes each, 2 strap handles, American, 11" H, 19th C. **$120-$175**

Candle mold, tin, 2 rows x 2 tubes with single strap handle, American, 8-1/2" L, 19th C. **$70-$100**

Candle mold, tin, 2 strap ear handles, 2 rows of 5 tubes each, American, 10" H, mid to late 19th C. **$150-$225**

Candle mold, tin, 4 angle feet, small handle, makes 4 candles, American, 6-1/8" H, mid 19th C. <u>Added value:</u> If it's odd, huge, small, signed, proveably old, etc., it's worth a lot. **$300-$400**

Candle mold, tin, for one candle, 1 tube with ring strap handle 1/3 way down from top, has very wide, ribbed flat lip, American, 5-1/2" L, mid 19th C. **$250-$300**

IV-89. Candle molds & candle dipping outfit. (T) *a set of tube molds, possibly pewter, set in wooden frame. Note wire rods with wicks, in place in tubes, ready for pouring the melted tallow. Note also the rack strung with many wicks. Engravings from unidentified book, dated 1820, found at a print shop.* **(M)** *Candle wicks tied to sticks, the strings twisted and taken one by one and coated first with tallow to give them weight and a surface easier to coat by dipping. Next a wooden box with a sheet iron or tin bottom turned up and tacked on the sides, and a lid, is put on the stove. Tallow is melted in it, deep enough for the dangling wicks. Each stick with as many tallow-rubbed wicks as wanted, is dipped three or four times slowly, until no more fat hardens on them. Each stick of dipped candles (rounded ends are seen on candle) is hung on a cooling frame. When completely cool, the first stick of slim candles can be dipped again, until the candles are fully built up. (Directions as well as bottom picture adapted from American Agriculturist, 11/1876. Interesting that the pictures from 56 years before fit the instructions!)* **(B)** *a typical pieced tin mold, for a dozen candles, with hanging ring, and the wicks in place.*

Reproduction alert I. A 6-tube mold of "pewter-finish" (in other words, rather dark and dull, imitative of old tin) tin, set 2 x 3 with almost flat bottom and top, very small strap handle near top, was advertised by Sturbridge Yankee Workshop, Sturbridge, MA, in the Oct. 1975 *Early American Life*. **Alert II**. The same issue had a very similar (identical?) 6-tube mold, 2 x 3, with nearly flat bottom & top, small strap handle, advertised by Hawthorne Products Co., Bloomington, IL. They also offered 8- & 12-tube molds. Both companies were selling the molds in candle-making kits. **Alert III**. Another ad in same issue presents a 6-tube mold, arranged 2 x 3, somewhat deeper rectangular base with incurved sides, top piece deeper too, and strap handle comes further down end. This was a "Lucky Eleven Americana Reproduction," made for "over 12 years" by tinsmith Irvin Hoover, Irvin's Craft Shop, Mt. Pleasant Mills, PA.

• • • •

Make Dripless Candles. *American Agriculturist* reprinted this tip (from a journal called *Exchange*) on homemade candles in October 1850: "If you manufacture your own candles, immerse the wicks in lime water, in which a little nitre (saltpetre) has been dissolved, and dry them before dipping. The light from such is much clearer, and the tallow will not 'run'."

Candle mold, tin, long fat single tube, top is soldered to large square flat lip, which serves also as stand for mold when not in use, strap handle connects tube to edge of lip, American, 21" L, mid 19th C.   **$200-$300**

Candle mold, tin, round, wire handle, makes 8 candles, on plaque on front it reads "MASON'S," English (?), 6-3/8" H x 4-3/8" diameter, c. mid 19th to early 20th (?) C.   **$125-$180**

Candle mold, tin, strap handle, 6 tubes in single row, arched bracket base, American, 10-1/2" H, 19th C.   **$75-$120**

Candle mold, wooden frame, 16 pewter or Britannia tubes fitted in frame, dealer (Hardings of Hancock) says this is marked by maker "K. Webb," American, prob. first half 19th C. • K. Webb was not known to Ledlie Laughlin, who does give a W. Webb, of NYC, "probably after 1810," as having signed two known pewter candle molds.   **$1200-$1500**

IV-90. Candle mold, *redware 12-tube in wooden frame. Impressed mark by maker, Alvin Wilcox, West Bloomfield, NY. 15" H x 10" L. Photo courtesy Litchfield Auction Gallery. Ex-Harold Corbin Collection, auctioned 1/1/1990, for $1200.* **$1000-$1500**

Candle mold, wooden frame with 18 pewter tubes, called by the inventor an "Improvement in Candle-Mould Apparatus," marked "Humiston," patented by Willis Humiston, West Troy, NY, patent #13,334, pat'd July 24, 1855.   **$1200-$1400**

Candle mold filler, ladle with long spout to bowl, forged iron with applied handle, American (?), 25-5/8" L overall, bowl is 2-5/8" deep and 4-3/4" diameter, early 19th C.   **$125-$140**

Candy crimper, a sort of fluter or mangle for candy, cast iron & brass, an oblong iron box with hinged lid revealing horizontal brass crimper drums, and brass gears, crank in side, L. T. Yoder, Pittsburgh, PA, 9" H x 15" L x 10" W, pat'd Dec. 3, 1883.   **$170-$225**

Candy crimper, for ribbon candy, "The Champion," square-based cast iron, brass crimpers turned by a wire belt & crank, has wooden trough that folds up. In original latched wooden box with hinged lid. Machine about 6" H, box is 7" H x 12" x 12". Pat'd March 1886, mfd. by The Champion Candy Machine Co., Philadelphia. Still making such machines in early 20th C., so impossible to date exactly.   **$170-$225**

Candy cutter, a sort of rolling pin, plated steel, barrel or drum set with 15 fixed sharp disc blades, fixed handles at both ends, used for cutting strips of candy for sticks or rolls, Sethness Co., Chicago, IL, barrel 1" L , blades set 3/4" apart, handles 2-1/2" L. (Choice of blades fixed at 7/8", 1", 1-1/4" & 1-1/2".) 1st quarter 20th C. Sethness also made to order cutters with 24" L barrels with fixed blades set in same choice of intervals as above. They also made adjustable cutters, with "revolving brass handles," packed with 12, 15, or 20 disc blades, plus washers to separate the blades, 2 cast iron wrenches for assembling, and extra blades. The Dec. 1925 *Sethness Candy Maker,* part catalog, part recipe book (for professional confectioners). **Corrugated wooden rolling pin**. The catalog also shows a corrugated wooden rolling pin, with turned handles, 18 sharp edged ridges set at 3/4" intervals, overall length 15", with the drum or barrel 4" in diameter. It is called a wooden marker and used to <u>mark off rows</u> for cutting with a knife, or for breaking apart. For more see "What're the Ridges For?" in the rolling pin entry, this chapter.   **$25-$45**

Candy cutter, for hoarhound, licorice or other hard chewy candies, looks like a miniature garden tiller or farm tool. Nickeled iron frame fitted with sharp disc blades, with a turned wooden handle. Used by rolling across spread-out pan or cooled puddle of candy to make long sticks of candy. Shorter pieces, even small lozenges, could be made by cutting across the original rows. American, last half 19th C.   **$25-$35**

IV-91. Candle mold. *Pieced tin, for making 6 candles. Ribbed strap handle. Shown "upside down," as they were stored if they didn't have a hanging ring. 10-1/4" H x 7" W. Early to mid 19th C.* **$125-$175**

"Hoarhound Candy. 7 lbs. sugar, white or brown; 1/4 oz. cream of tartar; 1 qt. water; 1/2 pint strong hoarhound tea; boil to the feather; grain against the sides of the pan with spoon, 2 or 3 minutes; then pour out onto slab; form into flat sticks, rolls or drops, with a hoarhound cutter, which are made in two styles, with movable knives or with fixed divisions." Henry Scammel, compiler, *Treasure House of Universal Knowledge,* 1891. "If, when the sugar is boiled, the skimmer is dipped in and shook over the pan, and then given a sudden flirt behind, the sugar will fly off like feathers; this is called the feathered stage." *ibid.*

Candy mold, boy riding slim free-range pig, an image dating back at least to early 18th C., presumably from an old nursery rhyme or song, and found in pen & ink calligraphy drawings too, one half missing, grainy wood stained dark. Looks like a modern fake: distressing on edge looks fake, too dark, it's pushing credulity to have the half that's remaining be the one with the value-adding signature initials, particularly since 2 other half-molds with the same troubling qualities have the same signature, "V. E.," on back, supposedly PA, but looks European (motif poss. Eastern European or Dutch), 4-1/2" H x 4-5/8" W, supposed to be mid or early 19th C., but could be as recent as 1970s or 1980s. Read carefully: probable value range, if wrong, is under $25; if right, much higher, at **$250-$400.**

IV-92. Candy curling machine. *For making candies "known to the trade as 'Opera Curls.'" Thomas Mills & Bro., Philadelphia, 1930 catalog.* **$75-$100**

IV-93. Candy cutters. (T) *"Circular batch cutter ... especially useful in handling caramel batches." Steel knife revolves between 2 wooden handles. 6" or 9" diameter knife, "larger sizes to order."* **(B)** *"Handy chip cutter ... used for cutting chips (hard boiled candy pulled thin as paper) made in a variety of colors and highly flavored. This will cut them into uniform pieces about 1-1/2" square, while at the same time permitting them to keep flat and glossy." Two sizes: 8" block, 1-1/2" W, and a 12" block with set-in steel blades 2" W. Mills, 1927.* **$25-$50**

IV-94. Candy marker & candy cutters. *Most are metal, and therefore not confusable with rolling pins., although I've seen them labeled "noodle cutters." From top:* **(1)** *Turned wood corrugated pin, called a* **"marker."** *15" L x 4" diameter, marking off 3/4" divisions. Sethness Candy Maker, 1925.This rolling marker is often called a cracker roller & is probably interchangeable in function with other concentrically ridged rolling pins.* **(2)** *Caramel cutter, steel blades or "knives." Could be had "adjustable," meaning you could get one with 8, 12 or 15 knives, and set them as close as desired; or "stationary," meaning with fixed blades, from 1/2" to 1" apart in 1/8" increments. Duparquet, Huot & Moneuse, c.1904-1910.* **(3)** *Bonbonschneidewalze (candy cutting roller) with tempered steel blades 3-1/4" diameter. You could order with 12, 18, 26 or 35 blades (also, cheaper, one with 26 tinned iron fixed blades). Catalog of A. Bertuch, Berlin, c.1904.* **(4)** *Brass revolving handles, 12 blades with spacers, for cutting caramels and other candies. Also could be had with 6" diameter blades. Mills, 1927.* **(5)** *Adjustable steel blades, 4" diameter, with spacer rings. Mills.* **(6)** *and* **(7)** *Movable steel cutters, for marking or cutting lengths of horehound sticks, butterscotch, peanut cakes, or bars, taffies, etc. Five 4" diameter knives (blades), with provision for adding blades.* **(7)** *has iron frame presumably for added weight bearing.* **(8)** *Horehound stick cutter with brass revolving handles & steel blades. "Designed to meet the demand for a cutter which will cut horehound and peanut sticks and add the beveled side and rounded top to the goods." 18" L plus handles. Last three all Mills, 1927.* **$35-$75**

Candy mold, dense, heavy yellowish wood, carvings include 2 well-carved human figures, front & back views, front of figures carved at very bottom of board so the little feet could actually stick out, may be <u>Robinson Crusoe & Man Friday</u> — a bearded sailor with dotted pants, and a caricatured thick-lipped "native" in short grass skirt. Dealer Teri Dziadul says these figures were used on cakes. Above are something like a corset cover or camisole, a dagger and two other small weapon-like things. On the back, the only really 3-D carvings are a pair of tiny wings! There's also a longish border design, a simple aeronautical balloon, and a sort of connect-the-dot geometric shed or hut, which probably was practice carving or a child's addition, English (?), 9-3/4" L x 3" W x 1" thick, mid 19th C. **The book**: Daniel Defoe's *The Life and Surprizing Adventures of Robinson Crusoe* was first published in 1719, but has been a classic ever since, so it does not really assist in dating this mold. **$400-$600**

Candy mold, dog, carved heavily grained wood, one half only, curly hair on body & legs, long & down-hanging curly-haired ear, short bobbed tail, probably a retriever (a popular dog in the decorative arts), this one looking rather like full figure Pennsylvania chalkware, carved wood and pottery dogs of the period, but because of fortuitous "coincidence" of the remaining half having a signature, plus the fact that in same auction another mold bearing same fakey faults & signature was bought, I doubt that this is what its maker hoped it would look like. Supposed maker's initials carved on back, "V. E.," looks Pennsylvania; may be Dutch, or an American or European fake, 3-3/4" H x 5-7/8" L, supposed to look mid 19th C.; I'm afraid it's a fake from 1970s or 1980s. Probable value range if a fake would be under $25; if for sure it's old, much higher: **$150-$200**

Old? What do you think? One bothersome thing about the dog mold in the listing above is the <u>wood used</u>, which is inconsistent with the dark color of its finish; also it is awfully <u>distressed</u> around edges <u>in an unrealistic manner</u> (and you really have to do a sort of method acting approach when examining wear and distress marks). It also just begins to <u>approach cuteness</u>, a deadly sin! But maybe the artisan was sentimental about the model. Garth's Auctions, Delaware, OH, pictured all the "V. E." molds in their catalog for the April 11-12, 1986 sale, and made no representations about the molds as to age, authenticity, etc. That is an auction house to love, with apparently hundreds of neat things appearing monthly, but buyers have to do some of the work for themselves. Better than always having to depend on a cataloguer's opinion.

Candy mold, man & woman, full length front views, he in long-skirted mucho-buttoned coat, with walking stick, and she in long-waisted, corseted dress, one half the mold only, back part missing, looks European (Polish or Czechoslovakian), 5" H x 5-1/4" W, 19th or 20th C. The style of the costumes makes it look older than it really is, I'm sure. Even when only one part is present, these candy molds can be distinguished from similarly carved wooden cookie molds by the fact that the bottom of the carving is flush with the bottom of the board. A sort of built-in funnel is formed if both halves are placed face to face & is carved so that the molten candy could be poured in. Sometimes there are small holes on the background for fitting the two halves together with small pins or pegs. When both halves are present, the value may be more than doubled. Sold for $105 at Garth's Auctions, Delaware, OH, April 11-12, 1986. As is: **$90-$145**

Candy mold, or some other kind of mold?, cast aluminum, fairly thin but nicely made, 2 rows of 4 egg-shaped cups each, hanging hole at one end, no mark at all, American (?), 13" L x 4-1/2" W, 20th C. **$22-$28**

Wormhole test. Back in the 1950s, "wormy chestnut" was the wood leading the pack when it came to the wood of choice for picture frames. Lots of what was holey was actually fake. But since then, and probably for decades before, one kind of distressing done to make wood look old was the drilling of wormholes. Fake wormholes are straight; you can put a piece of paperclip wire in and it keeps going, whereas a real worm hole will wiggle around starting right under the surface, so a wire poked in will be stopped before it's gone 1/16th of an inch.

IV-95. Candy & confectionery-modeling tools. *Carved boxwood with great detail. About 4-1/2" L. Especially good for marzipan candies and modeling leaves and flowers for cake decorating. A full set included 34 tools. In top row, the three round designs are meant to show what design is made by the end of the tool. Bertuch catalog, Berlin, c.1904. Value range given is for a small mixed collection of, say, 10 tools. See also IV-368.* **$50-$100**

IV-96. Candy & confectionery-modeling tool. *Carved boxwood, double-ended, similar to two in top row of previous picture. 4-1/2" L. Bertuch, c. 1904.* **$10-$20**

IV-97. "Ball or Gooseberry cutter," *being a hand-operated machine for cutting and rolling a "perfect round Ball or Gooseberry." Wood, with top part tracking along sides of lower part, rolling out candy balls. Stock sizes to make 5/8", 11/16", 3/4", 15/16", 1-1/8" and 1-1/4" balls. They also made them to order for larger balls, and for forming almond paste [marzipan]. Mills, 1927, but made for many years before that. Value would depend on patina and general appeal of appearance. Many people pay premiums for good lookin' wood.* **$45-$65**

Candy mold, pair of hands, flat, nickel alloy, 20th C. **$35-$40**

Candy mold, rabbit pair, seated, tin, 4" H, late 19th C. **$18-$25**

Candy mold, rabbit, standing, tin, 6" H, late 19th C. **$15-$20**

Candy mold, sheep, couchant, 2-part, redware, with good detail, orange glaze inside, outside of mold follows form inside, with a 2-1/4" peg handles sticking up from both rumps, thought by Earl Robacker to be "the only redware candy mold thus far reported" [that is, the 1960s], PA German, 5-5/8" H x 8" L x 4-1/2" W (when both halves put together), 19th C. Ex-Robacker, $500. **$500-700**

Candy mold, swan, carved wood, 2-piece, European or English, 3-1/8" H x 4-1/2" L, mid to late 19th C. **$185-$225**

Candy mold, swan in pleasingly plump shape, well-detailed up-lifted perky wings, carved wood in 2 peg-fit parts, English (?), each part is 3-1/8" H x 4-5/8" W, last quarter 19th C. Brought $210 at Garth's Auctions, Delaware, OH, April 11-12, 1986. **$200-$285**

IV-98. Candy press & dropper. (T) *Mint cake press, for "pressing balls into kisses." Wood lined with tinned iron. 24" L x 12" W or 15" W.* **(B)** *Chocolate wafer dropper, wood, 10" x 14". Wood with hinged upper box. Both T. Mills & Bro, 1920s, but probably made much earlier.* **$45-$65**

IV-99. Confectioners' presses. (T) *Sucker press, for making lollipops. Seven styles, including making 3 "faces on stick," a lemon slice, and oval, and a heart. Sizes of suckers varied from 1-1/2" diameter to 2-3/8".* **(B)** *Pop Corn Ball hand press, to make popcorn & caramel balls from 2" up to 4" diameter. Also had one for making egg-shaped balls. Both appear to be plated cast iron on boards. Mills, 1927.* **$65-$125**

Reproduction alert. In *House Beautiful*, in 1973, I found an ad from The Studio Barn in Wilton, CT, for a pair of "Aspic Mold Fish Sconces." Are you ready? The copy goes on: "A whimsical fish — deep-carved by early American seafarer — reproduced in Arrowood™ with wrought iron candle holders. Rich, dark finish, hand-done — initialled by proud craftsman. Each 4" W x 12" H." First of all, these were never aspic molds, and if there was an original two-part candy mold with a fish, it probably wasn't carved by an "early American seafarer." Arrowood™ is a fake compo wood like Syroco™ that is molded and can have a lot of detail, including wood-like graining, but probably wouldn't fool anyone. The mold has the "funnel" like carving on the edge of both halves, and there's a peg in corner of one and a hole in its facing half, so that the two halves could be fitted together and the melted candy poured in the funnel. The black iron candleholder is fixed to the tail end of both halves. The combination is a pretty desperate one, but still beats some other make-intos I've seen. While this pair of sconces cost $19.50 ppd in 1973, they shouldn't bring a fourth of that now.

IV-100. Fruit-drop frames. *Cranked machine with patterned rollers, for imprinting boiled sugar fruit-drop candies. Fully adjustable, and with scores of patterns, all interchangeable. You had to buy the frame before you could order the rollers. Rollers were from about 3-5/8" L up to 6" L, and all 2" diameter. Mills, 1927 catalog, but made earlier. Good condition, with interesting rollers (note fish in lower one) would increase collectible value. These are up-and-coming collectibles.* **$100-$200+**

IV-101. Rack & roller. (R) *A cast iron wall rack to hold pairs of rollers. Could be had to suit longer rollers and from 3 to 6 pairs.* **(L)** *A cast bronze roller with steel shaft, 5" L x 2" diameter, to make watermelon slice-shaped boiled sugar candies. Mills, 1927.* **$50-$175+**

Candy mold, top hats, 10 on flat metal tray, 14-1/2" L x 1-1/4" W, 20th C. **$25-$30**

Candy mold — See also maple sugar mold

Candy molds, various designs: nickeled cast iron, shapely concoction of scrolls, curling around each other, with runnels for candy or other confection. These curled & scrolled runnels, teardrops & "S" forms are not all connected; the manufacturer's instructions say, "It can be used for casting, moulding as well as baking . . . When all the pieces are casted, moulded or baked, stick them together with icing or caramel to the desired shape . . . The most attractive ornament can be made out of caramel of different colors, also out of nougat, fragrant paste, gelatine paste, macaroon, sponge cake, plaster of paris(!), etc." H. Hueg, *The Little Confectioner*, pub. c.1921. This mold was used to make showy pieces for bakery windows. H. Hueg & Co., Long Island City, NY, 14" L x 10" W x about 1" thick, pat'd 1896, but sold for decades thereafter. **$75-$125**

Hueg made another nickeled cast iron mold that is round and has 5 concentric channels surrounding a circle in the middle. Confectioners bought these molds in various sizes, in sets of a dozen, and packed the "fragrant paste" or whatever they were molding into the circles. Then followed the baking or whatever was needed, and the confectioners assembled baskets, pyramids, cornucopias, bowls and other hollow shapes that started small and got bigger and bigger, then smaller and smaller, or vice versa. "A very slight practice will enable anyone" to make or invent similar shapes, says the 1921 booklet! I've never seen one, and from the description I think the largest of these ring molds had an outside diameter of 8".

Candy pattern molds, cast plaster of paris, various small simple shapes — buttons, lumps, elliptical discs, hearts, little bananas, lozenges, leaves, diamonds, etc. — mold patterns, used with trays of corn starch. I've never seen one that I know of, but next week? Anyway, now you'll know those cast plaster "ornaments" you occasionally see may not be architectural, but possibly are candy mold patterns, used as described below. A supplier of candy tolls and ingredients, Sethness Co., Chicago, in their Dec. 1925 catalog, offered a page full of "Plaster of Paris Starch Mould Patterns," sold in dozen lots of one kind only — "plain, per dozen - 75¢" or "fancy, per dozen - $1." The patterns for making candy molds are interesting partly because of method of use. One maker in 1920s-1930s was J. Frauenberger & Co., Philadelphia, American, European, probably 1/2" to 4" or 5" L, 19th & early 20th C. $25+for board-full; or each worth about **$3-$10.**

IV-102. Stick candy machine. *"Five-Cent Stick" size, adjustable for different candy thicknesses. See example of what the candy looked like. Cast iron with cast bronze rollers. This one has a hand crank, but others could be had hooked up to an electric motor. Mills, 1927.* **$65-$150**

"Bon Bons. This name is given to cream goods, as described [below] in the manufacture of chocolate cream. Different varieties of shape, color & flavor are nearly all produced from the same formula.

"It is necessary to have an apparatus to mould the forms of the different varieties. The impressions are made in fine pulverized starch, which is put on boards usually two feet long by sixteen inches wide, having sides one and a half inches high, which are filled with the light starch and struck off even with the edges by a straight flat stick. The models of the bon bons are usually made from plaster of Paris, and are glued on a flat board about one or one and a half inches apart. When starch is ready the impressions are made by gently pressing the moulds [mold patterns] that are fastened to the board their full depth in the starch until all are full. Now, having all ready, the cream must next be prepared to pour in the impressions."

"Chocolate Bon Bons. 2 oz. finest assorted gum arabic, 2 lbs Icing sugar, 4 oz. Chocolate, 2 Whites of eggs. Flavor with vanilla. — Dissolve gum in a gill of hot water & strain through a piece of muslin; add the essence of vanilla; add icing sugar until the mass is quite stiff."

"Melt chocolate with a tablespoonful of water. Work it very smooth with a spoon, stir in the 2 egg whites & icing." [Then follows a method of making bon bon drops on sugar paper sheets, squeezed from a funnel in plops.]

"Vanilla Cream Bon Bons. — Pour a sufficient quantity [of the cream above] in a small copper pan & put it over the fire. Stir it until melted; add the vanilla. It is now ready to pour in the moulds. Confectioners use a funnel shapped vessel holding about a quart, with a handle at the upper end & a hole 1/4" in diameter at the small end, a long plug with a sharp point is fitted that can easily be moved up or down to regulate the flow of the cream. This is filled with cream, the plug prevents its escape or dripping, and by gently lifting the plug the cream is poured in each depression and shut on & off until all are filled. Let the cream remain until hard enough to handle without crushing, then empty the moulds, starch and contents in a sieve, and gently agitate until all starch is removed. Lay the bon bons in a moderately warm place for two or three days to harden, then they may be crystallized." All quotes from H. Hueg, *The Little Confectioner*, n.d. [c.1896].

"Charlotte Russe. Whip one quart rich cream to a stiff froth, and drain well on a nice sieve. To one scant pint of milk add six eggs beaten very lightly; make very sweet; flavor high with vanilla. Cook over hot water [ie. in a double boiler or bain marie] till it is a thick custard. Soak one full ounce Cox's gelatine in a very little water. When the custard is very cold, beat in lightly the gelatine and the whipped cream. Line the bottom of your mold with buttered paper, the sides with sponge-cake or lady-fingers fastened together with the white of an egg. Fill with the cream; put in a cold place, or in summer on ice. To turn out, dip the mould for a moment in hot water. In draining the whipped cream, all that drips through can be re-whipped." Miss Neill, in Gertrude Strohm's *The Every-day Cook-Book*, 1888.

Charlotte Russe mold, small, stamped & pieced polished tin, bottom has small disc-like flat foot, rest of bottom is fluted, not actually distinguishable from jelly molds or blancmange molds, and often in old catalogs you will see the same linecut used on different pages, to depict different items! These came in small individual sizes & in larger sizes more suitable to the recipe given below. French, English or American, 3-1/2" deep x 3" diameter, late 19th C. **$8-$20**

IV-103. Patterns for fruit-drop rollers. *Shown is a selection from many pages of patterns in Thomas Mills' 1927 catalog. The detail is probably greater than what came out embossed on the candy itself. They were all identified by name, and by how many of the fruit-drops it would take to make a pound of candy. These probably weren't even big enough to be penny candies. Of particular interest to me are the heart and hand (200 to the pound), the bowlegged clog dancer (there were 146 of these to the pound), the face drop above the fish at left, the boy scout, and the delightful* **Yellow Kid** *(big ears & nightgown), the first beloved comic strip character, originated by Richard Outcault about 1896. Individual rollers with multiple images range in value depending on image — of these, the Yellow Kid would be the most valuable by far, with crossover interest.* **$30-$200**

IV-104. Patterns of sugar toys, *that could be made by the electric-powered "Universal" sugar toy machine, used to make transparent, brightly colored, hard sucking candies, or decorations. "The animals turned out in this machine stand erect as if made in moulds, and run 65 to the pound." The machine was not like the stick candy one. The candy actually passed between two revolving wheels, both of which had the pattern cut into its smooth face. The candy toys went through "standing up," so to speak, making their bottoms flat and smooth. Actual size of the candies ranges from 1-1/4" to 1-1/2" H. If a hoard of these candies, perfectly preserved, were to be found — in an iceberg, say — they would be collectible, and could probably be freeze-dried for permanent preservation. Mills, 1927 (but patterns found in late 19th C. Mills' catalogs also). The machine:* **$50-$150+**

Cheese drainer, basket, large interstices, traces of blue paint, American, 4" H x 11" diameter, mid to late 19th C. **$200-$230**

Cheese drainer, basket, tightly woven sides connecting square bottom with round top, 2 handles, Windsor style, American, 6" H x 12-1/2" diameter, mid 19th C. **$225-$275**

Cheese drainer, basket, well-defined bottom, American, 4" H x 12-1/2" diameter, mid to late 19th C. **$175-$200**

Cheese drainer, natural wood with arrow-shaped slats leading from square base up to round hooped top rim, in so-called Windsor style, because general construction resembled that of Windsor chairs, American, fairly small example, only 5" H x 9-1/2" diameter, early 19th C. **$300-$400**

Cheese drainer, skinny peeled hickory or ash spindles from square base (integral part of ladder stretchers) up to large round hoop, Windsor style, American, nice and big, 10" deep x about 22" diameter, late 18th or early 19th C. **$400-$500**

Cheese drainer basket, rather limp basketry, American, 4" H x 10" D, mid 19th C. **$120-$140**

Cheese drainer mold, basket, beautiful weave forming 6 pointed stars, American, 3" H x 15" D, mid 19th C. **$225-$300**

Cheese drainer mold, heart-shaped, punctured tin, with presser plate, and — very unusual to find — a heart-shaped lid, the punctures in the bottom start as triangle in center and as each concentric row was added it got more & more swirly & rounded, American, prob. PA, approx. 6" x 6" x 2" deep, c. 3rd quarter 19th C. **$500-$700**

IV-105. Molded nougat, *meant to resemble a small footed bulge pot full of potatoes. A pretty little confection from Urbain-Dubois'* La Patisserie D'Aujourd'hui, *Paris, c.1860s-70s. Nougats are a sugar paste candy mixed with chopped fruits or nuts (in this case, almonds); this was made using accessory legs and bail handle.*

IV-106. Clear toy candy molds. *Hinged metal, making from 3 to 6 candies in the small molds, and singles in the larger ones. Sizes not given, but the small candies come out about 1" H; the larger ones up to about 3" H, or even bigger. The large ones were not made to be eaten, and were more likely to be saved (if possible) as holiday ornaments for a tree or table centerpiece (or shop window). Mills, 1927, but most of these are also found in late 19th C. Mills' catalogs.* **$40-$75**

IV-107. Sugar candy stamps, *for making leaves & flowers. Embossed cast lead on wire handles, with loop for hanging. Bottom one, looking like fairy parasol, is a flower mold, the deepest one. Several companies made them, main differences are in the handles. These from A. Bertuch, Berlin, Germany, c.1904.* **$12-$20**

IV-108. Cream egg molds. *At* **(T-R)** *is "lever press for making handmade cream eggs." This came in nine sizes, making eggs that would require from 3 to 22 to make up a pound.* **(L)** *Cast brass mold, with some resemblance to chocolate "bathtub" mold in IV-128. Made eggs of 5 sizes, from 25 to the pound up to 2 to the pound.* **(B-R)** *is a cast iron mold, in 9 sizes, making eggs from 5 to 1 per pound. All from Mills catalog, 1927.* **$20-$50**

IV-109. "Kiss machine." *Tin syringe with wooden pusher and various insert discs, for making candy kisses. Jaburg, 1908. See also French butter forcer (in with butter), and Jumble machine (with cookies).* **$50-$65**

IV-110. Cheese drainer baskets & ladders, *considered a type of cheese mold. These "Windsor"-style baskets were so-named because of resemblance of much of the construction to that of Windsor chairs. These baskets were lined with cheesecloth and the wet cheese put in. The basket was then set over a container to catch the whey. Some had built in "ladders"* **(T)** *, others needed a separate ladder or pair of sticks* **(L)** *. When completely drained, the cheese was formed into round shapes.* **(T)** *Drawn from unidentified ad in* Maine Antique Digest, *for ash & hickory piece 10" deep x about 23" diameter.* **(L)** *Drawn from ad of Evelyn Rue in M.A.D., 1981.* **(R)** *Drawn from ad of Jerard Paul Jordan in M.A.D., 1982. Value range mine.* **$375-$1000**

IV-111. Cheese mold. *Very fine pierced tin heart-shaped drainer-mold — liike a Valkyrie's breastplate armor! With hanging ring. About 12" H. American, c.1850s-70s. For making tsierkase, or "pressed egg" cheese, not so-called cottage cheese (smearkase). Photograph courtesy Gail Lettick, Pantry & Hearth, NYC.* **$800-$1000**

IV-113. Cheese molds. *Also called* **cheese strainers.** *Pierced tin.* **(L)** *Diamond shape, with 4 small feet, wire hanging loop. 3-3/8" H x 7-7/8" x 5-1/4".* **(R)** *Unusual truncated pyramid, with slanted sides, strap handles, 4 round feet, wire hanging loop. 5" H x 7-1/8" square at top. Ex-collection of Earl F. & Ada F. Robacker, auctioned by Horst Auctions, for $100 and $750.* **$100-$125; $600-$800**

IV-112. Cheese mold. *Pieced tin heart on 3 small feet, 2 strap handles, pierced in simple star-flower design. 4-1/2" H x 5-1/4" x 4-7/8". Pennsylvania German, 19th C. Ex-collection of Earl F. & Ada F. Robacker, auctioned by T. Glenn Horst, Horst Auctions, Farmersville, PA, 6/23-24/1989, for $775.* **$600-$800**

IV-114. Cheese mold. *Pierced tin, round, with 6-point star and concentric rings. Wide strap handles. Has also a slightly domed lid with strap handle. 4-1/4" H x 9-3/8" diameter at top. Ex-collection of Earl F. & Ada F. Robacker, auctioned by Horst Auctions, for $975.* **$800-$1000**

IV-115. Cheese mold. *Very unusual shape — a cloverleaf overlying a triangle. Drawn from picture in enlightening article by Mildred T. Bohne, "Tin Cheese Strainers," in [Ohio] Antique Review, 2/1985. Bohne calls these strainers a "specialized form of colander," which explains their function very well. Value probably* **$800-$1200**

"Lemon Cheese-Cake. 1 pound cottage cheese, 4 eggs (separate), 1 cup granulated sugar, 2 rounded teaspoons flour, grated rind and juice of a large lemon, 1 teaspoon cinnamon, almost 1/4 of a nutmeg, 1 tablespoon butter. — Cream the butter, add the sugar and egg yolks, and cream until light; next add the spices, flour, rind and juice of the lemon, and the cheese rubbed through a sieve or squeezed through a potato-ricer. Beat the whites to a stiff froth, stir them in lightly, and pour the mixture into a large pie-pan lined with rich pastry. Bake in a rather quick oven." *Womans Home Companion*, Jan. 1901. ["Quick" oven means a hot oven.]

Cheese drainer mold, heart-shaped, very wide at top lobes, tin, punctured and slit or slotted design of starbursts and holes, the holes nowhere near so close together as in more common slit & punctured heart molds, 3 strap feet, PA, pint-size, late 19th C. **$150-$200**

Cheese drainer mold, heart-shaped with 3 short feet, little hanging ring, pierced tin, nice old dark tin, prob. PA German, 19th C. **$250-$400**

Cheese drainer mold, lobed form, rather shallow sides, 6 lobes with 3 pointed rays & three rounds, intricate concentric rings of slits, some wavery to give effect of hot sun, triangular hanging ring of wire, punctured & pieced tin, extremely unusual, PA (?), 19th C. This one appeared in a picture in an interesting article by Mildred T. Bohne, "Tin Cheese Strainers," in *Antique Review* (formerly *Ohio Antique Review*), Feb. 1985. It is the only one I've ever seen with such unusual shape. The most common shape is round, the second most common is heart-shaped. Bohne writes that, "Although they have been described as having been made for draining cottage cheese [smearkase], they were really made for ... pressed egg cheese, tsierkase." The value given is not Bohne's. **$400-$600**

Cheese drainer mold, pieced & punctured tin with strap handles, possibly Shaker, 19th C. **$100-$130**

Cheese drainer mold, pierced copper, heart-shaped, 3 short feet, European (?), 19th C (?). This entry taken from an ad. It could be authentic (probably European) antique, or a fairly recent "decorator" take-off on traditional PA German heart-shaped tin molds for cheese curds. A mold in this form made of copper sends alarm signals. If old: **$225-$255**

IV-116. Cheese mold. *Handmade tin, perforated on bottom and lower sides of cylinder. Three short conical feet. Has round tin "foller" or presser, shown at left. Both parts have loop handles. 7-1/8" H with 1-1/4" H legs; 6-3/8" diameter. Pennsylvania, late 19th C. Courtesy Jean Hatt, Hatt's Hutt, Denver, PA.* **$300-$400**

Reproduction alert. Because of shape and origin, heart molds are very desirable. They are widely reproduced, not for fakery but for decorators, and sold in gift shops around the country. The country look in new kitchens, which began at the tail end of the 1970s and continues now, has encouraged this kind of reproduction. Study any drainer carefully. Heavier dark tin is older. Idiosyncracies in curlicue feet or evidence of hand-punctured holes are indications of age too. By the way, new ones are not necessarily shiny — they can be distressed. **Marked Reproductions**. Too few reproductions or "replicas" are marked at all, or marked with anything besides a stock or model number. To my mind, this is proof positive that the maker of the piece has the willingness, if not the intent, to deceive, by having his reproduction misrepresented and sold as the old thing it is a modern copy of. There are makers of cast metal wares who have names and numbers cast into the metal only to have a future seller file them off. Unfortunately very few collector periodicals have stringent rules or any enforced rules at all about advertising reproductions. One notable exception is *Antique-Week*, Knightstown, IN, with regional offices in Leesburg, VA, and Mechanicsburg, PA. They publish in every issue a "NOTICE ON REPRODUCTIONS," which tells all that "Items advertised in [this paper] are supposed to be old or antique unless it is stated that they are clearly and permanently marked reproductions . . . Please advise of cases where you received reproductions that are not advertised as such. There will be honest mistakes, and we will, therefore, not necessarily take one complaint as proof that an advertiser has been unethical or is in violation of postal regulations that forbid misrepresentation."

Cheese drainer mold, round, tin cylinder, 3 small tin peg feet, alternating rows of vertical slits & large round pierced holes, American, 4" H x 4-1/4" diameter, mid 19th C. **$150-$175**

Cheese drainer mold, round, punctured tin cup with 2 strap handles, American, 4" H x 4" D, 19th C. **$50-$65**

Cheese drainer mold, round & simple, but possibly handmade as spacing is eccentric, punctured tin hoop with flat bottom, design on bottom & sides are 5 circles of concentric rings of holes; on sides are 8 circles, marked "Weiss," American, early 20th C. **$45-$65**

Cheese drainer mold, round, tin, 2 strap handles, has wooden cheese ladder with it to rest over crock, American, late 19th C. **$65-$100**

IV-117. Chocolate or marzipan molds. *Also meant for fondants. Stamped tin. Upper ones are the "large" size, which came mounted "in plaques containing 6 moulds, all of one pattern" or with 12 the same. Size probably about 1" or 1-1/4". Lower set is "small" size, mounted same way. Probably about 3/4" to 1". From Mrs. A. B. Marshall's Larger Cookery Book, London, c.1902. Note flying fish — it and the dolphin, lower right, would probably bring the most.* **$10-$20**

Cheese mold, cow, round, carved wood, American, prob. WI, 10" diameter, early 20th C. **$45-$75**

Cheese mold, various carved wood motifs: dogs, cows, chickens, pigs, WI, three sizes: 10" D, 12" D, 14" D, late 19th C. **$60-$120**

Cheese-Chocolate-Pudding molds. A 1927 catalog from S. Joseph, NYC, of bakers' supplies, offers several heavy stamped tin, fully 3-D animal molds in several sizes, that were described as, "Imported chocolate or pudding molds, can also be used for cheese." So! The perfect definitions, distinctions and classifications which elude us as collectors, weren't even made when the molds were new!

Cheese press, oak, stands on floor, fancy turned legs, American, 38" H, 19th C. **$85-$150**

Cheese press, round, handmade, tin cylinder with 3 short conical legs, holes in bottom and first 2" around bottom sides, foller or press with little handle is tin, ring handle on side of cylinder, American, 7-1/8" H with 1-1/4" legs, 6-3/8" diameter, 19th C. **$150-$220**

Chocolate mold, alphabet, cast metal tray type with heavy tinning, all letters, numbers "1 - 0," and name, "AUERBACH," 12" x 6" x 3/4" thick, making chocolate wafers 3/16" thick, 20th C. **$60-$75**

Chocolate molds. This is a classic field of collecting and a surprising number of molds are available dating from the first half of this century. Older ones, of course, exist also. There are a couple or more reproduced catalogs: see the name Judene Divone in the bibliography. One of the appeals of closed molds is the secret treasure aspect. There is so much more detail on the inside of some chocolate molds, or ice cream molds for that matter, that I have called them the "Fabergé Eggs of Kitchendom!"

Prices of Chocolate Molds. Just to be old isn't enough. **Size** has a strong effect on value: large and very large molds (over 15" H, or over 20" H) seem to get about 250% more than the 5" or 7" H molds of the same subject, condition, and approximate age. Tiny molds may also command more money than the run of the middle ones, but only if the subject is desirable. **Subject** is very important, although chocolate mold collectors seem to have a slightly different idea of what's "special" than does the outsider amateur. Some subjects are predictable, because any collectible in that shape sells well: Scotties, teddy bears, Kewpies, Santas (Kris Kringle, St.

Nicholas, Belsnickel, Father Christmas), automobiles, poodles, bears, pigs, and especially rabbits dressed in clothes. The mold-designers often celebrated scientific or technological objects such as dirigibles, trains and rockets, or then-current cartoon characters — much the same way that tin windup toys celebrated such things for children. It would be an interesting study to do a crossover comparison, form by form, with chocolate and ice cream molds and children's toys of the first third of the 20th century. **Scarcity** is the other main ingredient of value. And only if you are an avid and active collector of the molds will you get a feel for what's rare. **Condition** and **completeness** almost go without saying, for most chocolate molds on the market today are in fine condition. **New looking?** Dealer Don Appelquist, Suckasunny, Morris County, NJ, explains that many of "those that look new are actually old. They were never used, and never had the edges cut or trimmed, and were never mounted in the protective strapping." **Rust** isn't necessarily a sign of age; neither are distress marks and dings. Before you buy something, look around the dealer's stock carefully. If there are a number of very similar things, especially if they are all rusted, weathered, or otherwise distressed, they are probably new reproductions. **Strap scaffolding**. Don Appelquist explained that in a candy shop, "when finished with a particular shape, having made as many as they wanted, they'd just toss the mold into a corner until needed next time." Most collectors remove the straps. **Copper & steel**. Two companies using copper and steel to make chocolate molds were Weygandt, of NYC, and the American Chocolate Mould Co., in business in the 1930s and 1940s. Their molds were made of copper-plated steel that was tinned.

IV-119. Chocolate molds, *"or pudding molds. Can also be used for cheese." Imported tin, with ribbony spring clips.* **(T-L)** *Rabbit made in 5 sizes, from 1/8 pint to 2 pts.* **(B-L)** *Lamb made in 1-1/2 pt. and 4-1/2 pt. sizes. Swan made only in 3 pint size. Worst and most unappetizing is the unhappy dead pig at bottom right. How anyone could think the agonized grimace on the intelligent face of an animal more easily trained than a dog would be fun to eat beats me, but it's an ancient style of mold. All from S. Joseph Co. catalog, c.1927.* **$45-$150**

IV-118. Chocolate mold. *Heavy tin in protective frame. Hinged, marked #34882. Weygandt Co., NYC, but made in Germany. They are just 3 monkeys — not hear no evil, see no evil, speak no evil, or . . . eat no evil. Collection of Meryle Evans.* **$100-$110**

3557 6027 4295

3565 .07 .088

9 3

IV-122. Chocolate mold. *Stamped heavy tin, hinged on side, with 2 clips opposite. Back and front views of female rabbit, ready for church and a potluck afterwards, with parasol, wicker basket on back which she supports with an arm behind her back. Apron has flipped hem. 7-1/4" H. Beautifully detailed. Marked #14037 and #2 down by bottom clip. Anton Reich. Collection of Margaret Upchurch & Kyle Goad.* **$90-$120**

IV-120. Chocolate molds. *Variety of 2-part stamped tin molds with clips, including two standing Santas and a standing turkey. The rabbit with flag could be used to celebrate a patriotic Easter I guess. All from Mills' catalog, 1927. I left numbers on in case you find molds stamped with those numbers. Santas cost the most.* **$40-$125**

IV-123. Chocolate mold. *Standing rabbit with apron and wicker backpack. Both sides the same. Hinged with one large clip. Well-detailed, 20" H. Courtesy of dealer Don Appelquist, Sussex County, NJ.* **$125-$200**

IV-121. Chocolate mold. *Elephant in hinged mold. Stamped #8306 and also #20. Anton Reiche, Dresden. About 4-3/4" H. Collection of Margaret Upchurch & Kyle Goad.* **$50-$65**

IV-124. Chocolate mold. *Man holding small ginger beer bottle; probably a Dutchman, because he's wearing a sailor's watch cap, with a leather bag under his long coat, and has a typical Van Dyke (also spelled Van Dyck) beard and a deep Dutch collar. His right hand is extended but holds nothing; maybe when they finished the choclate they stuck something in his hand? 9-3/8" H. Marked #84, and partial name "—zerhey & Co., Rotterdam." Collection of Margaret Upchurch, Kyle Goad & Amanda Carrotluv.* **$160-$175**

Chocolate mold, Army truck with tied-on canvas covering on back, "Vormenfabriek #15371," Tilberg, Holland, 1940s (?). **$60-$75**

Chocolate mold, baby standing with finger in mouth, very tubby, steel alloy, Anton Reiche, #17197, sold by T. C. Weygandt of NYC, made in Dresden, Germany, 6" x 3-1/8", early 20th C. **$80-$95**

Chocolate mold, baby, stark naked, one hand to mouth, one to belly, 2-part, heavy stamped tin or steel alloy, marked "Kunzig 17499, C. Weygandt," NYC, USA, Made in Germany, 12" H, early 20th C. **$125-$140**

Chocolate mold, birds in flight, cast aluminum, ornate, somewhat oxidized (with white powdery film), American (?), 7" H, post World War II. **$50-$70**

Chocolate mold, blacksmith snippers in rectangular frame, 2-part, clamped, well stamped metal, only 5" L, 20th C. • Representations of tools are particularly interesting. Other tools include a hammer and a scissor-action tool that looks like pliers. Masonic emblems also include tools. **$15-$25**

Chocolate mold, bowknots, flat tray multiple of 12 cups, nickel silver alloy, early 20th C. **$30-$40**

Chocolate mold, boy, small & fat, metal alloy, mfd. by Gesetze Geschutz, imported by Van Emden Co. of NYC, German, 2-1/2" x 4-1/4", c.1900 or early 20th C. **$70-$75**

Chocolate mold, bugle, stamped alloy, LeTang Fils #3919, 8-3/4" x 3-1/2". **$60-$65**

Chocolate mold, Bugs Bunny, double standing figures, 2 halves hinged, within heavy frame, with old clamps, marked "Warner Bros. Productions, Inc." in molds, so name would appear on finished chocolate Bugs, each rabbit 9-1/2" H x 3-3/4" W, mid 20th C. **$90-$120**

Chocolate mold, bull dog, 2 parts, wide flange, Weygardt Co., NYC, but "Made in Germany," 5-1/4" x 5", 1920s-1940s. **$60-$70**

Chocolate mold, bulldog, sitting, tin-plated nickel alloy, J. G. Laurosch, #4102, German, 5-1/4" H, 1920s-1940s. There are many **bulldog** chocolate molds — something to do with Teddy Roosevelt, who died in 1919 and was sometimes caricatured (because of his teeth & tenacity) as a bulldog. A popular dog of the period — maybe from a cartoon strip? **$55-$65**

Chocolate mold, candy bars, cast metal tray type makes 14, "Wilbur Candy Co.," 20th C. **$18-$22**

Chocolate mold, cartoon character "Jiggs," nickel silver, tinned, American, 20th C. **$60-$70**

Chocolate mold set, champagne bucket & bottle, stamped alloy, only bucket is marked: "Eppelsheimer #4580," bucket 2-3/4" H x 2-3/4" diameter; bottle 4-3/4" H, early 20th C. **$85-$100**

Chocolate mold, Charlie Chaplin figure, well-stamped metal alloy, marked "Dépose" (deposited or registered), French, 6" x 3-1/2", c.1920s (?). I had never seen this nor heard of it until browsing catalogs from dealer Teri Dziadul in Enfield, CT. Her 1986 asking price: $195. My price range: **$195-$235+**

Chocolate mold, chicken, tin, marked with Sommet's dolphin stamp and #2031, 4" H, turn of century. **$50-$60**

Chocolate mold, chicks standing on rim of nest, 2 figures, tin-plated nickel & copper alloy, Anton Reiche, #6543, Dresden, Germany, approx. 4-1/2" across, early 20th C. Little 'nipple' in the edge of this & many molds is called a locater, and helps to line up fronts & backs. **$75-$90**

Chocolate mold, child with cat, pewter, late 19th C. **$45-$55**

Chocolate mold, chimney sweep on roof holding his ladder, alloy, no marks, 4-1/2" x 2-3/4". **$95-$115**

Chocolate mold, cigars, makes 5 of solid chocolate, good details of wrapped leaves, when 2 parts are closed, there are 5 tubes to fill, may need special funnel, American (?), 5-1/8" H x 4-1/2" W, 20th C. **$40-$45**

Chocolate mold, dirigible, nickel silver, marked with name on dirigible, "Los Angeles" and "#1," German (?), 20th C. **$150-$170**

Chocolate mold, dog (poodle or water spaniel with poodle cut), sitting, heavy tinned nickel alloy, 2-part mold with clamps, Sommet #1306, Paris, 9" H, (also made 6-5/8" H), 1900 to 1950. **$200-$235**

Chocolate mold, duck, metal alloy, very full-formed for solid candy, with lid on bottom, American, 8" H, 20th C. **$58-$65**

Chocolate mold, Dutch boy, nickel alloy, tinned, Anton Reiche, #24247, 6" H, 1930s. **$75-$80**

Chocolate mold, Dutch boy & girl pair, Anton Reiche #17604 & 17605, 6" H, c.1930s. For the pair: **$175-$200**

Chocolate mold, Dutchman holding small ginger beer bottle, bearded man wearing sailor's watch cap, leather bag under long coat with Dutch collar, right hand held out but holding nothing, probably given a wooden cane or something after chocolate was taken from mold, "--zerhey & Co., No. 84," Rotterdam, 9-3/8" H, late 19th C. **$160-$175**

Chocolate mold, egg & grapes, tin-plated nickel silver alloy, Eppelsheimer & Co., #5024, 3-15/16" L, early 20th C. According to Judene Divone (see bibliography), Eppelsheimer used an alloy "very high in nickel." **$65-$80**

Chocolate mold, egg with design of jumping pig on side, heavy tin, no mark, 20th C. **$15-$18**

Chocolate mold, egg with image of Man in the Moon smoking his pipe, metal alloy, E. & Co. (Eppelsheimer), NYC, 4-1/4" x 3". **$70-$100**

Chocolate mold, electric iron, heavily tinned stamped metal, 2 parts with clamp, "Vormenfabriek," (reported once as Vormenfaberier -- maybe a French form of name?), Tilberg, Holland (often reported as Tilbury or Tilburg), 4" L, c.1930s-1940s. **$85-$100**

Chocolate mold, elephant, 2-part hinged, Anton Reiche #8306, also #20, turn of century. **$50-$65**

Chocolate mold, Father Christmas on donkey, early Santa character has traditional peaked cap & long robe with short jacket, 2-piece tin, German (?), 7" H, 19th or early 20th C. **$110-$160**

Chocolate mold, fish with many fins, huge & slightly stylized, dark gray nickel alloy with partial tinning, somewhat flimsy for the length, probably for making a confectioner's showpiece, German (?), 26" L, 19th C. **Straight Fish**. Unlike fish molds for jellies or aspics, which are curved, this mold and other fish chocolate molds are straight. I don't know the significance of the fish; obviously it's a Christian symbol, but usually having to do with Lent, which is hardly a time to be eating a 26" long chocolate fish! **$165-$220**

IV-125. Chocolate mold. *Stamped tin chicken, with large clip. Standing type, marked with small dolphin, and #2031, mfd. by Sommet, French, 4" H.* **$50-$60**

Chocolate mold, girl with watering can, 2-piece tin plated nickel alloy, Mistress Mary, quite contrary, English or German, 7-1/2" H, 19th C. or early 20th C. Good for a watering can collection! **$75-$95**

Chocolate mold, girl with watering can & large hairbow, "Little Jane," Anton Reiche, #24222, Dresden, Germany, 3" H, c.1930s. Little Jane is cute, but fortunately not so cute as the terminally-precious "Mary Jane" little-girls-with-big-bows also made by Reiche in the same period. **$75-$95**

Chocolate mold, half old man, half egg, pewter, 1-3/4" x 2-1/2", possibly Gustav Krieg, Hamburg, Germany, 19th or 20th C. **$30-$40**

Chocolate mold, half old woman, half egg, pewter, 1-3/4" x 2-1/2", may be Gustav Krieg, Hamburg, Germany, 19th or 20th C. **$30-$40**

Chocolate mold, hen on her nest, white metal alloy, Eppelsheimer & Co., #4688, NYC, 5-1/2" x 5", turn of century. **$60-$70**

Chocolate mold, horse, Anton Reiche #6872, 4" x 3", early 20th C. **$55-$75**

Chocolate mold, horse, Anton Reiche #8458, only 3-1/2" x 2-3/4", early 20th C. **$65-$75**

Chocolate mold, horse, extra soldering to make a little clip with wire, horse's legs are separate, not joined or filled in, 2-part, Anton Reiche #8, and #8760, 3-1/4" H, turn of century. **$65-$75**

Chocolate mold, hotdogs or sausage links, 5 in tray form, heavy metal, marked "Supe & Busch Dresden," Germany, 7-1/4" x 3-3/4", early 20th C (?). **$55-$65**

Chocolate mold, Jack & the Beanstalk, tinned copper, good detail, no mark, 8-1/4" x 5-1/4", turn of century (?). **$175-$185**

Chocolate mold, lamb, lying down (in heraldic terms <u>couchant</u>, meaning lying down with head up). Metal alloy, 2-part, Kanter Mfg. Co., Cleveland, OH, 8" H x 12" L, 20th C. **$65-$75**

Chocolate mold, lamb lying down (couchant), front legs are visible, longish tail curled around, lots of stylized detailing of wool, tin-plated nickel alloy, Anton Reiche, #6638, 7-1/4" L, early 20th C. **$125-$140**

Chocolate mold, lamb standing (which is unusual), steel & copper alloy, C. Weygandt, #381, NY, 2-3/8" L, mid 20th C. **$60-$70**

Chocolate mold, lion, "Anton Reiche #6869," 2-1/2" x 4-1/2", early 20th C. **$75-$85**

Chocolate mold, lion, sitting, slightly rusted metal, B.V. Vormenfabriek, #15281, Tilberg, Holland, 4-5/8" L, mid 20th C. **$60-$75**

Chocolate mold, locomotive, white metal alloy, Anton Reiche, #9959, 4-3/4" H x 6-1/4" L, early 20th C. **$125-$145**

Chocolate mold, man's striped tie with looped knot, stamped heavy tin, very flat rectangular frame, marked only #12680, American, 11-1/2" L, tie itself is 9" L, 20th C. **$50-$55**

Chocolate mold, monkey in hat, very impish, with round object (coconut?) between feet, stamped alloy, marked "H. Walter," Berlin, Germany, 5-1/4" x 3-1/4", early 20th C (?). **$85-$100**

Chocolate mold, monkeys, 3 sitting in a row, but they aren't "Hear no evil, See no evil, Speak no evil," just heavy metal monkeys, NYC, 3-3/4" H x 7" L in frame, turn of century. **$100-$110**

Chocolate mold, mouse boldly climbing cat's leg, 2-part stamped alloy, perhaps a reference to a fairy tale, marked "G. DeHaeck Gand," Holland, 20th C. **$80-$100**

Chocolate mold, nesting hen, stamped alloy, marked "Ger. Fontaine et -?-" [et Fils?], French, 2-1/2" x 1-3/4", early 20th C (?). **$40-$50**

Chocolate mold, nursing bottle with baby's face on front, stamped alloy, setting (?) sun behind mountains mark, #2050, 5" x 2-3/4", 20th C. **$75-$100**

Chocolate mold, owl on branch, tin-plated nickel alloy, Letang Fils, #1599, Paris, France, 2" H, turn of century into mid 20th C. Made over a long period, in different alloys; hard to find. **$85-$120**

Chocolate mold, patties, heavy cast metal tray type makes 28, "Wilbur Candy Co.," American, 20th C. **$22-$30**

Chocolate mold, penguin with top hat & spectacles, nickel alloy, Anton Reiche, 20th C. **$65-$80**

Chocolate mold, pretzel, stamped tin, 1-1/2" x 2", 20th C. **$7-$10**

Chocolate mold, rabbit, a blacksmith <u>occupational mold</u>, he's got one tool in his apron pocket & is standing at anvil, hammer at the ready, not marked, late 19th or early 20th C. From catalog of dealer Teri Dziadul in Enfield, CT, who called it a very rare subject. Extra valuable for collectors of iron, or blacksmithing tools. **$200-$255**

Chocolate mold, rabbit, crouched down, metal alloy, Eppelsheimer, #6183, NYC, 7-3/4" x 3-1/2", 20th C (?). **$100-$110**

Chocolate mold, rabbit, high sitting with basket on back, steel & copper alloy called <u>Platina</u>, C. Weygandt Co., #238, NYC, NY, 17-1/2" H, c.1950s. **$130-$150**

Chocolate mold, rabbit, high sitting with basket on back, tinned metal, hinged at top, Eppelsheimer & Co., NYC, 9" H x 4" W, Dec. 1935. U.S. Pat. No. 948146. **$130-$150**

Chocolate mold, rabbit, high sitting with one paw on basket, tinned nickel alloy, Heris, #417, Nüremberg, Germany, 12" H, pre-1950. **$75-$85**

Chocolate mold, rabbit, hiking with basket backpack, very detailed basket and features, marked "O. Darchambeau," 7-3/4" H x 4" W, turn of century. **$65-$80**

IV-126. Chocolate mold. *Santa in two parts, with registration dimples or bumps and 2 clips. Marked #76 (?). 7" H, heavy tin, early 20th C. Picture courtesy of the National Museum of American History, Smithsonian Museum, Washington, DC.* **$125-$150**

IV-127. Chocolate mold. *Stamped tin, 2 part, makes chocolate blacksmith's pincer tool. 5" H, no mark, late 19th or early 20th C.* **$20-$35**

Chocolate mold, rabbit in landscape, clothed & pulling wagon full of Easter eggs, "5 Miles to Go" signpost, houses, Eppelsheimer & Co., NYC, entire rectangle 5" H x 7-1/2" L, early 20th C. **$60-$65**

Chocolate mold, rabbit, lady ready for church with parasol, wicker basket on back is supported by arm held behind body, beautiful curved body, apron has flipped hem, hinged on side and with 2 clips, marked #14037 and #2, Anton Reiche, 7-1/4" H, late 19th C. **$90-$120**

Chocolate mold, rabbit pulling cart, cast aluminum, single hinge, flat bottom, American? 9" H, 20th C. One dealer, noted for selection of chocolate molds, says these are also for cakes. **$35-$45**

Chocolate mold, rabbit, sitting & looks surprised, rigid silvery alloy, Eppelsheimer & Co., NYC, NY, 10" H (this rabbit came in several sizes), mid 20th C. **$100-$120**

Chocolate mold, rabbit, sitting with basket, shiny alloy, J.G. Laurosch, #4032, German, 15" H, 1930s-1940s. **$100-$120**

Chocolate mold, rabbit, standing, pewter-like cast metal, heavy straps in sort of protective bridgework case around outside. American (?), prob. c.1930s. **$110-$125**

Chocolate mold, rabbit, striding on hind legs over clump of ferns, heavy stamped tin 2 parts, marked "Anton Reiche #24353," Dresden, Germany, and extraordinary size: 21-1/2" H x 11-7/8" W x 5" deep, early 20th C. **$350-$450**

Chocolate mold, rabbit with backpack, well detailed, for making solid chocolate, has clipped-on lid on bottom, unused and looks new, no mark, American (?), 20" H, early 20th C. **$125-$200**

Chocolate mold, rabbits on 4 eggs, for hollow chocolate, white metal alloy, American (?), 10-3/8" H, 20th C. **$70-$75**

Chocolate mold, rooster, heavy tin, 3 hinged sections, 10" H, late 19th C. **$125-$165**

Chocolate mold, rooster, steel & copper alloy with small rust spots, C. Weygandt #62, NY, 10" H, mid 20th C. **$125-$145**

Chocolate mold, roosters, 4 of them connected, steel alloy, C. Weygandt, NYC, 4" H, 20th C. **$75-$95**

Chocolate mold, Santa Claus, marked "solid nickel silver," also "B-M #44," 7-1/4" H, turn of century to c.1920s. **$110-$150**

Chocolate mold, Santa Claus with backpack, deeply-stamped metal alloy, clips on edges, American (?), 20th C. **$75-$100**

Santa Reproduction Alert. Two Santa chocolate molds, imported from Holland, were advertised in 1983. They are supposed to be "replicas," and are nickel-plated stamped metal. Both are 2-part, have wide flanges and 3 spring wire ring clips. The 6-1/2" H Santa, or Belsnickle, has long fur-trimmed coat, and soft bag over one hip, into which he reaches for gifts. The flange is stamped "Holland Handcrafts #15554." The 4-1/2" H Santa has short belted fur-trimmed coat, high boots, jolly elfin face. Number illegible. They sold for $27 and $23 in the catalog.

Chocolate mold, spaceship or rocket, shiny alloy, 2 parts, relatively flat, American, 9-1/2" x 6" W, 1960s-1970s. Don't mistake this, which has 2 rocket boosters on either side, for the rocket-shaped dirigible mold, one of which is embossed "Los Angeles" and dates from the late 1920s-1930s. **$50-$75**

Chocolate mold, squirrel with acorn, very bushy tail curled up over head, dark pewtery nickel silver alloy, fairly thin & light in weight, 2 parts, 15" H, c.1880s to1920s. **$150-$175**

Chocolate mold, St. Nicholas forms in high mitred hats, multiple 3-D old-fashioned type in hinged rectangular frame, called by collectors a book mold, metal alloy, 6-1/4" W x 13" L, individual figures are about 6-1/2" H, early 20th C. **$140-$170**

Chocolate mold, St. Nicholas on horseback, with rooftop above him, 2 parts, with clamps, Dutch, 8" H x 6" W, turn of century. **$185-$225**

Chocolate mold, stag, standing with left leg poised, heavy weight tin, marked "France 1313" with a dolphin and #48 within a diamond lozenge, Sommet, French, 12" x 10-1/2", late 19th or early 20th C. **$250-$300**

Chocolate mold, stars, 6 in a row, tray type, bronze-finished heavy metal, "A. F. Tool Co.," NYC, NY, 6" L x 1-1/2" W, 20th C. **$55-$85**

Chocolate mold, swan, 2-part heavy stamped tin, marked "Thos. Mills & Bro., Inc., Philadelphia," 8-1/2" H x 10-1/2" W, turn of century. **$165-$175**

Chocolate mold, swan, nickel alloy, tinned, Sommet, "#1756," with dolphin mark, Paris, France, 3-1/4" x 3-1/2", 20th C. **$75-$95**

Chocolate mold, swan, sitting (swimming), tin-plated nickel alloy, Eppelsheimer & Co., #6212, NYC, 3-1/2" L, 1919 to 1972. According to the excellent book by Judene Divone on *Chocolate Moulds* (see bibliography), this rather undistinguished looking mold (my judgment, not hers) was made over a very long period — 1919 to 1972. **$45-$55**

Chocolate mold, teddy bear standing (waiting to be picked up), stamped alloy, marked with new one on me, "E. I. Metro, -?- Anver," French, about 4-1/2" H, early 20th C. **$200-$235**

Chocolate mold, television, alloy looks like stainless steel, American (?), c.1960s. There are several really modern forms in these less-appealing molds. Radios and telephones are two that come to mind. Still, collectors pay rather high prices. **$40-$60**

Chocolate mold, toy soldier with high hat, tinned nickel alloy, Randell & Smith (?), the only English firm, or poss. American, 4" H, 20th C. **$25-$35**

Chocolate mold, turkey, tinned nickel silver, H. Walter, #8635, Berlin, Germany, 4-1/2" H, c. late 1940s, early 1950s. **$60-$65**

Chocolate mold, turkey, every feather shows, metal alloy, "Vormenfabriek, #15292," Tilberg, Holland, 4" x 4-1/2" L. **$70-$75**

Chocolate mold, turkeys, a pair posed tail-to-tail, alloy, American, 6" H x 9-5/8" W, 20th C. **$70-$80**

Chocolate mold, violin, stamped alloy, Anton Reiche #40034, 10-1/2" L x 3-3/4" W, 20th C. **$125-$140**

Chocolate mold, wheat sheaf, tinned copper, used for chocolate candies, "Harrod's Store, Ltd.," English, 3" H, turn of century. **$15-$18**

Chocolate (?) molds, figurals, described by dealer in ad as "nickel plated cast iron," with "6 figures in each" of the various molds, marked "Letang Fils," Paris, 6-3/4" L x 3-3/4" W x 1/2" thick, early 20th C. **Cast Iron?** Although this manufacturer made chocolate molds, I don't know if these are chocolate molds, having not seen them. I'm reporting to you to add to our data-

IV-128. Chocolate mold. *I've finally decided to call it a chocolate mold. 4-3/8" L. Looks like an egg's bathtub. Heavy cast iron with 3 legs. Something similar is shown in IV-108 for Cream eggs. Late 19th C.* **$20-$45**

base. "Cast iron" seems odd to me. Subjects as described in ad: child behind hi-button shoe marked "BeBe"; small girl, fancy dress, high button shoe, "Elegante" on bottom; "Jockey" in riding clothes, crop, spurs, "Chasseur." **$75-$100**

Chocolate molds, figures of stamped metal, tray type rows of repeat images, 20th C. Figures include sitting rabbits, turtles, ducks, roadsters, cigars, men in the moon, kewpies, frogs and beetles. Prices vary widely according to appeal of individual subjects as well as determined rarity. Prices range below for 5 nicely detailed frogs (modeled as if seen from above) to 4 army trucks in a row. **$85-$145**

Confection mold, cast brass, round with 2 loop handles, 13 small, finely detailed cups in traditional Chinese shapes, including butterfly, chrysanthemum, koi (carp), lion head, and other flowers and forms, very rough casting on underside. Received with the bottom "packed very hard with sand that appeared to have grease soaked into it." This mold was reported by collector Jim Holroyd, who has shared many things with me over the years. Bought in Singapore, 9" diameter x 2" deep, looks 19th C. Price range mine, not Holroyd's. **$80-$100**

Confectioner's mold — See molds, tin; listing for French pie mold

Cookie baking set, Dick Tracy motif, in original box, Pillsbury's "Comicooky," 1937. **$28-$35**

Cookie board, animals — carved wood with figures on both sides, oblong with regal lion, head at right, tail curled up over rump, one front leg on double arch tombstone, on other side is seated cat, dark color to wood, stone marked "Koning Van Dieren." Dutch? or NY or other Dutch-settled state? 8-3/4" H x 14" L, 19th C. look; poss. 20th C. Sold for $365 at Garth's Auctions, Delaware, OH, April 11-12, 1986. **$350-$450**

Cookie boards — See cake boards

Cookie board, "gingerbread mold" say ads for the **reproduction**. Hand-carved poplar wood board, figure of periwigged Punch, in fancy striped knee britches and fitted coat, holding walking stick, exaggerated nose and chin of the famous puppet, lots of details in buttons and pattern in textile of clothing, supposed to be a replica of an "18th century original now in Van Cortlandt Manor," NY, apparently not available in cast metal as was their other replica cookie board, ad is for American Heritage Museum Collection ... from Sleepy Hollow Restorations, NY, 28" H x 10" W, advertised in July/Aug. 1978 *Americana*. Original price was $165 plus shipping. The value has not gone up, but has instead gone down, even though it was nicely carved. **$20-$45**

Cookie board, St. Nicholas with his miter hat decorated with a cross, long beard, bishop's crook, ecclesiastical alb or surplice, bands, and chasuble, with basket of 3 baby dolls in bunting, "hand carved" wood, reproduction or "replica of an 18th century Dutch colonial mold..in Van Cortlandt Manor," American (?), 26" L x 11" W, the figure being 24" H, advertised in 1978 *Americana*. **Reproduction alert:** This reproduction was "also available in a polished cast metal version," which was 24" H x 8-3/4" W. The description comes from the Sept./Oct. 1978 *Americana* magazine's American Heritage catalog. The wooden one originally cost $165; the metal one (looks like cast aluminum) was under $50. The unfortunate realities are that some people will have bought these on the secondary market thinking they were getting a real antique, and the value has gone down, not up, unlike a real antique. A copy or reproduction, at least a nameless one, can not be expected to rise in value. Reproductions by Wallace Nutting and the Stickleys excepted. **$20-$45**

Cookie boards — See also springerle mold; cake board

Cookie & candy mold, cat, a new, large reddish brown mass-produced stoneware mold for making flat cookies or shortbread, finely detailed striped tiger cat with bow around neck, the outer rim of the mold almost follows the cat's outline, hanging hole at top, "Le Chat," mfd. by Hartstone, Inc., Zanesville, OH, 9-3/4" H x 5-1/4" W, (and also in larger size, 11-1/4" H x 6-1/2" W), 1980s. **$12-$15**

COLLECTING COOKIE CUTTERS

For Christmas over a hundred years ago, Pennsylvania German children in Lancaster County helped cut out and decorate foot-high cookies to stand in the front windows of their stone or brick houses. These cookie people — often gingerbread men and women iced with rows of buttons and big smiles — were a cheerful sight to snow-cold passersby. Figural cookie-making was practiced in Europe at least as far back as the sixteenth century — most of them were made using intaglio molds rather than with cutters.

Today, the holiday tradition is carried on by a vast legion of cookie cutter collectors who make large gingerbread folk as well as small shaped cookies, cutting the dough with old and new cutters. For most people, the joy of such cookies would be in the baking, eating, and giving of them. Collectors, however, are more interested in finding yet another whimsical lovebird or unicorn, or a different trotting horse to add to the already full corral.

Cookie cutter collectors are a democratic group who appreciate and buy cutters from all periods, from the nineteenth century to the present, from Europe and North America. With the phenomenally diverse forms, a huge menagerie of creatures, a galaxy of stars, a honeymoon of hearts, or a botanical garden of flowers can be assembled fairly easily.

Unlike many collectibles the "entry level" cost of cutters is low, and because the size is small, collections of hundreds of cutters can be assembled and displayed without vast funds or space. When starting a collection, it is helpful to have a unifying theme such as motif, material, or season.

Tin — Terne Plates & Roofs. Terne (from the French for dull) is a mixture of tin and lead and is actually a form of pewter, according to P. W. Flower, who wrote *A History of the Trade In Tin*, 1880. Flower said that terne plates were used to line wooden packing cases of certain products that had to be kept dry or sealed from the air. "Of the tin plates of commerce there are two general kinds: One is known as 'tin plate' or 'bright plate,' and the other as 'terne plate' or 'roofing plate.' The coating of the former is supposed to be pure tin, and the bright appearance which it presents gives it the name by which it is most commonly designated, 'bright plate.' The coating of the second kind is composed chiefly of lead, which, being dull, or dead, in appearance, gives it the name usually applied to it, 'terne,' that term being a French word signifying 'dull of appearance.' In considering tin plate for any purpose whatever, it is necessary to examine both the plate and the coating . . ." *The Metal Worker*, Sept. 23, 1882.

Tin cookie cutters of the nineteenth century are the most expensive type. They have many crossover devotees among folk art collectors. Old tin is relatively heavy and thick and almost always quite darkened in color. Most old tin cutters make 3/4" to 1-1/8" deep cuts (although they can be nearly two feet in height!), and almost all have flat backs with or without strap handles attached. Backs of old ones are fairly roughly trimmed to the shape of the cutter because the tinsmith conserved every possible bit, including odd jut-outs and skinny strips, to be used for other cutters or other small projects.

Holey Tole. In old cutters there are usually several air holes or push holes cut in the flat back, which aided in getting the dough free of the cutter. Small air holes allowed air to escape that would otherwise have been trapped in the cutter above the dough. Some holes are big enough to push your finger through.

How & When Were Holes Made? Evidence of how things were made gives clues to their earliest possible date, if not the latest. So far, cookie cutter holes don't add dating data. Holes are made in sheet metal by (**1**) drilling, (**2**) drilling or punching a start hole then sawing with hack or band saw, or (**3**) punching out or puncturing with something such as a nail, a small sharp-edged punch, or a die stamp (a form of punch). A hand-held hammer is needed to drive a nail or a small punch, and either a mechanical drop hammer is needed to provide the force required to strike a die stamp through a metal sheet, or a screwed or levered press must be used to perforate the metal. Holes made with a punch or die can be round, heart-shaped, diamond-shaped, or, in fact, any shape. Most cutters have round holes, some big enough to stick a forefinger in to push out the dough, some quite small, say 1/16" across. At least one cutter from the Robacker Collection had small air holes in a heart shape, which were struck with a tiny heart-shaped punch. The holes made by any method will have a slight burred edge, perhaps visible only with magnification. The burr is called a "barb" or "fin," to be filed smooth. Most familiar to us kitcheneers are barbs or fins on punctured tin or brass graters, or pie safe tins. Besides a barb, there is apt to be a distortion of the metal surrounding the hole. It may be very slight, or a pronounced warp, especially with thicker metals and larger die stamps. The larger the hole the more metal resists the strike, and if that is not delivered evenly, some distortion may occur. **Die stamps** for use by tinsmiths making cookie cutters were available at least since the early nineteenth century. I don't know how early a simple stamping press capable of making nickel- or quarter-sized holes in tin plate was widely available to tinsmiths. In general, assume a small town tinsmith would be restricted to small punches. A "Machine for Punching holes in metal" was patented by J. Sarchet in 1822. Many were patented in the 1850s to the 1870s. Small presses were available that screw-clamped to the workbench, using a levered ratchet. In the 1890s and perhaps before, "The Little Giant," American Tool Co., Cleveland, was capable of making a 7/8" hole in sheet iron 3/32" thick. It was marketed to tinsmiths for "small work" — just right for cookie cutters.

Motifs. Among the most popular cookie shapes are hearts, horses, rabbits, birds, long-dressed ladies and high-hatted men, horsemen, and shapes of common household items.

Leaves and flowers are also fairly common. Often these are very shallow cutters, and some have even shallower corrugated "veins" that mark but do not cut through the cookie dough. Such cutters would make cookies and also pastry plants to decorate pie tops (see also jagger-pastry stamps further on in this chapter).

Some Hints On Determining Age. In cookie cutters look for old dark tin, rather thick gauge, spotty soldering, irregularly trimmed flat backs usually without rolled edges, and other signs of hand manufacture. Spotty soldering used to be considered *de facto* proof of age, because it was adduced that solder in the good old days was too expensive to make a continuous solder seam. However, if a cutter was given a lot of use, and solder spots came loose, repairs at some later date would change the character of the soldering and throw off any calculations of age that were dependent on the appearance of the solder. If solder got cheaper, why could not a repaired old cutter have new continuous solder? **Depth Sounding**, or <u>Dating By Shallow or Deep.</u> It is possible that the old rule of thumb, that a very shallow (ie. 3/8" or less deep) always meant a twentieth-century cutter, is incorrect. A large number of interesting and apparently old cutters were sold at the first and second two-day sessions of the Horst auction of the Earl F. & Ada F. Robacker Collection, May and June l989. There were some extremely deep cutters with not any more apparent age than the larger number of cutters 1/2" or less in depth. The necessary depth would depend entirely on the kind of cookie dough being cut. To save tin, and make more economic use of scraps (which might often have been long straight strips), why make a cutter for an almost paper-thin Moravian ginger cookie any deeper than it had to be to raise the flat back off the dough while cutting? One of the cutters in the sale, almost 12" H, a full-length side profile of woman in big shoes, small topknot, and long skirt with pinked hem (or fringe), was very shallow and was thought by Robacker to be "probably oldest" in their collection. (That cutter brought $775.)

In the early popular collecting studies (and many of the more serious studies) of old kitchenwares, mainly in the 1920s and 1930s, many assumptions were made based on hearsay about many kinds of cooking utensils and tools, and judgements were highly colored by sloppy sentiment. Myth cannot be made Fact without direct evidence. In the case of cookie cutters, **two avenues of research need exploring: (1)** <u>Recipes</u> for cookies or "cake" (50 and more years ago these cutters were called cake cutters), which would predicate the need for cutters in contrast to molds (for springerle, marzipan, etc.); and **(2)** <u>Diaries, journals, receipt & account books</u>, in which might be found reference to such popularized figures as the itinerant tinsmith who created cutters to order for a meal. Many figural cookies dating back to the sixteenth century in Europe were created in carved wooden molds, not with cutters. Ad hoc cutters of some kind, such as canister lids or tumbler rims, were called for in eighteenth-century American cookbooks, but we don't know now at what point cutters made specifically for shaping dough, especially fancy and decorative shapes, gained widespread use. A useful start could be made using the extensive <u>Bibliography of Published and Manuscript & Unpublished Sources</u> in William Woys Weaver's *Sauerkraut Yankee: Pennsylvania German Foods & Foodways* (Philadelphia: U. of PA Press, 1983). (However, before your mouth starts to water, note that there is only one cookie recipe, and that related to Anglo-American culinary heritage, and it's for Hard Gingerbread. Apparently the down-to-earth and refreshingly unacademic food historian Weaver either found few cookie recipes or decided they were outside his purview.)

Tin cutters are still being made by various manufacturers and by craftspeople. The manufactured ones come in a fairly small range of shapes, are able to cut 1" dough, do not have flatbacks but sometimes have handles, are very shiny and rust easily with bright orange rust.

Prices for tin cutters. For most old tin cutters from the late nineteenth or early twentieth century, expect to pay between about $20 to $150. I know that's a wide range, but many flower and animals cutters can be had for around $35 or less. **The Robacker Effect:** Notable for all kinds of "dutch country" antiques but headlined by the unexpectedly high prices paid for cookie cutters, the first two of four Robacker Collection auctions (T. Glenn Horst, auctioneer, at Farmersville, PA, May 26-27, 1989, and then in June, 1989), have had a mixed effect on the cookie cutter market. Prices achieved at these auctions are hard to translate meaningfully because of the extraordinary cutters sold, but also because of one or two extraordinary collectors who went to the heights in order to buy the cutters they wanted. It is probable that if the same cutters were re-auctioned today that prices wouldn't get so high. But this doesn't mean that they have "lost value." In a funny way, the thousands spent on the very best Robacker cutters wasn't real money! Money just had to be the medium that would draw attention to the art value of the cutters in order to elevate those cutters to their rightful place in the pantheon of kitchen collectibles. One important result of the auction and the publicity about it is that serious attention is now given to really good old tin cutters — especially attention from top folk art collectors. As to current value, nearly a decade later there are a few marketplaces where the very top dollar might be attained: for instance, the high-quality folk art show held every fall in NYC. And even then, it probably would be only some of the dealers who could ask and get prices in the thousands. Then, too, the value of a Robacker provenance is not fully calculable. A cutter known for sure to have existed at a certain time in the Robacker Collection is known for sure not to be a reproduction or fake postdating that time. With more and more fakes and forgeries and repros entering the market-stream every year, this is valuable information.

The cutters sold at that auction are identified in the listings as "Ex-Robacker." The actual price achieved at the auction is given, then the estimated value range now. This range assumes two things: first, that there's been some long-term bounce from the Robacker auctions, and second, that the cutters are being sold in the highly competitive folk art market, not the "kitchen collectibles" market. Measurements given in the listings are taken from Clarence Spohn's catalog descriptions; other descriptions are entirely from my personal observation or from photographs appearing in one or the other of the Robackers' books, or articles from publications of the <u>Pennsylvania Folklife Society</u>. Some cookie cutters, ex-Robacker, that were small, rather insignificant in appearance or even unattractive, "late" (i.e.1920s or 1930s on), or not uncommon (such as simple fish, Christmas trees, flowers, ducks, chickens, dogs, birds, bears, donkeys, lions, rabbits, stars, clubs (as in bridge), hatchets, pigs, deer, etc.) — were sold in lots of 2 to 6 cutters. The lots averaged $25 or less each, just slightly over the money for similar cutters found at the average flea or show. **Another low-price factor** may have been buyer burnout. A chart of highs and lows of the cookie cutter lots, mixed in with sales of other things (including hot soup and doughnuts), might show some kind of alternating cycle of alertness and eagerness to buy followed by inattention and disinclination to shell out. The figural cutters were probably PA German but in some cases there's no known provenance; probably of various sizes, averaging about 3" to 4" H x 2" to 3-1/2" W. Most if not all are likely early twentieth century. One lot of 11 cutters (only 4 had backs) went for $150, and included a hippo, Santa, angel, shooting star, etc., and obviously this lot included some unusual forms.

Stamped aluminum cutters date back as far as about 1900, but most are from 1930 on. By far the most common one seen is the little gingerbread man with a belt and buttons. These are fun to look for because there are variations. I just found one in a cowboy outfit with holsters.

Usually the cutting edge of aluminum cutters is very shallow and not sharp, the detail is poor, and the pinch-it strap handles are punched-out slits or riveted-on strips. Some have a wooden knob riveted on. Many shapes are to be found, especially holiday shapes, and there are the so-called bridge sets with heart, diamond, spade and club. They were also used for cutting canapes for the bridge parties, and so were deep, one-inch cutters. The price ranges from about $1 to about $8.

Plastic cutters made in molds date back at least 50+ years, and plastic is the most common material used today, even by companies such as Hallmark, who periodically offer "collector editions" of cutters. From the 1940s come transparent red and green cutters that make deep cuts. Opaque designer colors such as aqua or royal blue date from the 1960s on and tend to be shallow cutters. Forms are truly infinite and celebrate religious holidays, cartoon characters, and national events from the Centennial for the Statue of Liberty to the Fourth of July to presidential elections. Wilton Enterprises has sold scores of designs of metal and plastic cookie cutters and still does. Some of the fun shapes include a "Looney Tunes" set, a computer-game-inspired "Mario Brothers," and even "Teenage Mutant Ninja Turtles," and "Barbie" cutters — all created with special licenses from originators of the characters. Ekco, a longtime kitchen manufacturer, offers many cutters. Midwestern Home Products offers cutters in varied shapes. Hallmark offers collectible plastic cutters often: some of their cutters from the late 1970s and early '80s are valued between $12 and $30. This is one collecting field where things that are made "for collectors" actually have a strong secondary market. Some plastic cutters are imported from China, Japan, Taiwan and Europe. For older plastic cutters, expect to pay 25¢ to as much as $25 or $30; new ones often come in sets, costing under $10.

Collecting Attitude, or, why collect what some people call "ugly" new cutters? First of all, I'm the first to say there are no absolutes about "beauty," and so there are many people who don't judge new cutters so harshly. And there is more than one way to collect anything. Some of the earliest documented collectors, many hundreds of years ago, assembled oddities and curiosities of Nature and put them in curiosity cabinets. Other collectors bought (or appropriated) objets of aesthetic "merit" or intrinsic worth, including jewelry, gold decorative pieces, marble sculptures, etc. Still other collectors added only objects with religious significance (artworks and relics) to their private collections. The curiosity collectors evolved into curators of science museums; the others became connoisseurs, who based all their judgments on immutable "facts" of proportion, style, grace, finish and other establishmentarian rules (which changed somewhat with fashion, though more slowly). In the history of the United States there have been eminent curiosity collectors like the Peale family and John James Audubon, who were scientists and artists. Also there have been many connoisseurs and pseudo-connoisseurs, of which the latter are most common and most enduring. The benefactors of many of our museums were either connoisseurs or they had lots of money and good advisors. It has not been popular outside of anthropology or sociology to collect curiosities of art until the twentieth centure, and even now it is often looked down upon by people who believe in a good-better-best (and not-so-good, worse, even awfuller) system of connoisseurship. (A rueful play on a dealer's appraisal of his wares as "good, better, and best" of each form, is that it is more likely "good, better, and 'in stock'.")

For the same reasons that a money standard is necessary, rules and calibrated values for objects need to be widely accepted, or your piece of artwork might be worthless in the very marketplace you needed it to be pricey. I mistrust any pontifican on art — fine, decorative or useful — who claims absolutes, and who says and believes "This is great; that is terrible." Absolute aesthetics are not objective, because there is no such thing as pure objectivity; this critical dilemma lies behind the ongoing argument over folk art (i.e. "Yes, but is it Art?"). Material culture collectors are often as interested in the use and context of something, the *reality* of it, as in the aesthetics. This is not to say that material culturists don't judge objects within a group or class, but they factor in a good deal of value based on purpose or function, or even current educational potential. It is unacceptable to me that even when an old-time connoisseur concedes that a thing is interesting, to him that quality is valueless.

What's in a Word? "Cookie" anyone? or "Cake"? Once there was a clear difference, related to size, kind of dough, and effect of baking. Diminutive suffixes -ey or -y or -ie indicate a cooky or cookie is a small cake (Dutch *koekje*). **English Usage:** The English (but not always the Scots) call crackers *biscuits* — small, dry, flat bread or cakes. Cookies are *cakes* (according to *Oxford English Dictionary,* "a comparatively small flattened sort of bread" [no mention of sugar]), and a cookie as "a small flat sweet cake" is a term "applicable" only in the U.S. (says the *OED*). Just for fun, and not part of the discussion here, a very funny term for a tea party is quoted in the *OED*, from the nineteenth-century English novelist Charles Reade: "<u>cooky-shine</u>."**American Usage:** In Noah Webster's *American Dictionary,* 1858, a biscuit is a "kind of bread, formed into cakes, and baked hard for seamen" or "a cake, variously made, for the use of private families." According to the same American wordman, a cake is "a small mass of dough baked; or a composition of flour, butter, sugar, or other ingredients, baked in a small mass," or "something in the form of a cake, rather flat than high, but roundish." Finally, Webster says that a "Cooky" is "a small cake moderately sweet" and adds that it's a "familiar word in New England." Pennsylvania was not part of New England so Pennsylvanians probably called them "cakes." **Nineteenth-century American cookbook authors** called cookies "cakes," and the cutters were "Cake cutters." Some cakes were thick, some thin, so that is no clue. In the 1920 catalog of The Central Stamping Co., NYC, there are a number of shallow-edge cutters with flat backs and handles called "Cake Cutters." These were offered in animal shapes or assorted "fancy" shapes with corrugated edges, and small inset marking designs. Marks would not stay on cookies (or cakes) that were thick or would rise and puff out in the oven. Another shown is suitable for a cookie that rises, has a deep-cutting corrugated or fluted-edge round cutter and a bracket strap handle, single air hole, available in four sizes from 2-1/2" to 4" diameter. It's termed a

"Cookey Cutter," while the one called a "Biscuit Cutter""is slightly shallower and doesn't have the flutes. The 1914 catalog of Shapleigh Hardware Co., St. Louis, shows several very shallow flatbacks called "Cake Cutters," with small air holes and no apparent strap handles, though the catalog copy says "Flat tin Handle," possibly referring to the overhanging flat backs(?). Their cake cutters have corrugated edges, with and without insets. Fancy inset ones could be ordered "extra fancy" (and weighed 25% more & cost accordingly). Shapleigh also offered animals, birds, fish, and a tantalizing unidentified "etc.," in their assorted sets of "Cake Cutters." Their cake cutters were shallow cutters with large roughly trimmed flat backs; no handles mentioned. Shapleigh showed simple round deep cutters with strap handles & termed them "Biscuit or Cake Cutters." Shapleigh's only cutter called a "Cookey Cutter," was also for biscuits; it is a simple wire and tin rotary or rolling cutter, for thick dough.

• • • •

Kinds of cookies. There are hundreds of kinds of cookies made with cutters and molds; some of the most important here are typical Pennsylvania German cookies — especially as they relate to particular motifs, or ones with a long European tradition. Old Penn Cookies: Ruth Hutchison, in *The New Pennsylvania Dutch Cook Book* (1958), gives 19 pages to late nineteenth- and early twentieth-century Pennsylvania German cookies. The selection includes raised and flat cookie recipes from old cookbooks and Pennsylvania housewives' collections, including some that are not necessarily traditional, though widely adopted. A selection follows. **"Moravian Brown Cookie,"** chilled overnight, rolled very thin & cut with "Christmas cookie cutters — men, deer, men on horseback, etc."; **"Mandelplaettchen"** or Almond Wafers, also rolled very thin & cut in shapes; **"Almond Cookies"** cut in "diamond shapes with jagging iron"; **"Lebkuchen,"** a spice cookie of a thick dough type, chilled, rolled and cut in "hearts or diamonds"; **"Spiced Ginger Cookies,"** stiff dough, rolled thin and cut in shapes; **"Molasses Cookies,"** stiff dough, chilled, "rolled very thin, & cut in animal shapes"; **"Butterthins,"** chilled, rolled thin and "cut in shapes;" and **"Sand Tarts"** [elsewhere called "Sand" or "Saint Hearts"] of two kinds, both rolled very thin and cut prior to baking, the second "cut in shapes — usually rounds, also hearts, stars & half moons." The rest are either drop cookies, or spooned & squashed (with tumbler bottom, wire potato masher or fork). No gingerbread boys, no zoomorphic or figural shapes.

In addition to those in Hutchison: **Speculaas,** also called **Speculatius,** are very spicy, relatively low-fat stiff cookies, traditionally made in the shape of a windmill. They are also imprinted with cookie molds made up of individual images about 2" x 1-1/2" — yes, the same as springerles. **Stiff & Spicy:** The thinnest, stiffest, most highly spiced cookies were best suited to hang for Christmas tree decorations, especially after icing; this was traditional in Germany, Sweden and Switzerland. Such cookies were hard and tended to be preserved by the ginger in them. See also cake boards; and springerle molds.

• • • •

Collector Newsletter: "COOKIES, A Newsletter Devoted to Cookies & Cookie Shaping," has been going strong since 1972. Founding editor, the late Phyllis Wetherill, did it through 1994, and since then the bi-monthly has been put out by Rosemary Henry. A subscription is under $12. • Please use an SASE when writing Mrs. Rosemary Henry, 9610 Greenview Lane, Manassas, VA 20109, about starting a subscription.
• A book on cookie cutters started by Mrs. Wetherill and building on her three previous books, with assistance from Mrs. Henry, is

now being completed by Mrs. Henry. It is *A Cookie Shapers' Bible.* An encyclopedic work on American and foreign cutters and molds, with an emphasis on 20th century pieces. There are alphabetical entries, by manufacturer or maker -- from a couple of lines to several pages -- with many many photographs and line drawings. At our press time, it's not out yet -- write Mrs. Henry at the above address for ordering information.

Club & newsletter: "Cookie Crumbs," which is the quarterly put out by the Cookie Cutter Collectors Club (membership is $12 a year). Phyllis Wetherill founded that club too -- with an appeal to readers in *Women's Circle* magazine in 1972. • Send an SASE for information on the club and "Cookie Crumbs" to Ruth Capper, 1167 Teal Rd., S.W., Dellroy, OH 44620.

Cookie cutter, angel, shown from side, with large wing, muttonchop sleeve, long dress, tiny feet, mounted on oblong tin back, but overlaps considerably, marked only "Germany," 9-1/2" H x about 5" W, c.1891-1915. **$125-$170**

Cookie cutters, animals — See also individual animals

Cookie cutters, animals in set, 7 small ones in simple outline, including pig, dog, cat, deer, horse, cat-like animal with large bushy tail (another cat?), & a pointy-eared short-tailed leaping animal that isn't a deer, all tin, in box, imported or American, c. 1870s or 1880s. **$45-$65**

Cookie cutters, animal set of 12: bird, cat, chicken, dog, duck, goat, goose, horse, pig, pigeon, sheep & swan, simple tin outlines, original printed cardboard box, "Barnyard Cooky Cutters," American, 1930s. **$30-$40**

Cookie cutters, animals from farm set, tin, 12 in original box with color picture of farm scene, American, 20th C. Added value for M.I.B. (mint in box). Sets in original boxes are desired by many collectors, although, of course, boxed sets are not comparable in value to older, handmade, non-commercial cutters. **$45-$55**

Cookie cutter, automobile of 1930s type, tin, flat back, strap handle, American, 4" L, 20th C. Automobiles were a fairly popular motif for early 20th C. cookie cutters and ice cream molds. I have also seen carved wooden cookie boards with the open top roaster type of car and a spiffy driver. **$25-$45**

IV-129. Cookie cutter. *Tin, strap handle, flat back with large hole. Hand motif very popular. 2-3/4" H, American, late 19th C. Picture courtesy of the National Museum of American History, Smithsonian Institution, Washington DC.* **$200-$350**

Catalog Cutters: A Lalance & Grosjean Mfg. Co., NYC, 1890 catalog has no biscuit or doughnut cutters. Under "Cake Cutters" is a 12-piece set of "retinned Animals," including a sitting cat, song-bird, horse, lion, sheep (?), leaping rabbit, rooster, donkey or dog (?), eagle, pig, rocking horse, and standing man with cap and insets under arms. The set could be had in three sizes: small, medium and large. Wholesale prices were $11.25 to $20 a gross, which might mean a gross of sets (1728 cutters), or of cutters (144 cutters). The price for the small cutters, then, was either about 8¢ a set or 8¢ a cutter. For the large about 14¢ per set or cutter. Since this was a wholesale catalog, and it was 1890, the price was probably from 8¢ to 14¢ per set, to retail at about twice that. • A 12-piece animal set of Cake Cutters found in a 1920 Central Stamping Co.'s catalog has a rooster, mule, parrot, cat, horse, lion, sitting dog, standing dog (?), bull (or other udderless ruminant), dromedary, a song bird and a long-necked, up-winged bird (eagle?). This set had two catalog numbers, possibly denoting size or gauge of tin. • A 1925 catalog from manufacturers Geuder, Paeschke & Frey Co., noted enamelware producers of Milwaukee, has a page of "cooky," biscuit, doughnut and cake cutters. The only cutter called a "Cooky Cutter" is tin, round with scalloped rim, "solid" back with air hole in center, arched strap handle. It came in two sizes: 3-1/2" and 4" diameter. The "Cake Cutters" came in a set of "Cream City Card Party" solid back cutters, rough cut to fit shape, hearts, diamonds, clubs, spades, air hole and no handle. These sets came in one size, respectively by shape: 2-3/4" x 3-3/4"; 2-1/2" x 2-3/4"; 2-3/4" x 3"; and 2-3/4" x 3". Also offered was a flatback star with 6 points, 3" diameter; and a heart, flatback, 3" diameter. The best set? Animal

Cake Cutters with 12 different designs: a squirrel, swan, lion, eagle, duck (?), rooster, fish, cat (?), parrot, song bird, another bird, and pig. All shallow cutters, they are flatbacks mounted to flat, very rounded oval tin backs, and are approximately 3" L. Such a set, which originally came in a paper bag, would be a nice find, worth possibly $120 or so, despite a relatively recent vintage.

Cookie cutter, bird, a small <u>distelfink</u> (gold finch or "thistle" finch: favorite food for all types of finches is thistle seeds), tin, flat back, prob. PA German, 3" L, late 19th C. **$15-$20**

Cookie cutter, bird, backward-looking, of type found in Pennsylvania German fraktur & other decorated paper documents as well on decorated stoneware, dark tin, flat back, PA (?), 4-1/2" L x 5/8" deep, 19th C. **$70-$85**

Cookie cutter, bird — See cookie cutter, chick; cookie cutter, parrot; cookie cutter, rooster

Cookie cutter, bootjack, tin, flat back, American, 3-1/4" L, turn of century. **$35-$45**

Cookie cutters, bridge cutters or what traditionally were called hearts, rounds & diamonds, ie. heart, diamond, spade & the trifoil club, tin, set of 4 in original box, rather deep cutters, with strap handles, these were also sold as sandwich cutters, for those little crustless dainties served at bridge parties, American, approx. 3" diameter, 1920s-1930s. **$22-$35**

IV-130. Cookie cutter. *Old dark tin, corrugated at wrist, folded-edge strap handle, small holes neatly placed in each finger and the heart. Heart-in-hand, 4-3/4" H x 3-1/2" W, mid 19th C. Picture courtesy of Museum of History and Technology, Smithsonian Institution.* **NOTE**: *Copies of this cutter have been made in quantity by tinsmiths Bill and Bob Cukla, Hammer Song Country Tinware, 221 S. Potomoc, Boonsboro, MD, 21713. Each copy is conscientiously and responsibly marked on the back of the thumb with "B. Cukla." Too bad more skilled artisans don't sign their work; when they don't, they are in partnership with the person who passes the item as antique. The size varies widely in the old ones, and size, age, patina and design as well as the sale venue influence price.* Old ones: **$750-$2000**

IV-131. Cookie cutters & mold. *Varieties of heart shapes in tin. Clockwise from top (L).* **(1)** *"Card Party" cutter, for cookies or sandwiches, in sets of four including club, spade & diamond. Ritzinger, Grasgreen catalog, c.1906-07.* **(2)** *Actually a heart mold, not a cutter, although it could be used to cut. 3" L x 2-1/2" W, fairly deep, with flat bottom, no handle of course, and no holes. D. J. Barry jobber catalog of housefurnishings, NYC, 1924. The following three are commercial bakery types, with thick palm-fitting handles:* **(3)** *is 3" across, with interior trefoil design. Central Stamping Co., 1920.* **(4)** *Three sizes, 2-1/2", 3-1/2" and 5-1/2" across. Jaburg, 1908.* **(5)** *Another scalloped one, 2-3/4" x 3" or 3" x 3-1/2", Jaburg.* **(6)** *Nested set of 7 cutters. Bertuch, c.1904.* **$10-$50**

German playing cards: Suits on German cards are an acorn, a tulip-shaped leaf, a heart, and a decorated ball. The suits correspond: acorn = club; leaf = spade; ball = diamond. I don't know if the idea of bridge party cookie cutters pertains in Germany.

Cookie cutter, bugler on horseback, in military charge position, tin, flat back, one of a very popular subject group, the genesis of which probably goes back to 17th C carved cookie boards found in several European countries, PA German, 7" H x 6-1/4" L, prob. 4th quarter 19th C. Ex-Robacker, $550. **$400-$600**

Cookie cutters, buildings, a set of 4 deep tin backless & strapless "cookie cutters" called "Cookie Village," consisting of 4 building-shaped cutters, including a hip roof & a salt box house, a church & a meeting house (the latter 2 with steeples). Directions tell how to make 24 different buildings by combining shapes (which you would fasten together with icing). You could make a 3-D building because you were using "firm plain

IV-132. Tin hearts. (L) *Pieced tin, rolled & flattened edge, carefully made, appears to be handmade. Perhaps is a small heart mold, as in IV-131, or a cutter. Only 7/8" deep x about 2-3/4" across. Late 19th C.* **(R)** *Commercial bakery cutter with scalloped edge. One advantage of big handle is extra air intake to drop those cookies out faster. Stamped 3-1/2" in two places on handle. Measures 7/8" deep x 3" x 3-1/2", and the heart is 3-1/4" x 3-1/4". Late 19th or early 20th C.* **$15-$25**

IV-133. *Side view of cutter in* **IV-132.**

cake, baked in one inch layers." Trees and bushes could be made for your cake village by using only the steeples. It was suggested that you could freeze the village, by wrapping each building in plastic, for future use. No mark on cutters, box with directions is clearly marked: "Fox Run Craftsmen," Lambertville, NJ, cutters 2-3/4" to 4" H, c.1960s. **$10-$20**

Cookie cutters, cartoon characters Dagwood, Blondie, the children, the dog Daisy, and her puppies, in original box, yellow plastic, Educational Products Co., Hope, NJ, c.1948. **$75-$100**

Cookie cutter, cartoon character figural of Blondie, yellow plastic, part of original set with Dagwood, etc., Educational Products Co., Hope, NJ, late 1940s. **$15-$20**

Cookie cutter, cat, sitting, tin, no handle, stamped "Davis Baking Powder," 7/8" deep cut x 4" L, early 20th C. **$18-$22**

Cookie cutter, cat, slightly pregnant, suspicious but eminently feline, short legs, shortish tail, head turned to gaze from almond eyes. The detail inset in the face created with small curls or loops of tin soldered inside outline of head, 2 very large finger push-out holes in flat back, PA German, 3-3/4" H x 7-3/4" L, 3rd to 4th quarter 19th C. Ex-Robacker, $650. Great subject. **$450-$750**

New Meows: An amusing pieced tin, flat back cookie cutter, which should be called "The Owl & the Pussycat Combined," a sort of 2-legged cat with large head & round inset eyes, inset beaky nose, and a bird-like tail, appears in *The International Cook's Catalogue*, (Random House, 1977). The cutter, which is 4-1/2" L x 3-1/4" H x 1/2" deep, is (at least in 1970s) imported from South America, where it was used to make a *galletita* honey & cornmeal cookie, in the form of a *gatito*, or little cat.

Cookie cutter, chick, simple & little, tin, flat back with several small release or air holes, American, 3" L, late 19th or early 20th C. **$15-$20**

Cookie cutter, Christmas tree, tin, no back, strap handle, with tiny narrow brace across cutter where trunk branches out, has a handmade look, but I've seen 2 exactly alike, German(?). Phyllis Wetherill writes that the brace is typically German, 1-1/8" deep x 5" L, late 19th or early 20th C. **$25-$45**

IV-134. Cookie cutter rolling pin patent. *Pat'd 10/31/1865, by Isaac N. Pyle, Decatur, IN. "I have invented a new and improved combined cake-cutter and rolling-pin." The pin was an ordinary rolling pin, with all-on-piece handles, or rigid handles. The cake cutters are made on a cylinder that will "envelop or partially envelop" the rolling pin, which you provide. "It will be understood that the roller is to be used as an ordinary roller for rolling out dough into sheets; that it can then be rubbed off and enveloped in the case. This can then be rolled over the sheet of dough, and the cakes will be cut out quickly and accurately. The cakes so soon as cut drop out of the cutters more readily than when ordinary flat-surfaced cake cutters are used." Official Gazette of the U.S. Patent Office. In the picture, the odd oblong shape represents the rolled out dough. Pyle said that of course it was understood that "several different cases, bearing different designs" could be used in succession, providing many varied cookies. If this was ever made, which is not known, it would have a high value:* **$250-$300**

The Christmas tree, because it is an evergreen, has been a Christian symbol, a sacred tree, at least as far back as the early 17th C. Many people believe its pagan origins go much further back, and that the evergreen was adopted, for obvious reasons, by Christians. The other sacred tree to Christians is the palm.

• • • •

Traditional New Years motifs: During at least the last half of the 19th C., from various items I've seen, German decorators or artisans consistently used 5 motifs: a gold horseshoe, a pig, a 4-leaf clover, a money bag, and a lady bird or lady bug. In addition, bells are frequently seen, but this is almost universally a symbol of change, including the coming of the New Year. I think we might find cookie cutters in these shapes.

CoCookie cutter, corncob, tin, flat back, 6" L, 19th C.   **$55-$65**
okie cutter, cow, tin, flat back, shallow cut, American, turn of century or early 20th C.   **$35-$45**

IV-135. Cake cutter patent. *Pat'd 11/17/1857, by G. R. Peckham, Worcester, MA. Has a separate section in center so that doughnuts, or the kind of jumble cookie that was ring-shaped, could be made. Official Gazette.*

IV-136. Cookie cutters. *All stamped aluminum, with riveted handles. "Mirro," mfd. by Aluminum Goods Mfg. Co., Manitowoc, WI, 1927 catalog.* **$3-$8**

Woodstove Christmas Cookies In the 19th Century. "At least a week before Christmas all the tin cooky cutters were brought from the cellar and scoured with wood ash until they shone. There were forms of every shape and description — birds, stars, hearts, horses and other animals. No one wanted to miss a chance at cutting out these lovely cookies. Usually mother would permit the children to use her thimble to cut a hole in the center of the cookies. The dough remaining in the thimble was baked into 'thimble' cookies, as the children called them. Often a dozen or more kinds of cookies were baked. The recipe book was in constant use. There were biscuits, sand tarts, ginger, and spice cookies . . . Store baskets, wash baskets, and lard cans were brought out and filled with newly-baked goodies. Many were needed, depending on how large one's family was or where he lived. If you lived in the city there was much company and many visitors to be treated. The poor had to be remembered and some cookies must be given to the friend who had lent mother a special cooky cutter." Katharine D. Christ, "Christmas in Pennsylvania," *Historical Review of Berks County,* Winter 1960-61.

Cookie cutter, crescent moon & heart, tin, fat cylindrical handle with palm-fitting convex cap, for bakery use, 5" diameter, c.1920s to 1930s.   **$40-$50**
Cookie cutter, daisy with 10 petals (the large number is fairly unusual), tin, American, late 19th C.   **$15-$18**

IV-137. Sandwich cutters, *or large cookie cutters. Pieced tin.* **(T)** *Simple strap-handled backless set of card suits, from S. Joseph catalog, c.1927.* **(B)** *Flatbacks with air holes. Ritzinger, Grasgreen catalog, c.1906-07. Value range for singles:* **$5-$15**

IV-138. "Bridge set" or "card party" cookie cutters, *all pieced tin.* **(L)** *All approximately 2-3/4" x 3", but the heart is the biggest at 2-3/4" x 3-3/4". Flat backs, trimmed roughly to follow outline.* **(R)** *Card party set plus a star and a crescent moon. About 2-1/2" x 2". Savory, c.1927-28. Singles:* **$5-$15**

Cookie cutter, daisy-like flower, many petaled, tin, flat back, strap handle, American, 3" diameter, late 19th C. **$25-$30**

Cookie cutter, deer, leaping, tail up, tin, flat back with 3 air release holes, PA German, 9-1/8" H x 12-1/2" L, 3rd to 4th quarter 19th C. "Leaping deer" sometimes translated as springerle. Ex-Robacker, $775. **$350-$600**

Cookie cutter, dog, standing large breed: Newfoundland? St. Bernard? Heavy gauge tin, with folded top edge, strap handle, deep cutter, American, 6" L, mid 19th C. **$50-$65**

Cookie cutter, dog, Scottie, shallow stamped aluminum with green wooden knob handle, American, 1930s-1940s. **$8-$10**

Dog Dates. The dog cutter above is the kind of cutter you could probably research to narrow down the date, if it is indeed a Scottie. When were Scotties really popular? The 1920s and increasingly so in the 1930s, and they were used as a motif in everything from weathervanes to boot scrapers to pocketbooks and slippers. The most famous Scottie was Fala, President Franklin D. Roosevelt's favorite pet, who often traveled with the President. Roosevelt was first elected in 1932. Scotties were overtaken by Fox Terriers, then Cockers and German Shepherds began to move up the charts. Surprisingly, the most popular dog in America in the 1880s and 1890s was the huge St. Bernard, which accounts for how many of them you see on old trade card illustrations, etc. Other very popular dogs featured in decorative arts (particularly ceramic figurines), in the eighteenth and nineteenth centuries were (1) the little "Comforter" or lap Spaniel, with big eyes, floppy big ears, and silky hair; (2) the Pug, another small, baby-faced dog meant for lap or silk cushion; (3) an intelligent working dog, the standard Poodle, whose poodle cut was known by the nineteenth century at least (from France), and whose tight curls, long ears, and cocky tail made great models for works of art or craft; (4) the watersport Retriever, a large dog also depicted with ringlets or curls; and (5) the Water Spaniel, another similar looking breed. **Dog Days a long time ago?** Although some advanced collectors of cookie cutters believe strongly that dog motif cutters didn't naturally fit into the early PA German repertoire of motifs, I believe that if they used dogs in watercolors, on quilts, for wood carvings (think of Mountz) and chalkware figures, why not cookie cutters? Cats may be another story; they are much less common in all decorative art until this century, though sometimes featured in portraits of people, or paintings of kitchen or barn interiors.

Cookie cutter, dog very like a Scottie, running pose, tin, flat back with strap handle, nice age, but probably all machine manufactured, American, 3" H x 4-1/2" L, 2nd quarter 20th C (?). **$20-$28**

Cookie cutter, dromedary (one hump, not two like a camel), tin, flat back, fairly thin sheet tin, shallow cut, 3-1/2" L, American. prob. early 20th C. **$20-$28**

Cookie cutter, dromedary, tin with arched strap handle from hump to belly, 2 legs, no flat back, offered as mail order premium by "Dromedary Cocoanut" which was mfd. by The Hills Brothers Co., NYC. Sold for 10¢, or 5¢ through 1915 ad. **$20-$30**

Cookie cutter, duck, tin, adv'g "Davis Baking Powder," American, 20th C. **$8-$12**

Cookie cutter, Dutch boy, odd small circles (that made holes) under his arms, tin, strap handle, turned edge, American (?), 5-1/8" L, 19th C. **$65-$85**

Jumbo the Elephant may have been the inspiration for this large cutter, which sold in New York City at a Pier Show for $250 or so in the mid 1980s. In 1883, circus entrepeneur Phineas T. Barnum bought a large African elephant from the London Zoological Gardens for exhibition in the United States. People were wild for Jumbo, and he not only came to be used as a wonderful advertising image (you'll see many 1880s chromolith trade cards with large elephants, some named Jumbo), but his very name became synonymous with very big. The next time you buy a jumbo-sized box of detergent, you've got P.T. Barnum to thank! But Barnum wasn't the first to bring an elephant to America. Probably the first, a three-year-old female, arrived in 1796, and was exhibited on the Eastern seaboard for an unknown length of time. Probably the second to come was a four-year-old male, exhibited in the same area, including Philadelphia and Newburyport, from 1797 for an unknown length of time. This elephant, whose name was not given, was advertised as eating 130 pounds of food a day, and drinking "all kinds of spirituous liquors; some days . . . 30 bottles of porter, drawing the cork with his trunk." Where were the teetotalers when we needed them? The third elephant, probably the first famous one, was "Old Bet," who was brought to America in 1815 by a sea captain & sold to Hachaliah Bailey who exhibted her around Putnam County, NY.

IV-139. Cookie cutters. *Flatbacks all cut round, with rolled edges. For making tea cookies. The scalloped one top right is a* **"Bolivar"** *cutter. I have not been able to track down just what a Bolivar cookie/cake is — Simon Bolivar, the South American leader who died in 1830, seems an unlikely eponym. Singles:* **$10-$20**

IV-140. Cookie cutters. *All with scalloped edges, and one — bottom right — called a "Bolivar" cutter by the distributer. Clockwise from top* **(L)**. *(1) Pieced tin, flatback with strap, 3-1/2" or 4" diameter. Buhl Sons hardware, c.1919. (2) Seamless stamped tin, bracket handle, 2-1/2", 3", 3-1/2" or 4" diameter. Central Stamping Co., 1920. (3) Baker's style of "Bolivar" cutter, Jaburg catalog, 1908. (4) Stamped aluminum with riveted handle, 3-1/4" diameter, Aluminum Goods "Mirro."* **$5-$15**

Cookie cutter, Dutchman in wooden shoes & wide pantaloons, tin, strap handle, 4-3/4" H, 20th C. **$25-$30**

Cookie cutter, eagle with spread wings, tin, flat back, 6-1/4" W x 1/2" deep, late 19th C. **$40-$55**

Cookie cutter, elephant, possibly related to P. T. Barnum's "Jumbo," tin, flat back with strap handle, PA German, desirable size: 6-3/8" H x 9-7/8" L, prob. 4th quarter 19th C. Ex-Robacker, $385. **$350-$500**

Cookie cutter, elephant, tin, strap handle, American, 9-1/8" W, 19th C, prob. 1880s. **$350-$500**

The **Belsnickel** is another Christmas character depicted in cookie cutters. By custom, the costumed Belsnickel came on Christmas Eve to decide which children had been good or bad (shades of Santa). "If one lived in the country, he expected to see . . . a weird-looking hobgoblin with a long beard & a blackened or false face, dressed in old clothing . . . often . . . torn and ragged. In one hand the Belsnickel carried a whip or a bundle of switches, & in the other a bag of nuts, snitz [dried apples], & occasionally candy.

"The Belsnickel always asked whether there were any children living there who had been naughty. Those who had recently raided the cooky basket or forgotten some chore had real cause to be frightened . . . Before he left, he would open his bag & strew his nuts, snitz, and candy all over the floor . . . Invariably, as a boy tried to get the candy, the whip would come down on his shoulders . . . Sometimes . . . he left a switch for the parents to use . . .

"The origin of the Belsnickel comes from *Pelz*, meaning fur, because St. Nicholas was always represented as a person dressed in a huge fur cap and a fur-trimmed suit. He, too, carried, thrown over his shoulders, a bag in which he had presents for good children. His servant, Knecht Rupert, had a blackened face and always carried a bundle of switches which he left for naughty children.

"The city Belsnickel was a somewhat different character. Often more than one Belsnickel visited a home. Sometimes there were as many as five or six in a group, led by a leader. Their visit was much the same as to their country cousins, except that these visitors, instead, looked for cookies as a treat. The city Belsnickels were dressed in all sorts of costumes & disguises. Among the group one was likely to find clowns, Indians, harlequins & anything imaginable. Often they carried a musical instrument such as a hand organ, accordian, guitar, trombone, banjo or musical bones." Katharine D. Christ, "Christmas in Pennsylvania," *Historical Review of Berks County*, Winter 1960-61.

The English counterpart of these musical characters were **Christmas Mummers** who still parade in Philadelphia. Many cookie cutters are found in the shape of Indians, humorous characters, & musical instruments; probably these cutters refer directly to the Belsnickel tradition. See also cookie cutter, Santa.

Cookie cutters, fairy tale set of five plastic cutters & embossers in original box, Hansel, Gretel, witch, pine tree, gingerbread house, American, 1947. **$55-$85**

Cookie cutter, Father Christmas (one precursor of what we call Santa Claus) with toy bag on back, beard & cap, long skirted robe, small feet, mounted to but overlaps the oblong flat back, tin, marked only "Germany," 9-1/2" H x about 5" W, c.1891-1915. **$155-$250**

Cookie cutters, figural set, airplane, star, heart, chicken & cloverleaf, 5 miniature cutters in original cardboard & tin box, Dixon Specialities, Inc. (or Specialties?), NYC, NY, box only 1-3/8" deep x 2-1/2" diameter, c.1940s. Ex-Robacker, $15. **$30-$40**

Cookie cutters, figurals, tin, new reproductions or facsimiles (?) of "Early American designs," assortment of 13 cutters: a boy, girl, rabbit, tree, star, dog, bell, turkey, owl, Santa, angel, heart

& deer. Advertised as made by "Pennsylvania craftsmen," small, 1980s. Might as well say it again: being new doesn't necessarily mean the value won't increase. New original designs appreciate in value. Reproductions don't. **$5-$10**

IV-141. "Rock Cake" stamp. *"The Handy," nickeled cast iron, wooden handle. "This little stamp is a great time and labor saver, it makes the cakes all alike, uniform and prevents burnt edges; it does away with the fork, and is invaluable to any bake shop." Hueg, c.1927.* **$25-$35**

IV-142. Shrewsbury Cake mold & cutter. *(L) Inverted scalloped edge, with almond-shaped flower design inside. Wood knob handle. "This Patent tool will cut, crimp and finish a Shrewsbury cake at one operation, and as fast as Sugar cake can be cut out; have them all perfect and uniform far superior to hand work. For very stiff doughs this tool may be used as a mould by simply unscrewing the handle." Hueg and Jaburg both sold it, c.1908 through 1920s at least. (R) Tin, 3-1/2" diameter. Note inverted scallops and fat handle. Jaburg, 1908.* **$25-$35; $15-$25**

IV-143. Nested cookie or cake cutters. *Leaves, flowers, and a few useful abstracts. Tin, in tin box. Sold in sets of 1, 2 or 3 dozen cutters. A. Bertuch, Berlin, 1908. These were very small, and the same or similar ones were sold as canape cutters and vegetable cutters (for decorating broth soups). Many of these round tin boxes of small cutters are still being sold, and were made at least since the 1940s, and probably continuously since the turn of the century or before. SEE the pictures of vegetable cutters near end of chapter.* **$30-$50**

IV-144. Cake cutters. *From top:* **(1)** *Fancy leaf with tulip inside, from Henry Scammell's Treasure-House of Knowledge, 1891.* **(2)** *"An assortment that shows a few of the many designs in cake cutters made of tin, to give fancy forms to cakes. They may be had of all house furnishings stores, and are among the luxuries of the kitchen — very nice where they can be afforded, and they are not very costly. The effect is pretty when different or even a single fancy form is used." Scammell's.* **(3)** *Next is a bakery version of a veined leaf cutter with a fat handle. Came in two sizes: 1-3/4" x 3-3/4" or 2-1/4" x 4-5/8". Joseph Middleby, Boston, 1927.* **(4)** *A round tin box of assorted flower shapes. Sometimes these sets are mistaken for toy cookie cutters. F. A. Walker catalog, c. 1870s.*

IV-145. Nested cookie or cake cutters. *Hearts, 6-point stars, 6-petaled flower, squared "flower." Ten cutters per box, sizes range from 1-1/4" to 4". S. Joseph, c.1927. Nested plain rounds and scalloped rounds, called "paste cutters" were sold at least as early as 1860.* **$20-$40**

IV-146. Cake cutters. *Assorted fancy shapes, crimped or corrugated edges, flat backs. Some with interior flower shapes. Central Stamping Co., 1920 catalog, but using much older linecut that may date to 1860s. Set:* **$40-$60**

Cookie cutters, figurals, tin, old. Animal, human & object forms, tin flat back that fits the simple outline perfectly, shallow cutting edge, a few have strap handles, factory-made, little detail. This kind of cutter is just primitive enough to look homemade, but it isn't. (Though probably they were handmade to some degree.) American, two general groups of sizes, about 3" to 4" L and about 4" to 7" L, late 19th C. or early 20th C. **$10-$50**

When Form Adds Value to factory-made cutters. Variables include collector interest in and charm or appeal of individual forms, detail (though for most cutters there isn't much), size and condition. Large, well-detailed popular forms always win and bring prices 3 to 4 times as much within this rather narrow field of factory-made cutters. For some examples, a boring eagle might be $20 while one of the same size with a little more zest might be $35; an armless long-skirted woman might be $20 while one with arms and a hat might be $45; a fat simple chicken with no cluck might be $10 while a rooster with a big tail or cocky head tilt might be $45. You get the idea.

Cookie cutter, fireman, poised while working, simple but effective profile, flat back, tin trimmed only approximately to fit outline. As with many cookie cutters it is hard to recognize the subject until you study it (and others), PA German (?), 7-1/4" H x 3-3/4" W, 3rd to 4th quarter 19th C. Ex-Robacker, $225: this price is under what we expected, so there were either no "fire fighter" collectors (hence no crossover interest) or the fireman wasn't detailed enough. **$225-$350**

Cookie cutter, fish, fairly ornate, tin, square or bracket strap handle, rectangular flat back with turned edges, American, fish is 5-1/2" L, makes only 1/2" deep cut, back is 6-1/2" L, late 19th C. The term **bracket strap handle** is easy to remember when you think of the squared parentheses-like punctuation marks called brackets [ ], which set off certain prescribed material in a sentence. Sometimes parentheses ( ) are called "round brackets," but we don't need that term in this book. **$50-$60**

Cookie cutter, fish, simple & stylized, with crimping top and bottom to represent fins, punched up half-moons as tab handle on back, tin, flat back size of playing card, American, cuts 1/2" deep, 4" L, late 19th C. **$35-$45**

Cookie cutter, fish, tin, flat back, American (?), vary from 4" L to about 6" L, most seem to be late 19th or early 20th C. **$15-$30**

Few Fish Flaunt Flair. I've never seen a really really nice fish cutter. Most are very shallow cutters and have open mouths, top and bottom fin & tail, but nothing particularly well-shaped. Also, I don't know why, most of the ones I've seen have very poor soldering and are coming apart. I can *imagine* a more intricate one, perhaps with nifty crimped edges to fins & tail. Fish cookies are almost certainly Christian religious symbols, Christ having been a "fisher of men" and also because He divided the loaves and the fishes to feed the multitude.

Cookie cutter, flame, very stylized, of the advertised stove, back stamped with ornate scrolled border & name, strap handle embossed with legend, stamped tin, shallow cutter in shape that looks like ruffle top tulip, "Garland Stoves & Ranges," and "The World's Best," 3-5/8" W, late 19th C. **$25-$45**

Cookie or cake cutters, floral & leaf designs, a tin box with 12 small tin cutters, from F. A. Walker catalog, c.1870s. (There are new ones, not too much different, in a tin box. They are shinier and not quite as nice as the old.) **$35-$50**

Cookie cutter, gingerbread boy, a classic form, though this one a more than insipid cutter, tin, strap handle attached to flat back, American, 5" H, late 19th C. **$15-$25**

GeeBees: English and European gingerbread bakers from the early Middle Ages (13th C.) into the first third of the 19th C. often made gingerbread men as well as other gingerbread forms. In fact, according to Max von Boehn in *Dolls and Puppets,* a revised edition of which was published in Boston in 1956, "The gingerbread doll had a tenacious life ... [and] the shapes which it assumed remained the same for centuries." According to Dan Foley in *Toys Through the Ages* (Philadelphia & NY: Chilton Books, 1962), "So popular was gingerbread in England that there were fairs where only gingerbread and toys were sold. Each year in Birmingham, two gingerbread fairs were held until well into the nineteenth century . . . Long lines of market stalls, filled with gingerbread in every imaginable shape and form, were interspersed with booths filled with toys." He goes on, **"Gingerbread men** were called 'husbands' at the English fairs, and were often referred to as 'Jim Crows' in nineteenth century America," where they had become popular since the eighteenth century. Foley cites Nathaniel Hawthorne's *House of Seven Gables* as a literary source for the mention of gingerbread elephants! Another popular and historical form for gingerbread was the edible horn book, modeled like the wooden or ivory ones, a sort of abecedarian paddle, sometimes with numbers, formed in ceramic or carved wooden molds before baking. Such **gingerbread horn books** were all said to be decorated with gold leaf, and were given children as rewards or inducements for learning.

Andrew W. Tuer, in *History of the Horn Book* (©1897, reprinted 1968 by Benjamin Blom, Inc; and 1979, Arno Press), devotes a chapter to gingerbread horn books. He writes, **"Halfpenny gingerbread** was made of flour, sugar, and treacle. In a white variety of cake stamped from the same moulds there was more sugar and the treacle was omitted. Pieces of gold foil were dabbed on both sorts . . . The white cakes being sweeter and dearer — they sold for a penny — were considered better and were . . . given as . . . rewards. It may be noted here that confectioners sold a white gingerbread of a better class of flour, butter, ground ginger, lemon rind, nutmeg, and loaf-sugar." Tuer believed the molds for gingerbread horn books dated to the mid-eighteenth century.

Cookie cutter, gingerbread boy, shallow stamped copper anodized aluminum, on original printed card, Color Craft Co. #89, Indianapolis, IN, 5-7/8" H x 3-1/2" W, prob. 1960s-1970s. **$3-$5**

Cookie cutter, gingerbread boy with barely discernible features (meant for the purchaser because the impression made on cookie dough would be fleeting to say the least), very shallow stamped aluminum, green painted strap handle riveted on, no marks, American, 5-7/8" H x 3-1/2" W, originated c.1930s, but prob. made for a long time. **$3-$5**

IV-147. Cake cutters. *Pieced tin with strap handles. Pretzel cutter, 3-7/16", and almond-cookie cutter, 3-1/4" diameter. Bertuch, c.1904.* **$40-$60; $20-$40**

Cookie cutters, gingerbread or "spice bread" (*pain d'épices*) — made by Letang Fils, Paris, and shown in their catalog from 1912. They show outlines plus interior lines delineating clothing, buttons, accessories, ribs, hair, scales. Really wonderful forms including bishop, gentleman, countryman, rabbit, dog, soldier, Arab, lady with buttoned 3/4 coat & flower, lady with more ornate clothing, lion, donkey, fish, gingham dog (!), pirate, Chinese man, four little men in hats, and four little grinning pigs. Value probably in this range for each: **$50-$80.**

Cookie cutters, hands — 3 tin flat backs on a theme: **(1)** hand with pointing finger, **(2)** hand & heart, and **(3)** heart with hand inside. The 2nd had a handle. The subject of hands, especially those with hearts, is very desirable, and these were nice but not spectacular cutters. Prob. PA German, about 4" x 3" or smaller, prob. Late 19th C. Ex-Robacker for three cutters, $1000. **$800-$1200**

IV-148. Multiple cake cutters. (T) *Rolling cutter, heavy cast metal drum, many contiguous designs, bird on branch, elf, bear, bell, rabbit, chicken, chick, Christmas tree, etc. Natural finish wood handle, 7-3/4" L, no marks, c.1960s-80.* **(R)** *Plastic cube is by EK-CO, with 4 bridge club motifs (heart, spade, diamond, club), plus half moon and star. 3-1/2" square, 1980.* **(B)** *Roller has yellow plastic drum on which are a cross, 6-pointed star, shamrock, circle, heart and a whatsit. 9-3/4" L, yellow wood handle. Marked "Made in Hong Kong." Early 1980s.* **$6-$15**

IV-149. Cake cutters. *Top* **(L)** *combination tool: apple corer, biscuit cutter, doughnut maker, fluted cookie cutter, strainer or sifter. You made doughnuts by first cutting with plain round, then cutting center with small tube seen at top. 6" L x 3" diameter, late 19th C.* **(R)** *deep star-shaped tin cutter, 4" diameter, 3-1/2" deep overall, cutter itself an unusual 2-1/2" deep.* **(B)** *lathe-turned wooden doughnut cutter, 4-1/2" L x 2-3/8" diameter. Late 19th or early 20th C. All Collection of Meryle Evans.* **$35-$50; $22-$30; $20-$35**

Cookie cutters, hands, old dark tin, flat backs with strap handle, American, from 2-1/2" H to about 7" H, strips forming cutting edge about 3/4" wide, at least, 19th C. Hand-shape cutters are extremely desirable, as are full figure and well-detailed human forms (particularly men, because of their legs and thus more detail) and to hearts and hands together. **$350-$1000**

Value-adding details. Simple outlines of inanimate objects, geometric forms and some animate forms, like some leaves, flowers and fish, are worth the least. Start adding details and the value goes up, sometimes disproportionately. This more complicated detail can be in the outline itself or within the outline or both.

The outline itself. Detail is added with a closer following of the natural outline, viz. sawtooth or serrated leaf edge, fingers on a hand, heels on shoes, a bun, crimps or curls on a head, a zigzag hem, coattails, apron strings, a tongue in the mouth, individual hairs on a tail, a nut in the paws of a squirrel, etc.

Within the outline. Details inside the outline are sometimes added with strips of tin the same depth as the outline, the ends of the strip joined, used to cut out small details or portions of the cookie. Sometimes the strips are not as deep as the outer cutting edge so that linear marks are made on the surface of the baked cookie which would, whether iced or not, make the form more readable or more interesting. Same depth cutter types include small curls of tin to cut out holes for eyes or buttons, or rounded triangles, arches and rectangles to cut out under arms akimbo, basket handles or windows. A variation of this include short meander strips cutting all the way through the cookie, used to make a strong but small mark, going all the way through the cookie, but short so as not to jeopardize the integrity of the cookie. A little "E" of tin, for example, was used to make a human ear. Shallower marking types include simple strips bent in a curve to indicate the line of an animal's back leg or the

veining of a leaf, to give dimension to the points of a star, define petals on a flower, or make a heart shape within a geometric or figural outline. Sometimes crimped tin strips are used. Final note: many stark and simple cutters with little detail are worthy of study and collection, and can be more dramatic artistic statements than those with more detail. Beware of the cute detail. If you want to collect cutters, study general books on folk art long and hard, and keep referring back to them after you've been out and have seen some cutters. If you aren't born with a sense of what folk art is, you can acquire it. You can also apply aesthetic knowledge and intuition achieved by studying all other kinds of art and design, from Japanese netsuke to African masks to the paintings of Miro to the wire art of Alexander Calder. A successful collector has gut feelings, backed up with exercised brains!

Cookie cutter, hatchet, with inscribed notation "George Washington's hatchet he used to cut down his Dad's favorite cherry tree," tin, signed "Robt. P. Frey," Cleona, Lebanon County, PA, 6-3/4" L, dated 1973. **$25-$35**

Cookie cutter, hatchets, a pair in one cutter, tin, fat cylindrical handle with convex cap, for commercial bakery use, 5-5/8" diameter, c.1920s to 1930s. **$45-$60**

Cookie cutter, heart design, corrugated tin, commercial bakery type, with large fat cylindrical handle that fits in palm of hand, convex cap on handle, stamped "3 1/2" in 2 places on handle, no maker's mark, (Jaburg Brothers was one company making them, NYC), measures 3" H x 3-1/2" W, heart itself measures 3-1/4" x 3-1/4" x 7/8" deep, early 20th C. **$20-$25**

Cookie cutter, heart, has interesting spring-action push-off rod that goes through the strap handle & is attached to the pusher plate inside, tin, American, heart is 3" from the point up to crack between lobes, late 19th C. **$95-$125**

Jingling Itinerant Tin Peddler Theory. In popular books on folk art, especially Pennsylvania Dutch, you often find the jingling itinerant tin peddler theory of cookie cutter origins, or **JITPTOCCO**. So far I haven't traced it to its first appearance; but somewhere someone first wrote, in effect, as Jean Lipman did in the following: "It must have been a red-letter day for the *hausfrau* when the itinerant tinsmith came by with his jingling cart and made her some newly designed cooky cutter, while the whole family watched his nimble fingers at work with shears and solder." (*American Folk Art in Wood, Metal and Stone*, 1948). In Earl F. Robacker's booklet about cookie cutters, he says, "The tinsmith, traveling from place to place, soon exhausted his ready-made stock, and profitably extended his trip by manufacturing a variety of buckets and pots and pans at farmsteads where they were needed . . . The smaller bits which fell from the shears were used up . . . in such items as children's toys . . . and cooky cutters." Robacker goes on at some length describing motifs, and then: "In later years, with the passing of the tinsmith's jingling cart, a specimen set of cutters would often be put on display

IV-150. Cookie cutter. *Farm draught horse, old tin, flatback, very large pushout holes, 5-1/2" H x 6-1/8" L, last quarter 19th C.* **$75-$100**

IV-151. Cookie cutter. *Tin horse on rough-trimmed conforming flatback. One of assorted animal, bird & fish forms in Montgomery Ward catalog, c.1895. 4¢ original cost!* **$25-$45**

IV-152. Cookie cutters. *Three tin flatbacks with small air holes offered by Joseph Middleby, in jobber's catalog, 1927. A "large man" cutter was 10-1/4" H; a "small" man was 5-1/2", whereas a large animal was only 5" H.* **$25-$45**

at a general store, and orders received there." (*Home Craft Course, Pennsylvania German Cooky Cutters and Cookies*, Plymouth Meeting, PA: 1946.) Margaret Coffin wrote: "In the country the tinker was apt to travel on horseback, saddlebags filled with solder, old lead, and a soldering iron, a spoon mold, a clock dial mold, and bits of tinplate . . . [to repair] a teakettle, mend a hole in a pan, or cast a spoon. He made cookie cutters to order to fit the [housewife's] fancy." (*History & Folklore of American Country Tinware, 1700 -1900,* NYC: Galahad Books, 1968.) Jeannette Lasansky's *To Cut, Piece and Solder, The Work of the Rural Pennsylvania Tinsmith,* (1982) includes so much in-depth information, interpretive of 10 tinsmiths' account books & cutters, that it could be called a book on cookie cutters, even though it covers all kinds of tinwares. According to her, even in the 1750s many Pennsylvania smiths had a shop. A 1793 ad for "gingerbread cutters," cited by Lasansky, gives a shop address. Lasansky does not, as far as I know, mention itinerant cookie cutter makers.

The 1832 Tinker. "Here comes the Tinker, — surgeon-general of pans and kettles in all the alleys and courts about town, as well as in all the villages in the neighbourhood. Yet, till the establishment of large manufactories, and the making of articles by wholesale, and the keeping of them in warehouses and shops, . . . the tinker was a man of no small importance: and the people had to wait his pleasure before they could cook their dinner. At that time, if any one wanted a pan or a kettle, the plan was to send for the tinker, who travelled with all the materials and tools necessary for his purpose; and, erecting his apparatus by the hedgeside in the summer, or in any shed or outhouse in the winter, the tinker worked away as blithe as a lark, well knowing that he should not be grudged his price, and a mug of ale to lighten his labour . . .

"The tinker, and the other men of the travelling workshop, learned [sic] to make the people themselves much more handy than they are now; and that was of far more advantage to them than would at first be believed. A labourer now, whether boy or man, has little opportunity of seeing the whole of any thing made; and . . . workmen in the great manufactories are not much better; very much of the work [which used to be made by a tinker] is done by machines . . .

"When the tinker went about in full employment, all the boys came to assist with his little furnace and forge; and there they learned to do many useful things . . . But can't the boys go and learn of the tinker still? [Now the tinker] has very little to teach them . . He used to be an iron-founder and a brass-founder; had . . . crucibles for melting his metals, bellows for blowing his fire, and hammers and pincers. He also knew how to mix his metals — could have made a fine-toned bell out of an old tin pot and copper kettle; and work up all the old tin, copper, and brass, for use again. He [made] solder and could give the seam of the kettle the degree of firmness that you wanted; if you wanted a kettle to stand a strong heat, the brass, zinc and copper filings were mixed in a moment, and iron was so firmly joined as to bear a red heat . . . Now the tinker has only a pot of coke, blown by means of holes in the bottom, a soldering iron, some soft solder and a pinch of rosin; and therefore his employment is as inferior as as himself." *Pinnock's Guide to Knowledge,* London, Sept. 8, 1832.

• • • •

Age Wrinkles. The earliest method for corrugating sheet metal was with the use of a corrugating or crimping swedge — a sort of little molding anvil to fit onto an anvil; an iron piece, cast with the requisite pattern of hills and valleys against which the metal could be hammered, thereby taking on the corrugations. As far as I can

determine, corrugating or crimping machines for tinsmiths were not patented until 1854. Therefore, cookie cutters (or other tinwares) that have extremely regular corrugations are almost undoubtedly from the second half of the nineteenth century or later. These hand-operated machines (one of which a friend and I found on the streets of NYC in the 1970s) look rather like large fluting machines, or some kind of interesting laundry mangle. The two rollers have corrugated surfaces, and the distance between the rollers is adjustable. The sheet of tin (or brass or other sheet metal) is fed through while the machine is cranked. • A very simple tool, actually a pair of long-handled tongs with special jaws with diagonal grooves on the inside, was available and advertised for "tinners, stove dealers, galvanized iron and cornice makers, and all workers in sheet metal." Tedious to crimp 200 feet of cornice for a house, maybe, but just the ticket for a cookie cutter. "Packham's Pipe & Sheet Metal Crimping Tongs," advertised in *The Metal Worker,* Aug. 12, 1882. Packham Crimper Co., Mechanicsburgh, OH, also had a cranked crimper which did the same jobs, only faster — a machine screw-clamped to the work table, had 2 narrow rollers and so could only crimp a narrow band of metal or the edge of something — perhaps 3" or 4" W. It was also advertised in 1882. • A tinsmith from Ohio wrote the *Metal Worker,* Sept. 9, 1882: "to suggest that all my brother <u>chips</u> [the nickname amongst themselves for tinners & tinsmiths] buy a machine specially devised for crimping stove pipes. It costs so little money that it is within the reach of every one, and a tool of this character is far preferable to a combination tool. A machine especially designed for the purpose is expensive only in the first cost. Experience demonstrates their great utility in the tin shop. Devices of this kind are very generally sold in the trade, and may be ordered from any tinners' suppliers. It also promotes morality, for it saves a lot of swearing over ill-fitting stove pipes."

IV-153. Cookie cutters. *Assorted fancy animals and geometrics, flatback tin. They could be had with "fancy centers" (that made indentations but did not cut through), as most are here, or plain. Animals (like the lion & horse at top) came in 3 approximate sizes: 2-3/4" H, 3-1/2" H and 4" H. Matthai-Ingram, c.1890.* **$20-$55**

Cookie cutter, heart-shaped, corrugated around outside, with inset in center to mark design of 3 petals, tin, flat back, strap handle, lots of little holes in back, American, 3-1/8" W at largest part, late 19th C. **$45-$55**

Cookie cutter, heart, deep cutter, no back or handle, homemade from old turquoise, printed tin "Maxwell House" coffee can, American, 1-3/4" deep x 3-1/2" L, c.1940s. Folk art crossover appeal. **$15-$22**

Cookie cutter, heart-shaped, homemade pieced tin, edges rolled on cutting edge as well as flat back, no handle, American, 7/8" deep x 2" x 2-3/4", late 19th C. **$15-$22**

Cookie cutter, heart with corrugated edge for a Valentine, bracket or strap handle on flat back, not real deep, or uncommon, but a nice shape, poss. PA, 3" x 3", late 19th C. **$28-$40**

Cookie cutter, heart with corrugated edge, strap handle, 3 airholes well-placed, perhaps unintentionally, so that the cutter resembles a modern artist's mask, American, 5" across, late 19th C. or early 20th C. **$75-$100**

IV-156. Cookie cutters. *Tin, solid oval backs of uniform shape, small air holes, about 3-1/2". Packed a dozen in a paper bag. Geuder, Paeschke & Frey, 1925.* **$15-$30**

IV-154. Cookie cutters. *Four of the 12 assorted "fancy animals" that were offered in a box for 80¢. Strap handles. All the animals have a folky rather than a mass-produced look. Ritzinger & Grasgreen, c.1906-07.* **$15-$25**

IV-155. Cookie cutters. *Tin, flatback with backs cut roughly to conform to contour. Sold in 3 sizes, small, medium & large. These, like those in IV-151, 152, 153, would be easily mistaken for handmade one-of-a-kind cutters. Lalance & Grosjean, 1890.* **$15-$35**

IV-157. Rabbit cookie cutters. *All tin. Strap handle, backless ones at top are about 3-1/2" L. Bottom one, with flat tin back, was about 6" L. It was offered in sitting, running & standing positions also, and was called a* **"gingerbread rabbit cutter."** *S. Joseph, c.1927.* **$15-$35**

Cookie cutters, heart in hand motif, a Shaker as well as a PA German motif. Old dark tin, flat backs with or without strap handles, airholes for releasing dough, relatively deep cutting edges, American, range from about 2-1/2" H to 6" H, mid 19th C. to 1890s or so. This is the second most avidly sought type of cookie cutter, after the full human form (mainly men) or vice versa, depending on the collector. Look for old tin of relatively thick gauge, signs of hand manufacture such as the edges of the strap handle meticulously but not machine turned. Reproductions of the example in the Smithsonian, made by tinsmiths Bill and Bob Cukla of Hammer Song, Boonsboro MD, are marked on the back of the thumb "B. Cukla." Other makers' reproductions should be marked, but may not be. **$700-$1500**

Cookie cutter, horse facing right, rectangular flat back, no handle, 2 airholes, nice & large, American, 8" x 6", c.1870s to 1880s. **$150-$175**

"Ginger Horse-Cakes. One quart of flour, one pint of best Orleans molasses, one cupful of sugar, tablespoonful and a half of ginger, two small teaspoons of soda, half a cupful of sour cream, and a heaping tablespoonful of lard. Sift the flour first, and then sprinkle the ginger well through it, add the sugar and molasses, putting in lastly the soda dissolved in the cream. Obtain from a tinner a cutter shaped like a horse, for cutting out the cakes." Gertrude Strohm, "Pies and Small Cakes," *The Universal Cookery Book*, NYC: 1888.

Cookie cutter, horse, long skinny & very short, facing left, very shallow cutting edge, tin, long bracket strap handle, American, horse is 3" H x 6" L, late 19th C. **$75-$100**

Cookie cutter, horse with high rump, high head and 4 little legs like the drawings in that charming 1963 book *A Leg At Each Corner: Guide to Equitation*, by Norman Thelwell. Tin, small thumb size strap handle, one tiny nail hole, probably to string on cord as it's not big enough to function as air release hole, American, 5-1/2" L, late 19th C. **$75-$100**

IV-158. Animal cake cutters. *Leaping rabbit was only one of many backless cutters offered by Jaburg, which included in "small" a horse, basket, scissors, pitcher, trumpet, bear, parrot, star, camel, and cat. A "small rat" and a "large man" were offered side by side. Other designs were "Jumbo" (elephant), horse & rider, Liberty Statue, Men and Women, watch, padlock, and eight sizes of hearts. The boxed set of 12 shown under the rabbit was also sold, and possibly made, by Central Stamping Co.. The same line-cuts were used over and over, and by several manufacturers at the same time. It is hard to say how much more (or less) primitive the catalog pictures are than the cutters themselves. These pictures, Jaburg Brothers, 1908.* **$15-$65**

Old Cookie Cutter Shapes. Ann Hark & Preston A. Barba, in *Pennsylvania German Cookery*, Allentown, PA: Schlechter's, 1950, give a recipe borrowed from Mrs. Robert A. Wertman, Sr., for **"Bellylaps** — An old-time Christmas cooky." Made of flour with lots of dark molasses, a small amount of butter, two eggs and some baking soda, they are rolled out to "about 1/4 inch thick on a lightly floured board. In the olden days it was customary to make large cookies of this particular dough and they were cut into the shapes of hearts, stars, eagles, horses and their riders." Bellylaps were also called belly-guts.

● ● ● ●

Batallion Day. Like the Civil War reenactments popular with some people today, there was an annual Battalion Day held in many Pennsylvania communities between 1783 and 1862. This day of parading, training and militia exercises included cavalry troops outfitted in uniforms at least similar to those of the Revolutionary War. So cookie cutters (and carved cake or marzipan boards) or any other decorative use of the horse-riding soldier, could as easily be inspired by latter day Battalion exercises as by the War of Independence. For more, see J. Ritchie Garrison's "Battalion Day: Militia Exercise and Frolic in Pennsylvania Before the Civil War," *Pennsylvania Folklife*, Winter 1976-77, Vol. XXVI, No. 2.

Cookie cutter, horse with horn-blowing rider, tin, flat back, PA German, 7" H x 6-3/4" W, 3rd to 4th quarter 19th C. See also cookie cutter, bugler. Ex-Robacker, $450. Current value probably **$450-$600.**

Cookie cutter, horse with very short, slightly bent legs, tin, homemade, primitive, rather deep 3/4" cutting edge, American, 7" L, late (?) 19th C. Full-figure horses are really popular forms. Less desirable are horse heads. The variety is tremendous. **$150-$200**

Cookie cutter, hunter wearing hat & holding gun, tin, flat back, American, 4-1/2" H, prob. 3rd quarter 19th C. **$125-$150**

Cookie cutter, Indian with raised tomahawk, tin, flat back, vigorous figure called "Threatening Indian" by the Robackers, PA German, 7-1/2" H x 4" W, 19th C. Ex-Robacker, $550. **$500-$750**

Cookie cutter, "jigsaw puzzle" interlocked figural cookies, makes 14 with 2 oddly shaped scraps left over, big cheap thin shiny rectangular frame of tin, with bent strips inside form shapes, American (?), 12-5/8" L x 9-3/4" W, mid 20th C. Related is a cutter comprised of a round band of tin, 12" in diameter, enclosing about 16 different outline cookie cutters ranging from a duck, a dog and a bird on a branch to a tulip and what appears to be a daffodil. All the cutters are soldered to one another so that all the various cookies (and the oddly shaped scraps left over) could be cut in one step. A number of them were seen in the late 1970s and early 1980s, and they are almost undoubtedly 20th C. **$5-$12**

Cookie cutter, leaf, corrugated outer edge, inset marking veins, with big cylindrical palm-fitting handle with convex cap, for commercial bakery use, tin, unusual because marked: "Wood & Selig" (or Selic?), which could be maker, dealer or bakery, NYC, 4" L x 2-1/4" W, cutter 5/8" deep, handle 2-3/8" H including cap dome, x 2-1/8" diameter, turn of century to early 20th. **$20-$30**

Cookie cutter, leaf, corrugated outside & 4 inset vein markers, tin, strap handle, Pennsylvania European heritage style, 4-3/4" L x 2-1/2" W, shallow cut, late 19th C. **$15-$22.**

Cookie cutters, leaves & flowers, tin, flat backs, shallow cut, with corrugated outside edges as well as even narrower corrugated interior inset strips for marking leaf veins or little pedula designs, once thought to be indubitably Pennsylvania German, and perhaps the first ones were. But they are found in later general manufacturers' catalogs, sometimes described as "Cake cutters," American, about 2" to 4" L x 3/8" to 1/2" deep, 1870s to 1920s. **Not So Old:** I once thought that these were at least 100 years old; they all look so old-fashioned, folky Victorian, dark and beat up. A very nice 3" shallow-cutting heart "Cake Cutter," with flat back, strap handle, corrugated edge, and even shallower 3-petal inset marking design appears in the 1920 manufacturers' catalog of The Central Stamping Co., NYC, NY. Central Stamping also had an assorted set of 12 fancy cutters, the simplest of which were a corrugated oval and a corrugated hexagon. There were also a diamond, 2 rounds, a square, an oblong, a 6-point star, an egg shape, and an oval with corrugated edges, all with insets, and finally an 8-point star with plain cutting edge. It's reasonable to assume that other companies made this type of cutter, possibly only hearts, diamonds & other geometrics, but possibly leaves and other designs too. They are probably dark because they were either scrubbed too hard or the tin plating was very thin; the rust and the dings came from neglect or hard usage. "The less expensive tin cake cutters in their multitudinous designs are very inexpensive and good tools. They are keen cutting and light and durable." Ethel R. Peyser, *House & Garden*, June 1922. **$15-$25**

Lions may originally have been borrowed from heraldry by cookie cutter makers or they may a religious symbol (the lion and the lamb shall lie down together; or a symbolic representation of Christ by a lion); or they may reflect an interest in the lion seen in early menageries or circuses. Probably the first African lion brought to America was the "Lyon of Barbary," which arrived in 1716 for exhibition in New England.

Cookie cutter, lion, very simple, tin, 3-1/2" L, 20th C.   **$15-$20**

Cookie cutter, Maid Marian figural, tin, advertising "Robin Hood Flour," 20th C.   **$10-$15**

Cookie cutter, male figure, standing strong man, arms down, feet out, heavy sheet iron or <u>terne plate</u> (a heavier tinplate with higher percentage of lead), flat back with airholes of 3 sizes at head, shoulders, chest, belly, thighs and ankles, unusual in that they are symetrical, which adds to visual appeal, or rather doesn't distract, as the holes in a cutter this big are very obvious, two strap handles behind knees and behind heart, American, unusually tall at 18-1/4" H, mid to late 19th C. A spectacular sculptural piece with great appeal to folk art collectors, and sold as such over a decade ago by dealers Roger Ricco & Frank Maresca. The piece was shown a few times, and the price kept going up.   **$3000-$4000**

Cookie cutter, man, hunched & elderly, with skinny walking stick, imagine making a cookie & not breaking off that walking stick, tin, flat back, PA German (?), 7" H x 4-1/4" W, late 19th C. Great folk art piece. Ex-Robacker, $275.   **$350-$450**

Cookie cutter, man in derby or bowler hat, full standing, soldered tin strips that form the cutting edge in 2 parts — top half of his body overlaps bottom half & solder joints are just below waist level on both sides, no strap handle, no back, "Nutbrown Product," a mark found on a number of housewares from manufacturer Thomas M. Nutbrown, Blackpool, England. About 5" H, mid 20th C.   **$20-$25**

Cookie cutter, man on horse, tin, flat back, small, marked "GHESCINERE MENIN"(?), (see next listing and a Santa cutter further on). French, Belgian, German, or Alsatian (?), 19th C. Ex-Dziadul.   **$300-$400**

Cookie cutter, man on horseback like a Revolutionary War Hessian soldier, tin, flat back, marked "GHESCINERE MENIN"(?). French, Belgian, German, or Alsatian (?), 11" H x 9" W (tail to nose), 19th C. Ex-Dziadul.   **$400-$600**

Cookie cutter, man, standing, tin, fat cylindrical handle with convex cap on end, for commercial bakery use, marked "Germany," 5-1/4" diameter, c.1920s to 1930s.   **$65-$80**

IV-159. Animal cake cutters. *Assorted set in two approximate sizes — 1" and 2-1/4". Tin, strap brace handles, boxed. S. Joseph, c.1927. Singles: $10-$35. Set:* **$80-$100**

IV-160. Cake cutter sets. **(T-L)** *is a "Noah's Ark Set" of 1" deep x 3" H cutters, that came in an "attractive cellophane wrapped box."* **(R)** *Standing tall is Savory's "Ginger Bread Man," who was 9-1/2" H x 5-3/4" W x 2" deep. I believe he must have had a flatback to which the features were soldered (or possibly that's the artist's improvisation to help sell the cutter.) Savory, c.1925-28.* **(B-L)** *Small set, with 12 designs about 3" H or long, from the Buhl Brothers Hardware Co., Detroit, c.1919. Singles:* **$12-$55**

Cookie cutter, man, tin, rather primitive, standing but no hat or cane, this not my idea of a gingerbread man, American, 7" H, 19th C. Some of these almost look like political figures. Humorous caricatures of people as well as animals were popular with PA German cookie makers. **$125-$175**

Cookie cutter, man, tin, flat back closely trimmed except between thighs and between back arm and back, an example of <u>Black Americana</u> called the "Runaway Slave" by Robackers and in auction catalog, obviously intended to be a running black man, with crimped hair on top of head, full lips. Small curl of tin for eye, another for ear, but not much detail in extremities. The figure, with its curved torso, appears naked, or at least there are no ridges or other indications of hems or cuffs. PA German (?). PA was destination for many runaway slaves. 12-1/8" H x 7-1/2" W, prob. 3rd or 4th quarter 19th C. Ex-Robacker, $7400, paid by a very discriminating collector of cookie cutters who will be writing a book. The almost unimaginably high price, even now almost a decade later, cannot be used to make judgments about any other cutters. The high price achieved for a fine cutter cannot be useful in determining the probable market value of any but the most closely comparable cutters. **$7000-$8000**

"Runaway Slave" Reproduction alert. Within a couple of months of the sale of the aforementioned cookie cutter, an enterprising person created a lookalike cutter (that doesn't really look like the original). "The Tinner," without consulting either the owner of the superb original or common sense, has turned out an awkwardly drawn (but perhaps well-executed) rip-off, in the same size, in "a rich, aged patina," and supposedly in a "marked and numbered limited edition" for $24.95 ppd. Thank heaven it's marked and numbered (I don't know how many are in the edition), and let's hope the marks are permanent & deep. In the original, the lines flow as if Picasso or Matisse had drawn them; in the copy, the back leg is bulging and muscular, the front one skinny, the fingers look like hooves, and the head is tiny and with a hatchet-like projection off the back, whereas the original has gorgeously simple crimped hair and a robust face. The inset ear on the new is oversized and poorly positioned; that on the original is a sort of squiggled "C" and in good proportion. "The Tinner," of Spencer, NC, has also advertised a heart-in-hand cutter, on a square flatback that measures 6" x 5". It only costs $8. Well . . . you know what my opinion is of fakes and most reproductions. Some are close to worthless, others have utilitarian value but no value as collectibles.

IV-161. Cake cutter set. *"Noah's Ark" assortment, 3-1/2" L. Could be had with or without handles. Shown here with what appear to be braces across body for strength. (They also made the rabbit set in IV-157, which shows handles clearly.) S. Joseph, c.1927. Singles:* **$10-$35**

Cookie cutter, man with hand raised to reach for something, small curl of tin for inset eye, tin, flat back, PA German, 9-7/8" H x 5-5/8" W, 3rd or 4th quarter 19th C. Great! Ex-Robacker, $425. **$350-$500**

Cookie cutter, man with hat, interior inset strips or curls of tin making line of his arm, also eye and ear, tin, flat back, together with a simple cutter of man in hat, PA German, 7-1/4" H x 3-5/8" W, and 7-5/8" H x 3-1/2" W, 3rd or 4th quarter 19th C. Ex-Robacker, for both cutters: $425. For both now: **$400-$500.**

Cookie cutter, man with hat, very primitive standing figure, tin, flat back, looks "right" & old, American, 8-1/2" H, 19th C. In the early 1980s this was for sale at a good antique show for a paltry $98. Gadz, what a fool I was not to have bought it. These hatted men cutters are extremely desirable, particularly in anything over 6" H. **$450-$500**

Cookie cutters, man, woman & child, tin, flat back, tallest is 5-1/2" H, late 19th C. Set: **$100-$150**

Cookie cutter, mermaid with upcurled tail, nice & robust, tin, flat back, PA German, 5-3/8" H x 5-5/8" L, prob. 3rd to 4th quarter 19th C. Ex-Robacker, $450. **$500-$600**

Cookie cutter, Mickey Mouse, stamped aluminum, riveted strap handle (there's a Minnie Mouse, same series), Disney licensed, 4", 20th C. **$30-$35**

Cookie cutters, multiple cutters that make several different cookies at once, an auction lot of 3 made of tin. **(1)** The most unusual is the combined flour container (according to Earl Robacker), nutmeg grater & 4 cutters. The body of the grater is cylindrical, with an oblong raised grating surface along one side. With the lid on, on both ends is a fancy cutter, inside lid is a 3" heart cutter, and finally, with the lid off, a round cookie could be cut with the cylinder's rim. **(2)** Another unusual one was a cube with different cutters on each of the 6 sides. **(3)** The third was a large oval cutter for making 13 different cookies at a time, American, poss. PA German, 1st is 4-1/2" H x 3-1/8" diameter; 2nd is 4-1/2" square; 3rd is 11-1/4" L x 7-1/2" W, the combination piece poss. 1870s to 1900; others 20th C. Robacker May 1989 price for the lot of three cutters was $800. A similar but more complex combination cutter than (1) is depicted in Brigitte ten Kate-von Eicken's *Küchengeräte um 1900*. It consists of a japanned tin cylinder with a perforated domed lid on one end, a fine grater and a medium grater soldered lengthwise on opposite sides of the can, with a finely crimped round fluted cookie cutter on end, a bracket strap handle going from close to the bottom to near the top, and opposite the vertical handle is a tin bracket with a fluted pastry jagger wheel. A stamped brass (?) medallion attached to the can above the jagger is not completely legible in the photo, but it appears to read "--RGAN COMP / MANDAL6 (or MANDAL'S) / LONDON," with a lot more that is completely illegible. Clearly it is English. It looks 1870s to 1890s and is probably the same age as the one in the Robacker sale. A collector in America says it is called a "Kitchen Magician," which may be a later appellation. Price range for rather complex tin combination baking tool cutters: **$175-$250**

IV-162. Cookie cutters. *Stamped aluminum with riveted bracket handles, about 4". "Mirro," Aluminum Goods Mfg. Co., 1927.* **$3-$8**

Cookie cutters, multiple — See also cookie cutters, rolling

Cookie cutter, oak leaf, tin with strap handle, 5-1/4" L, 20th C. **$25-$30**

Cookie cutter, parrot on a branch, sheet brass, very high arched strap handle on flat back, 4 holes, PA German (?), early 20th C (?). **$75-$100**

Cookie cutter, piper — man blowing pipe or horn, on back it reads "Eleven Pipers Piping," red plastic, very modernistic, ugly too, "Made by Chilton," Aluminum Specialty Co., Manitowa, WI, 5" H, 1978. **$1-$3**

Periodical research. I have not been able to track down a copy of the periodical, but in the September 1925 issue of *Industrial Education Magazine* there is a how-to article by an H. W. Paine entitled "Rotary Cookie Cutter." The reason I know there is an article, although I've not found it or read it, is because of the *Readers' Guide to Periodical Literature* subject & author index, which is in most if not all public libraries, and lists articles that appeared in magazines from last part of nineteenth century to date. The problem is that the library probably does not have a full set of the particular magazine you want to see. So make a list and contact used magazine dealers and look at flea markets and house sales.

Old Catalogs for Research. Nothing is so helpful to the collector as old illustrated manufacturers', wholesalers', and retailers' mail order catalogs. Especially nice is a small importer's catalog, c.1906, of the firm of <u>Ritzinger & Grasgreen</u>, NYC. Depicted in it are two of an "assortment of 12 Human Figures In Box," which sold (retail or wholesale not specified) for 80¢. They are tin outline cutters, top edge rolled, no flatback or strap handle. Two figures are depicted: the woman's ankles and heeled boots show under her hem, she wears a wide brimmed hat; the man's suit coat is just a bit longer than nowadays, with a more pronounced waist, and he wears a flat-crowned had. They were probably imported from Germany. The company also sold a 4-piece set of Sandwich Cutters, tin, flatback, strap handles, with air release holes in the center, in bridge sets, club, spade, diamond & heart. The set sold for $1.20 — a high price then. The look of the cutters, with flatbacks only roughly trimmed to shape, makes it easy to assume that many of the cutters sold as cookie cutters today may have originally been intended for cutting crustless luncheon sandwiches. There is also a deep cutter set of Card Party Cutters, "Hearts, Clubs, Spades, Diamonds," tin with rolled top edge, heavy duty strap arched handle. Another set offered by Ritzinger & Grasgreen is an "Assortment of 12 Animals in Box" for 80¢. Depicted in the catalog are 4 cutters, tin outlines, no backs, 3 with narrow strap handles (much narrower than the strap handles for the Humans). They are: an eagle, cat, dog and fish (no handle).

Cookie cutter, pitcher with nice shape & handle, tin, flat back, strap handle, American, 3-1/2"H, late 19th C. **$20-$30**

Cookie cutter, rabbit, tin, no handle — one of an animal set that includes a horse, goose, rabbit & cat, premium for "Davis Baking Powder," 7/8" deep x 4" L, Hoboken, NJ, 1926. **$15-$20**

Cookie cutter, rolling multiple type, makes a diamond, heart, club & spade, green wood handle, body of roller & cutters are crimped & riveted tin, no maker name, makes 1-1/4" cookies, overall length 6-1/8", 1932 patent #1855663. **$25-$40**

Cookie cutter, rolling multiple type, plated cast steel, 6 designs, marked "D. R. G. M.," German, mid 20th C. **$15-$30**

Cookie cutter, rolling multiple type, sheet metal, white wooden handle, "Rollemout" by American Cutter Co., Milwaukee, WI, 20th C., "Patent Applied For." The late Phyllis Wetherill, cookie cutter queen, showed a Rollemout with a twisted wire handle in her profusely illustrated book on 20th C. cookie cutters (see bibliography). I don't know which handle is earliest. See also doughnut cutter. **$15-$30**

IV-164. Gingerbread boys. (**L**) *Shiny thin tin, fairly recent manufacture, 8" H.* (**R**) *Stamped aluminum, with details that probably wouldn't show on finished cookie. Has strap handle created by slitting back. 5-3/4" H, 1940s.* **$3-$8**

IV-163. Cookie cutter. *A large flatback tin elephant, probably "Jumbo." Strap handle. Shallow cutter, exuberant trumpeting position. 9-1/8" W, 19th C. Collection of Charismatic Studio.* **$200-$400**

IV-165. Gingerbread boy & tree. (**L**) *Similar to one in IV-164, but here the bracket handle is riveted on, and there are no features. 6" x 3-3/4".* (**R**) *The tree is about 3-1/4", and the catalog pictures were not to scale. "Mirro" Aluminum Goods Mfg. Co., 1927.* **$3-$8**

Cookie cutter, rolling multiple type, tin, wire handle, 3 interchangeable barrels for making diamonds, waffling, or swirls, in original box, mfd. by Guirier, c.1930s. **$25-$35**

Cookie cutter, rolling multiple — See cookie cutter, multiple

Cookie cutter, rooster, all carved of wood, the cutting edge also of wood. It wouldn't really cut, per se, but would smush the form out from the rolled dough, PA German (?), 4-1/2" x 4-3/8", 19th C. Ex-Robacker, $250. **$250-$300**

Cookie cutter, rooster, of a type sometimes called a "maple sugar mold" — tin with wooden back, PA German, 5-1/2" x 6-5/8", 3rd to 4th quarter 19th C. Ex-Robacker, $750. **$300-$500**

Cookie cutter, rooster with high perky tail with 4 squared-off feathers, long open beak, 2 oblong legs with no feet, round bumptious rear end, iridescence to tin (possibly coated with something?), 4 small airholes & several small holes up in tail feathers, beak & legs, old type tin flat back, marked "A. J. B.," poss. PA, 5" H x 4" W x 5/8" deep, dealer tag said "not old." Prob. late 1970s or even 1980s. **$12-$18**

Cookie cutter, round, a circle with fluted edges, tin, strap handle, "Fries," American, 20th C. **$10-$18**

Cookie cutters, round, 4 graduated cutters with corrugated edges, in box with lid, all made of tin. "Merridale Works," English (?), box 4" diameter, 20th C. **$22-$30**

Cookie cutter, round with scalloped edge, tin, fat cylindrical handle has convex cap on end, for commercial bakery use. This one was called a <u>Bolivar cutter</u> by at least one company. (They also made one with inverted scallops called a <u>Shrewsbury cutter</u>), maker's name not marked, but Jaburg Brothers was one maker/importer (?), NYC, NY, 4-1/2" diameter, early 20th C. (**NOTE:** for another scalloped-edge cutter, see cookie cutter & doughnut cutter combo.) **$20-$30**

Cookie cutter, <u>sand tart</u> round, tin with corrugated outside cutting edge, inner ring plain, for ring "sand tart" cookies of type traditionally hung on indoor Christmas trees, strap handle, American, 3" diameter, late 19th C. **$15-$22**

Cookie cutter, Santa Claus, tin, flat back in oblong shape is not cutaway to follow outline, which is the more usual form. The figure's detailed outline includes hem of greatcoat, he carries small Christmas tree on his left shoulder (our's & the cookie's right), stands on block assumed to be the top of chimney, all in all the form & stance is very like Christmas postcards & other holiday images of Santa. This cookie would require much decorating in different colors to make form interesting. PA German, good size: 11" H x 5-1/2" W, late 19th C. See also cookie cutter, Father Christmas. Ex-Robacker, $850. **$350-$500**

Cookie cutter, Santa Claus with toy pack on his back & what cataloguer Clarence Spohn (and the Robackers) call a <u>tsipfel cap</u>, a liberty cap (though that's not the translation), tin, flat back,

IV-166. Santa Claus & Angel. *Tin profile cutters with rolled top edge (for stability) and strap brace handles. Santa is 4-1/2" H; not-to-scale angel is 5" H. S. Joseph catalog, c.1927.* **$10-$25**

"handle missing, solder loose," PA German, 9-1/2" H x 6" W, prob. 4th quarter 19th C. Ex-Robacker, $375. **$350-$500**

Cookie cutter, Santa Claus with very little appeal in detail or form, factory-made, tin, 3-1/2" H, 20th C. **$5-$7**

"Syrup Küchlein (Molasses Cakes). Two scant cupfuls of lard, two cupfuls of molasses, one egg, one teaspoonful of ground cloves, one teaspoonful of ground cinnamon, half a teaspoonful of salt, one teaspoonful of soda, and [probably about 3 1/2 pounds?] flour. Melt the lard; when cool add the molasses, spices, salt, and the soda dissolved in a little hot water. Stir thoroughly and add the flour, a little at a time, until the dough is very thick; roll out and cut in fancy shapes. These little cakes are always to be found on a German Christmas tree.

"Tin forms or cutters to cut little cakes into various shapes may easily be made at home. Get narrow strips of tin from a tinsmith. These strips should be about three-quarters of an inch wide; then cut off the length desired for the form. With the fingers bend and shape this narrow strip until it is the desired shape, then pinch the two ends over one another like a seam and the form is complete. These cutters do not require a handle or top; the sides alone are sufficient to cut out any animal desired. Figures of crows [sic -- possibly supposed to be cows?], elephants, birds, squirrels, dogs and cats, or the figure of Santa Claus, are easily made out of these simple strips of tin. However, these forms may be secured at many stores and at a very reasonable price." Lola D. Wangner, "Christmas Cakes of Germany," *Ladies Home Journal*, Dec. 1906.

Cookie cutters, Santa Claus & nicely detailed Christmas tree, tin, strap handles, a pair & very well-formed, American, 9" H, late 19th or early 20th C. **$140-$200**

Cookie cutter, Santa-related motif of St. Nicholas with mitred hat & long staff, tin, flat back, no handle, stamped with illegible name — MENIN is most likely, French, Belgian, German, or Alsatian (?), 11" H, 19th C. Dealer Teri Dziadul. Teri and I think the possible

IV-167. Men & women cutters. (T) *Part of what Ritzinger & Grasgreen refers to as an "assortment of 12 human figures." 3" H, without handles. About 1908.* **(B)** *Tin man & woman with brace handle, 3" H, S. Joseph Co., c. 1927. Slight variations from top one, but essentially the same.* **$30-$40**

201

variations of the visible letters are: "GHESCINERE MENIN" (or MERIN or MEKIN), or GHESCUIERE MENIN (or MERIN or MEKIN — note how all have same diagonals). (See also two horseman cutters and a woman cutter.) **$800-$1200**

Cookie cutters, shoes, a high-button pair, tin, flat back with trimmed edges, strap handles, prob. PA, 4-1/2" H, c.1880s to 1900. **Shoes** have been a symbolic love token for a long time (witness the old shoes tied on the back of the going-away car). These cutters maybe were a token of love or, even more likely, a tenth wedding anniversary gift. **$100-$125**

Cookie cutter, song bird, a small unidentifiable species, early heavy dark tin (probably terne — see cookie cutter introductory essays) with the satiny feel described by some writers as "greasy," flat back, no handle, prob. PA, 4-3/4" L x 2-1/2" W x 34" deep, 19th C. **$60-$80**

Cookie cutter, squirrel with small loop that cuts out eyehole, plus inset strips for detail in tail brush, tin, flat back, solder very bright (repair? late cutter of old tin? Probably the former). PA German, 7" H x 5-3/8" W, 3rd to 4th quarter 19th C. Ex-Robacker, $350. **$300-$450**

Cookie cutter, star, 5-pointed, unusually deep, flat back tin, strap handle, American, 2-1/2" deep x 4" diameter, 19th C. The tin is so sharp and the sides so deep that it's possible these were used for something other than cookie cutting. Can't think what, though. **$25-$40**

Cookie cutter, star, Moravian 10-point, tin, American, 2" diameter, late 19th C. For those delicate Moravian ginger cookies, thin as cardboard and crisp as chips (great with coffee icecream). **$25-$45**

Cookie cutter, tobacco pipe, modern briar type, tin, flat back, for Father's Day? American, 5-1/2" L, this one prob. 20th C., but pipes with long stem much earlier. **$35-$45**

IV-168. Cookie cutters. *Molded light blue plastic with fine interior details. Santa is 5" H; Christmas tree, 4-1/2" H. (These came in other colors.) Stanley Rome Products, 1950s-60s.* **$1-$3**

Cookie cutter, tulip, tin. Imagine an oval doughnut cutter which would make a tulip motif center hole instead of a round or oval one. The outer cutting edge is a ribbon of tin forming an oval, with a small central tulip with curved stem, 3 petals in design we think of as Pennsylvania German. This little tulip cutter is mounted to a capped cylinder which forms the handle, and this cylinder is held in place in the oval's center by 2 strap braces on the long axis, prob. American & commercially made, not PA German, 5-1/2" L oval, early 20th C. **$95-$125**

"**Kindergarten Sandwiches**. Remove crusts from a white and graham loaf and cut each in thin slices, lengthwise. Shape with round, round-fluted, elliptical [oval], cutlet-shaped, square or oblong cutters. Spread one-half the pieces generously with butter, which has been worked until creamy. From remaining pieces cut out shapes, using small flower, animal or fancy cutters, and refill cuts thus made with similar [matching] cuts of bread of contrasting color. Put together...and wrap in cheesecloth wrung out of hot water to keep moist until serving time." Fanny Merritt Farmer, *A New Book of Cookery*. Boston: Little, Brown, & Co., 1915 edition of 1912 book. • I found the "Kindergarten Sandwiches" instructions confusing, even when looking at the picture in the book, so will describe in other words. The "graham" bread is a dark whole-grain bread, and the other bread is white. A tulip "insert" cut out of dark bread is inserted into the identical cutout space in the white bread — like assembling a jigsaw puzzle from two identical sets, one light, one dark. Other sandwiches were done as mosaics, held together with butter. Peering closely at the picture of the various cutters in Farmer's book, you see they're are all tin, but different ages and origins. Some are deep-cutting, some shallow cutting, some flatback, some backless, some with a bracket strap handle, some with no handle. The most complicated one is the tulip & oval, which does two cuts at once.

Cookie cutter, tulip with curved stem with 2 small non-tulip leaves, very graceful form, strong & simple, 3-point large petals, tin, flat back, PA German (?), approx. 6-3/4" L x 4-1/8" W, 3rd to 4th quarter 19th C. **$400-$500**

Cookie cutters, tulip, a pistol, a guitar, and a wonderful saw, which alone might have brought the price, 4 in a lot, tin, all flat back, PA German. The saw: 7-3/8" L x 2-3/4" W, the guitar: 5-3/8" L x 2-1/8" W, 3rd to 4th quarter 19th C. Ex-Robacker, the lot: $775. **$700-$900**

Cookie cutters, twins, boy & girl in original box, "Avon," American, 20th C. **$12-$22**

Cookie cutter, twins, females, tin, outline with no detail, no back, no handle, American, 3-5/8" x 3-3/8", late 19th or early 20th C. This cutter may have extra value because there may be a story behind the twins. See below. **$40-$55**

Twins. Here's something to look for: a Biddendens "bun" mold, as described by Carl W. Drepperd in *A Dictionary of American Antiques*. He says that from the sixteenth to the eighteenth century carved molds depicting the charitable Chulkhurst twins, Elisa and Mary, of Biddenden, England (who were joined at hip and shoulder), were used to mark the buns (probably some form of cookie) that were distributed to the poor, under the terms of the twins' will. The legend, if that it is, dates back to the twelfth century.

Cookie cutter, Uncle Sam. Marvelous tall proud figure, with 5 little curls of tin for buttons down his coat front, one curl for the eye, a sort of E scroll of tin for the little ear, each finger delineated, unusual flat back, in that — according to cataloguer Clarence Spohn — it is the back of a tin wall sconce that was used. The edges of the backing are turned, and there is a little impressed bead molding around part of perimeter. PA German, 12-1/4" H x 4-1/4" W, 3rd to 4th quarter 19th C. Ex-Robacker, $3000. **$3000-$4000**

Cookie cutter, Uncle Sam, walking tall, in swallow tail coat that projects slightly over edge of flat back, high crowned head, beard, skinny legs with heeled boots, oblong flat back, very shallow cutter, one large push-out hole in hat, 2 small air release holes in body, PA German, 12-5/8" H x 3-1/8" W, 3rd to 4th quarter 19th C. Ex-Robacker, $725. **$900-$2500**

Cookie cutter, Uncle Sam, with flying coat tails & high hat, wonderful profile full figure, apparently old dark tin, flat back, American, 12-1/2" H, 19th C. **Reproduction alert**. These are widely reproduced, that is to say faked, now, to capitalize on the rage for folk art. You have to develop a feel. If they look too good, they are. If the drawing or outline seems just too hokey pokey folky, it is. If it's real cute, give it the boot. If it looks too distressed, it is. If the crudeness is overwhelming, it probably overwhelmed its 1970s or 1980s maker too. The rotter. A real one (and you'd have to be sure of yourself) would probably bring something in this range: **$1200-$1800**

Cookie cutter, woman in a long dress, copper, flat back, 2 large push-out holes (bigger than airholes & useful for thin dough cookies that might not drop out of their own weight), very plain geometric female form, with a small circle for head, larger circle for upper body, large triangle for skirt, no arms. Sounds boring, it is, sort of, but still it has more zip that can be described, if you think A R T. American, 8" H, late 19th C. Copper is a popular medium with modern crafts people, but was also used by cookie cutter makers in the 19th C, much, much less often than tin. **$95-$125**

Cookie cutter, woman, small, tin, flat back, "GHESCINERE MENIN" (? See St. Nicholas cookie cutter above), French, Belgian, German, or Alsatian (?), 6" H, 19th C. Cutter was Teri Dziadul's; price range mine: **$400-$450**

Cookie cutters, wood backs to which are tacked tin cutting sides, very uncommon, but 3 showed up in first auction of Robacker Collection: bird, 8-point star, heart. PA German, 3-1/4" x 4-3/4"; 3-1/4" diameter; and 3-3/4" x 4-1/4", 19th C. **NOTE:** Sometimes these cutters with the wood backs are labeled "maple sugar molds." Ex-Robacker, $250; $175; $100. **$200-$300; $150-$200; $100-$150**

Cookie cutter & doughnut cutter combined, tin & wire, round cutter with wire handle sticking out side and going through from one side to the other so that the wire supports a small doughnut hole cutter to be used with the plain cutting edge. Flip it over and it makes scalloped edge cookies, which some writers say is the traditional style of cutter for a Pennsylvania German cookie called an "Apee." American, 6-1/2" L x 3" diameter, c.1890s. **$15-$20**

"Making Moravian Christmas Cakes. With your sleeves rolled up & your aprons on, you and Mother begin to roll & cut out. Mother seems to get along well from the first, but at your end of the table there is more or less trouble . . . Your first tinful looks pale & ragged beside Mother's perfect, crinkly ovals . . . later you get the knack. All the extra boards are needed to hold the cakes . . . While Mother tests the oven, to see if the heat is low & steady, you survey with pride the hearts, stars, crescents, diamonds, squares, circles & different geometrical shapes, but you think more fondly still of the animals & the men and women that will be made after dinner . . . The afternoon baking is somewhat different from the morning session. You have packed the cakes away in the deep can, & have run over to borrow Mrs. Reed's animal cutters. It takes all Mother's skill to move a long-eared rabbit from board to tin, & the elephant with a curled trunk is troublesome too. There are horses, dogs, cats, roosters, ducks & many others. You are quite occupied holding your breath & making Ahs ! & Ohs! as each cake is successfully or unsuccessfully placed. Mother does not make as many of these delightful creatures as you could wish, & when it comes to the men & women cakes there is just one apiece for each of you children. Baking this last batch is more work for both Mother and you, but neither of you minds the extra trouble. You remove them from the tins with care bordering on reverence, & place them on top of the 'common' ones: not a few lose their limbs and have to be put in the boys' pile of 'brokens.' When the last fragile cookie is stored away and the lid closed over it you and Mother feel that the busiest, happiest and most profitable day of the year is past." Annie M. Stein, *Ladies Home Journal*, Dec. 1909. • This informative little fiction whimsy had a **Moravian molasses cookies** recipe, calling for 1 qt. of molasses, 12 oz. of butter & lard, 12 oz. of brown sugar, 1 oz each of soda, ginger & cinnamon, 1/2 oz. each of cloves & orange peel, and 4 lbs. of flour. The soda was mixed with a tablespoon of milk, & when all the other ingredients (except flour) were stirred into a sticky mass, the soda was added: "How the mass puffed up!" The flour was added last, mixed in, & the mixture covered & set to get cold, before rolling & cutting.

• • • •

"Apees. A pound of flour, sifted. Half a pound of butter. Half a glass of wine, and a table-spoonful of rose-water, mixed. Half a pound of powdered white sugar. A nutmeg, grated. A tea-spoonful of beaten cinnamon and mace. Three table-spoonfuls of carraway seeds. — Sift the flour into a broad pan, and cut up the butter in it. Add the carraways, sugar, and spice, and pour in the liquor by degrees, mixing it well with a knife; and add enough of cold water to make it a stiff dough. Spread some flour on your pasteboard, take out the dough, and knead it very well with your hands. Cut it into small pieces, and knead each separately, then put them all together, and knead the whole in one lump. Roll it out in a sheet about a quarter of an inch thick. Cut it out in round cakes, with the edge of a tumbler, or a tin of that size. Butter an iron pan, and lay the cakes in it, not too close together. Bake them a few minutes in a moderate oven, till they are very slightly colored, but not brown. If too much baked, they will entirely lose their flavor. Do not roll them out too thin. The top of the oven should be hotter than the bottom, or the cakes will lose their shape." Miss Leslie, of Philadelphia, *Seventy-Five Receipts for Pastry, Cakes, and Sweetmeats, Appended to The Cook's Own Book and Housekeeper's Register ....*, by a Boston Housekeeper. Boston: Munroe & Francis, 1833.

• • • •

Apees Anyone? Ann Hark & Preston A. Barba, in *Pennsylvania German Cookery*, Allentown, PA: Schlechter's, 1950, write that A.P.s are spelled "apees, apeas, apise and apiece." Marcus B. Lambert, in his *Pennsylvania German Dictionary*, enters it as "Eepies," and relates it to the French *pain d'épice*, spice bread or gingerbread). Ruth Hutchison's *The New Pennsylvania Dutch Cook Book* (1958), repeats a story from John F. Watson's *Annals of Philadelphia*, that in early Philadelphia, a "young woman named Ann Page had made the first of these cookies, scratching her initial on each one, hence AP's." The apee story may be yet another apocryphal pastry origin story, the most famous being about Sally Lunns. Stories: (1) They were first made by a young English woman named Sally Lunn; (2) they are of French origin, and because of their golden top crust & white underneath they were first called "Soleil et Lune" (sun and moon).

Cookie cutter & doughnut cutter, strainer & apple corer combined, ingeniously pieced tin and mesh, being essentially a cylinder of tin, one edge of which is corrugated or fluted, the other straight, in between a piece of mesh, and sticking out of the side at right angles is a 3" L corer tube. Further on around the edge sticks out a short tube used to cut the holes out of doughnuts. American, 6" L (including corer), 3" diameter main cutter, late 19th C. Nothing like these interesting combination tools to get a walkin' hawker's, traveling salesman's or agent's attention. They may have cost the salesman 2¢ wholesale, and he could sell them for 15¢. What a sales pitch too! **$22-$40**

Cookie or biscuit cutter, round, wrought iron, simple circle with very high arched handle. (See also biscuit or cookie cutter.) American, 2-3/8" H x 2-5/8" diameter, early 19th C. This extremely handsome wrought iron piece is in the Kyle Goad Collection, Virginia. Price range estimates probable current market value (colored by what I'd pay myself — it's that gorgeous!) **$100-$150**

Cookie cutters — See also a combo nutmeg grater in Chapter I.

Cookie machine, for bakery, 28 <u>speculas</u> (like springerle) cookie molds on rotary drum, German, 1910. **$175-$250**

Cookie machine, for bakery, side-by-side rows of springerle-type cookie molds on rotary drum, which is cranked on side, on iron frame, with long cloth conveyor belt, mfd. by Hengler & Cronemeyer, German, different sizes, to make multiple cookies at a time, laid out from 2x2 to at least 6x6, dated 1905, won awards in 1903 and 1904. **$225-$350**

Cookie machine, for making Chinese fortune cookies, American (?), prob. 20th C. I merely report this 1983 ad from the *Antique Trader Weekly*. The machine is described as "antique," in this case almost undoubtedly early 20th C. Dealer asking this price: **$1000.**

Cookie mold, basket of berries, cast iron, oval, gritty silvery look to iron which indicates it may be a modern cheap reproduction,

American (?), 5-3/4" L, if old, mid 19th C; if new prob. mid to late 20th C, and worth no more than $10. Many cast iron cookie molds are being reproduced, and some designs have been copied since the 1950s. **$50-$65**

Cookie mold, basket of holly, cast iron oval, casting gate in back, not in middle, mostly ground down flat, Christmas holly in theorum-like low, flared sides basket, no mark, prob. American, 5-7/8" L x 4" W x 1/4" deep, c.1840s to 1860s. **$125-$175**

Cookie mold, bee skip or skep, flat cast iron oval, prob. NY state, 19th C. A bee skip is a coiled and bound rush, straw or reed hive, placed on a wooden stand — a bench or table. They look like upside-down rush baskets with a hole in the side. **$150-$200**

Cookie mold, bird on branch, carved granite, two-sided, with flowers & monogram on other side, very rare, 4" x 6-1/2", early 19th C. Folk art collectors find stone carvings very desirable. **$250-$350**

Cookie mold, bird on branch with 5 stars, oval, cast iron, no handles, possibly a wafer mold: at least it could make thin wafer like "cookies." 5" x 3-1/2" oval, mid 19th C. Molds meant for cookies, without the reins or long handles of wafer molds, and resembling secular wafer molds in their designs, were made by foundries in NY state and probably elsewhere. Iron collector Joel Schiff terms these "'press & roll-over molds,' to distinguish them from cookie/biscuit/muffin pan molds. Old ones (often from England) were frequently large, very smooth and with classical motifs such as the pineapple, the Odd-Fellows chain links, Greek urns & lyres, basket of flowers, and bird-on-a-branch." **$150-$250**

Date by State, or Star-gazing. The look of the piece above is c.1840s to 1860s. But if you use a star chart as it relates to each state entering the Republic, it could mean this dated to 1788, when the 5th state (Connecticut) through the 11th state joined the union.

Cookie mold, butterfly, flat cast iron oval, Albany, NY, 5-1/2" L, early 19th C., and an extremely unusual motif. **$200-$275**

IV-169. Cookie mold. *Cast iron, oval, intaglio impression of what may be Christmas holly in a basket. Casting gate on back is mostly ground down. 5-7/8" L x 4" W x 1/4" deep. Possibly Albany or Troy, NY, 19th C.* **$150-$200**

IV-170. Cookie or marchpane molds. *"Marchpane" is the English equivalent of marzipan. Cast iron, elliptical or oval intaglio designs. Upper (L) Unusual design of boy with pipe in his mouth, sitting on chamber pot. 3-1/2" x 6". Border design of dots. The author's version is quite similar, though 1/4" smaller, and the child has no pipe. Mary Mac Franklin mused whether or not these molds might have been used for making sweet rewards for successful toilet training — the pipe version for a boy. This is probably the oldest of the three, and appears to be c.1840. (T-R) Songbird on branch, dotted elliptical border. 3-1/4" x 5-1/4". (B-R) Cornucopia, grapes, dot border, 5-3/4" x 4-1/4". Photo courtesy Litchfield Auction Gallery. Ex-Harold Corbin Collection. Auctioned 1/1/1990, $275; $170; $185. Now:* **$250-$350; $150-$250; $150-$250**

Cookie mold, cornucopia, cast iron, rounded oval, central cornucopia holding melon, pineapple, grapes, fat leaves spilling out, 2 star-like X marks, border entirely made up of small dots, rather close together, perhaps done by a stove foundry, looks like casting from Troy or Albany, NY, 4" L, c.1840s. **$125-$150**

Cookie mold, lyre, cast iron, oval, gritty silvery look to iron which indicates it is probably a modern cheap reproduction, American (?), 5-1/4" L. If old, mid 19th C; if new prob. mid 20th C, and worth under $10. **$50-$65**

Cookie mold, Odd Fellows, cast iron, oval with hanging hole, Odd Fellows symbols: 3 chain links (friendship, love & truth), hatchet, fireman's pike, 3 columns or pillars, hand with heart in palm, crossed swords, bow & arrow, American, 6-13/16" L x 5" W, 19th C. This thing looks like a firemark, but if it were it would have more than one hole, as it would have to be screwed or bolted to a building wall. For more information on Odd Fellows, see the paragraph regarding Fraternal Order motifs, in with the butter mold listings. **Reproduction alert**. There is evidence these are being reproduced. You've got to get to know what old cast iron and new cast iron look like. Remember, most new cast iron is not made with virgin ore but from all kinds of scrap iron, including whole engine blocks with other metals involved. Graininess, relatively light weight, slightly blurred details, somewhat lighter metal color and no patina are signals of newness. **$175-$300**

Cookie mold, Odd Fellows, cast iron, rounded oval, I.O.O.F. symbols almost the same as the other one, 3 linked chain, bow & 2 arrows, crossed swords, heart in palm of hand, and 3 pillars, no hanging hole. American, 6" L x 4-1/2" W, 19th C. **$175-$300**

Cookie mold, pineapple, cast iron, oval, Albany Foundry Co. (?), Albany, NY, 6" L x 4-1/2", looks much earlier in 19th C. than this company, which was est. in 1897. Turn-of-century dealer Thurnauer lists seven rectangular or square molds, five oval ones and three rounds. I wonder if the oval ones are the cast iron ovals with single designs seen in such quantity at antique shows in late 1980s. See also springerle mold. **$150-$200**

Cookie mold, pineapple, cast iron, oval, gritty silvery look to iron which indicates it's probably a modern cheap reproduction, American (?), 6" L, if old, mid 19th C; if new prob. mid 20th C. **Reproduction alert**. A very rounded oval pineapple mold, cast iron with enough matt black paint finish to hide any gritty surface (if it exists) front & back, is marked on the back with a permanent molded identification. In a small oval are initials "OSV" surrounded by words "Old Sturbridge Village," plus another mark with illegible numbers or letters, plus numbers

"5-50." This mold has a fairly large hole all the way through near the top for hanging. It is probably cast from a mold made from an original in their collection. If you've never been to Old Sturbridge in Massachusetts, do go; it's a wonderful place. And you could always "do Brimfield" before or after, as it's just a few miles away. **$50-$65**

Cookie mold, urn, cast iron, rectangular, intaglio design of neo-classical Greek urn with flowers; assumed to be NY state, but not marked. 4" x 2-3/4", mid 19th C (?). **$150-$175**

Cookie mold, bear, glazed redware, large bear with fur, claws & teeth all delineated, American, 3" x 5", early 19th C. **$300-$450**

Cookie mold, oblong tin mold, with 3 clamps along top, in section it is the shape of a spade (as in cards), and is for making icebox cookies, the dough of which was chilled then sliced. Heart-, club- and diamond-shaped molds were made too. This kind of metal mold was usually lined with paper (antique cookbooks say letter paper or parchment), to make removal easier. American, about 12" L x 2" across, 1930s. **$15-$30**

"Sliced or Icebox Cookies." These cookies cannot be mixed and baked immediately because they require thorough chilling in the refrigerator. Their great advantage for the small family which likes its cookies fresh is that the dough can be kept on hand and the cookies sliced and baked as needed. It is because the dough can be used over a period of a week or more that we suggest a fairly large recipe even for the small family. Icebox cookies are always of the crisp, buttery type. Marjorie Hesel'tine and Ula M. Dow, *Good Cooking Made Easy and Economical.* Boston: Houghton Mifflin, 1933.

Cookie mold, or **marchpane mold,** or even springerle mold. Good old cast iron, elliptical shape with a narrow channel around outside, plus 20 round concave dimples framing unusual subject — child on footed chamberpot or thundermug with handle, child has small pointy feet, almost look like boots with little heels, finely modeled, iron is right: very smooth & silky to feel, finely grained, no marks, prob. American, prob. NY state, maybe Troy or Albany: stove foundry towns. 5-3/4" L x 3-3/8" W x 1/2" deep, from look of child and chamberpot, I believe c.1840s-1850s. Most of these molds that are truly old and not grainy gray repros, may have come, as popular supposition has it, from New York State, possibly an Albany foundry, or even The Albany Foundry Co.

IV-171. Cookie or marchpane molds. *Swan in a circle, surrounded by dots, on oval mold, 4-3/4" x 5-3/4"; pineapple in Pennsylvania German style, though probably New York State. 6" x 4-1/2"; and oval with acorn and leaves, 4" x 5-3/4", the last being the thickest of all six molds auctioned. Mid 19th C. Photo courtesy Litchfield Auction Gallery. Ex-Harold Corbin Collection. Auctioned 1/1/1990, for $180; $85; $160. Now:* **$150-$250**

IV-172. Cookie mold. *Round, deeply carved mason's tools carved in wood, including a hammer, mallet, chisel, and sqaure. Also initials "I. D." 5-1/2" diameter x 7/8" thick. Dealer thought it might be a butter mold instead. I disagree.* **$150-$250**

(in existence only from 1897-1932), though late 19th C. or early 20th seems very late. This mold found by dealer Ed Boeyink, of Hilton, NY, in Eastern New York, between Albany and Syracuse, in a long-held private collection. **$200-$300**

"Butterscotch Cookies." (45 to 60 Cookies.) 3-1/2 cups flour. 3 teaspoons baking powder. 1 cup butter or other fat. 2 cups brown sugar. 2 eggs. 2 teaspoons vanilla. 1 to 1-1/2 cups chopped nuts. — Sift the flour and baking powder together. Cream the fat; stir in the sugar gradually; add the unbeaten eggs one at a time; add the vanilla; mix well; stir in the dry ingredients. The mixture will be a stiff dough.

"The cookies may be shaped in several ways as follows: (a) In butter cartons. Stand 1 pound butter cartons on end and pack the mixture firmly into the corners. (b) In a cracker box. Waxed fiber boxes need no lining; tin boxes should be lined with heavy waxed paper with the ends extending beyond the edge of the box. Pack the dough firmly into the box. (c) With floured hands shape the dough into rolls about 2 inches in diameter, wrap the rolls in heavy waxed paper, twisting the ends. The roll will settle to an elliptical shape on standing.

"Place the molded dough in an efficient refrigerator for several hours or until it is very hard. Remove the chilled dough from its wrappings; place on a molding board covered with heavy waxed paper; cut into slices about 1/8 inch thick. Place on a baking sheet (greasing is not necessary because of the large quantity of fat in the dough); bake on the top shelf in a moderate oven (375° F.) for 10 to 15 minutes." Marjorie Heseltine & Ula M. Dow, *Good Cooking Made Easy and Economical*. Boston: Houghton Mifflin, 1933.

Cookie mold, or possibly for something else, rough, crude light-colored fired clay, design is spreadwing eagle standing on something, slightly undercut, so how would it work as mold? Was the undercut effect the result of the edges slightly sagging or collapsing when the well-carved wood or perhaps cast metal stamp was withdrawn after being pushed into clay? Or perhaps it sagged during firing? Anything put in it for molding would have to withdraw from the sides of the deeply molded design in order to come out; found in home in Southern Ohio, 5/8" thick x 3-1/2" H x 4" W, c.1830s to 1850s (?). **$150-$200**

Cookie mold pan, cast aluminum, very light color & bright, 18 cups with 9 tulips & 9 scalloped rounds, Wilton Enterprises, Woo-

dridge, IL, 1980s. *The Wilton Cookie Maker Fancy Cookies* booklet, 1984, Wilton Enterprises, Inc., includes several catalog pages of aluminum baking pans, plastic cookie cutters, tartlet molds, cookie racks & sheets, icing & pastry bags & tips, mini muffin pans, & at least 6 cookie mold pans, 5 have 18 cups, one has 16, for Viennese, Bavarian, Marseilles (16 cups), Barcelona, Venetian & Parisian cookies. The catalog is worth as much as the pan. **$12-$18**

Cookie or jumble press, or butter press, or pastry tube, pieced tin, wing like side handles, nicely buttressed, turned wooden plunger with nicely flared out top, 5 plates to insert in business end, to create cookies in different shapes, from a half moon to a 10-point star, European (?), c.1870s. **$50-$65**

Cookie press, fat metal cylinder with plunger, & set of 6 cutout metal inserts to form everything from stars & flowers to corrugated rounds, made by icing decorator people, Ateco, The Thompsen Co., NYC, NY, c.1940. **$45-$65**

Cookie press, tin cylinder with wood plunger with 2 little side handles, also called a pastry tube or syringe, 19th C. **$45-$60**

Cookie press, tin tube, wood plunger but no handles, American, 12" L, early 20th C. **$20-$30**

IV-174. Cookie press or "Cake dropping machine." *A little metal stand with bag. Spring action. Came with various inserts to make all the different jumbles and cookies shown. Jaburg, 1908.* **$25-$45**

IV-173. Jumble machines, *or* **jumble syringes** *for making the cookies known as jumbles, which William Woys Weaver describes as "any kind of cookie twisted into rings, knots, or even bows." (T) Syringe in four sizes, with 2, 3 or 4 insert discs. Jaburg, 1908. (B) Pieced tin, wood plunger, various fancy-holed inserts. F. A. Walker import catalog, c.1870s. This style of jumble press required both hands (to hold the side handles) and a belly to push it against (which was achieved by eating jumbles).* **$25-$65**

IV-175. Syringes for cake dough & garnishes. (L) *A "Queenspritze," for cake dough. Crank action, 12 inserts. 14" L x 3-1/2" diameter.* **(R)** *A "Garnierspritze," only 3-7/8" L, and could be worked with one hand (the thumb pushing the plunger). Bertuch, c.1904.* **$25-$40**

"Jumballs. 8 oz. of Jordan almonds, 2 lb. 8 oz. of searched [sierced, sieved] sugar, about two whites of eggs. — Blanch and beat the almonds until there is not any particle of the almond to be seen; then rub in with the pestle two pounds of the sugar with whites of eggs; beat them well until smooth; that done, divide the paste into three parts, one for white, one pink, and the other yellow. The pink must be coloured with the best lake finely ground; and the yellow with strong prepared saffron; stiffen each with part of the sugar left; then put them through a jumball mould; and make them into rings about the size of a dollar. Lay them on dry paper, and bake them in a very slow oven. N.B. A jumball mould should be made of brass, in the shape of a butter squirt, with a star at the end, half an inch in diameter." Joseph Bell, *A Treatise on Confectionary*, Newcastle, England, 1817. [**Lake is lac**, the same red resinous secrection of the tiny scale insects <u>lacs</u> that's used to make lacquer.]

Corn bread skillet, cast iron, frying pan shape with short handle & teardrop hanging hole, cast with 8 dividing ridges to create 8 wedges, hole in center, mfd. by Lodge, South Pittsburgh, TN, 1" deep x 9" diameter, late 20th C. **Old Ones Too.** This type of corn bread mold has been made since about 1950. New versions have a hole in the center of the pan. Lehman's Hardware & Appliances, 4779 Kidron Rd., Kidron, OH 44636, offers the above-described mold pan in their "Non-Electric Good Neighbor Amish Country" catalog. Value range below includes the $12+ cost of the new one and assumes unmarked antique ones. Marked iron seems always to bring more than unmarked because a brand name means safe, if impersonal, investment.　　**$30-$35**

Corn bread skillet, cast iron, sectioned in wedges, marked "Corn Bread Skillet" on back, American, 9-1/8" diameter, 20th C.　　**$30-$35**

Corn or wheat stick pan, cast iron, 7 sticks with well-formed kernels, "Best Made Wheat & Corn Stick Pan, No. 1270," marked "S. R. & Co." (Sears, Roebuck, but mfd. by Griswold). 13-1/8" L x 5-5/8" W, 1927 design patent #73326.　　**$100-$125**

Corn or wheat stick pan, cast iron, wheat pattern, Griswold #282, Erie, PA, 20th C. (The Griswold #2800 corn stick pan is valued by collectors at around $1000-$2000!) The #282: **$200-$250**

Corn stick mold, gray graniteware, 5 cobs, American, early 20th C.　　**$85-$135**

Corn stick pan, cast aluminum, Wagner Ware, Sidney, OH, pat'd 1920.　　**$25-$45**

Corn stick pan, cast aluminum, "Krusty Korn Kobs," Wagner Ware, tea size, 7-1/8" L x 4-1/8" W, mid 20th C.　　**$25-$45**

Corn stick pan, cast aluminum, 7 ears alternating direction. The way they are patterned, with slight irregularities, I'm sure the original casting molds were real ears, probably of hard seed corn, Mullins Non-Ferrous Castings Corp., St. Louis, MO, 20th C.　　**$20-$25**

Corn stick pan, cast aluminum, odd cob-shaped cups but no kernels, just 3 long ridges in each cob cup, makes 7 sticks, medallion on back with "Wearever, No. 22---," "Made in U.S.A.," 13" L x 5-1/2" W, 20th C.　　**$15-$20**

IV-176. Corn cake or roll pan. *Called a* **"Russia Iron Roll**, *or corn cake pan.* — *Gives a handsome brown soft under-crust." Russia iron is heavy sheet iron, not cast iron. This appeared as a kitchen necessity in* American Home Cook Book, *1854.* **$50-$75**

Corn stick pan, cast iron, "Krispy Korn Mold," mfd. by Wagner, Sidney, OH, 7-1/8" L x 4-1/8" W <u>tea size</u>, very dainty tiny ears only 4-1/2" L x 1" W, 20th C.　　**$65-$95**

Corn stick pan, cast iron, Wagner Ware, Sidney, OH, 3 sizes: (1) <u>Tea</u> size, 7-1/8" L x 4-1/8" W; (2) <u>Senior</u> size, 13-3/4" L x 6-7/8" W; and (3) <u>Junior</u> size, 11-5/8" L x 5-7/8" W. 1920s.　　(1) **$65-$95**; (2) **$125-$150**; (3) **$45-$65**

Corn stick pan, cast iron, 5 ornate cobs with curly silk tassels at ends & scrolly husks, in wide bordered rectangular frame with fancy scroll handle at each end, stamped "John Wright" on back, with button affixed to one handle reading "Classic Gourmet," Wrightsville, PA, ©1984. **Reproduction alert**. Only one of the corn stick pans I've seen has retained the tiny white porcelain button on the front, affixed to one handle, that says "Classic Gourmet." And most have been badly (and deliberately) rusted. I saw one for $82, which is ridiculous at least until 2097! These are still being made — now without the button, making identification for new collectors even more difficult. Now for buttoned pans: **$35-$45**; unbuttoned newer: **$10-$15.**

Corn stick pan, cast iron, 7 alternating well-modeled corn cobs, in original lithographed box (sometimes found with wraparound cardboard label instead), "Junior Krusty Korn Kobs, #1319," (I've seen this reported as #1319D), Wagner Ware, Sidney, OH. Junior size is 11-5/8" L x 5-7/8" W, pat'd July 6, 1920, but made for many years.　　**$45-$65**

Corn stick pan, cast iron, 7 sticks all going same direction, Griswold "Crispy Corn #273" Erie, PA, 14" L x 7-5/8" W, 20th C.　　**$55-$65**

Corn stick pan, cast iron, 7 cobs facing same way, Griswold "Krispy Cornorwheat Stick Pan #262," also marked "825" and "13," Erie, PA, 8-1/2" L x 4-1/8" W, 1927 design patent #73326, made for many years.　　**$70-$85**

Reproduction alert. The #262 pan above has been reproduced fairly recently. **Lookalike alarm.** Lehman's Hardware & Appliances, 4779 Kidron Rd., Kidron, OH 44636, offer legitimate (not repro) cast iron 7-stick & 9-stick pans in their "Non-Electric Good Neighbor Amish Country" catalog. All sticks point same direction. Lehman's say that all their cast iron pieces, except a griddle that's the "Atlanta" brand, are "individually sand cast and finished by hand. All are produced in a family foundry — Lodge, in South Pittsburgh, TN — that dates back to 1896." The Lynchburg Hardware & General Store, Lynchburg, TN, the home of Jack Daniels, sells the same 7-stick Lodge pan. They say Lodge has been in business since 1872.

IV-177. Corn stick pans. (L) *Cast iron, "Griswold Krispy cornorwheat Stick Pan #262," Erie, PA. 8-1/2" L x 4-1/8" W. Makes 7 one-way sticks.* **(R)** *Molded heavy glass, Wagner Ware. 13" L x 6" W. Makes 7 which-a-way sticks. Which makes me wonder out loud, why did muffin and roll pans always make odd numbers? For luck? Collection of Meryle Evans.* **$22-$35; $55-$65**

Corn stick pan, cast iron, 7 well-defined head-to-toe ears, Griswold "Krispy CornorWheat Stick Pan, No. 270," also marked "#636," Erie, PA, 13-1/8" L x 5-5/8" W, 1927 design patent #73,326. **$250-$300**

Corn stick pan, cast iron, 7 well-defined head-to-toe ears, Griswold "Krispy CornorWheat Stick Pan, No. 280," with same patent as #270. 14" L x 7 5/8" W, c. 1927+. **$600-$800**

Corn stick pan, cast iron, 7 head-to-toe cobs, in original printed cardboard sleeve, advertising blurb reads: "Corn Cake Pan, Griswold Early American Quality Cast Iron. There's nothing like iron to cook in. By the makers of Griswold famous cast iron skillets. For almost 100 years, Americans have known Griswold." Griswold Mfg. Co., Erie, PA, this one c.1953. (Only $3.50 bought a new one in 1973.) **$55-$65**

Corn stick pan (only part of a corn dog maker & sausage grill), cast iron, hinged, wire handles, makes 2 full cobs, Wagner Ware, closed it is 15" L including handles x 6" W, makes approx. 1-3/4" x 5-1/2" L cobs, early 20th C. If this were complete with collar, base, grill & mold, it'd be $250-$350. But as is, only **$125-$175.**

Corn stick pan (only part of a corn dog maker & sausage grill), cast iron, hinged, wire handles, makes 4 full cobs, Wagner Ware, closed it is 20" L including handle x 12" W, finished breads approximately 5-1/2" x 1-3/4", early 20th C. If this were complete with collar, base, grill & mold, it'd be $350-$690. But as is, only **$125-$175.**

Corn stick pan, heavy molded glass, 7 cobs alternate directions, Wagner Ware, 13" L x 6" W, according to collector Jim Holroyd, between 1942 & 1947. This is obviously because of WWII and the metal drives. It's probably safe to assume most of the glass ones date to the same period. **$40-$65**

Corn stick pan, molded glass, "Beauty Bake," 20th C. **$15-$20**

IV-178. Corn dog baker. *"Krusty Korn Dog" baker, also sandwich toaster (grill) or steak fryer. "A big money maker! For use on gas, gasoline, oil or coal stoves. 'Krusty Korn Dogs' are novel and delicious. The hot dog is baked inside the corn batter, which as it bakes, moulds itself to resemble an ear of corn 6-3/8" L and 1-1/2" diameter. Easy to make: Red hots are first fried in butter, then placed in 'korn dog' sections together with required amount of batter, they are then quickly and thoroughly baked together. Baker is made of cast iron, smooth japanned finish, with heavy, sturdy wire coil pan handles. Heavy lifting handles at each end." Frame is 2-1/2" H x 10-1/4" x 21-1/4"; fryer pan (R) is 3/4" deep x 8-1/2" x 8-3/8". You bought the frame, and a fry pan (griddle), and a pair of the "Krusty Korn Sausage Dog Pans," each of which made two, separately to suit your business. In Pick-Barth wholesale catalog of many makers' hotel and restaurant supplies, 1929. See also IV-367. For the whole set-up:* **$550-$690**

Corn stick pan, molded glass, 6 ears, half of each ear made up of gracefully pulled back husk, "Miracle Maize," American, 12" L x 6-1/4" W, "Pat. Pend.," 20th C. See also wheat bread mold. **$35-$55**

Corn stick pan, chrome-plated cast iron, 7 cobs all same direction, Griswold "Crispy Corn Stick Pan," "No. 283," and at bottom, "931," 1930s. **$150-$200**

Corn stick pan, **poor reproduction**, cheap cast iron, 7 cobs all pointing same way, each letter of misspelled words on back impressed separately in the casting mold, marked "No. 252 CRISWOLD CRISPY CORNORWHEAT SNICK PAN" also "625," and address "ERIE PA USA," but made in Taiwan, 8" L x 4" W, 1980s (?). I was fortunate to see one with its original tiny gummy gold & black sticker on the front, reading "W. E. RHYNE CO., Made in TAIWAN." You would buy one of these only for your study collection. **$2-$4**

Corn stick pan — See also wheat bread mold pan

Cracker pricker, fat wooden knob with 12 iron pins or "nails," American (?), 4-1/4" H x 2" D, 19th C. **$45-$55**

Cracker pricker, or biscuit prick, carved wood, one-piece palm-fitting knob and rather elongated body, 7 thick pins or nails, American (?), 5" H, 19th C. These were necessary for soda crackers or biscuits & for beaten biscuits to prevent huge blisters or air pockets forming during baking. **$65-$95**

Cracker pricker, or biscuit prick, double-ended, fairly intricately carved body, with simple geometric designs, and the two heads have pricks carved from the wood in two different designs & lengths, 7-1/2" L, c. 1870s. **$75-$100**

Cracker pricker & cutter, cast iron, spring steel with wooden block that has little 2-pronged prickers stuck in it. Spring-loaded action, fat palm-fitting handle, it not only cuts out square crackers but makes the pricked marks in them essential to their success. Without the little holes, the soda crackers would swell up and be big fat pillows, instead of pleasingly tufted. American, made crackers just shy of 2" square, marked "Pat'd Dec. 13." Tuesday, patent-granting day, fell on Dec. 13 only 3 times in the possible time frame — 1864, 1892 and 1904. My patent subject index goes only to 1873, and it is not in that, so although the appearance is 1870s, I go with 1892. Now somebody else can do the rest of the legwork. **$30-$45**

Cracker pricker & stamp, carved wood, 3 nails to punch holes through cracker, depicts marvelous burning house with raging flames, house has big gothic window with tiny leaded panes, English, 1-9/16" x 1-1/4", c.1820-1830s. **$450-$600**

"**Crackers**. Take a large cupful of bread dough; roll out on the molding-board; spread on it a piece of butter and lard together, as large as a goose-egg; sprinkle a little flour over it; fold it up, and pound with something heavy a long time; take a small piece at a time; roll out very thin; stamp with a clock key, and bake very quickly." Henry Scammel, compiler, *Treasure House of Universal Knowledge*, 1891. (**NOTE:** In some turn of the century American cookbooks, the word "wafer" is used, to be served after dinner and before dessert, with cheese. I suspect the "wafers" are crackers.)

Cracker pricker & stamp, wood with many prickers & cast lead letters, commercial type, late 19th C. **$100-$140**

Cracker roller, wood, handles, corrugated drum or barrel, with corrugations going around the circumference of the drum, used to crumb crackers. 11" L, late 19th or early 20th C. Also used to crumb dry bread. See also rolling pins, wood. **$35-$45**

Cracker stamp, carved wood basket of flowers, English, 1-3/4" x 1-1/4", c.1840s. **$200-$300**

Cracker stamp, carved wood depicting sheep, 6 pricker nails, cracker name "INNOCENCE," religious symbolism for some kind of ceremony? English, 1-3/4" x 1-3/8", c.1840s. **$350-$400**

Cracker stamp, carved wood, double arched top like 2 tombstones, name of cracker "VICTORIA," English, 2" across. From appearance, it dates from Queen Victoria's 1837 ascendency as late as the 1860s or so. **$250-$300**

Cracker stamp, carved wood, looks like a dumbbell or a doggie bone, English (?), 1-7/8" across, mid 19th C. **$250-$300**

Cracker stamp, carved wood, makes 6-point star plus many pricker holes, American or English (?), 2-3/4" diameter, 19th C. **$150-$200**

Cracker stamp, wood carved with rose & thistle, name of cracker carved too: "UNION," from Great Britain — the rose signifying England, the thistle Scotland, 1-7/8" x 1-3/16", early 19th C. **$200-$300**

Crimper, cast aluminum, wooden handle, "Dandy," American, 6" L, pat'd April 22, 1925. **$15-$22**

Crimper, stamped aluminum, "Juice Tite Pie Sealer," 5-1/2" L, 20th C. **$15-$22**

Crimper or pie sealer, aluminum, "Just-Rite," Minneapolis, MN (?), 20th C. **$10-$15**

Crimper or pie sealer, brass & wood, no mark, American, early 20th, late 19th C. **$12-$15**

Crimper, turned wood handle in unvarnished pale wood, blue & white Meissen wheel, Dutch (?), late 19th C. **$85-$115**

Crimper, turned wooden handle, brass ferrule, wire axle with wide corrugated wooden roller wheel, American, turn of century. **$30-$40**

Crimper & trimmer, cast aluminum, relatively large wheel with corrugations & cutting edge, short pointed handle with large hanging loop, "Ateco," mfd. by August Thompsen & Co., NYC, NY, c.1920s. **$15-$22**

Crimper & trimmer, aluminum sealer, plastic cutting wheel, wood handle, "Dual Purpose," American, 20th C. **$15-$18**

Crimper & trimmer, big brass wheel, black molded phenolic resin handle, steel shaft, American, 20th C. **$20-$25**

Crimper & trimmer, nickel-plated shank, red wood handle, ingeniously stamped aluminum wheel, "Vaughn's Pie Trimmer & Sealer," Chicago, IL, 5-1/2" L, pat'd May 10, 1921; this one prob. c. 1940s. **$10-$13**

Crimper & trimmer, tin, wire, corrugated wide wheel, "The Ideal," mfr. unknown, American, marked pat'd March 10, 1908. **$10-$18**

Crimper & trimmer, cast aluminum, would trim as it corrugated the pie's edges to seal the top crust to the bottom one, no mark, American (?), 4-3/4" L, 1920s or 1930s. The ridged or corrugated edge of the pie, after being crimped, is what gives the name **piecrust edge** to quite a large number of butter stamps. On the other hand, a piecrust table, in furniture talk, is one with the kind of riffled edge given to a pie edge by pinching with the fingers & thumb. **$8-$15**

Crimper & grater & cutter combined, tin, tinned steel, wooden crust crimper wheel at one end, middle part punctured for grating nutmegs, probably, fatly pointed tip used to trim off excess dough around edge & to slash steam slits in top crust, American, 6-7/8" L, late 19th C. **$25-$30**

Crimper or sealer, turned varnished wooden handle, chrome-plated or stainless steel metal bracket and wheel, which has double tread design, for making fancy "tea and open sandwiches, delicious canapes for your luncheons, teas, and meetings . . . helps make turnovers, ravioli, pierogi, kreplach, strudel, dumplings. Free recipes furnished." "Krimpkut Sealer," mfr unknown, adv'd by Gemini House, Buffalo, NY, 1968 ad. Originally this tool, guaranteed to make you a "Sandwich Queen," cost only $2.15 ppd. **$2-$5**

Crimpers — See also jaggers. Some are combined jaggers (which cut) and crimpers (which squished & seal edges). Pictures are further on with jaggers.

Croquette mold — See molds, in tin mold listings

Cutlet molds — See molds, in tin mold listings

Dariel mold — See molds section, in tin mold listings

Dough board — See pastry board

Dough scraper, forged or wrought iron, short hollow socket handle, to be fitted with jammed-on wooden longer handle, American (?), early 19th C. **$70-$100**

Forged or Wrought? The terms mean fundamentally the same thing: both apply to objects that are worked (or wrought) at a forge. Because the usual understanding of wrought is of something iron, black and turned in scrolls, like a wrought iron fence or wrought iron lampstand, I prefer "forged." It is not enough to describe something as "handwrought," because the metal must be specified. Copper, pewter, silver, aluminum: all can be handwrought.

● ● ● ●

Whitesmithed. A whitesmith worked iron past the point that most blacksmiths worked it — they beat the black out of it, so to speak, making a silvery "white" metal from the forged iron.

IV-180. Dough scraper. *Wrought iron, polished and worked by a whitesmith to take on appearance of steel. Socket handle. About 3-3/4" L overall x 3" W. Early to mid 19th C. Not an uncommon type, and very simple. Collection of Mary Mac Franklin.* **$55-$70**

IV-179. Cutlet cutters & mold. *Two punctuation marks-like cutters, pieced tin, from F. A. Walker catalog, 1870s. I don't know if they had a flatback. Two sizes, probably about 4" and 6" L. Bottom one is a mold, in same catalog as the heart mold in with heart cookie cutters. Tin, 4" x 2-1/4". The top ones might be used to cut shapes from whole, as opposed to ground meat.* **$12-$20**

Dough scraper, brass blade, tapered tubular handle made of tin, capped with brass, copper rivets, very small, marked "J. B.," probably mid 19th C, and one of the most unusual I've ever seen. **$125-$180**

Dough scraper, cast & forged steel, simple blade, American, blade 3-3/4" L x 3" W, handle 4" L, mid 19th C. **$75-$100**

Dough scraper, forged iron, punchtooled maker's or recipient's initials, "H. B.," American (?), 4-1/2" L, early to mid 19th C. **$125-$185**

Dough scraper, forged iron, looks like small hoe with very short handle, mid 19th C. **$50-$70**

Dough scraper, forged iron, like a hoe but with a hollow handle socket, for a wooden handle of whatever length that was useful to the cook who owned it, and easily replaced by the cook. American, 19th C. **$65-$80**

Dough scraper, forged iron, skinny handle with twist at end, long-ish blade, American, 6-1/2" L, mid 19th C. **$30-$40**

Dough scraper, forged iron, thick solid handle set at angle, American, mid 19th C. **$45-$60**

Dough scraper, forged iron, whitesmithed & polished, PA, blade is 4-3/4" W, dated 1840. Ex-Robacker, $275. **$250-$325**

Dough scraper, forged iron, wooden handle & brass ferrule, American (?), very early 19th C. **$60-$75**

Dough scraper, forged steel, heart cutout in blade near tang, comfortable handle, PA (?), early 19th C. **$115-$135**

Dough scraper, forged steel with tubular copper handle, 4-1/2" L, late 18th or up to mid 19th C. **$100-$125**

Dough scraper, forged, whitesmithed iron, the blade a sort of hillock shape, a rounded top triangle, with a tapered peg handle set (riveted?) at right angles to the blade, near the "crest" of the hill marked "P. D." (for Peter Derr, a very desirable maker), Berks County, PA, blade 3-1/4" W, dated "1854," each number stamped separately. **$475 - $550**

Dough scraper, iron blade with short stubby wooden handle, quite primitive, early 19th C. It's possible, I think, that this is actually a primitive mason's tool, used for pointing bricks. You have to ask yourself questions like that: Is this really what the sales tag says? Or could it more likely be a (fill in the blank)? **$50-$75**

Dough scraper, machined brass, very beautiful tubular handle with bands of turned decoration, signed "P. D." by maker Peter Derr, Berks County, PA, dated 1848. Others by Derr are known. Early one dated 1832 was for sale for $375 in 1984. **$475-$575**

IV-181. Dough scrapers. *Long-handled one is wrought brass and iron, about 12" L, with split & twisted cage handle, with three marbles inside. Drawn from story on a March 1990 Pook & Pook sale at Chester, PA.* **(B-L)** *One in foreground is drawn from one seen at Pennsylvania show, about 4-1/2" W. It was made from one wrought piece, the handle being bent back between the "ears" of the blade. One* **(T-R)** *is simple triangle with separate tapered tubular socket handle riveted through hole in blade. Also about 4" W. There is a higher value if signed.* **$900-$1200; $150-$250; $55-$70**

Dough scraper, polished forged iron, decorated with etched tulip, shaped & slightly curved iron handle, marked with initials "C L" on blade's front, could be maker or owner, Pennsylvania (?), blade 4-1/4" W, early to mid 19th C. Ex-Robacker, $500. **$375-$600**

Dough scraper, tin, truncated wedge-shaped blade with side edges turned, set at angle to pieced tapered tubular handle, PA, 5" L x 3" W, late 19th C. **$65-$95**

Dough scraper, triangle of steel for the blade, a separate steel handle riveted on, American, mid 19th C. **$55-$85**

Dough scraper, whitesmith's work, polished, planished worked iron, heart cutout, beautiful detailing on hollow tubular handle, cap knob on end, design comprised of cross-hatching with lines of tiny drilled holes, American (?), 4-1/8" W, prob. 1st or 2nd quarter 19th C. **$350-$450**

Dough scraper, or cake turner or short peel, forged iron, keyhole-shaped blade with punch stippled profile bust of smiling man with high arched eyebrows & standing bird, rattail handle, length of handle marked with a triple row of punched dots, Pennsylvania in appearance, 3-1/8" L overall, blade is 5-3/4" L, appears to be mid 19th C, but I think it's a mid 20th C fake. I suspect this only because it's too much for the money. A portrait bust? plus a bird? both done in unusual manner, with gorgeous keyhole shape & 1989 selling price of only $100? If real, value should be much higher, such as **$450-$600.**

Dough scraper & jagging wheel combined, some alloy metal, wheel-to-point is 4-1/8" L, pat'd May 10, 1921. **$18-$25**

Doughnut cutter, 2-part, with insert for cutting doughnuts, tin, "E-A Company Flour Always All Right," Waseca, Minnesota, 2-3/4" D, 20th C. **$15-$20**

Dunkin Oly Koeks. As long ago as 1809, in *History of New York*, Washington Irving described some tasty treats: "An enormous dish of balls of sweetened dough, fried in hog's fat, and called dough nuts, or *oly koeks*." [The latter is the Dutch term.] See also Ebelskiver pans.

Doughnut cutter, one piece of lathe-turned wood, seen from side it's like a short ninepin or beetle, hollowed inside to make a thin cutting edge plus the hole cutter, American, 4-1/2" L x 2-3/8" diameter, 19th C. The more patina and smoothness, the higher the value. **$25-$45**

Doughnut cutter, one piece of turned wood, marked "Pat. Mar. 26, 190-" (1901 or 1907 if the Mar. 26 part is correct.) **$50-$60**

Doughnut cutter, one piece of turned wood, knob handle, possibly mass-produced in the kind of craftsman factory where butter stamps were made, American (?), 19th C. **$70-$85**

Doughnut cutter, rolling or "rotating" type, with aluminum cutting blades with small tubes, for cutting 2 doughnuts in one revolution, twisted wire & turned wooden handle available in different colors. This was one of a set of 4 for making "cookies,

IV-182. Doughnut or cruller cutter, *top and underneath view. Fluted or crimped & pieced tin, strap handle, pat'd 10/15/1889. Matches a similar biscuit cutter. From F. A. Walker catalog, c.1890.* **$15-$20**

210

doughnuts, rolls, scones and tarts." From editorial copy in *House Furnishing Review*, Jan. 1930, we learn about "rotating cutters having detachable blade for cleaning and edges flanged at a varying pitch so that the cutting edge cuts vertically, straight through the dough, leaving no dough sticking to the blades," and also the advice that the doughnut "Item [is] somewhat seasonal. Best buying months are February, March, April, September, October and November," and finally, "Six foot counter space is sufficient for demonstration." "Rollemout," by The American Cutter Co., Milwaukee, WI, being made at least by 1928. Price for one from set only: **$15-$22**

Doughnut cutter, shiny tin, strap handle, American, 1920s-1940s. **$4-$8**

Doughnut cutter, stainless steel with wood T-handle, "The Saturn," 1930s. **$10-$15**

Doughnut cutter, tin, fluted sides with strap handle, center hole cutter soldered on, handle soldered on, but main body is stamped, American, 3-1/2" diameter, pat'd Oct. 1, 1889. **$10-$15**

Doughnut cutter, tin, long cylindrical handle, closed on end, marked "Rumford," 3-7/8" H x 2-1/2" diameter, turn of century. **$18-$22**

Doughnut cutter, tin, strap handle, doughnut holer cylinder has 3 struts holding it to outside cylinder, mfd. by Fries, 3" H overall, cutting part 1-1/2" H x 3" diameter, early 20th C, poss. late 19th. **$15-$25**

IV-183. Doughnut cutters. *Clockwise, from top.* **(T-L)** *Tin, strap handle, deep cutting, no top, one size only, 3" diameter. Marked "Fries." From Sexton Stove & Mfg. catalog, c.1930.* **(T-C)** *Next is heavy tin one with rounded palm-fitting top, deep cutter, for bakeries. 3". Pick-Barth catalog, 1929.* **(R)** *combination cookie and doughnut cutter, with detachable center cutter. Aluminum, white painted wooden handle, 3" H overall x 2-3/4" diameter. "Mirro," Aluminum Goods Mfg., 1927.* **(B)** *the solid back tin one, either 3" or 3-1/2" diameter. Geuder, Paeschke & Frey, 1925.* **$8-$22**

IV-184. Ebelskiver or aebelskiver pan. *Also called a* **muffin pan,** *or an* **egg cooker,** *but really for ebelskivers, which are apple-chip pancakes. Cast iron, Griswold No. 32, #962, Erie, PA. Seven cups, 1-3/4" H x 9-1/4" diameter, with 4-3/4" L handle. Cups are 1-1/4" deep.* **$35-$60**

Doughnut cutter, tin, strap handle with center ridge for strength, edges folded over, one strap goes straight across as strut for the cylindrical hole cutter, American, 1-1/8" diameter, late 19th or early 20th C. **$15-$22**

Doughnut cutter & apple corer combined, tin, strap handle, the separate corer is removed from cutter's "hole" for use in making doughnuts, American, 3-7/8" L x 3" diameter, turn of century. **$15-$22**

Doughnut cutter & cookie cutter combined — See cookie cutter & doughnut cutter combined

Doughnut mold, hinged cast iron, long handles with wooden grips, looks like 3-leaf clover to make 3 doughnuts, used by filling then holding in boiling fat, "Ace Cloverleaf Donut," Ace Co., St. Louis, MO, 20th C. **$55-$75**

Ebelskiver or ebelskiver pans are of Scandinavian origin, at least in name. They are cast iron, round with a relatively short frying-pan-type handle, and have seven ball-like cups (I've never seen one with more or fewer cups). They are also called "muffin molds," "egg poachers," "apple pancake pans," "Danish cake pans," and "*olie-koeck* pans" (for "fat cakes" or fritters). For the latter, I'm indepted to William Woys Weaver and his highly readable cookbooks that are full of social history. On page 69 of *The Christmas Cook* (Harper Perennial, 1990) he writes, "Several nineteenth-century foundries in this country sold an implement they called an *olie-koeck* pan. Many signed examples bear the names of J. M. B. Davidson and Shear, Packard & Company of Albany, New York, or Griswold of Erie, Pennsyulvania. This pan is the same as the egg and *Krapfen* pans made in Germany." *Ebelskivers* are apple pancake balls made with apple slivers and batter.

• • • •

Ebelskiver Recipe. According to Rebecca Wood, who wrote the wonderful cookbook *Quinoa the Supergrain: Ancient Food for Today*, here is the way to make these "apple sliver pancakes." You make a smooth batter like pancake batter (she adds cardamom), then heat the ebelskiver pan (she spells it ableskiver) over medium heat. "Thoroughly oil wells. Fill each well 5/8 full of batter and allow to cook for several minutes or just until the surface contacting the pan has browned. With a bamboo skewer (or knitting needle or nut pick), pierce and lift the cooked side up to a right angle. The batter pours out to form a second surface. When the new surface browns, turn again. A total of four turns produces a round and hollow ball." She adds a small slice of apple (or other fruit) before making first turn.

Ebelskiver pan, cast iron, reproduction or at least new production, 7 cannonball cups, side handle, flat on top including handle, rim of pan follows outline of cups, giving it a rounded hexagonal shape, Emig Products, Inc., (but I don't know if it is marked with their name), Reading, PA, roughly 7-1/2" diameter with 3-1/2" L handle, weighs 3-1/2 lbs, in 1966 catalog. Most if not all the **reproduction cast iron** is finished with flat black paint, but this could be distressed or removed. 1966 new price for the ebelskiver: $3.50. Realistic asking price now up to $20. **Collector Hint.** You can expect lots of reproduction pieces, not always identified as such, in booths where there are a lot of newly made "country" pieces, or wooden cutout (or cute-out) sheep or pigs, painted in pastels, with real ribbons. This dealer is really a decorator, not an antiques dealer, and is supplying a demand for a Look. If you want more than a Look, you may find a sleeper in with the new stuff. Conversely, you may be asked to pay too much, because you are buying a Look. **$15-$20**

IV-185. Ebelskiver pan or egg poacher. *Cast iron, 7 cups, no feet. Only mark is "8." 1-1/2" H x 9" diameter with 5-3/4" L handle. I like this one much better than the Griswold, especially its bottom. Courtesy Jean Hatt, Hatt's Hutt, Denver, PA.* **$45-$65**

IV-186. *Detail of Ebelskiver in* **IV-185.**

IV-187. Ancient egg poachers & basin. *Cast bronze reproductions of cookwares found at Pompeii, during excavations at different times in the 19th C. (The basin at right, with bas-relief decoration of swimmers, was excavated June 5, 1880.) Large pan at left is 29 cavities for eggs; and measures 19-1/8" in diameter. The long-handled square pan for four eggs measures 17-1/4" L. They were offered in the "Pompei or the Herculanum" finishes. J. Chiurazzi & Fils & S. De Angelis & Fils, Fonderie Artistiche Riunite, Naples, Italy. Catalog from 1910-11.*

IV-188. French pie or pâte molds. *All hinged, most relatively shallow compared to diameter.* **(A)** *German hinged mold, simple flutes, in 5 sizes, from 5-1/2" to 8" diameter.* **(B)** *Similar, with ring border, ranges from 5-1/2" to 8-3/4" diameter.* **(C)** *Another German one in 8 sizes, from 4-3/8" to 9-3/4" diameter. All Bertuch, Berlin, c.1904.* **(D)** *Oval "pie mold," planished tin. 11-1/2", 12" and 13-1/2" diameter. John Van Range Co., Cincinnati, 1914.* **(E)** *Round, herringbone design, two sizes. English, from Mrs. A. B. Marshall's Cookery Book, c.1887-1900.* **(F)** *"French Oval Meat Pie Mould. — Opens at one end." American Home Cook Book, 1854.* **(G)** *"French Pie Mould," hinged tin, clamp, five sizes: 7", 8", 9", 10" and 12" L. From F. A. Walker catalog, Boston, c.1870s. Walker imported many cookwares from France.* **(H)** *"Pot-Pie Mould," bright tin. Made in 12 round sizes, from 4" to 13-5/8" diameter, and in 11 ovals, from 5-1/2" L to 15-5/8" L. Imported by Duparquet, Huot & Moneuse, NYC, c.1904-1910.* **$25-$75**

IV-189. Ice cream cone fryer. *Cast & plated iron, wooden knob handle. "Batter: 1 lb. soft flour, 4 oz. confectioner's sugar, 3/4 pt. beaten eggs, 3/4 pt. milk. Mix flour, sugar and eggs with an egg beater very good, then add milk gradually. In meantime have your oil heated to 370° to 375°. Put your spring iron in the oil, allow to get hot; then dip the iron into the mixture, but don't let the mixture run over the iron. Then take the iron out and put in the heated oil; in a few seconds the cake [cone] is baked. Take out and give it a knock on a piece of wood to remove the cakes from the iron. Put the iron in the oil again for a few seconds. Knock the adhering oil off, and continue the same way as before. If mixture gets thick, add a little more milk and eggs. A nice showy cake which has a fine taste if eaten fresh, but it will be dry the next day." Pat'd 1903 or before. H. Hueg catalog, 1910.* **$125-$175**

Ebelskiver pan, also referred to as a "muffin mold" or an "egg poacher," with 7 round-bottomed cups set in frying-pan-like straight-sided frame with short handle, marked both "Griswold No. 32," and "962," Erie, PA, cups 1-1/4" deep, pan is 1-3/4" H x 9-1/4" diameter with 4-3/4" L handle, as early as c.1918 or as late as the 1960s. **$45-$60**

Ebelskiver pan, cast iron, 3 peg feet, 7 cups, eye ring in handle, prob. Scandinavian, 7-3/8" diameter, 11" L overall, mid 19th C (?). **$85-$125**

Ebelskiver pan, cast iron, 7 cups with resting rings, "Product of Norway," 20th C. **$28-$35**

Ebelskiver pan, cast iron, 7 straight-sided, flat-bottomed cups, squared-off rim so shape is hexagonal to pan, slightly raised edge, side handle that is also raised at angle. This is a **reproduction or lookalike** sold through Cumberland General Store catalog, foundry unknown to me, prob. American, 7" diameter, handle approx. 3-1/2" or 4" L, shipping weight 5 lbs, 1980s. Approximate price for new one: **$15-$20**

Ebelskiver pan, heavy cast aluminum, plastic handle, 7 cups, marked on back "Ebelskiver Pan" also "Apple Pancake Balls," Northland Aluminum Products, Inc., Minneapolis, MN, 9" diameter, 20th C. I think this is the one sold under the "Nordic Ware" trade name. **$20-$25**

Ebelskiver pan, cast iron, round with short frying pan handle, 7 cups, no feet, only mark is "8," 1-1/2" deep x 9" diameter x 5-3/4" L handle, 19th C. **$60-$75**

Ebelskiver pan or muffin pan, cast iron, 7 shallow flat-bottom cups, more like muffin pan, short frying pan handle with teardrop hanging hole, the bottom is the really great part: instead of being perfectly flat, it reveals the shape & position of each cup and has interesting hollows and negative spaces. Two molds were required to cast this — one for top side and one for underneath. That in itself is not so unusual, but the shapes of the cups underneath are. American (?), 9-1/4" diameter, 6-1/2" L handle, turn of century. **$40-$50**

Ebelskiver pan — See also Plett kaker

Egg pan, with 12 round cups, often called a muffin or gem pan but patented as an egg pan, cast iron, marked "N. Waterman," patented by Nathaniel Waterman, Boston, MA, pat'd April 5, 1859, patent #23,517. Waterman was a fairly prolific inventor, beloved of collectors. Others of his patents include a coffee maker, a foot warmer, a match-stand, and a sad iron. This egg pan patent ended up covering baking pans of different shapes

IV-190. Ice cream cone baker. *Called a "Standard Cone Oven,"* *used on any style stove. Came with wooden conical roller for rolling* *into cone as soon as taken off the baker. T. Mills, 1915.* **$75-$120**

and sizes, despite the drawing of the 4-3-4 cup pan in the *Annual Report of the Commissioner of Patents* for 1859, the design for which the patent was granted. See article on cast iron pans by David Smith, at the end of this chapter. For more on Waterman see also photo IV-302. **$45-$65**

Food mold — See mold listings. And remember this is a huge field, with some molds suitable for cake, pudding, jelled sweet or savory dishes, aspics, and more.

Fortune-telling cake charms — See cake fortune-telling charms

French pie mold — See molds, tin

Fritter baker — See Ebelskiver pan

Frosting tubes in case, pieced tin, 6 tubes, case with conical hinged lid, French (?), case 6-1/4" L, 1870s or 1880s. **$60-$75**

Fruit or melon ballers — See entries in Chapter I.

Gem pan — See muffin or gem pan

Gingerbread cookie cutters — See among cookie cutters

Gingerbread man mold, heavy cast aluminum, 2-part, very 3-D, on his base it says "Gingerbread Man," very exaggerated features of man — possibly meant to be an African-American chef, hence might be appropriate for a "Black Americana" collection. About 8" H, maker unknown, ad found in *American Home*, Feb. 1949. **$60-$75**

Gingerbread molds — See cake boards and cookie boards

Goffering or gauffre iron — See wafer iron

Gugelhupf mold — See molds; Kugelhopf, tubed or spouted ceramic, and copper sections

Hoarhound cutter — See candy cutter, this chapter

Ice cream brick mold, tin, American, 7-1/2" L, early 20th C. **$45-$55**

Ice cream cone baker's mold, 6 cast iron heavy conical forms, hinged "cover," handle, c. 3rd quarter 19th C. Rare. **$350-$450**

A must-have book: Wayne Smith's *Ice Cream Dippers* and separate *Price Guide*. For both: $19.95 + $2.50 shipping (unless rates have gone up since this book went to press). *Price Guide* only is $4.95 + $1.75. Please use an SASE if you write for information. Wayne Smith, Box 418, Walkersville, MD 21793.

Club For You Who Scream For Ice Scream. Join the club and get the high-calorie newsletter *The Ice Screamer*. Write Don Snyder, Box 465, Warrington, PA 18976, and use a large SASE.

Ice cream dishers listed by type.
BANANA SPLIT ELONGATED BOWL, mechanical:

Ice cream disher, banana split type, elongated oval bowl of nickeled silver, thumb piece, black painted wooden handle, "Hamilton Beach #34," actually the Gilchrist #34 after HBCo. bought Gilchrist (1931), 30 scoops to a quart, bowl approx. 3-3/4" L x 1-3/8" W x 7/8" deep, c.1931-1934. **$550-$650**

Ice cream disher, banana split type, long oval, nickeled brass, wooden handle, long thumb lever, "United Products Co., Inc.," Chelsea, MA, 11-1/2" L, bowl 3-1/4" + L, 1930s.

Ice cream disher, banana split type, nickeled brass, wooden handle, elongated oval disher, Gilchrist #31 — just like the round-bowl one. 11-1/2" L, pat'd 1915. **$550-$650**

BOWL-SHAPED ROUND CUP, mechanical:

Ice cream disher, bowl cup, nickeled brass, wood handle, "Philcone Disher," 10" L, 1930s. **$50-$65**

Ice cream disher, bowl cup, nickeled brass, wooden handle, 30 dips to a quart size, "Indestructo #31," mfd. by Benedict Mfg. Co., East Syracuse, NY, 10-1/2" L, 1920s. **$60-$80**

Ice cream disher, bowl cup, all metal: buyer had choice of "best white metal," or cast aluminum; both had German silver/nickel-plated bowls. Thumb lever with quadrant gear, 6, 8, 10, 12, 16, and 20 scoops to a quart — i.e. the #6 would make the largest scoops. "Unique," mfd. by Mosteller Mfg. Co., Chicago, c.1908. **$150-$200**

Ice cream disher, bowl cup, cast aluminum bowl, cast metal quadrant gear & thumb lever, steel scraper inside bowl, clumsily shaped turned wood handle, no marks, prob. American, 8-1/2" L, bowl 2-1/2" diameter, c.1950s-1960s. **$10-$15**

Ice cream disher, bowl cup, cast aluminum, thumb press lever to release ice cream by making the little "golf tee" prod in bottom of bowl knock it out, squared handle, made in Japan, 7-1/2" L, 1950s. **$3-$8**

Futurewatch: While cheaply made, these odd mid twentieth-century dishers are some of the collectibles in this field to be looking for, even though they are not as exciting and well-engineered as the older ones. I must have a dozen different ones, picked up at yard sales and thrift shops, all under $3.

Ice cream disher, bowl cup, cast aluminum with golf-ball dimples cast in handle, "Scoop-Rite," patent pending, c. 1940s. **$15-$20**

Ice cream disher, bowl of chrome-plated brass, black Bakelite[a] handle, Model #66, mfd. by Hamilton Beach Mfg. Co., Racine, WI, pat'd 1920, with these handles prob. 1930s. Black Bakelite[a] looks like hard rubber and is one trade name for the generic molded phenolic resin plastic. Catalin[a] is another. **$22-$35**

Ice cream disher, bowl of chromed brass, wood handle, Hamilton Beach "No-Pak" #31, 10-1/3" L, pat'd 1932. (Please don't encourage strippers by buying "deplated" ones.) **$60-$75**

Ice cream disher, bowl cup, nickel-plated brass, two-way finger action, springless model sometimes referred to as the "Dover Springless," or the "Double Flip," Dover Mfg. Co., c.1928. **$75-$95**

Ice cream disher, bowl cup, nickel-plated brass, has unique slicing mechanism: when finger lever is operated a blade slices off excess ice cream, giving a perfect half-round mound of ice cream,

IV-191. Ice cream dishing spoons. *Also called* **ice cream spades**. *(A) nickeled metal with wood handle. Round bowl. Marked "Crandall & Cudahy" on handle, in Duparquet, Huot & Moneuse catalog, c.1904-10. (B) Tinned steel, shank riveted to wood handle. 2 sizes: 10" L and 12" L. From Pick-Barth, 1929. (C) All metal, round bowl. D,H & M, c.1904-10. (D) Oval paddle, tin, D,H & M. (E) Long-handled, "spade bowl," 10", 12" or 14" L, D. J. Barry catalog, 1924. (F) Spade bowl, all metal, nickel-plated cast metal (brass?). 11-1/2" L. Pick-Barth, 1929.* **$5-$18**

called "The Perfection" and the "New Method" disher in trade adv'g, although a much older "New Method" disher that measured portions was being sold in 1915. Marked on thumb lever "Dover Mfg. Co." with patent & place, Dover, NH, 10-15/16" L. Two models: one with a single finger lever, and a double with a lever for thumb and one for fore- or middle finger. Pat'd 1924 & 1928. At least some were sold through Perfection Disher Co., of Boston, hence the trade name. **$600-$700**

Ice cream disher, bowl cup, nickeled brass, fat wood knob on top, round cylindrical disher part has central vertical shaft, worked by pushing down on knob with palm, Fro-Zon Mfg. Co., Schenectady, NY, pat'd Feb. 24, 1925. **$500-$800**

Ice cream disher, bowl with point, probably nickeled brass, with plain shaped wood handle, thumb lever with spring return. The bowl has a small pointed protrusion on outside — the advertising copy from a June 1919 "Soda Fountain," reads "Our Service

IV-192. Ice cream conical or cornet dishers. *A cornet is sort of a small cornucopia — both come from a root word meaning horn. Paper cornets (like those pointed-bottom disposable paper cups) were used in the 18th & 19th C. for nuts or sweetmeats. All the dishers shown here have a blade that scrapes out the inside. Most are the simplest mechanical type — the* **"key scraper,"** *with a blade (sometimes called a knife) inside that is scraped around inside of cone by twisting the "key." All the conical types seem odd now because the conical scoop of ice cream faces the wrong way to fit into the wafer-like cone, but this style predates the baked cone, and was used to serve a conical serving of ice cream in a dish. From top: (A) "Chicago" disher, nickel-plated, one size only, 16 to the quart. It has a spring-loaded scraper activated by thumb piece on the long tubular handle. (B) "Clad's Improved," of seamless drawn steel, German silver knife, 4, 5, 8, 10, 12 and 16 to the quart. (C) "Delmonico Improved," cast iron handle, heavy spun brass bowl, all nickeled, interior cup removable. 6, 10 and 12 to quart. (D) Kingery's "Rapid," one-hand squeeze type — the blade moves when you squeeze the double handle. One-handed kitchen utensils, which probably started after the Civil War, when amputees needed such utensils, are an interesting broad-spectrum collectible. The "Rapid" has a nickel-plated spun brass bowl & blade, "Bessemer steel spring," in 4, 5, 6, 8, 10, 12 and 16 to quart. (A, B, C, D) from Albert Pick catalog, 1909. (E) "K-W-Cone" disher, mfd. by Keiner-Williams Stamping Co. Tinned bowl, malleable cast iron handle, with long slot. Several sizes. Cherry-Bassett catalog, 1921. (F) & (G) are two versions of the "Clewell" disher & measure: (F) Tin bowl, cast iron handle with small hanging hole, German silver knives, made in "standard sizes." Mfd. by V. Clad, Philadelphia. This one from an 1892 ad. (G) Bowl is seamless drawn steel. Note handle with long slot opening. 4, 5, 6, 8, 10, 12, 16 and 20 to quart. In 1915 and 1924 catalogs. "Rapid" about* **$175;** *the rest:* **$15-$75**

Disher has every good point any other disher ever had and a few points no other disher has. Once you see this disher with the point, the point will get you and you will 'get the point.'" Further: "Make a hollow in the top of the ice cream with the point on the back of the disher. Serve the syrup on the top of the cream where it will do the most good. Make every drop count. A little less fruit and syrup served this way looks like more and gives better satisfaction. All the syrup served this way is eaten with the cream and none is left in the bottom of the dish." Service Commodities Mfg. Co., Chicago, IL, c.1919+. **$475-$600**

Ice cream disher, bowl cup, nickeled brass, round bowl with scraper, spring & small thumb lever, flat, knurled metal handle embossed with patent date, manufacturer & trade name, "Clipper Disher," mfd. by Geer Mfg. Co., Troy, NY, 9-1/4" L, pat'd Feb. 7, 1905 by Rasmus Nielsen. Nielsen patented at least 10 dishers, some conical, some round, before 1921. **$200-$250**

Ice cream disher, bowl cup, nickeled brass, marked "Dairy Fresh," 20th C. According to Wayne Smith, this is a fool-the-collector item made in Taiwan (origin noted on a removeable paper label), that can be detected by its shoddy workmanship. **$9-$12**

Ice cream disher, bowl cup, nickeled brass, knurled metal handle that looks borrowed from a screwdriver, spring-operated with thumb lever, marked: "Myers Deluxe Disher," Chicago, IL, pat'd May 19, 1936 by Louis Myers. **$25-$40**

Ice cream disher, bowl cup, nickeled brass, shaft screwed into end of red painted wooden handle, not well made but interesting for the extreme simplicity of the gearing. There's a tight spring inside handle, the thumb piece has 5 holes & a little gear has 5 teeth; as you push thumb lever against teeth they move the scraper, Japan, 8" L, 20th C. **$7-$10**

Ice cream disher, bowl cup, nickeled aluminum bronze, with small gear, rack & spring halfway up shaft to bowl, rosewood handle, quite simple, even modern in look, hard to find, mfd. by Gem Spoon Co., Troy, NY, 10-1/2" L, sizes in 6, 8, 10, 12, 16, & 20 dips to the quart, pat'd by Bernice J. Noyes, May 7, 1895. The Noyes' Gem was possibly the first round bowl disher and predates the similar Gilchrist #3l, which was a decided improvement since the mechanical part was moved farther away from the ice cream itself. **$60-$80**

Ice cream disher, bowl, lever activated roll-over type, aluminum with German silver plated bowl, "Unique," Mosteller Mfg. Co., Chicago, IL, pat'd 7/3/1906. There was a white metal version with German silver bowl. **$800-$1200**

Ice cream disher, bowl cup, nickeled brass, wood handle, lever action, "Trojan No. 16," by Gem Spoon Co., Troy, NY (later Newark, NJ, after the 1920s), c.1911. **$60-$70**

Ice cream disher, bowl cup, nickeled brass & copper, squeeze action moves scraper inside bowl, Gilchrist #30, 10-1/2" L, c.1915-1930. **$35-$50**

Ice cream disher, bowl cup, nickeled brass, wooden handle, thumb lever with tiny gear, rack* and concealed spring, #3l, mfd. by Gilchrist Co., 11" L, pat'd March 23, 1915. This is the most common make & common size (#31) or model of all dippers — reflective of its great popularity when made. It was not patented until 7 years after Raymond Gilchrist filed for a patent, but was sold for many years beginning in 1908. The bowl in this model came in nine sizes: 6, 8, 10, 12, 16, 20, 24, 30, and 40 scoops to the quart. *The gear & rack provided "alternate rectilinear motion . . . to the rack-rod, by the continuous revolution of the . . . spur-gear, the spiral spring forcing the rod back to its original position on the teeth of the gear, quitting the rack," in terms taken from *Mechanical Movements*, first published in 1868, renewed in 1896, reprinted in 1933 in a "Century of Progress" special edition. Related collectible: Look for the *Saturday Evening Post*, June 27, 1953, with a colorful cover by American artist Amos Sewell. The genre depiction of an outdoor children's birthday party shows a harrassed mother holding what appears to be a Gilchrist #31. **Stripped to Death.** The Gilchrist ice cream servers have been the victims of nickel strippers for almost 20 years. It's a real bugabear of mine, the stripping of the original nickel plating from cast brass dippers. It's like taking the old finish off furniture. The price of these dippers was going up and UP, and not only in the 1970s and 1980s. But some dealer ads still reflect the trend towards stripping and unabashedly say "brass ice cream scoop." Such is the power of the golden-glow metal; brass glisters like gold, whereas nickel has no glamour unless it's on an old stove. I've often seen a Gilchrist #31 with its original plating, if somewhat worn, for $25 to $30. In the next booth, a highly polished, buffed, stripped one may be as high as $85. Hey! It's real brass! It is NOT a good investment to buy one like that. **Still a Classic.** For a long time the price range of $65 to $85 held at fancy antique shows, but these Gilchrist #31s had become a sort of token kitchen tool that was displayed with the pressed glass and Staffordshire. Real ice cream disher collectors know how common they are, and more exciting novelty dishers, manufactured originally in much, much smaller quantities, have grabbed the bucks. This Gilchrist, however, remains a classic. **$30-$45**

Ice cream disher, bowl-shaped cup, nickeled brass, turned wooden handle, one lever moves scraper inside bowl, Dover #20, Dover Mfg. Co., 10-1/2" L, c.1930s. **$35-$45**

Ice cream disher, bowl cup, one-piece scoop, with spring action thumb button in bowl's center, cast aluminum, Decatur Lloyd Disher Co., Decatur, IL, 1940. **$25-$35**

Ice cream disher, bowl cup, original nickel plating, thumb lever has only mark: "16-to-a-Quart," 20th C. **$12-$15**

IV-194. Ice cream measure. *"Perfection" was one name used; "Philadelphia" was a later name. Actually a Clewell patent of 5/3/1876, mfd. by Valentine Clad, Philadelphia, PA, in two sizes: 1 pint and 1 quart. This footed goblet shape with handle is from a 1915 catalog. Spun brass, nickel-plated outside, silver-plated inside (probably meaning German silver), with nickel-silver blade that scrapes out the portion. In cutaway linecut you can see the key in the base. An 1892 V. Clad ad mentions only German silver. The Cherry-Bassett Co., calling it a "Philadelphia" measure, has two versions — one "heavily tinned," and one silvered inside, nickeled out.* **$25-$75**

IV-193. Ice cream key scrapers. *Two types, tin with capped tubular handles. One has conical bowl, braced to handle. Other makes rounded serving. Bertuch, Berlin, c.1904.* **$25-$45**

Ice cream disher, bowl cup, pewter-like cast aluminum & nickel-plated steel, #16, Bohlig Mfg. Co., St. Paul, MN, pat'd Oct. 6, 1908. Martin Bohlig's patent uncannily resembles an 1884 patent. Extremely unusual disher used for filling ice cream cones; when handle is squeezed the bowl divides in half, opens like a steam shovel, and drops the ice cream through the bottom into the cone. Very rare. **$750-$950**

CONICAL OR CORNET, mechanical:

Ice cream disher, conical, what was called a <u>cornet disher</u> in the old parlance, key wind, heavy tin & galvanized metal, key at top turns the cornet itself rather than the scraper inside (reverse is true on most if not all other conical dishers), #10, American, about 8" L, Naylor's Patent of 6/19/1888. **$45-$55**

Ice cream disher, conical disher with vaguely heart- or valentine-shaped key, tin with tubular steel handle with brass cap on end bearing name & date, "Clewell's V. Clad Maker," mfd. by Valentine Clad Co., Philadelphia, 8-1/2" L, pat'd May 3, 1876. **$35-$50**

Ice cream disher, cone or cornet disher, heavily nickel plated, one-handed kind with fancy-looking embossed squeeze handles (like tongs) with a spring at the end. Handles look like those grip strengtheners you get at sports stores, "Kingery's Rapid," Kingery Mfg. Co., Cincinnati, OH, 8-1/2" L, pat'd 1894. **$150-$200**

Ice cream disher, cone disher, loop handle, ornate key release, tin & iron, "K W" in oval of key, Keiner-Williams Stamping Co., Richmond Hill, NY, 7-1/2" L, pat'd Nov. 7, 1905. **$35-$45**

Ice cream disher, cone disher, metal, "Safe-T-Cone," American, early 20th C. **$10-$15**

Cornet Key Names. The four initials or monograms found on the keys of this type of disher (known to me or Wayne Smith in his excellent first book on dippers) are **KW, BK, W, and G**. Most keys are plain open ovals, slightly fancier geometric open forms, or very fancy casting — like Delmonico's scroll. We would love to know of any other initial keys. I'd like to say also that although I read books, and talk to collectors, and try to learn, any mistakes I make here are due to too little knowledge on my part and in no way can they be dished up to my advisor Wayne Smith.

Ice cream disher, cone type, with key mechanism, key is letter "G," tinned steel, loop handle, Gilchrist Co., Newark, NJ, 7-1/2" L, c.1915 -1931. **$25-$30**

Ice cream disher, cone or pyramid-shaped disher, nickeled brass, wood handle, Gilchrist #33, with thumb lever like the #31, and concealed reciprocating gear & notched rod atop the pyramid, Newark, NJ, 10-1/2" L, pat'd Sept. 1, 1914. This one came in 6 sizes: 6, 8, 10, 12, 16 and 20 scoops per quart. **$100-$125**

Ice cream disher, cone shape, nickeled brass, spring on top of cone, pulled by pressure on long wide thumb lever, turned wood handle, "Quick and Easy #486," Edwin Walker's patent, mfd. by his company, Erie Specialty Co., Erie, PA, 10-1/2" L, pat'd May 11, 1915, but inventor filed application 5 years earlier, so it's possible at least some were made before the patent was granted. In 1909, this Quick & Easy was advertised as being made of cast aluminum (called by Erie "our cast aluminum near-silver metal" that "remains white like silver, insuring clean, attractive service"), and it came with a tiny little one-cone tray — #487 — used while filling cones, that looks like a miniature griddle with frying pan handle. Apparently you released the cone of ice cream, big end down on the little tray, then maneuvered the ice cream into the baked cone. The sales copy reads amusingly: "The distinctive feature of this cone disher is that the bottom of the cone is so shaped that the ice cream sets down solidly in the cone when released from the disher . . . This gives the appearance of having served the customer with an unusually liberal amount of ice cream." Unlike other "Quick & Easy" models, this one was solely for filling cones. **$275-$325**

Ice cream disher, cone-shaped nickeled "seamless pressed copper cup," german silver (scraper blades) "knives," nickeled malleable iron handle (three years later, in 1907, the handles were described as being cast bronze — the whole disher being heavily nickel-plated), thumb lever operates a rod atop cone which pulls knife or scraper around inside cone, ad states "This Disher

IV-196. Mechanical cornet dishers. *All with thumb levers that move the blade within.* (**L**) *Large one is "Gilchrist's No. 33 Pyramid" disher. "Bowl and scraper all made of German silver (nickel). Phosphor bronze spring fully concealed. Press button (arrow points to it) to take entire thing apart for cleaning or repairing. Six sizes: 6, 8, 10, 12, 16 or 20 to the quart."* (**R**) *Disher under the hand is C. L. Walker Co.'s "Quick and Easy" disher, formerly made by the Erie Specialty Co. Nine sizes: 6, 8, 10, 12, 14, 16, 20, 24 and 30 to the quart. First two from 1919 ads in* The Soda Fountain *trade magazine.* (**B-R**) *Bottom disher is the "Dandy." Two qualities — silver plated or tinned, with wood handle. 8, 10, 12, 16 to the quart. Pick catalog, 1909.* **$100-$150**

IV-195. Three types of mechanical ice cream dishers. (**T**) *Cast aluminum, thumb-lever spring action prod knocks ice cream out of bowl, 7-1/2" L, made in Japan, 1950s.* (**M**) *Longest one is a Dover Mfg. Co. #20, wooden handle, nickeled bowl. This has a leveling cutter that flattens scoop before it comes out. 10-1/2" L.* (**B**) *Cornet disher with key-wind, heavy tin, marked "#10." In this case, the key at top turns the cornet-shaped bowl, not the scraper inside, although the reverse is true of most (or all?) others. Pat'd 1883 (?). Last two collection of Meryle Evans.* (**T**) **$10-$15**; (**M**) **$600-$700**; (**B**) **$40-$50**

is used at the St. Louis Exposition," "Walker's No. 186," pat'd by Edwin Walker, mfd. by Erie Specialty Co., Erie, PA, six sizes of scoops-to-the-quart: 5, 6, 8, 10, 12, 16. By 1907 it was made up to size 20, advertised 1904. See listing above for Walker's patented 1915 brass disher. Walker's dishers also included a shallow round cup one (#386) with levered thumb piece, almost like this one; a simple key top conical one of tin (#184); and cast aluminum models. **$350-$550**

Ice cream disher, conical bowl, plated brass, "N. & Co., Delmonico," 8" L, turn of century. **$75-$100**

IV-197. Ice cream disher. *"Gilchrist #30," with squeeze action. Nickeled brass & copper — sometimes called "bronze metal," 10-1/2" L, c.1915-1930. $35-$50*

IV-198. Ice cream dishers. *Classic Gilchrist's #31, thumb lever. Made in nine sizes: 6, 8, 10, 12, 16, 20, 24, 30, 40 to the quart. Also sold for dishing out mashed potatoes! Nickel-plated "bronze metal." From 1930s catalog. CAUTION: These and the one above are the ones dealers like to engolden, by removing necessary nickel plating. $35-$55*

IV-199. Ice cream dishers. (T) *"Arnold," with nickel plating. End of handles marked with code colors for size. (So you could see them when they sat immersed in that bucket of disgusting bath-water scummy mess.)* **(M)** *The "Philcone," identified as a "patent chromium plated disher," in Jaburg catalog, 1915. Small-scoop sizes only, 12, 16, 20, 24 and 30 to the quart.* **(B)** *"Gem" disher, with bowl made of "aluminum bronze, heavily nickel plated." Rosewood handle; 6 to 20-to-the-quart sizes.* **$45-$65**

Ice cream disher, conical disher, tin with heavy wire handle, key-scraper, no mark, American, 7-5/8" L, turn of century. Wire handle is unusual, as most have a sheet metal or cast handle. **$22-$30**

Ice cream disher, conical, heavy tinned sheet metal, stamped sheet metal handle with long hole, key release/scraper is relatively big oval, American, 7-3/8" L, late 19th C. **$25-$35**

Ice cream disher, conical metal dish, squeeze action handle, "Squeeze Action," early 20th C. **$65-$8**

NON-MECHANICAL:

Ice cream disher, bowl of cast aluminum with colored anodized aluminum cap at end of tubular handle, non-mechanical. The "Zeroll" or "Roll Dipper" disher is filled with liquid that is supposed to chemically keep it warm enough to help scoop out very cold ice cream. Designed by Sherman Kelly, mfd. by Zeroll Co., Toledo, OH, 7" L, 1934 to present day. Called by the Museum the "Roll Dipper," this was chosen by the design curator to be in the Museum of Modern Art's Design Collection, NYC. Zeroll changed its name in 1953 to Roll Dippers, Inc. Other disher-dippers made by them in the 1940s and 1950s are the "Nuroll" and "Roldip." **$10-$15**

Ice cream disher, bowl of cast aluminum, non-mechanical, has smaller bowl & longer handle than the later award-winning "Roll Dipper," cap on end has blue finish, probably too early to be anodized, "Zeroll," Toledo, OH, #30, 1934 patent #1974051. **$15-$20**

Ice cream disher, bowl of cast aluminum, non-mechanical, no special fluid in handle, "Nuroll," Toledo, OH, made by Zeroll Co., 1950s. **$15-$20**

Ice cream disher, bowl of cast aluminum with ridged cigar-shaped handle & a bowl clunkier than similar "Roll Dipper," non-mechanical, marked "PROGRESSUS" (**NOTE:** some letters may be indistinct — mine reads only "...ESSUS"), made in Italy, 7-1/2" L, c.1960s. **$5-$12**

Ice cream disher, bowl of un-ID metal with wood handle, non-mechanical, "Arnold," pat'd 1928. **$20-$30**

Ice cream disher, nickeled brass, wooden handle, New Gem Mfg. Co., Newark, NJ, (affiliated with C. T. Williamson Wire Novelty Co., the corkscrewers), c.1932-1940. **$35-$45**

NOVELTY SHAPES, heart, cube, tube:

Ice cream disher, heart-shaped bowl, nickeled metal, shaft, & thumb lever, simple turned wood handgrip is stained red, makes heart-shaped servings, mfd. by the inventor, John Manos, Toronto, OH, 11" L, pat'd Nov. 17, 1925. Marked "Patented Nov. 1925" on back of heart-shaped pusher plate. Mr. Manos had molded glass heart-shaped dishes made in New Moundsville, WV, (a big glass center) to go with the ice cream, and because they would have suffered much higher casualties from use the dishes are valued at about $100 each. Price has skyrocketed for these dishers, and Wayne Smith, who actually had the great honor and pleasure to talk with Mr. Manos himself, reports directly from the inventor's mouth that there were only 1000 made. One of my concerns is that as the price goes up, it'll be profitable for a very skilled person to make fakes. After all, it's not platinum, so the material cost would be small, and it's not even really all that odd, except for that beautiful heart-shaped dipper bowl. One man in 1987 advertised his standing offer for $2500 for one. One sold at a Gaithersburg, MD, auction in February 1988 for $3000. At a Noel Barrett auction in New Hope, PA, in April 1988, someone paid (including 10% premium) an astounding $4620. At an auction in St. Louis, MO, in 1989, one brought $5500. For a while, Wayne Smith was carefully tracking the selling prices of the heart dishers: 15 sold between 1988 and

IV-200. Ice cream disher. *"Service" disher. The distinguishing feature is the pointed piece on top, and their ads are filled with word play on "the point." But it's a great idea: "Make a hollow in the top of the cream with the point on the back of the disher. Serve the syrup on the top of the cream where it will do the most good. Make every drop count. A little less fruit and syrup served this way looks like more and gives better satisfaction." Heh heh. Service Commodities Mfg. Co., Chicago. Ad in* The Soda Fountain, *1919.* **$125-$175**

A PERFECT CONE FILLER AND DISPENSER

IV-201. Ice cream disher. *"Unique," mfd. by Mosteller Mfg. Co., Chicago. "A perfect cone filler and dispenser, made in sizes 6, 8, 10, 12, 16 and 20 to Quart." Two styles, one of white metal, one of aluminum, both with German Silver bowls. Ad in* Iron Age, *1909.* **$800-$1200**

IV-202. Novelty ice cream dishers. (T) *Slice molder, "Handy," mfd. by Mayer Mfg. Corp., Chicago, c.1910s. Not a thumb lever, but a <u>forefinger</u> lever, as shown.* **(B)** *Banana split disher Gilchrist #34, long oval, 3-3/4" L x 1-3/8" W, 20 per quart. Both in Mills catalog, 1915.* **$120-$175; $500-$600**

1989, and 10 more were sold by 1991, with an average selling price of $3450. Since then, prices have leveled off, with an occasional "bargain" in the $2000 range. These high prices are, obviously, for dishers in Good+ condition, with no damage. It's impossible to say now whether this is a temporary stall in a price rise, or a signal of a downturn. If Manos' recollection is true, that only 1000 were made, this situation offers an almost unparalleled opportunity in any field of collecting to track the market for an appealing, attractive, strongly designed durable item over a period of years! We know that 1000 could not have survived. To be neither optimistic or conservative, say that between 1925 and 1940 half, or 500, were lost, melted for scrap, destroyed, or thrown out by accident. Then there would have been, in 1940, 500 awaiting disposition. Maybe 50 of those are accounted for. If you collect ice cream implements, specializing in dishers, you would see that old pool of possibles drying up in the sun, like a rain puddle in August. So my feeling is, the price hasn't really started to go down yet. Wayne tells me that there are over 1000 *known* collectors now in this field, which is rapidly expanding. A small percentage of those people would be able to afford to pay so much money for something. So who knows what the price range might become? And who knows how long it will take an entrepeneur with criminal intent to make, say, 10 copies? The price is really crazy, but it's hard to know what to say or if there's an absolute rule to apply to what you will be asked to pay, or what you "should" pay. For the rest of the century: **$2500-$5000**

Ice cream disher, cube, stainless steel, makes small 1-1/2" cube of ice cream, "P C Server," mfd. by Prince Castle Co., c.1950s. **$150-$250**

Ice cream disher, tubular novelty, nickeled metal, wood handle, 9-1/2" L lever, long cylinder makes a tube of ice cream that is inserted in chocolate covered "bun" — the dessert is called a "cold dog." Canadian, pat'd 1926. **$600-$750**

SANDWICH, SLAB OR PIE A LA MODE:

Ice cream disher, pie a la mode novelty, triangular wedge-shaped aluminum disher with angled wooden handle, "Pi-Alamoder," mfd. in St. Louis, MO, pat'd by Harlan Gardner and Alvin Olafson, Aug. 10, 1926. **$225-$300**

Ice cream disher, sandwich scoop, cast aluminum handle, stainless steel body, "Rainbow Ice Cream Dispenser Cake Cone Co., Inc.," St. Louis, MO, 10" L, sandwich part 2-7/8" x 3-3/8", 1920s. **$250-$300**

Ice cream disher, sandwich-type square disher, nickeled brass, nice big cog gear wheel, small thumb lever, wooden handle, "The 'Polar-Pak' Disher," mfd. by Philadelphia Ice Cream Cone Machinery Co., Phila. 10-1/2" L, pat'd July 26, 1932. Production started upon or before patent application was filed in 1928; disher is marked "Pat. Apl'd For." **$350-$400**

Ice cream disher, sandwich disher, rectangular with spring inside handle. "Ergos," nickel-plated brass, 3-3/4" x 2" x 5-1/2", English, 1920s. **$150-$200**

Ice cream disher, sandwich disher, adjustable to make three slab sizes, nickel silver (alloy), long shaft, wide-set thumb/forefinger lever, wooden handle, ads called it "Mayer's Handy Ice Cream Disher," marked on front "Mayer Mfg. Corp.," Chicago, IL, 12" L, "Patent pending" appears in a 1915 ad. "Mayer's Handy" is very like the Jiffy Dispenser dipper but doesn't have slightly curved disher, the wooden handle is slightly different proportion, and the thumb lever is not just slightly bent, it is cast and machined. The "Jiffy" (see below), which was sold by a Chicago company, and pat'd in 1925, is undoubtedly closely related. **$125-$175**

Ice cream disher, sandwich style, "German silver" (old name for nickel silver, which was an alloy of copper, zinc and nickel, used for flatware and some hospital equipment), nearly square, slightly bowed disher, wood handle, thumb lever, "Jiffy Dispenser Co.," distributed or possibly mfd. by Jiffy Sales Co., Aurora, IL (Jiffy Sales in Chicago), 12-1/2" L, pat'd Feb. 17, 1925. **$125-$175**

Ice cream sandwiches were very popular in the 1920s, especially as a soda fountain novelty. However, people could make their own at home with waffles and by slicing a brick of ice cream, which was slightly larger than an unquartered pound "brick" of butter or lard. Until bulk ice cream was available, these sandwich dippers were not especially useful in a home kitchen; sales pitches were directed to soda fountains and ice cream parlors. More than two dozen styles of sandwich dippers were made during the 1920s! All are highly collectible.

Ice cream disher, sandwich style, square disher of nickel silver alloy, with levered push-out, wooden handle, "ICYPI" (the trademark, pronounced "Icy-Pie," was patented in 1926), Automatic Cone Co., Cambridge, MA, 10" L, 2-1/2" x 2-1/2" slab, c.1926. This disher was used to fill "ICYPI" wafers — a special sandwich wafer with three sides enclosed to prevent dripping. It was, in effect, a flattened square cup. This popular ice cream treat was eaten by millions from about 1924 to 1930. **NOTE:** ICYPI is pronounced I-Cee-Pie & was usually spelled IcyPi by the company. An early ad for the Automatic Cone Co.'s "ICYPI" named the Pioneer Ice Cream Cone Mfg. Co. as the manufacturer: perhaps they meant of the wafer itself, not the dipper.
• For the wafer mold itself, see ice cream wafer mold, a few pages below. **$125-$175**

Ice cream disher, sandwich style, square disher of nickel silver, levered push-out, wooden handle, "McLaren's ICYPI," McLaren Consolidated Cone Corp, Dayton, OH, 10" L, 2-1/2" x 2-1/2" slab. In 1929, the McLaren Co. and also the United Products Co. (Chelsea, MA) were licensed by Automatic Cone Co., Cambridge, MA, to manufacture the highly successful ICYPI. **$125-$175**

IV-203. Ice cream sandwich molds. *"Pan-American," for "the very latest form in which Ice Cream is sold at Soda Fountains, Cafes, etc., is the Ice Cream Sandwich, composed to two oblong Biscuits with a thin cut of Ice Cream between them."* **(T)** *Style One is shown in 2 views with fancy cast iron base, 9"-10" H;* **(B)** *style two was handheld, 5" L. Apparently the "mold" holds the wafer or biscuit in place while ice cream slab is put on and topped. Thomas Mills, 1915 catalog.* **$100-$200**

Ice cream disher, sandwich/slab type, German silver, heavy wooden handle, makes a rectangular slab, "Sanitary Mould Co.," pat'd 3/17/1925. **$250-$350**

Ice cream disher, sandwich type, nickeled brass scoop, rectangular, broad & slightly curved or bowed, turned wood handle, thumb lever action, no marks, American, 12-1/2" L, c.1930s. This is like a cross between a Jiffy & the un-curved Mayer sandwich dishers. The wooden handle is shaped differently, as is the position & shape of the thumb lever. **$125-$150**

Ice cream disher, sandwich type, nickeled brass, spring inside handle, used to hold while being made, and then to serve ice cream sandwiches, "Reliance," 4-1/2" L, 2" x 3-1/2" slab. American, c.1920s. **$100-$150**

Ice cream measure, pieced tinned heavy sheet iron, footed goblet shape with generous strap handle on one side, key (which is hidden in concave base or ring foot) turns 2 scrapers that go all the way up inside of cup. Opposite the handle is an attached medallion, unfortunately rather smashed & illegible, "Clewell," mfd. by Valentine Clad, Philadelphia, pint-size: 5-1/2" H x 3-1/2" diameter, May 3, 1876 is the date on medallion. (The same patent date, May 3, 1876, as their disher). Used to measure ice cream for take-home consumption. Made in one quart and one pint sizes. Several companies made this type of measure: unfortunately few were marked. The "Perfection Ice Cream Measure," which was essentially the same as the Clewell except it was "made of hard spun metal, silver plated inside and nickel plated outside" with a "tempered nickel-silver" blade inside, was advertised by Thomas Mills & Brother, Inc., of Philadelphia, along with the "Clewell" cornet ice cream disher, in their Catalog #31, from the late 1920s. Value range for the Clewell as well as the others: **$25-$75**

ICE CREAM MOLDS

Most ice cream molds are a somewhat soft, gray, heavy metal called "pewter," although it's not the same proportionate mix of metals used in the eighteenth century for plates and hollowware. Many "white" metal alloys that could be formed with great detail were made in the nineteenth century as substitutes for pewter. The molds are mostly two-part, hinged and heavy, or relatively thick, so that they would hold the cold temperature longer while unmolding the ice cream. Many molds — perhaps most — are not as antique as we think they must be in this age of prepared foods and frozen novelty desserts. Prices have risen dramatically in the last decade or so, as have prices for all kinds of molds. **Figural, Animalistic, Zoomorphic:** In art-talk, something made in the shape of a human figure is called figural; if it's an animal or bird form it's animalistic or zoomorphic. I use the term figural throughout because it is the more widely (mis)used term; it is easier than zoomorphic; and animalistic is sometimes used to describe something sensual or even bestial, as opposed to what is "spiritualistic" in humans. Read the daily news for your dose of human spiritualism.

Some molds achieved their full effect only when accompanied by "decorations" of composition, printed paper or wire — such as leaves, stems, hats, golf clubs, flags, sails and tablewares. Krauss and also Jo-Lo offer these in their 1930s catalogs. There were also paper favor companies, like Dennison's, and novelty companies who offered extremely inexpensive little decorations. **Holidays:** With the twentieth century came the commercialized commemoration of more and more holidays. Special cards, decorations, objects, and also ice cream molds were made to help people celebrate (and to help companies sell more merchandise in seasons besides Christmas). This is especially true beginning in the 1920s. **Confusables:** Models or "Chalkware"? When looking at ice cream mold catalogs from the early twentieth century, it is interesting to note how many of the big molds (often represented by colored plaster or "composition" models used for display by the ice cream shoppe taking party orders) remind you of ceramic "cottage" figurines, or of chalkware. Most would not fool a chalkware collector, but people just getting started with carnival chalks, which are cruder and have more popular-culture subjects, might find these models (if they indeed have survived and surface in the market) very confusing. Especially the traditional animals — squirrels, rabbits, cats, pigs — and the holiday figures like Santa or George Washington. At this point, I have no idea of the probable collector market for these models and am not aware of a collector group for them, but I believe they should be collected and may command prices, if colored especially, higher than the molds themselves! My Krauss and my Jo-Lo catalogs show some really fabulous pieces. Jo-Lo's 1930s catalog even gives the price for each mold and also each model.

Evaluating the Molds. When looking at ice cream molds, remember that any damages (holes, small cracks, hinge damage) reduce value dramatically. Pewter is soft and easily damaged. Look for really good condition and fine interior detail. Interesting shapes or "collector cult" subjects add value too — subjects such as Christmas, teddy bears, Amerindians, character figures. **Old Style or Reproduction?** Tantalizing evidence exists in the 1932-33 *Thomas' Register of American Manufacturers*, that old-style ice cream molds were being made in the early 1930s by a company called Reproductions Co., Boston, MA. Alas, when you turn to the manufacturers' alphabetical listing, this company is not given. I tried "Ice Cream Mold Reproductions Co." and "Boston Reproductions," to no avail.

E-K-S: These are the big three — a handful of early twentieth-century American companies whose marks are amost always abbreviated to initials on the molds themselves, plus the style or design number (usually three or four digits), and abbreviated to single initials by collectors (for ads and collection lists). These are Eppelsheimer & Co., NYC & Brooklyn, a.k.a. "E & Co. N. Y.," or **E**; Krauss Co., Milford, PA, a.k.a. "K" or "Krauss," or **K**, established in 1860; and Schall & Co., NYC, a.k.a. "S & Co.," or **S**, the oldest company. (**NOTE:** Eppelsheimer & Co., in 1945 *Thomas' Register,* was listed as belonging to Warren Bros. Corp, Cranford, NJ.)

Krauss's catalog states that any molds made of "pure tin" would cost 20% more than the pewter. An article in *The Spinning Wheel,* Sept. 1965, by Duncan B. Wolcott, says that in 1965, moldmaker Walter Perry, who worked at Fr. Krauss in Milford, PA, used "61% tin and 39% lead" for his molds. This is cause for great concern, if true. Mr. Wolcott also writes, "If the [owner] plans it as an ash tray, will it lie flat? If he wants it for decoration or as a conversation piece, it should to a certain extent tell its own story. Many of today's collectors of pewter ice cream molds are actually using them to make up their own fancy individual ice cream desserts." Krauss also claimed that their moulded hinge construction was "exclusive" to them. "Unlike the common practice of soldering the hinge to the metal mould, we have perfect a manufacturing method of actually moulding the hinge as part of the mould itself . . . which makes for a much stronger and truer hinge construction."

Other American Mold Makers: There are many unmarked molds whose makers we cannot at this time identify. There are other molds that may or may not be marked by the following makers. • In the 1905-06 *Thomas' Register of American Manufacturers* I found: W. H. Sweeney Mfg. Co., Brooklyn (who made cake, ice cream, jelly, pudding molds); Crandall & Godley, NYC; Eppelsheimer & Co., NYC; William Hart, NYC (who also manufactured carved cake boards with engine turnings, springerle molds, jelly molds and copper pans as early as 1876); Lalance & Grosjean Mfg. Co., NYC; Valentine Clad & Sons, Philadelphia; and Thomas Mills & Bros., Pittsburg. • From the 1932-33 *Thomas' Register* come: Cherry-Burrell Corp., Chicago (later Cherry-Bassett); Reproductions Co., Boston; Fr. Krauss & Son, NYC (I don't know the relationship to Krauss Co., Milford, PA); James Y. Watkins & Son, NYC (a name known to us from the John Conger molds); August Kreamer, Brooklyn, who made many kinds of kitchenwares — al-

though I had not been aware of their ice cream molds; Eppelsheimer & Co., Brooklyn; Victor V. Clad, Philadelphia; and Thomas Mills & Brother, Inc., Philadelphia. • In the 1945 *Thomas' Register of American Manufacturers* are the following listings, some of which carry over from earlier directories: Cherry-Burrell; Ueding Ice Cream Mold Mfg. Co., Vincennes, IN; Warren Bros. Corp., Cranford, NJ; August Kreamer, Brooklyn; Grimm Mfg. Co., Cleveland, OH; Victor V. Clad; and Thomas Mills & Bro., Inc., Philadelphia. **Others:** One name known from a mold and a search of city directories is Jacob Ernst ("J. Ernst, N. York") a mold-maker in New York from 1858 through 1872. Not found in the Thomas' directories, but known: Jo-Lo (Joe Lowe Corp., Brooklyn), c.1930s catalog; T. C. Weygandt Co., NYC, 1930s & 1940s, who imported molds from Europe and also made their own for ice cream and chocolate; "D. & Co." — not known, probably twentieth century.

European mold makers. Some of these are taken from catalogs in my collection, others from molds themselves. **French:** M. Cadot et Cie, Paris (founded 1826; catalog c. 1900), marked "C C" on each mold. The double "C" appears within the trademark image of an old cranked ice cream freezer that looks exactly like a wishing well. Well . . . I wish for some ice cream too, n'c'est pas? • E. Compiègne, successor to Cadot, c.1904, also marked "C C" on each mold, tin and pewter. • A. Anthoine, Paris, late nineteenth-century catalog, probably in business from 1960s on, pewter & tin molds. • H. Trottier, Paris, (large geometric or vase-shaped tin molds, late nineteenth century. • Maison Letang Pentury catalog, but in business since 1832. **German:** "Joh: Reinölds" for Johannes Reinölds, Ulm. Letang Pére & Fils, Paris, using the mark "L. G.," early 20th century • Herrn Gustav Krieg, Hamburg, late nineteenth century to ? (I have c.1914 catalog). **Austrian:** "GE, Austria" is a mark on one mold I've seen but I don't know the company. **English:** Harton & Son, London, known to be working in 1878 to c.1890, successors to Harton & Watts, pewterers, London, prior to 1878. • Biertumpfel & Hepting, London, fl. 1860s (Maltese cross & orb mark). • A. B. Marshall, London, c.1860s to ? Mrs. Marshall ran a cooking school, wrote many cookbooks, and had a huge culinary supply store in London, which may have also handled imported wares.

NOTE: It's a good idea to remember, if you are researching European molds, that sizes in French & German catalogs are given in centimeters and litres. A centimeter (cm.) is .39 of an inch; a litre (lit.) is approximately 1.06 the size of a quart and therefore approximately equal to 2.12 pints.

1838 Ice Cream. From a letter to the editor of *The Magazine of Domestic Economy*, July 1838: "Mr. Editor, — Can you give me any practical **directions for making Ice creams?** I have this year an opportunity of procuring ice in a rough state, but being unacquainted with the management of it for cream, &c., I shall be obliged by your giving the necessary directions through your valuable Magazine; also as to what vessels are necessary for the general use of ice in a small family." The editor replied: "**Sorbetieres or moulds for cream** or fruit-ices, are made of two sorts of materials, block-tin and pewter; of these, the latter is the best, the substance to be iced congealing more gradually in it than in the former; an object much to be desired, as when the ice is formed too quickly, it is very apt to be rough, and full of lumps like hail, especially if it be not well worked with the spatula; the other utensils necessary for this operation are, a deep pail, with a cork at the bottom, and a wooden spatula about nine inches long; being so far provided, fill the pail with pounded ice, over which spread four handfuls of salt; then having filled the sorbetiere, or mould, with cream, &c. put on the cover, and immerse it in the centre of the ice-pail, taking care the ice touches the mould in all parts; throw in two more handfuls of salt, and leave it a quarter of an hour; then take the cover from the mould, and with the spatula stir the contents up together, so that those parts which touch the sides of the mould, and consequently congeal first, may be mixed with the liquid in the middle; work this about for seven or eight minutes; cover the mould, take the pail by the ears, and shake it round and round for a quarter of an hour; open the mould a second time, and stir as before; continue these operations alternately, until the cream, or whatever it may be, is entirely congealed, perfectly smooth, and free from lumps. Take care to let out the water, which will collect at the bottom of the pail, by means of the cork, and press the ice close to the sorbetiere with the spatula. When the cream is iced, take it from the pail, dip the mould in warm water, but not to let it remain an instant; dry it quickly, turn it out, and serve it as soon as possible."

Ice Cream Molds: A Note on How To Read the Listings.

For brevity, I've used the standard number notation style of mold collectors — the initials of the big three (E, K or S), hyphen and style number. Some listings have no maker and no number — for them, what information I have is included. Unless otherwise noted, molds are "pewter" or whatever pewter-like alloy passes for pewter. Unless otherwise noted, molds are the individual serving size — which varies, but is relatively small (usually 7-10 per quart) compared to a table service mold (holding 1 or 2 pints) or a banquet or centerpiece mold (which held 3 or 4 pints or more). I have chosen to list only the figural or zoomorphic molds rather than the geometric, architectectonic ice cream molds, which look more or less like other food molds. Most of them were made in heavily double-tinned sheet iron, partly stamped perhaps, but using the technique of piecing. That type of mold is mainly from the nineteenth century.

Ice cream mold, airplane, 8 to the quart, E-1132, (the larger one, 5 to a quart, is E-1131, c.1930s. Jo-Lo had the same one, same numbers, and offered a "gum paste aviator" at $12 per 100.) **$60-$75**

Ice cream mold, alligator, great detail, S-394. **$80-$90**

Ice cream mold, American flag, Jo-Lo-1160, 1930s. **$40-$45**

Ice cream mold, apple, Jo-Lo-240, 6 per quart, 1930s. **$45-$50**

Ice cream mold, apricot, hinged 2-part, only mark is a gouged "X" in hinge, late 19th C. **$35-$40**

"How to put Ice Cream into Moulds. Rub your moulds very bright; then fix on the top and bottom with writing paper; take off the top, and fill the mould with the frozen ice cream already prepared; it must be forced in very tight that no holes may appear when turned out; then lay on the writing paper, fix on the top, and immediately cover it well over with salted ice, go on in the same way until the whole is put into moulds; then lay them on one side, upon ice, in a tub with two bottoms; cover them well over with salted ice, which must be pressed tightly down; and in one hour it will be hard enough to turn out; but should it be wanted in a shorter time, a little salt petre beat small, and mixed with the salt, will be of great advantage to it. To put Ice Cream into Shapes, to represent ripe Fruits. — Your apricot moulds being ready for use, open them, and colour

IV-204. "Mold for Ice-Cream, Jellies, &c." patent. *Pat'd 8/19/1873, by Edgar Mason May, Fond Du Lac, WI. What is seen is a sectional view of the scissor-action mold. The mold is a round "pan or cup" with open ends facing each other. "Each cup as a curved piece cut from one side, so that when they are closed together they resemble a round box with an opening in the periphery." It was to be used by holding open and dipping in the cream, "or other substance to be molded, taking up as much as can be held. They are then forced together, pressing the cream into a compact mass, the surplus passing out through" that hole in the periphery! Cast or sheet metal, inner surfaces "corrugated, carved, or ornamented in any manner." Official Gazette of the U.S. Patent Office.*

the inside a pale yellow, with a small brush; then take another brush, and dip it in lake finely ground, colour the sides of the mould, in part, with it; then take a small bit of whisk, dip it in the lake, and spot the mould a little with it; after which, fill both sides very full, and put them together; wrap the shape in strong brown paper, to keep the salt from penetrating the opening of the mould; then immerse it well in salted ice. N. B. Peach, pear, or pine apple, must all be coloured in the same manner, well bedded with ice, beat small, and salted properly, as before." Joseph Bell, *A Treatise on Confectionary*. Newcastle, England, 1817.

● ● ● ●

"To turn Ice out of Shapes. When you wish to turn out your shapes, have every thing in readiness to receive them, and never turn it out before the moment it is wanted; take each mould and wash it well in plenty of cold water; then rub it dry with your towel; take a strong knife, and force off the top; rub the top very clean; then take away the paper, and place the top on; do the same with the other end; after which, take the mould between both your hands, (having previously taken off both top and bottom) and let the shape of ice drop on to the dish you serve it up to the table upon; repeat this with every mould, do it in as short a time as possible, and serve it to the table immediately. N. B. The ices in natural shapes must be turned out in the same way, and laid upon the dish, when you may put a natural stalk into each, and garnish them with their own leaves." *Ibid* .

IV-205. Bomb or bombé molds. *All for iced dessert dishes — ice cream, iced pudding. biscuit glacé, etc. I don't know what made this style so popular, maybe it was some exciting anarchist movement; it goes back at least two centuries. Clockwise from upper (**L**): (**1**) "Bomb," tinned copper, two sizes — 1 pint and 1 quart. Note the fuse opening. Pick-Barth, 1929. (**2**) Tinned copper, from William S. Adams, London, c.1860-61. (**3**) "Bombe Enflammée" mold, A. Anthoine, Paris, c.1900. (**4**) "Boulet," in four sizes, holding 1/2 litre, 1, 1-1/2 and 2 litres. Anthoine, c.1900. **NOTE:** An invaluable book for research into dishes is* Hering's Dictionary of Classical and Modern Cookery, *trans. by Walter Bickel, published in Germany. I have a 1974 edition. There are almost seven pages of recipes for Bombe, "a special ice concoction moulded ... and deep frozen. The mould is lined first with plain ice cream and the center filled with a bombe mixture of different flavor, to which may be added diced fruit and other ingredients. [Just like iced biscuit.] Fruit should be macerated in liqueur and sugar before being added to prevent it freezing too hard. Bombe mixture is made by whisking egg yolks with a syrup of 28 deg. first hot and then cold, blended with whipped cream and the desired flavor." Just for one example: "Zamora: lined with coffee ice: filled with Curacao- flavored bombe mixture."* **$55-$200**

Ice cream mold, artichoke, E-222 (and it's 22 to the qt.). **$35-$45**

Ice cream mold, artist (like baby or cupid, with beret & modest loincloth) leaning on palette as big as he is, ribbon banner below, on oval medallion, Jo-Lo-410, 14 to a quart, 1930s. **$65-$75**

Ice cream mold, baby in finery, K-286, 8 to qt. **$85-$95**

Ice cream mold, baby shoe, 20th C. **$35-$45**

Ice cream mold, banana, hinged 2 parts, smaller than life size, #157, American, c. 1920. **$45-$60**

Ice cream mold, banana, E-228. **$40-$45**

Ice cream mold, baseball player, K-555, 8 to qt. (They also sold little baseball bats to go with the players, for $3 a gross!) The mold: **$110-$125**

IV-206. "Bombe Sarah Bernhardt" mold. *Not all bombe molds are shaped like bombs. Some are conical; this one is a 6-point star, made of tin, with a close-fitting lid. It appears in Urbain Dubois' La Patisserie d'Aujourd'hui, published over long period, with illustrations from early editions, c.1860s-80s. A Sarah Bernhardt bombe, named after the French actress of the last half of the 19th C., had peaches, maraschino cherries, and vanilla mousse. (It is not in Hering's.)* **$40-$70**

IV-207. Melon molds. *Used for iced desserts and puddings.* **(T)** *The warty "Musk Melon" mould is tin, hinged, and came in 4-1/2", 5-1/2" and 6" diameters. S. Joseph, c.1927.* **(M)** *Plain melon, holding 1-1/2 pints. Mrs. A. B. Marshall's The Book of Ices., c.1900-02.* **(B)** *Two views of hinged pewter ice cream melon mold, for "fruits glacés." Urbain Dubois, c.1860s-80s. More familiar to us are the melon molds in a half-melon shape, pictured in IV-293.* **$60-$100**

Ice cream mold, basketball, showing segmented construction & lacing, Jo-Lo-1150, 8 to a quart, 1930s. **$40-$50**

Ice cream mold, battleship, E-1069 (also Jo-Lo-1069). **$90-$130**

Ice cream mold, battleship, K-513. **$90-$100**

Ice cream mold, battleship "Monitor" with turret top, for those Civil War Veterans or Widows luncheons, could get cannons & flags, Jo Lo-1068. **$100-$130**

Ice cream mold, beagle (not Snoopy), B-1412. **$55-$70**

Ice cream mold, beaver, E-644. **$60-$70**

Ice cream mold, bell, heavy tin, American, early 20th C. **$18-$25**

Ice cream mold, bell, "Marriage," K-285, mfd. by Krauss, Milford, PA, prior to 1930s? They also did a Liberty Bell, K-473. **$45-$50**

Ice cream mold, bicycle, simplified man's bike on oval, white iron, #3509, about 8-1/2" H, Letang Fils, Paris. **$70-$90**

Ice cream mold, bicyclist in knee britches & billed cap on bike, oval plinth, white iron, #3506, about 8-1/2" H, Letang Fils, Paris. **$80-$95**

Ice cream mold, bicyclists — lady riding is K-431; man riding is K-551. She is 7 to the quart; he is 8 to the quart! Each: **$90-$120**

Ice cream mold, boar or wild pig, E-647. May somehow relate to Teddy Roosevelt's hunting prowess. **$60-$65**

Ice cream mold, boar or wild pig on grassy plinth, white iron, #3518, about 6-3/4" H, Letang Fils, Paris. **$55-$60**

Ice cream mold, boar on grassy oval, double-tinned stamped sheet iron, Bertuch-541, in five sizes from four to a pint to total capacity of 1-1/4 pints, c. 1904. **$55-$65**

Ice cream mold, little boy climbing fat tree stump taller than he, round base, white iron, #3493, about 9" H, Letang Fils, Paris. **$75-$90**

Ice cream mold, bride & groom, K-627. **$40-$48**

Ice cream mold, bride & groom, 2 molds, chubby children — E-1148 bride with veil & short skirt, E-1149 groom with tails & top hat, cast white metal, quarter pint size, c.1929. (**NOTE:** shortly after, the same molds appear in the Joe Lowe, Jo-Lo, catalog with same numbers.) Each: **$70-$80**

Freezing • Coloring • Decorating. "The best results are obtained by using soft ice cream which works well into all parts of the mold and produces a finished model, perfect and distinct in every detail. **FREEZING** is done in a hardening room or with brine which is a mixture of three parts ice to one part salt by weight. If used in brine, it is advisable to seal the seams of the mold with butter or wrap the mold in wax paper to prevent the salt penetrating to the cream. In ten to twenty minutes the Ice Cream Form should be hard enough to remove from the mold by immersing in cold water and carefully lifting the form out of the mold. Hot water will destroy fine detail. **COLOR EFFECTS** are obtained by using different flavored ice cream, such as Vanilla for white, Pistachio for green, Strawberry for pink, Chocolate for brown, and so forth. These flavors are pressed into the various parts of the molds with a small knife or spatula. **COLORING** is also done by Painting, Spraying or Dipping the hardened Ice Cream Form into a certified food color. Color designs of rare beauty and attractiveness may be obtained by using one of the methods mentioned or a combination of them. The appearance of Ice Cream Forms may be further improved by the addition of "fixtures," such as artificial leaves, flags, ribbon, and so forth, some of which are suggested throughout this catalog. **FANCY DECORATING** with a tube, using ice cream or whipped cream is always attractive. It is advisable to do this work in a hardening room. Every tray, container or wax paper should be thoroughly chilled before placing an Ice Cream Form thereon so as to avoid the possibility of melting the resting side of the form." Joe Lowe Corp., Brooklyn, NY, 1930s catalog.

IV-208. Ice cream mold. *Looks like a tin quonset hut. Shown in 1 pt. and 2 pt. sizes. "An entirely new idea is worked out in the Silver Ice Cream mold. The housewife may send the receptacle to the* **cream saloon***, and have the ice cream packed in ready to use, or it may be packed in at home. In each instance it assumes the shape of the pan and makes a splendid appearance. The cream can be sliced at the sections. The results are very dainty and appetizing. ... It can be used also for gelatine, custards, etc." Compare with bread mold at IV-13, also by Silver & Co., Brooklyn, c.1910.* **$25-$40**

Ice cream mold, bridge sets — the lady having a bridge party could serve various playing-card-related ice creams with her bridge cookies! Krauss made rectangular "cards" on which were molded a Queen, a King, a Jack, or an Ace in any suit: ranged K-432 to K-447 or, for smaller ones, ranged K-526 to K-541. Then you could apply little "spots" or suit emblems, including hearts (K-355), spades (K-353), clubs (K-356), diamonds (K-354); or you could serve a bowl with one each of the largish 11-to-a-quart heart (K-213), spade (K-211), club (K-214), and diamond (K-212). For someone with the time or the maid, these could be gaily colored just like a playing card. Value range given for one card mold, with suit figure in relief: **$30-$35**

Ice cream mold, Brownie character with acorn lid cap, fat tummy, hands at side, K-389, 8 to qt. **$100-$120**

Ice cream mold, Buddha, #476, maker unknown. Ewwwwh, who would want to eat Buddha? **$50-$55**

Ice cream mold, buffalo on round (nickel-like) disc, S-586. **$65-$70**

Ice cream mold, buffalo, standing on patch of prairie, 9 to quart, Jo-L-418. **$65-$75**

Ice cream mold, bust of George Washington — See George Washington

Ice cream mold, bust of Admiral Byrd in his parka, 2-part tin, E-1165, 8 per quart, 1930. **$150-$175**

South Pole Crossover. A sales letter from Eppelsheimer dated June 1930 reads, "THE BYRD ANTARCTIC EXPEDITION RETURNS TO THE UNITED STATES DURING JUNE. It is expected that Admiral Byrd will tour the entire Country, giving lectures about his Expedition to the South Pole. There will doubtless be Banquets in his honor in every City he visits. Be prepared to supply Fancy Forms of Ice Cream of the BUST OF BYRD in his 'Parka' (fur-coat), mold No. 1165 and BYRD'S SHIP 'THE CITY OF NEW YORK', mold No. 1164. Molds for making the Fancy Ice Cream Forms, capacity 8 per quart, price $3 each, Display Models 60¢ each, less your usual discount. ORDER YOUR SUPPLY NOW."

The display models mentioned were molded composition figures that showed how the ice cream in a particular mold would look. They'd be extremely collectible. I don't think I've ever seen one for sale, but Eppelsheimer offered them as a sort of advertising premium to confectioners or ice cream parlors who ordered a quantity — usually a dozen — of a particular mold.

Ice cream mold, bust of General Grant, surrounded by laurel wreath & crossed bullets motif, heavy, no marks, American (?), 3-1/2" H, prob. last quarter 19th C. **$100-$125**

Ice cream mold, cabbage, S-162. **$45-$55**

Ice cream mold, calla lily, 3-part, #210. **$50-$60**

Ice cream mold, candle for Christmas, E-207. **$50-$55**

Ice cream mold, candlestick, low & decorated, which would hold a real candle — they also sold tapers at 12¢ a gross, K-207. **$50-$55**

Ice cream mold, candle & chamber candlestick, 6 to the quart, Jo-Lo-932. **$40-$50**

Ice cream mold, cards — See ice cream mold, bridge set

Ice cream mold, carnation (but looks like a rose), #193. **$55-$70**

Ice cream mold, carnation centered in small posy bouquet, K-554. **$50-$60**

Ice cream mold, carnation, E-361. **$50-$60**

Ice cream mold, carriage, #562, early 20th C. **$45-$55**

Ice cream mold, carrot, K-138, 10 to qt. **$35-$40**

Ice cream mold, cart, 3-piece mold, K-488. **$45-$50**

Ice cream mold, cat, large sitting realistic cat with head turned & front paw on ball, Jo-Lo-10, table service or centerpiece size holds 3 pints. The mold model for this, once painted, would fool many people into thinking it was a carnival chalkware piece. **$100-$130**

Ice cream mold, cat sitting on the lower curve of the Man in the Moon, on his beard, looking into his quizzical face, Jo-Lo-1180, 8 per quart. Wonderful image. **$90-$100**

IV-209. Ice cream mold. *Tin, long "bridge party" club motif, for slicing. Cherry-Bassett, 1921.* **$30-$60**

IV-210. Pyramid ice cream molds. *None look like the Egyptian pyramids, but the influence is there from the exciting archaeological digs in Egypt at various times in the 19th C.* **(L)** *Fancy patterned mold, 1 litre or 2 litre sizes, Anthoine, Paris, c.1900.* **(R)** *Looking like a stack of witch's hats, this style was made round (as here), square and octagon, with 1, 2 and 3 rings. Jaburg, 1908.* **(C)** *Stamped & pieced tin swirled like soft ice cream, with lid. Imported, possibly from England. 1-1/2 quart size: 6" H x 6-1/2" diameter; and 2-1/2 quarts: 8-1/2" H x 8" diameter. Joseph, c.1927.* **$40-$65**

Ice cream mold, cat with arched back, E-1175. **$80-$85**

Ice cream mold, cat, called "Puss in Boot" but not the fairytale character; instead, a cat in a big boot, head showing only, K-178. (**NOTE:** This design was also made in a large center-piece size, numbered K-2, that held two quarts of ice cream. It would bring twice that of the individual mold, or even more.) **$90-$110**

Ice cream mold, cat quartet on oval "stage" with 4 animated, well-modeled cat figures playing guitar, cello, flute and one holding music book & singing, Bertuch-593, holds nearly 2-3/4 pints, c. 1904. **$200-$225**

Ice cream mold, cello or violin, E & Co., late 19th C. **$40-$50**

Ice cream mold, champagne bottle modeled with cork & wires & foil, white iron, #3508, about 9-3/4" H, Letang Fils, Paris. **$50-$65**

Ice cream mold, champagne bottle in cooler, K-206. **$50-$60**

Ice cream mold, chariot, 3-piece mold, K-400. **$65-$70**

Ice cream mold, cherries, 4 to a mold, K-108. They sold as accessories, a gross of leaf-and-stem pieces for $1.50. **$50-$60**

Ice cream mold, chicken or hen, sitting (no nest), white iron, #3516, about 5-3/4" H, Letang Fils, Paris. **$40-$50**

Ice cream mold, Chinese man, turn of century. **$60-$70**

Ice cream mold, Christopher Columbus full figure, knee-britches, hand on globe on stool, Jo-Lo-1017, 7 to a quart. **$75-$85**

Ice cream mold, chrysanthemum, K-313. **$40-$50**

Ice cream mold, chrysanthemum, E-344. **$40-$50**

Ice cream mold, Christmas hearth/fireplace, E-1202. **$90-$115**

IV-211. Ice cream or ice pudding mold. (**L**) *is the tin mold, balanced on its bracket strap handle. The cylinder seen at top serves to hold the mold upside down while filling, and helps protect the stamped copper ornamental turk's-head top if the mold is handled carelessly during use.* (**R**) *is the "shape produced" by the mold. This mold was made in 1, 1-1/2, 2, 3 and 4 pint sizes.* Mrs. Marshall's Book of Ices, c.1902. **$40-$60**

IV-214. Jelly & Cream molds. *Copper, with lining inserts, so that a different color or flavor could be put into center of mold, and would show in the horizontal slices when served.* (**T**) *"Alexandra," in 2 sizes, and* (**R**) *"Brunswick Star," in 2 sizes.* Mrs. Marshall's Book of Ices, c.1902. *Design registered in England in the 1890s. For mold & insert:* **$200-$300**

IV-212. Ice cream or ice pudding molds. *All "pillar molds," of tin, possibly with stamped copper tops.* (**L**) *"Fruit Top," in 1, 1-1/2, 2 and 3-pt. sizes;* (**M**) *"With plinth" is sole description. 2 and 3-pts.* (**R**) *"Cherry top" in 1, 1-1/2 and 2 pts. Made to put maraschino cherries in. All from* Mrs. Marshall's Book of Ices, c.1902. **$50-$100**

IV-213. Ice cream or ice pudding molds. *Various tin ornate molds, 1 quart sizes. with nooks for fruit, lady fingers, etc. Probably all imported from England, c.1870s-90s.* **$60-$110**

IV-215. Ice cream molds — Transportation. *By theme is just one way to collect molds. The detailed drawings from catalogs are idealized versions of what the ice cream would look like when molded. Lots of exaggeration was allowed the artists: although many molds have great detail, not all of it shows on the ice cream. Accessories like wheels, flags, canes, etc., had to be added, and were made of paper, wood or metal. Top two pewter molds, for 1-1/2 and 1-1/3 litres, from Bertuch, Berlin, c.1904. Bottom two, in individual sizes of 7 to a quart are also pewter, pictures from Duparquet, Huot & Moneuse catalog, c.1904-1910. Bicycle also made in large 4-pint capacity. All train and bike motifs have good crossover interest. Molds:* **$95-$150**

Ice cream mold, Christmas tree, decorated, E-1154. **$90-$100**

Ice cream mold, Christmas wreath, E-1146. **$100-$110**

Ice cream mold, clover, hinged 2-part mold, with one half fluted pan shape, like a cake mold, the other half with well-defined 4-leaf clover to make design on top only, heavy, E-1039. **$55-$65**

Ice cream mold, clown head, E-1035. **$40-$50**

Ice cream mold, clown figure, hands in pockets, K-624. For $2.25, they sold a 100 clown hats to set on the unmolded ice cream serving. **$60-$70**

Ice cream mold, corn cob, E-219. **$45-$50**

Ice cream mold, corn cob, K-270. **$50-$55**

Ice cream mold, cornucopia, tin-washed copper, #287. **$40-$55**

Ice cream mold, cotton bale, Jo-Lo-1095, partly collectible today because it is a reminder of the inglorious Southern slavery past. Black Americana. (See also ice cream mold, "Darkey.") **$40-$45**

Ice cream mold, cow, head turned, low haunches, hinged 2-part centerpiece mold, "L. G." in oval, mfd. by Maison Letang P.,Paris, late 19th C. **$175-$200**

Ice cream mold, cowboy with lariat, K-1064. **$85-$90**

Ice cream mold, cradle, woven wicker basket on rockers, with babe & blanket inside, 3-piece, K-344. A hundred "baby faces" (presumably printed paper) could be bought for $4.50. **$50-$65**

Ice cream mold, crescent moon with face of Sphinx, marked "32nd Degree Shriner," dated 1905. **$55-$65**

Ice cream mold, cross, Maltese style for Masons or Knights of Columbus, K-296. **$30-$35**

Ice cream mold, crusader with cross & sword, #320, early 20th C. **$65-$75**

Ice cream molds, cup and scalloped saucer, 2 different molds. Cup is K-205, with capacity of 6 to a quart; saucer is K-198; capacity 10 to a quart. (**NOTE:** The saucer could be used to hold other "spot" or small molded bite-size ice creams: flowers, fruits, hearts, eggs, etc.) For the pair: **$100-$120**

Ice cream mold, cupid standing on rabbit — mixed holidays! K-561. **$85-$90**

Ice cream mold, cupid and anvil, K-467. **$60-$70**

Ice cream mold, cupid & fat heart, K-573. **$55-$60**

Ice cream mold, cupid, E-992. **$60-$70**

Ice cream mold, daisies, 3 in one mold, S-365. (See also wildflower mold.) **$45-$50**

Ice cream mold, daisy with perfectly detailed petals and center, hinged 2-part, no mark, 2-1/2" diameter, late 19th C. **$60-$65**

Ice cream mold, "Darkey," (I apologize for using the term that Jo-Lo used), a Black Americana image of man sitting on sack or carpet bag, Jo-Lo-1053, 9 to the quart, 1930s. Very collectible for the reasons that make it such a painful image of some awful history in this country. It sure makes you wonder who sat down and enjoyed ice cream made in these molds: some good ol' boys and segregationists? **$100-$130**

Ice cream mold, "Darkey stealing turkey," Jo-Lo-1089, 8 to quart. This one is an even worse example of Black Americana from the 1930s — not that long ago, really. The closer we get to the year 2000, the more horrible, sickening and unfathomable the dark American past seems. Maybe the field should be termed "UnAmericana Noir." **$100-$130**

Ice cream mold, deer standing on oval grassy plinth, white iron, #3490, about 11" H, Letang Fils, Paris. **$90-$110**

Ice cream mold, Diana the Huntress with dog, standing in her short Roman drapery with quiver of arrows, Bertuch-557, capacity of about 1-1/4 pints, c. 1904. **$100-$120**

Ice cream mold, dog (retriever? poodle?), large & seated on oval plinth, with very deep tightly curled mane, long ears, body shaved close except for muffs on front feet, mane and tale, huge head, ponderous (or patient?) visage, pewter, small stamped maker's mark of old cranked freezer (resembles a well), "C C" & "Marque Fabrique," according to catalog #13 it was in the #969 series, mfd. by M. Cadot et Cie, Paris, France, 3 pt. capacity, pre-1900. **$75-$100**

Curly dogs. I have a c. 1900 catalog of ice cream molds made by E. Compiègne, successor to Cadot. It says that "tous les moules portent ma marque C. C.": all molds are marked C. C. They had a poodle couchant with curly ears, the anatomy obviously that of a poodle rather than a retriever (although remember the poodle was originally bred as a retriever). Also a very short-haired hound dog, lying down with head pointed up. Letang Fils of Paris had nearly identical molds, which they advertised in their 1912 catalog as for "cake or ices."

Ice cream mold, dog, a sort of poodle with curly mane, sitting on hexagonal plinth, Bertuch-607, holds about 3/4 pint, c. 1904. **$60-$70**

Ice cream mold, dog, another curly retriever/poodle type, sitting on haunches on nearly square plinth, white iron, #3513, about 9" H, Letang Fils, Paris. **$90-$100**

Ice cream mold, doll's face in bonnet, E-963. **$85-$90**

Ice cream mold, donkey with bridle & saddle, standing on grassy plinth, white iron, #3491, about 11" H, Letang Fils, Paris. **$75-$90**

IV-216. Ice cream molds. *Pewter, various designs from a sample or "specimen" page of Mrs. Marshall's touted Book of Moulds. Late 19th C. The hen on nest, the swan, and fish probably would be worth the most.* **$45-$125**

Ice cream mold, donkey head, 3-part mold, early 20th C. **$35-$45**

Ice cream mold, doves, a cooing pair, E-655. **$65-$70**

Ice cream mold, drum, 3-part mold, K-511. **$55-$65**

Ice cream mold, duck riding little waves, white iron, #3514, about 6-3/4" H, Letang Fils, Paris. **$60-$70**

Ice cream mold, eagle on a disc-like medallion with an approximate national seal, American, late 19th C. **$85-$100**

Ice cream mold, eagle, #283, early 20th C. **$75-$90**

Ice cream mold, eagle, standing & looking over his left shoulder, lead, 2-part with 5 pinned clamps, linecut in F. A. Walker catalog shows mark of a tiny castle stamp, imported, c.1870s or 1880s. **$85-$110**

Ice cream mold, eagle with shield & swords, called "Trophy Eagle" by Krauss, K-517, early 20th C. **$80-$100**

Ice cream mold, eagle pair for Masons, K-613. **$100-$110**

Ice cream mold, eagle, spread wing, E-655. **$135-$150**

Ice cream mold, electric light bulb, pointed tip in Mazda style, Jo-Lo-990, 8 to quart, 1930s. Some crossover interest. (Another bulb with standard shape, #1112, was also offered.) **$50-$55**

Ice cream mold, elephant, E-656. **$60-$70**

Ice cream mold, elephant, S-169. (Krauss also used #169.) **$65-$70**

Ice cream mold, elephant on grassy oval plinth, trunk curled under, Bertuch-559, large capacity of almost 4 quarts, banquet size, turn of century. Really awe-inspiring. **$200-$250**

Ice cream mold, elephant standing on oval plinth, very muscular, with curled under trunk, white iron, #3519, about 8-1/2" H, Letang Fils, Paris. **$90-$110**

Ice cream mold, elk head, 3-piece, K-493. **$85-$90**

Ice cream mold, engagement ring with floral decoration & set diamond, ring mold type, cast white metal, E-1141, individual mold, a little more than 1/4 pint, c.1929. **$35-$40**

Ice cream mold, envelope for a "Valentine," K-506. **$50-$55**

Ice cream mold, Eskimo figure (probably from same period as the Admiral Byrd bust, K-510. This has been listed as "Arctic explorer" S-510). **$85-$95**

Ice cream mold, fairy, figure in drapery w/ leg showing, Jo-Lo-1032, 10 to a quart. **$60-$70**

IV-217. Ice cream molds — Pigs. *Two tin styles on bases.* **(T)** *1 litre $22, and 3/4 litre#1149. From Fabrique Spéciale de Moules en Etain ... Marque c.c., Paris France catalog, 1900. The "C.C." mark had a well with bucket and the initials "C.C." I will refer to molds from that catalog as "Marque C.C." from here on out.* **(B)** *This tin mold is from the same catalog, but you can see the design is different. It is advertised as the #832 "1/2 Glace" style; which I assume may mean there's dimensional modeling on only one side?* **$100-$150**

IV-218. Ice cream molds — Horses. *Top* **(L)** *appears to be the sea god Neptune, borne on the waves in a chariot. It and the large horse at* **(R)** *are 1-3/4 and 1-1/4 quart sizes. The jockey on left is 7 to a quart. First three tin molds all sold through Duparquet, Huot & Moneuse, early 20th C. Jockey lower right is pewter, 1-1/8 litre (a dry litre is about 9/10 of a quart; a liquid litre is just over 1 quart. Ice cream must be halfway between.) Bertuch, Berlin, c.1904.* **$150-$225**

IV-219. Ice cream molds — Lobsters, dolphins & a shrimp. *The dolphin, or* <u>dauphin</u>, *molds, a symbol of French royalty, were probably used for "Crownprince" bombes, with a hazelnut and kirsch mixture. Big lobster was described in catalog as a "Glace entière" as opposed to a "Demi-glace" (or half mold). Anthoine, Paris, c.1900. Small lobster found in Duparquet, Huot & Moneuse c.1904-10 catalog, in very small sizes, from 9 to 20 to the quart, and in a 5 pint size. Shrimp is #1090 in Marque C.C. catalog, 1900. Upper dauphin, #1180, is 2, 1-1/2 and 1-1/4 litres. Marque C.C. Large dauphin, #101, in 1 litre size. Anthoine, c.1900. Small lobster & shrimp:* **$45-$60.** *Large molds:* **$85-$125**

IV-220. Ice cream molds — Dogs. *Mainly poodles or retrievers. Top* (**T-L**) *#13, glace entière, tin. Marque C.C., 1900.* (**T-M**) *#3 in Series No. 969, tin, glace entière for 9 centilitres. Marque C.C.* (**T-R**) *#83, Anthoine, c.1900. Bottom* (**B-L**) *#8, Series No. 969, tin, glace entière, Marque C.C.* (**B-M**) *"Chien loup," No. 82, Anthoine.* (**B-R**) *Poodle with ball, #52, demi-glace, Anthoine.* **$65-$150**

IV-221. Ice cream molds — Cats. *Top* (**T-L**) *Pewter Cats' Quartet, the cats and podium, holding 2-1/2 litres. Complete with music stand. Apparently instruments were extra. Bertuch, c.1904.* (**T-R**) *#14 in Series No. 969, glace entière. Marque C.C., 1900. Bottom* (**B-L**) *and* (**B-M**), *#74 and #75. One on left is a wild or jungle cat. Both Anthoine c.1900.* (**B-R**) *Cat with ball, small size — 11 to quart. Duparquet, Huot & Moneuse, c.1904-10. The quartet:* **$200-$250**; *others:* **$65-$135**

IV-222. Ice cream molds — Squirrels. (**L**) *#18, Series No. 969, glace entière, Marque C.C., 1900.* (**M**) *#84, Anthoine, Paris, 1900.* (**R**) *Small one in several sizes, from 7-10 to the quart, 20 to quart, and 2 pints. Duparquet, Huot & Moneuse, c.1904-10.* **$60-$125**

Ice Cream Molds in 1803. In Ledlie Irwin Laughlin's massive, instructive *Pewter In America*, 3 volumes in one, American Legacy Press, 1981, there are but two references to ice cream molds. The first is in Vol. II, p. 54, and refers to the <u>1798 will inventory of pewterer William Will of Philadelphia</u>. Laughlin was surprised to find the listing, and said that the actual form itself, with a Will touch [mark], had not been found as of then (1940). In Vol. III, p. 111, Laughlin transcribes a July 25, 1803 newspaper advertisement placed by NYC pewterer George Coldwell. It reads: "Ice Cream Moulds, a few pair of pewter Ice-Cream Moulds are now finished and now offered for sale at the subscriber's work-shop No 7 Beekman-street. They contain one gallon, are well made of the best materials, very strong and infinitely more durable than those made of Tinned Iron . . ." Coldwell then enumerated his other products. Laughlin again states that as of the time of publication (1970) of Vol. III, he had yet to read of any other pewter ice cream molds, nor had he seen any [to recognize, we must add]. Such molds may so differ from what we might assume such a mold would look like (for example, it may look like a pudding mold, or a pail with a lid) that we may never know if we've seen one or not.

• • • •

Fruit Ice Cream Recipe. "Ice-cream is prepared by mixing three parts of cream with one part of the juice or jam of raspberries, currants, etc. The mixture is then well beaten; and after being strained through a cloth, is poured into a pewter mould or vessel, adding a small quantity of lemon-juice. The mould is now covered, and plunged into a pail about two-thirds full of ice, into which two handfuls of salt should be previously scattered. The vessel containing the cream is then briskly agitated for eight or ten minutes, after which it is suffered to stand for a similar space of time; the agitation is then repeated, and the cream allowed to subside for a half hour, when it is taken out of the mould and sent to table." Anthony Florian Madinzer Willich, *The Domestic Encyclopedia; or A Dictionary of Facts & Useful Knowledge....*, 1st American edition, Philadelphia: W. Y. Birch & A. Small, 1803-04.

IV-223. Ice cream molds — Chickens. *Top* (**T-L**) *Hen on high basket, #818, Marque C.C.* (**T-R**) *Hen on basket nest #55, demiglace, Anthoine.* (**B-R**) *Rooster, #49, sold glace entière and demiglace. Anthoine. I left out one that shows rooster mounting hen — hey! What occasion was that one for?* **$60-$95**

Ice cream mold, female near nude figure, K-401. (**NOTE:** This was not included in their "occasion index" — no, not under Maritime, nor Valentine's — not even with the mold they called "Foxy Grandpa," K-594!) 7 to a quart. **$100-$120**

Ice cream mold, fireman, K-340. You could order little firemen's hats as decorations, for $4.50 per 100. (That's about the price we pay for 16 party napkins. Too bad we can't get these cute little decorations now!) **$90-$110**

Ice cream mold, fleur-de-lis, K-507. **$35-$45**

Ice cream mold, football, 3-piece mold, K-381. **$55-$65**

Ice cream mold, frog sitting on tulip, K-578. Good crossover (or hop-over) interest from frog collectors. **$60-$65**

Ice cream mold, George Washington's bust on shield with flag, K-456. **$60-$70**

Ice cream mold, George Washington bust, E-1084. **$65-$70**

Ice cream mold, George Washington, standing, S-460. And its mate, Martha Washington, standing, S-461. (**NOTE:** Krauss made these too, using the same numbers.) Each: **$90-$95**

Ice cream mold, George Washington's hatchet, marked "G. W." in case you thought it might be Carrie Nation's, #243. **$32-$40**

Ice cream mold, George Washington's profile bust on hatchet or ax blade, E-1093. **$75-$80**

Ice cream mold, George Washington's profile bust on hatchet head (or, as Krauss put it in a sort of guillotineish way, "George Washington's head on an ax"), K-336. **$70-$75**

Ice cream mold, George Washington's profile bust, cameo-like on a hatchet shape mold, 2-part hinged, S-336, 4" H x 3-1/2" W x 1-1/2" thick, early 20th C. **$75-$80**

Ice cream mold, gnomes, two at a tavern table, tippling, Bertuch-633, capacity slightly over a pint, c. 1904. **$65-$75**

Ice cream mold, goat, rearing, E-639. **$75-$80**

Ice cream mold, golf bag with tips of clubs showing. K-622. You could buy extra clubs for $2.80 per gross. **$55-$65**

Ice cream mold, grape bunch, E-278. **$40-$50**

Ice cream mold, grape bunch, 2-part hinged mold, stylized with leaf, no mark, slightly bigger than walnut, late 19th C. **$50-$60**

Ice cream mold, grape bunch, cast white metal, marked "W. Hart," NYC, turn of century. An uncommon maker, but not a desirable enough form to raise the value much. **$45-$50**

Ice cream mold, grape bunch, S-159. **$40-$50**

Ice cream mold, grape leaf (to accompany grapes), E-256. **$25-$30**

Ice cream mold, hammock, 3-piece mold, K-470. **$60-$65**

Ice cream mold, hand with fancy cuff, S-289. A favorite decorative motif from the 1840s on, especially in the 1880s-1910s. **$60-$65**

Ice cream mold, hare — See ice cream mold, rabbit

Ice cream mold, heart with cupid inside, E-1102. (Unbelievably, one of these sold at Atlantique City show in the mid-1990s for $300. But it might have been a last minute engagement present.) **$65-$80**

Ice cream mold, hearts, 2 fat ones embossed with word "LOVE" and flames, almost like a religious symbol, called "Hearts Aflame" K-300. **$45-$55**

Ice cream mold, horse head, 3-piece mold, K-579. **$60-$70**

Ice cream mold, horse prancing on grassy plinth, white iron, #3495, about 8-3/4" L, Letang Fils, Paris. **$70-$80**

Ice cream mold, horse & rider in jumping position on oval plinth, white iron, #3496, about 8-3/4" L, Letang Fils, Paris. (**NOTE:** They did another jumping horse & rider, this one leaning forward over mane, #3505, that was 12-1/2" L x 9" H.) **$90-$110**

IV-225. Ice cream molds — Elephants, *perhaps based on Jumbo.* (**L**) *#559, pewter, 2-3/4 litre (almost 4 quarts) although looks teensy here. Bertuch. You could also order a canopy accessory.* (**R**) *#73, Anthoine.* **$200-$250; $70-$90**

IV-226. Ice cream molds — Lions. *Top* (**T-L**) *Lion couchant, with paw on ball (globe). #10, 9 centilitres. Marque C.C.* (**T-R**) *Another regal lion, #103, holding 1-1/2 or 3 litres, Anthoine. Middle* (**M-L**) *#84, Anthoine.* (**M-R**) *More realistic cut of a mold, showing the two hinged parts and the clamps. Lead or pewter mold, from F. A. Walker import flyer, c.1880s. Bottom* (**B-L**) *Box mold, tinned sheet iron, holding 1-1/2 liter. Bertuch.* (**R**) *Two sizes, 9 to quart, and 3-1/2 quarts, Duparquet, Huot & Moneuse.* **$60-$125**

IV-224. Ice cream molds — Rabbits. *Top* (**T-L**) *12 and 20 to quart; also 3 pint size. Duparquet, Huot & Moneuse.* (**T-R**) *Pewter, 2 pint size, Mrs. Marshall's Book of Ices. Middle* (**M-L**) *#16 in Series No. 969, glace entière, Marque C.C. Bottom* (**B-L**) *#78, Anthoine.* (**B-R**) *Standing in cabbage patch, pewter, 1-1/4 litre size. Bertuch.* **$60-$90;** *big one:* **$100-$125**

Ice cream mold, horseshoe, "Good Luck" inside, K-183. **$50-$55**

Ice cream mold, Indian chief, standing, K-458. **$120-$135**

Ice cream mold, Irish gent, K-387. $1 bought 144 pipes for them. **$70-$80**

Ice cream mold, Kewpie, E-1913, 6" H. For more on Kewpies, see the first entry under "Bride & groom figures," this chapter. Kewpie Krossover interest is strong. **$150-$165**

Ice cream mold, Kewpie on little mound w/ word "Kewpie," E-1115, early 20th C. (Jo-Lo has this with same number). **$125-$150**

Ice cream mold, Kewpie figures, 2, very fat bellied, T. C. Weygandt Co., 9-1/2" H x 7" W, 20th C. **$170-$200**

Ice cream mold, leaf, D-319. **$30-$40**

Ice cream mold, lemon, E-308. **$25-$30**

Ice cream mold, lettuce head, "Romaine," K-549. **$30-$35**

Ice cream mold, lighthouse showing some detail of stonework, Bertuch-561, capacity of a little over a pint, c. 1900. **$40-$50**

Ice cream mold, lily, Calla, 3-part, K-210. Krauss made seven lily molds — it would have been wonderful to see a "bunch" of lilies, all from different molds, in different colors of ice cream. (The numbers are K-235; K-210; K-472; K-548; K-457; K-386; and a lily pond 3-piece mold K-209.) **$45-$50**

Ice cream mold, lily, 3-part hinged, #354. **$55-$60**

Ice cream mold, lily, well-defined details, 3-part hinged, #472, early 20th C. **$55-$60**

Ice cream mold, lion couchant on lid of rectangular box mold, double-tinned pieced & stamped sheet metal, Bertuch-525, Berlin, capacity of 1-1/2 litres, or 1-2/3 pints. c.1904. **$70-$80**

Ice cream mold, lion, standing, 2-part lead mold with 6 pinned clamps, F. A. Walker catalog linecut shows mark of a tiny castle & some illegible initials on this mold, European (?), c.1870s, 1880s. **$100-$135**

Ice cream mold, lizard — chameleon with tight-curled-under tail, K-576. **$55-$65**

Ice cream mold, lobster, K-330, very small: 20 of these to the quart. **$15-$20**

Ice cream mold, locomotive, old steam type with barrel-like boiler body, whistle, cab, K-477. (**NOTE:** a generalist price guide lists a set that include a locomotive, tender, and two passenger sleeping cars, no number given, valued at over $500. The only trace I can find of anything but locomotives is a passenger car and locomotive from Bertuch, Berlin.) **$110-$120**

Ice cream mold, locomotive, old steam type, centerpiece size, Jo-Lo-155, holds 4 pints. **$175-$225**

Ice cream mold, magnolia, graceful, and esp. nice because not symetrical. K-348. **$35-$40**

Ice cream mold, mandolin, K-547, an instrument very popular among the college crowd in the 1920s (not to mention Tiny Tim!). **$80-$95**

Ice cream mold, Masonic compass & square, crossed to form a diamond inside, #323, American, early 20th C. **$45-$55**

Ice cream mold, Max & Moritz, a pair from German cartoon & book fame. Mold has a sort of "soap bar" plinth, with the 2 caricatured boys from the waist up, Bertuch-573, holds about 1-1/2 pints. **$100-$120**

Ice cream mold, Mikado, Japanesey full-length figure in flowingly draped kimono. This celebrated either the very popular comic opera by W. S. Gilbert & A. S. Sullivan from the late 19th C., or generally the craze for Japonism — a style movement in the late 19th C. **$45-$55**

Ice cream mold, Miss Liberty (not the Statue, but Miss Columbia), hinged 2-part, American, individual, turn of century. **$75-$100**

Ice cream mold, Miss Liberty (sometimes called Miss Columbia), bedraped & standing on globe and wearing crown, hinged 2-part centerpiece mold, marked "Joh: Reinöhl" for Johannes Reinöhl, Ulm, Germany, c. 1860s-70s. (This is not Statue of Liberty.) **$200-$250**

Ice cream mold, 3 Odd Fellows chain links, representing friendship, love and truth, #577. **$45-$55**

Ice cream mold, orange, hinged 2-part, #357. **$35-$45**

Ice cream mold, peach, in section, with almost a half cut away to reveal pit or stone, hinged 2-part, marked #13, late 19th C. **$50-$65**

Ice cream mold, pear, E-248. **$30-$35**

Ice cream mold, pedestal, square column with base and top, suitable for placing a small molded ice cream (of course, molds made by different companies were mixed and matched to create still-lifes and vignettes) or a composition "party favor" piece such as a composition bust of Lincoln or a cupid. K-571. **$25-$30**

Ice cream mold, pie slice in wedge shape, 8 to a quart, Jo-Lo-1097, 1930s. Wouldn't this be fun to make in layered fruit ice creams, and then put a pie á la mode wedge of ice cream on top using a novelty disher? **$30-$40**

Ice cream mold, pineapple, upright, white iron, #3498, about 8-1/4" H, Letang Fils, Paris. **$90-$110**

Ice cream mold, pineapple, K-337, small mold 20 to the quart, for which Krauss sold clusters of paper leaves, $12.60 per gross. **$15-$20**

Ice cream mold, pineapple, with lots of outside detail, 3-part hinged, heavy casting, marked "Harton & Son, London," c.1870s-1880s. **$95-$100**

Ice cream molds, playing cards — See ice cream mold, bridge sets

IV-228. Ice cream molds — Baskets. *Top* (**T-L**) *Basket of Fruits, with split pomegranate on top. 3 pint capacity.* (**T-R**) *Wheatsheaf, 8" H, 1 quart.* (**B-L**) *Basket of flowers, 1-1/2 pints.* (**B-R**) *Smaller fruit basket, only 1-1/2 pints. All from* Mrs. Marshall's Book of Ices. *English, late 19th C.* **$45-$85**

IV-227. Ice cream molds — Eagles. (**L**) *Small, 7 to a quart. Duparquet, Huot & Moneuse.* (**R**) *#0256, lead or pewter, with clamps, size not given. F. A. Walker, 1880s.* **$50-$80**

Ice cream mold, potato, E-244, c.1910s. **$35-$40**

Ice cream mold, potato, S-154. **$35-$40**

Ice cream mold, pretzel — a religious symbol for arms folded in supplication across the chest, #577, early 20th C. **$55-$65**

Ice cream mold, pumpkin, K-600. **$40-$45**

Ice cream mold, question mark, top part of 2-part hinged mold, bottom part is shallow oblong pan or tray with flared sides, top very high relief, heavy casting, no numbers or marks, 3-3/4" L x 2-1/4" W, exclusive of hinge, 20th C. As a writer and editor, believe me there can be crossover interest in objects like this! (Krauss had a question mark very like this, K-288.) **$30-$45**

Ice cream mold, rabbit running on grassy oval plinth, white iron, #3501, about 9-1/4" L, Letang Fils, Paris. **$70-$75**

Ice cream mold, rabbit or hare rising up out of enveloping kale leaves, Bertuch-567, holds about 1-1/2 pints, c. 1904. **$70-$80**

Ice cream mold, rabbit, S-189. **$70-$75**

Ice cream mold, rabbit, standing, with basket backpack, Eppelsheimer & Co., NYC, NY, about 12" H, 1934 patent #1948148. **$80-$100**

Ice cream mold, rabbit sitting up, alert with ears high and paws to chest, on oval plinth, white iron, #3517, about 12-1/4" H, Letang Fils, Paris. **$100-$120**

Ice cream mold, Radio Corporation of America "His Masters Voice" double joined medallions, with Nipper & phonograph & motto on right disc, and RCA with lighting bolt on left. Jo-Lo-1168. It's shown in their 1930s catalog, with the caption "Specially designed for the Radio Corporation of America through one of the large Ice Cream Manufacturers." There is no indication that this mold (probably an individual mold about 7 to 9 to the quart) was not available to the general public. I believe this would be a very valuable mold, with great crossover interest. **$200+**

Ice cream mold, roast turkey, marked "364" on turkey; "D & Co." on hinge. Another was marked S-364, 20th C. **$45-$55**

Ice cream mold, rose — See carnations, which often look like roses

Ice cream mold, Santa Claus, E-991, 20th C. **$90-$100**

Ice cream mold, Santa Claus, one hinge, E-166, 4-3/4" H, late 19th C. or early 20th. **$90-$100**

Ice cream mold, Santa & toy bag, plus wicker back pack, S-427, late 19th C. **$110-$125**

Ice cream mold, Santa, banquet size, E-194. (Joe Lowe also made this large, standing, old-fashioned, relatively skinny Santa,

with his long fur-trimmed coat and small shoulder bag of toys, and used the same number #194.) **$300-$375**

Ice cream mold, seashell, stamped tin, conical helical shell design, with screw-on tin lid & strap handle, marked "GE #920," Austria, 9" L, lid is 8" diameter, early 20th C. **$65-$75**

Ice cream mold, shoe, 3-part, late 19th C. The form of a shoe has long been a love token. **$60-$65**

Ice cream mold, sitting hen has egglike body, uplifted head on elongated neck, perky tail, single serving, early 1900s. **$65-$75**

Ice cream mold, skull & crossbones, hinged 2-piece, #508, 3-3/4" W x 4-1/2" with hinge, 1-3/4" thick, 20th C. **$90-$100**

Ice cream mold, skull, S. & Co., late 19th C. **$80-$95**

Ice cream mold, sleigh, 3-part mold, K-494. Meant to be used with small deer figures, which were $12 a gross. **$50-$55**

Ice cream mold, lady's slipper with back & heel (another was a backless slip-on mule with heel), 3-piece, "899A," 20th C. **$35-$45**

Ice cream mold, snowman, much more of a human figure than the rotund pile of balls we're used to, arms folded across chest to hold an accessory broom, a hat could be bought too, Bertuch-578, holds nearly 1-1/4 pints, c. 1904. **$55-$65**

Ice cream mold, squirrel sitting, large 2-pint table service mold, K-27. **$110-$135**

Chalkware Confusable. When I saw the plaster model made in the above large squirrel mold, I realized that it is quite possible that many of the so-called "carnival chalkwares," perhaps even the "19th century chalkwares" so hotly collected now may actually be ice cream mold models. Especially reminiscent are this squirrel, a cat, a lamb, a Santa and a rabbit standing with paw on stump.

Ice cream mold, squirrel sitting on round disc, holding nut up to mouth, very lively, Bertuch-608, capacity a little over a pint, c. 1904. **$60-$70**

Ice cream mold, squirrel, sitting on half a nutshell plinth. Possibly A. Anthoine #84, French, c.1900. **$65-$75**

Ice cream mold, squirrel holding nut to chest, sitting on small oval, white iron, #3504, about 8-1/2" H, Letang Fils, Paris. **$90-$110**

Ice cream mold, Struwelpeter, stamped tin, marvelously detailed figure of 19th C. German folktale bad boy "Struwelpeter": literally "shock-headed Peter," with a shock of long straw like hair sticking out all over in a bush. Everything Struwelpeter was told not to do he did; he was used in morals & manners tales as an example of what happened if you didn't behave. Bertuch-564, little over a pint capacity, turn of century. **$100-$125**

Ice cream mold, Statue of Liberty, centerpiece size, metal, 2-part, Jo-Lo-150, 10 pt. capacity, c.1930s-1940s. In their catalog they also offered this design on a pedestal, for sale or rental, with a 26-pint capacity, for large parties or banquets. It was 37" H. The mold was $30; for $10 you could get a display model made in it. **$260-$300**

Ice cream mold, stadium, rectangular w/ press box and banked rows of seats, Jo-Lo-1169, 1930s or 1940s. **$50-$55**

Ice cream mold, stocking or long sock, very detailed knitted pattern, hinged 2-part, S-590, turn of century. **$75-$85**

Ice cream mold, stork, American, 20th C. **$70-$90**

Ice cream mold, straw basket, 3-part, #598, early 20th C. **$45-$55**

Ice cream mold, teddy bear, little eyes, nose and every one of his hairs show perfectly inside, E-1103, late 19th C. **NOTE:** The one I saw had the numbers stamped into the pewter backwards, as if "3011;" this may help you decipher confusing numbers. **$120-$130**

IV-229. Ice cream molds — Flowers, *Hinged pewter. Beautiful detailing in 3-part lily mold, 5-1/4" L closed. No marks. Author's collection. Two-part carnation and tulip molds, collection of Meryle Evans. Late 19th into early 20th C. Made for long time.* **$50-$65**

Ice cream mold, thistle (?) is what it appears to be on inside, stamped sheet metal, letters say "20th Century" —possibly for a railroad?, marked "D. & Co.," 3-1/2" H. **$40-$50**

Ice cream mold, top hat, turn of century. **$40-$50**

Ice cream mold, tulip, 2 parts, unmarked, 2-1/2" L, 19th or early 20th C. **$35-$40**

Ice cream mold, tulips in pot, E-1199. **$45-$50**

Ice cream mold, turkey, E-650, early 20th C. **$60-$75**

Ice cream mold, Uncle Sam, standing, E-1073. **$120-$130**

Ice cream mold, watermelon, centerpiece size, Jo-Lo-108, holds 7 pints. **$75-$100**

Ice cream mold, wedding bell with cupid inside, E-1019. **$55-$60**

Ice cream mold, wheat sheaf, stalks forming pedestal base, with the top very rounded, 2-part, Biertumpfel & Hepting, with Maltese cross & orb mark, London, design registered July 22, 1868. **$40-$50**

Ice cream mold, Whistler's Mother, oval framed medallion showing woman in chair, drapery, picture on wall, and word "Mother," Jo-Lo-1187, 8 per quart. Really unusual. **$60-$70**

Ice cream mold, "wildflower" in catalog (black-eyed susan or fancy daisy), 10 big petals, rosette center, 2-part hinged, E-240, late 19th C? **$50-$60**

IV-230. Ice cream molds. *Pewter gnomes. #633, two of them at tavern table, holds 1 litre in all. #632, gnome pushing large nut . . . uphill?, holds 1-1/8 litre. Bertuch, Berlin, c.1904.* **$75-$100**

IV-231. Ice cream molds. *More fantasy figures in hinged pewter molds. (T-L) #578 Snowman, in 1-1/4 litre size. Broom & hat extra. (T-R) #564* **Struwelpeter,** *or Shock-headed Peter, the antihero of cautionary morality stories used to teach children manners and behavior in Germany. 1 litre. (B-M) #591* **Bachus,** *holding 1-1/2 litre. All Bertuch, c.1904.* **$65-$150**

Ice cream mold, witch on broom, E-1153. **$100-$110**

Ice cream mold, "Yellow Kid," the raggedy little street waif created by cartoonist Richard Outcault, whose strip ran in Hearst newspapers beginning in 1896 and was probably the first really popular American cartoon character. K-476, turn of century. **$150-$175**

Ice cream mold, Yule log, E-987. **$65-$70**

Ice cream mold or freezer, pressed glass cylinder, domed glass lid, perhaps has inner cylinder (?) of glass, wire clamp frame, exactly like the Fox mold but advertised as is the Dazey as a "freezer," and not described well enough to know if there is an inner chamber. Ad reads "No cranking, no gear, no dasher, no rust, no crank, no metal, no wood, no labor, just VELVET ICE CREAM." Reassuringly, it "Makes Ptomaine Poisoning impossible." "The Sanitary," mfd. by Consolidated Mfg. Co., Hartford, CT, probably about 9" H, advertised Jan. 1909, company still in business in 1915. **$125-$150**

Ice cream mold or freezer, pressed glass cylinder with slightly domed lid, footed base, tin inner chamber open at both ends, false bottom has small hole fitted with white glazed stoneware stopper & rubber washer, which is where you would use wooden dowel pusher to push ice cream out the open top. Wire clamp, which is also handle, holds lid & stopper on, marked "G. H. Fox" and patent dates, invented by George H. Fox, Bangor, ME, 8-1/2" H x 3-1/2" diameter, pat'd Feb. 14, 1899, and July 15, 1902. **$125-$150**

Ice cream mold or freezer, pressed glass cylindrical vessel, inner vessel (possibly tin, less probably glass, unclear from old ad picture), wire clamp to hold lid on & wire pusher to push round ball of molded ice cream out of inner cylinder for slicing, called a "freezer" in ad, "The Dazey Glass Freezer — The Freezer that Freezes Without Motion," probably mfd. by the churn people, probably about 9" H, depicted in *House Furnishing Review* as a "latest model" in 1911. **$125-$150**

Ice cream sandwich mould, cast iron, (1) ornate countertop style, or (2) simple wooden-handled hand-held style, to form an ice cream sandwich with two oblong biscuits and a "thin cut of ice cream between." "Pan-American," mfd. or sold by Thomas Mills & Bro., in 1915 catalog. (1) and (2): **$125-$175; $45-$60**

Ice cream wafer holder, metal, "Reliance," early 20th C. **$200-$250**

Jaggers. A jagger is a pastry cutter, generally one that makes a jagged (actually zigzag) edge. It could be used to cut or trim off the pie crust dough that hung over the edge of the pie pan, or to cut shapes out to lay on top in lieu of a top crust, or to cut strips for a lattice top. Of course jaggers could be used to cut other dough, such as for making free-form cookies. Jaggers are also called <u>pie wheels</u>, <u>pie rimmers</u>, <u>pie jiggers</u>, <u>pie cutters</u>, <u>jagging irons</u>, <u>gigling irons</u> (very archaic term), and probably other names. Some jaggers are made with separate **crimpers** (which squish and corrugate and seal the top and bottom crust edges together, for pies or tarts); sometimes the jagging wheel and the crimper are all-in-one wheel. Some jaggers — usually scrimshaw ones — have two fork-prong **prickers** for making steam release in the top crust. Some jaggers are made with a **pastry stamp** at the other end, a sort of small curvy cookie cutter used to cut out leaf shapes, used especially for the tops of savoury pies. Generally there are two kinds of collectors for pie jaggers — the patent collectors who seek patented late nineteenth-century pieces, and the folk art collectors who favor scrimshaw if they're rich, and old, interesting design, especially with old paint on handles, if they aren't so rich. Prices haven't really moved a lot: jaggers are a neglected corner (or outer edge) of both folk art and kitchen collectibles.

Ice cream wafer mold, cast iron, 3-piece, patterned to make a waffled design, with "ICYPI MADE IN USA" in pattern, ICYPI, mfd. by Automatic Cone Co., Cambridge, MA, 1920s. These molds were not necessarily used by each soda fountain owner, because already prepared & baked wafer sandwich "holders" could be bought in large quantities already made. They are open on one end only to receive a slab of ice cream made using the ICYPI mechanical ice cream dipper. (ICYPI is pronounced I-Cee-Pie & usually spelled IcyPi by the company.) See also the ICYPI ice cream disher under ice cream disher listed with other sandwich or slab dishers. See also wafer irons. **$350-$400**

BONE: (See also ivory; scrimshaw)

Jagger, bone wheel with turned maple handle, 4-1/2" L, 19th C. **$40-$55**

Jagger, bone, simple carving, American, 4" L, mid 19th C. **$45-$60**

Jagger, turned wood with bone wheel, steel pin, American, 5" L, 19th C. **$28-$38**

BRASS:

Jagger, brass shaft, small brass cutting wheel, big crimping wheel is cast iron, American, 6-1/2" L, late 19th C. **$75-$90**

Jagger, brass shaft & small brass wheel, cast iron sealing & trimming wheel, no marks, 6" L, late 19th C. **$30-$40**

Jagger, brass shank & fancily fashioned wheel, turned wood handle has original hang-up ring, American or English, 7-1/2" L, 19th C. **$125-$150**

Jagger, brass, lightweight brass wire shaft or frame, split to take a light sheet brass wheel at each end, American, 4" L, late 19th C. **$35-$45**

IV-232. **Jagging iron.** *Probably all metal, maybe cast and sheet iron, or brass. Drawn from tiny sketchy engraving in original kitchen interior print in Bartolomeo Scappi's* Opera di M. Bartolomeo Scappi, *a 1570 Italian cookbook. There's a trestle table holding a mound of dough or flour, rolled-out paste with a long slim rolling pin resting upon it, a craved wooden tool like a big molar tooth, used as a dough marker, and a clumpsy, large jagging iron with serrated wheel and relatively short shaft, with knops at center and end.*

IV-233. **Jaggers & pastry pinchers. (T)** *a "paste jigger," with smallish wheel and long pincers, corrugated lengthwise on the inside. Hard to say what material, either brass or iron are springy. Linecut from* Warne's Model Cookery, *London & NY: 1868.* **(M)** *Drawing adapted from the paste-pincher depicted in* Mrs. Beeton's Everyday Cooking, *1872 edition.* **(B)** *A spring steel pincher, from Duparquet, Huot & Moneuse catalog, c.1904-10. Pincher:* **$5-$10**; *Jaggers:* **$35-$100**

Jagger, brass shank, steel wheel, large but delicate, turned wooden handle, American or English, 9" L, 2nd quarter 19th C. **$75-$95**

Jagger, brass wheel, forged iron shank, wooden handle, American, 8" L, early to mid 19th C. **$45-$60**

Jagger, cast brass, wheel at one end, curved semi-circle cutter at other, turned brass shank, English or French, and imported in the late 19th C., between about 4-1/2" L and 7" L, 19th C. An all brass jagger, 4-3/4" L, with a slightly knobbed shank, curved stamp at one end and small jagging wheel with 4 drilled holes, was auctioned by Garth's in Sept. 1989. It was marked "Germany" — first I've heard of. **Brass Jaggers from India (?):** There are, upon examination, a great variety in these, even though most have the knop or thickening in the center of the shaft and the smallish corrugated or jagged wheel and the cutter or stamp at the other end. I have seen some rather crudely cast and finished ones, with extremely flimsy pins holding the wheels in place, that appear to be of recent manufacture. With all the brass coming in from India, that's my suspicion, though I've not seen "Made in India" marked on any of them. The best ones, most to be desired, have leaf stamps instead of simple corrugated curves. These stamps were used to cut out pastry leaves to be applied to the top crusts of tarts or pies. The curved pieces could be used to cut out circles or ovoid shapes, as well as sawtooth-edged elliptical leaves. **$28-$40**

Jagger, cast brass, nickel-plated & very heavy, piece looks like machinists' work, American, 6-1/4" L, turn of century. **$85-$95**

Jagger, turned brass, large wheel, extremely wide crimper piece at other end, English (?), 4-1/4" L, 1-5/8" W with 1-15/16" diameter wheel, mid 19th C. **$70-$90**

Jagger, brass wheel & shank, black painted wood handle, Alfred Andreson & Co., Minneapolis, MN, 20th C. **$20-$25**

Jagger, cast & machined brass, unusual because of long straight shank or handle with slight knob at end, American or European, 6" L, 19th C. **$35-$45**

Jagger, cast & turned brass shaft, brass wheels at each end, American, 4" L, late 19th C. **$35-$45**

Jagger & crimper, brass, American, pat'd 1871. **$40-$55**

IV-234. **Jagger & pie.** *Simplified jagging iron with a pie crust showing serrated edge, taken from Henry Scammell's* Treasure House of Useful Knowledge, *1891, a book compiled, often without credit, from all existing books available to the editor. The style of this engraving seems very old, even 18th C., and it is possible that the jagger was meant to have a pincing end, rather than what appears to be a horn or wood handle.*

IV-235. **Jagger with ornamenter.** *A very old style, back to the 1600s, wheel with a cutter that worked like a cookie cutter to make pastry leaves. Such leaves ornamented the top crust, or were baked, then laid upon the filling. Probably brass, English or French. Note knop (a mid-shaft knob) in center. F. A. Walker, Boston, import catalog, c.1870s.*

Jagger & crimper, heavy brass handle or shaft, 2 brass wheels at one end plus steel edge sealing stamp or edger at other end, patented as a "pie rimmer" by J. Stephen and W. Zeller, Womelsdorf, PA, 5-1/2" L, pat'd Sept. 11, 1866. **$95-$125**

Jagger & pastry stamp, brass wheels & stamp with turned wooden handle, American, or English (?), 6" L, 19th C. **$45-$55**

Jagger & pastry stamp, cast & machined brass, turned beechwood handle, cruciform with 2 stamps and wheel, English, 11" L, 2nd quarter 19th C. **$125-$150**

Jagger & pastry stamp, cruciform baker's tool, cast brass, includes jagging wheel, diamond shape stamp with 16 points laid out in rows of 4 x 4, round stamp also has 16 points, English, 7-5/8" L x 3-7/8" W, c.1810s. **$300-$350**

COPPER:

Jagger, wheel is a copper coin, Quebec, CAN, 1852, wooden handle. **$100-$150**

Jagger, copper?, heavy copper or bell metal wheel and shaft, turned wooden handle, very pretty, wheel drilled out with 4 holes, English (?), 6" L, 2nd quarter 19th C (?). **$110-$135**

IV-236. Jaggers & pincer. *Top* **(T-R)** *is a wood-handled jagger, from Lalance & Grosjean, 1890, as well as Duparquet, Huot & Moneuse, c.1904-10, catalogs. Other three pictures — pinchers, jagger with turned wood handle, and latticed pastry of some kind — from chapter on little cakes and petits fours, in Urbain Dubois, La Patisserie, pictures c.1860s-80s.*

IV-237. Jaggers. **(L)** & **(R)** *Cast iron long ones from Italy, 17th C., many tiers of turned knops and rings. Pieces on end are semi-circular cutters (see next picture.) 8-1/4" L.* **(M)** *is smaller, two-wheeled brass one, 18th or early 19th C., 5-1/2" L. Note the drilled holes in the brass one; these are often found, and I can only assume it had something to do with cost-per-ounce, either making or shipping costs. Courtesy Hillman Books.* **$125-$225**

IRON:

Jagger, cast iron shank with knops & the effect of turning, forged iron wheel, turned wooden handle, probably a one-off blacksmith's piece, American, 5" L, 19th C. A **knop** is like a knob only it's not on the end or top of something, but somewhere in the middle. **$55-$60**

Jagger, cast iron, wooden handle, quite simple, American, 9" L (which is exceptionally long, and indicates this may have been used in a bakery), late 19th C. **$25-$35**

Jagger, forged iron with file-decorated shaft & faceted ball knob end, one wheel, sometimes called a <u>gigling iron</u> in very old cookery books, American, 8-1/8" L, late 18th C. **$210-$250**

Jagger, forged iron, simple, forged or possibly drawn wire rod in square shape (nail stock?), which has been split at one end to admit a brass jagging wheel with 4 drilled out holes, and pinned through, handle end bent into sharp hook for quick hanging,

IV-238. Jaggers. **(T)** *cast brass, with long curved paste cutter for making circles, ovals, ellipses, leaves, etc. Five knops in center of shaft. This picture is from the 1908 Jaburg Brothers catalog for confectionery supplies. The style is very old. Similar ones, differing in workmanship, number of knops, length of cutter, style of serrated blades, and style of the straddling shaft for the wheel.* **(B)** *picture is from John Van Range, Cincinnati, catalog of 1914. Similar one-knoppers appear in 1865 catalog of Russell & Erwin Mfg. Co., New Britain, CT, and Lalance & Grosjean, 1890, as well as a 2-knopper made by Ekco, with 1" wheel, about 1925, and many modern cheap imports, principly from India. Caution: The lightweight, fairly crude ones are often way overpriced, and should be under $25. Pictured ones:* **$35-$55**

IV-239. Jagger. *Brass, with unusually curved cutter at one end. 6-1/4" L. Early to mid- 19th C.* **$25-$50**

IV-240. Jagger. *Cut pewter wheel, 4 spokes, set in turned and carved wood handle in old red paint, possibly overpainted on old green. 6-3/4" L, probably American, early to mid 18th C.* **$300-$400**

very utilitarian, American, 5-7/8" L, poss. early 19th C. **Holey Wheelies**. I cannot figure out why the holes are cut in the wheels. Surely not for decorative purposes. The only thing I can think is that even that little bit drilled out would mean saved brass (the filings or dust could be melted) or saved weight for shipping. **$65-$75**

Jagger, iron shank, brass wheel, wooden handle, American, 7-1/2" L, mid 19th C. **$45-$60**

Jagger & crimper, or pie trimmer & sealer, also called in ads a pie crimper & ornamenter, iron, with longish flat handle with 2 heart cutouts (top to top), corrugated wheel, 5 fork-like prongs to pierce upper crust to let steam out while baking, "Cinderella," mfd. by Mr. G. J. Capewell, Cheshire, CT, 4th quarter 19th C. **Handy to Have in the House**. "A well stocked house-furnishing store is to us a most interesting and instructive place to visit. It is wonderful to see the various contrivances for performing household operations, and the numerous little conveniences that go to make domestic matters run smoothly, but are classified under the general head of 'Notions.' ... [A rather] fanciful notion is the 'Cinderella,' which is a trade name for a new Pie crimper and Ornamenter. The grooved wheel is used for printing rosettes, and also to run along the edge of the pie to crimp it; on the other side, opposite the wheel [not at the other end of handle, but on the flip side], is a set of blades which cut ventilating holes in the crust in the form of a star. The manufacturer also makes tack hammers and various other articles handy to have in the house." *American Agriculturist*, Dec. 1876. **$55-$65**

Jagger, wrought iron wheel, turned wood shank, American, 6" L with 2" wheel diameter, early 19th C. **$70-$85**

Jaggers, forged iron, 8 different ones, wheels of different "gauges" of teeth, very simple rod handles, a few with half circle

IV-241. Jaggers. (L) *"Ivory" colored plastic wheel, asparagus-green shaped plastic handle, beautifully simple, c.1915-20s.* **(M)** *Machined brass, commercially made, possibly the Russell & Erwin one mentioned in IV-273. 3rd quarter 19th C.* **(R)** *Turned wood with ebony-like wheel, 19th C. All between 4-1/2" and 5-1/4" L. The most valuable is the plastic one.* **$35-$50; $25-$35; $25-$50**

cutters on one end, two with faceted knobs at end, American or European (maybe Italian), 6" to 8" L, with wheels 1" to 1-1/4" diameter, early to 3rd quarter 19th C. For the collection: about $500. Singles: **$90-$125**

IVORY: (See also bone; scrimshaw)

Jagger, ivory, elephant (not whale or walrus ivory), inset with ebony pins, metal hook on end, nothing special to look at but the material counts, 7" L, mid 19th C. **$600-$900**

PEWTER:

Jagger, pewter wheel, heavily carved wooden handle with old old red paint, possibly old green paint underneath, American (?), 6-3/4" L, early to mid 18th C. or even older. **$400-$435**

PLASTIC:

Jagger, plastic & aluminum, butterscotch yellow molded plastic handle, cast aluminum shank, bronze or copper well-defined corrugated wheel, American, 7-1/2" L, 20th C. **$25-$30**

Marketing information from *House Furnishing Review*, Jan. 1930, says that the "Relative popularity of **colors** is as follows: Green, 60%; red, 25%; yellow, 15%." Apparently blue was not a choice in 1930 (or any other time?).

Jagger, plastic, marbleized asparagus green plastic handle, with carved "ivory" plastic jagging wheel, steel pin, American, 5-1/4" L, 1930s. The rage for interesting and well-designed plastic, partly fueled by the book *Art Plastic*, by Andrea DiNoto (Abbeville Press, 1985), has caused prices for especially nice or particularly interesting plastic kitchen wares to go up. **$35-$60**

PORCELAIN:

Jagger, turned rosewood handle, with all-white porcelain wheel, English (?), 19th C. **$45-$60**

SCRIMSHAW: (whale and walrus ivory and bone): (See also bone; ivory)

Jagger, scrimshaw piecrust edger in form of horse with an elongated, curved fish or whale's tail, the head is fairly small & as abstract as Cycladic art from over 3000 years ago, the front legs arch downwards & grasp a jagging wheel, the 6 spokes

IV-242. Jaggers. *A pair of double-wheeled brass jaggers.* **(T)** *cast one with substantial knopped shaft, wheels not drilled out;* **(B)** *sheet brass wheels, 4 holes each (which may have had something to do with diecutting technique of making the wheels), and having a much thinner shaft — actually brass rod split at each end to accommodate wheels. 4" L each. 19th C. Courtesy Barbara Canter, Livingstone, NJ.* **$35-$45; $25-$35**

of which are cut in such a way to create 6 hearts, American, 5-3/4" L, early 19th C. At early 1980s auction of Barbara Johnson's scrimshaw collection, the jaggers, many architectural or geometric in style, went for high prices, from $750 to $1700. Others, highly ornamental but not figural or animalistic, ranged from $275 for one with a broken prong on the pricker part, to $1550. At another auction about the same time, some whale ivory and walrus ivory jagging wheels, none of them figural, realized between $225 and $650. Geometric was in, figural wasn't. Depending on the subject of the scrimshaw pieces, values have risen 100% to 1000%. At Richard A. Bourne Co.'s auction in July 1989, of the Jeffrey Cohen Collection of maritime antiques, two scrimshaw unicorn jaggers, each with a long bifurcated horn pricker and front legs that straddle wheel, sold for $8,000 & $10,000, plus 10% premium for buyer. **$2500-$3000**

Jagger, scrimshaw: carved whale bone with whale tooth wheel, mermaid with long wavy hair, smiling, slightly Negroid features so she almost resembles African carving, 3 brass nails hold on arms, American (?), 9-5/8" L with 2-1/16" diameter wheel, early 19th C. **$2000-$2300**

Jagger, scrimshaw, with detailed horse's head with bridle, leg-like extensions grasping wheel, the spokes of which are the 5 points of a star, American, 6" L, early 19th C. This one sold for $500 at auction a few years ago. **$1500-$2000**

Jagger, whale bone scrimshander work, sailor with hands on his midriff against his double-breasted buttoned jacket, straddling large fluted wheel (looks like he's riding a unicycle), wears lit-

tle black cap, a skimmer, eyes appear set in of ebony, but are possibly carved & painted, American, 6-1/2" L with 1-3/4" diameter wheel, c.1850s. **$2000-$3500**

Jagger, whale bone scrimshander's work, determined-looking mermaid, arms nailed on with tiny nails, long hair down back, American, 6" L, early 19th C. **$700-$900**

Jaggers, scrimshaw whale bone or walrus ivory, figural forms, American, 5" to 8" L, 19th C. Prices start at about $500. Especially prized are pieces with double wheels and a pricker (sometimes in the form of a unicorn horn). **$500 on up.**

STEEL:

Jagger, steel shank & wheel with bone handle, American, mid 19th C. **$45-$55**

Jagger, turned steel handle shaped like wood handles, brass shaft, nickeled brass wheel, American, 7-3/8" L, late 19th C. **$75-$85**

Jagger, steel, machined shaft & handle, brass wheel, very finely made, American (?), 7" L, early 19th C. **$125-$150**

Jagger, nickeled steel wheel & shaft with black-painted turned wood handle, American, 6" L, late 19th C. **$60-$75**

Jagger, steel wheel, hand carved & turned wooden shank, with original dark worn red paint, American, 8" L, late 18th or early 19th C. To identify these really old ones, study books on furniture styles, candlesticks & andirons, as they will give you a feel for the look of late 1700s turnings. Here, it's partly old red paint, partly magisterial (as in sceptre) look that increases value. **$300-$400**

Jagger, steel, **replica** of early 19th C. figural jagging wheel in the collection of Metropolitan Museum of Art, NYC, and created by them in their workshops. Roughly S-shaped shank with a simple bird at one end, a fishtail at the other, 10-1/2" L, 1980s. **Reproduction alert**. Sold through the beautiful Metropolitan Museum (NYC) catalog in the early 1980s for $170. Very hard to figure a resale value for this because it's a reproduction, not an original. The price had to be high for the reproduction because of the work involved in making it, but my feeling is that it is like new furniture in an old style: after you've had it a day it's simply secondhand furniture and it'll take a generation (more like a century) to become valuable again. I'd be very wary of such pieces, as the price for an original of this type might be in the high hundreds. I believe the Museum marked theirs. Anything offered you should be carefully examined with a magnifying glass — standard collector equipment. Get as powerful a one as you can find. The museum repro resale value: **$75-$100**

IV-243. Jagger. *Stamped brass wheel, something like those in previous picture, set into split iron square rod (nail stock?), that's hooked at end for easy hanging up. 5-7/8" L, 19th C.* **$25-$35**

IV-244. Jaggers & pie sealer. *Left to right:* **(1)** *Fat wood handle, thick, machined steel wheel, 6-1/4" L;* **(2)** *Nickeled steel shaft & wheel, black, turned wood handle;* **(3)** *Blue & white Meissen or Blue Onion porcelain wheel, light-colored handle, possibly boxwood, Dutch (?)* **(4)** *Steel handle, brass shaft, nickel-plated brass wheel;* **(5)** *turned wood handle, steel shaft, architecturally cut, steel wheel with very small serrations — possibly not a jagger but bookbinder's tool.* **(6)** *Next, very heavy cast brass, nickel-plated. Dealer thought a machinist might have made it for his wife;* **(7)** *Last, pie sealer, turned wood handle, brass ferrule, wire axle, corrugated wood crimper roller. This might be potter's coggler. Courtesy dealer Lenny Kislin, Bearsville, NY. Most valuable are (2), (3) and (6).* **$40-$125**

IV-245. Jagger. *Carved whalebone, 6" L, early 19th C.* **$150-$200**

IV-246. Commercial jaggers. *For bakeries.* **(T)** *Brass wheel, drilled holes, long shaft, turned wooden handle. 7-1/2" L with 1-1/8" wheel.* **(B)** *Shorter, stubbier, 6-3/4" L, 1-1/8" wheel with finer serrations. Both S. Joseph catalog for bakers, c.1927.* **$25-$35**

Jagger, wrought steel, lathe turned, American or English, 7-3/16" L, mid 19th C. Sometimes you will see the term <u>engine turning</u>, but strictly speaking that is lathe turning done on an eccentric lathe, one that could turn designs not merely concentric to the center axis. Spiral turned borders, fancy rosette-like turnings, etc., are engine turned. **$250-$300**

IV-247. Scrimshaw jagger. *Outstanding sailor of carved whale-bone, with ebony hat, high button shoes, pupils and buttons. He straddles the jagging wheel like a unicycle. 5-3/4" H. Courtesy Neil Blodgett, Higganum House, Higganum, CT.* **$2000-$3500+**

IV-248. Scrimshaw jagger. *Mermaid holding large wheel. Carved whalebone. Arms nailed on with tiny nails. Courtesy Sidney Getler, American Folk Art, NYC.* **$2500-$2800+**

IV-249. Scrimshaw jagger. *Carved whalebone mermaid holding large, beautifully carved wheel. Flowing hair, lots of face detail. Slightly Negroid features on smiling face. Three brass nails holding on arms. 9-5/8" L, wheel 2-1/16" diameter. Courtesy Neil Blodgett, Higganum House, Higganum, CT.* **$2000-$3000**

"Almond Filberts. 1 lb. of Valentia almonds, 1 lb. searched [sierced or sieved] sugar, about 2 yolks of eggs. — Blanch and beat the almonds very fine with yolk of egg; mix in the sugar and yolks, and beat them into a smooth paste with the pestle; roll the paste out thin, and cut it up with a proper cutter in lengths; then cut it so as to leave three points on each side; place a small almond on the middle point, and one opposite (being previously made wet with yolk of egg and water); roll them up, and put two across each other, and one on the top, which will form a filbert. Work up all your paste in this way; place them on a clean iron plate dusted with flour: bake them in a slow oven. NB. -- A proper cutter for filberts must be made of tin, in a zig-zag shape, with nine points on each side; when the paste is cut by it, it will make three nuts." Joseph Bell, *A Treatise on Confectionary*, Newcastle, England, 1817.

Imagine an oblong of pastry with 9 points of a zigzag on each side; cut this in thirds. And that's as far as I can get with this. If rolled up, with crosswise almonds sticking out, I imagine it looking rather formidable. Bell was confectioner to the Prince of Wales and the Duke of York before writing the book.

Jagger, machined steel wheel, fat wood handle, American, 6" L, late 19th C. **$60-$75**

Jagger, steel shank with very architectural turnings & planes, small-toothed wheel, turned wooden handle is possibly 19th C. replacement, American, 7-1/2" L, 1st to 2nd quarter 19th C. **$75-$85**

"Dough-Nuts. Three pounds of sifted flour. A pound of powdered sugar. Three quarters of a pound of butter. Four eggs. Half a large tea-cup full of best brewer's yeast. A pint and a half of milk. A teaspoonful of powdered cinnamon. A grated nutmeg. A table-spoon ful of rose-water. — Cut up the butter in the flour. Add the sugar, spice, and rose-water. Beat the eggs very light, and pour them into the mixture. Add the yeast, (half a tea-cup or two wine-glasses full,) and then stir in the milk by degrees, so as to make it a soft dough. Cover it, and set it to rise.

"When quite light, cut it in diamonds with a jagging-iron or a sharp knife, and fry them in lard. Grate loaf-sugar over them when done." Miss Leslie, of Philadelphia, *Seventy-Five Receipts for Pastry, Cakes, and Sweetmeats . Appended to The Cook's Own Book and Housekeeper's Register ....,* by a Boston Housekeeper. Boston: Munroe & Francis, 1833.

WOOD:

Jagger, turned fruitwood with ebony wheel, French (?), 4-3/4" L, c.1880s. <u>Added value:</u> One with really nice turning might bring a few dollars more, but this is a commonly found variety, and may even be made today. **$22-$32**

Jagger, carved bird's-eye maple, handle & wheel, American, 4-1/2" L, late 19th C. **$35-$40**

Jagger, grain painted wood handle, metal, "Ridgely," American, late 19th C. **$35-$40**

Jagger, hand-carved wood, big wooden wheel, American, 8" L, 1860s or 1870s. **$35-$50**

Jagger, lathe turned wood, 2 wheels of different size corrugations, one at each end, American, 8" L, mid 19th C. **$70-$90**

Jagger & pastry stamp, carved wood, very smooth, satiny patina, abstract flower incised on shank, stamp at one end is serrated, possibly American, more probably English, 6-3/8" L, mid to late 19th C. **$165-$185**

Jaggers & crimpers — See also crimpers
Jelly molds — See molds, especially the tin and copper ones
Jumble press — See cookie press, also pastry tube
Krum Kake mold, cast iron, "Andresen's," American, 20th C. **$35-$45**

Cornerfolds. "The handsomest way of ornamenting the edge of a pie or pudding is to cut the rim in large square notches, and then fold over triangularly one corner of every notch." Miss Leslie, of Philadelphia, *Seventy-Five Receipts for Pastry, Cakes, and Sweetmeats . Appended to The Cook's Own Book and Housekeeper's Register ....*, by a Boston Housekeeper. Boston: Munroe & Francis, 1833.

●　　●　　●　　●

"**Rhubarb Pies**. Gather a bundle of the leaf-stocks, sufficient quantity — cut off the leaf and peal [sic] the stock of the thin epidermis — cut in quarter inch pieces, and lay them into the crust — cover well with sugar, and add nutmeg, orange peal and spice to taste. The flavor is equal, and many deem it preferable to gooseberries. The pie-plant is perennial, herbaceous and very hardy. A dozen plants will afford a family a constant supply." *The Farmers' Cabinet*, Philadelphia, Aug. 1, 1836.

IV-250. Scrimshaw jaggers. *Sea horses.* **(T)** *Carved whalebone, star-shaped spokes to wheel. 6" L, early 19th C. Picture courtesy of Robert W. Skinner Inc., Auctioneers, Bolton, MA.* **(B)** *Carved whalebone, fishy tail, heart cutouts on wheel, 5-3/4" L. Picture courtesy of the National Museum of American History, Smithsonian Institution.* **$2000-$3500**

IV-251. Jagger. *Cast pewter rabbit or leaping hare, resembling cast pewter chocolate molds made by 19th C. makers such as Anton Reiche, Dresden, Germany. Charming, almost feminine look, 6-1/4" L, looked old — although nowadays there are so many "collectibles" made by the so-called limited edition companies, something similar could be made recently. That said, I wouldn't be surprised if this was made as a sideline by a chocolate mold manufacturer in Europe in the 2nd half of the 19th C.* **$200-$350**

Kugelhopf mold — See molds, kugelhopf, tubed or spouted, in ceramic and copper sections
Lady finger cutter, stamped tin, strap handle, 2 airholes, American (?), 2-7/8" L x 1" W, 19th C. **$28-$35**
Lady finger or madeline mold (both are a sort of small sponge cake), sheet tin, rather crudely made, 6 small elongated ovals, corrugated at each end, riveted to flat sheet, handle on one end, American or German, 9" L, each cup 4-1/4" L, 19th C. **$30-$40**

IV-252. Pastry & pizza cutters. *Sharp steel blades, in a variety of wooden handles. From top:* **(1)** *From Jaburg, 1908.* **(2)** *Long shafted one, in 3 sizes: 7-1/2" L with 1-1/2" wheel; 8" L with 2-1/4" wheel; 8-3/4" L with 3-1/4" wheel. S. Joseph, c.1927.* **(3)** *Lower left, a large-wheeled cutter, 6" diameter, with gauge; and* **(4)** *Right, a 4" or 6" diameter cutter, larger sizes to order. T. Mills, 1930. For candy, pizza, bread dough, etc.* **$5-$15**

IV-253. Pie crimper & ornamenter. *"Cinderella," invented & mfd. by Mr. G. J. Capewell, Cheshire, CT. Face of wheel used for printing rosettes; and also crimp; on the other side, opposite the wheel ... is a set of blades which cut ventilating holes in the crust in star shape. American Agriculturist ad, 12/1876. The broadside valued at about $10. The tool:* **$45-$55**

IV-254. Pie rimmer, crimper & pastry cutter. *Pat'd 9/11/1866, 5-1/2" L, brass. Mfd. by J. Stephen & W. Zeller, Womelsdorf, PA. Illustration is from flimsy printed broadside that advertised the rimmers. Note the little footstool on which the infant stands. Such little painted stools are found in many "country" collections. It would be fun to collect all the items seen in a period picture like this.* **$85-$125**

Lady finger pan, tin, stamped with elongated peanut shape cups, "Kreamer," Brooklyn, NY, early 20th C. **$20-$28**

Lady finger pan — See also sponge cake tin

Loaf pan, gray graniteware, oblong, high slanted sides, c.1930s. **$25-$35**

Loaf pan, white enamelware with cobalt trim, 8" L, 20th C. Sometimes these look suspiciously like some kind of sterilizing container from a medical supplier. **$15-$25**

Lollipop mold, cast iron, makes 5 octagonal lollies, with room for stick, American, 5-5/8" x 10-1/2" x 3/8" deep, late 19th C (?). **$65-$90**

Lollipop mold, makes 24, heavy stamped metal, American, 20th C. **$65-$85**

IV-255. Combination tools. (L) *Pieced tin, japanned finish, brass medallion appears to say "-organ —— Comp. Mandal 6 LONDON." (Probably "Morgan.") Sugar shaker or dredger, shape cutter (corrugated bottom), nutmeg grater, lemon grater or zester, and pastry jagger. Late 19th C.* **(R)** *A nearly identical piece patented as an "Improved Dredge-Box, Cake-Cutter and Grater," by Sydney Cooke, Bayonne City, NJ, April 26, 1870. Cooke describes his invention thus: "The lid of the box is a doughnut-cutter; the bottom of the box is a corrugated cake-cutter; the raised graters are attached to the sides of the box, one for nut megs, and the other for lemons, &c. The grates being raised from the surface of the box prevent the holes in them from getting clogged. The jagger iron or knife is attached to the front of the box." Official Gazette of the U.S. Patent Office. I do not know the story of how the Morgan one came to be licensed (or not).* **$85-$135**

IV-256. Crimpers & jagger. *Top (L) to bottom (R): (1) Large all wood wheel, set in wooden handle, 7" L, homemade? Collection of Meryle Evans. (2) galvanized tin sealer with plain wood handle, 6-1/2" L, possibly homemade with kitchen tool handle, late 19th, early 20th C. (3) cast aluminum, very cheapo, 4-3/4" L; (4) Cheapest of all is "Vaughn's Pie Trimmer & Sealer," pat'd 5/10/1921. Aluminum wheel, green painted wood handle. 6-1/2" L.* **$10-$25**

"Apple Bread. Boil a dozen good-sized apples that have been peeled and cored, until they are perfectly tender. While still warm, mash them in double the amount of flour, and add the proper proportion of yeast. The mass should then be thoroughly kneaded without water, as the apple juice will make it sufficiently soft. It should be left to rise 12 hours, then formed into loaves, and baked when quite light. Apple Bread was the invention of a scientific Frenchman, and it has always been highly commended for its healthfulness." *Ladies Home Journal*, Sept. 1896.

IV-257. Crimper & grater combined. *Tin, wood and cast metal. The grater was probably used for nutmeg. The pointed end may be a can opener, or for making slashes in top crust before baking. 6-7/8" L, American, late 19th C. Picture courtesy of the National Museum of American History, Smithsonian Institution.* **$35-$45**

IV-258. Crimper & pie cutter. *"Ideal," from Seastrand salesmen's catalog, c.1929. "Why not save time by using the Ideal? The only perfect pie cutter and crimper; it not only makes a cleaner cut and a neater crimp, but it presses both crusts firmly together, thus preventing the rich juices from boiling over." Wood and wire and tin, with edging trimmer. • About a similar cutter, was written "This simple little instrument trims off the surplus pie-crust that projects over the plate, and at the same time neatly ornaments the border. It is one of the indispensable conveniences of the kitchen after it has once been used. Pies can be made without it, but if ornamentation does not add to the nutriment, it pleases the eye and aids digestion, and pies are not famous for being the most digestible articles in the world, no matter how carefully made." Scammell's Treasure-House of Knowledge, 1891.* **$15-$30**

Lollipop or sucker mold, 2-part stamped metal, rough square with image of hen on basket, place for round stick in bottom, American (?), 3" x 3" square, c.1930s (?). **Reproduction alert**. For a while in the 1980s, lollipop molds were advertised as being a "warehouse find" of 1940s-1950s vintage, although they appeared to be brand new. • By spring 1989, a company in Vermont started advertising "Profitmaking Lollipop Molds! . . . genuine antique re-creations originally made up to 30 years ago . . . Each one-piece mold is made of heavy gauge tin for good detail and measures 2" to 6" high. Our assortments contain a wide variety of popular holiday designs and themes that SELL — for Easter, Mothers Day, Wash. B'day, Valentines, Thanksgiving, Halloween and Christmas, plus . . . animals galore . . . in addition to Santas and a clown. 30 different designs are included in our profitmaking assortments. Sugg. Ret[ail] up to $4.95 each." Wholesale price for 25 assorted was $55.50; and $189 for 100 of them. I will add only that "genuine antique recreations" is an oxymoron. So be careful, and don't be a . . . sucker. • In June 1989, another company, in Illinois, advertised "Old Metal Sucker/Candy Molds. Warehouse Find ca. 1950's ($4 Retail Value)." They are stamped metal, and can be ordered in a surprising variety of forms: angel in flower; baseball player; boy in sunsuit; car; cat on ball, Halloween cat, and playful cat; chicken; covered wagon; cowboy; daisy; doll head; 2 different elephants; Father Time; fish; four-leaf clover; heart; horse; 3 different Indians; Jiggs; jumping clown; owl; pumpkin; Statue of Liberty; several rabbits doing things; several Santas; a real and a toy soldier; a squirrel; a submarine; and a witch. Range for each: **$5-$15**

Madeline molds, stamped in tin in geometric, natural & figural shapes, individual serving sizes, used for baking the rich small sponge cakes (recalled so well by Marcel Proust in his 7-volume novel *Remembrance of Things Past,* 1913-1927). They are rather like pound cake, served plain or ornamented with frosting, nuts or fruit. Also called a dariole mold. No mark, French (?), a few inches wide, 1870s to 1880s, poss. earlier, but known from F. A. Walker catalogs. A horse's head, a rose, shells, a bunch of grapes, and a fluted flaring cup are among the forms known. **NOTE:** The traditional shape for madelines was a scallop shell, or a shallow fluted cup, but importers and dealers seem often to have felt free calling various things by the same name (not just madelines). See also a muffin pan further on. **$18-$30**

Maple sugar mold, all tin, with corrugated cups riveted to rectangular tin pan, American, 9" L x 6-1/4" W, small cups, 19th C. **$45-$65**

Maple sugar mold, carved block of wood set into tin stand or frame that holds it up as if on an easel, mold is heart-shaped, American or Canadian, 6-1/4" H with frame, mold itself is 4-1/4" W, 19th C. **$135-$170**

Maple sugar mold, carved maple, 2-part, makes 6 barrel-shaped candies, late 19th C. **$45-$60**

Maple sugar mold, carved wood, 2 hearts & a crescent moon, American? 15" L x 3-1/2" W, 19th C. **$120-$140**

Maple sugar mold, carved wood, 3 hearts, American, 14" L, late 19th C. **$100-$170**

Maple sugar mold, carved wood, a blue jay with crest, American or Canadian, 5-1/2" x 6-3/4", 20th C. **$30-$50**

Maple sugar mold, carved wood, beaver design, Canadian (?), 8-1/2" x 3-1/4", early 20th C. **$30-$50**

Maple sugar mold, carved wood, geometric forms, 8-3/4" H, early 20th C (?). **$25-$35**

Maple sugar mold, carved wood, heart, diamond, spade, American? 16" L x 4" W x 2" thick, 19th C. **$150-$185**

Maple sugar mold, carved wood, squirrel with thick curled tail, 6-1/2" x 5-1/4", 20th C. **$30-$50**

Maple sugar mold, carved wood with 3 designs: sunburst, heart, tulip, American or Canadian, 17" L x 5" W, 19th C. **$195-$250**

Maple sugar mold, carved wood with 3 stars, 15" L x 3-1/2" W, late 19th, early 20th C. **$125-$150**

Maple sugar mold, chip carved thick wood, one end cut away except for wedge-shaped handle (large part out), 3 cakes made in shallow fluted cups, Canadian or American, 11" L x 2" W, mid 19th C. **$55-$75**

Maple sugar mold, deeply carved wood, oblong plank, 3 hearts, with sides & bottom of cups further decorated with carving, Canadian (?), doesn't look American, 22" L x 7" W, early 19th C. **$300-$375**

Maple sugar mold, floral design, carved wood, American, 10" L, turn of century. **$75-$85**

Maple sugar mold, for making sugar pyramids, very tall & narrow, all wood, 4 side pieces are acute triangles held together with simple wooden clamp: a square cut out of oblong piece of wood, meant to fit down over assembled sides & be wedged in place, so mold could be filled at big open base end. The wedge also served as a sort of flange so the mold could be put in a rack or frame to harden, Canadian, about 10" H x 4-1/2" square at base, 19th C. **$50-$65**

Maple sugar mold, hand-carved, long & skinny, makes 14 hearts, 42" L, makes 2" H hearts, 19th C. **$135-$175**

Maple sugar mold, heavy terne plate (?) tin, prints 12 figures, viz. cornucopia, fleur-de-lis, pear, heart, daisy, oak leaf, shell, bell, fish, moon, flag, automobile & strawberry, "Jaburg Bros.," NYC, NY, 6" x 6-1/2", c.1930s (?). **$125-$150**

Maple sugar mold, large house, carved wood, 19th C. **$150-$170**

Maple sugar mold, long trough of wood, makes 5 oblong blocks of sugar candy, American, 18" L x 2-1/2" W overall, one block is about 4-1/2" L x 1" deep, other 4 are about 3-1/2" L x 1" deep, late 19th C. **$40-$50**

IV-259. Madeline molds. *Small molds of stamped tin. S. Joseph, c.1927.* **$8-$12**

IV-260. Madeline molds. *Stamped tin, from F. A. Walker catalog, c.1890. Probably imported.* **$7-$30**

IV-262. "Fancy Patty Pans *for baking ornamental tea cakes."* *These were probably indistinguishable from madeline molds.* American Home Cook Book, *1854.* **$8-$12**

IV-261. Madeline molds. (T) *set, stamped tin, from Pick-Barth catalog, 1929. A few sample sizes: top left one is 4" x 2-1/8"; the star one at right is 2-7/8" diameter.* **(B)** *set, imported tin molds, from G. M. Thurnauer & Bro., NYC dealers & importers.* House Furnishing Review *ad, 1/1903. Singles:* **$5-$10**; *Sets of 10-12:* **$50-$75**

IV-263. Petits fours molds. *Small, and pretty much similar designs as madeline molds, only somewhat deeper. S. Joseph, c.1927.* **$8-$15**

IV-264. Maple sugar mold — both halves. *Carved wood, horse, beaver, fish, square with plus & minus signs (?) Note pegs & holes, for holding halves together. Each half is 18" L x 4-1/2" W x 1-3/4" thick, American or Canadian, late 19th C. Photo from Jeannine Dobb's Country Folk Antiques, Merrimack, NH.* **$600-$850**

Maple sugar mold, looks like muffin pan, heavy sheet tin, blackened by use (or intentionally blackened by maker?), 8 round shallow cannonball cups, American, 12-3/4" L x 6" W, late 19th C.   **$35-$50**

Maple sugar mold, oblong of wood, 14 carved figures, including horse, diamond, 6-pointed star, hearts, houses, anvil, etc., very precisely & carefully cut, in contrast to many observed maple sugar molds with rather crude carvings, American, 32" L x 7" W x 2" thick, 19th C. The houses add particular interest. (Even more valuable are the rare house-shaped molds in 3 dimensions. These are in 2 or 4 parts: inside carving includes doors, windows, chimneys, etc. They're probably earlier than flat ones, and may be Canadian.) This one offered by the Jorgensens of Hallowell in 1983. Value range mine.   **$400-$550**

Maple sugar mold, or muffin pan, tin, 12 star-shaped cups with 6 points, riveted to rectangular pan, with round holes in bottom, of the type of pan often called a maple sugar mold, but possibly used for muffins, American, 15" L x 13" W, marked only with illegible patent date, "Pat'd Dec. 11, 19--". If the Dec. 11, 19-- was stamped accurately, or read correctly, that is if the 11th was a Tuesday in early 20th C., then the only years in the right period would be 1900, 1906, or possibly as late as 1917, even 1923. Ex-Robacker, $160.   **$150-$200**

Maple sugar mold, sheet tin, 7 individual shallow cups with hexagonal exteriors, round interiors, riveted together (this is the reason for the hexagonal edges) & giving the appearance of a piece of honeycomb, thin strap handle, (I identified this as a muffin pan in last edition), American, 9-1/8" diameter, 19th C. Maine

collector Joanne Wilson wrote to tell me that hers was "given to me by a lady who said it was used as a maple sugar mold on the farm where she grew up." I accept this new attribution, as it does seem too shallow for muffins, though not for some kind of small cake or cookie.   **$28-$40**

Maple sugar mold, strawberry, carved wood, American, 9-1/4"L x 5-1/2" W x 1-3/4" thick, 19th C.   **$135-$150**

Maple sugar mold, stamped tin, fluted shallow pan, small enough for doll tarts, American or import, late 19th or early 20th C.   **$5-$8**

Marzipan mold, also called a <u>marchpane</u> or <u>massepain</u> mold, heavy tin plated, 2 hinged sections, 3" x 3", German, 19th or 20th C.   **$30-$40**

Marzipan mold — See also the many cake boards and springerle boards and molds

MOLDS FOR ASPICS, BLANCMANGE, FOOD, JELLY, PUDDING, ETC.

I have grouped almost all the molds here which tend to have more depth than cake molds, or are useable for a variety of foods and might sometimes be termed "food molds," or are known as jelly molds or pudding molds. Not included, generally speaking, are cake, candy, chocolate, cookie and ice cream molds. There are also a few molds under "Bake molds" that might fit here. The greatest concentration in this long listing is for either jelly molds or pudding (sweet or savoury) molds.

IV-265. Nineteenth-Century Pastry Kitchen with Molds. *Unidentified highly detailed print, showing kitchen layout similar to those found 300 years before the mid-19th C., as well as today. From the (**L**), traveling around wall: cupboard with rolling pin, dredger, ban with scoop; range with 3 grated openings, above which are bracket shelves loaded with molds and sieves. In the middle of the back is some kind of cupboard or oven. Then more molds, with a balance scale on the table at right rear, and a large dresser with molds, and a churn in the near right corner. Probably English or French, probably about 1870-80.*

FANCY MOLDED FOOD

Each of the finely detailed nooks and crannies in food molds (stamped, or hand-beaten repoussé, or formed by piecing small shapes of copper or tin, or molded in ceramic) could be filled with a piece of food or a spoonful of differently colored gelatin so that when turned out, the surface of the fancy dish would be beautifully patterned. Little slices of carrots or lady fingers or olive slices or biscuits all had their places — usually after the entire mold was coated on the inside with clear jelly. Very contrived artifice, but in its way attractive — at least in chromolithographs of nineteenth-century cookbooks. Molded puddings and blancmanges might be decorated with bits of fruit and with a sauce or icing dribbled decoratively over the peaks like snow.

A Modern View of Artifice. Famous ex-patriot American cookbook author, French food expert and artist Richard Olney (*Simple French Food*, 1974; *The French Menu Cookbook*, 1970) told his interviewer, William Rice, for an article in *The Washington Post*, Dec. 12, 1974, that "... to be appetizing as well as attractive, food should always look like food, and we may be grateful that the chilly bits of baroque architecture with sumptuously inlaid facades of jewel-cut truffle, egg-white, and pimiento mosaic belong largely to the past. The grace of a field bouquet touches us more deeply today than the formal splendor of a funeral wreath."

TYPICAL MOLDED FOODS & WHY THEY SET UP IN SHAPES

Molds are not a necessary part of cooking. They are used to form food that will set up in one way or another and hold its fancy shape when you turn it out (unmold it) and serve it. Molded foods are, literally, *set pieces* — that is, "an often brilliantly exe-

IV-266. Photogravure plate of copper molds, etc., *which is # XXIX plate, in unidentified 19th C. German book. The molds are probably early 19th C. Note especially the turtle mold at bottom left. Such copper molds, particularly the turtle, are very collectible. The turtle mold might be valued:* **$200-$300**

cuted artistic work characterized by a formal pattern," as the *American Heritage Dictionary* defines the term.

Aspic is the word usually used for a meat- or fish-flavored jelled dish. It is made with something called "aspic jelly" which is gelatin, like any other, but savory, and cooked with onion and spices of choice and strained. It sets because of the gelatin. Sometimes aspic jelly was poured in a thin layer over some meat dishes, or was chilled and cut into fancy shapes to garnish a galantine dish.

Blancmange or Blanc Mange is a sort of pudding dessert — in some old books it may be classified as a pudding or a custard or an iced dessert. In a way it's all three. It sets up because of cooking milk and starch together with other ingredients. Starches included corn, rice, or arrowroot starch, or wheat flour. Some old recipes call for Irish Moss, which is Carrageen moss, a seaweed, from which a mucilaginous gummy substance can be extracted when it's cooked in water or milk. Carrageen is harvested today and used widely in commercial foods. After being cooked in a saucepan or double boiler, a blancmange is poured into molds, chilled, then turned out for saucing and serving.

Breads, cakes and muffins take shape because their ingredients include some form of starch, sometimes gluten, and liquid, and because they tend to expand during cooking. They will take the form of whatever they're baked in.

Custard sets up because of cooking egg and milk together, but it is usually eaten right out of custard cups or glasses, and is not turned out. Or it is cooked, then poured into puff paste, and baked. An exception would be custards such as flan, which are turned out of the cup in order to pour on the caramelized sauce. Mrs. A. P. Hill, in her *Receipt Book* of 1870, wrote about the difference between puddings and custards, "Puddings are baked without crusts and usually in deeper vessels; are generally served hot and eaten with sauces. Custards . . . as a general thing, are baked in rich paste, and usually served cold."

Ice cream and other frozen desserts set up because they are frozen — more or less assisted by the particular combination of ingredients. A century ago ice cream was either made with a custard base or with a gelatin base, both of which aided the binding. Today we get ice cream with lots of "fillers" including natural and artificial gums.

Jellies, that is, jelled or gelatinized dishes, set up by the use of gelatin or isinglass (a gelatin made from the air bladders of certain fish). Jellies are either sweet and based on fruits, or a savoury aspic of fish, meat, or vegetables. "Jelly" is a basic, presumed to be neutral in flavor, so aspic jelly defines what has been done to the basic jelly. Fruit jellies used today for toast set up mainly because of fruit pectin, found in apples, crabapples, and other fruits; some writers define this kind of jelly as strained jam.

Mousses set up because of the gelatin into which whipped cream and other puréed ingredients are whipped, and may be sweet dishes or savory. They are served chilled, and have a lot of air in them so they seem very light and fluffy. Soufflés are also whipped, but using a lot of egg whites.

Puddings set up because of the combination of ingredients cooked together, always some kind of starch (even as crumbled bread or crackers), and usually milk and egg. They may be hot or cold, sweet or savory. See custards.

TURNING OUT A MOLD

In an 1838 copy of *The Magazine of Domestic Economy*, published in London, is this query and answer: " 'Sir, — Every housekeeper, however practical, must, if candid, admit many failures in practice; one of my greatest is, that my jelly, of which I have to make much, never turns well or tolerably from the mould; though it is filled from cold water, of white stone

IV-269. Ancient animal-shaped molds. *Pictures not to scale vis a vis each other. These are old cast bronze reproductions of pastry and other molds found in excavations at Pompeii during the 19th C. Two at (L) are a leg of ham, 13-1/2" L, and a whole dead pig, 20-1/2" L. At right is a pig with handle, only 7-7/8" L. At bottom is a horrible flayed hare, each detail of its poor backbone dotting the length of the mold. 26-1/2" L. All were made at Fonderie Artistiche Riunite, by J. Chiurazzi & Fils & s. De Angelis & Fils, Naples, Italy. From their catalog, 1910-11.*

IV-267. Molded gelatin (jellied) dessert, *made with Rich's "Tryphosa" brand jelly mix. They had great flavors, including mint and coffee and wine (like Madeira). Turn of century booklet.*

IV-268. Dessert jelly ad. *"Bro-Man-Gel-On," mfd. by Stern & Saalberg, NYC.* Ladies' Home Journal, *11/1902.*

IV-270. *Outline drawings of molds in* **IV-269.**

ware, of each figure, &c., yet it never takes any form. The jelly is as invariably stiff, clear, and good, but some witchery always spoils its appearance. Can you help?' — We do not quite understand what our correspondent means; but we believe the sum of her complaint to be that her jelly does not turn out well from the mould. A **jelly-mould** may be made either of common tin, block tin, or of white earthen or stone ware. [Note no mention of copper!] If of one or other of the two first-mentioned materials, before the jelly is turned out, the outer surface of the mould should be rapidly wiped with a napkin dipped in hot water; if the mould is of earthenware, it should itself be dipped for an instant up to the edges in hot water. The jelly will then turn out well, provided it be well set, cold, and stiff."

Turn-out Two. "Take a pan or basin of hot water, of a temperature that you can only just bear your hand in. Dip the mould in, lift it out very quickly, and turn the shape out — this is with a tin or copper mould. An earthenware mould takes a little longer for the heat to get through." Katharine Mellish, *Cookery Book,* London & NY, 1901.

FOOD MOLD PARTS

The naming of parts of many collectible kitchen things is difficult, because sometimes manufacturers' terms are too technical or can't be understood intuitively, or because collectors and writers have used terms (which may or may not be accurate) for so long that they are understood widely.

The parts of a food mold (which itself is called a shape in England), in order of importance to the value, are the top, the part with the stamped design, which will be on top of the finished molded food; the sides or base, which is the deep part forming the walls of the mold, and which may or may not be stamped or hammered with its own designs or shapes; the skirt, which is a sort of shallow mirror image of the base, and which rims the top so that the mold may be set upside down while the food congeals or becomes firm; and, in some molds, a ring hanger; feet or similar levelling projections that perform same function as the skirt, to make the mold stable while the food is setting (these are found almost always on fish molds); and lid. In the middle of some molds you may find a tube or a spout, the former is capped or closed, the latter is open. As a mnemonic, think of a closed mailing tube and an open coffee pot spout.

KINDS OF MOLDS

Blancmange molds. Usually, blancmange molds are geometric tin or copper molds, possibly indistinguishable from other food and jelly molds in these listings. Basically, these intricate, relatively thin molds were used in forming dishes that were not baked or cooked in them. The only time I've really labeled them "blancmange" molds is if the mold could be matched up to an old catalog or cookbook picture so labeled. Sometimes, not only can I not tell the fine differences between similar molds, I wouldn't try, because so many nineteenth-century molds were used for all kinds of food. They were also used for flummery, and the tall-tiered architectural types were also called ice-cream pagodas or ice cream towers. Most are so tall that I can't imagine how they were served. Would you like to divide a tapering tower of frozen flummery into 12 precise portions before it all precipitously toppled? (Alliteration T. Agnew might have liked to try.)

Border or ring molds. These were oval or round, in various serving platter/plate sizes. Some were used to form a ring of cooked rice (which is sticky enough to take a molding) or mashed potatoes, or even some kinds of mashed or puréed vegetables like green peas. They were set around meat, or another kind and color of vegetable. Other ring molds were used for jellies or mousses or fancy ices.

Cake & bake molds. The main kind treated in this section are the fluted or turban head spouted or tubed ceramic molds, with a few tubed or spouted molds in other materials. For shapes such as lambs or rabbits see at the beginning of this chapter under

IV-271. Small molds, *for dariols and one bouche cup (bottom center). Stamped & pieced tin. Center of one at left is oval.* Mrs. A. B. Marshall's Larger Cookery Book, *1902.* **$15-$25**

cake molds or cake pans. It's hard at this time to differentiate between pudding and cake molds of the same type. In Germany, many ornate stamped copper or tin molds that we are accustomed to think of as jelly molds are called bake molds. For sponge cake molds, see ceramic, tubed or spouted molds.

Individual molds. Most are for single servings of jellies or little cakes of various kinds. Deeper ones are for either; the very shallow ones are meant to be used in quantities for making little shaped cakes or dessert elements like lady fingers, madelines, sponge cake — and often these little cakes were used to line the inside of much larger molds to create extravaganzas of dessert. You will note how each decorative element around the border of a pieced or stamped tin or copper geometric mold is exactly the size, say, of a lady finger.

Jelly molds. The most prized of these are eighteenth- or early nineteenth-century, elaborate pieced copper molds, well-tinned on the interior. Later ones are pieced or stamped tin, or stamped copper, or a combination of both metals in order to take advantage of copper's ability to take a finer-detailed design. Copper must be properly and completely tinned on the inside before use. Most of the metal molds have a simple rolled-edge skirt or raised edge ringing the design in the top, so that the mold would stand steady (upside down) while the gelatine set. These skirts serve the double purpose of protecting the fancy designs in the tops. Architectural and geometric designs could be rested on their peaks or hills or other "high" spots, without needing a skirt. See also cake and bake molds, above. There are also lovely ceramic jelly molds, which also have a skirt. They have several advantages for molded food — they take and hold a hot or a cold temperature, and their glaze helps in the unmolding process.

"**To ornament Jelly.** Jelly put into moulds should be particularly strong; a little stock from isinglass, mixed with the calf feet stock, will be of great use, when you intend to introduce fruit; fix your moulds in salt; then fill them half full of jelly; let it stand until set; place on it a large strawberry, just plucked, with the leaf and stalk on; fill up the mould with the jelly; you may also introduce in another mould cherries, and in another peaches, and so on; this, however, can only be done when fruit is in season; when it is not, wafer paper painted as such, or in landscapes, and laid upon the dish, and your shape of jelly turned upon it, have a very good effect." Joseph Bell, *A Treatise on Confectionary,* Newcastle, England, 1817. *Translation: Use extra strong gelatin when using fresh fruit (like now, the cautions against using fresh pineapple, as opposed to canned). Set the moulds down in a bed of salt — to stabilize and to chill (think ice cream makers). When the first layer is set, put in the fruit — if nothing's in season, then fill the whole mould with the flavored gelatin and paint fruit or a landscape (!) on a thin piece of paper, put it on the serving dish, and unmold the gelatin. If it's as clear as it's supposed to be, the painted fruit or landscape will show through the mound. Gadzooks!*

Pudding molds. Most pudding molds were used either to bake a pudding or to steam a pudding. This meant it had to take oven heat or would have to be set down in a larger container with water, which would steam when hot. However, a good number of pudding molds were used the same way gelatin molds were used — the ingredients were mixed and cooked in a saucepan, then transferred to the pudding mold to be chilled and set. Tin and ceramic molds are commonest. There are sweet dessert puddings (some served cold, some hot) as well as savoury puddings meant to be eaten with main courses, something like our "stove top stuffing." Many pudding molds have a spout (open) or tube (closed) in the center so that they could be cooked through and through at a more even rate. That kind of open-center mold also works best for some cakes (think of angel food cake or sponge cake). Some of the most desirable of all molds, and particularly of pudding molds, are late eighteenth, early to mid-nineteenth-century Pennsylvania German redware molds. One of the most spectacular ones I've ever seen was a huge (16" or 17" diameter) fluted mold that had been broken and repaired with metal staples and wire.

Vegetable or rice mold. Sometimes elaborate molds were used to mold cooked rice or puréed vegetables, not necessarily with anything added to make it take the molding. Presumably the dish was served hot. These were advertised in the 1870s and were very architectural tin molds indistinguishable from blancmange or ice cream or jelly molds.

American Made Copper Molds. Practically at the last minute, after reading 60 years' worth of New York City directories on microfiche, I found an extremely important listing in *Trow's Directory* for **1866-67**, which is confirmation of what seems logical — that some copper molds were made in America. The expanded listing in question is for <u>Louis Ottenheimer</u>, at 404 E. Houston, and 295 Second Street "near Union Market," NYC. It reads: "Ottenheimer Louis, tin, brass and copper works. Copper tea kettles, stew pans, sauce pans, confectioners' pans, <u>the only manufacturer in this country of Copper Sponge Cake and Jelly Moulds</u>; copper and brass urns for porterhouses, various styles; brass and copper drainers, copper funnels; tin, brass and copper measures."

Arrangement of listings: I have first divided the molds into the <u>material</u> they are made from — aluminum, cast iron, ceramic, copper, copper & tin, enamelware, glass, and tin. Then I have tried to indicate what <u>kind of mold</u> each one is; I've listed the sort of generic "unknowns" or undifferentiated simply as molds, and they come first in each section. I've listed tubed and spouted molds at the ends of each material section. If the opening has a closed end it's **tubed**. Tubes terminate in a top. If open it's **spouted**. Stand back if it's spouted; it can spout off!

ALUMINUM MOLDS:

Jelly mold, aluminum, stamped heart-shape individual size, marked "Jell-O," American, 20th C. Stacked sets are more valuable than singles. **$12-$15**

Jelly mold, stamped aluminum individual size cup with rolled rim, slightly flared sides, & large embossed block capital letter in bottom, mfd. by The Barnard Co., Boston, MA, 1/4 pint size (also came 12 to quart), c.1910. <u>Added value.</u> A single one wouldn't be worth much, but a set of six or 12 or especially 26 would be nice. Value would be affected also by the particular initial, whether or not it suited you. Originally you could order whatever initial you wanted. **$8-$15**

Jelly molds, copper-toned stamped aluminum, set of 5, most with fluted or pleated or scalloped sides, all with wire ring hanger, in various shapes with rather mushy-formed "soft" stamped design, viz. pentagram with bunch of grapes, heart with 3 cherries and twig, square with pear [hey! a pome, if not a pomme], diamond with seahorse [huh? an inedible motif], and a triangle with a crab. "Add a unique touch of beauty to your kitchen with these smart, new . . . molds . . . and the charm of decorating with copper color will be only part of the fun. You'll love them just as much for those distinctive gelatin salads and desserts they mold so beautifully. They're "specially formed to hold more of that fancy topping, too," reads the ad. West Bend Aluminum Co., West Bend, WI, c.1958. These have a certain value for a study or nostalgia collection, and they add interesting sidelight to the decayed art of making fine food molds. But they won't ever really be the "antiques of the future" as they look so . . . well, awful. **$7-$12**

Jelly molds, set of 4, stamped aluminum individual molds, anodized copper on outside, patterns stamped on tops are acorn & oak leaves, daisy or sunburst, 4-leaf clover, thistle & leaves, maker not known, offered as premium by Knox Gelatine, 5 oz. size, 1972. These are rather like the ones in preceding listing, but maker is unknown. A set is also known that says "Jell-O." Value for either set: **$6-$12**

Jelly molds, a set of 8 individual, stamped aluminum, fluted sides, for congealed salads or iced desserts or even Jell-O, American, 3-1/2" deep x 4" diameter, 1930s or 1940s. We have two tall wire racks to hold four filled individual molds on for the refrigerator. Two racks and 8 molds would bring the upper end of this price range. **$12-$18**

BRASS MOLDS:

Jelly mold, frame with 10 wonderful stamped fat well-detailed fish in 2 rows, all facing same direction, brass & tin, probably for individual fish mousses, English or American, each fish 5" L x 2" W, overall dimension is 10-1/2" x 10", late 19th C. **$145-$160**

CAST IRON MOLDS:

Generally cast iron is for baking, but iron holds cold temperatures as well as hot, so it is also useful in making some candies and even jelled dishes which must be "set." The downside is that a cast iron mold would be much more difficult to heat just enough to unmold, unless it is quite thin.

Mold, cast iron, oval, "M. & H. Schrenkeisan," NYC, NY, about 2-1/2" deep x 7-1/2" L, late 19th C. **$50-$60**

Mold, heavy thick cast iron, in bath tub shape without legs, probably candy — dealer thought it was a chocolate mold for cream eggs, cast on bottom is only "1 lb," American, late 19th C. **$18-$22**

Mold, heavy cast iron, amazing finny detail on curved fish, American, 2-3/8" deep x 12-13/16" L at widest, mid 19th C. **$120-$165**

CERAMIC MOLDS:

Mold, bake or pudding?, yellowware ceramic, oval with flat inside bottom, fluted sides, recessed inside foot, drippy brown Rockingham glaze outside, stamped clearly on bottom, advertising "L. B. Patterson Fire-Clay Ware Manufactory, Pottsville, PA," almost 4" deep x 9" L x 7" W, 19th C. **$165-$185**

Mold, red stoneware not glazed on outside, pale yellow glaze inside, green around chipcarved edge, figural of baby (Baby Jesus) in swaddling clothes, face rather well detailed, bundling has pattern of flowers. Although this is a newborn baby (which seems like Christmas), the bread baked in it is for Easter, or perhaps Lent, at least in Germany. Several versions of the ceramic "Wickelkinder" (swaddled babies) are depicted in German books on old kitchenwares. One has curly hair, a fluted ruff, and the swaddling is criss-crossed with a ribbon tied with a bow. A stamped tin one shown in one book looks like a chocolate mold & dates to the end of the 19th C. Southern German, 12" L x 5-1/2" W, c.1830s-1840s. **$165-$200**

Mold, cauliflower design, cream colored earthenware, "Alcock," English, 8" L, last quarter 19th C. **$75-$100**

Mold, cauliflower design, cream colored earthenware, "Alcock," English, 8" L, last quarter 19th C. **$75-$100**

IV-274. More cornucopias, *a popular form because it symbolizes bounteous harvests, plenty, prosperity. Ribbed one upper (T-L), 6-3/4" L. (B-R) with flower horn is much larger, about 10-3/4" L. (T-R) Small one was made in 4 sizes, from 4-3/4" to 11" L. All Bertuch, c.1904.* **$65-$125**

IV-272. Ceramic molds. *A page from the S. Joseph catalog, c.1927. These are fairly heavy creamware or stoneware, well-glazed; the star, turtle, lobster, corn, fish & melon all came in more than one size. The turtle mold would be the most valuable:* **$100-$125***; the rest:* **$75-$100**

IV-273. Cornucopia or Horn of Plenty molds. *For various foods. All are hinged. (T-L) shows a dessert, decorated with a molded cornucopia, from Urbain Dubois' La Patisserie. (T-R) Simple mold at top, made in 4 sizes, from 5-1/2" to 10-1/4" L, Duparquet, Huot & Moneuse, c.1904-10. (B-L) Decorated one at bottom is copper, 6-3/4" L, and imported (from Germany?), also D,H & M. (B-R) With gadrooning and braced curly tail is "French Horn of Plenty," 10-1/2" L with 7" opening, for ice cream. S. Joseph.* **$65-$125**

IMPORTED TIN FORMS.
For Glace, Nougat ou Sucre.
Many other designs kept in stock.

IV-275. Molds for glacé, nougat, etc. *Tall urn and fountain "forms" for a variety of fancy desserts. Page from Duparquet, Huot & Moneuse, c.1904-10.* **$200-$350**

"Yule-Dough, or dow [sic], a kind of baby, or little image of paste, was formerly baked [in England] at Christmas, and presented by bakers to their customers, 'in the same manner as the chandlers gave Christmas candles.' They are called yule cakes in the county of Durham. Anciently, 'at Rome, on the vigil of the nativity, sweetmeats were presented to the fathers in the Vatican, and all kinds of little images (no doubt of paste) were to be found at the confectioners' shops.' My correspondent, Mr. Brand, who mentions these usages, thinks, 'there is the greatest probability that we have had from hence both our yule-doughs, plum-porridge, and mince-pies, the latter of which are still in common use at this season. The yule-dough has perhaps been intended for an image of the child Jesus, with the Virgin Mary,' he adds, 'it is now, if I mistake not, pretty generally laid aside, or at most retained only by children.'" William Hone, *The Every-Day Book*, Vol. I, n.d. [1825 or 1826]. Lesley Gordon, *A Pageant of Dolls,* (NYC: Wynn, 1949), says that in the Yorkshire district of England, a "bread doll" was made "as nearly as possible to look like a real baby, with fingers and toes marked on it and a small dab of dough for a nose; this doughy infant was lightly baked and dressed in real white babyclothes."

Mold, pudding or bake?, brown glazed ceramic, celebrating the American Centennial, molded mark "1776-1876" inside, American, 1876. **$100-$125**

Mold, pudding or bake?, yellowware, ear of corn, American, 4-3/4" H x 8" L x 6" W, 19th C. **$75-$120**

"Corn Meal Pudding, No. 1. One pint of sifted meal, one tumbler [6-8 oz.] of good molasses, one pint of sweet milk [i.e. not butter-milk], a quarter of a pound of butter, grated lemon peel or powdered mace to flavor it. Boil the milk; while hot, pour it upon the meal, and mix well. Warm the butter. Stir to the molasses half a teaspoonful of [baking] soda. Beat the eggs separately; add the eggs when the mush is cold. Mix all well. Bake in a buttered dish. Eat with a rich liquid sauce." Mrs. A. P. Hill, *Receipt Book,* NYC, 1870.

Mold, corn design, ironstone, American or English, 10" L, 19th C. **$55-$75**

Mold, corn design, cream colored earthenware, English, 6" L, late 19th C. **$60-$80**

Mold, custard or pudding using milk?, ironstone, large size oval, fluted base, rare image of cow with man milking her, English, 19th C. **$200-$300**

Mold, so-called crown mold because of very deep molding (just as deep, wide molding along the ceiling is called crown molding), cream glazed ceramic, English, 3-3/4" H x 5-3/4" L x 4-1/4" W, mid 19th C. **$70-$80**

Mold, for a Lenten dish?, brown glazed redware, an unidentifiable, slightly curved, scaly fish with pleasant smile & pronounced double caudal or tail fin, no other fins, very primitive, somewhat lumpy ungraceful form, PA German, 11-5/8" L x 4-1/2" W, 19th C. Ex-Robacker, $350. **$300-$400**

Mold, redware fish, slightly curved with bifurcated short tail, no body fins, large exaggerated scales & smiling expression, Pennsylvania, 19th C. **$300-$400**

Mold, floral design, tan earthenware, oval, footed base, English or American, 19th C. **$60-$75**

Mold, rabbit design, earthenware, "Meakin," English, mid 19th C. **$60-$75**

Mold, redware glazed inside with dark brown, lots of detail, rooster with squirrel-scroll tail, small feet underneath hold it steady, American, rooster is 11-1/2" H x 11" W, mid 19th C. Ex-Jacqueline Hodgson Collection. **$800-$1100**

No More Breaks. "To prevent Glass, Earthen, Potter's and Iron[stone] Ware from being easily broken . . . put dishes, tumblers, and other glass articles into a kettle; cover them entirely with cold water, and put the kettle where it will soon boil. When it has boiled for a few minutes, set it aside, covered close. When the water is cold, take out the glass . . . Treat new earthen ware the same way. When potter's ware is boiled, a handful or two of bran should be thrown into the water, and the glazing will never be injured by acids or salts." Mrs. Cornelius, *The Young Housekeepers Friend or, A Guide to Domestic Economy and Comfort*, NY or Boston, 1846.

Mold, bread or pudding?, brown glazed pottery, slightly oval, fluted sides, very detailed swan, high tipped up tail, with reeds, English (?), about 7" L x 6" W x 3" deep, late 19th C. **$85-$120**

Mold, (cake? pudding?), redware, Turk's head, orange & brown glaze, a few flaky chips, 7" diameter, 19th C. **$140-$165**

Mold, glazed pottery, oval with flutes inside & scalloped rim, design is a tall footed urn, 4 feet on mold formed as flower petals, English, only 2" H x 6-1/4" L x 5-1/4" W, early 19th C. **$65-$75**

Blancmange mold, gray glazed pottery, very decorative molding with recipe for a blancmange pudding printed on side, advertising "Brown & Polsons Corn Flour," English, 7" x 5-1/2" x 5", turn of century. **$35-$45**

Jelly or aspic mold, armadillo design, white vitreous earthenware, "Shelley," Longton, England, c.1922. **$175-$200**

Jelly or aspic mold, white ceramic, asparagus bunch, Minton #41/6, English, mid 19th C. **$120-$130**

Jelly mold, saltglazed stoneware, basket of flowers, German, 20th C. **$30-$40**

Jelly mold, white glazed ceramic elephant, white body clay, English, 2" deep x 6-1/2" x 4-3/4", mid 19th C. **$175-$225**

Jelly mold, saltglazed stoneware, grape bunch, American, 19th C. **$45-$60**

Jelly mold, buff glazed heavy ceramic, deep molded bunch of grapes in top, American, 3-3/4" H x 8" L x 7" W, mid 19th C. **$75-$100**

Jelly mold, ceramic, grape cluster, brown ringed earthenware, English, 7" L, 19th C. **$60-$75**

Jelly mold, lobster, oval, earthenware, German, 19th C. **$65-$85**

Jelly or pudding mold, thick glazed ironstone, fluted sides, pineapple motif, English or American, 7" L, 19th C. **$45-$65**

Jelly mold, ceramic, glazed stoneware, rectangular, wonderful design made up of concentric borders of round tennis balls with crossed tennis rackets on top, "Copeland," English, turn of century. **$125-$150**

CERAMIC, SPOUTED OR TUBED:

I use the term tubed to mean a closed or capped tube, because I have several times seen such redware molds with an old cork stuck in the end of the tube. For some (perhaps now arcane) reason, apparently it was deemed useful to use one mold for different baking jobs — one requiring a closed tube, the other a spout. I suppose a mold set down in water for steaming might be corked, so that water wouldn't percolate up the spout and splish splash on the food.

Cake mold, also called a **sponge cake mold**, brown glazed earthenware, fluted, spouted, with side handle, American, prob. PA or Shenandoah Valley of VA or WV, 3-1/8" H x 9-1/2" diameter, 19th C. Any piece with clear provenance from a known potter would be worth much more than an anonymous piece like this. **$140-$180**

Sponge cake: A. H. Rice and John Baer Stoudt, in The Shenandoah Pottery, first published in Strasburg, VA, by The Shenandoah Publishing Co. in 1929, and reprinted in Berryville, VA in 1974, call this kind of glazed earthenware spiral fluted spouted mold a "Spiral sponge cake mould," in their catalog of Alvin Rice's huge personal collection. The meaning of sponge cake may differ from region to region, and from period to period, because while I can find Pennsylvania German (closely related to Shenandoah Virginian) recipes for sponge cake, they are all to be baked in square or oblong loaf pans. It is angel food cake which calls for the spout. And in one book there is something called **"Glory Cake,"** which is like angel food cake except that the yolks are used also, separated from the stiffly beaten whites. This cookbook is Ruth Hutchison's *The New Pennsylvania Dutch Cook Book*, NY: Harper & Bros., 1958. It was originally published in 1948. In William Woys Weaver's scholarly, entertaining *Sauerkraut Yankees*, which is based directly on historic nineteenth-century German American cookbooks rather than on modern housewife cooks in Pennsylvania like the ones Hutchison depended on, there is no Angel Food Cake but a Sponge Cake very similar to that "Glory Cake" in the earlier book. It calls for a square tin pan, with the batter an inch deep. In *Sauerkraut Yankees,* no cake recipes call for a spouted mold. In Weaver's book *America Eats* (1989) there is a picture of an 8-1/4" square tin cake pan, with spout and envelope ends, captioned "Original angel food cake pan" (p.140 of his book).

Pudding or kugelhopf mold, pottery with medium brown glaze, wheel thrown, fluted and spouted afterward, spout is corked with what is obviously contemporaneous cork, American, 3-3/4" H x 7-1/2" diameter, 19th C. **$55-$65**

Pudding mold, ceramic, glazed & hand-painted, apple design in relief, fluted sides, spouted, American (?), small size, only 3-3/4" x 4-3/4", 20th C. **$25-$35**

"Brown Betty Pudding. Take a cup of grated bread crumbs, 2 cups fine-chopped tart apples, 1/2 cup brown sugar, teaspoon cinnamon, one tablespoon butter, cut into bits. Butter a deep pudding dish, and put a layer of apples on bottom; then sprinkle with sugar, cinnamon and butter and cover with bread crumbs. Put in another layer of apples, and proceed as before until ingredients have been used, having a crumb layer last. Cover the dish and bake for 3/4 hour in moderate oven, then remove the cover and brown the top. Serve with sugar and cream." Maria Parloa, *Kitchen Companion,* Boston: Estes & Lauriat, 1887.

Pudding mold, redware, spouted turk's head, with "swirled fluted sides & finger crimped rim," palpably handmade, prob. PA, 9-1/2" diameter, 19th C. Only $25 because of "old chips & hairline" cracks, at Garth Auction, May 5-6, 1989, Delaware, OH. Worth four or five times as much in better condition. **$25-$175**

Pudding mold, redware with unusual black glaze, Turk's head or turban design, spouted, widely canted sides, American, 11" diameter, 19th C. **$150-$200**

Pudding mold, earthenware, spouted, has handle, American, 9-1/2" diameter, mid 19th C. **$120-$150**

Pudding or cake mold, fluted tubed redware with yellow glaze, marked "John Bell," Waynesboro, PA, 19th C. The earthenware & stoneware made by John Bell & his brother Samuel Bell is possibly, taken as a whole, the most desirable pottery in the history of America. John Bell's figural pieces, dogs,

and especially lions, bring many many thousands of dollars the rare occasions they come to auction. Most Bell pieces are probably safely (alack alas but fortunately) in museum or private collections. **$250-$350**

Pudding or cake mold, glazed earthenware, a mottled brown finish, conical spout, large swirled flutes, stamped "John Bell," Waynesboro, PA, 4" H x 10" diameter, c.1860s-1870s. **$600-$750**

Pudding or cake mold, Turk's head tubed mold, redware, American, 7-3/4" diameter, 19th C. **$140-$160**

Pudding or cake mold, Turk's head with spout, creamware, American, 9" diameter, 19th C. **$70-$90**

COPPER MOLDS:

Mold, copper, round with 2 handles, 9 shaped cups, very Oriental in feel, a fish, shell, leaf, melon, etc., sold as "French" but a new one bought in China was shown me recently, 12-1/4" diameter, dealer said c.1760; I think prob. late 19th C. to recent times. The dealer's price of $1400 was based on belief it was "18th C European." Price range is based on belief it is much newer. **$45-$85**

Mold, for a confection or candy?, heavy copper, tinned inside, well-defined thistle design, only mark is "194," 1" deep x 2-1/8" diameter, late 19th C. **$12-$18**

Mold, copper, 3-tier, fancy looking with petal-like top, no mark, English, 10" H x 8" diameter, c.1860. **$1000-$1200**

Blancmange mold, relatively thin pieced copper with tinned interior, 8-sided, very architectural, English (?), only 6" H, late 19th C. **$140-$160**

Blancmange mold, heavy pieced copper with tin lining, 6 columnar pieces form structure, 15" H, 1850s to 1870s. **$300-$320**

Border or ring mold, copper, stamped, tinned inside, rustic & exaggerated twiggy bird's nest design, English (?), 6-1/2" diameter, late 19th C. **$175-$200**

Border mold, copper, heavily tinned inside, geometric oval, makes an oval food "frame" for other food — say rice around peas on a platter. 7" L, late 19th C. Note that not all border molds were oval, although platters are oval. Many were round and were used on a big plate. **$175-$200**

Jelly or blancmange mold, 3 tiers, very architectural, copper, tinned inside, stamped "N & G 529," 4" H x 4" diameter, late 19th C. Dealer William Davis said that manufacturers used some very fine contemporary designers to design the molds, and that they also used architects. He said he had one mold that looks like the top of the Chrysler Building in NYC! **$165-$200**

IV-276. Biscuit, creme or jelly mold. *Stamped copper, tinned inside, oval, 7-1/4" L. Bertuch, Berlin, c.1904.* **$125-$175**

Jelly mold, pieced & stamped copper, tinned inside, architectural, each tier soldered together, tall "chef's hat" effect, 6-lobed top with swagged sides or base, marked only with stamped number 38, probably an inventory number, English, 8-1/2" H, c.1860. Inventory numbers were either scratched on the mold or were stamped using different combinations of single digit stamps, made of iron, and looking like a nailset or punch except that a small backwards number is on the tip. **$700-$1000**

Jelly mold, stamped or beaten into form, architectural, each of 4 tiers pieced & soldered together, copper, tinned inside, tall & with a sort of scalloped Jell-O mold look on top, marked "206 C," English, 8" H x 6-1/2" diameter, c.1860. **$375-$400**

Jelly or blancmange mold, copper, 3-tiered, the 2nd tier is fat columns into which lady fingers would fit nicely, top tier of fat turban twists, stamped with numeral "1," also initials of owner, "J. A. C.," English, 9" H x 8" diameter, c.1860s. **$800-$900**

Jelly mold, pieced copper, heavily tinned, hanging ring, corn design stamped in bottom (what becomes top of food), English, 8" L oval, late 19th C. **$85-$100**

Jelly mold, copper with heavily tinned inside, fluted sides, cornucopia in top, oval, 1-1/2" deep x 4-1/2" L x 3-1/2" W, late 19th C. **$55-$60**

Jelly mold, copper, tinned inside, crown-like with chain link effect on top, 5 lobes to sides, stamped "M 443," no other mark, English, 5-1/2" H x 5" diameter, c.1860. **$300-$350**

Jelly mold, copper, tinned inside, shallow oval mold in 3 tiers, diamonds on top, marked "Moulton Paddocks" and with initials "E. C," possibly the owner's initials, English, 2" H x 6-1/2" L, mid 19th C. **$115-$125**

Jelly mold, fish, copper, tinned inside, 3-1/2" L, late 19th C. **$55-$65**

Jelly mold, fish, stamped copper, tinned inside, "Kreamer," Brooklyn, NY, early 20th C. **$50-$65**

Jelly mold, copper with dovetail seams, scroll-petaled flower on top, round edges, slightly dented, stamped in mold, at least the top, marked only with #15, English, 6-1/2" H, mid 19th C. **$165-$200**

IV-277. Molds for biscuits, cremes, etc. *Copper. Many of these made in several sizes. All sizes range from 4" to 8" diameter. Bertuch, c.1904.* **$25-$150**

IV-279. Melon mold. *Very unusual mold with ribbed copper body, wrought iron handle. Note leveling foot where handle joins body. 18" L overall. European probably, early 19th C. Ex-Wiggins Tavern Collection, Northampton, MA. Photograph courtesy Luella McCloud Antiques, Shelburn Falls, MA.* **$400-$600**

IV-278. Jelly molds. *Ovals with various embossed designs. 6-1/2" to 7-1/2" L. Material not mentioned, possibly stamped steel as some others on same page of the catalog, or possibly copper with tin lining, or maybe just tin. S. Joseph, c.1927. Part of the value relates to subject; part to material. Stamped steel would be unusual, but probably not as valuable to collectors as copper.* **$35-$85**

IV-280. Macedoine molds. *Imported copper, 6-1/4" and 6-3/4" diameter at bottom. A* **macedoine** *is chopped fresh fruit, soaked in kirsch and maraschino cherry juice, mixed with cream and chilled. Duparquet catalog, c.1904-10. Copper molds very desirable.* **$100-$150**

Jelly mold, pieced & seamed copper, tinned inside, braided border & 8 tall fluted risers, unpolished old patina, only mark is "435," stamped in so it's either maker's mark or inventory mark from large kitchen, English, 6" H x 5-1/2" diameter, c.1840s to 1860s. **$250-$300**

Jelly mold, fruit pattern on top, copper, tinned inside, round shape, fluted sides, short rolled-edge skirt, late 19th C. **$45-$60**

Jelly mold, geometric, copper with tinned inside, oval ring mold, 9" L x 3" D x 5-1/2" W, 3rd quarter 19th C. **$130-$150**

Jelly mold, copper, tinned inside, oval ring, gothic arches, stamped with the #198 and a maltese cross and orb, sign of a Birmingham works, English, 2-3/4" H x 6" W oval, c.1870s to 1890s. Birmingham, England was a great copper mold manufacturing center from about 1840 to about 1910, according to mold dealer William Davis, of Wilmington, DE. Traditionally, Birmingham has been known for several centuries for brass-working. **$250-$300**

Jelly mold, copper, tinned inside, oval, makes hearts at the top of columns, pieced, with dovetailed seam, no mark, English, 6" W oval, c.1870s to 1880s. **$250-$300**

Jelly mold, copper, pieced & stamped, dovetail seam, tinned inside, high base or sides shaped like a fez, couchant lion on top, looking up, simple skirt, no discernible mark, English (?), 4-3/4" H exclusive of low lion, 7" L, c.1850s. **$450-$600**

Jelly mold, pear, copper, tinned inside, 3-1/2" L, late 19th C. **$38-$45**

Jelly mold, copper, tinned inside, rose design stamped in top, 7" L x 5" W, late 19th C. **$65-$80**

Jelly mold, rose design, stamped copper, tinned inside, 4-1/2" D, late 19th C. **$90-$120**

Jelly mold, seashell design, copper, tinned inside, 3-1/2" L, late 19th C. Could also be for a madeline. **$35-$45**

Jelly mold, starflowers, copper, tinned inside, individual size, 3-3/4" D, late 19th C. **$45-$65**

Jelly mold, pieced copper, dovetail seams, tinned inside, oval with swirled lobes, English (?), 4" deep x 4-1/2" x 7", c.1850s. **$145-$160**

Jelly mold, copper, simple design, besides the makers' mark, another mark is an 8-point star. The numbers "11/11" are also scratched in, probably a personal inventory number, perhaps meaning this mold was number eleven out of a set of eleven. Other marks are a stamped Maltese cross and orb, and "#458," Birmingham, England, 4" H, mid 19th C. **$165-$200**

Jelly mold, copper, tinned inside, stamped & pieced with zigzig edge, marked with Maltese cross and orb, and number "198," Birmingham, England, 19th C. **$250-$300**

Marks on Molds. Quoting dealer William Davis, of Wilmington, DE, the molds were marked because "they were very expensive when they were new. I have one with the coat of arms of the Duke of Bedford, one with those of the Earl of Selburne; these molds were marked and had inventory numbers too. Very frequently on the Birmingham ones, you'll find a star stamped in the side. This was a craftsman's signature, but I've not been able to identify the maker." He showed me another signature comprised of a cluster of 4 periods, a half moon and a tiny 8-pointed star.

• • • •

"Aspic Jelly. Aspic jelly is largely used in cold entrées such as boned chicken or turkey, game, vegetables or fish, the material being molded in the jelly. This means that the aspic must be brilliantly clear and of firm consistence. It also presupposes a foundation of strong stock made of veal or lean beef according as the finished jelly is to be of a light or dark color. For one quart of good strong stock

allow one box of granulated gelatine, two tablespoonsful of strained lemon juice, the whites of three eggs, one scant cupful of white wine, a bay leaf, two cloves, one dozen peppercorns, two sprigs of parsley, a sprig of thyme and one-quarter of a cupful each of chopped onion, celery and carrot.

"Put three-quarters of the cupful of wine, the seasonings and chopped vegetables into a saucepan, cover and simmer for ten minutes, then strain. Soak the gelatine in one cupful of the stock; when soft and swollen put into an agate [graniteware] saucepan with the lemon juice and the remainder of the stock, heat slowly; when warm season to taste with salt and cayenne. Whip the whites of the eggs to a soft froth, dilute with the liquid strained from the vegetables, add to the soup and bring rapidly to the boiling point, stirring constantly. Now put aside the spoon, let boil very gently for three minutes, draw to the side of the fire and let stand untouched for twenty minutes. Strain through doubled cheesecloth wrung out in cold water, being careful not to squeeze or the jelly will be clouded. Add the reserved wine and it is ready to use." [That is, to gently stir in the bits of meat or vegetables, to put into a mold, and chill until gelatinized firmly.] Cornelia C. Bedford, "Housekeepers Inquiries," *Table Talk,* Philadelphia, January 1903.

Jelly molds, tubed — See tubed copper molds, below

Pudding mold, so-called **beehive** type, copper, with brass screw-on base, ring handle on snug lid, concentric lines inside are tinning lines, according to dealer William Davis, no mark, 5-1/4" H x 4-1/2" diameter, 1840s to 1860s (?). I asked Delaware dealer William Davis about the tinning, and he said that in some instances the makers "began with tinned sheet copper; in others they were dipped. Frequently you'll find them tinned both inside and out. I had an eagle mold, the exterior was originally tinned but in the cleaning I had it removed — much more attractive." If all jelly or pudding molds had been tinned outside, I'd take the same purist stance on removing tinning that I do on "brassifying" ice cream dishers, which were tinned for health reasons. The molds did not have to be tinned on the outside, and if the housekeeper was willing to devote the time to polish them, because of their beauty, fine. **$175-$225**

Pudding mold, beehive mold, large rounded copper bowl on disproportionately tiny pedestal foot of tooled brass that screws on so it can stand upright, snug-fitting lid with ring handle, marked only #6, English, 6-1/2" H, mid 19th C. One similar to this had a bayonet fastening for the lid. **$140-$175**

Pudding mold, beehive type, copper, with small cast brass pedestal screw-on base, brass ring handle on snug-fitting copper lid, tinned inside, looks like a lifesize upside-down artichoke, marked "F. W. & Co. #1100," English, about 7" H overall, late 19th C. **$165-$180**

Pudding mold, copper, cylinder with slightly slanted shape, bayonet mounted lid with bracket strap handle, tinned inside, marked only with the Birmingham orb and Maltese cross, and "#195," English, 5-3/8" H exclusive of strap handle x 5-1/2" diameter, 1840s to 1860s (?). **$175-$225**

Pudding mold, copper, tinned inside, hanging ring, marked "Christian Wagner," German, 11" diameter, turn of century. **$75-$125**

COPPER, tubed or spouted:

Kugelhopf or *gugelhupf* mold, spouted (with a little cruciform opening in the spout, instead of being fully open with rolled rim), stamped copper with tinned interior, German, 4" deep x 10" diameter, late 19th C. Kugel or gugel is the German word for ball (the same word is used for glass Christmas balls); the hopf or hupf is harder to figure out — it means to hop. This kind of mold is surmounted by a ring of balls or round shapes, with successive layers less round. This one is a traditional kugelhopf mold. The word is used also for many different spouted or tubed stamped copper molds, even ones with grapes or flutes or swirls. One distinction might be made: the center may be tubed or spouted, but the diameter of the center part is relatively wide compared to angelfood cake pans. Older kugelhopfen: older molds from the late eighteenth or early nineteenth century are simpler, smaller (about 7" or 8" D), the ball or flute or other motif is partly hammered, partly pieced, and the molds have brazed seams. **$110-$150**

Mold, copper, tinned inside, flared sides, tubed Turk's head, poss. American, prob. European, 11" diameter, mid to late 19th C. **$115-$150**

"To ornament a Spunge Cake, as a Turban. — Provide a copper mould in this shape, and bake a spunge cake neatly in it; when cold, ornament it with some handsome borders on the foldings, cutting off the bottom part of the border to make them represent rich lace; then fix one or two feathers on the side, which will give it a neat effect." Joseph Bell, *A Treatise on Confectionary,* Newcastle, England, 1817.

Mold, spouted, copper, tinned inside, stamped turban-like pattern makes it look like a bundt pan, small metal ring for hanging, no mark, German, English or American, 5" H x 10-1/2" D, late 19th C. Aspics, and what were called "jellies" and other congealed or jellied foods, were made in such molds. **$125-$175**

Mold, spouted, copper, very simple fluted design, no marks at all, 10-1/2" diameter, mid 19th C. **$115-$145**

Mold, spouted, copper, very simple fluted design, American or German (?), only 6-1/4" diameter, mid 19th C. **$120-$150**

Mold, spouted, with 6 fluted cap-topped towers, heavy pieced copper, tinned inside, English, 5" H, c.1830s to 1850s (?). For collectors, the apparent aristocrats of copper molds are the architectural ones, the more sky-reaching and cloud-breaking the more fun, but actually these are later than the highly prized molds from early Victorian times. Extreme gothic aspirations, and thin gauge copper, date English molds to the 1880s or 1890s. **$185-$225**

Mold, heavy copper, pieced & hammered, spouted, Masonic (?) hammer mark and a "5S" over a "C," American (?), 19th C. **$230-$250**

Mold, heavy gauge copper, tinned inside, tubed oval, fluted sides, top has Turk's head effect, looks as if it has been wire brushed, which lowers its value, marked "LAGRE 448 M. TEBE. DE," Belgian or French?, 11", 19th C. **$150-$300**

Mold, tubed, copper, tinned inside, oval, 4" deep x 8" L, late 19th C. **$125-$145**

Mold, hammered copper, spouted, marked with a "P" over a 2-step mark, also "#205," 20th C. **$25-$35**

COPPER & TIN MOLDS:

Jelly mold, copper & tin, ear of corn deeply embossed on copper top, tin sides & skirt, American (?), 5-1/4" L, 19th C. **$135-$150**

Jelly mold, copper, tin skirt, corn design, oval 4" deep x 4" W x 6-1/2" L, 19th C. **$125-$140**

Jelly mold, tin sides & skirt, deeply repousséd copper top, grape bunch, 5-1/2" L, late 19th C. **$85-$100**

Jelly mold, pieced & stamped tin, copper top, oval, "picket" flutes around sides, seamed at each end, top is very high profile stamped copper lion couchant but looking over left shoulder (couchant sinistral? as opposed to couchant dextral) with distinctly bewildered expression, this lion poly-

chromed in old paint, metallic gold, shades of deep yellow, black, with red inside mouth & red border, very unusual and attractive, English, 5" H x 7-1/4" L, mid (?) 19th C. The paint, which I believe is period and original, accounts for about half the probable market value. **$300-$375**

Jelly mold, copper & tin, lion design, deep tin sides, shallow tin skirt, English, 7" L, 19th C. **$175-$210**

Jelly mold, tin skirt to support mold upside down while gelatin setting, tinned copper oval mold with slightly slanted sides, fairly common pineapple design, English or poss. American, 6-1/2" L x 5" W x 5" D, late 19th C. or early 20th. **$65-$75**

Jelly mold, tin sides & skirt, copper top with rose design, sides formed in a sort of cathedral arch design, "J. A. & Co.," 1 pt. capacity, 1-1/2" H skirt, mid 19th C. **$95-$120**

Jelly mold, copper with tin sides & tin skirt, rose design, 4" deep x 4" W x 6-1/2" L, 19th C. **$135-$150**

Jelly mold, copper & tin, thistle design, small, late 19th C. **$55-$60**

Jelly mold, shallow tin skirt with tin-plated copper mold, thistle pattern, almost as common as the pineapple, 8-1/2" L, English or American, 19th C. **$75-$110**

Jelly mold, tin with tinned copper mold part, nice wheat sheaf & sickle, prob. American, 19th C. Motif adds value. **$125-$135**

ENAMELWARE MOLDS:

Mold, enamelware, fluted gray graniteware, American (?), 2-1/2" deep x 7" diameter, late 19th C. **$28-$35**

Mold, gray graniteware, scalloped sides, 4" D, 19th C. **$35-$45**

Pudding mold, dark brown & white mottled enamelware, European, 2" H x 12-1/2" diameter, turn of century. **$85-$145**

Pudding or cake mold, gray & cobalt blue agate enamelware, slope sided, possibly Columbian Enameling & Stamping Co.'s "Dresden," Terre Haute, IN (?), 11" diameter, late 19th C. or very early 20th. **$90-$125**

"Boiled Puddings. — I omitted to mention in the proper place that a mould is sometimes used for boiling puddings. I greatly prefer a bag. When the mould is used it should have a well-fitting cover, or be carefully tied over with a strong linen cloth, as the smallest quantity of water getting in would spoil the pudding." Mrs. A. P. Hill, *Receipt Book,* NYC, 1870.

"Dr. Kitchiner's Plum Pudding. — Suet chopped fine, six ounces; raisins, seeded and cut, six ounces; the same of currants, washed and dried; bread crumbs, three ounces; the same of flour, three eggs, half a nutmeg, a teaspoonful of mace and cinnamon mixed, half a teaspoonful of salt, a tumbler of milk, four ounces of sugar, a little citron and orange peel. Beat the eggs well; add the spice; mix the milk in by degrees; then the rest of the ingredients. Boil in a cloth, in plenty of water. It must boil steadily, or the pudding will be heavy. Boil six hours. Prepare everything the day before it is wanted." Mrs. A. P. Hill, *Receipt Book,* NYC, 1870. Arrrrrghhhh.

Pudding mold, gray graniteware, a melon mold with plain tin close-fitting flat lid, 7" L, 19th C. Very attractive, and much less common than the all-tin melon mold. **$145-$175**

Pudding mold, gray enameled iron, fluted melon mold, footed to hold it stable, lid not made for this one, prob. European, late 19th C. **$95-$125**

Pudding mold, melon type, gray graniteware, flat tin lid, "L & G," mfd. by Lalance & Grosjean, Woodhaven, NY, late 19th C. An 1898 ad reads: "Cooking Utensils are Safe is stamped with trademark ["AGATE nickel steel ware]. Because to each article is attached chemist's certificates [a blue label], guaranteeing that it is free from arsenic, antimony, lead or any other poisonous ingredient." **$145-$175**

Pudding mold, cobalt enamelware, melon type with flat tin lid, last quarter (?) 19th C. **$150-$175**

Pudding mold, gray enamelware, with tin lid, marked "L. & G. Mfg. Co. No. 60, Extra Agate," Lalance & Grosjean, late 19th C., early 20th. **$60-$80**

ENAMELWARE, spouted or tubed:

Cake pan, round spouted, blue & white swirl enamelware, 11" D, 19th C. **$60-$80**

Cake pan, spouted, gray graniteware, American, 9" D, turn of century. **$35-$50**

Cake mold, angel food cake, octagonal blue & white swirled enamelware, with spout, no mark, American or European, turn of century. **$75-$90**

Cake mold, angel food cake, pale aqua & white enamelware, spouted, American (?), 9" diameter, early 20th C. **$25-$30**

Cake mold, octagonal, cobalt enamelware, spouted, American (?), turn of century. **$25-$35**

Pudding mold, gray graniteware, spouted Turk's head, American (?), 19th C. **$85-$100**

Mold, gray graniteware, spouted Turk's head, only 6-1/2" diameter, late 19th C. **$40-$48**

GLASS MOLD:

Jelly mold, pressed glass, for gelatin dish, oval, clear glass, paneled sides, English, 3-1/2" H x 7" L x 4" W, late 19th C. **$35-$55**

TIN MOLDS:

Blancmange molds, a pair, tin, deep scalloped base with octagonal "lighthouse" structure atop, tightly fitted lids on bottom, poss. English or French import, poss. American, 11-1/2" H x 5" diameter at base, c.1870s. **$55-$80**

Blancmange mold, high tin structure consisting of very pointed central pinnacle surrounded by 2 tiers of lower pointed peaks, European or American, 11" H, c.1870s. **$140-$160**

Blancmange or ice cream mold, pieced tin, straight sides with rolled edge, clumsy but charming corrugated cup in center with 6 small very pointed cones, one in each of the 6 large scalloped compartments around the center, American, 19th C. **$100-$125**

IV-281. Fish molds for various foods, *including iced, jellied and biscuit. Most of these probably for fish-flavored aspics or mousses. All about 7-1/2" to 13" L. Top two are from* Mrs. Marshall's Cookery Book, *c.1902; one in second row* **(R)** *is from S. Joseph, NYC, c.1927. Rest from Bertuch, Berlin, c.1904.* **$35-$75**

Border mold, tin, extraordinary form composed of 7 swirled (like soft ice cream) & pointed cones, wire hanging ring, German, 9" diameter (these came in various sizes with different numbers of cones), turn of century. **$55-$75**

Border or ring mold, stamped tin, marked "KREAMER 2," 9-1/2" L x 6-1/4" W oval, mfd. by A[ugust] Kreamer, Brooklyn, NY, early 20th C. The oval rice mold by Kreamer came in three sizes, and you could get them with snug lids. **$25-$35**

Border or ring mold, tin, with ring handle, "15" is only mark, 2-1/4" deep x 6" diameter, late 19th or early 20th C. **$15-$20**

Border mold, stamped & pieced tin, fruit design on top, plain sides, American, 10" diameter, early 20th C. **$18-$25**

"Ground Rice Flummery. — boil 1 quart milk, except that portion which you have reserved to wet a heaping teacup of rice. Stir this in when the milk boils up; put in 1 teaspoon of salt. When it has thickened, stir in a table spoonful or two of dry ground rice, let it boil up again all around, and take it off the fire as soon as you think the dry rice has become scalded. Have ready a bowl or blancmange mould, wet with a spoonful of milk or cold water, into which pour it. If it is of the right consistency, it will turn out after 15 or 20 minutes in good shape. Eat with sugar and milk or cream. For this and all similar milk preparations, peach leaves are better than any spice [to add an almondy flavor]. Boil in the milk 1/2 dozen fresh leaves from the tree. Remember to take them out before you stir in the rice." Mary Hooker Cornelius, *The Young Housekeepers Friend,* Boston, 1846. **NOTE:** Some flummery recipes use gelatin, but their distinguishing ingredient is almost always rice meal or flour. Katharine Mellish's cookbook *Cookery and Domestic Management. Including Economic & Middle Class Practical Cookery,* (London & NY, 1901), contains a recipe for "Corn Blancmange."

"Almond Charlotte. Blanch and chop fine one large cupful of almonds. Melt three tablespoonfuls of sugar in a frying pan — do not add any water — throw in the almonds and stir until browned, then turn out to cool and pound them quite fine. Put them in a double boiler with one cupful and a half of milk and heat slowly to the scalding point. Beat together three egg yolks and two-thirds of a cupful of sugar, add some of the hot milk, mix and turn into the [double] boiler, stirring until the mixture begins to thicken. Add one-half of a box of gelatine which has been soaked in one-half of a cupful of cold water and stir until it is dissolved; take from the fire, strain and set aside until beginning to cool and thicken. Add one pint of thick cream whipped to a solid froth, stir lightly until mixed, then turn into a fancy serving dish or into individual molds." Cornelia C. Bedford, "Housekeepers Inquiries," *Table Talk,* Philadelphia, January 1903.

IV-282. Fish mold, *for aspics, etc. Stamped tin, leveling "leg" at tail end, marked "Germany," c.1900-1920. Probably a Bertuch mold from Berlin. 2-3/4" deep x 13-1/2" L x 5-1/2" W. Ex-collection of NYC food stylist Grace Manney.* **$35-$45**

Border mold, tin, deep design of 13 connected hearts, American (?), 8-1/2" diameter, prob. early 20th C. **$100-$135**

Border mold, tin, scalloped outside edge with plain inside ring, 9" cake pan, round, stamped tin, Turk's head, spouted, 9" diameter, 20th C. **$15-$18**

Cake mold, tin, round with low sides, top stamped with very swirly design, sometimes called a "trois freres" mold after 3 French pastry chefs, French, 2" deep x 7-1/2" diameter, late 19th C. **$20-$35**

Cake or bake mold, looks like some kind of muffin mold, heavy tin, oblong shape, 6 V-shaped troughs side by side, triangular in section, for making "Waldorf Triangles," or "Golden Rod Cake," or "Orange Slice Cake" and many other fancy cakes, not marked (one company making them was Jaburg Brothers, NYC), about 13-1/2" L x 3-1/2" W, late 1890s to c.1920s. This size baked six one-penny sticks; another with only three "V" troughs to make 10¢ size "Golden Rods." **$15-$25**

Cake tin for sponge cakes, stamped tin, oblong tray with 6 elongated peanut-shaped or, as the catalog says, "finger shape" cups, in Harrod's Stores catalog, London, England, 11" L, late 19th C. **$18-$25**

Charlotte Russe mold — See entry under Charlotte Russe mold just after the big cake board section in this chapter

Croquette mold, tin, conical shape, 2 halves pinned lengthwise to release molded ground meat (ham, chicken, veal, fish) form to roll in crumbs before cooking, possibly made by Silver, marked "Brooklyn, NY," 4-3/4" L x 3" diameter at open end, c.1880s. According to Richard Hooker, who wrote the amusing, informative *History of Food and Drink in America*, meat choppers

in the 1860s and 1870s "opened to the housewife an entire school of dishes based on chopped foods: croquettes, timbales, patties, loafs, ..." etc. **$15-$25**

Cutlet molds, pieced tin, shaped like cutlets or big fat commas, deep straight sides, used to shape a mixture of minced meat, spices, onion & egg into shape of lampchop or drumstick, etc., before cooking, but not used to bake the cutlet in, American or European, about 5" L x 1" deep, from c.1870s to 1900. I've never seen the leg of mutton mold, made of pieced tin in the appropriate shape but with slanted rather than straight sides, but one was advertised in the F. A. Walker catalog of 1886. I suppose it is much larger, meant for forming a meatloaf for a family rather than an individual serving. **$10-$15**

Dariel mold, often spelled **dariole** in old catalogs, a little tin cup — slightly flared cylinder, flat bottom, rolled edge, side seam, for a particular kind of small cake or custard, very like a small tartlet cup found today in the frozen food section of grocery stores. F. A. Walker's 1870s catalog also called them "individual jelly

IV-285. Jelly molds. *Two at top have protective rims, to keep designs from being banged, and also to enable the mold to stand firmly, upside down, for filling and while setting. Tin with fluted skirts. Sizes from 1/2 to 2 pints, and 2 quarts. F. A. Walker catalog, 1880s. Bottom mold, with grape bunch on top, is also oval, in 2 sizes — 8" and 8-5/8" L. Bertuch, c.1904.* **$75-$125**

IV-283. Fish mold, *for aspics, etc. Stamped tin, simple head, wide flat edges. Wire leg at tail end. Stamped "Austria," and "CF" (?), also #499 over a #3. I cannot identify the maker. 2-1/4" deep x 9-1/8" L x 3-3/4" W. Ex-collection of NYC food stylist Grace Manney.* **$35-$45**

IV-286. Jelly mold. *Stamped & pieced tin, pineapple design, rim. Mold depth 4-7/8". Overall 6" H x 7" L. Ex-Collection of Grace Manney, NYC food stylist.* **$30-$45**

IV-284. Fish molds, *in animated curves. (T) called a "Dresden carp mold," stamped tin, with hanging ring at center, 8" or 11" diameter size, from S. Joseph, NYC, c.1927. (B) Stamped tin, 11" and 12" diameter, from Bertuch, Berlin, c.1904.* **$35-$45**

cups" ("jelly" meant a gelatinized sweet or savoury, not a big blob of grape jelly). The same Walker's catalog also had a cut of what looks exactly like a bouche iron, but called a dariole mold — a turned wooden handle set at right angle to corrugated, flared, solid cast iron mold to be dipped in batter before quickly deep frying. That type of mold molds on the outside rather than the inside. American or European, 2" H x 2-1/4" diameter, last half 19th C. F. A. Walker, in an 1886 sales brochure, advertised three sizes of dariel molds, viz. 1-3/4" H x 1-3/4" diameter; 1-7/8" H x 1-7/8" diameter; and this one. Not all had equal height & diameter. <u>Added value</u>: tinned copper would bring a bit more. **$7-$15**

French pie mold, or pâte mold, also called a confectioner's mold, round, stamped tin, hinged opposite the clamp, French, came in several sizes through the F. A. Walker catalog: 7", 9", 10" and 12" diameter, 1870s. Some of these had fluted sides, some were stamped with fruit and vine designs or other designs. The ring was in 2 parts so the sometimes concave designs on the sides could be released; rings were either hinged and pinned, or pinned in 2 places. **$30-$40**

Jelly or blancmange mold, stamped & pieced heavy tin, 3 tiers, architectural in appearance, hanging ring at rim, poss. American, 9" H, 19th C. **$55-$75**

Jelly mold, stamped tin, shape of stack of corn cobs, American, 1870s. An unusual version of the corn mold. **$70-$85**

Jelly mold, pieced tin, round, sides or base made in 3 parts, soldered to top, interlinked crabapple design on top, scored lozenges on sides, marked near ring hanger, initials that look like a capital "N" superimposed on a "C," also numbers 32 and 6, no country of origin, 3-1/2" deep x 8-1/8" diameter, late 19th C. **$15-$30**

Jelly mold, fish, stamped tin, for congealed (jellied, or gelatinized) dishes, although at least one dealer said it was for baking Lenten bread. American or German, 19th C. **$25-$30**

Jelly mold, stamped tin fish, simple head, wide flat edges, wire leveling leg, stamped "CF," also numbers "499" over "3," "AUSTRIA," 2-1/4" deep x 9-1/8" L x 4-1/4" W, c.1900 to 1920. **$20-$30**

Jelly mold, stamped tin, fish-shaped, fancy head, "G. M. T. Co., Czecho-Slovak," 1-5/8" deep x 9-1/4" L x 3-3/4" W, c.1900 to 1920. **$20-$30**

Jelly mold, stamped tin, fish-shaped, stamped on leveling 'leg' at tail end is "Germany," 2-3/4" deep x 13-1/2" L x 5-1/2" W, c.1900 to 1920s. **$25-$35**

Jelly mold, stamped & pieced tin, grape bunch design, 3-1/4" L x 2-3/4" W, late 19th or early 20th C. **$15-$20**

Decorating with figural molds: "The Accolade of the Pudding Mold. — Every year the harassed interior decorator is driven well nigh distracted in a vain endeavor to find some new idea in decoration. What shall it be? Eagerly he searches London, Paris, Berlin and Vienna in the chance hope of discovering some novelty that will fit in with the general furnishing scheme and make one room look different from a hundred others . . . Now an enterprising few, instead of scouring the foreign marts and exhibitions have stayed at home and looked around their own homes for inspiration. And at last they have found it . . . Strangely enough, the kitchen has been the chief source of inspiration; so the following suggestions for decoration are well within the reach of the slenderest purse.

"One of the most amusing of these ideas is the way in which the ordinary tin pudding molds can be used for decorative purposes . . . [Especially] interesting is the use of large jelly or pudding molds as mural decorations. For this purpose the molds selected should be rather important in design. Fortunately many enchanting patterns are obtainable. Some show fruit nestling in beds of vine leaves, while others reveal fantastic looking fish, such as one sees in old Japanese prints. Then there are animals — rabbits, chickens, and even squirrels — charming accessories for a child's room. More novel are the molds patterned in geometrical designs — a type particularly well suited to rooms furnished in the modernist taste. Hung upon the wall or above the mantlepiece, gleaming like dull silver and covered with unusual designs, they look like native masks or . . . modern sculpture." Derek Patmore, *House & Garden*, Aug. 1928.

IV-287. Jelly molds. *Sampling from ad of stamped tin molds sold by J. & C. Berrian, NYC. Ad in History of Prominent Mercantile & Manufacturing Firms in the U.S., Boston: 1857. The molds:* **$25-$65**

IV-288. Jelly molds. *Stamped & pieced tin. (**L**) Round, interlinked crabapple (?) design bordering top, scored lozenges on skirt. Skirt in 3 parts, soldered to top. Marked near hanging ring, looks like capital "N" superimposed on a C or H, with "32" and "6." No country of origin, could be pre-1892 if imported, or turn-of-century if American. 3-1/2" deep x 8-1/8" diameter. (**R**) Round, tin, shell design bordered by rope. Simple fluted skirt of 2 pieces soldered. Marked "France 296," 4" deep x 6-1/4" diameter. Ex-Collection of NYC food stylist Grace Manney.* **$30-$45**

Schooling Adds Value. I have to say, the more fish molds I see of these, and the more I think about hanging them all together in all their variety on the wall, the more I like them. Each one may be not be worth much, or even be all that exciting a form, but imagine a school of 20 or 30 of them, swimming across the wall! Gee! I can hardly wait.

● ● ● ●

"Fish Jelly. Take a two-pound haddock, one onion, and half rind lemon; just cover with water, and boil; remove all the bones and skin; flake the fish, or pound it in a mortar, with a tablespoonful of butter, pepper and salt to taste. Put back the bones, reduce the liquor to one pint, add a quarter of a packet of gelatine (previously dissolved in a quarter of a tumbler of cold water). Make some veal forcemeat, without suet, roll in small balls, and drop into boiling water; they will cook in seven minutes. Decorate a mould with the balls and rings of lemon, mix the strained liquid with the pounded fish, and, when nearly cold, pour into the mould. Hard-boiled eggs may be made over in this way." Gertrude Strohm, *The Universal Cookery Book*, 1888. If you do not like the idea of veal, for humanitarian or any other reasons, you can use ground turkey, or decorate the mould with mushroom caps and forget the meat except for the fish.

Jelly mold, tin, 2-part, with strap handle on lower section, strawberry, cherry, apple, pear, grapes & plum design, obviously for a congealed fruit salad! "Kreamer," early 20th C.   **$35-$50**

Jelly mold, stamped & pieced tin, round geometric, with castle turrets around sides & a pattern of blocks in the top, also called a town mold, because of its resemblance to an abstract medieval walled town, in a F. A. Walker catalog, most of whose things were French or English imports, 1870s to 1890s.   **$55-$70**

Jelly mold, stamped tin, bunch of grapes design not well-defined, small, probably imported, 1870s.   **$15-$20**

Jelly mold, tin, sharp edges almost as if it were to be a cutter, shape is outline of pineapple, bottom is separate & pushes through the shape, no mark, 2-13/16" deep x 7-1/4" L, turn of century.   **$30-$45**

Jelly mold, stamped & pieced tin, pineapple top, drape or "peacock eye" sides or base, simple skirt, American or English, mold depth 4-7/8", skirt is 6" x 7", turn of century.   **$28-$40**

Jelly mold, stamped tin, scroll shape, marked "SCT Co.," German, about 5-1/2" L, 20th C.   **$15-$22**

Jelly mold, stamped & pieced tin, round, 4 pieces soldered: the skirt & the simple fluted side or base made of 2 pieces, and the top, which is an embossed shell design, bordered by rope, marked "France 296," 4" deep x 6-1/4" diameter, turn of century.   **$15-$25**

Jelly mold, tin, oval with short skirt, 6-point star design, an individual mold size, for a fancy jellied dish, English or American, 2-1/2" H x 3-7/8" L x 2-1/4" W, 19th C.   **$35-$45**

Jelly mold, tin, thistle design on top fairly well-defined stamping, sides stamped in unnamed pattern, could be called "peacock eye" or "drape," made of 3 parts soldered together — the sides or base, the skirt or protective raised edge around fancy stamped top, and the top, American or English, mold depth 3-3/8", skirt 5-1/4" L x 3-3/4" H, c.1880s.   **$20-$35**

Jelly molds, stamped & pieced tin, oval, fluted base or side wall, simple rolled-edge raised edge ringing the top design. Well-defined, deeply stamped designs include flowers, fruits, vegetables & animals, as well as geometrics, imported in the late 19th C. from France, Germany or other countries, various sizes, holding 1/2, 1, 1-1/2, and 2 pints, and 2 quarts, 1870s or 1880s, prob. before and after too. These are usually found rather darkened, and with little bright tinning showing. Similar molds are made all of tin except for the top where the decorative motif is stamped; some of these are made of copper, which presumably took a deeper and more detailed stamp, and would avoid any tendency to rust in the creases or "cracks." Full range about: **$35-$125**

IV-289. Specimen page from Marshall's "Book of Moulds." *Tin molds in fancy shapes, mostly for jellies, from* Mrs. A. B. Marshall's Cookery Book, *London, c.1900 edition.*

IV-290. Specimen page from Marshall's "Book of Moulds." *From* Mrs. A. B. Marshall's Larger Cookery Book of Extra Recipes, *London, c.1902 edition.*

255

MOULDS FOR HOT & COLD ENTRÉES & SAVOURIES.

No. 215B.
BUTTERFLY MOULD.
Copper tinned,
10s. per doz.

No. 215C.
FANCY MOULD.
Copper tinned,
10s. per doz.

No. 215D.
FANCY MOULD.
Copper tinned,
10s. per doz.

No. 215E.
FANCY MOULD.
Copper tinned,
10s. per doz.

No. 215F.
FANCY MOULD.
Copper tinned,
10s. per doz.

No. 215G.
FANCY MOULD.
Copper tinned,
10s. per doz.

No. 215H.—COPPER BOMBE.
9s. per doz.

No. 217.—FLUTED FLEUR RING.
1s. each. Plain Fleur Rings, 6d. & 9d. each.

No. 209.—2s. and 3s. per doz.

No. 215I.
WALNUT MOULDS.
For Petits Fours, etc., 2s. per doz.

IV-291. Specimen page from Marshall's "Book of Moulds." *Molds for hot & cold entrées and savories, as well as a copper bombe mold. From* Mrs. A. B. Marshall's Cookery Book, *London, c.1900 edition.*

IV-292. Mold. *Stamped tin scroll, hanging ring, marked "SCT Co., Germany." 7" L, 20th C. Ex-Collection of NYC food stylist Grace Manney.* **$25-$35**

IV-293. Melon molds — for Pudding & Ice Cream. *Tin, oval. Three versions (you'll note that some never did have handles on the body).* **(T)** *"Pudding Mould. — Who likes boiled pudding can have it dry and light if cooked in one of these moulds."* American Home Cook Book, *1854.* **(M)** *"Fancy Quart and Two-Quart Ice Cream Mould."* Cherry-Bassett, 1921. **(B)** *With wire handle. Four sizes: for 2, 3, 2-1/2 and 4 pints. From 6-1/2" x 4-3/4" x 3-1/2" up to 8" x 6-1/8" x 4-1/8". Central Stamping Co., 1920. An even larger range of sizes, from 2 to 8 pints, was offered by Duparquet, about 1904. (SEE also the melon molds for ice cream, IV-207.)* **$25-$45**

IV-294. "Ice cream & pudding mold" patent. *Pat'd 11/10/1885, by Henry Eppelsheimer, NYC. Eppelsheimer, of course, was connected to the well-known American ice cream mold firm. This melon has two convex halves, with one serving as the snug-fitting "lid" to the other. Official Gazette of the U.S. Patent Office.* **$55-$65**

IV-295. "Hall of the Mountain King" molds ! *Stamped, pieced tin. Actually* (**L**) *is a "Jelly or Blanc Mange Mould," also for ice cream.* American Home Cook Book, *1854.* (**R**) *is a "Vegetable and Rice Mould," #229, for making decorative spires of cooked, mashed root veggies or rice. F. A. Walker catalog, c.1890. Nearly identical molds are still made, and sold in such all-inclusive kitchenware stores as Bridge's in NYC.* **$60-$100**

IV-299. Steamer molds, *for pudding and bread. All three, with spouts or plain, are for steaming pudding or brown bread. Bottom two have* **bayonet mount** *(put on and twist to secure) lids. Tin, in many sizes.* (**B-L**) *Spouted ones, mainly for pudding, are for 1 to 4 quarts.* (**B-R**) *Plain one, from 1-1/2 pint to 4 quart, from 4" x 4" to 8" x 6-1/2".* (**T**) *made by Dover Stamping Co., c.1899 (and before & after); others from D. J. Barry, 1924.* **$25-$45**

IV-296. Pudding mold. *Round tin* **"Turk's Head"** *or turban mold. (Could also be a turban squash — related to a melon!) I call this one the <u>laughing jockey</u>. F. A. Walker catalog, c.1890.* **$25-$45**

IV-297. Piccolo mold, *"... for making a fancy jellied dish called Little Piccolos. Line molds with 1/8" thick lemon jelly, and after lining, fill up the top parts with 2-colored creams, using forcing bags and plain pipes for the purpose, and partly fill up the bottom part of the moulds with finely-shredded blanched sweet almonds and pistachio nuts; in the centre of each put a little liquid jelly, then close up the moulds, place them on ice till set, and turn out on wet foolscap paper. Serve on a little plate, with chopped jelly around edges, and pour over a pale green cream made of whipped cream mixed with lemon jelly, rum, 'Noyeau' syrup, and coloring." From Mrs. A. B. Marshall's Larger Cookery Book, c. 1902. Picture from her 1900 book.* **$45-$65**

IV-300. Jelly molds, *and others, from William S. Adams & Son, London, ad in* Francatelli's Cook's Guide Advertiser, *c.1860-61.*

IV-298. Pudding molds. (T-L) *Stamped & pieced tin, imported by Duparquet, NYC. 4-3/4" diameter. Big flat bracket handle on lid. Hearts add value. C.1904-10.* (**R**) *Heavy tin, spouted, showing bayonet mount clearly. Four sizes, from 1-1/8 to 2-3/4 litre. Bertuch, c.1904.* **$45-$65**

Pudding molds, heavily-tinned, so-called melon style (imagine half an elongated acorn squash) with close-fitting flat lid that has an oval wire ring handle that folds flat, some of these are found marked "Kreamer" (made in Brooklyn, NY), others unmarked, American (poss. also English), various sizes, typical one is 6-1/2" L x 5" W x 3-3/4" deep (stamped 3 on lid), another is 7" L x 5-1/2" W x 4" deep, another 10" L x 5-5/8" W, late 19th C. to early 20th. The handles are sometimes missing, and the molds are sometimes found still brightly tinned outside but rusted inside, where dampness was trapped by the tight-fitting lid. Most have an oval wire loop soldered to the body of the mold so that you could grasp lid and body with your left and right hand and pull apart. If the ring was once there and is now missing (you can see the evidence by bits of solder in a roughly rectangular shape), subtract about $5 to $7. Extra large sizes cost the most. **$50-$60**

Pudding mold, melon shape, tin, 3 clips, marked only with 14 in a diamond and 127 on other half, 5-1/2" deep x 6" diameter, 19th C. I got the sparse description from an ad, so this is a hypothetical entry. I imagined a flat-top mold until reading that Henry Eppelsheimer, of the famous ice cream mold company, had patented a full-round "pudding and ice-cream mold" on Nov. 10, 1885. Patent drawing IV-294 looks like tops of 2 flat-lid melon molds fitted together, both with elongated oval wire handle. I think this one isn't Eppelsheimers (theirs have no need of clips), although it is possibly a full round. **$45-$55**

Pudding mold, stamped tin, flat close-fitting lid with round turban or turban squash mold, American or imported, about 6" or 7" diameter x 4" deep, c.1870s or 1880s. **$35-$45**

Pudding mold, heavy tin, hinged lid with clasp, German or American, 19th C. **$65-$85**

Vegetable or rice mold, pieced tin, an assemblage of pointed spires, almost spikes, the overall outline fitting into a cone shape, meant for molding cooked mashed root veggies or cooked rice, from F. A. Walker catalog, European (?), probably about 6" to 8" H, probably came in 2 or 3 sizes, late 19th C. **$60-$75**

TIN, spouted or tubed:

Mold, tubed, fluted tin, American, 7" D, turn of century. **$20-$30**

Cake mold, tin, fluted, tubed with closed end, American, 7" D, early 20th, late 19th C. Lots of cake and pudding molds turn out cakes or puddings with open centers. The tube or spout in the center of the mold allowed the heat (dry, steam or hot water) to cook the contents more evenly. **$25-$35**

Mold, Turk's head, spouted, tin, American, 7" deep x 9" diameter, late 19th C. **$22-$30**

Mold, tin, spouted with 9 sections shaped like Mr. Softee[a] ice cream cones, the flat-bottomed kind, hanging ring, American or imported, 9" diameter, 19th C. **$150-$200**

Mold or cake pan, round, 3-part, 2-way, deep tin cylinder, on which fits either a bottom with built-in tapered spout, or a plain bottom, "Gem," mfd. by American Machine Co., Philadelphia, PA, pat'd July 29, 1890. **$14-$25**

IV-301. Rice boiler, *or* **pudding mold.** *Fluted, tubed, closefit lid with strap handle. Tin. F. A. Walker, c.1890.* **$45-$65**

Molds or cake pans, pieced tin, spouted, American, 9-3/4" D, late 19th, early 20th C. Price is determined by shape (an octagonal or hexagonal mold usually costs more than a simple round one), apparent age, condition, general look, and workmanship if handmade. **$20-$55**

Mold, heavy pieced tin, very carefully made, tubed, 8 pronounced scallops, large diameter tube, ring hanger, American (?), 2" deep x 6-1/2" diameter, 1890s. **$20-$30**

Mold or cake pan, octagonal with tube, factory blackened tin, American, 13" diameter, 19th C. or early 20th. **$20-$25**

Mold or cake pan, pieced & hammered tin, side wall has very graceful flare with 10 generous scallops & folded rim, slightly conical seamed spout soldered to bottom. This is unusual because it was made in only 2 pieces instead of 3. Starting with a large round tin "doughnut" with a hole only 1-7/8" diameter in center, it was hammered or beaten up into pan with flat bottom & scalloped sides. Usually there is a seam or two on the side, as well as a seam around the bottom where the sides were joined, then a separate spout soldered on too. American, poss. VA, 3-1/2" deep x 10-1/4" diameter at top, 7-3/4" at bottom, 1870s, poss. earlier. **$45-$65**

Mold, "Savarin" cake mold, after famed chef Brillat-Savarin, used for other dishes too, ring-shaped, tin, large center opening, rounded "bottom" (which becomes cake's top), no mark, European or American, 9" diameter, late 19th or early 20th C. **$20-$25**

Mold or cake pan, pieced tin, 6-point star, spouted, hexagonal flat bottom with very angular points, rolled rim, for individual little cakes, Jaburg Brothers, NYC, NY, about 1-5/8" deep x about 4" diameter, early 20th C. **$10-$20**

Muffin & gem pans — See also bake molds. For related items, see bread stick pan; tart pan

Muffin baker, cast iron, 7 very shallow straight-sided indentations rather than cups, as this was for making muffins of the English muffin type, not the delicatessen bran muffin you may have visualized. Iron is heavily encrusted from use (a good sign when dating pieces), "JOHNSON" cast on handle, American, 10-1/2" diameter with 6-1/4" L handle, 19th C. These are often called "pancake pans" because small flapjacks can be made in the cups, and the design is quite similar to the Scandinavian plett-kakers. I am calling it a muffin baker after seeing a nearly identical one pictured in the 1872 *The New Cyclopedia of Domestic Economy.* Such a pan took the place of separate muffin rings (tin hoops sort of like tuna fish cans with both ends open) which were laid upon a hot griddle, and the batter poured in. The all-in-one version was both more and less convenient. **$50-$65**

Muffin, gem or popover pan, cast iron, only 6 cups, "Griswold No. 18," also #6141, 9-1/2" x 5-1/2", turn of century into 1930s or later. **$65-$95**

"**Gems.** These are the simplest form of bread, and if properly made are certain to be light and sweet. A hot oven and hot pans are prime essentials, and there must be no delay between making and baking. The coldest water, ice-water preferred, should be used. Use either whole-wheat or Graham flour, three parts of flour to one of water . . . For a dozen gems allow one large cup — a half pint — of ice water, one even teaspoon of salt, and three cups of flour. Stir in the flour slowly, beating hard and steadily, not less than ten minutes. The pans should have been set on top of the stove, and oiled or buttered. Fill them two thirds full, and bake about a half hour." Mrs. Helen Campbell's recipe, in *Good Housekeeping Discovery Book, No. 1,* 1905.

IV- 302. Egg pan and cake baker patents. *Both designed to be made of cast iron.* **(T)** *Design pat'd 7/18/1871, by Adam Reid, Buffalo, NY. Hearts, stars, plain & scalloped cups. This is the "Reid's Patent" that is sometimes found molded into the handles of certain cast iron pans we usually call* **muffin or gem pans.** **(B)** *"Egg Pan & Cake Baker," pat'd 4/5/1859, by the collector-revered Nathaniel Waterman, Boston, MA. His objective was to invent "a new or Improved Egg-Pan or Article for Cooking or Baking Eggs." Eleven cups, with flat bottoms. Waterman believed that the design of cups was necessary in order to allow for a strengthening (and convenient) handle at each end. "Open spaces are left between the cups to allow the currents of heat to pass upward between them so as to equalize the heat against their surfaces. The metallic connections of the cups serve as conveyors of heat from cup to cup." Official Gazette of the U.S. Patent Office.*

"Cleaning New Iron-Ware. I do not remember to have seen directions anywhere for preparing new cast-iron utensils for service in cooking. I know I had a deal of trouble with my first stove furniture, and whenever I have anything of the kind to deal with now I wonder if there is not some better way than I have learned. I have just been tackling a new set of iron gem-pans. I filled them with ashes and water and left them standing during the forenoon. I heated them on the stove before emptying them, and then gave them a good washing and rinsing. I think they will do for use to-morrow morning. I usually scour new kettles with ashes, then rub them over with a little grease, and wash them well with suds. To-day a lady told me that it was a good way to wash new irons with sour milk. I had no sour milk to use, but I do not see the philosophy of it. It is not rust with which we have to deal in cleaning new iron, but a fine sand, used in the casting." Correspondent to Editor, *American Agriculturist,* June 1874. **NOTE:** Wood ashes and water form a somewhat mild lye.

Muffin mold or gem pan, cast iron, shapely oblong with 13 variously shaped shallow cups, including 2 hearts, one at both ends, 2 6-point stars, one next to both hearts on the long axis, 4 rounds in corners plus one in the center, & 2 scalloped cups on each side, cutout tab handles at both ends, looks right, nice satiny smooth dark iron, no marks, American, 16-1/2" L x 8-1/2" W x 3/4" deep, late 19th C (?). **$95-$130**

Muffin or cookie pans, cast iron, fancy cups, in wide-bordered rectangular frame with fancy scroll handles, (a) 5 toy soldiers in same frame, (b) a number of small figural cups, "Classic Gourmet Series," mfd. by John Wright, Wrightsville, PA, © 1984. Probably still in production. **$10-$15**

Muffin or gem pan, actually patented as an egg pan, cast iron with gray graniteware on inside of 8 oval cups, N. Waterman (very unusual to find enameling inside a marked Waterman piece). Boston, MA, pat'd Apr. 5, 1859. (When ill-cast or worn, date looks like 1853 or 1858.) The problem here is that there isn't much of a following for enameled cast iron ware among collectors. In fact, some collectors have been known to remove enameling. Yikes!, sez the purist. The value to enamelware collectors would probably be quite a bit higher. **$85-$125**

Muffin or gem pan, cast iron, 11 shallow cups in 3 rows, curved handles at ends, "R. & E. Mfg. Co.," Russell & Erwin Mfg. Co., Nathaniel Waterman patent, 13" L x 8-3/4" W, each cup is 3-1/4" diameter x 1" deep, pat'd April 5, 1859, but made by R & E some years after that. This was actually patented as an **"Improved Egg Pan"** and described as a "new or improved manufacture of baking pan, or arrangement of cups, and a handle at each end of the series, all connected together and cast or founded in one solid piece of metal and with heat passages between the cups." This pan was not only made by Russell & Erwin, but also Hibbard, Spencer, Bartlett & Co. H,S,B & Co. made two sizes: (1) 11 cups 2-3/4" diameter, and (2) 11 at 3-1/4" diameter. • See article on cast iron muffin pans by David Smith, this chapter, pp.293-318. **$45-$65**

Muffin or gem pan, cast iron, 12 round bottom cups, what Griswold called a "golf-ball pan," tab handles, cutouts between each cup, Griswold No. 9, 10-1/8" L x 7" W, c.1920s-1930s. Gary M. Smith and his wife, collectors and dealers in New Jersey, tried making a gem recipe in one of these. "Used the lil' darlins as door stops. As my wife said, 'It sure sticks to your ribs!' We have a theory that it could also do double duty as a mini-cannon ball mold," wrote Gary back in 1984. Griswold also made a 6-cup golf-ball pan, the No. 19, which brings $15 to $20 more than the 12-cup. **$35-$55**

Muffin or gem pan, cast iron, 12 very shallow fluted Turk's head cups, cutout tab handles, Griswold #14, 13-1/8" L x 8-1/2" W, c.1920s on. **$350-$400**

Muffin or gem pan, cast iron, 5 hearts surrounding single star, has one short, holed, handle with opening for a pot-lifting tool. Griswold's "Heart-Star #100," 7-3/4" diameter, c.1926 or later. The game of bridge became extremely popular in the 1920s, and all sorts of kitchen- or cooking- or serving-related things used bridge motifs. Yes, I know; stars aren't taken from playing cards. (A smaller version of this pan was also made, #50, only 6-1/2" diameter and only 1/2" deep cups, which is valued by avid collectors between $1000 to $1500.) The smallest, and the largest, are often worth the most. For the #100: **$200-$275**

IV-303. Cake or egg baker. *This one follows almost exactly the design of Waterman. Cast iron, marked "W & L Mfg. Co.," pat'd 1867. So far I've been unable to ID "W & L," but I believe it must have been a short-lived (?) company owned by Nathaniel Waterman and someone unidentified. (SEE also CIBP-1 in David Smith's article following this chapter.) Picture courtesy of the Smithsonian Institution, Museum of History & Technology.*

Muffin or gem pan, cast iron, 6 fluted cups arranged 3 x 3, small handle at each end with small hanging hole, American, 8" L x 5" W, late 19th C. or early 20th. **$65-$85**

Muffin or gem pan, cast iron, 8 cups arranged 3, 2, 3, with 2 clubs, 2 diamonds, 2 spades and 2 hearts, called a "Grand Slam" mold. Shallow flat-bottom cups, almost square pan has cutout handles inside outer rim, rather than projecting out. About 9-1/2" L x 7-1/2" W. Not marked, but made by Lodge. American, early 20th C (?). Collector Jim Holroyd says some variation of these card suit pans were made by several foundries, although they don't look the same. **$80-$100**

Muffin or gem pan, cast iron, 8 figural fruit & vegetable cups, viz. pear, squash, apple, beet, turnip, cherries, & unidentifiable ones, and scrolled handles, 13" L x 8" W, 20th C (?). Collector Jim Holroyd sent me a picture of his, which has 3 very small holes which appear to be drilled down the center of the long axis. **$160-$185**

Muffin or gem pan, cast iron, oblong with flat top, 8 cups (they also made a 6 Gem pan) with deeply and neatly molded fruits all in a general round configuration: quince or pear, peach, cherries, leaves, rosette, and something like a pomegranate (?). Outside on the two long sides of the pan the edges scallop around the cups. Triangular cutouts, one at each end, between the end cups, no handles. The Schofield Mfg. Co., c.1900 brochure depicts this and calls it "Our Ornamental Gem Pan . . . made of finest gray iron." About 13" L x 8" W, c.1900. Later ones have scrolled handles — possibly made by Lodge. (**NOTE:** Volrath also made a pan like this, valued like the Schofield.) **$250-$300**

Schofield's catalog states, "They need no recommendation, as all housekeepers know that thin cast-iron bakes more evenly than tin or sheet iron, and the beauty of the design sells the 'gem.' The poor man's table, neatly arranged, is more appetizing than the richest luxuries improperly placed." **Reproduction alert:** These have been almost exactly reproduced in the last 25 years. An ad in *McCall's* magazine (date unknown, c.1970s-80s), shows an 8-cup mold and gives its dimensions as 1-3/4" deep x 7-1/2" W x 15" L, including scrolled handles. They claim it is an "1850s style." New, it sold for $16.95; value about same now. I suspect that most molds of this type found now are no older than the late 1950s, or even the 1970s. Price for new about 15% of price for old.

New cast iron looks entirely different from old wares, even after use, or even if old piece with which you make comparisons was never used. New: grayish, and grainy, poor casting edges, etc. And it doesn't cook well either. **Old Gray Iron**: I don't know how literally we can take it, but there were companies casting at the end of the nineteenth century who advertised "cast gray iron." But the older gray iron wasn't so terribly grainy or gritty. I don't know all (any?) of the secrets of making gray iron, but here's something on the subject from the Mar. 22, 1890 *Metal Worker* : "Aluminum in Cast Iron turns the combined carbon to graphite — that is, [it] makes the white iron gray and also [closes] the texture of the metal. [Aluminum] makes the metal . . . more fluid and susceptible of taking a better polish and retaining it. Aluminum will also increase the tensile strength of many grades of cast iron and aids in obtaining sound castings free from blow-holes. It has been used in preparations from 1/10 of 1% to 2%, with good results, with various grades of cast iron."

Muffin or gem pan, patented as an "egg pan," sold as gem pan by Russell & Erwin, cast iron, 12 round cups, interesting to examine handle ends, as slight roughness at 2 "bulge" points, both ends, make you think these could have been cast in long rows & snapped or chiseled apart at the handles, then ground smooth. Nathaniel

IV-304. Baking molds. (T) *Darkened tin made up of shallow, flat-bottomed round cups stamped into hexagon modules — here 7 have been riveted together, but the modular format meant that any number of them could have been assembled in a honeycomb fashion. A bent tin strap handle attached. 9-1/8" diameter, late 19th C. (This mold design has sometimes been called a maple sugar mold.)* **(B)** *Tin, seven scallop shells stamped in circular modules, riveted together, and further strengthened by a circumferential band of tin, 9" diameter. Late 19th C. Collection of Meryle Evans.* **$35-$45**

IV-305. Baking pans, *of stamped tin.* **(T)** *"Turk head pan," in 3 sizes: 11" x 7-1/4" with 6 cups; 14-1/2" x 7-1/4" with 8; and 14-1/4" x 11" with 12. Cups all same size. Geuder, Paeschke & Frey, 1925.* **(M)** *Unusual round "biscuit pan," on frame. Plain cups, 2-1/4" x 1-1/8" deep. Only one size, with 9 cups, 9-1/2" diameter. Central Stamping Co., 1920.* **(B)** *Oblong pan with detachable shallow flat bottom cups. Stamped tin. Delphos Can Co., Delphos, OH, a company that made oil cans and dustpans. Ad in* House Furnishing Review, *1/1906.* **$20-$35**

Waterman patent, mfd. by R & E Manfg Co., #6, 10-3/4" L x 7-1/8" W, pat'd April 5, 1859 — often looks like "1858" or "1853." Collector Beth Kidder, of Normal, IL, wrote in 1988 reporting that she had three similar cast iron molds, one each with round, oval, and oblong wells, all shallow, and all bought at local antique stores. She reports that the one with oblong wells "appeared not to have been used for baking, but it did have a light allover coating of a whitish substance which behaved like soap. The insides are pretty rough . . . I first heard these pans [all three styles] called soap molds in spring 1987," writes Beth, "at a privately operated museum called Little Norway, Rte 1, Blue Mounds, WI. The museum is a preserved pioneer homestead, built by the Norwegian immigrant Austin Haugen. I questioned the guide about the pan, and she was quite definite in her identification of it as a soap mold. I have since heard them called soap molds someplace else . . . possibly a local antique shop, I can't remember." Beth's husband suggests that people may have used baking molds, or gem pans, as soap molds because they worked so well for that purpose. Waterman's patent itself was granted under the name Egg-pan, but was described also as a Baking pan. **$45-$65**

Muffin or gem pan, stamped tin, 12 cups soldered into frame, ring in one corner to hang up, no discernable mark, late 19th C. **$15-$25**

Batter Pans. In 1824, in a Charlotte, NC, newspaper, as gleaned by James H. Craig (*The Arts and Crafts in North Carolina, 1699-1840*), an advertisement placed by Edward M. Bronson, who had a sheet iron and tin plate factory in Charlotte, reads ". . . Batter pans, of every description, Hearts, Diamonds, Scollops, &c. &c. . ." I suspect these were individual muffin molds, and as such would be the earliest I've found evidence of. Gosh! Get me a time machine! So many places to go; so little time. Muffins, of course, were known much much earlier, but were rather like what we know as English muffins, and were cooked in muffin rings on a griddle. Similar, or perhaps even identical, were flan rings, tin hoops set flat on a cookie sheet or flat pan and used for baking flan (custard). See "Royal Hearts" recipe at beginning of this chapter, in with bake mold entries.

● ● ● ●

Egg O' My Heart. F. A. Walker, the New York City supplier and importer of housewares, showed a cast iron "egg fryer" in an 1870s catalog. From the linecut picture it appears to be exactly the same as this Emig pan. Walker's catalog also had a stamped tin "egg fryer," with no handle, very shallow rolled rim, cups for 18 eggs. $8 to $12 for recent ones.

Muffin or other bake pan, cast iron, skillet shape with 6 heart-shaped cups, one center cup in shape of 6-point star, raised rim, side handle with pointed end and elongated hang up hole, Emig Products, Inc., but I don't know if marked, Reading, PA, 8-1/2" diameter with 6-1/2" L handle, weighs 4-3/4 lbs, from 1966 catalog. **$15-$20**

Muffin or popover pan, cast iron, 11 cups, Griswold spelled it "Pop-Over," Griswold #10, Pattern #949 (sometimes reported as 949-B), Erie, PA, 11-1/8" L x 7-5/8" W (given in company catalog as 11-1/4" x 7-1/2"), 20th C., ads for the pan in 1973 look just the same as earlier ones. In 1919, Griswold's full page ad in *House Furnishing Review* depicted one 11-cup pan with two large holes in both handle ends, and stated, "Griswold cast iron gem and muffin pans are made in 17 different shapes. Being heavier and thicker they retain the heat more evenly and longer than ordinary pans." In 1973, the price was only five dollars! **$45-$60**

Muffin pan, blue graniteware, 12 cups, early 20th C. **$115-$145**

Muffin pan, blue & white mottled enamelware, 8 cups, "Iris," Hibbard, Spencer & Bartlett, Chicago, IL, early 20th C. **$100-$150**

Muffin pan, cast aluminum, 6 cups shaped like Texas, no maker's mark, c.1970s or 1980s. **$15-$20**

Muffin pan, cast aluminum, very lightweight, 12 cups, marked "GRISWCLD" [sic], also "No. 9" and "809," not Griswold Mfg. Co., a cheap fake, prob. made in Taiwan or Japan, 20th C. **$10-$15**

Muffin pan, cast iron, 12 cups, "Petersen No. 11" marked on handle, 12-3/4" L x 7" W, late 19th C. **$35-$45**

Muffin pan, or corn bread pan, cast iron in shape of frying pan with handle and 3 short triangular legs, 7 shallow ebelskiver-type cups, one in center, casting gate in center on bottom, no marks, prob. American, 7" diameter with 4-1/4" L handle, c. mid 19th C. **$125-$160**

Muffin pan, cast iron, 12 flat bottom cups, many smoothed off casting marks on back, marked with either a "9" or a "6" on back, also patent date, 12" L x 7-3/16" W, pat'd April 8 (1913 or 1919?). **$22-$30**

Muffin pan, cast iron, 12 flat bottom cups, nicely formed interstices between cups, rather than the rough & sloppy ones found on repros, only mark is "F" on back of handles, 11" L x 6-3/4" W, late 19th C. **$22-$30**

Muffin pan, cast iron, 12 fluted cups in frame with handle, American, 14" L x 10" W, 20th C. **$80-$100**

Muffin pan, cast iron, 13 cups include 2 hearts, 2 6-point stars, 5 rounds & 4 fluted rounds, "Reids Patent," 16-1/2" L x 8-5/8", sometimes reported to have been pat'd Dec. 1870. But the design patent #5132 that I have a copy of says "pat'd Jul. 18, 1871" by Adam Reid. Collector Jim Holyroyd's pan is marked with the July 18 date on one handle and "Reids Patent" on other. Jim says this is called the "Four Seasons" pan. Collector LuAnn Funk writes that she has this pan, and on one handle it says "Reids Pan" (rather than Pat.), and on the other it says "Dec. 1870." **$160-$185**

Muffin pan, cast iron, 6 long cups, set side by side in threes, with tab handles at ends, for muffins but they look like rolls (in fact, Wagner made one very like it, with 12 cups, that made what they called "small sticks"), Griswold #17, 7-1/2" L x 6" W, c.1920s. Very similar Griswold #16 has deeper cups. Values for the #17; and the #16: **$75-$95; $180-$250**

Muffin pan, cast iron, 8 cups — leaf, clover, crescent moon, chicken, spade, 6-point star, house, scalloped — plus 3 smaller diamonds down center, heart-shaped handles at each end, 14" L x 6" W, mid 20th C. to 1980s. **$15-$25**

Muffin pan, cast iron, 8 shell-shaped muffins or gems, rather shallow, 19th C (?). The shell-shape was originally for making the little madeline cakes — this might be for that too, although I think mostly of tin pans not cast iron. See also madeline mold earlier in chapter, IV-261. **$45-$65**

Muffin pan, cast iron, bar handles, "G. F. Filley #10," mfd. by Excelsior Stove Works, St. Louis, MO, late 19th C. **$130-$155**

IV-306. Melon pans for baking. *Size not given, but a commercial bakery pan, stamped tin. The melons are probably about 5" L each. Jaburg, 1908.* **$30-$45**

Reproduction alert & Lookalike alarm. The gift & accessory trade wholesale catalog of Upper Deck Ltd., New Bedford, MA, which you may have seen advertised in the late 1980s in collector papers, has a selection of cast iron shallow cup figural muffin pans which they call "trivets." The cups on (A) and (B) are flat bottomed and probably 1/2" deep; cups on (C) and (D) are dimensional and somewhat deeper designs: **(A)** "Heart Trivet," 4 points-in hearts, with short frying pan handle, 5-1/2" diameter, 3" L handle. **(B)** "Folk Art Trivet," oblong with 8 cups in club, spade, star, rosette, round, house, Xmas tree & rooster shapes, scrolly handles at ends, with heart cutouts. 14" L x 6" W. **(C)** "Cookie Man Trivet," 6 cups of cookie boys with striped pants, star pendents, in 2 feet-center rows, joined like paperdolls. Scrolled handles, much openwork & only one that looks something like a trivet (which has lots of air flowing through it to cool the object put on it), 9" L x 6" W. **(D)** "Christmas Trivet," 6 detailed jolly squat Santa figures smoking pipes, rectangle with 2 simple arched handles at ends, 11" L x 8-1/4" W. Wholesale prices are extremely low, all below $5.50; the heart pan one 2 for $5. The pictures look good; I can't tell what kind of graininess there might be in the casting.

• • • •

"Giles F. Filley, Pioneer In Stove Trade. — Mr. Filley was born in 1815, and went to St. Louis from Connecticut, in 1836. Upon his arrival he sought employment with his brother, O. D. Filley, who was then conducting a tinsmith's shop . . . Later Giles F. Filley was taken into partnership with his brother, assuming a third interest in the business. In this connection he remained until 1841, at which time he [decided] that there was not enough in the business for two, and so he retired. In that same year he came to NY with the intention of buying trinkets to take to Oregon for the purpose of trading with the Indians. It was his original intention to take one of Astor's boats from NY to Astoria, OR, but changing his mind he purchased a stock of crockery, which was shipped to St. Louis, where he opened a crockery store in 1842, remaining in that business until 1849.

"In 1848 he concluded to engage in the business of manufacturing stoves, and in December of that year ground was broken for a stove foundry, the molding floor of which was 80 x 100 feet, and the warehouse 30 x 100 feet. The first casting was made in the foundry on Sept. 1, 1849 . . .

"The first stove made by Mr. Filley was what is known as a step stove, called the Prize Premium, and was sold to Stark Mauzy of Brunswick, MO. The first Charter Oak stove was turned out on March 18, 1852, and was purchased by a man who, coming along the street and seeing the stove standing on the sidewalk, asked Mr. Filley if it was for sale. Informed that such was the case, he purchased the stove and took it home to his farm, some miles back of Clarksville, MO. The first bill of Charter Oak stoves was afterward sold to C. G. Jones of St. Louis, MO, who was then conducting a stove store . . . At the time Mr. Filley took up his residence in St. Louis that city had a population of about 7300. The first theatrical performance was given in the upper part of an old salt warehouse, the entrance being by an outside stairway. The chandelier for this theater was made in Mr. Filley's shop and Mr. Filley personally superintended the work of putting it in place. It was a tin chandelier with petticoat lamps." *The Metal Worker*, Feb. 27, 1892.

Muffin pan, cast iron, cutouts between each shallow straight-sided, round, flat-bottomed cup, not for puffy kind of bran or corn muffins you buy at a deli, probably for English-style muffin, Wagner #1322, 11-3/8" L x 7-3/4", inside of cups only 5/8" deep, early 20th C. into 1920s. Not considered rare, but very attractive . . . and useful! **$25-$35**

Griswold Collectors. In a way, compared to all collecting fields except stamps and coins, and maybe dolls, new heights have been attained in knowledge of details and minute differences by collectors of Griswold (and to a much lesser extent, Wagner). It is way way beyond me, partly because my cataloguing instincts are more than satisfied by working on my books. So you won't find details like "slant TM" (meaning slanted trademark), or very much detailed notation of pattern numbers, especially what they signify (like "the 400 series indicates this was a ___," or "the 866 didn't appear on earlier ___," etc.). **Mags & Book:** If you are a specialist collector of Griswold, or Wagner, or Wapak, or other marked, catalogued, listed manufacturers, you will want to see about back issues of *Cast Iron Cookware News*, ed. by Steve Stephens. His address is 28 Angela Ave., San Anselmo, CA 94960. *Kettles 'n Cookware* is another newsletter. Get info from David Smith, Drawer B, Perrysburg, NY 14129. You'll want to buy David Smith's & Chuck Wafford's *Book of Griswold & Wagner*, Schiffer Pub., 1995. **Club:** Another group is the Southern Regional Chapter of Cast Iron Collectors. Contact Jim Bell, POB 355, Swainsboro, GA 30401. Always use an SASE.

IV-307. Baking pans. *Pieced and sheet tin.* **(L)** *12 hearts riveted to oblong blued steel sheet. 13-1/2" L x 6-1/4" W, each heart is 2-1/2" L. Maker unknown.* **(R)** *Other one makes 6 Lady Fingers, with fluted ends. Mold 9" L exclusive of handle; cups 4-1/4" L. Both late 19th or early 20th C. Collection of Meryle Evans.* **$75-$130; $30-$50**

Muffin pan, cast iron, makes 12 cakes or muffins in troughs, mold almost identical to 19th C. Nathaniel Waterman patent "French Roll" pan, made for many years by Hibbard, Spencer, Bartlett & Co. This one "Griswold #11," Erie, PA, 12-1/8" x 6-1/8", 20th C. **$45-$65**

Muffin pan, cast iron, round with 7 cups: 2 plain, 2 fluted, 2 hearts, one star cup in center, maker not stated in catalog, 9" measured across handles, 8" measured diagonally without handles, 20th C. **$20-$35**

Lookalike alarm. A new, interesting looking pan, sold through (among other places I'm sure) Cumberland General Store, Crossville, TN 38555. In 1983 they were selling it for $7. It seems to be going in the secondary market now for much more. Another, actually more attractive, with 9 heart-shaped cups (outside rows both go one way, inside row goes opposite direction, so all 9 fit neatly together, shaped sides, handles at both ends. It is 9-1/8" L x 7-1/2" W, and is seen in the Lehman's Hardware & Appliances (4779 Kidron Rd., Kidron, OH 44636) 1989 "Non-Electric Good Neighbor Amish Country" catalog ($2). It is possible that the Lodge foundry makes them; they don't say. Lehman also offers a 13" L x 7-3/8" W muffin pan with ribbed handles at each end, design of what looks like 11 interlocking animals, mostly rather exotic ones. Yet another has 8 teddy bears, and is 15-1/4" L x 7-1/2" W; another is the 8-cup one of fruits and vegetables, offered by other companies too, which is 15-1/8" x 7-1/2"; yet another, which contains 26 highly decorative letters of the alphabet, is 14-5/8" L x 7-5/8" W, and is for making "cookies." Finally, one more, with that same pair of handles, but double-sided, has a "durable no-stick coating," is 13-3/4" x 6-7/8", and allows you to make a gingerbread house & a gingerbread man & woman. One side makes a "Victorian home" and the spicy couple; the other side makes a log cabin, and 2 more folks. **$20-$35**

Muffin pan, rusted cast iron, overall shape is a sleigh, interior cups are in Christmas motifs: gift stocking, Santa's head, star, tree, snowman, toy soldier, no marks, possibly John Wright, Wrightsville, PA, 7" H at highest point x 15-3/4" L, c.1970s or 1980s. It looks neat, but it sure isn't worth the $350 a dealer at Brimfield had on it. **$25-$40**

Muffin pan, unusual glazed earthenware, handle on each end, 12 cups, ochre yellow glaze inside & on top, green glaze on bottom, minor chipping, touched up glaze on rim. Not very attractive, but an earthenware oddity. PA, 16-3/4" L x 11" W, 3rd to 4th quarter 19th C. Robacker May 1989 price of $650 is amazingly high. I just don't know enough about pottery to know every factor in this price, but suspect much of it is size and rare form, plus the Robacker provenance. **$500-$700**

Muffin pan, cobalt swirl enamelware, 8 cups, early 20th C. **$140-$160**

Muffin pan, cobalt & white swirl enamelware, 8 shallowish cups stamped (before enameling) in rectangular sheet metal, rolled rim, small hanging hole at one end, 1880s or so. **$185-$200**

Muffin pan, gray graniteware, 12 cups, joined by metal strips, marked "Agate Nickel Steel Ware," Lalance & Grosjean, turn of century. **$55-$75**

Muffin pan, gray graniteware, Turk's head, 8 cups, late 19th C. **$65-$75**

Muffin pan, soapstone block with 9 cups, from a Vermont dealer, prob. VT, 1-3/4" H x 11-3/4" L x 7-1/2" W, late 19th C. **$100-$125**

Muffin pan, also called a muffin tin, interesting raised rectangular tin tray has wire end handles, sides ventilated with penny-size holes, 6 shallow round cups set into holes in tray, Delphos Can Co., Delphos, OH, c.1905. **$15-$18**

Muffin or madeline pan, stamped heavy tin, 7 scalloped cups riveted together, crude strap frame, American, 9" diameter, turn of century. **$40-$50**

Muffin pan, or madeline pan, stamped tin, 7 scallop shell cups riveted together within circular frame, still rather brightly tinned, American, 9" diameter, 19th C. **$28-$40**

Muffin pan, pieced tin, 8 cups held together in thin flat tin frame, mfd. by Geuder, Paeschke & Frey, 1" deep x 14-1/4" L x 7-1/4" W, turn of century. **$10-$15**

Muffin pan, sheet iron, 12 cups, "Lockwood," Cincinnati, OH, early 20th C. **$25-$30**

Muffin pan, tin, 12 cups, "Minute Maid," American. **$15-$20**

Muffin pan, tin, "Pillsbury Health Bran," 20th C. **$12-$15**

Muffin pans — See also bake molds; molds; tart pans

Noodle cutter, called a "Pot Pie Noodle Cutter & Lifter" by dealer, corrugated tin wheels with wire handle, rolls along & cuts ruffled-edge lasagna-like noodles, pat'd by FELDT, Jamestown, NY, 8" L, no date, but looks c.1880s or 1890s. **$30-$35**

Noodle cutter, iron, wood & brass, mechanical, "Teek 1," German, turn of century. **$65-$85**

Noodle cutter, iron & wood, mechanical, 8" H, turn of century. **$35-$55**

Noodle cutter, metal, turned wooden handles, dated 1932. **$6-$8**

Noodle cutter, metal, wood, crank action, "A A L Werke," & "Mark AAL," German, 20th C. **$250-$300**

Noodle cutter, or noodle pin, a noodle cutting turned wooden rolling pin with sharp edged corrugations. German (?), 14" L, late 19th C. (?) or early 20th? **$22-$35**

Noodle cutter, rolling type, wire handle and frame, 14 sharp blades with plate to push cut noodles off blades as it is turned, "The Ideal," Toledo Cooker Co., Toledo, OH, c.1910. **$12-$15**

Noodle cutter or candy cutter (?), tin & wire, hand held & rolling, 10 blades, German, 20th C. **$7-$9**

Noodle cutter & pasta maker, cast iron frame with 4 long legs, mounted to wooden base, iron crank, kneading rollers like a

IV-308. Noodle cutter. *Hand-cranked, table top. "Vitantonio Mfg. Co., Cleveland, OH." Pat'd 2/13/1906 and 3/2/1920. Cast iron, tin and wood, roller attachment shown here, the "Zigzag #6," is iron, tin and has white rubber around axle. Pasta maker is screwed to piece of wood which would be clamped to table top. 7" H x 7" W. Company still in business, making similar machines. Most for those with extra attachments.* **$75-$100**

mangle or wringer action, white rubber on axle of cutter attachment, set with blades, "Vitantonio Mfg. Co.," Cleveland, OH, 7" H x 7" W, pat'd Feb. 13, 1906, March 2, 1920. I saw great ad in 1983 *Gourmet Retailer*, for Vitantonio, depicting Angelo Vitantonio and his "first American pasta machine." The company is in Eastlake, OH, now, still importing and manufacturing Italian cookery items — pizzelle irons, ravioli makers, cavatelli & gnocchi makers, tomato strainers, etc. **$65-$85**

Noodle making machine, cast iron with wood, screw clamps, cranks, no mark, 6-3/4" L, "patent pending," late 19th C (?). **$18-$22**

Noodle pin, for ravioli, carved wood, long body has 10 spool-like sections with corrugations around circumference and 4 long ridges end to end, 2 short turned handles. Two flat pieces of dough with the filling in blobs inside were rolled with this to seal the filling in the little squares of pastry. After drying a little they were broken apart & cooked in roiling boiling water, Italian, 24" L, 20th C. **$18-$25**

Noodle rolling pin — See rolling pins. Basically the drum part is relatively short and fat, and is usually ceramic.

Pancake pan — See the first muffin pan listing; also plett kaker

Pastry board, oak covered with tin, T. Mills & Brother, Philadelphia, PA, 23" x 14", late 19th or early 20th C. Mills made confectioners' and candy makers' tools. **$75-$90**

Pastry board, thick plank cut slightly oval, very slightly warped, but beautiful dark patina from all the butter rolled on it, small hanging handle with hole, American (?), 19" D, 19th C. **$165-$200**

Pastry or dough board, slate, very short arrow-shaped handle, with hanging hole, Pennsylvania, 17-1/2" diameter, 2nd half 19th C. Geologist Noel Moebs informs us that the slate dough or pastry board is "made from a very fine and unique type of slate that is still being quarried in Pennsylvania's Pen Argyl by Anthony Dally & Sons, Inc., and others." I saw several in 1983 & 1984, and only one since; it was stuck in the window of a photocopying place on lower Broadway in NYC. I wondered at the time if they were being made now? They all have a lovely mellow slate patina, thin (about 1/2"), and were pretty much all the same diameter, but varied widely in price, from $80 on up. I suspect that these pastry boards doubled as hot plates (see the historic paragraph next). And, hey! why not chalkboards for messages? **$300-$500**

"A **Black Board** should be in every kitchen, not to mark with chalk, but to place pots and kettles on when removing them from the fire. Make it about a foot square, and one inch thick. It need not be washed often merely for looks, as the corners will be unsoiled. Its use will save the tables, floor, sink, etc., from many unsightly marks." *American Agriculturist*, March 1865.

Pastry board & rolling pin, white enamelware, mounted to wall with iron brackets, board hinges down out of way & brackets fold inward, pin has turned wooden handles, Barnes Mfg. Co., Mansfield, OH, 27" x 28" with 6" H backplate, c.1914. **$350-$450**

Pastry boards & rolling pins of tin were made by several companies. The sets either have all-tin "boards" and rolling pins of wood with tin covering on the drum, or they have wood-baked tin boards and pins similar to the others. Prices have gotten as high as $675, but then it seemed as if more came out of the

IV-311. Pancake griddle iron. *"U Like 'Em" multiple griddle. Polished cast iron that "will not absorb fat." Reversible so "no turning of cakes required." Each 6" diameter pan works independently. Made in 3 sizes, for 4 cakes (originally 49¢), for 6 cakes (71¢) and 8 cakes (97¢). Albert Pick catalog for hoteliers, 1909.* **$250-$375**

IV-313. "Timbale sheet." *Twelve relatively deep cups riveted on sheet tin, made in four sizes. Sheet 8" x 6" with cups 1-3/4" x 1-1/2" up to 10" x 7-1/2" with cups 2-1/4" x 2". Sold through D. J. Barry catalog, 1924. Used in the United States for making little pastry cups to be filled with sweet or savoury fillings. (In England, timbales were almost always little layered aspics, which could also be made in dariole cups or "little bombe" moulds.* Mrs. A. B. Marshall's Cookery Book, *c.1900-1902, gives several aspic Timbale recipes.). In* Fannie Farmer's Boston Cooking-School Cook Book *of 1896, none of the timbales are aspic — and range from mounds of rice to creamed seafood in little baked pastry cases. For example:* "**Rice Timbales**. *Pack hot boiled rice in slightly buttered small tin moulds. Let stand in hot water ten minutes. Use as a garnish for curried meat, fricassee, or boiled fowl." Another Fannie oddity:* "**Macaroni Timbales**. *Line slightly buttered Dario moulds with boiled macaroni. Cut strips the length of height of mould, and place closely together around inside of mould. Fill with chicken, or Salmon Force-meat. Put in a pan, half surround with hot water, cover with buttered paper, and bake thirty minutes in a moderate oven. Serve with Lobster, Béchamel, or Hollandaise Sauce."* **$25-$45**

IV-312. Pastry "board" made of slate. *Also called a* **dough board**. *This beautiful thing with arrow tab handle is made of slate, not wood. Hole for hanging cord. 17-1/2" diameter, American, probably Pennsylvania, possibly early 19th C. Bigger than most I've seen. Picture courtesy of Robert W. Skinner Inc., Auctioneers, Bolton, MA.* **$300-$500**

woodwork. They are highly desirable, and with the paper label, in unused condition, would be worth another $100 or $150 on top of the value range given for the next four.

Pastry board & rolling pin, a set that could be hung on the wall. The board is wood, with a working surface of tin. According to the 2 partial paper labels on the back, "The metal plate ___ ___ the manufacture of th___ is a special composition ___ finished in pure palm of ___ therefore necessary before using the first time to wash it with soap and warm water to remove any oil that may have been left on the surface. The ___ of the board is made of ___lv ___ veneer, with the grain ___ crossed, and then ___ saturating entirely [with] pure boiled oil, this ___ it from spliting [sic] or ___." At the bottom is a wooden ledge, sort of like found on a blackboard, with 2 metal spring clips to hold the wooden rolling pin. The pin has 2 spool-turned handles. The American Bread and Pastry Board Co., Cambridge, OH, about 25" square, turn of century. **$350-$450**

Pastry board & rolling pin, all sheet tin, ring loop at center top for hanging on wall, bottom edge turned up to hold tinned pin (wooden handles), paper label reads "Union Manufacturing Co.," Cambridge, OH, 19th C. **$350-$450**

Pastry board & rolling pin, also called a cookie sheet, tin with tin rolling pin, partial label on back: "The Metallic Board — Only All Metal Bread & Pastry Board," American, 21-1/2" L x 8-1/2" W, pat'd 1893. **$350-$450**

Pastry board or sheet, tin, wooden back, trough of wood at bottom to hold rolling pin, which is missing, paper label on back "The Non-Absorbent Bread & Pastry Board," American, 21" L x 21-1/2" W, c. 3rd quarter 19th C. If this had the tin & wooden rolling pan with it it would be a lot more expensive. **$200-$250**

IV-314. Patty, rosette, timbale, or bouche irons. *For making little pastry cups, about 2" H, that could be filled with cremes, mousses, and savouries. From top* **(1)** *one with spiraled iron is a* **"Coiled Spring Cake"** *or* **sprungfedern** *iron. Turn-of-century catalog.* **(2)** *a plain and 4 fluted cups or "case fryers," is nickel plated, from S. Joseph, c.1927.* **(3)** *Crossed timbale irons, nickel plated, could be had as plain or fluted rounds, ovals, hearts, diamonds, spades or clubs. From Sexton Stove & Range Mfg., c.1930s. Both 2 & 3 would be used by Fannie Farmer to make pastry cases for Cream Oysters or the like.* **(4)** *&* **(5)** *Last two sets from Griswold. These you often find in original boxes.* **$20-$60**

Pastry board or sheet, tinned sheet iron, holds rolling pin in curved bottom edge, hangs on wall from little wire ring, American (?), 23" x 16", 19th C. **$350-$450**

Pastry board — See also dough board. And, if you're using the term to mean a mold, look also under cake board.

Pastry brush, turned wood handle, real hog bristles, attributed to Shakers, 8-1/4" L, 19th C. **$80-$120**

Pastry stamp, cast & lathe-turned brass, like a small meat tenderizer with 6 small pyramidal points on head, turned wood handle with original hanging ring, very heavy, English, 7-7/8" L x 4-1/4" W, c.1820s to 1830s. **$275-$325**

Pastry tube, also called a pastry syringe, or cookie press. White metal cylinder & funnel nose, wood plunger, German (?), late 19th C. **$25-$35**

Pastry tube, or cookie press, tin cylinder with wooden plunger, star-shaped opening, American, 10-1/2" L, late 19th C. **$30-$40**

Pastry tube, or cookie press, tin, small cylinder, with side wings used to hold it while pressing the plunger. Could be fitted with several different flat tin discs that have cutouts in various shapes — stars, rosettes, etc. — through which the dough was expressed in fancy shapes for making drop cookies in something besides blobs. Also used as a butter press for fancy pats, American, c.1870s. **$25-$35**

Pastry tube — See also cookie press

Pâte mold — See molds, tin section, French pie mold listing

Patty bowl, cast iron, bail handle, pouring lip, Griswold "Deep Patty Bowl," #72, 2-5/8" deep x 5" diameter. **$35-$50**

Patty iron set, cast iron, with long handle, 4 molds: 2 deep cups, 2 lacy open ones, in original box, Griswold Mfg. Co., Erie, PA, about 9" L with handle, early 20th C. **$55-$75**

Patty irons, cast iron, in original box, "Mrs. Wheelock's," American, 1920s. **$35-$50**

Brown, Then Serve. Even a scrap of newspaper found in a box can provide tidbits to spice up your general knowledge. A very yellowed piece torn out of a January (!) issue of an unidentifiable Richmond, VA, paper, dated probably c.1900-1905, has this delightfully odd tip: "**A Brown Luncheon.** — Just to vary the monotony of life there is the 'brown' luncheon. The creamed lobster is served in cups covered with brown tissue paper, the browned chops, browned fried potatoes, and browned rice croquettes on plates decorated with a design of brown oak leaves and acorns. The ice cream is chocolate frozen in shape of large English walnuts and the little squares of white cake bear the design of a leaf in tiny chocolate candies. The courses are served from large wooden trays ornamented in pyrographic work decorated in brown leaves and the water is poured from a little brown jug. All the decorations are brown, shading from seal to orange. The candles are yellow with autumn leaf shades. The name cards are placed inside little boxes decorated with pyrographic work and suitable for jewel boxes. The hostess wears a gown of panne velvet in the shade of brown known as 'burnt onion' and the maid's apron and headdress are decorated with brown bows."

Patty irons, cast iron, set of 2 deep cupped ones in original box, with one screw-in heavy wire handle. One cup heart shaped, one fluted round. These were cooked & then filled with cold or hot, savory or sweet fillings — very nice for luncheons! Mmmm, wish I had me one right now. Griswold, Erie, PA, round cup: 2-1/4" D; heart about 2-7/8" across, c.1926 on. **$35-$55**

Patty iron or patty mold, cast iron, heart, individual, Griswold #2. According to collector Joel Schiff, the patty and rosette irons (which are probably all 20th C.) were commonly sold in sets, unlike bouche and timbale case irons, which were sold individually. **$20-$35**

Patty mold set, cast iron, in original box, cast iron, little kettle with thin wire bail handle for boiling oil, just right size for dipping in the batter-coated lacy rosettes & patty irons, also a cast iron rosette, a mold with concentric rings with 4 spokes, a heart, & a patty shell or case mold, 2 screw-in threaded wire rod handles about 7" L. Chromolithograph inside box lid shows kettle on little electric hot plate. Griswold Mfg., Erie, PA. Oil kettle is 2-1/2" deep x 5-1/8" diameter, c.1940s-1950s from box image. **$85-$135**

Patty irons — See also rosette irons; wafflet molds

Pie birds — See Measure & Weigh chapter, p.333

Pie crimper or pie jagger — See crimper; jagger

Pie divider, tin, rim turned up, big strap handle, looks like a huge cookie cutter that cuts wedges, cuts only 5 pieces in an 8" pie, no maker's mark, American, about 4-1/4" L, 20th C. **$20-$25**

IV-317. Pie & Cake marker. *For professional bakers to mark portions. Screwed to wooden base, spring-loaded punch. Nickel-plated, or polished cast aluminum. It marked a dotted line where to cut pieces, and could be fitted with markers for from 4 to 12 slices for different sizes of pie or cake tins. D. J. Barry, 1924.* **$20-$55**

IV-315. Patty, Rosette, Timbale set. *"Enjoy 'Old World' pastry treats!" Cast aluminum, about 3" diameter. Double-stemmed handle meant you could make 2 at a time. By this time "timbale" had stretched to include case molds much wider than deep. Probably A. Andresen. Gift shop ad in* House Beautiful, *4/1964.* **$5-$12**

IV-318. "Cottage stamp." *"In place of moulding the Cottage in six pieces, mould them in one piece, place same in pans, when half raised dust them lightly with Rye flour and stamp with this tool." In Hueg and Jaburg catalogs, early 20th C. "Cottage" is hard to track down. It's probably the same as "Cottage Pudding," a cake-like confection, which Marjorie Heseltine, in* Good Cooking, *from early 20th C, says to bake in a pan and cut into squares. The stamp is for bakeries.* **$15-$25**

IV-316. Pie markers, *for bakeries to mark flavors on two crust pies.* **(T)** *Pie stamp, for putting initials on the upper crust and puncturing it to let steam escape. Full set of 7 letters: A, C, H, L, M, P, R. in H. Hueg catalog, c.1900-1921. Let's see: Apple, Cherry, Huckleberry, Lemon, Mince, Peach, Rhubarb?* **(B)** *This set from the same period, not only has letters (P, A, B, R, H, L, and M), also has picture designs to mark other pies with the same initial letters as basic ones. Jaburg, 1908. Singles:* **$8-$20.** *Sets:* **$15-$30**

IV-319. Pie pans or plates. *Shallow. With exception of* **(4)**, *these have slanted sides. (Layer cake pans have straight sides.) From top:* **(1)** *Scalloped, stamped tin, in one sizes, 8-9/16" diameter x 1-1/8" deep. Savory, c.1925-28.* **(2)** *Perforated tin, 9-3/4" x 1-1/16", also Savory.* **(3)** *"Greystone" gray graniteware plate in 5 sizes, from 7" to 11" diameter. Also came in slightly deeper versions, 9" to 11" diameter. Matthai-Ingram, c.1890.* **(4)** *A "Greystone Lebanon" pie plate, for deep dish pies. 7-3/4", 8-1/2" and 9-1/2" diameter. The "Lebanon" referring to an area of Pennsylvania. Also Matthai-Ingram.* **$6-$30**

Pie or cake pan, tin, round, slightly flared sides & wide rim, embossed "PY-O-MY Dutch Apple Cake Mix Baking Pan," 1-1/2" deep x 9" diameter, early 20th C. **$10-$14**

Pie pan, blue & white swirl enamelware, 9" D, turn of century. **$15-$20**

Pie pan, cobalt blue & white agate enamelware, 10" diameter, early 20th C. Another, only 8-1/2" diameter and with all white interior, about same price. **$12-$15**

Pie pan, green & white swirl enamelware, 9" D, 20th C. A cobalt & white swirl, 8", is same price range. **$12-$16**

Pie pan, pale blue & white swirl enamelware, 12" diameter, early 20th or late 19th C. In turquoise, a bit more desirable. **$12-$15**

Pie pan, stamped tin, "Goldblatt Brothers," 20th C. **$8-$12**

Pie pan, stamped tin, shallow very slightly slanted sides, attached metal cutter pivots from center, to cut pie out of pan, "Clipper Pie Plate," L. E. Brown & Co., Cincinnati, OH, 8" diameter, c.1880s. **$5-$7**

Pie pan, tin, "Mrs. Smith's," early 20th C. **$3-$5**

Pie pan, tin, flared sides, embossed "Manning" in script, 7-3/4" diameter, early 20th C. **$8-$11**

Pie pan, tin, slanted sides, embossed "New England Table Talk Flaky Crust — Mother's Only Rival," 1-1/4" deep x 9-5/8" diameter, early 20th C. **$10-$14**

Pie pan, tin, slanted sides, advertising would make you think it a cake pan, "Presto Self-Rising Cake Flour," pat'd 1924. **$12-$15**

Pie pan or pie plate, stoneware with brown glaze, corrugated edge, American, 9" diameter, 19th C. **$80-$90**

Pie pans — See also cake pans. Cake pans have straight sides, pie pans have flared or slanted sides.

IV-310. Plett kaker, or Pancake pan. *Also referred to as a* **"muffin baker"** *in the 1872 New Cyclopedia of Domestic Economy. "Muffin" as in the flat "English" muffin. Cast iron, 7 very shallow cups, with "JOHNSON" cast on handle. 10-1/2" diameter with 6-1/4" L handle. Lower picture shows interesting appearance of bottom. Note heavy incrustation. Ex-collection of NYC food stylist, Grace Manney.* **$75-$125**

Pie pan or pie plate, (usually the ceramic ones are called plates), PA German redware, with message in yellow slip, "A Good Apple Pie is the Best of All," PA, 9" diameter, late 19th C. **$650-$800**

Pie plate, spongeware pottery, "The Pure Food Sanitary Cooking Ware," American, early 20th C. **$125-$135**

Pie plate, stoneware, bright blue glaze inside only, maple leaves molded along sides, outside not glazed, "Cookin Ware," Neu-Deel Economy Health Cookin Ware, Canadian (?), 9" diameter, "Patent Office R & G," prob. 2nd quarter 20th C. **$25-$32**

"Shrimp Pie. Take a quart of shrimp, clean picked from the shells; if they are very salt in the boiling, season them only with a little cloves and mace; but if they want salt, shred two or three anchovies very fine, mix them with the spice, and season the shrimps. You may make a good crust, because they do not want much baking; put a pretty deal of butter over and under them, one glass of white wine, and sent it to the oven." Eliza F. Haywood, *A New Present for a Servant-Maid; Necessary Cautions and Precepts to Servant-Maids for Gaining Good-Will and Esteem*, Dublin, Ireland: 1771.

Pie top-crust mold, redware pottery, nearly square with hanging hold in top left corner, detailed round design in relief of eagle standing on a shield, arrow underneath, rope border, the outer wide border being 8 demilune swags. It was in the famed Titus Geesey Collection in Wilmington, DE, and was depicted on the cover of September 1953 *Spinning Wheel* collectors' magazine, and described within as being "possibly" made from an intaglio carved wooden cake board. The article also states that this mold was used to imprint the top pie crust. I never heard of such a thing before, but maybe! Probably Pennsylvania German, probably early 19th C. Probable value: **$2000-$3000**

IV-309. Plett kaker, or Pancake pan. *Cast iron, 7 shallow flat bottom very shallow cups, 3 legs. From ad of NYC dealer, J. & C. Berrian, in a book on prominent manufacturers of the U.S., 1857.* **$85-$125**

IV-320. Popover pans. *Actually these are referred to as* **"corn bread"** *pans in Hibbard, Spencer, Bartlett's catalog showing "Waterman's Cast Bake Pans," and as a "Gem Pan," in Griswold's catalogs.* **(T)** *#10, 11 pans, 2-3/4" diameter each. 1880s.* **(B)** *#10, cakes 2-1/2" x 1-3/4". Griswold, early 20th C.* **$45-$60**

Pizzelle iron — See wafer or pizzelle iron

Plett kaker or pancake pan, cast iron, 7 shallow cups & skillet handle with teardrop hanging hole, marked "Western Importing Co." (successor to Alfred Andresen), on bottom near handle. Andresen used the name along with his own to mark company products. Because this piece has only the Western Importing Co. mark, it's likely that this dates after Andresen's departure from the company in 1906. Cups 2-1/4" diameter, overall 8-3/4" diameter, prob. 1906+. • A **"plett"** is a Scandinavian word for "spot" — hence, small pancakes, maybe what we'd call silver dollar cakes. These pancake molds are rather plentiful, and are only now beginning to have a collector following — primarily, according to Joel Schiff, "as a result of the company's involvement with Griswold, who actually manufactured their forms from about 1904 on." Andresen originally imported, and used other companies to make their wares. **$40-$55**

One-Alarm Reproduction Alerts. A credible new popover pan is being made by Iron Craft Inc., Freedom, NH, in 2 sizes: 6- and 11-cup. They are cast iron, but cups are only 1-3/8" deep. Two "flower petal" cutouts at each handle end presumably serve not only as decorative touches, but also to slightly cool the iron just where a person would pick it up. • Lehman's Hardware & Appliances, 4779 Kidron Rd., Kidron, OH 44636 offer 6-cup and 11-cup "2 petal" hole handled popover pans, made by the Lodge foundry, South Pittsburgh, TN, in their "Non-Electric Good Neighbor Amish Country" catalog. Value for new: **$18-$30**

Plett kaker or pancake pan, cast iron, like griddle with 7 extremely shallow cups that are bigger than the ebelskiver cups, slightly raised edge, short upcurved handle with teardrop hanging hole, Griswold Mfg Co., after a Swedish type of pan, 9-1/2" diameter, with cups only 1/4" deep, each cake 3" diameter, made c.1918 on, for many years. **$40-$55**

Popover pan, cast iron, 11 deep, slightly slant-sided flat-bottomed cups, Wagner Ware #01 B, Sidney, OH, cups are 1-7/8" deep, 11" L x 7-1/2" W, late 19th or early 20th C. **$45-$55**

Popover pan, cast iron. It has been said that because Griswold bought Wagner in 1957, for a while both names appeared on some pans; Joel Schiff feels that pans with the Griswold/Wagner mark are more probably from after 1974, when General Housewares bought out the company. This pan, marked both "Griswold" & "Wagner Ware," probably 1974+. **$25-$40**

"Graham Gems. To one quart of Graham flour add one half pint fine white flour; enough milk or water, a little warm, to make a thick batter; no salt or baking powder; have the oven hotter than for biscuits; let gem-pans stand in the oven till you get ready; beat batter thoroughly; grease your pans; drop in while the irons are smoking hot; bake quickly a nice brown." Henry Scammel, compiler, *Treasure House of Useful Knowledge,* 1891. Graham flour was named after the Reverend Sylvester Graham (1794-1851), an American who was the first to recognize the value of eating whole wheat flour, bran and all. He spent a lot of his life trying to encourage housewives and cooks to use his flour, which we now welcome as high fiber. He was ridiculed as a mad faddist by some, but did attract a large, enthusiastic following. Many nineteenth-century recipes called for graham or "entire wheat" flour.

Popover pan, cast iron, tab handles, 2 casting gates on bottom, no mark, 8" x 12" L, turn of century. **$40-$50**

Popover pan, or gem pan, cast iron, tab handles solid not cutout, 11 cups, Wagner Ware, marked "B" on center cup on back, Sidney, OH, 11-1/4" L x 7-5/8" W x 1-7/8" deep, late 19th C (?). **$45-$55**

Pretzel cutter, also called a **bretzel cutter,** tin like a cookie cutter, flat back, strap handle, 5" across x 4", cuts out the dough in the crossed-arms-within-heart shape that is basically the pretzel shape, for deep fried dough. Not technically a pretzel, which is made by hand by rolling out a long "snake" of dough, bending it around into the heart, crossing the ends and laying them on the edge of the heart (a pretzel is supposed to represent praying arms). Late 19th C. or early 20th. **$35-$45**

Pretzel or *bretzel* mold — I've never seen one, but William Woys Weaver has illustrated a recipe for "Speculatius" with a carved wooden mold from Germany, oblong, with 12 simple pretzel intaglio carvings, on p. 150 of his *The Christmas Cook,* 1990.

Pudding molds — See molds, in various materials

Pudding pan, blue & white swirl enamelware, rectangular, 12" L, late 19th C. **$30-$35**

Pudding pan, gray graniteware, shallow, slightly flared sides, "Chef-ette Enameled Ware" on red paper label, American. **$55-$80**

"Indian-Meal Pudding. One cup of yellow Indian meal, one quart milk and a cupful of molasses, one generous tablespoonful of butter, one teaspoonful of salt, one pint of boiling water, half teasponful each of cinnamon and mace. Scald the salted meal with the water. Heat the milk in a farina-kettle [a double boiler]; stir in the scalded meal, and boil, stirring often, for half an hour. Beat the eggs light; put in the butter and molasses, stirred together until they are several shades lighter than at first; add the spice; lastly, the batter from the farina-kettle, beaten in a little at a time, until all the ingredients are thoroughly incorporated. Grease a pudding-dish; pour in the mixture, and bake, covered, in a steady oven, three-quarters of an hour. Remove the lid, and brown. This is the genuine, old-fashioned New-England 'Indian' pudding. Eat with sauce, or with cream and sugar. It is very nice." Marion Harland, *Universal Cookery Book,* 1887.

Rice ball, large perforated 2-part spun aluminum ball, clip fastening, chain to hang off pot's side, American, 7" diameter, 20th C. **$10-$16**

Rice ball, tin & wire screening ball, 2 parts unscrew, wire handle locks over edges to hold halves together, chain & hook for edge of pot, American, 5-1/4" diameter, marked with date, pat'd June 17, 1930. **$10-$18**

Rice boiler mold, stamped & pieced tin, flat-bottomed, tubed with slanted out fluted sides, close fitting slightly convex lid with big strap handle, small wire ring catches to attach lid, American or European import, about 5" to 7" H x about 3" to 4" diameter at top, c.1870s to 1880s. These look like pudding molds, and may have been used as such, but adv'd by F. A. Walker in their catalog as rice boilers. **$45-$55**

IV-321. **Rice ball boilers. (T-L)** *Perforated tin, for balls of "fried" farina, from Urbain Dubois, c.1860s-80s.* **(T-R)** *"Wire pea or vegetable boiler, for beas, beans, rice, boils dry and when taken out no grains are left in the pot." Small one at far right is a "tea boiler."* American Home Cook Book, 1854. **(B)** *Tinned screen or wire gauze, in one size, 5-1/2" diameter. Washborn "Androck" line, 1936.* **$10-$25**

Rice cake mold, carved wood paddle, good luck symbol & calligraphy, Chinese, 7" L, poss. 19th C., more likely a 20th C. sort of export souvenir. These started showing up, in vast quantities, about 1982 or 1983. Many of them do not have Chinese characters carved in them, but typically Chinese motifs such as koi (goldfish/carp), butterflies, chrysanthemums and fruit. They come in a sort of butter paddle shape, or in truncated and elongated ovals, often with hanging hole with leather thong tie. The first wholesaler ads for them listed them in six styles: (1) a long narrow one, 12" L x 1-3/4" W with 10 small images; (2) 8-1/2" L x 3-1/2" W paddle, with sort of flower clam design; (3) 8" L x 3" W, paddle, irregular head, with curvy fish design; (4) 12" L x 2-1/2" W board with four fruity designs; (5) & (6) 12" L x 3-1/2" W boards with either 2 strange flower-fruit butterfly carvings, or 2 fish. Nothing in ad identified them as being Chinese, but they were called "Molds, 75-100 years old," and were priced $23 to $32 each, with 50% discount if you bought 10 or more, which meant that a dealer could then resell them for about the wholesale for one. It didn't take many months before they began appearing. The resale price is often very high, if there is but one on display, as much as $85 or $95. Asking price usually at high end of range. **$15-$45**

Rice cake mold, large oblong paddle with smallish handle, probably used for some kind of rice confection, 6 carved out cups including 3 different fish, a bird, also 2 plant-like flowers, Chinese, 13" L x 6" W, late 19th C (?). **CAUTION:** This is the largest of the Chinese rice cake molds, which have been sold all over the United States since about 1983 as, variously, maple sugar molds,

IV-322. Rice molds from China. *Carved wood paddles, with typical Chinese motifs of fish, butterfly and lotus flower. Usually called "sugar molds" by dealers who don't know or aren't telling. These are actually imported from China, and may be old in some instances. Photograph from stock of Mary Colborn, Murrysville, PA.* **$15-$45**

cookie molds, or candy molds. This is not to say they are not nice molds, but you could be paying a premium for "early American" when it's probably "late Chinese." **$30-$40**

Ring mold — See above in molds, tin border molds

Collector Hint: Stop, Look, Listen . . . and Read. Some antiques people think that out of a given number of collectors, a very few are graced with "the eye," an ability to see and know what is good, to pick the treasure from the dross. Furthermore, some of the antiques experts firmly believe that you're either born with it or you'll never have it. I don't entirely believe that, although there is an element of natural talent involved. Lots and lots of studying, of subjects as diverse as Japanese woodblock prints, African masks, Fauvist paintings, Egyptian jewelry, Shenandoah pottery, Victorian valentines, Thonet chairs, and Christmas glass ornaments, will never be wasted. But you must absorb yourself in each subject, sit on the sofa with a pile of library books from call number 700's shelves, and look at all of them, back & forth. Don't say "I don't like African masks." Look at pictures of them, or best, real ones in museums, until you do like them. Don't say "Fiesta Ware is cheap and ugly." Look at it until you appreciate what there is about it that's perfectly done. This is not to say you have to like everything, or that everything is worthy of praise. But everything you study, go in with a Zen "don't know" mind. The open mind, the clean slate tabula rasa mind, will allow you to learn something you can apply to your butter molds, churns, tin trays, copper tea kettles, cast iron griddles. You will find yourself choosing, and knowing why.

I used to think that to study a piece (or to analyze your motive for wanting it) took the fun out, spoiled it, maybe even prevented its purchase (to question is to doubt). Now, because I know there are **many ways to study a piece or a field (aesthetically, socially, historically, functionally)** I know that study can only add to the pleasure. Harry Rinker wrote in a column on "Collectibles" in early 1989 that the "fun" of collecting is in the chase, not in the piece itself. If he really means that, I am diametrically in opposition. In collecting, a little (or no) knowledge is not only the dangerous thing and the foolhardy way, it's self-defeating in the long run, because the fun of the chase is diminished by a lack of awareness (of the other hunters, as well as the hunted). Then, after your treasure is up on the wall, mounted with the other trophies, there would be nothing to reflect on, no new way to re-appreciate, or re-evaluate. So keep on reading and looking, and exercise your own "eye."

Roll cutter, brass & iron, it rolls with 2 handles, like a rolling pin, cuts dough into oblongs, English, 4-3/4" diameter rolls or biscuits, English patent #16798 (19th C., prob. c.1880s). **$85-$100**

IV-323. "Elementary method of rolling layered pastry." *From Urbain Dubois La Patisserie, late 19th C. Note completely straight, slim, "French" rolling pin.*

Roll pan or bread stick pan, cast iron, 11 long troughs, 2 lengthwise casting marks, filed down, catty-corner on back, no maker mark, 13-1/4" L x 9-1/4" W, 19th C. **$35-$45**

Roll pan, cast iron, 6 cigar-shaped cups, many cutouts in frame, marked in cups: "Vienna Roll Bread Pan No. 6," Erie, early 20th C (?). **$85-$150**

Roll pan, cast iron, makes 12 French rolls in trough-like cups rounded on bottom & oblong in outline, in 2 rows 6 x 6, very similar to what Griswold called a muffin pan. American, dated 1850. No U.S. patent that year for bake pan, roll pan, muffin pan, gem pan or bread pan. This is very handsome, but according to Joel Schiff is the "most common pan in the United States!" **$25-$40**

American Agriculturist, Jan. 1868, had one of these illustrated, with a short article called **"Gems or Aerated Rolls.** — The only convenient article for cooking Gems is a French roll pan for baking, and we cannot warrant success in anything else. The pans are made of cast iron, and can be had at the large hardware and furnishing stores in the cities at about $4.50 per dozen, and 75¢ single. Put the pan upon the stove, heated nearly to redness. Take one cup of water, one cup of milk, and three cups of flour, of the best quality. Stir in the flour gradually, and with a spoon beat the mixture five minutes briskly. The object of the beating is to get as much air as possible into the batter. Put a piece of butter of the size of a pea into each of the moulds, and fill about two-thirds full with the batter. Put immediately into a very hot oven, and bake for 20 minutes, or until nicely browned.

"This form of unleavened bread is the best article for breakfast or tea we have ever found in that land of good housekeepers, Eastern Connecticut. It is exceedingly light, palatable, and nutritious, excellent for invalids and dyspeptics, and quite as good for people in sound health. They are so nice that we hope our readers will try the article for themselves. We bear no ill-will to hop growers, or venders of soda, saleratus, and other salts, but we have no doubt that the Gems once introduced into a family would greatly diminish the use of these unwholesome articles in cookery, and help to promote health and good digestion." (What I don't understand, is how you take this 2/3 full red hot pan weighing 4 pounds or so and get it quick into the hot oven.) **Gems:** Occasionally the word gem is associated with "aerated roll," meaning a non-yeast roll whose dough is raised with saleratus or baking powder, or by being "air whipped."

Roll pan, cast iron, very shallow, makes 8 oval rolls, only mark is "No. 5" on back, 7-3/8" W, turn of century. **Confusable:** What looks in pictures like a roll pan for making 4 oblong rolls and may look like one in real life (or it may be much smaller), is a solder mold. It is oblong with flat long handle coming from one end, the pan divided into 4 shallow oblongs. It is marked "C. S. Osborne" on the handle. I found it in Alfred Revill's *American Plumbing*, NY: Excelsior, 1984. The resemblance in picture is striking enough to make me add it in here. (Also very similar to baking pans, and approx. the same size, are cast iron molds with conical cups; these are assayers' slag molds, and have various numbers of cups (often 6) in an oblong frame. One has 'frying pan' handle off one end, and 2 rows of 3 cups. Another has a long single-file row of 6 conical cups; it has a wooden handle at one end. These molds were used as crucibles to melt finely ground ores to determine the percentage of gold or silver in a particular prospector's sample. Collector Jim Holroyd told me about them, sharing information he'd got from Jack Ward.) **$22-$30**

Roll pan, flat tin sheet with 6 curvy roll cups riveted to sheet, Silver & Co., Brooklyn, c.1916. **$12-$20**

Roll pan or Vienna baker, for what are called "Vienna Rolls," cast iron, 6 cigar-shaped cups set rather farther apart than usual, Griswold #26, about 12-1/2" L, turn of century or early 20th C. Wagner's was almost the same, 12" L x 6-1/2" W. Value range related to whether it is marked #6 or #26, and the company marking. Griswold higher than Wagner. **$50-$100**

Roll pan or Vienna baker, heavy tin, 9 oval shallow cups set in frame, with end handles, mfd. by Lalance & Grosjean Mfg. Co., late 19th C. **$20-$25**

Roll pan, cast iron, 11 shallow cups set 4 x 3 x 4, handle brace at each end, W & L Mfg. Co., 19th C. **$22-$35**

Rolling pins come in a wide range of styles and sizes. Some are truly just "pins" (like a sailor's belaying pin), slightly tapered at each end, used by rolling with the palms of both hands at each end. Some of these are quite long and thin, others fatter and short. Then there are the revolving barrel pins that have handles which are gripped in one position and pushed away or pulled toward the cook, across the dough. The barrels are made of various materials. I've divided the listings into sections according the material. See also some information in the cake board listings; also in the pastry board listings. See also noodle cutters and cracker rollers.

ROLLING PINS, advertising:

Rolling pin, blue & white pottery, adv'g "W. E. Neyland," Goliad, TX, late 19th C. **$150-$175**

Rolling pin, brown pottery, adv'g "Thompson's General Store," Grand Junction, IA, 19th C. **$160-$180**

IV-324. Rolling pins. *Fancy carved wooden pins, well-turned from one piece of wood. One with variegated wood, third from top, with bulbous handles and thick barrel, is possibly a Shaker piece. Note the 2 different ends on the long French pin — undoubtedly made to order for a cook with special needs. From about 15-1/4" L to 18-1/2" L. 19th C. Collection of Meryle Evans.* **$60-$125**

IV-325. Rolling pin. *Of type called a "draalhus" by the Pennsylvania Germans. Heavy wood with double-barred handle for extra strength and good grip. 11" L x 6-3/4" H as shown. 19th C. Collection Meryle Evans.* **$175-$250**

Rolling pin, crockery, adv'g "Robert F. McAfee, Dealer in Groceries, Augusta, IL," late 19th or early 20th C. Others noted: adv'g "John M. Merriot" (possibly John H.), Mt. Vernon, Iowa; "J. F. Reily Groceries, Hardware, Implements, Buggies & Wagons," Seaton, IL; "Dawson Furniture," Ziegler, IL (that one with blue stripe); "Thompson's General Store," Grand Junction, IA, (brown stripe); "Killian's," Wahoo, NE (brown stripe); "Peterson & Anderson," Pomeroy, IA; "Joseph Reuter, General Merchandise," Gilbertville, IA. Price is for main entry; full range would be $115 to $235 (most $150 to $185), mostly based on desirability & subject of advertising, meaningfulness of place, and condition & decoration, range is for others noted. **$160-$175**

Rolling pin, crockery, with bank or flour mill advertising maxim, "Save Your Dough," late 19th or early 20th C. **$120-$130**

Rolling pin, crockery, with brown bands & letters, adv'g "O. O. Hartley, Home of Quality Groceries, Phone 53, Roseville, IL," turn of century. **$185-$235**

Rolling pin, crockery, with brown stripe, "Perry & Buchanan General Merchandise, Quasqueton, IA," late 19th, early 20th C. **$150-$175**

Rolling pin, crockery with brown stripe, adv'g "White Swan Flour," Garrison, IA, late 19th or early 20th C. **$150-$175**

Rolling pin, white & blue pottery, "Ernest Nelson Sells the Flour that Makes the Dough Hump Great," American, late 19th C. **$150-$175**

Rolling pin, saltglazed stoneware with blue border with flowers, wooden handles, advertising message "Compliments of Berks County Democrat, a Newspaper," Boyertown, PA, 8-1/2" L excluding handles, late 19th C. This one has extra appeal to crossover collectors because it advertises a newspaper. **$275-$350**

Rolling pin, white pottery, "Kelvinator" — yes! the fridge people, the pin to be chilled before using, American, 20th C. **$45-$65**

Rolling pin, milk glass, wooden handles, advertising "Pekin Coal Fuel Co.," Pekin, NE, 19th C. Very unusual because most advertising pins are ceramic. **$100-$150**

Rolling pin, white "milk" glass, turned wooden handles, adv'g "Columbus Flour," late 19th C. **$115-$150**

Rolling pin, wood, with pyrographic, or hot poker work, advertising Custers Mills, Milton, PA, late 19th C. **$75-$100**

ROLLING PINS, aluminum, cast iron — See rolling pins, misc. metals

ROLLING PINS, ceramic:

Rolling pin, blue & white china, with blue painted wooden handles, "T. G. Green & Co., Ltd.," English, 18" L, late 19th C., early 20th. **$85-$100**

"Shrewsberry Cakes. 1 lb. butter, 1 lb. sugar, 2 lb. flour, and a few caraway seeds. — Rub the butter in with the flour; then put in the sugar and seeds, and mix them up into a paste, with a little milk; roll them out thin, cut them with a small round cutter, and bake them on iron plates in a good oven." Joseph Bell, *A Treatise on Confectionary*. Newcastle, England, 1817.

Rolling pin, blue & white Delft faience barrel with windmill scene, very heavy, has turned wooden handles & rod, English, German or Dutch, 9-3/16" L (overall 17-5/8" L), c.1870s. This is quite possibly a noodle roller, a *Nüdelrolle,* because of ratio of the barrel length to overall length. **$285-$350**

Rolling pin, blue & white pottery, "Harker," American, 20th C. **$35-$55**

Rolling pin, blue & white sponge decorated saltglazed stoneware, wooden handles, American (?), 15" L x 5-1/4" D (a very fat or thick roller drum, possibly for noodle dough), 19th C. **$165-$180**

Rolling pin, blue & white china, Blue Onion pattern, nicely turned wooden handles, 19th C. **$140-$200**

Rolling pin, blue-decorated white pottery, with Dutch windmill scene, turned wooden handles, English or Dutch, 15" L, 19th C. **CAUTION:** Sometimes the handles have been replaced. If the pottery shows wear, even small chips or hairline cracks, but the handles look unused, you shouldn't have to pay as much. **$175-$250**

Rolling pin, ceramic, to be filled with cold water, "Petit Point Rose" design, has original stopper, Harker China, American, 20th C. **$45-$60**

Rolling pin, crockery decorated with wildflowers, type found from Rodman, Iowa, also Milwaukee, WI, late 19th, early 20th C. **$145-$155**

Rolling pin, ironstone, long turned wooden handles, American (?), 9-1/2" L x 3-3/4" D pin, 4" L handles, 19th C. **$130-$150**

Rolling pin, white porcelain, with painted ship, "The Harkaway" & painted motto reading "A present for my cousin Rose Godsmark, 1861," also, "When this you see, remember me, and bear me in your mind. Let the world say what it will, speak of me as you find." (NO, it did not say ". . . as your friend."), open at one end,

IV-326. Rolling pins. *Two patented ones.* **(T)** *has its own compartment of dusting flour above in mesh cylinder. 20-1/4" L. This is Harlowe's "Do No Stick" pin, pat'd 12/1903.* **(B)** *double barrels or rollers, and beautifully formed handles, is 20" L, with rollers 11-3/4" L x 1-3/4" diameter. It is "Taylor's Patent Combination Rolling Pin" pat'd 7/16/1867. June Sprigg says it is a Shaker pin. The instruction sheet reads "The advantage of this Roller is, it will do the work in half the time it can be done with the single roller. It is worked with the greatest ease."* **$200-$300; $175-$250**

IV-327. Rolling pins. *Two wooden ones, with separate turned handles and an axle rod. 16-1/4" L and 18-1/2" L. Glass bottle pin has screw-on metal cap, and was meant to be filled with cold water or shaved ice. Many old old pins were glass — they could be chilled and this makes rolling fine pastry easier. c.1900 for wood; 1930s for glass.* **$15-$35**

English, 1861. Retyping this into the computer, something about the ship's name makes me wonder if this was sort of a generic seaman's gift, that he could get painted with his lady's name. "Harkaway" sounds more like a romantic story than a ship ("Hark! I'm away"). Can anyone out there report another pin like this one? Or news of a real ship by that name? **$125-$175**

Rolling pin, gray white saltglazed stoneware with blue circumferential rings, Clinton, OH, late 19th C. **$150-$175**

Rolling pin, pale tan or buff saltglazed stoneware, black eagle mark, turned oak handles, 9-3/4" L pin, 4-1/2" L handles, late 19th C., maybe even early 20th, I just can't say. It's very handsome, but somehow doesn't look quite right with the eagle. Perhaps this is a much later 20th C. piece for the "country look" market. If old: **$135-$150**

Rolling pin, saltglazed stoneware with blue flower design, European or American, 16" L, late 19th or 20th C. **$135-$165**

Rolling pin, saltglazed stoneware with orange bands, Red Wing pottery, 20th C. **$120-$150**

Rolling pin, saltglazed stoneware, wooden handles, motto "May peace and plenty/ Dwell on England and shore/ And there remain/ Till time shall be no more." English, late 19th C. **$200-$250**

Rolling pin, glazed stoneware roller, revolves on turned wooden handles, American, about 14" L, early 20th C. **$30-$55**

Rolling pin, white pottery, lavender & blue flower decoration, turned wooden handles, American or English, 19th C. **$120-$135**

Rolling pin, white saltglazed stoneware with blue floral & scroll bands near ends, T. G. Green & Co., Ltd., English, 18" L, 19th C. **$200-$225**

Rolling pin, yellowware, wood handles, 11" L barrel, plus handles, American, 19th C. Rolling pins are unusual in yellowware. **$200-$250**

Rolling pin, yellowware, oak handles, English or American, 11-1/4" L pin, 3-1/2" L handles, 19th C. **$200-$250**

ROLLING PINS, glass:

Rolling pin, amber glass, freeblown, knob ends — one with pontil, prob. American, 16" L, 19th C. **$85-$125**

Rolling pin, amethyst glass, freeblown with 2 knob handles, American, 15-1/2" L, 19th C. **$90-$130**

Rolling pin, blue & red spattered opaque white glass, white glass inside so possibly of a type called Nailsea, freeblown, double ball-knobbed, English, 14" L, 19th C. **$200-$265**

Rolling pin, blue & white loopy Nailsea glass, English, 20" L, 2nd or 3rd quarter 19th C. **$250-$275**

Rolling pin, clear glass with blobs of cobalt with blood red and brown glass blobs too, big knob ends, salt still inside, cork intact, prob. Nailsea, England, 14" L, prob. 2nd or 3rd quarter 19th C. A myth started up in the late 1980s about these glass salt pins — that they were used by sailors to "smuggle" salt. **$250-$280**

Rolling pin, clear glass, metal axle, turned wood handles, "Gem," 19-1/2" L, 20th C. **$65-$90**

Rolling pin, cobalt blue glass, enameled ship design, English, 13-3/4" L, dated 1854. You see so many with ships and flowers, you have to wonder how the decorative painting survived on so many. These pins, reported to be sailors' love tokens, were probably never actually used in the kitchen, but were decorative parlor pieces. **$120-$135**

Rolling pin, cobalt blue glass, freeblown knobbed "salt bottle" type, with corked end, English, 16" L, 19th C. **$175-$200**

Rolling pin, bottle green, very dark, freeblown, tapers to small knobs, lots of wear scratches show up on this very utilitarian but handsome pin. English or American, 14" L, 19th C. **$95-$125**

Rolling pin, Bristol glass, translucent rich blue with ship & other decorations in gilt, poss. Bristol, England, or other English glass center, 14" L, prob. early to mid 19th C. Practically all these rich cobalt blue rolling pins with traces of enameled decoration are called Bristol glass. According to Hampden Gordon (*The Lure of Antiques*), painted blue, emerald green and purple glass were all done at Bristol, Sunderland and "a number of other places." It's a field in which too little knowledge can do you in. Over a period of more than 100 years, the blue color was achieved several different ways, according to the supply of varying qualities of the cobalt mineral (or substitutes) with which a blue color could be created in glass. **$125-$160**

Rolling pin, marbleized or swirled cobalt blue & white glass, knob handles, American, 17-1/2" L, mid 19th C. **$145-$175**

Rolling pin, marbleized or swirled pink & white blown glass, knob handles, American, 16" L, mid 19th C. **$150-$200**

Rolling pin, milk glass, 2 smallish knobs, one rough, English, 19th C. May have had some stenciled paint decorations, flowers and the like, but completely worn off now. **$50-$65**

Rolling pin, milk glass, knobby ends, painted flowers & green leaves, had name on it, mostly rubbed off, English, 19th C. **$85-$100**

Rolling pin, milky, almost opalescent white Bristol glass, English (?), 13" L, 2nd or 3rd quarter 19th C. Nineteenth century opaque white glass (often called "milk glass," a term a lot of glass collectors don't like), is sometimes called Bristol glass, although it was made, wrote Hampden Gordon (*The Lure of Antiques*), " . . . in London & Stourbridge, Sunderland and on the Tyneside as well as at Bristol." **$275-$300**

IV-328. Rolling pin combination tool. *Pieced tin, with everything needed to cut cookies, churn syllabubs, funnel, strain and squirt. From Seastrand catalog, c.1912.* $55-$75

IV-329. Rolling pin. *Really odd red & white plastic one. The "Magnus," mfd. by Magnus Harmonica Corp, Newark, NJ. Arching handle across the 8 rollers makes it a one hander. Great conversation piece, or use for duet performances with a harmonica player. Photograph & information courtesy of great cookie cutter collector, Evelyn King.* $45-$65

Rolling pin, milky pastel green "Jadeite" glass, American, 1930s. June 1989 asking price: **$350**

Rolling pin, "Bristol" type opalescent white glass, turned wooden handles, Imperial Glass Mfg. Co., Cambridge, OH, 19" L, pat'd July 26, 1921. Rollers in opaque white glass (that people inaccurately call "milk glass") that is found with enameled and gilded decorations are also called by what is almost a generic term — Bristol glass, but was made probably at even more places than the decorated blue glass. **$75-$95**

Rolling pin, white opaque "milk glass," plump, with 2 very small knob handles, like little mushrooms, 16" L, English or American, 19th C. **$150-$200**

Rolling pin, white "milk" glass, well-turned wooden handles have plain wood knob close to pin with gripping part stained green, National Mfg. Co., Cambridge, OH, patented but I can't read date. Presumably late 19th or early 20th C. **$40-$65**

Rolling pin, clam broth glass (off-white murky mottled color, faintly tan), American or English, 19th C. **$50-$65**

Rolling pin, clear glass with screw-on black-painted metal lid, step-down ribbed glass handles, meant to be filled with ice water, American, 14-1/4" L x 2-3/4" diameter, c.1920s-1930s. **$15-$22**

Rolling pin, clear glass bottle type with screw-on metal cap, American, 13" L, 20th C. **$15-$22**

Rolling pin, clear glass bottle type, with white painted screw-on metal cap, "Roll-Rite," with the Good Housekeeping Institute Seal of Approval printed on cap, American, 14" L x 2-1/2" diameter, 20th C. **$22-$25**

Rolling pin, clear glass with cork stopper, American, 20th C. **$22-$35**

Rolling pin, clear glass with wooden axle rod & turned wooden handles, this one not a bottle, American, says pat'd July 28, 1921, but the 26th was Patent Tuesday that year. **$25-$50**

Rolling pin, custard glass with aluminum screw-on cap, American, 1930s. **$70-$85**

Rolling pin, green glass, fat & short, with small knob ends, European or American, 5-1/2" L, 19th C. **$60-$80**

Rolling pin, green glass, freeblown, lots of bubbles, American, 15" L, 19th C. **$75-$85**

Rolling pin, green & white Nailsea glass, big thick white swirls, freeblown, knob ends, prob. really from Nailsea, England, 14" L, 2nd or 3rd quarter 19th C. **$275-$300**

Rolling pin, heavy purple blown glass, knob handles, English or American, 15-1/2" L, 19th C. **$200-$250**

Rolling pin, Nailsea glass, blue with white loopy stripes, English, 15" L, 19th C. **$120-$135**

Rolling pin, Nailsea glass, red with white loops, knob at each end, unusual & very desirable in red or cranberry, English, 14-1/2" L, prob. mid to late 19th C. **$125-$150**

"Best Scotch Bread. 1 lb. butter, 1 lb. sugar, 1 lb. 8 oz. flour, 4 oz. cut almonds, 4 oz. lemon. — Cream the butter; then mix the other ingredients with it into stiff paste; you may cut it in different shapes; put caraway comfits and citron on the top; and bake it in a slow oven. **Scotch Bread, another Way.** 1 lb. 8 oz. butter, 1 lb. sugar, 2 lb. flour, a little mace. — The butter to be rubbed very fine with the flour; then add the sugar and spices; make it into stiff paste, with a little cream; roll half of it out, and lay upon it cut almonds, citron, and caraway comfits; then roll out the other half, and lay it upon the top; press it down; mark it in diamonds; cut it any shape you please; and bake it in a slow oven. It is most commonly cut in small diamonds, and mixed with rout biscuits." Joseph Bell, *A Treatise on Confectionary*, Newcastle, England, 1817.

Rolling pin, Nailsea-type glass, aquamarine with white loopy swirls, a handle at each end, remnant of ribbon hanger, prob. English, but poss. American, 9-1/2" L, prob. mid 19th C. **$200-$250**

Nailsea Glass. British antiques author, Hampden Gordon, wrote a no-nonsense, easy to follow, small book, *The Lure of Antique: Looking and Learning Today*, published first in 1961 by John Murray, London. The chapter "Variety in Old Glass" gave tips on Nailsea and Bristol glass, invaluable to those who fancy glass rolling pins. Nailsea glass is " . . . but a species of bottle glass, which was taxed at a lower rate . . . ," writes Gordon. Then, with but one passing reference to rolling pins, he explains that the glass-house at Nailsea was founded in 1788 by J. R. Lucas (a bottle maker from Bristol), and that typical "early work" was dark green with "splashes and loops of white." He goes on, "The style was changed in 1810 . . . [with a new owner], and "clear glass took the place of green with loops and stripes in white and pink and blue and other popular colours . . . About 1830, came the style in which the coloured loops are massed closely together, concealing the clear glass. Dating is very difficult; for the later Nailsea patterns, and particularly the quaint conceits such as walking-sticks and pipes and rolling-pins with inscriptions — great favourites on the fairground — were still immensely popular in late Victorian days." He goes on to say that the term "Nailsea" is almost a generic term for the white-swirled novelty glass that was made not only at Nailsea, but at Warrington, Stourbridge, and other glass-making towns.

Rolling pin, opaline glass, painted with ship & prayer, English, 14-1/2" L, 19th C. **$110-$130**

Rolling pin, opaque "black" or extremely dark green "Nailsea" glass with what appears as light blue & white splashes throughout, knob ends, prob. English, 12" L, 2nd to 3rd quarter 19th C. **$150-$175**

Rolling pin, pale turquoise opalescent glass, English, 14-1/2" L, 19th C. **$100-$125**

Rolling pin, robin's-egg blue freeblown glass, 29" L, 19th C. **$125-$135**

Rolling pin, Stourbridge glass, turquoise color, English, 13" L, 19th C. **$135-$145**

Rolling pin, turquoise green Bristol glass with gold & red painted floral decoration, cork missing, English or French Bristol, 15" L, c.1870s to 1880s. **$185-$220**

Rolling pin, very heavy glass, old style fat drum with fat knobby short handles, filled with bath salt crystals, "Clean Bath Salts," mfd. by the Clean Perfume Co., Chicago, 13" L, turn of century to c.1915 (?). **$35-$45**

ROLLING PINS, marble or stone:

Rolling pin, marble, all one piece including handles, very heavy, thick & cold, 16" L, 19th C. **$35-$50**

Rolling pin, marble with no handles, very smooth (but not finished like a statue would be), American (?), 17" L x 3" diameter, prob. 19th C. **$35-$50**

Reproduction alert. Repros, or rather new, marble pins, often have turned wood handles & highly polished finish.

ROLLING PINS, misc. metals:

Rolling pin, aluminum, "Mil-Bar Co.," Canton, OH, 20th C. **$25-$35**

Rolling pin cast iron, for candy makers because the iron can be so well chilled, wood handles, American, 24" L, early 20th C., or poss. late 19th. **$45-$75**

Rolling pin, nickeled metal pin, turned wooden handles, plus something inside that makes it rattle, perhaps lead shot to make it weigh more?, American, 15-1/2" L, c.1920. Another similar one, same value, has green stained wooden handles and is 15-3/4" L. **$15-$22**

Rolling pin, tin barrel, wood handles: most of these came in a set with a tin tray like pastry "board" which had a curved end to act as a holder for the pin when the set was wall-hung. Several manufacturers in late 19th C. Very desirable! See also pastry boards. **$575-$700**

ROLLING PINS, plastic:

Rolling pin, molded plastic, fixed handle arched across from one side to other, round red frame set with 8 white rolling cylinders, like cigar tubes of different lengths, side by side at right angles to the handle, which was held to push multiple rollers to & fro, "Magnus New Style Rolling Pin," mfd. by the Magnus Harmonica Corp., Newark, NJ, about 10" diameter, c.1940s (?). Yep, the harmonica-makers made this. The copy on the colorful box states, "Like Magic. Rolls the Dough with one Hand. Fluffier, Tastier Pies and Pastries." It doesn't have a lot of heft, but all those rollers, and the pressure of the hand directly above the center, does the work. **$35-$45**

ROLLING PINS, wood:

Rolling pin, carved tiger maple all one piece, with 2 long handles, American, 21" L including both 4" L handles, 19th C. I've seen several, and of course maple was the best wood after lignum vitae for rolling pins, because of weight & dense grain, which meant protection from moisture and cracks, and both resisted absorption of ingredients that might make the pin smelly or unsanitary. **$80-$115**

Rolling pin, double rollers with oval-ended frame & simple turned handles, maple, beautiful patina, paper label "Taylor's Patent Combination Rolling Pin," pat'd by A. L. Taylor, Springfield, VT, rollers 11-3/4" L x 1-3/4" diameter, overall length 20-1/2", pat'd July 16, 1867. This pin, because of the simplicity of form and shape of turned handles at each end has been incorrectly attributed by other writers to the Shakers. As the original spiel had it, "The Advantage of this Roller is, it will do the work in half the time it can be done with the single roller. It is worked with the greatest ease, as the Combination Rollers give double the surface bearing, and one roll following the other — making the Pastry of uniform thickness, and perfectly smooth and even finish." Original price was (you'll have to dust yourself off now!) only 50¢. **$175-$250**

Rolling pin, hardwood with turned bone handles, prob. American, 15" L, 19th C. **$175-$200**

Rolling pin, heavy, thick lignum vitae which is the hardest of all woods & nearly as dense as iron, meant to last forever. Probably a commercial baker's pin, American (?), 16" L, 4-1/2" D, 19th C. **$85-$100**

Rolling pin, heavy wood with heavy frame & 2 vertically held handles at ends, the type called by the PA Germans draalhus, American, 11" L x 6-3/4" H including upright handle frame, prob. late 19th C., and prob. patented. **$150-$175**

Rolling pin, maple with handles on axle rod, probably bakery or hotel kitchen ware, American, 27-1/2" L, early 20th C. **$40-$50**

Rolling pin, tapered wood, name marked in pyrography or hot poker burned letters, "Pie Maker," Harrisville, NH, late 19th or early 20th C. **$40-$50**

Rolling pin, turned & carved wood, barrel connected by a sort of stand-up frame with vertical ends as gripping handles. These uprights carved rather like simplified human forms. They're connected lengthwise not only by the pin's axle, but by a plain wooden dowel & a carved dowel, PA, 14" L x 5" H including pin & handle, 19th C. **$175-$250**

Rolling pin, turned from one piece of maple, including handles, American, 14" L x 3-1/2" diameter, 19th C. **$30-$50**

Rolling pin, turned maple, button or mushroom knob at one end, American, 12-1/2" L, 19th C. I believe these dense wooden pins, with one knob only, could also be used as pestles of a sort for such things as cooked apples or potatoes, although this is just a hunch. I suppose if the patina at the rounded no-knob end is different from the rest of pin, that might be considered evidence of such use. **$35-$50**

Rolling pin, turned maple, nylon ball bearings, length marked off in centimeters & inches, Rowoco Inc., Elmsford, NY, 18" L x 3-1/2" diameter, early 1980s. **$5-$10**

Rolling pin, wood with iron rod, turned handles painted green, set at right angles to pin itself, marked only "D. R. G. M.," German, 10-1/8" L with 5-1/2" L handles, pre-1918, prob. early 20th C. The initials **D. R. G. M.** are found on some German collectibles — prior to 1918 — and stand for Deutsches Reichs-Gebrauchsmuster, which meant that any trademark shown was a registered trademark of Germany. After 1918, and until the division of Germany after WWII, I believe at least one official mark used was **D. R. P.**, or Deutsches Reichspatent. See also an entry under coffee mills in Chapter XIV and a brass grater in the Chapter I. **$65-$85**

Rolling pin, pyrographic wood — See under advertising pins above

Rolling pin, wooden pin with wooden rod & handles, also wood & mesh self-dusting compartment above, "Harlowe's Do Not Stick," American, 20-1/4" L, pat'd Dec. 1903. **$200-$300**

Rolling pins, turned wood, handles or knobs all in one with pin, interesting woods & knob shapes, unusual lengths, American, from about 14" L to 20" L, 19th C. Look for variations of turned maple, for example, with particularly nice knobs. These may have mostly been one-off turnings meant as gifts. Some were commercially produced. Added value: Add another $20 or so if some feature is extra ultra — for example, extra long, or extra thick, or with extra nifty turning details, or great deep patina. **Reproduction alert.** At least 2 forms of new ones are being made and sold through Cumberland General Store. One is based on a "1907 design from Garland County Arkansas . . . made up in sassafras and various fruit woods from Cumberland County, TN, about 19" L x 2-1/4" diameter." The other is a "standard Old World style . . . made of smooth hardwood, 18" L" with short very ball-y knob handles, turned all-in-one. About $7-$9 for new ones. **$50-$85**

Rolling pin whatzit, hard wood, ridged or corrugated lengthwise rather than around the pin's circumference, this one carved of one piece of wood including handles at each end, nice patina, American, 14" L, this one poss. as early as mid 19th C. See also noodle cutter; also one candy cutter entry & picture this chapter. **$45-$85**

What're the Ridges For? In *Tri-State Trader* of Aug. 5 & Sept. 3, 1985, collector William Baader and Ralph & Terry Kovel had a rolling pin fight about what this was for. Is this [the one with ridges around circumference] for crushing crackers or stale bread to make crumbs? The Kovels, using Doreen Yarwood's *The British Kitchen* as their source, say it is for rolling out oat cakes (and allows "a current of air to pass beneath the oatcakes," says Yarwood). Baader claims it is for crushing oats to make oatmeal, using Edward Pinto's *Treen & Other Wooden Bygones* as his expert source. I say it is what it's used for. Many of us (at least in the 1950s) rolled graham crackers for pie crusts, or wheat cereal flakes for fried chicken or even Saltines for topping tuna casseroles. I've seen these pins used to pound meat (and therefore it could be called a tenderizer). Pins with the lengthwise ridges are also used for making croissants or other pastry with lots of butter that has to be layered into the dough. Pierre Franey's column on Kitchen Equipment in the *New*

York Times, 2/21/79, describes one thus: "The French-made Tutové pin, which has [longitudinal ridges the length of] its barrel and is excellent for distributing butter in puff paste, costs four or five times as much as . . . [another pin selling for $10 then]." **Ridges around circumference:** An ad in the July 1897 *Woman's Home Companion* depicts a rolling pin with a barrel about the same length as either of the two handles, ridged circumferentially. The ad copy reads "Noodles now made easily by the Lightning Noodle cutter. 'Cuts 'em quick and fine.' The cooks delight. Sent to any address for 35¢. Household Supply Co., Toledo, O."

Rolling pin, wood with carved surface — See springerle rolling pin

Rolling pin confusables, 2 types: (1) Wooden pin, with 6 corrugations & tapered ends, an axle & 2 handles, about 24" L. It is a very old leather tanner's tool for working the "bloom" off hides. (2) All-wood or wood & hard rubber pins with a waffled pattern, about 16" L, which are antique spot reducers or massagers. American, (1) late 1700s to early 1800s; (2) late 1800s — early 1900s. **$200-$300, $45-$100**

Rolling pin footstools seem to have been made in three periods: (1) early 19th century with "Windsor" style turned legs. These are probably all English, and are painted like Windsor chairs — green or black, with ochre or gold pin striping on legs; (2) late 19th century with carpet piece tacked onto barrel of the large pin; (3) from the 1950s or so, in fake "olde fashioned" maple varnish and tacked-on carpet on the pin. The oldest pin stools are very rare, and generally speaking are probably the largest (up to 22" L, and about 9" - 10" H). The 1870s-1890s ones are somewhat smaller and "fancier," but still seem to have been made with a real rolling pin with turned legs set in at a slightly less exaggerated splay. The 20th century ones are comparitively puny, and are obviously made to be footstoools, rather than adapted from real pins. Prices from newest to oldest: **$35-$55; $100-$125; $300-$400**

Rosette iron set, cast iron in original box, the star and wheel molds were dipped into thinnish batter, then plunged quickly into a deep pot of very hot cooking fat, cooked for a minute, dropped off the molds and drained on paper, making light crispy confections in the same shape as the molds, and served after dusting with powdered sugar, "Manufactured for Alfred Andresen & Co.," Minneapolis, MN, this one, from the box's design, is mid 20th C. They are a much older form. **$45-$65**

An Alfred Andresen ad in *Ladies Home Journal*, Dec. 1906, shows **"Rosette Wafers"** being cooked in a steaming stovetop sauce pan. They are described as the "daintiest, crispest little morsels that ever tempted an epicure, or delighted the fastidious. Light as a summer zephyr, and delicious as ambrosia. You can make forty of them in 20 minutes at a cost of ten cents with this simple little iron and the thinnest batter. A distinct novel delicacy for breakfast, luncheon and afternoon tea . . . sold by leading dealers at 50 cents per set." They offered to send a free recipe booklet, "illustrated in eight colors," plus an "interesting catalog of culinary novelties," and all you had to do was send your dealer's name. I wish it would work now; I'd love to have a catalog (which itself, incidentally, would be worth about $35 to $50).

Rosette irons, cast iron, set of 2 in original cardboard box, the "shallow pattern" openwork rosette irons, heavy gauge wire screw-in handle with wooden grip, Griswold, (there were several makers of these), Erie, PA, round rosette is 2-5/16" D; scalloped one (which looks like 4 hearts, arranged points in) is 3" D, c. 1926-1960s (?). **$35-$55**

Rosette & timbale mold combined, cast aluminum molds in set, screwed onto Y-shaped handle that looks like slingshot or wishbone, simple hotdog-shaped turned wood handle, meant that 2 could be dipped at once. One fluted round & one fluted square timbale or patty shell mold, plus one star & one wheel-like rosette mold. The patty shells could be filled with anything from fruit or custard to creamed chicken, very popular for luncheons, American, molds each about 3" diameter, 1960s. **$15-$20**

Modern rosette maker. Shown in an early 1980s kitchenware catalog is a cast aluminum desert rosette set, for making "waffle cookies & fruit filled patty shells," shrink-wrapped on printed card, mfd. or imported by Fairgrove, place illegible. It consists of slightly bent rod with handle, a patty iron with heart, spade, diamond & club, a butterfly & an 8-petal flower, the three things to be screwed to handle.

Rosette molds — See also wafflet mold

Sausage stuffers — See Chapter I

Sealer or crimper — See crimper or sealer; also tart sealer

Snow cone set, molded plastic & metal, snowman figure of white on white snowbank base, red plastic foller goes in hopper in top of head, eyes, nose & teeth of plastic "coal," red plastic shovel & funnel, red crank in back turns perforated metal cylinder against ice cube, shaved ice supposed to come out front & cascade picturesquely down front into snowbank so it could be shoveled into cups; set includes red & yellow squeeze bottles with flavoring syrup, small Dixie conical cups, in original box, with illustrated instruction folder, "Frosty Sno-Man Sno-Cone Machine," marked Hasbro, mfd. by Hassenfeld Bros., Inc., Central Falls, RI, 9-1/4" H, c. 1952. **$10-$15**

IV-330. Souse mold, *for a kind of spiced, pickled pork-head dish, yuck. Cast iron, 8-1/2" diameter x 2-3/4" deep. Photo & collection of David G. Smith.* **$150-$175**

Soap molds — See listing under muffin or gem pans for speculation on this extra use for such molds

Souse mold, for pork head-cheese (which dates back in America to at least 1801, from cookbook evidence). Cast iron, round with 2 handles, scalloped border design with sow's head including ears, in good detail, American, prob. PA (?), 11" diameter, late 19th C. to early 20th. Joel Schiff says he has never seen either a sprue or a gatemark on some 50 or more souse mold heads hc's seen. He believes they originated in the south, and were probably introduced closer to 1920 than 1900. He asks if I have any documents to help date the earlier-looking souse molds, but I don't, except a pig head mold (side view rather than head on) of bronze found at Pompeii, and dating to the first century C.E.   **$150-$175**

Souse mold, painted cast iron, pig's sad face, ears down, natural pink tones in what looks like old paint (see a lion mold in copper & tin molds, above), scalloped frame, loop handles cast in top & bottom, American, 8-1/2" diameter plus 1-1/4" handles, late 19th C.   **$150-$175**

Reproduction alert. Dating is hard to do. I believe I have seen two old ones (listed here); all the rest, in that easily detected orangey powder-rusted state, are either reproductions or something somebody came up with in the mid-twentieth century. I have never seen reference to a souse mold, and am still not convinced they are nineteenth century in origin. But if this one was old the value would be high. $15 ought to be enough for new ones.

• • • •

The worst thing I've seen in a grocery store ever is an arrangement of styrofoam trays with pigs' heads under the shrink wrap. It almost made me sick. I wouldn't eat pork, or beef, or lamb, or veal, or mutton (and haven't for 22 years) if you paid me a million dollars. Think about it: a pig is more intelligent than a dog, by far, and can be trained and housebroken (even to use a litter box), can be affectionate and naturally clean. Why not try soy protein "bacon" . . . it's very good. And, if you know of any pigs needing sanctuary, there's a wonderful place called PIGS, POB 629, Charles Town, WV, 25414.

Sponge cake tin — See molds, ladyfinger pans, etc., in tin section

SPRINGERLE BOARDS

Springerle boards are intaglio carved: that is, carved *into* rather than carved relievo (raised relief, where the background is carved away, leaving the design raised like a cameo). They are generally smaller than cake boards, although large ones were made, with border lines carved into the mold that would indicate where the individual springers were to be cut after molding and before baking. Some springerle boards are of cast iron or pewter.
Springerles — also spelt **Sprengerlies:** According to William Woys Weaver springerles are a so-called "water marzipan," a cheaper non-almond version of marzipan (p.116, *America Eats*). "The beauty of [these baked springerle] cookies, with their detailed designs in high relief, veritable cameos in dough, charms young and old," write Ann Hark & Preston A. Barba, in *Pennsylvania German Cookery*, Allentown, PA: Schlechter's ("Publishers for the Pennsylvania Germans since 1810"), 1950. They go on to say that the word *springerle* means "charger or horse" in "South German;" other sources say it means "small jumping horse" in German. But other sources say it means leaping deer — and perhaps as many deer as horses are depicted on the molds we know. *Sprengen,* related to the sprengerlie spelling found in an American cooking magazine of 1903, means both to blow up and to gallop! Hark & Barba note that "the man on horseback is a familiar figure among our old Christmas cooky cutters" and the image is common on cake boards and springerle molds too. They write that the "beautiful designs [are] delicately engraved into pearwood or some other hard or close-grained wood. Most of them are imported from Germany and are occasionally for sale in our large department stores."

Springerles: Wood to Iron & Pewter. I have read in various sources that these were sometimes cast from patterns made from original carved wooden springerle molds. Would be especially good for bakery, which could soon wear out a wooden mold. These metal springerle molds are also found in a heavy cast metal something like lead that is probably zinc. A book by Katherine Morrison McClinton states that marzipan molds were first made in carved wood, then of tin and cast iron. William Woys Weaver says that in the last half of the nineteenth century, bakery supply companies had made cast iron, and, later, pewter copies of the old carved molds.

What do you make of this? The Smithsonian was offered a puzzling mold with these same images. It is cast iron but with a strange variegated irridescent color appearing on the underside that makes you suspect impurities or unorthodox casting methods. On the mold's topside are 12 intaglio images laid out 3 across by 4 down: an apple basket, pear, turkey or peacock, cornucopia, bird in branch, oak leaves with acorn, fruit tree branch, horseshoe with blacksmith's hammer, large bird on branch, bushel basket with apples, grape leaves and tall cross — *identical* to the images described on a cast iron mold toward end of these listings. On the underside of this relatively thin metal slab, in relief, are the same images, backwards so to speak. Furthermore, four short peg feet, almost like casting sprues, extrude from the four corners. There is considerable appearance of damage to the underside image of the tall basket where the peg leg is joined, and also to the cross cookie, but it occurred before the casting was made, so it may have been on the original metal casting from which this apparent copy was made. Overall dimensions are slightly larger than the main one priced in the preceding entry, viz. 8-3/16" H x 4-13/16" W; each cookie is about 1-15/16" H x 1-7/16" W. The collection from which the mold came was rather old and select, so if this is a reproduction, it has some age. My suspicion is that the upper and underside images are somehow indicative of the exact method of production, a method that remains unknown.

Sources for Springerle Designs. It is hard to find identification of, or exact sources for, the designs, but if you keep your eyes open all the time, serendipity and diligence will sometimes give you clues. I picked up a Dover Publications book called *Catchpenny Prints: 163 Popular Engravings from the Eighteenth Century*, originally published in London by Bowles & Carver in the late 1780s and early 1790s (reprint published in 1970). A man with a whip, seen on one mold, is identified as a waggoner [sic] in a very similar picture in the catchpenny book. A man with a tall ladder is usually identified as a "Lamp-lighter," but sometimes I believe they may be chimney sweeps, at least if there is any hint of a long brush. Trades people, including butchers, shoe-makers, hat-makers, coopers, carpenters, etc., are somewhat common designs. **Costume fashions.** A good reference book on costume, including hair styles, shoes and hats, would be very valuable for collectors who specialize in decorated pieces or figural items. **Bird Watching.** Catchpenny prints and chapbooks for children are full of birds. The Dover reproduction of 1780s-1790s catchpenny prints, in one book, must have 100 bird pictures, tail up, tail down, straight beak, finch or parrot-like beak, open beak, closed beak. Each bird is labeled, but it is very difficult to decide which bird was used by the springerle mold carver. Some birds are more likely to have been used than others because of fable and song, viz. swan, peacock, turkey, sparrow, magpie, robin, wren, nightingale, magpie, swan, duck and goose. More unusual waterbirds such as cranes (herons?) and sandpipers are found on some items, like decorated stoneware.

Springerle Cookie Recipe. A basic recipe for these cookies requires 2 eggs, a cup of sugar, grated lemon rind, 2 cups of sifted flour with about a half teaspoon of baking powder, and 2 teaspoons of aniseed (it is this and the lemon that give the distinctive fragrance). All the recipes suggest beating the eggs first, then slowly beating in the sugar and adding the lemon rind. Then you start adding the flour and baking powder. Finally add the aniseed. The dough shouldn't be too soft; if it seems soft, stiffen by kneading in a little more sifted flour, and roll out thin (a quarter-inch thick) and lightly flour the surface. The mould has to be pressed onto the dough carefully to leave its impression. You can cut the cookies apart before baking, especially if you use a mold that doesn't have the dividing lines. Some molds are so made that the whole set can be baked whole and broken after being baked and cooled. The ones with a groove between each design probably should be cut before drying; the ones with a ridge, sometimes relatively wide, between each design can be left until after baking. Carefully lift the printed dough with a couple of spatulas or cake turners, and shift to greased then floured tin baking sheets. Cover with a dry towel overnight, so that they have a chance to set and dry out. They will bake in about 15 minutes at 325°, and should not be allowed to get brown.

Using a Springerle Board or Mold. A springerle board is usually used lying flat on a work surface, with the rolled dough pressed or rolled into it. It is sometimes used the other way, with the dough rolled out and the mold pressed down on the dough, and lifted off. Either way, the individual designs were cut apart with a jagger or knife, or baked whole to be broken apart, depending on the kind and depth of dividing line between each design.

Springerle board, carved hard wood, vertical rectangle with 12 designs, including woman in gathered skirt, holding 3-part burden on head; rooster; woman sowing seeds from apron; an arch of some kind with tree; cherry or current branch; bird on fruit tree branch; 2 handled posset cup or tyg with odd plant (?); alert deer; sprightly flower; man with whip, probably a wagoner; hunting horn with 2 tassels; and woman in native costume with brimmed hat, and multitiered gathered skirt, next to tree. The individual cookies have very narrow frames, separated by a narrow channel or runnel — the type to be cut apart before drying & baking. European, about 6-1/2" x 4", prob. 3rd quarter 19th C. **$110-$140**

"Sprengerlie. Each nation has its own way of celebrating the advent of the New Year, some custom in in private or public life. In this initial number for 1903 we illustrate a cake familiar to all Dutch and German housewives — sprengerlie. A very righ, sweet dough is rolled out and stamped with molds of quaint or familiar objects. Not long ago we were privileged to see two such molds at least a hundred years old; one was of iron, a four by six-inch oblong, with a dog on one side and a basket of roses on the other; the second was of some hard wood — a six-inch ellipse — and showed a reindeer with branching horns. The aged housewife who owned them also gave a practical exposition of the manner in which the dough was rolled on the molds, carefully detached then baked. Some modern molds are similarly made, but it is better when purchasing to buy a regular sprengerlie pin. This rolling pin is of hard wood and has the figures carved in it. In all cases the figures are sunken so that the patterns stand in relief on the dough. These cakes are very popular in various sections of the country, and molds or pins can be obtained from or through any first-class house furnisher. For the dough cream together one-half of a pound each of butter and sugar. Sift in one-half of a teaspoonful of salt and three-quarters of a pound of fine pastry flour,

IV-331. Springerle board. *Carved fine grained wood, 9-1/4" x 6-3/4" W, signed "F. G." American, Pennsylvania German, 1860s-70s. Note great variety of motifs, including man playing pipe while sitting on bench under a tree with curving branch (think of those butter molds), and the St. Nicholas and his reindeer. Ex-Keillor Collection.* **$500-$1000**

IV-332. Metal faced springerle boards. *Modern manufacture, both from ads of The House-On-The-Hill, Vermont, or Minnesota. Makee puffy little cookies. "Heavy metal mounted on hand-finished cherry-wood." With hanging rings to serve as "kitchen plaques." (L) Ad from* Gourmet, *10/1967; (R) ad from* Early American Life, *1975. Company has been bought and revived, so these are still being made. It's easy to pay too much thinking they're old. I did it several times, alas.* **$25-$65**

then add gradually two well-beaten eggs and one scant teaspoonful of vanilla. This will make a stiff dough (if the eggs are small a few drops of cold water may be added) which is turned out on a board and thoroughly kneaded. If flat molds are used the dough is rolled down to half an inch, laid on the mold and rolled until the even surface is but half as thick, carefully peeled from the mold and laid on a slightly-buttered flat pan. With a sprengerlie pin on hand, the ordinary pin is preferred until it is rolled almost thin enough, then the special pin is applied and the cakes cut apart with a jagging iron. When on the pan they are brushed with unbeaten white of egg and are often sprinkled with 'hundreds and thousands,' sugared caraways or cardamoms or similar tiny confections. The oven should be very moderate so that the cakes when done will not be much deeper in tint than a straw color. If placed in a tightly-covered tin box or pail they will keep crisp for a long time." *Table Talk,* Philadelphia, January 1903.

Springerle board, carved maple wood, 8 patterns laid out in 2 x 4 formation, including animals, fruit, flowers, German or poss. German American, 8-1/2" L x 3-1/2" W, 19th C.   **$135-$160**

Springerle board, carved walnut, large ornate wreath design of flowers & birds, "Harman's Bakery," Brunswick, ME, 9" square, early 20th C. If you're reading this and wonder why this isn't called a cake board or marzipan board, I can't answer you. I'm confident it's interchangeable. See also an entry under pie top mold.   **$250-$350**

Springerle board, carved wood, 6 designs: rooster, house, fruit compote, dog, shore bird, grape bunch, European (?), 7" H x 3-1/4" W, late 19th or early 20th C.   **$100-$120**

Springerle board, carved wood with 5 geometric designs on one side only, handle with hanging hole, European (?), late 19th C.   **$60-$75**

Springerle board, carved wood with a cherry, grapes, sailboat, poss. American, 5-3/4" x 3", late 19th or early 20th C.   **$100-$120**

Springerle board, hand-carved wood, images on both sides (as they usually were), designs include angel, pecking chicken, steamboat, castle, tricorn hat, unusual and small, 19th C. **$145-$165**

Springerle board, machine-carved wood, 4 squares on pale maple wood, American or European import, early 20th C.   **$35-$45**

Springerle board, or confectionary mold? carved wood, long & skinny, on one side is a woman carrying water, a ship, a mermaid, & a lion, on other side are 37 small carvings, mainly fish, some people, a dog, birds, griffin, European, 18" L, board is 1-5/8" thick, looks c.1800 to 1820.   **$200-$250**

Springerle board, worm-eaten fruitwood, carved on both sides, rooster, boar, squirrel & heart on one side, a cat, dog, horse & lion on the other, European, 5" x 9", prob. very early 19th C., though poss. late 18th C.   **$550-$600**

Springerle board, carved boxwood (?), 6 images laid out 2 x 3: foamy beer mug (?), long-skirted bustled lady with fan, a cupboard, a pig, a boy bowling or playing bocci, with 3 balls in pile behind him, & finally a stepped thing like a plant stand with tiny unreadable objects on the 3 shelves, European, 5-7/8" H x 4-1/8" W x 1" thick, 1870s when bustles were "in" or skip to mid or late 1880s.   **$160-$185**

Springerle mold, ceramic block, flat with 35 separate small impressed images, German, mid (?) 20th C. reproduction. **$30-$35**

Springerle mold, cast metal plate, probably zinc, attached to oak board. This one has 12 designs laid out 3 across by 4 down. The designs show **tradesmen or craftsmen & their tools** & products. Amazingly detailed images of Butcher (sausages, cleaver & chopping block); Cooper (barrel); Tailor (sitting cross-legged, 'tailor' fashion, on his table, scissors); Wheelwright (wheel & plane); Blacksmith (horseshoe & anvil);

IV-333. All cast metal springerle mold. *Heavy metal like pewter. Makes 15 individual designs, measures 5-3/4" x 3-1/2". House with well, dog, church, another church, bird, grapes, raspberries, 2 beeskips on bench, elk (?), duck in pond, heron, berries, hunter with gun & rabbit, man cooking over gypsy kettle, woman holding a boot (?) in one hand. Courtesy Lenny Kislin, Bearsville, NY.* **$200-$250**

IV-334. All cast iron springerle mold. *12 squares, slightly irregular, each cookie would be about 1-1/8" x 1-3/4". Basket with 3 apples, pear with 2 leaves, turkey or peacock, cornucopia, bird in branch, oak leaves with acorn, fruited branch, horseshoe with blacksmith's hammer, large bird on branch, tall basket with apples or peaches, grape leaves, a cross. Courtesy Lenny Kislin, Bearsville, NY. Now in Joel Schiff collection.* **$225-$350**

Stone Carver (blocks, pick & square); Druggist (scales & apothecary chest); Fisherman (net); Lamp-lighter (ladder); Carpenter (adze & sawbucks); Shoemaker (boots & shoes); Clockmaker (carrying case clock reading 10 to 2). All with dividing ridge, & herringbone chip-carved edges, American (?) or European — nothing here to rule out either. Measures 7-5/8" L x 4-3/8" W. Cookies are 1-15/16" x 1-3/5". Metal is 1/8" + thick, mounted to board (no screws visible) almost 5/8" thick, prob. repro from 1970s-1980s, although it looks c.1840s-1850s. There is some crossover interest from tool collectors. Price range is for an authentic old one; divide by 5 or 10 for value of repro. **$200-$275**

Reproduction Alert. I had quite a start when I found an ad in Dec. 1973 *Early American Life* for a "Beautiful springerle cookie mold . . . an exact reproduction of 18th century Pennsylvania German original. Makes 12 cookies picturing 12 different craftsmen. Mold is of heavy metal mounted on hand-finished cherry-wood. Also serves as a handsome and indestructible kitchen wall plaque. History and our own springerle recipe included. $15 ppd. The House-On-The-Hill, So. Strafford, Vermont 05070." Now. **Do I have a repro?** Probably. The small, dark & rather sharp ad photo shows the same 12 images, but there appear to be slight differences in the shapes of things, esp. the Fisherman's net. And mine is not mounted on cherry, and there are no signs of a once-attached hook for hanging on the kitchen wall. It's scary and very maddening; you buy something because it looks so right, then a bully kicks sand in your face with a 1973 ad.

Where to Get Springerle Reproductions Now, for use. The-House-On-The-Hill has been moved by collector Caroline K. Kallas to Villa Park, IL (POB 7003, 60181). You can order her catalog (about $3 ppd) as a reference and as a positive impetus to make your own springerle! The most helpful thing Ms. Kallas told me, in a letter, is if you find screw heads in the back of the wooden plaque, this indicates the metal face is screwed on and old — newer ones are glued onto the wood. Newer, pot metal molds, are first copper- then nickel-plated. Kallas's good-looking replica springerle molds are glued to a cherry wood back plate and have a brass hanging ring in the top edge. Subjects include the "Guildsman" (or Trades) mold (7-1/2" x 4-1/2"); "Musical & Variety" mold, flowers & trades & musical instruments (7-1/2" x 4-1/2"); the "Swan" mold, swan, bird, boater, fruit, churner & house (6" x 3-1/2"); "Petite," house, dog, church, church, bird, grapes, fruit, bee skips, goat on rocks, swan, peacock, flowers (5-3/4" x 4"); "Cornucopia," with cornucopia, flower, game beater, goat; "Heart," heart design with lovebirds & flowers (3-1/2" square); "Der Kinderbringer (The Child-bringer)," winged angel with baby (4" x 2-5/8"); 6 round designs — grapes, birds, flowers, birdhouse, female gardener (6" x 4"); 6 ovals designs, anchor, house, lovebirds, etc. (6" x 3-1/2"); "Architectural," 9 churches, buildings (6" x 6-1/4"); 15 designs, animals & people (8-3/4" x 4-3/4"); and others (mostly religious) imported from Switzerland. **For wax reproductions:** Historic Waxcraft, 176 Elmerston Rd, Rochester, NY 14620. **Where to get Springerle Lookalikes for use:** please use SASE with queries. Carved wooden molds: HOBI Handcrafts, POB 25, Belleville, IL 62222; and D. D. Dillon Carvings, 850 Meadow Lane, Camp Hill, PA 17011. Others: Laxa Family Molds, POB 76, Belmont, MA 02178. In a 1984 catalog of Maid of Scandinavia Co., Minneapolis, appeared a cast aluminum springerle mold with 12 designs, laid out three across, four down, with flowers, birds, fish, a ship, a windmill, fruit. It measures 8-1/4" H x 4-1/2" W and cost $16.25.

Springerle mold, cast metal, probably zinc, with 12 designs, L to R: crossed guitar & cornet; 3-berried plant; squirrel on stump eating nuts; lyre & laurel wreath; clump with 3 flowers; bird (magpie, mockingbird or nightingale?) on branch; dairymaid in long gathered skirt with ruffled bottom, carrying 2 pails; wild flower with 6 leaves and single stalk with tiny flowers; woman in long 2-tiered gathered skirt, possibly arranging flowers in pot on 3-legged stool; man (lamp lighter?) with tall ladder, hand in belt; lily of the valley type plant; & man in skirted hunting coat with gun under arm walking toward tree. Each design has chip carved herringbone frame, and was meant to be cut apart before baking. European, 6-1/8" x 3-3/4", mid 19th C (?). **$150-$175**

Springerle mold, cast metal sheet with 12 rectangular designs, 3 across by 4 down with dividing ridges & chip carved edges, mounted to oak board. The very heavy dark gray metal is not lead or iron, but probably cast zinc, as the detail is very good, and zinc was similarly used for electrotyping & printing plates. Designs, L to R: log church & pine tree; peacock (?) on shed roof (?); 2 grape bunches; strawberry plant; table with 2 bee skeps & 6 bees; downhill mountain goat; swan on pond; wild turkey (?); branch with 5 five petal flowers (jasmine?); man in hat, gun under arm & dead rabbit; butcher with sausages & butcher's block; short-skirted woman (man in skirted coat?) in kitchen with posnet, dead fowl & a fish in each hand & utensil rack (?). American (?), or European for American market, 3-5/8" L x 4-7/8" W, cookies 1-5/16" x 1-1/4". Metal is 1/8" + thick, mounted to board almost 5/8" thick, prob. 1840 to 1860. The originals of these molds were probably carved wood, used to make casting models for metal molds. The cast metal ones, whether zinc or iron, reveal their carved wood origins. Price range for old ones: **$150-$175**

Springerle mold, cast pewter mold mounted to wooden back for stability, 12 rectangular designs include people, plants & animals, European, 7-1/2" x 4-1/2", 19th C (?). **$165-$175**

IV-335. All cast metal springerle. *Probably cast pewter. 7-1/2" H, with musical, fruit, and household scenes. Note woman arranging flowers, 3rd down on far right. Late 19th C.* **$125-$175**

Springerle mold, heavy cast metal, probably zinc, makes 15 individual cookies to be cut or broken apart, designs are laid out 3 across x 5 down, & include house with well; dog; church; another church; bird; grapes; raspberries; 2 bee skips on outdoor table; elk (?); duck in pond; heron; berries; hunter with gun & rabbit; man cooking over gypsy kettle with hanging implements; woman holding something in one hand (broom?) & something unidentifiable in other hand, motifs could be English, American or German, 5-3/4" H x 3-1/2", mid 19th C. (?) This old one is not cast aluminum. **$240-$300**

Springerle mold, unidentified heavy cast metal, rectangle divided into 6 pieces including 2 birds on branches; perky flower; odd domed building; building with thing on top like TV aerial but possibly a lighthouse; and something like a mug on top of a drum; all these descriptions are based on a picture in a 1917 ad of imported metal molds brought into NYC by Otto Thurnauer, German, c.1917. Turn-of-century dealer Thurnauer lists seven rectangular or square molds, five oval ones and three rounds. Are the old oval ones the cast iron ovals with single designs seen in such quantity at antique shows in late 1980s? See also cookie mold. (**NOTE:** The Thurnauer firm still imports kitchen things — I bought a tin mold recently with their stamp.) **$100-$150**

Springerle mold, cast iron, 12 squares laid out 3 across by 4 down, each square slightly irregular in outline, depicts basket with 3 apples; pear with 2 leaves; turkey or peacock; cornucopia; bird in branch; oak leaves with acorn; fruit tree branch; horseshoe with blacksmith's hammer; large bird (parrot?) standing on branch; tall bushel basket with apples; grape leaves, a high cross; a stunning collection of images, European or American, each cookie would be about 1-1/8" x 1-3/4", mid (?) 19th C. **$250-$400**

Springerle molds — See also cake boards; cookie molds; pretzel mold

Springerle roller or rolling pin, carved drum (or barrel) about 3" L, with two turned handles about 3-3/4" L. Design of roses & leaves. Marked "J. Conger," one of only two Conger examples of this form that I have record of. The other appears on p.110 of *America Eats* by William Woys Weaver and belongs to the Henry Francis du Pont Winterthur Museum. Its design is also of roses and leaves, with a decorative edging motif on both ends of the barrel comprised of a sort of lacy border on either side of a narrow band of dots. That one is 12-3/8" L overall, 3" diameter. (**NOTE:** See the cake board listings for a lot more on Conger. For using a springerle roller, see the recipe above for "Sprengerlie.") **$700-$1000**

Springerle rolling pin, carved wood, relatively fat short barrel divided into 16 segments with flowers, animals, butterfly, fruit, other designs, yellow painted wood handles, American or European import?, c.1930s. (With original cookbooklet, maybe a bit more.) **$45-$55**

Springerle rolling pin, carved wooden wheel in slingshot-like handle, pineapples & leaves, with metal pin axle, German (?), 5-1/2" L, 19th C. Look for well carved designs, in unusual subjects, just as you would for butter molds. Rarest are those with 4 or 5 different designs, not a band of repeats. Look also for well-formed handles, old patina (butter & age contribute), condition and size. **More Lookalikes**. Almost all seen at recent shows are repeat patterns, rather simply (that is to say quickly & commercially) machine-carved, and in pale unpatinated wood; these are 20th C., perhaps country-look reproductions. Cumberland General Store has one with 16 pictures "deeply carved," and a "hard maple barrel with natural polished lacquer finish. Enameled handles . . . ivory or yellow." This new one about $10. Old ones: **$55-$80**

IV-336. Commercial quality carved wood springerle boards. (**L**) *"Wooden cake prints or Springerle Moulds," 6 prints to block, available "plain" or "fancy" (I don't know which this is), Ritzinger, Grasgreen c.1906-07.* (**M**) *One of several designs, which could be had on boards with from 2 to 12 designs, for from 15¢ to 80¢ each.* (**R**) *More fully detailed round designs on bigger board, but price was still under 80¢. Both from Jaburg catalog, 1908. Collector value now is higher than it should be for something mass-produced and machine carved.* **$35-$150**

IV-337. Another commercial springerle, *carved wood. With from 1 to 12 pictures, costing wholesale, from $2.50 to $8.64 a dozen!!! S. Joseph, c.1927.* **$35-$150**

IV-338. Springerle rolling pins & cake marker. *Some called "New Year's or Springerle Rolling Pins."* (**1**) *Top one has 12 designs, from Middleby, 1927.* (**2**) *has many designs, this one has 24, the picture cheats a bit on perspective. Jaburg Bro., 1908.* (**3-L**) *and* (**4-R**) *from Germany. All late 19th C to early 20th. No way to know how long a pattern could have been made in the same way.* **$130-$200**

280

IV-339. Whatsit press mold — for tortillas? *All wood, bent & carved. 16" L x 6-7/8" diameter. Practically without mark or stain, none inside, so probably not used. No drainage holes for cheese. No bloodstains, so not for meat patties. Collection of Meryle Evans.* **$25-$45**

IV-342. Vegetable cutters. *Three more sets, in round tin boxes. Top 2 sets are from S. Joseph. 1-1/2" cutters; and 2" cutters. Bottom set of 12 cutters, very like others, is in a tin box only 3-1/2" across. "Can use either end of cutters." This was given as a subscription premium for 1930* American Cookery *magazine.* **$20-$55**

IV-340. Vegetable cutters. *In this chapter, because while they are cutters, they are meant to create special shapes. Pieced tin. The pictures are primitive, as are many old catalog linecuts, but they show that you can cut a shamrock or 6-point star from a slice of root vegetable. Came in 20 styles, used for decorative veggies for inside molds, or for soop. F. A. Walker catalog, c.1890. SEE also IV-143. Julienne cutters are similar but are in Chapter I.* **$15-$25**

IV-343. Vegetable or "garnishing" cutters. *Also for pastry. Came in 50 patterns, in sizes 1", 1-3/16", 1-5/8", 1-3/4" and 2-1/8". Duparquet catalog. Per cutter:* **$10-$20**

IV-341. Vegetable cutters. *Set of tin cutters, showing available designs (note shamrock, etc.). Came in three sizes: 7/8", 1" and 1-1/4" diameter. Ordered as "macaroon cutters," the same set was made in 2" and 2-1/4" diameters. S. Joseph, c.1927. For a set:* **$35-$55**

IV-344. Nested garnish cutters. (L) *"Column cutters" or corers. Nested, tin, made in various shapes. Only about 7" H overall. F. A. Walker, c.1890s, but made before. Probably imported from France.* **(R)** *Many shapes, all geometrics. This shows the star set. For vegetables or pastries. Bertuch, c.1904.* **$25-$50**

Sugar cubes, gift box with white sugar cubes decorated in colorful sugar frosting, include candlestick, angel, snowman head, white wreath, green wreath, Christmas star, Star of Bethlehem, bells, Christmas tree, poinsettia, candy cane, praying angel & full-figure snowman, 1940s (?). **$4-$7**

Tart pan, fluted sides with ring holder, gray graniteware, only 3-3/4" D x 1-1/4" deep,19th C. **$55-$65**

Tart pan, sheet metal, "Parkersburg Iron & Steel Co., WV, turn of century. **$18-$25**

Tart pan or muffin pan, cast iron, 7 shallow cups in 4 shapes, including plain, fluted and with star in center, rounded hexagonal in shape with side handles, called a "four season pan," but there don't seem to be leaves in the design or snowflakes, don't know maker, sold through Cumberland General Store catalog, 9" diameter, 1980s. **$15-$20**

Tart pan or muffin pan, cast iron, 11 shallow turban mold cups, cut out between cups, maker or mark not known, sold in Cumberland General Store catalog, 9-1/2" L x 6" W, 1980s. **$15-$20**

Tart sealer, cast aluminum with wooden knob, spring-loaded action works scalloped inner ring to seal the tart while outer ring cuts round outline. Could be used for ravioli or tortellini too. Marked "Tart Master," approx. 4" diameter, pat'd 1938. A new "Tartmaster" [one word] was being made in the 1970s (still may be); looks the same except that knob is now a metal cap. Directions read "Roll out a sheet of dough, place small mounds of filling at regular intervals, cover with a second layer and then, with a quick push of plunger, punch out tarts or ravioli." **$8-$15**

Tortilla iron, looks like a cast iron stovetop waffle iron, low frame with very flared base, cutout short side handle like a skillet's, hinged press with long iron rod handle, used like a waffle iron only it bakes a thin cornmeal batter to make one tortilla at a time, not marked, American, or poss. Mexican?, 1870s to 1900. These were probably made in cast iron up to the 1960s or 1970s, then in cast aluminum, worth considerably less to collectors. **$45-$65**

Truffle cutter — See canape or truffle cutters this chapter; also julienne cutter in Chapter I

Vegetable cutters, for garnishes, small round tin box with 10 tiny, very fancy tin cutters with reinforced edges, designs include fleur-de-lis, rosettes, scrolls, & forms that look heraldic, "J. Y. Watkins," a house-furnishing shop in NYC that began in the 1830s when Watkins set up as a tinsmith. By the late 19th C., the firm was a wholesale supplier, and most likely an importer of European kitchen items. Can-like box for cutters only 4-1/2" diameter, c.1870s-1890s. Importer F. A. Walker advertised a single deep-cutting vegetable cutter, tin, flat back, in one of the almost figural "heraldic" designs found in the Watkins box. No size is given, but Walker was in business from the 1870s probably to c.1900. These could also be used for cutting out shapes in very firm jellies that would be used to decorate galantines or to insert in jelly molds before pouring another color of jelly. **$45-$65**

Vegetable or rice mold — See molds, tin

Vienna baker — See roll pan

IV-345. Vienna roll stamp, *for making vienna rolls the right way, marked in 5 sections. "May also be used for hot cross buns." Used when the yeast dough is "half proved." You mark them, turn them over, wash with water, and bake. Hueg, c.1905.* **$15-$20**

WAFER IRONS & WAFFLE IRONS

These are easy to tell apart. Wafers are "wafer thin," more or less crisp; waffles are thicker and "waffled" with a grid of little "niches" — square or other shape, such as hearts or diamonds — in an all-over pattern. Early wafer irons and early waffle irons both may have long handles, called reins. In fact, some twentieth-century wafer & pizzelle irons also have long reins. Wafer irons make one, round wafer at a time, whereas waffle irons may make just one, or make several break-apart waffles that are divided into wedges or squares or hearts, etc. In addition, there are "Hotel Waffle Irons," for hotels, restaurants or even large boarding houses, that were large two-burner cast iron rectangular frames, in which three or more 2-plate hinged "pans" making 3 small waffles each were arranged so they could be flipped individually to match orders. Other hotel irons were large oval or rectangular frames to fit over two burners or range eyes, which made six or more breakapart cakes.

Wafer types. We are accustomed to seeing pictures of round wafer irons with ecclesiastical or eagle and star motifs; the former probably used for religious ceremonies or occasions. Political or patriotic ones are harder to relegate, and yet there are proportionately many of them. (Perhaps some are skilled 1876 reproductions?). Albert H. Sonn, in his three-volume *Early American Wrought Iron,* NY: 1928, wrote that wafer irons were "used in making of holiday or wedding wafers": those with heart and flower motifs were probably for weddings. (Early heart-shaped waffle irons with reins probably were too.) Dr. Henry Mercer's "Wafer Irons," an article in Vol. V, Bucks County Historical Society publications, 1920, outlines **six types of wafers**: **(1)** ecclesiastical, **(2)** domestic, **(3)** documentary, **(4)** medicinal, **(5)** fish, and **(6)** confectioner wafers. This was related by Richard H. Shaner in his fact-filled article "Waffles and Wafers," *Pennsylvania Folklife,* Summer 1962, Vol. XII, No. 4, pp. 20-23. Shaner adds that the ecclesiastical ones were probably most common, because they were still being used in the twentieth century. He wrote that in 1920, "there were still Catholic churches in the area [Pennsylvania Dutch country] which were still making wafers from 18th century styled wafer irons." An extensive collection of wafer irons can be seen at the Mercer Museum (which you'll love for many reasons) in Doylestown, PA.

Lava wafers. A letter from John W. Wells to the *New York Pennsylvania Collector* in June 1984 relates a fascinating fact. In the early nineteenth century and for many years thereafter, American and English families made the "Grand Tour" of Europe, and included a climb of Mt. Vesuvius, from which molten lava would be descending in rivulets. According to Mr. Wells, some guides would "lift up a gob of moten lava with his 'wafer iron' . . . squeeze it for a moment, and out would drop a small slab of congealed, glistening lava bearing the impression of the iron." He has one about 3" x 4", a quarter of an inch thick, that reads "Salvatore Madonna" on one side and "1832" on the other.

Wafer irons are also called oble irons (probably from the German *oblaten,* or else an example of a phenomenon in the English language, of a dropped "n" word, in this case noble iron. Another example is the word apple, which was originally napple).

Goffering or gauffre irons or goofer irons. This use of the word goffer was a big surprise to me, because I never heard the term goffering iron used for anything but a ruffle-ironing implement used in the laundry. But in Silas Bent's *Machine Made Man* (Farrar & Rinehart, 1930), p. 26, is the following: "there were toasters, and boat-shaped troughs wherein coffee could be ground with two handled discs. And for pastries there were 'goffering irons.' These were stands bearing metal pods with removable discs, which could be heated in the coals; then replaced, they heated the metal so that pastry could be ironed over it." In a way this makes sense, if you think how wafers were first rolled into a conical shape to receive ice cream. Other words, in corrupted French or -?- are gaufriers, or gaufrettes, or goffer, and the word oublie for the wafer itself (related to German Oble). **Or Vice Versa**. To further confuse things, some nineteenth-century catalogs, from which storekeepers could order, used "Gauffre Irons" to mean waffle irons, along with "Wafer Irons" for those. See also the lengthy section on ice cream in this chapter.

WAFER IRONS:

Wafer iron, for hearth, cast & forged iron, intaglio design of heart within rectangular frame of criss-crossed lines, <u>long handles called reins</u>, marked "S. M. /ID ED," American, 5" x 8" head, 31-1/2" L overall, dated 1787. Originally in the Keillor Collection. **$1000-$1500**

Wafer iron, for hearth, with **13 stars** : I reported this in the last edition, fully believing that I had seen one and carefully counted the stars. I checked all my files and was unable to come up with original source documentation. Advanced collector Joel Schiff wrote me regarding this: "I have seen seven or eight of these, in three different styles. All had 16 stars. If this is a legitimate wafer iron, it would be very very rare, and probably worth significantly more than the 16 star variety."

Wafer iron, for hearth, cast iron, Great Seal of the U.S. design with eagle & shield with **16 stars**, "lips" or head 5-1/4" diameter, overall length 27-1/2", long rein handles, American (?) (Tennessee was admitted in 1796, and the 17th state, Ohio, in 1803.) However, as Joel Schiff wrote me, "While clearly not made before 1796, the 16 star types may have been made primarily in England, up to and even after the war of 1812, as an export item." One such iron was advertised in 1984 bearing the makers' mark "POPE & JONES" in a small oval, near where the each rein handle is joined to its disc. **$1000-$1200**

Dating by the Stars: <u>Antiquastrology</u>. There was never, officially, a flag with 16 stars, but at one time there were only 16 states. The state was Tennessee, and it was the 16th state from 1796 to 1803, when Ohio became the 17th state. There were <u>13 stars</u> to the first American flag, under the First Flag Act of 1777 and back to 13 stars on coins from the 1820s, 1830s, 1850s, 1860s and 1890s; there were <u>12 stars</u> in the Bon Homme Richard flag of 1779; there were <u>15 stars</u> in the flag under the Second Flag Act in 1795 and 15 stars on 1794 and 1797 Liberty coins; and <u>20 stars</u> in the design under the Act of 1818. This is useful information so far as it goes. Check a world almanac or encyclopedia if you are trying to determine origins or dates from the number of stars on a piece. Even then it could be a commemorative or patriotic piece that refers back to a date or period, rather than contemporaneous to it.

Wafer iron, for hearth, cast iron plates (sometimes called <u>lips</u>), long forged iron reins or handles, with figure 8 loop attached to one, a knob on other, the plates with finely detailed eagle & striped shield with **16 stars**, "E Pluribus Unum" in ribbon banner in eagle's mouth, one foot holding 8 arrows, one holding olive branch, American, 6-1/2" diameter, 31-7/8" L, c.1796 to 1803 or later. **$1200-$1500**

Wafer iron, for hearth, cast iron with forged reins, flower surrounded by concentric rings, American, 28" L, c.1800. **$300-$500**

Wafer iron, for hearth, forged iron with brass stamps inside the "lips" to ensure very fine detailing in finished wafers, & fast even heating, American or English, 2-1/2" x 4-1/2" wafer disks, and 14-1/2" L handles, 18th C or very early 19th C. **$250-$300**

Wafer iron, cast iron, hinged, on base, plates decorated with flowers & cornucopia, Wagner, 6-1/2" D iron, 9" D base, 1892. **$150-$200**

"Sweet Wafers. Two ounces of butter, half a pound of sugar, half a pound of flour, five eggs, beaten separately. Bake in wafer-irons well greased, and roll over a knife." Mrs. A. P. Hill, *Mrs. Hill's New Family Receipt Book*, NY: 1870.

• • • •

"Almond Wafers. Ingredients, 1/2 lb. of sweet almonds, 1/4 lb. of sifted sugar, 1 oz. of flour, and 2 eggs. Blanch and cut the almonds small, moisten them with the yolks and whites of eggs previously beaten. Sift into them the sugar and the flour, and mix the whole together with two drops of essence of lemon peel. Lightly butter a clean tin [apparently a square or rectangular baking pan], and spread the mixture over it as thin as possible. Bake it a light brown, and cut it with a knife, before it is cold, into long squares; roll them immediately on pieces of wood, to make them round and hollow. They are usually served to garnish creams." Webster & Parkes, *An Encyclopaedia of Domestic Economy*, 1848 NY edition of 1845 English book.

IV-347. Waffle-wafer iron detail. *Showing mold head only. Cast iron, forged iron handles. Commonly found, but quite appealing, an iron with rectangular heads for making a sort of waffled wafer combo. Thicker than wafers. 6 designs. Note bird in tree and various flowers. This one marked "H. & M." Others have been brought back from German trips, and found with no marks. Iron expert Joel Schiff says this is "generally thought of as Swiss."* **$125-$175**

IV-346. Wafer iron detail. *Wafer irons were used to make thin, crisp cookies called wafers. Cast iron, wrought handles. Eagle with shield body and 13 stars, possibly as early as 1800. 27-1/2" L x 5-1/4" diameter, American. Ex-Keillor Collection.* **$1200-$1500**

IV-348. Wafer iron detail. *Cast & wrought iron. Note design with wreath of leaves around border, and the sort of urn or vase design with stylized flowers. This one is usually known by collectors as the "Easter Lily" pattern. Compare with next picture. This photograph courtesy of the National Museum of American History, Smithsonian Institution.* **$150-$200**

IV-349. Waffle iron & wafer iron & detail. *Cast heads, long wrought handles called reins — note clips at end that hold the two handles together.* **(T)** *Simple waffle iron at top, 6" x 3-1/2" head.* **(B-L)** *&* **(B-R)** *this one particularly interesting because by blowing up the small, small picture in the Duparquet catalog, c.1904-10, I saw that the design of wreath and urn is the same as the Smithsonian one, which may help bracket the date from mid-19th C. to as late as the early 20th C.* **$100-$200**

IV-350. Gauffre & wafer irons. *Probably similar combination as the previous picture, the rectangular one making a waffle, or "gauffre" in France. William Adams & Son, London, c.1860-61 ad.* **$100-$200**

Wafer iron, cast iron, "Kornu Kopia Krum Kake" by Andresen, Minneapolis, MN, early 20th C. Ornate scross design on both sides, with center cartouche containing name. Meant to set down in low or high cast iron, 2-handled frame to set over heat source (high frame if gas, low if wood). These were meant to be removed from the iron when baked (a couple of minutes) and quickly rolled into a cone or a "cornucopia" using a separate tool that's an iron cone with a handle — looks like a gardener's dibble or planting stick.   **$75-$95**

Wafer iron, nickeled cast iron, floral wreath design inside plates, long rod-like reins, meant to be used in a frame with a sort of "frying pan" handle, just like a waffle iron of the period. Wagner #1451, Sidney, OH, c.1920s.   **$150-$200**

WAFER IRONS called Pizzelle irons:

Wafer iron, of type called a <u>pizzelle iron</u>, for hearth although modern, cast iron, with long handles, rectangle with diamond pattern waffling, Baccellieri Brothers Mfg. Co., Philadelphia, 20th C. These were made in iron up to 1950 or so, thereafter in aluminum. A pizzelle is an Italian hazlenut or anisette wafer that looks like a lacy doily when sprinkled with confectioners' sugar after baking.   **$35-$70**

Wafer or pizzelle iron, for hearth though modern, cast steel, rectangular, long handles, Ciunta Brothers, Philadelphia, 20th C.   **$35-$70**

Wafer or pizzelle iron, for hearth, forged iron long handles, cast iron plates with simple waffling criss-cross design, 23" L, late 19th C. or maybe early 20th C.   **$75-$100**

WAFFLE IRONS, for hearth:

Waffle iron, for hearth, cast iron heart-shaped head, forged reins & catch to hold ends together while baking, heart-shaped waffles, no mark, American, 21-1/2" L x 5-1/4" W, early 19th C.   **$275-$700**

Waffle iron, for hearth, cast iron, hinged 2-part with long handle, one part has small 1/8" lip that holds other half more securely in place, head is lovely 12-scallop edged circle, which when waffles are broken apart reveal that they form 6 hearts, simple waffling pattern, prob. American, 10-5/8" diameter head, 20-1/2" L overall, 19th C.   **$300-$500**

Waffle iron, for hearth, cast iron with forged iron handle, the iron is star-shaped, with small stars within the waffling grids. These small stars look punched; ironware collector Joel Schiff believes they were swaged: that is, while the cast iron was hot (or after reheating), the waffling grid was hammered on a sort of miniature anvil-like <u>swage block</u> with a small star design. I'm not sure the apparent accurately placed stars could have been achieved that way. American, prob. PA German, 6-1/2" diameter waffle, 34-1/4" L overall, late 18th C. Ex-Robacker, $1550.   **$1200-$1600**

Waffle iron, for hearth, cast iron with long forged iron handle, bottom part is pan-like, flattish lid, nice arrow-like hinge details, unusual patterns — top & bottom both have 4 different waffling patterns, almost a sampler of waffle patterns, no marks, American (?), waffling iron is 6-1/8" x 8-1/4" and bottom section is about 1-1/4" deep, overall length with handle is 27-1/8", early 19th C.   **$350-$450**

Waffle iron, for hearth, forged handles, cast rectangular iron, simple grid, American (?), 31-1/2" L, early 19th C.   **$75-$150**

Waffle iron, for hearth, forged iron handles, cast iron mold, beautiful decoration along top edge of one half of the mold's back depicts 2 Hessian soldiers on horses, & a pine tree, inside is a simple waffling grid, no maker's mark, American. Head is 6" W x 4-1/4" H, overall 26" L looks 18th C., but some Chathams resemble this.   **$250-$500**

Waffle iron, for hearth, long forged iron reins & rectangular plates with diamond waffle grid, "scissor" or pivot point levered handles rather than type with hinged head. Marked "Chatham," (probably B & W Co., or B. W. Co.), Chatham, -?- (Chathams in GA, CT, IL, IA, KY, MA, PA, NY, NC, VA), 24-1/2" L, early 19th C. **$135-$175**

Waffle iron, for hearth, heart-shaped cast iron head or mold, long forged reins with very small knobs on ends, simple waffling pattern, no mark, American, 31" L x 7" W, 18th C. **$350-$500**

IV-351. "Waffle furnace." *Of range-top type. Cast iron, with removable iron and handled low frame. This one is "A very ingenious article, making four good-sized waffles with less labor than is required in making one with the ordinary iron" [ie. the long handled kind]. From* American Home Cook Book, *1854. The artist drew the grid sketchily.* **$65-$100**

IV-352. Slightly later stove top waffle iron. *Cast iron 4 designs — hearts, diamonds, squares, X'es. Maker unknown. The linecut shows that each rectangular waffle has a different pattern on front and back. Ad of J. & C. Berrian, wholesalers & retailers of house furnishings, NYC. 1857 ad.* **$100-$200**

IV-353. Waffle irons. (T) *This is, as the catalog states, a "square" iron, for stove tops. For 1, 2 or 4 cakes. Similar to IV-352, but not as nice because it only has diamonds & rounds.* **(B)** *round, low frame, flipped with lid lifter tool. Four sizes (6" x 7", 7" x 8", 8" x 9" and 9" x 10" — sizes which I think refer to the diameter of the iron and then the frame) were offered by Stuart Peterson, 1875 and Leibrandt & McDowell Stove, 1861.* **$100-$200; $45-$55**

"Rice Waffles. Boil half a pint of rice and let it get cold, mix with it one-fourth pound butter and a little salt. Sift in it one and a half pints flour, beat five eggs separately, stir the yolks together with one quart milk, added whites beaten to a stiff froth, beat hard, and bake at once in waffle-irons." Mrs. S. C. Lee of Baltimore, in *Practical Housekeeping*, 1884.

Waffle iron, for hearth, rectangular cast iron head has rows of small dimpled squares for grid (looks like aerial view of city streets, from 10 miles up), set at right angles to long wrought reins, one ending with knob, other with free-moving loop to work as catch, marked "B. W. Co." also "Chatham" (see another above), approx. 15" L overall, head 6" x 4", early 19th C. "At auctions kitchen furniture is popularly supposed to go for a song . . . these things are usually sold in lots and a person needing a waffle-iron and muffin rings may find himself in possession of coal skuttles and dish-pans." *Appleton's Home Books*, 3 volumes, NY, 1881, 1884. **$135-$175**

WAFFLE IRONS, range or stove top:

Waffle iron, cast aluminum, handle replaced with piece of heavy black insulated cable, lid has smiling sun face, waffling pattern comprised of 6 stars & a crescent moon in each waffle, slightly corroded, "Mazie Lee," 8-1/8" diameter, 20th C. **$70-$90**

Waffle iron, cast aluminum high frame, multipurpose outfit that makes waffles & if you use the frame with omelette pans, it cooks eggs too. Wagner Ware #8, 20th C. **$140-$165**

Waffle iron, cast aluminum, oblong, makes 2 rectangular waffles, very simple grid with squares with a dimple in each, short stubby black painted wood handles, "Waffle Iron For Armstrong Table Stove," S. S. Co., Huntington, WV, 6-1/4" x 5-1/4" exclusive of handles, which are 3" L, early 20th C. (I'm not sure what S. S. is, but an interior pattern on another waffle iron, that looks like SS, was made by John Savery's Son & Co., of NYC.) **$30-$40**

Waffle iron, high frame, cast iron, Wagner Ware #7. **$140-$155**

Waffle iron, cast iron, hearts, diamonds, flowers, low frame, 2-part mold, long forged iron handles, Warnick & Leibrandt 8, 9", Philadelphia, PA, 3rd quarter 19th C. (This may be a long-handled conversion from their more commonly-made stove top irons.) **$75-$100**

Waffle iron, hinged waffle part only, frame missing, cast iron, turned black painted short wood handles, grid of 4 simple parts, "Crescent Waffle #8," Fanner & Co., Cleveland, OH, late 19th C. **$35-$55**

Waffle iron, rectangular 2-part hinged mold that sets into 4-legged frame with side handle, makes 3 waffles with patterns of little squares, little diamonds & little hearts, maker not marked, American, 5" H x 8" L x 5" W, c.1870s. **$125-$140**

Waffle iron, sits over range eye, 2 big looped bail handles, 4 waffling patterns, hearts, stars, diamonds & rounds, hinge is gorgeous cast leaf, New England Butt Co., Providence, RI, 9-3/4" diameter, makes 7" diameter waffles, mid 19th C. New England Butt Co., who were named for the butt hinges they made for doors, also made the various iron wares of Nathaniel Waterman. **$175-$225**

Waffle iron, square, cast iron, on low stand or frame (worth more than the high frame #11), 4-square waffling grids, Griswold #11 — "The American Waffle Iron," early 20th C. **$150-$170**

Waffle iron, stove top, cast iron, heart & star motif to grid, bail handle on frame, coiled heat dissipating handle on hinged mold, Griswold #18, pat'd May 18, 1920 & July 11, 1922. **$175-$200**

Waffle iron, cast iron, "X" geometric pattern with name inside, "Giles F. Filley," St. Louis, MO, prob. 3rd quarter 19th C. **$95-$125**

Waffle iron, cast iron, mfd. by Bridge & Beach Stove Co., dated 1865, but poss. made over long period. **$85-$150**

Here's what Mrs. S. C. Lee of Baltimore, wrote in her 1884 *Practical Housekeeping* about waffle irons: "The waffle iron is a very peculiar machine. The waffle is put in, locked up, baked on one side to a lovely brown, turned over, prison and all, until the other side is a still lovelier brown, and then released steaming hot ready for the table."

Waffle iron, cast iron, mfd. by Bridge & Beach Stove Co., dated 1865, but poss. made over long period. **$85-$150**

Waffle iron, cast iron, 2 parts & four plates — called a "waffle twin," hinged iron fits over range eye, makes 5 sectioned waffles, marked only "No. 14," American, 11-1/2" diameter, makes 8-1/4" waffles, 19th C. (**NOTE:** The regular home style worth $35-$60.) **$190-$270**

Waffle iron, cast iron, 2-piece with bail handle, Wagner Ware, 1920. An ad in the Dec. 10, 1892, *The Metal Worker*, claims that Wagner had just brought out in November the "only bailed and detachable hinge waffle iron in the market." Depicted in ad is a low frame mold, the socket joint hinge opposite the 2 turned wood handles, arched bail crosswise. **$35-$60**

Waffle iron, cast iron, 3 pieces, low frame with extra decorative frying pan handle, the 2-part waffle iron has openwork casting to dissipate heat, Majestic Mfg. Co., No. 885M, St. Louis, MO, 16" L with handle, pat'd 1908. (Much later, Majestic made electric waffle irons.) **$150-$200**

Waffle iron, cast iron, design of little girl & garden (Mistress Mary? Not contrary enough to not get her waffles?), 2 hinged round plates, quite possibly this was made by Stover, the windmill company, 20th C. Friend & collector Linda Fishbeck of Texas found this, the dealer said it was a waffle iron, and she didn't buy it, feeling there was something wrong about it. Sounds to me, some years later now, that it was probably just missing its frame, and that it possibly could even be late 19th C. In the future, one sure thing to look for would be the two side "pegs" that would fit into slots in the frame. **$50-$65**

IV-354. Waffle irons. *All could be flipped in their frames to evenly heat top and bottom.* (**L**) *This one in "new style," with fleur-de-lis designs, low frame for range or stove top,* (**T-R**) (**B-R**) *others with frames elevated on 3 or 4 legs, and with what were called "patent revolving" designs. All probably by Nathaniel Waterman. Russell & Erwin catalog, 1865.* (**L**) **$45-$60;** (**T-R**) **$130-$160;** (**B-R**) **$90-$130**

IV-356. Waffle iron patent. *Pat'd 8/23/1881, by Alexander S. Patton, Columbus, OH. Shows in several pictures the particular type of "hinge journal" used for turning the mold in the frame, and the upright handle that made opening the lid easy. Official Gazette of the U.S. Patent Office.*

IV-355. Waffle irons. *Stove top styles, cast iron.* (**T-L**) *Small one from Matthai-Ingram, c.1890, in sizes 6x7 to 9x10.* (**T-R**) *Big one from M. L. Filley, Troy, NY, c.1880.* (**B**) *Bottom one, with apparently fancy face that is probably just a bad drawing of diamonds, from unidentified 1880s cookbook.* **$100-$200**

IV-357. Waffle irons. *Griswold's "The New American Waffle Iron," probably both based on the 6/25/1893 patent, as described in the wholesaler's catalog.* (**T**) *High or "deep" frame, "specially adapted for vapor stoves," came in one size, "8D," with round "pan" 7-3/4" diameter, according to the Buhl catalog.* (**B**) *Low frame style came in "8" and "9," with "pan" diameters slightly less — 7-3/4" and 8-5/8", Buhl catalog, c.1912.* **$75-$100**

IV-358. Heart & star waffle irons. *Everybody wanted in on the heart act. These are Griswold's "Heart & Star Waffle irons," low and high frame, with 5 hearts surrounding a star, and a tiny star within the bigger one. The lid looks like a five-leaf clover! (NOTE: Griswold also made a 5-heart design, the lid of which looked like a 10-scallop-petaled flower, for Western Importing Co. after 1904. It had a wooden side handle, and a nifty cut-out cast iron handle on frame. It's worth under a hundred.) Cast iron, from c.1925 flyer with recipes. The handle design helped dissipate heat. The heart-star design was patented 5/18/1920 and 7/11/1922. Due to the vagaries of the Griswold collector market, the later heart-star is worth more than the earlier all heart, at least in cast iron:* **$200-$250**

IV-361. Waffle iron. *Griswold #9 "French Waffle Iron," for doing four pairs at a time. Hotel or restaurant (or large family) model. Note stubby wooden handles — short but sufficient. 22-1/2" L x 11-1/2" W, pat'd 6/29/1880. Ad in The Metal Worker, 6/20/1890.* **$1000-$1200**

IV-359. Wafer & waffle irons. *For stove top.* **(L)** *Kornu Kopia Krumb Kake wafer iron set in choice of high or low frame, with a fancy quasi-religious old-fashioned design. Note conical and cylindrical wooden rollers that came with the wafer iron, to roll the hot & still-soft wafers into cones or cylinders, for filling with ice cream.* **(R)** *5 waffles are heart-shaped. Also advertised was a brass pie trimmer with turned wood handle. Booklet from Alfred Andresen & Co., Minneapolis, c.1905. Booklet worth about $12 in ephemera market. Wafer iron (L):* **$75-$125;** *Waffle iron (R):* **$45-$65**

Waffle iron, cast iron, flower, heart & diamond design waffling plate, 2-part with stand, Francis Buckwalter & Co., Boyer's Ford, PA, pat'd Aug. 9, 1910. Also known as the "Pennsylvania card motif." **$45-$65**

Waffle iron, cast iron, frame has 2 high arched handles, hinged 2-part mold fits down in, has marvelous recipe for potato waffles in pretty hand-printed-looking letters cast intaglio on flat lid: **"Kartoffel Waffeln."** A translation of recipe: 1/2 lb. cooked grated potatoes, 1/4 lb. meal, 1/2 litre warm milk, 3 eggs, 50 grams butter, 20 grams yeast. Recipe is only marking, probably German not PA German, 11" diameter, late 19th C. **$90-$130**

Waffle iron, cast iron, high frame, Wapak #8, mfd. by William H. Howell Co., Geneva, IL, 20th C, marked with the Wapak Indian. High frames were for gas or coal or vapor stoves; low for wood. **$175-$250**

Waffle iron, cast iron, high frame, Harwi #8, American, early 20th C. **$30-$45**

Waffle iron, cast iron, high frame or base with bail handle, coiled-heat-dissipating handle on 2-part mold part, heart & star waffling pattern, Griswold #18, "928," pan: 7-3/4" D, pat'd May 18, 1920. **$160-$190**

Waffle iron, cast iron, low frame, Favorite Piqua #8, Favorite Stove & Range Co., Piqua, OH, late 19th or early 20th C. "Favorite" line introduced 1892. For crossover handle type: **$75-$100**

Waffle iron, cast iron, low frame, 2-part hinged round mold fits into it, simple grid pattern, Dover Stamping Co., about 8" diameter, c.1870s. **$75-$100**

Waffle iron, cast iron, low frame, 2 parts, hinged, 2 side handles on frame, mold divided into 4 wedges, design is fleur-de-lis & crosses, Norths, Harrison & Chase, #7, 8, Phila., late 19th C. A common pattern. **$45-$80**

Waffle iron, cast iron, low frame, 2-piece mold, coil handles, "American No. 8 885-B," Griswold Mfg. Co., pat'd Dec. 1, 1908. **WWI Waffles**. It was your patriotic duty during WWI to eat waffles. Early ads in 1918 & 1919 really pushed them as food, so that they could sell more waffle irons. What I don't understand is how they managed to get the iron to cast the waffle irons with; what about metal drives? In Sept. 1918 trade publication, *House Furnishing Review*, a Griswold ad stated "With housewives all over the country absorbed in menu problems, this is the time to feature your kitchen-ware!" Since this was aimed at retailers, they added "Our advertising, appealing to 550,000 readers, stimulates waffle-hunger." Stover, meanwhile, claimed that people were "Living on waffles." **$65-$85**

Waffle iron, cast iron, low frame with flat top, convex underside side handle, 2-part hinged waffle mold fits into this, extremely plain, not marked, American, makes 8" diameter waffle, overall length including handle 18-1/2", c. 1860s or 1870s. **$65-$75**

Waffle iron, cast iron, low frame with slightly up-angled frying pan handle, hinged round waffle mold set down inside with lifting ring upright on lid; you would need an extra tool, perhaps some kinds of stove lid lifters would work, to open it up, oh bother it all, must we have waffles again? Lid of waffle mold has beautifully crisp design of small daisy-like flower or stylized sun in center and a half-inch band of radiating lines around rim, not marked, American, frame is 9-1/2" diameter with 5-1/2" L handle, makes 6-1/2" diameter waffles, c.1870s or even 1860s. From **the look of the casting**, my hunch is this was cast by a stove maker, probably in Troy or Albany, NY, and possibly as early as the 1850s. There was a waffle iron patented by C. Swartwout of Troy, NY, Aug. 24, 1869. A really early waffle iron patent was a design patent granted Nathaniel Waterman of Boston, on July 5, 1853, but this isn't his. There were, I believe, no more than 5 waffle iron patents, including a design patent, granted before 1873. But I'm sure that many waffle irons were made, especially simple ones to go with specific ranges or stoves, without a pat'd design. **$65-$100**

Waffle iron, cast iron, low frame with very wide flange to accommodate a variety of range eyes, frying pan handle, 2-part, hinged mold has no handles but for a little tab with hole for lifting tool, hearts, diamonds, rosettes, circles and Xs — what the dealer called "Deck of Cards" pattern, more commonly known among collectors as the "Pennsylvania card pattern," Orr, Painter & Co., No. 6-7, Reading, PA, mold is 5-15/16" diameter, turn of century. Another, slightly larger, marked No. 7-8, with broken hinge, was priced $25. What use is a broken one? **$35-$45**

IV-362. Waffle irons. *All multiple range eye frames.* **(T-R)** *by John Van Range Co., Cincinnati, 8" and 9" made "to fit on all our Pacific, Maggie, Chimney Corner, and No. 130 Single Oven Ranges, but no other range." Of course they thought this meant people would want their waffle iron so much that they'd buy the range too — but that's a poor marketing strategy!* **(L)** *Griswold #7, 17-3/4" L x 7-1/2". Came in three sizes, this one the smallest. #9 was 21" L. The littlest kids in the family probably begged for the "ends." 1909 catalog.* **(B-R)** *Griswold #00, 10-1/4" x 7-3/4", makes 6 waffles with waffling patterns in hearts, squares, diamonds and rounds.* **$65-$75; $750-$1000; $525-$650**

IV-363. Waffle iron. *"Yum Yum" waffle iron, a Griswold hotel iron, the nickname was the cataloguers' (Albert Pick, 1909). While the "French" one sat over a stove, this one has its own stove. Other irons, say those from the "French," would fit this frame also. Three sizes: 2 pans, 4" diameter, frame 14-1/2" x 11-1/2"; or 3 pans, 4" pans, 20" L x 11-1/2" frame; or 4 pans in 22-1/2" x 11-1/2" frames. Pat'd 1901, 190-?* **$750-$950**

Waffle iron, cast iron, low frame with wide flange, longish "frying pan" handle, mold is hinged, 2-part with no handle, 4 designs: heart with 3 small diamonds inside; simple scrolls with 3 small diamonds between; 5 radiating broken lines; and a pattern of rather widely spaced small diamonds. Top mold has same 4 designs, only they're rotated 90¡ on the axis so that each waffle would have different patterns front & back. Lid has small iron ring near edge for lifting with small pot hook, unfortunately this has no mark at all but probably is the same as the marked "Augur & Lord" in next listing, American, 8" diameter, 9-1/2" L handle on frame, mid to 3rd quarter 19th C. **$120-$150**

Waffle iron, cast iron, round, 3 parts: flanged frame, hinged mold making 4 wedge waffles decorated with small: hearts, diamonds, scrolls, ridged rayed lines. Augur & Lord, Chester, CT, 8" diameter mold, mid to 3rd quarter 19th C. **$120-$150**

Waffle iron, cast iron, low frame with wire bail handle, coiled wire "Alaska" handles that kept cool by dissipating heat, simple waffling pattern. Base also was available with short cast "frying pan" handle. Griswold #8, Erie, PA, 2-part pan with 7-3/4" diameter, frame 10" diameter, makes 7-1/4" diameter waffle, c.1926. **$65-$85**

Waffle iron, cast iron, medium high frame with 2-part waffler, makes 4 small waffle wedges with pattern of fleur-de-lis & crosses, North, Chase & North, # 6, 7, Philadelphia, 5-3/4" diameter, 11-3/4" L with handle, late 19th C. Common pattern. **$55-$80**

Waffle iron, cast iron, range top, very low frame with flat rim, frying pan side handle, 2-part hinged mold fits into it, nice casting of scrolly wreath around center design of concentric rings on lid, American, 8" diameter, 14" L overall, marked "8/9/1910." Common pattern. **$40-$50**

Waffle iron, cast iron, range top, very low frame with frying pan handle, 2-part hinged mold, Orr Painter & Co. 7 & 8, Reading, PA, makes 6-3/4" diameter waffle,13" L overall with handle, 19th C. Common pattern. **$35-$45**

"Among **iron goods used in the kitchen** are frying pans, waffle-irons, roll-pans, griddles for batter cakes, large iron pots, etc. Sometimes some of these things are so highly polished that they only require to be washed in soap and water and rubbed dry . . . Griswold's American Waffle-irons are most satisfactory. They are comparatively new." Maria Parloa, *Kitchen Companion*, Boston: Estes & Lauriat, 1887. The text illustration is of a cast iron waffle iron, low frame, short "frying pan" handle with hanging hole, hinged mold has very short handles, the baking surfaces divided into 4 parts with simple waffling pattern of small raised square blocks with dimples.

Waffle iron, cast iron, round, 3 parts, wide flanged low frame with "frying pan" handle, hinged mold making 4 waffles in different patterns: small outlined hearts, small diamonds, small squares with pattern that could be interpreted as "SS" on surface, & small circles with pebbled surface, 8" diameter x 15" L with handle, John Savery's Son & Co., NYC, NY, c.1880s. (See also the waffle iron above for Armstrong Table Stove.) **$50-$75**

Waffle iron, cast iron, round (despite measurements given in their catalog, as transcribed below), 3-part with low frame with side frying pan handle, 2-part hinged mold fits into it, Matthai-Ingram Co., came in 4 sizes: 6" x 7", 7" x 8", 8" x 9" and 9" x 10", c.1890s. **$45-$55**

Waffle iron, cast iron, round head with 6-pointed PA German flowers on one side & waffled grid on other, no maker mark, prob. PA, 20th C. **$25-$45**

Waffle iron, cast iron, round or square high frame, Wagner Ware #8, turn of century. Round: **$50-$75**. Square: **$125-$145**

Waffle iron, cast iron, short-handled, makes 5 heart-shaped waffles, riveted-on leather handles probably replacements,

marked "MUSTAD #4," European, inside diameter 6-1/4", handle 7" L. prob. mid to late 20th C. Joel Schiff believes this is still in production. **$35-$55**

Waffle iron, cast iron, small flared, wide-flanged frame, hinged 2-part mold, wood handles, "Buster Waffle No. 8" cast in script on lid, depicts Buster Brown facing his dog Tige, who sits up to get treat. Mfd. by Andrew M. Anderson & Co., Chicago, pat'd 11/13/1906. One is depicted in Steve Stephens' "Cast Iron Cookware News," Nov. 1990 issue; it has coiled-wire, heat-dissipating handles. **$450-$600**

Waffle iron, cast iron turntable style, heart pattern waffling plates, Alfred Andresen & Co., 20th C. Common pattern. **$35-$45**

Waffle iron, cast iron, frame that sets over range is rounded corner square, but the waffling plate is rectangular and divided into three breakapart "gridded fields" per plate with 3 different waffle designs — hearts, squares, diamonds, Griswold #1, c. 1890s-1930s. (**NOTE:** The Griswold #2 is similar, only slightly smaller, and also makes 3 breakapart waffles with three patterns (front and backs different) and it's worth about $600-$800. The Griswold #0, slightly larger than the #1, makes four cakes, in 4 different breakapart waffles, in 4 designs: hearts, diamonds, squares, circles. It is worth about $500-$700.) **$450-$700**

Waffle iron, cast iron, elongated oval frame with long oval hinged waffle pan, divided into 10 breakapart waffles — the curved ends were divided into two wedges with rounded edges, and the central section made 6 oblong waffles. Hearts, squares, diamonds and circles. Griswold #7, pan is 17-3/4" L x 7-1/2" W, and most waffles are 4-7/8" x 2-3/8". Turn of century. Smith & Wafford show one in their great book on Griswold, complete with simple wire hook to lift lid. Griswold made this in 3 sizes, the largest is 21" L x 9-1/2". The #7 originally cost $1.35; the #8 cost $1.60; the #9 cost $1.95. Now? Eat your heart out, Standard & Poor! **$800-$1100**

IV-364. Waffle irons built into range. *This is a "griddle & waffle range combined," all sheet iron and cast iron. Range itself 4 feet long, with 2 waffle irons (one shown here closed, one open) and a griddle 21" square (you see corner at right). Duparquet, Huot & Moneuse, NYC, c.1904-10. Waffling patterns are hearts, diamonds, rounds & squares. The 6-waffle irons themselves would be valued at least* **$450**. *The whole set-up might be valued at more than* **$2000.**

Waffle iron, cast iron, with hearts, clubs, spades & diamonds waffling pattern, marked only "7," American, 20th C.   **$35-$45**

Waffle iron, cast iron with stand, Shapleigh #8, 20th C.   **$45-$55**

Waffle iron, cast iron with stand, "National," American, 20th C.   **$25-$40**

Waffle iron, cast iron with stand, hearts & diamonds waffling pattern, Abbott & Lawrence, 8-1/2" L, late 19th C.   **$45-$85**

Waffle iron, cast iron, with wonderful logos forming waffling pattern for 4 pie-wedge waffles, "Keen Kutter No. 8," E. C. Simmons Hardware, St. Louis, MO, 20th C. **Reproduction alert**. There are repros of this. Look closely, because it's a pretty good copy.   **$120-$150**

Waffle iron, commercial use, cast iron, makes 12 waffles, I have no idea what this looks like, having only read about it in a trade journal of 1892. Called "The Hotel Mammoth," mfd. by Stuart & Peterson Co., Philadelphia, adv'd Sept. 24, 1892, *The Metal Worker*. Collector Joel Schiff has one which he believes is twice as large (!!), and he's never seen or heard of another. I bet many of them went into war material. As a rule large commercial wares didn't get the same attention from collectors as regular family sized, or toy sized, until fairly recently. They do give you a lot of bang for your buck.   **$150-$250**

Waffles & Catfish. "Any one familiar with the suburbs of Philadelphia, may have seen at various small hotels near the Wissahickon, the notice posted in a conspicuous place, 'Catfish and Waffles.' Why such a forlorn little fish with such a repulsive name, except to Philadelphians, is associated with waffles, we are unable to discover. With flap-jack it would do very well, for what visions do flap-jacks suggest of elegant supper tables and shining silver. But the delicious waffles which are so seldom seen on private tables nowadays, bring to mind our childhood and grandmother, with her solid, old-fashioned silver, and well do we remember the little silver basket, with its equal parts of powdered sugar and cinnamon, the proper thing to spread is here offered for the benefit of those who do not know how to make these just right: 2 cups of milk; 2 eggs; 3 cups of flour; one teaspoonful of cream-tartar; one-half teaspoonful of soda; one saltspoonful of salt; one tablespoonful of melted butter." *American Agriculturist*, October 1883.

WAFFLE IRONS, electric:

Waffle iron, electric, aluminum base, chromed lid, shaped wood handles painted black, 3 Bakelite[a] or hard rubber feet, temperature dial in lid has mica covering, "Bersted Model 242," Bersted Mfg. Co., Chicago, IL, 12" overall diameter, 8-1/4" diameter grid, 1930s.   **$40-$50**

Waffle iron, electric, chrome all over except plastic side handles on octagonal base & hinged lid, various controls on base, "Wafflemaster," Waters-Genter Co., Minneapolis, MN, 1931.   **$45-$55**

Waffle iron, electric, nickeled cast metal, hinged mold raised off simple flat base, turned wooden spade handle on side, huge outlets in top & bottom plates for electric cord, General Electric Co., about 9" diameter, maybe a bit more, 1922-1923.   **$45-$55**

Waffle iron, electric, nickeled metal, fancy cutout pedestal base, side lifting handles, another handle for domed top plate of mold, "Universal," Landers, Frary & Clark, c.1920s.   **$35-$45**

Waffle iron, electric, plated metal, pedestal base, Bakelite or other phenolic resin handles, Manning-Bowman, Meriden, CT, early 20th C.   **$24-$30**

Wafflet molds: according to manufacturer the pieces in this cast aluminum set are "<u>combination rosette and patty shell</u>" molds, includes rod handle that screws into the 8 different heads — club, heart, diamond or spade rosette or patty — also available in a scalloped edge cup or flower, "Century," mfd. by U. S. Utilities, Chicago, IL, c.1933.   **$20-$30**

IV-365. **Electric waffle iron.** *One of earliest — very early 20th C. General Electric #293079. Cast iron frame and waffler. Note the spiral "cool" handles, and the two sets of screw-in power plugs that went into lightbulb sockets. Photo courtesy General Electric Corp. This is a good example of what's now being called a "tech-tique."* **$400-$500**

IV-366. **Electric waffle irons.** *Two more "tech-tiques."* (**T**) *"Westchester Automatic, Catalog #149Y183," by General Electric. Chromed finish, black enamel stripes, "old ivory marblette" handles and pendent drop handle. Fibre feet. Detachable cord. 11-3/4" diameter base. The rim you see is to catch batter overflow — great idea! From 1935-36 catalog.* (**B**) *The "Handy-hot" iron, No. 4704-H, by Chicago Electric Mfg. Co. Square overflow tray. 7-1/4" cast aluminum grids, chromium finish on outside, "rich looking walnut finished" handles. Chicago Electric catalog, 1938. Really cool Deco look.* **$80-$135**

"Gingerbread Waffles. 2 cups flour, 1 tsp ginger, 1 1/2 tsps cinnamon, 1/2 tsp salt, 1 tsp baking powder, 3/4 tsp soda, 1 cup molasses, 1/3 cup butter, 1/2 cup sour milk or buttermilk, 1 egg, well beaten. — Mix the dry ingredients. Put molasses and butter in a saucepan, let come to boil and remove from heat at once. Cool, then add milk and egg. Add mixture to dry ingredients and beat until light and smooth. Bake immediately on an Electric Waffle Iron which is not quite so hot as for ordinary waffles, for molasses burns easily. Serve with honey or sweetened whipped cream." Recipe from *"Waffles,"* Brooklyn Edison Co., Inc. Bureau of Home Economics, n.d. [c.1935 to 1940]. Included in this little booklet was information on: Saturday morning junior misses' cooking classes; how to arrange a waffle party for your club; and even Lamp Shade Making Classes. In those days, they had to urge the surge.

● ● ● ●

"A New Piece of China. The waffle plate is a great addition to the table ware. It may be had in plain china or handsomely decorated; the former costs one dollar, the latter from two to three dollars. The perforations in the top admit the escape of the steam so that the cakes may be kept warm yet free from moisture. the deep bowl gives ample space for the half-dozen circles of delicious brownness." *The Housewife*, NY, July 1891. This is a deep, widely flared bowl or dish, with perforated flat china top with knob handle.

Whatzit cutter or mold, stamped & pieced tin, partly corrugated deep sides, shaped like horseshoe & looks like a mold or some kind of cutter, "Acme Potato Implement Co.," Traverse City, MI, 1-7/8" deep, of which 3/4" is corrugated, 5" L, turn of century. **$8-$12**

Whatzit mold, or possibly something else, heavy cast iron, 3-legged, looks like a bath tub for an egg, and in fact has been advertised by at least one dealer as a toy bath tub, American, 4-3/8" L, c.1880s. **What Kind of Mold?** If this is a mold for chocolate, you would end up with only a half egg that might have to be joined to another half egg. Its weight and thickness argue against its being a chocolate mold, but stranger things have been true. I thought it was possibly something like a spoon rest when I first bought it, but that seems doubtful. **$25-$40**

Wheat stick pan, cast iron, 7 ears of wheat all same direction, two little knob feet on bottom at each end, "Puritan No. 1270," also marked #1513 on bottom, 13-1/8" L x 5-1/2" W, 20th C. **$95-$115**

Wheat stick pan, also called a wheat bread pan, cast iron, makes 6 same-direction wheat sticks showing beautifully delineated grainy head of wheat stalk. The oblong frame is cutaway around both ends of each cigar-shaped wheat stick, making a sort of thin lengthwise "rail." Marked on non-hole handle "GRISWOLD," and underneath: "No. 27, Whole Wheat Stick Pan Griswold Erie, PA., U.S.A. 638," 10-7/8" L x 5-7/8" W, 1926 on. (Another wheat stick pan, the same size, same No. 27, has on back "Wheat & Corn Stick Pan" and the well-used design patent #73,326. Griswold also made a solid-frame 7-wheat stick pan as No. 2700; and to further confuse things, there's a "Merit" 7-stick wheat pan with "No. 1270" on its back. This is a very, very exacting, precise field of collecting, and you absolutely must have *The Book of Griswold & Wagner*, by David G. Smith & Chuck Wafford. See the bibliography.) **$200-$275**

Wheat stick pan — See also corn stick pan

IV-367. "Hot Dog" patent. *This picture is from the June 1930 issue of* Science & Invention, *in their "Yankee Brains at Work" column about new inventions. This is Patent #1,742,945, issued to Peter S. Banff. "Relates to an electrical cooking device designed primarily for that type of sandwich termed 'hot dog.' However, it may be adapted for producing any article of food to which it is applicable." (The "hot dogs" on the plate look like big animal crackers, but the child appears to be eating a weiner/hot dog.) "The invention consists of an electrical cooking device with an open bottom upper casing and an open top lower casing, each adapted to contain a heating unit," and 2 facing molding plates detachably connected to the lid and the lower part of mold. Wow! Bow Wow! Wonder if it was ever made? See also IV-179.*

IV-368. Wax-flower modeling tools. *Pieced tin. This is an example of the kind of* **confusable** *item often mistaken for a cooking tool. Shown are dippers for molten wax, plus forms for cutting out petals. 19th C. Picture courtesy of the National Museum of American History, Smithsonian Institution. See also the vegetable cutters & nested cookie/cake cutters. A set approximately this size:* **$75-$125**

A FEW USES FOR CENTURY WAFFLETS

Century Wafflets can be served as wafers with hot or cold drinks. Serve with powdered sugar, Domino cinnamon sugar, maple syrup, jelly, honey, marmalade or whipped cream.

Serve them wherever toast is used—with poached eggs, spinach and egg, asparagus, creamed foods, etc.

They can be properly used for almost any part of the meal. The small Rosettes and appetizer designs form a delightful base for hors d'oeuver or canapes. Serve them instead of crackers for soup—first dust with salt or cover with grated cheese and toast in oven until hot.

For the main course, use for chicken a la king, creamed foods, etc. Place a slice of fried apple on Rosette and serve as side dish. Serve vegetables in Patty Shell. Fill Patty Shells with creamed oysters, chicken, lobster, crab meat, sweetbreads, chipped beef, mushrooms, etc.

Salads can be placed in Patty Shells or built up on the Rosettes.

Desserts can be arranged in great variety. Mince meat pies are made by placing hot mince meat between two Rosettes. Strawberries, sliced peaches, etc., can be served and decorated with whipped cream and a cherry. Custards, jellies, fresh, canned or crushed fruits, ice creams, etc., can be served over the Rosette or inside the Patty Shell.

Delicious Rosette sandwiches can be made. Marmalade or chopped preserved ginger are suggestive of many fillings.

The Heart design, with red or rose batter, is appropriate for engagement or wedding parties, or anniversaries. Also for St. Valentine parties. The Club design with green batter is ideal for St. Patrick's Day parties. The Bridge Set for Bridge parties. Butterfly design for social occasions, etc. Use them often for different parts of the meal.

File this in your 3x5 Recipe file

Century
DOUBLE PURPOSE
Wafflet Molds

COMBINATION DAINTY ROSETTES & PATTY SHELLS
(PATENTS PENDING)

Many attractive designs Including Beautiful Butterflies, Modern Rosettes and Bridge Sets.

MANUFACTURED BY
U. S. UTILITIES
2750 W. VAN BUREN ST.
CHICAGO

DAVID G. SMITH
11918 Second Street
P.O. Box B
Perrysburg, NY 14129

Advanced collector David G. Smith — **The Pan Man** — has a spectacular collection of old cast iron cookware. He also publishes the newsletter "Kettles 'n Cookware," and is co-author with Chuck Wafford of the recently released *The Book of Griswold & Wagner* (Schiffer, 1996). Mr. Smith carefully cleans, weighs, measures, catalogs and photographs each piece as it is acquired. All the photographs in this special article commissioned for this book were taken by Dave. Anyone wishing to correspond directly with him may use the address in the pan! Please use an SASE.

CAST IRON BAKING PANS
by David G. Smith

Muffin pans, gem pans, popover pans, breadstick pans, cornstick pans and French roll pans — baking pans with numerous compartments are called by many names. The names of the pans were influenced by era, culture and cookbook recipes, and then designated by the manufacturer. A *muffin* pan by one maker might be called a *gem* pan by another.

Cast iron baking pans were made in many hundreds, perhaps thousands, of foundries in the world. Some of the largest and most notable foundries that manufactured baking pans in the United States are **Wagner**, Sidney, OH; **Griswold**, Erie, PA; **Favorite Stove & Range Co. (Favorite Piqua)**, Piqua, OH; **Wapak**, Wapakoneta, OH; **R & E** (Russell & Erwin) **Mfg. Co.**, New Britain, CT; **G. F. Filley** (Excelsior Stove Works), St. Louis, MO; and **Lodge Mfg. Co.**, South Pittsburg, TN (which is still making cast iron wares). The identity of the makers of the baking pans illustrated in this article has been determined by markings on pans, reference to old trade catalogs, and/or design characteristics.

Shown here are dozens of styles and sizes, with many variations. Some are common, and some are very unusual — surviving, perhaps, in a single example.

Manufacturers:

Nathaniel Waterman and R & E Mfg. Co.

If any one person influenced the design and manufacture of baking pans, it was Nathaniel Waterman of Boston, MA. Waterman established in September 1825 a large kitchen furnishings jobbing house that sold many kitchen and housekeeping items. "Waterman Furnishing Store" at 5 & 7 Essex Street, is listed as a house-furnishing store in the 1869 *Boston Business Directory,* along with F. A. Walker & Co., at 83 & 85 Cornhill, and Edward W. Noyes & Co. at 1827 Washington, whose names are familiar to readers of this book. Waterman's goods included French-style coffee biggins, waffle irons, water filters, tea kettles, "ventilated refrigerators," and gridirons — under the name "Waterman's Patent." In 1858, Waterman designed and patented a series of roll pans to be used "for baking bread in small rolls." That patent was followed by his April 5, 1859 patent for an "Improved Egg Pan," which had openings between the cups "in order to allow currents of heat to pass upward between them, so as to equalize the heat against their surfaces."

Subsequent Waterman Roll Pans had this "egg pan" modification, and bear the April 5, 1859 date. Waterman designs set a standard that was followed by many foundries. The most common series found today are numbered from #1 to #11, and are marked either "Waterman - Boston," or "R & E Mfg. Co." The R & E Mfg. Co. was the Russell & Erwin Mfg. Co. (later Russwin) of New Britain, CT, which specialized in building hardware. As was common in the nineteenth century, indeed in the twentieth, inventors either sold sole rights or licensed other companies to manufacture their inventions. Designs were (and still are) pirated too. Notable foundries besides R & E apparently produced the Waterman patented designs but they were not marked as such.

Some of these are included in the illustrations of the Waterman Series in CIBP-1 through CIBP-11. Marked "Waterman" pans are not as plentiful as those marked "R & E Mfg.," and are therefore more desirable.

Standardization of Numbers & Letters: The five numbers that were standard with many manufacturers are **#3** (See CIBP-3, -63 and -82); **#5** (CIBP-5, 70, -80); **#9** (CIBP-9, -52); **#10** (CIBP-10, -42 through -44, -73); and **#11** (CIBP-11, -48, -49, -74). For the most part, foundries participated in this standardization of style numbers. Two major exceptions were Wagner, which preferred a letter designation; and G.F. Filley, which, except for one pattern, was very creative with their designs and did not follow the industry norm. Filley's two pans that did conform were their #5 and #3, which were like the Waterman #7 (See CIBP-71.)

CIBP-1. Roll pan. *"R & E Mfg. Co. #1." Also marked "Patent April 5, 1859." Eleven round very shallow cups. 12-1/2" x 8-5/8"; cups, 3-1/8" x 5/8" deep.* **$30-$50** *[Ed. note: This pan is very close to the Smithsonian-owned one that appears to be marked "W & L Mfg. Co." After looking at a number of the "R & E" pans under a loupe, I finally found one with wear marks that distorted the "R & E" just enough that it might somehow have been read as "W & L." This is only a clue — not a final judgment. LCF.]*

PHOTO CREDIT: *David G. Smith, this chapter's author, also provided the photos.* **VALUE GUIDE:** *The book's author overrode some of Smith's value ranges, which were prepared more than a year before this book went to press, by gathering collector price-paid information. This explains the sometimes wide range in value. Anything under the low is probably a really good buy, and even pieces 5% or 10% percent higher than the high may still be within acceptable range — allowing for geographical location, surges in demand, individual desire, and unknowable factors. This is true, actually, for all the value ranges in this entire book.*

CIBP-2. Roll pans. (T) *Underside of an otherwise unmarked "#2." Eleven round cups. 12-1/2" x 8-5/8"; cups, 3-1/8" x 5/8" deep.* **(B)** *"Detroit #6," with same handle as other. Eleven shallow cups in openwork frame. 12-5/8" x 8-1/2"; cups, 3" x 5/8" deep. Other makers call this a "#2" as above.* **$35-$50**

CIBP-3. Roll pan. *Underside of a "#3," showing small round "foot" to each cup. Eleven round cups. 12-3/15" x 8-11/16"; cups, 3-1/8" x 3/4" deep.* **$35-$50**

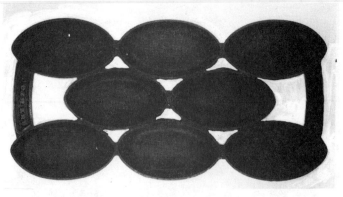

CIBP-4. Roll pan. *"R & E Mfg. Co. #4." Other handle marked with April 5, 1859 patent date. Eight elliptical cups. 13-7/8" x 7"; cups, 4-1/8" L x 2-3/4" W x 3/4" deep.* **$35-$55**

CIBP-5. Roll pan. *"N. Waterman Boston" #5. Also marked with April 5, 1859 patent date. Eight rounded oval cups. 12-1/4" x 7-3/8"; cups 4-1/8" x 2-3/4" x 3/4" deep.* **$35-$55**

CIBP-6. Roll pan. *"N. Waterman Boston" #6. Also has April 5, 1859 patent date. Twelve rectangular cups with rounded corners. 12-3/4" x 7-7/16"; cups, 3-1/4" x 2-1/8" x 9/17" deep.* **$40-$60**

CIBP-7. Roll pan. *"R & E Mfg. Co. #7." Russel & Erwin Mfg. Co. Patent date April 5, 1859. Eight rounded rectangular cups. 11-3/4" x 7-11/16"; cups, 3-1/2" x 2-1/2" x 11/16" deep.* **$40-$60**

CIBP-10. Popover pan. *"R & E Mfg. Co." Marked with patent date, that appears to say 1858, not 1859. Eleven cups with flat bottoms and flared sides. 12-3/8" x 8-1/8"; cups, 2-3/4" diameter x 1-3/4" deep.* **$35-$55**

CIBP-8. Roll pan. *"N. Waterman Boston" #8. With April 5, 1859 patent date. Eleven oval cups. 13-9/16" x 6-11/16"; cups, 3-3/8" x 2-5/8" x 5/8" deep.* **$35-$50**

CIBP-11. French roll pan. *"#11." Marked on handles with "Patent Apr 5, 1859." Twelve trough-shaped cups. 13-1/4" x 7-1/4"; cups, 3-3/8" x 2" x 1" deep.* **$20-$35**

CIBP-9. Roll or muffin pan. *"R & E Mnfg. Co." #9 "golf ball" pan. Also marked with April 5, 1859 patent date. Twelve round cups. 10-1/2" x 6-5/16"; cups, 2-5/16" diameter x 1-3/4" deep.* **$30-$50**

Wagner

Wagner Mfg. Co. of Sidney, OH, used a lettering system to identify their styles. In addition, they used a four-digit catalog number. Though the pan may not be marked with "Wagner" or "Wagner Ware," the letter or a combination of letters and numbers identify the piece as Wagner. The illustrations from CIBP-12 through CIBP-24 were all listed in Wagner's 1913 and/or 1924 catalogs.

CIBP-13. Gem pan, *commonly called a* **popover pan**. *"Wagner Ware," style "B." Note small hanging hole at both ends. 11-5/16" x 7-11/16"; cups, 2-3/4" x 1-3/4" deep.* **$30-$45**

CIBP-14. Vienna roll pan. *"Wagner Ware Sidney," style "I," also marked "Vienna Roll Pan" and with a 4-digit catalog number. Six fat cigar-shaped cups in solid frame. There is also one with an open frame. 11-1/2" x 6-1/2".* **$65-$80**

CIBP-12. Gem pans. (T) *"Wagner Ware" - "Little Slam Bridge Pan." Twelve figural shallow cups with three in each card suit. Widely spaced in solid rectangular pan with no handle, but with small hanging hole. 10-3/4" x 7-5/8"; cups, 2" x 2" x 1-1/4" deep.* **(B)** *Another very shallow cup pan. Wagner, style "A," c.1900-1920. Eleven flat bottom shallow cups. 11-3/16" x 7-5/8"; cups, 2-3/4" x 5/8" deep. Value range for (T) is for nickeled finish & plain iron.* **(T) $95-$150** *; (B)* **$45-$80**

CIBP-15. Gem or popover pan. *"Wagner Ware," style "Q." Five flat bottom cups. Recess for stove lid lifter. 7-1/2" x 5-5/8"; cups, 2-1/2" x 1-1/2" deep. Cups are easy-cleaning: where sides join bottoms is rounded.* **$50-$80**

CIBP-16. Gem pan. *"Wagner Ware," style "R." Eight flat bottom round cups. 8-1/2" x 7-3/8"; cups, 2-1/2" x 1-1/2" deep.* **$45-$65**

CIBP-18. Gem pan. *"Wagner Ware," style "T," commonly known as a* **"turk's head"** *or "turk head" pan, for the supposed resemblance to an ancient Turkish-style turban. Twelve cups in openwork frame, with handles. 14-7/8" x 10"; cups, 2-3/4" x 1" deep.* **$55-$80**

CIBP-17. Gem pans. (L) *"Wagner Ware," style "S," pattern #1428. Eleven flat bottom round cups in solid frame with stove lid lifter recesses. 10-3/4" x 7-1/4"; cups, 2-1/2" x 1-1/2" deep.* **(R)** *"Wagner Ware" - "Little Gem," style "C." Marked "pat. pending" on underside. Twelve round flat bottom cups in openwork frame. 9-5/8" x 7-1/8"; cups, 1-3/4" x 1-1/4" deep.* **$30-$50; $100-$125**

CIBP-19. Gem pan. *"Wagner Ware," style "K" (which may or may not appear on the mold), with five swirl-fluted cups, also sometimes called a "Turk's head" pan (more accurately, costume-wise, than the pan in CIBP-18, because the swirls more closely resemble the turban referred to). Unusual because of almost nonexistent frame. 7" x 5"; cups, 2-1/2" x 9/16" deep.* **$300-$450**

CIBP-22. Gem pan *with a short handle. "Wagner Ware #2." Three flat-bottomed cups like the popover pan cups. Including handle: 6-5/8" x 5-3/8"; cups, 2-1/2" x 1-1/2" deep. [Ed. note: This looks to me like a cloverleaf, and is the most charming pan that I've never seen. LCF.]* **$300-$400**

CIBP-20. Gem pan. *"Wagner Ware," style "L." This style is usually* __not__ *marked. Six bowl-like round cups. 6-3/4" x 4-1/2"; cups, 2-1/4" x 1" deep.* **$80-$160**

The 1924 Wagner catalog had this to say about the "Krusty Korn Kob" mold (CIBP-23): "One of the most delicious and pupular hot breads today is the 'Krusty Korn Kob' made in the Wagner mold. This mold produces delicate, crisp, golden brown cornbread, shaped just like an ear of corn, but infinitely more delicate and appetizing than old fashioned cornbread."

CIBP-21. Gem pan or French roll pan. *"Wagner Ware," style "O." This style may or may not be marked — marked are rarer. Five trough-shaped cups. 9-3/8" x 3-1/8"; cups, 3-1/2" x 1-3/4" x 7/8" deep.* **$90-$150**

CIBP-23. Cornstick mold, *also called a* **cornbread mold.** *"Wagner Ware Sidney" - "Krusty Korn Kob" - "Reg. in U.S. Pat. Off." — "Pat'd July 6, 1920" and with the catalog number "1318," plus the little outline cross. Seven well-delineated cobs, alternate directions. Tab handles with hanging holes. The "Senior" size: 13-1/4" x 6-7/8".* **$50-$80** *[NOTE: There's another "Krusty Korn Kob" senior-size pan (but catalog number 1319), marked "Pat. Pending," "Wagner Sydney." Has narrow oblong handles without holes & is worth about twice the "1318."]*

There were three sizes of the Krusty Korn Kob mold (CIBP-24). They are the "Krusty Korn Kob, Senior," which is 13-1/4" x 6-7/8"; the "Krusty Korn Kob, Junior," which is 11-5/8" x 5-7/8"; and the "Tea Size," which is 8-1/2" x 4-1/4".

CIBP-24. Cornstick molds, *showing the three sizes of "Krusty Korn Kob" pans. From the top: the "Senior" depicted in CIBP-23; the "Junior," 11-5/8" x 5-7/8"; and the "Tea Size," 8-1/2" x 4-1/4" . All have seven alternating cobs.* **$50-$80; $30-$50; $50-$80**

Lodge

The Lodge Mfg. Co. has been located in South Pittsburg, TN, since 1896. [Ed. note: At least one source gives an 1872 date. LCF] It is still producing cast iron cookware and other items. While Lodge did use a catalog numbering system, not all their baking pans are numbered. Some are marked with a letter.

There are two significant differences between the letters used by Wagner and those used by Lodge. The letters used by Wagner are usually located in the middle of the pan and are *intaglio* — they give the effect of being incised or indented into the surface because the casting mold had raised letters. Letters on a Lodge pan are usually raised, usually on the end or in a corner, and they also appear to have been placed at random. I do not know the purpose of the Lodge letters, and there are no references in their catalog to them. CIBP-25 through CIBP-33 are all of Lodge pans.

CIBP-25. Gem pan, or Vienna roll pan. *Lodge Mfg. Co. #18. Six fat cigar-shaped cups or sections in open frame. Handles almost like truncated hearts. 13-3/4" x 6-1/4" . (SEE also CIBP-14.)* **$65-$125**

CIBP-26. "Bridge" pan, *for making gems or little cakes in shape of card suits. Lodge #26, style "D." Eight flat-bottom shallow cups, hearts, diamonds, spades & clubs, in rectangular solid frame with generous cutouts for fingerholds at both ends. 9-7/8" x 8-3/8".* **$100-$150**

CIBP-27. Muffin or gem pan. *Lodge, style "R" turk's head pan. Six deeply fluted cups in solid, flat-top frame, with tab handles with hanging holes. 9-3/4" x 5-3/8"; cups, 2-1/2" x 3/4" deep. This one's still being made. Old ones:* **$35-$60**

CIBP-28. Muffin or gem pan. *Another Lodge turk's head molds, the #19. Six fluted cups in openwork recessed frame with the "truncated heart" handles. 13-3/4" x 8"; cups, 3" x 1" deep.* **$40-$60**

CIBP-29. Muffin or gem pan. *Lodge's largest turk's head pan, #20. Twelve fluted cups in openwork recessed frame. 16-1/8" x 11"; cups, 3-9/16" x 1-1/26".* **$50-$80**

CIBP-30. Muffin or gem pan. *Lodge turk's head pan, marked "R" on raised circle on back. Six fluted cups in solid, recessed frame, with bifurcated T handles. 12" x 7".* **$45-$70**

CIBP-31. Stick molds. (T) *The Acorn pan. Six cups in the form of the typically elongated acorns of the magnificent southern Live Oak tree. (This pattern has been vulgarly known as the "penis pan" among some collectors, and supposedly was withdrawn from manufacture for that reason.) This example is a particularly fine casting.* **Caution: reproductions** *are being made of this pan. 11-3/4" x 6-3/8"; cups, 6-1/8" x 1-5/8" x 5/8" deep.* **(B)** *Cornstick mold. Lodge, "V." Five cobs facing same direction in solid rectangular frame with arched handles the full width of the frame. 9" x 5-3/8".* **$200-$350+; $35-$45**

CIBP-32. Cornstick molds. *Both Lodge, but not marked. Identified by the typical Lodge handles. Both have cobs all facing same direction. Unusual nine stick pan: 15-5/8" x 5-1/2". It may be only 25 or 30 years old. Seven stick pan: 12-1/2" x 5-1/2".* **$25-$40; $45-$55**

CIBP-33. Cornstick mold. *No marks, but because of the shape of the handles, the texture of the casting, and the general shape of the pan, it is believed to have possibly been cast by Lodge. Seven square-ended cobs ... but not cast in the same direction. From L-R: Cobs 1, 2, 3, 6, and 7 are facing same direction; Cobs 4 and 5 are turned the other way. 11-3/4" L x 6-1/8" W; cobs, 5-7/8" x 1-1/4" x 5/8" deep. NOTE: Since this picture was taken, the collector has found another one, almost identical, marked "CAHIL" in a diamond cartouche, and #1507. It is slightly smaller: 11-1/2" x 6"; cobs, 5-5/8" x 1-1/4" x 5/8" deep. [Ed. note: There was a Cahill Co., a foundry specializing in fireplace furnishings, in Chattanooga, TN, at least in the 1930s. See CIBP-78, -79, and -80 for information on pieces supposedly made by "Chattanooga Iron." LCF.]* **$50-$80**

Griswold

In 1884, the Griswold Mfg. Co., Erie, PA, began manufacturing hollowware (the trade's name for cooking utensils, and found spelled as either one or two words). Early Griswold baking pans, when marked, were marked "Erie," but many were not marked either "Erie" or "Griswold." They are identifiable as Griswold, however, by a three-digit pattern number. Many of these pattern numbers appear to have been inscribed by hand in the mold (see further on CIBP-53, -54, -57). Griswold identified their baking pans by two methods: a style or catalog number, and a pattern number. For example, a #22 Breadstick pan is also identified by pattern number 954.

Of all the manufacturers, Griswold produced the greatest number of patterns, including variations. It is the variety that makes their molds so interesting and challenging to collectors. My book on Griswold and other founders' iron wares has a great deal of information on marks, and shows several hundred Griswold pieces.

Variations of the cornstick pan took several paths. (1) a difference in the designs of the kernels and cobs (CIBP-34 through CIBP-38). (2) Notice that all the cobs face in the same direction, with the exception of pattern #270 and #280. (3) Size is also a variable. Most of Griswold's cornstick patterns came in two sizes: 13-3/4" x 5-3/4", and 14" x 7-5/8".

CIBP-34. Cornstick mold, *called the "Crispy Corn Stick Pan." Griswold pan with seven cobs all facing same direction, and hanging hole in only one handle. This type came in three sizes. #273: 13-1/4" x 5-3/4"; #283: 14" x 7-5/8"; and #262: 8-1/2" x 4-1/8".* **$100-$135; $70-$90; $55-$65**

CIBP-35. Stick mold, *called the "Crispy Corn or Wheat Stick Pan." Griswold pan with seven sort of all-purpose cups (neither much like ears of corn or wheat) all facing same direction, and hanging hole in only one handle. This type came in two sizes. #272: 13-1/4" x 5-3/4"; and #282: 14" x 7-5/8".* **$150-$200; $200-$250**

CIBP-36. Stick mold, *called the "Crispy Corn or Wheat Stick Pan." Griswold pan with seven all-purpose corn or wheat ears, alternating directions, and hanging hole in only one handle. This type came in two sizes. #270: 13-1/4" x 5-3/4"; and #280: 14" x 7-5/8".* **$250-$300; $800-$1000**

CIBP-37. Stick mold, *called the "Wheat and Corn Stick Pan." Two views, of cups and of the bottom. Seven elliptical ears facing same direction. 13-1/4" x 5-3/4". Came with two pattern numbers, #2700 and #1270, the latter of which is not marked "Griswold," but rather "S.R. and Company Best Made," made for Sears, Roebuck & Co. #2700:* **$250-$350;** *#1270:* **$100-$120. NOTE:** *The similar #2800 would be the real find! Seven eliptical ears, pan measures 13-1/2" x 7-1/4" W (1-1/2" wider than the 2700), with same patent number but different pattern number: "633." This one is valued between* **$2000-$2500.**

CIBP-38. "Wheat Stick Pan," *marked "Griswold" on one handle. Six ears of wheat, all facing same direction in open frame. Note the "hairs" in the design of the kernels. One handle has hanging hole. Pan came in two sizes: #27 is 10-3/8" x 5-7/8"; and #28 is 12-5/8" x 7". Either size:* **$200-$250**

There was also an 8-1/2" x 4-1/8" "Tea Size," pattern #262, of the "Crispy Corn or Wheat" pan, shown at the bottom of CIBP-39.

The Griswold patterns #27 and #28 "Wheat Stick Pan" vary in size, and in marking. Both sizes may be marked either "Wheat & Corn," or "Whole Wheat." Judging from the quality of lettering, I believe the "Whole Wheat" marking is earlier. CIBP-41 illustrates both the size and lettering variations.

CIBP-41. Stick pans, *by Griswold, with size and marking variations. Both have six sticks in open frames.* **(T)** *pattern #638, is #27, "Wheat & Corn Stick Pan" - "Griswold" - "Erie, PA, U.S.A." - Pat. No. 73, 326. It measures 11" x 6"; cobs, 5-3/8" x 1-1/2" x 1/2" deep;* **(B)** *pattern #639, is #28, marked "Whole Wheat." 12-5/8" x 7"; cobs, 6-3/8" x 1-3/4" x 5/8" deep.* **$200-$250**

CIBP-39. Cornstick molds. *Griswold's "Crispy Corn or Wheat" stick pans, showing comparison of the three sizes. All have seven cobs facing same direction.* **(T)** *14" x 7-5/8";* **(M)** *13-1/4" x 5-3/4"; and* **(B)** *the "tea size" (pattern #262), 8-1/2" x 4-1/8", which is a quarter of an inch narrower than Wagner's "tea size."* **(T) $150-$200;** *(M)* **$40-$60;** *(B)* **$75-$125**

Without a doubt, the most common style muffin pan, whether Griswold or any other company made it, is the #10 eleven-cup popover pan. Griswold made several variations, of which CIBP-42, -43, and -44 illustrate but three. There were also variations in Griswold's #18, six-cup popover pan (CIBP-45, -46, -47).

Griswold also made "Puritan" wares. The kernel design of the Puritan (CIBP-40) is almost identical to the "Griswold" shown above in CIBP-37. The shape of the Puritan pan's handle is different from other cornstick pans, and their pan is also slightly smaller.

CIBP-42. Popover pan. *"Griswold's Erie" #10, pattern #948A. Eleven flat bottom cups in openwork frame. 11-1/4" x 7-3/4"; cups, 2-1/2" x 1-5/8" deep.* **$35-$40**

CIBP-40. Stick pan, *in "Wheat and Corn Stick" pattern, #1270. This one made by Griswold, but marked with a name they used, "Puritan" and "1533." Rounded tab handles, one with hanging hole. NOTE: The pattern number may be the same as the one Griswold used in making the pan for Sears, but the handles are quite different.* **$95-$115**

CIBP-45. Popover pan. *"Griswold's Erie No.18" marked on handles. Six flat bottom cups in openwork frame. 8-1/2" x 5-1/2"; cups, 2-1/2" x 1-5/8" deep.* **$125-$150**

CIBP-43. Popover pans. (T) *"Griswold" - "Erie, PA U.S.A.," #10, pattern #948. Eleven flat bottom cups in mostly solid frame with large fingerholds at both ends. 11-1/4" x 7-3/4"; cups, 2-1/2" x 1-5/8" deep.* **(B)** *"Best Made No.10" - "S. R. and Co." Pattern #1253. Eleven flat bottom cups in openwork frame with large fingerholds. This was made by Griswold for Sears, Roebuck & Co. 11-3/16" x 7-1/8"; cups 2-9/16" diameter x 1-1/2" deep.* **(T) $35;** *(B)* **$45-$65**

CIBP-46. Popover pan. *"Griswold's Erie No.18." Six flat bottom cups in openwork frame that differs substantially at handle ends from CIBP-45, therefore in length. 9-1/8" x 5-1/2"; cups, 2-1/2" x 1-5/8" deep.* **$75-$100**

CIBP-44. Popover pan. *"Griswold" - "Erie, PA U.S.A.," #10, pattern #949B. Eleven flat bottom cups in mostly solid frame with large fingerholds at both ends — note difference in their shape and those of CIBP-43, top. 11-1/8" x 7-5/8"; cups, 2-1/2" x 1-3/8" deep.* **$20-$30**

CIBP-47. Popover pan. *"Griswold," #18. Pattern #5141. Six flat bottom cups in openwork frame with yet another handle style. 9-1/8" x 5-1/2"; cups, 2-1/2" x 1-5/8" deep.* **$75-$100**

303

Many foundries produced a #11 muffin or roll pan. Griswold — being true to form — had its own variations (CIBP-48, -49). Another variation was a so-called half-sized version (CIBP-50). A larger version of their #11 was the #15 (CIBP-51). They also made a #16 — a "half-size" of the #15, but not illustrated here.

CIBP-48. French roll pan. *Griswold, #11. Twelve closely-regimented trough-shaped cups. 12-7/8" x 6-1/8"; cups, 2-7/8" x 1-3/4" x 7/8" deep. Frame is closed rather than partially cutout as in CIBP-11 (the early one from 1859, which overall seems more delicate and graceful).* **$35**

CIBP-49. French roll pan. *"Griswold" #11. This version has a dividing "aisle" of a half inch between the two rows of six trough-shaped cups. 12-7/8" x 6-5/8"; cups, 2-7/8" x 1-3/4" x 7/8" deep.* **$65**

CIBP-50. French roll pan. *Griswold #17. So-called "half-size" version. Six troughs. 7-1/2" x 6"; cups, 2-7/8" x 1-3/4" x 7/8" deep. [Ed. note: Although I haven't seen this in the flesh & bone, so to speak, it looks very lumpen prol to me compared to other Griswold pieces. LCF.]* **$100**

CIBP-51. French roll pan. *"Griswold" #15, pattern #6138. Twelve rather deep troughs, narrowly separated. 14-3/8" x 7-1/2"; cups, 3-1/2" x 2" x 1-1/4" deep.* **$200-$250**

Often referred to as the "golf-ball pan" is Griswold's #9, pattern #947, pan. In this instance, Griswold made design variations with the same pattern number. CIBP-52, -53, and -54 are all marked pattern #947. CIBP-53 is one of Griswold's early pans. CIBP-54 was probably made for a chain store's distribution.

CIBP-52. "Brownie Cake Pan," *also familiarly called* **"golf ball muffin pan."** *Griswold #9. Twelve bowl-like cups in skeletal frame. No hanging hole in handle, but none needed with those cutouts. 10-3/8" x 7"; cups, 2" diameter x 1" deep. Underside of each ball has a word or part of a word. 1925-1930s.* **$125-$175**

CIBP-53. Muffin pan. *Griswold pattern #947, marked at both ends on crosspieces in what appear to be hand-drawn numerals. Ten bowl-like cups in open frame. 9-1/2" x 7-1/8"; cups, 2" x 1" deep. c. 1890. [Ed. note: It's unusual to find a muffin pan of any kind with 10 cups. The more usual was 11 or 12 cups. There was certainly room for one more cup in the center row. But then, why did they make 11-cup molds, divisible only by one or eleven? Could this be some numerological tidbit that we don't know about? LCF.]* **$150-$200**

CIBP-54. Muffin pan, *another in the* **"golf ball"** *pattern #947. Griswold, 12 cups, 10-3/8" x 7-1/8"; cups, 2" x 1" deep, c.1890-1920.* **$75-$100**

Even the plain #22 Breadstick pan is interesting because of variations (CIBP-55).

CIBP-55. Breadstick pans. (T) *Griswold #22, pattern #954. Eleven long troughs. 14-1/2" x 7-3/8"; cups, 7-1/8" x 1-1/8" wide.* **(B)** *Marked "Corn Bread Pan" on bottom. Griswold, pattern #954-E. Eleven long troughs. 14-1/2" x 7-1/2"; cups, 7-1/8" x 1-1/8" wide. [Ed. note: This is the type of baking mold that bears close resemblance to cast iron molds with series of thin (or fat) troughs used by plumbers to cast lead sticks. I saw one just before this book went to press, and it was marked "LEAD" on one of the troughs, which may or may not have been customary. LCF.] NOTE: The #23/955, same size as the "E" 954, is worth two and a half times as much as the 22s.* **$35-$60**

A fancier Griswold pan is the "Heart-Star." See Griswold's and another company's versions in CIBP-56.

Another Griswold variation to look for are two pans with the same pattern number but different style numbers. The #6 Vienna Bread pan, pattern #958 was later designated style #26, with the same pattern #958 (CIBP-57). To add to the confusion, there's a #26 Bread Pan (CIBP-58), but it is pattern #960.

CIBP-56. Baking or Gem pans, *in two versions of a "Heart-Star" design.* **(T)** *Griswold #100, pattern #960. Five fat hearts with star in center. Short tab handle. 7-3/4" across including handle. Cups, about 2" x 1" deep. A 1925 Griswold flyer said "Use ... to bake gingerbread and simple cakes for the children's lunches. Also nice for jello and fudge molds. Just as easy to make as in any shape pan!"* **(B)** *This one is not Griswold, and is an unmarked pan with skillet handle with teardrop hanging hole. Six hearts surrounding 6-point star, recessed in round frame. 9" diameter plus 6" L handle; cups, approx. 2-1/2" x 2-1/2" x 1" deep; star is 3-1/2" W.* **(T):$500-$700; (B) $85-$125** *[Ed. note: Re: (B) This unmarked heart-star pan is almost surely an Alfred Andresen Co. pan, in almost continuous production since it was first featured in ads around the turn of the century. Old ones have a casting "gate" mark on bottom, and are worth the most. LCF].*

CIBP-57. Roll pans, *in the Vienna roll pan style, both are pattern #958, with six fat elliptical stogie-shaped cups. 12-1/2" x 6-7/8"; cups, 6-1/4" x 1-5/8". Note differences in lettering, and in the pairs of casting gates at each end.* **(T)** *Griswold #6, c. 1880s. Not always marked "Griswold," and worth more if it is.* **(B)** *Griswold #26, c. 1915-1930s.* **$75-$150** *[Ed. note: There is one rare, really fabulous Vienna Roll Pan, the #1, It has raised lettering inside "VIENNA ROLL PAN No. 1." It's 11-1/2" L x 3-3/4" W, and with the little gatelegs on the bottom, it looks exactly like one of those herb crushers or "herb boat" used for grinding herbs and spices, and pictured in Chapter I. LCF]*

CIBP-58. Bread pan. *"Griswold Erie" #26, pattern #960. This bread pan is listed in a 1905 Griswold catalog. Two long trough-like sections for two loaves. 13-7/8" x 6-1/2"; loaves, 12-1/8" x 3" W x 1-3/8" deep. Note undercurve of the handles at both ends. With the pattern number only it's worth less than with "Erie No. 26."* **$600-$1000**

Griswold made several other baking pans. Some had variations, some did not. A few more of their baking pans are illustrated below in CIBP-59 through -66.

CIBP-59. Muffin or gem pans. (T) *Griswold #8, pattern #946. Eight flat bottom shallow cups in openwork frame. 12-3/4" x 6-3/8"; cups, 3" x 7/8" deep. Note the Griswold trademark in the large outline cross within circles.* **(B)** *Griswold #2, pattern #941. Eleven flat bottom shallow cups in openwork frame. 12-1/2" x 8-1/2"; cups, 3" x 5/8" deep.* **$190-$200; $180-$200**

CIBP-60. Muffin or gem pans. (T) *"Erie #8," mfd. by Griswold. Pattern #946. Eight flat bottom cups in skeletal frame. 12-3/4" x 6-3/8"; cups, 3" x 7/8" deep, c.1890-$1920.* **(B)** *Griswold #1, pattern #940. Eleven round flat bottom cups in openwork frame. 11-1/2" x 8-1/2"; cups, 2-9/16" x 5/8" deep, c.1890-1910.* **$100-$130; $150-$200**

CIBP-61. Muffin or gem pans. *Above* **(L)** *Griswold #7, pattern #945. Eight flat bottom rectangular cups with rounded corners. 11-3/4" x 7-7/8"; cups, 3-1/2" x 2-1/4" x 5/8" deep. Worth more with pattern number than without.* **(M)** *Another Griswold #7, pattern #945. Eight rectangular cups, openwork frame. Note it measures differently: 11-3/4" x 7-5/8"; cups, 3-9/16" x 2-3/8" x 5/8" deep. Above* **(R)** *Griswold #6, pattern #944. Twelve rectangular cups with rounded corners. 11-3/4" x 7-3/4"; cups, 2-7/8" x 1-7/8" x 1/2" deep. Note lettering style of name "Griswold." The quality of casting of this one varies widely, affecting value.* **(T) $175-$250;** *(M)* **$150-$200;** *(B)* **$150-$250** *[NOTE: despite appearance on the page, these three are not the same size.]*

307

CIBP-62. Gem pan. *Griswold #12, pattern #951. A very delicate, beautiful pan. Eleven flat-bottom, straight-sided cups in interesting rectangular frame that conforms to 4-3-4 arrangement of cups. 11" x 7-1/4"; cups, 2-1/4" x 3/4".* **$175-$200**

CIBP-64. Gem pans *in turk's head design with fluted cups.* **(T)** *Griswold #130, pattern #634. Six cups in solid frame. Marked on underside of one large tab handle; hanging hole in other. 10" x 5-1/2"; cups, 2-5/8" x 7/8" deep.* **(B)** *Griswold #14, pattern #641. Twelve cups in openwork frame. 13-1/2" x 8-5/8"; cups, 2-1/4" x 7/8" deep.* **$400-$700; $400-$600**

CIBP-63. Gem pans. (T) *Griswold #3, pattern #942. Eleven bowl-like cups in openwork frame. 12-1/2" x 8-1/2"; cups, 2-3/4" x 3/4" deep. Note trademark.* **(B)** *Griswold #19, pattern #966. Six cup* **"golf ball"** *pan in very openwork frame. 7-3/4" x 4-5/8"; cups, 2" x 1" deep.* **$185-$300; $350-$500**

CIBP-65. Muffin pans. (T) *"Griswold" #20, Pattern #953. "Turk Head" pan, with swirled flutes. Eleven cups in openwork frame, the outer corners round to encompass the corner cups. 10-3/8" x 7-1/8"; cups, 2" x 3/4" deep, c.1900-1930.* **(B)** *"Detroit #33." Eleven turk's head cups in openwork frame. 10-3/8" x 7-1/8"; cups, 2-1/4" x 3/4" deep. [Ed. note: Did Griswold copy "Detroit," or vice versa? Or did Griswold produce this pan for "Detroit," which was maybe the stove company? LCF.]* **$250-$300; $85-$135**

CIBP-66. Muffin pan. *Griswold #140 "Turk Head" or "Queen Cake" pan, pattern #835. Twelve fluted flat-bottom cups (they actually look just like the stamped aluminum Jell-O molds). 12-5/8" x 8-1/4"; cups, 2-5/8" x 7/8" deep. (This pattern also came in the #240 size, which is 14-5/8" x 10"; cups, 2-3/4" x 7/8" deep, and has a raised rim, worth about $200-$250.) This one:* **$150-$200**

Filley / Excelsior / Davis

G. F. Filley / Excelsior / W. C. Davis. Baking pans marked "G. F. Filley" were manufactured by the Excelsior Mfg. Co., St. Louis, MO. The Excelsior Stove Works, incorporated in 1865 as the Excelsior Mfg. Co., was founded by Giles F. Filley. This explains the pans being marked with his name. Excelsior also made "Charter Oak" stoves and ranges.

Excelsior's 1884 catalog illustrates a line of "Excelsior Bakers' or Gem Pans," in #1 through #8, and #10, #11, and #12. It lists no #9; does one exist? The catalog also lists a #15, but with no illustration.

For the most part, Filley designs (CIBP-67 through -74) were very creative and did not follow the trade's standardization. The exception is their #5 (CIBP-71). Filley pans are highly desired by collectors.

CIBP-67. Muffin or gem pans. *(T) G. F. Filley #2, mfd. by Excelsior Mfg. Co. Hexagonal honeycomb design, quite possibly used for some kind of honey cake. Fourteen cups in oblong shape with zigzag sides. Two upraised handles with large openings. 12-3/8" x 7"; cups, 2-1/4" x 1/2" deep. (B) G. F. Filley #1. Fourteen diamond-shaped cups set in sort of herringbone pattern. 13" x 6-5/8"; cups, 2-1/4" x 2-1/8" x 3/4" deep. (T)* **$250-$350;** *(B)* **$150-$200**

CIBP-68. Gem or muffin pans. *More in the honeycomb hexagonal pattern. These by W. C. Davis, Cincinnati, OH. (T) Ten cups in roughly rectangular frame. Elongated tongue-like tab handles. 14-1/2" x 9-1/8"; cups, 3 1/8" x 1" deep. This pan was also made with thirteen cups ($275-$300). (B) Seven cups in roughly round pan, with elongated skillet handle with teardrop hanging hole. 9-5/8" diameter, plus 5" L handle; cups, 3-1/8" x 1" deep. Higher value is for marked pans. (T)* **$200-$250;** *(B)* **$150-$275**

CIBP-69. Muffin or gem pan. *G. F. Filley #4. Eight 4-petaled oblong cups — a unique shape amongst gem pans — with edge of frame conforming to edge of side cups. 14-3/8" x 6-5/8"; cups, 4-5/8" x 2-3/8" x 5/8" deep.* **$250-$350**

CIBP-70. Baking pans. (T) *G. F. Filley #12. Fourteen bowl-shaped cups in solid frame. 12-1/4" x 6-5/8"; cups, 2-1/4" diameter x 7/8" deep.* **(B)** *G. F. Filley #10. Eleven round cups with raised bottoms, in solid frame with cup-conforming outer edge. 12-1/2" x 8-1/2"; cups, 3" x 3/4" deep. [Ed. note: Probably used for making a small shortcake or spongecake that would be served upside down, the shallow depression caused by the raised bottom in the mold to be filled with berries. In today's grocery store, you'll see packaged spongecakes of this type sold with strawberries. LCF.]* **$175-$250; $100-$150**

CIBP-72. Muffin or gem pans. (T) *G. F. Filley #3. Eight simple rectangular flat-bottom cups with rounded sides & corners. Same angled upwards openwork handle grips. 11-3/4" x 7-5/8"; cups, 2-1/4" x 1/2" deep.* **(M)** & **(B)** *Two views of G. F. Filley #7. Eleven ribbed rectangular cups. 12-1/2" x 6-3/8"; cups, 3" x 2" x 9/16" deep.* **$100-$150; $350-$450**

CIBP-71. Muffin or gem pan. *G. F. Filley #5. Eight flat-bottom oval cups, with Filley's typical upraised handles, and cup-conforming sides to the pan. 11-5/8" x 7-1/8"; cups, 3-5/8" x 2-3/8" x 3/4" deep.* **$75-$150**

CIBP-73. Muffin or gem pan. *G. F. Filley #8. Eleven rectangular flat-bottom cups with canted sides. 13-1/8" x 6-1/8"; cups, 3-1/8" x 1-7/8" x 1" deep.* **$200-$350**

CIBP-74. Baking pan. *G. F. Filley #11. Eleven round cups [with bowl-like bottoms and a rounded molding ring around top half of cup that will result in a sort of "foot" or ring around the cake, that would be served upside down. LCF] 12-1/4" x 8-1/2"; cups, 3" x 3/4" deep. NOTE: There's also a G. F. Filley #6, with eleven oval cups & the same molding ring. It's 12-1/2" x 6-1/2"; cups, 3" x 2-1/4" x 9/16" deep (The #6 would be worth $185-$215.) For the #11:* **$250-$300**

Other Foundries.

The following baking pans (CIBP-75 through -92) are from various other foundries. Some have marks identifying the company, some do not. Some companies were prominent, some obscure. Encouraging to collectors is the fact that the variety goes on and on.

CIBP-75. French roll pan. *Unmarked. Unusually large, with twelve trough-like cups with interesting cutouts in the "aisle" between the rows. Shapely handles look like the ends of draughtsman's T-squares. 16-1/4" x 8-1/4"; cups, 3-3/4" x 2-1/4" x 1" deep.* **$45-$80**

CIBP-76. Muffin pan. *This example unmarked, but other known examples have been marked "Barstow Stove Co.," which was a 19th and early 20th C. stove foundry in Providence, RI. Twelve parallelogram cups set in an interesting pattern, with sides raised almost 1/4" above top surface of solid frame. No real handles, but because of angling of the cups, two cattycorner handles are effected. 11-1/2" x 7-1/2"; cups 2-1/2" x 2-1/2" x 1" deep.* **$100-$150**

CIBP-77. Popover pan. *"Favorite" "pop-over pan," mfd. in Piqua, OH. This is the largest of the popover pans. Nine cups in open-work frame with side handles. 10-1/2" x 10-1/2" plus handles that extend from edge of frame about 1-1/2". Cups: 3-1/8" diameter at top x 2-1/2" deep. Weight, 8 lbs, 12 oz.* **$150-$250**

CIBP-78. French roll pan. *Barstow Stove Co., Providence, RI. Twelve trough-like cups with bracket-shaped wire bail handle, hooked into holes in the "aisle" between the rows. Note handle shape. 14-1/8" x 8-1/4"; cups, 3-3/4" x 2-1/8" x 1-1/4" deep.* **$45-$65**

CIBP-79. Muffin or gem pan. *A #2, identified by fellow collector Chuck Wafford as made by "Chattanooga Iron." Eleven flat-bottom cups with rounded sides and cup-conforming frame edge. 12-5/8" x 8-5/8"; cups, 3" x 5/8" deep. [Ed. note: There was a Chattanooga Iron & Coal Co., in Chattanooga, TN, that made cast iron radiators; there was also a Chattanooga Stove & Foundry Co. In addition, see CIBP-33 for some information on a Cahil. Co. LCF.]* **$45-$70**

CIBP-80. Muffin or gem pan. *A #5, identified by fellow collector Chuck Wafford as made by Chattanooga Iron. Eight oval flat-bottom cups with rounded sides; solid frame whose outside shape conforms to the layout of the cups. 12-1/4" x 7-1/4"; cups, 3-3/4" x 2-1/2" x 3/4" deep. [Ed. note: Talk about restrained design and pure elegance. If the Japanese can be attracted to antique American kitchen utensils as a hot new collectible for the 21st century, this pan and the next, also by Chattanooga (?), may do the trick. LCF.]* **$50-$80**

CIBP-81. Muffin or gem pan. *A #8, identified by fellow collector Chuck Wafford as made by "Chattanooga Iron." Eleven oval flat-bottom cups in simple frame. 13-1/8" x 6-5/8"; cups, 3-1/8" x 2-1/4" x 3/4" deep. [Ed. note: There was a Chattanooga Iron & Coal Co., in Chattanooga, TN, that made cast iron radiators; there was also a Chattanooga Stove & Foundry Co. LCF.]* **$50-$75**

CIBP-82. Muffin or gem pan. *Unmarked #3, but from its appearance, probably from a Southern foundry. Eleven round flat-bottom cups in solid rectangular frame with oval handle openings (note raised edges). 13-1/8" x 9"; cups, 3" x 3/4" deep. (This design is found also in a smaller size, the #6, also with eleven cups. 12" x 8-3/8"; cups, 2-5/8" x 1/2" deep.)* **$50-$70**

CIBP-83. Ebelskiver or applecake pans. **(T)** *Hollow iron socket handle to accommodate a long wooden handle. Marked "NAC & Co." Seven bowl-shaped cups set in round recessed pan frame. 9-3/4" diameter with additional 7-3/4" L handle. Cups, 2-1/2" diameter x 1-1/4" deep.* **(B)** *This example is exactly the same size, and is also marked "NAC & Co." It has a rigid bracket handle of heavy steel wire, and was cast with reinforcements, specifically for taking this handle. Otherwise it is the same as the one above. [Ed. note: " NAC & Co." has not been identified. It is probably some precursor or variant of Northland Aluminum Co., Minneapolis, MN, even though this pan is made of cast iron and Northland is known for their cast aluminum ebelskivers. LCF.]* **$60-$85; $60-$70**

CIBP-84. Gem pan. *Unmarked and maker unknown. Crudely molded (or perhaps only crudely cast) oblong pan with eight oval cups with the stepback ring that will form a "foot" when the cake is turned and served upside down. Simple tab handles. Cloverleaf cutouts are interesting. 14-7/8" x 8-1/8"; cups, 4" x 2-1/2" x 3/4" deep.* **$65-$80**

CIBP-85. Vienna roll pan. *Unmarked. Four very fat cigar-shaped cups in openwork frame. No handles. 12-1/2" x 6-1/2"; cups, 5-7/8" x 2-5/8" x 1-1/8" deep. [Ed. note: Value range for this one was very wide: from $65 to $200! This sure looks like a Griswold #4 to me, which may explain why so many prices were gathered. The piece, however, is in David Smith's collection, and he does not identify it as a Griswold. LCF.]* **$75-$125**

CIBP-86. Roll or muffin pans. *All of the "French Roll" type.* **(T)** *Marked only "#14" under handle, but this is a Griswold pan, c.1890. Twelve rectangular flat-bottom cups in very modern-looking frame with slotted openings between the cups. 12-1/2" x 6-5/8"; cups, 2-1/2" x 1-7/8" x 3/4" deep.* **(M)** *Roll pan. "Shepard" - "Buffalo," #12. Twelve rectangular flat-bottom cups in frame with vent slots. Note recess in one handle that accommodates stove lid lifter. 15-3/4" x 6-3/4"; cups, 2-3/8" x 1-3/4" x 3/4" deep.* **(B)** *Marked "French Roll Pan No 11." Twelve trough-shaped cups in ventilated frame. 12-3/4" x 7-1/2"; cups, 2-3/4" x 1-7/8" x 7/8" deep. This has been found marked "Erie," and worth much more if marked.* **(T) $450-$600**; **(M) $100-$200**; **(B) $45-$75+**

CIBP-87. Roll pan. *Unmarked. Six oblong flat-bottom cups with canted sides, tab handles. 10-7/8" x 9-1/4"; cups 4-1/2" x 3" x 1" deep. [Ed. note: As a folk art collector, and a generalist collector, I am often attracted to handsome pieces that may or may not be valuable to a specialist collector. This pan is so perfect in form that I would rank its design with the best minimalist art of the 1980s or with nearly any Shaker cupboard. Therefore, I agree with the few who value this pan from $150-$200+ — it is art.* **An important point to make to new collectors: ultimately, the best rule of thumb vis a vis prices is pay what feels right for you.** *A dealer, of course, must pay less than what the customer will pay. LCF.]* **$50-$75**

CIBP-88. Muffin or roll pan. *Shepard Hardware, Buffalo, NY, #7. Manuf'd. c.1880. Eight oblong cups with rounded corners, in openwork frame with square recesses at ends to accommodate a stove lid lifter. 11-1/2" x 7-1/2"; cups, 3-5/8" x 2-3/8" x 5/8" deep.* **$60-$100**

CIBP-89. Roll pan. *Unmarked. <u>Unusually large</u> pan, with ten oblong cups with canted sides. Note fancy raised handles. 15-1/2" x 9-1/4"; cups, 4" x 1-1/4" x 1-1/4" deep. [Another one with a wide value range: $65-$200.]* **$70-$100**

CIBP-90. Muffin pan. *Schofield Mfg. Co., NYC, c.1890.* **Rare** *fruit and vegetable pattern, figural cups in openwork frame. 9-1/8" x 6-5/8".* **$250-$400**

CIBP-91. Gem or cake pan *or possibly a candy mold? Unmarked. Nine cups with crosshatched or lightly "waffled" bottoms; fancy, sort of pleated sides, joined to form the largest possible open spaces between cups [which is probably a clue to use, as this would allow more hot air to circulate]. Cups, 2-1/2" x 2-1/4" x 1/2" deep; handle, 2-1/2" L. [Ed. note: I don't think it's a candy mold, having seen nothing like it in any of the numerous trade catalogs I've searched. The cups are too big anyway. Since the last edition, collector Joel Schiff has come to believe this is a* **shortbread mold**. *He values it at around $200. LCF]* **$75-$125**

CIBP-92. Gem or muffin pan. *Unmarked. Rounded oblong frame with handles; twelve cups, with 9 flutes instead of the more usual 10 flutes. 15-3/4" x 10-1/2"; cups, 2-3/4" x 1" deep.* **$50-$75**

Reproductions of Baking Pans:

Reproductions and copies are increasingly a problem in today's antique and collectibles market, as originals become more difficult to find. Unfortunately, reproductions are sometimes sold as originals. For the novice, and sometimes even the experienced collector, it is difficult to recognize the difference. There are some indicators that can help determine an original from a reproduction.

Rust. Many originals, even if rusted, will have an accumulation of years of burned-on food and grease. Also, rust on an old piece will probably be uneven. This is caused by the protection the encrusted food has given parts of the metal. Rust on a new reproduction will usually be even, and often is bright orange.

Casting Quality. Craftsmen who carved the molds and cast the originals were proud of their work. Their products were precise. Today's mass-produced reproductions, for the most part, do not get the attention of human hands.

Patina. The illustration CIBP-A, below, shows a forgery of the Griswold #262 Tea Size Corn Stick Pan. Note how grainy the iron of the reproduction is (lower right) compared to the old original (upper left). Older iron has a patina, a satiny smoothness, which new castings don't have. Look at CIBP-B and note the difference in the detail of the kernels between the authentic original (top) and the reproduction (bottom).

CIBP-A. Stick pans — authentic vs reproduction. (L) *Authentic Griswold #262 "Crispy Corn or Wheat" pan.* **(R)** ***Reproduction*** *of same pan. This would be easier to see if you could lay the pieces down side by side. Get out your magnifying glass (What! You don't have one?) and notice that even with the "graininess" due to the printing process in this book, you can still see that the one on the left has a smoother finish.*

CIBP-B. Details of interiors of stick pans in CIBP-A. (T) *Detail of two cobs from* ***authentic*** *Griswold #262 from previous illustration. Note relatively smooth surface of frame and handle, sharp detail of kernels, clean hanging hole, .* **(B)** *Detail from* ***repro*** *Griswold. Note fuzzy kernels, ground-off breathing hole pin, evidence of other grinding on the handle, and the partly filled-in sloppy hole.*

Modern casting technique. Note the excess left by the breathing hole pin (CIBP-B, bottom). In one modern method of casting, breathing holes are punched into the cast to allow air to escape when the molten iron is poured into the mold. When the air escapes, the molten iron rises in these holes. These projecting "pins" are then broken off or ground down.

Inaccurate copying. CIBP-C illustrates an attempted copy (possibly of Far Eastern manufacture), not a reproduction. This pan is marked "CRISWOLD" (with a "C" not a "G") and says "SNICK" (with an "N" not a "T"). It also has the pattern number 252 (with a "5") instead of #262 of the Griswold original. This pan is commonly seen; there may be others. Buyer beware!

Grinding and finishing. Older, original castings were, for the most part, precise, therefore required very little "cleaning" — filing or grinding. Shoddy molding of repros is compensated for by grinding off excess metal, but sometimes the reproduction-maker doesn't even bother with that. CIBP-D shows the edge of an original casting at top, compared to the reproduction edge, bottom.

CIBP-D. Details of cup edges, *comparing the grinding-off of an* **authentic** *pan* **(L)** *and a* **reproduction** **(R)**.

Weight or Heft. Another sign of a reproduction relates to weight. Repros tend to be much heavier than old originals. The original in CIBP-D, top, for example, weighs 3 lbs, 6 oz. The reproduction, bottom, weighs 4 lbs, 14 oz — over a pound and a half more!

CIBP-C. Stick pan — reproduction. *Laughably inaccurate though not uncommon reproduction. Note misspellings in "Criswold" and "Snick" as well as incorrect pattern number.*

CIBP-E. Muffin pan — the real "Reid's Pat." *One of the most famous. An* **authentic**, *original "Reid's Pat.," dated "July 18, 1871." It is 16-1/4" x 8-3/4", and weighs 4 lbs., 11 oz. The reproduction of this pan is not marked and dated.* **$125-$185**

CIBP-F. Muffin pan — authentic half-size. *An authentic, half-size version of Reid's Pat. However, it is not marked or dated, and it's not been learned when these were first made. They have been in production for quite a while. The casting quality is the same as the large original pan. Seven cups: 2 fluted, 2 hearts, 2 plain rounds, surrounding a single 6-point star. 9-1/4" x 8-1/8"; weighs 2 lbs, 4 oz.* **$60-$80**

If a pan feels too heavy for its size, it may very well be a reproduction. Below (CIBP-E through CIBP-H) are some other old pans that are commonly reproduced, along with their weights and sizes.

CIBP-G. Muffin pan — authentic. *This is an authenic original in the twelve-cup heart pattern pan. 13-1/4" x 8-3/8"; weighs 4 lbs, 12 oz.* **$225-$275**

CIBP-H. Muffin pan — authentic. *This is an authentic original of the often-seen eight-cup fruit and vegetable pan. 16-5/8" x 8-1/4"; weighs 4 lbs, 9 oz. This has been reproduced for a long time — at least 40 years. One of the <u>reproductions is found with a tiny white enameled button</u> identifying it; that was the early John Wright repro. Later Wright repros don't have the button.* **$145-$185**

Signs of wear. Wear is a good indicator of an original. Being pushed in and out of an oven over a period of years polishes high points on the bottom of a muffin pan. CIBP-I illustrates these wear points on the bottom of the eight-cup fruit and vegetable pan.

CIBP-I. Detail of CIBP-H, *showing bottom of the fruit and vegetable pan cups. Notice how wear polishes the high points.*

Final judgment. Just one of the eight indicators of an original (encrusted food, uneven rusting, high quality casting, patina, weight, signs of wear) is probably not sufficient to positively determine what is an old original from what is a reproduction. The newer the repro, the easier the task becomes. Complicating matters is the existence of old and heavily used reproductions from 50, 60 or 70 years ago. A combination of several indicators is a pretty good guide.

Cleaning and Preserving Iron:

It is no easy task to clean a muffin pan, or any other iron cooking utensil, that has an accumulation of many years of burned-on grease, or rust from years of neglect. The result is worth the effort. If you have optimism and perserverence, the rest is elementary!

The first consideration is to <u>preserve the patina</u>. In cast iron, the patina is the natural smoothness of the surface, smoothness that has developed through years of use, especially by the slow absorption of oil or fat and the high heat. To preserve the patina, do not use anything abrasive; especially DO NOT SANDBLAST. Sandblasting destroys the old finish and the value, and often gives a pitted, grainy look that is no better than that of reproductions.

Soften & remove burned-on food. The first step of the cleaning process is to soften and remove the burned-on grease. This can be accomplished by applying an oven cleaner. Apply it as directed on the can, with plenty of fresh air, and let it set for several hours. Oven cleaner can burn your skin, so wear rubber gloves. After a few hours, wipe the deposit off and apply another coat. Repeat the process until all the burned-on grease is removed. Stubborn spots can be scraped with a putty knife or spoon. Be careful not to dig into the iron. [Ed. note: Some collectors will not use anything chemical on their old iron, and advise using wood or glass (like a heavy shard from a bottle) to scrape the metal. LCF.]

After removing burned-on grease, you may discover rust underneath.

Remove rust. The most difficult task is removing rust. The best way to remove it is with a wire brush. If you have an electric drill, many shapes and sizes of wire brushes are available — some are quite fine. Power brushing is much easier than hand brushing, but it is hard for some people to gain fine control over the brush, which may skip and bounce if it gets caught in a corner or cut-out. Do not use a coarse brush on a smooth surface. A coarse brush will scratch the surface and destroy the patina. Use a fine brush first. If this is not adequate, cautiously try a coarser brush. [Ed. note: Again, many collectors hate wire brushes in all forms and descriptions, but particularly the big unwieldy coarse ones often used to refinish (ie. ruin) old furniture. I've seen experienced people use a fine wire brush mounted on an electric motor, with beautiful results. I would advise practicing — maybe on a few of those repros you wish you hadn't bought. I tried using a fine brass-wire brush on heavily rusted old andirons, and ended up with a sort of golden sheen. LCF].

Severe, crusty rust may not come off with brushing. Crusted rust pods resemble barnacles. They can be broken by scraping them with a spoon or putty knife; then use the brush to remove them.

I do not like to use a rust-removing chemical (such as naval jelly) because it leaves the iron a dull gray and destroys patina. I have used it in severe cases — it does work. After removing the rust, I scrub the pan in a detergent with a brass brush to remove iron dust and the rest of the grease. After thoroughly drying the iron, you are ready to cure and preserve it.

Cure the iron. There are several methods you may use to cure and preserve an iron piece. Some use vegetable salad oil, some peanut oil and some mineral oil. All will protect against rust, and none are poisonous.

I prefer to cure a pan with solid Crisco, which works better than the oil. Apply it to the pan and put the pan in the oven at about 225 , and leave in for about 30 minutes. Remove the pan and wipe off the excess grease. Replace in the oven and leave for another 30 minutes, then shut off the heat and let it cool down. I think you will be pleased by the results. Vegetable oil — such as corn or peanut oil — tends to leave a sticky film on the pan, making it unsuitable for curing pieces meant for display only.

Considered only from the viewpoint of rust prevention, I have found that mineral oil works best. Wipe it on liberally and let it soak in for a few days, then wipe off. The mineral oil accents the patina and also tends to darken the color of the iron. It is also consumable, so you can cook with the pan later if you choose.

Care after use. After you have baked with a cured pan, don't scour it. Merely rinse it in clear hot water and wipe it out with a paper towel. Stubborn deposits may be dislodged by scraping with a spoon (start with a plastic or wooden spoon before resorting to metal). After the pan is clean and dry, apply a protective film of Crisco — it doesn't take much.

CARE OF CAST IRON:
by E. Lillian Hutchinson

(From her book *Department Store Merchandise Manual, New York University Housefurnishings Department,* NYC: 1918)

"...New cast iron ware, which is to be used for cooking, should be coated on the inside with tallow and allowed to stand for a few days, then heated until the fat melts, and washed in hot water and washing soda. Rinse in hot water and wipe dry, rubbing very hard." p. 11

MEASURING

V. WEIGHT, AMOUNT, SIZE, QUALITY, TIME & TEMPERATURE

Clocks and scales are the best-established categories in this chapter, but not necessarily from a kitchen collector's viewpoint. In fact, kitchen clocks of old or new vintage are hardly collected at all. I think a **futurewatch** on kitschy **figural kitchen clocks** might be in order for the new century.

Scales relating to food handling have a well-established market. Those with polished brass faces or interesting cast iron bases lead the category. However, scales are, for most advanced scale collectors, the only dip in the ocean of kitchen collectibles that they've ever taken. Strictly speaking, many, or most, scales aren't a "kitchen collectible" at all, but they are considered an attractive "go-with" and therefore belong in this book. **Scales** are primarily an important specialty in the scientific instrument collecting field, and have been featured as "men's antiques" for decades. **Egg scales** are virtually ignored by most scale collectors, but with kitchen collectors they are very popular, and — it is nice to report — still relatively inexpensive. There is a collectors' organization: **The International Society of Antique Scale Collectors**. Contact Bob Stein, 176 West Adams St., Suite 1706, Chicago, IL 60603, (312) 263-7500.

Many cupboards and pantries have been raided by collectors who have preferred (at least until very recently) to not acknowledge kitchen antiques as a serious and worthy field. The contents that have been "kidnapped" this way include most decorated tin (sometimes appropriately called "tôle" wares), most *polishable* brass and copper wares, and all woodenwares that could be attributed to the Shakers, or that could be given the name treen (also trein), which is a Scottish word for something made of wood. Although there is much disagreement about what "treen" includes, it usually applies to objects of turned wood, sometimes called turnery. Another theory of the word's origin is that it means something made from trees. At any rate, the way you will find turned and carved cider funnels or fine old scoops (or butter paddles, from Chapter II), will be to conduct your own raid into the treen market, which is altogether more posh than ours.

Another category in this chapter that has enjoyed a good deal of cachet is **measures** — most particularly liquid measures of copper (remember the unfortunate Law of Polishing: shine = decorative value) or pewter. Copper is considered here but not pewter, because that field of collecting is long established and requires years of specialized study. Green Depression glass measuring cups are also borrowed from glass — a specialist collecting field about which I know little. I don't (or should I say can't) do glass.

TABLE OF EQUIVALENT MEASURES

Not only do you need equivalent measures when working with very old or foreign recipes, but some of the kitchen antiques you collect were catalogued using metric measures or unfamiliar units. Sometimes you're at a flea market with no way to measure something: use a dollar bill, or your own thumb!

WEIGHTS:

1 dram	1/16 ounce
1 ounce	16 drams
1 pound	16 ounces
1 pint	1 pound ("A pint's a pound, the world around.")
1 stone	14 pounds (British usage)

LENGTH OR SIZE MEASURES:

1 inch	25.4 millimeters, or 2.54 centimeters
1 foot	30.48 centimeters
1 yard	3 feet, or 36 inches, or 0.91 meter
1 meter	39.24 inches, or 1.09 feet
1 centimeter	0.39 inches
1 dollar bill	6-1/16" x 2-9/16"
1st joint of thumb	1-1/4" to about 1-3/8"

COOKING MEASURES:

1 drop	1/60 to 1/76 teaspoon
15 drops	1/4 teaspoon
1 pinch	1/8 to 1/4 teaspoon
1 teaspoon	76 drops, or 1/3 tablespoon
1 tablespoon	3 teaspoons
1 dessert spoonful	2 teaspoons
1 cup	16 tablespoons, or 8 ounces, or 1/2 pint
1 tumbler	6 to 8 ounces
1 wineglass	4 to 6 ounces
2 2/3 cups	1 pound (brown sugar, oatmeal, corn meal)
1 pint	2 cups (a pound of butter, flour, granulated sugar)
1 quart	4 cups, or 2 pints
1 "goose-egg" butter	2 heaping tablespoons (about 2oz.)
9 large eggs	1 pound

DRY MEASURE VOLUME, U.S.
(British "Imperial" is about 1/5th more):

"Dry measures" may be marked with some of same quantities — pint, quart, gallon, barrel — as a "wet or liquid measure," but the weight & cubic inches when filled differ. For example, one dry pint has 33.6 cubic inches; whereas one wet pint has 28.875 cubic inches.

1 pint	1/2 quart
1 quart	2 pints
1 peck	8 quarts, or 1/4 bushel (Peter Piper picked a lot!)
1 bucket	2 pecks
1 bushel	2 buckets, or 4 pecks, or 64 pints
1 quarter	8 bushels
1 chaldron	36 bushels
1 barrel	2 kilders (or kilderkins), or 4 firkins
1 puncheon	2 barrels, or 4 kilderkins, or 8 firkins

LIQUID OR FLUID MEASURE, U.S.
(British "Imperial" is about 1/5th more):

1 ounce	1/16 pint	29.574 milliliters
1 gill	4 ounces	0.1183 liter
1 pint	16 ounces, (4 gills)	0.04732 liter
1 quart	2 pints	0.9463 liter
1 pottle	4 pints	
1 gallon	8 pints, (4 quarts)	3.7853 liters
1 bucket	2 gallons, (informally, 5 quarts or more)	
1 firkin	72 pints, (9 gallons)	

LIQUID OR FLUID MEASURE, U.S. (cont.)

1 bushel	74 pints	
1 kilderkin	2 firkins, (144 pints)	
1 runlet	1 kilderkin, (2 firkins, 144 pints)	
1 wine barrel	31-1/2 gallons, (252 pints)	119.24 liters
1 beer barrel	36 gallons	136.27 liters
1 oil barrel	42 gallons	158.98 liters
1 hogshead	63 gallons, (7.2 firkins, 9/10 puncheon)	
1 butt or pipe	126 gallons	
1 tun of wine	252 gallons	
1 tun of beer	259 gallons, (28.8 firkins)	

CONVERSION EXAMPLES:

You know:	Multiply by:	To find:
inches	2.54	centimeters
feet	30.48	centimeters
fluid ounces	29.57	milliliters
cups	0.24	liters
gallons	3.79	liters
centimeters	0.39	inches
liters	1.06	quarts
liters	0.26	gallons
liters	4.23	cups

Asparagus buncher, cast iron, painted dark red, mounted to board, has end plate, a U-shaped cradle for stalks & spring-loaded hinged piece to form bunch, "The Philadelphia Buncher," 5-1/2" H x 8-1/2" L exclusive of board, looks late 19th or early 20th C. **$95-$150**

Asparagus buncher, cast iron top of frame, slightly scrolled cutout wood adjustable for bunching the asparagus, brass spring clips & ratchet thumb catch (probably "The Philadelphia" model), mfr unknown to me, "PHILA." is only mark, buncher hoop is 4-3/4" diameter, base is 11-5/8" x 10", 3rd quarter to late 19th C. **$120-$175**

A simpler buncher, mostly of wood, with springy brass partial hoops in a wooden cradle, flat wood end piece against which to thump the bottom of the stalks, is depicted in the Feb. 1876 *American Agriculturist* as "Conover's Asparagus Buncher." They give advice on sorting by size and washing before bunching, and advised standing the finished bunches (held in the buncher until they can be tied in 2 places with string) on wet hay if they have to be "kept for some hours before packing" for market. This magazine was full of advice on marketing, and said once that it was easy to grow the food but hard to market it. For example: a delicious juicy watermelon couldn't be sold in New York City markets because it was too hard to carry under your arm, too big for a market basket, and New Yorkers "refused to" hoist them on their shoulders to carry home! After several years of disappointing sales, someone finally came up with a sort of bookstrap device with a wooden handle (shades of those nifty things we used to get attached to suit boxes), to provide what nature had neglected to provide — a way to carry a watermelon. In another article, from 1873, the editor noted that if one wanted to sell produce one had to "conform to the customs of that market . . . If a lot of loose asparagus, or strawberries in the large trays used in Cincinnati, were sent to the New York market, they would probably find their way into the garbage-cart." This is probably still true. I am dismayed by huge trays of strawberries (such as are found 125 years later in Charlottesville, VA) and wish for the small box style of New York City.

V-1. Asparagus buncher. *Cast iron hoops, hinged, mounted to oak (?) base. Joseph Breck & Sons catalog, 1903-05.* **$85-$100**

V-2. Asparagus bunchers. (L) *Oldest of French bunchers, consisting of "two pairs of wooden scissors with curved blades, to each short arm of one of these is fixed a wooden rod, which passes through a hole in the corresponding arm of the other, allowing the two to be placed at the desired distance apart." A string is used to hold the rods in place after the "scissors" are opened to the right size.* **(R)** *Conover's buncher, wood, hinged with lever (partially visible in vetical position), with brass strips inside. The fattest butt end of the stalks are pushed against the endboard at right. Both pictures from* American Agriculturist, *5/1876; and 2/1876.* **$45-$55; $85-$100**

V-3. Beer measures. *Copper, with glass viewing or indicator window, hinged flat lid with vent holes, strap handles.* **(L)** *A 2 quart size from Duparquet, Huot & Moneuse hotel & restaurant supply catalog, c.1904-1910.* **(R)** *One with a braced handle from the Manning & Bowman catalog, 1892. It came in 2, 3 & 4 quart sizes, either planished copper or nickel-plated copper. The catalog says it has a "strainer for pouring from bottom." These are found in other c.1900 catalogs.* **$135-$175**

Bean sizer or bean sorting frame — See Chapter III (Separate, Strain, Drain, Sift and Dredge)

Beer measure, copper slant-sided pitcher-like container with long "V" neck lip or spout originating at bottom, flared foot, strap handle, inset panel with 4 small arched glass windows down one side, hinged lid with small perforated hatch in middle, mfd. by E. Ketcham & Co., NYC, NY, 2 qt. capacity, c.1877. **$135-$175**

Bucket, for dry measure, tin, with handles, "Franklin," 1/2 bushel capacity, late 19th C. **$20-$28**

Bucket, dry measure, wood with old green paint, American, 2 gal. capacity, 19th C. "**Bucket**. The term is applied, in the South and West, to all kinds of pails and cans holding over one gallon." John Russell Bartlett, *Dictionary of Americanisms. A Glossary of Words and Phrases usually regarded as peculiar to the United States,* Boston: 2nd ed.1859 (1st ed. 1848). **$75-$85**

Candy scoops & thermometers — See scoop, candy; thermometer, candy

Clock, battery, decorated china plate, 6 herbal bouquets, Arabic numerals, General Electric, 9-1/2" diameter, c.1960. **$10-$18**

Time Isn't Ageless — "To the casual observer, today's smart kitchens seem perfect in their charm. Gay, sparkling, they are a whirl of matching color . . . harmonious in every detail . . . except the offending clock! Sometimes a crude, ungainly alarm. Often a makeshift relic of other days. . . . Miller has created an enchanting array. Clocks, bright as butterflies . . . perky-fresh and in perfect tune with the kitchen scene. Designed in a cheerful 'cottage-y' mood, these delightful time pieces are of gleaming porcelain . . . so charmingly right for the kitchen, so easy to keep twinkling and clean. . . . Either with the 8-day lever movement (which does away with the pendulum nuisance) or the new electric movement (which need never be wound or regulated)." Sept. 1930 ad, *House & Garden.*

Clock, ceramic, <u>Black Americana</u>, Aunt Jemima, works' manuf'r not known to me, pottery by Red Wing, MN, 20th C. **$125-$175**

Clock, electric, blue & white Delft china plate, Dutch scene, English, German or Dutch, 20th C. **$45-$55**

Clock, electric, colorful yellow china octagonal plate with blue & green flowers in border, center is clock face, Arabic numerals, insignia of windmill, "Cretonne," by Irving Miller & Co., NYC, NY, 9" diameter, 1930. **$12-$18**

Clock, electric, molded avocado green "antiqued" plastic, in shape of hutch cupboard, with 3 little metallic plastic "copper" plates on top shelf, a pot & 2 candlesticks on 2nd shelf, clock face on

front of lower doors, Arabic numerals, mfd. by Spartus, 12" H, 1960s? More charm than you'd think. Another version was made in wood tones, with blue & white plastic "Delft" wares, plates, etc., on the shelves & wonderful blue & white coffee pot. I wonder how many versions Spartus did. **$7-$15**

Clock, frying pan, keywound with regulator, a real stamped sheet steel frying pan, decal image of North & South America as voluptuous women's figures, mfd. for Expo in Buffalo, NY, a "Cold Handle Acme" pan, mfd. for the Pan-American Exposition Co. by the New York Stamping Co., NYC, 26" L including handle, 13" diameter, clock itself ©1899 for 1901 fair; but pan pat'd Nov. 14, 1876. There was at least one more "Pan" pan clock, but this is the most valuable. **$600-$800**

Clock, frying pan, black painted cast iron, sides have hammered look with bronzed finish, outside bottom of pan cast with raised numbers, painted white, electric or battery (?), unclear from catalog, Emig Products, Reading, PA, 8" diameter x 12" H overall, c.1966. Wholesale price then was $13. Asking price now isn't much higher. **$15-$25**

Clock, frying pan, cast iron, quartz battery motor, loop hanging hole, 2 pouring lips, 4 Arabic numerals & 8 dots as well as the hands are finished brass, has second hand, sold (& mfd?) by Clock Wise, Inc., Andrews, NC, 6" diameter frying pan bottom or clock face, advertised in 1983. **$10-$25**

Clock, frying pan, electric, enameled iron & tin, white pan, red screwed-on handle, red knife & fork (minute) hands, modern-looking sans serif Arabic numerals in white on white, "Made in Great Britain," c.1950s. In just a few years this has doubled in value because of great crossover interest in stuff from the 1940s and 1950s. **$60-$85**

Clock, frying pan, electric, molded plastic with copperoid finish, "Model 504," Herold Products Co., Chicago, IL, c.1950s. **$30-$40**

Clock, frying pan, electric, stamped tin, Sessions, Forrestville, CT, c.1920s. **$35-$55**

Clock, frying pan with inset clock. A nickel-plated, cast iron promotional piece for dealers. Hung by hole in short handle, with the bottom of the skillet facing out. 8-1/2" diameter. Cast with large-letter legend around clock, "ERIE UP TO TIME" and "We Sell Hollow Ware," Griswold Mfg. Co., Erie, PA, 1900 to early 20th C. High value because it's Griswold. Crossover advertising collectible. **$2500-$3200+**

Clock, frying pan, sheet metal, with knife & fork hands, this one German, early 20th C. **$75-$125+**

Clock, milk can figural, battery-operated, molded plastic, finished in a sort of brushed pewter or old tin look. Great thing about the casting is it successfully imitates a banged-up old milk can, with dents. Face with large Arabic numerals is on a flattened front, has sweep second hand. Called the "Milkmaid" clock in ads, "Seth Thomas" on face; inside, cast into plastic, it says "Ronthor R 60 3464," & "Seth Thomas 2436," NYC, NY, 11" H x 7-3/4" W, 1973 ad. **$10-$15**

Clock, pumpkin, 3-D stamped tin, round face has some 3-D dimension & modeling, painted in shaded orange, with black Arabic numerals, 2 hands. I saw this in an ad only, which doesn't mention works — probably some form of 7-day windup. Advertises in bold lettering on face: "None Such Mince Meat [&] Pumpkin-Squash Like Mother Used To Make," American, 10" diameter, early 20th C. **$550-$700**

Clock, refrigerator in shape of Monitor Top, electric works, heavy cast metal, painted white, black "hinges" on 2 doors, clock face on doors, Warren Telechron Co. mfd. this Electron clock for The General Electric Co., Ashland, MA, 8-3/4" H x 5" W x 3-1/8" deep, advertising piece made from 1928 to early 1931. Refrigerator collector Russell Wilson adds that these clocks were "an exclusive premium item given to managers (dealers) of

G.E. appliance stores selling the 'Monitor Top.' There were, according to G.E. only 21,460 made altogether during the years 1928 to 1931." **$400-$525+**

According to Russell Wilson, there were **four types of these GE Monitor Top clocks** made in 1928, 1929, 1930 and part of 1931, alike at a cursory glance, but differing in case, movement and numerals. For example, he said that the nameplate above the clock shrank on later models from 3-3/8" L to only 1-9/16" L; the coils of the condensor "monitor top" went from 16 down to 14 and vertical fins were added; numerals changed size too; and later movements were marked "Model No. M-1," with a serial number prefix "A." Wilson also said that a cast iron pennybank, 4-3/4" H, also exists. • According to Edwin P. Mampe, writing in the National Association of Watch & Clock Collectors Museum's *The Bulletin*, at least two versions of the clock were made — an earlier one with longer nameplate, larger Arabic numerals, legs "indented" at the joint with box so they appear separate, and the 16 condenser coils on top permanently affixed to the case. A later type has no indentation where the legs join and has a 14-coil condenser bolted to case and thus removable.

Clock, shelf, gingerbread oak case, brass works, key wound, William L. Gilbert Clock Co., original paper label "Tiger," Winsted, CT, late 19th C. **$175-$220**

Clock, teapot, chubby figural, stamped metal, electric movement, Arabic numerals, came in white, green, red or blue finish, Sessions, 7" H x 8-1/2" W, c.1940. **$35-$45**

Clock & inkwell combined, cast brass with cast round face, decorated with flour sacks, brooms, barrels or kegs & groceries, advertising 50th anniversary (1863 to 1913) of Joseph Spidel Grocery Co., mfd. by Mercedes, American, 1913. **$150-$175**

Coffee measure, metal, with sliding backwall to adjust capacity for 2, 4 or 6 cups, "Dix Coffee Meter," pat'd 1908. **$30-$45**

Coffee measure, tin, Bokar, 20th C. **$5-$10**

Dinner chimes, mahogany rectangular base with molded edges, 4 bell metal oblong keys mounted to base, raised above it a little, to be hit with little wooden ball on a stick. My grandmother, Grace Campbell Franklin, had one of these on her sideboard, and when we visited it was the greatest honor to be asked to ring the dinner chime. I usually played a version of "My dog has fleas." Originally such chimes came with a tune booklet — even "bugle calls" could be played on the chimes. Who knows — one tune might mean "Liver Tonight, Stay Upstairs," another "Buttered Biscuits Going Fast," another "Soup's On, Come Immediately." One company, Kohler-Liebich, made "Liberty" chimes, Chicago, IL, 1910s & 1920s. Others prob. much earlier. **$22-$45**

Dry measure, bentwood, handforged lap nails, painted old gray, American, 9-3/4" diameter, 19th C. **$40-$65**

Dry measure, bentwood, turned wood side handle, copper rivets & nails, American, 3-1/2" H x 5-1/2" diameter, 19th C. **$65-$85**

Dry measure, bentwood with copper rivets, for measuring dry weights as opposed to liquid amounts, "C.A. Wilkens," Henniker, NH, 8-3/4" D, 20th C. **$65-$85**

Dry measure, bentwood, with cover, supposedly Shaker, Maine, 8" diameter, 19th C. Cover is rarely found. **$150-$200**

Dry measure, bentwood with old red paint, wire bail handle, American, 19th C. **$60-$80**

Dry measure, bentwood with tin binding, American, 5-1/4" diameter, 1 qt. size, mid 19th C. **$60-$80**

Dry measure, dark green painted bentwood, 9" D diameter, late 19th C. **$75-$100**

Dry measure, for grain, marked "Dry 4 Quart, Frye," American, 20th C. **$20-$30**

Dry measure, for grain, wood with old mustard paint, American, 19th C. **$40-$55**

Dry measure, oak bentwood, "Daniel Cragin," Wilton, NH, 11-1/2" diameter, 19th C. Another by same maker, only 5-3/4" diameter: add 10% to 20% to value, because of rarer size. **$65-$85**

Dry measure, bentwood, copper nails, looks like saucepan with exaggeratedly uptilted handle, American, 6-1/2" diameter, 19th C. **$115-$140**

Dry measures, for grain, nested set of 4, old blue painted bentwood, American, 6" D to 12" D, late 19th C. **$250-$350**

Dry measures, set of 4 round graduated measures, bentwood, American, 6", 7", 9" and 11" diameter, late 19th C. **$120-$150**

Egg alarm timer, aluminum insert, in original box with instructions, whistles when egg is done, 20th C. **$20-$30**

Egg scales — See scale, egg grading

Egg tester or candler, pierced tin cylinder with strap handle, resembles a drinking cup, has hole in top for holding eggs to be candled using candle inside, "The Family Egg-Tester," American, 3" H, pat'd March 13, 1876. **$40-$65**

Egg timer, Black Americana, tin, color lithographed "Mammy," 3 hooks for potholders, 3 minute timer, American, early 20th C. **$55-$75**

Egg timer, cast iron frame with pedestal base, shaped like a cheval mirror, with small glass bulbs pivoting inside, from F. A. Walker catalog, American (?), or European import, about 4" H, c.1870s to 1880s. **$75-$125**

Egg timer, "Mauchlin ware" wood, with red plaid finish, simple square top & bottom with 4 corner columns, glass "hourglass" bulb inside this "cage." Scottish or German imitation, early 20th C. Early pieces of Mauchlin are highly collectible now. **$65-$85**

Egg timer, turned wood frame with old red paint, small glass bulbs inside, American, 4" H, 2nd to 3rd quarter 19th C. **$65-$85**

Egg timer, cast white metal, painted figural Amish woman with churn, glass bulbs off to side on pivot, John Wright Inc., Wrightsville, PA, 2" H x 3" W, c.1963. **$22-$30**

Egg timer, wall mounted, figural milk bottle backplate of enameled tin, attached flip timer with small glass bulbs, American, 6" H, turn of century. **$75-$100**

Egg timers, or **egg glasses,** figure-8 "hourglasses" but measuring a few minutes not an hour (or more), within frames of cast iron or turned wood, sold through F. A. Walker catalog, poss. European import, probably about 3" to 5" H, c.1880s. **$55-$75**

V-4. Teapot electric clock. *Stamped steel, finished in choice of colors: ivory, white, green, red or blue. 7" H x 8-1/2" W with 4" dial. Mfd. by Sessions. Advertised in various ladies magazines in 1941. SEE also V-101.* **$35-$45**

V-5. Egg timers. *At first glance, these appear identical. Both are obviously plaid, undoubtably Mauchlin ware.* **(L)** *Called an "egg glass," in "Scotch Wood," glass bulb. From 1870s-80s F. A. Walker kitchenware catalog.* **(R)** *3" H, in c.1909 A. Pick catalog.* **$65-$85**

V-6. Egg timers. (L) *Japanned cast iron pedestal-based frame with swiveling glass bulb, imported or American. Could be anywhere from about 4" H to 7" H. From F. A. Walker catalog, 1870s-80s.* **(R)** *also called a "time-glass for boiling eggs." Three turned wooden posts, wood disks for top and bottom, glass bulb. Virtually identical linecuts found in c.1870s-80s F. A. Walker and c.1909 Duparquet, Huot & Moneuse catalogs.* **(L) $75-$125**; **(R) $45-$65**

V-9. Egg timer— "The Signal." *This was found in the 2/1882* American Agriculturist: *"A short while ago we [the editor] visited Messrs. Baldwin & Co., Murray Street [NYC], for novelties. Among other things ... is the Signal Egg-timer. In this the sand-glass is suspended in a frame; ... and when sufficient sand has run into the lower part of the glass, its weight turns the glass and the hammer, shown at the top, falls down and strikes the bell below, informing the cook that the time is up. Below is a wedge-shaped counterpoise; by moving this, the alarm will be given at the end of two, three, or four minutes."* **$85-$125**

V-7. Egg timers. *Also called in latter years "telephone timers."* **(L)** *"Silver's Revolving Egg Timer," to hang on kitchen wall. Heavy printed fibre board with glass bulb containing fine white sand. Printed marks.* **(R)** *Brooklyn Egg Timer "is made of Bohemian glass with a sifted clear yellow imported time glass sand, that is absolutely reliable, never clogging, never stopping, and always indicating the correct time at the graduated points on the enameled board." 8-1/2" H x 1-1/2" W. These two are from the c.1910 catalog of Silver & Co., Brooklyn. (A similar one, valued at perhaps a third the value of the Silver's, is a 1920s German import, enameled metal frame (red, white or blue) which could be hooked at either end on wall.)* **$45-$60**

V-10. Egg testers. (L) *Turned wood with cup for egg, encircled by sheet tin or cardboard "frame" with a hole in the center about the size of the eggs tested. Black cloth or ribbon fills in space around edge of egg. The idea is to completely block light from escaping around edges of egg, in order to intensify the effect of the light shining through it. "A fresh or infertile one [is] perfectly clear, while a fertile one that has been incubated two days will show the embryo, as in the engraving. Infertile eggs may then be taken from the nest."* American Agriculturist, *early 1870s. I always had thought egg candling was done prior to selling the eggs. This implies that it's done when gathering, to leave fertile, viable eggs with the hen.* **(R)** *"Prairie State," pieced tin with small spirit lamp, a mirror inside reflects light through the egg. Joseph Breck catalog, 1905. The "spider" you see on the eggs is the embryonic chick.* **$40-$60+**

V-8. Egg timers. *Though similar in form,* **(L)** *is of turned wood, with portholes for viewing the sand bulbs, from S. Joseph catalog, c.1927;* **(R)** *is of pieced tin, japanned with background color and a few sprigs. Ritzinger & Grasgreen import catalog, c.1906-07. They look somewhat older than they are.* **$65-$85;$45-$55**

V-11. Egg detector. *Pieced tin, wire. Note arched piece in left of "dish" — this is the cutting edge. "By this machine you cut your shell; you do not smash it and get your batch full of small pieces. You do not make a mess on your table or bench; besides, you can break eggs much faster than in the old way, thereby saving valuable time." V. Clad & Sons pamphlet, c.1890-1900.* **$50-$75**

V-12. Faucets. *Turned wood faucets, leather- or cork-lined. For use with coopered vessels. J. Breck catalog, 1905.* **$3-$6**

Folk art sculpture, saxophone, made up of soldered together tin kitchen utensils: funnel, flour sifter, grater, and lots of tin ice cream spoons as the buttons & plates, almost full size, probably for hardware store display, American, very early 20th C. (Lavines say 1910). Dealers Jim & LuAnn Lavine in Geneseo, IL, advertised this in early 1989. Value range mine.   **$450-$600**

Funnels — So far these aren't avidly collected, but as we know, a collection of types, rich with variation, can be very attractive. A century ago, the word "tunnel" was sometimes used instead of funnel. In fact, the word "tunnel" is related to "tun," a large cask for wine, and one meaning of a tunnel was a pipe to draw off fluid from a tun! "Three tunnels [sic] are needed — a grocers tunnel for filling preserving jars, and one large and one small for filling bottles, jugs and cruets." Maria Parloa, *Kitchen Companion*, Boston: Estes & Lauriat, 1887.

FUNNELS, ceramic:
Fruit jar funnel, green sponged yellowware (unusual form in ceramic), small handle, American, 3" L x 5" D at top, wide neck, 19th C.   **$110-$135**

FUNNELS, enamelware:
Fruit jar filler or funnel, mottled gray graniteware, turn of century. See fruit jars & related items in Chapter XVI (Can, Dry and Preserve).   **$25-$35**

Fruit jar funnel, for canning jars, white enamelware, wide untapered neck, no mark, American (?), 5" L, late 19th or early 20th C.   **$20-$25**

Fruit jar funnel, large-throat size for canning jars or bulk meals & grains, also called a grocer's funnel, wide neck & mouth, cobalt & white swirled enamelware, 6" diameter, late 19th C.   **$75-$100**

Funnel, blue & white mottled enamelware, white interior, small strap handle, 5" L x 4" diameter, turn of century. Same approximate value for one in blue & white swirl enamelware.   **$55-$65**

Funnel, gray graniteware, crimped bottom, small side handle, 6" H, early 20th C. Another with elliptical mouth, same size. **$25-$40**

Funnel, white enamelware, small with relatively long neck, 4" H, early 20th C.   **$5-$10**

FUNNELS, glass:
Funnel, amethyst glass, flared sides, rolled lip, American (?), 5" L x 10" D, early 19th C.   **$150-$200**

Funnel, glass, bottom of neck is quite sharp, somehow looks like laboratory equipment, and it's not marked "Pyrex," which you would expect if it were a kitchen piece, 20th C (?).   **$5-$10**

FUNNELS, metal — aluminum, copper, tin:
Fruit jar funnel, for canning jars, spun aluminum, coffee-cup-like handle, wide cylindrical neck to fit into top of canning jar, 4-1/2" H x 5" diameter, late 19th C.   **$6-$9**

Funnel, spun aluminum, fat bowl, ring handle, shapely neck, about 4-1/2" H, late 19th C. The fat bowl is the charm & value.   **$6-$10**

Funnel, wide-mouthed, unusual brass in oval shape, American, mouth is 5" x 6-1/8", neck is 2" x 3", funnel is 7" H, 1860s.   **$55-$65**

Funnel, for brewers, copper with wire hanging loop, Eastern Bottlers Supply Co., 11" L x 9-1/4" D at top, c.1880s to 1900.   **$45-$65**

V-13. Steps in making a funnel. *From a series on the "Art of Coppersmithing" by long-time coppersmith John Fuller, Sr., in trade paper* The Metal Worker, *6/14/1890. (Fuller's articles were from his book published c.1889.) "Copper funnels were generally made brown, in size from pint to gallon. Let us make one to hold a half gallon; that is, one into which a half gallon of liquor may be dumped without running over. It will be found that an 8-inch cone whose slant hight is equal to its diameter will hold approx. a half gallon, Imperial measure. Funnels have always been of one style, and formed of one-half a disk whose radius is equal to the diameter of the mouth of the funnel." After assembling, it was scoured, tinned inside, and the outside rubbed with "Spanish brown." Note dovetailed seam; also fluted or furrowed neck providing air-escape route. Approximate value for late 19th C., pieced copper, 8" to 10" L funnel:* **$45+**

V-14. Cider funnel. *Turned wood, with 5-1/4" L neck. From 1983 Linden sale at Christie, Manson & Woods International Inc. Rather than round, oblong is the more usual shape for cider funnel bowls. Probably early 19th C.* **$125-$200**

V-15. Fruit jar funnels. *Obvious distinctive feature is large diameter neck. (Bag-filler funnels are big and have very large neck openings too.) Top* **(L)** *is plain, pieced tin, strap handle, shortish neck, 4-3/8" diameter cup with 2" diameter neck. Top* **(R)** *"Greystone" graniteware, same dimensions. Both Matthai-Ingram catalog, c.1890.* **(B)** *is spun & polished aluminum, riveted handle, with 1 pint capacity. 5-3/8" diameter cup; 2-1/8" diameter neck. "Mirro" Aluminum Goods Mfg., 1927. (If you thought aluminum was a post-20s thing, you'll be surprised to know there were many spun aluminum wares from about 1890 on. The older ones are noticeably more attractive than later ones, but value might be only a dollar or two more.)* **$10-$60**

V-16. Measuring funnel. *"Improved candy funnel," heavy tin, spiral spring ("no stick needed"), originally for confectioners. "Lately it found its way into restaurants and hotels for laying out griddle, wheat and buckwheat cakes." Henry Hueg, The Little Confectioner, c.1900-1921.* **$25-$40**

V-17. Measuring funnel patent. *"Combined graduated measure and funnel," pat'd 10/2/1877 by Simon Schippert, Burlington, IA. Has a stop valve to plug the mouth of the neck (seen within cutaway), activated by the thumb lever. Pieced tin.* Official Gazette.

V-19. Measuring funnel. *"Burke's Patent," copper that's tinned inside, strainer piece inside pouring nozzle. Two sizes: to measure from 1/2 pint to 1 quart; and 1/2 pint to 1/2 gallon. 1920s.* **$25-$40**

V-18. Measuring funnel combination tool, *called a "Combination Funnel Jigger," quadruple silverplated Britannia. Graduated inside to show 1/2, 1, 1-1/2 and 2 ounces. "Produced by one who has many years of experience in dispensing drinks, and he found a constant need for an article that would combine both all the uses of a graduated jigger and Pousse Cafe and Float making contrivance. ... It will make one dozen Pousse Cafes as easily as one. It is almost instantaneously in making a brandy, or other float ... and dispenses with the old-time method of using a spoon in order to float a liquid." A. Pick, 1909.. See also the "funnel droppers" in V-32 and V-33.* **$40-$50**

V-20. Funnels. **(L)** *Graniteware with large riveted side handle with grip, in 1 quart and 1/2 gallon sizes. Available through the Sethness Co. candy-maker's catalog, maker unknown. 1925.* **(R)** *White enameled steel without a seam, imported from Czechoslovakia. Five sizes: 3", 4", 4-3/4", 5-1/2" and 7-1/8", with capacities from 3 to 32 ounces. Pick-Barth catalog, 1929.* **$ 20-$40**

V-21. Funnels. *Clockwise from deep conical one at* **(B-L)***: Copper or brass, with strainer, in two weights — "light" and "strong" and six sizes from 1/2 to 2 pints.* **(T)** *— a large brewers' funnel, "brown" copper, with shapely bowl, in five sizes from 1/2 to 4 gallons.* **(R)** *Copper or brass, with strainer, in six sizes from 1/4 to 2 pints.* **(B-R)** *— a pewter strainer funnel, in two qualities: "best" and "common," five sizes from 1/4 to 2 pints. All four from catalog of Henry Rogers, Wolverhampton, England, 1914.* **$15-$100**

Funnel, copper for bartenders, advertising "Lash's Bitters," late 19th, early 20th C. **$65-$85**

Funnel, copper & tin, large tumbler-shaped cup with rolled rim, abruptly narrowing neck, "Schuyler's Improved Safety — Static Proof Filtering Funnel No. 1," Schuyler Mfg. Co., Springfield, OH, 8-1/2" H x 5-1/2" diameter, cup is 5" H, early 20th C. "pat. pending." I'm not convinced this is a kitchen piece — why the "static proof"? Maybe it's some kind of commercial piece that facilitated free-flowing contents. Or, it may be related to the late 19th, early 20th C. fascination with the powers of electricity — a company trying to cash in on that. **$30-$40**

Funnel, copper, tinned inside, American (?), cone-shape tapers from 6-1/2" D at mouth down to 2" at neck, late 19th C. This is lovely, but it's the kind of puff 'n' buff piece which is as much Brasso™ as anything else! I know I sound crazed on the subject of stripping and over-polishing brass and copper, but it drives me crazy. On the other hand, if a dealer has just retinned an old copper piece, I will pay extra, because it now costs over $1 a square inch to have it done. By the way, an old-fashioned way to polish copper was to keep a little saucer of sour milk (or buttermilk) near the stove, for wiping the copper pots every day. It tends to make a pinkish finish, at least at first. Try it; it almost always works, at least after more vigorous first-time cleaning. **$30-$40**

Funnel, copper, with brass spout & stopper, "Straiter," Boston, MA, pat'd Dec. 5, 1893. **$45-$55**

Funnel, copper with brass thumb piece that closes funnel, bulbous shape, "Straiter," Boston, MA, holds almost a quart, pat'd 1890. See also strainer funnels in Chapter III (Separate, strain, Drain, Sift and Dredge). **$65-$85**

Funnel, handwrought copper, dovetail seam construction, American, 10-1/2" L, early 19th C. **$120-$160**

V-22. Combination funnel, measuring cup/dipper, strainer, jar filler. *Spun aluminum. Has long "saucepan" handle, and the neck is a curved conical shape. Maker unknown, but from the Ritzinger & Grasgreen import catalog, c.1906-07.* **$20-$25**

V-23. Combination funnel. *Another, this one in pieced tin, with one brass strainer. Also Ritzinger & Grasgreen.* **$30-$45**

Funnel, for lamps, copper, embossed with name, a store premium or giveaway, for filling lamps with kerosene. (Coleman lamp funnels known in tin too; worth something less.) "Coleman Lamp & Stove Co." with paper label for "Steve's Furniture," turn of century. **$30-$45**

Funnel, pieced tin, interesting "around the corner" shape, 2 elbow joints that allow funnel to fit into hole otherwise unaccessible, looks like a Dogpatch hearing aid for Mammy Yokum, no mark, 14-1/2" L measured sort of diagonally, 5-1/2" diameter, late 19th C. Folk art crossover interest; why oh why didn't I buy it when I saw it!?! **$70-$90**

Fruit jar funnel, pieced tin, ring handle, early 20th C. **$10-$15**

Funnel, tin, with long cylindrical handle, capped & hooked, possibly for filling candle molds, American, 6" deep x 4-3/4" diameter, overall length 13-1/4", early 19th C. **$135-$175**

FUNNELS, wood:

Funnel, cider, carved from one piece of wood, American, 18" x 8-1/2" oblong x 3-1/2" deep, with 1" D hole in center of the oblong bowl, early to mid 19th C. These large, oblong (rather than round) cider funnels are very unusual looking, often primitive in style. They were meant to fit across the top of a cider keg. Prices range considerably, not so much because one is that much nicer than another, but because of knowledge of dealer, demand of collector, and general market conditions. A few cider funnels have dates or initials carved on them, which adds considerably to the value, as do any "finishing touches." Folk art crossover interest. **$150-$200**

V-24. Percolator funnel, *to put in top of coffee pot so that the flange held it in place. Cloth filter inside. 4-1/2" diameter. Graniteware mfd. by Matthai-Ingram, c.1890.* **$45-$65**

V-25. Funnel with stove polish. *You bought it with a quarter pound of C. W. Hart & Co., Troy, NY, paste stove polish inside. "all will readily perceive the convenience of the tube of the funnel, which serves as a handle, thereby making it possible to polish a stove without soiling the hands." You certainly didn't rub the funnel on the stove, and would need a brush too. "after the Polish is out of the Funnel, it can be used as a household article, always ready and convenient; therefore we utilize all, both the box and the blacking." Ad in* The Metal Worker, *10/7/1882. Collector value now is related to finding one with the marked tin cap or lid. Otherwise it's just a tin funnel with fluted neck.* **$20-$35**

V-29. Three-nose funnel, *for making butterscotch wafers. Pieced copper, with valve control ring visible coming up out of mouth. Braced tubular handle. Thomas Mills confectioners' catalog, 1930.* **$115-$150**

V-26. Droppers for candy-making. *Sort of a cross between a measuring funnel and a ladle, but put in this chapter because of relationship to droppers and fillers seen in the pictures.* **(T-L)** *is a "copper sugar dropper," in sizes from 5" to 10" diameter, tapered tubular handle without capped end. Bottom* **(L)** *is a "copper mint dropper, with one or two lips," 4" to 10" diameter, also tubular handle. They are in the Duparquet, Huot & Moneuse c.1904-1910 catalog.* **(T-R)** *is one of Lavoisier's chemistry instruments — made of copper or silver, for making a solution of salts in water. It dates to the 18th C.* **(B-R)** *is from a German confectioners' supply catalog of c.1904, a "Giesspfannen" [pouring pan] with two lips. A. Bertuch, Berlin. It is probably the same as the second one described above. Biggest have the most decorative value, and are valued as such.* **$50-$125**

V-30. Multi-nose or spouted funnels, *also known as* **"A. B. Runners,"** **"Candy Droppers,"** *or in German,* <u>Giesspfannen</u>, *or pouring pans. Five- to 8-spouters were depicted in several confectioners' supply catalogs. A c.1904 Bertuch catalog from Berlin offered them with 4, 6, 8 and 10 feststehenden Röhren, but depicted only a 5-spouter. Duparquet, Huot & Moneuse (c.1904-1910) also had a 5-spouter (with a beveled front edge like Bertuch's in the picture above) and 4, 6 or 8-spouters. The 1925 Sethness candy-making catalog picture (top) actually shows a Thomas Mills' runner with 8 spouts; Sethness offered only 5-spouters, but a 1930 Mills' catalog says they could be had with 4, 5, 6 or 8 spouts ... or "any size to order." An antique dealer's ad in 1990 called one of these a "rare candlemould filler," which it isn't.* **$125-$175**

V-27. Custard dippers or pie fillers. **(T-L)** *is from Duparquet, Huot & Moneuse, NYC, catalog c.1904-1910, and has extremely pronounced spouts. It came in 1, 2 and 3 quart sizes.* **(B-R)** *has braced tubular handle, and was available in 1 and 1-1/2 quart sizes. It's from the Jaburg Bros. candy-making supply catalog, 1908. Both probably made of heavy pieced tin.* **$50-$125**

V-31. Multi-nose or spouted funnel, *or "dropper for cream work," to be used in filling cream-filled pastries. Pieced tin, bail handle, seen curving around just above the 10 spouts. Turned wood handle above operates the bank of rubber stoppers. This could be had in "any size to order." Thomas Mills, 1930.* **$85-$135**

V-28. Pumpkin pie filler. *Pieced tin, with braced handle, two spouts, and a flared funnel-like hopper at top; 2, 3 & 4 quart capacity. The catalog had absolutely no explanation of how it's used, but at least you'll recognize one if you see it! Jaburg Bros., 1908. Has "folk art" appeal.* **$65-$ 85**

V-32. Funnel droppers. *All pieced tin.* **(T-L)** *from Sethness 1925 catalog, apparently mfd. by C. & B. S[ethness]. Co., with braced handle. 6" diameter at top, 3/8" opening.* **(B-L) Another** *that also came with a funnel stick, Thomas Mills' c.1915. The cone of this one came in four diameters and heights: 6-1/4" x 7"; 7-1/2" x 8-1/2"; 7" x 10"; and 10-1/2" x 12".* **(R)** *The biggest one in the picture is also Mills' — from 1930. It has a spring-lever built-in funnel stick, and was advertised as useful also "for cordial work." (A cordial was a filled candy, like chocolate cherries.) The funnel stick is used to push the creme material through the hole. SEE also the measuring funnels V-16 -19.* **$30-$50**

Funnel, cider, carved from two pieces of wood, oblong with rounded corners, has separate wooden spout fitted into center of bottom, American, 18-1/2" x 9" oblong x 4-1/2" deep, early 19th C. **$125-$150**

Funnel, cider, carved from one piece of wood, oblong wooden trencher (a sort of side-walled plate) with hole in bottom center, American, 21" x 8" oblong x 3" deep, early to mid 19th C. **$135-$160**

Funnel, for maple sap, barrel construction with iron band, American, 12" H x 11-1/2" D with 6" L cylindrical neck, 19th C. **$180-$225**

Funnel, turned wood, with nice lip, rather deep nicely rounded bowl, tapered neck, American, 5-1/4" L, early 19th C. **$110-$135**

FUNNELS, combination tools:

Funnel, corer, cookie cutter & grater combined, pieced tin, funnel has scalloped mouth for cutting cookies, the small end has sharp points for coring, the strap handle is partly punctured for grater & has one edge with sawteeth (I don't know what for). American, 5-3/4" L x 3-1/2" diameter, "pat. appl. for," c.1890s to 1915 (?). Collection of Carol Bohn. Price range mine. **$65-$85**

Funnel & dipper combined, tin, with 6 parts that fit together in various ways to create a funnel, sifter, dredger, measure, tea or coffee strainer, colander, ladle, clothes sprinkler, egg poacher, or funnel cake maker — considerably more than its name implies. The 6 parts are (1) main body or bowl, with handle, and bottom with screw threads; (2) funnel neck soldered to flat plate that fits hole in bottom of bowl; (3) screw threaded ring, like a canning jar ring; (4), (5), & (6) discs of perforated tin or wire mesh to provide various porosities. "Five-in-One," American, 5-1/4" H x 4-3/8" diameter x 8-1/2" L including long handle, c.1890s into 1910s. **$30-$45**

Funnel & measure combined — See measure & funnel combined

V-33. Funnel dropper. *For making cream wafers in 2, 3 or 4 colors (note dividing partitions within body of funnel). Pieced tin, capped tubular handle. Mills, 1930.* **$20-$30**

V-34. Cake filler, *or* **cream puff filler**. *Screw clamped to work table, mostly pieced tin. For a small set-up — in a shop with limited demand. Jaburg Bros., 1908.* **$45-$55**

Hourglass, glass funnel-like bulbs in wood frame, gilt & blue paint. (See also egg timers.) American (?), 7" H, early 19th C. **$180-$250**

Hourglass, simple 6-corner wooden cage-like frame, turned wooden "columns" at each corner, 2 glass flask-shaped bulbs fastened at waist with chamois leather, sometimes called a bottle glass, American (?), 8-5/8" H, early 19th C or late 18th. **$150-$200**

Hourglass, wood frame in old blue paint, glass with sand, American, mid 19th C. Added value: Old blue color more $$ than red; this one has nice detailing besides and a certain lopsided charm. **$85-$100**

Hourglass, wooden frame with rounded glass bulbous "funnels" joined at the small ends, 7-1/2" H, late 18th, early 19th C. **$150-$185**

Lamp funnel — See funnels, copper

Liquid measures are sometimes called **measuring pitchers** because they look and function like a pitcher, usually with a tapered body, wraparound lip & strap handle.

V-35. Cake filler. *"THE ANGER FILLER," is the great headline in the catalog. It sounds like a short story by Ray Bradbury! A cream puff filler which would "deliver large portions" or could be "regulated down to the smallest, which is 60 parts to a pound." I suspect it was about 16" H. Jaburg Bros., 1908.* **$50-$60**

V-36. Measuring device patent. *Pat'd 8/2/1887 by Elijah Truman, Parkersburg, WV. "The measure provided with a chamber closed on all exterior sides and partially covering the top of the measure, and having a discharge-nozzle, and a [spring-controlled] hinged cover to that portion of the top of the measure not covered by said chamber." Truman claimed as worthy of a patent "the combination of a measure having pins or axles below its center of gravity, and a support having standards provided with notches at different heights to receive the axles of the measure." The drawing alone makes this worth putting here. It's as surreal as a Man Ray or other Dada drawing. Patents were granted for many useless things; sometimes it seems as if patent examiners were charmed by the drawings as much as anything! If this were ever made, or if a patent model exists, I believe the collector value would be $300 or more. Official Gazette of the U.S. Patent Office.*

V-37. Measures. (L) *"Straight ale measure" in choice of "best pewter" or "common pewter," and in 1/2 pint, 1 pint or 2 pints.* **(R)** *Wine measure, in "best" or "common" pewter, and in "gun-metal." Many more sizes here: 1/16, 1/12, 1/8, 1/4 and 1/2 pint, 1 pint and 2 pints. Henry Rogers, Sons & Co., Wolverhampton, England, 1914. A full set of seven would be a good find, and would be over $200, despite lack of age.* **$45-$60**

V-40. Measures. *Pieced tin, partially wraparound lips, braced or reinforced handle for largest, 2-gallon, size. Smallest is 1/4 pint. F. A. Walker catalog, c.1890; same cut used to depict "Old Time" measures of heavy tin plate in the Matthai-Ingram catalog also c.1890. For each:* **$25-$65**

V-38. Measures. *Copper, tinned inside, with brass handles. From 3-3/8" H to 4-3/4" H — 1/2 pint to 2 pints, marked on small brass plates. Collection of Mary Mac Franklin.* **$60-$90**

V-41. Measures. *Quite similar to those in V-40, except that they are made of heavy tin with copper lips, and all, including the smallest, have reinforced strap handles. Sizes 1 gill, 1/2 and 1 pint, 1 quart, 2 quarts and 1 gallon. Duparquet, Huot & Moneuse, c.1904-1910. Extra value is for the "decorating" value of the copper.* **$25-$85**

V-39. Spirit measures. *Sometimes called "haystack measures." Both in the brown-finished copper described in Figure V-14. They could be had in many sizes: 1/8, 1/4, 1/2 and 1 pint, 2 or 4 pints, 1, 2, 3, 4 or 5 gallons. The* **(L)** *one is termed a "bottle necked" measure. H. Rogers, 1914. The value here is not in real age, but in the ancient form.* **$30-$70**

V-42. Measures. *Heavy tin, shown in 3 sizes:* **(L)** *2 quarts, which has a beautiful curved and reinforced handle to allow for pouring approximately four pounds of fluid,* **(R)** *1 pint,* **(M)** *1 quart, all with flared wraparound high lips. (A gallon size, with similar handle to 2-quart, was also available.) Notice the ribs or ridges denoting divisions within. Lisk Mfg. Co., 1896.* **$25-$45**

V-43. Measure. *Graniteware, gray & white. Completely wraparound lip, reinforced strap handle. Maker unknown, but was available in 4 sizes from Sethness: 1 pint, 1 quart, 1/2 gallon and 1 gallon. 1925 catalog, but probably virtually unchanged for 30 years before that.* **$60-$85**

Liquid measure, brass can, strap handle, American (?), 1 pint capacity, mid 19th C. **$45-$60**

Liquid measure, copper, flared complete wraparound lip, strap handle with semi-cylindrical inset for better grip, dinged, "Fleming Apple Distillery," Fairmount, NJ, 7-1/2" H, late 19th C. **$45-$65**

Liquid measure, copper, wraparound pouring lip, strap handle, American or English, 1 qt. capacity, 19th C. Sets of these were sold by candy makers' suppliers, at least as late as 1925. Copper ones were offered in six sizes, from 1 pt. to 1 gal., by the Sethness Co., Chicago. Theirs had a completely wraparound lip that was wider at the pouring "front" than over the handle. The largest one, which sold for only $2.50 in 1925, also had a strap handle with part of the loop filled in to make a hand grip. **$65-$85**

Liquid measure, copper, simple cylinder with strap handle, close-fitting lid with strap handle, "Stevens & Duncklee," Concord, NH, 5-1/2" H x 5" diameter, holds 52 oz. — an odd amount, neither here nor there, being 6-1/2 pints or 3-1/4 quarts. Possibly relates to a standard measure used for some now-unidentified liquid. Prob. 4th quarter 19th C. **$45-$60**

Liquid measure, copper, tinned inside, wraparound lip, reinforced strap handle, big dent in one side, no marks, American or English, 7-1/2" H, 1 quart capacity, 19th C. **$28-$40**

Liquid measures, copper & brass, elongated necks & widely-flared bodies (like skirts), English (?), 1 qt. & 1 gal. capacity, 19th C. Value for pair: **$200-$250**

Liquid measures, set of 3, tin-lined copper with small attached brass labels & brass strap handles in rounded rectangular shape, English (?), 1/2 pint size is 3-3/8" H x 3-1/8" diameter; 1 pt. — 3-7/8" H x 3-5/8" diameter; 2 pts. — 4-3/4" H x 4-1/2" diameter, mid (?) 19th C. Value range is for each, the way measures are usually found. **$45-$55**

Liquid measures, copper, tapering body & wraparound lip, strap handles, set of 6, "D. M. Smith," English or American, early 19th C. **$500-$650**

Liquid measure, gray graniteware, "NESCO," St. Louis, MO, 1 gal. capacity, 1st quarter 20th C. **$45-$55**

Liquid measure, gray graniteware, graduated stepped thirds, wire handle, American, 1 cup capacity, turn of century. **$25-$35**

Liquid measure, gray graniteware, pouring lip, slanted sides, 2 qt. capacity, late 19th C. **$45-$55**

Liquid measure, gray graniteware, riveted handle & lip, American, 1/2 pt. capacity, turn of century. **$40-$55**

Liquid measure, gray graniteware, straight sides, applied flaring wraparound pouring lip, strap handle, American, 2 qt. capacity, turn of century. (Pint size about 1/3 value, quart about 1/2.) **$60-$85**

Liquid measure, pieced tin, stepped sides, upside-down truncated cone, strap handle, marked "Kellerman's" (the mfr?), & "U. S. Standard," & "J. Coover," "Harrisburg, PA," 6-1/2" H, embossed 1 qt, 1 pt, 1/2 pt & 1 gill, pat'd Oct. 22, 1872. • Coover, of Chambersburgh, PA, invented the method for forming sheet-metal measures. **$45-$65**

Liquid measure, tin, bail handle, shaped like a small coal scuttle, marked "Pour Chaque Litre" & "Canneleure Correspondante," French, 1 decilitre capacity, mid to late 19th C. **$45-$55**

Liquid measure, pieced tin, Dover Mfg. Co., 1 qt. capacity, 19th C. **$18-$25**

Liquid measure, tin, flared wraparound lip, strap handle with brace, American, 8" H, 8 cup capacity, 19th C. **$18-$25**

Liquid measure, tin, high pouring rim, blobs of spelter or solder on it with marks stamped in the blobs, its size on a brass plate, and word "JOB" under plate. Square or bracket strap handle, strangest marks are letters stamped near handles, front & back: "Y Q A R C D F G H K M N P Q" (It's possible that "R" was a poorly punched "B"). Only 2" H x 2" diameter, marked "1 de-

ciliter," 19th C. As to the meaning of the string of 14 letters, I wonder if it indicates that the measure had been inspected 14 times, and each time the inspector used a different letter punch to indicate it had passed inspection? **$60-$75**

Liquid measure, tin, wraparound lip, generous strap handle, can part is perfectly cylindrical, marked with 3 ridges to divide it into fourths, looks like a coffee can, Matthai-Ingram was one mfr; I'm sure many others made similar wares, American, 4 sizes: 1 pt, 1 qt, 2 qts & 4 qts. The 1 quart size is 5" H x 3" diameter, c.1890 to 1910. **$15-$20**

Liquid measures, set of 6, pieced tin, slightly conical, wraparound lips, large strap handles, only one of which (the 2 gallon size) is reinforced, F. A. Walker catalog, American or imported, 1/4 pt. to 2 gal. capacity; that is, approx. 3" H to 15" H, c.1870s to 1890s. **$18-$30**

Liquid or dry measure, stamped tin, "Kreamer," 4 cup capacity, turn of century. **$15-$20**

Liquid or dry measures, set of 4 graduated cups with thumb tab handles, stamped tin, "Maryann's Accurate Measure," Chicago, IL, 1/4 cup to 1 cup, 20th C. For the set: **$15-$20**

Liquid measure, tin, with scrolly cast iron side handle, upside down conical shape with stepped divisions marking off 1 gill, 1/2 pint, 1 pint, 1 quart. Big flared fixed foot, I say prob. English, because on one 2-day trip to PA I saw at least a dozen of them, 6-3/4" H x 5-1/2" diameter at top, late 19th C. **$35-$45**

V-44. Vinegar measures & funnel. *Each piece scarped, hollowed, and finished from one piece of wood (not identified, but possibly maple or ash) in catalog of Joseph Breck, 1905. Style of all pieces is like much older examples. A set consisted of a pint, quart, 1/2 gallon measure and the funnel. Approx. value range for measures might tend to be higher than that for a funnel, which was probably about 7" H. Much of asking price would be based on patina and condition, and the presumption of great age that could be based on style and patina. For each:* **$35-$75**

V-45. "Utility" measures, *or* **combination measures**, *described in various catalogs as being a measure with an attached funnel. These appeared in several catalogs from about 1890 well into the 1920s (and probably later). Top one, shown being used to fill a bottle, is of pieced tin, in 5 sizes: 1/2 and 1 pint, 1 quart, 2 and 4 quarts. Matthai-Ingram, c.1890. Lower one is of polished tinned steel, with "tinned steel rests" on the bottom, reinforced handle. It came in 3 sizes: 1, 2 and 4 quarts. "Puritan" line, Central Stamping Co., 1920. Another one, almost identical but made of copper and available only in the 1-gallon size, is found in the Sethness publication of 1925. Value range for tin only; add from 50 to 100% for a copper one.* **$25-$45**

Measure, varnished, dark reddish brown wood-fiber & glue composition, rather thick-walled, cylindrical with raised edge for pouring lip opposite tin strap handle, bound with thin wire in 3 places, Indurated Fibre Ware, Cordley & Hayes, NYC, 9" H, late 19th or early 20th C. **$35-$45**

Measure, wooden, "Best Sealer," Henniker, NH, 6" D. **$15-$20**

Measure & funnel combined, called in catalogs a **utility measure**, a slightly tapered vessel, with strap handle hand grip, fitted with most of a funnel instead of pouring lip, copper, tinned on inside, American, 1 gal. capacity, late 19th into 2nd quarter 20th C. A similar one was sold in pieced tin in 5 sizes from 1/2 pint to one gallon by the Matthai-Ingram Co. The <u>funnel attachment</u>, as they called it, made it easy to fill small-mouthed vessels or to direct the stream in a particular place in a larger-mouthed vessel. The tin ones would bring only about half what the more "decorative" copper one would bring. **$60-$85**

Measuring cup, spun aluminum, "Swans Down Cake Flour Makes Better Cakes" embossed on side, American, 1 cup, 20th C. **$12-$15**

Measuring cup, cobalt blue & white mottled enamelware, "McClary," Ontario, Canada, 1 pt. capacity, early 20th C. **$75-$95**

Measuring cup, gray graniteware, heavy, applied pouring lip, strap handle, "Granite Iron Ware," mfd. by St. Louis Stamping Co., St. Louis, MO, 1 cup capacity, pat'd May 30, 1876, May 8, 1877. **$30-$40**

Measuring cup, embossed green Depression glass, Kellogg's, American, 1 cup capacity, 1930s. **$20-$30**

Measuring cup, embossed green Depression glass, 3-way pouring lips, straight sides, Hazel Atlas, 1 cup capacity, c.1930s. **$20-$35**

Measuring cup, embossed green Depression glass, one pouring lip, sides flare up slightly, Hazel Atlas, 1 cup capacity, c.1930s. **$20-$35**

Measuring cup, embossed green Depression glass, sides flare, modernistic or Art Deco stepped angular handle, rather tall, 3 pouring lips, c.1930s. **$30-$45**

Measuring cup, glass, "Faultless Diamond Starch," American, 1 cup capacity, 20th C. **$5-$7**

Measuring cup, heavy colorless glass, no pouring lip, marked on one side 1/4, 1/2, 3/4 & 1 cup; on other side 1/3, 2/3 & 1 cup, "Sellers," to go with their cabinets, pat'd Dec. 8, 1925. **$10-$18**

Measuring cup, stamped tin, "Rumford Baking Powder," 20th C. **$15-$20**

Measuring cup, stamped tin, "Cottolene" (shortening made from cottonseed oil), American, 1 cup, early 20th C. **$8-$15**

Measuring cup, stamped tin, embossed advertising message "Drink Barrington Hall Coffee," 1 cup, 20th C. **$6-$8**

Measuring cup, tin, deep wraparound lip, strap handle, American, 5" H, 2 cup size, late 19th C. **$12-$18**

Measuring cups, small tin flared side cups with tab handles, set of 4, "Mary Ann's Accurate Measure," mfd. by Katzinger Co., Chicago, measure 1/4 cup, 1/2 C, 1/3 C, and 1 C., c.1930s-40s (?). **$12-$15**

Measuring cup, turned maple, double ended with cups at each end, American, only 3-5/8" H, late 19th C. **$65-$85**

Measuring spoon, 4-way flip-over tool, stamped metal, 2 spoon bowls measure 1 TBS and 1 tsp, flip over & small concavities on back of bowls measure 1/2 tsp and 1/4 tsp, adv'g "Dr. Price's Baking Powder," 4-3/8" L, "patent pending," 20th C. **$12-$18**

Measuring spoon, 4-way flip-over tool, stamped metal, 2 spoon bowls measure 1 TBS and 1 tsp, flip over & small concavities on back of bowls measure 1/2 tsp and 1/4 tsp, adv'g "Dr. Price's Baking Powder," 4-3/8" L, "patent pending," 20th C. **$12-$18**

Measuring pans — I have seen cooking pans of bell metal and possibly also sheet iron (I can't recall now) with concentric rings on the inside bottom, as well as the sides. I thought it was some "accident" or evidence of the manufacturing process. But when I read in one of Soyer's 19th C. cookbooks about frying, and read to "place into the pan any oleaginous substance [viz. butter, lard], so that, when melted, it shall cover the bottom of the pan by about two lines . . ." I realized that the lines, even on the bottom, might be used for measuring. (It is also possible that a "line" is a unit of measurement, somehow related to line as a measure of length equalling 1/12 of an inch. In that case, Soyer would mean covering the bottom of the pan with lard enough to be 1/6 of an inch deep when melted.)

V-46. Measure. *Stamped & pieced tin, wraparound lip, strap handle, embossed graduations of 1-quart size. 5" H x 3" diameter. Maker unknown, c.1900.* **$15-$25**

V-47. Measure. *Copper, 5-gallon size only, with two tipping strap handles near the bottom, flared wraparound lip-rim or flange, swinging strap handle with reinforcement at center. Graduated with ribs. Sethness, 1925. Original price was $9.75 — talk about inflation!* **$45-$85**

Measuring spoon, aluminum, peculiar instrument with flat center handle strip, with propellor-like swiveling spoons at each end, measures 1/4 and 1/2 tsp, 1 tsp, and dessert spoon, "Level Measuring Spoon," mfd. by Barnard Co., Boston, MA, "patent applied for" c. 1920s. **$15-$20**

Measuring spoon, for coffee, molded yellow or red plastic, with "Mr. Peanut" handle. He stands on tablespoon coffee measure, and has smaller cup atop his head, Planters Peanuts, 20th C. **$10-$15**

Measuring spoon, silver-plated metal, beading around handle, with hanging hole, bowl of tablespoon-like spoon engraved with concentric oval rings for different measurements, with "Armour's Extract of Beef" engraved on bowl, picture of can of beef extract on handle, with label engraved "Armour & Co.," Chicago, U.S.A., c.1905. **$15-$22**

Measuring spoon, tin, "A & P," 20th C. **$6-$10**

Measuring spoons, stamped "malacca" tin of extremely simple construction, the handles of the three sort of riveted together with an open brass ring like a grommet, "Original," Landers, Frary & Clark, New Britain, CT, measured in teaspoons and drops: 1/4 teaspoon or 15 drops; 1/2 teaspoon or 30 drops; and 1 teaspoon or 60 drops, pat'd July 10, 1900. LFC showed the spoons at the Mechanic's Fair in Boston, fall of 1898, and said the three measurements "form the complete spoon measurements for any recipes." Also that the set "will hang by the eyelet on any convenient nail in your pantry when not in use." Ah, the simple claims of old-fashioned ads! I believe this may be the "original," of what we now take for granted. **$20-$25**

Oven thermometer, 2-part, heavy stamped brass-finished (or brass?) sheet metal with asbestos on bottom, & tilted upright frame with mercury thermometer, in original box, chromolithograph picture on front shows turn-of-century aproned woman putting food in oven with her thermometer, & legend "Always Use a Taylor Thermometer for Uniformity in Cooking & Baking." Also is an illustrated cookbooklet, *Taylor Homeset Cookbook. Bake & Cook the Thermometer Way,* with recipes. Woman on cookbook cover is of later date, but same box was probably used over a long period. "Taylor," model #5928, Rochester, NY, c.1920s. Added value: If the box were in good condition with a vibrantly colored, instead of faded & scuffed, picture, the set would sell for two or three times as much. **$10-$18**

Pie Birds, Vents & Chimneys — The earliest picture I've seen is of a pie vent was in a very early (probably pre-1710) chapbook/cookbook. (See illustration X-1 in Chapter X.) But I suspect that if I read Italian, I'd discover some kind of pie vent in use at least as early as the sixteenth century. In the 1890s there were a number of "pie funnels," "crust supports and ventilators for pies and pastry," "pie chimneys," "pie tubes," and "pie vents" patented in Great Britain and here. They may have been invented to cash in on a serious pie fad. Or to replace earlier specific pie vents, or modified ceramic or glass funnels used for the purpose of venting steam from a two-crust sweet or savory pie as it baked. The two requisites which help you recognize a pie vent, or even a figural pie "bird," are an arched opening in the base, and a vent-hole above the crust level — mouth, eyes, trunks, hats, chimneys, etc. There are many 3-1/2" to 6" H ceramic figural pieces which could be confused — until you note that they have no arched base and no definite vent-hole. Expert Lillian Cole dates the beginning of zoomorphic or human figurals (mainly in ceramic, a few in glass) to the 1930s, beginning with a blackbird. There are now many different blackbirds, almost the fabled "four & twenty blackbirds" baked in a nursery rhyme pie. Most of them look fairly similar and few are marked, although they come from potteries in several countries. There are dozens of other designs — most are the same motifs for which there are thousands of collectors, which include: hens & roosters, clowns, chefs, ladybugs, elves, pigs, dragons, snowmen, dogs, penguins, fish, owls, elephants, Santas, opera singers, bluebirds, cats, Wise Men, Mexican women, mushrooms, frogs, English "Bobbies," "Mammies," Dutch girls, angels, waiters, zebras, pelicans, ducklings, goslings, whales, bears, turtles and more. Some advertising pieces or licensed characters — like Donald Duck — may cost a lot, partly because of crossover interest. Most pie birds are collectible for under $50.

Pie bird, Black Americana figural "Mammy" with exuberant bandana turban, ceramic, American, about 4-1/2" H, c.1920s-1930s. **$50-$75**

Pie bird, ceramic, figural blackbird, in original box. The bird was positioned in the pie, a slit was cut in the top crust & it was put, serape-fashion, over the bird. Steam was supposed to be vented from within the pie, although it is possible that they didn't work as well as they were supposed to. This bird is marked "Royal Worcester." English, 4-1/2" H, 20th C. **$30-$50**

Pie bird, figural goose, pink ceramic, English, 20th C. **$25-$40**

Pie bird, pink ceramic figural of the "Pillsbury Twin," Pillsbury, 20th C. **$18-$30**

V-48. Measuring cup. *Molded lime glass, "annealed to prevent breaking from extremes of heat or cold. Graduated in thirds and fourths. Style called the "Brooklyn." One may hold it up to the light and see just the exact measurement." Silver & Co., c.1910.* **$15-$25**

V-49. Measuring spoons. *Aluminum, on a ring, a set of five including the midway measurement "**dessert spoon**," widely known in England, but not here anymore, although 19th C. American cookbooks use that measurement. Mfd. by the E. A. Fargo Co., Taunton, MA. An ad in* House Furnishing Review, *5/1915.* **$8-$12**

V-50. Measuring spoon. *A nickel-plated stamped steel mixing spoon with measuring graduations marked on bowl. Green plastic handle. Two sizes: 8-1/2" L and 10-3/4" L. "Androck" line, Washburn Co., 1936.* **$5-$8**

My friend Lillian Cole started a **newsletter for pie bird collectors** about the time the third edition of this book came out. Lillian has about 150 different birds (or other animals or people), most of which she believes are American-made. She probably knows more about them than anyone — partly because she has had incredible luck in tracking down people & potteries, in the U.S. and abroad, who have made them. For information, please write her at 14 Harmony School Rd., Flemington, NJ 08822, and enclose an SASE.

• • • •

New pie birds — For information and a color flyer, send $2.50 and a #10 SASE to one contemporary pie vent maker — Cupboard Classics, POB 373, Deer Trail, CO 80105.

• • • •

Huge Pie — The following appeared in the *Newcastle Chronicle*, 6th January 1770, in England: "Monday last was brought from Howick to Berwick, to be shipp'd for London, for Sir Hen. Grey, bart., a pie, the contents whereof are as follows: viz. 2 bushels of flour, 20 lbs. of butter, 4 geese, 2 turkies, 2 rabbits, 4 wild ducks, 2 woodcocks, 6 snipes, and 4 partridges; 2 neats' tongues, 2 curlews, 7 blackbirds, and 6 pigeons: it is supposed a very great curiosity, was made by Mrs. Dorothy Patterson, housekeeper at Howick. It was near nine feet in circumference at bottom, weighs about twelve stones [168 pounds], will take two men to present it to table; it is neatly fitted with a case, and four small wheels to facilitate its use to every guest that inclines to partake of its contents at table."

Pie bird, chef on a sort of pedestal, all white glaze, England. **$35-$45**

Pie bird, black chef, in green clothes, c.1940s. (Other color clothes worth a third or half.) **$150-$200**

Pie bird, crested head, blue glazed, eyes are the vents, 20th C. **$40-$50**

Pie bird, Donald Duck, cream color with pale blue sailor hat, bright yellow base & beak, marked "Walt Disney" and "Donald Duck," 1940s. **$150-$225**

Pie funnel, white china with wide brim, mfd. by Nut Brown, England, c.1920s. **$40-$50**

Pie vent or funnel, also called a **pie chimney**, white china, marked "Gourmet Pie Cup" with a crown, English, 1880s-1890s. There are several stoneware or white pottery pie vents, from England, Germany & the U.S. Names to look for are "Roe's Rosebud Patent;" "Cascade;" "The Improved Pie Funnel"; "Whitak-er's"; "Wilkinson's"; and "Foulds' & Smiths'." There are also glass & aluminum funnel vents. **$30-$45**

Room thermometer, stamped & painted tin, shaped like an urn, American, 1st quarter 20th C. **$15-$18**

Room thermometer, wall mounted, stamped sheet metal painted red, shaped like round teapot, has 2 simple hooks at bottom for hanging potholders, "Tel-Tru," Tel-Tru Thermometer Co., Rochester, NY, 5" H x 7" W, c.1930s to 1940s. **$12-$18**

Scale, balance, equal arm balance type, tin & iron, center post like a dinner horn, closed end possibly weighted with plaster or sand, beam is cast & looks European, 2 tin pans hung with string, probably homemade of assorted parts, American, 21" H, mid 19th C. Crossover folk art collectible. **$800-$1000**

Scale, bathroom, iron & brass, 'clock face' style standing on dimpled platform, spring balance type, "John Chatillon & Sons," NYC, NY, 1905. **$275-$325**

Scale, beam, cast iron, Dearborn Patent, 19th C. **$65-$95**

Scale, beam or balance, equal arm balance type, very elegant, decorated with restraint, cast brass, nickeled brass, sheet brass, marble base, adapted Byzantine central column of brass, weight pan attached to brass rods, goods scoop pan set on odd one-sided support, both rods & supports are on hooks, mfd. by one of finest American scalemakers, Henry Troemner, Philadelphia, PA, early 19th C. **Scientific instrument collecting**, for gents — scales of this class are probably not for foodstuffs. They form a collect-

V-52. Sap spouts. (T) *galvanized cast iron Eureka sap spout of 1869;* **(B)** *"improved" Eureka from 1870, mfd. by inventor, C. C. Post, Burlington, VT. "In the improved one, the bucket hangs by two points, so that it cannot swing like a pendulum, and in two narrow notches, so that it cannot twist nor wabble [sic]." W. J. Chamberlain, Hudson, OH, wrote in "Maple-Sugar Making," American Agriculturist, 2/1871: "Last year I recommended a wooden sap spout ... because it was, on the whole, better than any metallic one I had then seen. I find four or five different kinds are used in Vermont, but only one appears to me preferable to the turned, bored, and notched- in- three- places one in general use [in Ohio]. That is Post's Eureka." The marble-like "hemisphere 'hugs' against the outer edge of the hole" in the tree.* **$4-$8**

V-51. Pie birds. *Pastel-colored glazed china,* **(L)** *a blackbird or songbird, 5-1/8" H; the* **(R)** *one in the form of a baby bird asking for food is much heavier than the other, 5-3/8" H. 20th C. For those of you who wondered if you would recognize a pie bird vs. a bird figurine: note the cutouts in the base. Ex-collection Lillian Cole. The value range for these is very wide, depending on where you find them.* **$20-$40**

V-53. Sap spouts. *Here are C. C. Post's Eureka spouts after another 13 years! "The Sugar Maker's Friend. Over 6,000,000 sold, to replace various kinds." About 3-1/2" L. Note that he went back to the wire hanger for one style. The price in 1871 was described by Mr. Chamberlain as "high" at $4 for a hundred spouts. By the time of this ad, in American Agriculturist, 3/1883, the price was $4.25 and $4.50 per hundred. You could order a sample for three 3¢ U.S. stamps. Sounds like a postage cut would spur business growth a lot better than a tax cut!* **$4-$8**

ing field, along with microscopes, quadrants, telescopes and other precision scientific instruments, that exists in rather rarified air, and has been considered by realists as well as chauvinists, as of interest to men only. It's true, until recently, few women have collected such pieces. But then, many fewer women became scientists or pilots or astronomers, too. **$600-$850**

Scale, beam or balance, iron, chain hangers, tin pan, American?, 14" x 24", 19th C. **$25-$50**

Scale, candy, spring balance for countertop, cast iron, brass pan, counter top, "Brandon," American, about 14" L, pat'd 1867. **$70-$100**

Scale, candy of the spring balance type, tin base, brass pan, white enameled dial, Hanson Brothers, Chicago, IL, 12" H, late 19th C. **$75-$100**

Scale, candy or confectioners', <u>unequal arm balance</u> type, black painted cast iron, abstract fishtail or bird foot base, with 3 toes, brass pan, Fairbanks & Co., Philadelphia, PA, 1870s-1880s. Fairbanks also used a lot of red paint on cast iron bases. **$125-$160**

Scale, countertop, sometimes called a **platform scale**, unequal arm balance type, cast iron base with "fishtail" that keeps base stable, flat platform (for putting basket, box, bag or pieced brass pan of goods), oval brass pan with fixed ring base, sold through Montgomery Ward catalog, American, 1/2 oz to 25 lbs capacity, dated 1892. Platform scales of this type are **unequal arm balance scales** & have a long calibrated bar sticking out to the side, with a hook at the end from which a weight can be hung, plus a movable sliding weight that slides along the bar (like the scale at the doctor's office). The most commonly seen base design has an exaggerated fishtail (a sort of 2-toe chicken foot) sticking out at the bottom in the same direction as the bar; it helps keep base stable. **$80-$125**

Scale, egg grading, cast iron weight & balance painted red, cast iron base painted sky blue, aluminum egg pan & scale, brass pointer, very sculptural & aerospacey, "Zenith Egg Grader, #1002," also marked "1-F," Earlville, NY, 8" H, early 20th C. **$50-$75**

V-54. Sap spout. *Galvanized malleable iron, the "Breck" spout — "the invention of a practical sugar maker." Guaranteed not to break from being driven into the bored sap hole in the tree, and the cast-in hooks were made to "withstand the strain of high winds" which often caused buckets to twist off the hooks. They also sold the "Concord," "the common spout used largely in New Hampshire and Vermont, made of wood and steel." Joseph Breck, 1905.* **$4-$8**

V-55. Spice scale. *Of the <u>hanging equal arm balance</u> type. Japanned & pinstriped cast iron arm, (L) tin weight pan and scoop (R) for the loose spice being weighed. These cost only 75¢ for small size, or $1.25 for large, in Jaburg catalog, 1908.* **$25-$45**

Scale, egg grading, galvanized metal, stamped tin, "Oake's 'Sanitized' Equipment for every poultry need," Oakes Mfg. Co., Tipton, IN, 6-1/2" H x 6-1/2" W, 20th C. **$45-$60**

Scale, egg grading, painted heavy tin, Oakes Mfg. Co., Tipton, IN, 7" H x 7" L x 3-1/2" W, 20th C. **$30-$40**

Scale, egg grading, metal, "Mascot," American, 20th C. **$20-$25**

Scale, egg grading, metal, "Val-A," American, 20th C. **$20-$25**

Scale, egg grading, metal, "Montgomery Ward," American, turn of century. **$18-$25**

Scale, egg grading, metal, made in Toledo, OH, 20th C, could this be Toledo Scale Co.? **$15-$20**

Scale, egg grading, metal, "Unique," possibly made by the Steel Edge Stamping & Retinning Co., Boston, MA, 20th C. **$25-$35**

Scale, egg grading, painted sheet metal, red, green & white, "Jiffy-Way," "World's Largest Manufacturers of Egg Scales," Owatonna, MN, 5-3/4" H x 7-1/8" L, pat'd 1940 & still being made. <u>This is a commonly found egg grading scale.</u> It is a **spring balance scale** like many postal scales. The weight of the egg depresses a spring, which makes a pointer move to the calibration mark. New they cost about $18; "old" ones, if you can recognize them, are also: **$18-$25**

Scale, egg grading, polished metal, mounted on wooden board, has clip to hold egg, no mark, 20th C. **$65-$85**

Scale, egg grading, sheet metal base with spun brass egg cup, very simple modern frame, thumb screw adjustment, beautiful engraving of numbers on the scale, no marks, 9-7/8" H, 20th C. This is art, not just a egg scale. **$75-$110**

Scale, egg grading, stamped aluminum, wonderful soft slithery sound of the fulcrum as the egg is weighed, "Acme Egg Grading Scale," Specialty Mfg. Co., St. Paul, MN, 4-1/2" H x 10-1/2" L x 3-1/2" W, pat'd June 24, 1924. Some egg grading scales, like this one, are very like some postal scales, and are classed as <u>pendulum balances</u>. This one is fairly common, but it's a real classic. **$18-$28**

Scale, egg grading, tin box mounted to wooden base that's painted green, cup for egg, directions printed on it: "It is necessary that this scale is set level to weigh correctly. Clamp furnished is used when definite grade is desired. Place clamp on dial at grade wanted, and it will act as a stop to indicate for any . . . [weight]. This speeds up grading." "Reliable, Automatic Dial Egg Scale," Reliable Incubator & Brooder Co., Quincy, IL, 13" L, early 20th C. **$30-$40**

Scale, egg grading, painted sheet metal, extremely simple with cast metal counterweight, something like a Jiffy-Way, American, c.1910 to 1940. This is another "modern art," Alexander Calder-ish classic. Not rare, but a must-have. **$20-$30**

V-56. Spice scale, *or candy, grocers' or counter scale. At any rate, an <u>unequal arm balance scale</u> with a single beam. Black enameled cast iron with gold pinstriping, brass beam, cast iron weights and poise (the movable weight along the beam), and choice of brass or tin scoop (pan). Note the scoop pan in the picture has a high flared foot; the thing looks almost like a fancy hat. Round plate upon which the scoop sits is 8" diameter; scoop is 18" L x 8-1/4" W. Mfd. by Fairbanks — a high quality scale, and the price in the 1910 Norvell-Shapleigh catalog reflects that: $15.50 with the brass pan; a buck and a half less for tin.* **$95-$150**

V-57. Counter scale. *Japanned cast iron, bronze pinstriping, one type of so-called* **"fishtail" base**, *tin scoop pan, single beam, 25-pound capacity. Possibly a "Howe" scale; offered in the A. Pick catalog, 1909. The price then was only $3.60.* **$95-$150**

V-58. Counter scales, *unequal arm balance scales with single beam.* **(L)** *"Little Detective Pattern," probably Fairbanks, black japanned cast iron with brass beam. Tin scoop 12" x 6-3/4". Capacity 25 pounds. Norvell-Shapleigh 1910 catalog.* **(R)** *Painted and striped cast iron columnar base, capacity to 36 pounds, available with tin or brass scoop for the round plate. Available through, and possibly manufactured by, the John Van Range Co., Cincinnati, 1914.* **$95-$125**

V-59. "Union scales," *platform countertop, with single beam and slotted cast iron weights that slip over hanging weight rod. Painted and decorated cast iron, with pieced scoop (tin? brass?). Capacity from 1/2 ounce to 240 pounds. Jaburg catalog, 1908. The original cost was only $4, which seems absolutely impossible now.* **$100-$150**

V-60. John Wanamaker's Candy Department, *"from a photograph — showing four National Cash Registers in use," but also a unequal arm candy scale in foreground. From ad in Century, c.1880.*

V-61. Cake scale, *or platform scale with dial. Decorated cast iron, with oblong marble platform. Wonderful fluted columns. It came in three sizes: capacity 5 pounds, measured in 1/2 ounce increments; capacity 10 pounds, measured by 1 ounce; and capacity 20 pounds, by 2 ounces. Mfd. by John Chatillon & Sons, NYC; sold through Jaburg, 1908 catalog.* **$125-$150**

V-62. Cake scale, *of equal balance "trip" type. Japanned and decorated cast iron with 8" x 10" cool marble plate for the cake (or fudge?) being weighed. Jaburg, 1908.* **$135-$175**

V-63. Scale, *called a "ball scale" by Thomas Mills & Bro., in 1930 catalog. It is impossible to read the name plate because it wasn't engraved as real words, but it may have been made by Mills — and from the looks of it, long before 1930. Ornate cast iron with ball-shaped poises. Nickel-plated brass scoop. It could also be had with a plate (or platform) instead of a scoop. Capacity five pounds by quarter ounces. 1930 price with scoop was relatively high: $22.* **$175-$250**

V-64. Counter scale, a "double graduated 'arc scale' *that combines with Utility, both Beauty, and Convenience. Its primary object is to save the annoyance and expense [of] the loss of weights. It works [like] ordinary counter Scales, but in lieu of the plate for the ... weights, has a Graduated Arc, with a* **Permanently Attached Weight**, *through which an Index is passed, which [moves] over the Arc and denotes with great accuracy the weight of the commodity in the opposite dish. The scale is peculiarly adapted to Druggists, by having upon the Arc, a scale of Apothecaries' weights along with the ordinary Avoirdupois scale ... with an outer and inner index. ... The scale is also manufactured for Grocers, Tea Dealers & Confectioners." Buckelew & Waterman, Philadelphia, c.1840s-60s.* **$275-$350**

Scales, equal arm balance type sometimes referred to as a "balance scale," for countertop, cast iron base with hexagonal pyramid flanked by lyre shapes, pieced tin pan with fixed ring base, full set of 7 cast iron weights, in F. A. Walker catalog, American or import (?), about 6" H excluding pan, c.1880s. A **countertop equal arm balance scale** has a base that supports a sort of seesaw beam, each end of which has a platform. On one platform (or four-"fingered" support) goes the pan with the goods; on the other goes a weight or selection of weights in pounds & ounces, until the two platforms balance. This type is also sometimes called a platform scale, a country store scale, a countertop scale, or (if it's small enough) a candy scale. It should not be called simply a "balance scale" because all scales are balances — they are equal arm balances; unequal arm balances; spring balances (either platform or hanging); and pendulum balances. See the technical leaflet *"Scales and Weighing Devices"* that Albert R. Eaches wrote for the American Association for State and Local History. **$150-$200**

Scale, equal arm balance, countertop for candy, cast iron with brass pan, set of cast iron weights, "Dayton Style No. 166," (probably Dayton Standard Scale Co., Dayton, OH), late 19th C. Most candy scales are of the class called **equal arm balances.** They have a calibrated beam with arms of equal length, one end supporting a pan or scoop or platform for the thing being weighed, and a platform on which to pile weights that will counterbalance exactly that which is being weighed. Instead of being suspended from a hook, the calibrated beam is, in effect, suspended on its fulcrum, like a teeter-totter. When you are trying to remember just what kind of scale is a candy scale, visualize eating candy while playing on a seesaw. **$75-$150**

Scale, equal arm balance for candy, cast iron, painted black, with gold pinstriping, with brass pan, weights missing, no mark but date, 1915. So-called candy scales, or **countertop equal arm balances,** are the most collectible scales at this time, because of the dec-oration & form of the cast iron part, and the presence of a polished brass or interesting pieced tin pan or scoops. **$115-$150**

Scale, equal balance arm scale of unusual type, for candy or confectioners', cast iron stepped base, flat pan at one end, interesting half-circle horizontal graduated **arc with a sliding weight** on bar below arc, Buckelew & Waterman, Philadelphia, prior to 1867, but I can't find patent. This one is an equal balance arm scale, but the platform or pan for what is being weighed is balanced by a **permanent weight**, which causes a pointer to show weight on a calibrated arc. In addition, below this arc is a small calibrated beam with a small sliding poise, which is used to weigh the bottle or jar or small container that is to be filled. This prior weighing "automatically" adjusts the pointer on the arc. It really is quite ingenious, but I'm glad we don't have to use them at salad bars! **$175-$275+**

The 1867 advertisement for the above scale states that, "this novel invention combines with *Utility*, both *Beauty*, and *Convenience*. Its primary object is to save the annoyance and expense attendant upon the loss of weights. It works upon knife heads, as in ordinary Counter Scales, but in lieu of the plate for the reception of weights, has a graduated *Arc*, with a Permanently Attached Weight, through which an Index [pointer] is passed, which latter, moving over the Graduated Arc, denotes with great accuracy the commodity in the opposite dish [on the opposite platform]."

Scale, equal arm balance, countertop or "grocery" scales, green painted cast iron, brass scoop pan, Fairbanks, 11" L x 6-1/2" H, dated 1877. **$75-$85**

Scale, equal arm balance scale, countertop — sometimes called a country store scale, black finished cast iron with red & gold trim, tin pan, brass beam, American, late 19th C. **$95-$125**

Scale, equal arm balance type, countertop, red painted cast iron base, tin pan, with 1 lb & 2 lb weights, very handsome, Southwark Hardware Co., Philadelphia, PA, late 19th C. **$175-$215**

V-65. Counter scale, *equal arm balance type. Cast iron, meant to be used with weights piled on plate at left. The picture, of an "improved weighing balance," comes from the 1854* The American Home Cook Book, *which had many illustrations of recommended kitchen equipment.* **$150-$200**

V-66. Counter scale, *equal arm balance with plate, weights and scoop. Black japanned cast iron with fancy lyre-like Federal-inspired design. Weights 1/2 ounce to 4 pounds. This illustration from the F. A. Walker catalog, c.1890s. An identical linecut appeared in the 1875 Stuart, Peterson & Co.'s manufacturer's catalog, so they may have made them. Either this was the most popular style of scale at the turn of the century and several firms made them, or the artists doing the linecuts for catalogs all drew the same one just a bit different.* **$150-$250**

V-67. "French scales," *equal arm balance, with brass plate and index pointer. Capacity 4 and 5 kilograms. Imported from France, and sold by Duparquet, Huot & Moneuse, NYC, through their 1904-1910 catalog.* **$150-$250**

V-68. Counter scales, *equal arm balance scales with the lyre base, almost identical to the Stuart, Peterson/Walker scale.* **(T-L)** *"Hatch Pattern Even Balance" from the 1910 Norvell-Shapleigh Hardware Co. catalog. "a low priced scale for family use." 8-pound capacity, japanned cast iron frame 12-1/2" L, tin scoop is 16-3/4" L x 9-1/4" W. Original price $4.20.* **(B-R)** *"Iron Bearing Bakehouse Scales," cast iron. With the weights, in the 1908 Jaburg catalog, this was only $2.75. Hard to believe. — H. G. Wells, where are you when we need you!* **$150-$250**

"No kitchen outfit is complete without scales. Two kinds come for use in the household. The old-fashioned is the better, as there is nothing to get out of order. These scales [the equal arm balance type, with cast iron base] are more cumbersome than the dial scales, but the latter are likely to require repairing." Maria Parloa, *Kitchen Companion*, Boston: Estes & Lauriat, 1887.

• • • •

Scales of the **hanging spring balance** or **hook balance** type are probably the most commonly found scales at flea markets and antique malls. This is because so many of them, in a range of sizes, were used in Europe, Great Britain and North America — by grocers, butchers, farmers, feedstores, seed stores and housewives, and because they are so well made that a century or a century and a half later, they just keep on going! Those weighing up to 12 pounds are the commonest household size; up to 24 pounds worked for families and small tradesmen. Those with 50-pound capacities are commercial or at least for business use. "Landers, Frary & Clark" is the most common brand name scale found today in the U.S. "Salter's" is the commonest in England; "Chatillon" is a French name, but it's an American scale. Other makers include "Royal;" "Eagle Warranted;" and "Excelsior," mfd. by Sargent & Co. All those in a certain weight capacity group are pretty much worth the same thing,

unless there is something unusual about the brass face — fancy design or collectible advertising.

Hanging spring balance scales use a spring, but the weight hangs off the spring (with a hook) rather than being place on top of it to depress it, as in a dial scale. The face or dial of the scale, on which the pointer registers the weight, is usually long and rectangular and often brass, but it can be round, like a dial scale's face. There has to be a hanging ring at top, so the scale can be hung near where it's to be used. From the bottom comes a ring & hook, from which is hung the food to be weighed. A complete set might also have a round platform with a fixed bail handle to hang off the hook (some of these have porcelainized platforms and nickeled brass frames & bails), or a pieced tin pan with chains to hang off the hook.

In Albert R. Eaches' Technical Leaflet #59, *"Scales and Weighing Devices,"* he writes "a spring balance is a weighing device which utilizes the physical distortion of a piece of metal." In this case it's a steel spring, inside the cylindrical scale body, that is "distorted" or pulled to a looser spiral by what is hung from it, causing a little pointer to move on the calibrated face.

Asher & Adams' Pictorial Album of American Industry, published in 1876 as a gala advertisement and history for the U. S. Centennial, has a piece on the New York scale manufacturer Thomas Morton, in which they surveyed the **"origin" of [hanging] spring balances**, also called hook balance scales. "Since the invention, nearly half a century ago, of the spring balance by one George Salters, of West Bromwich, England, we suppose no article of a mechanical nature in itself has obtained so universal a practical character as this. Scarcely a butcher or grocer in any country . . . but finds its utility second only to his knife and hatchet. . . . When spring balances were first introduced in America our people had but little confidence in them. The principle of springs was deemed unreliable, but they soon began to work their way forward. As soon as their real value was known, competitors in the field . . . sprang

V-69. Counter scales. *Japanned and decorated cast iron frame, seamless stamped brass scoop 13" L x 6" W, rubber tips on the "fork" that holds the scoop. Thomas Mills catalog, 1930.* **$125-$175**

V-70. Counter scales, *also called* **even balance trip** *scales. Cast iron are enameled or japanned, and decorated, seamless brass scoops.* **(T-L)** *described as being "without tare beam," which means that you could not adjust it to take the weight of the commodity's container into account when weighing for contents. It came in four sizes.* **(B-R)** *a tare beam, and came in three sizes. Both from the 1908 Jaburg catalog for professional confectioners and bakers.* **$125-$175**

V-71. Scale or "weighing machine." *The "Registered" style, in three sizes, 1/4 ounce to 14 pound capacity; 1/4 ounce to 7 pound capacity; and 1 ounce to 4 pound. Cast iron, ornate, japanned base, octagonal scale plate, slightly dished pan. Harrod's Stores catalog, London, 1895.* **$175-$225**

V-72. Scale *or "weighing machine." Called "Family" style in England, although an American "Family" style scale was probably always a dial scale like those in V-84, -85, -86. Very simple cast iron frame, octagonal weight plate. Same three capacities as the "Registered" in V-73. Also from Harrod's, 1895 catalog.* **$125-$175**

up with great rapidity, and the market was flooded with unreliable scales and balances. . . . In 1842, in conjunction with Mr. A. A. Bremner, Mr. Thomas Morton introduced to the American public the first domestic made spring balance, the construction of which was based upon Salter's method. This was a hook balance scale to weigh up to 24 lbs. From that day to this the principle [of these scales] has remained intact, thought the number of varieties of spring scales now made by Mr. Morton amounts to more than 150, rising from balances that will weigh a ten cent stamp — whose weight by the way is only a quarter of a dram — up to heavy instruments capable of weighing accurately 2000 lbs. at a time. . . . Mr. Morton's goods rank with the best. None but the very best iron, steel and brass that can be bought are used in his manufacturers. . . . As a striking evidence of their excellence it might be remarked that one of the Morton & Bremner spring scales has been in use in the Boston market for the last twenty years, and has never faltered or required any repairs whatever. . . ." One of the scales pictured with the above is a jockey chair, a very elegant armchair without legs, hanging from a large round dial decorated with an eagle and the date 1866 — what a great big-bathroom accessory!

Scale, hanging spring balance, oblong brass face, 12 pound, "Landers, Frary & Clark," New Britain, CT, mid to late 19th C. **$30-$40**

Scale, hanging spring balance, for ice, iron with brass face, (Landers, Frary & Clark, as well as Wilson Mfg. Co., made ice scales of this type), American, c.1900. **$35-$40**

Scale, hanging spring balance, brass face, iron, "Frary's Improved Balance #2," mfd. by L, F & C, 50 lb capacity, late 19th C. **$35-$45**

Scale, hanging spring balance, brass & iron, "Chatillon," NYC, NY, 8" L x 1-3/8" W, 25 lb capacity, pat'd Dec. 10, 1867, Jan. 6, 1891, Jan. 26, 1892. **$35-$45**

Scale, hanging spring balance, brass plate, steel & iron, weighs up to 60 pounds, "For industrial use only," mfd. by Henry Boker, German, about 6" L, late 19th or early 20th C. **$35-$45**

Scale, hanging spring balance, cast steel, brass base & iron pan, "Class Two, Salters Improved Family Scale, No. 50," Silvers Patent, English, 14" H, late 19th C. **$90-$125**

Scale, hanging spring balance, iron ring, iron hook, brass face engraved with measurements, "Salter's Improved Spring Balance," mfd. by Salter & Co., West Midlands, England, 50 lb capacity, 2nd to 3rd quarter 19th C (?). **"Salter's improved Spring Balance.** — A very neat form of the instrument [known as the spring steelyard] has been recently brought before the public by Mr. Salter, under the name of the Improved Spring Balance. The spring is contained in the upper half of a cylinder behind the brass plate forming the face of the instrument; and the rod is fixed to the lower extremity of the spring, which is consequently extended, instead of being compressed, by the application of the weight. The divisions, each indicating half a pound, are engraved upon the face of the brass plate, and are pointed out by an index attached to the rod." Captain Henry Kater, *The Cabinet Cyclopædia. Conducted by the Rev. Dionysius Lardner.* Volume on *Natural Philosophy. Mechanics.* London: Longman, Rees, Orme, Brown, & Green, 1830. The engraving in the book looks exactly like the Salter's scales so often seen. It should be noted that the hook is forged iron; on later examples, the hook would be a heavy drawn wire, cut into a point and bent. **$55-$70**

Scale, hanging spring balance, iron with brass face, "Peck's," (Peck, Stow & Wilcox, Connecticut), turn of century. **$25-$45**

Scale, hanging spring balance, iron with large brass face, another brand of feed advertisement, legend reads "FEED KASCO FEEDS, weigh the milk, weigh the feed," Kasco Mills Inc., Waverly, NY, about 11" L, 20th C. **$150-$200**

Scale, hanging spring balance, iron with large crested brass face, decorated with checkerboard design top and bottom, legend reads "COW CHOW MAKES MORE MILK AT LESS COST, Don't guess — Use this Purina Milk Scale," Ralston Purina, (coincidentally there was a Ralston Scale Co.), American, face is 10-1/2" L x unusually wide 4-1/2" W, weighs to 30 lbs, 20th C. Who wouldn't want one of these! **$225-$450**

Scale, hanging spring balance, green painted steel case, "Viking #8910," Hanson Scale Co., 13" L, 100 lb capacity, 20th C. **$40-$60**

Scale, hanging spring balance, red, black & green finished iron, with white enamel face, 2 pointers, marked "Hanson Dairy" (not the name of a particular dairy, but a "dairy scale" by Hanson Scale Co.), American, 6-3/4" D face. **$115-$135**

Scale, hanging spring balance, brass plate, steel & iron, "Excelsior Improved Spring Balance," mfd. by Sargent & Co., American, about 6" L, 25 lb capacity, late 19th or early 20th C. **$50-$65**

Scale, hanging spring balance, brass face, iron, "Excelsior Spring," Sargent & Co., 50 lb capacity, late 19th C. **$60-$75**

Scale, spring, also called a **dial scale**, a **kitchen scale**, or a **family scale**, this one the boxy kind with pan or platform on top, meant for kitchen or household use, green painted iron, red & white enameled face, red pointer, tin pan, "American Family Scales," turn of century to 1920s. **$45-$65**

Scale, spring, for kitchen or household use, cast iron & stamped sheet iron, "Simmons Hardware Co.," 20th C. Crossover Simmons collectors. **$40-$50**

Scale, spring, kitchen balance with large brass dial face, Ariosa Coffee, 20 lb capacity, early 20th C. Advertising piece. **$75-$100+**

Scale, spring, kitchen or family scale, the boxy base with a large dial face on front, with the weight pan or forked support (almost like an upraised hand with fingers outspread) that holds a scoop or pan on top, sheet iron, partly painted, "Winchester," turn of century. You've got competition from Winchester collectors. **$75-$125**

Scale, spring, kitchen or household type, iron base, "Cat Tail," sold through Sears & Roebuck, American, turn of century. **$45-$60**

Scale, spring, metal with white face, red pointer, "Pelouze," 12" H x 6-1/2" D dial, 20th C. **$25-$35**

Scale, spring balance, cast iron 3-legged frame, round cast iron faceplate, very finely cast with calibrations, weighing platform on top, "Novelty Scale," "Turnbull's Patent," American, 7-3/4" H, 12 lb capacity, pat'd July 24, 1877. Just fabulous; this is the kind of neat cast iron piece that appeals to "iron" collectors, who dip in and out of many specialty fields of collecting — from garden to stable, hardware to kitchen, still banks to doorstops. **$200-$250+**

Scale, spring balance, family type, very graceful minimalist cast iron base, round deeply engraved brass face, beautifully formed shallow bowl is the attached weighing pan, "Salters Family Scale, No. 50, Class II Improved," about 13" H, weighs to 15 lbs, late 19th or very early 20th C. Pure sculpture. **$125-$175**

Scale, spring balance, family type, fancy cast iron, "Sutler #49," 12-1/2" H, turn of century. **$95-$130**

Scale, spring balance, countertop (despite brand name this is not the standard old fashioned "family" style scale), heavy sheet iron, finished black, very fancy dial plate, legs, flat platform, "Novelty Family Scale," sold by Montgomery Ward, Chicago, IL, late 19th C. **$65-$80**

Scale, spring balance, family or dial type, painted sheet metal, square base, round dial, square flat platform, American Family Scales, 9-3/4" H x 6" square, pat'd 1898, mfd. for years. Condition of paint is important here; these rusted easily, so inspect for repainting over rough, bumpy rust areas. **$18-$30**

V-73. Scale *with weights arrayed along front of cast iron frame. "as one of the great elements of success in cooking is preciseness in the proportions of ingredients, the cook should never be without a good pair of scales, and she should keep them in thorough order. In delicate dishes an uneuql proportion of an article inserted only to impart a certain flavour, will ruin the dish. The necessity as well as use of scales is therefore obvious." Picture and quote from* Warne's Model Cookery and Housekeeping Book, *compiled by Mary Jewry. London: 1868.* **$125-$175**

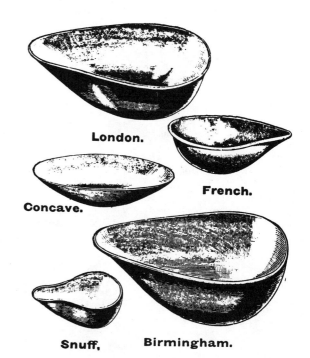

London.

French.

Concave.

Snuff.

Birmingham.

V-75. Scale pans or scoops. *All obviously unseamed (which means stamped) and probably brass. The five styles — London, Birmingham, French, Concave, and Snuff — were all offered in the 1914 Henry Rogers, Wolverhampton, England, catalog. Collectors will pay extra for brass pans, even if originally the scale had a tin pan, or if the brass pan was nickeled.* **$15-$30**

V-74. Scale scoop *for bakehouse scales. Heavy tin, pieced construction, footed. Came in three sizes: medium, large and extra large. 1908 Jaburg supply catalog.* **$15-$25**

FAIRBANKS' STANDARD SCALES.

BUY ONLY THE GENUINE.

V-76. Trade card *for Fairbanks scales, NYC. Chromolithograph depicting the showroom, with several gents looking over various sizes and types. Card from 1880s. For the card:* **$15-$20**

V-77. Weights *for bakehouse scales. Five materials, available singly or in sets of 8 or 9, from 1/2 ounce to 4 pounds or 1/4 ounce to 4 pounds. The five were nickel-plated brass, solid brass, cased brass, zinc, or cast iron. 1908 Jaburg catalog. Value mostly for sets of matching weights, even if the sets are incomplete. Per weight, with maybe a bit added for solid brass weights:* **$2-$8**

V-78. Weights *of two types.* **(L)** *"Nest of Brass French Weights" in wooden box, in kilograms.* **(R)** *"Nest of Iron American Weights," stacked, 1 ounce to 8 pounds. Duparquet, Huot & Moneuse, c.1904-1910. A full set of 10 French ones would be worth between $40-$60. For a set:* **$20-$50**

V-79. Weights. *Cast iron.* **(L)** *Flat weights, beveled edge, 9 in a set, from 1/4 ounce to 4 pounds. Top* **(M)** *Convex edge weights, same 9. Bottom* **(M)** *Plain flat weights.* **(R)** *Bell weight, in 10 sizes, from 1/4 ounce to 7 pounds (skips 5, 6 pounds). All in Henry Rogers, Wolverhampton, England, 1914 catalog. Individual weights:* **$2-$8**

V-80. Egg scale. *"Acme Egg Grading Scale," mfd. by Specialty Mfg. Co., St. Paul, MN, aluminum. 4-1/2" H x 10-1/2" L x 3-1/2" W, pat'd 6/24/1924. This one doesn't seem to get the price that the Jiffy-Way does, though to my mind it's far more desirable aesthetically and aurally.* **$18-$28**

V-81. Egg scale. *The most commonly found kind — mainly because it's been made continuously since being patented in 1940. "Jiffy-Way," green & red painted heavy sheet metal, 5-3/4" H x 7-1/8" L. Patent #2205917. Jiffy-Way Inc., Owatonna, MN — "World's largest manufacturers of egg scales." 1-1/2 ounces to 2-1/2 ounces.* **$18-$25**

V-82. Family scales, *also called* **dial scales.** *Both enameled and decorated sheet iron with flat platforms and round dials on front, all weigh to 24 pounds.* **(T-L)** *"Columbia," mfd. by Landers, Frary & Clark, New Britain, CT. In six models: black enamel; white enameled dial, square steel top; white enameled dial, steel top, tin scoop; brass plated scale; brass plated with white enameled dial and steel top; and the most desirable one — brass-plated body, brass dial, brass scoop, steel top. Joseph Breck catalog, 1905.* **(B-R)** *"Favorite," mfd. by John Chatillon & Sons, pat'd July 16 [?], 18—, "silver-plated" brass dial, "handsomely ornamented." 24-pound capacity. In 1924 D. J. Barry catalog.* **$45-$85**

V-83. Family scale. *Stamped sheet iron, white painted dial, 11" H with 8" diameter pan or tray attached on top, "The Daisy," maker unknown from the ad.* **$90-$125**

V-86. Hanging spring balance scale. *This is the most commonly found type of old scale; at least one appears at every show and flea market. This one is iron with brass face to the spring-housing, steel spring, white-enameled dial in front. Mfd. by Morton & Bremner (formerly Thomas Morton), NYC. In Asher & Adams Pictorial Album of American Industry, 1876.* **$50-$60**

V-84. Family scale. *Cast steel or iron with brass base and iron pan. "Class Two, Salters Improved Family Scale, No. 50," 14-pound capacity, about 14" H. English, late 19th C. Salters is one of three big names in scales, the others being Chatillon and Fairbanks.* **$125-$175**

V-87. Hanging spring balance scales. **(L)** *"Sargent Armored," black japanned steel case for spring, nickeled dial on both sides, steel spring, tinned steel hook & ring, 9-1/2" H x 2-1/2" W, overall length 14", 200-pound capacity in 5-pound graduations. Norvell-Shapleigh Hardware Co., 1910 catalog.* **(M)** *"Chatillon's Balance No. 2," iron case with curved back and nickel-plated brass front; also available with flat back, and a much broader index pointer. 25-pound capacity by 8-ounce increments. D. J. Barry catalog, 1925.* **(R)** *Called a "German Crab" scale in the Norvell-Shapleigh catalog, which refers to the side hooks, because its capacity is 300 pounds, in 5-pound graduations — not the thing for weighing crabs. Spring steel frame 3-3/4" x 3-1/2" , overall 10-1/2" L, polished brass demilune face with stamped lines & numbers, polished wrought steel hooks and ring.* **$35-$45**

V-85. Hanging spring balance scale. *Fancy japanned cast iron case with large white enameled dial, 7" diameter, with graduations enameled in black. 13" diameter pan suspended from tinned bow and swivel. Overall 31" H. 10-pound capacity. Norvell-Shapleigh, 1910 catalog.* **$100-$150**

V-88. Spring balance scale *and standard. Nickel-plated brass. Maker not shown, in catalog shot but probably Chatillon. Could be had with a double-faced dial, and the arched standard could be bought separately. Jaburg 1908 catalog.* **$125-$200**

Scale, spring balance, family scale type, sheet metal painted black with fancy trim, brass dial, tin pan, "Columbia," Landers, Frary & Clark, 24 lb capacity, turn of century.   **$55-$75**

Scale, spring balance, family type, slanted dial, stamped steel body enameled blue with pin striping, tin scoop fits on claw, "Triner Perfection," mfd. by Allsteel Scale Co., Inc., NYC, 24 lb capacity, 10" H x 6" W, pat'd May 1, 1906. Interesting looking.   **$30-$45**

Scales, spring balance, or dial scale, red painted cast iron base, brass pan & glass dial face, "Eureka," style C, 18" H x 15", pat'd Oct. 5, 1869. These spring balance scales have a base below the weighing platform or pan, and a large clock-like dial on the side of the base with an index pointer that indicates the weight. These usually have a little fine tuning wheel for resetting zero.   **$225-$250**

Steelyard scales, from the class of scales known as **unequal arm balances**, are the oldest type of scale, and examples from many parts of the world are known. It consists of a long flattened beam suspended from a hanger hook attached close to the thicker, shorter arm of the beam. There is a hanger hook underneath the short arm, from which the thing to be weighed is hung. The long arm of the beam is calibrated, in pounds or ounces, or metric units, and has on it a weight called a poise, which can be slid along the long arm to balance whatever is hung from the hook at the other end. The poise may be cast iron and somewhat decorative, and a steelyard scale might have several different poises. According to Albert R. Eaches, who wrote the invaluable Technical Leaflet #59, *"Scales and Weighing Devices,"* for the Association of State and Local History, these unequal arm balance scales got the name steelyards "when steel was first imported into England." He also explains that another type of unequal arm balance scale very like a steelyard, and sometimes even called a steelyard, should actually be called a <u>weighmasters beam scale</u>. These can be identified by the

Fig. 1.
—The Folding Family Scale.
Folded Flat Against the Wall.   **Fig. 2.**
—Scale Unfolded and Ready for Use.

V-89. Fold-away scale. *Called in* The Metal Worker *article about it a "folding family scale," but the term "family" is most usually associated with spring scales with platforms or pans above the dial. Ornamental cast iron bracket, brass pan, unequal arm balance type with poise and loose weights, 50-pound capacity by 1/2-ounce graduations. Mfd. by Folding Scale Co., Beloit, WI. "Heretofore persons having a family scale have been troubled by having no regular place for it that would not at times make it an inconvenience. This new device overcomes that difficulty, as the scale can be folded up against the wall or door to which it is attached." The Metal Worker, 5/31/1890.* **$150+**

rather large swooping hooked end (looks almost like an antique iceskating blade) of the short arm of the beam, and by two sets of calibration and two "separate poises to correspond" to these calibrations.

V-90. Ancient steelyard scales. *Excuse the poor quality of the picture: it is adapted from a 1910 catalog with shadowy photographs, of a foundry in Naples, Italy, that specialized in reproductions of ancient bronzes found at Pompeii and Herculaneum. Cast bronze. Two have hanging pans, one has a hook. This type of scale has changed little in 2000 years; the weights have changed (see Figure* **V-XXX**). *In this lengthy catalog, the date the archaeological find was made, and measurements of the originals are given. These steelyards were found the 31st of July, 1888, at Pompeii.* **(L)** *45 cm. or about 17-3/4" L;* **(M)** *40 cm. or about 15-3/4" L;* **(R)** *50 cm. or about 19-3/4" L. They were available in 2 finishes: blackened cast bronze (Herculaneum) or verdigris or green (Pompeii). Center figural* **weight** *for steelyard of ancient Pompeian type. Cast bronze, woman's bust, with waved hairstyle and draped bodice. It appears that a hook was cast on top of the heads — this one represents the weight of the scale at right — and hooked through a ring that hung from a chain fixed to the steelyard beam. The size is probably about 5-1/2" to 6" H. My drawing adapted from J. Chiurazzi & Fils-S. De Angelis & Fils catalog, 1910-11.*

V-91. Steelyard scale. *The round moveable weight is at* **(L)**, *the package being weighed is at* **(R)**. *Illustration (taken from a schoolbook of 1905, entitled* Natural Philosophy), *explains that the steelyard scale, also known as the* **Roman balance**, *"has no great sensitiveness" and is based on the <u>principle of a lever</u>. The fulcrum is the pivot point on the beam below where the hand is holding the hanging ring. The arm or beam to the left of the fulcrum is "graduated into equal parts," and the weight is moved along the sharp edge of the arm until a position is found in which it just counterbalances the load. The weight of the lever itself is allowed for in the graduations. For this type of manufactured scale the value is much less than that for a comparably sized hand-forged one.* **$35-$85**

Scale pan, pieced tin, oval with its own foot ring attached to the flat platform of balance scale, American (?), 4" deep x 14-1/8" L x 8" W, late 19th or early 20th C. Hard to evaluate because it is part of something else & might be worth a lot to someone trying to set up a spring balance scale. **$12-$22**

Scale, spring with beam, countertop, cast iron, brass scoop, 2 iron weights, includes scoop, 20th C. **$50-$65**

Scale, steelyard, or <u>stillyard</u> type, wrought iron, long rod with weight, hook at other end for the goods, nice detailing. When not in use, steelyard scales tend to look like a pile of iron bars & hooks. They only really come to life when they are hanging up & have the movable poise placed so it can balance the weight of the end with the hook or hooks, or when actually weighing something. For display, some scale collectors hang a heavy weight from the hook meant for the goods. According to Carl W. Drepperd, a small steelyard scale is called a <u>steel foot.</u> American, 25" L, 18th C. **$95-$125**

Steelyard caveat emptor — Being imported now from Turkey are a steelyard scale with single hanging dished pan and an equal balance scale with two pans hanging from the beam, which is suspended by a chain and hook. All the pans are hung with three chains and are made of copper and iron. Three sizes of each are being imported: of the first type, a 21" H with 8" pan; a 24" H with 10" pan; and a 27" H with 12" pan, ranging from $60 to $125.50 in price. Of the second type, a 17" H with two 5" pans; a 20" H with 8" pans, and a 27" H with 10" pans, ranging from $67.50 to $142.50 each. The ads of one of the two import companies never mentions country of origin and explains that "Some items have minor dents and old repairs that do not reduce their value." This company also sells various straight-sided pots, round-bottom pots, waisted pots with bails, flared-side shallow pans with covers (all preceding have 2 handles); also 3 sizes of copper "egg pans" with round cups, also plates, bowls, frying pans and long-handled pans with braces. In many sizes. One company sells by the piece; the one that mentions "Turkey" sells by weight.

Scale, steelyard, iron & brass, "Detector," American, 23" L, late 19th or early 20th C. **$35-$45**

Scale, steelyard, iron, with an iron weight that has a raised star design cast on it, American, 25 lb capacity, late 19th C. **$15-$25**

Scoop, adjustable, tin, has lever you push to shove backplate out, smooth-working, American (?), 10" L x 4" W, 19th C. **$135-$160**

V-92. Candy scoop. *Molded glass. From D. J. Barry 1924 catalog, but probably had been made for at least 30 years at that time.* **$20-$30**

V-93. Scoop. *Flat-bottomed, self-balancing, pieced brass, which could be had nickeled for a quarter extra. Tubular capped handle. Sizes 00, 0, 1, 2 & 3 (measurements not given, but probably ranging from about 5" L to 10" L). Jaburg 1908 catalog.* **$35-$65**

Scoop, adjustable, tin, inventor must have been still working on this one when he quit. You have to sort of wriggle the backplate out with your fingers, like a backplate in a really old style filing cabinet drawer. No marks, American (?), 13-1/2" L x 4-7/8" W, 19th C. **$75-$100**

Scoop, apple butter, carved wood, all one piece, open "D" handle, American, 4-1/2" x 11-1/2", late 19th C. **$135-$175**

Scoop, candy, a crude measure, pieced sheet brass, attached handle, small size, late 19th C. Some of these were made by candy scale makers, & match the pieced sheet brass scale pans. **$25-$30**

Candy scoop, japanned tin, tapered sides, small with braced tubular handle, late 19th or early 20th C. **$12-$15**

Scoop, candy, molded glass including handle, American, 6" L x 4" W, early 20th C. **$18-$25**

Scoop, carved & stained wood, probably walnut, folk art piece with largish oblong bowl, the handle is a gorilla with a snake twisted around it, supposedly made by an elderly black sailor, coastal New Jersey, 9-1/8" L, mid 20th C. I also bought a box with a sliding lid by the same man, a master carver with a sense of humor. Both pieces show a remarkable resemblance to some East African carvings. **$200-$250**

Scoop, carved wood, long bowl & longish handle, huge dry-wood or age check in wood is mended with tacked-on strap iron, bowl mended with waxed string — actually sewn together the two halves, American, 12" L, 19th C. This is a very collectible repaired piece. **$30-$60**

Scoop, cast aluminum, fairly smooth, rounded handle, marked "Wagner Ware" on handle, 11-1/4" L x about 4-1/2" deep, c.1930s (?). **$12-$18**

Lookalike alarm — Somebody is making these cast aluminum streamlined scoops today. Lehman's Hardware & Appliances, Kidron, OH, offer 5 sizes in their "Non-Electric Good Neighbor Amish Country" catalog. Old ones (of any type of scoop) will show damage to the lip of the scoop, the front edge that pushes against whatever is being measured out may be nicked, especially smoothed, even thinned out somewhat. I saw a picture of one in a c.1900 magazine that was said to have measured "over two and a half tons" of coffee beans during the preceding year, and the long "lower lip" of the scoop had been worn down and shortened so much that essentially the scoop was a can with a handle at one end.

Scoop, cast iron, sharply truncated cylinder with longish handle, meant for washing or cleaning compound, marked "4 ounce OAKITE," mfd. by Oakite Products Inc., NYC, NY, 6" L, late 19th C. **$15-$28**

V-94. Scoops. *From the top:* **(1)** *"French sugar scoop," from* American Home Cook Book, *1854.* **(2)** *Thumb scoop, tin with ring handle, in 2 sizes: 5" L x 3" W and 6" L x 3-1/4" W. Buhl Sons c.1919 catalog.* **(3)** *Spice scoop with ring handle, tin, in 3 unstated sizes, and* **(4)** *Tea or candy scoop with tubular handle, tin, in 2 sizes. Both from 1924 D. J. Barry catalog.* **$12-$25**

Scoop, coal, pieced brass, riveted-on wooden handle, nice curvy body, Brasscrafters, Syosset, NY, 16-3/4" L, 1980s, possibly before. If new, about **$20-$30**

Lookalike alarm — This is so nicely made and good-looking, as well as being old-fashioned in design, that it could easily be mistaken for an antique. I don't know if it is marked. It is always a good idea to get on the mailing list of such catalog houses as Yield House (which specializes in the country look), and keep a clip file of info on new pieces. That's why I never turn down even a 1950s or 1960s magazine such as *Good Housekeeping* or *House Beautiful*; I search the back pages for small display ads showing items that are likely, just 20 or 30 years later, to be taken as antique.

Scoop, coffee beans, cast aluminum, "Barrington Hall Coffee," 20th C. **$5-$12**

Scoop, coffee beans, tin, "Martinique Coffee Scoops Them All," Oct. 19, 1897. **$15-$20**

Scoop, coffee beans, probably for grocers, cast aluminum, "Blue Diamond - Sunbeam Best Coffees," 12" L x 4-1/2" W, 20th C. **$15-$20**

Scoop, flour, carved from one piece of wood, rounded short handle, American (?), 6-1/2" L, late 19th C. Small hole at end of handle, as well as handle's rounded shape, are evidence that this was at least partly lathe-turned, so probably from a manufactory. **$15-$22**

Scoop, flour, carved maple, nice long oval bowl with curved handle, American (?), 12-1/2" L, early 19th C. **$85-$125**

Scoop, flour, carved wood with fingerhold grip, primitive, very smooth finish, American (?), 7" L, 19th C. **$60-$75**

Scoop, flour, metal bowl with thick wire handles, handles stamped "Airy Fairy Kwik Bis-kit Flour," also "Airy Fairy Cake Flour," American, 7-1/2" L, early 20th C. A campy gotta-have. **$15-$22**

Scoop, flour, stamped metal, "Trisco Flour," 5-3/8" L, early 20th C. **$12-$18**

Scoop, flour, tin with turned wooden handle, American, 7" L, late 19th C. **$12-$18**

Scoop, gray graniteware, 7" L, late 19th C. **$20-$40**

Scoop, heavy, galvanized crimped sheet iron, brass rivets, cast iron heel, wooden handle, 8" L, early 20th C. **$15-$25**

V-95. Scoops in advertising. *The struggle to find a catchy advertising phrase has long been with us. (Now we would probably say "scoop this up.") Brass scoops in set of four, tubular capped handles, crimped back plate, apparently flat-bottomed self-balancing. These were manufactured by William Wrigley, Jr., & Co., Chicago & Philadelphia, the chewing-gum makers! They were offered as a "necessity in every retail store," and available as a free premium when the dealer sent in order for 120 five-cent packages of gum. Advertising card, printed in blue, c.1900. The scoops, singly:* **$20-$25**

Scoop, tin, strap handle, American, 3-3/4" L, turn of century. **$8-$10**

Scoop, tin with tubular handle, braced underneath at attachment. (This brace was called by tinsmiths the **boss**.) American, 9" L x 4-1/2" W, 19th C. **$25-$45**

Scoop, turned wooden handle, bentwood cup is enlongated half-round, brass nails like those used for pantry boxes, Shaker manufacture, 14" L x 6-3/4" W, 19th C. **$125-$160+**

Scoop, dry measure, carved wood, very shallow and long bowl, short hooked handle, marked "Tollard," American, 15-1/4" L, prob. last quarter 19th C. **$55-$75**

Sorghum meter or faucet, metal and wood, to be fitted into a keg, metal, pat'd 1878. **$30-$40**

Spigot for cider barrel, wood with pewter key, marked "John Sommer's Best Block Tin Key," English (?), 19th C. **$8-$15**

Futurewatch: Thermometers are certainly an unexplored collecting area, as far as I know. There is a great variety available, including candy, meat, deep fat and oven types, as well as kitcheny motif, wall-hung room temperature thermometers. Some companies besides those in listings include: "The Acme" oven thermometer, mfd. by Evans Stamping & Plating Co., Taunton, MA, early 20th C; oven thermometers by Ingram-Richardson Mfg. Co., Beaver Falls, PA, and Rochester Mfg. Co., Rochester, NY, both from the 1920s-1930s.

Thermometer, cast iron corncob, cast in 2- or possibly 4-part mold (possibly made from real cob), painted black, hand-engraved brass face along length is flat, rest of cob is full dimensional, American, 10-1/2" L, c.1870s. Wonderful for folk art, corn, cast iron collectors. **$200-$250**

Thermometer, for candy, tin with brass face, marked "Spirit, Boil, Simmer, Heat, Temple, Freezing" (stages for sugar cooking), mfd. by J. Kendall & Co., 6-1/2" L, 19th C (?). **$30-$45**

Thermometer, for candy, copper, "Moeller Instrument Co.," Brooklyn, NY, turn of century. **$55-$65**

Thermometer, for candy & jelly, long palette-knife-shaped calibrated metal plate with glass tube, and with marks giving stages in candy-making, tapered turned wooden handle, large hanging loop at end, Taylor Instrument Co., Rochester, NY, Toronto, CAN, mid 1930s. **$12-$18**

Thermometer, for candy & jelly, metal with light green wooden handle, "Taylor," c.1940s. **$12-$18**

V-96. Looks like a scoop — *but it's a* **bankers' money shovel**. *Copper, flat bottom, steel lip like certain dustpans, tubular handle is copper (available also in turned ebony), protective heel like a shoe! The size is not given, but presumably about 10" L or longer. English. Henry Rogers, Wolverhampton, England, l1914 catalog. This is sure to show up in the containerloads from England. Now you will know what it is!* **$30-$60**

V-97. Tea scoop. *Seamed brass with big rounded bowl, turned ebony handle. Four sizes that measured from 2 ounces to 1 pound of loose tea leaves. Henry Rogers, Wolverhampton, England, 1914.* **$45-$65**

V-98. Flour scoop. *Pieced tin, braced tubular capped handle, reinforced upper rim. Came in 2 sizes — small and large. Jaburg, 1908 catalog.* **$15-$22**

V-99. Sugar scoop. *Cast solid aluminum, 3 sizes: 11" L x 4" W; 12" L x 5" W; and 14" L x 5-1/2" W. Thomas Mills 1930 catalog.* **$8-$12**

V-100. Scoop or dry measure. *Carved from one piece of wood. Marked "TOLLARD" — which could as easily have been the store in which it was used as the maker. Short hooked handle. 15-1/4" L. c.1860s-80s. Picture courtesy of Christie, Manson & Woods International Inc.* **$55-$75**

V-102. Candy-makers' thermometers. (L) *for hard candy, with 5" L stem, 14-1/2" L overall.* **(M)** *"Wood stirring paddle with thermometer," this one at least we know was mfd. by Thomas Mills. 36" L.* **(R)** *Copper-cased with glass, 12" L, 14" L or 18" L.* **(M)** *"Improved boiling thermometer," turned wooden handle, in 2 sizes. First, for caramels, hard candy, etc., has a 14" L stem and is 32" L overall. All from 1930 Mills catalog.* **$12-$50**

V-101. Room thermometer. *Red-painted, stamped heavy tin in teapot shape. "Tel-Tru" Thermometer Co., Rochester, NY. 7" W, c.1930s-40s. (For you who are looking for backgrounds for photos — this is water-spritzed chipboard, an excellent mottled background for dark objects.) SEE kitchen clock in V-4.* **$20-$24**

V-103. Thermometers. *All have mercury stems.* **(L)** *Confectioners' thermometer, copper case. 12" L. Stamped maker's name looks like W. L. Inhagen & M. Espe, NYC. 1925 Sethness catalog.* **(M)** *Dough-mixing thermometer, turned wooden handle. 7" L case, approx. 21" L overall. Pat'd April 24, 1894. Made by Homann & Maurer (sp?), Rochester, NY. In 1908 Jaburg catalog.* **(R)** *Syrup hydrometer, also known as a saccharometer. Glass. Also Homann & Maurer. Sethness 1925 catalog.* **$12-$50**

Handy Oven Thermometer — "Many test their ovens in this way: if the hand can be held in from 20 to 35 seconds, it is a quick oven, from 35 to 45 seconds is moderate, and from 45 to 60 seconds is slow. 60 seconds is a good oven to begin with for large fruit cakes. All systematic housekeepers will hail the day when some enterprising, practical 'Dixie' girl shall invent a stove or range with a thermometer attached to the oven so that the heat may be regulated accurately and intelligently." *Practical Housekeeping*, 1884.•Thomas Masters of London invented what was probably the **first oven thermometer** about 1850. It was a glass ring with mercury and an indicator guide telling what to put in the oven when the mercury reached a particular point on the guide.

Thermometer, for oven, porcelainized iron in white, light blue, light green or orange, tall vertical tombstone shape set on flat round base, glass tube with degrees from 100 to 600 marked off, "Bake-Rite Portable Oven Thermometer No. 115," mfd. by American Thermometer Co., St. Louis, MO, 5-1/2" H, late 1920s, early 1930s. **$8-$12**

Thermometer, for oven, modeled almost exactly like the "Bake-Rite" but available only in white porcelainized metal, tombstone-shaped vertical face with glass tube, set on stamped round base marked with maker's name, registers from 200 to 800, & is also marked from "slow" (at 300) to "hot" (at 500): is the extra 300 degrees for people who fire pottery in their ovens? Taylor Instrument Companies, mid 1930s. **$5-$8**

Thermometer, for oven, painted wood, "Occident Flour," Russell-Miller Milling Co., Minneapolis, MN, early 20th C. **$30-$40**

Thermometer, printed metal, "Ward's Vitovim Bread," Ward Baking Co., NYC, etc., early 20th C. A store thermometer, although no doubt some would have been found just outside the kitchen door, maybe on the icebox porch. **$100-$150**

Timer for toaster, green marbleized plastic, chrome, green cord, to be hooked up to a Hotpoint toaster, "Hotpoint," Edison General Electric Appliance Co., Chicago, IL, 1930s. An interesting explanation for the name <u>The General Electric Co</u>, is found in Orra L. Stone's *History of Massachusetts Industries*, 1930. He says **THE** is a formal part of the name and is an acronym for Dr. Elihu **T**hompson and Dr. Edwin J. **H**ouston, who were co-founders of the American Electric Co., est. 1879 in Philadelphia, and a predecessor to GE, plus Thomas Alva **E**dison, whose Edison General Electric Co., est. 1881, merged with American Electric to become <u>The G. E. Co</u>. (This may be an apocryphal tale.) **$125-$140**

Utility measure — See measure & funnel combined

COOPERED WARES — HOW BIG?
Or, Twenty-nine Firkins of Beer on the Wall

In everyday eighteenth-century life, a knowledge of such exact measures as barrel, hogshead, tub or firkin was vital to any citizen who bought, sold or bartered grain, butter, ale, soap, tallow, cider or any other other dry or liquid stuff that was measured out in supposedly uniformly sized coopered (staved & bound wood) containers. Many of these containers (at least the smaller ones) are found in kitchen and country store collections today.

In America's earliest days we used British standards of measure. Later the legal capacity of coopered vessels differed (and still do) in England and America. To take just one early eighteenth-century liquid product — ale or beer — and give its <u>rounded off</u> old time British measures: one **tun** of ale equaled about four **hogsheads** or almost seven and a quarter **barrels**, or fourteen and a half **kilderkins**, or close to 29 **firkins**. A tun of ale held about 259 gallons, a firkin held only a little over nine gallons. A **keg** was a small ale or beer <u>cask</u> that held 10 gallons or less, so it was an inexact measure that might easily coincide with a firkin. (A **cask** usually referred to a generic coopered container, just as today we often use "barrel" to generally mean a big coopered container, or "keg" to mean a small one.) A **kilderkin** and a **runlet** had the same measurements — almost exactly 16" H x 20" diameter; a **firkin** was half that in both dimensions; a **butt** was twice as big.

HOLDING & HANDLING

VI. TRIVETS, STANDS, RACKS & POT HOLDERS

Is it a **trivet** or is it a **stand**? Trivet is the choice in common English usage — even for something with four legs. Trivets are three-legged, vaguely triangular stands meant for sadirons, and the word itself means three legs, but people are used to calling any sort of cooling stand a trivet. Most of the trivets and stands here are for hot pots or hot dishes. Most are technically stands, not trivets because they have four or more legs. Over the objections of some, I'm going to use the familiar word "trivet" for most of the pieces in this chapter.

Wire pieces are increasingly popular and have finally earned their own book (see bibliography). Many round, flat wire stands are actually countertop cooling racks for baked goods — either taken out of the pan or left in. The wire itself draws heat off the bottom of the pie pan, but it also allows cooking air to circulate; others are stands for teapots to be used at table, and they protect the finish. Wire can be twisted and bent into the desired scribbly design. It can be easily soldered (so many wire stands are a combination of soldered and twisted wires). It could even be twisted in spirals around lengths of wire, making the heat conductive potential even greater. The most wide-open and unexplored stands and trivets are homemade — of scrap copper, steel, tin, even wood.

This isn't a big area of collecting, and people are most familiar with the trivets or stands meant for sadirons. Handforged trivets are often very valuable. And some of the trivets for cast iron roasters or other pots and pans are important to collectors of Griswold, Wagner, etc. Oddly, many of those trivets are used inside the utensil to hold up tired roasts. Some are made of cast aluminum, to match the hollowware they were meant to be used in. Griswold, like many twentieth-century foundries, also made old style sadiron trivets in lacy cast iron — those are worth under $40. If Griswold had been thinking of collectors, surely they would have made a limited edition trivet or stand of their wonderful Griswold spider in a web. If that had ever been made, it might be worth more than $500. But they never did, so if you see one, you know it isn't a Griswold. (There is a very interesting 8-spoke spider-web-with-spider cast iron trivet, with webbed handle, 6" diameter, marked "Rd. No. 96845," which I believe is English. It's worth upwards of $125.) A fun go-with to look for is a 1954 catalog from Lily Mills Co., Shelby, NC, *Wrought Iron Crochet, Book #74,* which has 23 patterns for objects to be crocheted in black yarn, including several trivets! For **pot holders**, see the last section of this chapter; there's a book in the Bibliography by Doris Hoover.

Hot mat, variegated woods in pinwheel design, supposed to be Shaker because of the variegated woods (used for rolling pins & table mats), 8" diameter, came in other sizes, 1920s. New ones are made with strong fishline. **$20-$25**

Jelly maker's stand, cast iron, sort of like a trivet bench, 4 legs, top has 2 large holes — for 2 kettles, American, about 26" L, 19th C. **$150-$175**

Stand, cast iron, sand casting of a real hand, hanging (?) hole in wrist, American, 18th or early 19th C. This was seen in a dealer's (Rose W. Olstead, Madison, NJ) ad in *The Magazine*

ANTIQUES, July 1962. I suspect the price then was under $50. If you found such a piece now, if it was determined to be old, the price would be much higher, and it would be for sale by a folk art dealer. **$500-$1000**

Stand, for pots, and <u>combination tool</u> including meat tenderizer, tack hammer, stove lid lifter, pot lifter (hook fits around bail handle), pie crimper, candleholder (the last 2 dubiously efficacious), found in cast iron and cast bronze-like metal. Basically round, with 4 deep ridges (the tenderizer) shooting off at an angle, 2 round candle- or finger-sized holes, one longish curved piece (lid lifter), 3 short hooked pieces off bottom, viewed from right angle, it's an [unintentional] caricature of Groucho Marx. This is almost always found at fleas and shows on the tables of people dealing in knives, guns, Nazi

VI-1. Trivet. *Called a "farrier's whimsy" in the auction catalog. Steel and brass; a horse (or pony) shoe, fitted with three high laced boots as feet and decorated with miniature farrier's tools — anvil, tongs, hammer, etc. Approx. 5-3/4" W x about 1-1/2" H. Photo courtesy Litchfield Auction Gallery, Litchfield CT. Ex-Harold Corbin Collection.* **$700-$1000**

VI-2. Trivet or stand for pot. *Intricate cast iron, japanned finish (similar iron doilies often seen in enameled finish, white, blue or black). Russell & Erwin, mid-1860s.* **$30-$45**

memorabilia, camo junk, etc., and is usually labeled "brass knuckles," which it most assuredly isn't. "6-Way Trivet" is one; another American one is the "Seven Way Kitchen Aid," pat'd by W. H. Thayer, May 24, 1881. **$60-$85**

Trivet, also called a <u>dish rest</u>, cast iron, round with side handle, <u>3 legs</u>, heart motif with radiating spokes, heart end to handle, American, 11-3/8" L x 6-1/2" diameter, marked "1829" on handle. This has been reproduced by Virginia Metalcrafters in brass and iron. **$150-$175**

Trivet, brass, fire bar type that hooked onto the fire bar that went between 2 andirons, stylized thistle design, English (?), 19th C. **$150-$175**

Reproduction alert — A decorative hearthside trivet type frequently found nowadays, especially with English imports, is the brass lyre-top trivet with wrought strap iron legs or base, with heavy turned wooden handle. The better ones have shaped penny feet; usually the heavy strap iron is just bent to make a foot. Much to my amazement, I found a 1937 *House Beautiful* ad for a $4.50 reproduction, offered by H. Wiener, on Allen Street in NYC, which was the brass capitol of America from the late nineteenth century up to the 1960s!

Trivet, cast brass woman's head, Bradley & Hubbard, Meriden, CT, 3rd to 4th quarter 19th C. **$50-$65**

Trivet, cast iron, round with heart & rays design, 8" D, late 19th C. This is the kind of design reproduced widely. Use every bit of your iron-age-detecting knowledge before buying. **$55-$75**

Trivet, for Dutch oven #6, round, cast iron, pattern of round holes, "Griswold #204," Erie, PA, 12" D, turn of century. **NOTE:** #205 through #211 are all Griswold Dutch oven trivets in different sizes. **$20-$35**

Trivet, expanding, for hot dishes, copper & brass, prob. originally nickeled, "Manning-Bowman," American, 1st half 20th C. **$20-$25**

Trivet, for kettle or pot, cast iron square, 4 legs riveted on, at the knee of each leg is a flattened oval medallion with a relief profile of a

Roman warrier in helmet, all 4 the same, openwork top plate spells out name, "Houchin's Patent," NYC, NY, but T. W. Houchin lived in Morrisania, NY, 2-1/4" H x 5-3/8" square, prob. 1870s to 1890s. (Another Houchin trivet, probably for a portable kettle or other little vessel, has a very delicate cast iron top, probably brass plated or bronzed, is only 3-3/4" square with 3 shaped 1-1/4" H brass legs, round cutout design in top spells out H O U C H I N. (It is worth only $7 to $15.) **$75-$100**

Trivet, probably for pot, cast iron with bronzed finish, skeletal triangle with 3 longish feet, marked on underside "Thos. W. Houchin Co. 1898," NYC, 1-1/2" H x 4-1/4" sides, TOC. **$15-$20**

Trivet, for pot, beautiful cast iron in interesting flat-top piece with large hole cut in center, outside edge basically round with projections where 3 legs attached, largish tab handle (shaped like a porringer handle) has a hanging hole, English (?), only 2-5/8" H x 4-1/2" W at widest part, mid 19th C (?). **$35-$50**

Trivet, for pot, cast iron, advertises "Cinderella Stoves," early 20th C. **$25-$45**

Trivet, for pot, cast iron, letters form openwork design, "J. R. Clark Co.," Minneapolis, MN, late 19th C. or early 20th. **$25-$35**

Trivet, for pot, cheap metal cast to resemble bamboo, back bears motto "East or West - Campbell's Soups Are Best," Campbell Soup, c.1970s (?). **$7-$10**

Trivet, for pot, white enameled cast iron — a permanent doily, very ornate openwork, the center a sort of flowerette composed of 6 hearts joined at the points, the outside frame composed of 12 looped and rococo scrolls arranged so that 2 form a unit, all surrounded in delicately scalloped edge, peg feet, American, 18" diameter, prob. 1860s to 1880s. **$55-$90**

Trivet, for pots, cast iron, this one also called a <u>simmering cover,</u> to use on cookstove, Walker & Pratt Mfg. Co., "W & P," 7-3/4" D, 19th C. **$18-$22**

Trivet, for roaster, oval with 6 little tab feet, cast iron, with patten of three sizes of round holes, Griswold #7 (it came in 4 sizes: 3, 5, 7 & 9), "Oval Roaster Trivet" #276. **$90-$100**

Trivet, orange painted cast iron, advertising "Grain Belt" beer, early 20th C. **$25-$35**

Trivet, wire in a spiral, cross pieces form legs with a rivet, American, 6" diameter, c.1890s to 1910s. **$15-$20**

Stand, wire, for hot dishes, round, tight spiral of thin wire, reinforced and soldered by eight spokes radiating from center, with 8 little loops underneath as feet, several makers among the wire novelty companies, American, about 6-1/4" diameter, late 19th or early 20th C. **Variations:** This type has many variations, sometimes unsoldered and held together only by little twists of wire at each intersection of spiral and spoke. I have seen them as large as 8" diameter; others may be larger. Other variations of thin twisted wire stands include some that look like daisies, with each petal

VI-3. Stand or trivet for pots, *and a combination tool. This was patented May 24, 1881 by W. H. Thayer as a "seven-way" tool. It is often called a brass knuckle by those who don't know. Its seven functions are (1) trivet, (2) stove lid lifter, (3) pot bail hook, (4) meat tenderizer, (5) pie crimper, (6) bottle opener, and (7) candleholder. It is found most commonly in cast brass, and is worth a bit more in cast iron.* **$30-$45**

VI-4. Trivet. *Cast iron, spoked heart design. Dated "1829," which makes it very desirable, as well as the hearts. 11-3/8" L x 6-1/2" diameter. Picture courtesy of the National Museum of American History, Smithsonian Institution. NOTE: Virginia Metalcrafters made a repro of this in brass.* **$150-$175**

having its own little bent loop foot, and some with many spokes or rays but without the spirals but using heavier wire, twisted sometimes from two strands. **$15-$25**

Reproduction alert. This and other types of twisted wire stands have been heavily reproduced and sold to "country" dealers. I don't know what to tell you about telling the difference between new and old. I would say that the soldered are much more likely to be new, whereas no modern worker would spend the time twisting the tiny wire around some 90 to 100 intersections.

Trivet, real forged iron horseshoe, backed with disc of sheet metal from which a large V has been cut, with 3 forged short peg legs, American, 4-1/2" L, late 19th or early 20th C. I bought this for $2 from a dealer who said it was an "ashtray," but that is way under the money. And, no, I didn't argue. **$40-$55**

Trivet, for pot or kettle, a real wrought iron horseshoe welded to sheet iron, 3 feet, American, 19th C. There are enough of these, all one of a kind, to make a very handsome collection. **$100-$145**

Trivet, for pot, wrought iron, heart-shaped, with a scroll & heart inner design, 3 boot-shaped feet, like riding boots, stamped with a small eagle punch mark & a flower on the handle, maker's name marked too, "J. English," PA (?), 10-3/4" L x 4-1/4" W, early 19th C. Ex-Robacker Collection. Sold at Horst Auction, June 1989 for $1600. Because of the marks, the hearts & the boots: **$700-$1000**

The Composition of Price. Why did the Robacker trivet sell for so much? Surely a record for a trivet or stand. There are many elements that went into the price, which may or may not be the secondary market value for this trivet. I believe that factors (1) and (2) probably contributed to the price realized.

(1) It came from a famous, published collection, the Robacker Estate, and gains value from association, and from the fact that it had presumably been bought by a knowledgeable couple who wouldn't have bought a reproduction or fake.

(2) It was sold at auction, where the pace and fever of selling are conducive of high realized prices.

(3) It is marked. It not only had a maker's name, "J. English," but also a stamped American eagle with a shield and banner and a clutch of arrows. So far, nothing is known about the maker.

(4) There was a valuable multiplier motif in the design, in this case cutout hearts — usually good for multiplying price by 5X to 10X or more, meaning that without it, the price might be 1/10th to 1/20th.

(5) There was at least one figural element in the design. For me, personally (thanks to my 12AAAA understanding), the most enchanting factor is the boot feet. I already own one nice trivet with cast boot feet. I saw another trivet or stand, probably Pennsylvanian, in the Keillor Collection, when I was doing my first book. The Keillors' was 13" L, with a cutout cock or rooster and a very graceful and shaped handle. It is truly the most wonderful of the three, and I wish I owned it. I also wish that I could see all three next to each other; it'd be useful to compare the shape and exact size of all the boots.

(6) Size is the most easily overlooked factor in the composition of price, whether a piece is unusually large or small — especially if you are looking at pieces in a catalog or book. In this instance, it is largeness. The one we are discussing is nearly a foot long — a good-sized trivet, quite impressive.

Trivet, wrought iron in a tight coil, with handle, quite heavy, 10" L including handle, early 19th C. **$65-$80**

Trivet, for pot, wrought iron pony shoe mounted to black painted copper plate cut to fit shape, 3 wrought booted feet with rounded toes and heels, the boots resemble riding boots, American (?), 1-1/4" H x 4-7/8" x 4-7/8", early 19th C. **$175-$200**

Trivet, wrought iron, round long triangle outline, with pointed piece almost like a steeple, from point of trivet up into open space, topped by cutout bird form (like a weathervane), 3 feet in shape of boots, all pointing away from slightly curved skinny handle. This was in the Keillor Collection, auctioned in 1976, and may

VI-5. Trivet for frying pan, *or other long-handled pan. Forged iron, heart shape, long legs. Upright piece supports handle of pan — if it tilts up (which handles of most hearth utensils did to make them easier to hold and move for a person standing at the hearth). Continental European, possibly French or Portuguese. Late 18th or early 19th C. Photograph courtesy of Pat Guthman antiques, Southport, CT.* **$550+**

VI-6. Stand patent. *Pat'd 12/8/1885 by Joseph P. Hurley, Philadelphia, PA, #332,201. Called a "Kitchen utensil" by Hurley, and claimed to be "a new article, ... a metallic stand for kitchen utensils, consisting of two plates with connecting legs, all cast in one piece." I have a cast brass drain cover that looks almost exactly like this, although the center hole is much smaller and was meant for a screw. It has three stubby feet, and except for the fact I actually removed it from a drain in a building being razed, who would know? This from the Official Gazette of the U.S. Patent Office. If it were made:* **$25-$45**

VI-7. Kettle bottoms & meat rests. *A form of trivet, and often identified as such. They were meant to be used inside a pot or kettle. Both are tinned iron wire. The upper mesh one, with wires welded to the round frame, came in 6", 7", 8", 9" and 10" diameter. The bottom one was only made in 7" and 8-1/2" diameters. The Washburn Co., Worcester, MA. Sno-Cap catalog, 1927.* **$6-$10**

VI-10. Tea or coffee pot stands. *Twisted wire in various shapes, available in different sizes. Mfd. by Sherwood, Worcester, MA, mid 19th C. and made for long period.* **$20-$45**

VI-8. "Grates." *Much older than the ones in VI-5 are these three pastry or confectioner's grates, meant for cooling baked goods.* **(T)** *came in sizes from 6" to 16" diameter.* **(M)** *simpler center one was made in 5-1/2" to 15-3/4" diameters (or any size "to order").* **(B)** *This came 9" x 13", 10-1/2" x 15", and 12" x 16", or any size to order. From professional suppliers Duparquet, Huet & Moneuse, NYC, c.1904-1910. The form, and probably the linecuts used to illustrate the catalog, are from the 1860s or 1870s.* **$25-$45**

VI-11. "Tea or coffee pot stand." *Called that in the catalog, but looks more like a sadiron stand. Nickeled cast brass horseshoe design, with expected "Good Luck." Heinz & Munschauer, Buffalo, NY, 1882 catalog.* **$20-$30**

VI-9. Pot stand. *Twisted iron wire, originally tinned, 6-1/2" diameter. Probably French, but could also havde been made by Sherwood of Worcester, MA. Called also a "teapot stand." American Agriculturist, 11/1872.* **$20-$30**

be one of the finest trivets ever seen on the market, American or poss. French, 2" H x 13" L overall, early 19th C.   **$700-$1600**

Trivet, for pots or kettles, forged iron, with hearts in center, plus a 2-hearted handle, American, 12" L, date difficult to call. **Old Hearts** — With the heart motif's popularity and the proliferation of fake forged iron pieces of all kinds, this could be as recent as 1988. This one has convincing signs of wear, cleaning, polishing, & use, both on bottoms of feet, and on surface, and may be early 19th C.   **$120-$150**

Trivet, cast & wrought iron, 3-legged hearth style for pots, also called a <u>brandelette</u>, <u>brandiron</u> or <u>brandise</u>. American (?), 10" H, 18th C.   **$250-$275**

Trivet, for hearth, revolving, forged iron, American, 11" diameter, high legs, very early 1700s. The trivet, without a handle, is much rarer than the similar form, the revolving broiler (see Chapter X for those).   **$200-$300+**

Trivet, for hearth, with adjustable fork or handle support that works on the pawl & ratchet idea, forged & twisted iron "running man" piece with adjustable height to support fork or stirring spoon. Two long legs on either side of circle of trivet, one leg near end of handle, very handsome form that looks like what sculptor Alberto Giacometti would have done if he'd made 18th C. cooking utensils. 7-5/8" diameter x 24-5/16" L. Found in house on the Connecticut-Massachusetts border, 18th C.   **$450-$575**

Trivet, for hearth, wrought iron with sliding support for saucepan handle, 3 penny feet, 22-1/2" L, 18th C.   **$350-$450+**

Trivet, wrought iron, round with 3 legs & a long handle, for hearth use. American (?), 6" H x 8" diameter, with 11" L handle, late 1700s or early 1800s.   **$300-$400+**

POT HOLDERS
Or, Another Way to Handle a Hot Pot

A long time ago I discovered that the cheapest, most colorful, easily found kitchen collectible is the pot holder. The commonest is the woven rag strip kind made on a little square loom that is at least 60 years old. Most of them have no distinctive feature at all, but occasionally one with interesting color is seen.

The three most collectible types are **(1)** unique (not-pattern) nineteenth-century quilted and/or appliqued cotton or wool ones, or needlepointed wool ones, often in the shape of a butterfly or bird (so that wings can be folded around the handle). The old printed calicoes and chintzes make this type a good go-with for a quilt collection. Some of these old pot holders are actually meant to be used in the parlor, to pour tea from a hot teapot. **(2)** Twentieth-century (c.1900-1950s) figural appliqu, done in ginghams and calicoes and usually made from a pattern, or at least a how-to article in a ladies' magazine. **(3)** Twentieth-century crocheted pot holders: geometrics (c.1900-1950s), and figurals (c.1900-1950s, but mainly the '40s and '50s). Some crocheted pieces have very intricate, virtuoso stitches that make the flat pot holder into a 3-D work of textile art.

The colors most commonly found in the last two types are red and white; then green and white; then red, green and white; and finally colors like blue, yellow and pink. The first three combinations reflect the color schemes most favored in kitchens in the 1930s and 1940s, schemes that also inspired the implement handles in red, green, white, and — much more rarely — yellow and blue. Hanging loops were part of the holder in the late nineteenth century on, and rings seem to be a twentieth-century feature. Small circles of celluloid — called a "bone ring" — were stitched to an edge through the twentieth century; brass rings were also used. These rings are barely an inch across — they were used to make cafe curtains. Crocheted holders often have a ring crocheted only from the yarn, or crocheted over a "bone" or brass ring.

Every motif fad — from palm trees to seafood, from barbecue to tropical fruits — that was used for dishes, lamps, aprons, wallpaper, shelf paper, cabinet decals, juice glasses, bridge tallies, etc., also found expression in pot holders. Cheerily attractive finished pot holders were shown in color photography or duotone on the covers of crochet pattern books put out by such yarn and threadmakers as Coats & Clark's, American Thread Co., and The Spool Cotton Co., in the 1940s and 1950s. A needlework magazine with patterns for everything from tablecloths to bedroom booties was *The Work Basket,* published for about 40 years until 1971. These magazines and pattern books are great research sources and fun go-withs.

The introduction to a 1947 American Thread Co. pot holder pattern book says, "More Pot Luck — So many handicrafters loved our Star Pot Holder Book No. 32 — with recipes — that we decided to design another book with the same idea — but with oh-so-different patterns. We hope you'll like them — they look so bright and sparkling when made with Star Brand Cottons." So a recipe for "Crab meat au gratin" is accompanied by a fish-shaped pot holder, and another with a crab double-crocheted on a plain square. Accompanying a "Cheese cake" recipe are — you guessed it — "Panties Potholder #5512" and a "Slip Pot holder." "Indian Pudding" gets three designs, a "Navajo" geometric, a "Log Cabin" design something like the pieced-quilt pattern of that name, and "Indian Circle," like a pinwheel.

The twentieth-century holders are usually a lot dirtier and stained than the older ones, which weren't really meant for day-to-day kitchen use. Fortunately, the crochet yarns tend to be 100% cotton and colorfast to a high degree. They can be washed very successfully. An elderly needlewoman of my acquaintance is known to all her friends as a person who can *always* get an old textile clean. The "magic" potion she usually uses is "Biz™" or "Super Biz™" powdered detergent. A few tips: don't soak overnight because even strongly set dyes can begin to run. Do it in stages — be somewhat timid at first, soak a little, scrub with your fingers a little, rinse a lot, squeeze in a towel, and dry quickly. And do it again if the stain hasn't come out. Sometimes a paste of detergent and water can be applied to a stubborn stain, left to do its work for a short few minutes, then rinsed out. As for scorch? Nothing gets it out completely.

Only one collector magazine has published an article on this unheralded, but increasingly popular, field of collecting. That was "Handle with Care," by Cathy Cook, editor of *"Country Accents® Collectibles. Flea Market Finds,"* in the summer 1996 issue. Another article cited by Cook is by social historian Rachel Maines: "The Evolution of the Pot Holder from Technology to Popular Art," *Journal of Popular Culture,* July 1985.

Pot holder, appliquéd cotton, <u>Black Americana</u> cook or chef, American, 1940s or so. Probably not a pattern piece. **$12-$20**

Pot holder, appliquéd cotton, pig motif, 20th C.   **$7-$10**

Pot holder, appliquéd cotton, hearts and diamonds, red & green on white, brass hanging ring at corner, c.1930s.   **$5-$7**

Pot holder, appliquéd cat's head, very fanciful, c.1930s.   **$7-$10**

Pot holder, appliquéd & embroidered cat's head, c.1950s.   **$3-$5**

Pot holder, crocheted thick cotton yarn, deep red & green, with interesting wiggly woven look to top side, brass hanging ring sewed on corner, 4" x 4", c.1920s.   **$6-$9**

Pot holder, embroidered cotton cutout, depicts a house, c.1920s to 1930s.   **$10-$15**

Pot holder, crazy quilt silk & satin, embroidered, probably for parlor use while pouring tea or coffee, c.1870s to late 1800s.   **$18-$22**

Pot holder, bargello needlepoint, backed with printed cotton, geometric pattern, c.1880s.   **$10-$15**

Pot holder, appliquéd & cutout felt, odd, typically Amish, color combinations — modern-art in appearance, cotton flannel baking, all bound in red cotton tape, c.1880s to 1890s.   **$20-$30**

Pot holder, for teapot in parlor, needlepoint in dark green & red, brown polished cotton backing, design is a rebus poem, pictures given here in parentheses: **"Except the (Tea Kettle) Boiling (B), Filling the (Tea Pot) Spoils the (T),"** prob. American, close to 6" square, c.1830s to 1850s. **$85-$125**

Reproduction alert — a **Craft Lookalike** — In the Feb. 1925 *House Beautiful* there is a short piece on buying a commercial pattern for and making a cross-stitch (or maybe needlepoint?) pot holder with this re-bus puzzle motif. The illustration with the column is clear enough that a clever needleworker could make her own pattern, which would account for some slight variations. The editor writes, [We bring you a] "canvas pattern for a teapot holder which I am sure many of you will enjoy doing in cross-stitch. It is a pattern which our Grandmothers used, and I have one at home in crimson wool, with the figures in black, which is very old. The work is of the simplest, and I should think little girls would like to make these useful bits of needlework. The pattern itself is 6 inches square, and it is priced .35 cents."

Pot holder, tan wool flannel, red cotton tape binding, tiny red braid machine stitched in floral pattern on front, back plain (another example done on gray wool flannel), supposed to be Amish, c.1880s to 1890s. **$15-$18**

VI-12. Pot holder. *Appliquéd cotton cat, handsewn, with simple embroidery. Thin and barely stuffed at all — obviously for decoration.* **$3-$5**

VI-13. Pot holders. *Gingham & calico appliqué, handsewn, with simple embroidery. Picture from* McCall's Needlework *magazine, Summer 1941.* **$7-$10**

Reproduction alert — I heard in 1989 that some immigrants from India who settled in Pennsylvania are sewing things that are being sold as Amish. I don't know if they are using old cast-off materials, or things bought in thrift stores, or new fabrics.

Pot holder, chicken with stuffed upstanding neck & head, body folds around handle of teapot, mustard & ochre cotton sateen, green floss knots around neck, blue eyes, Mennonite, 5-3/8" diameter, c.1900-1920s. **$45-$60**

Pot holder, needlepoint, pink, red & blue, tree of life, printed brown calico backing, Mennonite, 5-3/8" x 5-5/8", c.1870s. **$45-$55**

Pot holder, printed cotton & muslin butterfly, the wings to be folded around the handle, 6" W wingspread, c.1920s. **$4-$7**

Pot holder, crocheted cotton, caricature face of an Oriental, yellow with red lips & black hair, yarn pigtail braided & attached, 6" diameter, c.1940s-1950s. **$7-$10**

Pot holder, fine needlepoint on canvas, one side is a rebus with ombré shaded lettering in red on green background, with black kettle picture, reads "Genie put the [kettle] on & we will all take tea," obverse has flowers, vases, dog, cat, pair of scissors & a wreath on black background, English (?), 5" x 4-3/16", c.1860s to 1880s. Being a rebus collector, this attracted my attention immediately. It is a fine piece of needlework, as well as being a puzzle, and has crossover appeal to various kinds of collectors. **$85-$125**

Pot holder, appliquéd in layers & embroidered, Black man's face, with frayed fringe hair, red wood jersey lips, white jersey eyes, flappy ears, not a nice caricature, but interesting handicraft in Black Americana mode, 8" diameter, c.1890s to 1910s. **$50-$70**

VI-14. Pot holder. *Colorful appliquéd cotton, handsewn, butterfly's body has extra stuffing. What's called a "bone" ring of celluloid. 1940s or 1930s.* **$3-$6**

VI-15. Pot holder. *A simple gingham butterfly with corded edge. Handsewn. Same idea, different species of butterfly! 1940s or 1930s.* **$3-$6**

VI-16. Pot holder. *Cotton gingham checks in two sizes, both red & white. Machine sewn. Probably 1950s.* **$3-$5**

VI-19. Pot holder. *There are those "Cheese cake" panties! This red & white pair is actually nicer & fancier than the Star pattern book version. This is probably the most commonly found crochet*

VI-17. Pot holders. *Really well-done crocheted holders with crocheted flowers done right on the background pieces. Red, green, yellow & white — very 1940s.* **$5-$8**

VI-20. Pot holder. *Crocheted red & white cottage, c.1940.* **$7-$10**

VI-18. Pot holder. *Crocheted caricature of Oriental woman's face. Yellow with red lips & black eyes & hair. Braided pigtail. C.1940s-1950s.* **$7-$10**

VI-21. Pot holders. *More red & white crochet from the 1940s. The one on the left actually somewhat resembles the wirework teapot trivet stands. The dress, which looks like a doll dress (Yo! Barbie, eat your heart out!), actually couldn't be a doll dress because the stitches connect back to front. Both with crocheted-over "bone" rings.* **$3-$6**

Pot holder, for handle of parlor teapots, velvet parrot without wings, only body, tail & simple head with beak, body folds over the handle, green velvet with pale tan silk lining, embroidered with mother of pearl button eyes, poss. English, certainly High Victorian, 7" L, c.1880s to 1890s. Another one, an inch longer, was teal blue velvet with beige silk lining. **$30-$35**

Pot holder, <u>Black Americana</u> needlepoint with simple depiction of a dancing black man & woman who nearly fill the space, also **"Any holder but a Slave holder,"** reputedly made for Frederick Douglass by Lena Irish, 5-1/2" H x 6-1/2" W, c.1860s-1870s. Dealer Bernie McManus, Woodbury House, Woodbury, CT, offered this punning piece in 1985, along with a letter by Douglass. In Feb.1989, Windham Antiques in Shepherdstown, WV, advertised a "potholder by freed slave (NC, circa 1865), red, black, white cross-stitch on gray wool (Confederate uniform)," red binding and hanging loop. It has a dancing Black man and woman very small in center, and the same motto, but with all 6 words with initial capital letters, and measures 5-1/2" x 6". **$250+**

Pot holder, crocheted bear head, black, crocheted contrasting trim that looks like rick-rack, appliqued felt eyes, 1950s. **$4-$8**

Pot holder, crocheted cotton bunch of bananas, yellow & brown, brass ring, 1950s. **$3-$5**

Pot holder, crocheted cotton, white with red outlines, little house shape with colored windows & door, crocheted hanging ring as chimney, about 5" H, patterns for these advertised 1940-1941. **$7-$10**

Pot holder, appliquéd cloth, blue & white gingham around edge, white cotton center, red stitching, a clock face with every other numeral, tab hanger at top, 5" diameter, pattern appeared for this in summer 1941 *McCall's Needlework* magazine. In the same how-to article appeared a wonderful cozy little armchair-shaped pot holder of calico. Also a great man's shirt with red tie, the sleeves and shirt tails forming irregular outline on basic round shape. I've never seen either one, but would like to! **$7-$10**

Pot holder, crocheted cotton, round, with appliquéd flowers & leaves crocheted separately from red, green & yellow cotton. Hanging ring of metal. American, 6" diameter, c.1930s-1940s. **$6-$12**

Pot holder, printed cloth, adv'g "Reddi Kilowatt," c.1920s-1930s. See electric chapter for more on Reddy. **$15-$22**

Pot holder rack, plywood cutout, <u>Black Americana</u> theme, a painted "Mammy" with blue & white gingham checked apron & kerchief of cloth, white thumbtack eyes, paper glued-on lips, thumbtacks in legs to hold 2 pot holders, American, 7" H, 1/4" thick ply, c.1940s. **$18-$22**

VI-22. Pot holders. *These are partly handmade — the fruit appliqués are sewn to squares of a manufactured dishcloth. Lined with layers of cotton, bound with cotton tape, and machine stitched around edges, with a loop made from the extra 2" of tape. c.1950s.* **$3-$5**

VI-23. Pot holder. *Cotton terrycloth souvenir of the 1939 World's Fair in Flushing, NY, showing the Trylon and Perisphere that towered over the exhibition buildings. 1938/39.* **$5-$7**

HOLDING & HANDLING:

VII. STORAGE & CONTAINERS,
With Several Important Essays on Metals
& Chronologies on Tin & Japanning.

This is literally a catch-all chapter — maybe because almost everyone has some kind of container collection. It's been said that women are great collectors of containers — boxes, jars, trunks — maybe there's a physiological basis for what is often an obsession! This chapter also has more kinds of things valued by "crossover collectors" (folk art, ceramics, baskets, glass, wooden wares) than probably any other.

To figure out which aspect to pursue yourself is "like trying to use a straw to drink from a fire hydrant," as some wag said about Congress and its legislative agenda. Probably half the stuff at any flea market or antique show might be classified as a container of some kind. Open or closed.

There are several subjects here that I've decided not to include to any extent: Cookie jars are very specialized, prices are difficult for an outsider (i.e. non-collector) to track meaningfully, and there are several books. I am excluding licensed-character lunchboxes for similar reasons. Novelty salt & pepper shakers have several colorful books, and a club: Novelty Salt & Pepper Shakers Club, Lula Fuller, POB 3617, Lantana, FL 33465. (561) 588-5368. In addition, there is a group who collects all sorts of antique salt shakers, including the patented Christmas salts, the Mt. Washington salts, etc.: Antique & Art Glass Salt Shaker Collectors Society, 2832 Rapidan Trail, Maitland, FL 32751. Please always use an SASE when writing.

Two areas where there's elbow room, and on which a **Futurewatch** has been placed, are **berry baskets** and **candy boxes**. Low to mid prices are still the rule, but by the time this fourth edition is published I may have to eat my berries. A broad and deep collecting base is essential to the long life and success of any collecting field, and is rather like a mountain lake fed by springs from the bottom and rain from the top.

Some areas are ripe for attention but may be too limited in scope for a broad following. If there isn't enough variety (in price as well as appearance or material), there's no fun. **Collapsible cups** and **string holders** are of interest, but I think probably only the latter might have enough variety to sustain a collector market.

Finally, I've included a sampling from two long-established collecting fields — **birdcages** and **candlesticks** — because of their obvious connection to the kitchen and the running of a household (in college, where I lived in a boarding house, our wonderful cook Melba Hamlet kept her parrot in a corner of the kitchen). Many birdcages are showing up at antique shows; a good many, I believe, originating in England and Europe as part of the trend toward commissioned container picking done by dealers who don't actually go overseas to shop themselves. There are also many many Far Eastern reproductions of the big "condo" birdcages — probably 99% of the big green and big purplish-brown ones are modern fakes. Candlesticks are merely glanced at in this chapter — just a hint of what might be added to a collection of useful household objects.

Finally, the most exciting and fully satisfying area of collecting in this chapter is that of **repaired pieces**, sometimes called "make-dos" — as in "Use it up, Wear it out, Make it do, Or do without!" It is a vast field waiting to be plowed and discovered. Gently, now . . . gently. Tools, as well as pitchers or bowls, were repaired to extend their lives. I suspect that housewives themselves did a lot of it — they were accustomed to using a soldering iron during canning, and there was always a kitchen drawer with twine, tack hammer, awl, baling wire, soldering iron (see Chapter XVI), nails, heavy staples, and other odds and ends that could be ingeniously used to repair something.

ABC plate, ironstone, transfer printed in black under glaze, depicts 2 small boys playing with small whips & a spinning top, decorated with red, green, yellow & blue, "Mekins," English, 5-1/4" diameter, mid 19th C. **$150-$175**

ABC plate, ceramic, decorated with Palmer Cox's Brownies, American, pat'd Feb. 11, 1896. Palmer Cox wasn't the only Brownie artist. He was the originator, but Brownie illustrations for ads were drawn by a team signing off as "Marr & Richards, Eng[graving]. Co., Milwaukee." So look for that name as well as Cox's. **$150-$200**

ABC plate, stamped tin, depiction of Palmer Cox's "Brownies," American, the "Brownies" pat'd 1896. **$140-$165**

ABC plate, stamped tin, alphabet border, nifty train design with cloud of smoke from smokestack, American, perhaps mid 19th C. Lots of potential crossover interest here. **$135-$165**

ABC plate, stamped tin, low relief sans serif alphabet letters, depicts girl & boy (both skirted) running with hoops, lots of landscape, American or English, toy — only 3" diameter, prob. 1840s-1860s. Wide value range due especially to kind of show at which it is sold. **$45-$150**

ABC plate, stamped tin, rolled rim with upper case letters, lower case letters surround profile portraits identified as "Oscar" & "Josephine," the man in military uniform with epaulette & Napoleonic curly short hair, the woman with a bead choker & neoclassical hairdo with trailing tendrils on shoulders. This was a puzzle until I turned to the 11th ed. *Encyclopædia Britannica,* which revealed Swedish King Oscar I & his wife Josephine; he reigned from 1844 to 1859. Swedish, 6-1/2" diameter, prob. 1844 to 1859, or later to commemorate something. **$65-$85**

Rolled rims — A rim or edge that is described as "rolled" may actually be rolled, such as this piece of tinware. The term is also used to describe the look of a rounded rim that couldn't possibly have been actually rolled — such as a turned wooden bowl or a ceramic piece.

ABC plate, stamped tin, serif alphabet letters around wide rim, depicts small dead Cock Robin lying at feet of large sparrow with bow; legend "Who killed Cock Robin. I said the sparrow with my bow and arrow, I killed Cock Robin" appears around picture. Could be American or English, no words that prove British spelling, 8-3/4" diameter, mid 19th C. up into early 20th C. (This plate was offered in an 8" size by L. H. Mace Co. of NYC, for 36¢ a dozen.) **$85-$125**

Elephantine Chronology — <u>Most famous</u>: In 1883, circus entrepeneur Phineas T. Barnum bought a large African elephant from the London Zoological Gardens for exhibition in the United States. People were wild for Jumbo, and he not only came to be used as a wonderful advertising image (you'll see many 1880s chromolith trade cards with large elephants, some named Jumbo), but his very name became synonymous with very big. The next time you buy a jumbo sized box of detergent, you've got P.T. Barnum to thank! But Barnum wasn't the first to bring an elephant to America. Probably the **first**, a three-year-old female, arrived in 1796 and was exhibited along Eastern seaboard for an unknown length of time. Probably the **second** was a four-year-old male, exhibited in the same area, including Philadelphia and Newburyport, from 1797 for an unknown period. This elephant, whose name was not given, was advertised as eating 130 pounds of food a day, and drinking "all kinds of spirituous liquors; some days . . . 30 bottles of porter, drawing the cork with his trunk." Where were the teetotalers when we needed them? The **third** elephant, probably the first famous one, was "Old Bet," who was brought to America in 1815 by a sea captain and sold to Hachaliah Bailey, who exhibited her around Putnam County, NY. A 6" diameter stamped tin "JUMBO" plate was offered by Central Stamping Co., NYC, in their 1920 catalog; obviously this type of plate was made over a long period. Only by collecting a few and comparing them could one discover the differences.

VII-1. ABC plate. *Stamped tin, round (though depiction is oval), Jumbo, an elephant famed in the 1880s. 6" diameter. Central Stamping Co., 1920 catalog.* **$65-$115**

VII-2. ABC plate. *Stamped tin, 6" diameter, Cock Robin depiction. This one probably late 19th C. This was offered in mail order catalog of Butler Brothers, 1899. It was offered in other catalogs through the 1920s, along with "Hi-Diddle-Diddle" nursery rhyme. Butler offered an undescribed one called "Harvard."* **$85-$125**

ABC plate, stamped tin, serif letters, delightful depiction of elephant & his name, "JUMBO," prob. American, could be pre-1883 English, 6-1/4" diameter, c.1880s to 1920s. **$65-$115**

ABC plate, stamped tin, somewhat runover looking, serif letters around rim, bust of George Washington, with name "Washington" underneath & 13 stars arched overhead, American, 6-1/8" diameter, 19th C. The condition depresses value here. **$70-$90**

ABC plate, stamped tin with rather ugly alphabet letters around rim, depicts cat playing fiddle, dog dancing, cow jumping over moon, dish & spoon hand in hand, legend reads "Hey Diddle Diddle," American or English, no words to check British spelling, 7-3/4" diameter, mid 19th C. Even if somewhat flattened, dinged & bent, and with plating loss, the value is still about $50. A perfect specimen would have to be suspect. **$85-$115**

Apple basket, oak staves painted yellow, wood bands, round double bottoms, wire bail handle with turned wood "spool" handle, poss. Edgerton Mfg. Co., Plymouth, IN, or Paoli, IN, half-bushel size, prob. early 20th C. Two 1920s catalogs show nearly identical baskets, natural finish oak. Established in 1849, Edgerton possibly made same baskets over a long period. They'd be surprised at today's prices. **$160-$185**

Apple box/basket, for market, nailed wood with slanted sides, painted green, 10" x 13", late 19th or early 20th C. **$135-$165**

VII-3. Produce or fruit basket. *Wood splints woven in flared shape almost like standing cornucopia. About 25" H . Photo of piece belonging to Arne Anton.* **$200-$300**

VII-4. Peach basket & Bushel basket, (L) *"standard Jersey & Delaware" type (there was also a "Michigan" type made without the hoops, holding 1 peck). Wood veneer with 3 hoops, came in 2, 4, 6 & 8 quart sizes. "The fruit-dealers in Chicago have a little 'dodge,' which we never saw elsewhere. Each basket of peaches is covered with a piece of tarletan or millinet, of a bright rose or scarlet color, which gives to the fruit a most attractive appearance, and at the same time prevents handling; this is put [also] over pears and other fruit."* American Agriculturist, *11/1875.* **(R)** *Elm staves, oak bottom & handles, galvanized iron hoops. Originally cost $4 per dozen! Both pictures are of old type baskets, from D. J. Barry & Co. catalog, 1924.* **$25-$45; $40-$65**

Apple butter jar, stoneware, dark brown Albany slip glaze inside, mug shape with round lip & slightly limp, applied "mug" handle, impressed mark, "F. H. Cowden" with place, "Harrisburg, PA," 7" H, c.3rd quarter 19th C. It looks very much like a stoneware chamber pot, except that the mouth is slightly smaller than the largest circumference of the vessel's body, whereas in a chamber pot the mouth widens out slightly. I would rather collect apple butter jars than chamber pots. In "The Shape of Stoneware," an article by James Mitchell, of the William Penn Memorial Museum (Harrisburg, PA), in *Early American Life*, Oct. 1978, we are told that "Sanitaryware is generally not found made from stoneware, but chamberpots are sometimes encountered. There are at least three marked examples. . . . One dated "1776" was excavated from the site of the James Morgan Pottery in Cheesequake, Middlesex County, NJ. . . . Another marked "Charlestown" belongs to the Smithsonian. . . . The third is marked "Hawthorne Pottery Co [Hawthorne, PA]" and is in the . . . William Penn Memorial Museum." **$85-$135**

Apple tray, tôle — painted tin, square bottom, widely slanted arch-topped sides, intact original paint in red, green and yellow, on dark asphaltum background, prob. CT, 13" x 8", mid 19th C. **$950-$1500**

Apple tray, tôle, oval, amber crystalized inner bottom, large hand hold cutouts at both ends, simple flowers & leaves in red, salmon, pink, yellow, green, black & white, American, 2-3/4" deep x 12-5/8" L x 7-3/4" W, early to mid 19th C. **$3000-$4000**

Apple tray, tôle, rectangular bottom with high arched & slanted ends & slanted sides, crystalized & colored gold inside on bottom, sides japanned dark brown with flowers & leaves in yellow, white, blue, red & black, in extremely good condition, American, 2-3/4" deep x 12-5/8" L x 8" W, mid 19th C. (See more on trays at end of chapter.) **$1800-$2000**

Barrel, for store, wood staves with paper label on side, "Davis Baking Powder," 23-1/2" H x 15" diameter, early 20th C. **$150-$175**

Barrel, made from hollowed tree trunk, American, 30" H x 19" diameter, early 19th C. Folk art crossover interest. **$250-$400**

Basket, for berries, round, vertical strips of prettily cutout wood veneer bound with wire, wood bottom with hole, crimped tin edge (some found with wooden hoop at top), often called a "Shaker" basket but many examples have a non-Shaker mfr's name stamped on the bottom — "D. Cook's," with patent date, or "L. Cook & Co.," with place name. Others stamped "Union Manufacturing" & place, New Haven, CT, at least two sizes, pint (4-3/4" H) & quart (taller & much bigger in diameter), pat'd July 12, 1859, but prob. made over a long period. **$125-$155**

Basket, for berries, wood splits, galvanized tin rim, American, 1/2 pint size, 3-1/8" H, late 19th C. Dealer Mickie Carpenter of Lousiville, KY, told an amusing story about the "spice balls" she often fills such baskets with in booth displays. Her friend Kathie Hill makes the balls of ground spices mixed with a paste of some kind and stuck with cloves. Once she had a small bowl full at a show and a man wandered into the booth, picked a spice ball up and bit into it, and made a very sour face. "Do you have anything I can spit this into?" he asked. She told him there was a waste can down the aisle, but allowed the taste alone to chastise him. **$125-$155**

Basket, for berries, flared sides, very small but not delicate. Bottom is round wood disc with hole, strips of split wood almost as thin as veneer tacked to disc and to strip that forms rim with small-head brass tacks, American, only 2-1/2" H x 4" diameter, c.1860s-1880s. **$75-$95**

Baskets, for berries, 2 very unusual, charming round, smoothly turned, bark baskets. Sides gently flared, with very skinny high arched cutouts, little finger size, from base up. Most appealingly, both baskets have been repaired. One with a small tin patch bent over the round rim, and tacked; the other with cord actually sewn back & forth across a long crack. Impressed in a 3/4" band close to the top is the name. "Mellish Patent," mfd. by Baird & Roper, Norfolk, VA, 4" H x 5-1/2" diameter, pat'd Feb. 23, 1869. **$100-$140**

Baskets, for fruit, various brands & very utilitarian: (1) thin split wood, constructed with 3 criss-cross strips joined at the base and bent up to form sides, purple stained band of wood at top; (2) essentially the same as the first but slightly different look, name stamped in purple; (3) wooden bottom, criss-crossed narrow strips of wood, bound with wire, one marked "Webster," Webster Basket Co., Webster, NY, 1/2 peck, turn of century to c.1930s or 1940s. **$10-$12**

Basket, for fruit, decorative, not utilitarian, twisted wire, 4 very unusual cabriole legs, bowl with 8 fancy petals with scrolls inside, American or French, about 9-3/4" diameter, 1870s to 1890s. **$250-$275**

Basket, for fruit display on sideboard or dining table, delicate, lacy twisted wire, sometimes painted dark green, very dark red, or white, 3-ply wire pedestal base, handles, French or American, 14" H, 1870s-1880s. Like wirework egg stands meant for table use, these could be imports from France, not American, even though the USA had several thriving wiregoods firms. **$165-$200**

Basket, for fruit, woven, looped, soldered wire, a footed compote with swags around top, for all the world like a line drawing of a cut glass compote, showing where the fancy wedge cuts would be made by the cutter, American, about 8" H (these are hard to measure sometimes because wire squushes), 1870s to 1890s. **$135-$175**

VII-5. Fruit baskets. (L) *"Mellish" patent, for berries, peaches, etc., in various sizes. Wood bark with unusual appearance. Illustration from David Lyman ad in* American Agriculturist, *7/1868 and later. Mellish baskets also manufactured by Baird, Roper & Co., Norfolk, VA, and advertised in same magazine after May 1870. Very hard to find — I've only seen two in 10 years.* **(R)** *Square, veneer with nailed rim, meant for strawberries. "Thoroughly ventilated, remarkably attractive when filled with fruit — and can box." Capacity one quart; they also made crates to hold from 12 to 96 quart baskets!* American Basket Co., New Haven, CT. American Agriculturist, *6/1865.* **$120-$160; $20-$40**

The Rochester Berry Basket.

[Patented 1870.]

1 quart.   1 pint.   ½ quart.

The best ventilated and neatest Basket made.

Fits in Beecher Crates.

VII-6. Berry baskets. *Interesting wood veneer construction, nailed rims, pat'd 1870. Collins, Geddes & Co., Moorestown, NJ. Ad in* American Agriculturist, *5/1872.* **$60-$100**

Beecher Baskets.

Star Basket.

QUART.   PINT.
PATENTED DECEMBER 17, 1872.

IMPROVED Square Basket.
Patented Feb. 26, 1878.

VENEER BASKETS. Patented May 31, 1864.
For circular of description, &c., address
THE BEECHER BASKET COMPANY,
Westville, Conn.

VII-7. Berry & fruit baskets. *The baskets in the last picture were advertised as fitting "in Beecher crates." Here are some real Beecher Basket Co. baskets. Various shapes and sizes, pat'd 5/31/1864; 12/17/1872; and 2/26/1878. Westville, CT. American Agriculturist ad, 5/1878. Thirteen years before, C. Beecher & Sons, advertised their widely-acclaimed "Veneer Fruit Basket," being "neat, stylish, durable and cheap." As well as close-nesting when empty. It was similar to the 1864 patent basket shown at bottom, only sides didn't curve at all.* **$20-$60**

The above cuts show the form and some of the uses of the Sugar-trough Gourd. They grow by the acre to hold two bucketfuls each, and I have raised them to hold over eleven gallons each. My Catalogue tells how to grow them, and illustrates and describes over 200 varieties of choice vegetable and flower seeds. Send stamp for Catalogue, or 25 cents for it and package of the Gourd seed.
Address WALDO F. BROWN, P. O. Box 2, Oxford, Butler Co., Ohio.

VII-8. Useful gourds. *Ad placed by Waldo F. Brown, Oxford, OH, to sell his gourd seeds and a booklet. Note two baskets made from the gourd, which he said could be grown to hold 2 gallons! American Agriculturist, 2/1892. Old containers made from gourds are often found varnished, but you should see the beautiful painted ones! Basket made from gourd:* **$20-$100**

VII-9. Berry basket. *Wood veneer, wood bottom, sheet metal rim. Type often called a "Shaker" basket, but it probably isn't. Many marked "D. Cook's," or "L. Cook & Co." or "Union Manufacturing, New Haven, CT." Pat'd 7/12/1859, but made over long period. 4-3/4" H.* **$125-$155**

VII-10. Berry basket. *Very similar to VII-9. Wood veneer splits, galvanized metal rim & hoop at bottom. Only 3-1/8" H . Courtesy Mickie Carpenter.* **$125-$155**

VII-11. Wire baskets: *fruit compotes, cake stand, flower-holder centerpiece. The linecuts are all "Sherwood's Standard White Lustral Wire Ware" from the catalog of Woods, Sherwood & Co., Lowell, MA, as it appeared in a book from 1876. In 1872, the same linecuts were used in an article on "tinned twisted wire" household goods, based on French originals, in 11/1872 American Agriculturist.* **$85-$200**

The Convertible Basket

The Most Wonderful Invention of the Twentieth Century.

VII-12. Convertible basket, *made of nickeled iron wire, and used as a lamp shade, flower stand, egg boiler, hanging lamp, ladies' work basket, [sad] iron stand, card holder, cake stand, fruit basket, etc. Novelty catalog of A. E. Rayment Supply Co., Rockford, IL, c.1910-20s. (One of these, looking confusingly but appropriately old, was for sale for $265 in 1997!)* **$18-$30**

358

Lookalike alarm — A good design can't be improved, and wire things have eye appeal matched only by pen and ink drawings. Giulio Cappellini, a designer in Milan, Italy, has a line of accessories called "Filo di Ferro" [wire of iron]. He makes "reinterpretations" of French wire fruit dishes, high footed compotes, low baskets, stemmed candleholders (for votive candles in glass jars), and various plate and platter trays — all of exquisitely twisted iron wire. To my eye, at least in photographs, they look just like the pieces from 100+ years ago; soon, differences will be impossible to detect.

Basket, for gathering fruit or vegetables, round wooden bottom, with a sort of picket fence of tongue depressors, wirebound, forming flared sides, folding wire & wood handles, Shaker, made in KY, 14-1/2" diameter, 19th C. Two others have been seen: one with rectangular bottom (with slightly rounded long sides) & handle at each end, 20" x 12-3/4", and elongated oval-bottomed one with very flared sides, 32" L x 20" W. Ovals up to twice the price for rounds. **$185-$225**

Basket, half bushel size, oak splint, a zinc hoop plus wooden hoops & bottom, bentwood oak handle grips with both ends cut to pointed wedges & driven into woven bands near top, extremely handsome, perfectly made, American, late 19th C. **$125-$150**

Basket, hickory splint, swing handle, American, 13" diameter, early 20th C. **$175-$225**

Basket, hickory splint with wooden handles, bushel size, American, late 19th or early 20th C. Patina costs! **$85-$135**

Basket, homemade from green-painted motor oil can, cut from rim down close to bottom so sides could be made to flare out, edges bent around copper wire rim, high arched copper wire handle, basket 6" H, can from c.1920s-1930s. Folk art crossover. **$40-$65**

Basket-framed plate, interwoven lacy twisted wire, shallow basket with widely flared sides in dish shape, wires frame a molded pressed amber glass plate, "Hobnail" pattern with nipple-like projections. American, about 2-1/4" deep x 7-1/4" diameter, with 4-1/4" diameter plate, last quarter 19th C. I have several of these, one in amber glass, one with a nice hand-painted china plate, all amost exactly the same size. They look less fussily Victorian when displayed with plain wire fruit compotes & other woven wire objects. Crossover glass & china collectors help set price. **$50-$125+**

Basket-framed lithograph, intricate woven wire with chromo cardboard center depicting fruit, poss. American, prob. German, only 1-1/4" deep x 6" diameter, turn of century. **$30-$40**

Basket, miniature splint, 2 handles, American, only 3-1/2" x 3", 19th C. **$35-$45**

Basket, tin, footed, with twisted, corrugated rim, base & handle, American, 11-1/2" H, c.1870s. Tin household objects or items of apparel from shoes to baskets to hats were commissioned from tinsmiths as 10th anniversary gifts. Surprisingly few have surfaced, although many are hidden away or on display at museums. The more detail the better. **$1600-$2000**

Basket, tin, woven, 10th anniversary piece, high handle, American, 5" diameter, 19th C. **$275-$400**

Basket, wire in form of chicken, very intricate weaving, wires are close together, painted tin trim, viz. red comb, yellow eyes, with wooden beak, carrying handle of heavier wire, prob. American, 8-1/2" H x 12" L, 19th C. **Cheep chicken** — This isn't the common 1950s chicken basket, perfectly rounded & made from somewhat heavy wire not too close together, soldered joints. That kind shouldn't be more than $15-$20. This one: **$350-$400**

Basket, woven splint, miniature melon, Tennessee, only 5-3/4" across, c.1850s. **$275-$325**

Perhaps a Futurewatch? — On Jan. 1, 1988, the Litchfield Auction Galleries, CT, sold the James & Nancy Clokey collection of folk art, including **10th anniversary tin pieces.** I wish I'd been there. The *Maine Antique Digest* reporter summed up the disappointing take by saying that the Clokey's "enthusiasm never rubbed off on others." I, and everyone else who might have smidges of the Clokey's *joi*, so overestimated what the pieces would bring that I (we?) didn't bid. A square basket of woven strips of tin, with a fancy wrapped hoop handle and edges, and four sproingy loops at each corner, filled with polychromed stone fruit (which alone should have brought the price) sold for only $425, plus 10% premium. A punch decorated pudding mold sold for $900 (plus 10%); the decoration probably accounted for most of the money. A life-size Windsor chair, all tin, went for a shockingly low $525 (plus 10%). A cake box, round with slanted sides, domed lid with nifty funnel finial and applied 3-D tin flowers, which *MAD* reported the Clokeys paid over $4000 for when they bought it, went for a paltry $1200 (plus 10%). I don't know what this bodes for the future of anniversary tin, but surely that isn't true market value.

Basket, woven splint (& reed?), large, straight-sided, colored green, blue, orange & yellow with potato stamp designs, American — possibly Native American, 20" H x 24" diameter, 19th C. **$500-$700**

VII-13. Market basket. *Dyed straw, 14" H x 14-1/2" L, Tennessee, 1930s-40s. Collection of Mary Mac & Robert Franklin.* **$25-$35**

VII-14. Beer pot or pitcher. *Graniteware, reinforced strap handle, wire bail handle with turned wood. Lalance & Grosjean Mfg. Co., NYC, 1890.* **$60-$90+**

Baskets, painted sheets of perforated tin, the perforations square and rather close together, one basket is a small oblong with very high, trellis-like square cornered double handles; the other is sort of a canoe shape with single high bracket handle, for flower arrangements, American, about 9" to 11" H, 1920s. **$30-$50**

Batter jugs — See Chapter II (Mix, Beat, Stir, Churn and Blend)

Beater jars — See Chapter II (Mix, Beat, Stir, Churn and Blend)

Berry box tray, green painted wood, very flat with low sides, high arched bentwood handle, meant for holding 12 berry boxes, American, 1-1/4" H sides x 17" x 12", 19th C. These came in various sizes & proportions, but most seem to have been meant for 8 or 12 small square berry boxes. Some had four little block feet, one at each corner. Many were left unpainted, but old green, gray, blue and red are found. **$145-$175**

Lookalike alarm — To cash in on country-look lust, some entrepeneurs have recently made up crude berry box trays from old crates or other weathered old wood. You get a feeling for them after a while, but many have tell-tale fresh sawn edges, easily visible.

Berry container, also for dried fruit, made of wood fiber, dipped in paraffin, used with a special sealing tool, square or oblong, round air holes in top & lids, "Seal-Tite Weis Fibre Containers," mfd. by American Container Co., NYC, NY, five sizes, from half pint to quart, 1918. **$6-$10**

Early Paper Containers — as outlined in Jan. 7, 1888 *Chamber's Journal*: "An attempt now being made on an extended scale to introduce bottles made of paper into this country [England] merits some passing notice. The paper-bottle industry, which has achieved considerable success in Chicago, and is gradually extending throughout the United States, has not yet obtained any development on this side of the Atlantic. Foremost amongst the advantages accruing from this new adaptation of paper is the fact that the bottles are unbreakable; whilst the cost at which they can be placed on the market is considerably lower than that of articles of the same size in glass, stoneware, or tin. A great saving in weight is moreover effected, a desideratum of no small moment where cost of carriage of large numbers has to be taken into consideration; whilst the cost of packing is reduced to a minimum, for breakage in transit, which is a constant source of loss with glass bottles, is obviously impossible. Special machinery is employed in the manufacture of paper bottles. A long strip of paper of requisite thickness having been formed into a tube by bending around a circular 'mandrel,' is covered externally with an outer glazed sheet, bearing any printed labels to be employed; the tube is then cut into short lengths, to the ends of which are added tops, bottoms, and necks of paper — or of wood, if special strength is desired — nothing further being necessary beyond pouring in and lining the insides with a composition, which on setting will effectively resist the action of acids, spirits, inks, dyes, & c." Milk cartons are taken for granted now; we never see milk bottles.

Berry pail, blue & white swirl enamelware, with lid, straight sides, 7" H, turn of century. **$100-$135**

Birdcage, brass cage, molded opaque white "milk" glass cups, cast iron stand with small bird design on base, American or German, mid 19th C. Required equipment for many late 19th C or early 20th C kitchens was a bird, plus cage. Housewares stores & departments stocked birds & cages; unfortunately, the practice continues in some dimestores today. **$165-$200**

Birdcage, brass wires & sheet brass, arched top, simple bottom with 4 squatty feet, scrolly hanger on top "Colonial," mfd. by American Cage Co., Racine, WI, 1920s. **$20-$40**

Birdcage, globular pumpkin form, tin top, bottom & center band, bars of tin going from "North Pole" to "South Pole," conical finial on top with wire hanging ring, top, band & bottom painted blue, bands/bars painted white, a lovely form but awful to think of a bird living its life inside this. Birds should live outside, in their natural habitat. No mark, prob. New England, 14" H, early 19th C. **$175-$200**

Birdcage, heavy green, ochre & red painted tin, tin roof in peaked form, decoratively pierced with tiny quatrefoils, wire sides, no marks, American, 18" H x 15" L x 9" W, 19th C. **$125-$150**

Birdcage, high beehive or haystack shape, iron wire, longitudinal wires bound by latitudinal wires twisted at each intersection, very deep straight-sided pan, almost like a cake pan, bottom, hanging ring of wire at top, not painted, American (?), about 13" H x 10" diameter, prob. mid 19th C. **$120-$150**

Birdcage, japanned & decorated perforated & plain tin, brass wire, in shape of large mansion with mansard "French" roof with widow's walk on top, large arched "entry," with 2 interior staircases, solid back, on scalloped base with 4 conical feet, Heinz & Munschauer, Buffalo, NY, about 16" H x 12-3/4" W x 8-1/2" deep, c.1880. **$175-$235**

Birdcage, on pedestal stand, round with double dome top, brass wires finished in colored enamel, large brass finial, stand looks like bottom 4/5ths of a floor lamp from same period, it is marbelized with paint, Crucet Mfg. Co., NYC, NY, early 1920s. They offered in their ads a booklet I'd love to see: "<u>Lovely Cages</u>." The ads pack a lot of decorating value into a bird cage: "Introducing a harmonious assortment of exquisitely decorated cages with pedestals to match decorative surroundings of home. There is a wide variety of finishes to suit exacting, individual tastes or requirements, among which are: New dandeli-

VII-15. Birdcage & ground squirrel (chipmunk) cage. (L) *Wheel cage with painted iron wire and stamped tin front & trim. 19" H x 13-1/4" x 6-1/2" body (tray base is 16-1/4" x 12"). (R) Enameled iron wire & stamped & perforated sheet metal, 18" H x 11" x 7-3/4". Both in catalog of Norvell-Shapleigh Hardware Co., St. Louis, 1910. $90-$175+. FAKE ALERT.— The most commonly found repro (or shall we say fake) birdcage is the big (36" H x 28" L x 9" deep), dark green or brown, three-domed, wood & wire bird condo, with a fake clock above the arched front door. Asian-made, deliberately aged and distressed to make it look antique, it's been imported by the thousands, along with fake carousel horses, wicker baby buggies, hobbie horses, ad nauseum. Gift catalogs offer them retail for $300; antique dealers have them for up to $500. The intent is to bilk the gullible, not house the homeless. My opinion of the "value" of this cage is a big ZERO. Don't encourage them & don't buy 'em, please.*

VII-18. Pickled food bottle. *Green glass in the so-called* "**Cathedral**" *design with gothic arched hexagonal sides. 13" H, American 19th C., mold-blown. Photo courtesy of Robert W. Skinner Inc., Auctioneers, Bolton, MA.* **$300-$600+**

VII-16. Pen & ink original drawing. *"The Warm Weather — Terrific explosion of a Ginger Beer Truck." Signed K. Gregory (?), c.1880. 11-1/8" H x 8-1/4" W. A primitive, spirited drawing. Note corkscrew in vendor's hand, and the exploding thick stoneware ginger pop bottles, which are about 7" to 9" H. The simple, mass-produced tan & ochre bottles are worth about $30-$45. The drawing:* **$75-$125+**

VII-17. Stoneware bottles. (M) *a root or ginger beer bottle, big lip, initials in cobalt blue "D B," 10" H.* **(L)** *A Gin bottle, with handle, made by Wingender, in NJ, cobalt blue flower & bands, 10" H.* **(R)** *Another Wingender gin. Photo courtesy Litchfield Auction Gallery, Litchfield CT. Ex-Corbin Collection, 1990 sale prices: $175; $120; $130. Now:* **$125-$225**

VII-19. Novelty bar bottles. *All are molded figurals with etched details. From (L) to (R):* **(1)** *Mermaid;* **(2)** *Portrait bottle of champion heavyweight pugilist* **Jim Jeffries**, *who boxed from 1896 to 1904, and 1910 to 1921. This design shows "champion ready for an engagement," probably was done after his first retirement. Bottle has etched tights, body is painted flesh color. Catalog states "best and only representation of a pugilist made in the form of a bottle."* **(3)** *"Never Rip" decanter ... "They like to pour from it." A touch of soft porn, as in many late Victorian things.* **(4)** *Elephant's head & trunk, "cleverly gotten up for back bar display." All from the hotel & bar supply catalog of Albert Pick & Co., Chicago, 1909 (with some items going back to 1905).* (1) **$70-$100;** (2) **$500-$600+;** (3) **$80-$125;** (4) **$80-$125**

on and black ivory and colors. Roman gold and marble effect. Antique walnut and gold. Black and gold. These alluringly new and charming cages are a decided relief from ordinary, unsightly bird cage in general use. You will have a pride in the lasting beauty of the distinctive Crucet." **$65-$90**

Birdcage, pierced & pieced sheet metal, Art Deco, large canister cylinder, snap-on bottom, witch's cap conial top, sides and top all cutout so as to form a pattern of oblongs divided into 3 triangles, each triangle with diagonal lines going different direction from its neighbors, very effective & looks somewhat like abstractions of spider webs — a motif popular in the 1920s & 1930s. Little sliding door for bird egress & entrance, & for filling water & feed dishes. This one almost well enough made to look like a professional commercial craftsman made multiples of the design, but not quite. I think it's a one-off piece made skillfully in a home workshop. Prob. American, 18" H x 12" diameter, prob. late 1920s or early 1930s. Folk art. **$165-$200**

Birdcage, slightly peaked roof, wire sides, unusual feature being a sort of canopy of tied-back curtains actually made of polka-dot painted cutout tin, zigzag bottom, meant to hang from a holder, French, mid 1930s. **$115-$130**

Birdcage, stamped, japanned & decorated tin, wire, reticulated footed pedestal base also stamped with human figures, hexagonal dome-topped cage with reticulated gallery 2/3 way up, "cornice" decorations at corners made of stamped metal, Heinz & Munschauer, Buffalo, NY, 18" H x 9" diameter, c.1880. Many cages from this period are painted in vivid color combinations of cobalt blue, a bright medium green, an almost fire engine red (or a maroony red), and a sort of acid yellow. The blue is sometimes chalky in appearance; exactly like bright blue paints used by kindergartners. Some cages are decorated with small floral decals on the peaks; they resemble lithographed paper-covered dollhouses of same period. **$250-$350**

Bottles — A few are pictured, but better to consult specialty bottle books.

Bottles, for pickles, mold blown green or aquamarine glass, all with collared mouths, molded in the Gothic-arch-sided style called "cathedral" jars, ranging from pale green to rather dark green, collection of 5, as follows: **(1)** short squat one with 3 arches, extra decoration on front, plain arch in back has columns on either side, 8-1/4" H; **(2)** 4 sides, 3 arches with extra designs, 8-1/2" H; **(3)** 8 sided jar with arches, 11" H; **(4)** dark green, 4 sides with upside down crown around neck of jar, very simplified designs on body, 11-3/8" H; **(5)** large version of first one, crude mold, lots of bubbles, 4 sides, 3 arches filled with designs, 14-1/4" H. Quite extraordinary range of sizes. American, mid 19th C. According to Steven Van Rensselaer, who wrote *Check List of Early American Bottles and Flasks* (Southampton, NY: Cracker Barrel Press, 1921), "It is probable that most of the glass works made them, but it is known that they were made at the Willington Glass Works [in] East Willington, CT." Individual prices might range from $250 to $800. This set was $2000 in 1985. Now more likely to fall within higher range: **$2200-$2500**

Bottle carrier, green painted sheet iron, holds 6 bottles around outside, one in center, cap end of bottles fit into "dimples" in lid, kept cool with packed ice, for Nehi bottles, mfd. by Universal Container Co., Toledo, OH, about 8-1/2" H x 7-1/4" diameter, 20th C. **$40-$65**

Bottle carrier, soldered wire, 6 bottle "silos" 2 x 3 formation, high arched twisted wire carrying handle, from an F. A. Walker catalog, (also came in 2 & 4 bottle sizes), French?, c.1870s. **$125-$175**

Bowl, burl, deep, waxy-feeling wood, 2 small checks [dryness or age cracks, naturally occuring as wood dries out], one check filled with an old repair composition material, bowl slightly warped, American, 4-1/4" H x 11" diameter at widest part, late 18th or early 19th C. **$750-$900**

Burls — abnormal protuberant wart-like growths occuring on the trunks & large limbs of trees — usually found on hardwood or semi-hardwood trees, but can occur on any tree. The cause is "imperfectly understood," to use wood-mensch Albert Constantine, Jr.'s phrase. Speculations as to cause include injury (fire, frost, nail holes or other violent physical contact), and irritation from bacteria, fungi or viruses, says Constantine. I have heard people explain them as the effect of wasp stings; Constantine relates the belief that woodpeckers may cause burls to form. Different writers list different trees as most probable to have burls, especially those burls valuable to wood turners or cabinetmakers. Most lists include walnut, oak, cherry, sugar maple, mahogany, myrtle (i.e. acacia), thuja (i.e. thuya), various ash, yellow poplar, olive, mountain laurel, arbutus (i.e. madrone burl), birch, Norway burl birch, English elm, redwood, and box. Early settlers and nineteenth-century artisans in Europe and the United States prized highly figured burls, especially for making bowls. American Indians used burls to make bowls, some with handles carved in figural or animalistic forms. According to Constantine, some species of burls check and warp easily, maybe even requiring repair before using. This may explain why some burl bowls are so decidedly warped and cracked. Most burl wood can be very highly polished, sometimes without the addition of any wax or oil. To read more about wood, and to better understand color and figure (pattern of eyes, swirls and loops) of all woods, I recommend *Know Your Woods*, by Albert Constantine, Jr., (NY: Charles Scribner's Sons, 1959; revised by Harry J. Hobbs, 1975). Constantine is a name well known to twentieth-century wood artisans, because the firm has supplied craftspeople with woods, veneers and other materials for many years.

Bowl, burl, large, well-figured oval, 2 small handles are part of rim, very good patina, small crack with old repair done with metal staple or brad (when I use "staple" in this context, I don't mean Swingline™), not signed, but known to be from Bergen County, northeastern NJ, 6-1/2" H x 19" L x 15" W, early 19th C. **$2000-$2700**

Bowl, burl, lathe-turned bands on outside, cracks fill-fixed with solder, American, 15" diameter, early 19th C. **$1500-$1800**

Bowl, burl, lathe-turned decorative bands, American, 10-3/4" diameter, early 19th C. **$600-$800**

Bowl, burl, birds'-eye maple (?), 2 bands turned around top, American, 5-1/4" H x 13-3/8" diameter, early 19th C. **$700-$900**

Bowl, burl, oval shape, finely figured, old iron staple repair holds short age check, American, 19" L x 15" W x 6-1/2" H, late 18th or early 19th C. See picture IX-22 for several prized mended pieces. **$2300+**

VII-20. Bottle carrier. *Tinned iron wire, twisted & soldered, made for 2, 4 or 6 bottles. From F. A. Walker catalog, 1870s-80s. SEE also VII-145.* **$125-$175**

Bowl, burl, small age check or crack in rim, very good patina, American, 5" deep x 10" diameter, 19th C. Many burl bowls with a rounded lip or rim are described as having a "rolled" rim, a term only for metalwares where the metal has actually been rolled, usually around a wire core, to give stability. **$750-$1000**

Bowl, burl with old tin patch repair, American, 9" D, 19th C. **$275-$300**

Wood knots — "In the back country . . . cups, bowls, and trenchers were cut out of wood and served everyday table purposes. White ash knots were used for . . . bowls and constantly the woodworkers were grubbing around the forests for knots in old sugar maples, soft maples, ash, beech, and birch trees. A single large knot would make a whole nest of bowls. Such wood was referred to as '**dish timber**.'" Richardson Wright, *Hawkers & Walkers in Early-America*, 1927.

Bowl, cast iron, American, unusually deep, 7" deep x 9" diameter, 2nd to 3rd quarter 19th C. **$125-$145**

Bowl, cast iron, deep, with rounded rim and ring base, American, 3-1/2" deep x 9" diameter, 18th C. You see very few of these advertised for sale. The only dealer I know of who ever consistently comes up with them is Clara Jean Davis of Concord, NH. She is a direct descendent of Joseph Jenks (Jencks), first iron founder in America. **$125-$200**

Bowls, cast iron, most without foot, some with ring base, slanted straight sides or slightly rounded sides, earliest have round sprue marks on bottom, later ones (late 18th, early 19th C.) have straight sprue gate mark. No recorded marks known, American, varying heights from about 3" to 4-3/4" H, varying diameters from about 7" to 12", 18th or 19th C. **$125-$250**

Iron bowls are fabulous. One dealer described one of hers as having "a ring like bell metal." Clara Jean Davis of Hopkinton, NH, has described her offerings as being nicknamed "poor man's pewter." Another dealer called hers a "slave bowl." In my *300 Years of Housekeeping Collectibles,* page 205, you'll see two cast iron bowls that were called "**wash hand basins**" in the 1861 trade catalog I found the pictures in. One is bell-shaped with flared rim and with a small foot, and came in three sizes: 3-1/4" H x 8-1/2"; 3-1/2" H x 9-1/2"; and 3-3/4" H x 10" diameter. They could be had in plain cast iron, tinned, or porcelainized. The other one is proportioned more like a mixing bowl, with small foot, and came in five sizes, plain or tinned: 3-3/4" H x 9-1/2"; 4-1/4" H x 10-3/4"; 4-5/8" H x 11-3/4"; and 5-3/8" H x 13-1/2". Both styles were from Leibrandt & Mcdowell Stove Works and Hollow-Ware Foundries, Baltimore & Philadelphia.

Bowl, called a Scotch bowl or Scotch kettle, cast iron with forged falling bail handle, long casting gate on bottom, irregular reinforcing band around outside, just under slightly flared lip. The Scotch bowl did not necessarily have a lid that came with it, although if you've cooked oatmeal, grits or Cream of Wheat™ you'll recall how the bubbling surface sends up small volcanic eruptions of scalding hot meal to burn your stirring hand. Not

VII-21. Burl bowl. *Old, original red paint on exterior, about 16-1/2" diameter but slightly warped as usual. First half 19th C. Photo & information courtesy Jeannine Dobbs' Country/Folk/Antiques, Merrimack, NH. A sublime form, good sized.* **$2000-$3000**

VII-22. Burls still growing on tree. *This particular tree is near Mt. Crawford, VA, in the Blue Ridge area. In many places in Virginia and New Jersey (two states I know of) there are huge trees growing with a full supply of burls.*

marked, American, 2-7/8" H x 10-3/4" diameter, c.1830s to 1850s. According to Carl W. Drepperd's *A Dictionary of American Antiques,* a cast iron, cup-shaped cooking pot about the size of a Scotch bowl but without the flared sides is called a <u>Yankee bowl</u>. **$40-$55**

Bowl, for eating, turned wood, slightly warped, with faded old blue paint on outside, it has acquired a lovely patina inside from "wet" food, oils & greases, American, 7" D, early 1800s. **$225-$350**

Bowl, probably for fruit, painted turned wood, tulip on grayish old rose background, probably <u>Lehnware</u>, named for Joseph Lehn (also found spelled Lehne), Lititz, Manheim Township, Lancaster County, PA, 5" H, mid 19th C. (Joseph Lehn lived 1798-1892, & worked c.1856-1892). For comparison, see entry for a turned wooden sugar bowl made by Pease. **$700-$850**

Bowl, turned wood, rather thick, old gray paint on outside, American, 17-1/2" diameter, mid 19th C. My idea about all <u>old gray paint</u> seen on 19th C. pieces is that when you mix lots of leftover colors together and add white, it is always a shade of gray. Perhaps old batches of mixed paints were used up in painting utilitarian pieces. Otherwise it seems odd to pick gray, unless it was because it didn't show dirt. For modern collectors, it's a boon — grays seem very contemporary and cool and allow the form to lead. **$275-$325**

Bowl covers, for storage in refrigerator, made of "washable, airtight oil silk, with Lastex bands," looks like rubberized parachute silk. A complete set would include a zippered pouch for bread & small covers for bottles and jellies, Blossom Mfg. Co., NYC, NY, late 1930s. **$2-$5**

Bowl or trencher, hand-hewn thick wood in oblong shape, with old red paint on outside, American, 29" L x 13" x 6" D, early 19th C. Size, age, patina and paint = added value. **$350-$400**

VII-23. Bread box. *"Roll-A-Way" style with choice of decorations. This one is "Early American Girl Moderne," in ivory with green trim, or ivory with red trim, or white with red. "Betsy Ross Moderne" was not shown in ad. Mfd. by E. M. Meder Co. 1935 ad. Bread boxes, especially from the '30s and '40s, are increasingly in demand because of the millions of people using their own bread machines.* **$25-$65**

VII-24. Bread raiser. *"With ventilated cover." Heavy tin, riveted strap handle, 4 sizes in same odd-seeming choice of quart capacities — 10, 14, 17 and 21. Small ones suited for families, the largest for hotel kitchens or bakeries. Approx. sizes: from 6-5/8" H x 14-5/8" diameter to hold 10 quarts, to 8-1/4" H x 19-1/4" diameter (21 quarts). Central Stamping Co., 1920. Very similar bread raisers were made by Sexton Stove in Baltimore, Savory of Newark, NJ, and Geuder, Paeschke & Frey Co., Milwaukee, WI in the 1920s-30s. Graniteware ones may bring a lot more.* **$75-$125**

Bowls for mixing — See Chapter II (Mix, Beat, Stir, Churn and Blend)

Box, bentwood, straight lap with copper tacks, constructed with wooden pegs, wire bail handle with wooden grip, original varnish in golden color, stamped "Weston Sherwin & Co.," Winchendon, MA, 2-3/4" H x 4-3/4" diameter, 19th C. See also pantry boxes. **$550-$625**

Bread box, a sort of quonset hut, with rollup lid, painted tin with little design of long-skirted woman with parasol, painted ivory with green trim, ivory with red, or white with red, "Betsy Ross Roll-A-Way," mfd. by E. M. Meder Co., c.1935. **$25-$65**

Bread box, for diner or big household, holds 4 loaves stacked on end, tin, and with baked-on white enamel, lid has knob and holde, word "BREAD" stenciled on, motto reads "The All Welded, Rigid, for strength and durability. Built like a bridge," English, provisional patent #29069/24. Others are white; green; a white one with no stenciling. **$40+**

Bread box, japanned tin, imitation oak graining design in ochre and brown, wire handles, stenciled "BREAD," flat top, side wire handles, hasp closing, Matthai-Ingram Co., American, came in nests of three: 10", 11" and 12" deep x 13-1/4", 15-1/4" and 16-1/2" long x 9-1/2", 10-1/2" and 11-1/2" wide, late 19th C. Separately, maybe $25-$40 each. For original nest of three: **$100-$135**

Bread box, square punctured & slitted tin box, with roof-like lid with cast iron handle at top, design on front of box rather like pie safe tins, stars in each corner as spandrels, band across center has initials, probably of owner, "K. M. B.," prob. PA, 15" H x 14" square, mid 19th C. **$500-$650**

Bread & cake box, painted tin, 2 white porcelain knobs, roll-top with cake drawer below, 2 wire side handles, stenciled "BREAD" and "CAKE." (This came in ivory, white, blue, green, gray, red or yellow painted tin.) C. B. Porter Co., American, 14-1/2" H x 16" L x 11-1/2" W, turn of century, early 20th C. **$45-$70**

Bread & cake box, tin japanned in brown, words "Bread & Cake" in yellow stencil, has roll-top front lid, fold-down wire handles at side, "Kreamer," 13-1/2" H x 12" x 11", 20th C. **$90-$120**

Bread raiser, gray graniteware, with tin lid, small base, 16" D, turn of century. (This form more often found in tin.) **$125-$175**

Bucket, cobalt & white enamelware, wire & wood bail, late 19th C. **$165-$225**

Bucket, composition wood fiber & glue, wire & wood, bail handle, "Indurated Fibre Ware," agented by Cordley & Hayes, later called "Fibrotta," NYC, NY, 9-1/4" H, 1883, 1884, 1885 and 1886 patents, s.i.b. 1915. **$45-$55**

Bucket, coopered wood painted with diagonal smoke graining, iron bound at bottom, middle and near top, bands daubed with paint, falling wire bail with simple wood grip with beading at each end — a subtle detail that probably translated into a few hundred $$$ of total, it's perhaps the *punctum,* or telling point. Joseph Lehn, 9-1/2" H, 19th C. Lehnware is highly prized. **$4500-$5500**

VII-25. Bread trough & dough scraper. *Oblong wooden box with slanted sides. This was used the way the raisers were later used. I just love these old pictures from* American Home Cook Book, *written "by an American lady." NY, 1854. The crooked-handle scraper is not described, but it appears to be one of the wrought iron ones — a sort of dough hoe. I've never seen a carved wooden dough scraper, but it could also be that.* **$125-$250**

Fibre Ware History — After years of thinking Cordley & Hayes were manufacturers, I read in *The Metal Worker* that they were agents for The United Indurated Fibre Co., Lockport, NY. "A good substitute for wooden pails is what is called wood-pulp ware. Pails, dishpans, wash-bowls, etc., are made of this. [It is] light; no hoops to rust or loosen, and can be kept dry and clean easily." Maria Parloa, *Kitchen Companion*, Boston: Estes & Lauriat, 1887. Other products were fruit bowls, keelers, slop jars, commode pails, spittoons, cuspidors, mats and trays. Other fibreware companies were The Standard Fiber-Ware Co., Mankato, MN, which made a line of pails and basins, etc., of flax fiber c.1891; and Delaware Hard Fibre Co., Wilmington, DE, c.1905. The wares varied considerably, and included things to be left outside, filled with water! Anything in this somewhat vulnerable pressed wood-pulp composition is rare, because it first lost its protective varnish after long exposure to water and hot sun, and then would crack. An especially odd item is a deep straight-sided basket with high hoop handle, the entire body being perforated. This was made in 1890s for industrial use. They were called "dip baskets" and meant for use by brass foundries, nickel plating works, etc. They replaced stoneware baskets because they were thought to be more durable.

Bucket, emerald green & white enamelware, bail handle with wooden grip, turn of century. **$175-$225**

Bucket, extraordinarily bold, handsome small wooden bucket, painted dark green, with 3 wide lapped fingers in rather high relief, 2 large arched lugs for pegged bentwood bail, said to be Shaker, about 7" H x about 7" diameter, 19th C. The 1988 price ($3050) is what George Morrill paid at a Mike True auction. Collector & auctioneer Morrill said, "When you find impeccable color, you just have to go for it." **$3000-$4500**

"A Rightness in Green" — Cornelius Weygandt wrote in *The Heart of New Hampshire; Things Held Dear by Folks of the Old Stocks* (NY: Putnam's, 1944), a delightful chapter entitled "Why Woodenware is Painted Green: for Leslie Joy." He searches, wonders, and asks all around; he notes that "Most cooperage is left unpainted, fully three-quarters of it. If twenty-five percent is painted, fifteen of that . . . is green, five madder red, and five a blue so light it is almost gray, a blue even lighter than the Amish blue of barns and houses in Pennsylvania Dutchland." He describes many pieces of painted "cooperage" in his collection, some "painted the characteristic dark green." One is a "spice box seven inches long, five inches broad, and three inches high. It is oval in shape and redolent of . . . spices. . . . Its top and bottom are pumpkin pine and the sides of both base and cap look and feel like brown ash. The sides are pegged to top and bottom. Each is one piece of thin brown ash bent around on itself and sewed together with linen thread. . . . Some folks would write it down as Shaker made, but there were good artisans aplenty in the long ago outside the Shaker communities as well as within them. Its sides, rubbed in places, reveal a green much lighter in color than the characteristic dull dark green traditional for such pieces. This lighter green is, perhaps, a priming coat." Finally, Weygandt talks to a "lady of Newbury across the Connecticut in Vermont" who says, "There has never been any question in the matter. Since Vermont has been Vermont it has been proper to keep white sugar in green buckets, brown sugar in red buckets and soft maple sugar in unpainted buckets." Weygandt concludes by suggesting ". . . there seems, somehow, a rightness in green for cooperage."

Bucket, for sugar storage, not to hang on a maple tree, slanted sides with fitted & turned staves, 3 decoratively painted bands, lid has rounded edge, turned bands on flat top, possibly original white porcelain mushroom knob with screw, painted with orangey salmon background, white, red, yellow, green & black leaf & vine decoration, what is now called "Lehnware," made by Joseph Lehn, Lititz, Manheim Township, Lancaster County, PA, 8-1/2" H x 7-1/2" diameter at top, mid 19th C. **$900- $1200**

Joseph Lehn's Turned Wooden Wares — Lita Solis-Cohen, in her *Maine Antique Digest* report on the Musselman auction of 1985, wrote that Lehn was a "farmer-woodworker from Hammer Creek Valley, Elizabethtown Township, Lancaster County, . . . active from 1850 to 1890." I can't find any Gazetteer that locates an Elizabethtown Township in Pennsylvania. Carl W. Drepperd, in an article in May 1954 *Spinning Wheel* speaks of Lititz (or Litiz), as an "old Moravian Community," and, furthermore, places Joseph Lehn at a hamlet called Clay, "some four miles north of Litiz," where he made a "fairly scrumptious living as a wood turner, selling plain turned things. Then he had the idea of painting the woodenware somewhat after the manner of tinware painters of an earlier day." He also used Staffordshire wares and "Gaudy" wares for motifs. Drepperd tells us that Lehn's special favorite was his own design of pussy willows. Mildred T. Bohne, in *Ohio Antique Review* (now *Antique Review*), June 1984, wrote that Lehn settled in Clay, "close to Ephrata," and that he started making barrels about 1856 to supplement his farm income, and also small turned woodenwares. She goes on to say that "his small shop was at the back of the house he built at Hammer Creek, a little south of Clay." [Notice how we keep inching south?] Bohne describes many of the forms, from buckets to small covered spice & saffron containers and trinket containers in the shape of footed goblets, and also explains that Lehn "had trouble keeping up with his decorating" and resorted to a combination of paint and decalcomania, and that he also "contracted out some decorating to William Helich, an Ephrata chairmaker, and to John Sechrist."

Bucket, for sugar, wood staves with bentwood hoops & pegged handle, double band at bottom, closefitted bentwood frame lid, marked on lid "Our Centennial Best, 1776-1886," 12" H x 12-3/8" diameter at base, 1876. **$145- $175**

Bucket, or sugar firkin, original bluish green paint, staved, bail handle of split ash, bent to hoop, wooden cover, branded on bottom "D. C. & G. Bissell," American, 11-3/8" diameter, 19th C. **$175- $225**

VII-26. "Dutch bucket." *Pieced tin, footed, japanned on outside, 4 sizes from 8 to 14 quart capacity. Matthai-Ingram Co., Baltimore, c.1890. SEE also the pails in VII-98.* **$25-$50**

Butter box, pine bentwood, bentwood strap handle, iron hardware locks when box is lifted! American, 12" D, 19th C. **$125- $150**

Butter carrier, round bentwood with original blue paint, wire bail handle, wooden grip, American, 9-3/4" D, turn of century. When it comes to value, blue's the hue that is true! **$150- $175**

Butter carrier, with cover, red painted wood, with wire bail handle, 12" D, 19th C. **$125- $155**

Butter crock, also called a butter pot, saltglazed stoneware with indigo blue on bluish gray, depicts Utica's characteristic bird on branch, marked "White's Utica," Utica, NY, 3 lb. size, 3rd quarter 19th C. **$250- $375**

Butter crock, apricot saltglazed stoneware, with original lid & wire bail handle, 9" D, late 19th C. **$200- $300**

VII-27. Butter boxes. *"Bradley's" patented boxes, made of spruce or oak veneer "sewed together," tin bands at top and bottom. Used after scalding, by packing tightly with butter, overlaid with a disc of wax paper. American Agriculturist, 1/1880.* **$45-$125**

VII-28. Butter jar or crock. *Stoneware, with applied ear handles, slightly domed lid with self knob. Made in 11 sizes: 1/4, 1/2, 1, 2, 3, 4, 5, 6, 8, 10, and 12 gallons. The ones made in bigger sizes, from 15 to 50 gallons, were for meat. and did not have lids. Duparquet, Huot & Moneuse, hotel supplier, c.1904-1910 catalog.* **$40-$150**

VII-29. Butter chip holder. *You're right, it looks just like a poker chip holder. We don't know which came first. Wood (looks to be some kind of plywood), holding 6 stacks of butter chips or patties on what appear to be little pans or saucers. From V. Clad & Sons, Inc., c.1890-1900 pamphlet.* **$25-$45**

Stoneware Investment — The most valuable American or Canadian saltglaze stoneware dates to the late eighteenth or early nineteenth century, and has incised decorations filled in with cobalt blue or brushed with blue before the stage in firing when salt is thrown into top of the kiln. These pieces are very rare. Not so rare are stoneware forms with elaborate "quill traced" cobalt decoration (liquid slip applied through the narrow opening of a quill fitted as a sort of funnel into the mouth of a "slip cup," a small, squushed-sided bottle filled with liquid slip, powdered cobalt mixed with a flux and a binder and some water, and used sort of like modern day tubes of fabric decorating fluids, by drawing with tip of quill, leaving a trail of blue slip. The commonest cobalt decorated wares have brushed decorations, distinguishable because the lines tend to be broader, softer and reveal strokes of the stiff brushes used. Birds, animals, flowers, anthropomorphized suns, moons & stars, and often humorous portraits of people are all found in all three types of decoration, though mainly the second and third types. While collectors like crocks and jugs that have the maker's stamp impressed in clay before firing, or marked in blue under the glaze, wonderful stoneware forms can be found that are unmarked. It is advisable to study books that offer advice, and to pick up and look at and think about stoneware that is available for sale at antique shows, auctions and flea markets, and always to ask questions. The best book to my mind is Donald Blake Webster's Decorated Stoneware Pottery of North America , Rutland, VT: Charles E. Tuttle, 1971. It will be hard to find and worth whatever you have to pay if you intend to seriously collect stoneware.

Butter crock, blue & cream saltglazed stoneware, original lid, wire bail handle, 10-1/2" D, late 19th C. **$125-$175**

Butter crock, brown "Rockingham" glazed pottery, with original lid, 8-1/2" D x 6-1/2" H, 3rd to 4th quarter 19th C. **$100-$150**

Cake box, also called a cake tin, chromolithographed tin, round with close-fitting lid, three extremely collectible images: Santa Claus holding a bird toy, with a teddy bear & a Golliwog in his toy pack, border of holly leaves, one of the best ever, "Rich Iced Christmas Cake," Debus Bakeries, 3-3/4" diameter, c.1910s to 1920s. **$130-$165**

Cake box, for Christmas fruitcake, lithographed tin, depicts an Art Deco Santa Claus, American, 1930s. Added value — The most collectible boxes have Santa images, especially if the art is in a very pronounced style, such as Art Deco, where image of Santa has been manipulated to fit art style. **$55-$75**

Cake box, round with hinged, slightly domed lid with hasp closing, very deep & looks like a hat box, japanned & stenciled with scrolls & word "CAKE," from F. A. Walker catalog, American or imported, deep relative to diameter, c.1870s. **$50-$65**

Cake box, stenciled tin, red background, black & gold design, slant-front drop lid with porcelain knob, marked "CAKE BOX," with Schepp's Cocoanut advertising inside lid: "The object of this can is to serve as a Cake Box — the convenience of which will be readily seen at a glance. The cover opening in front and letting down, does not necessitate the trouble of pulling the box out from under the shelf and almost any Lady would cheerfully pay twice the price of one in preference to the unhandy old style box. "PRICE 60 CENTS." Early 20th C. A two-shelf Schepp's box, with blue finish, was also made and is worth just about the same. Price now depends heavily on condition, as it does for most if not all chromolithographed tin containers. **$75-$100**

Cake box or safe, japanned & stenciled tin with cast iron carrying handle on top, 2 shelves, swing-out door that could be ordered with a lock, from F. A. Walker catalog, poss. imported from Europe, or American, about 24" H (?), c.1870s. **$80-$115**

VII-30. Butter dishes. *Both in "Perfection" granite ironware with choice of white metal or nickel plated mountings & protection bands. Both have two small hooks on lip to hold butter knife. Manning, Bowman & Co., c.1892 catalog.* **$100-$150**

VII-31. Cake box. *"The japanned tin boxes keep cake, bread, &c., perfectly fresh without the undesirable moisture of the stone jar." American Home Cook Book, 1854. Thirty years later, similar ones were being offered by the kitchen supplier F. A. Walker, Boston.* **$50-$75**

VII-32. "Pastry closet" or cake safe. *Sometimes called an "upright cake box." Round corner, black or white japanned stamped tin, 6 compartments. 15-1/2" H x 11-1/4" x 10-1/8". Central Stamping Co., 1920 catalog.* **$30-$50**

VII-33. Cake & pie box. *"a new idea in making a receptacle for pie and cake. In this box may be placed pie and cake in separate compartments perfectly safe from insects of all kinds, and yet thoroughly ventilated and aerated by its patented construction." One size only: 8" H x 12-1/2" square. Three finishes: brown japanning with gold stenciling; oak grained with gold; white enamel with gold. Silver & Co., Brooklyn, NY, c.1910 catalog.* **$60-$75**

Candle box, brown japanned tin, cylindrical shape with shield-shaped back with hanging holes, not uncommon, prob. American, 19th C. These were still being sold at least as late as 1900. **$150-$250**

Candle box, heavy tinned sheet iron, in cylindrical shape with hinged lid, not of common storebought style (such as one with shield-shaped back), American, 18" L, early to mid-19th C. **$300-$350**

Reproduction alert — A "handcrafted reproduction of box used in 1800's," made in copper (natural or burnished), plain tin, "pewter finished tin," or "raw tin for toleware painting" were all available from Craft House in Tiverton, RI. This candle box was a long cylinder with hinged, pierced lid with single hasp, 2 tabs with holes for hanging on wall, and was 13-1/2" L x 4-1/2" diameter. They were offered for $16 and $9.25 in Dec. 1973, and $20.75 and $12 in Oct. 1975 editions of *Early American Life.*

Candle box, wood in old red paint, base molding, open with no lid, skinny high backplate with large round top and hanging hole, looks like a doughnut on a stick or a lollipop, American, 11" H x 12" L x 7" W, early 19th C. **$375-$450**

Candle box, wood with grain painting, slanted sides, old cut nail, cutout half moon in arched (sometimes called a "tombstone") back board, American (?), 6" H x 11" L, 19th C. **$250-$275**

Candlestick, cast iron, 2 parts: square base about 1" H, fluted column for candle, no mark, American, 5-3/4" H, c.1840-1860s. **$70-$95**

Candlestick, hogscraper type, tinned sheet iron, hanging hook, marked "Merriam, Harris, Wheeler, and Merriam," American, 5-3/15" H, marked "Patented 1853" on thumbpiece, pat'd ap. 2, 1853. **$120-$200**

Candlestick, sheet iron with touch of brass, a push-up type referred to as a hogscraper stick as well as a wedding band stick (now being widely reproduced); the former for resemblance to a butchering tool, the latter for narrow brass band about 5/8 the way up from bottom. (Much rarer are hogscrapers with double bands.) This stick has most commonly found mark, "SHAW," on push-up thumbpiece, Birmingham, England, 6-1/2" H, mid 19th C. A rarer version has an iron ring instead of the brass. **$150-$275**

Candlesticks, pair of "hogscraper type," tinned sheet iron, broad inverted saucer-like base, push-up in shaft, marked "S. T. Barnes," Columbus, OH, only 5-1/2" H, pat'd July 19, 1853. **$175-$250**

Candlestick of type called "chamberstick," white enameled stamped steel, blue edge, small ring handle on saucer base, short candleholder with wide flared flat rim, marked underneath with a medallion with balance scales, "KJAB," the "Scale Brand" mfd. by the Kockum Enamel Works, imported by Markt & Co. of NYC, made in Sweden, 6-1/4" diameter, turn of century. **$55-$70**

VII-34. Candlesticks. *Japanned stamped tin, all with black finish. At (L) is a "save-all" with the bottom of the candle accessible to the saver of scrap candles. (T-R) is 6-1/2" diameter with deep saucer base for runny candles. (B-R) came in two sizes — 4-7/8" and 5-1/2" diameter. Central Stamping Co., 1920 catalog.* **$25-$50**

Enameling Process — "When the vessels in the stamping works are of the right shape they are sent to the magnificent enameling department. It is here that the ware receives its ornamental, porcelainous [sic] appearance. The various utensils are first placed on large carriages and run into the enormous ovens, in which process a quantity of oil and other matter is thrown off. They emerge from this heat black and ugly, and are then dipped into tubs of stain and are afterward boiled and washed quite clean. They are now ready to receive their first coating of enamel, and afterward to be enameled white or blue. In order to receive the first coating the vessels are dipped in a thick, creamy enamel paste, but this first coating however, must be burned in, and for this purpose, after being thoroughly dried, they are placed on iron cars and run into red-hot ovens, in which they remain from eight to ten minutes. The wares are once more placed in the enamel to obtain the outer coating; the edges of white wares are coated blue, the handles of water cans, etc., are coated and all the other articles are given their proper appearance. By a most ingenious method the so-called granite effect is obtained in the coating. This is brought about by the vessel being dipped in enamel, the specific gravity of which is different, so that when the vessel is lifted out the enamel runs off, gets hard and certain attractive markings appear. Once the vessels have been fully enameled they are once more burned, this time becoming quite hard and glossy. They are then assorted and sent to the warehouse. The daily output from the Kockum factory [established in 1859, and also maker of "Flag Brand" wares] is as high as 20,000 vessels." *House Furnishing Review*, Feb. 1907.

Candy box, heart-shaped cardboard, lid covered with padded red satin, diecut white paper cupid glued on top, red satin ribbon edges, no name, 5" across, 1910s or 1920s (?), maybe later. **$15-$20**

Candy box, heart-shaped cardboard, top is chromolith of exuberant roses in turquoise vase, gilt paper on edges, box maker unknown, held Schrafft's candy, 2 lb box, 13" across x 1" deep, 1940s. **$15-$25**

VII-36. Candlesticks. *I found a 1925 Pearson-Page Co., Ltd., catalog of "cast and sheet brass reproductions," art and novelty items. Pearson-Page was in Birmingham, England, the catalog bore the NYC importer's name. Many of the pieces are now labeled "antiques," but I know different. Clockwise from top (L): (1) Pan type of sheet brass, riveted handle, 5-5/8" diameter. (2) 7-1/2" diameter pan. Note thumb rest on curled handle. (3) 7" diameter pan decorated with chased designs around floor of pan and on handle. Shallow sides have perforated design. (B-R) (4) 8-1/2" diameter pan with square strap handle, probably a new art style, not a reproduction. (B-L) (5) Version of chamberstick, 6-1/2" H x 7" diameter pan. Could be had plain or with chased decoration.* **$30-$70**

VII-37. Candy box. *Papier mâché turkey, "colored to represent a roasted turkey." Bottom opening. 4" L . From Slack Mfg. Co. novelty catalog, c.1925. Originally cost $9.50 for a gross.* **$55-$75**

VII-35. Candle holder. *Forged iron "pigtail" holder, on tripod base. 10" H . Maker's mark on rim of underside of base, "Samuel Yellin." Philadelphia, early 20th C. [Yes, the 1900s, not a misprint.] Photo courtesy Litchfield Auction Gallery, Litchfield CT. Ex-Harold Corbin Collection, auctioned 1/1/1990. Price realized: $2100.* **$1200-$2000**

VII-38. Candy boxes, *for Christmas. Lithographed cardboard, frosted with mica sprinkles for snow. Candy fits into opening in bottom of each. Originally cost $5 a gross. From Slack Mfg. Co. novelty catalog, c.1925.* **$75-$150**

Candy boxes, cardboard. A selection of rectangular ones from just one manufacturer's catalog: 1 lb, 2 lb, 3 lb & 5 lb decorated boxes, some with overhung lid & bottom. (1) Allover spiderweb stained glass look & trompe l'oeuil ribbon; (2) moiré sunray stripes behind buxom lass; (3) 2-tone background with chromolith woman in picture hat; (4) Art Nouveau scrolly "frame" with snowy sleigh scene; (5) twinkly Christmas candles in holly wreath; (6) Art Deco teal & orange design with framed pretty lady portrait; (7) overall subdued "raindrops in pond" pattern & trompe l'oeuil ribbon; (8) silhouetted Indian horseman against sky; (9) bubbles background with Beardsleyesque girl; (10) befringed "girlie" holding breast (gadz, who would you give this to?); & more. "Masterbuilt," F. J. Schleicher Paper Box Co., St. Louis, MO, company est. c.1900, these boxes c.1930s. Most spectacular are square ones in brilliant colors like Lautrec posters, mostly of women. Original prices for all types, wholesale, ranged from about 4¢ each for simplest litho ones, through 18¢ each for pretty ones, to 90¢ each for a 2-layer Christmas candle rect. one 5 lbs. Most expensive were red satin-covered heart-shaped boxes, some of which, the 2-layer 5 lb kind, with hand painting or embossing, cost as much as $2 each wholesale. All prices applied for purchase of lots of 100 boxes. The candy probably cost less than the boxes. Condition is of major importance in pricing old candy boxes. **$5-$30**

Candy boxes, cardboard, some covered in printed or colored paper (desirable motifs include "pretty ladies" & certain animals like cats, pigs, bunnies), some have satin or other cloth or paper ribbons, some are shaped (hearts probably best), some with paper-hinged lids, some retaining paper lace flaps inside, various candy makers, but not all have a name & were possibly identified with paste-on paper label, American, German, English, French, Swiss. Sizes from miniatures (like little Whitman Sampler™ boxes) to large 10 lb. chocolate boxes, late 19th C to 1950s. Price range for boxes only. **$5-$50**

Futurewatch — This may become an attractive collecting field. Old candy boxes have been used as perfect containers for trinkets, buttons, pencils, greeting cards, etc., and have often been just too good to throw away. Candy box manufacturers' catalogs and old candy advertisements would round out a collection.

Candy bucket, miniature turned wooden bucket with flat lid, bound with wire, with wire bail handle, originally filled with maple sugar hearts, "Sap Bucket," Maple Grove Candies, Inc., St. Johnsbury, VT, 21 oz. capacity, c.1930. **$10-$20**

VII-39. Candy boxes, *for Hallowe'en. All in orange & black, cardboard & tissue. The ones in the top row are small size; the lower row has big ones. From Slack Mfg. Co. novelty catalog, c.1925.* **$30-$150**

Candy container, cobalt blue glass, form of a dog, poss. c.1940s-1950s, as most early ones were clear colorless glass. **$35-$50**

Candy container, glass kettle with 3 little feet, paper cover, "Boston Beans Candy," mfd. by T. H. Stough Co., Jeannette, PA, 1st quarter 20th C. **$150-$175**

Candy container, molded clear glass rabbit, marked "J. H. Millstein Co.," Jeannette, PA, 6-1/2" H, "pat. appl. for" (prob. 1st quarter 20th C.). **$40-$60**

Embossed marks — According to William C. Ketcham, in "The Collectible Glass Candy Container," *Americana*, July 1976, ". . . since 1912 the manufacturers of the containers have been required by law to emboss their names — Victory Glass, Eagle Glass, & J. B. Higbee Glass are a few of most common ones — on their bottles." I suppose this had to do with some Food & Drug law.

Candy container, molded clear glass Scottie dog, tin cap, J. C. Crosetti Co., Jeannette, PA, 2-1/2" H, 1962. **$15-$20**

Candy container, molded glass rolling pin, metal cap, turned wood handles, "V G Co." (Victory Glass Co.), Jeannette, PA, 7" L, holds 3 oz., early 20th C. **$150-$200**

Candy container, molded glass vacuum cleaner, wire handle & tin wheels, "Dolly Sweeper No. 2862," West Brothers, Grapeville, PA, 3" x 2-1/4", early 20th C. **$300-$400**

VII-40. Candy boxes. *For fancy chocolates or candy assortments. All were oversized for actual contents held — meant to fool recipient. Chromolith paper covers in "beautiful assortment of art pictures," with real ribbon. One at left, 15-1/2" x 9", has classy deep flange. Catalog says "This is positively the biggest flash on the market." Two at right came in 3 sizes: 1/2 lb. box, 10-1/2" x 4-1/2"; 1 lb. box, 10" x 6"; and 18 oz. box, 12-1/2" x 5-1/4" which "looks like a 2 lb. box." From Slack Mfg. Co. novelty catalog, c.1925.* **$7-$20**

VII-41. Canister set. *Yellowware "Dandy-Line," mfd. by Brush-McCoy Pottery Co., Zanesville, OH. Included spice containers (on top row), those for sugar, salt, butter & flour, tea & coffee, and also bread & cereal & cake jars, rolling pin, mixing bowls, milk pitchers, and nappies (the smallest bowl on table). Various kinds of knobs and handles, not really matching. Ad in* House Furnishing Review, *8/1915.*

Candy container, papier mâché in shape of roast turkey, opening in bottom with cloth tape hinged cover, 4-3/8" L, late 19th or early 20th C.   **$80-$95**

Candy container, extremely realistic miniature smoked ham, polychromed papier mâché, smoothed out with plaster, with hanging hole in "bone" & a twist of cord knotted through it, German (?), 4" L x 2" W, late 19th C.   **$65-$85**

Candy container, full-size hen, tail up & head down in pecking position, head comes off at neck, painted paper and glue composition, extremely well-detailed, German (?), 12-1/2" L, turn of century.   **$300-$350**

Candy container, papier mâché turkey, molded & painted, Pulp Reproduction Co., Milwaukee, WI, 5-1/4" H, 1st third 20th C. Sometimes found in folk art dealer booths.   **$55-$75**

Candy container, red, white & blue paper, in shape of George Washington's hatchet, marked "I Cannot Tell a Lie," poss. imported, prob. American, early 20th C.   **$12-$15**

Canister, embossed stamped tin with stylized overall chrysanthemums in *Japonisme* style, truncated conical top with close-fitting lid, japanned in bronze color, American, 6-1/4" H, 19th C.   **$18-$25**

Canister, japanned tin, hinged dome top, stenciled "TEA" or "COFFEE," 6" H, American 19th C.   **$30-$40**

Japonisme — This French word describes a style of decorative arts (or decoration on useful objects) that show direct influence from various arts of Japan, (as well as China and the rest of the exotic Orient). "Japanese" motifs such as chrysanthemums, butterflies, fans, parasols and bamboo are found on Japanese screens, kimono cloth, inlaid metalwork and other domestic goods; the same motifs can be found in westernized versions that Japanese artisans devised for export to Europe and U.S. since the mid-nineteenth century. These imports were further westernized & interpreted (diluted or exaggerated) by Western artisans, who used them as models for making goods for their consumers. *Japonisme* as a movement is usually dated from the 1870s to 1890s, although some people push up the tail end of it as far as WWI; a design movement with some similararities is "The Eastlake Style," named for aesthetician Charles Eastlake, whose influential theories about good design and applied decoration were widely subscribed to. Both correspond somewhat in period and inspiration to the flowering of Art Nouveau. **Activating the "Japanese Movement"** — Nineteenth-century American interest in Japanese-like decorative motifs actually began with Commodore Perry's 1850s voyages to Japan, which were meant to open trade with Japan. This interest became a very popular fashion in the 1870s, long before Gilbert & Sullivan wrote *The Mikado* (which was first seen, in London, in 1885); the musical only fanned the flames. The Centennial Exhibition in 1876 also added to interest in Japanese style. **Enamelware decoration** — By 1890, such a huge manufacturer as Manning-Bowman satisfied popular demand for the look with a large selection of enamelware designs influenced by Japanese motifs; at about the same time, David Block, a New York manufacturer of stamped tin housewares, sold "Chinese Pattern Embossed Goods," which were Western forms, the surfaces of which were covered with a dense Westernized hodgepodge of Oriental motifs. Many late Victorian artisans in all fields adopted the coloration of *Japonisme*, especially vivid colors against dark backgrounds. Examples are seen in black velvet crazy quilts and chromolithographic commercial arts such as trade cards or greeting cards. By WWI, the "Movement" was over, having been supplanted by the Arts & Crafts Movement, Art Nouveau, and early stirrings of Art Deco.

Japanning Is Something Different — Japanning is much older than *Japonisme*, and it is another thing entirely, though much of it is characterized by vivid coloring against a dark background, adapted from Oriental lacquerware color schemes. By the early 1600s imported Chinese Coromandel screens and lacquered furniture were known in the West, including Britain, where some of the finest early japanning was done. Many of these Oriental wares had dark (black or brown) or "Chinese" red backgrounds, with decorative motifs in color & gold or bronze, plus inlays of colored stone or mother of pearl. Imitation "Japan" finishes were applied to papier mâché & wooden furniture & trays, as well as sheet metal coal vases, trays, coffee urns, etc. In the eighteenth century fashionable ladies in England and America (and probably in Europe) took up japanning — that is, "the Art of covering bodies by grounds of opake colours in varnish, which may be either afterwards decorated by painting or gilding, or left plain. . . . ," according to Robert Dossie, in *Handmaid to the Arts*, published in 1758. Ground [background] colors were browns, reds, maroons & blues. In the 1854 *Dictionary of Arts, Sciences and Manufacturers*, by James Smith, **"japanning"** is defined as "the art of varnishing in colours, and is frequently combined with painting . . . [on] wood, metal, paper, and leather." But in practice, by mid-nineteenth century, "japanning" mostly meant semi-translucent, heat-resistant lacquers on <u>tin</u>, like most pieces in this book. Oxidized tinted linseed oil or baked-on **asphaltum** (a sort of petroleum) were used. Dark maroon-y brown is the commonest color. Other colors included red, crimson, pink, yellow, green, blue, white, black and a browny-black "tortoise shell." See Chapter XIV.

Chinoiserie or **de Chine** — These are French terms used in the decorative arts to describe Western decorative motifs considered or *supposed* to be typical of, or related to, Chinese arts. Western artisans got inspiration from Chinese porcelains, some of which were made by Chinese potters in designs and with decorations *ordered* by Western importers (especially those in Holland) and even based on European designs: a real cultural exchange twice over. For the most part, *Chinoiserie* motifs are only "supposed" — that is, they are often not authentic, but are based on exotic decorations taken more from European engravings in travel books about China than from real Chinese arts. The term is related to *Japonisme*. In applied decorations, there are many Chinese and Japanese motifs common in name if not in appearance, including depictions of nature (flowers, bamboo, birds, water) and of manmade objects (fans, kimonos, stools, vases). One marked difference is that Chinese arts have more motifs that appear geometric or abstract, and Japanese arts may have more even allover patterns. Cross-pollination, i.e. the influence upon Oriental art by Western arts and vice versa, as well as the cross-cultural influences between China and Japan and the rest of the "Orient" (including India) is common to both decorative movements *Japonisme* and *Chinoiserie*.

Bug Out — "Tin cans of meal and sugar, stone jars of salt. . ..Tin boxes are best receptacles for food that would attract mice and weevils. They are, to be sure, more expensive than wooden buckets, but they are lasting and perfectly secure. Should have labels, and if they are made to order, have labels painted on them at the same time. Such boxes as cracker manufacturers use will answer this purpose and may be obtained through the grocer." Maria Parloa, *Kitchen Companion*, 1887.

Canister or pantry set, 10 emerald green glass jars, slanted ribs, rectangular, metal screw-on lids, name labels for Cereal, Flour, Sugar, etc., mfd. by Owens Illinois Glass Co., Toledo, OH, c.1920s or very early 1930s. A Greenie's Dream Set ! **$200-$250**

Canister for cookies, looks like small corrugated garbage can but was described as an "artistic shape," it's impressed "COOKIES" on side, came in 4 colored glazes, green, canary, ivory or blue, "Kolorkraft No. 344," mfd. by Brush Pottery Co., Zanesville, OH, about 8" H, introduced Dec. 1928. **Color Fashions** — The jar was an editorial feature in *House Furnishing Review* in February 1930. At the time it was said "Colors harmonize with kitchen and pantry. Colors available and their relative popularity is as follows: Green, 65%; canary, 20%; ivory, 10%; blue, 5%." (This was to guide the retailer in his ordering). Furthermore, "Best quantity buying months are those preceding the spring, Thanksgiving and Christmas seasons." **$40-$55**

Canister set, also called a <u>cereal set</u>, decorated earthenware, sort of ovoid rectangles, domed lids with huge hand grips, glazed with light cream background with a sort of happy-go-lucky plaid effect in blue and black in horizontal band near tops, entire set has

15 pieces, often you find just the big 6, marked on the fronts: "Tea, Coffee, Sugar, Rice, Barley, Farina," or maybe 7, with the "Salt" box with hinged wooden lid. Jug-like cruets are marked "Vinegar" and "Oil." Six half-size smalls are for spices: "Ginger, Cloves, Nutmeg, Cinnamon, Allspice, Pepper." imported from Czechoslovakia, early 1920s. **$125-$200**

Canister set, glazed china, red & white checkerboard design below, with much smaller diagonal checkerboard border, oblong, with china lids, marked on front in French for contents, the largest canister being for SUCRE. Very attractive, even when worn. French, the smallest about 4-1/2" H, the largest about 8" H, c.1920s (?). **$100-$150**

Canning jars — See Chapter XVI

Carrier, divided pan, perhaps a utensil or cutlery carrier for clearing the table, made of indurated fiber ware, cutout centerboard for hand grip, marbleized green-blue and cream paint on outside, cream inside, American (?), 4" H x 8-13/16" diameter, c.1870s. **$85-$125**

VII-42. Canister set. *Decorated china with patented rack with built-in metal lids. Made in Germany and imported by housewares wholesaler G. M. Thurnauer, NYC. House Furnishing Review, 8/1910.* **$100-$200**

VII-43. Table caster patent, *for small bottles — oil, vinegar, perhaps a bottled catsup or sauce too. Pat'd 11/10/1874, by Daniel Sherwood, Lowell, MA, assignor to Woods, Sherwood & Co., who were huge manufacturers of wire goods. This was the patent drawing, but it looks like the catalog linecuts too. The real thing:* **$65-$100**

VII-44. Cheese cradle. *Tôle — or japanned tin, with birds & flowers in ochre, white and gray on dark ground. A lovely form that almost looks like a doll-size Roman lounging chaise. 14" x 6". The form looks Welsh; the decoration too. Courtesy The Abrahams, Langhorne, PA.* **$450-$500**

VII-48. Public drinking cup, *as depicted for c.1908-1910 campaign to improve sanitation in public places. The cups this caricatured were simple enamelware or tin cups, or dippers such as we've seen in movies being used. Frightening health campaigns helped companies like Dixie Cup, who made one-use throwaway cups, as well as the collapsion cup companies, who made cups for each person to carry around with them. This from an "Educational Sheet" distributed by the Minnesota State Board of Health, published by Pioneer Press, St. Paul, MN.*

VII-49. (Was VII-52 and 53 in 3rd ed.) Collapsing or portable drinking cups. *From (L) to (R):* **(1)** & **(2)** *"Vest pocket drinking cup, shown closed with embossed lid, and fully extended. Stamped metal, nickel-plated. "Indispensable for fishing and picnic parties, tourists, etc." Rayment catalog, c.1910-20s.* **(3)** *"Collapsion cup," "pure white metal, finished in the finest style; warranted non-corrosive; holds half-pint; incased in screw top nickel case." Robert H. Ingersoll & Bro., NYC. c.1900 ad.* **(4)** *Embossed aluminum, polished finish, 2-1/2" diameter at top. "Mirro" made by Aluminum Goods Mfg. Co., c.1910s.* **$10-$15**

Carrier box, unusual, round bentwood sided box, with thickish wood bottom and 4 sections formed by 2 cross-piece dividers, one of which serves as centerboard with handhold cutout, held together with small nails or brads, prob. European, poss. English, almost certainly not American, about 4" deep x 11" diameter, prob. mid 19th C. **$85-$135**

Cheese baskets — See Chapter IV

Cheese box, bent basswood, painted in shades of yellow, American, 9" H x 15-3/4" D, 19th C., perhaps early 20th. **$125-$155**

Coffee can, tin pail with fitted lid, lithographed elephant, wire bail handle, "Elephant Coffee," Jewitt & Sherman Co., 4 lb. can, turn of century. **$95-$125**

Coffee can, wonderful barrel-shaped lithographed tin can, fitted lid, "Cafe Gruzerio Extra," Rio De Janeiro, Brazil, 5 lb. can, late 19th or early 20th C. **$60-$90**

Collapsible cup, also called a <u>collapsion cup</u>, divided into telescoping sections of nickel-plated brass, engraved with scrolls, 5 telescoping bands, marked on top in fancy script "Vest Pocket Cup," Scovill Mfg. Co., Waterbury, CT, pat'd Feb. 23, 1897. **$15-$20**

Collapsible cup, metal, Rumpp & Son, (a leather goods firm; this probably had a leather case), Philadelphia, PA, late 19th C. **$15-$20**

Collapsible cup, metal with depiction of couple on tandem bike, these are also called <u>cyclist cups</u>, American, late 19th or early 20th C. **$35-$50**

VII-45. Cracker or pretzel jar. *Sponged decoration in blue on white ironstone. Nickeled copper bottom & top rims, and nickeled brass hinged lids. 7-1/2" H x 12-1/4" diameter. Late 19th C. Courtesy The Abrahams, Langhorne, PA.* **$200-$250+**

VII-46. Creamery vessels. (L) *Milk jug or ewer for 3 quarts of milk, earthenware, unglazed outside. German type; made also in 19th C. U.S.A. Lid fit into top like butter crock top.* **(M)** *Large milk vessel. "Filled with milk and set into water in pans or tubs — or other crocks. ... Water is renewed as often as ... convenient. The outside is so porous that the water, if it once wets the surface, is continually drawn up by capillary attraction. It evaporates all the time, thus notably cooling the milk."* **(R)** *Process called "Slipping the cream," whereby "after the milk is two days old, in ordinary weather, the cream may be loosened from the sides of the pan," and slips from the pans into a cooler that has a spigot at the bottom. American Agriculturist, 5/1880.*

Collapsible cup, nickel-plated Britannia, 3 narrow & one wide telescoping band, footed base like a wine goblet, engraved, Meriden Britannia Co., Meriden, CT, 1886-87. **$20-$30**

Collapsible cup, nickeled brass, pat'd by John Lines, mfd. by Scovill Mfg. Co., Waterbury, CT, pat'd Feb. 23, 1897. **$15-$20**

Collapsible cup, nickeled brass, very small — good for one shot, embossed flowers & scrolls on cover, American, only 1" H, perhaps a traveling medicine cup? pat'd Dec. 23, 1896. **$20-$25**

Collapsible cup, tin, 3 telescoping bands, engraved lid, name "Clement" engraved on lid, which could be owner, late 19th C. There was a Clement Mfg. Co. that made cutlery, etc., in Northampton, MA. **$15-$22**

Comb pocket or rack, also called a **tidy rack** or simply a **tidy**, wall hung, heavy embossed brass, with flowers, scrolls & sentiment "Remember Me," arched top with 2 holes for hanging, American, 13" L, 19th C. Nice to think of this as a love gift, given by a person courting a cook or a maid! **$125-$150**

Comb rack, tin with embossed design of mermaid, 10" W, 19th C. **$30-$45**

Comb rack, embossed tin, design of Japanese fans & ribbons, 3 pockets & a mirror set on angle in center, hung on wall, American, 6-3/4" x 7", turn of century. **$30-$45**

Comb rack, for comb or oddments, carved & painted wood, with relief motif of horse in pasture, and young girl, on other side of fence, some painting, American, 16" W, turn of century. **$150-$185**

Crock, saltglazed stoneware, 2 applied ear handles, flat rim with slight lip, pale ochre or tan glaze with black and cobalt blue decoration, of bosomy bustle-y young woman, from knees up, walking small black dog, who has just made his contribution to the footpath, with large very pretty script remark, "Oh my?" [question mark rather than exclamation mark], a wonderful example of humor, though of course a strange subject for a food crock, although possibly this was for vegetable

VII-47. Stoneware crock. *Pale gray glazed stoneware, 10" H , wire bail handle with turned wood grip, 10" H , c.1900. This is plain, well-designed, serviceable, but there's no oomph and no decoration to add value.* **$20-$40**

scraps bound for the compost heap, also stamped "J. B. Pfal-tzgraff & Co.," York, PA. 7-1/4" H x 8" diameter, last quarter 19th C, prob. late 1880s. Pfaltzgraff began business c.1840 and is still in business. Robacker May 1989 auction price (it's the humorous figures that brought most of the money — an absolute folk art prize): **$19,000**

Crock, saltglazed stoneware, blue quill-traced, very calligraphic decoration of bird, Millers, Boston, MA, 3 gal. capacity, mid to 3rd quarter 19th C (?). **$600-$750**

"Apples, in small quantities, may be preserved by the following. First, completely dry a glazed jar, then put a few pebbles at the bottom, fill it with Apples, and cover it with a piece of wood exactly fitted, and fill up the interstices with a little fresh mortar. The pebbles attract the moisture of the apples, while the mortar excludes the air from the jar and secures the fruit from pressure." Anthony Florian Madinzer Willich, *The Domestic Encyclopedia; or A Dictionary of Facts & Useful Knowledge*, 1st American edition, Philadelphia: W. Y. Birch & A. Small, 1803-04.

VII-50. Cutlery tray. *Cutout thin wood, fancy centerboard handle, scalloped base, canted sides, typical Deco decoration of greyhounds, but possibly earlier. Four dogs on long sides, 2 on short. 13" L x 7-3/4" W. From booth of The Silver Flag, folk art dealers.* **$275-$350**

VII-51. Cutlery tray. *Cutout bent veneer finished in silky honey-color, turned wood grip and bull's-eye knobby decorations, green baize bottom lining, 2-1/2" H exclusive of handle & centerboard x 11-1/4" L x 7-1/2" W, c.1890. Since the publication of the last edition, the Smithsonian has acquired a wonderful sewing stand made like this. If any of you have seen other pieces which seem to be of the same type, please let us know!* **$150-$225**

Crock, saltglazed stoneware with 2 flowers in blue, marked "J. Fisher & Co." (Jacob Fisher), Lyons, NY, 3 gal. capacity, late 19th C. **$175-$2255**

Crock, stoneware, gray with blue band 5/8 of way down side, with legend, "WESSON OIL — For making good things to eat." 5-1/2" H x 4-1/4" diameter, 20th C. **$95-$115**

Cutlery tray, also called a **knife box** or **cutlery box**, this one a bent-wood oval with copper nails, straight lapped, original (?) light green paint, bent nail or wire hinges for the 2 center-hinged lids, 3-arch centerboard has handhold cutout, possibly Shaker, 2-7/8" H handle, body is 3" H x 12-3/4" L, c.1870s (?). **$200-$250**

Cutlery trays (also called knife boxes, knife & fork trays, cutlery trays, flatware trays, knife carriers, silverware trays or spoon boxes) from the nineteenth and early twentieth century all seem to be divided into only two compartments. Rarely can an old one be found with three sections, though the twentieth-century plastic or wooden cutlery trays we keep in our kitchen drawers always have 4, and sometimes 5 or 6 sections. Certainly knives, forks and spoons were all in wide use during the eighteenth and nineteenth centuries.

Cutlery tray, bentwood with border decoration of cutout holes, bottom edge cut so as to form 4 feet in middle of sides, turned wood "curtain rod" grip handle, lapped ends fastened with nails and turned balls of wood, green baize lining of both compartments, highly decorative, American, 4-1/4" H at center x 11" L x 7-1/4" W, 19th C. The Smithsonian, Museum of American History, Domestic Division, has a sewing stand made the same way, with near-matching features, probably made by the same, unknown, company. **$150-$225**

Cutlery tray, cutout wood, carved twisted rope or cable edging, handle carved to look like a twisted 3-strand rope, simple cutouts resemble hearts & acorns, canted sides, American (?), 11" L, 19th C. **$150-$180**

Cutlery tray, cutout wood, slanted sides, 4 greyhounds on both long sides, 2 on short sides, fancy cutout centerboard handle, American (?), 13" L x 7-3/4" W, late 19th C. **$300-$450**

Cutlery tray, dovetailed pine, faint traces of red paint, high double arch centerboard with heart cutout, American, 11" L, 19th C. **$200-$225**

Cutlery tray, flat base which forms low foot, deeply canted sides set back from edge of base, cutout centerboard, painted blue inside, American, 11" L, late 19th C. **$150-$175**

Cutlery tray, inlaid, stamped & stained design in top ridge of handle, high centerboard carved with 2 stars, cirles & heart, 2 scrolls, dart designs with shields, nice molded foot, American, 10-1/2" L x 8-1/2" W, mid 19th C. **$650-$800**

Cutlery tray, made of woven wire & a sheet metal frame, 2 sections, American, 10-1/4" L x 6-3/4" W x 2" deep, c.1900. **$35-$50**

Cutlery tray, painted pine with imitation graining in shades of ochre & brown, very fanciful with knots & extreme grain pattern, American, 13" L x 6-1/4" W, mid 19th C. The graining qualifies it for some folk art collectors. **$125-$160**

VII-52. Cutlery tray or knife box. *Japanned tin, hinged lids on either side, handle with reinforced grip. "a knife box should be large enough to hold the knives and forks in every day use, and nothing more. ... The handle should be large and sensible, and the partition through the middle of the box always separate the knives from the forks; there should be a lid to each side, to keep out the dust." American Agriculturist, 8/1879.* **$55-$95**

"Folk Art" Caveat: Folk art is a catch-all term meant to describe a certain naiveté in vision or execution, and it's sometimes used to lend distinction (and extra $$) to things better or more accurately described as "handmade" or "crude" or "old magazine craft project style." Folk art is the **exceptional not the ordinary artwork** of "folk"; the emphasis is on art. It is practically impossible to come up with an all-purpose definition. You must develop your own taste and eye for it; conjure up a vision of all the handmade objects you have (or have seen) that were made by people who considered themselves craftsmen or artists but whose work doesn't fall into the mainstream of academic art of the period in which they worked. Then sift out what you believe to be the very best examples — the pieces that are definitely art, which have something about them you may not be able to describe in words. You probably have a few pieces that qualify as folk art. The secret is to refine your own taste even if you can't define it out loud. When someone else, like me, tells you it's folk art, never take our word for granted. Start at the beginning & figure out why.

Cutlery tray, pieced tin, horizontal tubular handle soldered to centerboard, American, 11-3/4" L, c.1850s to 1870s(?). Fairly common. **$125-$150**

Cutlery tray, pine, old red paint, molding nailed to top edge, high arched centerboard, handle cutout, American, 12" L, 19th C. **$125-$140**

Cutlery tray, pine with geometric pattern pressed into sides & ends (looks like pyrography, but probably done like the steamed &

VII-53. Cutlery tray. *Wood, slanted sides, well-shaped centerboard handgrip, painted in bright colors like a game board. 14-3/4" x 7-3/4". In booth of Stephen Score, Essex, MA — a high end dealer who's recognized this as folk art. Wide value range reflects the importance of where a piece is for sale. A very high price could be expected at one of the big Americana antique shows. The lower price might be expected at a small regional show — and believe me, stuff is still coming out.* **$400-$1200**

VII-54. Cutlery trays. (T-L) *stamped sheet metal;* **(M)** *pieced sheet metal japanned & pinstriped, with tubular grip;* **(R)** *wicker work, lined with tin. All from 1895 catalog of Harrod's Stores, Ltd., Brompton, England.* **$30-$50**

pressed wooden kitchen chairs), cutout handle, American, 2-1/2" H at sides x 11-3/4" L x 7-1/4" W, early 20th C. **$25-$40**

Cutlery tray, red stained pine, straight sides, centerboard carved with simple alligator as grip, with head & tail curved slightly up, prob. American, 19th C. **$600-$800**

Dinner pail, stacking sections, pieced tin, lower straight-sided pail with short oil-can like spout holds a deep pan with slightly flared sides, then a pie-pan-like piece, then domed lid. Wire bail with wood grip to lower pail, metal clip strap holds parts together & can be locked with small padlock or kept closed with a peg, W. F. Janeway, Columbus, OH, 1890s. The editor of *The Metal Worker,* May 28, 1892, described the pail thus: "The pail is used for tea or coffee, the lower pan for the main dinner and the shallow pan for pie or cake. It is made of heavy stock, nicely finished. The pail is also furnished without the strap or shallow pan. . . . The pail is designed for miners, railroad men and others who carry a large quantity of tea or coffee. Instead of being obliged to remove the dinner in the mine, and getting dirt into it, the miner can drink his fill by drawing it through the spout, as the spout terminates in a hole at the bottom of the pail. The lock strap prevents the cover being knocked off when hitting the pail in getting off and on cars, and prevents the dinner being stolen, by locking the pail. The large space for carrying the coffee is referred to as a desirable feature, and a great improvement over a flask, or a shallow receptacle attached to the lid of the pail. The point is emphasized that drawing the coffee through the spout is much pleasanter and more desirable than drinking from a pail or cup also that with this spout there is no danger of any of the coffee being wasted. The lock strap and spout add but 15¢ at retail to the price of a pail. These pails are sold so they may be retailed at 45¢ to 75¢, according to the size of pail and number of pans." **$30-$55**

Dinner pail, tin, 4 stacking compartments that set down into each other, high wire rack handle, from F. A. Walker catalog, c.1890s. "The tin pail is a badge of work, generally honest work, always productive work, and work is the root of all that we have. We, the people, the rich, the society people, the literary people, the talkers and writers who make so much fuss in type and pretend to rule — or ruin — the world, all depend on the workers who are represented in force in 'the tin pail brigade.'" *The Metal Worker,* Sept. 2, 1882. **$35-$55**

Dish covers or fly screens; called fly walks by the Shakers. Wire screening, stamped into dome shape, with narrow japanned tin frame & disc for black-painted turned wood knob, made in rounds or ovals, to fit plates, dishes, pans, etc. Japanning was red, green, blue or asphaltum brown, perhaps other colors I've not seen. Matthai-Ingram was one manufacturer, American,

VII-55. Dish covers. *Also called fly screens or fly covers. People who have these always price them very highly, but the price is unwarranted. They were made over a very long period. The top picture, of a cover in oval shape, is made of "closely knitted wire, blue steel coloring." It was "especially adapted to Free Lunch Counters," and came in 10", 12", 14", 16" and 18" lengths. Round ones came in a series from 8" to 14" diameter. From Albert Pick catalog, 1909. At bottom is a stack of "wire dish covers. — To cover meats, pastry, milk, butter, &c., from dust, flies, &c., in the pantry or on the table." The picture is from the* American Home Cook Book, *1854. Prices sometimes unreasonably high.* **$30-$75**

their nested sets all about 5"-7" H; ovals 8" to 18" L ; 6" to 14" D rounds, c.1870s to 1910s. Other manufacturers of the period were: Bromwell; Gibbert & Bennett; Frederick J. Myers; Joseph Scheider; W. H. Sweeney; Wickwire Brothers. All the products probably were very similar. These have gone up incredibly. Range covers most asking prices: **$40-$95**

Dish covers, heavy pieced planished tin, high domed, oblong or oval in shape to fit over serving dishes or platters, with cast iron handles that are sometimes heavily tinned, American, 19th C. **$30-$40**

Dog biscuit canister, round cylinder, snug lid, enameled in bright red, black silhouette of Scotty in begging position, labeled "Biscuits," American, 7-1/4" H x 7" diameter, c.1930. Scotty crossover collectors will bark your shins for this one. **$10-$18**

Dog feeding dish, crockery glazed in green, with depiction of dogs, 20th C. **$12-$15**

Dog feeding dish, heavy glass, with glass lid for putting in fridge, if you know a dog who wouldn't gobble it all up at once! Red logo & adv'g, "Ideal Dog Food," 20th C. **$25-$35**

Ever wonder about **dog food, when it started**? Here's an historical tidbit or kibble: "One of the oldest industries in Chelsea [MA] is the Austin Dog Bread & Animal Food Company . . . a subsidiary of the Loose-Wiles Biscuit Company, 2nd largest in the U.S. . . . In 1864, following a serious fire in Lynn, C. F. Austin & Co. moved to Chelsea, manufacturing ship and pilot bread. In 1885, regular biscuits were manufactured with dog bread as a sideline, but in 1908, when part of the plant was removed to Boston, the Chelsea division became principally noted for its dog bread and animal food. . . . It is said that the first dog bread ever manufactured in the United States was made by this concern, the process of manufacture being similar to that used in the general baking industry. Three large ovens consume approximately 100 barrels of flour a day and more than 500 pounds of cereal. Fresh meat is an important part of the ingredients. The modern equipment, consisting of flour mixers, ovens, meat boilers, conveyors, cylinder, kibbling and automatic weighing machines, etc., produce the bulk and package commodities, which are distributed throughout the U. S. One-third of the product of dog bread flakes, dog bread, puppy bread and cat food is shipped in packages." Orra L. Stone, *History of Massachusetts Industries*, Boston: S. J. Clarke, 1930, Volume II (of II).

Dog feeding dish, yellowware, with nipple-shaped protrusions up from the bottom, made especially for weaning puppies, who would learn to suck 'n' eat at the same time, American, 9" D, 19th C. Only one I ever saw. **$125-$150**

Dog feeding trough, cast iron, rather thin walls, very smooth dark finish, really looks like a miniature hog trough, with 2 divisions

VII-56. Egg baskets, *for gathering.* (L) *Iron wire, in 5 sizes (6", 7", 8", 9" and 10" diameter), is from Duparquet, Huot & Moneuse catalog, c.1904-1910.* (R) *Retinned wire, looks like wastebasket, even in dimensions — 15" H x 12" diameter at top. "Keeping eggs in our wire basket has the advantage of locating broken ones instantly." From Albert Pick catalog, 1909.* **$20-$40; $50-$75+**

— for water & kibbles, no marks, American or English, 15" L, late 19th C. This looks very old and finely made. I thought it was much older, until I found reprint of the Harrod's Stores, Ltd., 1895 catalog, which shows a very similar one. Harrod's offered 4 sizes: 12" L without the division, 15" L, 18" L and 24" L, all with the division. I did see a tag saying "Cat trough" on a small one at a PA group shop. **$35-$55**

Feed pan, heavy galvanized sheet metal, round, fluted flared sides, looks like large fluted cake mold, mfd.. by Milcor Steel Co., Canton, OH, 3-1/2" deep x 17" top diameter, c.1930. **$20-$35**

Firkin, wood, painted mocha, finger-lapped, American, 9-1/2" H, 19th C. **$60-$75**

VII-57. Flour bins. *Japanned tin, with more or less decoration, in gold.* (L) *Black background with gold Japanese-influenced motifs, c.1880s.* (M) *Japanned brown, 50 lb. capacity. Buhl Brothers, c.1919.* (R) *Black with simple border design, in three sizes: 15" H x 10-1/2" diameter; 21-5/8" H x 12-1/2" diameter; 27-1/8" H x 15".* *Central Stamping Co., 1920.* **$50-$150+**

VII-58. Flour canister, *3-part, with sifting tray inside. Tin-lined copper, 7" H x 6-3/4" diameter, wooden knob. 19th C. Collection of Mary Mac Franklin.* **$70-$100**

Firkin, wood with dark green paint, finger-lapped construction, probably for liquids, American, 12" H, 19th C. **$50-$60**

Firkin, wooden staves, painted putty color, 4 wood bands with copper fasteners, wooden bail handle, made by cooper, probably Shaker manufacture, American, 9-1/2" H x 9-1/2" D, 19th C. **$230+**

History in Small Things — "I embrace the common, I explore and sit at the feet of the familiar, the low. Give me insight into today, and you may have the antique and future worlds. What would we really know the meaning of? The meal in the firkin; the milk in the pan; the ballad in the street; the news of the boat; the glance of the eye; the form and the gait of the body." Ralph Waldo Emerson, *"American Scholar,"* 1837.

Fly screens — See dish covers

Fruit jars — See Chapter XVI

Ginger beer bottles, tan saltglazed stoneware, banded in ochre (usually top half is ochre), thick flat mouth, rather roughly finished. Used for holding explosive homemade drinks that built

VII-59. Food holder. *"Crystal," mfd. by Ware-Standard Mfg. Co., NYC. For sugar, coffee, rice, salt, Indian meal, hominy, etc. Clear glass in metal bracket. This one shown with wall bracket; also was made to slide into brackets mounted to underside of shelf, so that they would hang down from the shelf. Made in 3 sizes, for 3-1/2, 7 and 14 lbs of dry food. "Turn the knob and the food runs out." Ad in* House Furnishing Review, *5/1905.* **$35-$50**

VII-60. Lehnware goblets. *Carved & painted wood.* **(L)** *Red & green paint, with snake wrapped around it, 3" H.* **(R)** *Flowers & vines, typical of Joseph Lehn, Lancaster County, PA. 2-1/2" H. Photo courtesy Litchfield Auction Gallery, Litchfield CT. Ex-Harold Corbin Collection, auctioned 1/1/1990 for $550 & $400.* **$600-$750+; $500-$600+**

up pressure and needed to have the corks tied down. The overhanging lip serves to anchor the string or twine. These bottles are a common type often seen at flea markets. American, English, about 7" to 9" H, 19th C. **$10-$50**

"Ginger Beer (superior) — To six quarts of water add one ounce of cream of tartar, and two ounces of white Jamaica ginger; boil it ten minutes. Strain it; add to the liquor a pound of loaf sugar. Put it on the fire; let it simmer until the sugar is dissolved. Pour into an earthen vessel, into which has been put two ounces of tartaric acid and the rind of one lemon. When lukewarm, add half a tumbler of strong hop yeast. Stir all well together, and bottle; tie down the corks tightly. Use in a few days." Mrs. A. P. Hill, *Mrs. Hill's New Family Receipt Book*, NY: 1870.

• • • •

"Imperial Pop — Three ounces of cream of tartar, an ounce of bruised ginger, a pound and a half of loaf sugar, half a tumbler of lemon juice, a gallon and a half of water, a wineglass of yeast. Shake well together; bottle, and cork well." *ibid.*

• • • •

"Ginger Beer — Boil together four gallons of water, one pint of hops, twenty races of ginger, beaten. Boil briskly half an hour; keep the vessel covered; strain; sweeten with good molasses. When tepid, add a pint of brisk yeast. Cover it closely with a thick cloth until morning; then bottle, and cork tight. Scald the corks, and drive them in, and tie down with twine. Keep in a cool place. It will be ready for use the third day. Less yeast may be used if the taste is not liked." *Ibid.*

Implement rack, blue & white enamelware, trough along bottom edge, late 19th C. **$140-$175**

Implement rack, fancy scribed & carved wood, European, 28" L, late 19th C. These are often termed "utensil racks," but actually a utensil is a hollowware cooking pot or such, and these are really implement racks. **$125-$150**

Implement rack, gray graniteware, somewhat shield-shaped, with spoon, dipper & skimmer, 19" H, turn of century. **$155-$200**

Implement rack, tall with drip catcher at bottom, utensils: ladle, tasting ladle, small ladle or gravy spoon and skimmer, teal blue enamelware, all have a gold pin stripe on handle, inside of bowls are white, European, late 19th or early 20th C. **$225-$275**

Implement rack, turquoise enamelware, no mark, prob. European import, early 20th C (?). **$125-$165**

Implement rack, wall hung, with high stepped backplate and shallow oval drip catcher, strap bar near top with skimmer, tasting spoon, ladle and dipper hanging from it, all matching teal blue & white enamelware with fancy gold pinstriping, skimmer holes are concentric & close-set, prob. European import, late 19th C. Gold trim was used in Europe, but as far as I know not on American enamelwares. **$225-$275**

VII-61. Herb tray. *Japanned tin, iron central handle, compartments. Picture from ad of William S. Adams & Son, London, in Francatelli's* Cook's Guide *Advertiser, c.1860-61.* **$70-$120**

VII-62. Housemaids' box, *for carrying little cleaning tools, polishes & rags, pieced tin, high handle in addition to the centerboard with the handgrip cutout. Japanned to resemble oak. From Harrod's Stores, Ltd. 1895 catalog.* **$40-$60**

VII-63. Housekeeper's safe patent. *Pat'd 2/10/1880, by Ebnezar H. Sturges, Wing's Station, NY. It has many compartments, not only for cleaning tools but for cooking tools too. The top box is for knives. Spices were apparently meant for the hinged compartment in the front, where the nutmeg grater is mounted. Official Gazette of the U.S. Patent Office.*

VII-65. Implement racks. *All imported from Germany, about 1904. "German manufacturers of house furnishings have devised a great variety of racks or sets for holding articles of kitchen utility. They are decorative and practical, some bearing appropriate designs in the panels, while others are plain, the panels finished in Delft tile. The woodwork is of grained oak or of a softer wood heavily enameled in white. ... The vogue for these sets has gained great headway abroad, and the demand is also extending in this country. The sets pictured retail for from $4.50 to $6.50, with all the accessories." The only metal one is at lower right, with the curved dripping trough at bottom. Though the article, in* House Furnishings Review, *doesn't mention Thurnauer, it was probably that NYC firm that imported these. The German words for spices and staples didn't seem to deter sales.* **$100-$200+**

VII-64. Implement hook, *bought with ladle probably not original to it. Heavy brass, cutout in large-eyed bird form. Oval plate to be mounted to wall or woodwork of fireplace surround. 7-1/4" H x 8" W. Early 19th C English. Collection of Mary Mac Franklin.* **$250-$325**

VII-66. Make-do "Bail for a Water Jug." *Drawing in* American Agriculturist, *4/1881, showing how "a jug, having lost its handle, was provided with a substitute in the form of a bail, as follows: Two wire 'rings' were made, one to go below the largest part of the jug, and the other and smaller one near the neck. these were held together by four wires passing between them. 'Ears' were put on opposite sides of the upper ring, and a stout wire bail attached; this bail was provided with a wooden handle through which the wire passed. From experience we can say it is more convenient to carry than a jug with the ordinary, one-sided handle." A repaired piece like this would probably sell for upwards of* **$200**

Implement rack, white enamelware, wall mounted, with matching small & large ladles & 2 skimmers, 21-1/4" H, c.1900. **$150-$200**

Implement rack, with implements, japanned tin, black-finished wood-handled meat fork, cake turner, can opener, carving knife, cake knife, strainer-spoon, sharpening "steel," paring knife, mixing spoon, cleaver. "Perfect Kitchen Set," American, 23" L, 20th C. **$95-$140**

Implement rack, wood, scrolled crested top, forged iron hooks, prob. not American, a bit too ornate along top, 24-1/2" W, early 19th C., perhaps late 18th C. **$150-$175**

Implement rack, wooden framed round plate-like wall hung piece with round Delft tile in center, wooden piece at bottom has 6 holes for handles of tools, including skimmer, ladle, spoons, etc., German, c.1904. **$95-$125**

Jar, earthenware, glazed with a reddish brown, cream body clay, charmingly marked in nice big letters on side "PLUMBS" [sic], English, 5-1/4" H, mid 19th C. **$120-$150**

Jug, gray saltglazed stoneware with cobalt scrolling & leaves, "New York Stoneware Co.," Ft. Edward, NY, 2 gal. capacity, c. 3rd quarter 19th C. Added value — A hand-carved wood **jug stopper** can be worth more than the jug itself, if it's good folk art and figural. Some to hope for are a black man's head; a dog's, cat's or mule's head; or a coiled snake (perhaps made from a root). Doris Axtell, dealer in Deposit, NY, advertised one in May 1989 that sounds great: "carved wooden hand & wrist jug stopper, old natural patina, well-defined sculpture, 7-1/4" L overall." She had it at $750, and if you had the right jug (as sculpture base), you'd really have something. It is exceptionally large. **$165-$200**

Jug, hammered copper, pewter lined (looks like tin), shaped somewhat like water pitcher but with back & front pouring lips, with crosswise falling bail high arched handle, based on Russian de-

VII-68. Jug. *Redware with brown crackle glaze, provocative lady's leg in high laced boot forms the angled handle. 8-1/2" H . 19th C., New England. Photo courtesy Litchfield Auction Galleries, Litchfield CT. Ex-Harold Corbin Collection, auctioned 1/1/1990, for $450.* **$550-$750**

VII-67. Jug with frame. *"Brackett's Revolving Jug," stoneware jug in cast iron frame making it easy to pour from. A beautiful, elegant form. Probably 1870s-80s. This was sold way under the money to my mind in 1985, for only $150. Photo courtesy Penny Sanders, Sanders Auctioneers, Wilton, NH.* **$350-$450**

VII-69. Jug. *Definitely a plumber's whimsy, as it's made of lead. Softened lead worked like clay to make decoration around neck and handle. I forgot to measure it, but seem to recall about 7" or 8" H . Courtesy Lenny Kislin, Bearsville, NY.* **$175-$250**

sign, B. Paleschuck, NYC, NY, 7" H, 2 qt. capacity, early 1930s, poss. based on 19th C. form. **$25-$35**

Jug or pitcher, hammered heavy gauge brass with 3 copper bands, tall, with very slanted sides, flat bottom, high arching lip is balanced by nicely arched handle, foreign looking & "reminiscent of old world ties is this Russian pitcher jug," also made in copper with brass bands, Adolph Silverstone, Inc., another Allen Street brass company like Palechuck, NYC, NY, 9" H, one qt. capacity (also 12" H, 2 qt. capacity), early 1930s, prob. based on 19th C. form. **$25-$40**

Jug, pieced copper, tin lined, unusual shape with the body having slightly slanted sides for most of its height, narrowing in dramatically, then rising straight up again for high neck, tiny lip, forged iron handle riveted at rim & curves down to narrowing part of body. Jug actually "looks" foreign, and it is a Syrian form, 11-1/2" H, 7" diameter at base, 3" at neck, made c. 1930 from much older form. **$15-$25**

Reproduction alert — Not only are collectors being confused by recent imports of elderly Turkish copper and iron cookwares, we now have a further Middle East Muddle. I have seen a few jugs (which I thought of as pitchers) generally answering this description. I could tell they came from a slightly Eastern-influenced country — they actually look Moorish, and could date to the fifteenth or sixteenth centuries. Not long ago, I found a 60-year-old editorial note about one in the Sept. 1930 *House Beautiful,* as follows: "One day when poking around among some odds and ends of old Syrian copper [seen in profusion in the late nineteenth and early twentieth century on Allen Street, NYC] I came upon the original of a jug [as described above]. I said I thought that copies of it would be both good-looking and extremely useful. I hoped it would be ready to show you early in the summer, when you might have used it as a water pitcher or as a vase for field flowers, but the business of copying takes time, and fall is now on the way. Perhaps,

after all, it is just as good now to hold sprays of bittersweet, or honesty, or even to have fitted up for a lamp base. . . . The proportions are excellent. It is of lustrous copper lined with pewter [?] (in case you want to use it as a water pitcher) and it is fitted with a handle of half-polished iron. With very little work, and the right shade, this could be converted into a stunning and important-looking lamp. The price is $7.75 . . . at B. Paleschuck, 22 Allen St., NYC." Palechuck was established in 1897, and sold real antiques and also made reproductions of antiques, mostly from Russia and the Middle East, made of brass, copper, pewter and iron. Paleschuck was but one of many similar companies.

● ● ● ●

"Miss Matilda's Ginger Cakes. — Three quarts of flour, one teacup of lard, one quart of molasses, one tablespoonful of soda beat into the molasses, half a teacup of sour milk, the same of water, and three tablespoonfuls of ginger. Roll half an inch thick; cut in any shape, and brush over with the white of an egg." Mrs. A. P. Hill, *Mrs. Hill's New Family Receipt Book*, NY: 1870.

Jug, saltglazed stoneware, applied handle at neck, 2 peg-like projections on either side, halfway down body, that fit into cast iron swing frame, so that the jug can be tipped to pour without picking it up, rather like modern whisky-pouring bottles in frames, "Brackett's Revolving Jug," American, c.1880s (?). Sold at auction by Sanders Auctioneers & Appraisers, Wilton, NH. **$400-$450**

Juice dispenser, octagonal painted tin base, decals of lemons & grape clusters, brass fittings, 2 glass containers, ice goes inside to chill drinks, American, 30" H, late 19th, early 20th C. **$400-$500**

Keeler, staved wood, with 2 handles, low sided tub for cooling liquids, American, 5-1/2" H x 12-1/2" D, very early 19th C. **$165-$200**

Lard jar, gray saltglazed stoneware with funnel top, American, 1/2 gal. capacity, 19th C. **$45-$55**

Lunch box, a sort of suitcase that looks like an old camera box of the period, imitation pebbled leatherette with strap handle, side folds down to reveal 3 heavy tin square trays, an oblong flask, & spirit lamp, "Bon-Vee-Von Lunch Box", mfd. by Union Luncheon Box Co., NYC, 7" H x 8" W x 5" deep, c.1903. Boy! Those bon vivants really used to have lunch! **$35-$45**

VII-70. Jugs. (L) Shoulder jug, *for liquor. Four sizes, from 1 qt. to 2 gal. capacity. Sure seems amazing that there was an actual type of jug to go with those "hillbilly" cartoons from 50+ years ago.* **(M) "Common shape"** *jug, "the kind that has been in use for many years. The demand for this old-style jug is ever increasing." In 7 sizes, from 1 qt. to 5 gal.* **(R) Bailed jug**, *"a new style." 2-1/4" diameter opening, 3 sizes — 1/4, 1/2 and 1 gal. (SEE VII-47.) From Albert Pick catalog, 1909. Makers unknown.* **$40-$75**

VII-71. Keeler. *Staved shallow tub, made in pie or cedar. Came in 4 sizes: 9-3/4" , 12", 15" and 16-1/2" diameter. Duparquet, Huot & Moneuse, c.1904-1910 catalog. At first, this kind of coopered staved shallow tub (such as seen here) was a "keeler" — a cooler — used in a brewery, or probably also in a dairy. By the 1850s, the keeler or "keeler tub" was a tub in which dishes were washed.* **$40-$70**

VII-72. Tine. *A Norwegian lunch box, bentwood oval with vertical wooden supports at each end, lapped, 10" L , painted black then carved through to make design. Lid swivels on a sort of wooden button at left end. Others are very colorful, and may have a swinging strap handle. 19th C., but a form that goes back much further. Courtesy R. C. Bowen.* **$250-$350**

VII-73. Lunch carriers in disguise. (L) *Lunch satchel for seam-stresses & excursionists, etc. "In outward appearance it is not to be distinguished from any other Leather Satchel for the use of working men and women, bookkeepers, clerks, engineers, conductors, drivers, school-teachers, dressmakers, seamstresses, excursionists, and all persons whose business requires their absence from home during the dinner-hour. It will hold a sufficient quantity of meat, vegetable, bread, and pie, coffee, tea or milk for one person's dinner, properly secured in their places, without napkin or paper, perfectly ventilated, and with an independent arrangement for heating them. They are made in different colors and in two sizes." Disguised brought-from-home lunches seem to have been important at the time. Peck & Snyder ad in* Century Monthly, *3/1883.* **(R)** *Best seller! This is a tin box made to look like a book, and is japanned in assorted colors, in "imitation of Morocco Leather." The spine reads "MID DAY EXERCISES." This has some extra appeal because there are collectors of book-shaped objects. 2-1/4" x 7-3/8" x 4-7/8" . Lalance & Grosjean catalog, 1890. Before reading this, if you'd seen one, would it truly have had as much appeal as it does now? This is why I have so much background info — it adds to the longrun appeal of any antique.* **$25-$35; $40-$65**

VII-75. Dinner carriers. (L) *Carrier in style called "decked." That is, the compartments — 2, 3 or 4, depending on how many courses — stack. Tin. From F. A. Walker catalog, 1890s.* **(R)** *Dinner pail, "New England" style. "Sterling" gray enamelware, by Central Stamping Co. Wire bail with wooden grip, and lid, which "shuts over outside" has wooden knob. Three sizes, holding 1-3/4 qts, 2-1/2 qts or 3-1/4 qts, and that's a lotta lunch. 1920.* **$30-$50; $60-$85+**

VII-76. Sandwich box. *Tin with hinged lid. I'd like to find a source for these, newly made. They would be very useful. From Harrod's Stores 1895 catalog.* **$20-$35**

VII-74. Folding lunch box patent. *Pat'd 11/4/1884, by Alfred Brown & Alvin Lightner, Kansas City, MO. Sides and end are hinged, and the cover has slots for the straps of the handle. Official Gazette of the U.S. Patent Office.*

VII-77. Lunch kit. *Black finished steel box with sliding compartment, steel & aluminum bottle, tinned steel drinking cup, with extra nested aluminum food trays to fit inside. 7-1/2" H x 10" L x 5" W . D. J. Barry catalog, 1924. In the 1970s and 1990s there as been crossover appeal to faddish teens, to use as pocketbooks.* **$25-$40**

VII-78. Dinner pail, *with trays & pie plate. "Saulson," in 2 sizes, 6-1/2" x 6", and 6-3/4" x 7-1/8" . Central Stamping Co., 1920.* **$25-$40**

Lunch box, bentwood, oval, well-fitted lid, swing handles, American, 8" L x 5" W, 19th C. **$30-$40**

Lunch box, brown pasteboard with leather strap handle, a tobacco box, "Sensation," late 19th C (?). **$25-$30**

Lunch box, called a *tine*, bentwood oval, lid swivels on peg at one end and then snaps when you push down on the little knoblike projection with your thumb and pull up on lid with your fingers to make lid come up, painted black then carved through to wood, Norwegian, 10" H, 19th C. Norwegian *tines* came in various shapes, from slightly oval to very oval, to round and rectangular. Most were decorated with a hot poker in stylized designs. Some were colored. Some were painted then carved through to the light wood underneath. **$275-$300**

Lunch box, embossed in small diamonds & japanned tin, book-shaped box, with name on spine, hinged lid (front cover), "Larrabee's Lunch Box," 8-1/2" H x 5-1/2" W x 3" deep, late 19th C (?). **$50-$65**

Lunch box, litho'd tin, "Sensible Tobacco," turn of century. It may seem strange now, in the increasingly smokefree atmosphere of the 1990s, but some tobacco tins 100 years ago were especially designed to have a second life as lunch boxes. Some names to look for include "Winner Cut Plug," "Just Suits," "Pedro," "Redicut, "Dixie Queen," "Patterson's," "U.S. Marine Cut Plug," and "Union Blend." **$45-$100**

Lunch bucket, brown & white mottled enamelware, wire bail handle, prob. "Onyx," Columbian Enameling & Stamping Co., turn of century. **$120-$160**

Lunch bucket, gray graniteware, 3 parts, with bail handle, American, turn of century. **$135-$175**

Lunch bucket, tin with 2 inner trays, cup fits onto oval domed lid, wire bail handle with wood grip, "Lisk," Canandaigua, NY, 9-1/2" x 6-3/8" oval, late 19th C. **$50-$60**

Lunch or dinner pail, tin, wire bail handle, 2 compartments, plus lid is a flask for hot coffee (or tea), the opening is capped with a tin mug, giving the whole thing the name "cup-top kettle," American, late 19th C. **$35-$55**

Lunch pail, better called a dinner pail, gray graniteware, miner's type with tray & cup inside, wire bail handle, late 19th C. **$75-$100**

Dinner Pails — In the 1850s and 1860s, "the dinner pail was a simple two-quart tin pail, with a cover. The food was packed in it as well as the space would permit and the skill of the housewife allow. And sometimes it was a queer mess when lunch time came around. The bread-and-butter slices at the bottom of the pail, and the corned-beef sandwich that made the next layer, were saturated with the juices of the apple pie and mince pie on the top, which had gradually settled and become compressed by the joltings of carrying, and the entire dinner tasted of a conglomeration of flavors that only exactive hunger could render palatable. No provision was made in this miscalled dinner pail for the reception of drink or the carrying of a knife and fork and spoon. If these were carried, they were bestowed in pockets in the clothes, as was also fruit, or else were made up into a separate parcel.

"The first true dinner pail came years after this makeshift had proved inadequate. It was a pail with removable compartments — or at least one removable receptacle. About half way from top to bottom was a projection to receive a cup fitting the interior of the pail, the cup to hold coffee or tea, while the lower space received the solid food. On top of the cover was a cylindrical ring that was a receptacle for salt, or salt and pepper in desirable proportions, and this ring was covered with a half-gill cup, with handle, into which the coffee or the tea might be poured. Subsequently were added a plain disk or diaphragm of sheet tin to separate the bread from the pie, or the dry from the moist . . ., and on the outside of the pail were fixed tin straps that served as sheaths to a fork, spoon and knife.

"But a still more important advance has been made . . . If one will take a run west of New York to Paterson, NJ, and beyond, and can spend time at prominent railroad centers, or the mining regions of Pennsylvania, he will observe workmen departing in the morning carrying a tin trunk of considerable size. With some curiosity he will inquire what these peddlers are vending, and will be told that these tin trunks contain rations for one and sometimes two days. These trunks are arranged for hungry men. They are divided into partitions, each with its cover, and each cover nearly air-tight. At one end is the removable receptacle for drink." *The Metal Worker,* Sept. 2, 1882.

VII-79. Lunch box. *Chromolithographed tin, oval, close-fitting lid, swing strap handle. This small box pictures characters from Peter Rabbit, as illustrated by Harrison Cady. Mfd. by Tindeco in the 1920s. A similar, more commonly found box has square corners. This one is 2-1/4" H x 4-1/2" x 3-1/2". Photo and collection of Robert Carr. Value range mine, not Carr's.* **$75-$125+**

VII-80. Lunch box. *Mickey Mouse, color lithographed tin, with "Bull Dog" wire handles, mfd. by Geuder, Paeschke & Frey, Milwaukee, in 1935. 4-3/4" H x 8-1/4" L x 5" W . This is the earliest known comic character lunch box, and while it has an interior tray, it never had a thermos bottle. It was made by a firm that had specialized in tin- and enamel- wares of many kinds for at least 55 years. Photo and collection of Robert Carr. Value range mine, not Carr's.* **$700+**

VII-84. Match holders. (L) & **(M)** *These were advertised as "safety match safes" because of the cylindrical "receptacle at the bottom to hold" burnt matches, and which was effectively closed by turning the inner cylinder. The term* **match safe** *usually refers to a fireproof receptacle in which the unburnt matches are kept, with a lid that would contain fire if by rubbing together they ignited. These japanned and decorated tin ones were pat'd 8/6/1895, and sold by Dover Stamping Co., Boston.* **(R)** *Stamped sheet steel enameled in "dull gunmetal finish." 5-3/4" diameter. The Washburn Co., Worcester, MA, 1927. Some of collector appeal comes from colorful decoration.* **$20-$45+**

VII-81. Make-do "catch-all." *A hanging repository for "burnt matches, bits of thread, paper, etc.," made from the broken top part of a footed goblet. All the rage in 1874-1875, so much so that "crockery stores were beseiged for broken goblets, and when none were left, it is hinted that some store-keepers broke them on purpose."* American Agriculturist, *3/1875. The article told how to make a pincushion of the bottom half, then how you could use the top part too, with bits of cardboard, silver paper, crocheted bag & tassels.* **$25-$100**

VII-85. Match holders. *All wall-hung, and all stamped tin, japanned in variety of colors,* **(L)** *type called a "twin," with scalloped bottom and "assorted colored enameled pockets." Linecut differs only slightly from a 1899 Butler Brothers catalog that sold theirs for 17¢ a dozen, wholesale!* **(R)** *Two with lids, properly called* **match safes**. **(B-R)** *is "self-closing." Three sizes: 5" x 4-1/2" x 1"; 3-3/4" x 2-1/2" x 1-5/8"; and 4-1/4" x 2-3/8" x 3". Central Stamping Co., 1920.* **$25-$50**

VII-82. Spill cups, *an early version of match holders for long matches called spills. These particular 1920s repros don't predate striking matches, but were meant for "Colonial" decoration, all the rage at the time. Embossed, pieced sheet brass, with fleur-de-lis, Adams' wreath, heraldic device. All 10-1/2" H x 5" W. From Pearson-Page 1925 catalog. My mother has one with a tall skinny bottle in it, with water, for flowers.* **$20-$45**

VII-83. Match holder patent. *Pat'd 3/13/1877, by J. A. Kratt, Buffalo, NY. Wall-hung, carved wood, fancy backplate, 2 turned half-cups. The feature claimed by the patentee is the fact that the "box plate" is hinged to a back-plate, and is "provided on the rear side with a friction-surface." I can see the spilled matches now.* Official Gazette.

VII-86. Match safe. *"Lusk," with choice of oxidized copper, nickel-plated, or brushed brass finish. Two advertised features were a "spark guard" along side the protected against flying sparks, and also that a "Lusk will save its cost many times over in keeping the wall paper and polished woodwork from being marred by matches, as the scratcher is always handy." In traveling salesman's supplier catalog put out by F. W. Seastrand, c.1910s. Great thing about reading original catalog copy is the glimpse into everyday life long ago. Here you can imagine the loutish ne'er-do-well striking his big fat match on mama's pretty flowered wallpaper until she was ready to scream. Then here comes a knock at the door, and it's the traveling salesman!* **$25-$45**

Match dispenser, cast iron alligator with lots of detail, "Monon Route," late 19th C. **$225-$275**

Match holder, 2 fluted urns, mostly black painted cast iron, 3 parts, crested fancy openwork backplate, urn fronts riveted on, striking panel with light colored gritty substance between feet of urns, white inside flutes, wall hung, American, 7-1/2" H x 5-1/2" W (another is 6" H), pat'd Jan. 16, 1867, but not in *Subject Index to Patents*. **$65-$85**

Reproduction alert — This urn has been reproduced in cast brass, and is in a 1989 catalog of a reproduction wholesale company in Massachusetts. The striking panel does not have any grit. One clue not always applicable, is that antiques that are made of cast iron are often reproduced in cast brass (partly because work can be cheaply done in India, and other countries), but mostly because brass is considered decorative by a broader market, whose primary interest is in decoration, not collecting. Remember: "All that glisters is not" old!

Match holder, 2 urns with grapes, cast iron, "Bradley & Hubbard," Meriden, CT, dated 1868. **$85-$115**

Match holder, 2 pockets with openwork shield backplate, flowers & scrolls, wall hung, cast iron, 5-1/2" x 6-1/2", late 19th C (?). **$65-$95**

Match holder, for the mantle as an ornament, a miniature hearth with crane & swinging kettle, sheet brass, double pockets — for used & unused matches, English, about 6" H x 3-1/8" W, 19th C. **$115-$135**

Match holder, frying pan, handle up, half an eggshell sticks out from middle of pan, oxidized silvery finish, wall hung, black enameled cast brass, 7-1/2" H x 4-1/2" W, c.1890s. **$140-$165**

Match holder, wall hung, crimped tin resembling pair of scallop shells under cylindrical pockets for matches, striking surface below, originally japanned or painted, often found in sort of salmon color; one sold by big catalog house, Butler Brothers, at the turn-of-the-century, had a crested stamped backplate with striking panel between 2 pockets with a scalloped top, and scallop shells underneath. It was called the "Twin," and came in assorted colors of "enameled" tin. Another type had the 2 shell decorated open pockets, mounted to a back plate of brass-finished tin, which I think was probably a transparent yellow japan or varnish. This one, pat'd in 1859, is the most valuable of this style. American, 4-1/2" H x 7" W, another is 4" H x 8" W, c.1860s-1910. The fairly common scallop shell match pockets are a *de rigeur* classic for kitchenarians, often unrealistically priced $100 or more. **$30-$60**

The History of Matches up to 1882 — "The 50th anniversary of the invention of matches by three Austrians was recently celebrated in Vienna. The inventor of the lucifer match lives in every country under the sun, so Austria will do as well as another. Fifty years ago [1832], in England, matches had only reached the stage known as 'lucifers,' and were clumsy and inconvenient. Fox, Burke & Dr. Johnson used to light their candles with flint & steel, though practice probably made them more skillful than we would be at such an operation. About the beginning of the century long brimstone matches took the place of tinder. About 6 inches long, tipped with sulphur, they caught fire easily from the spark of a flint.

"In 1825 an apparatus called the 'eupyrion' was used in most cities. This was a large-mouthed bottle containing sulphuric acid, soaked in fibrous asbestos, and the matches, about 2 inches long, were tipped with a chemical combination, of which chlorate of potash was the principle ingredient. When the match's end was dipped in the acid & rap-

idly withdrawn, fire was produced, but the acid was inconvenient, the matches easily spoiled by damp. Next came the 'pyrophoros,' the pneumatic tinder-box, and Doberlenier's hydrogen lamp.

"In 1832 the first friction match was made. It was jokingly called a lucifer. Lucifers were substantially the same as present matches, pulled through a piece of sandpaper. Since then, it has been altered from a silent to a noisy match . . . the safety fusée, which ignites only when rubbed upon chemically-treated paper. This safety match was patented in England in 1856." *The Metal Worker*, Nov. 4, 1882.

The **first American friction matches**, or lucifers, were made by Daniel Chapin & Alonzo Dwight Phillips of Massachusetts. Phillips received a patent on phosphorous friction matches on Oct. 24, 1836. The nickname "lucifer" was apt: the head was coated with a composition of powdered chalk, phosphorous, brimstone & glue. **Boon or bonfire** — The friction match saved trouble except when two of them accidentally rubbed together and caught on fire. Safety matches required a special striking surface, so open-top match holders (as differentiated from match safes — match holders with a lid, especially if self-closing) could be safely used. In 1858, a short cautionary tale in *Scientific Artisan* went like this: "Were I an insurance agent, remarks a writer in an exchange, I would make it an imperative rule, that every house insured by me should be provided by metal or earthen boxes, in which matches should be kept. They are often seen lying loosely upon the shelf or in the closet, where a careless servant, or an unthinking child or even a mischievous mouse, may produce disastrous results with them. A little incident has made me very careful in this matter. One day, when about closing my room, I hastily threw a key into a drawer where were several loose papers and miscellaneous articles, and closed it; but just as it was closed, there was a glimmer of light within the drawer, which attracted my attention from its novelty. Opening it, I found that the key had struck the end of a friction match and fired it." The 1881 edition of *Practical Housekeeping*, advised that "The only proper place to put matches is in a metal box with a self-closing lid." Then the 1884 *Practical Housekeeping* advised that **"Friction Matches** — should never be left where the mice will get them, as they carry them to their nests, and sometimes ignite them. They are poison to children, and are dangerous to women, who ignite them by stepping on them, and endangering their clothing from fire." Of course, a match safe wouldn't take care of all the dangers.

VII-87. Match holders. (L) *Fry pan wall-hung holder, black-enameled cast brass, with egg shell given an oxidized "silver" finish.* **(M)** *Owls on stone wall were a popular Victorian motif. Both from Montgomery Ward catalog, c.1895.* **(R)** *"Just out and the funniest novelty of the season. A perfect pair of miniature pantaloons, but five inches in length, made from the finest cassimere.* A pair of silk suspenders attached to the buttons on pants can be used to hang it on the wall. It will hold a full box." Sandpaper patches 1-3/4" across. A. E. Rayment Supply Co., c.1910-1920s. * Cassimere is, and was, a wool twill used for men's suits. See also VII-115.* **$45-$90**

Match safe, blue japanned tin with golden pinstriping, American (?), 3" x 4", 19th C. **$65-$85**

Match safe, cast iron, "Self Closing," mfd. by D. M. & Co., New Haven, CT, 19th C. **$55-$65**

Match safe, cast iron, bin with lid, embossed flowers on sides, spring dispenses matches, "IDEAL," 5" x 3", 19th C. **$65-$75**

Match safe, cast iron, with lid, in shape of fireplace, American, 1871. Being dated adds value for many collectors. **$90-$100**

Matchbox holder, boxy cat, painted wood, with metal buttons for eyes, painted nose & whiskers, and the upward curving tail serves to hang it to wall, American, 20th C. I have seen enough of these, all slightly different, to think it must have been one of those home workbench projects described in a magazine, around the 1920s or 1930s. Anyone know exactly? **$25-$45**

Matchbox holder, red painted tin, embossed "MATCHES," hangs on wall, turn of century or early 20th. **$18-$22**

Milk bottle, molded glass with large round cream top embossed as baby face. Those without the baby face, but with large round cream top and sloping shoulders are also called bubble tops, or Mae Wests. "Brookfield Dairy," small half-pint size, early 20th C. **$30-$45**

Glass cleaning collector hint — At a flea I overheard a dealer telling a customer to try Efferdent™ inside a bottle with discoloration or fogging. I wouldn't try it on a great rarity, not until you try it on something else. Some people use bits of copper shaken inside; I've used beebees.

VII-88. Matchbox holder. *Cutout plywood, green with black trim, furniture leg skids for eyes. Typical of home craft project holders, usually animals or people. 1920s-40s. Cats probably valued highest, if folky.* **$25-$45**

VII-89. Milk bottle. *"Warren," pat'd 3/23/1880, mfd. by Warren Glass Works Co., NYC. Advertised* American Agriculturist, *1882.* **$15-$25**

Milk bottle cover, stamped metal, convex ring that fits down inside mouth of milk bottle to increase the tightness of seal, marked "Frigidaire" with their crest 3" diameter, early 20th C. **$15-$20**

Milk holder, for condensed milk — meant to turn a can into a table cream pitcher, silverplate, figural fox on lid, inside lid is adv'g for "Wisconsin's Fox Brand Condensed Milk," late 19th C. **$65-$75**

Milk pail, blue ombré [shaded] enamelware, wire bail, probably Shapleigh Hardware Co., late 19th or early 20th C. Added value — Green "Shamrock" ombré finish worth a bit more, & purple "Thistle" ombré worth half again as much. **$120-$150**

Milk pan, pieced tin, handmade, slanted sides, 3-1/2" deep x 15" diameter at top, late 19th C. **$12-$20**

Milk pan, redware with brown glaze, relatively shallow compared to diameter, slanted sides, American, 16-1/2" diameter, 19th C. **$175-$200**

Earthenware vs. Stoneware, or Lead vs. Salt — "Before the glorious Revolution . . . here and there were scattered Potteries of Earthen-ware, infamously bad and unwholesome, from their being partially glazed with a thin, cheap washing of Lead. The best of Lead-glazing is esteemed unwholesome, by observing people. The Mischievous effects of it, fall chiefly on the country people and the poor everywhere. Even when it is firm enough so as not to scale off, it is yet imperceptably eaten away by every acid matter: and mixing with the drinks and meats of the people becomes a slow but sure poison.

"It is wished the Legislature would consider of means for discountenancing the use of Lead in glazing Earthen-ware, and encourage the application of the most perfect and wholesome glazing, produced only from Sand and Salts . . . A small bounty, or exemption, on this might be sufficient to the end. But, what if public encouragement was to be given on homemade Stone-ware, rather than on Earthen-ware? In Stoneware, Lead is never used; no other glazing need be used for stone than what is produced by a little common salt strewed over the ware, which operates as a flux to the particles of sand that stick on the sides of the Ware, whilst it is in the furnace.

"Stoneware is now scarce and dear amongst us, as the housewife knows. This is owing to its great bulk and low value, that scarcely affords to pay the freight." *Pennsylvania Mercury*, Feb. 4, 1785.

Napkin rings — Made of many materials, viz. carved wood, molded plastic, woven straw, but most spectacularly, Victorian silverplate, especially figural ones, little sculpturinos with animals and/or people cleverly disporting themselves on a platform (sometimes wheeled), including a cylindrical holder for the cloth napkin. This is a highly specialized field, especially the silverplated figurals, which I will not attempt to include in this book. Look for Dorothy Rainwater's books on silver & silverplate, some published by Schiffer, and Victor Schnadig's *American Victorian Figural Napkin Rings,* Wallace-Homestead, 1971, out of print. American, European, Oriental, c.1850s (?) through present time. "Napkins are never supposed to appear a second time before washing, hence napkin rings are domestic secrets and not for company." Todd S. Goodholme, *Domestic Cyclopedia of Practical Information*, NY: Henry Holt, 1877. **25¢-$500+**

Newspaper rack, not for newstand use like I always thought, but for a "hubby" who buries his face in the paper at table. "Keeps the daily news out of the breakfast butter. So good-looking that even wives like it. In English bronze, or brass and copper" reads the ad. A tabletop easel of wire, with a cutout silhouette of a cock, & word "NEWS," Chase Brass & Copper Co., Waterbury, CT, mid 1930s. **$85-$125**

The *Milk Can Server* is simple to operate. Cut or tear away paper label where spout closes, place can in container (see illustration), clasp tightly in one hand, bring spout to place with quick, firm motion and close down top. This action punctures a vent hole in top of can and locks spout in place, ready for instant service.

VII-90. Milk can server. *Provided an "attractive pitcher that harmonizes with the most richly appointed table service." Probably stainless steel. Pat'd 1915 & 1916. Liquid Container and Server Corp., Los Angeles, CA.* **$10-$20**

VII-91. Milk pail & teapot. (L) *Teapot cobalt blue enamelware with gold trim & white flowers, hinged lid. Probably European, late 19th C.* **(R)** *Pail in plain gray enamel, turned wooden know, bail handle, about 10" H. Courtesy Mainland Antiques, Mainland, PA.* **$65-$90; $60-$80**

VII-92. Milk pail holder. *(Not for use with milk pail of type in VII-91.) Hoop iron with riveted knee pieces, homemade, not commercially sold. American Agriculturist, 7/1873, had directions for making it. Workmanship of individual piece would determine value.* **$30-$50**

VII-93. Molasses pitcher. *Japanned pieced tin, strap handle, flip lid. Two sizes: holding 1 or 2 pints. Central Stamping Co.;1920 catalog, but easily thought much older.* **$40-$65**

VII-94. Two nappies & a pudding dish. *Lipped, "square" and round, all earthenware. "Very neat milk pans, made of yellow or white ware, are sometimes used and are by far the best round shallow pans. They are called by the trade 'nappies,' and are round or oval. The convenient sizes hold 4 to 6 quarts; the 8-quart ones are heavy to handle. The round ones with a lip were formerly made extensively for the southern trade, but less so now. Square dishes of the same ware are called 'puddings;' they are rectangular with somewhat rounded corners, and in common use as pudding dishes, but are admirable milk-pans when small quantities of milk only are kept." American Agriculturist, 5/1880.* **$40-$100**

VII-95. Nappy or nappie. *Yellowware, in 10 sizes, from only 3" to 12" diameter. Note slanted sides. In modern dictionaries, the general definition of a <u>nappie</u>, or <u>nappy</u>, is a small, shallow, slant-sided bowl used for cooking, said to derive from a Middle English word, nap, meaning bowl. (It's also a nickname for napkins, hence for diapers.) Some sources say they are for cooking, and some nappies have fluted bottoms or sides. Obviously, from the quote in the previous caption, to some people nappies were milk pans of a fairly large size. Although 20th C. ads show glass nappies, most are ceramic. This linecut from Duparquet, Huot & Moneuse hotelier supplies catalog, c.1904-1910.* **$35-$160**

VII-96. Nursing bottle. *Burr patent "medallion feeder," glass flattish bottle, glass "straw," rubber tube & nipple. Embossed eagle in medallion, M. S. Burr Co. From Butler Brothers 1899 catalog. This type of flask-like nurser, though not this brand, dates to at least the 1830s. The tubes may have been made of bone or pewter or porcelain. Nipples were bone, wood, ivory, pewter (hopefully without lead) and finally rubber in the last half of the 19th C.* **American Collectors of Infant Feeders,** *SASE to Jo Ann Todd, 5161 W. 59th St., Indianapolis, IN, 46254.* **$60-$120**

VII-97. Oiler sets — confusables. *Here because they're as elegant as cruet sets for the dining room, and possibly confusable.* **(L)** *Engineers' oiler set with oval tray and set of 4 oiler cans. Two sizes: trays 14" x 8-1/2" and 16" x 11-1/2" , the larger having 5 cans. They could be had in brass or nickeled brass finishes. Note little wheeled casters on the trays.* **(R)** *set on either 14" x 9" tray with four cans or 17-1/4" x 11" with five. Both are McNab & Harlin Mfg. Co., NYC, 1898 catalog. (NOTE: There are rather elegant pieced tin cans with small spouts seen at antique shows & fleas that turn out to be 1990s olive oil cans from kitchenware catalogs. These oilers are valuable — there are many collectors.) Values for individuals; for sets:* **$10-$40; $55-$125**

VII-98. Pails. (L) *Staved wooden pail of cedar (10, 12 or 14 qts) or pine (12 qts only). Iron bound, wire bail, wood grip. Duparquet, Huot & Moneuse 1904-1910 catalog.* **(M)** *Pieced tin, flared sides, wood grip, in 6 qt. (6-1/4" H), 8 qt. (6-3/4" H) and 10 qt. (7-7/8" H) sizes. Savory, Inc., c.1925-28. Tin one least valuable, although even rusted ones sometimes are priced high.* **(R)** *Graniteware water pail in 12 qt. size only. From Sethness Co. catalog, 1925. SEE also VII-26.* **$20-$100**

VII-102. Pepper bottle. *"a charming, life-like representation of a funny, knowing little pug dog. It is entirely of frosted silver, and will never fail to receive admiring attention. The pepper is shaken out through the tiny holes in the top of the dog's head." Original cost only $2, c.1883-84. Value range assuming bottle really made of silverplate.* **$70-$125**

VII-99. "Milk-Jug and Water-Pail." *An 1858 cautionary morality fable in the form of a conversation:*

MILK-JUG: *Water-pail, how can we two agree?/What are you, pray, sir, compared to me?/You'd better be gone, to drudge about, /For, if you stay, I shall turn you out.*

WATER-PAIL. *My dear little Jug, mind what you do;/Fine things are brittle, and so are you.*

The milk-jug thought always of his worth,/He look'd so handsome upon the hearth;/But the cook she crack'd him, which made him leak,/And he lay on the dust-bin that very week;/But the plain old water-pail held his own/Full three years after the jug fell down.

—— Picture Fables, *drawn by Otto Speckter, translated from German rhymes of F. Hey. NY: Appleton, 1858.*

VII-100. Paper candy cases, *or cups for candy or other small confections. Fluted colored paper in a variety of forms — mostly kitcheny things. Note the heart; the "staved" keeler at right of second row; the coffee cup; the low pail, bucket or firkin; the washtub; the basket! All from Duparquet, Huot & Moneuse catalog, c.1904-1910, from which hoteliers and shops bought supplies.* **$3-$15**

Pepper Box.

VII-101. Pepper boxes & a salt "box." *These were also called* **casters** *— a container to be shaken, hence to cast out from, a condiment.* **(L)** *Made in pieced & stamped tin, or better, in Britannia metal. From Harrod's Stores, Brompton, England, 1895 catalog.* **(T-R)** *is a relatively flat-top salt "box," 3" H ;* **(B-R)** *is dome-topped pepper box, 3-3/4" H . Both in Duparquet, Huot & Moneuse catalog, c.1904-1910.* **$10-$50**

Pail, blue & white agate enamelware, with tin lid, wire bail handle, late 19th C. **$55-$75**

Pail, deep blue & gray enamelware, cover, wire bail handle, probably Columbian's "Dresden," 19th C. **$140-$165**

Pail, marbleized midnight blue & white enamelware, 19th C. **$70-$115**

Pail, straight sided, with pouring lip, copper, with thick copper bail handle, American, 4 gal. capacity, mid 19th C. **$95-$110**

Pail, white enamelware, wire bail, white pail cover, 20th C. Pails with lids often used as **slop jars**, kept on kitchen counter near sink for scraping dishes into. Some food was put in as slops for pigs, although some pig farmers decried this practice. Some liquids used to make vinegar, including cider, hard cider & leftover wine, were put in separate jar or pail, left to turn to vinegar via the action of that gooey blob called "mother." **$180- $30**

Pantry box, bentwood painted robin's egg blue, 2 finger laps, 5-1/2" L oval, 19th C. **$200-$275**

Pantry box, bentwood, deep green paint, 3 finger laps, 1 finger lap lid, 7" diameter, 19th C. Value is in all those finger laps. **$500-$600**

Pepper pot, turned wood, pedestal base, English, 6-1/4" H, early 19th C., poss. late 18th. (Pepper pots were also made of tin, and looked like flour dredgers.) **$225-$300**

Changes in Climate — One thing I worry about, when there's nothing else, is all the old, old treen that's recently been imported into the USA from abroad, where climatic conditions are quite different and have been for centuries. Suddenly a nice old turned wood pepper pot finds itself sitting in a hot Arizona or Baltimore collection, unprepared for the considerable change in humidity and temperature. What happens to it? Does anyone have personal experiences to share with recent imported wooden smalls?

Pickle bottles — See bottles, for pickles

Pickle jar, stoneware glazed inside and out, levered bail clamp-on lid, Weir Pottery Co., Monmouth, IL, 14" H x 8" diameter, 19th C. into early 20th C. In a 1902 ad in *Ladies Home Journal*, a note was added at bottom of ad that "Heinz, the pickle man, has just ordered 500,000 Weir Jars." The H. J. Heinz Co., by the way, founded in 1867, has a museum of artifacts and memorabilia numbering in the thousands. It is at company headquarters in Pittsburgh, but is so far not open to the public, alas. **$40-$60**

VII-105. Picnic basket patents. (L) *"Lunch-box," pat'd 7/26/1881, by Sarah A. Hoskins, Bangor, ME. With a "hinged & folded table, each leaf of which has a pair of hinged legs crossing one another." Fitted compartments.* **(R)** *"Refrigerator-basket," pat'd 10/28/1884, by John R. Hare, Baltimore, MD. "a waterproof bag [is] placed between the felt filling and the wicker-work casing" to act as an insulator. Official Gazette of U.S. Patent Office. (NOTE: Well-fitted-out picnic baskets, many from England, go for upwards of $65.)*

VII-103. Picnic or market baskets. (L) *Called a "chip-basket," which is "made of neatly interwoven wooden splits, with strongly-framed flat covers, which shut down closely, and are fastened by catches." Rounded corners. American Agriculturist, 5/1871.* **(M)** *Refrigerator basket, made of rattan, with layer of asbestos (!) and layer of felt between rattan body and inside metal lining. Ice compartment shown at near end, which is removable for cleaning. Called the "Everybody," and came in 2 sizes: 12" H x 21" x 10", or 14-1/2" H x 22" x 10".* **(R)** *is woven of ash, plywood top, lined of material, and "made for the sole purpose of keeping out sand and dirt." 11" H x 19-1/2" L x 11" W. Both in 1930s Abercrombie & Fitch catalog of outdoors goods.* **$30-$60**

VII-106. Picnic basket. *Handsome form, said to be Shaker. Tightly woven ash splint over reed. 10" H x 16" L, 2 lids, woven handle slightly unravelled. Late 19th C. probably.* **$250-$350**

VII-104. Hanaper. *I found this word by accident, along with the hard-to decipher picture. It was in the 1903 Century Dictionary Encyclopedia. A Middle English word, hanypere, or Old French word hanapier, hannepier, etc. meaning "a case for a **hanap** or drinking-cup, or for other vessels. ... It was often made of wicker-work, and sometimes covered with leather." It is obviously where the word hamper, used for a picnic basket, came from.*

Picnic or automobile lunch kit, blackened tin, in wood case, "Model 4 Auto-Cook-Kit," by Prentiss-Wabers Products Co., Wisconsin Rapids, WI, 5" H x 16-1/2" L x 9" W, early 20th C. Automobilia collectors are probably well aware of such things, but it's a new branch of kitchen collecting. **$40-$65**

Pie carrier, plywood, homemade, 7 tiers of cutout "C" pieces of plywood, plus full circle top & bottom pieces, American, 20" H x 10" diameter, c.1950s. **$12-$15**

Pie rack, 4 tiers, twisted wire, not painted black (as some repros are), no mark, problematic to date. Could be late 19th C. — could be 1980s. If old: **$35-$100**

Reproduction alert — I see these pie racks advertised all the time, but haven't examined any. Common sense would tell you to look for signs (using a magnifier) of wear — pie pans scraping in and out for years, scuff marks on bottom from being moved, polishing marks. From other repro wire pieces, I know they use wire of the same gauge for uprights and rests. Don't pay for a descriptive tag that tries to assure you "early" or "old," unless you are sure.

VII-107. Pie holder & cooler. *Tinned wire, made in 5 styles. The 4 plate style was made with light gauge and heavy gauge wire. This one, from a 1915 catalog, is exactly like one that has been in our possession for over 30 years, maybe even 35, and is probably old because it predates the repros seen everywhere now. Ours measures 10-3/4" H x 12-1/4" W at bottom. Pie plate rings are 7-11/16" outside diameter. The wire is 3/16" diameter. Linecut is of a style dating to the late 19th or early 20th C. Other styles in catalog are made entirely of heavy gauge wire, for 6, 12 and even 24 pie plates for a bakery. From catalog of Wire Goods Co., 1915.* **Caution**: *Some reproductions of these are sometimes hard to tell, being of heavy wire. Most are painted dull black, but then so are some of the old ones. Ones with bright orange rust are undoubtedly repros, as are any with some kind of heart twist. I can't guarantee a description of an old one, but I'd say if you have one you've had for at least 25-30 years, it's probably old.* **$20-$100**

VII-108. Piggin, *with lid, which is unusual. 9-1/2" H overall. Early 19th C., either North American or European. Patina and original exterior paint add value.* **$150-$400**

Pie rack, iron, mounts to wall, dated 1874. **$150-$200**

Piggin, for liquids, staved pine, ash "buttonhole" hoops top and bottom, overlapped & fastened with wooden button-like peg, the distinguishing feature making this a piggin is the one elongated stave handle, this one beautifully shaped like long-stemmed mushroom, to give the hand a good purchase, has unusual flat cover with flange inside, finished outside & in with dark brown stain, possibly walnut stain (?), New England (?), or poss. Canadian, 6" H x 9" diameter plus 4" L handle stave, early 19th C. **Piggins** are described sometimes as small wooden buckets. The elongated stave for the handle, for most of them, is quite simple & it may have a hanging hole in it. They are not often found with their lids. See salt box picture VII-115.. **$200-$250**

Pitcher, repaired Bennington-type brown glazed stoneware, originally one of the pitchers with molded old man's face under lip. Handle broken off, repaired neatly with wide tinsmithed bands (with turned edges) forming a sort of harness around the body of the vessel, with a wide braced tin strap handle. Prob. VT pitcher, with New England (?) repair, 12" H, pitcher maybe 1840s to 1860s, repair poss. 1860s to 1880s. **$350-$500**

"Handles for Pitchers — A jug or pitcher without a handle is often considered past its usefulness. An economical person, believing a few pennies saved are equal to so many earned, may re-handle a jug or a pitcher with great ease, in the manner shown in the engraving. . . ." (a thin tin harness around neck & under belly, vertical strap in front, strap handle connects top & bottom band.) *American Agriculturist* , July 1885. Repaired pieces are now in great demand. A book, *Waste Not, Want Not: The Art of the Make-Do* was published in 1986 about the broken goblets, lamps, pitchers, etc., repaired or fitted out with new parts of different materials; such pieces are called <u>fractures</u> or <u>make-dos</u>. In the book there is heavy emphasis on pincushions made from broken goblets or hurricane lamp bases, and not a lot of other types of things. The book was available from the author, Don Naetzker, 205 S. Main St., Fairport, NY 14450. If you write, use an SASE. The name **"make-do"** comes from the thrifty ditty: "Use it up, Wear it out, Make it do, Or do without." I think the repaired piece, or the one made into something else (maybe, "make it do a new service"), has an ancient lineage. The mid to late Victorian urge to make a kickshaw or gimcrack out of every possible material object, from acorn to felt scraps, from ribbon to paper lace doiley, fed into this lineage and added things like the pincushions mentioned above. (I bought one recently with a goblet foot and stem, ground off at top of stem, & fitted with a human hair-filled pillow in old patterned silk.)

The *American Agriculturist,* a journal for farm families published in NYC, had an article in March 1875 on, **"How to Make a Catch-all** — Some clever person has contrived a use for broken goblets. They were so popular near last Christmas, that crockery stores were besieged for broken goblets, and when none were left, it is hinted that some storekeepers were so obliging as to break them on purpose. Here [a picture of the goblet top and its broken off stem & foot, and a picture of a sort of crocheted hanging basket on a wall hook] you have a picture of the fractured article — the bowl and the foot. Of course you all know how to make a pincushion of the base of the glass; and now I am going to tell you how to utilize the upper part. Take a strip of silver perforated cardboard, 9 holes deep (cutting it through the 1st and 11th row of holes). Measure the top of the goblet, and allow the strip to lap over 1 or 2 holes. Fit it snugly, now [needle] work upon the cardboard in any colored worsted you like, the 'Roman Key,' or any other pattern . . . through the holes." Then you crochet the bag and make a tassel, and you can "hang it up by your bureau or other convenient place for burnt matches, bits of thread, paper, etc." Sort of like a small wall wastebasket. Hmmm. See also picture of "Uses for Old Tin Cans" in Chapter XVI.

Plate, deep dish, almost a bowl, cast iron, marvelous patina, American, 4" deep x 7-3/4" diameter, late 1700s, early 1800s. **$130-$150**

Porringer, cast iron, fanned or ribbed openwork short handle, shallow recess underneath bottom edge, long casting gate on bottom, "Kenrick #0" marked on bottom, along with size, West Bromwich, England, 4-1/8" D, 1/2 pint, the smallest size, early 19th, late 18th C. Many porringers marked "Kenrick" are found in this country, as well as coffee mills & a few other iron-monger wares. Alex Ames, in his book on old iron, identifies the first "Kenrick" maker as Archibald Kenrick, of West Bromwich, who established his foundry in 1791, and is still in business as A. Kenrick & Sons. Distinctive openwork fan-ribbed handle was prob. copied by American founders. **$125-$160**

VII-109. Pitcher, *missing its original handle, economically repaired with soldered tin. Drawing was sent to* American Agriculturist, *7/1885, by C. F. Alkire, Madison County, OH. Value depends on artfulness of repair, as well as original interest & value of the pitcher.* **$125-$400+**

Porringer, cast iron, openwork ribbed fan handle, "Kenrick," English, 6-3/4" D, early 19th C. **$135-$175**

Portable pantry, also called a security safe, black japanned pieced tin, countertop, with almost turret-like bins on either side of large central rounded "silo" part which contains 5 stacked spice containers, lids out, coffee mill on right side, compartments in bottom with white porcelain knobs, center bottom door labeled "The Kitchen Secretary," American, about 40" H, 19th C. **$750-$1000**

Portable pantries were an important bridge product — self-contained storage units, usually with an integral flour sifter, and some with a windup clock. *Before* the advent of portable pantries, housewives and cooks stored staples and spices in assorted canisters, tins, bins, bags, boxes, drawers, and various racks and shelves — on the wall, floor, table and pantry. *After* these useful store-alls came the "Hoosier"-type, moveable work station — a sort of media center for cooking, where everything was stored within in various drawers and canisters, and where the housewife had built-in work surfaces — even pastry boards. The "portable" pantry was so-called not because it was put on a buggy and taken somewhere, but because it was moveable, and could be placed on any table or cupboard shelf that suited the individual. Of course, preparations for a big church social would have been made easier if the lucky church lady in charge could commandeer somebody's portable pantry for temporary use in the church kitchen!

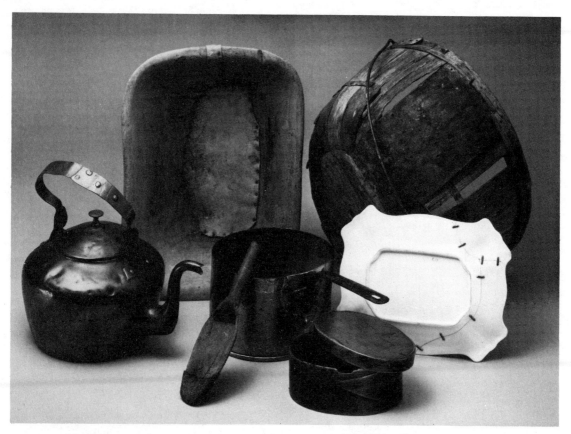

VII-110. Repaired pieces. *This is probably my favorite picture in the whole book. These were from an exhibition of repaired pieces, "On the Mend," held by Bonnie Grossman, The Ames Gallery of American Folk Art, in 1988. As she wrote, "examples are leather-patched, tin-patched, gut-sewn, stapled, and glued with sawdust paste." Also as Bonnie wrote, these are very "endearing" pieces, comfortable to live with. Photograph by Ben Blackwell. All objects courtesy Ames Gallery of American Folk Art, Berkeley, CA, and are valued upwards of $250 each. Of related interest is the Japanese Zen Buddhist aesthetic concept known as* **wabi-sabi**. *It celebrates the beauty of objects that are imperfect, incomplete, and impermanent. A book explaining this design tenet is Leonard Koren's* Wabi-Sabi for Artists, Designers, Poets & Philosophers, *Stone Bridge Press, 1993.*

VII-111. Porringer — two views. *Cast iron, half-pint size and so-marked on underside. Mfd. by the ubiquitous West Bromwich, England, founder, A. Kenrick, with distinctive fan-like tab handle. 4-1/8" diameter, long casting gate. Some in this size are marked "No. 0" but this one appears to be marked "No. 3." Photo courtesy of Oveda Maurer Antiques, San Anselmo, CA.* **$125-$160**

VII-112. Portable pantries. *Clockwise from upper* (L). (1) *"The Perfect Pantry," pat'd 1904. Some have a clock frame on top, although I believe the user supplied the clock.* (2) *Maker unknown, flour compartment in center, with sifter built in, spice containers along sides.* (3) *"Security Safe," pat'd in 1900 and 1901, 38" H x 31" W. Japanned dark brown with flowers and gilt stenciling.* (4) *Possibly a "Globe Cabinet," though similar in some respects to the "Queen Safe." 42" H x 31" W x 21" deep. Note opening for a clock, and also curved fronts of lower compartment. What's different from named examples I've seen are the two different-sized round spice compartments down center. Value goes down, and identification is hard, when pantries have been painted.* **$475-$1200**

Portable pantry, black japanned tin, wheat design stamped in the tin, big bins on top for coffee, flour & corn meal, coffee grinder on right side, flour sifter in center works by moving lever left & right back & forth, 6 spice canisters with double lids, including inner shaker lid, in "stacked" position, lids out, down center, 2 heavily encrusted compartments at bottom, almost as if used as an oven, but that couldn't be, mark so worn & rubbed it can't be read (except by infrared maybe?), probably a "Queen Safe," 50" H x 36" W, late19th C. **$750-$1200**

Portable pantry, tin, black with gold & silver decorations, bins in top, central vertical row of 6 spice cans, coffee mill on right side with crank, shelves for pies (?) below, waist high, marked "Queen Safe" in large serif letters, mfd. by Cincinnati Stamping Co., Cincinnati, OH, 42" H x 29" W, late 19th C. **$750-$1200**

Portable pantry, dark asphaltum japanned tin with ochre stenciling in Japanese-derived (*Japonisme*) bamboo and birds and butterflies motif, basically straight sides with front slanted out at bottom, usual bins for flour & coffee beans, with built in flour sifter & coffee mill (crank on side), 5 vertically stacked spice canisters in center, compartments below for flour, sugar & meal, marked "Manufactured for the Standard Cabinet Co. by B. Hunt Stamping Works," Kansas City, MO, 34" H x 26" W, pat'd 1893. Collector Mike Murrish of California sent me the information on this one. **$600-$800+**

Portable pantry, japanned black tin, with stenciled letters & bouquets of roses, also containers or canisters stenciled GINGER, CLOVES, CINNAMON, SPICE, MUSTARD, TAPIOCA, RICE, HOMINY, BARLEY, and one that's unreadable, crank on side for coffee mill, 2 lower bins labeled CAKE & BREAD, the 2 above those for SUGAR and MEAL, with flour sifter in center, "Security Safe," 38" H x 31" W, pat'd 1900 and 1901. **$900-$1200**

Portable pantry, japanned & stenciled tin, sort of *Chinoiserie* designs, top has 2 half-round bins with hinged lids on top that reveal compartments for flour sifting & coffee grinding with pans to catch the grounds, doors in bottom section reveal 2 sifters (flour & sugar[?]), center section has vertical row of spice canisters with screw-on tops, divided compartment below has 2 small pans like miniature loaf pans, originally there was a mirrored door covering the spice containers, there seems to be storage for baking pans or implements too, stenciled in script on lower doors is "Globe Cabinet," 41" H x 27" W, on a wooden base possibly added later, with 8" H legs, 1880s-1890s. Collector Geraldine Hoven is to be thanked for description & pictures of this heretofore unknown portable pantry, which was her grandparents' in Iowa. **$900-$1200**

VII-113. A "Salt" — a container called by what it contains. *Turned then chip-carved wood in abstract form of pineapple or osage orange, perhaps even a sort of inside-on-outside pomegranate. Green paint on outside, red inside, 5" H. Photo courtesy Litchfield Auction Gallery, Litchfield CT. Ex-Harold Corbin Collection, auctioned 1/1/1990, for only $750.* **$900-$1250**

VII-114. Salt box. *Two colors of turned wood, with bull's-eye backplate hanger, hinged lid. Word "Salt" in little ribbon design on front. Imported from Germany by G. M. Thurnauer, NYC. Ad in* House Furnishings Review, *1/1911.* **$90-$150**

VII-117. Salt shaker. *The "Crown," with device that could be lifted to pull rods up through holes to break up clogged salt. (By the way, you can put a few big grains of rice in a salt shaker, and that prevents most clogging.) Heavy glass, with silver-plated brass embossed top. H. & H. Mfg. Co., NYC.* House Furnishings Review *ad, 5/1907.* **$15-$20**

VII-115. Salt boxes. (L) *Turned wood, no lid, painted to simulate ceramic mocha ware (which may have been what some graniteware designs were meant to resemble), with gilt rim. Only 3-1/2" H. Photo courtesy Litchfield Auction Gallery. Ex-Harold Corbin Collection, autioned 1/1/1990 for only $175.* **(R)** *A wall-hung salt in the form of a piggin, with one long stave forming the hanger handle. Wood, iron hoops. Norwegian, 12" H overall & 4-3/4" diameter, mid (?) 19th C. Picture courtesy of the National Museum of American History, Smithsonian Institution. This one would have more value in the U.S. if it were made here.* **$250-$500; $100-$225**

VII-118. Salt shaker. *Another anti-clogging one called the "Kant-Klog." "Crystal" and "non-corrosive white metal." Humboldt Mfg. Co., Brooklyn, NY.* House Furnishings Review *ad, 10/1915.* **$20-$30**

VII-116. Salt box & match safe. *Red & white checkered enamelware, probably German, possibly French, late 19th C. Photographed in booth of Steve Smith, Country Bumpkin Antiques. You will often find these staples canisters from Europe with the German or French words for the contents on the front — such as "Salz" or "Sel." Fairly common to find these or similar attractive checkered pieces because of increasing numbers of imported antiques. The more that are imported, the less "rarity" eye appeal they have, hence the lower the collector value. For the pair:* **$150-$250**

VII-119. Salt & pepper dispenser. *Glass containers screwed into green plastic stand. Two buttons: push white one to release salt; black one for pepper. 2" H x 2-3/8" W . Imperial Metal Mfg. Co., pat'd 8/5/1939, #1,772,041. There are several varieties of this type.* **$12-$20**

Portable pantry, japanned tin, painted with flowers, butterflies, etc., compartments for all staples — flour (with sifter), sugar, etc. — spices, coffee (with grinder), unusual swing-out scale on side, missing the clock. scale marked "F & C" on face; cabinet marked "The Standard Cabinet Co., B. Hunt Stamping Co., Kansas City" [MO], early 20th C.   **$800-$1200**

Portable pantry, set on table, or well-braced shelf, not hung on wall, japanned & flower stenciled tin with name on 2 lower doors covering shelves, bins or containers for flour, corn meal, sugar, built-in coffee grinder on right side with crank sticking out side, white porcelain knobs on doors & spice canisters, clock in center top, "Perfect Pantry Co.," St. Louis, MO, about 50" H, pat'd 1904.   **$800-$1200**

Portable pantry, simple black finished tin with stenciled labels for various compartments, 2 tall side "silos" flanking center section with 6 stacked spice containers with double lids (one for shaking), topped with opening for clock (I've never actually seen one with the clock intact; maybe you had to furnish your own? or maybe you put a portrait of the cook in it!), 2 match safes, lower compartments for flour, meal & sugar, coffee grinder on right, bottom compartment like most of the portable pantries has hinged lids with curved fronts that make base larger & steadier, stenciled "Portable Pantry" on front, 42" H x 31" W x 21" D, 19th C.   **$900-$1200**

Portable pantry, simplest most economical kind, white painted metal chest with hinged cover, compartments inside hold 5 lbs sugar, 5 lbs flour, 3 lbs coffee, on front are 3 pull-out small catch drawers, with crank for flour sifter, & lever for releasing sugar & coffee, "Service Master," 10" H x 15" W x 8" D, 20th C.   **$85-$125**

Salt box, blue enamelware with wooden hinged lid, prob. imported in 1880s-1900 from Germany, late 19th C.   **$125-$165**

Salt box, gray & cobalt saltglazed stoneware, wall hung, round with flattened back, the German "SALTZ" written on front, German, late 19th C.   **$100-$135**

Salt box, green glazed ceramic, nice box with chamfered corners & scalloped backplate, varnished & stained wooden lid, large hanging hole, marked only "SALT," Bavaria, c.1900-1930.   **$115-$150**

Salt box, wall hung, copper with glass insert, hinged cover, "Kreamer," Brooklyn, NY, 9" H, early 20th C.   **$120-$150**

Salt & pepper dispenser, glass silo-like containers on green plastic base, has center plastic control panel with a black & a white push button to open plugs in bottom of respective containers, Imperial Metal Mfg. Corp., Long Island City, NY, 2" H x 2-3/8" W, pat'd Aug. 5, 1939.   **$15-$20**

Salt & pepper shakers, Catalan™ colored plastic, pepper is yellow with black top, salt is red with green top — each is half a cylinder & fit together into a little round tray that holds them together, American, in all 2" H x 1-1/2" diameter, c.1930s.   **$15-$20**

Salt & pepper shakers, panelled glass , slightly tapered sides, screw-on chrome cap has built in shaker device to keep holes clear, "Never-Klogg" mfd. by Reiner Products, Inc., NYC, NY, c.1929-1930.   **$7-$15**

Salt shaker, shapely molded clear glass jar with screw-on white metal lid with knob in top. Twist knob back & forth & it moves spiraled wire auger inside jar, "Kant-Klog," Humboldt Mfg. Co., Brooklyn, NY, c.1915.   **$12-$18**

Salt shaker, known by collectors as a <u>Christmas Salt</u> because of patent date, a bright blue clear blown molded glass honey pot or barrel shaped jar, screw-on pewter or Britannia lid with high acorn knob that you twist to turn the inside agitator device, like little metal fingers, some pointing down, some up, to break up damp salt, marked on lid, "Dana K. Alden. Boston." Glass by Boston & Sandwich Glass Co.; agitator by Alden Salt Caster Co., Sandwich, MA, and Boston, MA, respectively, 2-1/2" H, pat'd by Hiram J. White, Dec. 25, 1877. These came in different colors and in a taller panelled shape. There were sets with a pepper shaker too, sometimes found in a caster with ring handle. There are other old versions, patented by other inventors. Value is partly determined by color. Range for the type: **$275-$600**

Salt & pepper shakers — figurals or novelties. There are as many figural S & Ps as grains of salt in one of them. Most are molded plastic or ceramic, some are cast slush metal. These novelties seem to have started in the 1930s when kitchens began to get fun, with bright colors, lots of motifs used in decals, curtains, potholders. Before then, clever push-button mechanical devices were in demand. Most figurals are under $20 a pair; exceptions would be for certain name brand or character advertising pieces, but they're worth a lot more only if rarely found. A hint at what's available follows: • 2 little Schlitz beer cans in cardboard 2-pack,

VII-120. Salt & pepper shakers, *originally meant for lunch kit or picnics. Spun aluminum, 2" H x 1-5/8" diameter, "Mirro." Mfd. by Aluminum Goods Mfg. Co., 1925 catalog.* **$4-$8**

VII-121. Salt & pepper shakers. *Cactuses of molded plaster, painted green, with red and yellow flowers. 2" H , they sit in base made of real cactus wood. Souvenir of Benson, AZ, c.1940s. Value may increase slightly with renewed interest in Western motifs.* **$10-$15**

VII-122. Salt & pepper shakers. *Novelty plastic power lawnmower in original box. Red & white plastic, black rubber-like wheels. Says "Tiny Power Mower," but no maker's mark or origin. When you push mower, the eccentric axle underneath alternately pushes up the pepper then the salt. 1950s.* **$20-$30**

lithographed tin, 1957; • China boy chef, adv'g Tappan Ranges; • Stainless steel hotplate, plastic knobs & 2 burners, 2 very realistic glass drip coffee makers, 1950s; • Die molded colored plastic, Aunt Jemima & Uncle Mose F & F Mold & Die Works, Dayton, 5-1/2" H (also 3-1/2" H size); • Pair of opera glasses, knurled focus knob that actually controls whether the salt or the pepper side is open, c.1903; • "Milk glass" Monitor top refrigerators, cork plugs, tiny GE stickers, made for, if not by, General Electric, c.1930s; • Black & white plastic washer ("laundramat" is salt) & front load dryer (pepper), red plastic indicator "lights," clear plastic windows in doors, rubber plug in bottom, "Ideal Models," Detroit, MI, 4" H, 1950s-1960s (this set worth up to $30+); • Copper & chrome finish molded plastic frying pans, 1960s; • Molded plastic nude female forms, a lá Venus de Milo, one black & one white, marked "H. F. & Co." in diamond, 4" H, 1940s (worth up to $25+); • Plastic washing machine with wringers, machine body is a sugar bowl, wringers are salt & pepper, "Made in U. S. A.," "patent pending," c.1950s; • red & white plastic power mower with black rubber wheels, when you pull it the eccentric bends in the wire axle under the shakers alternately pushes up the pepper shaker then the salt; in original box, "Tiny Power Mower" but no maker's name, c.1950s; • Cast white metal, 2-wheel countertop coffee mills crudely formed, black & white, colored tulip & heart decorations, John Wright Inc., Wrightsville, PA, c.1963. • Other 1963 Wright castings are sadirons, a woman & cow, woman or man in rocking chair, a horse & buggy, and boy & wheelbarrow; • Cast white metal (also called pot or slush metal) coffee pots, white with red & green decoration, mid 20th C; • Cast white metal dog/salt, cat/pepper, adv'g "Friskies," Dayton, OH, 20th C., worth $30-$40; • Yellow dog & black cat, colored features, supposed to be Fido & Fifi, for Ken-L Ration, F & F Mold & Die Works, Dayton, OH, 20th C, common, but real works of plastic art; etc. Most of these are: **$10-$30+**

Soup Tureen Museum — The Campbell Museum, Campbell Place, Camden, NJ 08101, has hundreds of American & European tureens, ladles, spoons, trays, etc., made of ceramics, pewter, silver, etc. Call ahead for further information.

• • • •

Finials or knobs for tea or coffee pots, were shown in 1869 Dover Stamping Co. catalog., which had many **tinsmiths' supplies**, as well as housewares. They offered a "bright bird," a simple dovelike bird on grass; a "bright acorn," a pair of acorns sticking up from leaf; several round and rosette models were offered in a choice of finishes: **"black"** (sheet iron without tinning) or **"bright"** tinned.

Slop jar, gray graniteware, slightly rounded body, with wire bail & wooden grip, lid. Kept in the kitchen next to the sink, these held dish scrapings & veggie juice & parings used to "slop" the pigs, although there was disagreement about how much "garbage" was really good for a pig. 12" H, turn of century. **$75-$100**

VII-123. Slop jars. *All "Greystone" enameled ware by Matthai-Ingram, c.1890. (L) Has tin lid, wire & wood bail, tipping handle near bottom. (M) Two handles, footed; (R) bailed & footed. "Slop" was not contents of chamberpot. It was, in the toilette set, for the used wash water from the basin; and in the kitchen, it could either be the soggy remains on a plate — to be "slopped" to the pigs, or more discretely, it could be only leftover vinegar, wine, apple or grape juices, which with what's called "mother," turn into vinegar.* **$75-$125**

VII-125. Soup tureen. *"Patent Perfection Granite Iron," round tureen with nickel-plated or silver-plated mountings. 6-pint or 8-pint capacity. Manning, Bowman & Co., c.1892. See also VII-146.* **$250-$350**

VII-124. Soda glass holders, or zarfs, *two views each. Both are adjustable, and made of nickel-plated spring brass. Bottom one has a base. or foot From Cherry-Bassett Co., Baltimore & Philadelphia, 1921 supply catalog.* **$3-$10**

VII-126. Soup tureen. *Tin, with cast iron handles and lid finial. "Bite" out of lid for ladle. 10" H x 15-1/2" L x 9-1/2" W oval. Ex-Keillor Family Collection. The exact same tureen, even with the vertical lines on the body (which I thought were shading), appeared in the F. A. Walker catalog from the 1870s. It was available in five sizes — for 3, 4, 6, 8 and 10 quarts. (Another very similar tin vessel, with rim foot, in 4, 6, 8, 10, 13 and 18 quart capacities, was in a catalog meant for hoteliers, c.1904-1910.)* **$125-$160**

Soda glass holder, also called a **zarf**, nickeled brass, openwork with cup handle, used in soda fountains, American, about 3-1/2" H, late 19th C. through mid 20th C. **$8-$15**

Soup tureen, stamped & pieced tin with ornate cast iron finial & handles, lid has a "bite" opening in edge for ladle, from F. A. Walker catalog, American, or English (?), came in several sizes: 3, 4, 6, 8 and 10 quarts. One example seen is 10" H x 15-1/2" L x 9-1/2" W oval, c.1870s. **$125-$150**

TIN AND TIN-PLATING

"**Tin-plate**, or <u>tinned plate</u>, or, as the French people call it, *fer blanc* or '**white iron,**' is a material which, in a converted shape, is familiar to everyone under the name of tin; but outside of those unfortunate enough to be engaged in the manufacture, or are fortunate enough to deal in or convert this useful metal, few, indeed, of the world are aware that their so-called 'BLOCK-TIN' tea pot, kettle or dish-cover, is made of nine parts iron, and one part tin.

"Tin plates vary in size, in substance, in toughness, and in the nature of their coatings: in sizes they vary from a sheet of 10" x 14", suitable for a one-pound tin of provisions, to a sheet of 40" x 28", adapted for roofing purposes in the western states of America; in substance they differ from a sheet of <u>taggers</u>, as thin as paper itself, to a plate of ten times that thickness, adopted for the dish covers of ordinary use . . . . Coating varies with the purposes for which the tinplates are required, the lightest covering is sufficient for mustard & biscuit purposes; the heaviest possible coating is [best] for dish-covers, which have to stand planishing in conversion, and will be subsequently subject to the inevitable ceaseless 'rubbing' of every careful household." P. W. Flower, *History of the Trade In Tin*, London: G. Bell & Sons, 1880.

Tinware Origins & Tin Tariffs. — It's hard to tell the origin of some tin items because until the early 1900s there were almost no tinned iron or steel "plates" (or sheets of what we call <u>tin</u>) manufactured in the U.S. We didn't have the rolling mills for it, and probably 99.9% was imported as raw material for hundreds of stamping and/or piecing tinware factories in the U.S. Virtually everything from pie pans to cans for peaches to pails and pudding pans were made of imported plates or sheets of tinned iron (or steel). Many tin housewares were imported from Europe or England ready to sell.

William McKinley, a Republican Congressman (elected president in 1897), introduced a protectionist tariff bill, which passed in the fall of 1890 and went into effect March 1, 1891. It had at least three provisions of interest to collectors:

(1) <u>country of origin</u> must be marked on all import items
(2) imposition of a <u>higher tariff on import tin plate</u>
(3) a huge <u>tariff on import enamelwares</u>

Collectors have been thankful for the country of origin provision, although it is of limited value to us when temporary stickum or glued paper labels are allowed to satisfy the law.

The imposition of the tin plate tax occasioned long editorials and heated fights in the House because it would raise prices of finished goods made by Americans by an estimated 5% to 25%. Republicans hoped to use the tariff to encourage the infant industry of rolling tin plate in this country (sort of an early "trickle down" theory). Democrats argued that the increase of prices on canned goods & housewares would be an "unfortunate burden for the working man." One of many long *The New York Times* articles in 1890 laid out a chart of examples of how prices would rise. A four-quart coffee pot now costing 20¢ would cost 18¢ with no tariff at all, but 23¢ with the new tariff. An 11-1/4" colander costing 15¢ would be 14¢ or rise to 17¢. A 4" pie plate now 5¢ could cost 4¢ or rise to 7¢. An 1890 ad for Wanamaker's, Philadelphia, said "Tinware is advancing in cost, and very soon the manufacturers [!] will have their way and you and we will have to pay very much more. In view of this . . . we made some time since a large purchase of

kitchen tinware at what was a low price then and would be far lower now. **Bread Raisers**, 10 qt., with cover & ventilator in lid 58¢; tin-frame **Flour sieves** 9¢; tubed **Cake molds** 10¢; small **Tea Kettles** 20¢; Japanned **Nutmeg Graters** 1¢; Japanned Nests of **Spice Boxes** 30¢. . . ."

Shortly after the McKinley Tariff went into effect in 1891, a budding industry of rolling and plating iron and steel plates needed to grow quickly to satisfy enormous demands of tinsmiths and factory makers of pots, pans and cans.

A year after the tariff, the following article appeared in Jan. 1892 *The Metal Worker:* "**Tin Plate Sizes.** — Tin-plate manufacturers are still feeling their way with reference to sizes and gauges and nomenclature in general. A few concerns are turning out 14" x 20" and 20" x 28" plates of IC and IX gauge [a common grade and a better but not best grade], but greater thought is being given to the wants of the consumers in this matter than any one outside of a very small circle would suppose.

"No one seems inclined to erect tin plate works which shall be restricted to the sizes of plates heretofore current, which would make it impossible to produce larger sizes on occasion. All want to turn out whatever a consumer may desire. 1892 will, no doubt, decide many of the questions which are still open. Gauge designations have already been partially established upon a basis differing from that of British manufacturers." Next the journal listed all the "tin-plate works in operation and projected" — a scant 32 of them, mostly in Ohio & Pennsylvania.

To give the other side, the journal quoted from a circular sent out by a group of tinsmiths and factory owners: "If the tin-plate industry can be transferred to this country within a reasonable time and without damage to our business and the hundreds of thousands of workmen employed at our factories, and if we can get raw material as cheap as that obtained before the increased tax was levied on it, we will be the greatest beneficiaries. . . . Since the bill passed, we have had to pay over ten million dollars more for the tin plates we use in our factories and workshops, and every year the tariff will add over 15 million to the cost of our material.

"At the present moment [Dec. 10, 1892], . . . the present output of American rolling mills and platers . . . is less than 1% of the entire [requisite] of tin plate in America."

Tin Plate or Sheet Tin Sizes May Be Clues to Age. — All the major writers on tin agree that imported sheets of tin plate were small from the 1700s to about 1890. They disagree, however, on exact sizes of imported sheet tin during that period, although it's hard to compare exactly because of different reference dates. Most if not all tinwares used in America prior to the 1720s, at least, were finished wares imported from England (sometimes made with German/Bohemian tinplate). **A knowledge of maximum sizes** would possibly help in judging age of large pieces. You can make your own rough paper patterns of pieced wares, or measure with a cloth tape measure.

The six sources quoted below are listed chronologically by their period of research. W. D. John and Anne Simcox, twentieth-century historians of tinplate industries; Jeannette Lasansky, a twentieth-century historian of craft processes; Shirley Spaulding DeVoe, a twentieth-century domestic historian; Andrew Ure, an early nineteenth-century encyclopedist; Philip William Flower, a late nineteenth-century historian of industry; and *The Metal Worker*, a late nineteenth-century trade newspaper. (See bibliography for works.)

John and Anne Simcox: Their studies included tinplating in early Bohemia, France, and Wales, leading to Pontypool.

<u>c.1697-c.1760s (?) single size:</u>	12" x 9"
<u>c.1697-c.1760s (?) doubles:</u>	18" x 12"

DeVoe: She relied on a size chart from c.1817, of imports from Wales & Germany.

c.1817 Common size:	10" x 13-3/4"
c. 1817 Heavier plate:	15" x 11"

"When or if the early tinsmith ever used a tin sheet larger than 15" x 11"," DeVoe writes, "cannot be determined, but it was probably first imported when tin was admitted duty-free by the Tariff Act of 1833." (p. 126, DeVoe's *The Art of the Tinsmith, English and American*.)

Ure: Writing about English tin plate sizes, which at that time were imported to the United States.

1838 Standard, "Common No. 1":	10" x 13-3/4"
1838 Other sizes:	9-1/4" x 10-1/4"
	9-1/2" x 12-3/4"
	12-1/2" x 16-3/4"
	5" x 11"
	3-3/4" x 10"

The standard was marked on crates "C1" & called "Common No. 1." A box of 225 Common No.1 plates weighed exactly 100 lbs; it thus was the "standard" for measuring other plates. C1 comprised the thinnest iron plate, coated with thickest layer of tin — best to resist rust. The only other box of tin plate that weighed exactly 100 lbs was a box of "Waster's Common No. 1" — small "seconds." All other grades and sizes were measured in qrs. (quarters of 100 lbs), and lbs (pounds). The biggest plates ("Common Doubles") came 100 to a box weighing 3 qrs. 21 lbs (96 lbs).

Flower:

1870 plates for cans:	10" x 14"
1870 plates for roofing:	40" x 28"

(p. 156, Flower's *History of the Trade In Tin*, 1880).

1880 Tin Containers. — "We have not referred to the large uses for tea and coffee, matches, tobacco, jams, and bonbons, soup, fish, arrowroot, revalenta, baking powder, blacking, and the many other articles in daily use, which handsomely covered with paper labels, or still more handsomely finished by the new decorating process [direct lithography on tin], are to be seen in shop windows wherever you pass, for it would be useless, and wearisome to follow in detail the almost endless purposes [for tin plate]." Philip William Flower, *A History of the Trade In Tin*, London: G. Bell & Sons, 1880.

The Metal Worker: This was an American trade paper, and they described English tin plates of the time. They used the terminology "Common No. 1" in "XXX" (best grade) sizes, but instead of just one size there are nine!

1892 Standard, or Common #1:	10" x 14"
	10" x 10"
	11" x 11"
	12" x 12"
	13" x 13"
	14" x 14"
	15" x 15"
	16" x 16"
	20" x 20"

Surprising to find so many small increments — not much left over for cookie cutters or children's toys if the figuring was so close.

Lasansky:

c.1720s-1840s tin plates:	16" x 16"
1915 Standard:	14" x 20"

"Terneplate [roofing tin plated with a lead & tin alloy, not for cookware] came . . . as large as 28" x 40". These larger sizes meant that some shapes could be cut out in one piece, but generally the tinsmith was always restricted in this regard, having to make many of his forms out of seamed pieces." (p.76, Lasansky's *To Cut, Piece, & Solder*).

Spice box, 6 containers inside, all tin, "Kreamer," Brooklyn, NY, turn of century. Very interesting, rare Kreamer piece. **$75- $100**

Spice box, 6 round cans, oblong japanned heavy stamped tin box, cast iron handle on hinged lid, hasp closing, American (?), 9" L x 6-1/8" W, c.1890s. **$65-$100**

Spice box, japanned & pinstriped tin, 2 hinged lids on either side of center handle, each open to reveal 3 compartments, Dover Stamping Co., 19th C. **$100-$150**

Spice box, japanned & pinstriped tin, oblong two-tier chest, with small collapsing cast iron handle on top, 10 almost square drawers — 5 on each side (3 above, 2 slightly larger below), all stenciled with name, the bigger drawers for commonly used spices like salt, pepper, sugar, etc., Dover Stamping Co., 6-1/2" H x 9-1/2" L x 6-1/2" W, 1860s to 1880s. **$200-$250**

VII-127. Spice boxes. (T-L) *is a "Cooks' tin spice box" that came with 4 or 6 compartments. Duparquet, Huot & Moneuse, c.1904-1910.* **(R)** *"The Spice Box.— Has six separate boxes that take out, so that whole or ground spices may be kept nice and separate." Note the nutmeg grater in the lid. American Home Cook Book, 1854.* **(B-L)** *"Extra heavy XXXX tin, highly polished, heavy wired edges top and bottom." 3" H x 9-1/2" x 12-1/2" with 4 compartments, or 15" L with 6. Pick-Barth catalog, 1929.* **$60-$175**

VII-128. Seasoning box. *Japanned tin, hinged lid, cast iron handles. William S. Adams & Son, London, ad in* Francatelli's Cook's Guide Advertiser, *c.1860-61.* **$120-$200**

VII-129. Spice caddy patent. *Pat'd 10/14/1879, by William B. Hartley, Washington, DC. "The invention consists in a caddy consisting of a main or stock receptacle or vessel constructed of suitable material, and of any desired capacity, to hold the articles [tea, coffee, spices] in bulk, [and] being provided at the bottom with a series of hoppers, each with a sliding partition or cut-off, beneath which are arranged a series of removable drawers of varying sizes." Official Gazette, U.S. Patent Office.*

Spice box, japanned & pinstriped tin, oblong, hinged hasp-closing lid, cast iron handle, round, 7 round stenciled containers: Ginger, Cloves, Pepper, Allspice, Mace, Nutmeg & Cinnamon, American, 19th C. **$165+**

Spice box, japanned & pinstriped tin box, stamped lid imitates wood molding, with hasp lid that has nutmeg grater clipped inside, containing 6 square tin containers with stenciled names "Mace, Allspice, Cloves, Cinnamon, Ginger, Nutmeg." American, box: 10" L x 7", individual tins: 2-3/4" H x 3-1/4" x 3-1/4", late 19th C. Hasp closings are a remnant of earlier days when spices & tea were actually locked up, albeit in portable (therefore easily stealable) small containers. This isn't old enough to probably ever have been really locked. **$125-$150**

Spice box, japanned tin, rectangular stamped tin, inside hinged lid is a little scoop, 6 containers for Allspice, Cinnamon, Ginger, Mace, Nutmeg, Cloves, 8-1/2" x 6-1/2", American (?), 19th C. First I've seen with scoop. **$125-$150**

"**Nutmeg & Mace,** as we know them, are the dried seed or stone of the Nutmeg fruit, which is one of the most beautiful fruits that nature produces. It is about as large as a peach, and of a pale orange color. While ripening, it splits open lengthwise into halves, showing within the fleshy, bright, orange-crimson network of the Mace. Although a part of the Nutmeg fruit, it is considered and handled as an individual spice. Next, inside, is a brown shell of no market value. Within this shell is the center or seed of the whole fruit — the Nutmeg itself. Both the Mace and the Nutmeg are dried in the sun, and then graded for quality and size. As there is comparatively a small amount of Mace in each Nutmeg fruit, Mace is much higher in price than Nutmegs. The flavor is also much more delicate." Jos. Middleby, Jr., Inc., Bakers' Supplies catalog, 1927.

Spice box, lithographed tin, red, white & yellow with gold pinstriping, "Nutmeg, Ginger, Cloves" marked on outside, hinged cover holds clip-in nutmeg grater, box has 4 spice containers, American or European, 5-1/2" D, 19th C. Lots of spice boxes & containers of all sorts were imported in the 1870s through the teens, before WWI. Many were German; that trade stopped with the war. After that, probably the wide availability of packaged spices in small shaker tins, obviated the need for this kind of old-fashioned spice containers. **$125-$150**

Spice box, tin, round, domed hinged lid, cast iron fancy knob, hasp closing, japanned with gold pinstripes, divided into 6 wedge compartments, with central tube for nutmeg & grater, English (?), prob. made for 30 or more years, it appears in Harrod's 1895 catalog. **$125-$155**

Spice box, round tin box with 7 small containers, "Chautauqua," American, late 19th C. **$90-$120**

VII-130. Spice box. *Dark japanned tin, hinged hasp-closing lid, iron finial. Round box with 7 containers, all stenciled: "Ginger, Cloves, Pepper, Allspice, Mace, Nutmeg, Cinnamon." F. A. Walker catalog, c.1880s.* **$155-$175**

Spice box, round, with gold decorations & japanning, 4 cans inside for Ginger, Allspice, Cloves & Nutmeg, "The Model Spice Box" on center of lid, framed by flowers & leaves, very small, only 4-3/8" diameter, 19th C. **$125-$175**

Spice box, japanned tin with gold pinstriping, side handles, hinged lid with knob on edge, 16 spice canisters, for all the usuals, plus Saffron, Laurel Leaves, Mustard Seed, Kimmel, & Sundries, mfd. by Silver & Co., Brooklyn, NY, 3" H x 8-1/2" L, c.1909. **$155- $175**

Spice box, japanned tin with gold & red pinstripes on asphaltum background, 6 square cans for Nutmeg, Cloves, Mace, Ginger, Allspice, Cinnamon, plus nutmeg grater inside lid, American (?), 9" L x 6-1/8" W, 19th C. **$130-$165**

1840: "**For spice boxes**, it is best to keep different sorts in small, separate painted tin boxes, each with tight lid and handle to hang it by, to nails driven along the edge of dresser shelf. Each box to have name painted on side. These are better than large boxes, in which, not withstanding the division, the spices are very apt to get mixed." Miss Eliza. Leslie, *Housebook*, 1840.

1887: "**Spice boxes** come in many forms. Little boxes labelled with various kinds of spice are fitted into one large box. If they were well made they would be very desirable, but they are so poorly made it is difficult to take covers off or put them on. The illustration [of an oblong tin box with two "roof top" lids, hinged at center or "peak," inside divided into 3 compartments per side, hasp closing] shows good one with three compartments on each side; the only objection being that the spices are not so well protected as in the case of little boxes within one large box. However, one does not keep much spice at a time in these pantry boxes, and the saving of time and patience is a consideration." Maria Parloa, *Kitchen Companion*, Boston: Estes & Lauriat, 1887.

Spice box, tin, punched (not punctured) tin design on hinged lid, inside are 4 compartments with largish round open center for nutmeg & grater, tin ring legs, very delicate & pretty, American, 3-1/4" H x 6-3/16" L x 3-11/16" W, mid 19th C. **$225-$260**

Spice box, tin with asphaltum japanning, domed lid with brass knob, inside partitioned into wedges for 6 loose spices, nutmegs & grater fit in hole in center of wedges, American, 6-1/2" diameter, 19th C. **$115-$165**

Spice box, tin, with stamped design of morning glories, 4 spice compartments & 2 graters for bread & nutmegs. American (?), late 19th C. **$75-$125**

VII-131. Spice boxes. (L) *Japanned tin with gold border, radiating compartments, hinged close-fit lid with cast iron finial, hasp. Center hole, where axle would be in a wheel, is where nutmeg grater fit.* **(R)** *Open spice basket-type carrier for canisters. Decorated in "art colours with gold border." Both from Harrod's Stores, Brompton, England, catalog of 1895, but much older style.* **$125-$175**

Spice box, tin with brass handle on domed lid, holds 6 small containers, American, 6-3/4" diameter, 19th C. **$85-$120**

Spice cabinet, 8 drawers, stenciled tin on gray background, arched top, American (?), 19th C. **$150-$200**

Spice cabinet, red painted tin, 8 drawers, scalloped top edge, wall hung, late 19th C. **$145-$175**

Spice cabinet, tin, wall hung, 8 drawers, nicely shaped pediment top, American, 13-1/2" H, 19th C. **$200-$250**

Spice cabinet, for wall, bronze japanned tin, sort of Art Nouveau arched top, 6 drawers labeled Vanilla, Ginger, Cloves, Cinnamon, Pepper, Nutmeg, American or European, turn of century. **$150-$175**

Spice box, tin-banded varnished round bentwood box with 8 individual bentwood boxes inside. Stenciled "SPICE" on lid of outer box & names of spices on containers, American, 3-1/2" deep x 9" diameter, 3rd quarter 19th C. **$175-$200**

Spice box, thin quarter sawn maple bent into round, tin rim to lid and bottom, 7 round canisters with spices marked on lids, largest, for

VII-132. Spice boxes. *Both from Silver & Co., Brooklyn, catalog of c.1910.* **(L)** *Spice & condiment box, with hinged lid and drawer has 12 spice boxes and a compartment for 6 bottles of extracts for flavoring. Tin, finished brown & gold, oak-grained & gold, or white and gold, with white porcelain knobs and 2 handles. 8" H x 10-1/2" x 11-1/4".* **(R)** *Round spice box is "neat, roomy" and has 8 small canisters. 3" H x 10" diameter in brown japanning with gold, oak grained with gold, or white with gold. An 8" diameter one was offered in brown only. There are specialized Silver & Co. collectors.* **$125-$175+**

VII-133. Spice cabinets. **(L)** *Ash with oil finish, 8 small marked drawers, shaped backplate for wall-hanging. 18" H x 12" W. Sold originally through Montgomery Ward, c.1895, for only 90¢.* **(R)** *Wooden with carved fancy arched pediment top. Eight marked drawers. Imported from Germany, and with English spice names, by G. M. Thurnauer, NYC, 1903. These aren't rare, were mass-produced, but they have the look that appeals to collectors & decorators.* **$150-$200**

Cloves, in center, bottoms of canisters marked Patent Packing Co., Newark, NJ, pat'd Aug. 31, 1858. This is one of at least 3 versions of "bentwood" boxes with seven canisters. **$175-$200**

Spice box, varnished thin wood with metal bands, black stencilling on lid of outer box, lids & sides of all 8 inner boxes, American, 9" to 9-1/2" diameter, pat'd 1858. You often see orphaned spice containers from expensive sets, which would have 8 containers in the big box. The singles are relatively cheap — $15 to $20 @. **$175-$200**

Spice box, hickory split round box, varnished, 7 round spice containers inside, all stenciled, 8" diameter box, 19th C. **$145-$160**

Spice box, mechanical, figural, painted & brass-mounted wooden box shaped like book lying on table, side handle on "spine," dial selection on top, little carved & painted man on one end raises lid of little keg to reveal your choice, English, 18th C. **Crossover collecting** competition with automaton and folk art collectors. Offered for sale in early 1986 by Pat Guthman Antiques & Accessories for the Kitchen & Keeping Room, of Southport, CT. Value range mine. **$750-$1000**

Spice cabinet, 7 drawers, wood, with scroll-shaped pewter or white metal drawer labels. Bottom drawer marked "Nutmeg Grater," small, mid to late 19th C. **$175-$225**

"Franklin Cake — Mix together a pint of molasses and 1/2 pint milk in which cut up 1/2 pound butter. Warm just enough to melt butter, and stir in 6 ounces brown sugar, adding 3 tablespoons of ginger, 1 tablespoon powdered cinnamon, 1 teaspoon powdered cloves, and a grated nutmeg. Beat 7 eggs very light, and stir them gradually into the mixture, in turn with a pound and 2 ounces sifted flour. Add the grated peel and juice of 2 lemons. Stir very hard. Put in buttered tins and bake in moderate oven." "Old Time Thanksgiving Dainties," *Ladies Home Journal*, 11/1889.

Spice cabinet, hanging, 6 drawers, pine with white porcelain knobs, stamped tin labels, American, 12" H x 8" W, late 19th C. **$125-$150**

Spice cabinet, maple, 6 drawers with white porcelain knobs & whitish pewter-like or Babbitt labels which allowed penciled IDs to be wiped off, American (?), mid 19th C. **$250-$325**

Spice cabinet, oak, 16 drawers, wall hung, late 19th or early 20th C. These are way over-priced, but the market seems to bear it. **$150-$200**

Reproduction alert — A Wisconsin firm advertised in 1983 four "solid pine" versions, "exact copies of original models" and all nailed "no staples," stained & finished, all with white knobs and incised ring around knobs. Four drawer (not seen in antique ones): 7" H x 9-1/2" W; six drawer with shaped backplate, 13-1/2" H x 9-1/2" W; eight drawer same backplate, 16" H x 9-1/2" W, all three 4-1/2" deep; nine drawer "counter top" model is 9-1/2" H x 14" W x 5" deep. These sold for $15 to $23 each, with quantity discounts.

VII-134. Spice cabinet. *Simplest wooden type, 6 marked drawers, varnished finish. 13" H x 9" W x 5" deep. D. J. Barry catalog, 1924, maker unknown.* **$75-$125**

Spice cabinet or chest, dark green painted wood, dovetail construction, 8 drawers, countertop not wall hung, American, 19" H x 27-1/2" L, 2nd quarter 19th C.   **$550-$700**

Spice cabinet, pine, early green & red paint, 8 butt-joint drawers in simple frame, American , 11" H x 9" W, mid 19th C. **$350-$450**

Spice cabinet, various woods with original yellow paint, 6 labeled drawers for "Bay Leaf, Allspice, Cinnamon, Ginger, Cel. Seed, Mus. Seed," shaped backboard, American, early 19th C.   **$650-$800**

What Was In Old Spice Boxes? — The term "Spice box" seems to limit the contents, but these cased sets of small drawers were useful for saving many kinds of treasures. In the early 1980s I bought a small beat-up leatherbound book published in 1807 that was an account of the shipping trades of Russia, Prussia, Sweden, Denmark, and Germany, with a bit on the United Kingdom and even the United States. Particularly interesting is a list of merchandise imported in 1802 into Hamburg, Germany — at that time the busiest port in Europe. The list goes on for pages, always edifying and intriguing for its glimpses and whiffs of trade and the social scene almost 200 years ago. A selection from that list gives some idea of what might have been in the drawers of an eighteenth-century spice box:

Amber	Medicines
Beads	Natural curiosities**
Buckles	Perfumery
Buttons	Pepper
Cassia*	Quills
Cinnamon	Saffron
Cloves	Sealing-wax
Incense	Snuff & snuff boxes
Lemon peel	Tinsel
Mace-bloom	Watches
Mace-nuts (Nutmegs)	

* Cassia is used as a cinnamon substitute.

** Natural curiosities consisted of fossils, shells, stuffed birds, petrified wood, bones, skulls, mounted insects, geodes, meteorites, attractive mineral specimens, etc.

VII-135. Spice cabinets. (L) *Another imported carved wooden one, this with 4 small feet, to set on top of table or counter. It had tinned, embossed name plates — here, the catalog linecut was fudged so that the words (which I believe are in German) can't be read. G. M. Thurnauer & Bro., NYC,* House Furnishings Review, *1/1911.* **(R)** *Japanned tin, bronzed or "fancy decorations." Made in 2 sizes, with 6 or 8 drawers. Jobber's ad in* House Furnishings Review, *8/1913, maker unknown. This is the tin cabinet you'll sometimes see described, inaccurately, as "Pennsylvania German" or "early tin." Still, the look is great.* **$150-$200**

Spice cabinet, dovetailed wood, old dark wood finish, 12 drawers with nice turned knobs, counter top or wall hung, American, 17" H x 19" W x 6-1/2" deep, early 19th C. **Fake colors** — Unfortunately, the rise of craft stores has encouraged people to put fake old paint finishes on newer wooden pieces. Rubbed, scrubbed, nicked and marred they are hard to detect. You have to get a feel for the true old colors; the modern "olde" colors tend to be "antiqued" (dulled, grayed) versions of colors.   **$500-$600**

Spice cabinet, oak, 8 small drawers with set-in turned knobs, tombstone back, 2 hanging holes, American, c.1880s to 1890s.   **$180-$250**

Spice cabinet, walnut with brass knobs, hanging, 6 drawers, American (?), 11-1/2" H x 8" W x 8" D, 1870s. **$175-$250**

Spice cabinet, wood, 6 small drawers, one wide drawer at bottom, celluloid drawer labels (could be written on with pencil & washed off for changes) in imitation or as a modern adaptation of older ivory or pewter labels, American (?) or German, late 19th C.   **$250-$300**

"Currie — Imitation of the India Currie. — 3 ounces coriander seed, 3 ounces turmeric, 1 ounce black pepper, 1 ounce ginger, 1 ounce mustard, 1/2 ounce lesser cardamoms, 1/4 ounce each of cayenne pepper, cinnamon and cummin. Pound fine and mix well." Mrs. Cornelius, *The Young Housekeepers Friend, or, A Guide to Domestic Economy & Comfort,* Boston & NY: 1846.

Spice cabinet, wood, arched backplate, white porcelain knobs, 9 small named spice drawers, a shelf above & 2 long drawers at bottom for tea & coffee, wall hung, Pure Food Co., Cincinnati, OH, 24" H x 10" W, turn of century.   **$275-$325**

Spice cabinet, yellow varnished natural wood, marvelously shaped & engineered, wall hung, with 6 tin & wooden drawers, paired 2 x 2 with centerboard between, making a double bow front, shaped backplate, pin goes through from top to bottom on both sides & round drawer compartments pivot out on the pin, pat'd by J. T. Carter and J. Park, Lowell, MA, about 9" to 10" H, pat'd Dec. 10, 1867.   **$375-$425**

Spice cabinet or chest, wood, outside grain painted dull brown, with gold pinstripes, inside (surprise!) red & green with yellow varnished drawer fronts, 2 doors with one remaining knob of turned ivory, lock missing, 12 drawers inside, 10 with paper la-

VII-136. Spice & pasta cabinet, *advertised as a* **"pasta 'n' pizza rack."** *Philippine mahogany, earthenware drawers are hand-painted. 13" H x 11" W. This is hard to value. On the one hand you can say "it's only 40 years old" (advertised in* House Beautiful, *9/1960), and think of it as rummage sale material worth under $25. Or you could say, "it's already almost 40 years old, and awfully neat looking." The 21st C. isn't that far off, so let me upgrade value from price listing to:* **$75-$100**

bels with ink handwritten names "Cinnamon, Pudding Spice, Nutmegs, Carraway Seeds, Black Peppers, Mace, Cloves, Cayenne Pepper, White Pepper, Long Pepper," English, 10-1/2" H x 12-5/8" W, c.1840s to 1860s. **$500-$600**

Spice chest, and Pasta 'n Pizza Rack. Wall hung, Philippine mahogany chest with crested backplate, 2 long earthenware-fronted labeled drawers full width at bottom, for linguine & some other spaghetti, above that 2 half-width drawers for macaroni & noodles, 4 small spice drawers at top for oregano, bay leaf, rosemary & basil. All "hand-painted under glaze with Venetian gondolier designs," European for American market, 13" H x 11" W, c.1960. **$75-$100**

Spice & condiment containers, glass with PA German designs, possibly an incomplete set with only 5 pieces: marked "Cocoa, Salt, Spice, Sugar, Nutmeats," American, 4-3/4" H, 20th C. **$35-$45**

Spice container, green ribbed glass, screwtop aluminum lid, Hazel Atlas, who also made canning jars, 20th C. A set of six would cost more than six times the single price: **$8-$12**

Spice containers, glass with metal shaker tops, set of 6, McCormick & Co., Baltimore, 2nd quarter 20th C. **$20-$30**

Spice containers, tin, lithographed in blue & white with Dutch scenes, 5 square cans, 3" H x 2-1/2" square, 20th C. Set: **$25-$30**

Spice containers in rack, 9 containers, wood rack, "Black Cat" ceramic, American, mid 20th C. **$30-$45**

Spice & cookie set, <u>Black Americana</u> Aunt Jemima, colored plastic, American, 20th C. Aunt Jemima is a created human food character (like Betty Crocker or Ann Page), she was advertising every time she was seen. She is probably the oldest of the females — 100 years old in 1989. Set includes cookie jar, cream & sugar, 6 spice containers, a large & a small set of salt & pepper shakers. Usually seen as individual pieces. **$275-$300**

Spice rack, black painted cast iron one shelf with flying eagle above, 8 labeled glass jars with stoppers, "Ironmaster," possibly made by H. E. Hitt, Roslyn, PA, 15" L, c.1968. **$30-$45**

Spice rack, turned & varnished wood wall rack, with fancy cut pediment and 2 small drawers at bottom, made with small feet so it could be kept on counter, fitted with 6 blue & white porcelain spice jars with little knobbed lids, German, c.1904. **$85-$125**

Spice rack, wire in shape of crossed spoon & fork, with 4 hooks for hanging 4 china chefs with painted faces, paper labels & hanging loops on top of chef caps, Made in Japan, 3-1/2" H x 9" L, chefs are 3-1/2" H, c.1950s. **$45-$75**

Spice rack, with 12 milk glass square shaker jars with black metal lids, Griffith Laboratories, Chicago, IL, each jar 4-3/8" H, patent #2,107,697 (1938), being advertised in early 1940s. This also came with green lids & lettering; Griffith made a set with little honeypot-shaped jars with lift-out shaker piece under lid. **$75-$115**

Spice rack, with 8 jars, painted red wire rack for wall or countertop, square white glass jars with blue Dutch figures & scenes plus the spice names fused into the glass, Frank Tea & Spice Co., Cincinnati, OH, c.1941. The one I seem to find by itself is "Pepper" with the windmill. Singly they go for about $3. The original price was $1.25 for all, but now for a racked set: **$18-$30**

Spice rack tray, japanned tin tray has crimped railing, high crimped & scrolled strap handle, holds 6 japanned canisters, lots of soul, American, 8" H x 7-1/2" L, 1850s-1870s. **$200-$300**

Spice shaker, bulbous big-breasted blownmold glass, metal shaker lid, flat backside to sit on stove shelf, c.1870s-1880s. **$30-$40**

Spice tower, 3 sectioned varnished turned wood, decal labels are light yellow with black engraving, this one for "Mace, Cloves, Nutmeg," English, about 6" H, 19th C. **$175-$250**

Spice tower, turned wood, lovely light yellowy color, 5 stacked powder box size containers, all screw together, one on top of the other. This particular tower has Cloves, Nutmegs, Cinnamon, Allspice & an undesignated box, English, different sizes & number of boxes, this one 9-1/2" H, with each container 1-1/2" deep x 2-1/2" diameter, 19th C. **$175-$275**

Spice tower, varnished wood, lid & base painted or stained red, green paper labels engraved with black, stripes on lid & base, 3 tiers: Nutmegs, Mace, Cloves. Very unusual for coloring. English, 19th C. **$150-$175**

Spice tray, japanned tin, 6 canisters with slightly convex shaker lids in carrying tray with low sides & strap handle, English (the flat-topped set, very similar, was American), c.1860s-1870s. **$30-$50**

Spice tray, japanned tin, strap handle, 6 small round cans with snug lids, American (?), tray is 5-1/2" x 4-3/4", cans are 2-7/8" H x 1-3/4" diameter, late 19th C. **$35-$50**

Spoon rack, tulip poplar, painted red, carved pinwheels & geometrics, wall hung, holds 5 spoons, New England, 18th C. **$1200-$1500+**

Spoon rack, wood, with drawer below, late 19th C. Only the really remarkable 18th C. ones, with interesting chip carving and excellent patina, bring a lot. Some of the ones seen now are not very old, certainly not very well- or attractively made. Look at construction methods in drawers, and especially look at back, for signs of machine sanding/planing, or for much older and perhaps slightly uneven hand planing or shaving. **$35-$45**

Storage containers, mostly for the refrigerator, molded polyethylene plastic the inventor first called "Poly-T," with snap-on lids, also other forms, "Tupperware," originally called "Wonder Bowl," named after inventor Earl Silas Tupper, Orlando, FL, 1931 to present. An entertaining *Washington Post Magazine* article, Jan. 22, 1989, written by Vic Sussman ("I was a Middle-Aged Tupper Virgin"), tells about Tupperware **International's Museum of Historic Food Containers**, where, he says, "you can inspect everything from prehistoric vessels to

VII-137. Spice tower or turret. *Stacked spice boxes, turned wood, pale honey-color hardwood. Decalcomania labels in light yellow with black engraved letters for Cinnamon, Ginger, Cloves, Nutmeg. 7-1/8" H . English, 19th C. Courtesy R.. C. Bowen. (Another one has 5 boxes: Cloves, Nutmegs, Cinnamon, Allspice, and an unlabeled one. 9-1/2" H overall; each box is 1-1/2" deep x 2-1/2" diameter on inside. English, 19th C.)* **$175-$250**

VII-138. Spoon dripper. *A wall rack for hanging ladles, tasting spoons & basters. Copper, 28" H x 21" W. Mfd. by Henry Rogers, Sons & Co., Wolverhampton, England, 1914 catalog. Likely to be sold as older than it is — the form may be 40 or 50 years earlier.* **$90-$150**

the latest in Tupperware." Tupperware World Headquarters, Box 2353, Orlando, FL 32802. Call ahead for further information. Price range for resale "collectible market" not new Tupperware™. **50¢-$4**

Stove-blacking holder that looks like a trivet, adjustable, cast iron, 3 feet, figural head like a bulldog or even odd human, adjustable with thumb screw, and has lip to fit over edge of pan (?) or something to hold it securely, J & W. Cairns, 10" L x 2-3/4" W at widest point, pat'd Jan. 13, 1857. **$75-$100**

String holder, black painted cast iron, oval wall plaque with arched bracket with hook, holding round 2-part ball with oval holes, "old-fashioned" but probably not strictly a reproduction but an adaptation. Tolerton & Warfield Co., Sioux City, IA, advertised c. 1900 a cast iron ball, hinged 2-part twine holder, suspended from hook or bracket (?) by hoop of wire. Mfd. by Emig Products, Reading, PA, 4" diameter x 8" L, weighs 1-3/4 pounds, c.1966. Price in the 1960s was $3 for a pair, wholesale. The secondary market asking price now, which may not really be "value," is much higher. **$28-$35**

String holder, cast iron, beehive shape, one of more commonly found forms, but quite desirable, American, 19th C. **Reproduction alert** — Detail in repros is not good, usually has flat black paint, is slightly lighter in weight than it looks like it ought to be. **$125-$150**

VII-139. String holders, *or* **twine boxes**. **(L)** *Brass ball, nickeled, on stepped base.* **(M)** *Nickeled brass with embossed design.* **(R)** *Cast iron, on stand. Finished with copper or with japanning. All from Jaburg Brothers catalog, maker unknown, 1908. In a store or bakery, there would be spools of regular twine, as well as colored, gold and silver tinsel twine, were available.* **$125-$200**

VII-140. String holders. *Two hanging types, two counter tops types. All are cast iron, either japanned or finished in black paint. Most are about 3-3/8" diameter.* **(T-L)** *and* **(T-R)** *from Albert Pick catalog, 1909; others from D. J. Barry catalog, 1924. Considering lack of age on these, I think they are usually overpriced.* **(B-L)** *and* **(B-R)** *The only one with a name is the "beehive," 4" H x 4-1/2". Thomas Mills & Bro., c.1930.* **$95-$150**

String holder, cast iron, black finish, in shape of gypsy kettle with 3 little legs & wire bail handle, advertising motto embossed on both sides, "Use Jaxon's Soap," American, 4-1/2" H x 4-1/2" diameter, late 19th C. or early 20th. **$155-$190**

String holder, cast iron, gypsy kettle shape, 3 peg feet, openwork cast iron lid that fits down just inside rim, the openwork design actually comprises 3 "S"s, adv'g "S. S. S. for the Blood," American, about 4-1/2" H, late 19th C. or early 20th. **$165-$200**

String holder, cast iron, nickel-plated, round with heavy wire frame with counterweight, so after string is pulled & cut, it rights itself to pull back extra twine, marked only: "Pat. Sept. 9, 1890." **$80-$100**

String holder, cast iron, unusual fish shape, American (?), prob. 3rd or 4th quarter 19th C. **$150-$200**

String holder, cast iron with old red paint, sphere or globe on high foot, surmounted by comic open-mouthed woman's face with hole for string, American, 8-1/4" H, 19th C. **$350-$450**

String holder, hand holding twine ball, cast iron, American, late 19th C. **$150-$200**

Sugar bowl, gray graniteware, with Britannia mountings, nice round body, high domed lid with finial, 19th C. **$175-$200**

Sugar bowl, milk glass in shape of Monitor Top refrigerator, adv'g General Electric, c.1930s. **$65-$80**

White metals — What is often called "pewter" in modern dealers' ads is either an unnamed white metal (as described in the mfrs' own catalogs) or Britannia (sometimes seen spelled Brittania), which was a British, and later American, white metal substitute for pewter (and very close to it in composition and appearance), that contained no lead, but rather tin, antimony and copper. An American white metal compounded of the same 3 metals, invented about 1825 by Isaac Babbitt, of Taunton, MA, was known as "Babbitt Metal."

VII-141. Sugar bucket. *Staved wood, bentwood hoops and handle. Fitted lid. 9-3/4" H x 10-1/2" diameter at base. From Massachusetts, 19th C. Photo courtesy of the National Museum of American History, Smithsonian Institution.*

Sugar bowl, nickeled stamped metal base with 3 stamped cabriole legs, side ear handles, bowl is molded glass, rather like a melon with scalloped flutes, flat top, sliding lever in base releases sugar, "Sanitary," mfd. by Ideal Sanitary Sugar Bowl Co., NYC, NY, 2 lb. capacity, c.1915. **$25-$50**

Sugar bowl, painted tin, double stepped foot ring, slightly domed lid has 3 tiny joined tin cylinders for a knob, black ground with red, yellow & green flowers, super looking, American, 3-3/4" H x 4" diameter, early 19th C. **$500-$600**

Sugar bowl, robin's-egg-blue enamelware with black trim, including knob, rim & handles, probably Lisk Mfg. Co., Canandaigua, NY, 4-1/2" H x 4" D, 20th C. **$115-$145**

Sugar bowl, with fitted lid, beautifully patinaed turned wood in bulbous shape, nice finial, called Peaseware, made by Hiram Pease, (& other Peases ?), Painesville, Lake County, OH, 4-1/2" x 5", worked c.1850-1890. **$275-$350**

Sugar dispenser, green Depression glass jar, cylindrical shape, conical metal lid, mechanical measuring unit inside, "One Spoon At a Time," c.1930s. Also came with clear glass, called "crystal" by Depression glass people. **$125-$150**

Sugar jar, yellowware with turned bands, lid with set-in knob, Brush-McCoy Pottery Co., Zanesville, OH, 10 lb. size, c.1915. **$30-$50**

VII-142. Sugar bowl. *"Sanitary," with lever to release measure of sugar. Holds 2 lbs. Clear glass with nickel-plated base. Ideal Sanitary Sugar Bowl Co., NYC. 1915 ad.* **$55-$100**

VII-143. Syrup pitchers. *Also called simply* **syrups**. *All but first have "patented central spout and cut-off," from Manning, Bowman c.1892 catalog. Clockwise from (**T-L**): (**1**) Decorated enamelware one, with separate* drip plate*, with nickeled or silvered mountings. (**2**) "Pearl Agate" in assorted soft tints in mauve, brown, green, etc. (**3**) "Decorated Opal," with Grecian finial. (**4**) Chased quadruple silver plate. (**5**) Another chased design, nickel or silverplate.* **$150-$250**

Peaseware — The **turned wood containers** made by Pease(s) closely resemble woodenware covered bowls by other makers such as Paine. Some are footed goblet shapes, like the Lehnware trinket and saffron containers, and open eggcups. Some, with small flared footed base, have thin wire falling bail handles with simple wooden grips, with slightly convex lids with (mostly) acorn finials of wood. At some point, the company was Pease & Brown. Products of this partnership are rising in value, especially large lidded pieces, which may bring up to $1500. (At this time, collectors value more the distinctive, colorfully painted turned and footed woodenwares of Joseph Lehn of Lancaster County, PA, which can bring more than $3000 for certain covered forms.)

Sugar server, clear glass, "Tilt-A-Spoon," early 20th, late 19th C. **$20-$30**

Sugar server, old-fashioned looking heavy glass bottle with nickel trim, fat bottom, narrow neck, cast-in narrowing part in neck to measure out one teaspoon of sugar each time you turn it over, "Sanitary," c.1915. **$10-$20**

Tidy rack — See comb rack

Tray, elongated oval, reticulated sides pieced from 2 sheets of tin, large half-moon cutouts for handles at both ends, black japanned ground & painted with flowers in red, yellow & green, of a type of decoration & workmanship known to come from workshops in Stevens Plains, ME, 13-1/2" L x almost 4" deep, c.1820s-1830s. **$400-$650**

VII-144. Tin containers. (L) *A mini top hat, painted tin, and not a container except when upside down. 3-1/4" H .* **(R)** *Pieced tin in form of farrier's anvil, the lid having a horseshoe-shaped handle. Decalcomania transfer shows horseshoeing scene. English tea container, 6-1/2" H . Photo courtesy Litchfield Auction Gallery. Ex-Harold Corbin Collection, auctioned 1/1/1990, for $425 & $450.* **$425-$575**

VII-145. Child's tray, *for clipping to table edge. Assorted colors and fancy designs on chromolithographed stamped tin, spring steel clip. This one shows children playing outside on lawn, somewhat dangerously with bows and arrows. 15-3/8" x 10-1/2". Central Stamping Co., 1920, in design from 19th C.* **$30-$100**

Tray, japanned and flower-painted tin, raised slanted gallery around edge, called <u>octangonal</u> (a rectangle with 8 corners), also called a <u>coffin tray</u>, pieced from 2 sheets of tin (vertical seam on minor axis), near perfect unrestored condition, possibly Zachariah Stevens, Stevens Plains, ME, 23" L, c.1830s.   **$750-$1000**

Tray, japanned, stenciled & painted tin, with fruit compote still-life in theorum style, rectangular with rounded corners, broad convex rim with handle cutouts in elongated ovals with small heart-points toward center, very good condition with some alligatoring to varnish, attributed to Emma J. Cady, East Chatham, NY, early 19th C.   **$850-$1000**

Tray, or <u>waiter</u>, tin, with crystalized center and japanned, stenciled and painted border design of large grape leaves, spiral tendrils, outer border is a chain of comma or teardrop shapes, elongated octagon (rectangle with truncated ends to make 8 corners or sides) or coffin tray, no handle cutouts, could be NY, CT or PA, 32" L x 17" W, 2nd quarter 19th C.   **$850-$1000**

Tray, tôle, with flowers, Pennsylvania-European heritage motifs, not strictly PA Dutch, 18" L, late 19th C.   **$200-$250**

Tumbler, blue & white swirl enamelware, 20th C. A <u>tumbler</u> is a drinking glass without a stem or a footed base. Apparently hundreds of years ago, such a drinking glass was made with a rounded bottom that would actually tumble if you set it down. Whether it was to make you drink less or more, I don't know.   **$10-$17**

VII-146. Tumbler and bottle carriers. *Made of tinned wire, plain with twisted handle at* (**L**), *for 4, 6 or 9 bottles, or all twisted construction* (**R**) *for 2, 3, 4, 6, 8 or 12 tumblers and ranging in size from 6-1/2" x 3-1/2" up to 12-3/4" x 9-1/2". Wire Goods Co., "Sherwood" products. 1915. SEE also VII-20.* **$50-$85**

VII-147. Vegetable dish. *"Patent Perfection Granite Ironware," with white metal mountings. Came in 3 sizes, 11"L, 13" L and 15" L. Manning, Bowman & Co., c.1892. SEE also VII-124.* **$250-$350**

VII-148. Water can. *Not a watering can for gardens, but a hot water can for adding hot water to wash basin, or for other uses. Enameled sheet iron, white inside & out. Harrod's Stores, Brompton, England, 1895 catalog.* **$125-$200**

Crystal Gazing — Provenance of waiter/tray (left) is hard to know because <u>crystalization</u> used by tin decorators in 3 states. Grape leaves (vineyards?) may be clues. Earl Robacker, who thinks Pennsylvania, wrote that "the effect of crystals [is] obtained by washes such as aqua fortis and sal ammoniac before the varnish was applied in japanning."

"<u>Moirée Metallique</u>, called in this country [U.S.A.] **crystallized tin-plate**, is a variegated primrose appearance, produced upon the surface of tin-plate, by applying to it in a heated state some dilute nitro-muriatic acid for a few seconds, then washing it with water, drying, and coating it with lacker. The figures are more or less beautiful and diversified, according to the degree of heat, and relative dilution of the acid. This mode of ornamenting tin-plate is much less in vogue now than it was a few years ago." Andre Ure, M.D., *A Dictionary of Arts, Manufactures, and Mines; Containing a Clear Exposition of Their Principles and Practice.* NY: Appleton & Co., 1854, in 2 volumes reprinted from the "last" corrected English edition. "Less in vogue *now*" may be 1830s or 1840s. Ure explains chemical aspects of this decorative technique in his "Tin-Plate" entry: "It seems that the acid merely lays bare the crystalline structure really present on every sheet [of tin plate], but masked by a film of redundant tin. Though this showy article has become of late years vulgarized by its cheapness, it is still interesting to a practical chemist. The English tin-plates marked F answer well for producing the *Moirée*, by the following process. Place the tin-plate, slightly heated, over a tub of water, and rub its surface with a sponge holding one part of common salt or sal ammoniac in solution. Whenever the crystalline spangles seem to be thoroughly brought out, the plate must be immersed in water, washed either with a feather or a little cotton (taking care not to rub off the film of tin that forms the feathering), forthwith dried with a low heat, and coated with a lacker varnish, otherwise it loses its lustre in the air. If the whole surface is not plunged at once in cold water, but . . . is partially cooled by sprinkling water on it, the crystallization will be finely variegated with large and small figures. . . . A variety of delineations may be traced, by playing over the surface of the plate with the pointed flame of a blowpipe." *Ibid.*

VII-149. Water pitchers, *for hot and cold water. Wild designs, "painted in bright and subdued colors; superb adjuncts to summer or city houses." F. A. Walker, 1886 catalog supplement.* **$50-$200+**

Tôle peinte collector hint — If you are going to buy painted or decorated objects of household decoration, especially things made of tin, elegant enough to be termed tôle in this country, you must carefully read a how-to and history book long out of print. It is Esther Stevens Brazer's *Early American Decoration,* Springfield, MA: Pond-Ekburg Co., 1940, 1947. It is an extraordinarily fine and useful book on painted decoration on tin, papier mâché, wood, etc., used to make trays, chairs, floors, apple trays, bellows, candle sconces, coffee pots, dower chests, etc. Brazer covers subjects such as gold leaf and "floating" color, various kinds of graining — smoked, feathered, sponged, feathered or brushed, and has especially valuable information on "How to collect designs" [in order to reproduce them yourself], "searching for an old design beneath outer prints," "faint traces," etc. This book was intended to assist the skilled home crafts person to successfully decorate the surface of many kinds of decorative accessories as well as furniture, and has detailed drawings and patterns, which might help identify a piece you aren't sure of. Pieces done then are now 50+ years old, and with ordinary wear & cleaning could fool just about anybody.

Utensil racks — See implement racks

Utility rack, red enamelware with gold trim & with white lettering on each of 3 separate cups for dishwashing chores: "Zeep, Zand, Soda," meaning Soap, Sand & Soda, Dutch, 20th C. **$150-$200**

Utility rack, wall hung, white enamelware with blue lettering marking contents of each of 3 separate cups, "Zand, Soda, Zeep," materials used in washing dishes, pots & pans. Dutch, turn of century. Mine's in the bathroom, with combs in one cup, toothbrushes in another, and I have temporarily shelved the 3rd cup, as the hole provides a "holster" for a hair drier. **$100-$130**

Water pitcher, blue & white mottled enamelware, bulbous body, ice lip, turn of century. **$75-$125**

Water pitcher, cast aluminum, hammered surface, black Bakelite™ or other molded phenolic resin handles & knob, "Club Aluminum," Chicago IL, 10" H, c.1930s. **$25-$35**

Date Enamelware By Weight — One clue in dating enamelware is the weight of the underlying steel or iron. Reproductions or lookalikes, as well as most regular wares made since the end of WWI, are rather considerably lighter in weight than older pieces. If you recall, in the 1970s a lot of bright new wares, in very colorful blue, turquoise, green, red, orange or yellow, were imported and sold in warehouse stores specializing in fun, inexpensive, household wares. If you have such a piece, compare its heft with that of a piece you are trying to date. New pieces also seem to make a sort of tinny scratchy sound when pulled across a stainless steel sink or other resonating surface. You can develop a list of sensory tests for many categories of collectibles — sound (when struck with wooden spoon, tapped with fingernail, dragged on a metal surface); feel or touch (the surface, especially when you can run your thumb opposing your middle finger on the inside and outside of something; appearance of magnified surface examined with high power loupe or magnifier); weight or heft; and even taste and smell sometimes.

Water pitcher, chrome, yellow Catalin™ plastic (or other molded phenolic resin) handle, ice guard across lip to prevent bombing cubes, Chase Brass & Copper, with centaur logo, Waterbury, CT, 9" H, 1940s (?). **$25-$35**

Water pitcher, polished aluminum alloy, has ice lip, round body with flared conical top, handle is 2 slender twisted aluminum rods with spiraled tendrils top & bottom and bud-like terminals, "B. W." flanking a picture of castle turret, also "Buenilum," "Made in U. S. A.," 9" H, c.1940s. Gorgeous! **$20-$35**

VII-150. Wine coolers. *Bottom* (**L**) *is oldest. It's japanned tin, with cast iron handle. From* American Home Cook Book, *1854. Other two are from Duparquet, Huot & Moneuse, 1904-1910 catalog.* (**T**) *is japanned tin;* (**R**) *is galvanized sheet metal for one bottle.* **$50-$250**

VII-151. Oooops! *Center picture is from a humorous story in* Century, *6/1878. The officer from the War of 1812 has fallen backwards "plump into the sour-tub." The term* **sour-tub** *does not appear in any dictionary of Americanisms I have. I suspect it may be the same as* (**R**) **yeast tub,** *from the Duparquet, Huot & Moneuse catalog, c.1904-1910. It was made to hold 12, 16, 24, 30, 35 and 40 gallons.* (**T-L**) *a* **yeast pail,** *holding 10, 12, 14 or 16 quarts. Both of oak staves.*

HOLDING & HANDLING

VIII. TOOLS THAT OPEN & CLOSE

In this chapter are the ingenious devices used to open — and close — bottles, cans, jars, and milk bottles.

Arguably, the most elegant group is **corkscrews** (long ago called <u>wormes</u>, <u>scrues</u>, or <u>bottlescrews</u>), which have been collected for many years. Whether or not it is true today, corkscrews have gained their cachet because of the wine found within *most* bottles with corks. Anybody who would pay $4000 or $20,000 or even more for an historic aged bottle of wine (whether or not it would be potable), would want the very finest antique corkscrews. As W. C. Fields put it, "We lost our corkscrew and were compelled to live on food and water for several days."

One of the most select of all collector societies is devoted to these clever metal pigtails: The **International Correspondence of Corkscrew Addicts**. Their president is called the "Right" — as in, "I'd rather be right than president." Their international membership is limited to 50, with a long waiting list — an organization that's obviously very exclusive. If you seriously collect corkscrews, you may want to get on the list by writing Donald A. Bull, I.C.C.A. Right, 20 Fairway Drive, Stamford, CT 06903. Another group, with open membership, is the **Canadian Corkscrew Collectors Club**. They have a newsletter, "The Quarterly Worme." Write Milt Becker, P.O.B. 9863, Englewood, NJ 07631 for information. Always use an SASE, please. The collection of Brother Timothy (the ICCA's first Right) is on display at Christian Brothers Winery in St. Helena, CA.

The only jar openers here are a few meant for pickle jars or peanut butter jars, etc., with tightly screwed-on lids. **Jar wrenches**, on the other hand, are usually considered a "go-with" for collectors of canning or fruit jars, and other related canning equipment, and are to be found in Chapter XVI, in the Preserving Section.

"Bottle opener" as a term now refers almost exclusively to a prying tool for opening crown caps (1894-on). Collectors of **bottle openers** generally fall into two groups seeking: patented simple or combination-tool openers, especially those bearing advertising (and which may be shaped like something); or more decorative figural openers. A club with a quarterly newsletter for people who collect bottle openers and corkscrews is **Just for Openers**. Contact John Stanley, POB 64, Chapel Hill, NC 27514. Another club with a quarterly is the **Figural Bottle Opener Collector's Club**. Contact Nancy Robb, 3 Avenue "A," Latrobe, PA 15650, or Charles Lesser, 1953 Sugar Stick Rd., Harrington, DE 19952. Please always use an SASE.

Can openers — rigid and mechanical — are probably more widely popular with American collectors than are corkscrews. There is great variety in mechanical types — from one moving part to a series of gears. As I write this, a new/old concept of can opener is being advertised on TV: the "Safety Can Opener," which easily shears off the lid with the rim intact! According to the ad, you can re-use the lid to close up "pet food cans." There are many rigid openers — of which the majority look like simple tools, the minority have figural handles. As more collectors specialize in can openers, prices will rise. When unknown types are discovered, and other collectors find out, this will set off a search for multiple examples. The numbers so far are encouraging. When collectors Joe and Jackie Young started back in the 1970s, they thought "How many more could there be?" after their first 25 or so. Now, 4000+ can openers later, they *still* don't know, and the world's their oyster . . . can! A much newer collector, Bill Griffiths, has well over 1000 openers, most of them from the United States.

It is a good field for a beginning collector because of variety, quality and quantity. For some reason prices are still very very reasonable. The Youngs have over 1200 U.S. patents and 500+ English patents and haven't started to get copies of other European patents. All of this sets the ideal collecting scene because there is also an opportunity to trade up and to specialize. I keep expecting a club, and, please, at least one book on them, because it's such a richly rewarding subject, but as of 1997 there's nothing. Come on, you guys! As Christine Frederick wrote in 1929, in *Selling Mrs. Consumer,* **"The modern housewife is no longer a cook — she is a can-opener."**

There *is* a book on beer can openers, by Don Bull; this is a very specialized field whose devotées seek out those marked with rare breweries.

• • • •

Bar set, molded white plastic & metal, skeleton & bone figurals, includes bottle opener, corkscrew, 6 drink stirrers are skull on top of femur bone, "Name Your Poison," 1950s (?). Motif has value. **$10-$25**

Bottle cap, steel, rubber seal, knurled knob, "Sta-a-liv," for use with fizzy soda bottles. American, 1947-48. **$1**

Yo, Gyro! I just had to include this because of the ephemera that came with it. My friend Brenda "keep-it-for-at-least-20-years-then-consider-getting-rid-of-it" Woodward sent me an old flyer from the **Gadget-of-the-Month Club**, Hollywood, CA, whose motto was "easier living for everyone . . . thru new products." On one side we see "the best gadget of 1948" — the 1948 "gadget of the year" — "Sta-a-liv" bottle cap for a dollar each. On the reverse are a set of four plastic "Levelors" — self-leveling skids for chair legs, etc — "adjustable to meet almost any kind of 'unbalanced situation' in your home."

Bottle cappers are divided into two types: **(1)** were used to crimp a tin foil cap over a cork already in a bottle, and **(2)** were used to put on crown caps — the metal caps with crimped edges so widely used today in all parts of the world that it seems incredible that they weren't patented til 1894! For the home bottler, such a set-up made easy work of bottling a couple dozen bottles of home brew. The second type are common, and simple versions are still being made and sold to home brewers. Mostly, their value is connected to their present-day usefulness. The first type are much more collectable.

Bottle capper, cast iron, lever action, countertop, "Big Ben," English, late 19th or early 20th C. For use with a tin foil cap which was placed over the cork. **$30-$50**

Bottle capper, cast iron mounted to wood oblong, compound lever, countertop, works like a cork press to compress a cork.

Not really for home use — the liquor dealer put a heavy tin foil cap over the cork in the bottle's mouth, then placed it in the rubber-lined trough-like depression, pulled the lever to lower the top, which also has a rubber-lined trough, that crimped cap firmly in place, "Ideal," American, c. 1910. Not attractive, but looks something like a cork press, or even a nutcracker, until properly mounted. **$40-$50**

Bottle capper, rather decorative cast iron, mounted to oak oblong, simple knurled lever is pulled to crimp tin foil caps on corked bottles, embossed "CAPPEE," Manning & Bowman Co., c.1901. **$50-$65**

Bottle capper & cork press combined, cast iron mounted to wood, lever used to press three sizes of corks and/or to crimp a foil cap within a rubber-lined cylindrical opening. "Gem Capper," American, "pat. appl. for," early 20th C. **$50-$65**

Bottle corkers — See cork or corking press, cork drivers

Bottle, jar & screw cap opener combined, rubber gripper to protect & assist hand, "EZY-GRIP," Sieberling Latex Products Co., Akron, OH, early 20th C. **$4-$8**

BOTTLE OPENERS: The English call these openers **crown cork openers**, after the shape of a bottle cap, which within living memory was lined with cork for a tight seal. (Remember making badges or pins of Coca-Cola caps by prying out the cork and pressing the two halves back together with a thin layer of clothing in between?). The **crown cap** (crown cork) was invented by William Painter of Baltimore, in 1894. For some reason, Americans call the double-ended can & bottle opener a **church key**, but I don't know of anyone who calls other can and/or bottle openers that. Do you?

VIII-1. Bottle & can opener. *"Yankee," Nickel-plated. Pat'd 1/28/1902 & 12/26/1906, and mfd. by Taylor Mfg. Co., Hartford, CT. (SEE also the combination tools further on.)* **$5-$10**

VIII-2. Bottle stoppers. *Molded colored celluloid. Modernized versions, with more detail, of familiar carved & painted wooden stoppers — many of them also from Germany. Albert Pick, 1909. Most valuable in pairs; priced each.* **$10-$20+**

BOTTLE OPENERS, advertising or utilitarian:

Bottle opener, also called a **cap lifter**, adv'g "Rumford," early 20th C. **$10-$15**

Bottle opener, "Baltimore Cork & Screw," MD, 1908. **$15-$20**

Bottle opener, wall mounted with 2 screws, cast and tin plated iron with red lettering: "Coca-Cola," "The Starr X," pat'd 1925. **$10-$15**

Reproduction alert — At one time these Coca-Cola openers were hot: then someone claimed to have found a huge warehouse supply and then (or simulataneously, or instead of finding them) someone started reproducing them, so the value hasn't risen. In early 1989 I noticed an ad for a repro, which may have first been offered long ago. A company in Clarksville, AR, adv'd "Coca-Cola cast iron wall type bottle openers $21 doz.," but we don't know if this is a new repro, or by now a "Warehouse find" of an old cache of old repros. Arggh. Many collectors are not in a position to watch one particular item over the long crucial period between, say, 1960 and 1990 . . . either because it's not their specialty, or they aren't old enough! I've never wanted one of these openers, but used to see at least 10, in original boxes, every Saturday during the 1960s that I went to Englishtown Flea Market in south central NJ. To see them still for sale, for the same price or a little more, is proof that when something is available in large quantities, and has nothing going for it beyond the name, it just won't increase in value.

Bottle opener, cast steel, "Anchor Opener," 4" L, c.1910. **$7-$12**

Bottle opener, double-ended, flat steel, adv'g "Stone Malt Co.," 7-1/2" L, 20th C. **$7-$12**

Bottle opener, flat plated steel, key-like double-ended with open mouth cap lifter, and peanut-shape cutout that's marked "Pat. Feb. 19, 1901." "A.W. Stephens Mfg. Co., Waltham, Mass." on one side, "Trade > Picnic < Mark Reg. U.S. Pat. Off." on other. Pat'd by F. W. Lyons, Louisville, KY, 3-1/8" L. Many are known, most adv'g beer. These could be ordered by a brewery stamped with any name or slogan, so the collector fun is finding new names. Research into the pre-Prohibition brews helps date. Marked examples include "Duquesne Silver Top Beer," "East Tennessee Brewing Co.," "Grand Rapids Brewing Co." **$8-$20+**

Bottle opener, flat steel, adv'g Coca-Cola's "Sprite Boy," late 20th C. **$5-$8**

Bottle opener, steel business end, nicely tooled, with turned wood handle, "Havell," Irvington, N.J, 5" L, c.1900. **$10-$15**

Bottle opener, steel, green painted wood handle, dated 1933. **$5-$8**

Bottle opener, plated steel flat cutout of baseball player, the toe of one lifted foot creates the "hook" for opening, pat'd 1914. A clever figural, but considered an advertising piece. **$35-$45+**

Bottle opener, pointing hand, flat plated steel, "Effinger Beer," Baraboo, WI, 20th C. **$35-$55+**

BOTTLE OPENERS, figural, souvenir or decorative:

Bottle opener, alligator, polychromed cast iron, 20th C. **$20-$35**

Bottle opener, automobile jack figural, iron, American, c.1915 to 1925. **$25-$35**

Bottle opener, baseball cap, cast metal, painted black & orange, souvenir of "Mets," NYC, NY, late 20th C. **$10-$12**

Bottle opener, billy goat with great horns sits atop opener, polychromed cast iron, 20th C. **$30-$40**

Bottle opener, brass with antler handle, prob. 20th C. **$10-$15**

Bottle opener, steel with horn handle, sterling silver applied decoration, American, 7-1/4" L, pat'd 1864. **$30-$35**

Antlers or Tusks — An antler is a renewable resource; people walking through the woods in early spring can find deer antlers wherever deer live. A tusk — whether it's an elephant, walrus, rhinocerous, or boar tusk — as well as a buffalo or cattle horn, is not renewable, and requires the savage mutilation and painful death of the animal from which it is taken. For me, it is bad karma to have anything obtained in the brutal way all tusks are obtained. Doing research in nineteenth-century business directories for NYC and other cities, I found horrifying and truly sickening illustrated ads for ivory, showing "natives" fighting with elephants, blood and gore pouring from wounds in the elephant, the native triumphant in his fight to obtain the ivory tusk for the decorative trades in the Western and Eastern worlds. Old directories list many men whose occupation is described as "turner, in ivory and wood." It's imperative that the vast numbers of people who make up the collecting world become responsible and respectful "harvesters."

Plastic — Although 30 or so years ago I absolutely hated plastic, thinking it beneath consideration because it was a fake something else, I believe that the reason I have come to appreciate plastic objects so much in the last decade is because they may represent a saved elephant, a spared tree, a cow that wasn't turned into a pocketbook. Think about it.

Bottle openers, chromium, very stylized Art Deco/modernist, the figures of each style are mounted to a large "C" which is the business end of the opener. A rearing horse, a Scottie, an elephant. American, c.1931. **$40-$65**

Bottle opener, clown's head with **open mouth as opener**, cast iron, painted colorfully with polka-dotted tie, wall mounted, poss. made by John Wright Inc., or maybe earlier by another company, 4-1/2" L x 4" W, weighs 14 oz, when finish is worn it looks like a 1930s piece. This design is in Wright's 1963 catalog. Old ones from 1920s or 1930s get up to $75 or more, but there are so many now 30- and 40-year-old repros that it's hard to advise how to buy. 1963 wholesale price was 60¢. See the lobster bottle opener for remarks on evaluating new things.

Bottle opener, dachsund, cast brass, no mark, 20th C. **$45-$65**

Bottle opener, dachsund, nickeled-iron, adv'g "Medford Lager Beer," German (?) made for American brewery?, 20th C. **$30-$55**

Bottle opener, dog with open mouth, cast brass, probably Riverside Brass, Canadian, mid 20th C. **$25-$30**

Bottle opener, donkey, cast iron, 20th C. **$30-$45**

Bottle opener, drunk or lovelorn cowboy embracing a cactus, cast iron, painted, souvenir type, 20th C. **$20-$25**

Bottle opener, drunk & palm tree, cast iron, painted, 20th C. Drunks aren't funny, but they are collectible. The palm tree drunkard is

VIII-3. Bottle stoppers. *Figural heads, all mounted to corks.* **(L)** *Dour Uncle Sam, of "elegant china bisque ... finely colored."* **(M)** *Carved wooden bulldog, decorated with pyrography.* **(R)** *Best: comical colored rubber clown, whose tongue protrudes when squeezed. This might be a Futurewatch! I've never seen any of these. Albert Pick, 1909. Lots of crossover potential in this type.* **$12-$30+**

rarer than the lamppost ones. While the original price might have been a dollar, now the asking price is much higher. **$20-$35**

Bottle opener, drunkard leaning on signpost, colorfully painted cast iron, poss. made by John Wright Inc., Wrightsville, PA, 4" H x 2-1/2" W, weighs 7 oz, in 1963 Wright catalog, but poss. theirs is repro of earlier one. Souvenir type; sign was painted with different placenames such as St. Petersburg, FL, or Hershey, PA. More common is the drunk on lamp post, which usually did not have a place name. That one weighs only 6-1/2 oz. The 1963 wholesale price of either was 40¢. Asking prices now are partly dependent on place name. **$12-$20**

Bottle opener, duck's head, painted cast iron, American, early 20th C. **$45-$60**

Bottle opener, guitar, heavy metal, with opening in body of guitar, Japan, c.1960s. **$7-$12**

Bottle opener, hunting dog, cast iron, mid 20th C. **$20-$30**

Bottle opener, lizard (or baby alligator?), realistic small figural of cast bell metal or bronze painted in shades of brown; curled tail with a loop near end works as the cap lever, looks European from fineness of detail, poss. Austrian? (Vienna?), 4-3/4" L, early 20th C. If this were a Vienna Bronze, and the dealer knew it, the price would be four times the asking price of $50. Price range here is what I've seen for 3 offered examples at big shows. **$55-$150**

Bottle opener, lobster, red painted cast iron, possibly a reproduction of an early 20th C opener, poss. made by John Wright Inc., Wrightsville, PA, 3-1/2" L x 2-1/4" W, Wright's weighs 7 oz., shown in 1963 Wright catalog. The difference in real value and asking price for reproductions is very difficult to determine. By now, those Wright pieces which are assumed to not be repros, that were made in 1963, are almost 40 years old, easily qualifying under any criteria as collectibles. The difficulty comes when a piece is a reproduction, for it would take much, much longer than 40 years to become valuable in its own right. 1963 wholesale price was 30¢. **$15-$20**

Bottle opener, nude with arms stretched above head, cast brass & steel, 4" L, mid 20th C. This motif fits in with lots of 1950s collectibles, many of which are tacky, which is a big collector field. **$15-$25**

Bottle opener, nude with upstretched arms, white metal, plated with brass? marked "Herbert," prob. mfd. by Herbert Specialty Mfg. Co., makers of toys & novelties, Chicago, IL, 4-1/2" L, 1st third 20th C. **$25-$35**

Reproduction Figurals — A longtime collector of figural openers, Dale Deckert of Orlando, FL, announced in 1996 that he was going to try to reproduce over 40 figurals originally made by Riverside Brass of Canada, from their "plates." Instead of cast iron or brass, they will be cast aluminum, ready to paint or plate by the purchaser. These include an alligator, various birds including parrots, cats +, dogs +, donkey, elephants, fisherman, fish, goat, lamb, liquor bottles, raccoon, squirrels, etc.

Bottle opener, pelican, painted cast iron, souvenir type, mid 20th C. **$10-$20**

Bottle opener, reclining nude, chromed iron, 20th C. **$35-$55**

Bottle opener, rhinoceros, chunky & low to the ground, cast iron, mid 20th C (?). **$100-$150**

Bottle opener, shark, cast aluminum, American, 1930s. **$15-$25**

Bottle opener, spaniel dog, painted cast iron, mid 1900s. **$30-$40**

Bottle opener, steer head, handsome very Cubist sculptural form — somehow goes with Picasso's "Guernica" painting, cast iron with bronzed finish, no mark, 7" L, 1920s-1930s. **$50-$75**

Bottle opener, swordfish, painted cast metal, mid 20th C. **$20-$35**

Bottle opener, parrot or macaw on perch, cast iron, painted in bright colors, may or may not be reproduction, poss. made by John Wright Inc., 5" H x 2-1/2" W, weighs 7-1/2 oz, 20th C. **Reproduction alert?** — If there was an "original" it may date to 1920s or 1930s, but there definitely is one in Wright's 1963 catalog for 40¢. **$18-$25**

Bottle opener combination tools — See combination tools

Bottle opener for milk bottles — See milk bottle opener

A Brief History of Canning
— or, Bully Beef For You, Too!

You can't find two histories of canning that give all the same names, dates and information. I am footnoting this article (which first appeared in my newsletter, *Kitchen Collectibles News,* Jan/Feb 1985), to facilitate retracing the various authors' research. See footnotes following article and table of patents.

It is agreed, however, by all sources, that in 1809 — in response to General Napoleon's challenge to find a way to keep food fresh, or safe to eat, for his fighting troops — the concept of the supposedly longterm, airless preservation of food became practical. The French confectioner, chef, pickler and bottler Nicholas Appert won a 12,000-franc award by devising a way to put food up in glass containers. In 1810, he published the results of his studies, to fulfill the stipulations of the awarders. At the same time, the Englishman Peter Durand was awarded a patent for his technique of putting food up in glass containers, but he included tin cannisters in his patent.[1]

These early glass, wide-necked canning jars or bottles were filled with food, immersed up to the neck in a bath of boiling water until the contents were also boiling, then corked with waxed corks. The corks were then secured with wire. But these bottles cracked easily during the boiling process, or were broken later, and they were not perfectly sanitary because of the porous corks, which would admit bacteria (a danger unknown to Appert or Durand). Certainly not a handy way to preseve food for soldiers in the field or sailors on the high seas.

In 1811, Englishmen Bryan Donkin and his partner John Hall — mentioned in a few sources — patented a similar technique, and then in 1813 or so[2], they changed to handformed tin canisters. Through a smallish hole in the top, minced or diced food was put into the cans, the cans were set in boiling water baths (like a French *bain marie*) until the food boiled. A little cap-like disc was set on the hole and soldered in place. Though Donkin and Hall worked about the same time as Appert and Durand, it was this unheralded pair who actually set up the first factory for canning meat; in 1818, the products were being sold — including to career officers who could afford this luxurious new convenience food.[3]

Meanwhile, in America, tin-canning of fish was begun in New York City about 1819[4], and glass jar "canning" was patented in 1825[5] by Ezra Daggett and Thomas Kensett. The reported dates are fuzzy, but the two men's names are certain, as is that of William Underwood, who about the same time began

putting up vegetables in glass jars. One source[6] says that all three changed from glass to tin in 1839.

Can-makers, who frequently were also the food processors who filled the cans, went from small enterprises that could turn out a few score cans a day, by hand, to factories that could produce hundreds of cans. The Winslow Brothers of Portland, ME had a can factory in the 1840s[7] that made cans with a filling hole 1-1/2" across. Each worker could make about 60 cans a day. By the end of the 1850s, there were machines involving stamping of one-piece blanks that boosted production to 1000 cans a man (though not necessarily in the Winslows' operation). A man named Colonel Silas Ilsley made cans in Brooklyn[8] in the 1860s, as did Joseph Campbell (Soup's on!), and Abram A. Anderson in Camden, NJ[9]. Two Libby Brothers and their partner Archibald McNeill moved from Portland, ME, to Chicago — where the stockyards were — and began canning corned beef and other meats in 1872. Business was booming in canned goods, and the early pioneers of canning often became big names in canned goods later names still known today from the grocery store shelves!

But there's more to the story between the 1830s and the 1860s and 1870s. One reason for the popularity of canned foods before the Civil War was the huge number of people travelling westward, including Gold Rush miners. About 30 years after the gold-panning Forty-Niners rushed across the American continent, Philip William Flower wrote his *History of the Trade in Tin* [10], and described huge rusting dumps of empty tin cans left by the miners and other westward-ho'ers. He also told of the astounding number of tinned goods leaving the major canning city of Baltimore in just one year: 45 million one-pound cans, primarily of oysters and peaches!

Different ways of opening cans were possible — using simple tools, or even no tools at all. Early hole-and-cap cans sometimes had rings soldered on with the cap, and when pulled they were able to cut through the relatively soft solder and re-open the hole. (The problem was then to get the food out of the hole. To digress — once on an ill-planned trip from New Orleans to Memphis, in my adventurous twenties, all we had in the car were a couple of cans of baked beans, a heavy jackknife, and no money even for 15¢ McDonald's. But we had a nice roadside picnic by punching a hole in the cans and drawing out the beans, one at a time, with September-stiff weed stalks. Very ad hoc, very subsistence, very memorable.)

Some cans were opened with a chisel and hammer in the early days. But by 1858 there was probably a usable can opener: a patent model exists, though production has not been proved, of Ezra J. Warner's can opener of January 5, 1858.[11] By the 1870s, some cans could be opened by cutting the thin tops off with a knife, or by pulling off a tin strip — a lá Quaker Oats boxes — to loosen a cap.[12].

Invented can openers worked on two principles: either Stab-and-Saw-Open; or Stab-Twist-and-Behead. Collector Joe Young wrote up a list of the first 10 can opener patents granted in the United States for an article in my newsletter[13]. I have combined his list with one that I had assembled in an earlier issue of the newsletter.[14]

[1]. Bragdon, Charles R. *Metal Decorating from Start to Finishes,* Freeport, ME: Bond Wheelwright Co., 1961. Page 81.

[2]. Clark, Hyla. *The Tin Can Book,* NYC: New American Library, 1977. Page 13.

[3]. Ritchie, Carson I. A. *Food in Civilization. How History Has Been Affected by Human Tastes,* NYC/Toronto: Beaufort Books, 1981. Page 144.

[4]. Clark. Page 11.

[5]. Bragdon. Page 81.

[6]. Bragdon. Page 82.

[7]. Bragdon. Page 82.

[8]. Clark. Page 11.

[9]. Bragdon. Page 83.

[10]. Flower, Philip William. *History of the Trade in Tin.* London: G. Bell & Sons, 1880.

[11]. Young, Joe. "Some Notes on Early Can Openers", *Kitchen Collectibles News,* March/April 1985. Page 23.

[12]. Clark. Page 19.

[13]. Young. *Loc. cit.*

[14]. Franklin, L. C. "Bully Beef for You, Too!" *Kitchen Collectibles News,* Jan/Feb. 1985. Page 8.

First Ten Years of U.S. Patented Can Openers

INVENTOR'S NAME	RESIDENCE	DATE	NUMBER
1. Ezra J. Warner	Waterbury, CT	Jan 05, 1858	19,063 **
2. William C. Dick	New York, NY	Nov 01, 1864	44,856
3. Charles A. Ruff	Providence, RI	Mar 07, 1865	46,709
4. Eben T. Orne	Chicago, IL	Mar 13, 1866	53,173 ***
5. W. K. Baldwin	Chicago, IL	May 15, 1866	54,668
6. O. J. Livermore	Worcester, MA	Jun 26, 1866	55,878
7. Seth P. Chapin	Atlantic, NJ	Jul 17, 1866	56,368
8. John Willard	Norwich, CT	Aug 21, 1866	57,422 ***
9. J. Osterhoudt	New York, NY	Oct 02, 1866	58,554 **
10. William McGill	Cincinnati, OH	Jan 08, 1867	61,080 ***
11. S. O. Church[a]	West Meriden, CT	Jan 15, 1867	61,161
12. S. E. Totten	Brooklyn, NY	Jan 22, 1867	61,484
13. T. A. McFarland	Meadville, PA	May 21, 1867	64,891
14. W. L. Hubbell	Brooklyn, NY	Oct 22, 1867	69,996
15. W. H. Forker	Meadville, PA	Oct 29, 1867	70,188
16. G. A. Dickson	Woodcock Twnsp, PA	Dec 24, 1867	72,464
17. M. T. McCormick	Meadville, PA	Apr 07, 1868	76,490
18. N. F. Stone	Chicago, IL	Apr 14, 1868	76,669
19. C. F. Ritchel	Chicago, IL	May 12, 1868	77,916 ***
20. F. S. Wyman	Chicago, IL	Jul 28, 1868	80,326
21. G. C. Humphrey[s]	Washington, DC	Nov 17, 1868	84,122

a. *Is it possible that the expression <u>Church Key</u> came from this?*

** Patent models for these are known to exist.

*** Examples of these can openers are known to exist.

NOTE: The listings, which cover the first 10 years, were patented under various names, most commonly "Can opener" or "Tin can opener." My original failure to check under "Tin can" led me to miss several early patents.

Can opener combination tools — See combination tools

Can opener, alligator & black man, cast iron, obnoxious racist <u>Black Americana</u>, undoubtedly American, alas, and even worse, it's 20th C. **$25-$35**

VIII-4. Early cans. *Both of pieced tin plate.* (**L**) *"Cotton's Preserve Can," pat'd 12/21/1859 by P. H. Cotton, Demopolis, AL. Lid slightly concave to form recess for wax or cement poured in to make air tight. Bent wires hold lid on while cement hardens.* (**R**) *"Manley's Preserve Can," pat'd 8/3/1858 by E. Manley, Marion, NY. According to* Scientific American, *no can* "surpasses this one for cheapness ..., simplicity and perfection." *Slightly concave top is removed to put food in; can then placed in hot water to expel air from inside; cover replaced & center cup fitted into top to hold the cement. "To open the can ... pour hot water into the cup, which melts the cement."* Scientific American, 2/26/1859 and 9/25/1858. **$20-$30**

Collectibles That Offend — There's no "right way" to deal with these things. For a collector, many things do not come with intrinsic moralities or value judgments. I just know <u>what I wouldn't want around the house</u>, and that includes offensive racist things, Nazi collectibles, animal traps of all kinds (you'll note I have never put a mousetrap into one of my books — I hate them), and meat-tools of the kitchen, such as cleavers, meat grinders, etc. *De gustibus non est disputandum,* it's your choice, of course.

VIII-5. Early cans. *Pieced tin; various kinds of air-tight openings.* (**T-L**) *a "rip patch can" from 1875, which required a hole to be opened, and a hook to pull off squarish patch.* (**T-R**) *a squarish can with canted sides, called a "pyramidal can," 1879.* (**B-L**) *a "rip side can," 1879, and* (**B-R**) *a fruit can with bulge-pot sides and large opening for lid, 1879. Drawings adapted from* Wonders of Modern Industry, 1938. **$20-$30**

VIII-6. Can opener. *Called a "sardine opener, to open tin boxes of sardines, preserved meats, preserves, &c." Wood & steel. American Home Cook Book, 1854. This may actually be an English import, as its appearance in this book predates the first patented American can opener by four years.* **$10-$20**

VIII-7. Can opener patent. *Pat'd 5/21/1867 by Thomas A. McFarland, Meadville, PA. For opening oyster, fruit and other tin cans — "a cheap, simple, and effective implement for cutting an opening in a can by a single blow" by its "curved pointed teeth" which enter the lid easily, and as it is forced downward "the cutting continues, the cutting edges expand until they meet ... and thus punch out a ... disk or plug" of lid. McFarland wrote "I am aware that it has been proposed to open cans by the use of a single cutter operating like the single blade of a shear; ... also that cutters have been used in combination with separate spring handles sliding through a ring, and thus compressing the cutters to cut a plug out of a cork." Official Gazette. This and most other patent drawings that follow represent pieces that might or might not have been manufactured. Values for these patent "ghosts" are speculative. If it exists:* **$20-$35**

Can opener, black painted cast iron, thick ring at business end, longish handle with large hangup hole, circular blade, marked only "MARVEL," 7-1/4" L, blade is 2-5/8" diameter, early 20th C. **$45-$60**

Can opener, black painted cast malleable iron, all vertical, loop handle, double blades in arrowhead shape, "Heysinger's," 5-1/4" L, pat'd Oct. 24, 1876. **$55-$65**

Can opener, bull's head with looped tail handle, cast iron (sometimes nickel-plated, sometimes bronzed), English. Usually about 6" to 6-1/2" L, last quarter 19th C. through WWII at least. **$65-$80**

Can opener, bull's head & partial body, cast iron in 2 halves, spike & blade one piece screwed in to head, not much detailing in casting, English, 6" L, late 19th C. or early 20th. **$50-$60**

Bull openers — One early major canned food was tinned beef, also called "bully beef" (at least by the British Army), but surprisingly, the first known patented can opener shaped like a bull was pat'd in 1875 by J. A. Wilson, of Chicago, IL. His and others of these openers — strong as a bull themselves — utilize a play on words. There are many variations; makes a nice collection. Look for variations in expression, eyes, horns, hair detail, collar (not often present), tail, body shape. Because they are included in present-day container-loads of "smalls" from England, I assume that many of them are English. Perhaps they were exported from the U.S. to England? An example depicted in Evan Perry's *Collecting Antique Metalware* (London: Hamlyn, 1974) has a spike cast with the head, and the steel blade is marked with an undecipherable work's name, plus "Sheffield," which I assume was, as usual, England. One avenue of exploration would be for evidence that American manufacturers pirated the word "Sheffield" to imply fine-quality cutlery steel.

Can opener, bull's head & partial body, cast iron in 2 halves, spike cast in top of head, nice round eyes & ears, long hairs go straight back in line with body, English, 6" L, late 19th C. to 1930s? **$60-$80**

Can opener, bull's head & partial body, cast iron in 2 halves, very pronounced horns, particularly when seen from front, upper jaw's crosswise ridges look like teeth from side; blade & spike are one piece & screw in; interestingly, while the horns & ears are the same, the hair on the 2 halves is different, evidently the mold maker didn't use the same carving technique for both sides, little details like this make this small area of collecting very interesting, spike is marked "H L 43," English, 6" L, late 19th to early 20th C. **$50-$60**

Can opener, bull's head with very curly hair, cast iron, 6" L, 19th C. **$60-$75**

Can opener, cast iron, "Yankee," c.1900. **$12-$15**

Can opener, cast iron, "Indestructo," early 20th C. (?) **$5-$8**

Can opener, cast iron, "King," pat'd 1895. **$15-$18**

Can opener, cast iron, "A. S. & Co., Columbia," NY or PA or CT, pat'd July 25, 1899. There were many towns & villages named Columbia all over the U.S. by this time, the most likely manufacturing center being in NY, PA or CT. (Bill Griffiths has one marked "Columbia," like a Keen Kutter handle & blade, with design patent by Meisselbach, Sept. 26, 1893.) **$60-$70**

Can opener, cast iron, cigar-shaped wood handle stamped with name, "Keen Kutter," Simmons Hardware Co., c. WWI. Griffiths has two with similar blades, different handles. Also another that has a bottle opener. Crossover Keen Kutter collector interest. **$35-$45**

Can opener, cast iron, counter top, possibly for a restaurant, maybe a big family's kitchen, with an eagle on the top, mounted to heavy block of wood. This is a double opener that will open short cans on the side, taller cans in the back. Long curved lever works a small blade in the front to open a tuna fish size can, while the back blade is large & sort of heart-shaped. I thought this was Enterprise because of the eagle, but it doesn't appear in any Enterprise catalog known to collector Bill Griffiths. 7-1/2" H; lever is 12" L. Griffiths believes this is probably the Williams' patents of Jan. 8, 1878, and Oct. 29, 1878. **$600+**

Heavyweight Champion can opener — Bill Griffiths wrote me about a *really rare* model of the above opener: instead of an eagle, it has a figure of the famous heavyweight champion boxer John L. Sullivan on top. Champion for an entire decade, 1882 to 1892, Sullivan fought the last bare knuckle title bout in 1888. This is probably a commemorative piece, either from 1888 or 1892. It's worth at least: **$1000+**

Can opener, cast iron, handle has cross-hatch knurling pattern like Disston tools, adjustable blade, no mark, maybe Disston, 5-1/2" L including blade, poss. #2080, pat'd April 19, 1887. **$18-$22**

VIII-8. Can openers. *Clockwise, starting at top:* **(1)** *Cast iron & steel, 2 handles, pushed into lid then rotated to cut off whole top. 10" L.* **(2)** *Cast iron & steel, sliding adjustment for blade, embossed "World's Best, Pittsburgh, PA," 6-3/4" L., pat'd 6/6/1899 by Frederick C. Smalstig, Allegheny, PA.* **(3)** *Cast iron & steel, (very like #2) marked on it: "U.S. Can Opener, Made in Pittsburgh PA, Pat'd May 7, 1895." 6" L. Collector Joe Young says this is a Smalstig & Mayer patent of 8/4/1896.* **(4)** *Cast iron, 2 pivoting handles. Poke tip in, swivel it around. Marked only "patent applied for." 7-3/4" L.* **(5)** *Nickel-plated cast iron, steel, 6-1/2" L, "The Safety," Coles' patent, 5/12/1914.* **(6)** *Cast iron, pointed tip at right was punched into can's top by tapping on little knob at other end with small hammer. 7-5/8" L. Unmarked, but identified as the Elgin Wood (Toronto, Canada) Wood (or Woodward?) patent, 8/19/1890. All six located by the Primitive Man, Bob Cahn, Carmel, NY.* (1) **$200**; (2) **$30-$40**;(3) **$40**; (4) **$40-$60**; (5) **$30-$40**; (6) **$40-$50**

VIII-9. Can openers. *From left* **(1)** *Most unusual is slingshot "Y." Steel, turquoise wood handle. 7-1/2" L. This had 2 different handle styles. Both marked "Pat. Pend."* **(2)** *To me, neatest is top combo: knife sharpener between eye-like wheels, glass cutter, can & jar or crown cap bottle opener.* **(3)** *Center, serpentine handle, painted cast iron, steel blade. "The Improved Peerless, Austria, U.S. Patent Pending."* **(4)** *Just below it, also with curved handle, is cast iron "Delmonico," with cross-hatched handle, pat'd 2/11/1890. by Schofield.* **(5)** *At right: simple fat wood handle, large blade, mfd. by Cassady-Fairbanks, Chicago.* **(6)** *Combo tool with circular jar wrench, mfd. by "J. C. Forster & Son, Pittsburgh." Pat'd 9/13/1910. 6-3/4" L.* **(7)** *Big blade & pivoting guide, shaped wood handle. Meant primarily for opening square or oblong cans, as of sardines. c. 1880s. Probably a Sprague variant, pat'd 7/21/1874. Collector Bill Griffiths has one with a cast iron loop handle. All Collection of Meryle Evans.* (1) **$10** ; (2) **$10**; (3) **$10-$15**; (4) **$15**; (5) **$20**; (6) **$20**; (7) **$30**

VIII-10. Can opener. *Cast iron mechanical type, with large turning screw something like Baumgartner opener. Spikes & blade underneath. Marked only "Pat. Appl. For" on handle. 7-1/2" L. This is either the patent of Oscar E. Braconier (Rockford, IL), 12/8/1908., or the Lyons patent of 12/4/1888, depending on who you ask! Collection of Peggy Wainscott.* **$100-$150**

VIII-11. Can opener. *The Baumgartner side cutter, pat'd in Canada, 1896. As shown 9-3/4" L. Ex-Keillor Family Collection. (A similar opener with 3 "ears" is marked "ABC PAT NOV 27, '94.")* **$120-$150**

Can opener, cast iron, adjustable blued steel blade, round ridged wheel with crosspieces (looks just like miniature steering wheel), center pin was punched into can's center, then cutting blade moved to position at edge of can — whatever the can's diameter (within reason). Name & date cast into crosspieces: "Hopper's Can Opener," about 4-3/8" diameter, marked "Pat. Dec. 22, 1896." This was Charles S. Hopper's first can opener patent. **$65-$85**

Can opener, cast iron, longer steel blade with greater adjustability, looks pretty much same as earlier version, slightly finer-looking casting of outer wheel-like ring with 4 "spokes" and sort of scalloped edges as if they were very worn gear teeth, marked on crosspieces "Hopper's Can Opener," with date, pat'd Oct. 3, 1899. This was Hopper's second patent. 4-1/2" diameter. Another (probably later version) is identical but for the marked snappy new name, "Safety First." Mfd. by Cuspidore Mfg. Co., Newark, NJ, and possibly others. **$50-$75**

Can opener, cast iron loopy handle with tool steel blade, "Peerless," 6-1/2" L, Schofield patent, Feb.11, 1890 (same patent date as "Delmonico"). (**Note:** the "Peerless" combo bottle & can openers/knife sharpeners below in "Combination tools" are a different patent.) (Another interesting note: Collector Alan Wilder has a can opener like this that definitely is marked "Fearless" and "Made in U.S.A." A mystery to investigate.) **$10-$15**

Can opener, cast iron, skinny short snake of curved metal with blade, with screwed on simple cutting blade, "The Delmonico," 7" L, pat'd Feb. 11, 1890 by Schofield (same date as one of "Peerless"). Collector Joe Young says the manufacturer probably tried to capitalize on the name of the popular NYC restaurant. He and his wife also have a champagne tap marked "The Delmonico." **$10-$15**

Can opener, cast iron, mechanical, "Bunker Clancy," late 19th or early 20th C. Please ID this for me if you can. **$7-$10**

Can opener, cast iron, mounted on its original card, "Vaughn's Safety Roll Junior," Chicago, IL, 20th C. **$8-$10**

Can opener, iron, with corkscrew, "Opens All," mfd. by Vaughan, 1930s. Just one of many Vaughn openers. **$8-$10**

Can opener, cast iron, openwork handle has sliding blade to adjust to different can sizes, "World's Best," Pittsburgh, PA, 6-3/4" L, pat'd June 6, 1899 by Frederick C. Smalstig, Allegheny, PA. Collector Bill Griffiths has this with 4 different logos. Very similar to the "U.S. Can Opener," and because both were made in Pittsburgh, probably one is an improvement or later edition of the other. **$30-$40**

Can opener, cast iron, sliding blade adjusts to fit different size cans, not very spectacular to look at, but still a nice one, "U.S. Can Opener," Pittsburgh, PA, 6" L, Smalstig patent, May 7, 1895. **$35-$40**

Can opener, cast iron ring, with ratchet clamp to hold can, separate cutter on another pivoting ring, long loopy handles, "Champion," maybe a Peterson patent (?), pat'd 1873. **$75-$100**

Can opener, cast iron; the knob at end opposite sharp pointed blade serves as place for tapping with hammer to drive point in before starting to cut, very graceful & interesting, unmarked, American, 7-5/8" L, late 19th C. **$30-$40**

Can opener, cast iron & tool steel, vertical mechanical type, 2 blades — one rounded, one straight for sardine cans, lever attaches to either of 2 pivot points, "Bleakley" (?) or "Blakesley" (?), American, about 16" to 18" H, pat'd May 1888 (?). Collector Bill Griffiths says it doesn't fit either Blakesley patent he knows — April 28, 1891, nor June 25, 1869. I don't have a picture, just notes from an antique show. I don't think this is a "phantom" can opener, and am listing it in hopes of clearing up mystery. **$120-$150**

Can opener, cast iron, has adjustable blade in sliding frame, big "nail head" or spike on end to pound hole into can top, and a great screw-action works, with rat-sized "Mickey Mouse" ears on a disc, "Baumgarten," American, 9-3/4" L, 1896. This description is from the only one I've handled — from the Keillor Family Collection — back in 1973, so I can't check. Collector Bill Griffiths writes: "A similar opener, with 3 'ears' on top is marked "ABC Pat Nov 27 '94." He says that a "Baumgartner" opener in his collection has part of a patent date near the center hub "Nov 2. . ..," and wonders if the ABC and this "Baumgartner/Baumgarten" patent are the same. **$130-$150**

Can opener, mechanical, cast iron, with handle something like a skillet handle, fitted onto end with a vertical screw, & several sharp points underneath, similar to the Baumgarten patent opener, only mark is "Pat Appl For," American, 7-1/2" L, c.1900. Lyons' patent, Dec. 4, 1888. **$100-$150**

Can opener, cast iron with gritty cast no-slip surface on handle, simple pointed blade, curved handle, no marks, 6-3/4" L, c.1900. **$10-$12**

VIII-12. Can opener. *Cast iron mechanical type. Looks like a Nardi steering wheel! Marked "Safety First." Mfd. by the Cuspidore Mfg. Co., Newark, NJ; there may have been other manufacturers too. This is Charles S. Hopper (Philadelphia, PA) second patent, of 10/31/1899. (Hopper's first patent was 12/12/1896.) 4 1/4" diameter. Collection of Peggy Wainscott.* **$70-$80**

VIII-13. Can opener. *Cast iron, "V" blade, cast eagle on top. This is a double opener — small short cans cut on side seen here; taller cans in the back. Snaky lever works small blade in front to open a tuna fish-size can. Large, heart-shaped blade in back. Only 7-1/2" H with 12" L lever. Pat'd by Chas. M. Williams, Bethel, KY, 1/8/1878. Collection of Meryle Evans.* **$600+**

VIII-14. Can opener patent. *Pat'd 5/29/1877 by David F. Fetter, NYC. A "pair of spring-pliers, with a slotted convex jaw, notched or serrated on either side of the slot, and pivoted therein; a curved blade having concave cutting-edge, terminating in an upwardly-turned point; the handles authoritatively thrown open by a spring, and held together, when not in use, by a wire loop at their extremities." Official Gazette. Compare this with the Wheeler Patent Co. opener in the next picture.* **$30-$40**

VIII-15. Can opener. *Cutlery steel blade, malleable iron handles, steel spring. Mfd. by Wheeler Patent Can Opener Co., St. Louis, MO, and introduced in mid 1890. Looks very like the Fetter patent. Makers claimed the Wheeler "is the only can opener that will cut off the top of paint pails. ... It cuts stove pipe, tin pipe, &c." Also cut square cans (center corned beef can below). The Metal Worker, 1890.* **$30**

VIII-16. Can opener. *One of three malleable cast iron openers pat'd 5/7/1889 by John Kaylor, assigned to G. W. Lehman, Decatur, IL. This is the Lehman No. 3. After point at bottom left side of ring is stuck into top of can near the edge, the opener is "pressed down upon the top of the can until the spur [blade] penetrates the top. Then the moving handle is rotated and the top is cut off." Mfd. by G. W. Lehman & Co., later Lehman, Bowman & Co. Their No. 1 and No. 2, with wingnuts on top, are seen in VIII-17.* **$80-$90**

VIII-17. Can openers. *Two Lehman top openers, with wingnuts, based on Kaylor patent of 5/7/1889. No. 1 (L) is at top of piece of stationery dated July 8, 1890,. No. 2 (R) appears on a business card. From photocopies of ephemera in the Phyllis & Jim Moffet collection. The ephemera almost as valuable as the real things.* **$70-$80**

VIII-18. Can opener patent. *Pat'd 8/30/1887 by William J. Hammer, Boston, MA. A "spring clasping-holder" with handle, and a "standard extending over the top with a pointed turning rod sliding through" it, and a "knife," with a blade at each end, moved by the turning handle above. Looks extremely efficient. Official Gazette.* **$40-$60**

VIII-19. Can opener patent. *Pat'd 12/29/1885 by Charles W. Acker, Watertown, NY. Patent application was accompanied by a patent model. This one includes a frame into which the can sits, while the blade is carried by a rotary ring above.* Official Gazette. **$40-$60**

VIII-20. Can opener patent. *Combined jar-wrench & can-opener, pat'd 6/9/1885 by Alexander Van Slyke, Fort Plain, NY. The wrench part is easy to see, but heaven knows how it cuts a can's top unless the handles are used like levers to advance the blade seen at the fulcrum. (More jar wrenches in Canning chapter.)* Official Gazette. **$10-$15**

VIII-22. Can opener. *Or* **tin opener,** *as it would be called in its native England. Cast iron, with looped tail. Spike & blade one piece of steel, adjustable or removable for cleaning. 6" L. 19th C. There are many variations on this — enough for a herd. Many have spikes cast as part of iron body, with adjustable blade (lower "jaw") of steel.* **$35-$60**

VIII-23. Can openers. *Cast iron fish.* **(T)** *adjustable blade & spike-in-one. Probably English. 5" L. Late 1800s.* **(B)** *well-defined scales and eye, original dark green paint. Only 4" L. Meant for opening sardine or herring tins. English. 3rd or 4th quarter 19th C.* **$70-$80; $90-$100**

VIII-21. Can opener patent model. *Cast iron, pat'd 11/15/1887 by Walter B. Nutter. Appears to fit over top of can, and worked with rotary motion. Pieces in foreground look like size adaptors — one on right may be a blade. Picture courtesy of the National Museum of American History, Smithsonian Institution. Possible value if opener was ever made: $200-$300. Value of patent model:* **$1000+**

Can opener, malleable cast iron with 2 long, openwork, two loopy pivoting handles, one has adjustable blade in it to fit the size of the can; poke tip in center, adjust blade to match the lid's radius, and while holding one handle stationary as a sort of lever against which you can push, you swivel the other handle with the cutting blade around, American, 7-3/4" L, marked "patent applied for," late 1880s. See next two entries. **$30-$40**

Malleable cast iron — I feel uncomfortable using this term without a clear understanding of how to look at something and know if it's plain cast pig iron or malleable cast iron. The latter has less carbon in it than pig iron but more than wrought iron, and is extremely "malleable" or workable by hammering or rolling. When I have found documentation for an object, such as an ad, booklet or flyer, and the metal is described as "malleable cast iron," I have added it to the description (of what I count as only 11 pieces in this whole book). One source describes it as an "alloy of steel." Another has a simple definition that states that, "Malleable iron is able to be shaped or formed by hammering or pressure." An editorial answer to query in the May 31, 1890 *Metal Worker*, says that, "The work of making malleable iron castings necessarily involves considerable time, and they cannot be turned out with the rapidity of gray castings." This was to explain the higher cost. The most important aspect when using malleable cast iron for a can opener that had to be tapped into the can lid, is that it can keep its strength and integrity when subjected to "hammering or pressure." Therefore, an object with a lever action, for example, could hold up well without fracturing like ordinary cast iron might, and without tending to bend, as some wrought iron might if the pressure were great enough. An economic advantage is that casting is cheaper than forging, and scrap is an integral part of the alloy. Many, probably most, of modern objects made of cast iron, unless otherwise noted, are made with re-founded scrap cast iron. This scrap, which is composed in great part of old cracked car engine blocks, will not be "picked over" before founding, and so will also contain small quantities of aluminum and brass.

Can opener, malleable cast & sheet iron, with 2 openwork "loop" handles, opposite each other on the outside of the cutting blade, a full circle of sharpened iron, push down circular blade on can lid & rotate entire opener, while pushing downward, no mark, but surely the one mfd. by Lehman, Bolen & Co., of Decatur, IL, 10" L, advertised c.1890 as their "No. 3," so fits with the John Kaylor patent date of May 7, 1889. **$80-$90**

Can opener, malleable cast iron, with 2 pivoting loopy handles — upper one with steel cutting blade that you push in circle around can top, with lower ring as guide, the other handle, which is attached to a ring-shaped piece that roughly fits within top of can, has a point at end opposite handle. That pointed piece is a punch for puncturing the can top to start the cutting and to hold the can. Ad copy says this is a "double lever patent can opener & holder, combined. You hold the can firm with one handle, while you cut the top out with one stroke with the other." A little rickety — from age or imperfect manufacture, but terrific looking. ads identify this as "Lehman #9," mfd. by G. W. Lehman & Co. (later? Lehman, Bolen & Co.), Decatur, IL, 8-1/2" L with ring 3-1/4" diameter, no mark except John Kaylor patent date, May 7, 1889. **$80-$90**

Can opener, countertop for restaurant, cast iron with deep-blue painted spool-like wooden handle, "Heavy Duty Can Opener, No. A-123," also No. 134, mfd. by Dazey Churn Co., St. Louis, MO, 12-1/2" H x 11-1/2" W, 20th C. **$40-$60**

VIII-24. Advertisement. *Franco-American can shows one version of a can ready-made for easier opening. One tactic used to complement the search for better can openers was to make cans themselves easier to open.* Century, *5/1893.*

VIII-25. Can opener. *"Best Yet," mfd. by Hasbrouck Alliger, NYC, pat'd 7/29/1890. Malleable iron, steel blade. Point is driven into the top near center, then it's levered down to almost horizontal position to force chisel-like blade into rim. Then, holding the two parts firmly in the right hand, while holding the can in the left, one "carries the two handles around in a circle" as one either cuts off one's left thumb or the can's lid. Alliger claimed "It is so shaped that the blade will not work up, and [it] has no thumbscrew ... but fastens in the desired place by an automatic lock."* The Metal Worker, *8/30/1890.* **$20-$30**

VIII-26. Can opener. (T) *"The Acme," mfd. by the Goodell Co., Antrim, NH. "The blade is alluded to as being made of extra quality steel, and not to be confounded with the Cheap John affairs, of which there are many. ... It is designed to open any shaped can; to cut close to the edge, allowing the contents to be removed without breaking. The bend in the blade allows the handle to come down on the outside of the can, to secure a long leverage and a long cut." Wooden handle. Made by one of the best companies, so it probably was good.* The Metal Worker, *7/5/1890.* **(M)** *The "Stand-by," steel blade riveted on, not adjustable. c.1899.* **(B)** *"Peerless," pat'd 2/11/1890, by Scofield. An editorial note in* House Furnishing Review, *1/1903, stated "This is truly an age of little conveniences and ... here is one of those little devices that save the housewife time and trouble, and probably her husband much profanity." Nickel-plated, cutlery steel blade riveted to loop handle, toothed gripper "to prevent slipping."* **$15-$25; $5-$10; $5-$10**

Can opener, crowing rooster, cast iron, American, 20th C. $15-$20

Can opener, fish, cast iron, blade set in with screw to remove for sharpening, English, 5" L, late 19th C. $70-$80

Can opener, fish, like a sardine, with slender slightly curved body, dark-green-painted cast iron, very exaggerated and beautiful scales & front fins, gills bold too, large ring around eyes (where blade can be unscrewed for cleaning or sharpening), rather small tail ending in large ball, no mark, English, 4" L, c.1870s. $90-$100

Can opener, flat wood handle, brass ferrule, marked "T N & S," English, 6-1/2" L, turn of century. $15-$20

Can opener, flat wood handle, bulbous head, brass ferrule, marked on cutting blade, "Wynn & Timmins," English, 6" L, c.1900. $15-$20

Can opener, flat-sided shaped wood handle that's flat sided — probably flattened after turning on lathe, steel blade, "Midget," American, 6-1/8" L, (another reported was only 5-3/4" L), White & Winkler patent, July 19, 1904. $10-$18

Can opener — called a **sardine opener**, for sardine cans, tempered tool steel blade in turned wooden handle, with distinctive & typical sardine-opener's long evil-looking blade, prob. American, about 8" L, 1870s. (Some sardine openers have a scissor action, and have a leaf spring between the two handles to facilitate cutting.) $15-$22

Can opener, sort of like sardine [can] shears, a levered, 2-handle iron & steel cutter that gnawed its way through the tin after starter hole was made, tension of handles achieved with leaf spring. They claimed it could be used for cutting stove pipe also. Wheeler Patent Can Opener Co., St. Louis, MO, introduced 1890. $15-$22

Can opener, green enameled wood handles, one to hold, one to turn, steel mechanism & blade, "Edlund Junior," mfd. by Edlund Co., Burlington, VT, 6-1/4" L, pat'd April 21, 1925, May 12, 1925, June 18, 1929. $12-$18

Can opener, hardened steel hooked blade, simple turned wood handle, ferrule, "Handy," mfd. by Handy Things Mfg. Co., Ludington, MI, Franken patent, June 11, 1895. $12-$15

Can opener, iron, "The Jewel." Found with several different logos. Pat'd July 10, 1923. $15-$18

Can opener, iron, "Lowe," early 20th C (?). $8-$10

Can opener, iron, loop-handled, with corkscrew folded inside handle, "Dixie," 1930s. $4-$10

Can opener, iron, with gears, "Enbay," early 20th C. (?) $20-$35

Can opener, iron with wood handle, "Clean Cut," early 20th C. (?) $8-$12

Can opener, iron & wood, "A & J Miracle," Binghamton, NY, 6-1/4" L, 1930s. The all metal one is slightly less. $10-$12

Can opener, nickeled steel shaft, tempered steel blade, turned wood handle, "A & J," Edward Katzinger Co., Chicago, IL, 8-1/2" L, 1940. $12-$15

Can opener, metal, with little lifting spout slightly inset to catch drips, "For Karo Cans Only," very small, pat'd 1935. $10-$15

Can opener, nickel-plated iron, very modern-looking, with graceful curve, & relatively big head, "The Safety" marked on end of handle, American, 6-1/2" L, Cole's patent, May 12, 1914. $30-$40

VIII-27. Can opener. *"Handy," made of hardened steel, for round or square cans. An "improved" version of original pat'd 6/11/1895., by Robert Franken, Pico Heights, CA. Mfd. by Handy Things Mfg. Co., Ludington, MI, and sold originally for only a nickel!* House Furnishing Review, *1/1903. It's sometimes marked, sad to say, "KKK" — for Kalifornia Kan Kutter.* $8-$12

Can opener, pistol-shaped, loop handle, cast iron, adjustable steel blade, American, 8-1/4" L diagonally, Way & Clarke patent, Mar. 9, 1886. $80-$100

Can opener, plated & black painted cast iron, adjustable, long shaft with round head with 3 big ribs, "ABC," 7" L in closed up position, 9-1/2" L fully extended, Blen patent, Nov. 27, 1894. $120-$150

Can opener, rearing horse, cast iron, American, 20th C. $40-$55

Can opener, screw clamps on shelf or table edge, nickeled iron works with horizontal gears, blue wood knob, "Blue Streak," Turner & Seymour Mfg. Co., Torrington, CT, 4" H x 7" L, pat'd Oct. 1, 1921, Aug. 8, 1922, & Apr. 10, 1923. Sold into 1930s. Patented 7 years before 1st wall mount opener. $20-$30

Can opener, several small triangular steel blades to puncture can, turned wood handle with mushroom-like knob, J. Kaufman, NYC, NY, 6" L x 3-1/4" diameter, Kaufman patent, Sept. 6, 1870. $85-$125

Can opener, skeletal steel frame, point at smaller end for sticking in center of can, then the cutting blade can be moved along slide of shaft to fit can's radius, then whole thing is rotated to cut off most of lid, marked on sliding blade part "Hercules" with Hawks' patent date, Aug. 12, 1902. (See the "Peerless" openers too.) I wonder what the tetanus or botulism death rates were when such openers were in wide use? At least nobody trade-named an opener "The Lockjaw." $15-$20

VIII-28. Can opener. *"Hercules" — "A Giant of Strength." Pat'd 8/12/1902, by M. L. Hawks. Skeletal steel with adjustable blade position. Manufacturer unknown.* House Furnishing Review, *2/1904.* $10-$12

VIII-29. Can openers. (T) *all-metal loop handle version of the "Never Slip" — one of many similar openers meant to give a good grip and a leveraged cutting angle. Browne & Benton patent, 5/17/1892;* **(M)** *simple all steel "King" combo corkscrew & can opener. A cheaper version of it (not shown) is the "Dean."* **(B)** *wooden handled "Improved" version. All in April 1905 catalog of Joseph Breck & Sons, Boston.* $10-$15; $5-$10; $5-$10

VIII-30. Can openers. *Variety, some all metal, some with wooden handles — all made by same company, W. G. Browne Mfg. Co., Kingston, NY, who also made ice picks, potato mashers, tack hammers & "The Cyclone" eggbeater.* **(T)** *"The Shear Cut Clipper;"* **(M-1)** *"None Such" with crown cap opener (Browne's best seller — "The Best" — opened crown caps & corks too. It looks like the "None Such" except there's a bottle cap hook on top.)* **(M-2)** *all metal one with a tack puller;* **(B)** *"IXL." House Furnishing Review,10/1902. (Note: There's a "Clipper" patent from 1926, but this one was pictured & named 24 years earlier.)* **$10-$20**

VIII-32. Can opener. *"Joy" — "One Shove Does the Act" (sounds like a "Columbo" episode!). Metal with wooden grip. If kept sharp, it probably worked very well. Mfd. by Beveridge Mfg. Co., Baltimore, where tin-canning got started a 150 years ago. House Furnishing Review, 2/1915.* **$15-$25**

VIII-31. Can opener. *"Sure Cut," long shank with sliding blade, wooden handle, for round & square cans. Pat'd 7/19/1904. by White & Winkler. Mfd. by Ira F. White & Son, Newark, NJ. Came in several different sizes. House Furnishing Review, 5/1906.* **$5-$12**

VIII-34. Can openers shown closed & open. *(T-1, T-2) combined with a bottle opener, "Peerless," nickeled carbon steel, turned wood handle enameled black. (B-1, B-2) the "So-Easy." Houck patent. Mfd. by Hardware Specialty Mfg. Co., Chicago, IL. House Furnishing Review, 1/1914.* **$8-$12**

VIII-35. Can opener. *"Slick-Ope," very similar to "Sure Cut" in VIII-31. Adjustable, sliding blade on shank has locking device. Pat'd 11/1/1910., by Hall. Mfd. by Irwin Mfg. Co., NYC. House Furnishing Review,1915.* **$8-$12**

VIII-33. Can opener. *"Stork" combo can opener & jar sealer. All metal. Consists of a movable slide inserted in a handle. One side has flanges to grip the jar top when lever in handle is pressed. Mfd. by The Stork Mfg. Co., Dayton, OH. House Furnishing Review, 5/1905.* **$5-$10**

Can opener, steel blade & malleable cast iron, 2 parts, with long handle & toothed piecc, plus a shorter handle with chisel-like blade. The tip of long piece is stuck into middle of can, then the chisel blade is moved along the teeth until the blade lines up with edge of can. It is then stuck into can top at edge, and pushed down to lock into position. Then it is pulled around the can top, presumably while turning the can counterclockwise with left hand. Could be used only with right hand, and does not live up to name at all. "Best Yet," Hasbrouck Alliger, NYC, NY, pat'd Jul. 29, 1890. **$20-$30**

Can opener, steel, long black painted wooden handle, "Sterling," 7-1/2" L, Duncan patent Aug. 26, 1902. **$15-$18**

Can opener, steel, of type sold at the grocery now, a real cheapo type that actually works well, "Tilt-Top O-Matic," American, 3" L, c.1920. **$4-$7**

Can opener, steel with turned wood handle, brass ferrule, riveted 2-part blade with snub "nose" marked "ERIE, 227,761." Mfd. by Griswold Mfg. Co., Erie, PA, c.1930s according to David Smith, but the number, which looks like a patent number, would date it to 1880, and it looks like can openers from the latter part of the 19th C. **$150-$175**

Can opener, steel with turned wood handle, and sliding piece on shaft, "Vulcan Cut Can & Bottle Opener," American, 8-7/8" L, 1910. **$12-$18**

Can opener, steel, wood handle, "Sure Cut," came in several sizes, White & Winkler patent, 7/19/1904. **$5-$12**

Can opener, steel & wood, mark on blade is a small diamond with "SR" inside, also a shield that says "Our Label" above it, and "M. P. B. D. BM. & S. W. U. of N. A." which John Lambert, a few years ago, guessed might stand for "Massachusetts Professional Bottlers and Professional Bottle-Makers Brotherhood & Skilled Workers Union of North America." Inside is motto "Unity, Mutual Assistance and Education." Marked by manufacturer's (?) name: "S. Richard, Southbridge, MA," 5-7/8" L, late 19th C. Collector Bill Griffiths has two, only one with the shield & initials. Possibly Richard made them for different groups? **$20-$28**

Can opener, tinned or nickel-plated steel with turned wooden handle, painted turquoise (some found with clear lacquered finish), shaped like a slingshot "Y," 7-1/2" L, marked "Pat. Pend." — prob. 1930s. **$10-$15**

Can opener, unusual 2 steel blades, deep V-shape, fitted to horizontal suitcase grip turned wood handle, the whole thing pushed into top of can, "One shove does the act," as the ad said. "This is not the usual or average cheap 'cut around the edges' can opener or one that 'pulls around in a circle.' The Joy Can Opener cuts out a complete circle with one shove or one downward pressure and leaves a tiny part of the opening uncut, which acts as a hinge, so that the cutout part can be pressed back again, for a covering." "Joy Can Opener," mfd. by W. E. Beveridge Mfg. Co., Baltimore, MD, not adjustable for different size cans, would make cut about 4" diameter, c.1915. **$40-$50**

Can opener, wall mounted, "Dazey," by churn company, St. Louis, 20th C. **$10-$12**

Can opener punch, red & yellow painted wood bottle-shaped tool with little metal punch to open can, "Pet Milk Irradiated Can Opener," 4" L, early 20th C. See? People could have had to worry about "irradiated" food 50 or so years ago, but then it seemed healing, magic. I wouldn't eat it if you paid me. **$8-$15**

VIII-36. Can openers. *Two with fat wood handles.* (**T**) *is marked* "TN & S." *6" L.* (**B**) *Bulbous one marked on steel cutting blade* "Wynn & Timmins," *6-1/2" L. English, early 20th C.* **$15-$20**

VIII-38. Can opener. *The "P-38," U.S. Army issue. Steel, hinged triangular blade. Stamped "USA Shelby Corp." 1-1/2" L. According to Joe Young, this was first pat'd in 1886., although that seems very early. During WWII they were sold to the Government by the barrel. (In the 1935 Thomas' Register of American Manufacturers, a hinge company, Shelby Metal Products Co., Shelby, OH, was listed — perhaps it's the one, that by WWII became Shelby Corp.) Collection of Jim Holroyd, Oregon.* **$3-$6**

VIII-37. Can openers. (**L**) *"Blue Streak" shelf-clamp opener. Nickeled steel, blue wood knob, household size: about 4" H. Pat'd early '20s.* (**R**) *"Hotel Blue Streak," with metal stake & adjustable platform to support large heavy cans, about 7" L (plus crank). Mfd. by Turner & Seymour Mfg. Co., Torrington, CT, 1920s. Illustrations from c.1927 S. Joseph catalog of kitchen & bar wares.* **$20-$50**

VIII-39. Can opener. *Edlund Jr., steel, painted wood handle. Made over many years, and 1930 version almost exactly same as this 1944 version. Substantial, works great, not too sanitary. Lots of handle variants.* **$5-$15**

Combination tools — mainly bottle and can openers and cork-screws, with a variety of extras: knives, glass cutters, jiggers, etc. It was a popular concept by inventor, manufacturer and marketer to combine as many things as possible in order to increase opportunities for sales. Some of the wildest patents in the history of the U.S. Patent Office are combinations (many include beds!): combined bedstead, chair, secretary & wardrobe; combined call bell & slop jar; combined birdhouse & clothesline support; churn & washing machine; headrest & umbrella; etc.

Bottle opener & cake server combined, possibly for weddings? wire and sheet metal, the most peculiar combination ever, 11-5/8" L, pat'd Nov. 24, 1914. **$35-$40**

Bottle opener & can opener combo, fish, cast metal, adv'g "C. G. Richardson Oils, Gas & Machinery," Patten, ME, late 19th C. **$30-$45**

Bottle opener & corkscrew combo, adv'g "Green River Whiskey," 20th C. **$15-$20**

Bottle opener, knife sharpener & glass cutter combo, cast iron, "Apex," c.1900. **$8-$15**

Bottle opener & slotted spoon combo, wire & sheet metal, 10-1/2" L, pat'd Feb. 23, 1915. **$15-$22**

Bottle opener & spoon-stirrer combo, iron, "Firestone." **$5-$10**

Bottle opener, wrench & meat cleaver combo, iron, "Kitchen Klever Kleever," American, I'm sure. Late 19th, early 20th C. As in Leave it to Klever Kleever — a short of homey horror show. **$20-$30**

Bottle & can opener, steel with black painted wooden handle, "Peerless," 8-3/4" L, Houck patent, Oct. 29, 1912. **$12-$20**

Bottle & can opener & knife sharpener combo, cast iron, exaggerated fish-bird fantasy shape (as if drawn by abstract artist), "Peerless," 6-1/2" L, pat'd Aug. 12, 1902, Mar. 31, 1903. **$15-$20**

Bottle & can opener, knife sharpener, glass cutter combined, cast & sheet iron, long & very neat with 2 knife-sharpening emory wheels at one tip, the eyes of an insect, less like a fish than the other combo openers, this is like a 6-1/2" length of backbone, "The Improved Peerless," Austria, "patent pending" in U. S., probably after 1903. **$12-$20**

Well? What is it? The next listing is here because it is a constant source of disagreement. Mostly the arguments are about whether these have a "can opener" in their repertory. I maintain they do, using advertising of the period; collector Bill Griffiths says categorically "This is not a can opener." Collector Joe Young argues that what I've called a "putty knife" (based on ads) is really a "can opener" (which also appears in the ads).

Bottle & can opener, knife sharpener & glazier's tool combined, mostly cast iron, American, 5-1/2" L, pat'd June 8, 1869 by S. G. Monce, Bristol, CT as a "Glass-cutting tool." Monce later patented another "glazier's tool" July 1, 1973. The late Marion Levy led me to this idea. He identified the parts, left to right: tiny roundel glass cutter at tip, tapper, 2 nippers (top edge), knife sharpener, putty knife with spacer pins, and corkscrew to pull cork on linseed oil bottle to be mixed with whiting to make the putty. But then the putty may also by then have come in a can, so . . .? Combo can opener/ knife sharpeners were also patented by F. W. Echternach & M. J. Welch of Philadelphia, 2/6/1872 with the added feature of a "fork cleaner"; and S. C. Stokes, Manchester, NH, 2/15/1872. **$12-$20**

Bottle opener, can opener & corkscrew combined, also knife sharpener & glass cutter, cast iron, American, pat'd Aug. 17, 1875 by Woodward, as marked on frame. This is especially interesting because of the tiny peggy "feet" underneath the neck of the "arrowhead" blade and at the other end too. This combo tool is a mirror image, almost, of one in previous entry, and is owned by collector John Lambert. **$20-$35**

Bottle & can opener, corkscrew, glass cutter, knife sharpener combination, cast iron, with wire screw, no marks, English. 5-1/2" L, late 19th C. Evan Perry, author of a Shire Album book, *Corkscrews & Bottle Openers* (see bibliography), said about a similar multipurpose tool that it was "the nastiest corkscrew ever issued." (His example was very like this, except that it also had a screw gauge and a 3" ruler, was 6-1/2" L, and had a British patent.) **$20-$30**

VIII-41. Combined can & crown cap opener. *"Nuform," carbon steel & cocobolo wood handle, modern beveled design. Its makers, The Lo-Vis Co., Kalamazoo, MI, were given the Good Housekeeping Seal of Approval. House Furnishing Review, 1/1917. Probably went out of business during war, or turned to making other things.* **$5-$8**

VIII-40. Combination can openers. *From top:* **(1)** *Can opener, crown cap opener & -?-, wood handle, c.1930.* **(2)** *Small c. 1915 "Norlunds 3-in-1" with knife sharpener wheels center shaft, broad head to tap other end into can.* **(3)** *Wide nickeled "Ten-in-One," mfd. by New Jersey Patent Novelty Co., c.1910. It scales fish, opens bottles, slices carrots, severs twine, chops veggies, does screwdriver duty, and more.* **$10-$20**

VIII-42. Combination can opener. *Scissor model pictured. A bottle opener & knife sharpener combo tool made by The Boye Needle Co. (whose nutmeg grater is more notable). Pat'd 9/10/1912 and 18/12/1913. (Although an ad shows a different date: 12/16/1917). This is a little double-sided printed flyer that was sent out with the products. A non-scissors model from Boye bears patent dates 8/19/1913 and 5/6/1920.* **$20-$30**

Bottle & can opener, knife sharpener combined, hooked iron blade with knife sharpener sticking up sort of like wings above, wood handle, Boye Needle Co., Chicago, about 7-1/2" L, pat'd Sept. 10, 1912 & Dec. 18, 1917 (?). One Bill Griffiths has has the Sept 1912 date, also "Aug. 12, 1913." He also has a different-looking Boye, with dates Aug. 19, 1913 (Morrell patent), Apr. 6, 1920, and June 15, 1920. Boye made nutmeg graters, apple corers, screwdrivers & various needles, and still makes crochet hooks, etc. **$20-$30**

Bottle & can opener, knife sharpener combined, steel, "Norlunds 3-in-1," O. A. Norlund, Williamsport, PA, 4-1/2" L, c.1915. **$15-$18**

Bottle & can opener, knife sharpener combo, wood handle, iron top, "Sharp Easy," Premier Mfg. Co., Detroit, MI, pat'd 1922. **$18-$25**

Bottle & can opener, corkscrew, fork combination, iron, marked "B.M. Shipman Importer New York," and "Bon Accord Mackerel" "Bon Accord Herring," 6-1/4" L, American, c.1900. **$20-$30**

Bottle & can opener combined tool, with fish scaler, screwdriver, chopper, carrot slicer, etc., steel, "Ten-In-One," New Jersey Patent Novelty Co., Passaic, NJ, 7-1/2" L, c.1900. Extremely clumsy & weird; if Evan Perry ever saw this one, I'm sure he'd say that *it* was the "nastiest" combo tool he'd ever seen. And it doesn't do windows, because there's no glass cutter on it! **$12-$15**

Bottle & can opener combination, nickeled steel parts riveted together, corkscrew secured in looped handle, hook to remove crown caps, "Yankee," pat'd Jan. 28, 1902 and Dec. 26, 1906, Taylor Mfg. Co., Hartford, CT. Looks very like the "Best" by W. G. Browne. **$1-$3**

Bottle & jar opener, sheet steel, "4-in-1," J. C. Forster & Son, Pittsburgh, PA, about 6-3/4" or 7" L, pat'd Sept. 13, 1910. **$15-$22**

Bottle opener & corkscrew combined, nickeled steel, looks sort of like can opener except the cap-lifter part isn't at all sharp, screw folds within open loop handle, pat'd by H. A. Chippendale, American, turn of century. **$125-$150**

Bottle opener & corkscrew combined, Volstead figural, shape of stern top-hatted man (**Andrew Volstead**, who authored the **Prohibition Act**) with beaky nose, black hat, huge shoes, clasped hands, corkscrew pivots up out of tail coat in back, now and piece on chest are bottle opener, hat comes off and reveals small space — for a jigger of liquor (?), base marked "Old Snifter," mfd. by Demley, American, c.1919 to 1933 (period of Prohibition). Many corkscrews incorporated Volstead's caricatured image. **$175-$250**

VIII-43. Combined can & bottle openers. (T) *8" L, a 2-way type with sliding knife on long shank.* **(B)** *6-1/2" L. Nickeled metal & painted handles in choice of green, yellow, red, green with ivory band, and yellow with blue band. Washburn Co., "Androck" line catalog, 1936.* **$5-$10**

VIII-44. Combination novelty glazier's tool. *This one happens to be the Monce patent of 6/7/1869. It's 5-1/2" L and is complete as shown. According to the late Marion Levy, whose apple parers appear elsewhere in this book, from L to R are glass cutter roundel, tapper, 2 nippers (for edge of glass), knife sharpening stone, corkscrew for pulling linseed oil bottle cork, and at end, the arrowhead shape, putty knife with "two spacer bars." Almost identical are the "Excelsior Glazing Tool," which called the arrowhead-shaped end a "putty knife;" the "Centennial Combination Tool," with glass cutter, knife sharpener, can opener, wrench, tack hammer, tack puller, screw driver and needle straightener." Both made by the New England Novelty Works, F. R. Woodward, proprietor, Hill, NH. These, and two other products (viz. "Our Household Tool" had the "arrowhead" as an ice pick and a can opener), had glass cutting element patented by Woodward on Aug. 24, 1875. Another variant was a cast iron can opener, knife sharpener & polisher, called a "Centennial Novelty," but pat'd four years before: (2/6/1872) by F. W. Echternach & M. J. Welch, Philadelphia. Yet another is depicted in a novelty catalog aimed at traveling salesmen, c.1880. It is a more streamlined version based on Clark's glass cutter patent, called a "Combination Novelty Tool," consisting of glass cutter (which could be used as a paper pattern cutter too), scissors & knife sharpener, glass nippers, can opener (the "arrowhead"), and graduated wrench (the long slot in the center).* **$20-$40**

VIII-45. Cork-pulling appliance patent. *Pat'd 12/2/1890 by Alfred J. Parker, NYC. Composed of a flexible strap (to put foot through) passed through a "flexible yoke" (spoked piece lower right) with a hole in center for the bottle's neck. The appliance was to be used to aid the person pulling the cork by holding the bottle secure. I doubt if it was ever produced. Official Gazette.*

VIII-46. Cork-extractor patent. *Pat'd 8/9/1881 by Frederick Mann, Milwaukee, WI. A tubular sheet metal handle with long slot. Cap at left is removed & the vertical slender arm or rod on left is taken out from inside tube, passed through the slot, and cap is somehow used to fix it to tubular handle. The right arm "pivots and swings" or can be made to be detachable and kept inside also. If this looks feasible to you, you must be knocking the tops off bottles to open them now. Official Gazette. If it exists, the value should be quite high because of construction and material.* **$30-$45**

Bottle opener, corkscrew & jigger combined, chromed brass, handle unscrews to reveal screw & bottle opener, Chase Brass & Copper, with centaur logo, Waterbury, CT, 1930s. Chase's flashy Deco home bar products (ice buckets, shakers, trays, etc.) and other kitchen-related things, are a popular separate field for collectors. Not all bright chromed cocktail accessories are Chase. West Bend, Farberware, Manning-Bowman, and a Canadian company, whose name I don't know, made similar wares. **$15-$20**

Can opener & corkscrew combined, nickeled steel, screw folds up into space between handle loop, a style commonly seen today, & prob. being made from original design, "Browne Line None Such," mfd. by The Browne & Dowd Mfg. Co., Meriden, CT, Fenn patent, Nov. 3, 1908. The **trade name** situation a century ago was quite different from today's and several companies might use the same or similar names, for all kinds of products. "None Such" was a popular name — like "Uneek," "Non Pareil," "Ne Plus Ultra," "Best Yet," "None Better," etc., — and was used by at least five companies for such widely different products as blankets, mince meat, canned corn (see the Lehman Can Opener picture), can openers, and chain pumps, to name a few! **$12-$15**

Can opener & jar wrench combined, sheet steel, "4-in-1," mfd. by J. C. Forster & Son, Pittsburgh, PA, about 6-3/4" or 7" L, Forster patent, Sept. 13, 1910. **$20-$22**

Corkscrew, buttonhook & pick combined, steel frame, folding tool in harp, French or English, 3-1/2" L, 19th C. **$20-$30**

Corkscrew & cork combined, cork with wire passed through the cork from top to bottom, bent at ends, not as airtight as needed for wine, probably, invented by William H. Towers, poss. mfd. by The Union Pin Mfg. Co., Boston, MA, 1862. Towers also invented a machine for opening oysters, a new kind of broom, and a straight pin that wouldn't fall out. **$8-$15**

Corkscrew & jigger combined, Volstead figural of the Senator, "Old Snifter" with beaky nose, corkscrew pivots up in front when head is turned, hat comes off as jigger, "Old Snifter," mfd. by Neghaur, NYC, NY, c.1919 to 1933 (era of Prohibition). **$175-$250**

Cork, which grows principally in Spain, Portugal, Algeria and other Mediterranean countries, is not wood per se, but the bark of an evergreen oak, *Quercus suber*. A cork tree reaches sufficient maturity after 15 years that two or three inches of its thick bark can be stripped off without killing the tree! After eight more years, another "crop" is ready, and this harvesting can go on for 80 or more years. Cork has been used since ancient times — but not always for stopping up bottles and jars. All the writers on corkscrews speculate on just how long "corks" have been used — thus necessitating all sorts of cork cutters, compressors, drivers, and extractors, including corkscrews or bottlescrews. Tools are only needed for *really* tight-fitting corks, and it is hard to know how early cork's great compressibility was taken advantage of. A fascinating article appeared in the January 21, 1854 issue of Great Britain's *Chamber's Journal,* in which the author relates a story told by the ancient Roman natural historian, Pliny the elder, about a Roman courier who escaped the Gauls by putting pieces of cork under his arms and swimming the Tiber River. He further writes, "The ancients kept their wine in casks and jars which were stopped with pitch, clay, gypsum, potter's earth, and other substances; and the wine was drawn from these vessels into open cups or pitchers, which were brought to table; but when, in the fourteenth century, it became customary to keep wine in small bottles, then did also become prevalent the method of securing these bottles with small bits of cork-bark, which bits very soon acquired the name of corks. . . . it is very compressible and elastic; and it is easily cut — hence cork possesses remarkable qualities for bottle-stoppers." [Vol. I, No. 3.] But another writer, Henning Webb Prentis, Jr., in his 1939 Newcomen address on Armstrong cork, contradicts the *Chamber's* article. "The poet, Horace, is quoted as having told a friend, about 25 B.C., that on the occasion of a coming anniversary banquet he expects to 'remove the cork sealed with pitch' from a jar of a rare vintage of forty-six years earlier."

Old Corks — A long article in *The Metal Worker,* Aug. 5, 1882, on the secondhand bottle market in America, includes some new (to me) information on corkselling. "That bottles should be used again is not so much of a wonder when considered, but that old corks should be is something to marvel at. In a low, wooden building in Mulberry street old corks are made 'as good as new.' This is the only place in New York where they are dealt in. The dealer buys the corks by the barrel, and pays from $1 to $3. His trade is mostly in champagne corks. The best and cleanest of these he sorts out and sells to American champagne makers [who, the article explains, also bought used foreign champagne bottles, being unable at that time to make them strong enough in America]. The bottom of the cork where the first bottler's brand appears is shaved off and the name of the second stamped on them. These corks were cut expressly for champagne bottles, and as they can be bought much more cheaply than new ones, the bottlers purchase them. The old cork dealers obtain 25 cents a dozen for them, and make a handsome profit.

"The broken and dirty corks go through a peculiar process. They are first subjected to a sort of Turkish bath to clean them, and after they are dried are cut down. They are put in a machine and turned, while a sharp knife runs across them and takes off a portion. They can be cut to any size, and with the solid surface removed look as bright as when new. The corks cut down are purchased by root beer and soda water makers, who use smaller bottles. They can save a considerable amount by purchasing old corks, which, as it is easy to see, will do as well as new ones. The 'old cork man' is rushed with business. The champagne and root beer and soda water bottles take all the corks that he can furnish. He gets his supply at the hotels and elsewhere. . . . No demand has yet developed for small corks. The druggists are compelled to use new corks, but the dealer talking on the subject thought that manufacturers of ink, mucilage and the like, might use old corks as well as not." I wish the article had mentioned what they did about corkscrew holes.

Corking apparatus — "We have recently seen in the [NYC] House-furnishing establishment of J. H. Baldwin, a German contrivance for compressing the corks in bottling. It is essentially a conical tube with a plunger. The apparatus is set upon the neck of a bottle, the plunger lifted, and a cork introduced at the opening [partway down the tube]. The cork drops into the cavity which tapers downwards; it is lined with metal. By striking upon the top of the plunger with a mallet, the cork is driven downwards, and so much compressed in its passage, that it enters the neck of the bottle with ease. Good corks should be procured and soaked in warm water, to render them pliant, and then be pressed and driven in with a wooden driver; a flat piece of heavy wood or a mallet will answer. In filling the bottle it should not be so full that the cork will touch the liquid, as the bottle will be broken in driving the cork. there should be a space of an inch or more between the surface of the liquid and the bottom of the cork; this will prevent breaking." Editor, "The Household," *American Agriculturist,* August 1870. **Refer to these instructions for the next six $ listings.**

Cork drawer — See cork puller or drawer

Cork driver or corking press, turned wood (looks sort of like a nautical belaying pin), 2-part, with copper insert in bottom tapered part, opening is fitted over bottle with a soaked cork put in the side opening, not marked, 10-1/4" L when completely closed, German (?) late (?)19th C. Similar drivers still being made in Germany. **$150-$225**

Cork driver, turned wood with beautiful patina, metal lined, has four sections, including the plunger rod with its fat wood knob, so the appearance is confusable because it looks like a whimsy, a toy or a musical percussion instrument. About 9" L, late 19th C. **$250-$350**

Cork driver or corking press, turned walnut with simple shape, arched opening in side, tapered "chute" partially copper lined, marked "F. Amos," 10-1/4" L, English (?), mid 19th C. **$275-$325**

Cork driver, turned wood with great patina, overall bottle shape, wide cavity opening, stamped on side "The Star" "John Summer's Patent," late 19th C. **$200-$250**

Cork driver, turned wood, highly polished finish, "Best Star of Bottling," John Sommers, Newark, NJ, 11-3/4" L unextended, pat'd Aug. 25, 1885. **$155-$200**

Cork driver or bottle corker, turned wood, non-bulbous plunger top — actually it's shaped like a tapered cork, very graceful reeding. Bottom of plunger has screw-on pewter cap, tapered interior is brass lined. 12" L extends to 17", German, c.1870s. **$175-$225**

Cork driver, turned maple, "Redlich Mfg. Co.," Chicago, IL, early 20th C into 1930s. **$75-$115**

Cork driver or corking machine, cast iron with some fancy embossing, painted & pinstriped, screw clamps, lever with big wood knob, "Yankee." Works by holding the bottle by its neck in exact position to receive the cork which is put in a sort of "hopper," and plunged downward by force of the lever. About 13" L, late 9th C. **$125-$175**

Cork driver or corking machine, malleable cast iron, not attractive industrial design, but very efficient for setting corks at any depth. Screw clamps to shelf or counter, one lever sets cork, one lever holds bottle, "Corkee," pat'd Feb. 19, 1901. **$75-$95**

Cork driver or corking machine, cast iron, screw clamps to shelf, horizontal dog-leg lever to built-in cork compressor connected to bottle clamp underneath, another cranked lever drives cork, "Invincible," c.1910. **$75-$95**

Cork press, alligator with head looking up and tail lever up, regular pattern of warty stripes to represent the hide extends in diminishing size from neck to end of tail, red-painted cast iron, hinged at chest, holes drilled in feet so that it could be screwed to countertop or a plank, would press four sizes of corks. By "press" is meant compression. A water-soaked cork slightly larger than was needed would be put in the press to compress it

so that it could quickly be inserted in the bottle before it expanded to its original cut size. American, 3rd quarter (?)19th C. There are at least three different alligator presses. This one has a variation where the "warts" end partway up the tail, to be taken over by a sort of crosshatch knurling (see picture). Another is perfectly charming, truly a cute little 'gator modeled much less realistically, with the three "sections" all the same length: head & jaws, body, and tail. Also does four corks — probably for pharmaceuticals, not liquor. These are all essential for a good alligator collection, which would also include a lawn sprinkler and a couple of nutcrackers. **$475-$600+**

Cork press, cast iron in shape of playful setter dog, undoubtedly made by same company that made the head- and tail-up alligator presses. Does four sizes. American, last quarter 19th C. (?). I've never seen one of these, but it is pictured in the September 1971 issue of *Spinning Wheel*, p. 44. **$350-$450+**

Cork press, cast iron, mounted to wooden base, half-circle cradle with levered 6-spoked ridged wheel. Called a "rotary" cork press, and originally sold for 50¢. Late 19th, early 20th C. The most commonly found type. **$75-$125**

Cork press, cast iron finished with japanning or bronze, leaf-like design to lever, 3 legs with mounting holes, 3 corks. Russell & Erwin, c.1875. **$95-$125**

Cork press, cast iron, japanned or bronzed, 3 scrolly legs, scrolly, leafy top with shapely lever, does 4 corks, including very small one for pharmacies. Originally cost only $2.25 per dozen, wholesale! Probably Russell & Erwin, c.1875. **$125-$175**

Cork press, cast iron, "Whitall-Tatum," Philadelphia, 19th C. into early 20th. Probably for pharmeceutical bottle corks. **$45-$65**

Cork press — See also bottle capper & cork press

Corking machines — See cork driver or corking machine

Corking presses — See cork driver or corking machine

Cork extractor, iron & wood, looks much like a button hook with a T-handle. "B.J. Greely," c.1880s. **$15-$25**

Cork puller, nickeled steel (advertised also as coming "silver plated," but was it really silver?), extremely simple small device that mounts vertically to wall, cupboard or door jamb. You hold the bottle in place, then raise the lever so the centercut screw

VIII-48. Rotary cork press. *Cast iron, wooden base, rotary motion compresses cork to reduce its diameter long enough to stick it in bottle neck. A. Pick & Co. hotel & bar supplies catalog, c.1905-09, but press design may be much older.* **$85-$125**

VIII-47. Cork drawer or puller. *"Yankee-6," cast iron in choice of finish: bronze or nickel plate. Fancy casting of mechanism housing. Bottle is clamped into position underneath, and handle is worked up & then then down. There was also a "Yankee-7," also to be clamped either to counter, shelf or work board. Its handle started in vertical down position, and was moved up only, but traveled the same overall distance as the #6. The bottle clamp was optional. Mfd. by the Gilchrist Co., Newark, NJ, early 1900s.* **$90-$150**

VIII-49. Cork press. *Figural alligator, well-detailed cast iron. Mounted to shaped oak board, screwed through feet. Does four sizes of corks. Picture courtesy James & Phyllis Moffet.* **$400-$500**

enters the cork, then lower the lever to withdraw cork, "Yankee #1," Gilchrist Co., c.1890s-1915. (The Yankee #2 of steel mounted to a shelf edge with a screw clamp.) **$20-$30**

Cork puller, nickeled cast iron (also found bronze-plated), with fancy scrolled design on sides. Mounted to shelf, counter or other horizontal surface, has bottle holder clamp, upward lever action, "Yankee #7 ," The Gilchrist Co., Newark, NJ, c.1892. (There's also a Yankee #6 that's pretty much the same but it operates with an upward then downward motion of the knobbed lever. Originally they cost about $1.95 — this is another one of those time-machine shopping list items.) **$225-$275**

Cork pullers don't just grab the cork and pull it out, as the name may seem to apply. They incorporate a corkscrew, but use a (usually) levered action to facilitate pulling out the cork after the screw has engaged it.

Cork puller or cork drawer, cast iron, fancy embossed design, bronzed or nickel-plated, screw clamps to shelf or counter edge, has device to hold bottle (like one in picture of the "Yankee 6"), lever is pulled up to draw cork out. "PULLMEE," probably Manning Bowman/ Freeport Novelty Co., c. 1913. **$95-$150**

Cork puller, cast iron, overall fancy embossing, nickeled finish only. Attachment so that cork can be half or fully pulled.

VIII-50. Corkscrews. *The cheapest kind, but perfectly efficient for many kinds of corked bottles. These came with single ring of wire for the fingerhole, or double ring for strength. Simple one at top could also be had with two kinds of tubes. Center one has wooden tube with no printed advertising. The wholesale price was 250 of them for $3.75. At bottom is one showing printed wooden tube, meant as giveaway. They were only 25¢ more! Made at Albert Pick & Co.'s Pennsylvania factory. A. Pick, 1905-09. Value affected by advertising.* **$1-$10**

VIII-51. Corkscrew. *Figural "Old Snifter" caricature of Senator "Prohibition" Volstead. Corkscrew tail, bottle opener hook under chin. Hat removes — purpose not known, not big enough to hold much but a sniff. Painted cast metal (brass?). Many versions of this, some without cap opener or removable hat. C. 1920s.* **$85-$150**

"SHOMEE," marked "Freeport Novelty Co.," as well as "Manning Bowman," "Meriden, CT." **$100-$150**

Cork puller, cast iron, screw clamps to shelf or bar, angled lever with long turned black wood handle, embossed brass facing plate with vines & flowers, "Champion Bar Screw," mfd. by Chas. Brown & Sons, San Francisco, pat'd 1896. **$225-$275**

Cork puller, screw clamps to table edge, for bar or butlery, nickeled cast iron, steel, wooden knob on crank, nicely eared wingnut on clamp, helical worm, "Infanta No. 8," pat'd 1895. **$290-$350**

Cork puller **reproduction alert**, screw clamps to bar edge, cast brass with lots of cupids, replica of 1890s cork puller, one lever clamps to bottle neck, larger one, with turned wooden handle like the "Champion," used to draw out cork, recorks by reversing motion, says "VINTNER" in vertical letters on main body, c.1985. **Alert #2:** — A simpler version, of cast aluminum & called the "Estate," has knurled bottle clamp that looks like the old "Yankees" but lever like the "Champion," mounted to vertical iron rod and board instead of screw clamp, is less than half the price. Well-made enough to probably pass for much older, if the wood and metal is distressed. New price from 1985 "Wine Enthusiast" mail order catalog: **$159.90**

Cork puller, or cork extractor, mechanical, for bars or restaurants, cast metal, screw clamps to bar edge, "Edie Patent," Smith & Egge Mfg. Co., Bridgeport, CT, pat'd Feb. 4, 1890 by Alexander Edie. **$120-$150**

Cork puller, screw clamps to edge, mostly for bar or restaurant use, fancy openwork cast iron, nickel plated usually, lever, "Phoenix," 1887. **$175-$225**

First American Corkscrew Patent. — The late Raymond Townsend wrote an article in *Fine Tool Journal*, Sep/Oct 1989, saying that it has been incorrectly thought that the earliest American corkscrew patent is that of Philos Blake (a nephew of Eli Whitney from New Haven, CT), granted March 27, 1860. (**NOTE:** Actually, Joe Kane, *Famous First Facts,* wrote that the first was rec'd by M. L. Byrn, # 27, 615, on March 27, 1860. Same date. Hmmm.) According to Ray, the first was George Blanchard's combined nutmeg grater & corkscrew, July 15, 1856 (See nutmeg graters in Chapter I). The claim of Blake was that, "This invention is a new and improved manufacture of cork extractor, as made not only with a lever head applied to its lifting screw, but with a lever screw nut applied on such screw and to the cap of the heck stand, in such a manner that it may rotate and screw on the lifting screw and either rotate against or within said cap."

Corkscrews — some collector hints.— The 1854 *Chamber's Journal* writer who wrote on cork didn't speculate on the age of corkscrews. Recent writers date the first corkscrew to the late seventeenth century, when it was called a "bottle scrue" or "steel worme." I like to speculate that several factors (the ancient knowledge of cork's properties, the ancient manufacture of relatively small bottles, the ancient consumption of wine and beer, and — essential to my premise — Archimedes' invention of the giant screw to draw up liquids from wells, etc.) would naturally have led to the idea of a small-scale tapping screw that could be used, like a champagne tap is used now, to draw out fermenting or sparkling wine, and on from that to a screw to draw out a tight cork. Failing proof of that, I bet that older examples of the wrought iron L-shaped corkscrews (see illustration VIII-57) used by cellar masters, may date at least to the 1500s, possibly even earlier.

The aristocrats of corkscrews are patented mechanical ones from the nineteenth century; next in desirability would be rigid wrought iron or other metal ones dating back to the seventeenth or eighteenth centuries — pure functional form that you could imagine Leonardo da Vinci using. Least costly, though widely and popularly collected, are late nineteenth-century and all twentieth-century corkscrews, figural and mechanical.

In any mechanical corkscrew collection, the patient and patented search for improvement is evident, and while handmade and one-of-a-kind screws are valuable additions to a collection, the patented examples excite the most collector interest. All sorts of mechanical movements used in huge engines of the Industrial Revolution are found on a small scale in corkscrews: rack-and-pinion gears, levers, cams and clutches.

The screws themselves vary, although most people call all of them "worms" or "screws." These are the types of worms: (1) single **wire helix** (spiral), and the rarer (2) double or **duplex helix** (one is much shorter than the other), both found in relatively lighter or heavier gauge wire; (3) **augured worm screw** (looking like a cross between a wire helix and a wood screw); (4) **fluted wire helix** (which is made of relatively heavy gauge wire and has a channel or "flute" scoring the outer side of the entire worm's length); (5) **bladed worm** (on this, the outer side of the wire helix or spiral has a sort of sharp edge or blade to it); (6) **center-** or **solid-cut worm** — sometimes called an **Archimedean** screw— (which has, in effect, a straight center shaft with a spiraling blade the entire length, at first easily confused with the bladed worm until you get the hang of it); (7) **steep-pitched center worm** — called a "speed worm"— (which is like 6 but with fewer spirals per inch [s.p.i.] so the "pitch" or angle of the blade edge is greater); (8) **cyphered wire helix** (which I can't find a definition of, but in pictures it is a peg-and-worm two-part tool, the "peg" has a straight center shaft, around which fits a tightly-fit spiral wire worm); and (9) **flat twist worm** is a term appearing in a c.1904 Duparquet Moneuse & Huot catalog to describe a corkscrew that looks like it could be a center-cut worm or a bladed worm.

Other variations have to do with size and finish. A corkscrew can be either (**a**) an un-tapered worm or (**b**) a tapered worm (much less common, and refers either to the tapering of the wire itself, or tapering of the radius of the spirals). It can have a (**c**) **point** (i.e., it is terminated by drawing the tip into a point that lines up vertically with the shaft), or a (**d**) **tip** (not pointed, but simply terminated in the spiral so the point — yes, there is a pointed end — is of the same curve and pitch as the helix/spiral). Other terms used to define corkscrews are (**e**) **radius** (screws have different turning radii), (**f**) **pitch** (different pitches — what I call s.p.i. or spirals per inch. The fewer s.p.i., the faster the worm could be screwed through the cork), and finally (**g**) **length**: the length of the screw or worm varies depending on the intended use (viz. wine corks or medicine bottle corks, pocket, pantry, picnic, or wine cellar, etc.). Finally, there are many other terms to describe the **forms** or **types**: barreled, open cage, spring barrel, bell-cap, moving bell, spiked flange, swivel-over collar, duck bill cap, flared moving bell, Columbus type expanding frame, sprung frame, split-ring frame, folding, folding fulcrum, bow or harp, picnic; the **handles**: eyebrows, twisted wire, T-handle [which can be wood, metal, bone, ivory, horn, plastic], 2-finger pull, 3-finger pull, 4-finger pull, ring, figural; the **mechanical principles**: double-levered, rack and pinion, spring action, concertina, screw and lever; and **additional features**: cap lifter, pick, brush, wire cutter or breaker, wax cutter.

Inventors. — Three English corkscrew inventors, whose corkscrews are avidly collected, are Sir Edward **Thomason**, who patented what he called the "King's Screw" in 1802; William **Lund**, probably the most prolific inventor of corkscrews: his designs vary considerably in mechanical principle; and James **Heeley**. The four most famous American names are C[ornelius] T[itus] **Williamson** — inventor and founder of a long-lasting company — and his son and successor, William A. **Williamson**; William R. **Clough**, whose simple ring-handled, one-finger, wire and wood corkscrews, each with its own cylindrical wooden "sheath" meant to be stamped with an advertising message, are ubiquitous; and Edwin **Walker**, who patented many types of corkscrews, including an 1894 extractor or cork puller, which incorporated a corkscrew. The entire field, American and European, is vast, and only a hint of the range is given in this chapter.

VIII-52. Bawdy folding corkscrews. (L) *"leg puller," Enameled striped stockings in red & white, blue & white, etc. Crucible steel worm. 2-1/2" L folded; 5" L open. One example of popular type. Original wholesale price was $7.25 a dozen!* **(R)** *folding lady. "An imported novelty, beautifully enameled in colors." Tempered crucible steel worm. I wonder if the real one has such a dour expression? The legs look just like the catalog cut, but I've never seen this one. Both from catalog of A. Pick, 1905-09.* **$65-$125**

VIII-53. Corkscrews. *Combination folding pocket types. Large one* **(L)** *is a "Champagne Opener," and has button hook (nothing to do with bottle-opening) and a curved wire-cutting blade in addition to worm;* **(R)** *smaller one has extra worm, and a pick. F. A. Walker catalog, 1870s.* **$20-$35**

VIII-54. Corkscrew. *Another folding type, the "Handy Pocket Cork Screw," mfd. by the Little Giant Letterpress Co., NYC. Nickel-plated. You worked it by holding the tip of the screw worm to the cork with one hand, then pulling up on upper half of handle, which "forces the screw down." It would, of course, if it worked at all, force it straight into the cork without screwing. I don't see how it would work, but it was sold. The Metal Worker, 7/28/1892.* **$18-$30**

Corkscrew, "bar screw" — See cork puller

Corkscrew combination tools — See combination tools

CORKSCREWS, advertising & souvenir (some are folding or figural):

Corkscrew, cheap metal, very small folding type, worm folds into handle loop, for "Carter's Ink," pat'd 1894. **$10-$15**

Corkscrew, adv'g folding type, flimsy yellow & black printed tin, "Listerine," mfd. for them by unidentified novelty company, about 1-1/2" L folded, c.1900 to 1920s. **$10-$15**

Corkscrew, adv'g type in printed wooden tube sheath, "Kellerstrass Distilling Co., Kansas City," 1900. **$15-$20**

Corkscrew, flimsy lithographed metal, adv'g "Welch's Grape Juice," 20th C. **$15-$20**

Corkscrew, steel, painted wood handle adv'g "Welch Grape Juice," bell-cap, c. 1887 Williamson patent, prob. early 20th C. **$25-$35**

Corkscrew, disguised within World's Fair key that opens, "Century of Progress," 1939. **$65-$85**

Corkscrew, steel in wooden tube, small, meant for the corks in flavoring extract bottles, advertising printed on tube: "Chamberlain's Pure Extracts," c.1900. **$8-$15**

CORKSCREWS, figural & decorative (note that some folding and some lever corkscrews are also figural):

Corkscrew, alligator of carved staghorn, steel worm, prob. American because of motif, early (?) 20th C. **$150-$200**

Corkscrew, antler tip handle with sterling silver fittings, very small and may have had a sheath for pocket, 3" L, 19th C. **$65-$85**

Corkscrew, baby's upper torso, cast brass, French, c.1900. Why a baby? Maybe it was the infant Bacchus. **$85-$125**

Corkscrew, bottle shape, nickeled, with brass plate showing logo & date, "Anheuser Busch," dated 1897. **$40-$60**

Corkscrew, cat with screw as the tail, brass & steel, 3-3/4" L, c.1910. **$45-$55**

Corkscrew, Cheshire cat, cast brass & steel, English (?), late 19th C. **$100-$125**

VIII-55. Corkscrews. (L) *A so-called self-puller with cap to fit over mouth of bottle.* **(R)** *A flat twist helical worm, and slender wooden handle reinforced with a metal ring at each end. About 6-1/2" L. D, H & M catalog, c.1904-10.* **$4-$10**

VIII-56. Corkscrew. *A simple one with turned, stained wood handle, hardened steel wire, attached to handle by winding. More expensive versions upgraded step by step: nickeled wire, varnished wood; then tempered steel, brace, and imitation rosewood handle; then "best tempered steel," wire cutter and polished hardwood. They were mounted to a card, 12 at a time, and originally wholesaled for from 30¢ doz. to $1.75 doz. Butler Brothers catalog, 1899.* **$3-$10**

VIII-57. Corkscrews. *Called* **cellar corkscrews.** *Forged iron, twists at top provided leverage for turning. Italian, late 18th C. 6-3/4" L and 8-3/8" L. Collection Hillman Books.* **$100-$150**

Corkscrew, clown head, molded plastic — very moderne, 4-1/2" L, 20th C. **$65-$75**

Corkscrew, elephant head, ivory handle, glass eyes, sterling silver ferrule, English, 8-1/8" L, c.1900. **$50-$75**

Corkscrew, grotesque head of cast brass, steel helical worm, head is mythological hairy beast adapted from Durham Cathedral doorknocker, possibly a souvenir, marked only "DURHAM," English, 7-1/4" L including hanging ring on head's top, c.1930s. **$70-$90**

Corkscrew, iron with curlique, thick real grapevine handle, 19th or 20th C. **$15-$30**

Corkscrew, key of heavy cast brass, shaped like a very old-fashioned, ornate door key, probably a sommelier's corkscrew — the key signifying his control of the locked door to the wine cellar. (Some people have speculated the key just stands for hospitality.) Marked "G E A Bochum," European, late 19th C (?). **$75-$115**

Corkscrew, pixie figure carrying lantern, cast copper, simple helical worm screw, English, 6" L, late 19th C. **$65-$80**

Corkscrew, sailing ship, cast brass, 20th C., prob. 1950s. **$25-$35**

Corkscrew, Shriner's cap, cast aluminum, 6" L, 20th C. **$45-$65**

Corkscrew, sommelier, man dressed as aproned waiter or sommelier holding green bottle, looks like carved and painted wood, but is molded wood composition, head and shoulders pull out to reveal corkscrew and bell cap, "Syroco," mfd. by Syracuse Ornamental Co., Syracuse, NY, 8" H, c.1930s-1950s. **$40-$55**

Corkscrew, sommelier, a formally dressed wine-serving man of carved & painted wood, with steel, European (?), 20th C (?). **$30-$50**

Corkscrew, squirrel, steel helical worm, cast brass acorn with huge-tailed squirrel perched on nut, hanging ring at top, English (?), 6-1/2" L, late 19th C. **$125-$175**

Corkscrew, steel with boar's tusk handle, silver & ivory trim, European, late 19th C. **$95-$125**

Corkscrew, tomahawk or hatchet, wood handle, iron works, American (?), c.1900. **$25-$40**

Corkscrew, tree stump figural handle, iron, 6" L. **$25-$30**

Corkscrew, Viking ship with mythological Griffin heads, remove single sail to reveal screw, nickel- or chrome-plated cast iron, 3-1/2" H x 4-1/4" L, 20th C. **$30-$55**

CORKSCREWS, folding (see also advertising):

Corkscrew, Gay '90s lady's legs, bent at knees, wearing red & white striped stockings (they also came in charcoal-gray stripes and green stripes), partly nickel-plated, with high top laced boots, very elegantly risqué, German, 3" L, late 19th C. - 1910. (A similar one, 2-1/2" L folded, has striped stockings from boot-top to just above knee, thigh enameled "flesh" color, c.

1910, and probably imported from Germany, came in red/white, blue/white, green/white stripes, and wholesaled for 59¢ each! Value now under $175.)   **$250-$325**

Corkscrew, folding women's legs, plated metal with enameled red & black stockings, 5-1/2" L when folded, German, c. 1900.   **$95-$135**

Corkscrew, folding, "The Davis," pat'd 1891.   **$15-$20**

CORKSCREWS, "functional" (*not* figural, decorative, levered or mechanical — and of course we hope *all* corkscrews function):

Corkscrew, brass barrel with turned ivory handle with black bristles, 6-1/4" L, "Thomason," English, mid (?) 19th C.   **$500-$700**

Corkscrew, brass & bone or ivory, with dust & cobweb brush in one end of handle, Thomason type, English, 7-3/8" L, mid 19th C. Estimated at a 1983 Christie's sale to get $80 to $120, because such corkscrews had brought that before, this one got $440. Often auction prices are reported in trade papers with "Caution: Auction Price," but auctions can go anywhere — up or down — depending on the people bidding.   **$500-$700**

Corkscrew, brass shank with large ring below turned wood T-handle, helical worm, marked "The Twin" on ring, Wolverson patent, reg. #310265, English, 1877. Very elegant. **$125-$175**

VIII-58. Corkscrews. *All forged iron, all helical worms. European, probably Italian.* (**L**) *folding harp with a center cut worm, 2-7/8" L folded. The "T"-handle ones are 4-3/8" L, 4-5/8" L and 3-1/2" L. Mid to late 18th C. Collection Hillman Books.* **$85-$120**

VIII-59. Corkscrews. *For "vest pocket." Top two are the screw and the cap for it, to be assembled by putting the rod through hole and using as handle to twist. Nickeled steel, 3" L. Next is simple heavy twisted nickeled steel wire & metal tube, 3-1/4" L. At bottom is a neat one with screw kept inside, then fitted into position for use. Nickeled steel. 2-3/4" L in tube. A. Pick, 1905-09.* **$15-$22**

Corkscrew, cast iron, wood handle, Archimedean screw in cage, cast iron, wood handle, 1883.   **$65-$85**

Corkscrew, forged iron, very elegant L-shape for cellar use, long worm, Italian, 9-1/4" L, 18th C.   **$100-$135**

Corkscrew, Archimedean screw, steel, "Diamant J P Paris" [J. H. Perille], c.1900.   **$100-$150**

Corkscrew, for beer bottle, wooden cigar-shaped T-handle, nickeled shaft, short bell-shaped cap lifter of iron, design pat'd by William. A. Williamson, for Anheuser Busch, pat'd Dec. 13, 1898.   **$18-$25**

Corkscrew, "peg & worm" pocket or travelling type, polished cut steel with some lathe turning, and faceted peg, English, 4" L, 19th C. **Peg and Worm** — The "peg" is the handle, a cross piece with a knob or handle (in this case) either plain or decorated; the peg fits into the twist at the end of the screw. These came in little tubular sheaths, making them safe to carry about in trouser pockets. $65-$95 for really simple peg & worms. This turned steel one: **$125-$150**

Corkscrew, steel & wood, with cap that fits over bottle mouth, "W. Williamson" patent, American, 5-3/4" L, pat'd 1887. **$35-$55**

CORKSCREWS, levered (single, double, compound):

Corkscrew, lever action, cast iron with brass maker's plate, "The Royal Club," pat'd by Charles Hull, English (?), 1864.   **$300-$350**

Corkscrew, lever — Bacchus' head with wild curly hair, double lever type, levers are arms, the "body" that fits over bottle neck is cast brass to look like Greek tunic, with grapes, mfd. by Godinger, c.1983.   **$30-$45**

Corkscrew, iron, 2 parts, a plier-like lever with a bell cap to fit over cork, and with a worm or screw that fits on the end. The worm was twisted into the cork, and then the plier-lever was hooked on. The screw is commonly found by itself, having lost the plier part, "Lund's Lever," English, patent #736, pat'd 1855. **Classic** — According to Watney & Babbidge's *Corkscrews for Collectors,* variations of Lund's Lever were made by "a number of firms over the years," and were sold through the "Army and Navy Catalogue" as late as 1925-26."   **$180-$250**

Corkscrew, lever, single — steel, single arm pump lever type works like handle of water pump, marked "W.W. Tucker," Hartford, CT, pat'd Sept. 3, 1878.   **$800-$1200**

Corkscrew, lever, tangent lever mechanism, iron, originally enameled black, brass, separate worm is iron with metallic copper finish, "Spong & Co.," London, England, 7-3/8" L, registered Nov. 4, 1873.   **$125-$165**

Corkscrew, compound lever type — multiplied leverage achieved by two- or three-jointed criss-crossed arms, called "concertina" or "lazy tongs," named the "American Reliable Concertina," turn of century.   **$165-$200**

VIII-60. Corkscrew. *Mechanical "Lund's Lever" 2-part , 2-step opener. The 2 parts are plier-like lever and the screw, the shaft of which has a hole that fits over hook at top of plier/lever. The 2 steps are: screw the 3-1/2" L worm into cork, then fit bell cap over mouth of bottle and hook lever through hole in worm. The screw part is commonly orphaned, and mistaken for small pocket corkscrew. English. In importer F. A. Walker's catalog, 1870s, but pat'd 1855.* **$125-$175**

Corkscrew, compound lever type with criss-crossed arms with 4 lever points, also called "lazy tongs" or concertina type corkscrew, forged steel with bronze finish, "Wier's Patent," mfd. by J. Heeley & Sons, English, 14" L fully extended, patent #12804, pat'd Sept. 25, 1884. A **classic**. This corkscrew, bronzed or nickel-plated, was sold as late as 1939-40 in Army

VIII-61. Corkscrew. *A modern figural: Bacchus, mfd. by Godinger, cast brass. C. 1983-84.* **$25-$35**

VIII-62. Corkscrew. *Turned bone handle (possibly ivory), dark bristle dust & cobweb brush intact, cast & turned brass cylindrical sheath covering mechanism. Thomason type. Patented, 19th C. English. 7-3/8" L as shown. Picture courtesy of Christie, Manson & Woods International, Inc.* **$400-$500**

VIII-63. Corkscrew. *Another of Lund's patents from 1855. Bone crossbar handle, steel cage, helical worm, hanging ring at top, missing the dust brush. About 7-1/4" H as shown. English.* **$120-$185**

& Navy Stores Limited catalog, London, England. We suppose it was offered for a long time after, too.   **$100-$150**

Corkscrew, compound lever (lazy tong or concertina) style, steel, "Zig Zag, No. 38," also marked "Bte S.G.D.G. Fr & Et M & M. DER," French, 10-1/4" L fully extended, 1870s. **Marks on French Items** — **Bte** is an abbreviation for *Breveté,* or patentee. **S. G. D. G**. stands for *Sans Garantie Du Gouvernement,* or, registered, but without warranty by the government. In this case, it seems to say registered without warranty by the government of France and someplace else, I don't know where. The **Et** may be an abbreviation for *Étalage,* in the sense of a retail shop. In other words, "sold by," although I can't find that exact idiomatic use.   **$140-$200+**

Corkscrew, nickel-plated metal, cap fits over bottle's mouth & cork, action consists of a compound lever — a "jointed extension" like a lazy tongs, with 3 crossed or zigzag arms, used by screwing in worm, then pulling on handle, which pulls cork as it extends, "Zig-Zag Corkscrew," American, late 1920s. Probably related to the French one in more than name & works.   **$60-$75**

Corkscrew, compound lever modified "concertina" type like two very long arms held akimbo, then only one more pair of shorter "elbows," nickeled steel, oval ring handle, steep pitched center cut screw, "The Irresistible," pat'd by Armstrong, English, late 19th C.   **$100-$135**

Corkscrew, mechanical double lever type, bronzed iron, broad-shouldered levers (in down position), wingnut-like top, steel helical worm, marked "Heeley's Patent A-1 Double Lever 1888," and "James Heeley & Sons, 5006 Patent Double Lever," English, 6-1/2" L, 1888. Marvelous looking — a collector's **classic**.   **$150-$175**

Corkscrew, lever, cast & machined brass, with cog & rachet mechanism, and wingy top that looks almost like a maple tree seed, has a collar to grasp top of cork, Rosati's patent, Italy, 6-1/2" L, 20th C.   **$45-$65**

Corkscrew, lever, shiny tinned iron, "Magic Lever Cork Drawer," English, 5-3/4" L in closed position (levers down), turn of century — marked "pat. appd for."   **$125-$150**

Corkscrew, lever — nude "bionic" man, brass with red faceted glass eyes, looks more like a hood ornament than a corkscrew. Mid-late 20th C. Yuck (I say that now, but from experience I know that yesterday's "yuck" is often tomorrow's "yummy.") **$20-$35**

Corkscrew, lever — sommelier, double lever type, silver-plated metal, little man's body fits over neck of bottle, modeled with wescot & sommelier's medallion on chain, shoulders are where the levers pivot, the levers are his 2 arms, round bald head with big ears, called "Pierre le Sommelier," French import, 8" H, c.1980.   **$15-$35**

Corkscrew, lever — owl's head, with large eyes, plated metal, lever type, the 2 lever arms rather like wings, the words "HOOTCH-OWL" cast into body, pat'd by R. G. Smythe, American, pat'd 1935.   **$200-$225**

CORKSCREWS, mechanical other than lever:

Corkscrew, clutch mechanism, steel with open barrel cage, turned wooden (or fancier bone) handle, Coney & Co.'s "THE KING" (not Thomason's King's Screw), Birmingham, England, pat'd 1904. Handle affects price.   **$160-$250**

Corkscrew, double-action mechanical type with so-called "hermaphrodite raising screw" that goes one way then another, steel screw, brass barrel ornately decorated with the fruits & plants of wine & beer making, turned bone handle. Also has intact brush at one end of T-handle, Thomason patent, English, 1802.   **$400-$650**

Corkscrew, rack & pinion mechanism, blued steel (some have brass barrels or cages) with lathe-turned bone-ivory handle at top, plain steel smaller side handle, "King's Screw," or with only "King's" capitalized. Patented in 1802 by Sir Edward Thomason. Two English makers of are Mapplebeck & Lowe, and Dowler, English, about 7" L (hard to measure mechanical in a uniform way — open, half open or closed), 19th C. **Classic.**— Those with double bone or ivory handles cost more. Messrs. Watney & Babbidge, in *Corkscrews for Collectors* (see bibliography), say at least 24 manufacturers have been identified as making Thomason's "King's Screw," which is highly regarded as one of the handsomest and finest of the rack & pinion types. **$450-$650**

Corkscrew, rack & pinion type, long steel frame with turned wooden handle, brush intact, "London Rack, Lund Maker, Cornhill & Fleet Street, London," England, mid 19th C. **$180-$230**

Glass cutter combination tool — See bottle & can opener, knife sharpener & glazier's tool combined

Jar opener, cast iron, "H. L. Jenney," Greenfield, MA, undated late 19th C. "Pat. Appl'd For." **$35-$50**

"Pat. Appl'd For," which dealer Bob Cahn always refers to as "that famous inventor — Pat Apple," was marked on gadgets, or used in advertising, in an attempt to protect them at least long enough for the inventor to make some money. Sometimes it wasn't even true; but usually it seems to have meant production could go on for a few months or even one or two years, *before* a patent was granted (or possibly rejected, something the inventor would hardly emboss on the side of his invention). Similarly, **"Pat. Pending"** indicated the patent

had been applied for, and the inventor was optimistic of its chances! **Patent dates** found embossed or stamped on a device may or may not be the actual date the patent was granted. The date may also be the date the patent was applied for, usually many months prior to the granting. There's also the chance that the date is accidentally wrong, perhaps an error during marking.

Jar opener, iron with screw-action adjustable hook, "Best," mfd. by H. & E. Sanborn, Portland, ME, 3" L, "patent applied for," c.1920s (?). **$7-$10**

Jar opener, mechanical, tinned cast iron, meant to be wall mounted with (missing) bracket, vertical frame with "faucet" knob to screw one of 2 corrugated jaws to fit lid, "#A100" on moving jaw, "Speedo," Central States Mfg. Co., St. Louis, MO, 6" L, c.1900 to 1912 "patents pending." Worth a lot more with wall bracket. **$20-$35**

Jar opener, or jar wrench, nickeled iron oblong frame for geared jaws, which are set by turning the cigar-shaped wood handle clockwise until the jaws fit the jar lid, then turning the other way to twist the lid off, handle painted red or green, or varnished, "Top Off Jar & Bottle Screw Top Opener," Edlund Co., Burlington, VT, gear moves jaws from 1-1/8" to 4-3/8"; width of metal part of tool is 1-5/8". 1933, but made for some years, with various handles. **$5-$10**

Knife sharpener & glass cutter — See bottle & can opener, knife sharpener & glazier's tool

Milk bottle cap opener, iron, "Jack Spratt," turn of century. **$4-$8**

Milk bottle opener, metal with wood handle, adv'g "White Lily Milk," 5" L. **$4-$10**

Milk bottle opener, to open paper cap wires, looks like a cross between a buttonhook and a pick, embossed with the dairy's name, 1920s?-1930s? As a child in the '40s, how I loved to open (with my bare fingers) the wires on those pleated paper caps. The wires went in a kitchen drawer, like the twisties do now, for future repair jobs. My parents still use an aluminum pan lid that lost its ring, which Daddy fixed with two of those milk bottle wire twists. **$3-$10**

VIII-64. Corkscrew. *Double lever corkscrew with ratchet wheel, and side turning handle, in the style of the King screw. Probably steel with bone or wood handle, fitted with dust brush. From F. A. Walker import catalog, 1870s.* **$200-$300**

VIII-65. Corkscrews. (L) *"The Challenge," French-style, locking "fly nut" at top, cast steel open cage, helical worm. 6-1/2" L fully extended.* **(R)** *Steel & wood "Columbus," with spring around shank between cage & turned wood handle — referred to as a "sprung shank" type. 6-1/2" L. The "Challenge" worth $20 to $40 more than other. Full range of value:* **$85-$165**

VIII-67. Jar opener. *Malleable iron, thumbscrew adjusts tension. Paper label "Best," Portland, ME. 3" L. "Pat. Appl.," early 20th C, maybe 1920s.* **$7-$12**

VIII-66. Corkscrews. *And crown cap opener combined. Protrusion is a wire breaker. Pocket advertising type, shown with & without printed wooden tube. (Also came with metal tube). A. Pick, 1905-09.* **$4-$10**

VIII-68. Milk bottle cap lift. *Steel, handle stamped with name of dairy. Cherry-Bassett Co. catalog of supplies for dairies, 1921.* **$3-$8**

HOLDING & HANDLING

IX. WASH, REPAIR, & SHARPEN

This short chapter has tools and racks used for washing dishes and draining them dry; others for sharpening knives (although a few *combination* can openers and knife sharpeners are found in the previous chapter).

Knife sharpeners, which have the most variety, are probably the most popular tools here. If you include the contrivances used for cleaning or polishing knives, there's something for everyone — from an eighteenth-century knife-cleaning or scouring box, to a strange revolving wooden drum, like some magician's trick machine, with slots for the knives.

My personal favorites are the **soap savers**, but I'm afraid the field is quite small. I prefer the homemade ones, but they're hard to find. A surprise field, closely related to advertising collectibles, and just a tiny bit out of my purview, are the small flat chromolithographed sheet metal **pot scrapers**. Some astoundingly high prices were achieved at an auction where a number of them were sold a decade ago. I have said about other fields, and say about this one, I can't put an up-to-the-minute market range on a field that has achieved astronomical prices with little warning. We'd have to know the full story about the buyer(s) of the scrapers. If it was one person, aiming for a book along about now, then buying the "illustrations," so to speak, was a smart move.

Cutlery trays — See Chapter VII (Storage and Containers)

Dish drainer, 2-piece, wire with sheet metal soap tray, turn of century. **$25-$35**

Dish drainer, all wire, for 12 plates, resembles today's dish drainers except for wire trough at end for cutlery, "Loop Weld Model No. A-4," by Marlboro Wire Goods Co., 3-7/8" H x 18-3/4" L x 12" W, c.1910. A child's toy version was made exactly the same way and just as well, differing in the number of loops & plate arches. It's only 6-1/8" L x 3-5/8" W. It's valued about $30-$45. The bigger one: **$25-$45**

Dish drainer, blackened tin & wire, with fold-down cutlery draining trough with 8 drain holes along gutter of it, wire rack lengthwise down center for plates & saucers, Androck No. 199, 3-7/8" H x 19-1/2" L x 12" W, early 20th C. Rusts like crazy! There was, in the 1870s or so, a wire rack that looks like a dish drainer, but was advertised as a dish warmer, pictured sitting over 2 range eyes, lids on. This one would have served well to warm plates, but then it wouldn't have had the cutlery compartment. **$45-$50**

Dish drainer, round dish drainer, very substantial heavy plated wire, wide metal rim to help hold shape, round cutlery basket in center, Utility Mfg. Co., Baltimore, MD, about 15" diameter, c.1920s. **$25-$35**

Dish drainer, round, open woven wire, detachable cutlery holder suspended in center has much finer wire mesh bottom, Androck, Washburn Co., 5-1/4" H x 15" diameter, c.1930s. When I first saw one of these I mistakenly thought it was just a discard from an old dishwashing machine, and by "old" I meant, say, the 1950s. **$35-$45**

Dish drainer, soldered wire, T-shape with cross bar for flatware, or tumblers if tall narrow loops used, longer piece has loops for plates, American, 16" L, c.1890s to 1910s. **$45-$55**

Dish drainer, pine with woven wire screen & wooden dividers, American, 1880s. **$35-$55**

Dish drainer, water- & soap-bleached pine, 2 rows of nearly vertical dowel pegs to hold plates, a third of the drainer has crosspieces of dowels for flatware, small white rubber knobs on 4 feet, American, 2-3/4" H x 17-3/4" L x 11-1/2" W, 1890s to 1920s (?). **$35-$55**

Dish mop, cotton thrum with slender broomstick handle, Shaker construction, 9" L, mid- to late 19th C. **Thrum** is the word for loose ends of warp threads, left when the finished weaving is cut off the loom — hence for short pieces of scrap thread or yarn. **$35-$55**

Dish pans or wash basins — See paragraph on iron bowls in Chapter VII.

Dish warmer, usable also as a drainer, all wire oblong trough-shaped rack, made so it's flat on top, with vertical slots for a dozen or so plates or shallow dishes, to be set over 2 lidded range eyes for warm air to rise & dry or warm plates, American, 15" L, mid to late 19th C. **$35-$55**

IX-1. Kitchen interior with sink & stove. *Charmingly exaggerated spaciousness. Note slanted sink drain. Hot & cold running water. Mosely Folding Bathtub Co., Chicago, IL, 1896 catalog. "We have heard of a dish-washing machine, and seen an engraving. After it was invented, and pictured in one of the papers devoted to inventions, that was probably the last of it, for we never heard of one in use, and never expect to. The great trouble about a machine is that it can not think, and will give the same treatment to a delicate China saucer that it would to a large heavy platter. Dish-washing does not demand a high order of intellect, but it requires some thought."* American Agriculturist, 7/1875.

Dish mop, turned wooden handle, cotton mop head tied on. In 1904, *House Furnishing Review* commented, "Not one housewife in 25 knows how useful a . . . dish mop is in the kitchen. . . . Women who as girls were taught to immerse their hands in hot, greasy dish water are not prone to leave the beaten path of drudgery. They say the old way is good enough. As most of us have graduated from the tallow candle and the stage coach to the electric light and trolley car, why not improve in the same ratio in minor things?" In the same article, the largest American manufacturer was identified as J. H. Estes & Sons, Fall River, MA, with 4 styles, 5 sizes each. This company began making them c.1900. We often see dish mops at antique shows labeled "Shaker." Indeed, the Shakers made dish mops, using cotton thrum or the warp weaving threads cut off the looms. The simple turned wood handles and the bound cotton threads used in all the early ones would make it hard to know which were Shaker, which were J. H. Estes or other company. **$3-$10**

Dish scraper — See plate or dish scraper

Dishcloth holder, wire, 4 hooked fingers, the handle end is a coil and twist of the wires, a slip ring makes the fingers hold cloth in a tight grasp, American, 10-3/4" L, c.1890s. **$15-$20**

Dishcloth holder & cork puller combined, wire & wood, slip ring & 4 wire prongs which grasp cloth, American, 12" L, c.1880s to 1910. **$15-$20**

IX-2. Brushes, mostly for cleaning. (A) *Sink brush, bound natural fibers.* **(B)** *Scrub brush, wooden back. Note gap between bristles & different angle & set of bristles.* **(C)** *Stove brush, arched wood handle. Note gap.* **(D)** *Curved plate brush, made with 2, 3, 4, or 5 rows.* **(E)** *Baker's wash brush.* **(F)** *Steel wire brush for kitchen tables & butcher blocks.* (A) - (F) all from Duparquet wholesale supply catalog, c.1904-1910. **(G)** *Purée sieve brush. Looks like sign-painter's stencil brush. Jaburg Bros., NY, 1908.* **(H)** *Glass-washing brush, of "best Russia boar's bristles, drawn with copper wire."* **(I)** *Another, of horsehair, for tumblers. "Each little bunch ... bound with copper wire."* **(J)** *Another for tumblers, also Russia bristles. These 3 styles came in 3 sizes: "pony," "medium," and "large." Albert Pick & Co. wholesale catalog, 1909.* **(K)** *Yeast tub brush, of tampico (a plant) fiber. 11" L x 2-3/4" W. Jaburg & D. J. Barry catalogs,1908, 1924.* **(L)** *"Imperial" ox fiber scrub brush, 11" L x 6" W. Barry, 1924.* **(M)** *"Boxwood scrub-brush. — To clean beautifully unpainted wood, table tops, meat and pastry boards." American Home Cook Book, 1854. Lots of crossover interest in brushes, partly because of their appealing zoömorphic appearance.* **$6-$40**

Dish pans were often made in enamelware in the late 1800s-early 1900s, although the finish chipped and cracked easily. Dish pans *almost always* have two handles (heavy wire, strap, ear), have a relatively broad flat bottom, deep slanted sides, and are at least 12" in diameter. Smaller ones without handles were some other kind of basin — a child's wash basin or a pan for making a pudding. Very **similar are wash basins**, used with a pitcher, in rooms without running water. In imitation of fancier ceramic pieces, some wash basins were footed or had a small flared base, and had sort of rounded or "bowled" sides. The flat part is smaller in diameter than that of a dish pan. Collectors of enamelware are well-organized,

and buy and sell frequently, making the market hard to track for an outsider. In determining value, condition is very important, color is next, unless the pan has a very unusual rare color but is not in near perfect condition. Manufacturer marks are also important to collectors. Below is a list to give some idea of value per color. First is listed the body color(s) — then rim & handle color:

Blue & white mottled — dark blue:	**$100-$125**
So-called "end of day" swirls of white, pale green, light blue, brown — black:	**$145-$165**
Cobalt blue spots & blobs on white — black:	**$125-$135**
Dark green & white in short jabby swirls — black:	**$133-$150**
Brown & white speckly, white inside (attractive, but relatively new & lightweight) — white:	**$30-$45**
Red & white speckles & lines — red & white:	**$60-$75**
Gray graniteware (looks like stone) — gray:	**$30-$45**

Dishcloth holder & vegetable skimmer combined, wire, with 4 hooked prongs at one end, an openwork twisted wire spoon at other end, slip ring to tighten prongs, American, 12" L, turn of century. **$15-$25**

Dishwasher, tinned sheet iron, wooden lever handle, basket inside, "Whirlpool Sanitary Dishwasher," mfd. by Hershey-Sexton Mfg. Co., pat'd July 28, 1914. A "Whirlpool" washer was being made by the Nineteen Hundred Corp., of Binghampton, NY, in early 1930s. I can't find any better clues to maker. **$65-$85**

IX-3. Dish drainer. *Water & soap-bleached wood with dowel pegs, 2-3/4" H x 17-3/4" L x 11-1/2" W. White rubber feet. American, 1890s.* **$35-$55**

IX-4. Dish drainers & dish warmer. (T-L) *Dish warmer or dryer. Galvanized iron wire rack, to hold plates, and "set upon stove or in front of a fire, or over a hot-air register."* American Agriculturist, *3/1872.* **(T-R)** *Dish drainer, round, wire, with mesh cutlery drainer in center. 5-1/4" H x 15" diameter. Pat'd in 1901 by Marie L. Price, Chicago, who assigned one third rights to Bertha A. Price. Pat.# 646,128. Similar one with detachable silverware basket, was sold through Washburn-Androck in 1936, as something "good for country trade as drainer will fit inside round dish pan for draining dishes." (Note that this would require a dishpan at least 16" diameter.)* **(B)** *Full-size and toy. "Loop Weld" iron wire, Marlboro Wire Goods Co. 3-7/8" H x 18-3/4" L x 12" W. Child's sample version, on original cardboard mount, is 6-1/8" L x 3-5/8" W. Such miniatures, made carefully and with all the parts miniaturized, were used in a way as a mail order sales force — the intent was to sell the housewife on a full-sized version. Both c. 1910-15.* **$35-$50; $35-$45; $25-$35; $25-$45**

To Wash Dishes. "Dishes should be rinsed in clear, hot water after having been washed in soap suds. It is necessary from a sanitary point of view [because] the caustic alkali is corrosive and unwholesome, and the grease often impure. A rack made of narrow strips of half-inch board is a device frequently used for draining dishes, thus saving the trouble of wiping them. This rack placed on a shelf inclining towards and adjoining the sink holds the dishes securely while they are drying. Milk is a substitute for soap in the kitchen. A little put into hot water will soften it, give the dishes a fine gloss, and will not injure the hands. China and glass (when very dirty) are best cleaned with finely powdered fuller's-earth and warm water, afterwards rinsing it well in clean water. All china that has any gilding upon it may on no account be rubbed with a cloth of any kind, but merely rinsed, first in hot and afterwards in cold water, and then left to drain till dry. Cups and saucers which have become stained with coffee or tea can be easily cleaned by scouring them with baking soda." Henry Scammell, *Treasure-House of Knowledge,* 1891.

IX-5. Dish Dryer. *"Androck #199." 3-7/8" H x 19-1/2" L x 12" W, with fold-down perforated cutlery drainer tray. From Washburn Co., Andrews Division, catalog, 1936. A similar blackened "charcoal" tin one had an attached wire cutlery basket instead of tray.* **$45-$50**

Dishwashing brush, glass cylindrical bottle to be filled with soapy water, one threaded end has a turned wood handle that is hollow but has remnants of red rubber — probably a squeeze bulb; the other threaded end has screw-on zinc cap with small perforations on top, & a wood doughnut-shaped brush set with tampico fiber bristles, embossed on glass "CLIMAX Dish Dash Washer", American, 10" L, "pat. pending," c.1920s. Collection of Carol Bohn. Price range mine. **$35-$45**

Draining pan for sink, royal blue & white enamelware, 12" D, turn of century or early 20th. **$65-$80**

Draining pan for sink, white enamelware, triangular to fit into sink corner, 3 short legs, turn of century. **$20-$30**

Homemade drainer — An idea which has proved "most reliable in my own home, . . . I send along. A round piece of tin which one can easily procure, when punched full of holes (which you can easily do with hammer and nails) makes a capital arrangement to put in the opening of the pipe which leads from the butler's pantry sink. This of course prevents many things from going down and stopping up the drain." *The Housewife Magazine,* Feb. 1910, NYC: A. D. Porter.

IX-6. Dishcloth holders & vegetable servers. *Twisted wire, slip-ringed prongs. Longest one is 13-1/2" L. No perfect chapter for these combination tools — see others in Chapter III. One at* (**R**) *collection of Meryle Evans.* **$15-$25**

IX-7. Dish swab. *Type often described as "Shaker," because of short cotton pieces called* **thrum.** *Turned wood handle, cotton strings. The one shown was store-bought at a "house-furnishing store," but the circa 1870s description that follows is for a homemade one. "The swab may be made on any smooth round stick, about a foot long, and an inch in diameter. About two inches from one end cut a groove; take candle-wicking, white carpet-chain, or even strips of strong cotton cloth, and cut or fold about eight inches in length; tie this material firmly into the groove at the middle, and turn down and tie firmly at the end of the stick, and you will have a 'machine,' which will last many weeks, and go into boiling soap-suds, or even lye, without cringing."* **$3-$15**

Gloves, "India rubber," gauntlet style, apparently stitched together, Goodyear's India Rubber Glove Mfg Co., NYC, NY, advertised 1870. (I don't know if any of these could have survived, but if you thought gardening or dishwashing rubber gloves were fairly new, look at the date on these!) At least by 1901, Faultless Rubber Co. of Akron was making molded rubber gloves, which you could order by glove size, and finger length — long or short. "Rubber gloves for kitchenette and kitchen use save the hands and are worth their weight in radium. If more women used them the housework problem would be less like martyrdom. They preserve the hands' health and beauty." Ethel R. Peyser, "Tinware, Rubber and Paper for the Kitchen," *House & Garden,* June 1922. People do collect rubber stuff: bathing caps, bathtub toys, dog toys, galoshes! **$7-$15**

Knife cleaner, cast iron square frame screw clamps to table. A crank at side turns 2 geared & cranked felt-covered rollers, making them rub together; they adjust for even snugger contiguation with 2 set screws. The device is used by inserting tip of knife blade between rollers, then turning crank, probably while pushing blade all the way through. I imagine the felt rollers were possibly dressed with some kind of scouring material too, pumice or **brickstone**. This scouring powder probably fell off the rollers into the bottom of the device, which has sides that form an inch deep well. The felt was in round discs, like washers, put on (like beads on a string) the rollers' axles. I guess so that individual ones could be replaced if badly cut or worn. Pat'd as a "Machine for Scouring Knives, Etc." by G. M. Morris and J. Newton, Watertown, CT, base 4-3/8" square, rollers approx. 2" diameter and 2-1/2" L, overall height 7-1/2", including screw clamp, only mark is the patent date, Dec. 4, 1855. **Detective Serendipity Identifies Whatzit:** I got this at auction, and thought it was a pea sheller — that pea pods were cranked through the presumably once-soft felt rollers, popping them open so the peas would fall in the well. Oh dear, such fantasizing. The 1855 patent

IX-8. Rubber glove. *From 1870* American Agriculturist *ad of Goodyear's I[ndia] R[ubber] Glove Mfg. Co., NYC, in business at least since 1866. I don't know if you'd ever find a pair not dried out or shrunk in on themselves and sticky, but a collector of rubber bathtub toys & hot water bottles suggests treating them with Neat's Foot Oil and carefully stuffing with polyester fiber fill from a craft store "pillow-making" supplies.* **$7-$15**

IX-9. Rotary knife cleaners. (**L**) *Cranked machine (the interior moved, not the outer part with the knives stuck out of holes), on table-like frame. "Knife-cleaning machine. — By the use of which knives need never be put in water, and are kept bright with less time or trouble than in the old fashioned way."* American Home Cook Book, *1854.* (**R**) *"Kent's" patented rotary cleaner, originally pat'd in England. Made to hold 3, 4, 5, 6, 7, 8, 9 or 10 knives, including a carving knife. This one is tabletop style with cast iron frame and wooden drum. Very similar one mfd. in England by Spong & Co. Sold well into 20th C. for hotels and restaurants. This picture from V. Clad catalog, c.1890.* **$165-$350**

date was too early for the *Official Gazette,* which didn't start until 1873. The thing wasn't listed under Pea Shellers in my subject index to patents up to 1873. By chance, browsing in a Patent Office book picturing agricultural and mechanical patents of 1855, I found a recognizable drawing of a knife scourer, and it immediately made perfect sense! Nice to identify a Whatzit. **$30-$50**

Knife cleaner, polishing-stone blade, green wooden handle, probably A & J, 7" L, c.1930s to 1940s. **$4-$8**

Knife cleaner, tabletop style, cast iron frame with wooden drum slotted for inserting knives so several can be done at once. Inside, a rubber roller (like wringer) polishes blades, with aid of a polishing powder, "Kents," London, England, various sizes for different numbers of knives, pat'd 1882. Kents' common "Improved Patent" was pat'd 1890. In *Knights' Cyclopaedia of the Industry of All Nations* (London, 1851), appears this: "... a machine has been invented to perform the operation of cleaning table-knives; in which the cleaner has simply to turn a handle, instead of bestowing arm-movement in a somewhat laborious way. There are two rival patented machines for this purpose, Kent's and Masters'; both relate to a machine which was invented by an American, and was introduced into this country [England] ... by the parties above-named. The machine consists of a flat cylinder, or drum, in the inside of which are brushes placed in contact; holes are made round the drum, in which are placed from four to twelve knives, according to the size of the machine. The blades of the knives pass between the brushes; and when the brushes are made to roate by a handle worked from without, the blades of the knives are exposed to an amount of friction sufficient to clean their surfaces." **$185-$350**

"Slow Tunes and Quick Tunes — I have heard the anecdote attributed to Rowland Hill; who, being annoyed at his footboy singing profane songs whilst cleaning the knives and forks, ordered him, under the penalty of dismissal, to sing hymns. But as the work proceeded only to the tune of the solemn yet slow measure, Mr. Hill was compelled to tell the boy to return to his old style of profane music, otherwise his knives and forks would not have been ready for dinner." Alfred John Dunkin, to British periodical *Notes and Queries,* 3rd Series, Volume VII, April 8, 1865.

IX-10. Knife scouring or cleaning boxes. *Also called* **knife boards.** *A bath brick or other suitably fine grit was kept in the box-like part; knives were laid on the long part of* (**1**)*, or slanted part of* (**2**) *and* (**3**)*, and rubbed with rag, brush or large cork. Knives polished by moving back & forth between leather-covered hinged parts of* (**4**)*, while pressing down to make tight fit. All between about 16" to 26" L.* (**1**) *and* (**2**) *F. A. Walker catalog, c.1870s.* (**3**) *and* (**4**) *both from* American Agriculturist, *6/1876 and 8/1875. It was advised to "wipe knives with woolen cloth after rinsing." This was to impart a bit of anti-rust lanolin to the metal. Old paint, attractive patina and decorative cutouts, etc., would add value.* **$40-$150**

Knife cleaner & polisher, cast iron frame, screw clamps to table edge, other screws adjust distance between white rubber fat rollers, works like a mangle, "Spong's UneeK," English, about 9" L, 19th C. **$100-$150**

Knife & scissor grinder, japanned cast iron, screw clamps to table edge, "sapphire" carborundum wheel is turned by crank, & with each turn passes through cooling water compartment below. Both of the 2 wire clips, one on each side, are put in position for one side of knife blade (but are raised out of way when doing scissors). 3 toothed gears "gear up" action so that one turn of crank turns wheel 6 times. "Clipper," mfd. by Montgomery & Co., NYC, wheel 4" diameter x 1" thick, entire grinder about 7" H, 1890. **$35-$50**

Knife scouring board or box, also called simply a **knife board**, used for cleaning blades, painted wood with bath brick in compartment, heart cutout at top end, prob. PA, 38" L x 5-1/2" W, mid 19th C. **$250-$350+**

Knife scouring box, pine with original green paint on outside, simple box attached to footed scouring platform, American, mid 19th C. **$250-$350+**

Knife scouring box, wood, long board with compartment at one end for bath brick powder or other abrasive that was spread on board so that when the flats of the knife blades were rubbed up & down, sort of a lá razor stropping, they would be polished. American, 34" L x 5-1/2" W (they vary in length from about 30" to 40", and in width from about 4-1/2" to 6"), 19th C. Added value — Those with old painted surfaces outside, fancy cutting to sides of compartment, or hangup hole in fancy cutout (especially a heart), could bring up to five times as much as this: **$100-$150**

Knife sharpener, bentwood drum, vertically mounted (like a one-man band's drum beat with the foot pedal) on iron frame, iron crank, with leather polishing leaves inside on a wheel. Used with polishing powder, mildly abrasive, "Self-adjusting Stag," mfd. by Spong & Co. Ltd., English, tabletop model (others floor standing and more expensive), late 19th C. Spong also made the earlier "The Servant's Friend Patent Knife Cleaner," circa 1880. **$200-$300**

Knife sharpener, cast iron with 3 legs, spring steel in bottom allows adjustment of the 2 bars that sharpen, American, 6" L, pat'd Oct. 1891. **$55-$65**

Knife sharpener, for scissors too, cast iron fishtail-like piece at one end with sharpening stone, attached to a longish pointed "steel" [a rod with very fine crosshatched surface texture] for sharpening large chef's or butcher's knives, mfd. by Goodell Co., about 13" L, turn of century. **$40-$55**

Knife sharpener, homemade tools with 2 squares of steel screwed to wooden handle, resembles a patented sharpener of same type, American, 5-1/2" L, late 19th C. **$30-$40**

Knife sharpener, iron & carborundum, "Winchester," New Haven, CT, early 20th C. **$65-$85**

Knife sharpener, iron with wood handle, "Eversharp," Tungsten Tool Co., NYC, NY, early 20th C. **$20-$25**

IX-11. Razor sharpener. *The "Expeditious" is a modification of American table-knife sharpener of 1830s. Two smooth cast steel balls in brass frame with ivory handle; blade was drawn between the balls, which were 3/4" to 1" diameter and had a hole drilled through the center. Screw at right "added for the purpose of keeping the balls in contact, and if the pivots are ... a little loose in frame, the balls may be turned and again fixed. The balls are made as hard as possible, and polished in a direction opposite to that of their axes."* Journal of the Franklin Institute, *1837.* **$50-$100**

Knife sharpener, large bench style, has 6 carborundum sticks in a wheel at top, adjustable, red painted cast iron with black & yellow pinstriping, oil can attached, "Blankner's Knife Sharpener," mfd. by Blankner Knife Sharpener Co., Cleveland, OH, 9-1/2" H x 11" L, "patent pending" (c.1880s), and marked on wheel 0-5-4-3-2-1. I don't know why, but these numbers may work like the number used to designate printings in books, which are removed one by one each time book goes back to press. **$250-$350**

Knife sharpener, simple turned wood handle with screwed-on adjustable steel pieces, brass tip, American, 7-1/4" L, late 19th C. **$25-$30**

Knife sharpener, looks homemade, brass with some iron, stamped with individual letter stamps to read "M A R Y E Z I L," only 3-5/8" L, late 19th C (?). **$25-$30**

Knife sharpener, metal, adv'g "Crescent Hill Milk," 1920s. **$10-$15**

Knife sharpener, metal, "Sharpeit," mfd. by Dazey Churn Co., St. Louis, pat'd 1925. **$20-$25**

Knife sharpener, metal, "Lil Sharpy," mfd. by Milwaukee File Co., WI, late 19th or early 20th C. **$10-$20**

Knife sharpener, nickeled cast metal, 2 sharpening stones, screw clamps to table, lever works the 2 upright "Y" sharpening stones mounted to metal, H. L. Johnson, 6-7/8" H, pat'd July 24, 1888 & Sept. 2, 1890. **$45-$65**

Knife sharpener, nickeled steel with wooden knob handle, J. B. Foote Foundry Co., Fredericktown, OH, about 5" H, 1906. **$20-$30**

Knife sharpener, steel frame & "roof"-like housing, "corundum" wheel, wall mounted, access through 2 guide slots on top, crank turns wheel, "Wulff Knife Sharpener," Hone-Rite, 1941 patent #2257407. **$5-$10**

Knife sharpener, tabletop, iron frame with iron water trough to catch the water used to cool as it worked, cranked grindstone, mounted on wooden plank base, American, 8" diameter grindstone (other sizes from 6" to12" diameter), turn of century. **$35-$50**

Knife sharpener, turned wood handle & frame, partly cut through from use, 2 small square iron plates bolted in position to create a V-opening for sharpening knife, loosen them & rotate edges of plates, American, 5-3/8" L, mid 19th C. to 1870s. **$30-$45**

Stove & Knife Sharpener Combined — A candidate for most unusual, although very logical, combination tool is F. & L. Kahn's c.1890 range or stove top of cast iron, with a special beveled edge in the front to be used like a knife sharpening steel to clean up burry edges of a knife. Sturdy — that's for sure. The ads claimed "Always ready. Always Sharp! Always useful." Kahn, I believe, sold rights to stove companies to manufacture their own stoves or ranges with the Kahn's patented edge.

Plate or dish scraper, hard white rubber, green rubber handle, "Daisy," mfd. by Schact Rubber Mfg. Co., Huntington, IN, 5-3/4" L, 1933 patent #1898690. **$5-$8**

Plate or dish scraper, rubber with wood handle, "A & J," but mfd. by company that took over A & J, Edward Katzinger Co., Chicago, IL, c.1940. **$5-$8**

Plate or dish scraper, white rubber blade in stamped metal holder, turned wooden painted handle, marked "WB/W," I think it's probably Waterbury Button & Mfg. Co., (thought by Don Thornton to be Washburn Bros.), Waterbury, CT, 5-3/4" L, c.1925. A number of hard rubber & metal plate scrapers were made by different companies. Lasher Mfg. of Davenport, IA, made one around 1909-1910 with turned wooden handle, half-moon metal plate with rubber scraper part, called the "Kitchen Kumfort." Around 1915 Cassady-Fairbank Mfg. of Chicago made the "Foskett" scraper, almost identical in form. **$5-$8**

IX-12. Knife sharpeners. (T-L) *has three cast iron legs, and spring steel in bottom allows adjustment of twocrisscross sharpening bars. 6" H. Pat'd 10/1891.* **(T-R)** *is homemade, wood handle with 2 squares of steel screwed to wood, the wood almost cut through by many sharpenings. 5-1/2" L. Late 19th C.* **(B)** *in foreground is turned wood with 2 crisscrossed, adjustable steel sticks. 7-1/4" L.* **$25-$65**

IX-13. Knife sharpeners. (L) *"Silver Duplex," silver & Co., Brooklyn, c.1910. Small screw-clamped cast iron frame, 2 steel sharpening sticks.* **(R)** *Nickeled steel with knobby wood handle. J. B. Foote Foundry Co., 1906.* **$25-$35**

IX-14. Knife sharpeners & scissor sharpener. *Clockwise from top:* **(1)** *"Clipper," for knives & scissors. Shown with wire clip for doing knives. Cranked, screw clamped to table, pat'd 5/18/1886. Widely advertised 1880s to 1910s.* **(2)** *"Handy" sharpener for scissors. Eastman & Co., NYC. 1895 ad.* **(3)** *"American," mfd. by Mossberg Wrench Co., Mfrs of Novelties, Attleboro, MA. Pat'd 2/23/1892. Two discs between which blade was pulled.* **(4)** *"Peerless" combo sharpener & can opener. Early 20th C.* **$6-$45**

Polish, for aluminum, paper canister with silvery printed label, "Silver-Seal Polish, esp. prepared for Silver-Seal Kitchen Equipment," mfd. by Century Metalcraft Corp., Detroit, MI, (Chicago office named on label), early 20th C. **$5-$12**

Pot cleaner, stamped sheet steel, parallelogram almost square, with short handle from one corner, 2 corrugated edges, one edge with bristles set along it, "The Korker Sink & Pot Cleaner," about 4" square, turn of century. **$25-$40**

IX-15. Plate or dish scrapers. (L) *"Foskett's," wood, tin, rubber, 5-3/4" L, pat'd 6/26/1906. Sold through Wire Goods Co., Worcester, MA, 1915 catalog.* **(M)** *Wood handle, tin riveted clamp for rubber blade. Marked "WB/W." (Perhaps Waterbury Button & Mfg. Co., because hard rubber buttons were common at the time; or, Washburn Brothers.) 5-3/4" L, c.1925. I buy these scrapers all the time because they look so much like small African sculptures when held blade side up.* **(B)** *Rubber with green wood handle, 9-1/2" L. Androck, 1927.* **$4-$10**

IX-16. Pot chains or pot scrubbers. *Not shown to scale; assembled from various catalogues. All chain mail — iron rings linked into flexible pads (or a ball with a handle).* **(1)** *double rings, 4 sizes, from 3-1/2" x 5-1/2" to 8-1/2" x 11", with 1/2" or 3/4" rings. Washburn Co., 1936.* **(2)** *13" x 7", double mesh, hanging ring. Matthai-Ingram, c.1890.* **(3)** *"In some parts of the country, a pot-scrubber made of iron rings, as shown, is used, but it is by no means so well known as it ought to be. We do not know who the manufacturer is, but it is for sale at some of the hardware stores in New York City."* American Agriculturist, 7/1877. *Over a century later, in the 1980s, some were being made in midwest by an elderly man who had made them in a factory ages ago.* **(4)** *also Matthai-Ingram.* **(5)** *"Sensible," all nickel-plated, iron handle is also a scraper. 5/8" double rings, 5-1/2" x 3-1/4". Excel c.1916 catalog, and Washburn, 1936. Caution: Various styles are being reproduced.* **$18-$50**

Metal Polishing Recipes — "Common irons may be brightened by rubbing them first with a rag dipped in vinegar and the ashes, then with an oily rag, and after that with scouring paper, rotten stone, or white brick; but, if possible, red-brick should not be used, for it makes sad work. This method of cleaning serves for all sorts of common irons or brasses, tho' some prefer goose-grease to oil, or any other sort of grease, and do not use scouring-paper to brasses. If these should be very fine steel stoves and fenders, they should be first rubbed with oil, then with emery, till clear and bright, and next with scouring paper, which is an excellent thing to rub irons with that are not in constant use, every two or three days." Eliza F. Haywood, *A New Present for a Servant-Maid; Necessary Cautions and Precepts to Servant-Maids for Gaining Good-Will and Esteem*, Dublin, Ireland: 1771. Whew! and for a wage of a few pounds a year!

Pot cleaner, wire rings like chain mail, wire loop handle, some have iron loop handle, made first in the late 19th C., but now widely reproduced. "The 'chain-cloth' a net work of steel rings resembling an old fashioned reticule is of great service in cleaning burned kettles." Todd S. Goodholme, *Domestic Cyclopedia of Practical Information*, NY: Henry Holt, 1877. **$18-$50**

Pot mender, tube holding a small sharp metal reamer and white metal (relatively soft) rivets. Only a hammer was needed. Paper label on tube reads: "For tin, enamelled & Aluminum ware. Saves money — double life of ware. Directions. Rivets in the handle. Ream hole to fit rivet. Hammer in place. . . ." Arco Sanitary Mender, 7" L, 1910. **$9-$15**

IX-17. Pot menders. *"Mendets," Collette Mfg. Co., Amsterdam, NY. A metal patch, a tiny "bolt," and a small triangular wrench, mounted on chromolithographed card. This one c.1940. Fun to collect a variety from different periods; in 1908 they called them "Collette's Patent Patches." By 1910 they had name "Mendets." They're still sold, but card graphics are ugly.* **$6-$20**

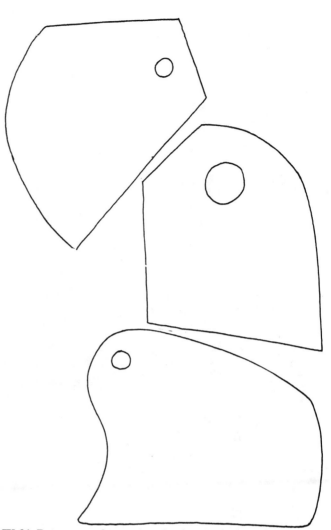

IX-18. Scrapers of various kinds. (1) *and* **(2)** *are* **dough scrapers**. **(1)** *Wood handle, 5", 6", 7", or 8" W;* **(2)** *Tubular handle, all iron, 4", 5" or 6" W. Duparquet, Huot & Moneuse, c.1904-1910.* **(3) Candy-makers' crystallizing pan scraper.** *Sethness, 1925.* **(4)** *Often sold as chopper, but is kettle or* **pan scraper,** *all steel, tubular handle. T. Mills, 1930 catalog of candy-makers' supplies.* **(5)** *Bench or* **butcher block scraper,** *all steel.* **(6) Broiler scraper,** *triangular blade, wood handle.* **(5)** *&* **(6)** *look quite old, and the forms may be, but they both are in a c.1904-1910 catalog.* **$15-$45**

IX-19. Pot, pan and kettle scraper. *Note that this is almost exactly the same as the potscraper shape most commonly found with lithographed advertising. The early date of the following story by a magazine editor predates the chromolithed scrapers it so resembles by 25 to 35 years. "A curious thing came by mail. It was a piece of galvanized iron, of about 2 inches length, and had attached to it a label which read: 'Pot, Pan, and Kettle Scraper. Please accept, with the compliments of the season, from John Furbish, dealer in kitchen furnishing goods, stoves, etc., Main street, Brunswick, ME. December 25, 1871.' It seems that Furbish did not, as many stupid people do, go and patent a simple thing. He had tried it, found it good, had a lot made, and gave one to every holiday customer. The piece of sheet-iron is so shaped that it will meet all possible angles, and save no end of knives and spoons. ... First rate, and I wish I had had one before." American Agriculturist editor, 5/1872.* **$6-$8**

IX-21. Pot scraper shapes. *Actual reduced tracings of three types in the Karol Atkinson Collection.* **(T)** *Small hanging hole, approx. 3-1/2" across.* **(M)** *Larger hanging hole, commonest shape ("Admiral Coffee," "Ward's Remedies, Extracts, ..." "Mt. Penn Stove Works," Red Wing Milling Co.," "Sharples," and "Dove Brand" ham & bacon). Approx. 3-7/8" across;* **(B)** *Small hanging hole, most curvaceous shape, "Junket" dessert powders is in this shape. Approx. 2-9/16" x 3".*

IX-20. Pot & pan scraper. *"Instantly cleans pots, pans, pails, cake tins, cake griddles, dough boards, etc." Picture copyrighted 1909 by "Peale Hdw. Co." or possibly "Pease Hdw. Co." From door-to-door salesman's catalog, F. W. Seastrand, c.1910s.* **$6-$8**

IX-22. "POT & PAN SCRAPER FITS ALL CORNERS." *Chromolithographed sheet metal (tinned steel), flat, approx. 3-1/2" across. "Dove Brand" ham & bacon, Cincinnati, OH. Picture courtesy Karol Atkinson Collection. Rhymes in segments along edges tell how it's used: "Here's to the girls/ who cook and bake/ and from the pans/ take out the cakes./ And also to her/ who fries the ham/ and turns it often/ in the skillet pan./ After all/ when the work was well done/ this little instrument/ did help some." C. 1910s.* **$125-$200**

IX-23. Pot scraper. *"Sharples Tubular Cream Separator." Beautifully color lithographed scene. Reverse is in cobalt blue and depicts the separator. Approximately 3-1/2" across. Picture courtesy Karol Atkinson Collection. 1909. These are essentially advertising collectibles, which is why the values are so high for examples in extremely good condition.* **$175-$250+**

IX-24. Pot scraper. *Color lithographed sheet metal. "Red Wing Milling Co.," Red Wing, MN. A name known to many collectors of decorated stoneware crocks, jugs, and beater jars from all the consortium of Red Wing potteries. These are another crossover collectible, sought by three schools of collectors — kitchen, advertising, Red Wing. Picture courtesy Karol Atkinson Collection.* **$275-$375+**

Pot menders, soft metal patches with tiny rivet or bolt, small triangular wrench, mounted on chromolithographed card, "Mendets," Collette Mfg. Co., Amsterdam, NY, different sizes & different number of patches, pat'd 1922, several different cards through the years, and still being made. **$5-$12**

Pot menders, wooden box with little metal discs and special "wrench," "Mendet's," pat'd 1922. **$5-$15**

Pot scraper, green, cream & black lithographed sheet tin, advertising type. "Mount Penn Stove Works, Penn Pots & Pan Scraper, Fits any corner of pot or pan," printer/mfr W. D. Beach Co., Coshocton, OH. This and one for Henkel's Flour are two most common scrapers. Of all the pot scrapers, this is the only one I run into fairly often. Still — this, like anything else — won't get less rare with time. **$65-$90**

Pot scrapers are small flat pieces of metal, approximately 3" across, plain or lithographed with advertising (sometimes on both sides). They usually are found in one of three shapes that have curves and corners meant to dig crud or crust out of any shaped pan. Collector Karol Atkinson, who wrote an article on pot scrapers for my second and third editions, has only found two different manufactuer's marks on the advertising type: W. D. Beach Co., Coshocton, OH; and Passaic Metal Ware Co., Passaic, NJ. Crossover collector interest has raised the asking price of two sought by graniteware collectors — the NESCO, and the "Royal Granite Ware" — to over $350 sometimes! The one with a fabulous color depiction of a sack of Red Wing Milling flour, with the wonderful red wing, has also greatly increased in value because it's desired by Red Wing ceramics collectors. One that has eluded Atkinson is a lithographed tin one depicting Buster Brown, and advertising "Buster Brown Bread," made by Schmidt's Bakeries, Harrisburg, PA.

Pot scraper, lithographed tin, "Royal Granite Ware," late 19th C. This one achieved at the George Haney auction in April 1988, an amazing $225. High auction records don't set future market prices in stone, but they sure affect them. This qualifies as an advertising piece, and is highly desirable to enamelware collectors. **$250-$375**

Pot scraper, lithographed tin, depicts flour sack with big red wing, "Red Wing Milling Co., Red Wing, MN", c.1910. A lot of crossover interest because of "Red Wing" stonewares. **$250-$375**

Pot scraper, color lithographed tin, nice depiction of dairy maid entering stone-floored dairy house, carrying her bucket, and preparing to use the advertised cream separator, near the door, "Sharples Tubular Cream Separator," c. 1910. **$175-$250**

Pot scraper, nickel plated steel, shaped to fit crevices & corners of pots and pans, marked "Jack the Scraper," mfd. by Bauer Utensil Mfg. Co., Cleveland, OH, c.1914. That name alone is collectible! **$15-$25**

Pot scraper, tin, triangular with hang up hole, no advertising — possibly scoured off long ago, late 19th C. **$12-$15**

"A **clam shell** is more convenient for scraping kettles and frying pans than a knife. It does the work in less time." Emma Babcock, *Household Hints*, 1881.

Scissors sharpener, adv'g "Monarch Malleable Ranges," turn of century to 1920s. **$25-$35**

Sink brush, tin, steel wire bristles, simple wood handle, fan-shaped, also cleans crevices in pots & pans, marked "Y-R," mfd. by Rice Mfg. Co., New Durham, NH, 9-1/4" L x 4" W, pat'd 2/27/1900. **$12-$18**

IX-27. Soap saver. *Wire mesh box, twisted wire handle with slip ring, wood grip. 10" L, c.1920-40s. Collection of the Disshuls.* **$8-$15**

IX-26. Sink brush. *Wire with wood handle. Marked "Y-R," pat'd 2/27/1900, mfd. by Rice Mfg. Co., New Durham, NH. 9-1/4" L.* **$12-$18**

IX-25. Sinks. (T) *"Wash Sink for Kitchen," suggested to improve the "unpleasant features" of dish washing. Sink is "lined with sheet-iron instead of zinc, and is made with two divisions." Removable wooden racks. American Agriculturist, 4/1883.* **(B)** *"Sanitas" kitchen sink, fancy cast iron legs (which are now very valuable to restorers). From Alfred Revill's American Plumbing, NYC, 1894.*

Soap cleanser canister, green paint enameled metal canister with shaker holes in top, side embossed with image of Dutch Girl, screw-on bottom is black, "Old Dutch Cleanser," c.1930s-1950s. **$15-$25**

Soap cleanser canister, tin, color lithographed, "Bon Ami" 12 oz. capacity, 1940s. When I was about 2-1/2, I started a combined scrapbook and sketchbook. The color ads for the Bon Ami chick — "Hasn't scratched yet" — were my favorite, and the scrapbook is full of Bon Ami ads. **$30-$45**

Soap saver, homemade sheet steel, nice perforated box with long handle, fill with soap scraps to swish in dishpan, American, 13-3/4" L, turn of century. **$25-$35**

Soap saver, or <u>suds whipper</u>, woven wire like a bustle making 2 fat pillows with a long wooden handle, American, 10-5/8" L, early 20th C. **$20-$30**

Soap saver, round perforated tin box , 2 equal parts held together with slip ring on long spring wire handle, Matthai-Ingram Co., about 11" L, pat'd Sept. 14, 1875, but sold for decades. **$12-$20**

Soap saver, spring steel wire with stamped mesh holder for soap scraps, 2 round biscuit-shape halves of the soap compartment clamped together by slip ring on long wire handle, American, 19th C. **$12-$20**

Soap saver, tin frame with twisted wire handle & hanging loop, wire mesh container for the soap, 3-1/2" x 2-1/2" with 7" L handle, turn of century. **$18-$25**

Soap saver, wire mesh box, wooden handle, box is hinged 2 parts, with little hook closing that slips under ring on shaft of handle, 10" L, c.1920s to 1940s. **$10-$15**

Soap shaver, tin with wire arch handle, looks like a vegetable grater but the openings are like little crescent moons or smiles, embossed "Sunny Monday — Saves Soap & Labor," 10-3/4" L x 4" W, c.1900 to 1920. **$15-$20**

Stove blacking brush, iron handle, black bristles, "People's," turn of century. **$18-$25**

Stove polish can, colorful lithographed tin, depicts devils cavorting on black iron cookstove, "X-Ray Stove Polish," turn of century to 1910s. **$35-$45**

IX-28. Soap savers. *Soap scraps are put into the boxes or cages, and tool is swished through dishwater to make suds. Works great. (L) to (R) from top:* **(1)** & **(2)** *Tin with fine wire mesh, 2 different handles. Both are 1-1/2" deep x 2-3/8" diameter x 12" L. Wire Goods Co., 1915.* **(3)** *Matthai-Ingram, pat'd 9/14/1875. c.1890 catalog.* **(4)** *"New Standard," from unID c.1900 flyer.* **(5)** & **(6)** *Tinned wire, different meshes offered.* **(5)** *Came in 4 box sizes, 11" L or 16" L.* **(6)** *Only in wide mesh, 8-1/2" L overall.* **(7)** *With "cups of wire gauze," was described in* American Agriculturist, *1881.* **(8)** *Welded wire, tinned, green handle, 10-1/2" L. Washburn, 1936.* **$10—$30**

COOKING

X. HEARTHS & FIREPLACES

The increasing interest in practical hearth-cooking and the revival of walk-in fireplaces built to order by specialists, as well as the generally separable goals of collectors of hearth wares and those of cast iron stove or range wares, have persuaded me to make this a chapter on its own. Most pieces here are from the eighteenth and nineteenth centuries.

I apologize for the lack of a chapter devoted to late nineteenth- and twentieth-century pots and pans. Simply put, there is no room, and there is coverage by other writers. There are several excellent books on enamelware, including pots and pans, and there are a few devoted to, or including, cast iron hollowware. So far, there is little collector interest in aluminum wares. This chapter, in its fourth incarnation, will not have the extensive section devoted to andirons that were in the third edition. It is a fascinating subject, and much of the research I did would help dealers and collectors of figural nineteenth- and early twentieth-century andirons. But this is a book for cooking antiques, and few andirons are part of a kitchen's equipment.

You may be confused at times. Some **hollowwares** and some implements, that are very old and were meant to be used in hearth cooking, were carried over to cast iron cooking ranges, which were coming into use by the first quarter of the nineteenth century in some urban houses, while the old-fashioned hearth cooking techniques were still being practiced late in the nineteenth century in many rural homes. I've put the hollowwares and the "sad" wares like griddles in this chapter, and many implements, such as flesh forks or tasting spoons (although they started life as hearth-cooking implements), in Chapter XIII. Old tea kettles used in the hearth are in Chapter XIV (Coffee, Tea and Chocolate).

One caution about collecting hearth-cooking tools, from whirling broilers to spiders to trammels: a good percentage (not calculable at this point, but perhaps as much as 75%) of the *old* forged iron, cast bronze, or cast iron pieces have been brought over in the last two decades from Europe and the Middle East. The first wave of modern immigrant hearthiana came, as did the *Mayflower* 300+ years ago, from the British Isles. Then wares from Germany, Holland, Italy, France, and other areas such as Scandinavia began to be imported in vast quantities. Then the great boneyard of old iron that must lie in every cellar and outbuilding in Portugal was discovered, resulting in a good deal of Portuguese iron here now — much of it quite attractive and decorative. In fact, "decorative" is the quality of much of this container-loaded old iron that enables us to recognize it as European. Where a simple curve might have been used on an American pot rack, for example, a splendiferous (splen-

di-ferrous?) scrolly crest would more likely have been the choice of a European artisan.

The application of decorative motifs to everyday household items came relatively late in Pennsylvania German craft (a delay attributed to the lengthy struggle just to meet purely utilitarian needs). Decoration for art's sake also came late to other immigrant communities throughout this country. When one blacksmith might have to do for an entire village, pounding out necessaries like horseshoes and cranes, does it stand to reason that he would have labored an extra amount of time to add curliques and furbelows while six horses that had thrown their shoes waited out front? Since the last edition in 1991, an alarming number of outright fakes have been imported from Indonesia. They're pretty good craftspeople, too.

It's Later Than You Think — I have acquired an 1895 Harrod's catalog from Great Britain, which offers many hearth-cooking pieces virtually identical in appearance to old ones — tin kitchens, cranes, bird roasters, etc. These weren't reproductions: they were meant to be ordered by a country crofter living in a home that was already 200 or 300 years old, or by a colonial living in more "primitive" conditions halfway around the world.

Regardless of provenance and age problems, the future for this field looks bright. Many collectors actively use their collections, and it's an interior decoration idea still in ascendency. The field still needs sorting out. We are faced, somewhat more directly than is often the case, with the questions of how much value do we place on provenance — how much are origins worth; how much extra value do we chauvinistically place on American origins; how much information will we demand from dealers who sell us old iron trammels and three-legged kettles? From a somewhat academic point of view, I think origins mean a lot, for two reasons. Not only are we usually asked to pay a premium for things "made in the U.S.A." (or the American Colonies, if they predate the Revolution), but our clear view of the background of a thing is obscured when either we aren't told where it is from, or when its origins are deliberately misrepresented. I feel it is necessary to continually stress the substance of things because I value meaning as much as, perhaps more than, appearance, which is why I write so much: in order to give you background to enrich your collecting.

There are many specialty dealers and hearth-cooking teachers around the country. Dealers advertise in such collector newspapers as *Maine Antique Digest,* Waldeboro, ME, often with several photographs of interesting pieces. For hearth-cooking classes in your community, contact your historical society or any restoration village nearby.

Adapter ring, looks like legless pot stand or trivet. Forged iron ring with a long angled-up handle with hanging loop, meant to fit over hole or eye of an early range to support handleless utensils of different circumferences. A versatile handle, useful in late 18th or early 19th C. on the brick ranges of the time, which had iron tops pierced with rows of holes (or eyes) for the utensils. These tops were set into the top of a brick structure which was the firebox. The fire was fed through doors set in the brick; ovens, drafts and dampers were also brick-set. This kind of cooking range was something midway between a fireplace or hearth and a cast iron cooking stove, where the firebox too was made of iron. American or European, about 19" L overall, 8" diameter ring, late 18th or early 19th C. **$30-$40**

Ale boot, shoe shaped, pointed toe, pieced copper, strap handle, pushed into hot ashes to warm ale, American, late 18th C. **$250-$350**

Ale boot or shoe, pieced copper, hinged fitted lid, strap handle, tinned inside, English, 7-1/2" L, late 18th or early 19th C. **$300-$450**

Ale shoe, pieced tin with cast white metal knob on hinged cover, English or American, 9" L, early 19th C. **$200-$275**

Ale warmer, conical, copper with wrought iron handle, tinned inside, English or American, 11" L, early 19th even late 18th. **$225-$250**

Copper caveat — "When taken into the human body, copper acts as a violent emetic, and is generally considered as poisonous; though it has occasionally been prescribed by physicians, it is always an unsafe and hazardous remedy. Hence, the greatest precaution is necessary in using this metal, of which so many kitchen utensils are manufactured. Besides the most scrupulous attention to cleanliness, it is extremely improper to leave any liquid to cool in a copper vessel; for this metal is more easily decomposed by liquids, when cold, than in a heated state.

"In order to prevent the deleterious effects of copper, the vessels made of it are usually covered with tin, on the inside. Nevertheless it is justly complained, that the tinning of copper vessels is not sufficient to defend them from the action of the air, moisture and saline substances; because, even when strongly coated, they are liable to rust [sic]. This may be remedied by a thicker coating of tin; and a manufacturer of this kind was established a few years hence in Edinburgh; in which. . .the surface of the copper is made very rough. . .;

then a thick coat of tin is laid in, and the copper hammered smooth as before." Anthony Florian Madinzer Willich, *The Domestic Encyclopedia; or A Dictionary of Facts & Useful Knowledge*. 1st American edition, Philadelphia: W. Y. Birch & A. Small, 1803-04.

• • • •

Andirons & Firedogs — According to Alice Morse Earle, *Customs & Fashions in Old New England* (Scribner's, 1893): "The **andirons** added to the fireplace their homely charm. **Fire-dogs** appear in the earliest inventories under many names of various spelling, and were of many metals — copper, steel, iron, and brass. Sometimes a fireplace had three sets of andirons of different sizes, to hold logs at different heights. **Cob irons** had hooks to hold a spit and dripping-pan. Sometimes the 'Handirons' also had brackets. **Creepers** were low irons placed between the great fire-dogs. They are mentioned in many early wills and lists of possessions among items of fireplace furnishings, as, for instance, the list of Captain Tyng's furniture, made in Boston in 1653." **Creepers** apparently once had at least four meanings in early America that are at all related to our subject here: **(1)** A Dutch oven; **(2)** "An iron used to slide along the grate in kitchens" Noah Webster, *An American Dictionary*, 1858; **(3)** "An instrument of iron with hooks or claws, for drawing up things from the bottom of a well, river, or harbor." *ibid.* ; and **(4)** "A small, low iron, or dog, between the andirons" — given as an obsolete meaning in *Webster's New International Dictionary*, 1931.

• • • •

New Iron Falsely Aged & Its Telltale Rust — Lester Beitz wrote in an August 1975 article in *Early American Life:* "[Recently] I came upon sets of the renowned Hessian Soldier & General Washington cast iron andirons in the same shop — which made me mighty suspicious. . . . Close examination revealed . . . top quality recasts, complete with that <u>peculiar rust effect</u>, circa 1974, caused by immersion in a solution of vinegar & nitric acid, caustic soda, sal ammoniac, or car battery acid — any number of concoctions which produce the desired effects. . . . the overly large, thin flakes of rust resulting from such treatment are . . . a dead giveaway." And new iron's rust seems to always come out orange.

X-1. Kitchen scenes, c.1690-1700. *Both English, from an early chapbook [cheap book]. Two spits and a legless bulge pot are seen in the first picture. Note plate rack and small-paned windows, which would not have appeared at the time in America. Note the apparent pie funnel in the other picture (above cook's right hand.) Undated chapbook entitled* A Choice Collection of Cookery Receipts, *printed c.1700 at Newcastle, England.*

X-2. Art as "Kitchen Maid" and "Cook Maid," *made up irresistably of kitchen tools. The real master of this style was a 16th C. Italian artist, Archimboldo. SEE chapter on implements for his version. Kitchen Maid has tea kettle head, tong upper body, coal "skuttle" skirt, ash shovel and poker arms. Note brush tucked into tipping handle on the scuttle. The Cook Maid has lid hat, colander face, bellows upper body, frying pan and gridiron arms, soup kettle or cauldron lower body, peel and flesh fork legs and I don't know what her shoulders are. From William Hone's* The Every-Day Book, *Vol. II, London, 1827.*

Andirons, for baking potatoes in hearth, also called **oven andirons**, cast iron, no upright post, mainly comprised of horizontal log supports that are actually hollow slant-sided 'tunnels' with slide-out drawers or ovens for 4 to 6 potatoes to be pushed back within the tunnel. The drawer fronts are shaped, and have a small projection bottom front for hooking with a log hook or other tool to pull drawer out. Both bars have a high toothed ridge cast the length of the top — like a stegosaur's spine plates — to hold logs. No marks mentioned, American, about 5" or 6" H x about 5" or 6" W, about 14" or 15"L, poss. as early as the 1st quarter 19th C., but could be 2nd, even 3rd quarter. These unusual andirons were pictured in an article on "Pre-Stove Cooking," by Edwin C. Whittemore, in *The Spinning Wheel*, March 1965, and have never appeared in any other publication, nor been seen by anyone I've ever talked to. I am guessing at dimensions from the photograph. They are a wonderful idea, and somebody ought to make them now for use in living room fireplaces. **$450-$600+**

Apple butter kettles, hammered copper, flat bottom, side ear handles of iron, American, range from 15 or so gallons up to 40 gallons or more. Imagine lifting this, full or empty. You couldn't! 2nd quarter 19th C. See also stirrers in Chapter II. **$450-$800**

X-3. Adapter ring. *A ring of flat iron with a long handle used to adapt the opening in an early brick raised-hearth range to a vessel somewhat smaller than the opening. Something similar, a stand with legs (bottom left) was used to hold a legless cooking vessel over coals in the hearth.*

X-4. Ale or beer warmers. (T) *two conical ones are of copper, with bow handle or turned wood handle. Sometimes called ale spikes. Came in 1, 2, 3, and 4 pt. sizes; Henry Rogers Sons & Co., Wolverhampton, England, 1914.* **(B-L)** & **(B-R)** *Other two, with and without lids, are called* **ale boots***, ale shoes or ale slippers, also made of copper, although some sheet iron ones are known. The shoes were easier to use than the conical ones which had to be held, or stuck into some kind of trivet or stand.* **(B-L)** *about 9" to 11" L exclusive of handle;* **(B-R)** *is 6" H x 18" L overall. It is from reproduction catalog of Pearson-Page Co., Birmingham & London, England, 1925. Only old ones worth much.* **$100-$375**

Apple Butter Making.— In the Sept. 1847 *American Agriculturalist*, writer E. S. notes "The large copper kettle (my kettle holds half a barrel of cider) three-quarters full of new sweet cider, made from sound apples, is set over the fire before five o'clock in the morning. I let it boil two hours, and then put in as many apples, which were peeled, cored, and cut up the night before, as will fill the kettle, and at the same time, I throw in about two quarts of nicely cleaned peach-stones, which by sinking to the bottom, and being moved about incessantly by the stirrer, prevent the fruit from settling and burning, which would spoil the whole. I take care in selecting the apples to secure a large proportion of sour ones; for, as the cider is sweet, unless this precaution be taken, the sauce will have a vapid taste that nothing can remove. . . . On the hearth, around the fire, I place numerous pans and pots of apples and cider, simmering and stewing, which I empty into the kettle as fast in succession as the contents boil away enough to make room for them; but after twelve o'clock I never allow any more to be added to the mass. The boiling must be continued steadily until the whole is reduced to a smooth, thick marmalade, of a dark, rich brown color, and no cider separates when a small portion is cooled for trial.

"From the moment the first apples are put into the boiling cider, the whole must be stirred without a moment's intermission, otherwise it will settle and burn; but the handle of the stirrer must be passed from hand to hand as often as fatigue or inclination makes a change desirable.

"My kettle holds half a barrel of cider, which, with the first apples in it, begins to boil about nine o'clock in the morning, and the whole is done enough by eight o'clock in the evening, when a sufficient quantity of powdered all-spice, cloves and cinnamon may be added to season it to your taste. The apple-butter must be dipped out as soon as possible when it stops boiling; for, if it cools in the copper or brass, it is in danger of becoming poisonous, as may be detected even by the unpleasant taste imparted by the action of the acid upon the copper. I prefer sweet stone, or earthen-ware pots to keep it in, but where the quantity made is very large, a barrel may be employed."

X-5. Andiron bake oven. *Cast iron, with sliding oven "drawer" for baking potatoes or other food. It is relatively low and rather short, appearing to be about a foot to 15" L in the photograph. This drawing is taken from the only picture I've ever seen of this type of andiron — it appeared in "Pre-Stove Cooking," by Edwin C. Whittemore, Spinning Wheel, 3/1965. The brontosaurus ridge holds the logs above and also conducts heat from every point touching the burning log. Hot ashes are pushed up against the tunnel. Possibly as late as mid 19th C., but probably much earlier. Collector Joel Schiff saw a recently made adaptation of this made of gritty cast iron, and with a cast woman's head bolted on to the front of the drawer. It was not a good casting at all, sharp edges and no finish, and yet the dealer asked $600.* **$450-$600+**

A. M. Thomas, of Flemington, NJ, wrote a query to *Americana* magazine in July/Aug. 1989, about the effects of making **apple butter in cast iron**. She wrote "of the experience of a woman in this area who made apple butter in a large ironware pot, only to find that her teeth turned black after she ate the apple butter. A food scientist at Rutgers University explained that tartaric acid from the apples combined with iron from the pot to produce iron tartrate salts." Maybe all those witches depicted cooking over a pot, grinning through their black teeth, were fond of butter of apple, not eye of newt.

Apple roaster, dark heavy gauge old-looking tin reflecting oven, 3 shelves, shaped feet, 2 little strap handles on side, about the size for pippins, American, only 7-3/8" H x 6" W, mid- to late 19th C.(?) These were made in 18th and throughout entire 19th centuries. **$300-$400**

Apple roaster, tin hearth reflector, on top is a bracket strap handle, 2 shelves, upper shelf is <u>perforated</u> with long eye- or almond-shaped slots, the only such roaster that dealer Joe Dziadul has ever seen. American, 9-1/8" H x 9-5/8" W, early 19th C. **$450-$600**

Apple roaster, tin & iron, wooden handle, looks sort of like a silent butler or a fat-hooded dustpan, American, c.1870s. **$125-$175**

Apple roaster, tin, open front reflecting oven with adjustable tray, American, early to mid-19th C. (?) **$300-$400+**

Bannock board, thick plank of unidentified wood with smooth face, set with stubby wooden handle in back that props it at about a 40 degree angle, used for making corn meal cakes called bannocks. American (?), 12" L x 8" W, handle 6" L, early 19th C., poss. later. **$40-$60**

> **Bannock** (Gaelic: <u>bonnach</u>. Irish: <u>boinneag</u>.): In Scotland, a cake of oatmeal, baked on an iron plate.
>
> Behind the door a bag of meal;
> And in the kist was plenty
> Of good hard cakes his mither bakes;
> And bannocks were nae scanty.
>
> *Scotch Songs,* II. 71.

"In New England, cakes of Indian meal [cornmeal], fried in lard, are called bannocks." John Russell Bartlett, *Dictionary of Americanisms. A Glossary of Words and Phrases usually regarded as peculiar to the United States* . Boston: 2nd ed.1859 (1st ed. 1848).

• • • •

Recipes for Bannocks — (1) "Into one pint of Indian meal stir a pint of buttermilk; 1/2 teaspoon of salt; one teaspoon of molasses; one of butter; and add two well-beaten eggs; one pint of wheat flour; thin with milk to a thin batter; last, stir in two large teaspoons of soda dissolved in hot water; pour into buttered shallow pans; bake one hour in quick oven which bakes top and bottom brown." This recipe, which sounds like corn muffins, appeared in *Treasure-House of Useful Knowledge,* compiled by Henry B. Scammel, who pirated recipes from many earlier cookbooks.

(2) "To one quart sour milk, put a teaspoon of salaeratus, dissolved in water; warm the milk slightly, beat up an egg, and put in corn meal enough to make it thick as pudding batter, and some salt; grease a pan and bake it, or you may put it in six or eight saucers." Elizabeth Lea, *Domestic Cookery,* Baltimore, 1851, 1859.

(3) **"Irish Bread** — 4 cupfuls flour, 1/2 cupful butter, 1 1/2 cupfuls milk, 1/2 teaspoonful salt, 3 teaspoonfuls Calumet baking powder. Mix the ingredients to a soft dough; roll an inch thick, shape into cakes, six inches across, with a large cooky cutter, and bake on a hot griddle. Before taking from the fire, be sure they are baked to the heart. Split in two, butter and serve hot." Sidney Morse, *Household Discoveries,* c.1909. When I made bannocks (on a plank in front of a huge fire), I used the latter recipe, substituting cornmeal for half the flour. They were rolled to about half an inch thickness, and slapped on the board rather smartly. They cooked through, "to the heart," before they lost their precarious hold on the plank. If I tried them again, I'd experiment with using a little brown rice or oat flour (from health food store), which are quite sticky.

Fire-Cakes — "There never was anything that tasted better than my mother's 'fire-cake,' — a short-cake spread on a smooth piece of board, and set up with a flat-iron before the blaze, browned on one side, and then turned over to be browned on the other. (It required some sleight of hand to do that.) If I could only be allowed to blow the bellows — the very old people called them 'belluses' — when the fire began to get low, I was a happy girl." Lucy Larcom, in *A New England Girlhood,* Boston: 1890.

Bellows, various types: **(1)** small, hand-held decorative leather & painted wood, turned handles, brass trim, for parlor use; **(2)** larger, simpler wood & leather, for kitchen hearth or small blacksmith's hearth; and **(3)** mechanical bellows, keywound or cranked, wood & metal without accordian action, more like a fan. All 3 types are collected; at present, mechanicals are most desired by collectors. For example: iron fitted, wood-cased belt-drive type in 2 parts: a sort of bellows-shape body, awkwardly held in left hand by short turned wood handle or set on hearth pointing brass "hose" nozzle at embers, upper wheel cranked to motivate fan blades in lower part, drawing air in side vents & exhaling it from nozzle, French, 21" H, early 19th C. **$400-$2000+**

X-6. Bellows. *"Buffalo" bellows, mfd. by Joseph Churchyard, Buffalo Bellows Factory, Buffalo, NY. Under his direction, "skilled worken" made "warranted bellows of the Eastern, Southern and Pittsburgh Patterns ... of the best materials." He also repaired them. Ad in Thomas'* Buffalo City Directory, *1866.*

X-7. Bellows. *"Antique oak" in six sizes, and "complete assortment of other styles." German import advertised by G. M. Thurnauer & Brother, NYC, 11/1909. Many companies made bellows in a deliberately old-fashioned style, some complete with painted boards and fancy trims.*

Bird roaster, heavy gauge tin reflecting oven with triangular sides with strap handles, looks like a pup tent, the back pivots at the crest of the "tent" and flips to cover open side, so you don't have to take the birds off the 2 hooks to turn them, you simply flip the reflecting back & turn the roaster, American, 7" H x 8" L, 19th C.   **$300-$400+**

Reproduction alert for bellows — A very large number of old-looking decorated bellows were sold during the heartily hearth-conscious Colonial Revival 1920s and 1930s. The leather of these repro or fake old bellows were painted, studded with brass, or fitted with repoussé brass in the same shape of the bellows. They used to cost under $10 usually, and worked perfectly for their purpose. A worn and battered bellows found now might be but 60 or 70 years old.

X-8. Standing bellows. *Mechanical type with adjustable front leg to deliver the blast where it was needed. 27" H x 38" L, probably English, early 19th C. From ad of James II, in James Robinson's gallery, NYC.* **$1800+**

X-9. Bird roaster, reflecting oven. *Pieced tin, 4 hooks under hood, strap handle. Drip pan has two birdbeak pouring spouts at corners. 10" H. Photo courtesy Litchfield Auction Gallery, CT. Ex-Harold Corbin Collection, auctioned 1/1/1990, for $375.* **$300-$425**

Bird roaster, tin reflector oven for hearthside use, hooks for 4 birds, triangular shape with side strap handles, from F. A. Walker catalog, prob. English, c.1870s.   **$200-$300**

Bird roaster, tin, very simple arched top with 4 hooks, no legs or feet, American, 10" H x 10" W x 8" deep, 19th C.   **$200-$300**

Bird roaster, tin, with hooks inside, short strap legs & strap handles, American, 7" H x 11" L, 19th C. By *birds* they didn't mean chickens or Butterball™ turkeys, but very small field birds. **$250-$325**

Bird roaster, tinned sheet iron, seen from side looks like bent-over L, generously looped strap handle, 6 hooks in pairs of 2, one pair top center, 2 pairs on lower row on either side of top pair, hooks reinforced on backside of this small reflecting oven, rimmed drip pan below, American, 11-1/2" H x 9" W x 4-1/4" deep, early to mid (?)19th C.   **$275-$400**

Bird roaster, wrought iron, dangle type which was hung on crane by its own hook, with sliding hoop with 2 hooks, poss. NY state?, 16" L, 18th or very early 19th C. I'm glad we don't eat little birds that fly by nowadays. Imagine hooking a robin, a lark or a nice fat chickadee to such a thing. Yuck. I don't even like to eat chickens. (You never know where you'll read a plea for vegetarianism, do you?)   **$450-$650**

Bird roaster trammel, wrought iron and brass, marked with stars & other punched designs, stamped all over it is "PATENTEE PATENTEE PATENTEE," French, 18-1/4" L at its least extension, adjusts in half-inch increments, mid 19th C.   **$400-$550**

Bird trammel, 2 hooks, for hanging a large trussed bird from for roasting, American or English, adjustable from 16" to 23" fully extended, 18th C.   **$350-$450**

X-10. Bird roaster, *of reversible type. Sheet tin. Hooks for 4 birds; small bracket handles on sides. Nowhere near as desirable as one in X-5. From F. A. Walker import catalog, 1870s-80s.* **$150-$175**

X-11. Bird roasters. (L) "Toaster and Trivet." *Picture from Warne's Model Cookery and Housekeeping Book, London: 1868. Wrought iron, and it looks as if it may even have a brass finial.* **(R) Bird roaster or bird spit.** *Wrought iron, with small drip or grease cup. Note Isle-of-Man type motif of the whirling spit, and the heart at the other end. Drawn from ad of Milk Street Antiques, Portland, ME. Value range mine not Milk Street's.* **$600-$1200**

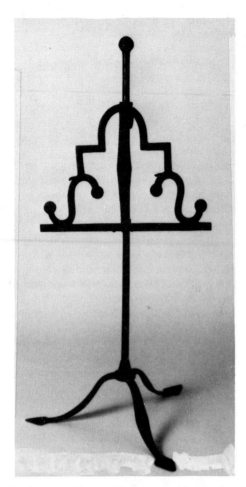

X-12. Bird spit. *Tripod base with pronounced snake feet. Wrought iron, interesting "easel" hanger with six double spits. 30" H, 18th C. Photo courtesy Litchfield Auction Gallery, Litchfield, CT. Ex-Harold Corbin Collection, auctioned 1/1/1989, for $1600.* **$1500-$1800**

X-13. Scotch broiler, *also called a* **brander.** *Easel-back upright broiler, forged iron, serpentine grids. Probably Scottish, 18th C. Photograph courtesy of Pat Guthman Antiques, Southport, CT. She has a large and very fine selection of kitchen-related antiques, almost exclusively related to hearth or early brickset range cookery, and writes a food column in the* Newtown Bee's *"Antiques & Arts Weekly,"* Newtown, CT. **$800+**

Age Will Out? — Just when you feel a little secure about the probable age of these old reflecting ovens, you find, as I did, a copy of the wonderful 1895 Harrod's Stores, Ltd. (London) catalog, reprinted by St. Martin's Press in 1972. (The actual title, which is probably how you'd find it at the library, is *Victorian Shopping.*) Over a thousand pages with terrific linecuts of everything anyone would want for house, home, body, yard, barn or buggy. There are several tin reflecting ovens, called generically "Broilers," in the Ironmongery & Turnery department pages. (For their "Cheese Toaster" see another entry in this chapter.) A pup tent "Game Oven," with hinged front lid, three wire hooks, and a strap handle on the two triangular ends, could be ordered 9" W, 11" W, 12" W or 14" W. Another, not pictured, but described as "strong," came in three sizes: 11" W, 13" W and 15" W. Presumably "strong" means thicker gauge tin as well as more substantial structure. Also available was an "Improved Broiler" oven with rather tall squared body, hinged domed hood with strap handle, four wire hooks, and a heavy wire hook support to hang on fender bar. It came 9" W and 12" W. Another was a "Cheese Oven," with hood and strap handle fixed to a large rectangular double pan. Another, the "American Oven," was made of tin, a large rectangular box, with a lift-out tray with wire handles, set onto a shelf, about 2/3 way up from bottom, hinged lift-off hood or lid, and the most distinguishing feature, a sheet of tin set at 15° from front to back, which reflected the heat to the underside of the shelf and tray. Behind this reflector, rather like underneath a flight of stairs, is an open space supported by side pieces of tin. Another was Harrod's "Dutch Oven," with open straight front, round back and domed lid, strap handle on top, three hooks over a reticulated removable shelf midway from top to bottom. Long pins at both ends allowed you to take this partly apart for cleaning. It came 9" W, 10" W, 12" W and 13" W. Harrod's shipped all over the world — from Smyrna to Switzerland, from Tahiti to Tripoli. Apparently in 1895 they did not ship to the United States, as "Parcel Post [is] not in operation." Hmmm.

Brander or **Scotch broiler**, also called a **brandiron**, a grill or gridiron held nearly vertical to the fire on a sort of easel. Wrought iron, 15" H, six serpentine & flat bars, probably Scottish, late 18th C. **$750+**

Brander, or Scotch broiler, wrought iron, horseshoe-shaped standing tripod type, American, 15-3/4" H x 12" W, late 18th, early 19th C. The design of the near-vertical broiler face & tripod, and condition of the iron contributes to value. Added value given by penny feet & extra iron scroll. **$250-$400**

BROILERS, stationary:

Broiler, wrought iron, front legs with penny feet, back legs are double-toed, beautiful long handle with rattail loop, American, 18th C. **$500-$650**

Broiler, wrought iron, 4 serpentine bars, very simple feet, handle ends in "doughnut" hole, American (?), 17" L, early 19th C. **$275-$375**

Broiler, wrought iron, 4 short feet, ram's horn handle, American (?), 30" L x 17" W, 18th or 19th C. **$300-$400**

BROILERS, whirling or revolving (called rotary or rotating broilers or whirling broilers, also rotary grills, rotary gridirons — ingenious pieces with a frame, legs and handle that remain stationery when placed on the hearth, while the round grid of the broiler can be rotated to evenly expose all parts of the steak or other cut of meat to the hot coals over which the broiler may be placed, as well as to the flames within the fireplace. See also toasters, pivoting and toasters, revolving):

Broiler, rotary, cast iron wheel with 19 spokes, each fluted or runneled with a concavity — a sort of grease arroyo — directing hot drippings to reservoir in handle, next to broiler, 3 legs, hanging hole in handle, handle marked only "PATENT," American, 12" diameter, 25-1/4" L overall, c.1830s. Cast iron is unusual for a revolving broiler, but not for a patented broiler. Casting made it a production piece. **$250-$450**

Broiler, rotary, wrought iron, long handle with rattail loop, round grill with double serpentine design, 3-footed, 18th C., American (?), 9" diameter x 18" L overall, 18th C. **$450+**

Broiler, rotary, wrought iron, round wavy grid, American (?), quite small, 7" diameter, 19th C. **$300+**

Broiler, rotary, alternating scalloped & straight bars, 3 legs, American or English, 3" H x 11" diameter, 11-3/4" L handle, early 19th C. **$550+**

Broiler, rotary and upright — a sort of merry-go-round grill, wrought iron with fleur-de-lis pattern formed by flat bars of iron making the grill's surface with unusual scalloped "fence" or edge around circumference, short penny feet, European, prob. French, 10" diameter, 18-1/2" L overall, 18th C. **$800+**

Broiler, rotary, wheel-like grill with radiating spokes fairly close together, lubricating grease cup below center pivot pin, "Y" handle — the 2 arms of the Y support the grill, plus nice long handle with grease catching cup, forged iron, 3 feet, American, 13-1/2" diameter, 25" L overall, prob. 18th C. **Lookalike alarm** — This has been reproduced with a brass center nut & bolt. **$450+**

Broiler, rotary, forged iron, very plain with neat perky upraised handle, long legs, American or English, 3-3/4" H x 12-3/8" diameter with 14-3/8" L handle, early 19th C. **$475+**

Broiler, rotary, grids made from square bars turned at angle so a sharp edge is along the top, English (?), 24-1/2" L x 12-1/4" diameter, early 19th C. **$250-$350**

Broiler, rotary, wrought iron, quite simple with straight bars on grill, long handle, American, 10" diameter, 21" L, 19th C. **$200-$250**

Broiler, rotary, wrought iron, round broiler or grill has alternating straight & undulating flat bars, 3 feet, longish handle, American, Canadian or English, 13" D, 18th or early 19th C. This type, with the wavy & straight line design, is most common, and apparently added just a touch of decorative quality to satisfy the original customer. There are many variations on the wavy straight theme. French whirling broilers or French Canadian ones tend to be fancier, and incorporate variations of fleur-de-lis for the broiling surface. When I see one with snakes, I'll buy it. **$550+**

Camp stoves — See Chapter XI (Stoves and Ranges)

X-14. Various hearth broilers. *All forged iron. (T) & (R) are meant to sit flat. One at right has very decorative, probably European, hearts and scrolls, and 3 legs. Bottom left is another brander or Scotch broiler, startlingly anthropomorphic. All late 18th C. Photograph courtesy of Pat Guthman Antiques, Southport, CT.* **$350-$750**

X-15. Whirling broiler or rotary grill. *Forged iron. Note serpentine grid and rattail hanging loop. 18" L x 9" diameter, American, 18th C. Ex-Keillor Family Collection. SEE also the revolving gridirons.* **$400+**

X-16. Whirling broiler. *Forged iron, with upright handle in center, and hooks for hanging small birds (?) around rim of wheel. French fleur-de-lis design, probably French, or possibly French Canadian. 16" diameter, late 18th C., probably prior to the Revolution. Courtesy Sestienne Collection.* **$800+**

X-17. Whirling broiler or grill. *Forged iron with unusual twisted-for-strength grids. Very nice penny diamond handle. Photograph courtesy of Pat Guthman Antiques, Southport, CT.* **$450+**

X-20. Hearth scene, *with large cast iron cauldron in background on 3 long legs, cast iron tea kettle* **S-hook** *hanging from chain probably hanging from* **lug pole** *rather than crane, ash shovel and tongs in foreground. The little story told in this 1858 children's book is remarkably humane. The little mouse explains she has stolen sugar to feed her babies, and the lady smiles and says "Well, Mouse, you may keep your prize;/ For I am going, just like you,/ To feed my child, who is hungry too."* Picture Fables, *drawn by Otto Speckter, from German rhymes by F. Hey. NY: Appleton, 1858.*

X-18. Whirling broiler or grill. *Forged iron piece, with alternating straight and serpentine bars. Late 18th or early 19th C., probably American. Photo courtesy of Oveda Maurer Antiques, San Anselmo, CA — who, like Pat Guthman, often sells through the mail.* **$350+**

X-21. Cheese toasters. (L) *"Cheese toaster to make Welsh Rarebits, with double bottom for hot water."* American Home Cook Book, *1854.* **(R)** *Cheese toaster, with wooden handle, from F. A. Walker catalog, 1870s-80s. Both of pieced tin.* **$125-$200**

X-19. Cauldron or caldron. *Riveted bronze, from ancient Ireland, 8th C. The illustration is from an article "The Old Poetic Guild in Ireland," by Charles de Kay,* Century, *4/1890. The story told in the article is about a "band of poets" who traveled all around and carried with them a "large pot, or caldron, called* **'The Pot of Avarice.'** *This was the sign of their intention to claim food from the chief they visited, although in legend it was meant for the gold and silver they expected as prerequisites. ... From a caldron like this one, king, poet, and hero obtained their porridge, their boiled beef and mutton, and their venison, which they ate without forks, using" short knives and their fingers. This one is one of several in the Dublin Museum.*

X-22. Cheese roaster or toaster — reflecting oven. *Hangs on fender of fireplace, for roasting birds, chops, apples, or for melting cheese — perhaps on a porringer of soup. From F. A. Walker catalog, 1870s-80s.* **$200-$300**

446

Chestnut roaster, cast iron, iron legs, European or poss. American, 4" deep x 12-1/2" diameter, mid 19th C. **$175-$225**

Chestnut roaster, copper pan with pierced design in cover, twisted wrought iron shaft and wooden handle, American (?), 13-1/2" diameter, 18th C. I cannot tell you why this is a chestnut roaster and not a bed warmer. It seems a bit big for the former, but that's what the dealer said. **$500-$750**

Chestnut roaster, copper pot with slightly flared foot, turned wood handle, hinged lid with ring knob or handle, many pea-size perforations cut in lid, English, 13" H, late 18th or early 19th C. **$1200-$1500**

Chestnut roaster, like a bed warmer, sort of, hexagonal pieced brass pan with a pierced lid, long flat handle, very shapely and with cutouts, English or poss. American, early 19th C. **$300-$375**

Chestnut roaster, pierced brass, long wooden handle, prob. English but could be American, 17" L, early 19th C. **$275-$350**

X-23. Chestnut roaster. *In extremely unusual heart shape. Long thin handle, twisted for strength. 28-1/2" L. Pennsylvania, 18th C. Photo courtesy Litchfield Auction Gallery, Litchfield, CT. Ex-Harold Corbin Collection, auctioned 1/1/1989 for $900.* **$800-$1000**

Reproduction alert — Arthur Todhunter, NYC, NY, made "quaint & useful gifts," mainly for use around the fireplace, that were "reproductions of Old England and Colonial wrought iron work and fire place furnishings." In a Dec. 1921 *House & Garden* ad, we see a "chestnut roaster," which is a round brass pan, pierced lid with slight convexity to center of it, with what appears to be a simple turned wooden handle. The size is not given, but is probably about 20" to 30" L. For the old, upwards of **$225**.

Chestnut roaster, steel with decorative engraving, wooden handle, American or English, 12" diameter, c.1810-1830. **$275-$350**

Clock or clockwork jack — See bottle jack, also: jack, clock and picture of smoke jack

Cook pot, also called a **flesh pot**, cast iron, very globular body, high straight-sided neck with triangular ears, forged and twisted iron falling bail, very long splayed legs, very handsome, American, 14-1/4" H, late 18th or early 19th C. **$200-$275**

A cooking pot is one form of cast iron **hollowware**, or hollow ware. Kettles, tea kettles, skillets, posnets, saucepans, porringers, spiders, Dutch ovens, the bowls of large ladles, and other wares with "hollow" insides are called hollowware. Some had to be cast in two, three, even four part-molds because the mouth or rim was smaller in diameter than the belly or middle. The term is also used for pewter, silver, brass, bell metal, copper and bronze wares. **Sadware** is applied to cast objects that are flat and cast in a one-part mold (or a relatively flat mold), as opposed to hollowware. Griddles, sadirons (or flat irons) are sadware.

X-24. Box style chestnut roasters. *"For fireside decoration." All are reproductions or meant-to-look-old decorative brass items all made by Pearson-Page, Birmingham, England, 1925 catalog. You could choose a brightly polished or an "old colour" finish. Upper row, left to right:* **(1)** *"The Battersea," 20-1/2" L;* **(2)** *"The Bishop," 20-1/2" L;* **(3)** *"The Musician," made round, square or octagon, 22" L. Bottom row, left to right:* **(4)** *"The Christy," 17" L, the oldest-looking one;* **(5)** *"The Graham," 16" L;* **(6)** *"The Wells," 16" L;* **(7)** *"The Colchester," 18" L;* **(8)** *and the oval "The Stratford," 19" L. Value range is for exactly what they were made to be — decorative items, with no claim to authenticity. They are, of course, almost old enough to be considered "antiques."* **$75-$175**

Crane, cast iron, simple and small, American, late 19th or early 20th C. This is not strictly a fake or reproduction but is a revivalist piece that was made to satisfy decorators' demands during a renaissance of Colonial accessories that got underway in the 1880s- 90s (and again in the 1920s). A "blanket crane" swung out from fireplace and was used for drying blankets, or heating them to wrap up a person with the ague. **$125-$150**

Crane, forged iron, curved brace, very simple, American or European, brace is 34" H, crane is 26" L, prob. 18th C. **$550-$675**

Crane, forged bar iron, curved bracket, very very simple, American (?), only 19" L, 19th C. "The lug-pole, though made of green wood, sometimes became brittle or charred by too long use over the fire and careless neglect of replacement, and broke under its weighty burden of food and metal; hence accidents became so frequent, to the detriment of precious cooking utensils, and even to the destruction of human safety and life, that a Yankee invention of an iron crane brought convenience and simplicty, and added a new grace to the kitchen hearth." Alice Morse Earle, *Customs & Fashions in Old New England,* Scribner's, 1893. **$450-$575**

Crane, forged iron, simple design with ram's horn tip to tapered bar, American (?), 21" L, 19th C. **$650-$800**

Cranes start at under $75 for simple small ones of late manufacture. Added value — The bigger, more interestingly forged cranes bring more, up to $2000+ if anything zoomorphic or figural has been done with the iron. **Reproduction alert** — Yes, that little crane that doesn't look old *is* wrought iron, but it is easily perceived as new. The iron is merely a scrolled piece of perfectly uniform 3/4" W, 1/8" or 3/16" thick flat wrought iron bar. • A 1970s fireplace crane & barbecue grill set, comprised of a vertical tension bar, a fixed fire bowl of sheet iron (like a big 24" diameter, shallow, slightly round-bottomed pan), above which is a grill (round with 10 cross bars of plated iron wire). Above the grill is the scrolled bracket crane with hook, from which to suspend a cooking pot. Sold as part of this 5-piece set was a small gypsy kettle with 2 quart capacity — a cast iron 3-legged, round-bottomed pot with the old type casting band around the widest part, wire bail handle. The whole set was made by Malone's Creative Products (formerly Malone's Metalcraft) of McMinnville, TN, prior to 1973, and sold for $49.50. The little pot or kettle could be bought separately for $8.50. The June 1973 ad states that they made "hundreds of other items": wish I had a catalog. • The will inventory of Jacob Alleweins, Berks County, PA, who died in 1781, listed a brass crane — very unusual.

X-25. Quadrant crane & kettle tilter, *with tea kettle. Forged iron, beautifully detailed and well-finished. Lever caught under one of six pegs (one missing). 18th or very early 19th C. Photograph courtesy of Pat Guthman Antiques, Southport, CT. Value range is solely mine, not Guthman's.* **$1200-$2000**

X-26. Standing crane with utensils. *Cast iron pot at left, cast and wrought girdle plate, and wonderful 18th C. English cast bronze pot. Photograph courtesy of Pat Guthman Antiques, Southport, CT. Unusual crane.*

Cranes, forged iron, a pair of floor-standing cranes with penny feet, T-bar, American or English, 35" H, 18th C. Very rare. **$2500-$3000+**

Creeper — See a spider entry

Curfew, from the French _couvre-feu_, or fire-cover. A sort of half dome, or quarter sphere — think of a baby buggy hood. They are usually at least 10" across, sometimes larger, made of sheet brass, copper or iron. This one is forged sheet iron, somewhat pitted, with a vertical twisted forged iron handle from the top down to the bottom, with a curl at the bottom tail. This hearth essential was pushed against the back or side of the fireplace, with the glowing embers of a wood fire within, to shut off the air. In the morning, the curfew was removed and the fire could be quickly restarted with a few puffs of the bellows. American (?), 10" H x 13" W, late 18th or early 19th C. Added value — Although I prefer iron, there will probably be more brass ones shown (mostly European imports), and because their decorative value is considered greater, their price would be higher by 10% to maybe 50% over that for the iron. **$175-$300**

Curfew or sleeper, wrought iron, 2 penny feet, gooseneck, American, 9-1/2" H x 10-1/2" L, 18th C. **$165-$225**

Dangle spit, steel, horizontal serpentine winglike governor at the top of a steel vertical rod with 6 holes at one-inch intervals, with a much thinner rod with a small hook at its top and 3 very sharp bigger hooks at the bottom to hold the meat or game bird to be roasted. The small hook at the top could be set into one of the holes to adjust the height off the fire. The whole thing was suspended by a stout twine or cord from the edge of the mantle, and it was set in rotary motion by twisting, so that when released, it would twirl as it unwound, thereby winding itself up again. English or American, 16" L fully extended, early 19th C. Added value for any filed or engraved decoration, or a date or initials. **$375-$575**

Dippers — See Chapter XIII (Implements that Turn, Spoon and Flip)

Dutch oven, cast iron, 3-footed, ear handles to use with pot lifter hooks, lid with raised edge to contain coals, lid has a few triangular "chips" along edge, marked only "Baltimore," 8-1/2" H x 12" D, early 19th C. Dutch ovens marked "Baltimore" show up fairly often. It is not known who made them, but there are three good possibilities: William Baer & Co., established prior to 1817, or the Cast-Iron Manufactory (which might have also been called Baltimore Cast-Iron Manufactory), established by 1803, and Hayward, Bartlett & Co., established 1844. The look of these is definitely _early_ 19th C., so the latter is _perhaps_ the least probable choice. **$200-$250**

Perhaps or Maybe: Why Ifs, Ands & Buts Are Necessary — Throughout this book I have tried to be as accurate as possible about provenance or dates. You will notice lots of question marks in parentheses after dates and places. You will also find a good number of "looks like" or "possibly" [poss.], or "probably" [prob.], and a few "perhaps." The appeal of objects with marks and patent dates obviously lies in the certainty such identification gives the collector. In fact, I believe that's why the two most popular fields of collecting worldwide, all totaled, are stamps and coins, because they have dates, provenance and well-established histories. Our field has its marked pieces too, but probably more pieces are mysterious and require research and study.

Dutch oven, cast iron, 3 peg feet, deep raised edge on lid, small interior flange to make a good fit in kettle, very handsome, particularly in this big size, American, 11" H, early 19th C. For some comments on a utensil called a creeper, see notes, p. 473, under spider, as well as "Andirons & Firedogs," p. 440. **$200-$250**

Dutch oven, cast iron, forged bail handle, 3 legs, high lipped lid, American, 14" diameter, early to mid 19th C. **$200-$250**

Dutch oven, cast iron, forged falling bail handle, 3 stubby legs, nice deep flange or raised edge on lid, American, 6-3/4" H x 9-1/4" diameter, early 19th C. **$250-$350**

X-27. Curfew, or coeuvre-feu. _Used to cover hot coals in fireplace. This one illustrated an article in William Hone's_ The Every-Day Book, _1825-26. About it was written: "It is of copper, rivetted together, as solder would have been liable to melt with the heat. It is 10" high, 16" wide, and 9" deep. The Rev. Mr. Gostling, to whom it belongs, says it has been in his family for time immemorial."_

X-28. Double boiler. _Copper kettle inside, with forged iron bail handle, hung from an S-pothook in double arch of fixed handle of outer iron kettle. Could be used with a crane in the fireplace, and later on a range. 16-1/2" H overall x 13-1/2" diameter. 1830s-50s. Ex-Keillor Family Collection._ **$600+**

X-29. Dripping pan and ladle. *Sheet iron, placed under spitted meat to catch the drippings, which were used for making sauces, gravies, soups, or for rendering for a purer fat.* Warne's Model Cookery, *London, 1868.* **$55+**

X-30. Dutch oven in use. *Somewhat romanticized illustration from the 1880s of a somewhat earlier housewife piling hot coals on the dished lid of her long-legged dutch oven, to bake something within. Note stationary crane in fireplace, with chain trammel — the most primitive kind. Also the ring atop the andiron. Its mate also had a ring, and a spit could be suspended thus between the andirons.*

X-31. Dutch oven. *Cast iron, bail handle, 3 shortish legs, very well-fitted and undoubtedly original lid with deep flange. 8-3/4" H x 9-1/4" diameter. American, probably early 19th C. Picture courtesy of Robert W. Skinner Inc., Auctioneers, Bolton, MA. It has been claimed by at least one writer that the Pilgrims, who spent some years in Holland before departing for the new land, brought "Dutch ovens" with them and used them on shipboard. An old oval Dutch oven would bring twice this or more.* **$190-$250+**

X-32. Cooking pot, *something like a Dutch oven, which may or may not have the distinctive high flange on lid. This charming illustration, is but one of at least 32, in a French book about a Monsieur Vieux Bois (Old Man Wood), who has many household adventures. Apparently the food cooking in this pot caught on fire, and was ruined, so Monsieur Bois carried it up on the roof so the dog could eat it. We all have known such dogs, n'c'est pas? Unfortunately, the bookshop where I found this in NYC tears many non-valuable books apart and sells the pictures as decorations. But those of us who use the pictures as part of our research, as well as those who just love an intact book, squirm at such practices.*

X-35. Dutch oven/skillet. *Called simply "skillet" in the catalog. Cast iron, "plain finish, unground." "Furnished in deep or shallow patterns." Seven sizes, from 8" to 14" diameter, from 2-1/2" to 3" deep for the shallow ones, and 3" to 3-1/4" D for the deep ones. National Stoves & Ranges. c.1916.* **$150+**

X-33. Dutch oven. *Cast iron, very unusual with the raised handles for the bail. Late 18th or early 19th C. Photograph courtesy of Pat Guthman Antiques, Southport, CT. Joel Schiff believes the odd bail handle had an added loop on either side, to slip over the ear handles, and then secured with a pin or wedge, sort of like a cotter pin.* **$400-$550+**

X-36. Biscuit baker. *Cast iron, very like the Dutch oven. 12" and 14" diameter, from Stuart, Peterson & Co. catalog of cast iron hollowware, 1866. No explanation is given, time travelers are supposed to know these things. See three legs on lid, and the two little stubby knobs obviously used to flip it over. Perhaps this could be used with both parts upside down, or the way shown here.* **$250+**

X-34. Dutch ovens or French bake pans. *Clockwise from* (**T-L**) *"French Bake Pan of wrought iron, to put fire or embers on the cover if needful."* American Home Cook Book, *1854.* (**T-R**) *"A Bake-kettle, or Skillet." "When cooking stoves came in, the bake-kettle, or covered skillet, went out, and with it went a large part of what was good in our American cookery. How many of your readers [*American Agriculturist, *9/1870] ever saw a* **bake-kettle**? *Probably only those who enjoy the blessing of a wood fire to cook by. Just send an artist down to the backwoods of Maine or away 'out west,' and have a drawing made of this most capital kitchen utensil. 'Pioneers' will know what I mean; it is a shallow kettle with a lid, which has a turned-up edge, and upon which coals are placed; and the thing to be cooked is 'between two fires.'"* (**B-R**) *Cast iron, unground, shallow or deep pattern, in sizes from 8" to 14" diameter, from 2-1/2"-3-1/2" D for shallow and 3-1/2"-5-1/4" D for deep. National Stoves & Ranges, c.1916. Note triangular ears, generally thought to be a sign of great age.* (**B-L**) *"French bake kettle," cast iron, note there is no flange at all on the lid. Henry N. Clark, Boston, MA, 1884 catalog.* **$125+**

X-37. Frying pan. *Wrought iron, 50" L x 14-1/2" diameter. American, 18th or early 19th C. Ex-Keillor Family Collection.* **$180-$250+**

Lookalike alarm — Calling it a "**camp oven**," Lehman's Hardware & Appliances, Kidron, OH, offer 5 sizes of cast iron Dutch ovens, made at the Lodge foundry, in their *Non-Electric Good Neighbor Amish Country* catalog. The utensils have 2, 4, 6, 8, and 12 qt. Capacities. All have "integral" legs, flanged lids & falling bails. In order they are: 8", 10", 12", 14", & 16" diameter, & weigh from 10 lbs. to 32 lbs. Without further explanation, Lehman's says they range from 3-1/2" to 4-1/2" deep, 5-1/2" to 7-1/2" high (which sounds like 2" & 3" legs, but in the picture they look short & peggy). They also have what they call a "**Dutch Oven**," which is for stovetop use and has a somewhat domed lid with no flange. Lynchburg Hardware & General Store, Lynchburg, TN, offers the Lodge Foundry Dutch oven with legs, in the 4 qt. size, 10" diameter; & one without legs in 9 qt. size, 13" diameter.

• • • •

The word "Dutch" is sometimes used to indicate that something is a substitute for something else. A <u>Dutch wife</u> (or husband) is the long torso size or bolster pillow that you use to drape your arm and knee over when sleeping on your side. <u>Dutch gold</u> is golden in color, but is actually a cheap alloy, tombac, made of copper and zinc, which is beaten to a foil and used to gild certain toys or knicknacks. A <u>Dutch treat</u> is not really a treat, because you are paying for yourself. A <u>Dutch uncle</u> is a person who isn't your uncle, but takes it upon himself to reprehend you. And a **Dutch oven** is a substitute for a built-in bake oven. The chief characteristic is the raised edge around the lid — meant to hold hot coals so that while the oven sat on the hearth, or in the embers, getting heat from below, it was also getting heat from above.

X-38. "Captain Warren's Bachelor's Frying Pan." *"Invented by Captain Warren" and it retains heat because of the heavy flutes inside. "It shuts and can be turned over from one side to the other, as the cook pleases."* Note how long wrought iron handles have a slip right — exactly like that on long-handled waffle irons, from which Captain Warren may have received his inspiration. From Warne's Model Cookery, London, 1868. **$200+**

• • • •

"To make Yankee Bread — Take two measures of Indian and one of Rye meal, mix with milk or water, to the consistency of stiff hasty pudding, and add yeast — bake in <u>iron pans</u>* or <u>iron kettles</u>** four or five hours. Eat with fresh butter, or other food, and if eaten while warm the better. Yankee bread is very good or very bad, according to the manner in which it is made. We commend it to dyspeptics. The Indian meal should be either bottled or sifted." *The Farmers' Cabinet,* Philadelphia, Aug.1, 1836. *What's Meant by **"Iron Pan"?** — I can't guarantee what is meant by "<u>iron pans.</u>" Although from the context it sounds as if an iron pan might be a cast iron gem or muffin pan, the recipe is way too early for that. So I believe them to be sheet iron, flat-bottomed pans, rather deeper than pie pans but with slightly flared sides, which are rarely found today. It is possible that they are cast iron Scotch or Maslin kettles of some kind, especially as the other utensil of choice is a kettle. ****"Iron kettles"** I'm presuming to be Dutch ovens. Another possibility is that iron pans and iron kettles are the same thing, and both refer to **Dutch ovens**, because Beecher & Stowe, in their 1869 *The American Woman's Home*, list among requisite iron wares, "a <u>Dutch Oven</u>, called also a <u>bake-pan</u>." As for "<u>bottled cornmeal</u>," I'm confident that this was a dialectical version of "beetled," or pounded. A <u>beetle</u> is a pestle-like wooden implement with a big head and a handle. And a very old low German word for maul is *bötel*.

• • • •

Dutch ovens. These were called *four de campagnes* in French, literally country oven. Many recipes in Alexandre Dumas' classic *Le Grand Dictionnaire de Cuisine* call for such a utensil, and called for the "braising pot" to be set in hot coals with the special lid with raised edge to be piled with coals. Close reading of some recipes seem to indicate that the *four de campagne* sometimes referred to what was called a tin kitchen in America. So perhaps the confused American usage of the term "dutch oven" dates to a similar French ambivalence.

Why "Dutch"? — One reasonable explanation for the name is given by Louise Peet and Lenore Sater in *Household Equipment,* NY: John Wiley, 1934, 1940. They wrote: "Dutch ovens were brought to America by the Pilgrims. As is well known, the Pilgrims spent some years in Holland before coming to America. The Mayflower was a tiny vessel and baggage limited. The dutch oven could be used for such a variety of cookery that it took the place of several other pots and pans and was, therefore, a favorite utensil of the early settlers."

Dutch oven, & lid, sometimes called a <u>braising pot</u>, <u>bake kettle</u>, <u>camp oven</u>, or <u>bake oven</u>, cast iron, with 3 short legs, raised edge on lid, small interior flange to keep lid in place. "Kentucky Stove Co.," KY, 10" D, early 19th C. **$350+**

Fish broiler, flips like swiveling hearth toasters, wrought iron footed frame with spikes to hold fish, even a small arch under handle to hold it up off hearth, American (?), 18th C. **$450-$650**

Fish grill, forged iron, elongated grid, long handle, prob. American, 30-1/2" L x 3-1/2" W, early 19th C. **$200-$250**

Frying pan, forged iron, long handle, American (?), 10" D with 11" L handle, early 19th C. **$70-$90**

Frying pan, cast iron, three 1-7/8" H legs, American, 6" diameter, early to mid 19th C. **$50-$65**

Frying pan, cast iron, three 2" H legs, American, 10-1/2" diameter, early to mid 19th C. These 3-legged ones could have been used on an early brickset range too. **$60-$75**

Terminology varies — What started out as a clearer-cut difference between a frying pan and a skillet in the eighteenth century, based on the form, became at some time a regional difference in language usage (in my experience Ohio and New York people say **frying pan**, Tennessee said **skillet**) not catalogued anywhere. Then there's a chronological difference; a skillet in the eighteenth century and early nineteenth century is more like what we might think of as a saucepan with legs. And a frying pan was also called a **spider**. Besides place and age, there's trade terminology — the names used by the manufacturers. Griswold, from Pennsylvania, used "skillet," as did Ohio's Wagner. Your choice.

Frying pan, cast iron, three 2-1/2" H legs, forged iron replaced handle that was riveted on to chipped edge of pan, long casting gate, this isn't a new pan but there is an odd gray glittery look to the iron on the bottom, possibly because of heat generated by welding to replace handle after pan cracked and original cast handle broke off. Marked only "No. 8, 12 in." on bottom, American, actually 11-1/2" diameter, overall length with new handle is 21-5/8" L, early to mid 19th C (?).   **$80-$150**

Frying pan, & lid, cast iron, pan has three 2-1/4" H legs, lid has raised edge like for Dutch oven, marked "1 N," G. T. Glascook & Son, Greensboro, NC, 12" diameter, mid (?)19th C. **$65-$90**

Frying pan, repaired sheet iron, hand wrought handle is extremely long, the 2 repairs to pan — one a rectangle of brass, one of copper — are riveted on, American, pan 14" diameter, handle about 38" L, late 18th or early 19th C. By virtue of its repair, this has become a folk art piece, and its value no longer relates solely to it as a utensil.   **$400+**

X-39. Girdle plate or griddle, *hanging type with swiveling trammel ring. Deep rim, with chip (not a pouring lip), crudely cast iron. 16" H x 13" diameter, American, late 18th C. Photo courtesy of Robert W. Skinner Inc., Auctioneers, Bolton, MA.* **$250-$300+**

"Flannel Cakes or Crumpets — Two pounds of flour, sifted. Four eggs. Three tables-spoonfuls of the best brewer's yeast, or four and a half of home-made yeast. A pint of milk. — Mix a tea-spoonful of salt with the flour, and set the pan before the fire. Then warm the milk, and stir into it the flour, so as to make a stiff batter. Beat the eggs very light, and stir them into the yeast. Add the eggs and yeast to the batter, and beat all well together. If it is too stiff, add a little more warm milk.

"Cover the pan closely and set it to rise near the fire. Bake it, when quite light.

"Have your baking-iron hot. Grease it, and pour on a ladle-full of batter. Let it bake slowly, . . . when done on one side, turn it on the other.

"Butter the cakes, cut them across, and send them to table hot." Miss Leslie, of Philadelphia, *Seventy-Five Receipts for Pastry, Cakes, and Sweetmeats . Appended to The Cook's Own Book and Housekeeper's Register . . ..,* by a Boston Housekeeper. Boston: Munroe & Francis, 1833.

X-40. Girdle plates or griddles. (A) (B) *Cast iron, Pennsylvania. 11" diameter, early 19th C. Three legs, with leg under handle nearly twice height of other two, intentional, I'm sure to get more reflected heat when placed on hearth. Simple crisscross on handle of* **(B)** *is cast in; it has no rim.* **(C)** *Full-bailed plate, with short feet. Cast and wrought, with side ears for the bail. 15-1/2" diameter. Early 19th C.* **(D)** *Both are quarter-hoop hanging girdles, probably English or Scottish. Forged iron, with plates almost 17" diameter. One on right, missing part of the ring bolt, sold at 1986 auction for $700.* **(E)** *Cast &forged iron, hearth-standing or hanging, central handle, late 18th, early 19th C. (E) From ad of Pat Guthman Antiques, Southport, CT.* **$125-$700**

453

Frying pan, wrought iron, rattail handle, American, 12" diameter, 14" L handle, early 19th C. **$95-$150**

Girdle or griddle plate, cast iron, no legs or feet, rigid bail handle by which it was hung on a pothook from a crane, American (?), 14-3/16" diameter, c.1830s. **$80-$150**

Girdle plate, cast iron, half-hoop fixed handle with large ring on top end, to be hung from crane, English or Scottish, small size, only 9" diameter, early 19th C. **$250-$400**

Griddle or girdle plate, also called a <u>backstone</u> [bakestone] in old inventories, forged iron, fixed bail handle with swivel ring, American, 10" diameter, mid to late 18th C. **$150-$200**

Griddle, cast iron, long handle, 3 long legs — 3-1/4" H, American, 12" diameter, 2nd quarter 19th C. **$100-$125**

Griddle, cast iron, round with short keyhole-shaped handle with hanging hole, no legs, cool, smooth, seductive, slate-like finish, American (?), 11-3/4" D with 2-1/2" L handle, very early 19th C. **$150-$200**

"Best Batter Cakes, or **Mush Cakes** — Beat the yolks of eggs very light, add one pint milk, two pints mush almost cold, 1 1/2 pints flour, one tea-spoonful salt, three table-spoonsful melted butter. To be well beaten together. Just before frying them, whip the whites to a strong froth, and stir it lightly into the batter. For frying all kinds of batter cakes, use no more lard than is necessary to make them turn well. . . But the usual mode is to boil hominy twice a week, and put it into a wooden or stone vessel, and set it in a cool place to prevent its becoming musty. When wanted for use, take the quantity necessary for breakfast or dinner, and having put a small quantity of lard into an oven, let it become hot; put in the hominy and mash it well, adding some salt; when well heated it is ready for the table. Some persons allow it to bake at the bottom, and turn the crust over the hominy when put on the dish. Be careful to have no smoke under the pot while boiling, or when frying for the table. Few things require more care or nicety in their preparation than hominy. (These pints were all measured with the common tin cup.)" *The Farmers' Cabinet, Devoted to Agriculture, Horticulture and Rural Economy* . Philadelphia: Vol. II, No. 1, Aug. 1, 1837.

Bucket Double Boiler.— "Let me suggest for the comfort of those who stir [mush] an hour or two, and then labor a great while to wash out the pot in which they boil it, that all this trouble may be saved by cooking it in a tin pail, set in a pot of boiling water, and after it has cooked, letting it cool in the same, after which it will slip out in a mass, leaving all clean behind it. Whosoever tries this plan will never try the old one again, for it prevents the possibility of burning the mush, and dispenses with all care and trouble except occasionally to replenish the water in which the pail is set to boil." *Farmer and Mechanic,* April 1853.

X-41. Gridiron or grill. *Forged iron, with grease trough. Late 18th, early 19th C. Probably American. Photograph courtesy of Pat Guthman Antiques, Southport, CT.***$250-$350+**

1865 — "I looked over a whole batch of recipes sent in by readers, and though I don't doubt they are good of their kind, it is the kind that don't suit me. The only thing the title of which tempts me at all is **Johnny cake**. I open the recipe, and find that though the mixture may be good, it is baked in an *oven*! Shade of my grandmother! a Johnny cake in an *oven* ! Don't you see that when it is baked in an oven, though it may be something good, it isn't Johnny cake? That must be baked on the middle piece of the **head of a flour barrel** (Beach's brand preferred), with a hole in the north-east corner. The cake is placed on this, and set up against a flat iron in front of a bed of hickory coals, to bake, and nothing short of this can be Johnny cake — but as I sometime intend to make a cook-book, I won't say anything more about it. — If I do make a cook book, I won't have any mince pies, any sausages, nor cakes, nor puddings, nor anything sweet, nor any saleratus; but just you wait and see what I do put in." A Bachelor, "Household Department," *American Agriculturist,* Feb. 1865.

• • • •

Jonakin, Jonikin or "**Jonny Cake** derives its name from <u>Jaunny</u>, the name of Pequots and Narragansets for Maise or Indian Corn. As this was a new grain to the Pilgrims, they very naturally adopted the Indian name, and called the bread made of it Jaunny Cake. After these once powerful Indian tribes were destroyed and forgotten, the origin of this name was forgotten also, and from similarity of sound, became corrupted into Jonny Cake." *Journal of the American Institute,* NYC, March 1839, p.336.

"Superior Johnny Cake — The following receipt will make a Johnny cake fit for an alderman, a mayor, an editor or any other dignitary in the land: Take one quart of milk, three eggs, one tea-spoonful saleratus, one tea cup of wheat flour and Indian meal, sufficient to make a batter to the consistency of pancakes. Bake quick in pans* previously buttered, and eat warm with butter or milk. The addition of wheat flour will be found a great improvement in the art of making these cakes." *The Farmers' Cabinet,* Aug. 1, 1836. (*Pans aren't further identified. *Subject-Matter Index of Patents for Inventions* has an intriguing early patent for a "baking-iron," records of which burned in fires at patent office 1836 or 1877, which was granted E. Skinner on Oct. 1, 1830. Was a baking-iron a Dutch oven with lid? a dripping pan?)

"Journey Cake — Pour boiling water on a quart of meal, put in a little lard and salt, and mix it well; have an oak board with a rim of iron at the bottom, and an iron handle fastened to it that will prop it up to the fire; put some of the dough on it, dip your hand in cold water and smooth it over; score it with a knife, and set it before the coals to bake." Elizabeth Ellicott Lea, *Domestic Cookery,* 1859.

"Johnny-Cake — Sift one quart of Indian meal into a pan; make a hole in the middle, and pour in a pint of warm water, adding one teaspoon of salt; with a spoon mix the meal and water gradually into a soft dough; stir it very briskly for a quarter of an hour or more, till it becomes light and spongy; then spread the dough smooth and evenly on a straight, flat board (a piece of the head of a flour-barrel will serve for this purpose); place the board nearly upright before an open fire, and put an iron against the back to support it; bake it well; when done, cut it in squares; send it hot to table, split and buttered." Mary Stuart Smith, *Virginia Cookery-Book* (as reprinted in G. Strohm's 1888 *Universal Cookery Book*).

Griddle, forged iron, 3 longish legs, long handle with hanging hole, found in Virginia, 11-11/16" diameter, overall length 23-1/4", late 18th or early 19th C. **$300-$350**

Griddle, forged iron, to hang from crane, with bail handle and swivel ring at apex of arch of handle, American (?), 14-1/2" D, 19th C. **$175-$250**

Griddle, rotating, wrought iron, long handle has heart-shaped loop, 3 peg feet, American, 25" L, 19th C. **$175-$250**

Griddle or girdle plate, forged iron, fixed forged iron handle forms quarter circle hoop, swivel ring to hang from trammel or pot hook, 3 peg feet, American, 13" diameter, 18th C. If Jonathan Winters were writing the copy for this, he'd make a crack about needing a girdle after you'd eaten a few of the flapjacks made on this, but actually girdle meaning encircle is the word origin. Metathesis — transposition of letters, such as "r"and "i" to make girdle into griddle — was typical for the English language for centuries, and is seen in the way some other languages, French, Italian, German, are changed when they join the English language. **$175-$300**

Gridiron, cast iron, 3 legs, long handle, drip cup midway along handle, cast along back of handle is the name, each word looks as if it were carved on separate narrow plaques that could be used in the casting mold arranged in a horizontal line or stacked, depending on requirements of various castings, "Campbell Foundry Co.," Harrison, NJ, 28-3/8" L x 16-5/8" W, c.1850s. **$95-$150**

Gridiron, cast iron, enameled white inside, 3 legs, grease cup, "A. Kenrick & Sons," also either numeral 9 or 6, West Bromwich, England, 1-1/2" H legs, 21-3/4" L including handle, mid to 3rd quarter 19th C. **$95-$150**

X-42. Hearth utensils. (T-L) *Skimmer of brass with iron and wood handle, c.1800-1820;* **(T-R)** *grill or gridiron hanging at top right, c.1790-1810. Bottom row: left to right:* **(L-1)** *Small cast iron bowl;* **(L-2)** *large cast iron bowl;* **(L-3)** *small posnet or skillet, cast iron, c.1820s-30.* **(L-4)** *Long-legged cast iron frying pan, c.1830. Picture courtesy of Georgia G. Levett, Levett's Antiques, Camden, ME. Probably the bowls are worth the most.* **$100-$450+**

1884 Steak — "Place the steak on a hot, well-greased gridiron, turn often so that the outside may be seared at once; when done, which will require from five to ten minutes, dish on a hot platter, season with salt and pepper and bits of butter.... A small pair of tongs are best to turn steaks, as piercing with a fork frees the juices. If fat drips on the coals below, the blaze may be extinguished by sprinkling with salt, always withdrawing the gridiron to prevent the steak from acquiring a smoky flavor. Always have a brisk fire, whether you cook in a patent broiler directly over the fire, or on a gridiron over a bed of live coals.... A steel gridiron with slender bars is best, as the common broad, flat iron bars fry and scorch the meat, imparting a disagreeable flavor." *Practical Housekeeping*, Minneapolis, 1884.

• • • •

Some English foundry names that may appear on hollowwares or other cast iron wares, all from the eighteenth & nineteenth centuries, are: Baldwin, Son & Co., Stowport; "Beatrice" — John Harper; Carron Co.; Coalbrookdale, Abraham Darby, Shropshire; Cockrane & Co.; A. Kenrick; Walter Macfarlane & Co., Saracen Foundry, Glasgow; Richard Rowbotham, Providence Foundry; and J. & J. Siddons, West Bromwich.

Gridiron, cast iron, grease drip basin in back, 2 short front feet, short handle, American, 13" x 16", 19th C. **$80+**

Gridiron, cast iron, grease trap and spouted to pour, grid is 10 runneled strips, two legs in front, one in back, shortish handle, American (?), handle about 6" L, mid 19th C. **$55+**

Gridiron, forged iron, almost square top with 12 very slightly concave bars, long front legs, back legs curved and much shorter, detachable grease catcher hooked along back edge, longish upcurved handle with large ring at end, American (?), grid is 11-1/4" x 12-1/2", overall length 23", late 18th or early 19th C. **$350+**

Gridiron, forged iron, simple rectangular grid of flat bars, short leg in each corner, the hind legs are a bit shorter than the front, medium-length fishtail handle with grab bar along top, detachable grease catcher like hook-on trough along back edge, American, 17" W x 23" L overall, 18th C. **$500-$700**

Gridiron, or "cooking furnace gridiron," as the inventor called it. Round, has runneled (fluted or concave) bars or ribs, gravy trough "all around, on the outer edge, having a spout on one side

X-43. Hearth utensils. *"The sow came in with the saddle, The little pig rock'd the cradle/ The dish jump'd up on the table/ To see the pot swallow the ladle./ The spit that stood behind the door/ Threw the pudding stick on the floor./ Odsplut! said the gridiron, Can't you agree?/ I'm the head constable, Bring them to me."* [*"Odsplut" is a very old way to swear "God's blood" without actually saying it.*] Mother Goose's Melodies, *1833.*

for discharging the gravy," handle on one side. "It may be made of cast-iron, or wrought, or sheet-iron, or any other material, and may be varied in form, size, or shape, as convenience may require, with, or without legs, for so I make them," wrote the inventor, Jonathan Powers, Lansingburgh, Rensselaer County, NY, who pat'd it Aug. 10, 1829. The Editor of the *Journal of the Franklin Institute* commented about this gridiron: "We are again at a loss to know what is intended to be patented. It certainly cannot be a round gridiron, as these have been made by the thousand. The fluted, or concave bars, and gravy trough, we have known for upwards of forty years [ie. c.1780s]: these, therefore, are not new. But, as the patentee has not chosen to tell his claim, it is not our business to do so; we therefore leave the discovery to others." It would obviously be hard to know if you'd found a Powers' gridiron, but I include all this as instructive of workings of the patent office, and of the infinite potential for finding interesting pieces, perhaps signed somewhere. **$200+**

Short Legs — I have three theories of why one of three legs, or two of four, would be considerably shorter than the others: (**1**) they were worn, broken off, or burned off by accident; (**2**) they were intentionally ground down so as to tilt the utensil and collect, pool, or puddle juices or fats to assist in basting or making gravy or sauce; or, (**3**) they were shortened intentionally so that face of utensil (and food on it) addresses the heat (coals or flames) more directly. These shorter legs are found on griddles, grilles, spiders, and various saucepans and skillets. (By the way, one old meaning of pot-leg is of a short piece of iron, such as a broken-off or ground-off pot leg, used as shrapnel-like shot in a shotgun.)

Gridiron, wrought iron, 2 penny feet plus foot at base of long handle, fixed grid, New England, 2-1/4" H x 19-1/8" L, late 18th or early 19th C. **$250+**

Gridiron, wrought iron, 4 small peg feet, long handle, American, 10-1/2" x 11" rectangle, with 11" L handle, early 19th C. **$250+**

X-44. Gridirons or grills. None all that old. (A) *"Fluted gridiron," fluted steel bars, "fat pan" or grease trough along back edge, under bars. Notched back feet to hook onto fender; 7, 8, 9, 10, 11, & 12 bars.* **(B)** *"London gridiron," a more economical model in same range of sizes.* **(C)** *"Double-hanging gridiron," with tinned iron wire (or with wrought iron, tinned all over "after made.") 8", 9", 10", 11" & 12" (or for wrought one, 10, 11, 12, 13, & 14 bars).* **(A-C)** *from Harrod's Stores, Ltd., Brompton, England, 1895 catalog.* **(D)** *"Heavy gridiron" in iron, 6 sizes, from 8-1/2" x 12" to 13" x 16-3/4", the smaller three for families, others for hotels. Duparquet, Huot & Moneuse, c.1904- 1910.* **(E)** *Tinned sheet iron, 15-1/2" x 9-1/8" to 16-3/4" x 13". Lalance & Grosjean, 1890.* **$75-$200+**

Grill, or broiler, forged iron, large square with shaped flat forged iron handle with rattail, the grill bars alternating plain with little loops & hearts, the whole giving an effect of iron ribbon cleverly tied, French or Belgian, or poss. French Canadian, about 12" square, handle 10" L, late 18th C (?). **$800-$1000**

Grill, revolving or rotary — See broiler, rotary

Grisette, wrought iron, long canoe-shaped, rather shallow bowl, with long forged iron handle set at right angles from middle of long axis, the handle terminating in a right angle bend forming

X-45. Revolving & stationary gridirons. (T-L) *Cast iron, 12" diameter, catches grease underneath.* **(M-R)** *Rectangular slightly convex, cast iron. Both Russell & Erwin, 1865.* **(B-L)** *"Revolving enamelled gridiron with fluted bars to convey the gravy to the cup" [which is seen mid-handle].* American Home Cook Book, *1854.* **$165-$200**

X-46. Gridiron patent. *Pat'd 11/14/1836, by Amasa Sizer and George Sizer, Meriden, CT.* **"Combined gridiron and spider."** *"The nature of our invention consists in uniting a gridiron and spider in one instrument in such manner that both may be used together or each separately at the same time, the juices of the broiling meat being conducted into the spider or when the spider is separately used, into a receiver placed within it. To enable others skilled in the art to make, and use our invention we describe its construction as follows: The form may be square, circular, or oval when open for use, or a half square, or parallelogram, or a semicircle when folded. The model deposited in the Patent Office is semicircular when folded. The spider (A) and gridiron (B) are each cast whole in separate castings, and united in the following manner. The spider is formed with legs and a handle, and on each end of the spider around the corners of the side approaching the fire is a projecting ear (C), having a staple of wire set in the casting to receive the pintle or gudgeon of the gridiron, and on which it turns. Near each of these ears is a spout (D) on each end. The gridiron is cast with fluted bars, and rim, on the end of the bar, which joins the spider, gudgeons or pintles are extended, which when connected form a hinge. When the two parts are used separately, and at the same time, a narrow tin pan is placed under the edge of the gridiron and within the basin of the spider, to receive the drip. When folded, the tin pan may be used as a chafing dish."* Official Gazette.

a supporting leg. This was used in the 18th C. for dipping lengths of rush into melted fat, to coat the stalks as crude "candles," American, "boat" bowl is 7" L x 3" W x 1" deep, handle 21" L, 18th C. <u>Confusable</u> — This is here because it could be mistaken for some kind of fish cooker or cooking ladle; or for a herb crusher (see Chapter I). **$550-$700**

Gypsy pot or kettle, cast iron, with 3 casting ribs around circumference, cast in 3-part mold, American, 11-3/4" H x 12-7/8" diameter, early 19th or late 18th C. **$275-$375**

"Preparing Homminy for the Table — It must be thoroughly washed in cold water, rubbing it well with the hands; then washed in the same way in warm water, changing the water several times. Put it into a large pot of cold water, and boil steadily eight or ten hours, keeping it closely covered. Add hot water frequently while boiling, otherwise the homminy will burn and be dark colored. When homminy beans are used, one pint to a gallon of homminy, to be put in when the homminy is put on. If it is put on the first thing in the morning, and kept briskly boiling, it will be ready for dinner at two o'clock. Season with butter and send it to the table hot. (These pints were all measured with the common tin cup.)" *The Farmers' Cabinet, Devoted to Agriculture, Horticulture and Rural Economy* . Philadelphia: Vol. II, No. 1, 8/1/1837.

Hake, forged iron, an "S" hook for hanging pots or kettles from crane, American (?), 6" L, 18th or early 19th C. — but hard to date now because so many are being made by artisan blacksmiths. With these, the best you could hope for would be something zoomorphic: for example, the hook ending in a snake's head or dog's head. Multiply price below by 30 to 100 if you should find such a thing. **$15+**

Ham hook — See hook, ham or meat

X-47. Standing gridirons. *Wrought iron. 18th C. Photograph courtesy of Pat Guthman Antiques, Southport, CT. Each:* **$450+**

Hearth warming shelf, wrought iron bracket, hung on nails in side of fireplace, American, 9" H x 13" W, 18th C. These are extremely rare, and might be mistaken for regular wall bracket shelves. **$275+**

Hoes, forged iron, broad-bladed, tilted sockets without their long wooden handles, sometimes struck with maker's mark, American, early to mid 19th C. **$15-$25**

Hoe downs & ups — Looking at a modern hoe, it is not easy to imagine propping one up at such a slant in front of the fire that a corn cake could actually be slapped upon it and baked. But the nineteenth century had a variety of hoes, for purposes such as weeding or grubbing, with shank sockets set at different angles, and blades of different dimensions. Hoes varied from region to region too. I have not yet seen a perfect description of a hoe suitable for hoe cakes.

• • • •

"Virginia Hoe Cake — Pour warm water on a quart of Indian meal; stir in a spoonful of lard or butter, some salt, make it stiff, and work it for 10 minutes; have a board about the size of a barrel head, (or the middle piece of the head will answer,) wet the board with water, and spread on the dough with your hand; place it before the fire; prop it aslant with a flat-iron, bake it slowly; when one side is nicely brown, take it up and turn it, by running a thread between the cake and the board, then put it back, and let the other side brown. These cakes used to be baked in Virginia on a large iron hoe, from whence they derive their name." Elizabeth E. Lea, *Useful Receipts and Hints to Young Housekeepers,* 10th ed., Baltimore, 1859 (1st ed. 1851).

X-48. Grill. *Wrought iron, well-finished. Heart decorations add much to value. 26" L overall x 13" W. Probably English, late 18th C.* **$450+**

X-49. Hoe blades. *Forged iron, potentially used for baking hoe cakes in front of coals or fire. When laid down, the shank socket would serve as a little foot that would raise one end toward the fire. Blades about 6" to 8" W.* (**T-L**) *is a* <u>Virginia</u> *style weeding hoe;* (**B-R**) *is a* <u>Carolina</u> *style hoe. Both made as "plantation" hoes in Sheffield, England, c.1816.*

Hoe Pones — E. Scott Boyce, in *Economic and Social History of Chowan County, North Carolina, 1880-1915,* published by Columbia University, 1917, wrote about this odd cooking utensil of the 1880s: "The '**hoe-cake**' — a pone of corn-bread baked on a hoe that had already lived out it's usefulness as a farm utensil — in Chowan had not yet passed into the realms of fiction." [p.223 of this really neat book.]

Hook, forged iron, 4 points, flattened, dealer Dorothy Lyon said she was told it was used for roasting small game birds and the flattened ends were supposed to keep the juices from dripping, American, prob. Richmond, VA, 9"L, late 18th or early 19th C. **$90-$110**

Hook, ham or meat, braided wrought iron, with eye at top and but one hook. Sides or large cuts of meat (such as hams) were hung in smokehouse from these. Sometimes the meat was rubbed in ashes, or wrapped in cloth before hanging. 9" L, American, late 18th, early 19th C. **$75-$100**

Hook, ham or meat, braided wrought iron, 4 hooks, 7-1/2" L, the hooks reach out 10" W. Impeccable provenance: it was formerly in the Keillor Family Collection, found installed in the chimney of a house built in Plymouth, MA, in 1711. **$400+**

Hook, ham or meat, forged iron with 4 graceful hooks, ring for hanging at top. Made from 2 twisted lengths of bar iron, heated & pounded together. Could be from anywhere, no stylistic details tie it to a country, 24" H, each hook 7-1/4" H, prob. late 1700s, early 1800s. Hard to date. So many turn up, you wonder if somebody has a blacksmith in the backyard. **$75+**

Hook, pot — See pot hook

Hot water kettle — See tea kitchens

Jack, type called **bottle jack**, brass with forged iron hook, rotary action provided by a clockwork movement, spring wound, concealed within the cylindrical bottle shaped drum above the hook.

X-50. Bottle jack. *Japanned sheet iron, or brass (which were much more expensive). Clockwork inside, but named for its overall shape. From Harrod's Stores Ltd., Brompton, England, 1895 catalog. They also cleaned and repaired bottle jacks, as probably many clock repairers did too. SEE also the reflecting oven meat screens, which were made for use with bottle jacks.* **$200-$350**

The key hole for winding is in the side, near the bottom of the cylinder. "Salter's Warranted Economical Bottle Jack," mark is a mariner's knot pierced by an arrow, & the initial "S," English, 12" H, c.1820s (?). A Mr. Salter (probably the same one) made brass-faced hanging spring balance scales. **$350-$450**

The Smoke-house of Col. M'Allister in 1828, Fort Turner, on the Susquehanna, above Harrisburg. "A convenience worthy of imitation," reported visitor Judge Buel. "The Smoke-house was a wooden octagon building, perhaps 16 feet in diameter, perfectly tight, except the door-way. The peculiarities of this building were, it was set a foot or more above the ground, and was perfectly dry, and bacon, hams, &c., were kept hanging around its walls all summer without becoming damp or mouldy, or being injured by flies; and in the second place, no fire was admitted into the building, the smoke being conveyed into it through a tube from the outside, where it was generated." *The Farmers' Cabinet,* Vol. I, No. 1, Philadelphia, July 1, 1836.

Jack clamp for bottle jack — a mantle clamp, also called a jack rack, cast & worked brass, a simple screw clamp, sliding jack hook, acorn finial to screw, English or poss. American, late 18th or early 19th C. (Those in elegant whitesmithed steel about same value.) **$250-$375**

Jack, clock or clockwork, brass & iron, iron weight, English, 8-11/16" H exclusive of wheel at top, early 19th C. **$1200-$1550**

Jack, clock, forged iron, spoked wheel, scrolled front plate, arched wall bracket, 3 gears and spool, American or English, 14" H, late 18th or early 19th C. **$1750-$2000**

Jack, clock, steel, cast, wrought & machined brass beautifully scrolled front plate, clean clockwork, the word "jack" in the name, standing for the assistant or spit turner who is no longer necessary, English, 18th C. **$1200-$1500**

X-51. Clock jack. *Skeletal iron frame, brass front. 8-11/16" H excluding governor wheel at top. Cast iron weight. Photographed from stock of Mark & Margery Allen, Putnam Valley, NY.* **$1800-$2500**

Planetarium stove — In the *Journal of the Franklin Institute..and Mechanics' Register* [Philadelphia], of 1839, appeared a report of a patent obtained July 12, 1838 by Samuel Pierce of NYC for an "Apparatus for Roasting Meat and other Articles." The *Journal* editor writes as follows: "This apparatus is denominated the 'manifold roaster, or planetarium stove,' and the patentee says, 'the main object of my improvement is to combine together a number of spits, or jacks, each of which is to sustain a joint of meat, a fowl, or other article to be roasted; and each of which spits is to be suspended by a hook over its appropriate dripping pan, the whole of which spits may be made to revolve simultaneously by wheel work, properly geared, either before an ordinary fire, or more perfectly by being placed around a stove constructed for that purpose; in which latter case the spits not only revolve on their own axes, but have an orbicular revolution round the stove. The effect of the heat is, in either case, to be promoted by means of reflectors. When the planetarium stove is complete, and in operation, its external appearance is that of an ordinary cylindrical stove of large diameter, the external cylinder being a case (usually made double) which surrounds the stove, and which also surrounds the system of spits which revolve round said stove.'" Pierce went on to claim that the originality of this invention was in the multiple vertical spits revolving simultaneously. I'm not convinced this was anywhere near the first of this type, although the older English ones seen in pictures were horizontal spits.

Jack or spit engine, clockwork mechanism for driving spit, brass face, wrought iron frame, English (?), 18th C. Appearance, workability (or at least repairable condition), completeness add value. **$1500-$2500**

Jack & crown spit, also called a spit engine, cast & machined brass, forged iron, marked "John Linwood," English (?), 18th C. **$1200-$1500**

Jack & spit, standing floor model clockwork jack, timer bell, vertical oblong housing for works, lion's paw feet to 4 short legs, carrying handle on top, cast iron & steel, cranked to wind, can motivate 3 long spits, one end hooked to jack, other supported

on wrought iron stand, French, 48" H, early 19th C. I don't know maker of this, it's not marked, but another French one, with clockworks inside a small 4-legged pedestal base, that drives a spit in a tin reflector oven with rounded back, and tapered tubular tin legs, was made in the mid 19th C. by Viville of Paris. Not only did the spit turn, but some system of "rotating spoons" kept basting the meat as it turned. The clockwork has bells that ring when it's winding down. It was exhibited at an antique show in 1988 by Larry Melvin, Springfield, OH, who was asking $950 for it then. **$1000+**

A spectacular mechanical spit was reported in William Hone's *The Every-Day Book,* 1827: "**The most singular spit in the world** is that of the Count de Castel Maria, one of the most opulent lords of Treviso. This spit turns one hundred and thirty different roasts at once, and plays twenty-four tunes, and whatever it plays, corresponds to a certain degree of cooking, which is perfectly understood by the cook. Thus, a leg of mutton à lá anglaise, will be excellent at the 12th air; a fowl à lá Flamande, will be juicy at the 18th, and so on. It would be difficult, perhaps, to carry farther the love of music and gormandizing."

Kettle, also spelled cettell, or kittel in old records, this one of cast iron, 3 short feet, slightly flared out sides, reinforced with one inch wide wrought iron band near top, American (?), 7-1/2" H, 18th C. Every once in a while you see such pieces with the wrought band, which may be as narrow as 3/8". **$125-$150+**

Kettle, cast iron with 3 legs, heavy twisted forged iron bail handle, domed lid, 3 longish feet, circumferential ribs or ridges, bulge-pot type that looks like a "gypsy kettle," American, 6-1/4" H x 4-1/4" diameter, late 18th C. **$275-$350**

Kettle, cast iron, with 3 legs, rare in this small size — only 4" H, American, early 19th C. **$125-$150**

X-53. Kettle tilter with kettle. *Forged iron with cast kettle. Photograph courtesy of Pat Guthman Antiques, Southport, CT.(SEE also a quadrant crane with kettle & kettle tilter.)* **$400+**

X-52. Smoke jack. *18th C. drawing cut (by dealer, not me) from unID book of plates. "A. Bell" was the engraver, and this is the "Smoke" plate, No. CCCCLXXI, so it was a big book. Note gears. This interesting invention worked by using the heated air (smoke) updraft which caused the vanes to turn, which turned the shaft which turned the spit. Archie Keillor told me, when I worked on my first book, that you couldn't collect these — unless you caught a sight of one, peering up an old chimney in an English manor home.*

Kettle, with lid, heavy copper with wrought iron swing handle, slightly convex bottom, meant to hang on a fireplace crane, American (?), 15" D, early 19th C. **$200-$375**

Department of Transportation & Sanitation Department find new uses for landfill! I have read of a seventeenth & eighteenth century practice called "kettlin' the roads," which involved dragging old, probably holey, iron kettles and pots behind a sleigh in order to destroy the potentially dangerous slick iced-over tracks of sleigh runners on snowy roads.

● ● ● ●

Lookalike alarm — Lehman's Hardware & Appliances, Kidron, OH, offers a full range of hammered copper kettles with extra bottoms brazed in, cast iron or cast brass lug ears, and steel bail handles, in their "Non-Electric Good Neighbor Amish Country" catalog. These are apple butter kettles and flat bottom kettles; the former come in 8, 10, 12, 15, 20, 25, 30, 40 and 50 gallon capacities, from about $175 to $450+. I believe the stamped trademark is "MAKERS" on the side. The flat bottom kettles come in 1, 2, 4, 6, 8, 10 quart sizes, and 3, 5 and 8 gallon. They have a "tough, tarnish & weather-resistent polyurethan coating" which must be removed with paint remover for cooking. Price range is for fairly small antiques; $$$ goes up in quantum leaps for large ones.

● ● ● ●

Spun brass & copper kettles — Until about 1852, copper and brass kettles were made by hammering sheet metal over a form, or by a combination of hammering and piecing (usually with a dovetailed joint). But in 1852, an inventor named J. F. Flanders was granted patent #8627 for a new method, a patent he granted to Roys & Wilcox, whose names appear on the bottom of many kettles made by this wonderful new way. It was described in the report of the Commissioner of Patents for the year 1852: "An automatic machine for performing, on a large scale, the well known metallurgic operation of spinning up cups, platters, and such like articles, from a flat disk in a lathe, is worthy of notice. In this machine, large copper kettles, known in the shops as brass batteries, and usually shaped by repeated blows of a small hand hammer, are formed with great rapidity, and with a beauty and finish never attained by the handmade article. A species of burnisher, sometimes provided with a friction roller, is forced, by means of curved slots acting in connexion with screws and guides, to travel in tolerably close contact with the exterior of a revolving conical mandril formed of cast-iron. The flat sheet of metal is clamped upon the apex of this conical-former, revolves with it, and is gradually, by the action of the burnisher, forced to conform exactly to its shape. Several formers, each deviating more from a disk, and approaching more nearly to the form of the finished kettle, are used before the operation is completed, in order to bring the metal gradually, and by successive stages, into its new shape, and avoid all straining that might be injurious to the finished article.

"This contrivance is now in use. Its productions will speak for themselves, and will, on account of their superior beauty, have the preference over the old article, even if the inventor should not reduce the price to that extent which the labor-saving qualities of his machine would fully warrant." p. 385, *Ex. Doc. 65*, 32d Congress. Washington: Robert Armstrong, Printer, 1853.

Kettle tilter, also called a tipper or a lazy elbow, or idle back, used to assist the cook in pouring from a heavy kettle (especially a tea kettle or hot water kettle) suspended over a fire in the hearth, wrought iron, no marks, English or American, late 18th C. **$175-$250**

Kettle tilter, forged iron, monkey-tail handle, American or English, 19-1/2" L, 18th C. **$225-$300**

Kettle tilter, forged iron, nice swivel loop to hang from hook, pleasantly curved handle, American or English, hard to measure exactly, but about 8-1/2" H x 14" L, 18th or early 19th C. **$250-$350**

Kettle tilter, forged iron, swivel ring and brass knob on end of curved handle, poss. American, more prob. English, 21" L, 18th or early 19th C. **$300-$350**

Kettle tilter, forged iron, swivel ring, nice formed brass knob on handle and swivel ring, English (?), 23" L, c.1800. **$400-$500**

Kettle tilter, forged iron, swivel ring top with acorn finial, nice swoopy thin handle, American (?), about 13" across, late 18th or early 19th C. **$350-$425**

Ladles — See Chapter XIII

Meat hooks — See hook, ham

Meat screens — See reflecting oven — meat screeen

Mulling iron, forged iron, wooden handle, paddle-like end, American (?), 16" L, 18th or early 19th C. **$125-$175**

Mulling iron, wrought iron, a hook at one end, a sort of curved blade, almost a paddle, at the other end, English or American, 18" L, 18th or 19th C. **$125-$175**

Peels — See Chapter XIII

Plate warmer, sheet iron cabinet, plain decoration, tall and cylindrical with door, small chamber at bottom with air vents, not for putting in charcoal — the air vents just drew hot air from hearth up into cylinder, American (?), 3 feet H x 13" diameter, early 19th C. **$375-$550**

Plate warmer, sheet iron with original red paint with flowers in ochre, cast brass side handles, elegant slim cast iron cabriole legs with penny feet, arched top, door, prob. English, 32" H, c.1800 to 1830. **$650+**

Plate warmer, wire & forged iron, concentric wire rings form platform, meant to hang in fireplace, American (?), 15" diameter, early to mid 19th C. **$175-$250**

X-54. "A simple feed cooker." *A large cast iron kettle, "large enough to admit the chine of a meat barrel or tierce, and arranged with a fire-place beneath it. A number of holes are bored in the bottom of the barrel, and two strong rings are affixed to the sides. The barrel is placed upon the kettle, fitting closely inside the rim, and is filled with roots and meal. A close cover is fitted to the top, and the contents of the barrel are cooked by the steam from the kettle. The barrel may be lifted off when the feed is cooked, by means of a small crane and windlass, and placed upon a wheelbarrow to be carried where it is to be used." Imagine doing that every day!* American Agriculturist, *6/1878.*

X-55. Plate warmer or dish warmer. *Sheet iron with japanned finish, and with cast iron cabriole legs with lion's paws. Cast handles at sides. This kind was slightly more versitile than the closed top kind, although heat escaped out of the top. American (?), mid 19th C. Courtesy William Hodges.* **$350+**

X-56. Plate warmer. *Japanned and decorated tin, most of decoration and finish burned off. With sheet iron legs bolted on. Brass decorative side handles. 28-1/2" H x 13-1/4" W, 2 inserted shelves. Other side open to the fire. Probably English, late 19th C. Photographed at booth of Jill Oltz, Mountainville, NJ, at a Pier show in NYC.* **$300-$450+**

X-57. Plate warmers. *Both japanned tin with decorative cat iron legs and handles. Both with open backs to fire. Both probably imports from England.* **(L)** *From ad of J. & C. Berrian, NYC dealer, in History of Prominent Mercantile & Mfg. Firms in the U.S., 1857.* **(R)** *From F. A. Walker catalog, 18701-80s.* **$450-$600**

X-58. Posnet. *Cast bronze, 3 legs, one under handle longest by far so tilts forward. Long horizontal handle flat on top, half-round in section. Cast along top of handle: "W. C : NEWPORT. C [?]." 9-1/16" H x 8-1/16" diameter x 17-5/16" L with handle. Picture courtesy of the National Museum of American History, Smithsonian Institution, John Paul Remensnyder estate.* **$1200+**

Plate warming cabinet, japanned sheet metal with domed top, shaped like a firescreen, 2 wire shelves inside, in F. A. Walker catalog, American (?), c.1870s. **$175-$250**

Plate warming cabinet, sheet iron with cast iron legs bolted on, brass side handles, most of japanned and painted decoration burned off long ago, 3 shelves, nice front door (facing out to room) & open of course in front though braced with bars of metal, prob. made at the Usk, Monmouthshire works in Wales, 28-1/2" H x 13-1/4" W, c.1800- to 1815. **$575+**

Plate warming cabinet, tin & cast iron, 3 well-shaped cabriole legs with lion's paw feet, mostly open at top with wide inner lip, one shelf, side handles, no door, American (?), about 28" H, early 19th C. **$375+**

Plate warming cabinet, japanned tin with bronzed cast iron decorative trim, high cast iron cabriole legs, lion's paw feet, English (?), 30" H x 15" W, 19th C. **$475**

Plate warming cabinets, japanned tin with high cabriole cast iron legs & side handles, back (or front) open to fire or stove, plates & dishes heated on shelves inside, from F. A. Walker catalog, made by various companies, American & English, about 25" to 30" H, c.1870s. **$375+**

Posnet, cast iron, 3 feet, slightly upslanted side handle, no mark, American (?), 5" H x 5" D, early early 19th C. The way to collect these is to look for variations in handles and feet, or to get a range of sizes (maybe starting with the darling miniature ones about 2-1/2" H), or — this appeals most to me — to get only repaired ones. **$75-$175**

Posnet, cast iron, rather shallow, with 3 short legs and long handle, American, 3" H including legs, 7" D bowl plus 6" handle, 18th C. **$100-$165**

Posnet or skillet, bell metal, long handle, 3 peg feet, "Austin & Crocker," Boston, MA, 18th C. Sold at the 1980 Garbisch collection auction for $3100. Price related to the metal, the mark, and a prestigous and renowned collector (of folk arts). **$3100+**

Posnet or skillet, cast bell metal or bronze, 3-legged with long handle, used like a saucepan, marked "Wasbrough No. 6," 7" H x 7-1/2" D with 11-1/2" L handle, 5-1/4" H legs, 18th or very early 19th C. **$475+**

Posnet or skillet, cast bell metal, 3 legs, longish handle, marked "Wasbrough No. 2," 15" L, early 19th C. **$500+**

Posnet or skillet, cast iron, 3 legs, long handle, repaired in very entertaining way: one leg seems to have dropped out leaving hole or else broke off, and hole was ground out. Then a bolt was stuck through the hole with a washer, and it was all hammered up around to fit the curve of the pot, then a pin, sort of like the cotter pin idea, was driven through a hole in the bolt to hold it tightly in place. American, 5-1/4" diameter, with handle 11-1/16" L, legs are 1-1/4" H, early 19th C. I love things like this, but paid only $19 for it. I honestly don't know if I would have bought it if it had been much more; I have very deep pockets but very short arms when it comes to collecting. <u>My advice is go for the old old repairs, as they are truly unique and add worlds of romance to a piece.</u> **$75+**

Skillet or Posnet? Both the posnet and skillet were used rather like sauce pans. A posnet is probably the smaller of the two. You do not find clear distinctions in old inventories or even cookery books, and certainly no exact sizes given anywhere. Alice Morse Earle, writing in a chapter called "Table Plenishings," in *Customs & Fashions in Old New England* (NY: Scribner's, 1893) has rather a lot to say about posnets, although a lot of it is now discounted because of her tying posnets and porringers together. It's possible that 300 years ago they weren't so careful. Generally we think of porringers as something to eat out of, and a posnet as a small cooking utensil. The etymology Earle relates is interesting: A posnet "was spelt, in various colonial documents, *posned, possnet, posnett, porsnet, pocneit, posnert, possenette, postnett, and parsnett.* It is derived from the Welsh *posned,* a porringer or little dish. In 1641 Edward Skinner left a 'Postnett' by will; this was apparently of pewter. In 1653 Governor Haynes, of Hartford, left an 'Iron Posnet' by will. In the inventory of the estate of Robert Daniel, of Cambridge, in 1655, we learn that 'a Little Porsenett' of his was worth five shillings. In 1693 Governor Caleb Carr, of Providence, bequeathed to his wife a 'silver possnet & the cover belonging to it.' By these records we see that posnets were of various metals, and sometimes had covers. I have found no advertisements of them in early American newspapers, even with all their varied array of utensils and vessels. I fancy the name fell quickly into disuse in this country." p. 141.

X-59. Posnet & Closeup of handle. (T) *Cast bell metal, 3 long legs, long flat handle slightly tapered at end, flat on top, round in section. Made by Robert Crocker & Richard (?) Austin, Boston, late 18th or very early 19th C. 8-1/2" H x 8-3/4" diameter x 19-5/8" L including handle. Picture courtesy of the National Museum of American History, Smithsonian Institution, John Paul Remensnyder estate.* **(B)** *"Austin & Crocker, Boston" in floriate scroll border, which is very unusual. Picture courtesy of the National Museum of American History, Smithsonian Institution, John Paul Remensnyder estate.* **$2500-$3000**

X-60. Posnet. *Cast bell metal. Maker, known more for andirons, is James Davis, who was working in the last quarter of the 18th C. and first quarter of the 19th C. Marked "J. Davis Boston." Photographed from stock of Jay Kohler & Louise Rozene, Sunset Mountain Farm, Amherst, VA.* **$1000+**

Posnet or skillet, cast iron, 3 tall tapered legs, long handle, marked "N. S." (possibly Nathaniel Starbuck), American, 12" L including handle, 18th or very early 19th C. **$175+**

Posnet or skillet, cast iron, nice deep bowl with 3 legs, flat top handle, American, 5-1/2" H x 6-5/8" diameter plus 6-1/2" handle, 18th C. **$175+**

Pot, also found spelled <u>pott</u> in old records, this one cast iron, bulbous body, 3 legs, with cast iron cover with generous curved loop handle, wrought bail handle, straight sprue gate mark on bottom, American (?), unusual heighth to width ratio: 10" H x 8" D, 18th C. This is a wonderful piece offered for sale several years ago by Clara Jean Davis of Concord, NH. She loves old iron and it shows in the pieces she finds. **$175-$225**

Pot, cast iron, with lid, oval shape with plump rounded sides, forged bail handle, English (?), or poss. American, about 11" L the major axis, late 18th or early 19th C. **$155+**

Pot, "gypsy kettle" type with globular body, sometimes called a <u>bulge pot</u> in some founders' price lists, flared rim, pitted cast iron, 2 lug handles of triangular shape with "elbows" that are almost straight out from side and partly curved inside, 3 circumferential or horizontal mold rings on belly and one around flared neck, as well as a "latitudinal" or vertical casting line from the "equatorial line" to the rim on both sides between the handles, long casting gate on bottom, 3 tapered legs that are flat on side facing in and deeply rounded on outside, this example with beautiful especially high, full half-circle wrought bail, which — when up — exactly copies the curve of the unusually large and high arched handle riveted to the flat, hammered sheet iron lid, which is probably original. No mark, American, 7-1/8" H x 7-3/4" diameter at top, legs are 1-5/8" H, late 18th or early 19th C. For me, a good deal of the charm (and value) of this particular pot lies in the lid, and the matched arches of lid and bail. **$175+**

Pot chain, forged iron, to hang pot over fire, hook at each end, 25 nice big round links, by using the hooks in different ways the effectual length of the chain is changed, could be American or European, 41" L, 18th C. See also trammels. **$65-$85**

Iron imports in 1775 — A New York City importer named George Ball advertised in the newspaper in 1775 that he had just received some "useful and wholesome iron utensils, so much recommended by physicians for their safety, and so generally and justly preferred to copper, by all the best housekeepers in England, for two of the best reasons in the world, viz. that they are entirely free from that dangerous, poisonous property [verdigris], from which so many fatal accidents have been known to arise amongst those who use copper vessels, and because they never want tinning. . . ." He goes on to enumerate the imports, including "<u>Tea kettles</u> from three quarts to six, four-gallon pots with covers, to five quarts, Pie pans, two gallon oval pots, <u>stew pans and covers</u>, of several different sizes, <u>Fish kettles</u> of six different sizes, with strainers, <u>Saucepans</u>, from six quarts to one pint. For cabin use on board of shipping, they are far preferable to copper, as no danger (however careless the cook, or long the voyage) can possibly happen from using them, as too often has through these causes, from the use of copper. They are all wrought according to the most approved pattern now used in London. . . ." Ball had no doubt of a warm, anglophilic reception to his ad: the British used New York City as its base of operations during the Revolutionary War from 1776 to 1783. New York had been a British stronghold since the 1660s, after taking over from the Dutch; about two thirds of the population was either British or Loyalist. The New York area did become the site for many battles between Americans fighting for independence and British forces.

X-62. Bulge pot, *of type sometimes called a* **"gypsy kettle."** *Cast iron, squat bulging body, 2 vertical seams, long casting gate on bottom, 3 longish legs, 3 vertical bands in relief around circumference. Marked on side "No. 1. 2 QTS. SAVERY & Co. Philadelphia." 6" H x 9-5/16" diameter. Photo by Jennifer Oka. Picture courtesy of the National Museum of American History, Smithsonian Institution, John Paul Remensnyder estate.* **$225-$275**

X-61. Posnets. *A delightful family of cast bell metal posnets in five sizes. Note brace, which may be an old repair, to handle at far right. Posnets are relatively deep and have flat bottoms (skillets have rounded bottoms). Photograph courtesy of Pat Guthman Antiques, Southport, CT. Assembled set:* **$1800+**

The most authoritative writing — all new articles and books included — I've found **on dating really old iron pots and kettles** was done by John D. Tyler, Curator of Science, Industry, and Technology at the Pennsylvania Historical and Museum Commission. He wrote two similar articles, one in *The Magazine ANTIQUES*, Aug. 1971, and another in the April 1978 *Early American Life*. The latter is somewhat more helpful, because it has a chart of the lug or ear handles. Both have a lot of information tying English and American technology to evidence found on the pots themselves — casting mold and seam lines, and sprues and casting gates (the former round and older, the latter a narrow oblong) through which the molten iron was poured into the molds. Tyler says that the rounded legs are typically American; the "triangular" ones English. We can all wish there were a Tyler book to read and reread.

• • • •

A **superstition** reported in William Hone's *The Year Book* (London, 1845 edition), reports: "Professor Playfair, in a letter to Mr. Brand, dated St. Andrew's, January 26, 1801, mentioning the superstitions of his neighborhood, says: '. . . mischievous elves cannot enter into a house at night, if, before bed-time, the lower end of the crook, or iron chain, by which a vessel is suspended over the fire, be raised up a few links.'"

Pot hooks, also called **racking crooks,** forged iron "S," hooked over pot chain, trammel, crane, or another pot hook, with a bail-handle or hoop-handle kettle, pot or griddle hung from the lower crook. Alice Morse Earle, in *Customs & Fashions in Old New England* (1893), writes "In earlier days the great **lug-pole** [made of green wood, to withstand the heat & flames], or, as it was called in England, the **back-bar,** stretched from ledge to ledge, or lug to lug, high up the yawning chimney, and held a motley collection of pot-hooks and trammels, of gib-crokes (or jib-crooks), twicrokes, and hakes, which in turn suspended at various heights over the fire, pots, and kettles and other cooking utensils" (p.130). **Cotrall** is another term. American or European, from about 6" L to 9" L, any age up to end of 19th C. **Reproduction alert** — I suspect many of the ones found laid out on the hopsacking for the unwary are newly forged. Look at the "grain" of the beaten iron, the texture, and particularly the two tips, which should not look as if they'd been snipped off with very powerful cutters. The blacksmith of the past might have used pincers, but would have cut then hammered again to finish the tips. If you ever see a pot hook with a snake's head, buy it. (And sell it to me?) Some of Earle's terms are not to be found in 19th C. dictionaries and glossaries of Americanisms, of which I have not a few. I believe **croke** is a corruption of crook, and a **gib-croke** would be a side hook. I think **twicroke** could be either a 2-hooked crook, or possibly a twisted hook. <u>Hake</u> is a kind of fish, but probably here it's a corruption of hook.   **$6-$15**

X-64. Hearth scene, *showing anthropomorphized food and utensils. Sausage is cooking in a frying pan over the coals. The covered vessels in rear are not identified. One on stand is probably made of heavy earthenware; smaller one with lid looks like a small skillet with lid, of cast iron. From* Picture Fables, *drawn by Otto Speckter, 1858.*

X-63. Pot, or "gypsy kettle." *Cast iron, 3 legs, twisted forged iron bail, domed lid with loop handle. 6-1/2" H x 4-1/4" diameter — beautiful small size. American, late 18th C. Picture courtesy of Robert W. Skinner Inc., Auctioneers, Bolton, MA.* **$350+**

X-65. Gypsy kettle or pot, *cast iron, 2 vertical seams, bail handle. A little beauty. Early 19th C. Photo courtesy of Oveda Maurer Antiques, San Anselmo, CA.* **$275+**

X-66. Pot hook. *Best one ever. Finely whitesmithed steel hook with beautifully shaped long slender forearm and hand grasping where loop comes around. 5-15/16" x 4-1/4", American (?), early 19th C. Photo by Jennifer Oka. Picture courtesy of the National Museum of American History, Smithsonian Institution, John Paul Remensnyder estate. There would be much excited crossover interest from folk art collectors if this were actually for sale!* **$800+**

X-67. Bulge pot, two views. *with pieced tin slightly domed lid. Cast iron, wire bail handle, 3 short feet. 9-1/2" H x 10-3/4" diameter. Note that wonderful pieced edge at bottom of lid photo. From stock of Jean Hatt, Hatt's Hutt, Denver, PA.* **$275+**

X-68. Similar pot in use. *"To bed, to bed, says Sleepy-Head; Let's stay awhile, says Slow; Put on the pot, says Greedy-Gut, We'll sup before we go."* Mother Goose's Melodies, 1833. *Many of these moralistic fable books for children have delightfully detailed engravings or woodcuts, which show such things as dress and household accoutrements. Note here what appears to be either a frying pan or a bed warmer leaning against the surround. Note the figural andiron of man in tricorn hat.*

X-69. Meat screen — reflecting oven, *sometimes called a* **tin kitchen**. *Of type specifically for a hanging jack of some kind, especially a bottle jack. This one has a dangle spit with 6 weighted rods — a flywheel — spoked out to assist the backward and forward spinning. Sheet iron with crown-like or harped superstructure. We see it as we would from the fire, the door in back is for the cook to view the proceedings and to baste. Vertical forged iron spit with hooks. Front left leg propped up on wood support indicating piece was either customized to fit a particular hearth, or that one leg has broken, or possibly that the other three legs were lengthened. c.1790 to 1840. Picture courtesy of the National Museum of American History, Smithsonian Institution.* **$1000+**

Pot lid, copper with relatively short forged iron handle with hanging hole chiseled out, leather, wood or horn gasket to insulate iron handle where it is riveted to the lid, copper rivets, tinned inside, raised edge to fit saucepan rim, marked "M. W."; inventory numbers "226, 7225, 2573"; plus initial "E" scratched lightly on surface near handle, English, 6-3/4" diameter, 3-5/8" L handle, early 19th C. Another one marked "M. W.," bought at same time, is much smaller (4-1/2" diameter with 2-1/2" L handle), and has one number the same, "7225," with some scratchmarks under the first two making it look like a "5," and a small "6" under the long number, probably left over from some other time, plus the "E." It was only when closely examining these lids, which my mother has owned for years, preparatory to photographing them and writing these descriptions, that I noticed the faint scratched inventory numbers, and the heat-insulating gasket on the larger one. <u>Close examination when you clean or draw something seems to work better to uncover unnoticed details than just looking at it</u>. That is, until you learn how to look.   **$25-$40**

Collector Tip — You know those little black plastic hooks that some socks come attached to at the store? Well, don't let the cashier throw them away. They are perfect for hooking over wrought iron dutch crown pot racks to hold extra pieces that aren't too heavy.

Pot lifter or pot bail, wrought iron, 2 "hinging" or swiveling curved arms with hooked ends, forming a sort of wishbone shape, used to hook under ears of kettle or pot, for lifting. 14" L, late 18th or early 19th C. With a huge iron pot full of boiling food, I'd hate to have to depend on a pot bail. Besides childbirth, accidents at the hearth — especially catching on fire, or other burns — caused most women's deaths in the 18th C.   **$65-$120**

"To extinguish Ladies' Clothes, catching Fire — We often hear, and read in newspapers, when one of those deplorable accidents has happened, which generally deprive us of the youthful and most lovely of our kind, dry recommendations, that ladies, whose dresses may catch fire, should lie down. This, though undoubtedly the right method of extinguishing a flame, is better illustrated, and imprinted more deeply on our recollection, by the following experiment. Take two pieces of muslin, (the article which usually catches fire), or paper, or any other light ignitable substance, and having set on fire the lower part of both, hold one piece upright, as female dresses are worn; it will burn out in about one minute, blazing up to a great height, where the neck and face may be supposed to be burnt. Meantime, fling the other piece of burning muslin on the ground; it will burn slowly, the flame at no time ascending more than an inch or two, and although the burning article might not be moved — as must happen when a living person is enveloped in it — nearly ten minutes would elapse before it would be consumed. In short, it is evident that a perpendicular female dress, though fifty feet high, would burn out with a destructive flame in less time than a single yard of the same material laid in a horizontal position. It results, therefore, from the foregoing experiment, that as soon as a lady's dress is discovered to be on fire, she should instantly lie down; and she may then call for assistance, or confidently set about extinguishing the flame herself. N.B. A current of air always prevails near the floor, particularly between the door and fire-place, and therefore it must be kept in mind, not to run out of the room, nor to open a window, in such cases, as that would be fatal." *The Young Man's Book of Amusement, Containing the Most Interesting and Instructive Experiments In Various Branches of Science.* London: 1850.

Pot lifter, wrought iron, 2 hinged arms ending in inward bent flat & wide hooks that could fit under outside lip of pot or kettle, or under some types of ear handles, American, prob. PA, 15" L each arm, 18th C. **$95-$155**

Pot lifter, wrought iron, 2 hinged & slightly curved arms with hooks at ends, meant to fit any size pot or vessel with ear handles, American (?), each arm 13" L, 18th or very early 19th C. **$65-$100**

Pot or kettle lifter, forged iron, 2 long arms twisted partway for tensile strength, hung on ring, arms end in curved pieces that act as your curved fingers would to fit under rim of pot, Pennsylvania, 17-1/8" L, mid to late 18th C. **$165-$200**

Pot lifter, forged iron, wooden handle, rather like a longshoreman's bale hook, early 19th C. **$55-$75**

Pot pusher, forged iron, 3 legs and curled handle, semi-circle cradles pot and makes it easy to push pot steadily and farther into the hot coals on floor of fireplace, rather ornate, American (?), 5" H x 6" W, 18th C. Very simple ones, with no detailing, go for between $60 and $90. The fancier ones, perhaps with interesting long handles or good penny feet are **$165+**

Pot pusher, wrought iron, chiseled zigzag decoration on handle, English or poss. American, 6-1/8" W at farthest reach of 2 arms, which means it wouldn't push a very big pot, early 19th C. or late 18th C. **$125-$175**

Pot pusher, wrought iron, pot-fitting wide open "horseshoe" of iron, with the ends bent into legs, short twisted handle supported by another leg, used to push posnets or bulge pots or other cooking vessels deeper into the coals or hot ashes. The height, of course, couldn't be so great as to push against the pot above about the lower third of its height. American (?), 3-1/2" H x 7-1/4" W x 9" L including handle, 18th C. or very early 19th C. **$165+**

Potato rake, for pulling potatoes from ashes in fireplace (or some kind of scraping tool, like for scraping out pumpkins), forged iron, straight toothed blade curved around so it would fit inside something like a pumpkin, longish handle with rattail end, American (?), 13" L, early 19th C. **$145-$165**

Reflecting or reflector oven, also called a <u>Yankee baker</u> (by Henry Thoreau), or a <u>tin kitchen</u>, small, tin, horizontal blimp shape, 4 V-strap legs, crank for spit at one end, 2 strap carrying handles on top, oval hinged lift-down door in back to check progress of food, English or German, 12-1/2" H x 14" L exclusive of crank, late 19th C. **$375+**

Reflector oven, sheet iron, has a crank spit, grease spout to pour off accumulation in bottom and 4 feet, American, 11" W, 19th C. **$275-$450+**

X-72. Meat screens & bottle jacks. *You may think I've got too many of these, but I found it fascinating that something so ancient looking could be relatively new. Both are tin, with clockwound bottle jacks in place.* **(L)** "**Roasting screen** *and jack. The screen is adapted to the ranges and cooking stoves in general use. The jack is wound up and runs so as to keep the meat constantly turning til cooked." American Home Cook Book, 1854.* **(R)** *"Roasting oven with jack." Two sizes — 18" W and 24" W ovens, jacks able to turn 25 lbs and 40 lbs. Note key for bottle jack on floor. Duparquet, Huot & Moneuse, hoteliers' supply catalog, c.1904-1910.*

X-70. Meat screen — just 100 years old. *Note striking resemblance to one from Smithsonian Collection in last picture. They may have to revise estimated age. This one came in three widths: 19", 21" and 24". Note lid on grease trap. Harrod's Stores, Ltd., Brompton, England, 1895.* **$500+**

X-71. Meat screen. *Tin, with bottle jack in place. William S. Adams & Son, London, c.1860-61 ad in Francatelli's* Cook's Guide Advertiser. *Note that all of these have a basin -like depression in the bottom for drippings.* **$500+**

X-73. Reflecting oven. *Called in English catalog a "<u>Dutch oven</u>," which was another common name for a tin kitchen reflecting oven. Came in four sizes, from 9" to 13" W. Harrod's Stores, 1895. SEE also the Bird roasters. Because we know these were made very late in the 19th C., and probably into the 20th C., the valuing of any piece depends on appearance, patina, source and practical need — maybe the buyer is cooking on the hearth at home.* **$150+**

At Walden Pond — In Henry David Thoreau's 1854 *Walden, or Life in the Woods,* in the "House-Warming" chapter, we read, "The next winter [1846] I used a small cooking-stove for economy, since I did not own the forest; but it did not keep fire so well as the open fire-place. Cooking was then, for the most part, no longer a poetic, but merely a chemic process. It will soon be forgotten, in these days of stoves, that we used to roast potatoes in the ashes, after the Indian fashion. The stove not only took up room and scented the house, but it concealed the fire, and I felt as if I had lost a companion. You can always see a face in the fire."

Reflector oven, heavy tin plates soldered together, with spit, strap handle and strap legs at each corner, basting door in back, American, 16" H x 20" L, late 18th or early 19th C. **$350-$450+**

Reflector oven, heavy tin, with spit, American, 17" H x 25" L, 19th C. If you want to read a very old-fashioned but sweet storybook, featuring as the protagonist one of these neat old reflecting ovens, look for *The Tin Kitchen,* by J. Hatton Weeks, published in New York and Boston by Thomas Y. Crowell & Co., in 1896. The pro-

X-74. Reflecting oven, *also called here a* **"Dutch oven for baking before the fire."** *Tin, boxy, not very attractive. F. A. Walker catalog, 1870s-80s.* **$125-$175**

X-75. New England kitchen interior, *as depicted on frontispiece of Esther Allen Howland's* The New England Economical Housekeeper, and Family Receipt Book. *Worcester, MA: S. A. Howland, 2nd edition, 1845. Note light walls and well-lit room. This is obviously not a very old house; neither is it new or it would have a brick- set range if not a cooking stove. Note dead animals hanging on walls — yikes. At* **(A)** *is a spit leaning against work counter. She is probably going to spit the goose, and fix it with a skewer, lying on counter. At* **(B)** *far back is black cast iron kettle hanging on crane.* **(B)** *At hearth, placed out a short distance, is a tin kitchen, a reflecting oven of good size, while foreground shows requisite bountiful-harvest basket with spilled veggies. At* **(C)** *are more iron 3-legged pots.*

tagonist — a tin kitchen — relates the job of cooking an old gander as brown and juicy as possible for the parson's visit.   **$475+**

Reflector oven, tin, meant for biscuits with 2 shallow shelves, American, 14" W, c.1840 to 1850.   **$150+**

Reflector oven, tin, with strap handles on top, 4 strap legs, spit & crank handle, "back door" for basting, American, 10" H x 12" L, 1830s-1840s. In many old cookbooks, these are confusingly also called "Dutch ovens."   **$450+**

Reflector oven or tin kitchen, heavy sheet tin, cranked spit, door in back, 4 short strap legs, pour-off grease spout at side bottom, American, 17" H x 19" W, 19th C.   **$450+**

In 1797, a Tin Plate worker by the name of Dewsbury Crawley, of New York City, advertised in the paper that "a very capital improvement [has been made] on the tin roasting ovens so universally in use, by making easy what was thought the most difficult task in using them, [the former mode of basting] which by the improvement is done on the top by means of a hopper and strainer, which causes the fat to drip gradually on the victuals roasting." I've never seen one; I'm sure we could recognize it by the built-in hopper and strainer in the top. At the time Crawley was working, tin was imported in small plates, measuring about 8" x 14", from Wales for the most part. This is why really early tin kitchens are made of pieced-together plates if they are over 14" L. For more [conflicting] information on sizes of tin plate, look in index.

X-76. Reflecting oven — "Tin kitchen." *Sheet iron, made from rectangles of tin soldered together, indicating an early date — late 18th or early 19th C. They were known and documented by the late 18th, and were considered novel and very useful. Wrought iron spit could be used at three different levels. There are tiny slots in the spit and they took the ends of skewers which secured meat to the spit. 13-1/4" H x 18-5/8" L. Picture courtesy of the National Museum of American History, Smithsonian Institution.* **$550+**

X-77. Tin kitchen. *Pieced tin, four iron hooks, spit and crank. Back door opens to allow basting. Came in three sizes, 20", 24" and 26" W. F. A. Walker catalog, 1870s-80s.* **$375+**

Reflector oven or tin kitchen, heavy sheet tin large cylinder, on 4 high iron legs, spit crank in side, hinged door in back for basting, etc., not marked, 38" H, c.1820s to 1840s. **$475-$650**

Reflector oven or tin kitchen, tin, angled "reflective" back, strap handle and 2 strap back legs, front legs twisted wire, extentions of the wire that went around edge of whole body, over which tin was folded at the edge, pouring spout at bottom right, forged iron spit, American, 14" W, mid 19th C. **$275-$350+**

Reflecting Ovens & Dutch Ovens — You will find in some early cookbooks and other writings, as well as ads by some twentieth-century dealers, that a tin kitchen reflecting oven is sometimes called a Dutch oven. The underlying meaning of "substitute for oven" makes both uses appropriate. I use "Dutch oven" only for a cast iron kettle with a lid with raised edges. Recently I found that John Russell Bartlett defined Dutch oven in the 1889 (4th) edition of his *Dictionary of Americanisms,* whereas he did not in the 1859 (2nd) edition. Bartlett writes, "**Dutch Oven**. A tin screen placed before a kitchen range, or open wood fire, within which is the meat to be roasted." He doesn't define tin kitchen in either edition. An English book from the 1860s, in its American edition of 1870, has three line engravings of types of reflecting ovens. **(1)** "The well-known **Dutch oven**" is a reflecting oven with a rounded back and back sides, therefore having a half-circle "footprint." "It is usually made with a little dripping-pan in the bottom, and it has a [slotted] shelf in the middle to place anything upon that requires to be warmed or browned; a small meat cut, or a bird, may be roasted by removing this shelf, and suspending the article by one of the hooks, which are made to turn to expose the different sides of the meat." **(2)** Next, the "**The Yorkshire oven**". . . differing from the Dutch in "being higher in proportion to its width, giving more room for anything suspended to be roasted; and by a slit in the handle, the meat may be moved farther from the fire, or nearer to it. There is likewise a door in the back for access to the meat. The shelf is only placed occasionally. . . ." The back side of this one is flat, and it is the top that is a rounded arch from side to side. **(3)** Last is "**The American oven** . . . an improvement on the Dutch. By means of a bottom slanting upward, and the top slanting downward, the reflection of heat is still stronger. In this case, the meat, or other article, is laid in an iron tray, which is movable, and may be lifted out by two handles, the top [of the oven] moving back on hinges; beneath the false bottom is a place for warming plates. This apparatus is coming much into use, being found extremely convenient for roasting & baking bread, cakes, &c." Carl W. Drepperd, in *A Dictionary of American Antiques,* (Doubleday, 1952), used the term "American oven," saying that it was invented in America c.1790. American collectors usually see types (1) and (3), especially the slanted one. It may not always have a slanted bottom, with a hidey-hole or sort of plate shed behind.

● ● ● ●

A utensil suitable for summer, or shipboard or camp cooking, was the **Salisbury portable kitchen**, an enclosed brazier invented in 1780 by an Englishman, William Redman. He described it thus: "For roasting, boiling, or baking of any kind of provision. The body or furnace is made oval or round, of wrought or cast iron, tin or copper. Within it is placed a grate for the fire, and in the upper part a pot for boiling with water or steam, or a plate for baking. Underneath the fire is a vacuity open in the front, serving as a receptacle for the ashes and admitting a current of air to pass through the fire, thereby carrying off any smoke or dust through a tube or funnell affixed. A front is fixed to the furnace before the fire, which joins close to a reflector, purposely to confine the heat so as to roast and boil, or do either separately with a very small quantity of fire. The reflector is made of tin, brass, or copper. A spit goes through it, and at the bottom a dripping pan is so fixed as to draw off the gravy, that the meat may be easily basted at a door which is made on the top or any convenient part. A gridiron may be fixed occasionally in the place of the spit for broiling, with an additional reflector placed obliquely underneath it, or occasionally an iron plate may be placed in the reflector for the purpose of baking. They may also be made with two reflectors, to fix to the same body, for roasting two or more joints at once." *Abridgments of Specifications Relating to Cooking, Bread-Making, and the Preparation of Confectionery A.D. 1634-1866.* London: Office of the Commissioner of Patents, abridged edition, 1873.

Reflecting oven — tin kitchen, with bottle jack, pieced sheet iron, tall domed oven on 4 cylindrical tin legs, balloon shaped tin structure above, of strap tin, supports windup jack inside, flywheel inside has 6 counterweights, door in back for basting or checking doneness, sometimes this type of vertical tin kitchen was called a <u>niche screen roaster</u>, and the English called it a <u>meat screen for bottle jack</u>, American, about 30" H, c.1790 to 1840. **$1000-$1500+**

Revolving toasters — See toaster, revolving

Lookalike alarm — Just when you thought you were safe with an oldie. Harrod's Stores, Ltd., the great London department store, depicted one of these "Meat Screens, for Bottle Jack" that looks like it ought to be a couple hundred years old, not a hundred! But there it is, in their 1895 retail catalog. It has a sort of lyre-shaped tin rack above the round dome top, that was for suspending the windup jack. It also has a lidded grease or fat well in the bottom, the tubular tin legs are braced, and it was offered in three sizes: 19" H, 21" H and 24" H. They also made one they described as "Extra strong, with enclosed Bottom for Hot Closet, to order, 21 in., 24 in." These were almost twice as expensive. I guess a "hot closet" is a sort of warming oven compartment under there, probably with access from the back, just like the hinged door in the back of the meat screen.

X-78. Salamanders. *Wrought or cast iron. They were heated to red hot in the fire, then set over a dish to radiate the heat and brown a meringue, pudding, or whatever else needed it. Even in 1891, they were still being called for in recipes, although you could use a "hot stove lid" instead.* **(T)** *Wrought iron, 34" L, 6-1/2" diameter, English, 18th C. Ex-Keillor Collection.* **(M)** *Drawing to show how used.* **(B)** *Newfangled style, adjustable in height — it probably turned on a threaded post.* Warne's Model Cookery, *London, 1868.* **$125-$300+**

Roaster, steel, iron & brass, square shaft, fully adjustable for distance to fire, hung over grate, handle unscrews, 6 hooks, English (?), approx. 18-1/4" L, early 19th C. **$250-$350**

Roaster, wrought iron vertical frame with penny feet, adjustable hooked rack, brass finials, "Bainbridge," English or American, 31" H, dated June 22, 1833 — not a patent date, because that year, June 22 was Sunday, and patents aren't issued on Sunday no matter what country. The name sort of "sounds English," but lots of 18th & 19th C. American names did too! A cursory search of the index to the *Official Patent Gazette,* for numbered & unnumbered patents, fails to turn up a Bainbridge. **$600-$700**

Roasters — See also broilers, gridirons, grills

Roasting fork — See Chapter XIII

Rotating broiler — See broiler, revolving

Salamander, forged iron, beautiful trifed feet, English (?), 6-1/2" diameter disk, 34" L, 18th C. **$250-$350**

Salamander, wrought iron, file decorated, short knee-out legs at join of disc and handle, American, 16" L, 18th or very early 19th C. **$350+**

A "wrought iron" **salamander** was offered in five (unstated) sizes in the Harrod's Stores, Ltd, of London, 1895 retail catalog. It is a bit thicker looking than the old ones, with a nearly round head and neck, with a thinner long handle with knob at the end. Apparently some could be ordered with a stand, and these salamanders have a different neck, with a hole through it that slips over the top of the stand. The stand has a heavy stepped base that suports a shortish vertical rod about the same thickness as the salamander's handle. You could thereby heat the salamander, slip it on the stand on your work table, and pivot it over your meringue or whatever it was you were lightly browning, and leave it there while you tended something else. When you read catalogs, particularly those from the very late nineteenth or early twentieth century, you cannot believe how many things you supposed long gone by then were still offered for sale and actual use. This is not the same as reproductions or fakes meant for decoration.

X-80. Skewer rack & skewers. *Forged iron with very fine cutting & filing. Thought to be possibly from East Windsor, CT, c.1760. Drawn from photograph of piece exhibited at Wadsworth Atheneum. From unID private collection.* **$500+**

X-81. Skewer racks & skewers. *Wrought iron, 18th & 19th C forms. Almost all skewer holders or racks are variations on two themes:* (**B**) *and* (**D**) *a diamond shaft, or* (**A**) *and* (**F**) *somewhat bulbous shaft and with upraised arms.* (**E**) *The tulip-like form of is very unusual, but probably wouldn't have the presence to command a top price. Value depends on age, size, and design. Don't worry about a "matched" or "original" set of skewers, because even in the 18th and 19th C. a set would be built up of varous skewers made for specific purposes. Special forms and beautiful detailing, such as extra fine rattail loops or twisted* (**C**) *iron add value.* **$175 and up for racks.**

X-79. Skewer rack & skewers. *Wrought iron, early 18th C. Picture courtesy of the Smithsonian Institution, Museum of History & Technology.* **$600+**

X-82. Skewer racks & skewers. *Even commercial sets might have well-shaped racks.* **(L)** *Iron, from Henry Adams & Son, London, c.1860-61 ad.* **(R)** *"Steel skewers. Round, 3 to 9 inches. Oval, 3 to 11 inches, and 4 to 12 inches." Look at that rack. Would you guess Duparquet, Huot & Moneuse, c.1904-1910? Although they could just have picked up an earlier linecut to use in their catalog. Still, the style looks early 19th or late 18th C.* **$125-$200**

X-83. Skewer pullers patent. *Pat'd 10/30/1877, by F. A. Will and Julius Finck, San Francisco, CA. Consists of a handle, a permanent jaw, a movable jaw operated by the thumb-lever. Shown with skewer stuck in it.* Official Gazette.

X-84. Fancy skewers. *All are French, with possible exception of center one, the bull's-head, which came from* Mrs. A. B. Marshall's Cookery Book, *London, c.1900. The others from Duparquet, Huot & Moneuse, c.1904-1910.* **$22+**

X-85. Skillets. *Cast iron, rounded bottoms, 3 legs, long handles flat on top, half round in section. Used sitting over raked coals in fireplace. 18th or early 19th C. Picture courtesy of the National Museum of American History, Smithsonian Institution.* **$125-$275+**

X-86. Skillet — note the round bottom. *Cast iron, long, more angular legs and handle. Longish casting gate on bottom. 4" H x 13-3/4" L overall. Picture courtesy of the National Museum of American History, Smithsonian Institution, John Paul Remensnyder estate.* **$325+**

X-87. Skillets & spiders — all with legs. *All cast iron.* **(A)** *"Lipped frying spider," in light or medium weight, both in 4 sizes, 8", 9-1/2", 11" and 12-1/2" diameter.* **(B)** *"Biscuit spider with lid." Also in light or medium weight, and 11", 12" or 13" diameters.* **(C)** *"Plain cake spider." Light or medium, four sizes from 8" to 12-1/2" diameter. All from Russell & Erwin Mfg. Co., New Britain, CT, 1865.* **(D)** *"Shallow spider" [flanged lid make it also a* Dutch oven) *in six sizes from 8" to 13" diameter.* **(E)** *"Skillet," which came nested in 3 sizes (not given); and* **(F)** *"Deep spider," in six sizes from 8" to 13". Note flat-top handles and half-round undersides of handles. Also note the flanged lid — making this also a* Dutch oven. *Stuart, Peterson & Co., 1866 catalog.* **$175+**

"Chocolate Custard — Scald a quart of milk; stir in 4 heaping tablespoonsful of grated chocolate and simmer two minutes to dissolve it; beat up the yolks of 6 eggs with 1 cup of sugar; add to the milk and chocolate; stir for one minute; then add vanilla flavoring and pour into your custard cups, which should be waiting in pan half full of boiling water in the oven; cook until you see that the custards are done; let them cool and then grate sweet almonds over the top; make a meringue of the whites of the 6 eggs and a little sugar; pile it on the top of each custard; grate more sweet almonds over that; set them in the oven to brown a little, or brown by holding a salamander or hot stove lid over them." Henry Scammel, compiler, *Treasure-House,* 1891 (filled with recipes from unidentified older sources).

Scotch broiler — See brander
Skewer holder & skewers, forged iron, ring top to boldly-shaped
    rack, American, 8" H, 18th C.   **$700-$1000**

Skewer value — Provenance and attractiveness are important to skewer rack values. A plain unexceptional example, relatively late, would bring $75-$100 at best. An early Pennsylvania German rack, with skewers, in some unusual or desirable design like a heart would bring lots more. One or two cautionary notes: you can't know if skewers are original to a particular rack, so you should neither pay for "matching," nor should you expect it. Blacksmith's marks may identify maker or owner. **Reproduction alert** — Also, there's a high probability of finding recently made holders and skewers, made not with the intent to deceive, necessarily, but as part of Colonial Revivalism. Twentieth-century blacksmithing craftsmen's books usually include a skewer design or two. There's no way to tell the difference if someone clever means to trick you. Some collectors feel that there's a general falling off in the buying of the simple forged iron early pieces because of this fact that they can be easily reproduced. Then aged with only a little more care and skill. Such collectors go on to say that perhaps this explains the fast-track approach of later nineteenth-century patented gadgets, etc., which cost a lot to reproduce and are therefore not. (So far.) The cost of molds and the whole casting process probably means that until antique cast iron things start selling for $1000 or more, we won't have many reproductions of things with moving parts, although cast iron toys have been profitably reproduced for years.

Skewer rack & skewers, holder is tulip pattern with wide arms, all
    4 skewers have end bent for hooking to holder's arms, 2 are
    twisted for strength, one has very very sharpened point,
    American (?), holder 4" H x 4" W, early 19th C.   **$400-$600+**
Skewer rack & skewers, the rack also called a skewer fraime,
    wrought iron, familiar elongated diamond with bull's eye
    above, upcurving horns or arms, 5 assorted skewers, no mark,
    American or European, holder or rack is 6" H, skewers range
    from about 5-3/4" to 11" L, late 18th C. for rack, skewers may
    be 18th & 19th C. Look for special forms & beautiful detailing
    in rack. Be somewhat suspicious of figural or zoomorphic or
    animalistic rack forms, such as open-beaked birds or eagles.
    Probably too good to be true.   **$350-$500+**
Skillet, cast iron, 3 peg feet, cast into handle is "13 IN," also
    "Cleveland TN," 13" diameter, 2nd quarter 19th C. **$175-$200**
Skillet, cast iron, 3 stubby feet, long handle, shallow rounded bowl,
    American (?), 19th C.   **$100-$150**
Skillet, cast iron, with 3 legs, American, only 6" D, 18th C. or early
    19th. These skillets look like what we would think of as <u>a</u>

saucepan with legs. A **hearth skillet** has been described as a utensil shaped like a shallow kettle, that is, pretty much cylindrical with the mouth being about as large in diameter as the bottom. (A silver skillet, on the other hand, used for warming liqueurs in the 18th C., has a mouth slightly smaller than the largest diameter of the body.)   **$125-$150**
Skillet, forged iron, 3 legs, American (?), 6" H x 6-1/2" D x 5" L handle, late 18th, early 19th C. From the small size of so many of the very early skillets, the following reference is puzzling: "Some three families cook and bake in one skillet, called the **cook-all**." W. Faux, *Memorial Days,* London: 1823.   **$125-$150**
Skillet, forged iron, perfectly round-bottomed, 3" L legs, long handle, American (?), 5-1/2" H x 7-1/2" diameter, with 3" L legs, 11" L handle, mid to late 18th C. A skillet for hearth cooking very rarely had a flat bottom, unlike a spider.   **$225-$300**
Skillet, forged iron with long handle, dished bowl, 3 stubby feet, American (?), 4" diameter, 18th C. In a fascinating book entitled *History Cast in Metal. The Founders of North America,* by Clyde A. Sanders & Dudley C. Gould (n.p.: Cast Metals Institute, American Foundrymen's Society, 1976), the authors show a cast iron pot, bellied body, triangular lug handles, three longish feet, which they describe as an English-made posnet. They go on to say that a four-legged pot was a skillet, or, in Northern England, a **stufnet**. I have yet to see the absolutely dependable definitive explanation of a skillet or posnet.   **$125-$150**
Skillet, wrought iron, long handle, 3 long legs, "G. W. Ibach," PA. 17-1/2" L including handle, 5" H, 18th or very early 19th C.   **$200-$235**
Skillet, ring handle, iron, "W. Foster, #8," early 19th C. **$150-$200**

X-88. Spit set-up in hearth. Basket spit, spit-dogs & clock jack. *A clockwork jack, with heavy weight to drive it (like a tallcase clock.) It moved the chain, which moved the pulley wheel ,which turned the spit,— on which was the roast that Jack turned. Spit height adjustable by hooking it on at different levels of the andirons. Cup-like tops were for caudle cups, to heat a milk & mead or other hot drink. From ad of now defunct B. Altman & Co., 6/1957. Longtime buyer for Altman's antiques was a wonderful Scotsman, Archie Keillor, who traveled all over the world looking for things. It was his family collection that was featured in my first book on old kitchen things, now out of print. I'm sure he found these items.* **$4500+**

Skillet, forged iron with pouring spout and fixed arched handle with trammel ring, American, 12-1/2" H including handle x 12" diameter, 19th C. **$200-$275**

Skillets, cast iron, set of 6 in different sizes, long handles and 3-legged, to use on hearth. American, late 18th C. This rare & wonderful set was sold by Lillian Blankley Cogan, one of the earliest dealers in kitchen "primitives," in 1988 for only: **$1800**

Sleeper — See curfew

Spider, cast bell metal, long handle at 40 degrees off the horizon, 3 long splayed peg legs, handle marked "20 Warner," American or English, about 7" H x 7-1/4" diameter with 9-1/2" L handle, late 18th or early 19th C. **$175-$250**

Spider, so named for the long legs, wrought iron, 3 legs, flat bottom, repaired, American, prob. PA, 6" H x 6-1/2" diameter with 10-1/2" L handle, 18th or early 19th C. **$120-$145**

Spider, cast iron, 3 short peg legs, flat bottom, American, 9" diameter with 5-1/2" L handle, mid 19th C. **$125-$150**

Spider, cast iron with 3 legs, long handle, straight sides and flat bottom, American, 5" H x 10-3/4" diameter pan, 9" L handle, 18th C. **$75-$125**

"**Poached eggs** — Have ready a kettle of boiling water, pour it in a pan or speeder, which is set on coals; have the eggs at hand; put a little salt in water, and break them in, one at a time. Let remain till white is set and take them out with an egg spoon." Elizabeth E. Lea, *Useful Receipts and Hints to Young Housekeepers,* 10th ed., Baltimore, 1859 (1st ed. 1851).

● ● ● ●

Creepy spider — A "**creeper**" is described in W. Scott Boyce's *Economic and Social History of Chowan County:* "The principal cooking utensils, even of most of the best families, were a pot, a creeper (a spider) or two, a long-handle frying pan, a tea-kettle, a griddle, and two or three wornout hoes" [p.222]. It sounds the same as a Dutch oven, but is a spider according to Boyce. He writes that "most baking . . . was done in the creeper. . . . To bake in the creeper, it was set on the fire and coals heaped on the lid. It was in this receptacle that was cooked that famous dyspepsia-producing Southern dish known as 'hot biscuit.' The much-prized apple and peach 'jacks' (kinds of pies — the New England 'turnovers') were cooked either in this or in the frying-pan" [p.223]. while "some few had big ovens for baking sweet potatoes, and some were baked in creepers, but probably the bigger half was roasted on the hearth before the fire. . .or in the hot ashes." *loc sit*. He further describes "The creeper at this time [1880s] ..as a heavy cast-iron pan some 3" or 4" deep, covered with a lid, [that] stood on three legs about three inches high. The handle was from 12" to 15" long." W. Scott Boyce, *Economic and Social History of Chowan County, North Carolina, 1880-1915,* submitted as a doctoral thesis at Columbia University, and published in New York City in 1917. It is a marvelous book, with many valuable nuggets of information.

Spider, wrought iron, flat bottom, long handle, "Whitfield" marked on handle, American (?) or English (?), 8" H x 14" diameter with 17" L handle, early 19th or late 18th C. **$175-$250**

Spider, wrought iron with 3 legs, flat bottom, American, 7-3/4" D, late 18th or early 19th C. **$125-$150**

Spit rack, wrought iron with penny feet (round & flat, usually somewhat bigger than a modern American penny — more like an English penny in size — they were formed by hammering flat the terminals of the legs). Adjustable vertical spit with hooks, American or English, 28" H, 18th C. **$750-$1000**

Spit, basket, also called a **cradle spit**, forged iron, a cage-like "basket" of iron centered on long spit rod, for holding any roast meat that might come apart if just skewered to a plain spit. This one complete with hinges & pulley, English (?), late 18th C. (**NOTE:** Another kind of spit with provision for holding the roast was called a **spit with holdfast**, a fixed two-pronged fork against which the spitted meat was rammed.) **$700-$1000**

X-89. Spits. *Wrought iron.* **Basket or cradle spit** & "**spit with Holdfast**." *The basket or cradle type was used to hold small game birds or animals or joints of other meat which it was better to keep unskewered so that it would remain moist inside instead of dripping out all its juice. The one with the holdfast was supplemented with skewers, which went through the meat and through holes (which you can't see here) in the thicker part of the shaft. From William S. Adams & Son catalog, London, c.1860-61.* **$150+**

X-90. Dangle spit. *Probably for birds. It was hung from a cord (which had to be replaced every so often from charring) and then twisted. The longish curved wings or governors helped to keep it twisting and turning, first one way then the other. Steel, 16" L, fully extended (shown here about half extended), American, early 19th C. Ex-Keillor Family Collection.* **$375-$575**

X-91. Spit driven by dog power. "Dog-Wheel. — *Both the turnspit-dog and apparatus for cooking are now nearly out of use. The example here was sketched in Glouscestershire about five years since." Hone's* Every-Day Book, *1850. What a horrible thing to do to a dog. And probably breathing smoke the whole time.*

X-92. Turnspit dog in his cage. *Depicted in* The Comic Offering; or Ladies' Melange of Literary Mirth for 1835. *London: 1835. Oh, yeah — Hah hah hah.*

X-93. "The Turnspit." *Illustration from the magazine* Frank Leslie's Boy's & Girl's Weekly, *8/7/1869. "Not long since, a wheel in a circular box was brought from an old house to a railroad station in England, with a lot of old trumpery. The other articles attracted little attention, but this puzzled all the group. There were old men and women, too, but none remembered seeing such a thing in use. At last, a blacksmith of a neighboring village said it was a turnspit's wheel, such as he remembered to have seen in use. It seems a hard lot for the dog to be kept at his work for, perhaps, three hours, till the joint was done, and we do not wonder the custom at last fell into disuse." Special short-legged, barrel-chested dogs were bred for this. The illustration here is a somewhat simplified engraving of a Thomas Rowlandson print, which shows more details.*

X-94. "Kitchen Fire-Place at Windsor Castle." *"The open fireplace measures 6 x 8 feet in size, the products of combustion passing up the chimney in such a way as to operate a kind of fan wheel [smoke jack], which is connected by means of belting and gears and revolve with the long spits placed before the fire. On these spits are various kinds of joints and poultry, while beneath is a large pan for the purpose of collecting the drippings from the various kinds of food in process of cooking." The drawing is an engraving, made from a pencil sketch, that a "gentleman connected with the [stovemaking] firm" of Rathbone, Sard & Co., Albany, NY, made on a trip to England in 1889.* The Metal Worker, *4/5/1890.*

Striker, for striking against a flintstone to make a spark to start a fire, would be kept in an early home in a tinder box (probably tin or wood), with a stone, a piece of charred linen. This striker is slightly different from most I've seen — flat narrow bar of forged iron, bent in a very tight hairpin curve with both tips curled in at the open end, American or European, 3-3/4" L, 18th or very early 19th C. Other strikers I've seen include something almost as wide open as a small horseshoe with no attempt to finish off the tips at the open end; rather loosely curved striker with one "arm" decidedly shorter than other, both tips curled; and various strikers with file and chisel decoration. The value range below would not include the decorated ones, which would add another $25-$50 to the high value.   **$40-$95**

"New England Fire Cakes — Make a pie crust not quite so rich as for puff paste. Cut off small pieces and roll out thin about the size of a breakfast plate, as nearly round as possible. Have a griddle over the fire, and bake a nice brown, turning it when done on one side and browning nicely on the other. When done, put on a plate and butter it well. Have ready another cake, and bake, piling one upon the other, and buttering each piece, until all you have made are cooked. Serve them quite hot, cutting down through all the layers. This is very nice if, as you butter each piece, preserved strawberries or raspberries are spread upon each layer. It is an old-fashioned New England cake, and in olden times was cooked in iron spiders, propped up before the kitchen fire; hence its name. It is a very nice short cake, to be eaten hot, for supper or breakfast." Mrs. F. D. J., in *Home Cook Book,* 1876.

Striker, forged iron, flat, form appears to be a "rocking fox," the rocker blade with both ends curled rather tightly, like old ice skate blades, incised lines to indicate the separation of 2 front legs and 2 back legs, also the eyes and mouth, brush tail out straight behind, American (?), poss. CT, VA ?, prob. not PA, 2-3/4" H x 4-7/8" L, early 19th C (?). This is the first figural striker I've ever seen, so don't know how to judge it. The dealer is from CT, the show in VA, a lot of very interesting iron in his booth. It is possible that this is European; some people say most of his wares are Portuguese; iron is getting all mixed up nowadays.   **$275-$400+**

Tea kitchen, a sort of kettle, also called a <u>covered cauldron</u>, copper, tinned inside, slightly round-breasted body, sturdy bail handle with pivot ring, small central opening with lid, copper and brass spigot sticks out straight from side, right at bottom, spigot as long as kettle is in diameter, to be hung on trammel or pot hook in fireplace for ready supply of hot water, English, 10" H x 10-1/2" diameter, late 18th C. A slightly later variation of this was adapted, or created, for use on top of a range, with the spigot sticking out off to side of range, as supply of hot water. This type is generally somewhat larger, and because it stood on its

own, was made to balance more safely by being taller and having shorter spigot relative to diameter. The 1895 Harrod's Stores catalog depicts two of these, cylindrical bodies, slightly domed top, with fitted lid with strap bracket handle, long spigot spout, falling wire bail handle. Made of cast iron or "London Wrought Iron," they were called **Tea Kitchens** or **Boiler for Fire** in the Harrod's catalog. In cast iron, there were three sizes: 2, 3 & 4 gallons; in wrought iron: 2 & 3 gallons.   **$350-$500+**

Tin kitchen — See reflecting oven — tin kitchen

TOASTERS, fixed:

Toaster, fancy brass single slice toaster for hearth use, probably for tea time in the parlor, with pivoting lazy elbow handle, scalloped-edge heavy gauge brass plate with 2 curved arches of brass rod to hold bread, English almost undoubtedly, c.1830s.   **$175-$225**

Toaster, forged iron, long slightly arched handle fixed to pair of footed arches with hook support underneath for one thick slab of bread, English, 12-1/2" L x 5" W, 18th C.   **$375-$425**

TOASTERS, pivoting or swiveling:

Toaster, pivoting, also called a **flip toaster**, forged iron, 2 sets of 3 twisted arches, European (?), toaster frame 13" L with 13" L handle, early 19th C. So many of these flip-over type are appearing at fleas and shows that I believe most are probably coming in from Europe in container loads.   **$275+**

Toaster, pivoting or swiveling, the kind you have to pick up the handle & move it to swivel the toast frame, very decorative wrought iron arches and handle, American (?), more likely French Canadian or European, late 18th C.   **$400+**

X-96. Revolving toaster, *also called a* **toe toaster**, *because instead of leaning over to turn it, you could turn it with your foot. Wrought iron, wooden grip on handle, possibly mid 19th C. Wooden handle grip is the puzzler — it just doesn't look old. Picture courtesy of the National Museum of American History, Smithsonian Institution.* **$300+**

X-97. Revolving toaster. *Wrought iron, strong spirals, extremely well-made. 3-3/4" H x 11" L overall x 7" W. American, early 19th C. Ex-Keillor Collection.* **$650+**

X-95. Pivoting toaster. *Wrought iron, 30" L x 13" W, possibly English, early 19th C. Ex-Keillor Family Collection. All you had to do was pick it up by the long handle, do a neat sort of flip with the handle, and set it down again.* **$300+**

Toaster, pivoting or swiveling, wrought iron, 4 rectangular arches, American (?), late 18th C. or early 19th. **$300+**

A recipe for a **"Method of Making Toast Water"** appeared in the Aug. 1851 issue of *American Agriculturist*. "Take a slice of fine and stale loaf bread, cut thin, (thin as toast is ever cut,) and let it be carefully toasted on both sides, until it be completely browned all oaver, but nowise blackened nor burned in any way. Put this into a common, deep stone or China pitcher, and pour over it, from the teakettle, as much clean boiling water as you wish to make into drink. Much depends on the water being actually in a boiling state. Cover the pitcher with a saucer or plate, and let the drink cool until it is quite cold; it is then fit to be used. The fresher it is made, the better, and of course, the more agreeable. The above will be found a pleasant, light and highly diuretic drink. It is peculiarly grateful to the stomach, and excellent for carrying off the effects of excessive bile."

Toaster, pivoting, wrought iron and wire, 4 pairs of arches, arched penny feet on toast frame, American or European, 40" L overall, early 19th C. **$400+**

Toaster, swiveling type with long handle, forged iron, heart design supports, from Maine coast, frame is 12-5/8" W x 5-1/4" deep, with 18-5/8" L handle, late 18th C. **$550+**

Toaster, pivoting, wrought iron with 4 twisted arches on footed frame, can be flipped at swivel-hinged junction of long handle and toaster, American (?), late 18th, early 19th C. The fancier the iron work on these, the more likely they are to be English or European. Most have iron handles; occasionally you find one with a wooden handle. **$500+**

TOASTER, revolving:

Toaster, revolving, or **toe toaster**, so-called because instead of having to lean over to turn the toast, you could just give it a tap with your foot and the rack would turn to face the other way. Forged iron, with unusual sprouted corn-stalk-shaped supports for the bread, within the double arches more commonly found, American, late 18th or early 19th C. You're never too old to learn: I learned the toe toaster term by accident, watching an episode of "Reading Rainbow" in August 1987, which featured a visit to Sturbridge Village in Massachusetts. **$250-$350**

Toaster, revolving, wrought iron with 2 sets of double arches, nice handle with hanging eye, American, 19" L, early 19th C. **$250-$350**

Toaster, forged iron, revolving, double arch holder on frame with long handle, 2 sets of double tree-like sprays of iron within arches that hold bread fit into holes, one on each side adjusts for various size of slices, American, c.1770s. **$450+**

X-98. Revolving toaster. *Wrought iron, with a two sets of four arches, big and small. 19" L, early 19th C. Ex-Keillor Collection.* **$425+**

Toaster, rotating type, frame has 4 sets of double rams' horns to hold 2 slices of bread, 4 little deep kneebend legs, and very unusual tiller handle rising up for convenient handling, wooden grip, signed "N. B." New England (?), 8-1/2" x 12", late 18th C. **$400+**

Toaster, wrought iron, for one slice, rotating head with 4 "horns" or antennae curving up from swivel point. Two legs under head or frame, one leg partway back on handle, reminds you of an abstract beetle or other animal, American (?), 12-1/2" L x 5" W frame, 18th C. Again, this was found by Clara Jean Davis; the description is based on hers, price range is mine. **$450+**

Toasting forks — See Chapter XIII

Tongs, forged iron, one arm is twisted, small head, American, prob. PA, 17-5/8" L, mid to late 18th C. **$140-$160**

Trammel, chain, forged iron, 50" L, early 19th C. **$120-$180**

Trammel, chain, strong twisted wrought iron hook, 70" L, early 19th C. **$150-$225**

Trammel, for fireplace, wrought & polished steel, nice filework, swiveling hook, English (?), 13" to 21", closed & open lengths, late 18th, early 19th C. **$335-$450**

X-99. Revolving toaster. *Wrought iron, with unusual "corn sprout" supports for bread, in addition to double arches. Late 18th or early 19th C. Picture courtesy of the National Museum of American History, Smithsonian Institution. (A very similar one, with 3 simple legs, was offered by Oveda Maurer Antiques, San Anselmo, CA, for $595 in 1987.)* **$750+**

X-100. Revolving toaster. *Wrought iron, another one with the "corn sprouts." Ram's horn handle. 17-1/2" L x 13-1/2" W, American, late 18th C. Picture courtesy of Robert W. Skinner Inc., Auctioneers, Bolton, MA.* **$550+**

X-101. Fender toaster or trivet. *Described in* Warne's Model Cookery, *London, 1868, as an "improved revolving toaster, also available as a hanging Trivet, for Kettle, Saucepan, or Plate." Hmmm.* **$150+**

"Polishing Metals — The polishing of metals differs according to the kind of metal and the kind of manufacture; [but] there are some general principles to be attended to as being common to all, of which it [is] useful to have a clear idea. All polishing is begun, in the first instance, by rubbing down the surface by some hard substance that will produce a number of scratches in all directions, the level of which is nearly the same, and which will obliterate the marks of the file, scraper, or turning tool. . .first employed. For this purpose coarse emery is used, or pumice and water, or sand and water, applied upon a piece of soft wood, or of felt, skin, or some similar material. When these first coarse marks have been thus removed, they next proceed to remove the marks left by the pumice-stone of finely powdered pumice-stown ground up with olive oil, or by finer emery and oil. In some cases, certain polishing stones are employed, as a kind of hard slate, used with water. To proceed with the polishing, still finer powders are used, as Tripoli & rotten-stone, which is still finer, and is found only in Derbyshire. Putty of tin & crocus martis are also used for high degrees of polish. But the fact is, in respect to polishing, that the whole process consists . . . in removing coarse scratches by substituting those which are finer & finer, until they are no longer visible to the naked eye; and . . . if the surface be examined by a microsope, it will be seen that what appeared without any scratches is covered . . . with an infinity of them, but so minute that they require a high magnifier to be discovered. The operator. . . who understands this principle, will. . .vary his polishing substances according to the nature of the article he wishes to polish. . . . His polishing material must be able to scratch, in a coarser or finer manner, the substance he is desirous of polishing, for wearing down is only effected by producing minute cuttings or scratches. It is evident . . . that great care must be taken to have the last polishing material uniformly fine, for a single grain . . . of any coarse substance mixed with it will produce some visible scratches instead of a perfectly polished surface. . . . Polishing materials: coarsest are emery, sand, glass-paper, whiting, or chalk, putty of tin, & black-lead" usually mixed with oil. Webster & Parkes, *An Encyclopædia of Domestic Economy,* 1848 NY edition of English book of 1845.

Trammel, forged iron, 2 piece flat bar iron, one with holes, one with rod to fit into any hole of other part, with hook at bottom, American, adjusts from 35" L to 60" L, so for very large fireplace, late 18th C. Unless these have some kind of spiffy form or decoration or hook or look, they are really rather dull. I like the sawtooth trammels much better, or the hand wrought chain ones. **$250-$350**

Trammel, forged iron, chain with long hook, knobbed lugpole hook, American or English, early 19th C. See also pot chain. **$325+**

Trammel, forged iron, sawtooth style, for big fireplace, American (?), 32" L to 41" L extended, late 18th or early 19th C. **$325-$450**

Trammel, forged iron, sawtooth type, simple keeper attached to hook through rattail loop, 11 usual-sized teeth, somewhat (and appealingly) different in angle and size, American, 21-1/4" L extends to approximately 32" L, early 19th or late 18th C. $250, a rather good price, at the Garth Auction, May 5-6, 1989, Delaware, OH. **$275-$400**

Trammel, possibly for a lamp, steel, English, 20-7/8" L sans hook, dated with individual punches or stamps, "ANNO 1774." **$300-$350**

X-103. Trammels. *Both wrought iron, 18th C., probably not American.* **(L)** *Pawl & ratchet type, with crank action. 36" L as shown.* **(R)** *Elaborate sawtooth style, probably earlier than other one. 56" L as shown. Ex-Keillor Collection.* **$300-$400; $900-$1500**

X-102. Trammel. *Wrought iron, finely done. Saw-tooth style with crane ring, extension 45" to 61" L. Probably American, early 19th C. Ex-Keillor Family Collection. The faint numbers you may see at top of "blade" are Keillor's acquisition numbers, not a mark.* **$425+**

Many trammels go for under $100 because they don't excite much visual interest unless they are very fine examples. But look again: workmanship, when you lean over and study them or clean them, begins to add up to higher value. Of course, you have to love iron. Several trammels would have been found hanging from the lug pole or crane in early kitchens. Some are surprisingly long. Added value — Some are very decorative, with scrolling curves and fanciful sawteeth or hook-and-eye elements; chains can be gussied up too. The finest go for upwards of $550. Containerloaded — Many, maybe most, antique trammels for sale in the U.S. today probably just arrived on these shores from England or Europe. Is there a difference if a French trammel got here in 1780 or 1980? You have to decide.

Trammel, sawtooth ratchet, cut out of heavy sheet brass, with a cutout flat finial decoration of a cock, English (?), extends 20" to 35" L, looks 2nd to 3rd quarter 19th C. It's possibly a containerload piece, or maybe it was a decorative piece made in the 20th C. There's something about it that just looks wrong. **$200-$300**

Trammel — See also bird trammel

Trammel, very large wrought iron sawtooth type, large hanging ring at top, 24 relatively small sawteeth (the 12th down broken off), decorative keeper and hook, heart cutout in crested top of the wide "blade," very unusual low relief decoration top to bottom of vines & tulips, poss. PA German, 47" L unextended, early 19th C (?). **$1500-$2200**

Trammel, wrought iron, hook & eye type, adjustable from 31" to 47" L, early 19th or late 18th C. **$350-$450**

Trivet, for hearth, with adjustable fork or handle support that works on the pawl & ratchet idea, forged & twisted iron "running man" piece with adjustable height to hold fork or spoon, 2 long legs on either side of circle of trivet, one leg near end of handle, very handsome form that looks like what sculptor Alberto Giacometti would have done, if he'd made 18th-C. cooking utensils. Found in house on the Connecticut-Massachusetts line, 24-5/16" L, trivet is 7-5/8" diameter, maybe mid 18th C. **$550-$700**

Trivet, for hearth, wrought iron with sliding support for saucepan handle, 3 penny feet, 22-1/2" L, 18th C. **$300-$400**

Trivet, wrought iron, round with 3 legs & a long handle, for use on the hearth, American (?), 6" H x 8" diameter with 11" L handle, 18th or early 19th C. **$225-$300**

Trivets not for hearth use — See trivets, Chapter VI

Wafer & waffle irons for hearth use — See Chapter IV

COOKING

XI. STOVES & RANGES

Stoves are still not widely collected, but people who do collect them are fervent. One long-time organization is the **Antique Stove Information Clearinghouse** (417 N. Main St., Monticello, IN 47960). Then there are dealers across the country who specialize in refitting, renovating and selling old stoves and ranges — such as **Macy's Texas Stove Works** (2617 Riverside Dr., Houston, TX 77004). Macy Stern also hosts the **Antique Stove Association**, for serious stove people as well as those approaching the subject obliquely. For a members' directory, she asks new members to circle categories, including: "Collector, Restorer-Dealer, Library, Owner-User, Pattern-maker, Re-porcelaining shop, Toy stove collector," etc. Two members I know of are Clifford Boram, who wrote the article following this chapter, and David G. Smith, who wrote on muffin pans a few chapters back.

Futurewatch: A related category is hot water **radiators** with built-in warming ovens, from the late nineteenth to early twentieth centuries, meant for cold, high-ceilinged dining rooms where eating dinner took an hour or more. These are going to be the hardest things to find; they haven't been given the sort of safety net that a lot of other old things have (either because they weren't important enough to notice and throw away, or they were too useful or too noticeable to discard). Probably several million radiators, many of them attractive works of cast iron art, have been junked or melted down in the last 70 or 80 years, gone forever.

The Yellow Pages in your town may help you locate a nearby source. There are many hundreds of people seriously into old stoves — especially for cooking, as well as heating. Thank heaven the collectors came along at the right time, and fortunately an adequate supply of stoves survived wartime metal drives and modernizations of dwellings.

Antique cook stoves and ranges probably have a slight edge on popularity, but there are some fantastically beautiful parlor heating stoves that deserve more attention, especially ones that look like large sculptures of urban Victorian buildings.

Some people collect **stove parts**. I knew somebody in New York City who used to climb into dumpsters (where they throw all kinds of eminently collectible stuff when renovating old buildings) to dig out cast iron gas-stove jet rings, which come in cast forms as varied as flowers in a garden, or coronets at a turn-of-the-century gathering of the crowned heads of Europe. When I lived in NYC, I often rescued porcelainized cast iron knobs, drop pulls and handles, even decorated oven fronts, while walking my dog.

Some people collect **stove tools and accessories** — from ash shovels and lid lifters to scuttles and stovepipe "flue stops" or flue covers. I've seen enough flue stops (those things that look like brass luncheon plates) to know that there is a satisfactory diversity and range to give a collector a run for the money. A lot of **stove lid lifters** are competently designed, even handsome, and some are figural. I've only got one — a cast iron female figural one described in this chapter, which I was fortunate enough to see listed in an *Antique Trader Weekly* classified. Another desirable one is a bent Victorian lady's leg with booted foot.

An adjunctive category is **camp stoves**: appealing, perhaps, because of the increasing interest in hearth cooking and portable "stoves" from braziers to chafing dishes. You might find a wrought iron one at a militaria show, from a dealer in Revolutionary War or Civil War equipment. Smart collectors, no matter what their specialties are, will not depend solely on specialist dealers within their fields but will imaginatively try to find connections to other specialties where treasures may lie hidden. For you, it might be a dumpster, a scrap yard, a gun show that will yield up something grand — maybe even a splendid "kitchen piano," a nickname for magnificent ornate cooking ranges — their ebony gleam coming from locomotive black finish, the twinkle coming from the nickeled trim.

Ash shovel, wrought iron, curved bifurcated <u>ram's horn</u> handle, 18" L, early 19th C. **$55-$85**

Ash sifter shovel, wood & wire, instead of steel blade with the typical shovel rounded shoulder, it's made of welded heavy wires, going lengthwise and joined at shoveling edge, and at top, steel "ferrule" fasted to long wooden handle, for shoveling through ashes to clear out clinkers or unburned debris from furnaces, or perhaps even large stoves. Androck, 50" L overall, "blade" is 14" L x 8-1/2" W, 1930s. These were made by different wiregoods companies, some with patterns of braced crisscrosses — very graphic, but all for same purpose. Even the blades alone are collectible; the handles are often missing or broken. A shorter version, almost identical, was called a <u>potato scoop</u>. Its handle was 30" L and the shoulder of the blade was solid steel, so the wires were shorter. **$12-$35**

Blacking box holders — See stove blacking box holders

Camp stove, small portable type called <u>Revolutionary War soldier's stove</u>, penny feet, sheet iron & forged iron, wood handle, for all the world like a modern day Sterno™, American, 6-1/2" H x 5" D, 18th C. or early 19th C. **$650-$850+**

Camp stove, wrought iron with turned wooden handle and hanging ring, 4 small penny feet, rectangular body or firebox, with rack or grid above, plus 4 corner supports for pot, works like a brazier — as a portable fire. American, 5-1/4" H x 6" W x 12" L, 19th C. **$600-$800**

Camp stove, boxy iron body, supposed to burn a special fuel, 4 squatty, fat-knee cabriole legs, adjustable air vent on side, single hole on top fitted with lid notched for lid lifter, wire bail handle, turned wooden grip, "Carbonite," The American Safety Fuel Co., NYC, 10" H x 10-1/2" square, with 6" hole & lid (also came in 7" or 8"), early 1890s. **$60-$75**

Camp stove — or charcoal stove, one burner, cast iron fire/coal vessel with flared sides and wide lip, bail handle, 6-point openwork grill, on wonderful little cast iron 4-legged hearth, Griswold's "Eldorado," late 19th, early 20th C. **$450-$650**

Coal carrier, brass with wood & wire carrying handle on side, like little suitcase, sheet iron bottom, called a <u>stoker</u>, small knob slides in slot to regulate vent opening in top, several marks stamped on lid, "Girodon & Cie. Fabnts. Déposé a Villeurbanne Lyon; Breveté en France" & "A l'Etranger Stoker S.G.D.B.," Lyon, France, 1-7/8" deep x 7-1/4" L x 5-1/2" W, c.1870s (?). *Breveté en France* means <u>Patented in France</u>; *S. G. D. B.* stands for *Sans Garantie Du Gouvernement,* or, registered with, but not warranted by, the government. **$65-$95**

Coal hod, wood with tin interior, cast brass handles, English, mid to late 19th C. **$65-$75**

Coal hod or scuttle, japanned & tôle-decorated heavy sheet tin with original tin liner, for the parlor, flowers & scrolls on black background, cast brass handles on side, nice feet, slanted hinged lid, this was the type of coal vase called a <u>purdonium</u>, back stenciled "Mfd. by Sidney Shepards Co.," Buffalo, NY, 23" H, 3rd quarter 19th C. **$275-$325**

Reproduction alert — Exactly this bin type of drop-front coal container was made by the thousands in the late 1920s and early 1930s during that phase of Colonial Revivalism. They were sold as magazine holders, kindling boxes and especially for fireside decoration.

Continuing tradition — John Fuller, Sr., author of occasional articles in a series called "Art of Coppersmithing," in *The Metal Worker,* wrote about "coal scoops and coal hods" as well as "coal scoopettes" (yikes), in article XVIII, Nov. 15, 1890. Some interesting terminology is used, which may either explain or confuse our notions of what's what. A number of horizontal coal containers with long "lower lips," like pelicans or pouters, all have flared feet and Fuller calls them all "<u>coal scoops.</u>" Only two designs are called "<u>coal hods</u>" — one is a vertical cylinder with tipping handle, arched falling handle and a roller coaster top edge to form a scoop mouth when held horizontally; the other looks almost identical to another that is called a scoop. Finally, the little scoop shovel used to remove coal from the receptacle is called a "<u>scoopette.</u>" All the designs, which Fuller encourages metal workers to make, have names. (As usual in his articles, Fuller mixes past & present tenses.) He writes: "Coal scoops were made in a number

XI-1. Leg base range, with parts identified, *on one turn of century Sears' catalog page. Was accompanied by lots of text extolling virtues.*

of fashions, among which, besides the common hod, were the round mouthed scoop; the square mouthed or flat bottom; the Tudor; the Florence; the Nautilus; the Royal; the Boat; and the Helmet. Some of these names are variable, according to the factories in which they are made, while others have had the same name from the time they were first designed. The hod has always been a hod, and the common round mouth shape [he calls it a hod] has never received any other cognomen."

Fuller goes on to say, that "we will now endeavor to describe the manufacture of several scoops in which we participated some forty years since [ie. c.1850], and while there have been deviations made during this long time . . . it would seem that nothing of any marked importance has been introduced to inconvenience one from resuming work as of yore." Most of the designs he describes measure 12" diameter at front, 13-1/2" at back, and are 18" long. He says "the ears may be cast or wrought" and the tubular handles are bent of 3/4" pipe, "filled and bent, then filed and burnished." (pp. 28-29).

Lookalike alarm — Many old copper and brass things are now imported from Holland, so if the next scuttle were distressed and the lacquer finish gone, it might be good enough to fool you into thinking it was old. Take every opportunity to look at old pieces of copper and brass, that have been in collections for several decades; this will help you pick up on the little details that are wrong. The gauge of the wire of the back handle, the way the pieces and parts are assembled, all are important. This advice goes for all kinds of antiques. The advertised prices of these three sizes, in 1973, were: $18.75, $29.75, and $39.75, all marked down about $16 from earlier prices.

Coal scuttle, hammered & pieced rounded copper body with brass base, large "gravy boat" type pouring lip, lion's head fittings for swinging handle, blue and white Delft porcelain hand grips on back handle & large swinging handle, supposed to be a "traditional Dutch Coal Scuttle," made in Holland, three sizes: 9-1/2" H, 12-1/4" H, 15-3/4" H, all measured to lip, sold through

XI-2. Camp stove, *to be used like a brazier. These could be used by anyone needing a small portable stove. Wrought iron with turned wooden handle. For use with charcoal. Four resting pads on the corners of the top accommodated whatever needed heating, and raised it slightly above level of detachable grill. 5-1/4" H x 12" L overall x 6" W. This type is late 18th or early 19th C.; later ones were cast iron. Picture courtesy of Robert W. Skinner Auctioneers, Bolton, MA.* **$500-$800**

XI-4. "Improved coal-scuttle." *For a base-burner stove or top-fed stove. Amount of effort required to raise to a pouring level (note tilting handle on right side near bottom) was much less than a conventional scuttle because it did not need to be "lifted through a large part of a circle."* American Agriculturist, *2/1881.* **$20-$40**

XI-3. Brazier or camp stove. *Cast iron footed body with wire bail. Lift-out grid has heart with radiating lines (symbolizing warmth of heart). 7-1/2" H x 10-5/8" diameter. Sold at Ada F. & Earl F. Robacker auction, Horst Auctions, 7/21-22/1989, for only $275. SEE also the spoked heart trivet in Chapter VI.* **$300-$500**

XI-5. "Coal scoops." *I have no idea why these are scoops and similar ones are hods. The primary difference seems to be the rounded, hooded tops. These illustrations accompanied a series of practical articles, "Art of Coppersmithing," serialized in* The Metal Worker, *from John Fuller's 1889 book on the same subject. These copper coal containers, "considered an adornment for the parlor," were made in these traditional shapes some 40 years before Fuller related his long experience in crafting all manner of copper household articles. The names, clockwise from top (**T-L**) are "The Florence," "The Nautilus," "The Boat," and "The Royal."* The Metal Worker, *11/15/1890. Value would depend on condition and material (copper would be highly prized.)* **$35-$65+**

the mail in 1973 ads in *House Beautiful,* etc. Value now is for the look, not as antique. **$55-$125**

Coal scuttle or vase, japanned & stenciled tin, highly decorative, cast iron feet & handle on pull-down bin front, counterweighted so as to be self-closing, holds small supply of coal for parlor heating stove, from F. A. Walker catalog, English (?), c.1870s. Chance of finding one with japanning & stenciling intact, and without major dings & dents, equals that of finding a Model-T in factory condition. **$115-$135**

XI-6. Coal vases. *Japanned and "handsomely ornamented." (L) Three cast iron fancy feet, fire iron attachment in back, and a half-cylindrical "vase" decorated in Japanese motifs, after the high (and low) fashion of the day. The "japanned" finish, by the way, does refer to the country Japan, but only because of its attempted resemblance to the fine lacquer finish used by generations of Japanese artisans. Japoniste motifs, also imitative, decorated all kinds of minor and major decorative arts in America, beginning with the 1850's opening of Japan to U.S. trade, and then in full bloom after the 1876 world fair. Mfd. by Heinz & Munschauer, noted for their birdcages, depicted in 1882 catalog. (R) Patent self-closing vase, cast feet, from F. A. Walker import catalog, 1870s. Valuable only if finish is in very good condition.* **$125-$350**

XI-7. "Patent Hand Revolving Pan," *or confectioners' nut roaster. "It will pay the Retailer to manufacture Cream, Jordon and Burnt Almonds, which can be made fresh everyday. The goods made in this pan are more like the Hand-made goods. The sugar coating does not become so hard and brittle. This pan will also do three times the work of the old-fashioned swinging pan. ... Put one in your store window and set a boy to work making goods." Broadside signed by Thomas Burkhard, date unknown, but looks to be 1860s-80s. I looked under everything I could think of in the patent index to find exact date, but couldn't find anything.* **$400-$600+**

Coal scuttle or vase, pieced sheet metal, painted black, flower-like pressed white glass knob on tight fitting lid, bail handle with wooden grip, little decorative cast iron feet, American, 13-3/4" H, c.1870s to 1880s. **$25-$40**

Coal scuttle or vase, tôle (decorated tin), footed helmet-shaped basket with high arched handle, domed lid with cast iron finial, cast brass lion's head side handles, could possibly be a chestnut urn, used to carry hot chestnuts to the table, but none depicted in book on Pontypool & Usk. Japanned wares shows a handle like this one, from Pontypool or Usk, or Wolverhampton, 25" H, c.1800 to 1810. **$500-$750+**

Coal shovel, cast iron, for stoves, "Boss," Indiana Stove Co., turn of century. **$18-$25**

Coal shovel, heavy cast iron, "DMI Co.," American, late 19th C (?). The only companies I could find fitting this at all were "Detroit - Michigan Stove Co.," from the 1930s, and Matthai-Ingram, much earlier. **$12-$15**

American Coal Scuttles — "Thomas Darby & Son, 160 Bowery [NYC], exhibited specimens of brass and copper coal scuttles, at the late fair, and obtained a premium. Mr. Darby claims to have first carried this manufacture into successful operation in this country, and offers them of as good quality and as cheap as the imported. They are articles required in almost every family. We hail the successful commencement of the manufacture of every new article of general use and necessity, as the commencement of a new era in the history of our productive industry, and the name of the pioneer should be enrolled on the catalogue of benefactors. Let any one just ask the question — what will be the difference to the country, whether a coal scuttle is made and sold here, or imported from England and sold. It is, simply, that in the one case the money is in the country, and in the other, it is out of the country. We hope every American will purchase Mr. Darby's coal scuttles, as long as he sells as good and as cheap scuttles as the imported." From a report in the Dec. 1838 *Journal of the American Institute* on the 11th annual Fair, Oct. 1838, sponsored by the American Institute, NYC, which fostered knowledge of invention and the improvement of manufactures.

Coal tongs, cast iron, small & decorative, turn of century. **$18-$25**

Coal tongs, cast iron with spring in hinge, possibly mfd. by Matthai-Ingram, American, 12" L, late 19th C. **$20-$28**

"COOK STOVE" or "RANGE"?

Like many people, I tend to use the word "stove" somewhat indiscriminately, when I might actually mean "range." It's easy to learn the difference between a mid-nineteenth-century range and stove, but not so easy in the twentieth century, when the two terms often seem to be a regional choice meaning the same thing.

First came fireplaces or **hearths**. Then came what are called **brick-set ranges** — actually an "arrangement" such as a row, or, say, a set of three holes by two holes in the brick top of a brick cabinet or box, with air intake along the floor level, and cast iron doors for the oven(s), for feeding the fire, and for taking out ashes and coals. Pots and griddles could be set over, or down into, the holes (called **range eyes**, or **boiling holes**), or raised above them. (See the adaptor ring in Chapter X.) These brick-set ranges may have been built into the old hearth where cooking took place at an earlier time, or might be along a wall. Then came a cast iron stove, assembled as a sort of cooking box from "plates" of cast iron. These were somewhat more movable than brick-set ranges, but otherwise they were very like.

Then came cast iron ranges and cook stoves, which could be set all the way or partly into the old fireplace to make use of the flue and chimney. This is when I think the nomenclature problem began. A wide fireplace could take a free-standing " leg base range," or a "cabinet base range," and a really wide fireplace could accommodate a cook stove. Visualize these: a range is an oblong with one of the long sides against a wall or fireplace back; and a cook stove is an oblong with a short side against wall or fireplace.

Got the flue? The three interrelated, telling differences between a range and a cook stove are (1) positioning and layout of oven(s); (2) placement of oven door(s); and (3) placement of flue.

According to stove/range expert Cliff Boram and the *stove* industry, what defines a **range** is its <u>smoke collar</u> for the flue(s), which is on the back long side of the top, and a <u>front-opening oven door</u> where the cook would stand. A range may have four, six, or eight holes, or "range eyes." (Or even more for hotels.)

A **cook stove** — according to Boram and the nineteenth-century stove industry — has *its* smoke collar (hence, flue) on the back short side of the top, with the oven running through the short axis and a door on either end of the oven, so that if the cook stood in front of the stove she would go around to either side to open the oven. And it appears that a cook stove usually has only four holes. (A box stove has one, or maybe two.) The stove industry actually used both words "stove" and "range" in advertising copy for ranges, but not vice versa.

Nowadays, depending on what part of the country you live in, you call your gas or electric cooking-station either a stove or a range. And if you cook on a wood-burner, you probably call it a "wood stove," even if technically it's a range. Just to complicate things, in England the word "cooker" was widely used for what appear to be both ranges and stoves. Also, some dealers, who primarily are in business to help people who want one old stove to use in their kitchens, aren't as fussy about terminology as collectors.

XI-A. Range vs. Stove. *Top view illustrating the differences between a range and a stove.*

PRICING OLD STOVES & RANGES. This is really beyond the scope of this book: it's almost like the antique car market. Prices for most of these stoves reflect value for stoves that have been restored and are in good working order. Added value for stoves completely re-nickeled. Generally speaking, if you want to buy a nice looking, somewhat ornate, nickeled-and-shined cast iron range or stove of any size or age, rebuilt so that it all works, you can expect to pay <u>at least</u> $1500. The fanciest of these kitchen pianos may have colored enameling, fancy re-nickeled trimmings, overhead ovens, ornate hob shelves — the works, and if they have been rebuilt or refurbished, expect to pay between at least $3000 and $6000 or more. These prices are mainly for coal or wood stoves. For early twentieth-century gas ranges, expect to pay up to $4000, depending on the features; some may be a lot more. Wood and coal stoves can also be converted to work with gas or electricity, while retaining the outward appearance of its original state. Add about $500 to $1800 for conversions. The days of finding a fabulous-looking 100-year-old relic from a bygone kitchen for under $100 (and it wasn't all that long ago) are past.

Heating stoves such as parlor stoves and base burners, from the mid- to late-nineteenth century, with some of the same trim and pizzazz of the cook stoves, generally cost less than cooking stoves.

XI-8. "Mennonite Woman Cooking at a Hearth." *A raised hearth, almost a range. Note hams and sausages hanging high up to be smoked; also the trivet or stand on which the center utensil rests, with the fire underneath. The flat-bottomed frying pan at right has three rather tall legs and a long handle. The tall, round-bottomed pot at left also has legs. "The most primitive cooking arrangement was seen in Harvey County [Kansas]. This is merely a block of adobe or masonry, 2 feet high, built in the base of an ordinary chimney. Cooking is done by building straw and corncob fires under each vessel, like persons camping out." Article on Mennonites, based on observances of Mr. H. Worrall, Shawnee County, KS, in* American Agriculturist, *12/1878.*

XI-9. "Interior of Mennonite Kitchen." *Also in Kansas. Note adobe or brick cooking range at right, and wash or laundry range at left, and the ubiquitous huge basket of corncob fuel. What look like ovens in the ranges are "fire doors" through which fuel was added. Baking ovens are seen as dark rectangles in the back wall, which is actually part of the main chimney. According to the* American Agriculturist, *12/1878, one Mennonite settler asserted: "Americans burn money; we burn straw." Still true, alas.*

Cook stove, cast iron, oblong box, rather fancy "bath tub" legs, 4 holes on top, oven & firebox doors on side, no maker's or founder's name, American, c.1840s-1850s. **$850-$1000**

So many Trojans — According to the 1860 census, Troy had three brass and bell founders, three iron works, eight stove manufacturers and 20 tinware manufacturers. That year, in the entire United States there were some 290 cast iron stove and hollowware foundries, at least among those counted in the census. Think how many hundreds of thousands of collectible objects were made that year alone!

E. Scott Boyce wrote, in *Economic & Social History of Chowan County, North Carolina, 1880-1915* (NY: 1917) that in the studied area, by 1915, "probably 90% of home owners and 50% of all other families now have sewing machines; for cook-stoves, the percentage is about 98 and 75, respectively." So some people were still cooking over fires, probably still using the "creepers" Boyce wrote about [see Chapter X].

● ● ● ●

In the *American Agriculturist* of Nov. 1847 comes the following lamentation, along with a **kudo for a new cooking-stove**. "Stoves are now so generally used all over the Middle and Northern portions of the United States for cooking, that one is to be found in almost every dwelling. Common as they are, the mass of them are defective, and in many cases very poor. We feel that we are doing a great service to our readers by recommending them to the use of proper stoves for cooking, particularly the planters of the South whose system of economy in cooking is very bad at present, incurring a vast deal of labor and expense for fuel, to say nothing of the imperfect manner in which it is often done. In fulfilment of our promise in the October [1847] number, we would now call attention to Granger's iron-witch air-tight cooking-stove . . . the main object of which has been to get as perfect and convenient an implement as possible, and at the same time to have it simple and without complication of flues, dampers, &c. The front of the stove is lined with brick, which keeps up that steady even heat, which is so desirable in baking, and in which particular cast-iron ovens are found so defective. By means of the brick in this stove, the baking is more like the old fashioned brick-oven, which it is universally acknowledged bakes in the best manner. A summer-furnace on the hearth is also attached to the stove with two boiler holes on which any and all the boilers fit. The furnace will be found very desirable for summer use, when but little fire is wanted; as a few chips or charcoal will do the cooking. The furnace can also be used at the same time with the stove, giving six boiler holes. A gridiron is also well fitted to the hearth for broiling, by raking the coals directly from the fire-chamber on to the grate. The grate in the fire-chamber is omitted, and the wood is burned directly on the bed of ashes, by which means the fire can be covered up and kept over night, which cannot be done on a grate; the expense of purchasing new grates is thus avoided."

● ● ● ●

The **conservation of fuel** that so occupied the minds of some nineteenth-century editors and inventors was not based on any ecological or environmental beliefs or ideals. It was purely a matter of economics, of supply and transport. Heavily populated areas, especially, needed to use as little fuel, wood or coal, as possible.

XI-10. Brickset range. *"Union Range," which won many medals and awards at the world's fair in London, and at others in U.S. and Canada. Moses Pond & Co., Boston, MA. Ad in American Portrait Gallery, 1856. Note ovens, large oval boiler at left on range, and huge hot water kettle. Standing at right is a hot water heater, with pipes leading to upstairs!*

XI-11. Range & stove. *Cast iron. (L) a brickset range, probably set into old high walk-in fireplace recess. Two flues — one at each back corner. Note decorative castings on doors. Cast by Sanders & Wolfe, successors to A. T. Dunham & Co., Troy, NY. Range pat'd 1853. (R) a cook stove. Note hearth and decorative casting. Also Sanders & Wolfe, 1855 or 1856 ad.*

XI-12. Box stove, *with four legs, but otherwise identical to a three-legged one that once belonged to trade-catalog-cataloguer Lawrence B. Romaine. Cast iron, 16" H x 23" L x 13" W, cast by Tyson Furnace, Plymouth, VT, dated 1839. This one was drawn from an Old Brookfield Tavern, Danbury, CT, ad in The Magazine ANTIQUES, from 11/1929. (L) The side view shows the ships that gave it its name "Mayflower" stove. (R) Bird's-eye view. The 3-legged version is depicted in Josephine Peirce's* Fire On the Hearth, *published in 1951. "Very rare" in 1929 ad, and "very popular design, possibly made other places [besides at Tyson], according to Peirce.*

Cook stove, cast iron, small oven, 4 burners, large flat hearth, 4 legs, design of front is like 6 fluted columns close together, "Summer and Winter Cooking Stove No. 4," invented by famed stove designer Philo Penfield Stewart, Troy, NY, 41" H x 36" W, pat'd Sept. 1838 (he was still patenting stoves 20 years later). **$3500-$5000**

Cook stove, of type called a <u>covered wagon stove</u>, though not old enough to be for a covered wagon, cast iron, oval with slanted sides, flat top with 2 eyes, looks sort of like bath tub with little grate in side, 4 short legs, mfd. by Fischer Leaf Co., Louisville, KY, 12" H x 18" W x 12" deep, pat'd 1879. **$250-$350**

XI-13. Cook stove. *Cast iron, ornate all over in designs not dissimilar to pressed glass designs from the same period, which came from molds also. Mold-makers and other kinds of carvers all drew on patterns common to furniture, architectural ornament, woven Jacquard textiles, etc. See more on space-filling patterns in the mini-chapter on pie safes. Maker of this cook stove not mentioned, but I believe this is the "New World Air-Tight" cooking stove, mfd. by Vose & Co., Albany, NY. From a dealer's ad in Johnston's De-troit City Directory, 1857-58.*

XI-14. Air-tight stove, *toted by Uncle Sam-like figure, on top of advertising flyer dated 1872. C. H. Tyler, a dealer, referred to himself as "U. R. Uncle," and was located on Davis St., in Greenfield, MA.*

Cook stove, electric, cast iron boxy body, flexible tubes coming up from back to attach to wall mounted box with switches & dials, ancient styling for hinges on oven door, 4 eyes, the lids of which make an even or flush working surface stove not in when not in use, oven has inner glass windowed door, "Carron," English, c.1912. **$700-$900**

Gobbledecook — To share with you the charm of technical journalism 100 years before this stove was a gleam in the eye of its inventor, I will transcribe a few paragraphs on an invention granted John J. Hess from an 1829 issue of the *Journal of the Franklin Institute* [Philadelphia]. "For an Economical Cooking Stove; John J. Hess, Philadelphia, March 19 [1829]." The inventor claims "This stove consists of seventeen pieces, or plates, independent of eight doors, and three grates, all resting upon four feet, which, when properly applied, and put together, form a perfect, whole, and entire construction, capable of performing, with rare economy, a great variety of cooking operations, together with numberless other services in housewifery, being heated by a very small portion of wood, or anthracite coal." The *JFI* editor advises that "The foregoing is the exordium of the specification, and the following is its peroration." Then back to Hess: "With this apparatus, and attentive care in its operations, great economy must be preserved in the consuming material used for fuel. Steam is generated from the boilers, and when received into proper vessels, can be applied to all the delicate cookery of luxurious dishes, without the aid of assistants; and important advantage to families. Boiling water is always in readiness; and with the same fire, baking of meats, and bread, or fruit, roasting, broiling, stewing, frying, boiling, and fricaseeing, are expeditiously going on, at one and the same time!"

The editor adds "There is a something so stimulating in the foregoing enumeration of properties and results, as to make us wish to anticipate the usual 'hour of prime'; and had we one of Mr. Hess's stoves, we certainly should hurry the cook. As it is impossible to describe this stove without engravings, and as most of our readers, like ourselves, are more inclined to partake of a good dinner than to study the means of preparing it, we will merely give them the address of the patentee, who resides at No. 237 North Second Street, Philadelphia, who is prepared to gratify the taste of those who will apply to him."

XI-15. "Anti-clinker" stove, *the "Fearless No. 8" made by Rathbone, Sard & Co., Albany, NY, 1873. Called a "plain top" cook stove, it is shown here without the reservoir for hot water and the warming closet which would be attached at the right side. Clinkers are rock-hard pieces of coal which will not ignite, and had to be removed.*

XI-16. Kitchens of "Notable People," *abbreviated from article in* The Metal Worker, *2/8/1890, detailing importance of the "French range" instead of a stove, for the wealthy.* **(T-L)** *"Fred Vanderbilt's Kitchen, showing end of servants' dining table."* Frederick Vanderbilt, *459 Fifth Avenue, NYC. "This kitchen is an old-fashioned one, is below the street and is dark and damp. Gas is burning all day long. The servants when at dinner sit at two long tables in the kitchen. There is no chef here. His place is occupied by a French woman, who has the girth of a typical cook." I bet the servants of "Fred Vanderbilt" were a diseased, unhappy lot.* **(T-R)** *"Kitchen of W. W. Astor."* William Waldorf Astor, *8 E. 33rd Street, NYC. The kitchen "is comparatively small, but there is a separate dining-room for the servants, so the chef has it all to himself. Here the cooking dishes are of porcelain, the French cook considering porcelain more wholesome for use than copper. Hardwood floor, polished to the smoothness of glass."* **(B-L)** *A. M. Palmer's kitchen, 25 E. 65th St., NYC. "The most beautiful, light and clean kitchen imaginable, and in it is a cook who makes one think of the old days when in mother's kitchen at home he reveled in doughnut horses and gingerbread men. It is typical of those of New England, with its oaken floor and shining tins, and one looks instinctively for the cat that should be purring before the fire."* **(B-R)** *"Kitchen of Cornelius Vanderbilt." 1 W. 57th St., NYC. It was the largest private kitchen in New York, and considered very fine. Floor of brown & white marble; pressed brick walls, one side and end with glass-doored cupboards. "This kitchen is beautifully lighted, as it is in the front part of the basement, on a level with the street, and has two very large stained glass windows." German chef used copper because "copper is cleaner than anything else."*

XI-17. "Ship's camboose," *or caboose, or cabin stove. This is the remaining top third of sales receipt of F. D. Chase, Boston, MA, dated Feb. 5, 1862. Note the fairly high brass rail or gallery which would keep the utensils from falling to the lower deck.*

Cook & parlor stove, cast iron, actually a parlor stove but known as a <u>dining room helper</u> because the top is a small oven, "Oven Parlor No. 7," mfd. by Newberry, Filley & Co., Troy, NY, c.1854 to 1858. **$1000-$1800**

Cook stoves — See also ranges

Cook stove nameplate, from oven door, multicolor enameled metal rectangle, "Glenwood," 8" x 10", turn of century. **$12-$15**

Door for oven, cast iron, fancy casting, "F. Earl Landis, Brunerville Foundry," Brunerville, Land County, PA, late 19th C. **$75-$125**

Door for bake oven, cast iron with hinged plump heart with sliding vent & motto "Heart of the Home" cast on it, dealer Emanon Corner Antiques says it was made in Ringoes, NJ, first half 19th C. It has <u>high collecting value for several reasons</u>. First, the heart and the motto. Second because it is not just for decoration. More and more colonial revivalists have bake ovens and walk-in hearths built in their twentieth-century homes, to use for cooking the old way. Price range mine, not Emanon Corner's. **$700-$1000**

Door for oven, for built-in hearth oven, cast iron, strap latch, pintail hinges, draft plate, design of 5 fluted fans, "Lincoln Foundry," Bath, ME, 11-1/2" x 15" , early 19th C. These so rarely come on the market it's hard to tell what might happen to the prices. Some doors have cast designs that appeal to folk art collectors. **$475-$675**

Door for stove, cast iron, depicts man clearing wood, "Leibrandt & McDowell Stove Co.," Philadelphia & Baltimore, mid 19th C. **$175-$200+**

Drying oven, tall oblong box with small smokestack on top, galvanized iron, 2 sets of double doors, stacked one over other, reveal drying or baking shelves, used on top of range or stove, "Zimmerman Fruit & Vegetable Dryer & Bake Oven," mfd. by Zimmerman Fruit Dryer Co., Cincinnati, OH. In May 1880 there were "over 11,000 in use." **$45-$75**

Fireless cooker, metal box with 2 wells containing original **soapstone** heater discs (the most common material because it holds heat so well), 2 lids, with clip fasteners, stones were heated on range then put in the cooker, then the special deep pan was set over the disc, "Thermatic," American, turn of century. Because some of these were insulated with straw, at least the homemade ones, they were also known as **haybox cookers**. **$50-$75**

XI-18. Range with attachments. *Drying & towel rack, of walnut or maple rods, fits on stovepipe. The shelves, also were fitted to the pipe, and available in sets of 2 or 4, were meant for "dishes while taking up dinner," for keeping plates warm, or for raising bread. "Always Handy" accessories mfd. by American Manufacturing Co., New Haven, CT. American Agriculturist, 12/1874. Possibly a Vose "wide oven" stove.*

XI-20. Humorous post card. *That stove is giving all it's got! But what I love are the sleeping chickens, which "Paw" has to turn to face the wall before retiring. Published by Asheville Post Card Co., Asheville, NC, in the 1950s, and an example of stove-related non-advertising paper available to collectors.* **$2-$4**

XI-19. Cook stove. *"Original Troy Charter Oak." M. L. Filley, Troy, NY. 1882 ad in* The Metal Worker, *reading "We offer our celebrated Charter Oak, manufactured by us since 1854. Entirely remodeled and with the improvements usually found in first-class wood stoves. In altering it we have retained all the good features that have made this stove so famous, and added those that experience has shown the trade demanded."*

XI-21. Modern cooking, *as depicted in* The Metal Worker, *6/18/1892. At left is a hot old smoky wood stove, with what appear to be corncobs [now coming back as a clean fuel] all over floor, a squawling baby fallen into the coal hod, and the chauvinist husband stalking out instead of helping. A "Fire King" gas stove, mfd. by A. Weiskittel & Son, Baltimore, with tin plate from the factory of Coates & Co., Baltimore, has made everyone happy.*

XI-22. Gas range. *"Caloric," in pale green porcelainized finish with ivory trim, in kitchen with marbled dark forest green & white floor. Note stacked ovens, warming closet above them, and overall streamlining of design.* House & Garden, *1930 ad. An article in* House Beautiful *of the time said "The kitchen range may be said now to have reached the robot stage, since it works with the minimum of human control or manual guidance! The mere pressing of a button or manipulation of cock or switch, and the 'die is cast' for an economically cooked meal.... The first thing that strikes the beholder is their modern air! The new ranges have taken unto themselves a new beauty! In some cases, we admit there is an effort at ornament which defeats itself in overelaboration and bewildering design and mottlings, but on the whole, every manufacturer has models beautiful enough to capture the eye of the most fastidious. Whereas we used to have woeful black, squatty, graceless ranges, to-day we have console models, with legs slender but firm, and with cabinets as attractive as are many chests of drawers. We have them enduringly enameled in white with gray, blue, green, and other colored trim, and finished in chromium rather than nickel." "The Robot of the Kitchen,"* House Beautiful, *May 1931.*

XI-23. Oil-burning range. *"Perfection #R-869," by Perfection Stove Co., Cleveland, OH. The ad goes on to tout kerosene, not mentioning oil at all except to identify model. Ultimate simplicity — probably would be collectible by moderne collectors seeking a look.* Farm Journal & Farmer's Wife, *5/1939.*

XI-24. Tabletop gas stove. *"No.2 Junior," mfd. by Cleveland Foundry — who also made the oil range in XI-23. Ad in* The Metal Worker, *2/6/1892. (NOTE: This is one commonly understood meaning of "tabletop." Stove makers in the early part of the 20th C. sometimes used "tabletop" range to mean a flat-top range with nothing, such as an oven, raised above the cooking surface.)* **$40-$50**

XI-27. Electric cooker, two views. *"Gilbert," mfd. in England.* **(L)** *View with hinged shelf down at side, and top raised for work surface, showing underside of the four round "boiling discs." Note controls for each of discs. Two ovens — one with two heating elements, one with three — explain the row of five control dials.* **(R)** *In position for cooking. Picture from Maud Lancaster's* Electric Cooking, *1914.*

XI-25. Oil stove. *"Royal #44," mfd. by The Perry Stove Co.'s Argan Stoves & Ranges, Albany, NY. Nickel-plated cast iron. Pat'd 1890. This was a small stove, but size isn't given in ad.* The Metal Worker, *6/28/1890.*

XI-26. Gasoline stove. *"Quick Meal Cabinet Range, #924," mfd. by the Quick Meal Stove Co., St. Louis, MO. "Among the features may be mentioned glass tubes which show the dripping of gasoline when the stove is in use, German silver needle points and a rim on the gasoline burner top extending over the burner drums and tubes, thus protecting them against the dripping from cooking vessels. All the pipes are anti-rusting material. [This model] is a new pattern, nicely japanned and ornamented."* The Metal Worker, *2/6/1892. This kind of stove may be in "low demand" among stove collectors, but I imagine there are collectors of japanned wares who would like to have it — not functioning — in their kitchens.*

XI-28. Electric cooker. *"Electroyl," mfd. by Purcell & Nobbs, London, England. Picture shows how it is set up in front of a fireplace, with some kind of crinkled stuffing filling the hearth opening. Cast iron frame, steel oven, with oven 23" x 16" x 16". Two 8" boiling discs flush on top, also one 6", and a griller/toaster. The area between the top and the oven is a "hot closet" or warming oven, for keeping plates and food warm. The control panel is mounted to the wall. Maud Lancaster's* Electric Cooking, *1914.*

Fireless cooker, oak chest with 2 lids, each covering a metal-lined well with a soapstone disc at the bottom that was heated in or on the stove, plopped in, the food in cylindrical vessels put in on top, for slow cooking without fire! This one with its original vessels & their lids, "Caloric" — "Hygienic, Scientific, Economical," Caloric Fireless Cookstove Co., Janesville, WI, 14" H x 29" L x 15" deep, the vessels shy of 12" diameter, early 20th C.   **$75-$135**

Fireless cooker, wooden box with all aluminum inside, including pots, pans, racks & lids, 2 holes with soapstone heater discs, "The Ideal," Toledo Cooker Co., Toledo, OH, early 20th C. They also made cookers with wooden boxes & steam cookers.   **$30-$45**

Fireless cooker, oak box like blanket chest, 3 wells, enamelware kettles with lids that lock on when twisted like a bayonet mount, "The Auto Cook," mfd. by Caloric Fireless Cookstove Co., Grand Rapids, MI, 17" H x 36" L x 15" W, c.1905.   **$50-$65**

Fireless cooker, metal box printed to look like wood, 3 holes with aluminum lining, single chest lid, "Rapid," mfd. by William Campbell Co., Detroit, MI, c.1919.   **$25-$45**

Fireless cooker range, looks like small apartment stove, electric powered rather than the heated stone type, pull-out drawer or bin below with insulated box that looks like old-fashioned fireless cooker, oven above that with Pyrex™ window, hotplate-grill style top. The usual concept behind a "fireless cooker" is that the food is partly cooked on some other stove, prior to being put for finishing in the cooker. This "Campbell's Rapid," invented by William Campbell, is combo range & cooker, with a thermostat that turns electricity on and off as needed to maintain the temperature. The fireless cooker part is in the lower pull-out bin. There's an oven above that, and a stove top grill on top.William Campbell Co., Alliance, OH, & Georgetown, Ontario, Canada, c.1925.   **$55-$85**

XI-29. Fireless cooker. *"Caloric — the Auto Cook." Caloric Fireless Cookstove Co., Grand Rapids, MI. 17" H x 36" L x 15" W, "solid quartered oak, furnished complete with German-made enamel ware, patent revolving bar-lock covers." On casters. Ladies' Home Journal ad, 4/1906. The collector value here is quite a bit due to the oak, which is a nice go-with for quarter-sawn oak tables and chairs in today's family room kitchens.* **$50-$65**

XI-30. Fireless cooker. *"Two vessels, one inside the other, separated by sawdust, asbestos, or other poor conducting material. Foods are heated in the usual way to the boiling point or to a high temperature, and are then placed in the inner vessel. The heat of the food cannot escape through the non-conducting material which surrounds it, and hence remains in the food and slowly cooks it." Bertha M. Clark, General Science, NY: American Book Co., 1912.* **$20-$30**

Flue cover, also called a **chimney hole cover** or **flue stop**, very decorative cast iron, probably made by a stove foundry to match a particular line of stoves, late 19th C. These have gotten very collectible, as more people collect "architectural elements."   **$25-$65**

Flue cover, japanned tin, brown color, put in place when cook or heat stove was dismantled for summer, leaving hole where stovepipe would ordinarily go. The trade name reflects the marketing magic of an exciting new source of power: "Electric," American, 14-1/2" D, pat'd Jan. 7, 1890.   **$10-$15**

Flue cover, brass colored metal frame, hanging brass-color chain, 2 girls in bonnets under glass, 19th C. or early 20th C. **$20-$25**

Flue cover, brass frame, chromolith depiction of lovely girl in garden, German, late 19th or early 20th C.   **$20-$25**

Flue cover, brass frame, chromolithograph of dancing Victorian children, music by a bug orchestra, American, litho prob. German, 9-1/2" D, c.1880s. This cute conceit, of the cheerful bugs playing music, is found on all kinds of color lithographed commercial art of the period. It always amazes me how peculiar some Victorian art is. Dancing bug pictures nowadays would be featured in the before panel on a Raid™ ad, I'm afraid.   **$35-$40**

Flue cover, brass frame, color depiction of English countryside with lots of teensy flowers, only 5" diameter, 19th C. or early 20th C.   **$20-$25**

Flue cover, brass frame, decoratively stamped border, chromolith picture of Little Boy Blue, American, 9" D, turn of century. **$15-$20**

Flue cover, brass frame, litho of 2 curly-headed little girls, clip back, American (?), 7-1/2" D, late 19th or early 20th C. **$15-$20**

Flue cover, brass frame, litho of 2 girls on a lake, swans around the boat, clip back, German-(?), turn of century. These fancified brass frame flue covers were available with stove pipe collars that has matching stamped flanges. **$20-$25**

Flue cover, brass frame, lithograph of wintery church scene glued in center, American, 8-1/2" D, turn of century to 1920s. **$10-$15**

Flue cover, brass frame, lithographed picture of horses & stable, American (?), 19th C. or early 20th C. **Reproduction Alert** — A company in Missouri makes reproduction flue covers. If you collect them, I suggest you send for their catalog. Write: NU-HL, 2113 Nottingham, Cape Girardeau, MO 63701. **$15-$20**

XI-31. Flue covers, *for covering hole in wall where stovepipe (usually parlor or heating stove) goes through, when the stove is taken down for the summer.* **(T-L)** *Stamped tin, with brass-like finish, cheap chromolith picture. From Lalance & Grosjean, 1890.* **(R)** *A similar one, called a "crystal flue stop ... the handsomest now on the market. Gold and silver finish." Pat'd 7/19/1887, 9/4/1888, and 4/9/1889. Haslet, Flanagen & Co., Philadelphia. The Metal Worker, 4/12/1890.* **(B-L)** *"Gold lacquered, wide flange" flue stopper, with "fancy picture." 8-1/4", steel spring to snap into hole. Wheeling Corrugating Co., 1921.* **$10-$15**

XI-32. Flue covers, *showing different types of hoops.* **(A)** *Spring steel. Sears & Roebuck, c.1900.* **(B)** *"Higgins Perfect" flue stops, with 5/8" double hoops, brass-lacquered embossed cover, 6" diameter.* **(C)** *Androck Folding, with flat cover for papering over. Green enamel finish.* **(D)** *"Gold lacquered" disc with no picture, single coiled flat spring. Central Stamping Co., 1920.* **(E)** *A "Higgins Single Hoop Star Cover," embossed and "brass lacquered," no picture.* **(F)** *"Edward's Tip-Top" flue stop, with double folding spring steel hoop, colored pictures, embossed metal disc, lacquered. brass 9-3/4" diameter. B, C, E and F all from The Washburn Co., Rockford, IL, catalog from 1927.* **$7-$15**

Flue stops — An ad in *The Metal Worker,* April 12, 1890, shows a flue stop tradenamed the "Crystal," made by Haslet, Flanagen & Co. of Philadelphia, and patented July 19, 1887; Sept. 4, 1888; and April 9, 1889. They were packed for wholesale trade 12 to a box, half "gold," half "silver," and were 8-3/8" diameter. The one in the ad has a gadrooned border surrounding a picture of an old mill, bridge and trees. A supplier's catalog put out by Buhl Sons Co., Detroit, c. 1919, shows several "Flue Stops." Two have stamped brass frames, with a sort of egg and dart design to the brass part. The centers, as shown, both have a snowy scene of a tall steepled church. One, "The Royal," which has a double figure-8 spring wire fastener on the back that popped into the stovepipe hole, was available either in a brass finish or "fancy assorted [lacquered] colors." The 2nd flue cover, "The Perfect," came in a brass finish with "fancy assorted centers." This cover had two spring wire ears, sticking out both sides, which were bent into the stove pipe opening. A third type, "The Gem is a Flat Stop which can be papered over if desired. It has a Patent Fastener at the center" (the double figure-8 wire one). It came painted gray with "fancy assorted centers" — presumably the same cheap chromolith landscapes, etc., that the other(s) came with. Any of you who have been in a store offering supplies for wood-burning stoves have seen modern flue covers. They are stamped metal, very yellow; they are brass-plated rather than brass, or may have an off-white or beige baked-on paint finish, with exceedingly ugly, poorly printed color pictures glued on the centers. You could do better with a picture cut from any magazine.

Flue cover, brass frame, reverse painting of sylvan scene on glass, late 19th C. **$35-$55**

Flue cover, brass frame, stamped & beaded border, chain hanger, well-done, "naive" hand-painted snow scene in oils, depicts shed, bar, trees, lots of snow, & large black dog walking across center of scene, American, large — 12" diameter, late 19th C. **$50-$75+**

Flue cover, brass frame, with beading around outside, oil painting of pug dog inside, no mark, 12" D, turn of century. You compete here with crossover dog & folk art collectors, so cheap prices (such as this one was marked) are probably because those collectors haven't yet harvested the flue cover field. **$60-$85+**

Flue cover, glass & color-tinfoil, brass chain hanger, depiction of kitchen with little girls paring apples by hand, prob. European, big 12-1/2" D, late 19th or early 20th C. Not very many flue covers have kitchen depictions, as the fancier ones were meant to cover the hole when the parlor stove was knocked down for the summer. **$25-$35**

Flue cover, glass & colored tinfoil, brass hanging chain, religious depiction of 2 children watched over by an angel, European, 12" D, late 19th or early 20th C. **$18-$25**

Flue cover, tin frame, stamped with design, center picture painted in oils of child feeding cat, 19th C. **$75-$125**

Flue cover, tin, chromolithograph picture of garden girl with red roses, spring clips to hold in hole, 8" D, turn of century. **$18-$25**

Flue cover, tin, stamped & painted, with chromolith farm scene on paper center, 19th C. or early 20th C. **$12-$18**

Flue cover, tinsel frame in dark blue, brass chain, center depicts young woman with water jug, Belgian, late 19th or early 20th C. I believe that the flue covers with chains are as a rule older than the spring clip ones. They fit in better with the Victorian conceit of hanging as many decorative things on the wall as possible. **$20-$30**

Flue cover, tinsel frame, rich red color, brass chain hanger, chromolith family scene in center, European, early 20th C. **$20-$30**

Flue cover, brass frame, small blond boy's portrait bust wearing red winter cap, American or European, 8" D, turn of century. **$20-$25**

Flue cover, brass with glass cover, depicts bust of young girl surrounded by flowers, 19th C. **$30-$40**

Grate shaker, ornate cast iron tool, used to move the grate & shake out the ashes & small clinkers to the floor of the stove's firebox for cleaning. Bements Stove Co., late 19th or early 20th C. **$7-$10**

Heating stove, enameled sheet iron, best described as Arts & Crafts lighthouse shape, beautiful rich medium blue, the base & 6 short legs & the hexagonal frame of lid are black, with large & small ventilating holes, ruby glass is behind larger double row of holdes in front, hole in back near top for small stovepipe, lid has acorn finial, lifts off to reveal small surface, for a tea kettle, front embossed "Quick Comfort," lid: "Quick Meal Stove Co., Div. of Am. Stove Co.," 23-1/2" H, turn of century to 1910s. **$225-$250**

XI-33. Garbage carbonizer, *to fit in stovepipe "between the stove and the flue of the chimney, and becomes a permanent fixture. It is a horizontal cylinder about 1/3 larger in diameter than the stovepipe. One end is removable, and attached thereto, on the inside, is a semi-circular pan or scoop, perforated along both sides and having solid ends and a tight bottom." The scoop is filled with the garbage and slid into place, where the heat eventually carbonizes it. "The carbon which remains is utilized as fuel," wrote Fannie Merritt Farmer from her Boston Cooking School, in praise of the gadget. Mfd. by New England Sanitary Co., Boston. American Kitchen Magazine, 4/1896.* **$5-$15**

XI-34. Parlor stoves, *with fancy cast iron finials. From the "Madison Square Series," mfd. by Southard, Robertson & Co., NYC. Madison Square lies just north of 23rd Street, east of 5th Avenue, and it was a fashionable area. While these stoves were "very moderate in price" in 1890 when advertised, they would cost a small fortune today, especially the building-shaped one with the horse. It is spectacular and highly desirable, especially now that there's been an upsurge of interest in collecting building-shaped banks, souvenirs, lamps, etc. A dancing gypsy with tamborine tops the other stove. Note low-set foot rails which look like carrying handles. In fact, at least one turn of the century parlor stove maker, Moore, advertised "Easy to carry; invert the foot rails and use them as carriers." Collectors for these would probably come from the folk art sector rather than the true stove collecting population.* **$3000-$5000+**

XI-35. Two photographic stereoptican card panels, *making entertainment out of what was a no-joking-matter affecting many husbands and wives in the 19th and early 20th centuries. (T) Busy one shows wife admonishing husband, who's ready to throw soot-caked elbow pipe on floor. Note: flue cover is already in place (above wife's head); also ladder, mad wallpaper, coal hod. "Have patience, dear, don't swear" caption is repeated on back in several foreign languages. ©1897 by Strohmeyer & Wyman, pub'd by Underwood & Underwood. (B) Simpler one is posed so man has stovepipe legs. "Oh, Dear! Don't Swear" is the caption. ©1892 by B. L. Singley, pub'd by Keystone View Co. How-to columns advised an aid to a "felicitous putting up" by numbering both ends of each section of pipe. Several more versions — mainly photographic — of the cards exist. For photographic ones:* **$6-$12**

Portable oven, sheet steel & cast iron, nickeled hinges & fittings, see-through glass window in drop-down door shows 2 shelves in one oven, came in two sizes — 13-1/4" W (#125), and 21" W (#140), "Bolo," mfd. by Griswold Mfg Co., Erie, PA, c.1920. Another Bolo I've read about but not seen is about 22" H x 13-1/4" W, two ovens connected by a flue. In the 1930s, Griswold made a "pie oven," with a black finish, slightly smaller than the #125 Bolo, worth about the same. **$75-$135**

Portable stove, folding "pocket" stove, black painted hinged and folding sheet metal 3-sided base, with stamped brass & tin fuel cup, in original box, with directions: "Use only Alcohol, pour in slowly through the wire gauze, one or two table-spoons full and light it. The Best Folding Pocket Cook Stove in the World." "Climax Patent Folding Pocket Cook Stove No. 888," Houchin Mfg. Co., NYC, NY, 4-1/2" H x cup 3-1/2" D, trademark reg. May 18, 1875, with patents earlier & later. Pat'd Sept. 17, 1872; May 4, 1875; July 27, 1875; Jan. 29, 1878; Mar. 20, 1883. **$15-$35**

Portable canal boat stove, cast iron, 2 burners, 3-legged, small hearth, American or English (?), 18" H, late 19th C. **$400-$550**

Portable stove, for fishing vessels or whaling ships, small cast iron wide-lipped fire pot with inset rack for putting cooking vessel on, forged iron bail handle, fits on base that has 3 legs and a little hearth, American, 9-1/2" H x 13" diameter, 19th C. **$500-$800**

Radiator, ornate cast iron, meant for dining room with 2 compartments called <u>hot closets</u> built right into it for keeping food warm, spectacular item — and think how many are rusted out in dumps or melted down during two World Wars. American, late 1880s to 1890s. **$425-$575**

Futurewatch.— I predict that even as this book is being printed there will be a number of people discovering & collecting ornate old steam & hot water radiators, and the salesmen's samples of them.

Range, gas, wood or coal. Finished in light gray blue (almost like so-called Wedgwood blue) enamel over the cast iron, re-nickeled, fitted with safety pilot for gas, given fiberglass insulation. Gas oven & broiler on right above door with built-in temperature gauge, a woodstove oven below with temperature gauge in door, range eyes fueled by gas, United Premier Boston Stove Foundry, Reading, MA, c.1926. **$3400-$4000+**

Range, cast iron, completely refurbished, re-nickeled, & painted with black high temperature paint (what used to be called "locomotive paint"), marked "Glenwood F" and "Glenwood Range #108," Perry & Co., Albany, NY, c.1906. **$1900-$2500**

Nickel-plating — Dealer Dave Erickson, of Erickson's Antique Stoves, at the Depot (Littleton, MA, 01460), explained nickel-plating this way: the plater grinds and polishes the surface to be plated, then puts a heavy copperplate layer on and buffs that. The copper gives a warm glow to the nickel tone and also is a "primer" to fill in minor imperfections. A good nickel-plater always puts the copper on first, then nickels the surface. Poor nickel-plating is obvious when you sight down the nickeled part from an extreme oblique angle and you see ridges, ripples, sanding and filing marks.

Range, cast iron, "Imperial Clarion 8-20," mfd. by Wood & Bishop, Bangor, ME, late 19th C. **$2500+**

Range, cast iron, nickeled copper, 6 burners, oven, warming oven, hot water reservoir, and all original accessory tools, "Copper Clad," 5 feet high, 19th C. **$2500+**

Range, cast iron, nickeled iron decorative pieces with acorn motif, very substantial base with cabriole legs, oven above, fold-down nickeled shelves on either side of flue, refurbished, "Crown Acorn," mfd. by Rathbone, Sard & Co., Albany, NY, 61" H x 64" W, pat'd April 18, 1907 & Sept. 17, 1907. **$3000+**

Range, cast iron, quite simple, "Home Clarion," mfd. by Wood & Bishop, Bangor, ME, late 19th C. **$900-$1200**

Range, white gas/gasoline, blue porcelainized iron, nickel trim, "Quick Meal," Ringen Stove Co., early 20th C. (in the late 19th and early 20th C., the maker's name was "Quick Meal Stove Co.") **$900-$1400**

XI-36. "Heating Stoves of 1990." *In the trade magazine* The Metal Worker, *8/16/1890, was printed a teasing piece on parlor or heating stoves of the future, based on the un-stovelike appearance being exaggerated beyond reason by contemporary stove designers. An abridged version of a spoof newspaper account, supposedly from 1990, of the purchase of this stove in the shape of a Newfoundland dog (cast iron with glass eyes on a nickel-plated base) follows: "I, being in need of a new base burner, called on Jones & Johnson for the purpose of purchasing a stove. Upon entering, I was bewildered at the glittering array of samples of artistic stoves spread before me. The place would hardly be taken for a stove store on account of the peculiarity of the designs. One would sooner imagine he was in a zoo or taxidermist's place of business, or possibly Barnum's winter quarters. There were cook stoves in the form of turtles, alligators, camels; heating stoves representing Bismarck, General Washington, Uncle Sam, dogs, cats, bears, tigers, elephants, lions, and, in fact, almost every conceivable object. The huge elephant stove is for school houses and public institutions. ... One beautiful pattern was George Washington. Standing as he did, he looked as if he might indeed be the father of the world. He was mounted on a platform or box with the word 'Liberty' in large raised letters across the front of the ashpit section. His right hand rested on the Western hemisphere of a bronze atlas which was placed at his side. His left hand held a statuette of the Goddess of Liberty Enlightening the World. The look upon his face was that of success achieved. A gentle pressure upon his right shoulder would cause his head to fall back, exposing the top into which the fuel was put to replenish the fire." A George Washington heating stove was actually made — and sold as a "dumb radiating stove" (furnishing heat created elsewhere) and also a garden statue. Made by their inventor, Alonzo Blanchard, from the 1840s, and later by J. L. Mott Foundry, they have sold to collectors for upwards of $15,000. Any other fanciful form described above, if it had ever been made, would be worth many thousands to collectors of cast iron and folk art.*

Range, white gas/gasoline, cast iron, sheet iron, 3 side-by-side large burners & oven, burns white gas. Has white porcelainized panels on doors, ornate nickel trim & on the fancy versions there are small grill work doors that flip down to reveal niches for warming a bun or two or for keeping salt & pepper shakers, or perhaps a flour dredger, or some crackers to keep them crisp. Towel rack on side. A smaller one has one oven, no storage cupboard, no salt & pepper niche. All have a japanned tin & cast iron fuel tank & filter, with 4 cocks with air intake valves, connect with rubber tubes to the burners & oven, "Quick Meal," Ringen Stove Co., pat'd Sept. 15, 1903; March 31, 1908; Dec. 21, 1909. Collector Dewayne Ziegler has explained to me that, "the long tubes on the end fill up with gas. Pull them out, light them, and shove them in a hole in your burner." Sounds like no easy feat to me! **$1900-$2800**

Range, cast iron, ornate, lots of shiny trim, "Atlantic Grand," Portland Stove Foundry Co., Portland, ME, after 1880. **$2500-$3500+**

Range, cast iron, very square & geometric designs typical of designs on paper goods from the same period, no really rounded forms, exhibits the mold-makers' jigsaw gingerbread rather than more voluptuous hand-carving, oven, large water reservoir at side, nice hob shelf with cutout brackets, "Happy Thought," mfd. by Pittston Stove Co., Pittston, PA, dated 1884. Call it good karma or conversation piece, this stove has got a great collectible name. (There was also a "Grand Happy Thought," for the power of positive cooking.) **$2000-$2500**

Range, ornate cast iron, warming ovens above, urn pedestals on either side of flue, 6 holes, water reservoir on side, "Grand Windsor," Windsor Stoves and Ranges, in Montgomery Ward catalog, and made at one of their foundries, late 19th C. **$2500+**

Range, white & baby blue porcelainized cast iron, gas, "Windsor," early 20th C. **$2000+**

What's In a Name? — I suspect that there are other collectors, like me, who would pay extra, a sort of premium, because something had a really great name right on the front. A personal short list of favorite names for cooking stoves or ranges include: "Legal Tender," "Busy Bee," "Early Breakfast," "Merry Christmas," "Reindeer," "Shoo-Fly," "Alligator Range," and your choice of "Woman's Rights" or the "New Cinderella."

• • • •

"Right and Left-Hand Ranges. — It is somewhat difficult to tell just what the custom may be in different parts of the country or among different manufacturers or dealers. Ranges are made of several kinds. Some are double ranges with a fire-pot in the center and an oven on each side. Others are single ranges with a fire-pot on the left side and oven on the right. Other single ranges are made with fire-pot on right and oven on left. . . . The one in ordinary use has the fire-pot on the left, oven on the right. The question arises, is this a right or a left-hand range? As the vast majority of people are right-handed, it seems . . . natural to suppose that the range most widely used would be constructed so as to be most convenient for them and would therefore be a right hand range. Yet this view is not taken by many manufacturers, who curiously enough regard the range in common use as a left-hand range, insisting that the location of the fire-pot fixes the name. Fuller & Warren's catalogue, for instance, says about their Diamond B range: 'This range has the fire-box constructed at the right side of the oven, hence it is termed a right-hand range, and for that reason it can often be used to advantage when a left-hand range or cook stove could not be used conveniently.'

"This peculiarity in naming ranges gives rise to a great deal of uncertainty in filling orders. One stove manufacturer, whose ranges are all made with fire-pots at the left, says that when he is asked by a customer for a left-hand range he invariably replies that he does not make them. While all his ranges are really left-hand, according to [Fuller & Warren's usage], he knows that his customer is seeking a range of a different type from those in common use, even if he does not use the term 'left-hand.' Other manufacturers, however, do not reason in the same way, but fill the order according to their own acceptation of the term. . . . Among dealers it is very probable that the custom exists of calling a range right or left hand according to the oven.

"It would be most interesting to have the opinions of the trade on this question in nomenclature and their reasons for adopting the name . . . they regard as correct. . . . What say you? Is a right-hand range one with the oven on the right or the fire-pot on the right, and why?" Editor, *The Metal Worker,* March 15, 1890.

• • • •

Classic Ranges & Antique Stoves — Once a woman named Macy Stern was asked to buy used appliances for about 500 apartments. Her client took the newer pieces, leaving Ms. Stern with heavy older ranges, etc. This led to **Macy's Texas Stove Works, 5515 Almeda Rd., Houston, TX 77004, (713)-521-0934.** As she defines it, "classic" or "vintage" ranges are those made since the 1930s, while "antique" ranges were made earlier. Ms. Stern admires them all, but you probably won't find a wider array of interesting 50- and 60-year-olds at an A.A.R.P. meeting! These gas and electric ranges — Chambers, Anderson, Magic Chef, Tappan, Roper, Royal Chef, Glenwood, etc. — are just old enough to have belonged to the grandmothers of those of us who are "vintage" ourselves! **Publications:** For $15 a year, you can subscribe to More Classic Ranges, a tabloid-size newspaper full of pictures, "parts wanted" ads, and offers of privately owned stoves and ranges, including what state they're located in, the sales of which are brokered by MTSW. If you have a vintage or antique range or stove, you can send a photo, description, and $50, and Ms. Stern will run the picture in More Classic Ranges until it's sold. And/or you can join the Antique Stove Association and get its quarterly newsletter. MTSW also sells reprints of stove literature, as available. **Repairs & Fabrications** — MTSW restores, rebuilds and fabricates parts for old ranges, and also parlor stoves, including re-porcelainizing, and of course is only one of many companies doing such revival work. Always use an SASE, please, when writing anyone for information.

Range, gas, cast iron, 6-burner, two ovens, vertical broiler, warming closet above side oven, fully restored "Magic Chef," c.1937. A few years ago, this would have been valued about the same as a comparable range by another maker. According to Clifford Boram, "there have been a considerable number of magazine articles about antique gas ranges in the last few of years. They all illustrate the big Magic Chefs, so all the free-spenders have been paying through the nose for them." That is, the demand has driven the price. Boram reports the following prices: 8-burner, **$10,000+**; 6-burner, **$6,000+**

Range, gas, colorful enameled cast iron, main body in white with a Chinese red trim (manufacturer called it "Mandarin Red"), long red legs, ovens to side with heat control on inner side wall over range top, Estate Stove Co., Hamilton, OH, c.1928. Estate also made electric ranges, and color combinations were a rich "King's Blue" and white, and "Jade Green" and white. You could get the oven and broiler on left or right side of range surface. **$1500+**

Range, gas, looks almost like a fancy sideboard or buffet for dining room, oblong box on slightly cabriole legs, enameled in tan, with fronts of ovens & control panels in black & white marbleized enameled iron, green Bakelite™ pendant pulls on all doors & utensil drawer, extremely handsome, "Magic Chef Patrician Model," mfd. by American Stove Co., St. Louis, MO, late 1920s. $200 was the original price! **$3000+**

Stove Coloring — "Retail store equipment used to be painted red in most instances and for a time there was a fad in scales and meat grinders for gold lacquer. Machine tools were painted at the whim of the manufacturer until the conglomeration of hues in factories became absurd. . . . When the cast-iron stove was replaced by the more modern sheet-metal variety, the industry went chiefly to white. For a period of four or five years white in turn gave way to a variety of pastel colors, applied with fancy crystal, cloud, and wood-grain effects. This fad finally ran its course, and white again became the overwhelming choice of most women." Harold Van Doren, *Industrial Design, A Practical Guide* . NYC: McGraw-Hill, 1940.

"More color in Kitchens.— About a year ago colored kitchen utensils burst upon the horizon, pots and pans as well as the handles of flat ware assuming such gay tints as vermilion, sea green, ultramarine and daffodil yellow. As a result, kitchens bloomed, decoratively speaking. Housewives, proud of their softly tinted walls, hangings and pots and pans, brought their guests into the kitchen to demonstrate the superiority of this colorful room over the all-white interiors of yore. The cook, stimulated by all this novelty, looked contentedly around and cooked a better meal, and even the family cat blinked more contentedly on a hearth made of brightly-hued tiles. Now a manufacturer has gone a step further and created colored plumbing fixtures. Enameled sinks for kitchens are now available in such engaging tints as horizon blue, West Point gray, spring green, lavender, old ivory and autumn, the latter being a deep, pinkish beige tone." Editorial, *House & Garden,* Aug. 1928. Just two years later, someone of the same ilk was saying that "severity should, perhaps," be the rule for the kitchen. That engaging whimsy drained out very quickly.

XI-37. Pocket stove. *"Houchin's Improved Patent," with gridiron and boiler (with folding handles) holding nearly one quart, which can be used as a drinking cup. Will "boil water in five minutes to make 2 or 3 cups of Tea, Coffee, or Chocolate, Boil Eggs, Stew Oysters, etc." Fueled with two tablespoonsful of alcohol; "the Lamp being filled with indestructible packing will not spill or explode." Houchin Mfg. Co., NYC. 1877 ad.* **$15-$35**

XI-38. Dining room radiator — two views. *"Perfection," mfd. by Michigan Radiator & Iron Mfg. Co., Detroit. Shown open it reveals the oven or "hot closet" above with a slotted shelf, and the smaller one below. Top "oven" is about 18" H x 21" W. Radiator came in seven sizes, from 35" to 65" L. The Metal Worker, 8/23/1890. Since 1991 I have seen three of these installed in old houses.* **$425-$575+**

Range, gas, streamlined clean design, 4-burner, white enameled steel, pendant or drop pulls, broiler drawer under 6 control dials, "Magic Chef," American Stove Co., St. Louis, MO, c.1934. **$1000+**

An old ad for this range started off with words sure to shrivel the heart of a collector of today: **"The Modern Housewife discarded the old Coffee Mill Years Ago** . . . Isn't it about time to discard that old-fashioned range of yours? The sound of the old coffee mill is no longer heard in the modern kitchen. Progress has relegated this outmoded appliance to the junk pile. Yet thousands of women who wouldn't keep a coffee grinder in the house, except as a relic, continue to use a gas range that is just as out of date. Don't cheat the junk pile and yourself any longer. . . . Replace the antiquated range with a modern automatic Magic Chef."

Range, gas, ivory & green enameled iron, 4 burner, "Magic Chef," c. 1939. **$900+**

Range, huge black cast iron range with its own enclosure, lintel and heating shelf, to be "brickset" into fireplace, with flues to go up chimney. David Foulis, Edinburgh, Scotland, whole assembly about 55" H x 54" W, c.1875. **$1200-$2800**

Range, range in the home — A complaint aired March 1839 in the *Journal of the Franklin Institute* of Philadelphia, goes, "The greatest objection to the kitchen ranges devised by various ingenious projectors, is the want of simplicity. Cooks will not take the trouble of learning to use them, or, which is necessary, to keep in order the various novel articles by which they are accompanied." By the 1870s, probably most cooks were either supplied with simpler ranges or experience as their teacher.

● ● ● ●

"Smoothtop" ranges — These are a 1930s transitional form made to assist cooks who were used to nineteenth- and early twentieth-century wood/coal stoves that had a flat smooth top, closed by stove lids and the "cut long center" and the "short center" — which fit around the round stove lids, like a jigsaw puzzle, to make a perfectly smooth surface. The "Smoothtop" ranges are gas ranges, and you can remove parts of the smooth top to reveal the gas ring below, or even — for slow-cooking — set the pan down on the cover, with the gas fire going below it.

Range, peach enameled cast iron, nickel trim, 2 warming ovens above, oven & broiler below, 6 eyes with one having smaller eye in middle of lid, 2 lids in center lift out along with the fat I-shaped piece between them, to open up a long, round-end oblong suitable for a 2-hole gridiron or boiler, etc. "Copper Clad," early 20th C. Unrestored. **$1200+**

Range, gas, cast & sheet iron, box with fancy side valves, "The Sun Dial," mfd. by Goodwin Meter Co., South Carolina Power Co., SC, c.1946. **$250-$375**

Simmering cover, cast iron round "trivet" to set into range eye to reduce heat, openwork 6-wedge design, with slots for lid lifter, marked "Simmering Cover, W & P Mfg. Co.," Walker & Pratt Mfg. Co., 7-1/2" diameter, turn of century. **$20-$30**

Stove blacking, in tin container, red, white & blue label with flag design, "The Union Blacking," turn of century. **$15-$18**

Stove blacking holder, also called a blacking box holder, cast iron, 3 peg feet, open handle, scrolly biparte end, dog's head on springtensioned slider, 9" L x 2-3/4" W, marked "J. & W. Cairns," and "1857," pat'd Jan. 13, 1857, by J. &W. Cairns, Jersey City, NJ, pat. #16,374. An almost identical one, minus the dog, was patented by G. W. Taylor, Springfield, VT, June 1, 1867. This has been advertised by a dealer in "country items" as a "rare mechanical four-way trivet," which it isn't. **$75-$125+**

Stove door — See door, stove.

Stove knobs, nickeled cast iron, one an elongated blimp shape with the pointed tips of metal, the middle half transparent blue glass; the round one having an orb of blue glass fitted into a metal base with 2 arms for holding bolt through glass, "Jewel," Greene & Mallett, manufacturers of stove trimmings, Troy, NY, came in 10 sizes and styles, and also in amber glass, Jan. 1892 ad in *Metal Worker*. It's likely these would be sold not as stove knobs but as bureau knobs. The blue color especially desirable to collectors. Each: **$5-$15+**

Stove knobs — Most knobs, pendant drop handles, and bracket handles are either nickeled cast iron, or nickeled iron wire coils (such as made by the Troy Nickel Works), or are cast iron enameled in white. I still think that if you can't save the stove, save the knobs. In NYC it is not so common as it once was to find a stove thrown out on the street for pickup that day by the Sanitation Department, and most stoves are vintage 1920s, but there are still goodies to pick up. **$3-$15**

Stove lid lifter — also called a **democrat**, or a **stove dexter**, cast iron, design of heat-dissipating handle formed of handsome cutout letters, "ESTATE #33," American, 10" L, turn of century. **$12-$18**

Stove lid lifter, cast iron, nickel-plated, coil handle and head of Jack Frost at the business end, "Alaska" brand, mfd. by Troy Nickel Works, Troy, NY, about 10" L, late 19th to early 20th C. **$30-$55**

Stove lid lifter, cast iron in form of slender, attentuated but voluptuous long-haired and long-gowned woman wearing a crown, which, with her upraised arms, forms part of the pot lid lifter at her head end, the stove lid lifter being at her foot, odd monobuttock rear, unmarked, American, 8-5/16" L, c.1850s or 1860s. **$250+**

Stove lid lifter, cast iron in form of Victorian booted lady's leg, unmarked, 9" L, American, c.1850s or 1860s. Not for your home range. It'd be interesting to know what market these were aimed at. **$250+**

Stove lid lifter, nickeled cast iron, working hook end is a bull's head, handle is tight coil to dissipate heat and stay cool, hence name, "Alaska" brand, sold through Montgomery Ward as well as other stores, mfd. by Troy Nickel Works, Troy, NY, about 10" L, late 19th C. **$25-$45**

Stove lid lifter, openwork cast iron, the central motif being a heart outline, with a sort of fish outline coming from between the lobes, & a sort of banner from the point, there being useful tips at both ends, the banner or streamer contains the initials "J P A" & date, mfd. by J. P. Abbott, Cleveland, OH, 1882. **$40-$55+**

XI-39. Stove door. *Oval, cast iron, "Liberty & Union," with 26 stars, which would date it to between 1837 (when Michigan became the 26th state) and 1845. 11" H x 13" L. Photo courtesy Litchfield Auction Gallery, Litchfield, CT. Ex-Harold Corbin Collection, auctioned 1/1/1989 for $450.* **$400-$600**

XI-40. Stove handle. *"Alaska. Always Cold," mfd. by Troy Nickel Works, Troy, NY. All their coiled handles were called "Alaska," as a trade name, and they had at least three figurals at the end of their heat-dissipating handles: a bull's head symbolizing strength (?), a Jack Frost (?) head, symbolizing cold, and this Egyptian's head, symbolizing desert heat. Note echo of the coils in the stylized hairdo. Ad in* The Metal Worker, *8/6/1890.* **$18-$30**

XI-41. Stove lid lifter. *Spectacular voluptuous female form, cast iron. Surely not for a housewife's cook stove; probably for the stove on a railroad caboose or the like. 8-5/16" L, c.1850s-80s. I have seen another figural lifter in folk art dealer Marion Harris's stock. It was a woman's bent leg, in high button boots, and with a garter above her knee.* **$250+**

XI-42. Stove lid lifters. (T) *japanned cast iron shank, brass ferrule, and red-stained turned wood handle, 11" L. The two little curved side arms are for lifting pails. From unidentified catalog page, c.1870s-90s.* **(M)** *A "cool handle" one, nickeled cast iron, mfd. by Cleveland Foundry, OH. 1892 ad.* **(B)** *A heart-and-ellipse one, openwork handle, cast iron. Letters in cutout form are "J.P.A." flanked by "18" and "82." Mfd. by J. P. Abbott, Cleveland, OH, in 1882 ad, claiming this is "the best, the handsomest and easiest selling stove lid lifter is the Abbott Cold Handle." Although it doesn't mention it, the bifurcated end* **(R)** *was probably meant as a tack claw. Crossover folk art interest in hearts.* **(T) & (M)** **$8-$12***; **(B)** **$65-$100**

XI-45. Stove polish ad. *"X-Ray," mfd. by Lamont, Corliss & Co. Ladies' Home Journal, 10/1904. (Wilhelm Konrad Roentgen discovered X-rays in 1895, and it was so revolutionary an idea that companies grabbed the name even though it had nothing to do with their product. A raisin seeder in the first chapter is called the "X-ray" seeder.) Blacking wasn't just a cosmetic, or a way to hold heat; it protected against rust.*

XI-43. Stove lid lifters. *(A) - (F) are from Excelsior Stove & Mfg. Co., c.1916.* **(A)** *and* **(C)** *are cast iron with a "coppered" finish.* **(B), (D), (E)** *and* **(F)** *are nickeled cast iron.* **(F)** *is a combination lifter and grate shaker.* **(G)** *and* **(H)** *are openwork castings of cast iron, offered in "coppered" finish. Heinz & Munschauer, Buffalo, NY, 1882.* **$8-$12**

XI-46. Stove blacking box. *A homemade wooden box, 4" H x 7" L, with a screw-on cover with handle, and a place for a cake of polish, the brush, and the "mixing plate or dish"* **(E)** *for mixing in the naptha or gasoline. "The cover has an opening* **(C)***, which comes directly over the mixing dish. Across this opening is placed an old knife blade, or a bit of iron filed sharp. The cake of polish is pushed across this blade until a sufficient quantity for use is scraped off, and falls directly into the dish, where it is to be mixed."*

XI-44. Stove lid lifters, etc. (T) *Four tools comprise the entire ad of Troy Nickel Works, Troy, NY, who made the cool coil "Alaska" line. The bent tool at top is a poker. The small hammer is for tacks — note tack-pulling tip to handle. Hardware News, 2/25/1895, but made much earlier.* **(B)** *a coiled-wire lifter — perhaps one of those "infringers" of patents warned against by Troy. It was mfd. by L. M. Devore, Freeport, IL. He calls it a "non-heating wire handle." The Metal Worker, 1892.* **$5-$15**

XI-47. Stove polishes in cans. *"Black Silk" paste "to be mixed with naptha, benzine or gasoline." "Vulcanol," was a cream ready for instant use. These were applied with special blacking brushes, sometimes called daubers, which look rather like the shoe blacking brushes you can still buy. Offered by Excelsior Stove & Mfg. Co., c.1916.*

XI-48. Stove blacking box-holder patents. (T) *indicating the round can with dotted line, pat'd 1/13/1857, and mfd. by J. & W. Cairns, of Jersey City, NJ. It was made, and is cast iron, with three peg feet and a figural dog head on the slider. 9-3/4" L. Pat'd Jan. 13, 1857, by J. &W. Cairns, Jersey City, NJ, pat. #16,374.* **(B)** *Showing spring tension slider, is G. W. Taylor's patent #60962, of 1/1/1867. Springfield, VT. Official Gazette. The dog holder:* **$75-$125**

Stove lid lifter, cast iron with coiled wire loop handle, "Stover," late 19th C. **$7-$13**

Stove lid lifter, crudely finished cast iron, marked on one "Horn" with initials M A, American, 9-3/8" L, turn of century. **$8-$12**

Stove lid lifter, cast iron, in combination with a pot lid lifter at other end, quite simple form, made by an unknown stove company, American, 9" L, 19th C. There were a number of combination stove tools patented, some with various curved projections for lifting pot lids, carrying bail handled pots, pulling tacks. **$10-$18**

Stove lid lifter, coppered cast iron, handle is thick tube with a number of holes cast in it to help disperse heat by helping air circulate around it, fairly straight long shank, "The Zero," sold through Montgomery Ward, late 19th C. **$12-$15**

Stove lid lifter, wrought iron bar, handle split into 6 narrow strips then loosely woven together to form heat dissipating handle, really beautiful, American, 14" L, early 19th C. **$125-$150**

Stove lid & trivet, cast iron in slightly raised design of sort of ruffly edged nautilus shell, on the underside are 2 short peg feet plus the slot where you stick in the lid lifter which forms the third foot, extremely handsome piece of cast iron, marked on back "K O 118," might be Kiechle & Oberdorfer stove company, or even the O. K. Stove Works, 9-1/16" diameter, 19th C. **$25-$30**

Stove ornament or "urn," brass plated cast pot or slush metal, marvelous standing Indian with feather headdress, framing him is sort of wreath of elongated pin oak leaves, stands up on round base, doesn't need to be on a stove for great effect, "Round Oak" stoves, Doe-Wah-Jack, 11" H, very early 20th C. There are several ver-

XI-49. Stove urns, *of stamped metal trimmed with delicate cast handles & finials.* **(T-L)** *available from 5-1/2" to 8-1/2" H; next one 7" H;* **(T-R)** *8-5/8" H and 9-1/4" H;* **(B-L)** *10-5/8" H and 11-3/4" H;* **(M)** *11-1/4" H and 12" H;* **(B-R)** *12" and 13" H. They made more — up to 14-3/4" H. National Stoves, Ranges & Furnaces, of Excelsior Stove & Mfg. Co., Quincy, IL, c.1916. Another crossover — some people buy these as objet d'art, even if they aren't interested in stoves. Most desirable are figural finials, that may bring five times as much as the above Some stove urns actually held water, to help humidify the room.* **$20+**

XI-50. Stovetop and tabletop ovens. (L) *Electric "Stanley Ovenette," Stanley Savage Mfg. Co.,1935 ad.* **(R)** *"Kantburn Kooker," or ovenless baker. Sheet metal. Also mfd by Stanley Savage. 1913.* **$15-$35**

sions of this, some with the Indian figure, some with urns or other shapes surrounded by stylized oak leaf wreath. **$160-$200**

Stove urns, cast iron, footed open top compote-like vessel that fit on hob shelves of some stoves and was filled with water that evaporated, humidifying the dry kitchen. Some were enameled inside; some were nickel-plated or "bronzed." No foundry mark on many of these, although sometimes there's a part number cast in, American, about 5-1/2" to 6-1/2" H, about 6" diameter, mid to late 19th C. **$55-$150**

Stove pipe oven, or drum oven, blued sheet iron, fits into stovepipe and hot air passing by bakes biscuits or cookies, there's a crank in the back to clear the pipe of soot, "Sootless Sue," mfd. by Stratton & Terstegge, Louisville, KY, 1890s-1910s. **$50-$65**

Stove pipe plate, cast iron, "Adams," American, pat'd 1897, 15-3/4" D, rim 6-1/4" W. **$45-$55**

Stove pipe trivet, airy fine cast iron, very openwork design within round frame, of 6 stars, touching at points to each other and frame, one projection, just like a lid lifter, fits into ring that goes around pipe. Ring could hold several. No mark, American, 6-5/8" diameter, late 19th C. **$75-$125**

Stove plate, from early cook stove made up of plates, like a prefab house. Depicts 2 tall men with guns, wearing Liberty caps, and 2 bearded men in frock coats shaking hands, from the Hudson River Valley, NY, 24" H x 25-1/2" L, late 18th or early 19th C. **$1200-$1500+**

Stovetop oven — actually a sort of cooking utensil, shaped like a cake carrier, aluminum with iron bottom & wire rack, with thermometer in lid, "West Bend Ovenette," by West Bend Aluminum Co., West Bend, WI, 10-1/2" diameter, c. 1940s. In NYC, I could bake a pair of sweet potatoes in this much faster than I could clear out the cast iron wares I keep in my oven. A mouse lived in the oven too, sometimes, and I hated to disturb him. **$7-$10**

Stovetop oven, heavy tin, has heat indicator in lid, "Bake Queen," early 20th C. **$7-$15**

Stovetop oven, tin , rack inside, one half of the oven, sides and top, is on a pivot and swings around inside other half, no mark, American, 6-1/2" H x 10-3/4" diameter, 19th C. or very early 20th. **$35-$45**

Stovetop oven, tin with copper bottom, 2-door, "Conservo," Schwarzbaugh Co., Toledo, OH, 20th C. Some people call stovetop ovens "Dutch ovens"; other people call reflector ovens "Dutch ovens." I've reserved the name for the cast iron kettle with a lid with high flanged sides (see Chapter X.) **$18-$25**

XI-51. Stovetop toasters. (T-L) *"Worcester," tin & wire, folds flat, 8-7/8" diameter, Washburn Co., 1936;* **(T-R)** *"Jim's Toaster," convex tin bottom with wire, heat-throwing cone. does 5 slices. Excelsior Stove & Mfg. Co., c.1916;* **(B-L)** *"Kitchen Kumfort," 2-sided, steel, with prferated radiator base, 5" H x 8-1/2" diameter. Washburn Co., 1927;* **(B-R)** *"Brooklyn Bread Toaster," heavy sheet steel, wire supports on 4 sides, 6" H x 8" square, Silver co., Brooklyn, NY, c.1910.* **$3-$5; $7-$10; 5-$7; $10-$15**

Trivet, attaches to back of stove for a place to put a teapot, cast iron, deer design, American, early 20th C.   **$70-$115**

Trivet or hot plate, folding, nickel-plated cast iron, to be wall mounted near stove, marked "A. Cast 14," 8" diameter, 19th C.   **$45-$65**

XI-52. Whatzit that's not a cook stove accessory. *This is here because of slight resemblance to the similarly well-cast, beautifully patinated cast iron accessories that went around a stovepipe. Collector Joel Schiff and I believe that this is probably Korean or Vietnamese (something similar though a single "dish" is called* le hap *in Vietnam). Cast iron, 2 parts: what you see is all one part — the central "bowl" (not a brazier because there's no vent holes in bottom) has five dogwood-like "petals" that tilt slight down toward the cups cast at each tip. The little points have a tiny groove that has to be just decorative because you couldn't pour out of one without spilling the other four. Marks on back of bowl look like numbers in reverse, and read from right to left 073342 or 073345, with a definite Oriental character at each end. Center bowl: 6-5/8" diameter; overall diameter is 19", hole in underneath part is 5-5/8" diameter, and has 5 slots to keep bowl from rotating, when you set this iron "flower" down into it. Dealer Lenny Kislin, Bear, NY, had this at a Pier show in NYC. It's probably 20th C.* **$200+**

NOTE: The following article was first published in "*The Antique Trader Weekly*," February 8, 1984. This is a revised version by its author. It is an excellent article to read to understand the difficulties of stating "market value" for all kinds of kitchen antiques — and most other fields too, although the market for many things would be "thick" as opposed to "thin" for stoves. Clifford Boram and the **Antique Stove Information Clearinghouse** may be reached at 417 North Main St., Monticello, IN 47960, (219) 583-6465. Services include putting buyers and sellers together, finding parts, and consulting on stove restorations. A number of helpful publications — especially catalog reprints — are available at reasonable cost from Mr. Boram. Publications include a **Nationwide List of Antique Stove Restorers**, and a very helpful Association yearbook: **Antique toy stoves and Salesmen's Samples**. Send an SASE for a complete booklist and an introductory sheet on the Association. **SASE** could mean SEND ALWAYS STAMPED ENVELOPES — it's a big part of mail order etiquette.

WHAT IS MY ANTIQUE STOVE WORTH?
by Clifford Boram

"What is my antique stove worth?" If someone answered your question with, "It's worth whatever you can get for it," you'd think he was being evasive or flippant, but let's take a closer look at your question to see if it's asking too much.

The question seems to say, "I'm not familiar with the market for antique stoves, but I take it for granted there's a going price for stoves like mine, regardless of circumstances, if only I can find out what it is." Sorry, but the assumption is not correct. The market for antique stoves is too thin for a consensus on a going price to emerge. In a market this thin, even the experts are at sea. In the course of long experience, they've resigned themselves to the very unhelpful truth that an antique stove isn't "worth": it's only worth something *to somebody*.

Time is one of the circumstances that influence a stove's price. In 1972, before the energy shortage and the suddenly renewed popularity of old stoves, they were being sold for scrap at one cent a pound. Later, their increasing popularity happened to coincide with a period of high inflation when the price of all collectibles was being driven skyward. In 1982, when inflation appeared to be under control and a recession had made many buyers tight-fisted, the price of antique stoves edged back down. Whoever wants the best price must time her sale to the economic cycle.

WIMSW-1. Wood- or coal-burning cook stove. *Example: "Valley Queen." Such a stove can retail for about* **$800** *when fully restored. At a country auction, the rusty, neglected veteran, complete but with some warped and cracked parts, would bring about* **$50**. *(Ed. note: Prices here are subject to all factors mentioned in text of Clifford Boram's article. Any discrepencies between his and my valuations in Chapter XI should be decided in favor of Boram, with reference to actual market conditions in your community.)*

WIMSW-2. Range. *An attractive all-cast-iron range from the 1890s will often be priced at over $2000 in a restorer-dealer's shop. But this 1891 "New Adonis" range, Buckwalter Stove Co., is so spectacular that it deserves a price of* **$3000+**.

Time of year also influences prices. Spring is the worst season to sell your stove; demand is slight. Late August through December are the months of heavy demand. Antique stove restorer-dealers are often overstocked and short of money in July, so they're only buying at bargain prices, if at all.

Time is also a factor in another way: are you in a hurry to sell your stove, or can you afford to wait for the right buyer to come along? If you have to sell the stove by tomorrow, you'll pretty well have to take whatever an antique dealer will give you for it, which is often surprisingly little. A dealer who specializes in dolls and glassware won't offer as much for your stove as one who trades in hard goods. And no dealer's offer will be even close to the price he expects to get by waiting — a year or more, if necessary — for the right buyer.

Place is another circumstance impacting on the price. There's a thin but continuous stream of desirable stoves being shipped to the lucrative Pacific Coast market. Prices in the Midwest are comparatively very affordable. New England is a hotbed of interest in antique stoves. Interest is practically zero in the deep South, and Southerners are taken aback when they hear New England prices. Although New York City is notorious for its high prices on antiques, the demand for antique wood/coal stoves is small, since New Yorkers aren't in a position to store such fuels, the cost of firewood is prohibitive, and not many people have chimnies or flues. In New York City, antique stoves would only be used as decorative pieces, and their bulk and weight keep them from being popular even for that purpose.

Place also matters where restorer-dealers aren't evenly spaced in a region. A restorer-dealer in Rhode Island tells us he never has to pay more that a few hundred dollars for even the most desirable unrestored stove in perfectly good condition. With no other restorer-dealers competing for stoves in his area, he has the market to himself. Farther north in New England, where there's more competition, restorer-dealers have to pay more.

Place also makes a difference when an antique stove is being sold in its own home town. An Indiana stove made by Madison Stove Works is just another out-of-state stove to a buyer in Iowa. But take it back to Madison, Indiana, and the demand will be greater for an object of local interest. The same holds true in much lesser degree for stoves sold in their home state.

Artistic value is an important influence on an antique stove's price. There are plenty of people, especially older and less educated ones, who fail to realize the beauty (if any) in their old stove. Either they sell the stove at a scandalously low price to the first bargain-hunter who happens to come along, or they're flabbergasted to see the high price it brings at auction. By contrast, there are other people, not educated about old stoves, who have heard of an antique stove that brought a premium price and who are quite incensed when someone offers them a realistic price for their very plain and uninteresting one. In general, a stove that's generously

ornamented with raised designs on the castings and has some nickel-plated parts is worth more than a plain one. The more mica windows it has, the better. One or more ceramic tile cameos attached to the castings are another desirable feature. And the less sheet metal, the better. Desirable options like a high warming-closet, water reservoir, and gas side attachment on a wood/coal range also add to the value.

If the stove was originally cast from fresh patterns, the designs will have a crispness that may add a little to the price. Many stoves were cast from old, cracked, and carelessly repaired patterns. The traces of these defects often show on the castings, and may lead a choosy buyer to pass the stove by.

The **age** of a stove influences its price, but it's not completely true that the older a stove is, the greater its value. There was a golden age of stovemaking, say from 1870 to 1910, during which art and technology both reached a peak. An 1820 stove is interesting, but not as efficient or useful as the improved 1890 models. A 1930 stove is just as useful as an 1890, but not so pretty. Most people who admire old stoves want to use them too. If a stove isn't very useful, the people who would want to buy it are fewer, and the price suffers. Hardly anyone is a really serious stove collector: the great bulk of demand comes from admirers who have only a few stoves at most.

The golden age of stoves ended as stoves became smoother, plainer, and easier to wipe clean. In general, stoves with a porcelain finish are more modern, and hence less desirable, than the bare-iron "black" stoves, but some of the earliest porcelainized ranges, still shaped in the old style, are raving beauties that will make your eyes pop. White is the least desirable color for porcelain. Chrome trim, rather than nickel, is the sure mark of a stove too modern to be interesting.

WIMSW-4. Range. *Numerous rivet heads identify steel ranges like this 1899 "Majestic #251." They're exceptionally difficult to restore, but in top condition they can bring over* **$1200** *at the right auction.*

WIMSW-5. Wood-, coal-and-gas combination range. *New England restorer-dealers have lately been getting* **$2000+** *for fine combination ranges like this 1927 "Magee National." In 1984, at the wrong auction in Indiana, an unrestored one in average condition sold for $15 because no-one in the crowd was interested in cooking. The buyer was an elderly woman who needed something to heat her garage.*

WIMSW-3. Range. *This porcelainized cast iron range, a 1922 "Peninsular," is typical of the plain style that became the predominant favorite in the early decades of this century. Restorer-dealers often price these very common ranges well* **below $1000** *in Midwest markets;* **below $1300** *in New England.*

WIMSW-6. Base-burner. *Dealers have been known to ask* **over $5000** *for a fully-restored square base-burner, such as the classic 1904 "Art Andes." The "piggyback" oven, seen at center back, is a desirable option.*

WIMSW-7. Base-burner. *The 1886 Argand round temple-like base-burner with the Roman warrior finial is awesome, though many round base-burners are plainer and too small to be really spectacular. Note the piggyback oven here, too. Value probably* **$5000+**.

WIMSW-8. Base-burner. *The 1931 "Columbian Art" reflector base-burner typifies the twiglight of the base-burner era: the desirable Victorian fancywork has been smoothed away, leaving only a handsome structure that priced even* **below $2000** *would have trouble finding a buyer in some markets.*

WIMSW-9. Heating stoves. *Two extremes of the oak stove desirability spectrum are shown by* **(L)** *E. Bement & Sons' 1892 "Capital Oak" and* **(R)** *Auto Stove Works' 1937 "Sun." The "Capital Oak" is blessed with mica windows, fancy ornamentation, and even a cast iron jacket — a deluxe option preferable to the "Sun's" sheet steel jacket. Larger skirt rails and a pair of nickel-plated wings beside the feed door would also be desirable in Bement's stove, but those features belong to the 1900 to 1930 era. Even though the "Sun" is now over 60 years old, its Art Deco styling denies it any claim to an antique premium above its utility value; it's a modern stove. (Ed. note: Always the optimist, I keep thinking that perhaps there exists a stove of that period which inadvertently rather than deliberately was artfully designed. And I have to say I like those stepped legs.)*

WIMSW-10. Gas ranges. *The recent surge of interest in gas ranges has driven some prices over $3000+ for fully-restored, top-of-the-line models. It should be obvious that the 1921 double-oven Chambers* **(L)** *is infinitely more desirable of the two shown here. The 1928 Tappan* **(R)** *shows the routine antique gas range configuration. A price of $150 for a good unrestored one would be a realistic minimum price paid by a dealer. Even later gas ranges, from the 1930s, with no high structure, are so close in form to modern ones that they have trouble commanding a significant antique premium. See the note in Chapter XI on the "Magic Chef" phenomenon. (L)* **$3000**; *(R)* **$150+**

Rarity of a particular stove may have a modest influence on its price, but perhaps not in the way you'd expect. Rarity may be undesirable to a buyer concerned about the parts situation. A kitchen range by the Majestic Mfg. Co., of St. Louis, MO, may command a premium over an equivalent model by the Cedar Grove Stove Co., of Cedar Grove, WI (a small and obscure manufacturer). Majestic parts are available; Cedar Grove parts would have to be fabricated. Certain common makes, such as Glenwood and Monarch, have a reputation for quality that gives them preference over an unknown make.

The only time rarity helps the price of a stove is when the buyer is looking for a particular type or model. For years, a serious collector has been searching for a hay-burning stove, and has been willing to pay a premium price for it, because it's the only type he doesn't have. The Nott's Patent stove would be another such example. Its historic significance as the first base-burner combines with its rarity to make it prized by collectors.

Some **types** of antique stoves are more in demand than others. Base burners are the most coveted type, because of their beauty. The 1900 to 1915 base burners are most often seen for sale, but once you've met an 1890 square base-burner, you'll know why it commands a higher premium. Wood parlor stoves, cooking stoves, and the upright, steel-jacketed "oak" stoves go begging, and are so common that there's some agreement on a correct price. One restorer-dealer offered to bury another's house in oval air-tights for $25 to $30 apiece.

Material counts too: restorers prefer cast iron stoves, which are bolted together and hence easy to take apart for repair. Steel ranges, on the other hand, are riveted together. If their sheet steel panels are rusted through or otherwise damaged, most buyers just aren't interested.

As for **fuel** types, wood-burning and coal-burning stoves are the usual favorites in demand. A wood and gas combination range often receives a modest premium over a comparable wood-only range because of its greater utility: a wood range makes the kitchen uncomfortably hot in summertime. Gas stoves are less in demand. There has lately been increasing in antique gas ranges, which are at a considerable advantage in metropolitan areas, and which some cooks find more satisfactory than the modern type. Antique gas heater stoves are trailing behind, with only one restorer-dealer, in Texas, specializing in them. The first, tentative demand for antique electric ranges has just begun to appear in a few areas. Significant demand for antique kerosene ranges is limited to Amish country. Gasoline ranges go begging.

WIMSW-12. Cannon or "pot-belly" stoves. *These too are considered of low value to most antique stove collectors. Popularly called "pot-belly" stoves, but termed* **cannon, globe,** *or* **egg stoves** *by the industry, most of these were among a manufacturer's cheaper goods — comparatively plain and simple stoves with no pretensions to the fancy, nickel-plated, mica-windowed parlor stove category that antique enthusiasts admire and pay high prices for today. Plenty of first quality, heavy, and substantial cannons were made too, but they were for depots, schools, offices, and other commercial situations, rather than for homes. Only a few achieved artistic merit, despite the limitations of their type, by adopting parlor stove features. Within the cannon category, it's possible to distinguish differences in desirability, and hence value. Lowest in interest and value is the utterly utilitarian and totally uninteresting little cannon, picture* **#0** *above. Such a stove's value depends entirely on its usefulness, not on the fact that it may be 70 years old. It would generally bring less than* **$40** *at auction, although you might see it priced at more than* **$100** *in a shop.* **#1,** *still low on the scale of desirability, is the sort of cannon most often seen. It has a bit of ornamentation, and isn't unattractive, but it lacks any features that would make it stand out from the crowd.* **#2,** *with its ribbed design and fender ring, begins to be more desirable.* **#3,** *with both foot rails and a fender ring, is a fine, handsome cannon, as cannons go, but would benefit still more from cheery mica windows in its feed door, through which to view the fire.* **#4,** *an artistic jewel among cannons, has mica windows in its feed door and three mica doors just above grate level. Its foot rail, deep ribs, and rich, angular design also contribute to its great desirability. It would be a bargain at* **$300+,** *especially in its larger sizes. Occasionally a sheet metal extension drum or even a cast iron extension containing a self-feeding magazine for coal would be added to the top of a cannon stove.* **#5** *has one [not the ornamental "urn" on top, but the cylindrical part below that], and is thus a* base-burning cannon. *The ornate extension must be considered desirable, although it makes this stove more spectacular and odd than beautifully proportioned.* **$150+**

WIMSW-11. Various low-demand stoves. (B-L) *Large black one is a kerosene range. Top row* **(T-L)** *to* **(T-R)** *are a sheet iron oval "Air-Tight," a kitchen heater, and a cast iron circulator.* **(B-M)** *cast iron laundry stove and* **(B-R)** *gasoline range with its small fuel tank raised above. (Ed. note: Perhaps it's the influence of collectors who want, in effect, whatnot shelves for their collectible utensils, but the kerosene and gasoline stoves sometimes find appreciative buyers — in some regions, by non-stove collectors. Collectors as a rule, don't want them. Many laundry stoves are very handsomely designed, and are considered natural adjuncts to sad-iron collections. Wherever in this book that you see "Ed. note" that means written by and expressing the opinions solely of the author of this book — Linda C. Franklin.)*

In evaluating a stove's **condition**, first see if its defects impair its beauty. Some buyers, who only want a stove for show, will disregard the most shocking internal damage if only the stove looks good. To take account of a stove's condition, run down this checklist:

1) Is there rust? Are the rust pits so deep they'll be a problem to fill? Are any parts rusted through? (Remove ashes and soot to be sure.)
2) Are there any cracks in the cast iron?
3) Have any hooks, tips, etc., been cracked off?
4) Are any parts warped or burnt out?
5) Is the firebrick (if any) intact and sound?
6) If there's a porcelain finish, has it been badly chipped?
7) Are there any bolt holes or mounting tabs that suggest missing accessories or controls?
8) Do all parts fit together nicely? Is anything loose? Do moving parts work smoothly?
9) If repairs have been made, are they neatly and professionally done, or are they crudely finagled with putty and incorrect substitution of materials or parts?
10) Are the correct stove tools (ash shovel, soot rake, poker, lid lifter and grate-shaker handle) included, and are they marked with the stove's name? Is there a teakettle or other hollowware marked with the stovemaker's name? Is there an original manufacturer's catalog or official cookbook showing the stove?
11) Is the stove's history known?

Are you still wondering what your antique stove is "worth"? A better wording for the question would be, "What have stoves like mine been selling for lately . . . around here?" But even this may not get you a really useful answer. The gamut of prices that any particular stove might sell for is just too great. It sounds simplistic, but a buyer who wants that stove has to be there — at an antique shop or an auction.

Normally, the auction price is lower than the retail price. Auctions are where antique dealers get a lot of their wares, and their mark-up from the auction price often approaches 200%. But if collectors attend the auction, they may bid some prices up to the retail level, or even higher. The fact that a certain stove once sold for a certain price at a certain auction doesn't mean that's the price you should charge for yours.

Turning to an antiques price guide for the value of your stove doesn't work because there are too many variables.

Perhaps you'd like to look in an antique stove restorer-dealer's shop to see the prices on restored stoves? You'll find that he's based the prices on a number of factors, including cost of restoration supplies, overhead, hours of labor; utility value of a new stove of equivalent size and type; and the decorative/artistic desirability of the antique. Most of these factors have a going price but the art value doesn't. And that's the one that matters most to a buyer. That's why some types of stoves aren't worth restoring.

A complication arises when a dealer is also a collector. He may like some of his merchandise so much that he really isn't particularly interested in selling it. In such cases, he may put an unreasonably high price on those items. It's his way of saying, "If you're crazy enough to pay me that kind of money for my stove, I'd be crazy not to accept; otherwise it's a keeper." Don't expect to get an exorbitant price for your stove. You'll have to price yours to sell — if you want to sell it.

Perhaps you'd like to ask an antique stove restorer-dealer for an appraisal? Many are willing to appraise a stove by mail from a photo if you tell them its condition in detail. There may be a charge of $10 or more for this service. And how much good will it do you? Thin-market appraisals are properly used for estate tax calculation and insurance inventory valuations. They're *not* properly used to set a price.

So What Shall You Do To Set A Price? The foregoing observations you've just read aren't meant to keep you from examining the market. They're only intended to keep you from being intimidated by it and to help you understand that in a market this thin, *you are the market*, to a surprisingly large degree.

• Start by figuring out what the stove is worth to *you*. That is, how much worse off would you be without it? This will be your minimum price. Be sure to take into account the stove's desirability.

• Next find the right buyer: a high-incentive buyer with enough income to let her pay generously for what she wants. The amount of time and effort you put into finding her has a lot to do with how much you wind up getting.

• Help this buyer decide her maximum price for the stove by asking how much better off she'd be with it.

• Have her write her price on a slip of paper while you write yours on another, and then exchange papers. The correct price is halfway between your minimum and her maximum; that way you'll both be pleased.

This is negotiation, the most satisfactory pricing technique in a thin market. There's no reason why the burden of setting the price should be borne entirely by the seller!

COOKING

XII. POTS, PANS & HOLLOWWARE

This chapter was abbreviated drastically in the last edition. I still have a space constraint, so again you get only the tiniest tidbit.

The decision was made because good resource books already exist for both cast iron cookware and enamelware (usually called "graniteware" after one of the most popular stone-like mottled gray finishes). Enamelware has been collected for decades, and some people have huge, gorgeous collections. The organization for enamelware collectors is the **National Graniteware Society**, POB 10013, Cedar Rapids, IA, 52410.

Cast iron cookware is a well-established, active, competitive "thick" market (the opposite of what stove-meister Clifford Boram calls antique stoves' thin market). See the introduction to the Stove chapter (Chapter XI) for information on the Antique Stove Association, which welcomes members interested also in cast iron cookware.

In a way, there's more variation in value here than in any other field of kitchen collecting. This is because of the comparative rarity and desirability of different sizes. A nine-inch (#9) frying pan might be worth a tenth of a #13; a pot with a certain style of logo on its bottom may be worth four times what the same pot with a different style logo is. If you expect to collect and pay fair, going prices for things you want, join organizations and subscribe to specialist papers. In 1991, I read an ad for **Kitchen Cast Iron Newsletter**, offered by dealer Bill Hahn, Bel Air, MD; I've never

actually seen one. In 1992, a bimonthly newsletter started up. As of 1997 it's still going: **Kettles 'n Cookware**, David G. Smith, editor, Drawer B, Perrysburg, NY 14129. The **Griswold & Cast Iron Cookware Association** is named to feature Griswold, which, for better or worse, is the focus of many collectors of cast iron. Write Joanie Baldini, 654 W. 26th St., Erie, PA 16508.

XII-1. Bain marie set. *Tall, straight-sided pans, long handles, for setting in large pan called a "box" of water. Bain marie means "bath pool." This set, copper with iron handles, from* Mrs. A. B. Marshall's Cookbook, *c.1900.* **$200-$650**

XII-2. Broiler & fry-pan combined. *"Tracy's The Triumph," Maltby, Henley & Co., Rocky Hill, CT. Stamped steel frying pan-lid detaches. Broiler is cast iron with grooved ribs. One of many such openwork stovetop broilers. 1890 ad. Joel Schiff has never found one of these intact. If intact:* **$75-$150**

XII-3. Chafing dish. *Copper, bronze & silver, turned oak handle with applied silver, and round oak plinth. Arts & Crafts period, very desirable. Three beautifully modeled , cast bronze standing hares — punning decoration for "Welsh rarebit" — hold the edge of the frame of the chafing dish pan. Tripartite "burner" underneath. 11" H x 13-1/2" diameter. One of three that have been advertised since the 1980s. Photo courtesy Michael Cable, Woodside Antiques, Greenville, NC.* **$1350-$1800+**

XII-4. Corn popper folk art. *Sheet steel, forged iron handles with strengthening twist, heavy wire baskets. Marked with a tree-oak-leaf stamp & name "W. Irving." Other Irving pieces known include a "Saratoga Jabber," & "Saratoga Frizzler" — for french fries. These two, slightly different corn poppers are for hearth use, or backyard cookouts.* Courtesy Aarne Anton, American Primitive Gallery, NYC. **$1000+**

XII-5. Cruller or potato fryers for deep frying. *Also called* **frying baskets** *or* **double fry pans.** *Heavy wire or perforated metal baskets suspended in various sizes of pans.* **(L)** *pat'd 7/8/1879 and mfd. by Matthai-Ingram, Lalance & Grosjean, etc.* **(R)** *Up to 20" diameter wrought steel, Duparquet, Huot, Moneuse, c.1900-1910.* **$75-$150**

XII-6. Double or farina boilers & valved saucepan. (T) *"French Milk Sauce Pan," with valves in lid.* **(L)** *Farina boiler for custard, corn starch, milk. Note spouting for water in lower part.* **(B)** *"Sauce Pan & Potato Steamer," from* American Home Cook Book, *1854.* **(T-R)** *Milk saucepan, tin with thick, white earthenware inner pan. Still being sold today, in nearly same form, also imported from France. This picture from an 1870s-1880s Walker import catalog.* **$35-$125**

XII-7. Egg poachers. (L) *Tin, 3-cup stack, loose cups in arched iron frame.* American Home Cook Book, *1854.* **(T-R)** *A "Maryland" poacher, with catch at top of handle. Used in a stew pan or skillet, c.1890.* **(R)** *Tin with iron handle, from F. A. Walker 1870s-1880s import catalog.* **$15-$50**

XII-8. Frying pan patent. *Pat'd 9/20/1864, by S. B. Sexton, Baltimore. Cast iron with integral venting tube or flue. Use with a domed lid. Sexton manufactured stoves & hollowwares into the 1930s, so this was probably made.* **$65+**

XII-9. Frying pans. *Cast iron.* **(L)** *"Common spider, ventilated handle," made in 6" to 10" diameters. Henry N. Clark, Boston, 1864.* **(R)** *Idealized drawing of Wapak Ware Indian on skillet bottom. Actually there's a smallish medallion in the center bottom of the skillets, with the Indian head. This Wapak Indian skillet is being reproduced, poorly, today. Value depends on the size, generally $100-$200, except for the 13" diameter one.* **(L)** **$50-$75;** *(R) in size #13:* **$850+**

XII-10. Soapstone griddles. *Iron rims, bail & ear handles. Used for grease-free, even cooking, especially good for pancakes.* **(L)** *"Hodges' Superior," William Hodges & Co., Philadelphia, c.1880s-1920.* **(R)** *From 12" to 16" diameter. Buhl Sons, c.1919 hardware catalog.* **$30-$65**

XII-11. Griswold's "Erie" spider logo. Spider *is another word for frying pan. From an 1890s ad in trade magazine for the founders, Erie Hollow-Ware Works, Griswold Mfg. Co., Erie, PA. The actual "spider" spider has two pouring lips in rim, and a frying-pan shaped spider & web in a round center medallion, with "Erie" and "8" marks.* **$1000+**

XII-15. Pots & pans of blue enameled ware. *"Complete outfit . . . true blue." Sets sized for the range-eye sizes of 7", 8" and 9". Tea kettle, coffee pot, Berlin kettle (bottom right), saucepan, pudding pan (top left), double boiler (bottom left), dish pan (center), soap dish (top right), basting spoon & soup ladle (crossed in front of dish pan), Windsor dipper (in dish pan), two pie plates (for baking pies in). $4.58 for all, Sears Roebuck, 1908. In perfect condition, probably 200 times as much or more.*

XII-12. Brass & enameled kettles & a cast iron bulge pot. (L) *Cast iron bulge pot, with bail, tipping ring handle, 3 short feet. "Favorite Piqua," Favorite Stove & Range, Piqua, OH, 1890 ad.* **(M)** *Spun brass preserve kettle, made in sizes 2 to 14 gallons, iron bail, c.1900. The form, and the method of manufacturing dates to H. W. Hayden's 12/16/1851 brass-spinning patent.* **(R)** *"Sterling" gray enamelware, 10 sizes up to 15" diameter. Pouring lip, tipping handle, falling bail with wood grip. Central Stamping, 1920.* **$40-$125**

XII-16. Potato baking rack. *Stamped tin with cutout & bent-up tabs to stab into potatoes, wire handle, 15-1/4" L, c.1900.* **$35-$60**

XII-13. Saucepans — most are age-deceptive old forms. (L) *Copper or wrought iron, tubular handle, pouring lip. From Harrod's of London catalog, 1895.* **(2)** *Cast iron, tinned or enameled inside, 1 to 20 quarts, Duparquet, Huot & Moneuse, NYC, early 1900s.* **(3)** *"London" shape, iron or copper, no lip. Also Harrod's.* **(R)** *"Sugar boiler," tinned copper, straight sides, William Adams, London, c.1860-61. The same forms lasted many many decades.* **$25-$125**

XII-14. Stock pots with brass spigots near bottom. (L) *"Gotham," seamless agateware (enamelware), stamped tin cover, two lug handles, brass strainer inside, 10-1/4" to 15-1/2" diameter. Central Stamping, 1920.* **(R)** *Choice of copper, brazed iron, or seamless steel, snug lid with its own set of lug handles. English, c.1900, but in style going back at least to 1840s.* **$60-$150+**

XII-17. Soup digesters, *an early form of* **pressure cooker. (L)** *Papin's Digester — "La Marmite" — a cylindrical vessel ["M"] with a firmly screw-clamped lid. "To close the vessel hermetically, sheet lead is placed between the edges of the cover and the vessel. In the cover there is a hole which is closed by a rod kept in place by a cylindrical guide ["u"] which presses against a lever. Pressure may be regulated by means of a weight ["p"], movable on the lever [between "d" and "b"]. The lever is so weighted that when the pressure in the interior is equal to six atmospheres, for example, the valve rises and the vapour escapes. The destruction of the apparatus is thus avoided, and the mechanism has hence received the name of safety valve. The digester is filled about two-thirds with water, and is heated by a large Bunsen burner." Denis Papin, French scientist, invented this digester in 1679 — over three hundred years ago! Picture from D. Atkinson's* Natural Philosophy, *1905. That lead seal! And we worry about cooking in aluminum?* **(T-R)** *This Digester produces "a larger quantity of wholesome and nourishing food" than any other. This was claimed because in it bones and gristle could be softened completely, for eating in a soup. Argghh! Two size ranges given as from 1 to 8 quarts, and from 4 quarts to 8 gallons.* American Home Cook Book, *1854.* **(B-R)** *cast iron, from 2 to 6 gallons, Duparquet, Huot catalog for hoteliers, 1909.* **$30-$400+**

COOKING

XIII. IMPLEMENTS THAT TURN, SPOON, FLIP & DIP

The title of this chapter says it all. These are handheld, non-mechanical cooking tools (correctly called implements, not utensils) of the most basic type. These tools are extensions of the cook's hands that help the cook move food or food particles from one utensil or container to another. Many are variations on a spoon theme (spoon, ladle, dipper); others are forks of various types and sizes; most of the others have blades — narrow or wide, metal or wood — that will slide under cooked food so that it can be turned over or retrieved from kettle, griddle or oven.

There are some things that might have appeared in this chapter but were moved to a chapter more related to function.

Some butter paddles are in the Form, Mold, Shape & Decorate chapter (Chapter IV); skimmers, as well as wire vegetable skimmers or "pea ladles," are all in Chapter III; scoops are in Chapter V.

In the last edition, I wrote that **cake turners** were the most generally popular category within this chapter. This is still true for collectors of twentieth-century kitchenwares. The enormous increase in collectors of metal and wooden Colonial and hearth-cooking implements has meant more interest in ladles and cooking spoons, although I know of no one who collects them as a "category." Collectors of enameled implements are legion; primarily they are material collectors, not form collectors.

"Forged" or **"wrought"?** These terms mean the same thing, although "wrought" is the more common. A blacksmith or whitesmith uses a forge to heat the metal he's going to hammer (or sometimes chisel) into shape. That blacksmith is a "wright" who wroughts. I believe that because "wrought" has been so common, and used by all and sundry to describe all sorts of neo-Colonial hammered iron pieces, that today's dealers are more inclined to use the word "forged," just to set their wares apart. Furthermore, "hand-forged" and "hand-wrought" are used to distinguish generally older pieces from those made with mechanical hammers.

Basting spoon, or baster, heavily tinned iron, deep bowl, possibly mfd. by Lalance & Grosjean, Woodhaven, LI, NY, 19" L, turn of century. **$8-$12**

Basting spoon, speckled black & white agateware, deep bowl, pointed end, American or European, 13" L, turn of century. **$20-$40**

Basting spoon, though rather shallow bowl, cast aluminum, marked "Mueller & Co.," Hagen, Germany, 14" L, turn of century. **$6-$12**

Beefsteak tongs — See tongs

Butter hands — See Chapter IV

Cake server, wide trowel-like tin blade but otherwise with same stamped embossed wire handle as the cake turner or spatula of same make, both adv'g "Rumford, the Wholesome Baking Powder," possibly mfd. by Pilgrim Novelty Co., American, early 20th C. The value spread is wide because some people price it as a "Rumford" collectible, and some as a simple cake server. **$12-$38**

Cake turner (or small peel, perhaps even a dough scraper, though without the latter's customary angled handle). This is whitesmithed iron, nifty large hanging ring, American, prob. PA, 12-1/4" L, late 18th C. **$135-$175**

Whitesmith or Brightsmith Work — The silvery surface comes from being worked, filed, polished, planished and hammered. The hammering and polishing, which gave the surface a very fine texture, is called **planishing**. Sometimes the smith who did this work was known as a whitesmith or brightsmith. According to Carl W. Drepperd, in *Primer of American Antiques*, originally a whitesmith was the same as a **whitster**, who was a "Planisher, one who hammered iron white," and only later did a "whitesmith" come to mean a worker in tin, tin plate, or any other white metal.

XIII-1. Asparagus holder. *"Champion" wire tongs, 3-1/2", 4-1/2", 5-1/2" diameter. Asparagus actually cooked in holder. Mfd. by A. H. Brinkmann & Co., Baltimore, MD. House Furnishing Review, 1903. SEE Chapter V for Asparagus bunchers.* **$15-$20**

XIII-2. Basting spoons. *Distinguishing feature of most is a rather shallow bowl with horizontal long handle.* **(T)** *Stamped steel with "threaded" handle — a ridge stamped in lengthwise for strength. 10", 12", 14" or 16" L, Central Stamping Co., 1920.* **(B)** *Crossed "French Basting spoons are deep and with side handles," American Home Cook Book, 1854. Probably iron. Note shaped handles, and hooked ends.* **$8-$20**

White Sediment on Iron — Every once in a while I come upon an old iron piece with this white substance, which really isn't powdery. I wonder if it's some sort of flux used when working the iron, and if its presence indicates a piece was never finished and therefore never used? Anyone know? Here's a possibility, just found in a Southern recipe book:

To Prevent Rust in Iron Utensils. — "To prevent their rusting when not in use: Mix half a pound of lime with a quart of warm water; add sweet oil until it looks like cream. Rub the article with this; when dry, wrap in paper, or put over another coat." Mrs. A. P. Hill, *Mrs. Hill's New Family Receipt Book,* NY: 1870.

Cake turner, polished, filed, shaped & decorated forged iron, handle has round hanging loop, copper inlaid along handle, small blade with very rounded shoulders & tips, no cutouts, marked "B. H" with date, PA. Blade is 4" x 3-7/8", with 12" L handle, dated "1821." Robacker May 1989 price: $850.   **$800+**

Cake turner, or <u>keyhole spatula</u>, blade of whitesmithed iron is shaped like a fat large keyhole, there's a cutout cross in the "ball" of blade, American (?), 8-3/4" L, very early 19th C.   **$75-$125**

Cake turner, keyhole spatula, twisted forged iron handle, all filed & polished whitesmith's work, pretty silvery appearance, American, 11" L, very early 19th C. This keyhole shape, sometimes called a <u>thistle shape </u>(with bulbous part down), was used in much later cake turners too — especially in enamelware.   **$100-$150**

XIII-3. Cake turners or short peels. *All are forged iron.* **(L)** *Heart-shaped shoulders, turned wood handle possibly newer than others. 16" L. Mid 19th C. Collection of Meryle Evans.* **(M)** *and* **(R)** *have hooked handles. One with spatulate blade, 17-1/2" L, other with cut & filed decorated handle, including abstract heart or arrowpoint at center. Oblong blade unusual. 22" L. Both late 18th, early 19th C. Photo courtesy Litchfield Auction Gallery, Litchfield, CT. Ex-Harold Corbin Collection, auctioned 1/1/1989, for $425.* **$125-$150; $175+; $350+**

Cake turner, forged iron, smallish flat blade with marvelous wing-like shoulders, long shaft that is straight for first few inches, then twisted with big-fat & little-tight twists, rattail loop at end, American, 17" L, 18th C.   **$275-$400**

Shrove Tuesday Flapjacks & Pancake Bells — William Hone's 1845 edition of *The Year Book,* for Feb. 3, Shrovetide, relays a quote from "Taylor, the water-poet, in his works, 1630" — "Shrove Tuesday, at whose entrance in the morning all the whole kingdom is inquiet; but by that time the clocke strikes eleven, which .. is commonly before nine, then there is a bell rung, cal'd the pancake bell, the sound whereof makes thousands of people distracted, and forgetful either of manners or humanitie; then there is a thing called wheaten floure, which the cookes do mingle with water, egges, spice, and other tragicall, magicall inchantments; and then they put it, by little and little, into a frying-pan of boiling suet, where it makes a confused dismall hissing, untill at last, by the skill of the cooke, it is transformed into the forme of a flip-jack call'd a pancake, which ominous incantation the ignorant people doe devoure very greedily."

XIII-4. Cake turner, *often also called a* **spatula**. *Wrought iron, rat-tail handle, twisted shank for strength, 8" L. American, late 18th C. Picture courtesy of Robert W. Skinner Inc., Auctioneers, Bolton, MA.* **$90-$150**

XIII-5. Cake turners & egg slices. *Crossed implements at top, by blade position:* **(T-L)** *All metal egg slice, 17" L, c.1904-1910;* **(T-R)** *Wood handled one at is 21" L, a "hotel" cake turner. c.1901-10;* **(B)** *egg slice, blade 4-3/4" x 4-1/8" with perforated blade, c.1904-10.* **(M-L)** *pear-shaped nickel-plated blade is the "Kitchen Kumfort Trowel," with rubberoid tiller handle. "The old fashioned turner was originally invented to lift and turn cakes on an old fashioned flat griddle. Now as the number of articles which are either fried or cooked in hot fat, such as croquettes, meat balls, omelets, etc., have increased, the cake turner has been used to handle such articles simply because there was no other utensil at hand. Experiments with a turner having the handle elevated about two inches from the blade resulted in [this] lifter." Lasher Mfg. Co., Davenport, IA, 1911 ad.* **(M-R)** *is the "Jewel," with "flat serpentine handle that gives a good grip." Steel, Arcade Mfg. Co.,1905.* **$10-$25**

Cake turner, forged iron, whitesmithed, polished & filed yet dark in color, shapely strong handle, end has teardrop hanging hole, shovel-shaped rectangular blade with rounded shoulders, slightly flared sides, bold cutouts of rather large diamond near center with four round holes near each corner, signed "E. P. Sebastian" on handle. Edward Sebastian was noted for openwork "spatulas." Host, Berks County, PA, blade 6-1/4" x 5-1/2" with 14-1/2" L handle, c. 1850s-1880s. Ex-Robacker collection, auctioned May 1989, for $1400 — in good part because of the Robacker provenance. **$500+**

Cake turner, forged iron with wide flat blade, relatively short handle, American (?), 13-1/2" L, mid 19th C. **$75-$125**

Cake turner, forged & polished iron, long handle with small heart cutout in end near rattail loop, American; PA (?), 18-1/2" L, early 19th C. **$150-$250**

Cake turner or peel (for removing bread from oven), nicely shaped wrought iron blade with heart-top (or shoulder-padded) shoulders, turned wood handle, shortish shaft, American, 12" L, 19th C. **$125-$165**

Cake turner or peel, very small round disc blade, interesting long handle with short chevron and bull's eye hole, marked "Levi Lewis," prob. PA, 14-3/4" L, 19th C. **$135-$175**

Cake turner or peel, whitesmithed forged iron, well-formed shoulder, initials "A. W." inlaid in brass on handle. From near Stroudsburgh, PA, 13-13/16" L, early 1800s. Marked pieces very desirable. **$200-$400**

Cake turner, or perhaps peel, forged iron, whitesmithed & polished, long handle with broad end & rattail loop, decorated with cut lines & bull's eyes. Round blade has cutout 6-point star or petaled flower, 3/4" wide border decorated with 6 bull's eyes, American, 20-1/2" L overall, blade is 4" diameter, 18th C. Good size & decoration. **$300-$400+**

Fake Brass Inlays — Jeannette Lasansky (Oral Traditions Project, Court House, Lewisburg, PA 17837) is author of several meticulously researched books on old Pennsylvania crafts. In "Collectors' notes," Nov. 1980 *The Magazine ANTIQUES,* she shared her discovery of a number of fake brass inlays found in a disparate group of eighteenth- or early nineteenth-century forged iron implements from different collections. The faking was done at some point after 1860 (determined from fluorescence analysis of the brass involved), and probably in the twentieth century. Pieces included cake turners, flesh forks, tasters, ladles and a skimmer, all common forms, with stylistic differences in the design of the forged iron. The significant thing, what brought Lasansky's attention to the fraud, is that **"On all the pieces the brass-inlay technique is identical and the motifs, repetitive."** The three types of decoration done by the faker are (1) narrow bands with minimal engraved design; (2) wide bands with engraved initials and/or dates (Lasansky says they are all from 1823 through 1829); and (3) wide bands or inset "lozenges" with images (hearts, eagles or tulips) engraved on them. From the pictures shown in that article, of pieces in the Titus Geesey Collection at the Philadelphia Museum, and the Abby Aldrich Rockefeller Folk Art Center, Williamsburg, VA, it seems that without Lasansky's eagle eye, and the sharing of artifacts made possible by exhibits, photographs and books, we would never have known. The engraving is of the bright cut variety from the early nineteenth century, and the style of letters, numbers and pictures mimics the eagerness and slight primitiveness of examples of authentic period engraving. It's scary. I've not seen an update, though Lasansky asked collectors and curators to closely examine their collections. One thing apparent from the pictures is that the pitting, scarring and surface distressing of the polished iron of the handles of the various implements is in sharp contrast to the virtually untouched surfaces of the brass inlays. I must stress that no item from the Earl F. & Ada F. Robacker Collection was said to have a fake twentieth-century inlay, and the sharing of Lasansky's observations is not meant to impinge on the value or authenticity of any inlaid piece auctioned by T. Glenn Horst.

• • • •

1875 "Tin Weddings. — Passing an extensive house furnishing store twice daily, we most always give a glance at the show-window. Some months ago we saw a most beautifully fashioned shoe on exhibition, which appeared to be made of the finest planished tin. We wondered what it could be for; it was too large for a smoker's ash-receiver, and could hardly be an article for kitchen or table use; several days after, and before we had time to step in and solve the matter, there appeared by the side of the shoe an elegant fan of the same material, at least so far as fine workmanship could make a tin fan elegant; this added to the mystery, but in a day or two all was made plain by the displaying of a card reading 'Articles for Tin Weddings.' All that we know of 'tin weddings' is that the tenth anniversary of marriage is by some people celebrated, as a sort of burlesque upon silver weddings, by a party, at which the guests made presents of tinware. The presents were formerly of useful articles, but now it seems that the burlesque itself is travestied, and much ingenuity is expended in making articles for tin weddings which can be of no possible use to those who receive them. Quite a large number of these articles are now imported from France; two of these have already been named above; besides these we found on inquiry there were ridiculous bouquets of tin flowers; preposterous necklaces, and other jewelry of skillful workmanship, but all of the same cheap material; a tin saw and other tools for a mechanic; instruments supposed to be emblematic of the medical profession, and other curious, expensive, and equally useless articles are offered. Now we believe in innocent amusement, and if any fun can be had out of a tin wedding — if the parties most concerned are so disposed — so be it, but there should be some sense even to our nonsense, and we must say that we regard this matter of tin shoes, tin bouquets, and the like, as carrying the matter just a little too far."

— Anonymous editor, *American Agriculturist,* July 1875, NYC, where this tinwares store must have been. The editor would be astounded to see with what high regard collectors today hold these "nonsensical" tin objects.

XIII-6. Homemade cake turner. *My personal favorite. Made from flattened & trimmed tin can, whittled stick, wire & a nail, 16" L. Found by Oregon collector Jim Holroyd, at "a camp on the Skyline Trail in the Oregon Cascades, c.1965."* **$10-$18**

Cake turner, forged & polished iron, unusual sideways rectangular blade almost size of playing card, with rounded corners, thin graceful forged iron handle, with small hanging loop, fine inlaid brass floral designs. PA. Blade 4" x 5-1/4" W, with 16" L handle, dated "1854." Price achieved at May 1989 Horst auction of Robacker collection: **$325**

Cake turner, handsomely formed tin, with tiny pie-wedge cutouts, stylized heart & bird decorations, ribbed cylindrical handle with little strap hanger, possibly made as a tenth wedding anniversary gift, found in Bradford or Sullivan County, NY, 13-3/8" L x 2-1/2" W at widest point, c.1860s to 1880s. **$165-$200**

Cake turner, probably a tenth anniversary piece, not for use. Described by the Robackers as a "Pie peel," but the blade isn't large enough. The blade is bent to create angled-up shoulder, & is crudely soldered to long dented cylindrical handle, the only redeeming feature being the punctured tin decoration (& that done with no finesse) comprised of a squat, typically Pennsylvania German heart, with the initials "L" and "S" inside, the heart surmounted by a wavy line indicating a leaf scroll with a small flower in the center, PA, 21-5/8" L, with blade about 6-1/4" L x 4-1/2" W, late 19th C. Robacker May 1989 price is way over the money in my opinion. **$450**

Cake turner, homemade, a flattened tin can side, carefully cutout in a truncated wedge shape, front edge bent, nailed to a peeled & partly whittled stick, extremely well-worn, great patina on handle, wire wrapped around handle as a sort of ferrule, Oregon, 16" L, found around 1965, dates poss. to c.1940s. Found by collector James R. Holroyd of Oregon, discarded at a camp on the Skyline Trail in the Oregon Cascades. **$10-$20**

Cake turner, also called a **kitchen trowel** by manufacturer, ovoid unperforated blade, nickel plated steel, tiller handle "Elevated about two inches from the blade," in trowel fashion, rubberoid handle grip, "Kitchen Kumfort Trowel," mfd. by Lasher Mfg. Co., Davenport, IA, about 10" L, patent applied for by 1911. **$10-$15**

Cake turner, wrought iron handle with brass blade, perforations in blade form the initials "L. H.," which were probably those of the owner (or recipient of this handmade gift). American, 9-7/8" L, 1850s to 1870s. **$175-$225**

Cake turner, brass with forged iron handle, "F. B. S.," Canton, OH, 14-1/2" L, pat'd 1886. The style of these looks much older, and there are LOTS of them around, accounting for wide value range, because they look much older, & some people may not be aware of supply. **$50-$150**

XIII-7. Cake turners. *Both cast aluminum.* **(T)** *marked "Royal Bra—", probably Royal Brand, and "Made in Germany." 12-1/2" L, c.1910. (B) Angled straight-front blade. Word "Aluminum" appears in hammer-shaped mark on back, also "D.R.G.M. Germany." 10-1/4" L, c.1910s.* **$12-$20**

"Cake turners" or "Spatulas." Cake turners are often called spatulas, although this is technically incorrect, or at least debatable. On the one hand, when you talk about the shape of some fingertips, or certain petals or leaves, they are *spatulate* if they broaden at the tip in a spade-like way. That is the classic cake turner blade shape. A [pan]cake turner has a blade which is almost always longer than it is wide, about 5" L x 4" or 4-1/2" W, and the blade is also almost always slotted or perforated with a number of holes. A cake turner is used to flip food like flapjacks (flatjacks, pancakes, hotcakes), fried eggs, grilled cheese sandwiches, crab cakes or banana fritters. Many people specialize in the numerous cake turners of the A & J Co, later Edward Katzinger Co. (now EKCO), or of Androck. For the most part, a spatula is like a wide, flexible or limber dinner knife blade only bigger — about 1-1/4" W. The long slender blade is rounded on the end end, and the most common kitchen uses are icing cakes or scraping work surfaces or grills or cleaning the curved insides of bowls. Some spatulas are also perforated, but longness and flexibility are the basic attributes. What we might take as our final arbiters, the manufacturers' catalogs of the nineteenth and twentieth century, are divided on terminology.

Cake turner, tinned sheet metal, wire handle stamped flat with embossed design and "Rumford," blade simple with small heart-shaped hole near the riveted joint of handle & blade, "Rumford Baking Powder" adv'g piece, but poss. mfd. by Pilgrim Novelty Co., American, 10-3/4" L x 2-3/4" W, c. 1914 (?). You find this same turner without an adv'g message too, but worth less that way. **$18-$25**

Cake turner, enameled sheet iron, white with pale blue pattern of "Chicken wire," tubular handle, hanging ring, blade spatulate in shape with rounded "shoulder," pattern of perforations is two double rows of stylized wheat berries along outside blade edges, American (?) or European, 13" L, turn of century. This came in various color combinations. The "Chicken wire" effect adds a lot to value here; one with black or dark red handle and plain white blade would be a fourth or third as much. **$95-$125**

Cake turner, nickel-plated steel with wire shank, blue & ivory painted wood handle, perforation pattern is center straight line of holes flanked by an outward curving line of holes on each side, "Blutip," A & J, Binghamton, NY, 14-1/4" L, c. 1940s. Price reflects poor condition of paint. The two-tone ones, especially with ivory, seemed to flake off in big chips more readily than the red or green finishes. Even in good condition these don't bring much. **$5-$8**

Cake turner, oblong tin blade, sharp front corners, rounded corners at heel of blade, 2 elongated corrugations lengthwise on blade — according to the ads, "So the cake cannot slide sidewise." Paint-enameled turned wood handle, mfd. by Handy Things Co., Ludington, MI, blade is 3-1/2" L x 2-7/8" W, overall length 11-1/4", c.1904. Remember, "Cake" refers to pancake, not layer cake. **$7-$12**

Cake turner, perforated tinned steel & wire, the heavy wire handle wiggles & snakes off at the tip, an elegant solution to heat dispersal problem. "A good cook will quickly see the merits of this cake turner. The grease passes through it instantly and leaves the food light and tempting. The handle gives a firm, cool grip and is easily cleaned," say the ads of the time. mfd. by Arcade Mfg. Co. (famed toy mfrs), Freeport, IL, 14-3/4" L, c. 1905. **$15-$25**

Cake turner, stamped sheet metal, handle riveted to simple blade round shoulder, no finesse to design, but it wouldn't look bad in that Bouquet-of-turner-tulips stuck handle down in a crock, no mark, American, 13" L, c.1890 to 1900. **$6-$8**

Cake turner, tin, adv'g "Quick Meal Ranges," for Ringen Stove Co., but prob. not made by them, early 20th C. **$15-$20**

Cake turner, tin & green finished wood, blade is stamped with ridges to add rigidity and is perforated with highly decorative pattern of holes that form a heart reminiscent of Pennsylvania German designs, American, 11-3/4" L, 20th C. **$8-$15**

Cake turner, tin with knobby turned wooden handle, baked on white enamel finish with 1/6th of handle at end dipped in rich medium blue, wire shank, shapely shouldered blade with 3 graduated rows of perforations, "Blutip," A & J Mfg. Co. (Div. of Edward Katzinger), Binghamton, NY, 13-1/4" L, c.1930. **$12-$15**

Cake turner, tin with wire, has 3 long oblong blades with large holes, they are stacked 1 2 3, but when fanned out when you pull the thumb release they almost triple the width of the useable blade. This way you can adjust the width to suit the griddle or frying pan you are using as well as the pancake or omelet, marked "Coradon," (the one in Jane Celehar's book was made by Gadget Mfg. Co.), NYC, 12-1/2" L, blade: 6-1/2" L x 2-5/8" W, spreads to 8-1/2" W, pat'd Dec. 8, 1936, by Minnie Greene & Lois Udey. **Flap the Jack, Mac, Lookalike alarm** — Lehman's Hardware & Appliances, Kidron, OH, offer a very similar one with stainless steel blades in their "Non-Electric Good Neighbor Amish Country" catalog. Another mechanical type has a trigger that you pull that flips the blade; talk about a "lazy elbow" (as the nickname goes for kettle tilters from hearth cooking days)! **$12-$18**

Cake turner, tinned blade, embossed handle, "Aurora Ice Cream," early 20th C. **$12-$15+**

Cake turner, tinned iron, adv'g "Ira Egger General Merchandise," American, early 20th C. **$7-$12**

Cake turner, tinned iron with bottle opener handle, adv'g "Clyde Milling Co.," Clyde, KS, early 20th C. **$7-$12**

Cake turner, tinned iron with bottle opener handle, adv'g "Farmers Mercantile Co.," pat'd Nov. 24, 1914. **$7-$12**

Cake turner, tinned metal, heart-shaped blade with very small heart cutout, bottle opener at other end of handle, looks rather like a Rumford turner, adv'g "Metropolitan Furniture Co. — A Good Place to Trade," American, pat'd Nov. 24, 1914. **$22-$32**

Cake turner, tinned steel blade in pear shape with straight front edge, slightly elevated tiller handle with turned wood grip, Cronk & Carrier Mfg. Co., Geneva, OH, 12-1/2" L x 4" W, c.1920s. **$15-$20**

XIII-8. Cake turners. *All nickel-plated steel, with turned wood handles with "three coats of highest grade enamel" in 2-tone Blutip colors. All made with or without holes.* **(L)** *perforated blade with "shoulders," 13" L.* **(M)** *Plain small one is 11-1/4" L.* **(R)** *Long perforated "kitchen tool" with tiller handle, 11" L overall. All "Ekco," Edward Katzinger Co., Chicago, in "A & J Blutip Kitchen Tools" catalog, 1930. A & J was division of Ekco.* **$6-$15**

Cake turner, tinned steel blade, wire shank, turned wooden handle. The blade is unperforated & if the turner is held upright, blade up, it looks like an abstract tulip. In fact, if someone could come up with an unobtrusive base, which would hold unaltered cake turners much as a flower frog holds roses and carnations, you could have a very wonderful bouquet of cake turners. I'm afraid the base would either obscure the handles, however, or the handles would have to be drilled. Hmmm . . . Aarne Anton, wanna try? Marked "WB/W," I believe this is probably Waterbury Button & Mfg. Co., Waterbury, CT, 14-1/4" L, c.1910-1930. **$10-$15**

Cake turner, tinned steel blade with as many perforations as a sieve, nicely turned wooden handle left natural, American, 15" L, c.1910. **$10-$15**

Cake turner, tinned steel blade with rounded "Fins" at the back end, 3 rows of perforated holes, center one straight, side ones curved out, stamped "Stainless" (which it wasn't), so they crossed that out & stamped it "Rustless" (which it wasn't either), A & J Mfg. Co., Binghamton, NY, 13-1/4" L x 3-1/2" W, c.1935. Some of value here is in the social history aspect of the stamped marks. **$12-$20**

Cake turner, tinned steel long oblong blade with 2 sizes of perforations forming diamond pattern, nice shoulder to blade, turned wooden handle, American, 12" L x 3" W, c.1920s. **$8-$15**

Brand names — The reality of collecting is that people still pay more for "Brand names" than unmarked pieces, but I firmly believe that in the long run this is a less successful way to collect. Remember that <u>unknown art always has to be discovered</u>.

Cake turner, tinned steel with wood handle, odd extremely rigid near-round blade with truncated end & no perforations, American, 14-1/4" L x 4" W, c.1910s. **$7-$15**

Cake turner, cast aluminum, angled slots in blade, 4 holes at front edge, marked with word "Aluminum" inside a hammer outline, also "D. R. G. M." (for *Deutsches Reichs-Gebrauchsmuster*), German, 10-1/4" L, early 20th C., prior to 1918, when the mark "D. R. G. M." was superceded. **$15-$20**

Cake turner, cast aluminum with sort of rayed design or perforations, hanging hole in handle, "Royal Brand," German, 12-1/2" L x 3-3/4" W, I used to think these were c.1930s; now I think c.1910s. **$15-$20**

Country of Origin Marks — Part of the widely debated <u>McKinley Tariff Act</u>, passed by the 51st Congress on October 1, 1890, is of interest to all collectors. From Chapter 1244, Section 6: "That on and after the first day of March, 1891, <u>all articles of foreign manufacture, such as are usually or ordinarily marked, stamped, branded, or labeled, and all packages containing such or other imported articles, shall, respectively, be plainly marked, stamped, branded, or labeled in legible English words, so as to indicate the country of their origin</u>; and unless so marked, stamped, branded, or labeled they shall not be admitted to entry." The name "England" often appeared stamped on export china after 1875, and many English potteries marked "England" after 1880, but *all* did after 1891.

Cake turner, shapely tinned steel blade with 3 parallel rows of large to small graduated perforations, wooden handle, A & J, Binghamton, NY, 13-1/4" L, 1930s. These A & J cake turners came in a variety of sizes and patterns of perforations. Condition of the paint on the wooden handle & size are important to value. **$7-$15**

Cake turner, tinned steel, wire, wood, blade has pretty design of radiating petal-like lines and small holes, shapely shoulder to blade, marked "WB/W," probably Waterbury Button & Mfg. Co., 12-1/2" L x 3-1/8" W, c.1915-1920. **$12-$15**

Cooking implements, set of 4 in original box, sheet metal with green wooden handles, "Samson Cutlery," Rochester, NY, 20th C. See also implement racks in Chapter VII. **$20-$35+**

Cooking set, handcrafted, a cleaver, large spoon, carving knife & sharpening or butcher's steel, flesh fork, handles are assembled bands of ivory, pipestone & onyx. American, mid 20th C. **$100-$150**

Cooking spoon, metal, adv'g "Monarch Stoves," turn of century. **$20-$25**

Corn cob handles, cast sterling silver, in shape of husked cobs, set of 12, 2-3/4" L, late 19th or early 20th C. Part of the value of any sterling piece is its intrinsic silver bullion value, so it's hard to judge. People have been making these for a long time, but I'm not sure many people ever use them. You have to handle that hot cob to push the handles in, and you might as well go on and lift the cob to your mouth by then. **$45-$85**

Cream dipper or ladle — See dipper or ladle for cream

Dipper, brass bowl with forged iron handle hooked on end, American (?), 15-1/4" L, late 18th or early 19th C. **$200-$235**

Dipper, agateware, mottled gray, "Windsor" type, large straight-sided & flat-bottomed bowl with slightly angled, turned wood handle painted black, four sizes, from 4-1/4" diameter x 3" deep, to 6-3/4" diameter x 3-3/4" deep, handles 5" L, American, 1880s-1890s. **$45-$75**

Dipper, brown enameled ware, "Windsor" style, flat bottom bowl, flat handle, 18" L handle, late 19th C. **$35-$60**

XIII-9. Bon Bon dips or dipping forks, *tinned iron or brass wire, to lift candies out of coating. Plain ones from candymakers' supplier S. Joseph Co. catalog, c.1927. Fancy ones from T. Mills, Philadelphia, 1930. Almost identical ones date well back into 19th C.* **$4-$20**

XIII-10. Candy egg dipper, *or* **egg hook,** *for coating cream eggs with chocolate. Heavy tinned wire, with hanging loop (to hang on rack). "Small" to accommodate 6 eggs, for 1¢, 2¢, 3¢ or 5¢ eggs; and "large" for 4 eggs of 10¢ size. Mills, 1930.* **$8-$12**

Corny Advice — *The American Agriculturist,* Sept. 1846, published a tip on **"How to Boil Green Corn,"** with advice on eating it too. "The proper state in which to eat green corn, is, at the time that the milk flows upon pressing the kernels with the thumb nail. It is best when boiled in the ear with the husks on, the latter of which should be stripped off when brought to the table. The ears should then be covered with butter, with a little salt added, and the grains eaten off the cob. Over-refined people think this vulgar, and shave them off, but in so doing they lose much of their sweetness."

Dipper, gray graniteware, bent-tip flat handle, deep but small bowl, a few dings & chips, 12" L overall, turn of century. **$10-$20**

Dipper, gray graniteware, "Windsor" style, rolled rim, long tubular handle riveted on at almost 45 angle. A "Windsor" has a flat bottom, and somewhat slanted sides, so that the dipper almost looks like a very small if long-handled saucepan. American (?), 13" L overall, turn of century. **$35-$55**

Dipper, robin's-egg-blue enamelware with black trim, black enameled tubular handle, probably Lisk Mfg. Co., Canandaigua, NY, 14" L, 20th C. **$20-$35**

Dipper, speckled burgundy enamel, 18" L, early 1900s. **$95-$125**

Dipper, mottled brown & white enamelware, a few slight dings, possibly "Onyx," Columbian Enameling & Stamping Co., or European, 5-1/4" diameter bowl, handle 14-1/2" L, late 19th C. **$22-$35**

Dipper, often called a <u>cocoa dipper</u>, characterized by round cup/bowl, small bowl relative to overall size, and a rim that is very slightly smaller than the widest part of the bowl. Enameled gray & black mottled outside of round-bottom bowl, black rim, black inside bowl, turned wood handle painted black, set into socket fixed at about 40 to bowl, prob. American, cup 3-5/8" diameter, 11" L overall, late 19th C. to turn of century. **$125-$175+**

Dipper, forged iron, stamped on handle is maker's name, "H. W. Weaver," 23-1/2" L, early 19th C. **$75-$100**

Dipper, forged iron, huge round-bottom bowl with 2 qt. capacity, long handle with hooked end, American, 24" L handle, early to mid 19th C. **$75-$130**

Dipper, forged iron with rattail handle, American, 15" L, early 19th C. **$45-$60**

Dipper, carved ash burl, beautiful patina, turned handle, American, bowl is 3" deep x 6" x 5-1/2", slightly warped oval, unusual 13" L handle, early 19th or late 18th C. **$180-$250**

Dipper, coconut, small, highly polished after stripped of husk, turned wood long handle set at about 30 angle, pointed tip, pewter ferrule, marked "Cleveland Brothers, Providence, RI," mid 19th C. **$250-$300**

XIII-11. Cheese scoop. *Steel mechanical scoop, bone or ivory handle (shaped like table knife handle). Tiny rivet has cut decorations & facets. Thumbscrew (small piece where arrow points) holds follower on track inside spade-like scoop and can be turned to lift follower for thorough cleaning. 10-1/16" L overall; scoop 1-5/8" L x 1-1/4" W. English, 19th C. Courtesy Louise Bibb, of Virginia.* **$40-$55**

Dippers were often made of "ready-made" raw materials like burls, coconuts and gourds. A very nice collection could be made of them. Such **dried gourd dippers** were made by many so-called "Native" cultures as well as by country North Americans. An old gourd dipper from Mexico or Central America might be expected to have some decoration carved into its surface, or a more colorful dyed wool cord, or perhaps the gourd itself might be painted on the outside. Now that I need the information, I can't find it, but I believe I read somewhere years ago that the growing of such gourds for making dippers & scoops (as well as birdhouses) once was a cottage industry in certain parts of the country. If you're interested in growing gourds to make dippers, birdhouses, bowls, rattles, whatever, the organization for you is the **American Gourd Society**, Box 274, Mount Gilead, OH 43338.

• • • •

Out Of Your Gourd — W. Scott Boyce's *Economic and Social History of Chowan County, North Carolina, 1880-1915,* published in NYC by Columbia University, 1917, says about the 1880s country person: "They improvised by far the greater number of their own dippers, occasionally from conch shells, more frequently from cocoanut hulls, but largely from the common gourd, which was cut, scraped, boiled, scrubbed, and sunned to remove the 'gourdy' taste and smell — said taste and smell, however, in spite of all these efforts, remaining to a more or less degree just as long as there was a piece of the gourd." [p.109].

XIII-12. Dipper. *Dried gourd. Late 19th C. Picture courtesy of the National Museum of American History, Smithsonian Institution. Value for similar pieces:* **$50-$90**

XIII-13. Dippers. (L) *Pieced tin, both with flat bottoms and braced tubular handles. Top has long handle with shovel-like half-loop handle. 1-3/8 quart capacity; bowl 3-5/8" H x 6-1/2" diameter. Central Stamping co., 1920.* **(R)** *Bent maple with turned maple handle & pine bottom. Copper tacks hold lap joint together. Shaker, mid to third quarter19th C.* **$15-$30; $250+**

Dipper, dried gourd of ornamental variety, long skinny neck, large hole cut out of main body, it's scraped clean & then dried, old cord through hole at tip of natural handle, American, 10" L, 19th C. The price for this one is in the gorgeous patina: **$80-$100**

Dipper, dried gourd, polished, ornamental variety, big bowl, curved neck with enough hook to end to hang over edge of bucket, American, 8" L x 3" deep, 19th C. **$65-$90**

Dipper, dried gourd, straight-necked ornamental variety, American, 4-7/8" deep x 9-1/2" L, 19th C. **$40-$65**

Dipper, tin, of flat-bottomed type called a cup dipper, smaller than a "Windsor," stamped tin, slightly bulging sides, rolled rim, long forged iron handle with hanging hole, set about 45 angle to edge of cup. This kind of dipper could be filled, then set down without spilling, with the handle propped against something. Matthai-Ingram Co., 5-1/8" diameter cup, 14" L handle, late 19th C. **$15-$25**

Dipper, pieced tin with tubular handle set at angle, American, 9-1/2" L, 2-cup capacity, 19th C. **$30-$38**

Dipper, tin, unusual for the stamped message: "Stolen from State Bank," Springfield, MN, looks turn of century. **$18-$25**

Dipper, tin, flat tinned iron handle with hook at end, American, 14" L with 5" diameter bowl, 19th C. **$22-$25**

Dipper, tin, long handled, tubular handle, with half-moon mount, blue paper label with black printing states "Made of Best Quality Charcoal-Plate, Warranted not to rust," "Reed One-Pint," mfd. solely by the Reed Mfg. Co., Newark, New York (not NJ), 14" L, dipper is 5-1/8" W x 3-1/4" H, pat'd Nov. 17, 1896. **$20-$35**

Dipper or ladle for cream, for using with milk bottles, tin, small conical bowl, vertical wire handle with slight curved hook on end, looks rather like a candle snuffer in form and size, mfd. by C. A. Chapman, Geneva, NY, c.1908. **$7-$12**

Dipper/ladle for cream, stamped tin, American, dated 1924. **$7-$12**

Dipper/ladle for cream, stamped tin, "Sweet Clover Condensed Milk," 20th C. **$7-$15**

Dipper/ladle for cream, stamped tin, for milk bottles to dip off cream that rose to top before homogenization, small like a gravy ladle for table use as it had to fit down in mouth of milk bottle, "Cream Top," pat'd Setp. 2, 1924, Mar. 3, 1925. **$7-$15**

XIII-14. Dippers, *most with round-bottomed bowls. From* **(T-L)***:* **(1)** *Tin, tubular handle, 2 qt. size. From Butler Brothers catalog, 1899.* **(2)** *Large water dipper in "Pearl Agate," which came in different pale colors, all with black- enameled wood handle, nickel or silver plated fittings. Manning, Bowman & Co., c.1892.* **(3)** *Smaller gray enamelware handle, very like the previous one, but not so well made — at least, original wholesale price was 5¢ each, as opposed to $1.10 each. Butler, 1899.* **(4)** *"Copper dipper," with tubular socket handle. Sizes from 4" to 10" diameter. Duparquet, Huot & Moneuse, c.1904-1910.* **(R)** *Flat-bottomed one is "Windsor" type, Agateware, turned wood handle; 4 sizes from 3" H x 4-1/4" diameter to 3-3/4" H x 6-3/4". Lalance & Grosjean, c.1890.* **$30-$130**

Dipper & skimmer, a pair, forged iron, polished, filed and decorated, stamped on both handles is maker's name, "W. Werntz," 19" L, early 19th C. **$150-$200**

Dipper & skimmer, a pair, wrought iron, arrow handle with hooked end, large shallow bowls, the skimmer pierced with concentric rings of small holes, the handles inlaid with brass bands, engraved with initials "T. L." and "1823" (see note below), American, 19-1/4" L. This pair sold at Garth's Auctions, Delaware, OH, April 11-12, 1986, for $1200. Probable value range now is extremely difficult to assess. If they are a recently decorated iron pair, they're good only for a study collection, and valued under $30. If they are legitimate (and I'm not doing anything here but *speculating* that they might not be) the range for a pair with brass inlay would be: **$1000-$1500**

Uh-oh, the Dreaded "1823" — While the two implements may be genuinely old (and they do have authentic-looking distressing, pitting, tiny scratches, etc.), the inlaid brass date & maker bands are possibly modern *en-forgings,* to coin a phrase. Jeannette Lasansky did some work on the modern addition of faked brass inlays to old implements. She found that the faked dates all fall within the limited range of 1823 through 1827.

XIII-15. Suds dipper. *Pieced tin, for laundry work. Tin, two sizes, 3-5/8" x 6-1/2" and 4" H x 6-7/8". Savory, Inc., Newark, c.1925-28.* **$15-$30**

XIII-16. Doughnut lifter, *used to "turn, lift and remove doughnuts and such from the hot cooking oil." 8" H, pat'd 4/14/1908. Should have been in Disney movie* Dark Crystal — *as a moonwater strider. Collection of Meryle Evans. This is a wide value spread, but they are uncommon, and most kitchen collectors want this* **classic** *for their collections!* **$175-$350**

For other skimmers — See Chapter III.

Doughnut lifter, bowed or curved slender wand of wood, with turned handle, for poking into kettles of boiling fat to remove doughnuts when they are just so, Mennonite, 30" L, 19th C. **$125-$150**

Doughnut lifter, scissor action multi-lever type with 4 long hooked prongs, cast iron & wire. Used to "Turn, lift & remove doughnuts & such from the hot cooking oil." American, about 10" L, pat'd April 14, 1908. **$175-$350**

Dried fruit or sugar auger, or dried fruit loosener, forged iron, with wooden crossbar handle (like on an old push lawnmower), two twirly prongs with straight pointed prong extension of handle, looks like a dancing post hole auger, pat'd by H. J. White, sometimes called the "Hiddleson's Dried Fruit Auger," agented by S. W. Sheldon, NYC (but we don't know where made), 16-1/4" to 17" L (measured examples), pat'd July 27, 1875. (In the last edition, I said 1873 or 1875, because the mark wasn't clear. Now I've seen 2 more that also appear to say 1873, so it is possible that a fault in the casting was made. July 27 was on Tuesday in 1875, and Tuesday is patent-awarding day in America.) Also called a **sugar devil,** obviously because of its whirling dervish appearance. (Or ballet dancer, for the gentler soul). Also called & used as a "Fruit lifter," to tear into a keg of hard sugar, or stuck-together dried fruit, to break it up. I've seen one other version of these. **$125-$175**

Dried fruit or sugar auger, wrought iron, 2 curved out-and-in prongs, wooden "T" handle like old lawnmower handle, pat'd by William McCormick, Blair, NE, about 16" L, pat'd May 23, 1876. Another type was made by Enterprise Mfg. Co. in Philadelphia, PA. It has a "T" handle, long shaft with crosspiece at bottom with short prong in center, and 4 curved short wider blades along the bar. Enterprise prob. 1890s. **$125-$175**

Egg lifter, spring steel wire, squeeze action, the 2 clasping ends are concave coils of wire, looks like some sort of exoskeleton, American, 12-1/2" L, c.1890s to 1920s. **$20-$35**

XIII-17. Dried fruit lifter or sugar auger. *Looks like a whirling dervish. Malleable cast iron, wood handles, 16-3/4" L. Pat'd 7/27/1875. Used to extricate stuck-together dried apricots or apples from a keg or barrel, or similarly, for damp-stuck sugar. Stab it in & twist. Collection of Meryle Evans.* **$120-$175**

Fish slice, enameled steel, cobalt blue tubular handle that is relatively short compared to white blade, diamond pattern of 9 perforations in center, blade and handle stamped out of one piece, some dimension given to blade, handle curled to make tube, American or European, 11-1/2" L, turn of century. **$65-$85**

Fish slice, perforated tin with wooden handle, wire hanging ring, design is a fabulous outline of fish with 2 fins, gill, eye in the small holes on blade, American, 12-1/2" L, late 19th C. **$95-$125**

Flesh fork, for hearth, forged iron, twisted & stepped handle with elongated chevron, rattail loop, 3 tines — 2 outer straight & simple, center one partly split or reticulated, finished by whitesmith, American, 18-1/2" L, late 18th or early 19th C. **$150-$200**

Flesh fork, forged iron, 2 prongs, long handle is arrow-shaped — from arrowhead point (where it joins tines) to fletch. At end of handle is heart with small hanging hole; smaller heart punched into flat surface near end of handle, American, 16-1/4" L, early 19th C. **$450+**

Flesh fork, forged iron, 2 tines, shaped handle, end shaped like fletching on an arrow (the trimmed feather part), prob. PA, 16-3/4" L, early 19th C. **Lookalike alarm** — You'll see a lot of iron flesh forks for sale, for about $15, which have little or no detailing, & the handles of which are an expeditiously hammered rod. Often they seem to be *painted* black. They are new, decorator items, not necessarily made to fool you. **$450+**

Flesh fork, forged iron, 2 tines, elongated chevron and bull's eye handle, American (?), late 18th or early 19th C. **$150+**

Flesh fork, forged iron, 2 tines, elongated diamond & bull's eye end to handle, plus heart, very decorative, signed "Nathan Putnam," prob. PA, dated 1749. **$550+**

Flesh fork, forged iron, very long handle with figural finial of man's head with pop eyes & porkpie hat, large hanging ring cutout a few inches below head, 2 tines, not signed, prob. PA, 29-1/8" L, prob. 1840s-1870s. Offered for sale in 1981 by David A. Schorsch, Greenwich, CT. Price range mine — as an upscale folk art piece. **$3500+**

Flesh fork, wrought iron, 2 prong, with arrow shape handle or shaft, terminating in marvelous generous heart with a small hanging hole. Almost too good to be true. American (?), PA (?), 16-1/2" L, 19th C or poss. late 18th. **$350+**

Flesh fork, forged iron, ring handle, 2 long tines, American (?), 21" L, early 19th C. Impossible, I believe, to determine origin of these pieces. There have been many brought in by dealers from other countries in the last few years. **$65+**

XIII-21. Flesh fork & tasting spoon. *Forged iron fork, late 18th C. Brass bowl & iron handle spoon, c.1800. Picture courtesy of Georgia G. Levett, Levett's Antiques, Camden, ME.* **$100-$150**

XIII-22. Forks *with mechanical actions.* **(T)** *Sandwich fork, with lazy-elbow push-off. Blue & white Meissen handle, came in small and large size. Ritzinger & Grasgreen, importers, c.1906-07.* **(B)** *"Duplex Serving Fork," wire spring, steel tines, nickeled handle. "For lifting vegetables from boiling water; for lifting fruit jars in canning; for serving." 10-1/2" L. Washburn Co., 1927.* **$8-$25**

XIII-18. Egg lifter. *Or* **egg tongs**. *Spring wire, for retrieving hard-boiled eggs — or dumplings! 12-1/2" L, c.1890-1920. Collection of Meryle Evans.* **$12-$18**

XIII-19. Egg slices, *or slicers. Completely tinned perforated copper blades & iron handles.* **(T)** *Nine sizes, from 3" to 7" diameter.* **(B)** *only two sizes: 4" and 4-1/2" diameter. Henry Rogers, Sons & Co., Wolverhampton, England, 1914 catalog.* **$20-$45**

XIII-23. Fork *with push-off, for serving hot potatoes, or meat slices. All wire, 9-1/4" L, pat'd 6/11/1895. Collection of Meryle Evans.* **$20-$35**

XIII-20. Fish slice, *also called a* **fish carver**. *Shape of blade fairly typical of fish slices. Tin with turned wood handle, perforated design of fish, 12-1/2" L, late 19th C. Very unusual. Collection of Meryle Evans.* **$115+**

XIII-24. Flesh fork. *Forged iron, 3-tined, twisted & stepped handle with chevron echoes space in reticulated center tine. Perfect rat-tail loop. 18-1/2" L. Late 18th C. Picture courtesy of Robert W. Skinner Inc., Auctioneers, Bolton, MA.* **$150-$200**

Flesh fork, planished forged iron, light-color, whitesmith work, 2 tines, ring handle, American (?), 15" L, early 19th C. **$65+**

Flesh fork, wrought iron, unusual with *four* tines of type found on much later dinner forks, rattail hanging loop, decoratively marked handle, 21" L, 18th C. or early 19th. **$275+**

Flesh Fork Variations: • Very simple with no nifty touches • Simple but with some nice detail like a rattail handle • Some punch design to shaft • Very elegantly finished by a whitesmith (planisher) with some decorations, nice handle & maybe something special about the shoulder to the fork.

Flesh or meat fork, tinned sheet metal, "Rumford," American, 20th C. **$18-$25**

Flesh fork — See also roasting fork

Foam scraper, for beer suds, molded celluloid, adv'g "Grain Belt Beer," 20th C. **$12-$15**

Fork, cast iron handle with simple scroll design, meant for table, American, 7-1/2" L, mid 19th C. Love that cast iron. **$15+**

Fork, twisted wire, ingenious push-off action when handles are squeezed, 2 tines, American, 9-1/4" L, pat'd June 11, 1895. **$20-$35**

Implements — See implement racks in Chapter VII.

Ladle, brass bowl, iron shaft with turned wood handle, American, 16" L, 19th C. **$75-$90**

Ladle, brass bowl, rattail iron handle, marked "J. Whitman," Reading, PA, 20" L, c.1800 to 1830. **$250+**

Ladle, brass bowl with flat steel handle with hanging hole at end, unmarked, American (?), 13" L, 19th C. **$125+**

Ladle, brass bowl, wrought iron handle has ring loop at end, American (?), dated "1835." **$250+**

Ladle, brass bowl with wrought iron handle, American, 14-1/2" L, 19th C. **$125+**

Ladle, cast aluminum, marked "G. M. T. & Bro." (G. M. Thurnauer, listed in *Thomas' Register* as a "Manufacturer," this was probably made in Germany *for* Thurnauer? & imported, as most GMT wares were.) Turn of century. **$10-$22**

XIII-25. Implements & rack. *Forged iron. Rack with decorative hearts riveted on, has sharp ends to be driven into wall. Narrow-bladed cake turner & flesh fork have decorative detailing, done with chisel or file, on handles. Not a set, but that would have been rare even in late 18th or early 19th C. when these were made. Probably Pennsylvania. Photo courtesy of Pat Guthman Antiques, Southport, CT. Rack:* **$175+***; 3 implements:* **$250+**

XIII-26. Implements. **(T)** *Skimmer, ladle, strainer ladle & cake turner (view show crooked handle) are stamped aluminum. "Mirro," Aluminum Goods Mfg. Co., 1927.* **(B)** *Catalog describes "1. "Slice" or cake turner with tinned-copper blade. 2. Sauce Ladle. 3. Spoon with Fork. 4. Spoon with Slice. 5. Double Spoon. 6. Pierced Spoon. 7. Stock Ladle." All tinned iron, William S. Adams & Son, London, England. c.1860-61. Sets:* **$20-$35; $50-$70**

XIII-27. Implement sets. **(T)** *"American Kitchen Friend," "our new flat handled kitchen outfit," with japanned tin rack, tinned steel blades, wood handles, brass rivets. Imported, probably German. Thurnauer wholesaler ad from* House Furnishing Review, *12/1909.* **(B)** *Almost 50 years later: "Flint Stainless Steel Kitchen Tools — tall, tapered, and terrific. So good they're guaranteed for fifteen years." From "Flint" line of Ekco, mfd. by Ekco Products Co. 1958. Racked sets:* **$60+; $15+**

XIII-28. "Instruments of Human Sustenance: Cooking." *Etching done in 1569 by an artist in "circle of" Guiseppe Archimboldo — the Italian artist who specialized in surreal assemblages of objects or fruits to resemble human figures. Painting which inspired etching was done by Giovanni da Monte Cramasco. Part of the verse translates "This is not an image, this is not a figure. It is the noble makings in the art of cooking." Photo courtesy of The Metropolitan Museum of Art, Elisha Whittelsey Collection, The Elisha Whittelsey Fund, and Harris Brisbane Dick Fund, by exchange, 1977.*

XIII-30. Ladles & packers for dairies. *Wood, in familiar forms we see today often described as mid or early 19th C. All from* **1921** *Cherry-Bassett Co. catalog of dairy supplies except top right, a hooked-handle butter ladle "in the New York Style." 1905 catalog.* **(T-L)** *is "transfer ladle" for icecream or butter. Other pieces include butter hands, dairy & factory size ladles, from 12" to 16" L, butter fork 11-1/4" L. A striker for tubs or printer looks like a rolling pin in picture; 27-1/2" L. Also assorted square & round dairy packers, etc. Value range shown is what it should be for such recent items, but wear & patina may make age impossible to determine, and even with such mass-produced items, there's always the chance that some inadvertently handsome piece of wood was used and now looks older. SEE also Chapter IV.* **$10-$50**

XIII-29. Strainer ladle, ladle & cake turner or peel. (T) *Wonderful long-beaked tin strainer has wood handle set into tubular socket. 13-1/4" L overall.* **(R)** *Brass ladle has steel or whitesmithed iron handle, marked "8" only. 13" L.* **(L)** *Cake turner or short peel is steel, marked "Levi Lewis," 14-3/4" L. Early 1800s. Strainer ladle is best piece. Collection of Meryle Evans.* **$175-$275; $100-$150**

XIII-31. Ladles. (L) *From "Androck Balanced" line. Oval with pouring lip at each end, nickel plated, upright handle with tapered enameled wood grip. 10-1/2" L, with handle in choice of green, yellow, red, green with ivory band, or yellow with blue band. Washburn Co., 1936.* **(T-R)** *Tinned iron "French Gravy Ladle," 3 sizes with bowls 1-3/8" deep, from 2-3/8" to 3-1/8" diameter. Sexton Stove & Mfg. Co., Baltimore, c.1930s, but this is much older cut.* **(R-M)** *Tin soup ladle, threaded handle, bowl 3-3/4" diameter. Central Stamping Co., 1920.* **(R-B)** *Welded iron handle with hook, tinned all over, 4 sizes from 3-1/4" to 4-1/16" diameter. Savory, c.1925-28.* **$5-$20**

XIII-32. Syrup ladles. *Tinned, with riveted iron socket handles to take long wooden handles.* **(L)** *Advertised for "sugar planters." Matthai-Ingram, c.1890.* **(R)** *More common spouted form for syrup ladles. From Urbain Debois'* La Patisserie D'Aujourd'hui, *Paris, c.1860s-90.* **$30-$60+**

XIII-33. Syrup ladle. *Copper with socket handle (Meant for any useful length of wooden handle) & 2 spouts. Iron bail. 7" H x 9" diameter. Ex-Wiggins Tavern Collection, Northampton, MA. Courtesy Glenna Fitzgerald. Photograph Luella McCloud Antiques, Shelburne Falls, MA.* **$95+**

XIII-34. Leg of mutton holder. *Nickeled steel or iron, wood handle. Fitted over end of bone and tightened, this allowed you to hold it securely for carving. Ritzinger Grasgreen importers' catalog, c.1906-07.* **$8-$15**

XIII-35. Lifter. *Twisted wire. 15-1/4" L, c.1900. From stock of Carol Bohn, Mifflinburg, PA.* **$25-$35**

XIII-36. Short peels or cake turners, *and one baker's shovel 2nd from right. Forged iron, late 18th or early 19th C. From 10-1/2" to 14-1/2" L. Ex-Linden collection. Photo courtesy Christie, Manson & Woods, International Inc. Each:* **$60-$150+**

XIII-37. Tasting spoon, cake turner or peel, flesh fork. *Forged iron.* **(L)** *Tasting spoon with incised zigzags, whitesmith finished handle, 18" L.* **(M)** *Cake turner with wonderful winged shoulders to the blade, 17" L.* **(R)** *Fork with 3 tongs, 16-3/4" L. American, late 18th or early 19th C. The most remarkable piece, the cake turner, would probably be valued above* **$350,** *but we don't know the reason behind its high price a decade ago. Photo courtesy Robert W. Skinner, Inc., Auctioneers, Bolton, MA. Sold at auction in early 1980s for* **$125; $600;** *and* **$75.**

"Ladle" or "Dipper"? — Euphony? Capacity? First of all, twentieth-century dictionaries don't seem to make much of a thing about defining the differences. In fact, the terrific Webster's *Second* even gives as one of the definitions of dipper — "A ladle," and for ladle, they say it is used to ladle out or dip out liquids — from soup to molten iron! In fact, popular usage over a long period seem to decide the question of whether it's a ladle or a dipper. "Soup" and "punch," for example, seem to be coupled with "ladle," while "chocolate" and "water" go with "dipper." Did someone long ago decide that "soup dipper" sounded strange? And how'd you like to gaze up into the night sky at the "Big Ladle"? There is, to some extent, a hint of quantification about the two words, so that "dipper" implies a smaller amount (dip, sip, nip, pip), while "ladle" imples a greater amount. Richard H. Thornton, in *An American Glossary, Being An Attempt to Illustrate Certain Americanisms Upon Historical Principles,* London: Francis & Co., 1912, lists "Dipper" with the meaning "A ladle," first citation of usage 1801. He doesn't give "Ladle" its own listing. John Bartlett's *Dictionary of Americanisms. A Glossary of Words and Phrases Usually Regarded As Peculiar to the United States,* Boston: Little Brown, 1887, defines a dipper as "A vessel, generally with a handle, used to dip water or other liquor." "Ladle" is not accorded a definition. In the 1859 edition of Bartlett's book, "dipper" is not listed. Checking out the *Oxford English Dictionary,* I found (as also cited in Bartlett) that the first printed reference to "dipper" belongs to George Mason's *A Supplement to Samuel Johnson's Dictionary.* In 1801, Mason said a dipper was "A spoon made in a certain form. Being a modern invention, it is not often mentioned in books." So he gave no printed earlier source, but by inference we can assume it to be earlier. It's not that a word "dipper" hadn't existed before, it's just that the meaning was different. The *OED* cites a 1611 use — for a person who dips, or moistens (as in Dippin' Donuts).

Get a handle on the differences. Nowadays, it seems that the primary difference lies in the angle of the handle. Both dippers and ladles have handles long in relation to bowl size, but the ladle's handle is set either at right angles (90°) to the bowl, or on the same horizontal plane as the rim of the bowl. A dipper seems to be set at between 15° and about 40°. Size of bowl probably has something to do with the definition, ladles being generally larger than dippers. See also the "Windsor" style dippers in the listings above.

Ladle, cast aluminum, ovoid bowl, long upright handle with short prong off side about 4 inches from end, to hook on side of kettle, German, 10-3/4" L, c.1910-1915. **$10-$22**

Ladle, cast aluminum, ovoid bowl, with one side distinctly more rounded that other side, long handle has cast-in ridge in center, set upright at almost right angles to bowl. Type sometimes only marked with country of origin, "Made in Germany," 10-3/4" L, c. 1910-1915. **$9-$18**

Ladle, dark blue spattered enamelware, 13" L, late 19th C. **$28-$40**

Ladle, enamelware, long black hooked handle, bowl is white inside outside with blue blobs with brown & white veining called "Turtle," "Tortoise" or "Chickenwire" by collectors, but "Duchess" by manufacturer, Vollrath Co., Sheboygan, WI, c.1900. "Now architects and decorators decree that beauty belongs in the kitchen too! . . . that even pots and pans can be interesting and attractive." Vollrath ad, 1928. **$50-$85**

Ladle, pewter bowl with socket-fitted turned wood handle, American (?), 15" L, mid 19th C. **$90-$125**

Ladle, possibly a <u>tallow spoon</u>, wrought iron, wonderful upcurving long handle with arched foot toward end, rather deep bowl with

pouring spout that rests perfectly horizontally on hearth or table, American, 4-1/2" D bowl, 19-1/2" L overall, 18th or very early 19th C. This is another rarity found by Clara Jean Davis. My description is adapted from her sale list, in which she also says "Rather crudely made, doubtless a country blacksmith, however, interesting work. . . . Done all in one piece of iron pounded out to make the bowl. . . . Most likely used as tallow spoon. Very early iron, impure, likely 18th C." Price range is not Davis'. **$200+**

Ladle, tan enamelware with green trim, 1930s. **$10-$18**

Love spoon, carved wood, painted & decorated, 5 glass windows set into wood over 4 printed blue & brown calico scraps plus a damask pink & white scrap; carved hex signs, little XXX borders & a tree of life, plus the initials, are picked out in red paint or lac (possibly mixed with sweetgum or wax), Welsh, 11" L, 18th or very early 19th C. I think this is the most extraordinary Welsh love spoon I've ever seen, I guess it's the charm of the little pieces of material set under glass that does it for me. **$1500+**

Marrow spoon, carved & decorated wood (possibly cherry), American (?), 10" L, late 18th C. **$85+**

Marrow spoon, very fine-grained wood with good patina, lathe turning on end of handle, American or English, 11-1/4" L, late 18th or early 19th C. **$85+**

Meat fork — See flesh fork

Olive fork, for pickles, cherries, olives, nickeled iron, long rod looped at one end to make a grip, end split to make 2 short sharp tines, mounted on original card, "No. 185-M," "Just the Tool for Small Mouth Bottles," American, 8" L, c.1915. **$2-$5**

Olive or pickle fork, twisted wire, American, 10" L, prob. late 19th C. **$4-$10**

Peel, carved pine, somewhat charred on blade end, nice used patina on handle, for removing bread from oven, American, 51" L, 19th C. **$110+**

Peel, carved wood, probably pine, European (?), blade only 13" L, with 5" L handle, late 19th C. **$35+**

Peel, for bread or pies, wrought iron, long handle with a fat ball end, American (?), 48" L, late 1700s. **$150+**

Peel, made in one piece instead of joined handle, wooden, with very long bakery handle, front edge of blade straight & thinned, 54" L, c.1800. **$150+**

Peel, short handled, one piece wooden, rather like a round paddle with hole for hanging, good patina & slight scorching. 15-1/4" L, of which only about 5-1/4" is handle. 19th C. **$75+**

Peel, wrought iron, fat knob on end of long handle, American (?), 51" L, late 18th or early 19th C. This peel, being 51" L, is obviously not going to be confused with a cake turner, but that is a possibility for short-handled & small-bladed peels. In fact, I don't know how to tell you it couldn't be a cake turner. And who knows? Maybe those skilled cooks back in the 1780s or the 1810s used small peels for all kinds of purposes. **$150+**

XIII-38. Peel blade & peel for bakers. *Replaceable tapered blades, which wore down & chipped along front edge, came in five sizes: 6", 8", 10", 12" and 14" wide. Replacement handles were — get this! — 12 feet long, and slipped into blade socket. c.1904-1910. Very similar wooden pieces, albeit narrower in blade, were candy stirring paddles & scrapers. Many were from 36" to 46" L.* **$20-$40**

Peel, forged iron, long handled with ram's horn finial. This is most unusual, with a church & cemetery actually painted on the peel's blade, in what appears to be about 50 to 70 years after the peel itself was made, American (?), about 50" L overall, with 10" x 8" blade, c.1740-1790. This piece was sold, I believe way under the money, at the Christies East (NYC) auction of the property of artist Violette de Mazia, April 26, 1989, for $1300 plus 10% premium. **$1300+**

Peel, wrought iron, ram's horn handle, wide blade, "Londonderry" (NH?), 35" L, late 18th C. **$200+**

Peels, wrought iron, long ram's horn handle, the commonest type found, ranging in size widely. American (?), 22" L; 25" L; 29-1/2" L; 35" L, early 19th C. First price range for about 2 feet long & under; second range for 2 feet & over, esp. over 4 feet long. **$40-$65; $75-$250**

Peels — See also cake turner or peel

Picnic fork, shaped thin wood with 3 stubby tines, pencil writing on back from souvenir-saving child reads, charmingly, "September, 8, 1942, Sun Set Large" [sic], mark burned into handle "Bentwood Forks," with a daisy, American, 4-7/8" L, c.1941. Believe it or not, this is a nice little subfield for collectors — wooden picnic spoons and forks. I have quite a number of them, but this is the first marked one. **$1-$3**

Pie lifter, forged iron, 2 widely spaced tines to support the pie (though not so's I'd want to depend on it when taking a hot one from the oven), twisted handle, broken-ring loop at end, American, 14" L, c.1840s. **$125-$150+**

Pie lifter, blackened sheet steel, like a big oblong pan or cookie sheet, & possibly used as such, rounded front end like some oven peels have, very low raised sides, the end, or handle, raised at about 45° angle with end curled under, embossed on handle "I. W. MCNESS," American, 15" L x 10" W, looks early 20th C., but may be later. **$20+**

Pie lifter, heavy spring steel wire with cast iron fingers, & sliding hook that slides along handle & grips pie pan, American, 16" L, pat'd 1883. **$65+**

XIII-39. Pie plate lifter. *"Eureka." Wooden handle with 2 wire prongs with stamped tin support for pie plate. Heinz & Munschauer's, Buffalo, 1882, who were famous for their birdcages.* **$15-$30**

XIII-40. Pie plate lifters. *All wire & spring action.* **(T-L)** *has finger & thumb holes, and works okay as long as pie isn't heavy. (And what pie, sigh, isn't?) 14-3/4" L.* **(T-R)** *Slightly springier; no stronger. 14-3/4" L.* **(B)** *is least trustworthy. I wouldn't carry a mud pie with it. 16-1/2" L. Collection of Meryle Evans.* **$25-$110**

Pie lifter, tinned metal combination tool, with long handle with crown cap opener at one end, & narrow rounded cake-serving knife flat blade, with small heart cutout, at other end. Stamped into the two narrow parts of handle's shank is "Use Omar Wonder Flour. Puts Magic In Your Baking," early 20th C. **$20-$25+**

Pie lifter, hexagonal tin platform to support pie, green wooden handle, adjustable side grips, "Sure-Grip," American, 20" L, turn of century. **$25+**

Pie lifter, wire with wooden handle, a sort of fork, with 2 long prongs that fit under the pie plate, American (?), 17-1/2" L, 19th C. **$25+**

Pie lifter, wooden handle, heavy gauge wire, turn of century. **$25+**

XIII-41. Plate lifter patents. **(1)** *"Improvement in Forks for Handling Heated Plates." Pat'd 11/11/1856. G. W. Hyatt.* **(2)** *A "plate or dish lifter" pat'd 11/6/1877, William Beattie, Portage, WI. Looks like a grip strengthener.* **(3)** *"Pie turner," pat'd 9/27/1887, George H. Thomas, Chicopee Falls, MA. Has "spirally-grooved rod," (dark part between the "plate engaging arms").* **(4)** *"Pie plate holder," pat'd 9/22/1874, Joseph L. Daugherty, Newry, PA. To fit in narrow column of* Official Gazette, *his handles were cut off in drawing. Even so, it still looks unworkable.* **(5)** *Plate Lifter, pat'd 3/5/1867, Daniel Welch, Lowell, MA, assignor to H. A. Hildreth, Lowell, & W. J. Johnson, Newton, MA. One jaw fixed, other adjustable "to accommodate itself to varying plates."*

XIII-42. Pie turner & lifter. *"Locke's Automatic," W. E. Thomas & Co., Boston, MA. "The wire jaws are put around the pie plate, and the weight of the pie when lifted causes it to turn, on account of the ingenious spiral attached to the handle." I'd call this "Tenterhooks Hopeful Pie Lifter." The Metal Worker, 11/15/1890.* **$75-$125**

Pie lifter & lid lifter combined, hinged cast iron, with hook ends, openwork casting in handles, 8" L, c.1880s. $70-$95

Pie lifter or hot pan lifter, heavy wire flapping wings or arms, black-painted turned wood handle, spring action thumb piece to work the arms, which we hope won't flap while you carry your blue ribbon pie from oven to table, American, 12-1/2" L x 6" W (each wing), late 19th or early 20th C. $50+

Pie or hot plate lifter, heavy spring steel wire arms & long double-shaft wood handle, looks like it ought to have something to do with clothes hangers. Actually it grips around opposite sides of pie plate (or other hot plate), "Triumph," sold through Montgomery Ward, or imprinted with adv'g for a store, American, 13-1/2" L, c.1890s. $35+

Pie or cake slice segmenter guide, wire, sets down over a pie or single layer of cake to create a guide for a separate (not included) knife to cut 8 equal wedges, turn of century. $25+

Pie server, metal, left in pan under the pie during baking, wedge-shaped & bent to conform to sides of pie pan, Shera Corp., Hohokus, NJ, for a 9" pie pan, but the peculiar thing is that it is so wide it only allows for 5 wedges, "Patent applied for," c.1940s (?). $5-$10

> "An apple-pie without some cheese
> Is like a kiss without a squeeze."
>
> *Old English rhyme*

Pie server, tinned metal, green wood tiller handle, cutouts in blade, adv'g "Rumford," manufacturer not known, early 1900s. $7-$12

Punch bowl hook, twisted steel wire with large curve at one end to fit over edge of punch bowl, smaller end is hooked for punch cup, plated in nickel, made by mfr, C. T. Williamson Wire Novelty Co., Newark, NJ, early 20th C. $2-$3

Roasting fork or roaster, forged iron, looks like a sort of lizard skeleton, with 2 straight prongs flanking a central wiggly one, 2 penny feet not far from forked end, a beautiful if damaged ram's horn loop at end, American, 26" L, late 18th or early 19th C. $350+

Roasting fork, for hearth, brass & steel, 3 tines, telescoping handle with some turning & detail, hanging ring, English (?), 12" extends to 20" L, 19th C. For a while in the late 1970s you saw a good number of these at antique shows; they don't appear much anymore, maybe the sources have dried up. See also flesh fork. $55-$100

XIII-43. Woodenware street seller print. *The man holds a grass rake. Note woman's woodenwares, from* (**L**) *to* (**R**): *Mixing spoons; knobbed chocolate mullers; —?—, perforated spoons; rolling pins. UnID engraving, "Publish'd as the Act directs June 1773. Published by John Heywood & Son. Excelsior Works, Manchester. [England]."*

Sauerkraut auger, very like a sugar auger, probably interchangeable, iron & wood, with twirled tongs that were stuck into kraut barrel, twisted, & used to bring up big batch of dripping sauerkraut to transfer to pot or serving dish, American, 3rd quarter 19th C. $150-$225

Serving fork, aluminum, graceful bold handle of twisted aluminum rod, with tendril & bud terminal, "Buenilum - Made in U. S. A.," 8" L, c.1940s. There are several pieces in this neat pattern. $10-$18

Skewers & skewer frames — See Chapter X

Skimmers — See Chapter III

Spatula, embossed metal, message is "Merry Christmas, Happy New Year," 10" L, 20th C. $15-$25

Spatula, embossed metal (name has been seen spelled two ways), "Swans Down Makes Better Cakes," also "Swansdown," Igleheart Brothers, Evansville, IN, 12" L x 1-1/4" W, 20th C. $15-$25

Spoon, carved from horn, very old repair with riveted iron bands, American, 7" L, late 18th or early 19th C. $55-$75

Spoon, for stirring powdered seltzer into water, long handle, marked "Bromo Seltzer Cures Headache!," c.1920s. $20-$25

Spoon, pressed wood fiber, end of handle has 4 crosses marked on it, shaft stamped "Sanispoon," mfd. by American Container Co., NYC, NY, 5" L (they also made a 3-1/2" L one), 1918. $3-$5

XIII-44. Spoons, ladles, tableware. *All cast aluminum, "Clover Brand." Mfd. by W. Seibel, Metmann, Germany, who also made Britannia wares. House Furnishing Review, 3/1914. Small tableware:* **$3+**; *implements:* **$12+**

Spoon, wrought iron, round bowl, rattail back attachment where handle is forged to bowl, American (?), 7" L, late 18th C. **$45-$60**

Spoon, wrought iron spoon, very crude, possibly not finished, some white stuff in crevices, American, 9-1/8" L, early 19th C. **$18-$22**

Spoon & fork combined, scissor action, carved of whale baleen with ivory pin, English or American whaling vessel product, 8-1/4" L, second half 19th C. **$125-$150+**

Spoon & ladle set, blue & white speckled enamelware, hanging holes in both handles, 20th C. For the pair: **$55-$90**

Spoon rest, stamped aluminum, instructions: "Place on kitchen table or range. Easy to clean. Unbreakable. Burn proof." American, 20th C. **$2-$3**

Spoon rest, stamped tin, with loop hook for side of pot or pan, egg-shaped bowl with 7 drain holes, adv'g "Rumford the Wholesome Baking Powder," 3" L, early 20th C. **$30-$40**

Suckit spoon, a spoon & fork combination — one at each end, light-colored whitesmithed iron, shallow bowl, Pennsylvania version of an English form, 16-3/8" L with 2-5/8" diameter spoon, early 19th C. **$500+**

Taster, also called a <u>tasting spoon</u>, for hearth use originally, but a type of spoon still in use, forged iron, smallish bowl, long straight shank with widening at end, rattail hook, incised with zigzags & highly polished or planished by whitesmith, also called a <u>brightsmith</u>, American, 18" L, late 18th C. **$125-$175**

Taster, forged iron, long straight handle ends in rattail loop, shallow bowl is turnip-shaped, American, 21" L, early 19th C. **$75-$100+**

Taster, ovoid bowl, very long handle with ridge up center, set in almost horizontal position to bowl, for right-handed cooks to pour from small end of bowl into mouth, "Made in Germany," 13-1/2" L, c.1910-1915. **$10-$20**

XIII-45. Roaster & toaster. *Forged iron.* **(T)** *Serpentine tine makes it useful as roaster. Damaged ram's-horn handle. 26" L, late 18th C. Ex-Keillor Collection.* **(B)** *Toasting fork, 3 prongs, 22" L. Early 19th C. SEE Hearth chapter.* **$250-$350+**

XIII-46. "Home-made Toasting Fork." *"A fork that will hold bread, cakes, muffins, or even chops, steaks and slices of bacon, that are to be toasted, before a fire, made be made of any refuse piece of tin, as the bottom of a sardine box, or the side of a fruit can. A piece of tin of convenient size, 6 to 8 inches long, and 3 to 4 inches wide, for instance, is flattened out; the corners are cut off, and the edges are turned up as shown in the engraving. This is done to make it stiffer, so that it will hold its shape. Three angular [triangular] pieces are then cut and bent up, and three wires are fastened into the holes, and then twisted to form a handle. This is a little useful thing for the boys to exercise their ingenuity on."* American Agriculturist, 7/1877. SEE also the potato baking rack in Chapter XI. **$10-$20**

Taster, small brass bowl, riveted to forged iron long handle, American (?), about 18" L, early 19th C. **$100+**

Taster, tinned brass, or latten bowl, forged iron handle riveted to bowl in 3 places, very attractive shape to tapered flat handle with hooked end, crudely engraved, and dated, American, 7-3/4" L, "1862." Sold for $375 at Garth's Auctions, Delaware, OH, April 11-12, 1986. **$350-$450**

Pennsylvania? — Everyone likes to know where a piece comes from, and some places are "sexier" than others hype-wise. Pennsylvania as provenance has been very popular for a long time; Ohio, South Carolina, Alabama, Georgia, Texas, West Virginia and Tennessee are up-comers. And there are probably many more out West, though we in the East are last to hear about it. But you have to think. People everywhere used utensils and implements, and there was a constant emigration, generally westward, all through the nineteenth century — when most of *our* antiques were made. The combination of brass and iron often proves to be Pennsylvanian; but the tasting spoon above could be a "country" piece from practically anywhere.

Taster, tinned brass spoon bowl, wrought iron handle, American, 7-3/4" L, dated 1"862." <u>Added value</u> — Pricier with tinning & date. Other tasters, with brass or copper bowls, might bring slightly less. A taster has a somewhat shallow and perfectly round spoon bowl, riveted to the perfectly straight handle that lies along the same horizontal plane as the bowl. The shallow bowl means the food to be tasted didn't have to be cooled a long time (and the cook didn't have to eat a lot). **$185+**

Taster & scraper (?), forged iron, with spoon at one end, a sort of cake turner, scraper at other end, marked "C. Monk," American (?), 7" L, 19th C. **$50+**

Toasting fork, 3-ply heavy twisted wire, decorative handle, of a sort of toasting fork made in England in the 1800s; but dealer found it in Ohio & said that 3 strands & the heaviness of the wire were "Typical of Ohio work," so prob. Ohio, 17-3/8" L, c.1860s to 1880s. I happen to have bought this one, & like it a lot better than the ones I've seen that were admittedly English imports. The wire is more substantial. **$100+**

Toasting fork, 3 tines, decorative long handle, forged iron, 23-3/8" L, c.1820s to 1830s. **$175+**

Toasting fork, for hearth cooking, wrought iron with wooden handle, 3 tines, American (?), 55" L, early 19th C, poss. late 18th C. **$100+**

XIII-47. Toasting fork patent & toasters. **(T)** *Patent drawing of 5-point star "Toaster & broiler," with squeeze handles, pat'd 9/18/1877, by Samuel Poole, Brooklyn, NY;* **(M)** *Star toaster, wire wood, 19" L x 5-1/8", c.1910. Courtesy Carmille S. Zaino.* **(B)** *Wire, wood, cloverleaf, 16-1/2" L x 4-3/4" W, late 19th C. Ex-Keillor Collection. When used, these left a lighter pattern on the bread slices, so a decorative design was a selling plus.* **$35-$75**

Toasting fork, forged iron, long handle with ball finial, 3 crooked tines separated from handle by a flat cutout heart that looks as if it would be a heat deflector, but is probably just a decorative way to join the tines to the handle, this tool could be set down vertically, tines down, on hearth, prob. English 22" L, 18th C. This piece was imported by B. Altman & Co., NYC, probably found by Archie Keillor, who traveled & bought for the antiques department there. It was advertised for $29.95 in a 1957 ad. Oh for a time machine! **$250+**

Toasting fork, forged iron, simple form with 2 tines, supporting arch forms 2 short legs, loop at end of handle acts as leg, American (?), 15-1/4" L, 18th or early 19th C. **$200+**

Toasting fork, forged iron, turned wooden handle, brass hanging hook, 4 prongs describe a cubic space, American or English, 26" L, 19th C. **$150-$175+**

Toasting fork, twisted 2-ply wire handle forms hanging ring at end, little metal sleeve or collar pulls down to release or open its prongs, English, 20-1/8" L, c.1880s (?). **$35-$45+**

Toasting forks, set of 4, all forged iron with 2 tines. **(1)** The tines on the "Marshmallow fork" are long, very slender, slightly curved, with suggestion of hooks at ends, the rod of the shaft is twisted 1/3 of way up from tines, and looped handle is twisted around shaft. **(2)** The "Little Colonial Fork" is very light-weight, has short tines, loop ring with tip twisted around shaft, which has another twist above tines. **(3)** The "Twist rod fork" is made of a length of iron rod, the ends forming the tines, a loop for hanging, the shaft's 2 wires twisted in 2 places to hold together. **(4)** The "Twist handle fork" has beaten tines to flatten and broaden them somewhat, loop handle, 2 twists to shaft. A "Colonial" set for "Bungalow & camping parties." The Arden Forge, Arden, DE, respectively: 30" L, 15" L, 24" L and 30" L, adv'd in Sept. 1923 *House Beautiful.*

Lookalike alarm — You'd not know which were made by Arden Forge (I'm sure other Colonial Revival forges made similar forks for fireplace or campfire), unless you found in original packaging with name. But this listing will alert you to the fact that even the least of old kitchen implements were replicated or approximated by 20th century commercial companies. Similar forks are still being made in 1990s. Re-sale price range for 20th C. set. **$12-$25+**

Tongs, for cooking, metal, adv'g "Ney's Restaurant," Bad Axe, MI, early 20th C. **$7-$15**

Tongs, iron, adv'g "Only Gas Costs Less," early 20th C. **$7-$12**

Whatzit spoon & fork, wooden spoon at one end, 3 tined fork at other. Spoon is like a scoop & when dealer accidentally set implement in sunny place, tallow came out. The chip carving forms zigzags, hole in broad part of fork for hanging up, English (?), 20-7/8" L, with 6" L tines, mid 1800s (?). **$55-$75**

XIII-48. Beefsteak tongs. (L) *Simplest pair from* American Home Cook Book, *1854. "To turn a steak, to avoid puncturing holes with a fork, which lets the juice escape."* **(M-1)** *are "spring tongs," 18" L, from Duparquet, Huot & Moneuse, c.1904-1910.* **(M-2)** *Next to last are from* Warne's Model Cookery, *ed. by Mary Jewry. London: 1868.* **(R)** *for "taking various articles out of boiling water, roasting oysters, taking fish out of brine, ... as a dish-washer, and particularly to wash out the inside of fruit jars, pitchers." Spring activated, long wooden handles. "Ladies' Favorite," mfd. and invented by Mr. G. J. Capewell, Cheshire, CT.* American Agriculturist, *12/1876.* **$40-$70**

COOKING

XIV. COFFEE, TEA & CHOCOLATE
with a lot about enameled wares

Well, it's about time to take a break and have a cuppa. This chapter has two of the most popular collecting fields in it: **coffee mills** (or grinders), and **enamelware** tea kettles and coffee pots. Many people who collect food-related items are attracted to coffee, tea and chocolate. They use books on coffee-growing, the tea ceremony or the history of the chocolate trade, to broaden the historical and social interest of their collections. Trade cards are an important part of chocolate collecting. An amazing 1300+ page **book on coffee mills** has come out recently: Joseph MacMillan's *MacMillan Index of Antique Coffee Mills* (see bibliography). A collector group — **Association of Coffee Mill Enthusiasts (ACME)** — now has a quarterly newsletter. For book and ACME information contact Joe MacMillan, 657 Old Mountain Rd., NW, Marietta, GA 30064.

The growing market in exotic blends of imported coffees and the proliferation of specialized coffee bean shops around the country is accompanied by increased interest in coffee utensils and gadgets. Apparently there are many new **theme collectors** of coffee-related stuff . . . including caterers and owners of the bean shops. They like to assemble old roasters and mills, sometimes for window-decorating potential, which is not to say they aren't truly interested in the objects themselves. There has been a shift in collecting from primarily late nineteenth- or early twentieth-century mills to much earlier pieces. Consequently, prices have gone up across the board.

The **enamelware**, or — more popularly — "graniteware" market has shot up amazingly in the last ten years. There is still some shaking out to do, which means that ready buyers have to be found for the most expensive pieces and the commonest and least sought-after forms have to have a price drop. Still, among the most desirable and expensive pieces are coffeepots, teapots or kettles. Chocolate pots are very high on collectors' lists. There's still room for entry level collectors to acquire the kinds of things in this chapter, such as smaller pieces like **tea balls**, **tea steepers** and **tea strainers**.

Advertising teapot, miniature size, saltglazed stoneware, 2-color decoration, "Van Dyke Coffee & Tea Co.," early 1900s.   **$75-$90**

Bracket for tea kettle, backplate is cutout heavy gauge copper in form of simple 2-handled ewer, 4 holes to screw to wall. Coming from center is a swinging bracket that pivots full 180 , sliding hook for tea kettle or teapot handle, English (?), 6-3/16" H x 6-1/8" W, with 7-7/8" L swinging bracket, 2nd to 3rd quarter 19th C.   **$110-$135**

XIV-1. Chocolate pots & a muddler. *Both have typical rounded bottom, which accommodated the muddler (stirrer).* **(L)** *Cast & turned brass, pyriform body (sometimes called "pear-shaped") with 3 ball feet, side spout, hinged lid with thumb-piece, ebonized wooden handle, 8-7/8" H. Probably French or Swiss, c.1730. Drawn from ad of reknowned brass antique dealer, Rupert Gentle, Wiltshire, England.* **(R)** *Pieced tin with hinged lid, slender gooseneck side spout, wooden handle. Probably American, early 19th C. Drawn from ad of Pat Guthman Antiques, Southport, CT.* **(B)** *Mexican all-in-one-piece carved wood muller or muddler, about 8-1/2" L. The three rings marked with "•" dots are loose, and twirl when the stick, held vertically, is rubbed between the palms. The rings do not slip off end. Note corrugated wide bands at bottom. Chocolate, of course, originated in South America. Pots:* **$175-$500***; muddlers:* **$5-$35+**

Chocolate grater — See Chapter I

Chocolate molds — See Chapter IV

Chocolate pot, copper with steel handle, with what could be original wood muller (or muddler), English, 7" H, mid 18th C. **$180-$210**

Chocolate pot, in its own nickel-plated castor, brown & white agateware with nickeled collar, lid & spout, "Manning Patent," Manning & Bowman, American, 11" H, turn of century.   **$200-$300**

Chocolate pot, pear-shaped body, cast & machined brass, 3 brazed-on short legs with fat ball feet, side handle of heavy ebonized turned wood, hinged spout lid, lid with finial & thumb hinge, French or Swiss, 8-7/8" H, c.1730s.   **$325-$475**

Chocolate pot, tin, side handle with turned wood grip, small "trap-door" in lid to allow muddler, American, c.1870.   **$150-$165**

Chocolate pot, brown sponged enamelware, nickeled copper, nickel plated lid, spout & handle, Manning, Bowman & Co., late 19th C.   **$250-$350**

Chocolate sauce pan, gray graniteware, pouring lip, American, 9-1/4" diameter, late 19th C.   **$35-$50**

Coffee Biggins: the original drip style coffee maker, invented by a Mr. Biggin around 1800: "Two cylindrical tin vessels, one fitting into the other; the bottom of the upper one is a fine strainer, another coarser strainer is placed on this with a rod running upwards from its center; the finely ground coffee is put in, and then another strainer is slipped on the rod, over the coffee, the boiling water is poured on the upper sieve and falls in a shower upon the coffee, filtering through it to the coarse strainer at the bottom, which prevents the coffee from filling up the holes of the finer strainer below it." *Practical Housekeeping*, Minneapolis: 1884. • "If you use a coffee-biggin, let the coffee be ground very fine and packed tight in the strainer; pour on boiling water, stop the spout of the pot, shut the lid close, and place it upon a heater kept for the purpose. This is made at table." Mrs. Cornelius, *The Young Housekeepers Friend, or, A Guide to Domestic Economy & Comfort*, Boston & NY: 1846.

Coffee biggin, French style, tall cylindrical body, enameled a soft sage green with black chicken wire design overlaid, with rows of white dogwood blossoms, partially fluted nickeled white metal mountings — spout & handle, tall white metal insert & domed lid, enameled white inside, Manning, Bowman & Co., Meriden, CT, capacity 2 pts., c. 1880s. Price on these highly decorative pieces is hard to determine. Partly this is because many advanced collectors prefer the subtleties of plainer wares, but to the "outsider" it seems as if the fancy ones ought to bring the most. **$250-$400**

Coffee biggin, gray graniteware pot with gooseneck spout, tin cylindrical vessel (the biggin part) with domed top, this one from Matthai-Ingram catalog and American, others imported, came in different sizes for capacities from 1/2 to 5 qts., this one about 8" H plus another 5" for tin part, c.1870s or 1880s. **$125-$200**

Coffee biggin, tin, cast white metal handle originally painted black. There's a cork stopper which is kept in a little dead end funnel on the straight spout's bridge or brace strut, except when it's transferred to spout when coffee has to be kept hot inside, "Chesterman's Coffee Pot," W. Chesterman, Centralia, IA, 9-3/8" H, pat'd July 19, 1859, & Jan. 24, 1860. **$85-$100**

Coffee biggin, silvery plated (tin? Britannia?) copper, straight-sided cylindrical lower body, slightly smaller diameter drip top, curved handle, straight spout, large round knob on lid, American, prob. CT, 11" H, mid to 3rd quarter 19th C. **$200-$235**

Coffee pot, a sort of combined French biggin & drip percolator, conical metal body with long straight spout originating near bottom of pot, fancy openwork scrolled cast iron handle, long "stove pipe" drip cylinder, with wooden rod or pressure block used to force hot water through the grounds placed in the perforated interior strainer, Manning-Bowman & Co., Meriden, CT, pat'd 1873. **$100-$135**

Coffee Boilers: These have tapered sides and big bodies, with smallish V-neck spouts. Typically seen in movie cowboy campfire scenes.

Coffee boiler, blue agateware, wire bail handle & fixed side handle, tapered body, American, 10" H x 8-3/4" diameter at base, late 19th C. **$90-$135**

Coffee boiler, blue & white swirl enamelware, with small V-neck lip or spout, American or European, late 19th C. **$75-$135**

Coffee boiler, gray graniteware, bail handle with wooden grip, American, 1-1/2 gal. capacity, late 19th or early 20th C. A one-gallon size almost same price range. Condition is all. **$50-$85**

Coffee boiler, gray graniteware, with typical V-neck lip or spout, "Granite Iron Ware," mfd. by St. Louis Stamping Co., St. Louis, MO, 8-1/2" H, pat'd May 30, 1876, May 8, 1877. **$55-$125**

Coffee boiler, mottled blue enamelware, enamelware lid with wooden finial, enameled handle, American or European, late 19th or early 20th C. **$75-$115**

XIV-18. Biggin Coffee makers. *When the factories of Manning-Bowman & Co., at Meriden, CT., were remodeled in the early 20th C., a "vault was discovered that had become bricked up at some time in the past and forgotten. In this vault were found a large number of coffee percolators and other household apparatus, which was made by Manning-Bowman & Co. as far back as the Civil War." (The company was started back in 1849.) Shown here, and in the article in* House Furnishing Review, *8/1911, are* (**L**) *a* <u>combined French biggin & drip percolator</u>, *pat'd in 1873. The coffee was "extracted by pressure of a wooden block forced down by wet coffee grounds."* (**R**) *"A nearer approach to the modern coffee* <u>percolator</u>*, made by Manning-Bowman in 1875 and patented in 1876. It proves quite conclusively that contrary to general belief [in 1911], the percolator is not a recent contraption. This model has a center tube with spray top, and a water spreader on the cover to distribute the water that is forced up through the tube. It differs radically from the present day percolators in the fact that the water, after it is poured in the funnel shaped aperture on the side" is percolated only once through the grounds, instead of "making a continuous percolation as the modern ones do."* **$85-$150+**

XIV-19. Biggin "French coffee pot." *Graniteware with planished tin. White metal or nickel-plated mountings. Made in 5 sizes — from 2 to 6 pints. Manning, Bowman & Co., 1892.* **$120-$250**

XIV-20. Biggin coffee pot patent. *Pat'd 12/29/1885, by Philip A. Covington, Fort Worth, TX, assignor of one-half to Albert H. Iverson. "A coffee-pot having a cone-shaped chamber perforated and provided with an upright tube, a perforated cup surrounding the same, a flaring cap connected to the tube and bottom of cup, a perforated retaining-plate, and a condensing-vessel formed with a convex bottom." For making a type of percolated coffee.* Official Gazette.

Coffee boiler, powder blue & white speckled enamelware, tin lid, wire bail handle with wooden grip, large size, early 20th C. **$80-$130**

Coffee boiler, tin with wide strap handle, plus small strap "tipper" opposite lip to ease pouring, from F. A. Walker catalog, imported or American, different sizes, including 6, 8, 10 & 12 qt. capacity, c.1870s. **$35+**

Coffee boiler, white & blue enameled sheet metal, V-neck spout, wire bail handle as well as large strap tipping handle opposite lip, American, early 20th C. **$65-$100**

Coffee boiler, white & brown speckled enamelware, nickeled base & lid, wood finial & fancy handle, Manning, Bowman & Co., 9" H, pat'd 1889. **$175-$225**

Coffee boiler, white & sky blue marbleized enamelware, bail handle with turned wooden grip, American, 13" H, late 19th or early 20th C. **$155-$225**

Coffee pot, thresher's boiler type — that is, a very big one for the harvest crew, green & white swirl enamelware, American (?), turn of century. **$165-$200**

Coffee boilers — See also coffee pots

Coffee cup, china, large size, with caricature of NYC's Boss Tweed and a spoofing quote, on other side, from the time of the Tammany Hall political boss's downfall. Quote in tradition of 200 years of politically related engravings & plates & cups. "I am not greedy, but I like a lot." American, early 1870s (?). Crossover with political collectors. Price probably less in areas of the country with no interest in Boss Tweed, although his name became nationally synonymous with political graft. **$325+**

XIV-21. Biggin coffee pot. *"Chesterman's," stamped & pieced tin, with fabulous air vent in cross-piece, with original cork stuck in it. Cast iron handle. Embossed stamped brass oval is the label — such stamped brass plates are found on many things, including many coffee mills of the period. Pat'd 7/19/1859 and 1/24/1860 by W. Chesterman, Centralia, IA. 9-3/8" H.* **$85-$135**

XIV-22. Biggin "French coffee pot." *Nickel-plated copper, "extra well made and the up-to-date thing." Hinged cover, ebony [perhaps ebonized] handle. 1 pt. or 2 pts. From Albert Pick catalog, 1909. You know if you see one in an antique shop now, the nickel [oooh, icky proletarian] plating will have been surgically removed to reveal the copper and improve the price.* **$40-$65**

"The Tin Pan Nuisance. — 'If I were Duke of this country,' began a friend, as we rode through an elegant section of the country, 'I would punish with banishment every man or woman who threw tin trumpery into the street.' — 'Amen,' said I, 'and send them out of the country with a string of oyster cans for a necklace.' This was no new spectacle — we had seen the like a hundred times before — but in this instance it was especially aggravating. There was a large country-house, with a beautiful lawn extending to the fashionable avenue, and at one side to a public road, not fashionable, but greatly traveled, and in a small ravine that made a gap under the fence and opened into the roadside gutter, was tumbled a mélange of old tinware — coffee and tea-pots, pans, cups, watering pots, innumerable fruit and vegetable cans, and broken crockery. It was an ugly blotch on the otherwise fair beauty of the place.... What to do with such old trumpery, that cannot be burnt, seems to be an unsolved riddle with the majority of country people. In cities, the housemaid stuffs it in a barrel, which the ash and garbage-men carry away. In the country, it is commonly pitched into some out of the way place, under porch floors, into vacant cellars, under currant bushes, etc., but always where in some moment it will be discovered....

"So far as I know, there is no better way to dispose of broken and worn out wares, than to put them into a well dug for the purpose — one which has a cover, and which, when full, can be earthed and grassed over. Such a receptacle has its advantages — one always knows where to look for old basins and pans, if they are needed, for broken pottery when pieces are required for drainage, while bits of glass are thus put forever out of the way of children's feet.

"The sight of old tin 'lying around loose' [must] have a charm for some people, judging from the way they distribute it in their backyards and front ditches. A man's back-yard is his private property; if he chooses to make it a hideous looking place, it is his own affair; but the man who makes a public highway the receptacle of his trumpery, should be prosecuted by the Commissioner of Roads, and punished as a polluter of public morals. It is as manifest [an] indelicacy to allow such broken & worn out domestic utensils to public view, as to throw old shoes in the street." — MWF, *American Agriculturist,* April 1878.

Coffee cup or mug, graniteware, white background with dark green (or black?) transfer picture of pine tree, etc., adv'g "Dickenson's Ace Clover, Extra-Recleaned, A Trade Winner" & "Dickenson's 'Pine Tree' Timothy Seed, Average Purity Test, 99 1/2%, It Stands Alone" (the lone pine tree symbolizes this). Dickenson's, American, 19th C. They must have made a lot of these, because you see them fairly regularly. See also Chapter VII. **$45-$75**

Coffee dispenser, wall built-in, aluminum, "Club Aluminum Utensil Co.," Chicago, IL, 2nd quarter 20th C. **$10-$15**

Coffee drip maker, individual size, aluminum, little non-folding legs, one of which serves as handle, snug-fitting lid, put coffee grounds in cup, which is marked with measuring line on side, pour water in, put lid on, no maker name, 3" H x 3-7/16" diameter, 1940s. My mother's note inside reads, "In the early days of WWII, a teacher at Hutchinson School (Memphis) gave me this to send to my mother to make her one-cuppa." **$4-$6**

Coffee & hot beverage urn, for restaurants & hotels, copper & brass, "Mason's," American, 18" H, including little feet, turn of century. These were used for hot water, coffee, even clam broth. Some of these were nickel-plated. **$150-$250**

Coffee maker, electric drip style, chrome 4-legged urn, the sides flaring up & out, drop ring handles on each side, 2 side by side spigots — one for coffee, one for hot water to "dilute to taste" or for making tea, "Edicraft Menlo Siphonator," mfd. in the Laboratories of Thomas A. Edison, Inc., Orange, NJ, 9 cup capacity, c.1930. The original cost was $45 — a very high price in Depression years. For $42.50 more you could also get a sugar, creamer & a sort of truncated oval tray to match. For other electric wares not related to coffee, see Chapter XVIII (Gadgets and Appliances). **$45-$65**

Coffee maker, for dining room, on stand with 4 cabriole legs, over alcohol lamp, all copper except for "fishbowl" glass globe top through which passes the vertical tube which circulated the boiling water through the grounds, "Empress Ware, No. 2," New York Stamping Co., Brooklyn, NY, pat'd March 2, 1893 and Sept. 17, 1895. **Very similar pieces** with alcohol lamps were made by other companies. Manning-Bowman made the "Meteor Circulating Coffee Percolator," with a sort of sugar-bowl-shaped glass top; another was the "American Coffee & Tea Extractor," by Buffalo Mfg. Co., Buffalo, NY, advertised in January 1903; a third was the "Auto Vac Glass Coffee Filter," maker unknown, advertised in 1917; then the "Paramount Percolator," NYC, with a glass top and bottom, advertised in 1915; a fifth was advertised by F. A. Walker, "housefurnishers" in Boston who imported many of their goods. This was the "French Steam Coffee Pot," of copper or silver-plated copper, with a glass sugar-bowl like top part. It came in sizes from 2 cups to 20. Sternau, a NYC company known to us for "Sterno," made a handsome coffee maker outfit on a stand with columns at each corner of the stand & a sugar-bowl-shaped top part. Sternau got a Feb. 17, 1865 patent for the fuel part, and a Nov. 10, 1908 patent for the rest. All such decorative wares were aimed at the new market that liked to cook at the table — newly servantless hostesses, who could also set up chafing dishes, waffle makers, and other pieces heated by alcohol lamps or electricity. **$45-$65**

Coffee maker, tin with turned wood handle, strainer inside, American, c.1910 to 1915. **$15-$20**

Coffee maker, vacuum type, 2 globular glass sections, glass rod filter, black plastic handle, measuring cup & lid, Cory Glass Coffee Brewer Co., Chicago, IL, early 1940s. **$5-$12**

Coffee measure, stamped aluminum, adv'g "Schillings Best," for A. & C. Schilling, San Francisco, CA, c. 1930s. **$12-$15**

Coffee mills, box type: — also called **table mills**, **lap mills** or **French mills**, but many early catalogs called them "box mills" to differentiate them from wall-mounted side mills or those that clamped to a table top.

Coffee mill, box type, mahogany (or cherry?), pewter hopper, cast iron crank handle, "Selsor, Cook & Co.," Philadelphia, 3rd quarter 19th C. I turned to MacMillan's wonderful tome on mills and got date info & place from it. Furthermore, apparently I've seen a marked mill (probably at a Pennsylvania flea market that I used to attend many times a year — before their pigeon shoots) but Joe found his references in a catalog. I wish *he'd* seen it rather than me! Listed but not described in the 1870 catalog are two basic types of Selsor, Cook mills: "Friction" and "Anti-Friction." Turning to one of my books on mechanical movements (used by inventors), I learn that friction was one way of driving one wheel with another. The surface is sometimes gritty, or faced with rubber or leather, to give it some grab. Another way to get grab, and increase the amount of touching surfaces, was to V-groove the wheels around their circumference, so that instead of 1/2-inch-wide area of each wheel touching, the surface would be doubled, by having V-grooves with two 1/2-inch sides. This **frictional grooved gearing** was said to be "comparatively recent" in the 1868 book. As to "anti-friction," the only thing I could find in this book is an **anti-friction bearing** — the drawing clearly shows **ball bearings**. Hey, you engineers — help us out please! **$125+**

XIV-2. Box type coffee mill. *Box type, also called a "lap" mill, cast iron with closed-top hopper, tin drawer slides underneath. Key at side for taking apart for cleaning. Screwed to oblong board with shaped ends and 3 holes at each end, perhaps for fingerholds for carrying? Mill 6-3/4" H exclusive of crank; base 5-1/2" x 5-7/8", Pennsylvania, mid 19th C. Courtesy of the late Darryl G. Dudash, Alaquippa, PA, who had a great eye, a lucky way of finding great things, and is sorely missed. He specialized in Pennsylvania cast iron.* **$350-$450**

XIV-3. Box type coffee mill. *"No. 1050 Improved." mfd. by John M. Waddel Mfg. Co., Greenfield, OH. "This is designed for a good, low priced mill, with burr and shell so constructed as to grind coffee very fine. The point is made of a new feature in this mill, consisting of a device for firmly locking the grinding shell and large retinned hopper to the box, holding the shell firmly to its place and making a bearing for the burr shaft." Open the door and a round tin receiver cup automatically slides out — this feature was typical of Waddel mills. From writeup in* The Metal Worker, *8/16/1890.* **$140-$180**

XIV-4. English box mill. *Raised hopper, wooden box with ornate cast iron top and slanted sides, shallow drawer. Marked on medallion above door, but I can't read. Both Kenrick (West Bromwich, England) and T. & C. Clark (later named Wolverhampton & Clark, Wolverhampton, England) made similar box mills. This one is probably a T. & C. Clark. It's wonderful to have Joe Mac-Millan's book to try to match up mills unidentified in old catalogs. From Harrod's Stores 1895 catalog.* **$140-$200**

Coffee mill, box type, brass with wooden handle, European (?), c.1920s. **$40-$50**

Coffee mill, box type, cast iron, pat'd by J. R. Adams, NYC, NY, Dec. 1, 1867. **$125-$165**

Barbed Wire Connection.— Joseph F. Glidden, who invented barbed wire, may have had an Adams' mill. Stephen L. Goodale, *Chronology of Iron and Steel* (Pittsburgh: Pittsburgh Iron & Steel Foundries, 1920), wrote about Glidden's two 1874 patents for barbed wire: "The first barbs were made on an old coffee mill, and the wire was twisted with the crank of an old grindstone. The barbs were put on one at a time, and set in place with a hammer. It was first manufactured under the name Barb Fence Co., at De Kalb, Illinois." (p. 185).

• • • •

Reproduction alert I — This extremely simple box style with bowl-like hopper is being made today. One that's being sold by Cumberland General Store of Crossville, TN, has "satin black finish" cast iron, is 6" H x 4" square, & sells for about $35. **Alert II** — Lehman's Hardware & Appliances, Kidron, OH, offers a 7" H x 4-3/4" square box mill with "dovetailed corners" (which are actually box jointed) in their "Non-Electric Good Neighbor" catalog meant for the Amish market. **Alert III** — A 1968 ad in *McCall's Needlework & Crafts* shows a box-joint wooden coffee mill, drawer with wood knob, ornate cast iron top, top crank with white porcelain knob, handle grip, hopper inside box, described by "The Country Cousin" dealer as "Decorative coffee mill really works, has a hand-rubbed antique walnut finish. 7" high. $9.95 ppd."

Coffee mill, box type, cast iron & wood with box joints, hopper & crank on top, very plain, probably a cheap proprietary model made for a mail order house, American, turn of century or early 20th C. **$35-$40**

XIV-5. Box mills. (T-L) *"Favorite No. 700." raised hopper with cover, and with handle for firm grip, wood box-jointed body with drawer, box 4-1/4" H x 6-1/4" square. Pat'd 1880 & 1888.* **(T-R)** *"Imperial No. 147," sunken hopper with hinged cover, white walnut box, cast iron top finished with "French gold bronze." 4-3/4" H x 7" square, pat'd 1888.* **(B)** *Simplest type of raised hopper box mill, "No. 257," japanned iron open hopper, hardwood box, 3-1/4" H x 6" square. All Manning, Bowman & Co., Meriden, CT, from their 1892 catalog.* **$100-$150**

Coffee mill, box type, cast iron & wood, side crank out of side of wooden box instead of more usually seen out of top of hopper, side handle, "Parkers Columbia Rapid Grinder, No. 260," sold through Montgomery Ward catalog, Meriden, CT, 1 lb. size, c.1890s. A very desirable mill. **$160-$220**

Coffee mill, box type, chromolithographed tin depicts coffee plant on front & convivial scene of man & woman drinking the brew on the sides, sunken hopper with crank, small drawer, "None-Such mfd. by Bronson-Walton Co.," Cleveland, OH, c.1904. **$75-$85**

Coffee mill, box type, dovetailed cherry wood, cast iron, American, 8-1/4" H x 7" x 7", 19th C. **$75-$85**

Coffee mill, box type, dovetailed hardwood, entire top is cast iron finished in bronze lacquer, sunken hopper has pivoting cover, handle on top, "Imperial Mill No. 705," mfd. by Arcade Mfg. Co., Freeport, IL, box 5" H x 6" square, c.1903-04. **$90-$110**

Coffee mill, box type, dovetailed wood, japanned cast iron, "Parker's Union Coffee Mill No. 25," 6-1/4" H, c.1908. **$40-$60**

Coffee mill, box type, dovetailed wood, with drawer, iron handle, brass hopper, American, 15" H x 8-1/2" square, 19th C. **$250-$300**

Coffee mill, box type, forged iron box on base plate supporting 4 corner columns with brass fleur-de-lis finials, large capacity high mortar-shaped hopper also houses mill, with serpentine scroll supports & side handle of flat iron also shaped like fleur-de-lis, central crank has turned wooden knob, French, 16" H. If for home use, certainly not for small family (although Emile Zola drank 40+ cups a day), late 1600s or early 1700s. **$650-$900**

Coffee mill, box type, "French style" with raised hopper, wood with ornate cast iron top, bad condition, with warped wood, poor finish, drawer knob missing, Amerian, 19th C. Even with everything wrong, still can bring real money as decorative shelf piece. **$25-$40**

Coffee mill, box type, grain painted tin in bold red & black, hopper filled at top, but bottom has a snap-on hinged lid that you open to release the ground coffee from the box, sort of like how you empty crumbs from a toaster, marked only "P B" on front, in block letters, "P.B. Machina Accaiai [or Acciaia]," Italian, 4-1/2" square, late 19th C or early 20th. The dealer had another like it, somewhat smaller, rather dully finished in brown paint, for much less. **$90-$100**

Coffee mill, box type, hand wrought iron bowl & crank, American, mid 19th C. **$80-$95+**

XIV-6. Box coffee mills. (L) *"None-Such," mfd. by Bronson-Walton Co., Cleveland, OH. Chromolithographed decorative box with scene of coffee-drinkers. Domed hopper with top crank.* **(R)** *"Universal No. 110," mfd. by Landers, Frary & Clark, New Britain, CT. Black enameled sheet steel with iron handle & crank. 8-1/2" H. Both in ads from 1905. The colorful one is more attractive than the plain one, but has a narrower value range. (L)* **$95-$120**; *(R)* **$75-$150**

"**A French coffee-mill**, which is simple and durable, is a necessity where filtered coffee is made. This will grind coarse or exceedingly fine. Easily adjusted and so simple that a child can use it." Maria Parloa, *Kitchen Companion,* Boston: Estes & Lauriat, 1887. **NOTE:** A "French" mill was another way of saying a box or lap mill with a hopper above the box, not within it.

Coffee mill, box type, heavy cast iron, square with slightly slanted sides, 2 cast-in flanges for bolting to board or table, cast iron drawer, brass hopper, brass oval medallion with regal looking rampant lion, "A Kenrick & Sons Patented Coffee Mill," England, 6-1/2" H, prob. c.1860s to 1880s. **$110-$160**

Coffee mill, box type, cast iron, wood, side handle on side & crank on other side, drawer, "Arcade IXL," proportion somewhat different from most box mills, being 11" H on a 7-1/2" square base, Arcade Mfg. Co., Freeport, IL, late 19th C. **$150-$165**

Coffee mill, box type, low wooden box with box joints, cast iron mill, hopper inside, cranked on top with "self adjusting spiral spring drawer for grounds," "Chicago Double Grinder, No. 60," Chicago Coffee Mill Co., IL, pat'd Oct. 19, 1886, but began making in 1890. **$90-$100**

Coffee mill, box type modern style, dark maroon Bakelite™ (or other molded phenolic resin plastic), nickel-plated handle, metal works inside, wooden knob, "The PE-DE Coffee Grinder," "Dienes-Reform D. R. G. M. R. P." German, 8" H, 1930s. The last two letters, **R. P.**, probably stand for *Reichspatent*. The **D. R. G. M.** stands for *Deutsches Reichs-Gebrauchsmuster* (or Registered Trademark of Germany). *Dienes-Reform* means Reformed Office. The whole thing (probably meaning Reformed Office of German Registered Trademarks and Patents) might have been used between WWI, when D. R. G. M. was used by itself, and WWII, after which Germany was divided. **$85-$100**

Coffee mill, box type, ornate cast iron top & dovetailed wood, tin drawer with wooden front & knob, top handle, "Challenge Fast Grinder," Sun Mfg. Co., Greenfield, OH, 1 pound size, late 19th C. In 1891 Jno. M. Waddel Mfg. Co., also of Greenfield, OH, sent out letters informing dealers that the Sun Novelty Works of Greenfield was infringing their patents on their "Greenfield" mill. **$70-$100**

Coffee mill, box type, with wide shelf base & lid, cast iron sunken hopper, lid, crank & top grip, door below swings out to reveal tin pan on little shelf that pivots out when you open the door, "Greenfield Coffee Mill, No. 91," mfd. by Jon. M. Waddel Mfg. Co., Greenfield, OH, 9-1/2" H, prior to 1890. See the similar mill by Sun Mfg. Co. **$110-$140**

Coffee mill, box type, painted wood, turned wooden hopper, iron works & crank, not marked, American (?), turn of century. **$100-$125**

Coffee mill, box type, plain, pale beech wood, drawer below, chromed-plated stamped sheet metal top, chromed top crank, German, c.1961. This box mill was offered in *House Beautiful* ad; also cherry or walnut. The 3 woods cost $4.95, $7.95 and $8.95 originally. **$12-$18**

Coffee mill, box type, stamped steel with black enamel finish, sunken hopper, crank on top, wood knob, "Universal #109," Landers, Frary & Clark, New Britain, CT, 5-1/4" H x 5-1/4" square box, pat'd Feb. 15, 1905. **$75-$90**

Coffee mill, box type, very ornate beautifully carved wood, probably mahogany, decorated with angel's heads at each corner of the lower box part, then carved into tower part housing mill works, with acanthus leaves coming down from top, 4 tiny feet, iron screw-on top with graceful iron crank with turned wood knob, ring handle on little drawer. This mill — with the almost furniture-like look, and the tall tower broadening out with un-

dulations into the little box — is what is called a "Louis XIV" type mill because that is when this style appeared, marked "Tivelier Jeune" [Tivelier Jr.], St. Etienne, France, 10-3/8" H, c.1830s-1850s. **$400-$600**

Coffee mill, box type, wood & cast iron, original red paint, pinstriping & other decoration on iron, "Landers, Frary & Clark," New Britain, CT, 12" H, late 19th C. **$200-$250**

Coffee mill, box type, wood drawer with brass pull, lid, sunken hopper, cast iron crank & mill works, nice surface decoration, American, late 19th C. **$75-$90**

Reproduction alert — A very close reproduction of this type is being made and sold now through Cumberland General Store (and probably other outlets). Like this one there's a 3/4" wide border around varnished wood box base, side grip handle cast as one piece with cast iron top. There's a double lock nut regulator, which is between the crank and the top. This repro box is 5" x 5" square, 5" H exclusive of handle. The new one goes for about $40.

Coffee mill, box type, wood & iron, original paper label on box, "Home Coffee Mill #767," mfd. by Arcade Mfg. Co., pat'd June 5, 1884. **$90-$100**

Coffee mill, box type, wood with chamfered top, turned cast brass tower, called a "collar," forged iron crank with turned wood knob, iron decoration on 4 sides of box, & brass ring handle on little drawer, Austrian or Hungarian, about 8" H, early 18th C. **$350-$400**

Coffee mill, box type, wooden, cast iron finished with thin copper plating, sunken hopper, crank in top, "Parker's National Coffee Mill No. 430," only 4-1/2" H, turn of century. **$75-$100**

Coffee mill, box type, wooden with pewter hopper bowl, American, box 5" H x 7" x 7", early 19th C. **$115-$135**

Coffee mills, electric:

Coffee mill, electric, cast iron painted white, with glass jar, looks almost like some modern flashlight & birdfeeder combined, "KitchenAid," division of Hobart Mfg. Co., Troy, Ohio, 1938. **$40-$50**

Coffee mill, electric, enameled cast iron base, screw-on clear glass bean holder above, a glass tumbler marked off in measures sits under chute in left side, "KitchenAid," early 1940s. **$40-$50**

Wartime dates — It is problematic to date any American, Canadian, English, French, Italian product to the years of the World Wars. **WWI** had been going on for three long years before the U.S. declared against Germany. I suspect that all metals, as well as glass and cloth, were in short supply for making housewares in any involved country between 1914 and 1918. Ads in trade magazines such as *House Furnishing Review* reflect the trade restrictions imposed on products of the Central Powers. **WWII** really started long before Germany invaded Poland in 1939. I'd like to read a study of trade practices between what became the Allied Nations and the main Axis powers, Germany and Italy, starting, say, in 1935. At any rate, the war was almost two years old when the U.S. landed troops in Iceland, and over two years old when we declared war in December 1941. Probably a great percentage of manufacturers of household appliances and wares suspended domestic production to turn to suitable war materiel manufacturing. Strategic raw materials were severely restricted. Many ads of the early 1940s talk about what goodies would come after the war was over. Any products made of vital materials (iron, steel, copper, rubber, etc.) sold in the U.S. between c.1940 and 1946 may have been made before that period. I don't know what the government did during the metal and rubber drives when objects made of metal or rubber were solicited from the general populace . . . whether or not they asked the same thing of manufacturers and their warehoused finished products. In a September 1944 ad in *Better Homes & Gardens,* the headline is "War or no war — Mrs. Jones keeps 'selling' KitchenAids! KitchenAid has gone to war — but enthusiastic KitchenAid users haven't stopped 'selling' their friends. What do they say? They say that a KitchenAid is more than a kitchen 'gadget.' It's a kitchen machine, strong enough and powerful enough to take the elbow-grease out of the really hard . . . jobs — mixing, mashing, juicing, whipping, and such. . . . They say — but why go on? The fact remains there still isn't a single KitchenAid to sell. But someday there will be — and then remember to talk to a KitchenAid user before you buy any mixer."

Coffee mill, electric, enameled cast iron, with glass top, "KitchenAid No. A-9," Hobart Mfg. Co., Troy, OH, 1938. **$50-$65**

Coffee mill, electric, for supermarket (and U.S. Navy!) use — known to mill collectors as the "Big Pot," in shape of big fancy coffee pot with high domed lid & curved short 'duckneck' spout, has 4 grinds — coarse, boil, perk & drip. Panel lights up in back to tell what grind to use: "Extra fine (maybe put through twice?) for glass maker, fine for drip, medium for perk, coarse for pot." "American Duplex Electric Coffee Cutter," mfd. by American Duplex Co., Louisville, KY, 30"H, c.1936-1940. It is one of 350 made. I've actually seen several; maybe a store chain (or a fleet) suddenly closed up a few years ago, releasing these into the atmosphere? **Duckneck spout:** What better name for a short, almost vestigial gooseneck spout than duckneck? **$500-$1500**

Coffee mills, globe:

Coffee mill, tabletop, orange painted cast iron globe mill with curved top crank with fat wood knob; top-hinged lid to drawer compartment, in slat-side base, is embossed: "Grand Union Tea Company." GUTCo was in Brooklyn, NY; mill mfd. by Griswold Mfg. Co., Erie, PA, for Grand Union, 10-3/4" H, c.1920. Much of the value is due to Griswold collectors, not mill collectors. (**NOTE:** In the 1920s Griswold made a virtually identical mill, bearing "The Griswold Mfg. Co. Erie PA." embossed on the drawer front, with black wood knob. This style eliminated the need for a hinged lid. It's worth $1000+.) GUTCo mill: **$400-$600**

Coffee mill, cast iron globe on iron strut-like frame, half-lid hinged in flat top, large ungainly crank comes out of side. Globe is embossed with concentric rings around the longitude lines from North Pole to South Pole, and its two halves are bolted together. Marked on the globe, above the crank shaft "ADAMS" and on the opposite side "CENTENNIAL." A very petite mill — only 6-1/2" H to lid; "belly" of globe only 3-3/4" across, crank handle about 5-1/4" L. This was located by the archaeologist of iron, Bob Cahn, and is in the collection of Neuman & Bogdonoff, NYC. Another was advertised by Golden Lane Antiques, New Oxford, PA, in 1994. The "Centennial" is most surely the U.S.'s in 1876. There was a mill pat'd by Calvin Adams July 18, 1876, but I think maybe this got a *design* patent (probably in 1875 or 1874). An inventor named Increase Adams got a patent for a "machine for breaking the husks of coffee berries on Jan. 13, 1835" according to Joe MacMillan, but this wouldn't be that. The mill itself looks rather English, but the "Centennial" is America's. **$500+**

Coffee mills, screw clamp to table:

Coffee mill, clamps to table, wood & iron, "S. H. Co." (Simmons Hardware), St. Louis, MO, turn of century. **$140-$160**

Coffee mill, screw clamps to table, cast iron, decorative decal, "Universal #30," Landers, Frary & Clark, turn of century. **$45-$60**

Coffee mill, japanned & stenciled cast iron, like the #00 but with screw clamp, hopper built in, but a bowl must be put below chute during use, "Enterprise #0," Enterprise Mfg. Co., 11-1/2" H, c.1898. **$45-$50**

Coffee mills, telephone novelty:

Coffee mill, telephone novelty type, wall mounted, side crank, all wood with side crank, of course it looks like an old oak wall crank telephone dating only a few years before the mill itself. Brass plate gives name and dates, "The Telephone Coffee Mill," pat'd by F. J. Hollis, Kansas City, MO, 16" H x 6-1/4" W, pat'd April 18, 1892 (2 years after Arcade's desirable telephone mill). **$600-$800**

Coffee mill, telephone novelty type, wall or shelf mounted, ornate cast iron front to wooden box, "Telephone Mill," mfd. by Arcade Mfg. Co., Freeport, IL, 13" H, pat'd Sept. 25, 1888; April 15, 1890; & April 11, 1898. **Thanks** to collector Dorothy Bloom for measurements & other information. **$450-$600**

Coffee mills, wall or side mount:

Coffee mill, cabinet side mount, cast iron, folding handle, marked "Geo. W. M. Vandecrift," American, c.1870s-1880s, though it looks older. Very desirable. **$200-$300**

Coffee mill, japanned & stenciled cast iron, wall mount side mill with hopper above balanced by receiving cup below, crank in middle, one of their many "rapid grinding and pulverizing mills" possibly usable as spice mill, "Enterprise Mfg. Co. #00," 9" H, hopper holds 4 oz., "pat. applied," for shown in their 1898 catalog-cookbook. **$30-$40**

Coffee mill, wall-mounted side mill (hereafter "wall/side"), sheet & cast iron, painted black & mounted to natural-finish wood block that's partly carved & painted so that it "mirrors" shape of the sheet iron hopper front, brass ID plate reads: "Wilson's Improved Patent Coffee-Mill," mfd. by Increase Wilson, or Wilson's Foundry, New London, CT, mill and hopper are 6" H, hopper is 4" W, crank is 4-1/2" L,1840s to 1860s (?). The only dated Increase Wilson coffee mill patent I found was March 6, 1818, and this mill is based on the old patent, though the mill itself isn't anywhere near that old. **$80-$100+**

XIV-7. "Mr. Garnet Terry's Mill" & another old one. (L) *A hand mill, for coffee beans, spices, etc., of wood and sheet iron. Invented by Londoner Garnet Terry, c.1800-01. Illustration published in Anthony Willich's* The Domestic Encyclopedia, *1803-04, which was a practical work meant for men who were used to making most of their own tools and household items.* **(R)** *Coffee or spice mill, "but will grind grain of any kind. It is sold without a frame, and is so constructed as to be fastened to a post or board in any part of the house, or it can be attached to a simple frame." Sheet iron with revolving cast iron corrugated "plates" which could be ordered separately. From article in* Journal of the American Institute, *9/1841. Its most recognizable features for a search are the apparently straight crank handle, and the 2-fingered back-plate for screwing to wall. It predates 1841, so it could be Ammi Clark's mill, Berlin CT, pat'd Aug. 4, 1833. But it really looks like the #2 side mill of the Lane Bros. - Swift Co., pat'd by Beriah Swift, Aug. 16, 1845. It may indeed be that it was in circulation before a patent was applied for or granted.* **$200+**

Coffee mill, wall/side, looks rather like the Wilson mill but backplate is cast iron as is the hopper & there is a thumb-screwed "friction piece" called a "collet," a sort of washer to regulate coarseness of grind, marked "James Carrington, Wallingford, CT," pat'd April 3, 1829. From a record of the patent claims in the *Journal of the Franklin Institute,* April 1829, comes this, which might help explain our question over **"friction and anti-friction"**: "I claim as my invention, and as very important improvements, the cast iron plate and hopper, and the collet in the plate in aid of the thumbscrew, to regulate the machine. By means of the friction piece, or collet, that screw will hold its place, and not yield to the motion of the crank, or be subject to wear by friction; and the runner, having a more extensive bearing, will run more true, perform its work more perfectly, be less liable to get out of order, and the whole machine being thus made of iron, not only assumes a more elegant form, but is free from shrinking, warping, and other effect of weather?" **$165-$200**

Coffee mill, wall/side, cast iron works in heavy stamped tin housing or body, triangular tin hopper, mounted on wooden board with three holes. Marked "S.J.," looks turn of century. I saw this a long time ago, and my flea-market notes weren't any more detailed. A search in Joe MacMillan's rewarding opus on mills, did turn up, finally, an "S. J." The description fits with a "pressed sheet metal" side mill on p. 632 of MacMillan, mfd. by Theodore Frank Parker, who was in business, c.1891, with a man named "S. J. Goff." There's more to the story, I'm sure, and we hope you will come up with more info! **$75+**

Coffee mill, wall/side, cast iron bean box above iron mill housing, spring & screw clamp holder below for cut crystal container for the grounds. Ornate casting depicts a hand bell surrounded with Art Nouveau scrolls, etc., & the word "BELL," one of 70 styles mfd. by Arcade Mfg. Co., in their "Crystal" line, Freeport, IL, c.1908. **$250-$300**

An **1841** article on side mills *(Journal of the American Institute),* the design of which hardly changed for 60 or 70 years, says, "It is sold without a frame, & is so constructed as to be fastened to a post or board in any part of the house, or it can be attached to a simple frame."

"Wood back" mills — Lots of side mills are found mounted to a board, sometimes with three holes in a staggered pattern on one side. This way, the mill could easily be put up on the side of a cupboard, or the wall of a pantry or kitchen, and moved more easily. Joe MacMillan terms these "wood back" mills.

XIV-8. Wall-mounted coffee mill. *"The Crystal," so-named because of glass hopper/canister and receiving cup. Ornate cast iron mill. Arcade Mfg. Co., Freeport, IL. Ad in* Thomas' Register of American Manufacturers ... Buyers' Guide, 1905-06. *(Complete with the Arcade receiver this value would be higher.)* **$120-$140+**

Coffee mill, wall/side, cast iron mill housing & crank & bracket, finished in black, white or blue enamel, clear glass upper bean container has screw-on lid on top & its bottom screws into iron center part, with clear glass grounds holder below, "Enterprise Mfg. Co. #100," 14-1/2" H, early 20th C. Complete with bracket: **$200-$300**

Coffee mill, wall/side, cast iron with glass canister, marked "Crystal No. 3," on glass, mfd. by Arcade, American, turn of century. Arcades are the most commonly found coffee mills, in various models & sizes. Having "Crystal" on glass canister adds value, as they are easily broken, and could be replaced with other glass jars. **$120-$140**

Coffee mill, wall/side, Delft blue & white pottery, iron works & crank, Dutch, English or German — prob. the latter, 1930s. **$75-$100**

Coffee mill, wall/side, glass & cast iron, "Arcade #3," Arcade Mfg. Co., late 19th C. **$100-$135**

Coffee mill, wall/side, cast iron, decorated tin cylindrical hopper (like upside down bottle screwed into top of iron body), "Regal #44," Landers, Frary & Clark, early 20th C. **$60-$70**

Coffee mill, wall/side, mounted on board, iron, large glass canister with red lettering "Koffie," Dutch (?), turn of century. **$90-$100**

Coffee mill, wall/side, mounted to board, blue, red, green & white lithographed tin oblong canister above, depicts fat Dutch girl & sea scenery, cast iron mill & catch-can below in bracket, marked "Holland Beauty" under woman's image, mfd. by Bronson-Walton Co., Cleveland, OH, pat'd July 9, 1901. Value is mostly in the fine condition of the lithographed tin canister. **$95-$120**

Coffee mill, wall/side, on board, sheet iron hopper, cast iron mill & "S" crank, no lid on hopper, but doesn't appear there ever was one, embossed "L. Holts Improved Coffee Mill," eagle & banner saying "Patent." Looks 1850s; no patent record for a Holt between 1790 and 1873 — under "Coffee-berries, Machine for breaking," "Coffee mill," "Mill," or "Grinding machine." According to MacMillan, this should be "E. Holt" ("E" for Elias, but my notes do say "L"). E. Holt worked with Charles Parker: In 1829, Charles Parker "went into business for himself. He contracted with [Patrick] Lewis & [Elias] Holt [Meriden, CT] to deliver a certain number of coffee mills every month." Un-

XIV-9. Coffee mills. (L) *"Bell," ornate cast iron fron to oak box. Glass receptacle inside.* **(M)** *"X-Ray," with glass box above ornate cast iron mill. Ads in* House Furnishing Review, 1908. **(R)** *"The Telephone Mill" for coffee or spices. "Made of hard wood, highly finished and nickel trimmed, and is the only boxed mill which can be fastened equally well on Table, Shelf or Wall. ... It is easily regulated to pulverize if desired." Name plate says "The Telephone Mill. Ring Up For Coffee. Freeport, Ill." Arcade Mfg. Co., appeared in Manning-Bowman 1892 catalog. Original price in 1890 was only $2.50. More desirable one has fancy cast iron front. Arcade Mfg. Co. made 70 "different varieties of coffee mills and 400 house furnishing specialties." (L) & (M)* **$250-$300**; *(R)* **$500-$700**

fortunately for this mystery, those mills were box or lap mills, not side mills for mounting to the wall. Help! **$75-$85**

Coffee mill, wall/side, painted or bronzed japanned cast iron, oblong upper box holds beans above grinder, cast iron front has shield cutout with glass window to show beans, below mill is spring-tension screw with plate that holds cup or can tightly against bottom of mill to catch grounds, "Golden Rule Blend Coffee. The Finest Blend in the World," Citizen's Wholesale Supply Co., Columbus, OH, 17-1/2" H, early 20th C. **$225-$250**

Coffee mill, wall/side, red & black sheet tin canister & cup, cast iron mill housing, "Aroma #9," Bronson & Walton Co., Cleveland, OH, early 1900s. **$75-$90**

Coffee mill, wall/side, screwed to board, oblong lithographed sheet metal canister top, in exaggerated grainy wood design, oval glass viewing window, below is plain cast iron mill housing & crank, with grounds cup that matches top, "Oplex #10," mfd. by Bronson Walton Co., Cleveland, OH, pat'd July 9, 1901, with other patents pending. A fancier version has little cast iron support for the grounds catcher cup. **$70-$80**

Coffee mill, wall/side, screwed to board, oblong lithographed tin canister above, cast iron mill housing, canister marked "Silver Lake" with four-leaf clover, mfd. by Bronson Walton Co., c.1901-1905. The works & the shape were, I think, patented July 9, 1901. I'm sure that different styles or decorations for the lithographed canister were introduced at least yearly. **$70-$80**

Coffee mill, wall/side, screwed to board, sheet & cast iron, cast iron crank, marked "P. S. & W. Co. No. 6," Peck, Stow & Wilcox, CT, 5-1/2" H, 3rd to 4th quarter 19th C. **$60-$70**

Coffee mill, wall/side, screwed to piece of wood which is then screwed to the wall, japanned cast iron, "Sun No. 94," Sun Mfg. Co., Greenfield, OH, c.1900. **$90-$100**

Coffee mill, wall/side, sheet metal & cast iron, screwed to board, oblong box with a small drawer below the mill to catch the grounds, & a larger storage drawer for the coffee beans on the side, cast iron X crank handle, brass plate on mill's hopper embossed "John Luther's Coffee Mill, Warren, RI," 12" H x 16" L overall, "pat'd Aug. 11, 1848." **$175-$200**

Coffee mill, wall/side, sheet steel canister painted black, cast iron crank & grinder, wood knob, green & white label on can, "Universal, #0012," Landers, Frary & Clark, 13-1/4" H, pat'd Feb. 14, 1905. **$65-$90**

Coffee mill, wall/side, tin & iron, "Parker #60," Meriden, CT, c.1860s to 1900. This looks like the Eagle side mill pat'd by J. & E. Parker, Meriden, on Feb. 7, 1860, and so marked on round stamped brass ID disc on hopper. The "Eagle" came in four sizes: #50, #60, #70 & #80, and sold in the Dover Stamping Co. catalog of 1869. **$50-$65**

Coffee mill, wall/side, unusual fold down type, adjustable mill parts, deep hopper & crank of cast iron, these 3 basic elements fitted to a wooden platform that is hinged to fold up against the wall. It would have to be mounted somewhere where a receptacle could be placed, & may have seemed more ingenious than it was in practice, "Lone Star," J. M. Waddel Mfg. Co., c.1890. Very desirable. **$200-$250**

Coffee mill, wall/side, with crank handle coming out of wooden box. This is a new one, being made today, & has an iron hopper and a "walnut stained hardwood body" mounted to a board & decorated with molding, described as being "Colonial styled with antique finish." American-made (?), 1980s. **Lookalike** advertised in Cumberland General Store catalog. New price about: **$30**

Coffee mill, wall/side, wood, drawer & crank have white china knobs, signed "I. D. Post, Lahaska, PA," last quarter 19th C. **$220-$240**

XIV-10. Coffee mill. *"Lone Star Side Mill." which "may readily be attached to the face of a door, window casing, or the wall" and may be "folded up when not in use." Projects 4" from wall when folded. John M. Waddel Mfg. Co., Greenfield, OH, article in* The Metal Worker, *6/14/1890.* $200-$250

XIV-11. Coffee mill. *Shelf or table-mounted. Cast iron with bell-shaped hopper. Maker not known; picture from Harrod's Stores 1895 catalog, London.* $50-$75

"ENTERPRISE"
Rapid Grinding and
Pulverizing Mills

Capacity of Hoppers—1 lb. of Coffee

Mills illustrated on this page will "Pulverize"

Will Granulate ¾ lb. of Coffee per minute.

Adapted for Steamboats, Butchers, Lumber Camps or wherever it is desirable to save space.

No. 350, $3.50
Height, - - 16½ inches
Weight, 17 lbs.

No. 235, $8.00
Height, 18 in., Diam. of Wheel, 17 in.
Weight, 29 lbs.
The No. 235 was designed especially for Butchers' use in grinding spices.

No. 450, $4.50
Height, - - 21 inches
Weight, 19½ lbs.

XIV-12. Coffee mills. *Various grinding & pulverizing styles of cast iron mills mfd. by Enterprise Mfg. Co., Philadelphia. Early 20th C. catalog. Note that top one is "adapted for Steamboats, Butchers, Lumber Camps" and will "granulate 3/4 pound of coffee per minute." (And, presumably, make hamburger & sawdust too!)* $350-$450

Coffee mill, wall/side, wooden box with iron lid & with one glass side for viewing the beans above the cast iron mill housing and crank, simple iron receptacle for grounds below. Advertised as "A reliable grinder at a very low price . . . for customers of limited means." "X-Ray Mill," mfd. by Arcade Mfg. Co., Freeport, IL, c.1908. **$120-$180**

Coffee mills urns, with 1 or 2 wheels, countertop (mostly for stores):

Coffee mill, for home use — like the "wheelers" but no wheels on this smallest model, cast iron, painted black with some fancy gold trim & stencils, urn body & hopper breaks [comes apart] at fattest part, where crank is, for cleaning, etc. Capacity of hopper is only 4 oz. of coffee, "Enterprise #1," American, 12-

1/2" H, crank 6" L, turn of century. $2.25 was the original cost. Good condition: **$400-$500**

Coffee mill, cast iron with original paint & stenciled designs, double wheel, drawer below, body "breaks" in center, hopper lid surmounted by eagle, "Enterprise #7," 21-1/2" H, 17" diameter wheel, dated 1873, still selling, with replacement parts, at least as late as c.1905. **$600-$800**

Coffee mill, cast iron & wood, double wheel, painted blue, "S. H. Co." (Simmons Hardware Co.), St. Louis, MO, 13" H, late 19th C. **$300-$450**

Replacement parts for coffee mills — Every part was replaceable. Perhaps of most interest to the general collector is the fact that 20 eagles were offered, from 25¢ each for the small mills up to 60¢ for larger ones. Looking closely at catalog pages, you can see **differences in eagles**: (1) Flying with wings spread wide & up curved; (2) flying, wings out in downstroke position; (3) standing with wings way out; or (4) tucked in partway, heads left, heads right. What a warehouse find these spare part eagles would be!

XIV-13. Coffee mill. (L) *"Double Grinding" mill for tabletop use. Decorated cast iron. Silver & Co., Brooklyn, c.1910. It came in two sizes, which affect price. It gets its name by being "a new departure in 'Grinding Mills.' Has two inlets for the Coffee Bean and two outlets for the Ground Coffee." Adjustable for coarse to powdered grinds.* **(R)** *"Crown No. 11." mfd. by Landers, Frary & Clark, New Britain, CT. Painted & decorated cast iron, 12-1/2" H, drawer in base. From Pick catalog, 1909. (L) #1:* **$250-$350***; (L) #2:* **$350-$400***; (R) good condition:* **$250***; (R) poor paint:* **$90-$125**

XIV-15. Coffee mill, *on high stand. Ornate, painted & decorated cast iron. Enterprise Mfg. Co., Philadelphia, late 19th C. This is so coveted by collectors that even one in poor condition (mainly paint, but may include dents & dings to hopper) brings serious money.* Poor: **$600-$900**; *good :* **$1100-$1800**; *excellent*: **$3000+**

XIV-14. Coffee mills. (L) *Enterprise Mfg. Co. No. 8, with double cast-iron flywheels, brass canister/hopper (sometimes nickel-plated), eagle finial, bulbous cast iron mill housing hinged in center. Three sizes in this style: 8, 10, & 210, which would grind 1 lb., 1-1/2 lbs., & 1-3/4 lbs. per minute. Offered in Duparquet, Huot & Moneuse catalog, c.1904-1910. (NOTE: from the same period, an almost identical red & gold one [except for decorations on the cast iron mill-housing] is Landers, Frary & Clark's "Crown No. 80." which has a nickeled hopper/canister.)* **(R)** *"Swift Mill," Lane Brothers. Large, double-wheeled mill, painted cast iron with drawer in box base. About 22" H. Early 20th C. ad, but mill dates to 1870s. (L)* **$400-$700**; *(L) original paint:* **$900**; *(R)* **$400-$600**

XIV-16. Coffee mills. *Small cylindrical mills of wood, about 7" to 9" H.* **(L)** *A simple turned wood mill made in Provence district of France, in very early 18th C. It was supposedly based on earlier Italian models.* **(R)** *Carved wood mill from the 18th C. It looks as if it could have been made by a furniture or frame-carver. Both are drawn from a wonderful article, "Les moulins à café," by Edith Mannoni, that appeared in the French magazine* Art & Décoration, *August/September 1982. It is filled with unusual mills, mostly unfamiliar to American collectors. I tried to get photographs, but the collection is private, and the pictures were not available to me.* **$125-$200**

Coffee mill, countertop type with double flywheels, painted & decorated cast iron, hinged lid for hopper, drawer below, "Coles No. 2," mfd. by Coles Mfg. Co., Philadelphia, PA, c.1906. Coles also made smaller & larger mills, for coffee & spices. **$500-$800**

Coffee mill, countertop, cast iron, double wheel with openwork 5-petal flower gear design, shapely body painted red and black, with gold pinstripes, wheels, with name cast around outside rim, rich dark blue with letters picked out in gold, the vase-shaped hopper above is painted light & dark blue with design of sun's rays in red on top, instead of being polished brass. Eagle & flag decals on body. "Elgin National Coffee Mill," 26" H, 1880s to turn of century. **$600-$900**

Coffee mill, countertop double wheel type, openwork wheels with 6-petal flower, red painted cast iron, brass knobs on pull-out drawer, & hopper lid, wood crank handle, marked on wheel "John Wright, Wrightsville, PA," 11" H x 7" W, advertised in 1973. **$120-$200**

Coffee mill, countertop for commercial use, red painted cast iron, spectacular double wheels, stately plinth base, cylindrical bean hopper with domed lid, with blue & yellow paint trim, & applied landscape & portrait bust decals on hopper & grounds box, "Lane Brothers & Co. #15," Poughkeepsie, NY, 29-1/2" H, wheels 16-1/2", pat'd Feb. 9, 1875. **$900-$1300**

Coffee mill, counter or tabletop, small 2-wheeler, painted cast iron, mfd. by "Swift," Poughkeepsie, NY, turn of century. **$350-$450**

Coffee mill, countertop for home, painted & decorated cast iron, double wheel, drawer in base, breaks apart in middle, no eagle on hopper top, "Family Mill No. 2," Enterprise Mfg. Co., 4 oz. hopper, 12-1/2" H, 8-3/4" wheels, late 19th C. Condition very important. **$400-$1100**

Lookalike alarm — Hammacher Schlemmer advertises a single wheel grinder thus: "Exact replica of the coffee grinder used during the turn-of-the-century. Fire engine red body and black wheel, topped with chrome hopper. Hardwood base drawer and handle. 12" H, 7" square base." It sells for about $40. Well! Even it it weren't for the chrome hopper, you'd never mistake this for an old one, and I cannot, after diligent search, find what this one is an "exact replica" of. Anyway, it works and it's fine as long as you aren't misled.

● ● ● ●

Reproduction alert — Cumberland General Store has a 2-wheeler, cast iron with wooden drawer, daisy petal spoked wheels, that comes in red with ivory trim or black with gold. It's 11" H x 7" square, and sells for over $100.

Coffee mill, countertop store model, 2 wheels, cast iron, original red & black paint, "Landers, Frary & Clark," New Britain, CT, 10-1/2" D wheels, turn of century. **$400-$600**

Coffee mill, double wheel store model, countertop but with funnel opening to lower compartment instead of drawer, painted & stenciled cast iron, eagle on top same as others, "Enterprise No. 12," Enterprise Mfg. Co., 32" H with 25" diameter wheel, late 19th C., but sold into 20th C. **$600-$1000**

Coffee mill, store model for countertop, cast iron painted red & stenciled, with 2 large daisy petal spoked wheels, convex round hopper has domed top, with cast eagle on top, white porcelain knob on drawer below, regulated to grind coarse or fine, "seventy-five turns by hand will granulate a pound of Coffee as fine as required" . . . "and by power (larger Grinders being supplied) fifty turns." "Enterprise Mfg. Co., #9," wheels are 19-1/2" D, overall 24" H, turn of century. This is the 4th from biggest overall size of this type with lower drawer. The **larger** are the #10, 28"H, 19-1/2" wheel, concave flared urn hopper; and #209 & #210, which both have 25" D wheels. #209, 33" H, has an iron wheel, fat, urn-shaped hopper surmounted with an eagle with wings spread. #210, 37" H, is even more spectacular, as it has a nickel-plated hopper, in a concave-sided urn-shape, surmounted by eagle with wings partly folded down. There are also **smaller** ones. The full range of capacity is 1-3/4 lbs. to 7-1/2 lbs. coffee. Then there are floor-standing models with their own fancy cast iron bases. For those, the added value would be considerable, probably triple, the countertop styles. **$500+**

Coffee mills, floor-standing wheelers:

Coffee mill, floor model on 4 legs, ornate cast iron base in original paint, huge double flywheels, flared vase-shaped hopper is right, I believe, but looks rather small for the wheels, stepped dome lid with wings-up eagle, "Enterprise #18," 5 feet 8" H, 31" wheels, turn of century. I've seen one advertised as size 18-1/2"; could this be a later model? If you think you'll buy one through the mail, it weighs 233 lbs, and was originally "packed in two crates and one box." **$1500-$2000**

Coffee mill, floor standing model on intricate cast iron base, 2 wheels. Cast iron with brass hopper & tall finial, "John C. Dell & Son," American, 33" D wheels, pat'd 1884. Dell mills very rare. **$1500-$2000**

Coffee mill, floor standing store model, 2 wheels, cast iron with all original black & red paint, "Elgin National," mfd. by Woodruff & Edwards Co., Elgin, IL, 65" H x 27-1/2" W, turn of century. **$1300-$1600**

Coffee mill, floor standing store model, ornate lyre base, double flywheels (the petal spokes of which are much fatter than on the Enterprise), large brass hopper with eagle finial, all original red paint, "Elgin National Coffee Mills," 60" H, turn of century. **$1000-$1300**

Coffee mills, miscellaneous:

Coffee mill, cast iron, 4-legged, frame screwed to long board with 3 fingerholes at each end, huge crank, tin drawer slides underneath between the legs, key at side to take works apart for cleaning, cup-shaped hopper, an extraordinarily handsome mill, not marked, Pennsylvania (?) or maybe Austrian (?), mill is 6-3/4" H (exclusive of crank) x 5-1/2" x 5-7/8", mid 19th C. **$150-$200**

XIV-17. "Turkish" style coffee mill. *Actually marked "The Turkish Coffee Mill" on decorative center band. "Patterned after Oriental models, heavily japanned, has black enamel finish, and is handsomely decorated. The grinders are of highest grade and grind the coffee to a fine powder, which is especially suited for making 'after dinner' coffee." 13" H, mfd. by Landers, Frary & Clark, picture from Albert Pick catalog, 1909. According to Joe MacMillan, there's a great variety of old and new ones, and wide value range:* **$45-$150**

Coffee mill, cast iron, brass, looks something like a cannon with an "S" crank where the cannon ball would come out, drawer below, "Persepolis Coffee Grinder," Metropolitan Brass Foundry, NYC, according to Joe MacMillan, prob. made only between 1902-1910. **$800-$1000**

Coffee mill, cast iron cup or hopper & bracket to screw to board, this example mounted to thick wooden paddle, porcelain knob on crank, sawtoothed opening in bottom of hopper, marked "ADAMS" on handle, opposite the word "PATENT," 12-1/2" L with 4-1/2" diameter hopper, date "1840" on underside. Dealer Bob "Primitive Man" Cahn found it. He discovered that ADAMS also made paint mills of a portable kind (perhaps also larger sizes). Again, Joe MacMillan to the rescue: This was patented by Calvin Adams, Pittsburgh, PA, on Sept. 25, 1840, #1,795. **$400-$600**

Coffee mill, very primitive wooden body with punched iron decorative sides, wide flaring hopper with crank, the whole thing mounted to seat-sized paddle. It is, in fact, a seat, to be straddled while working. Turkish, 18th C. **$350-$550**

Turkish Imports — I include a Turkish mill because in the last three or four years of the 1980s, lots of kitchen antiques began showing up in flea markets, imported from Turkey. At the time of this writing, most of these antique imports are copper frying pans with interestingly braced iron handles, or similar saucepans, or the more familiar exotic coffee pots. Some wholesalers are pricing these by the pound. In addition, around the turn of the century, many wares, mostly copper and brass, were imported to the U.S., and sold chiefly by dealers in New York City's brass district, down on Allen Street. This was true well into the 1960s, and people shopped there for samovars for 60 years or more. Turkey shared a border with Russia, so it is likely that some Turkish wares showed up in the emigré shops. Other Turkish coffee mills are much fancier, reflecting ancient Byzantine and Persian crafts of inlay and mosaic; some are made of several kinds of wood, even with bone decoration and brass fittings. A star and crescent moon decoration easily identify a piece as Turkish, but this symbol was not adopted for their flag until 1936. I don't know how long ago the symbols were popularly used. To confuse things, a popular American fraternal order, the **Shriners**, use as their emblem a Turkish scimitar (curve upwards) with a downpointing crescent moon with 5-point star pendent from the scimitar's blade. The Shriners wear a fez, which is also Turkish. Some decorative arts of American origin have the scimitar insignia or emblem.

Turkomania — In 1743, a young (and presumably attractive) Turkish ambassador arrived in France. This excited the French to an even higher excitement about all things Turkish — a fad that had been around for two or three decades. Everything Turkish was desirable: rugs, book designs, music, theater, coffee — and, presumably, coffee mills. Ersatz potentates and sultanas had their portraits painted in turbans and Turkish costumes. The end of the fad came, as the Revolution came, with the end of the century.

Coffee mill, wood base, vertical post that supports sheet iron hopper with snap-on hinged lid. Below the hopper are the horizontal works in a cylinder, with side crank; very delicate looking, George Washington had one almost the same that is now in the Smithsonian, possibly made from an illustration & description in the famed 1750s Diderot's *Encyclopedia,* French or even poss. American, about 23" H, late 18th C. **$600-$800**

"Coffee" mill, stump- or box-top, cast iron, with one wheel, simple angular open cast body, shallow wide hopper, for cracking bones, shells, corn, etc., for poultry feed, "Enterprise #750," 17-1/4" H, with 19" D wheel, turn of century. **Confusable.** — "Coffee" is in quotes, because this **Bone, Shell, Root, Bark, Salt & Corn Grinder** is sometimes confused with a coffee grinder. Enterprise made 3 of these grinders — one wall-mounted, the #650, which was 11" H; the #750, as above; & the #550 with a crank, instead of a flywheel, which was also 17-1/4" H. The ID number is on the hopper. **$200-$400**

Coffee or teapot, pieced tin lighthouse-shape body, made of 8 soldered vertical strips, thin strap handle, straight spout originating almost halfway up body, American, mid 19th C. **$100-$125**

Coffee or teapot, straight sides, Britannia trim and curved fluted spout, fancy handle, celadon green enamelware body with blue & pink morning glories with green leaves, Manning-Bowman, Meriden, CT, 9" H, 1890s. **$250-$350**

"Where the ebullition is most violent."— "Among the new inventions that may prove of advantage to housekeepers is a contrivance known as a 'percolator,' though the term does not accurately describe its operation. It consists of a small cage or basket of perforated tin or of fine wire-gauze attached to an air-tight tin float. The float forms a sort of cover for the cage and is easily detachable. A bent wire at the top of the float serves as a handle. The finely-ground coffee, as much as required, is placed in the cage, and the whole is then lowered into the water. The float keeps the coffee near the surface of the water where the ebullition is most violent, and the strength is very quickly extracted." *Appleton's Annual Cyclopaedia & Registry of Important Events of the Year 1887.* The writer goes on the say that the "cage" of coffee grounds in effect "floats" so that water can keep being passed through it, instead of the grounds sinking to the bottom, waterlogged, if in a "cambric bag" as of old.

Coffee percolator, aluminum, green Depression glass percolator lid, turned wood handle, 4 little feet, no mark, 14" H, 1930s. **$18-$22**

Coffee percolator, copper & brass, urn shaped with wooden handles, finial & spigot handle, nice footed base, on stand, Manning & Bowman, 13" H, pat'd 1906. **$85-$110**

Coffee percolator, dark blue spattered graniteware, early 1900s. **$75+**

Coffee percolator, electric, 2 glass globes with red phenolic plastic handles & swingaway or swivel lid for lower globe, black plastic base, percolating tube goes up through center, very handsome, "Silex" glass, "Automatic Coffee Percolator" mfd. by General Electric, c.1940s (?). Crossover interest from modernist collectors. **$85-$100+**

Coffee percolator, electric, chrome-plated brass & copper ball on high flared foot, with funny tapered perky spout, balanced on opposite side by arched white plastic handle, knurled knob on lid, "Table Electric" by Chase Brass & Copper Co., Inc., division of Kennecott Copper Corp., 7-cup capacity, c.1937. A non-electric companion was a tea kettle, a large chromium ball, same kind of tapered spout, much smaller ring foot, white plastic handle forms arches a few inches from spout to backside, describing an arch approx. 1/5 of kettle's diameter. **$65-$85**

Coffee percolator, electric, round, Labelle Silver Co., Brooklyn, NY, 1950s. **$20-$30**

Coffee percolator, light blue speckled enamelware, "Universal," L. F. & C., Landers, Frary & Clark, pat'd first in 1894. **$165+**

Coffee percolator, pale green enameled iron, nickeled copper lid & trim, paneled body, tubular handle painted black, aluminum basket, glass top, called in catalog the "High Pattern-Cold Water Type," glass insert in lid is "Fire King," function of the odd little tippy pedestal base was to draw heat up, separating the pedestal from the top is some kind of insulating material, Reed Mfg. Co., Newark, New York (not NJ), 9-7/8" H, 6-cup capacity, c. 1927. (It also came in white.) This particular color, sometimes called <u>closet green</u> by stove manufacturers, was called "blue" in the Reed catalog.   **$45-$75**

Coffee percolator, red & white swirled enamelware, glass insert in lid, 20th C. Red & white enamelware is high among the most sought-after colors.   **$150+**

Coffee percolator, stamped aluminum, paneled sides, domed percolator lid set with green glass, turned wood handle, V-neck spout or lip, "A. A. W. Peerless Co., The Better Ware," American Aluminum Ware Co., Newark, NJ, 9" H x 4-7/8" diameter, c.1915-1930.   **$10-$15**

Coffee percolator, stamped aluminum, slanting sides rounded at bottom, percolator lid, clear glass, somewhat straightened out gooseneck spout, C-shaped black-finished wood handle, No. 69, Landers, Frary & Clark, 7-1/2" H x 5-3/4" diameter, c.1915-1930.   **$10-$15**

Coffee percolator, straight sides, green & tan enamelware, green glass in lid, all interior parts present, American, 1930s.   **$35**

Coffee percolator, with rather fat slant-sided metal body, long tapered straight spout originating near bottom, simple strap handle above which is an attached tin funnel — the aperture through which water is poured into a sort of pocket inside pot. Above is a short cylinder, with hinged lid, where the grounds are & where the tube with perforated top terminates. Pour water in, it's forced up tube & percolates out strainer through coffee grounds. A 1911 article told the difference between this early percolator & later ones: in the 1875 one the water only dripped through one time, instead of over & over. Manning-Bowman & Co., Meriden, CT, for sale in 1875, but pat'd in 1876.   **$100+**

Archaeological Find — In a large ad featuring a brand new percolator for 1911, come three tantalizing paragraphs in small print, entitled "A Chance Discovery and Its Meaning." **(1)** While making changes in our factory at Meriden a short time ago, workmen opened up a long forgotten vault in the wall. **(2)** In the vault were a number of Manning-Bowman Coffee Percolators made from 1865 to 1876. Weird productions compared with modern designs, they show the wonderful progress we have made in Coffee Percolator building since 40 years ago. **(3)** The next time you are in Meriden, or New York, do not fail to drop in and inspect them." Oh boy, wouldn't you love to have that time machine now?

Coffee percolator, yellow enamelware with green trim, glass top, 20th C.   **$30-$45**

Coffee percolating drip type, nickeled copper, straight-sided cylinder with beading around top edge, straight tapered spout set midway up, vertical bracket handle of ebonized turned wood, ball valve in spout is a real marble, very fine wire mesh (called wire gauze) filter compartment gets filled with grounds & put down in pot, then strainer with vertical pipe — the "air tube" — put in on top of filter. Domed cover with knob. Medallion on side: "Marion Harland Tea & Coffee Pot," mfd. by Silver & Co., Brooklyn, NY, 4-cup capacity, c.1890, but made over a 30-year period or more. This also came in polished copper (tinned inside), or in what they called "Old English" finish, which was not defined in catalogs or ads. Possibly a sort of dull pewtery finish? This pot was also advertised with curved "question mark" handle.   **$35+**

Coffee percolator, plated metal tripod base, double-globe glass coffee maker in 2 parts — the filter part & the serving part, both decorated with leaves, scrolls & chrysanthemums in "silver deposit" on clear glass. The glass parts sit over alcohol heater in base, or can be used on a gas, coal or electric stove, "Auto Vac Glass Coffee Filter," mfd. by Auto Vacuum Freezer Co., NYC, NY, c.1917.   **$35-$45**

Coffee percolator, tin, perfectly cylindrical shape, with a perforated grounds cup insert, percolating funnel tube, slightly tapered straight spout originating near bottom, slightly domed lid with pretty little cast metal finial, graceful question-mark-shaped handle. Manufacturer's brochure states that "In using a new pot a slight taste of tin impairs the flavor of the coffee. After a few times using, (or after boiling coffee in the pot a few hours) this entirely disappears." Also stated is that the 2 extra pieces, filtering cup & tubed funnel, "are of a form easily kept clean, durable, and, if necessary, easily repaired or renewed by an ordinary tinsmith." "The Windsor," mfd. by Hubbard & McClary, Windsor, CT, 9 sizes — from one to 16 qts., c.1870s.   **$30-$45**

"Burnett's Coffee Clearer. A Woman's Invention. A patented combination of Cod Fish Skins and White of Eggs. The Best article for Settling Coffee. Eggs saved and no patent coffee pots needed. At a daily expense of less than 1/2¢ per family." Feb. 1889 ad of Joseph Burnett & Co., Boston.

● ● ● ●

Extracts from unsolicited letters used in manufacturers' brochures make informative reading. Some Hubbard & McClary extracts are transcribed here: "I have never seen, before, a coffee-pot which suspended the coffee midway between the top and the bottom, and then sent a continuous circulating current of water down through the ground powder, ascending by a separate channel to be again sent down through the grounds, and so on, over and over, until the nutritive matter of the ground coffee was so thoroughly leached and extracted as to leave the grounds about as tasteless as sawdust. This is just what your coffee-pot does." * * * "I weighed out one ounce of ground coffee, and placing it in the pot I added six cups of boiling water and boiled it five minutes; the result was six cups of coffee, which was consumed without any settling material, and which was so strong as to excite comment from the family, which was kept in ignorance of the way it had been prepared. The grounds, when collected and dried, changed from the original dark, to a light brown color. These exhausted grounds I placed in a paper marked 'A'. I next secured a quantity of grounds from the common coffee-pot, after breakfast, and dried them to a deep brown color. I then weighed out one ounce of these, which I placed in a paper 'B'. I next placed 'A' in your pot, and adding six cups of boiling water, I boiled it five minutes; the result barely colored the water, and no recognized taste of coffee was perceptible in the liquid. Cleaning out the pot, I put in 'B', — added six cups of boiling water, and boiled for five minutes; the result was a TOLERABLE cup of coffee — wanting in richness, but quite as good as one gets on steamboats or at R.R. stations, and fully confirming your declaration, that at least one-third saving in the coffee required may be effected."

"Tinkering Made Easy. — Holes in sauce pans or other tinwares, is a small thing. Those who will take the trouble to learn, can easily do small jobs at soldering, but many have not the needed gumption, and spoil the job. These will find the 'Magical Patching Plate' a great convenience. It is a thin sheet of solder prepared for the purpose, from which a bit is to be cut out large enough to well cover the hole; the surface of the ware is scraped bright, the patch put on, a poker or other hot iron held upon it, and when the solder melts, the job is done." *American Agriculturist,* 1877.

Coffee percolator or maker, 2 fishbowl-shaped glass globes, one above the other, scalloped red plastic "skirt" for the lower globe, part of the handle assembly, cover of top globe is also red, has odd little tabletop "gas" stove, with 2 handles, called the "Bride's Special," with "Pyrex" glass, "Moldex" plastic, mfd. by The Silex Co., Hartford, CT, about 18" H, late 1930s. **Silex made several models** — gas & electric — at the time. A fancy "De Luxe Lido" model had chrome instead of the "Moldex" & a sort of saucered chrome base. Another model, the "Buffet Service," for parties, had 2 bottom pouring pots, with one top globe. This model came on a 2-burner electric stove with black plastic base & small black handles at each end. **$18-$25+**

Coffee percolators — See also percolator urn

Coffee pots, biggins — See Coffee biggins

Coffee pots, aluminum:

Coffee pot, aluminum with Bakelite™ or other molded phenolic resin handle, 2 parts, top is "biggin" drip container, lower has V-neck pouring spout. (Another version, reportedly only 11" H, has green wooden finial and handle.) "Drip-O-Lator, The Better Coffee Maker," Enterprise Aluminum Co., Massillon, OH, 12" H, pat'd by R. F. Krause, Jan. 14, 1930. **$20-$22**

XIV-23. Drip coffee pot. *"French style," cast aluminum, 3 parts with inner basket, 3-pt. capacity. Mfd. by Wagner, Sidney, OH. "It makes coffee without boiling by the French [drip] method. It keeps coffee hot for a long time. The pot also is a beautiful pitcher. It will keep lemonade, etc., cold for a long period. It may be used for ice water by putting the cracked ice in the basket." 1930 ad. Similar pots with the scalloped bottom edge were made by other companies.* **$60+**

XIV-24. Biggin coffee maker, *and possibly a lamp filler, both in pieced tin. Note the delightful* **zigzag brace** *to the long spout at right. 19th C. Photograph courtesy Oveda Maurer Antiques, San Anselmo, CA.* **$85.00-$100; $75-$100**

Coffee pot, polished cast aluminum, sort of egg-shaped body, flat on bottom, in what manufacturer called a "graceful Dutch shape," hinged stepped lid made with perforated strainer appendage that fits exactly over small lip or spout, turned wooden handle, "which can readily be replaced if accidentally charred" (and I've seen quite a few with the handles charred on the lower end). "Monarcast," mfd. by Monarch Aluminum Ware Co., Cleveland, OH, c.1915. **$20-$25**

Coffee pot, so-called <u>French style</u> (Biggin dripper), cast aluminum in 4 parts, viz. lid (which looks like a fat biscuit cutter), perforated drip insert, urn shaped pot with black handle & funny fat little spout or lip up at top rim, separate sort of flared ruffled base, "makes coffee without boiling" by putting ground coffee in the cylindrical insert and pouring in water. Wagner Ware, 3 pt. capacity, 1930. A nearly identical pot, except for a more traditional gooseneck spout & rounder handle, was reported by collector Mozelle Bamber, of MA. Hers, which is marked on the bottom "Super Maid Cook-Ware," is 10-1/2" H or 11-1/4" H on base, which is about 4" diameter. Another collector from New Hampshire wrote to report one that is unmarked except for "Made in Canada." **$30-$40**

Coffee pots, copper & nickeled copper:

Coffee pot, copper, hinged lid, green Depression glass insert in lid, mark is indistinct, looks like "MERID—," could be name Meriden or possibly the place, Meriden, CT, 1925. **$15-$18**

Coffee pot, copper, roundish body, wood finial & handle, Manning & Bowman, makes only one cup, late 19th C. **$30-$45**

Coffee pot, copper with brass hinge, wood finial on lid & wood handle, brass ferrule on handle, crooked neck spout, "James S. Shaw Co.," 5-1/2" H, 19th C. **$70-$85**

Coffee pot, lighthouse (slant-sided) style, copper, wire bail & turned wood handle, ring finial on lid, 10-cup capacity, mid 19th C. **$65-$75**

Coffee pot, copper, with brass trim, & nifty turned wood handles painted black, American, 11-1/2" H, turn of century. **$45-$55**

Coffee pot, copper, with Britannia (pewter-like) lid, gooseneck spout & handle, very fancy, American, late 19th or early 20th. **$75-$85**

Coffee pot, hammered copper, pewter-lined (looks like tin), foreign-looking pot with round globular lower body, small ring foot, topped by slightly flared high neck with big beak spout, domed lid, thin handle curves out from near rim and "falls" inward to middle of globe, a reproduction based on a Russian pot from sometime in 19th C., which in turn reflects Middle Eastern & Turkish influence, B. Paleschuck, NYC, NY, 10" H, one qt. capacity, early 1930s, based on 19th C. form. **$25-$35+**

Coffee pot, slant-sided, copper, tin lid with unusual copper ring finial, wire bail with wood grip, American, mid 1800s. **$75-$100**

Coffee pot, nickel-plated copper, covered spout, turned wood handle & knob on lid, "Rome 4" on bottom, Rome, NY, early 20th C. **$18-$28**

Coffee pots, electric:

Coffee pot, electric, chrome, with sugar & creamer to match, "Edison General Electric Hotpoint," 20th C. **$22-$30**

Coffee pot, electric, chrome with tan handles & spigot, shaped like a football, "Forman Brothers Inc.," Brooklyn, NY, 2nd quarter, 20th C. **$20-$25**

Coffee pot, electric, copper, makes 4 cups, 20th C. **$25-$35**

Coffee pot, electric, floral patterned china, chrome base & spigot, matching creamer and covered sugar bowl, (china by Fraunfelter) "Royal Rochester," mfd. by Robeson Rochester Corp., (Zanesville, OH), Rochester, NY, pat'd Aug. 12, 1924. **$135-$150**

Coffee pots, enamelware:

Coffee pot, black & white enamelware, American, large size, c.1910 to 1930s. **$40-$65**

Coffee pot, blue & white enamelware in slant-sided shape, with moss roses on both sides, doesn't look like Manning-Bowman wares, prob. European, late 19th C. **$165-$250**

Coffee pot, blue & white enamelware with flower design, tin lid, gooseneck spout, European or American, late 1800s. **$155-$220**

Coffee pot, bluish-gray graniteware, tin top with wooden finial, unusual one-cup size, late 19th C. **$65-$120**

Coffee pot, robin's egg blue & white agateware, gooseneck spout, American, 19th C. **$125-$165**

Coffee pot, sky blue & white speckled enamelware, gooseneck spout, bail handle with wood grip, late 19th C., early 20th. **$130-$185**

Coffee pot, teal & white swirled agateware, 11-1/2" H, turn of century. **$200-$300**

Coffee pot, turquoise & white spattered enamel with deep blue trim, American, late 19th or early 20th C. **$250+**

Coffee pot, dark turquoise enamelware, with gooseneck spout, European or American, turn of century. **$150+**

Coffee pot, peacock blue & white enamelware, gooseneck spout, American, early 20th C. **$140-$175**

Coffee pot, brown graniteware with a few chips. 12" H, 19th C. Nice color, but a **shelf piece**, as they say, although that refers more accurately to something with a rusted out bottom, or a hopelessly calcium-clogged inside. **$25-$30**

Coffee pot, brown speckled enamelware, with Britannia mountings, including lid, handle & spout. Protective band around base is brass — undoubtedly once nickel-plated, probably Manning, Bowman & Co., c.1890-1900. **$155-$225**

Coffee pot, brown & white agateware, white metal lid, copper base, shell & column motif on throat of spout & handle, probably Manning & Bowman, 10" H, late 19th C. **$275-$350**

Coffee pot, brown & white spattered agateware, domed "golden" pewter lid, spout & handle, golden-colored tin "skirt," possibly colored by japanning. American, 11-3/8" H, late 19th C. **$300-$375**

XIV-25. Coffee boiler & tea pot & biggin. (L) & (M) *Enameled graniteware, with paint-enameled turned wooden handles, gadrooned domed hinged lids. St. Louis Stamping Co., St. Louis, MO. Ad in* The Metal Worker, *8/20/1892.; (R) Biggin, for drip-style coffee making, which was also known as "French style." Graniteware and tin, from Matthai-Ingram catalog, c.1890.* **$95-$125; $125-$150**

XIV-26. Souvenirs *of huge coffee pot in Winston-Salem, NC. Black-painted cast pot (spelter or zinc) metal, and cast brass version, both 5-1/4" H. I suspect brass one is older, maybe from the 1930s.* **$5-$15**

XIV-27. Post card of "The Big Coffee Pot" *in Winston-Salem, NC. Color lithograph, reprinted over fairly long period. This one was mailed in 1940. The conical coffee pot itself, with the braced crooked neck spout and handle with reinforced grip, is made of painted tin and was erected in 1858 and still stands today, off Main Street. Merchant Julius Mickey, who wanted to attract custom to his roofing, tin and stove business, had it built (or perhaps built it himself). Fortunately, it lasted through two metal drives and various vicissitudes. The pot, probably based on a Moravian style, is 87" H x 27" diameter at top & 64" diameter at bottom. It is calculated that it would hold 740-1/2 gallons of coffee.*

Coffee pot, brown & white speckled enamelware, gooseneck spout, nickeled white metal mountings, probably Manning, Bowman, late 19th C. **$140-$190**

Coffee pot, brown & white swirled enamelware, gooseneck spout, probably "Onyx," Columbian Enameling & Stamping Co., turn of century. **$150-$190**

Coffee pot, dark brown enamelware flecked with white, hinged lid, possibly "Onyx" by Columbian Stamping, or possibly Manning, Bowman & Co., or even none of above, and, instead, European, early 20th C. **$90-$150**

Coffee pot, cobalt enamelware, with gold trim, gooseneck spout, prob. European, late 19th C. **$115-$165**

Coffee pot, gray spotted graniteware, two-tone, pewter spout, base, trim, handle, crown collar & lid, American (?), 8-3/4" H, 19th C. **$135-$175**

Coffee pot, gray graniteware, tin cover, graceful shape, American, 9" H, early 20th C. **$85-$135**

Coffee pot, gray graniteware, tin lid with white porcelain knob, hollow cast iron handle was originally painted black, American (?), 8-1/2" H, late 19th or early 20th C. **$85-$135**

Coffee pot, gray graniteware with tin lid, brass ring around base, a few dings, late 19th C. **$45-$65**

Coffee pot, gray spattered graniteware, tin lid, large size, late 19th C. **$125-$160**

Coffee pot, green & white striped enamelware, small size, European, prob. Czechoslovakian, early 20th C. to 1930s. **$135-$145**

Coffee pot, lavender or mauve (Hey! What would you call mauve? Oscar Wilde said it was pink trying to be lavender, and Thomas Beer, who in 1926 wrote *The Mauve Decade* about the 1890s in America, said it was "pink turning to purple." Some dictionaries say mauve is lilac.) Anyway, pale browny lavender speckled enamelware, tin spout & tin lid with turned wood finial, wood handle, probably Manning & Bowman, American, 9" H, late 19th C. **$200-$250**

Coffee pot, mulberry enamelware, lighthouse shape, black-painted turned wood handle & wood finial, 9" H, c.1890-1900. **$150-$250**

Coffee pot, pink agateware with handpainted petunias, nickeled brass & copper trim including breast-band, spout, lid & base, probably Manning & Bowman, late 19th C. **$225-$350**

Coffee pot, purplish brown enamelware, domed enameled top, turned wooden handle, possibly Manning, Bowman & Co., 9" H, late 19th C. **$180-$255**

Coffee pot, red enamelware, gooseneck, nickeled lid, 20th C. **$75-$120**

Coffee pot, white & black enamelware, tall & thin, American, 19th C. **$150-$170**

Coffee pot, enamelware with colorful depiction of Statue of Liberty, ornate pewter spout, domed lid & handle, American, Statue of Liberty Commemorative, 1886. **Would Have Been A Great Investment:** Offered in 1982 for sale by Al & Nancy Schlegel, Willow Hollow, Penacook, NH. The price then was only $225. It most likely would have doubled in 1986, the centennial of the statue. Probable value now: **$1000+**

Coffee pot, enamelware with white background & floral design, white metal mountings at collar, gooseneck spout, base, handle (these were also offered with nickel-plated mountings at a slight extra cost), Manning-Bowman, pat'd June 5, 1883, registered Jan. 13, 1885. **$175-$225**

"New Art Enameled Ware. Beautiful Creations That Prophesy Great Developments in Ornamental Novelties of Steel. — It is refreshing to turn away for a brief while from . . . ordinary enameled ware . . . & contemplate the possibilities that lie in enameled ware as an article for decorating & beautifying homes. Not much of the latter is yet shown in this country, & probably none of it will ever be made by the American manufacturer whose mind runs more toward the question of profit than the production of truly artistic wares.[!] But the Austrians have devoted considerable time of late to the making of beautifully decorated vases, pitchers, urns, mugs, etc., that at first glance can scarcely be distinguished from pottery or fine china, although made of drawn steel.

"It is decorative in every sense of the word and possesses all the charm of . . . ceramic . . . [plus] indestructability, for this new art enameled ware can be dropped to the floor or knocked about with impunity. . . . [On display at a NY firm, Stransky & Co., is a collection of] various kinds of enameled ware that are sold in foreign countries. In America the housewife is satisfied with her white and white, blue and white, gray mottled, etc., but abroad . . . tastes are more exacting, and each country demands its own particular designs.

"In Japan, for example, the vogue is for flowery patterns in all the pleasing colors of the Sunrise Kingdom, and the Stransky collection contains a series of basins bearing characteristic pictures. Some are purely floral but others portray boating scenes and sketches of Japanese life, every detail being worked out even more minutely than is possible on pottery.

"If the limits of this article permitted, it would be highly interesting to describe separately the enameled ware fashions of each country: China, Little Asia, Turkey, Singapore, Siam, the Balkan States, Hungary, etc., all have their individuality, running the gamut from the fantastic dragon patterns of China to the thick, heavy designs of Russia. It is amazing how well the colors are produced, and the effect of real china is so cleverly simulated that even a trained eye could be readily deceived. The Stransky collection will be appreciated by those of the trade who are interested in something more than enameled ware which sells at nineteen cents, marked down from a quarter." *House Furnishing Review,* Feb. 1906.

Coffee pots, tin: painted, punched and plain:

Color & Added Value — Generally speaking, blue background is $$$$$, red is $$$$, yellow $$$, black $$, & brown $.

Crooked-spout Coffee Pots — A pattern for fraud. In the mid-1980s, an expert in early painted tin (sometimes called tôle) noticed something chilling. Libby Spencer, writing in *New York-Pennsylvania Collector,* December 1985, recounted the sighting, within a four-week period, of almost a dozen painted tin, **crooked-spout** coffee pots — which are considered rare. Further, all were **black**, with flowers & scrolls in red, yellow and green. All had the **cut-back spout tip** that looks like an open bird beak. All had **hinged domed lids** with small **mushroom finial**. All had a **braced strap handle**. All had **orangey rust**. All had **"signs" of wear** — not too little to look new, not too much to turn off a sucker who'd want to pay $800 to $1000 to add one to a collection. The value of a real, 150-year-old pot of this type, could be well over $1000 — definitely a critical-mass triggering fakers, especially if there's only one fabricator to make them, and one "fence" to pass them off to dealers. Using a common market equation, the *cost* of something is multiplied by about two to arrive at wholesale, and multiplied by either four or five to arrive at *retail*. In this case, it would imply a *cost* of between $200 and $250, and a wholesale price to an unsuspecting (we hope) dealer that would include another $200 to $250 — or $400 to $500. Not only is the collector, and the hobby, a loser, but so is the poor schlub talented enough to make such a thing, and desperate or crooked enough to be willing to. I'm sorry, but my advice is don't buy this form unless the provenance is absolutely foolproof. The value ranges are as they were reported or seen in the last few years. The plain colored ones are probably OK, and possibly the brown asphaltum ones are OK, unless the faker thought he better sprinkle in a few more common examples. (These descriptions will probably make some of you nervous about your pots!)

Coffee pot, lighthouse shape, decorated tin, or tôle. Dark brown japanned background (least desirable color) with polychromatic flowers & swagged border, strap handle with grip, crooked spout, stepped low dome lid with brass knob finial, **amazingly unworn finish**, American, 10-5/8" H, 19th C. pot with period decoration, though faked finishes are known. Brought $3700 at Garth's Auctions, Delaware, OH, April 11-12, 1986. **$3000-$4000**

XIV-28. Coffee pot. *Pieced tin, squared short curved spout, unusual fanciful curve to handle. Brass mushroom finial to convex lid, 10" H. Pennsylvania, mid 19th C. Courtesy Carol Bohn, Mifflinburg, PA. Value range mine, not Bohn's. While this one is not decorated on the surface, the extra* **wiggle** *in the handle adds great sculptural charm, which many people pay extra for. (SEE XIV-24, -31, -34 for more odd spout braces. What a wonderful collection theme that would be!)* **$170-$300**

XIV-29. Coffee pots —wriggled & punched. *Both Pennsylvanian pieced tin with inverted cone bodies and crooked-neck spouts.* **(L)** *Pot with flared footed base. Its funnel-like conical hinged lid, which gives it a slightly comical appearance, is very uncommon. Note extra brace to handle. The style of decoration is called "**wriggled**." Signed with serpentine maker's mark, early to mid 19th C. 10-3/4" H.* **(R)** *A jauntier pot, 11-3/4" H, has maker's smoothly domed lid. Its decoration called "**punchwork**." Signed in beautiful capital serif letters by "W[illoughy] Shade for Mary Shade," and dated March 18,1848. We do not know who Mary was, but such coffee pots were usually, if not always, presentation pieces given to brides. In* <u>wrigglework</u>, *the graving tool was skidded across surface, making a jiggedy mark to outline & fill shapes of flowers, leaves, etc.* <u>Punchwork</u> *is done with a punch, but although it is hit hard enough to make a dimple on the tin's surface, it is not allowed to puncture or pierce it. Photograph courtesy Sotheby Parke-Bernet, NYC. Prices realized at 10/26/1984 auction.* **$2200; $2400**

Coffee pot, lighthouse shape with crooked neck spout, domed lid with brass knob, braced strap handle with grip, painted tin with flowers, fruits, leaves in **color on black** asphaltum background, American, 11-1/2" H, mid 19th C. **$800+**

Black grounds — "Black grounds may be formed on metal, by drying linseed oil only, when mixed with a little lamp-black. The work is then exposed in a stove to a heat which will render the oil black. The heat should be low at first, and increased very gradually, or it will blister. This kind of japan requires no polishing. It is extensively used for defending articles of ironmongery from rust." James Smith, *The Dictionary of Arts, Sciences and Manufacturers.* Vol. II, p. 795. Boston: Phillips, Sampson & Co., 1854.

XIV-30. Pieced tinwares, *including coffee pots, and unusual conical vessel. Compare the dark pot in the very back with the pot in XIV-28 Note the two-handled cup or sugar bowl, and the punctured tin cheese mold in foreground. Photograph courtesy of Oveda Maurer Antiques, San Anselmo, CA.* **$125+**

XIV-31. Tinwares. *Note low-originating straight spout on coffee pot at right. But for me, of special interest is the funny spout and its* **serpentine brace** *on the vessel at left. It appears to be an oiler or lamp filler of some kind. (Cup or sugar bowl is same as one in previous picture.) This dealer always has unusual metalwares. Photograph courtesy Oveda Maurer Antiques, San Anselmo, CA.* **$125+**

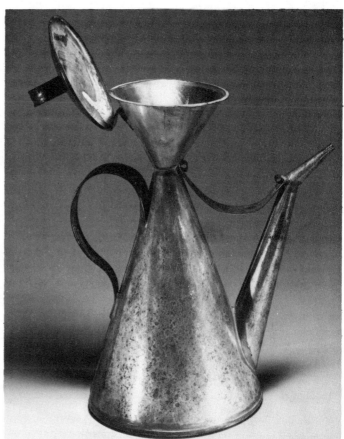

XIV-32. Coffee pot. *Paint-decorated tin, (I don't know the color, which would be important in determining value — see text for relative color values). Short straight spout, hinged lid with curled-tin knob. Note diagonal piecing seam under handle, indicative of small sheets of tin. Note also the faint light circle behind the flowers: this is thought by some to be near-proof of Pennsylvania origins, and yet coffee pots having this circle and with exactly this kind of border near the top are said by others to be typical of Connecticut provenance. Generally speaking, it seems that the straight spout tends to be Connecticut, while the crooked spout is Pennsylvanian. Remember: wares were made in CT for "Western" trades, and peddled in NY & PA. 8-7/8" H, 19th C. Picture courtesy of the National Museum of American History, Smithsonian Institution.*

XIV-33. Coffee pot? *At least so identified by the Smithsonian. I believe it may be a large lamp filler. At any rate, a tinsmith's work of art. Funnel top (for making drip coffee? for safer filling with the lamp oil?). Hinged lid, strap handle,* **swag-braced spout.** *I think it's a lamp filler because of the smallness of the spout's tip, and the angle of the spout. 11" H, 19th C. Picture courtesy of the National Museum of American History, Smithsonian Institution.* **$165+**

XIV-35. "Student's coffee pot." *Brass and tin, with wood side handle. 2, 4, 6 and 8 cups. From F. A. Walker catalog, c.1870s.* **$45-$60**

XIV-34. "Infuser for tea or coffee," *two views. "By the insertion of the stopper into the spout of the pot, the water poured into the [upper chamber] infuser is retained there until it has dissolved all the desirable properties of the tea or coffee. By withdrawing the stopper the prepared beverage is allowed to run into the pot, from which it may be served in the usual way. This infuser is made in three styles — tin, enameled ware and stoneware, and it comes in various sizes." Imported from Europe by G. M. Thurnauer & Bro., NYC wholesalers of housewares. Article in* House Furnishing Review, *7/1905.*

XIV-36. Coffee pot — Turkish style, *easily confused with a butter melter or some other saucepan. Copper, in the "Turkish pattern," made in six sizes, holding from 1 to 6 cups. Henry Rogers Sons & Co., Wolverhampton, England, 1914 catalog.* **$20-$30**

Coffee pot, lighthouse (tapering toward top with straight sides) style, tin with black japanning, crooked neck spout, slightly domed hinged lid with brass knob, American, poss. CT, 10" H, 19th C. Not as desirable to collectors as would be one with either a red background, or painted decorations over the japanned background. **$325+**

Coffee pot, lighthouse style with perky — even impertinent — pieced, crooked neck spout & extra large curved handle, dark brown japanning & polychrome flowers, brass mushroom finial to lid, American, 10-5/8" H, 19th C. Not as desirable as one with red or blue japanned background color. But **surface is very good**, & looks original. **$2500+**

Spouts — I use the term <u>crooked neck</u> or <u>crook-neck</u>, or <u>crooked spout</u> only with an angled spout having a seam at the elbow (to mix similes), occasionally at "wrist" also. Sometimes these are called <u>cock's head spouts</u>. Many crooked spouts on copper tea kettles look just as angular, but do not have a circumferential elbow seam. These are called <u>gooseneck spouts</u>, and there is a wide latitude in the use of the term. Some goosenecks are more stuck-out, curious, and aggressive than others, more ganderish; some are more graceful and plump at the bend; others are small and timid, perhaps goslings? The crooked neck spout is, I'm sure, tinsmiths' version of coppersmiths' gooseneck spout, which could not be copied exactly, because it was impossible to hammer out the extreme angle in tin plate and keep the plating's integrity.

Coffee pot, lighthouse type with tapered sides, painted tin with scrolls & flowers on dark green ground, somewhat worn, nice scrolled strap handle, deep conical lid, very handsome, American, 11" H, mid 19th C. **$800-$1500**

Coffee pot, painted tin or tôle, decorations in **perfect condition**, red, yellow & green on **black asphaltum ground**, braced strap handle, attractive finial, American, looks mid 19th C. **$1000-$2000**

Coffee pot, engraved tin, with designs including tulips, eagle, flag, peacock, vines & leaves, PA German, prob. mid 19th C. **$3000+**

Coffee pot, punched tin, slightly battered but still graceful crooked neck spout, design of small pot with large tulip & leaves punched on one side (perhaps on both?), braced strap handle, traces of "old black paint & light rust." **Punched tin is not punctured tin**. It refers to a very rare form of decoration, done by tapping a small punch along the outlines of flowers, urns, birds, eagles, on what will be the inside of the vessel, in order to make a raised beaded line. Pennsylvania, 11" H, mid 19th C. Sold at Garth's, July 28, 1989 for: **$2600**

Coffee pot, punched tin, simply decorated with strong tulip and leaves on upper part of body, flowers with 6 petals below, spiraled ring border around flared foot, crooked spout, braced strap handle, nearly flat lid with button finial, out & in body pieced from 2 truncated cones (also called an inverted cone body by some cataloguers), the shorter below, joined at the "waist," 1/3 way from bottom, marked with two initials "A" and "R," probably those of owners, Pennsylvania, about 10" H, dated 1867. This piece from the Lamb collection was sold at Pennypacker's in 1976. Price then was $2,300. A similar pot, 11" H, with punched design of flower pots with tulips, very attractive curve to spout, was in the Richard Withington March 4, 1989 auction at Andover, MA, and sold for a low $1100. Very surprising. **$3000+**

Coffee pot, for students, tin with brass trim, wooden handle sticks straight out halfway down cylindrical body, straight side spout attached at bottom of pot, looks sort of like an espresso coffee pot, from F. A. Walker catalog, four sizes: 2, 4, 6 and 8 cup capacity, c.1870s or 1880s. I have always thought that F. A. Walker was only an importer & wholesaler. But here's an enlightening news item from *The Metal Worker*, Oct. 21, 1882. "Messrs. F. A. Walker & Co., 83 Cornhill, Boston, <u>manufacturers and refinishers</u> of brass goods, have a very fine display of brass fenders, fire screens, fire sets, coal vases, tea urns, placques, brass-trimmed bellows, &c. Several specimens of Benerez brasswork shown by this firm are very fine indeed, and attract marked attention." **$30-$45**

Coffee pot, large tin one with unusual copper bottom coming 2 inches up sides. The copper protected the tin solder & conducted heat better besides, American, 19th C. **$35-$45**

Coffee pot, pieced tin, tall & thin, extreme conical body with funnel top, strap handle, hinged lid with strap handle, curved spout support from neck where cone meets funnel, for drip coffee, extraordinary piece. American, 12" H, early 19th C. **$500+**

Coffee pot, pieced tin with diagonal seams, straight spout with thin brace at top, slanted sides, braced handle. If this is not early 19th C., at least it was made from small pieces of tin. (Tin was only available in small sheets during 18th & early 19th Cs, imported, mostly from England. But nothing would stop a frugal tinsmith from using pieced scrap tin from larger, later sheets.) Style sometimes called "Shaker," American, 9-1/2" H, early 19th C. See also reflector oven in Chapter X, and information on tin plate in Chapter VII. **$250+**

Coffee pot, straight-sided, tin, with copper bottom, turned wooden handle painted black, American, late 19th C. **$45-$55**

Coffee pot, tin, 3-loop tin finial on the lid, prob. CT, 6" H, c.1830s to 1850. **$95-$125**

Coffee pot, tin, conical shape with straight side spout, strap handle, simple but very unusual, the design as spare & elegant as the sleek Italian designs of 100 years later, American, 8-3/4" H, prob. 2nd quarter 19th C. **$95-$125**

The Kin-Hee Coffee Pot

is a triumph of genius. It is unlike other Coffee Pots. If you can boil water you can in one minute make Coffee in it fit for a king. By actual test it costs only seven-tenths of a cent per cup. It is, therefore, the best to drink and the least expensive.

Demonstrated at Pan-American Exposition

This shows the coffee pot upside down, the top filled with boiling water and coffee submerged. It stands for one minute, straining cloth is put on, then the bottom. Then the entire pot is turned right side up and the coffee is ready to serve. A child can do it. *Patented May 22, 1900.*

XIV-37. Coffee pot. *"Kin-Hee" pot, mfd. by James Heekin & Co, Cincinnati, OH, and in Canada, The Eby, Blain Co., Ltd., Toronto. They also sold a mocha-java coffee blend in 1 lb. cans.* **$20+**

XIV-38. Tea & coffee pot. *"Marion Harland" pot, mfd. by Silver & Co., Brooklyn, NC. In their c.1910 catalog. Made of copper with ebonized wood handles. Could be had in plain, nickel-plated or "Old English" finish. Tinned inside. It was sort of a percolating infuser. Marion Harland ran a cooking school in the late 19th C, and wrote cookbooks too.* **$25-$45**

The Thirteenth Annual Report of the Commissioner of Labor. *1898. Hand and Machine Labor,* Volume 1 (Washington: GPO, 1899) compares two methods of making a 2-quart coffee pot from tin. The conical pot above is about the same age as the "primitive" one described below. "Under the modern method the bodies of the pots were cut with a steam cutting machine in 15 minutes. Under the primitive method the tin was cut with stock shears by hand and required 4 hours, but before the tin could be cut . . . it was necessary to mark it out, and this required an additional . . . 2 hours and 40 minutes, so that . . . the hand work required nearly 27 times as long as the machine work." The "primitive" method dates to 1840; the machine method to 1895. *The Report* lists a tinsmith's 30 production steps — using tools from an awl & hatchet stake to swage & peening hammer — in order on the left below. The 22 steps for machine-making, taken by 27 different workers with 18 job descriptions, are on the right.

● ● ● ●

1840 PRODUCTION STEPS "Primitive Method"	1895 PRODUCTION STEPS "Factory Method"
marking out bodies of pots	cutting out bodies
cutting out bodies	perforating for spouts
turning top edges for wire	edging bodies for wire
putting in wire	forming bodies
peening down top edges	groving bodies together
swaging bead around tops	wiring top
forming bodies	notching bodies for hinge
cutting out handles, spouts, rims	boring bodies for bottom
forming spouts	cutting out bottoms
turning edges of handles for wire	double-seaming bodies
putting in wire and forming hinges	cutting out spouts
peening down edges of handles	forming spouts
cutting out hinges	cutting out handles
forming tin lips on hinges	beading handles
forming handles	forming handles
marking out covers	cutting out covers
cutting out covers	drawing covers
raising covers	crimping covers
turning edges of covers	notching covers
peening down edges of covers	punching covers
putting knobs on covers	& putting in knobs
soldering spouts and seams in bodies	soldering all seams*
turning edges for bottoms	testing pots
marking out bottoms	
cutting out bottoms	*plus overseeing*
edging bottoms	*establishment;*
snapping on bottoms	*furnishing power; and*
peening down edges of bottoms	*firing boiler*
double-seaming bottoms	*[for steam power].*
soldering all seams	

*Note that soldering was also done by hand in the factory setting of 1895.

Coffee pot, tin, finial is a grape cluster, brass ID plate with an eagle, and reads "The National Tea and Coffee Pot Company," J. B. Smith's, Milwaukee, WI, 1859 patent #22737 (or 22787?), & Nov. 19, 1867's #71236 & #71237. Smith patented this & at least two more coffee pots later. **$85-$100**

Coffee pot, tin, lighthouse (or slanted sides) shape, with domed lid & ring finial, wire bail handle, great braced handle, 3 qt. capacity, American, early to mid 19th C. Even plain, this is quite a looker, especially the braced handle. A lot of modern designers

— even (or especially?) architects — could learn something by studying such a coffee pot as this. **$75+**

Coffee pot, tin, "out-and-in" hourglass body of 2 different height truncated cones, the bottom one upside down, joined at the large ends around the "waist" in a sort of collet, with crooked spout originating in lower part, braced strap handle with grip, hinged high conical lid with scrolled double ring finial, rather high foot. Elaborately decorated with an eagle (?) & foliage in **wrigglework** or <u>wriggle work</u>, accomplished by tapping a small chisel-like tool with a mallet or hammer so that it makes tiny bounces or skips & cuts a sort of chased zigzaggy line in the metal somewhat similar to brightwork engraving on silver. This is probably the most highly desired type of tinware, more than painted tin, and is sometimes called <u>wrigglesware</u>. Unmarked, but if Lasansky is correct, "M.B." is the maker, therefore prob. PA, 10-3/4" H, 19th C. According to Jeannette Lasansky, in her *To Cut, Piece, and Solder,* "Only one maker of tinware used this [wriggle work] technique . . . unfortunately . . . [his] identity . . . remains a mystery — only two of his pieces have initials (M.B.), and none are dated." (p.72) Her book shows four pieces. **$5000-$7000**

Coffee pot, tin, slanted sides, straight spout, scroll-y handle with spur lid rest, American, mid 19th C. **$70-$85**

Coffee pot, tin, brass ID plate reads "The Young America," American, dated 1859. There's a town in Minnesota, known to devoteés of sweepstakes, called "Young America," but I couldn't find, among the several coffee pots patented in 1859, any from that state. **$100+**

Coffee pot, tin with copper bottom to aid heat conduction, American, late 19th or early 20th C. **$45+**

Coffee pot, tin with fluted spout, delicate mushroom finial on lid, cast iron handle with spur lid rest, beautifully made, elegant detail, American, late 19th C. **$125-$160**

Coffee roaster, cast iron, 3 part, pot with 3 legs, wire bail handle, pivoting agitator with tall vertical handle, slotted lid, pat'd by F. Humphrey of Philadelphia, mfd. by I. A. Sheppard & Co., marked Philadelphia, PA (Baltimore was another Sheppard location). Size #1: 5-1/4" H x 8-1/2" diameter, pat'd Mar. 13, 1866. **$275+**

XIV-39. "Self-pouring" tea or coffee pot. *"Royle's Patent," this "Boston No. 1" model was sold by Paine, Diehl & Co., Philadelphia, out of their 1888 catalog. It was probably made for them by William Vogel & Brothers, Brooklyn. The patent was granted 4/3/1888 in America, but two years earlier in England. There, the self-pourers were made by James Dixon & Sons, Sheffield, for the patentee, J. J. Royle, Manchester. Wherever made, most seem to be made of Britannia metal, which could be left plain, or plated with nickel or silver. Meriden Britannia Co. and The Boston Co. were other makers in the US. It was sometimes called a* **mother's helper** *because "mother" (the person designated to pour tea at tea-time) needed only pull up the pump in the top of the finial, place the cup under the spout, and push the piston down. I imagine it took a bit of practice.* **$75-$135**

XIV-43. Coffee percolator-urn *and server. Chrome, electric, mfd by Labelle Silver Co., Brooklyn, NY, c.1950s. It's possible that this company is related to Silver & Co. And it's possible you can see me taking the photo at a NYC street fair.* **$40-$60**

XIV-40. Canal or barge coffee pot, *"gaudy" decorated, with glazed applied posies. Rockingham ceramic called "barge" or "canal craft," used on British canal barges. Besides the flowers and the mini-pot finial is the legend "A Present from a Friend" on the side. 10-1/2" H x 6-1/2" W, English, 19th C. Ex-Keillor Collection.*

XIV-41. Coffee & tea filtering system. *"Boston," all glass, mfd. by The Silex Co., Boston, MA. Came in 4 and 6 cup sizes.* House Furnishing Review, *5/1917.* **$70-$150+**

XIV-44. Coffee roaster. *Cast embossed marks: "Woods Patent, Roys & Wilcox Co., Harrington's Import, Berlin Ct. Pat'd 5/17/1859." Oddly, the T. R. Wood's Patent was granted 4/17/1849, so actually this is dated as J. D. Harrington's patent, not Wood's. Wood lived in Cincinnati, OH; Harrington in Rochester, NY. The word "Import" is another mystery. The unknown missing "chapter" might be found by searching the* Official Gazette *for the not-infrequent reports on infringement suits, etc., between 1849 and 1859. Cast iron, hinged "cannon ball" in frame, with bail handle & 3 legs. Ball has long handles, which clamp together by the crank. Frame 2-3/4" H x 9" diameter; ball 6-1/2" diameter with 5-1/4" L handles. Courtesy the late Darryl G. Dudash, Alaquippa, PA. Prices vary widely; range given here is general average.* **$500+**

XIV-42. "Tricolator" coffee maker. *Filtering percolation pot, the "Norfolk" 9-cup electric. Mfd. by Tricolator Co., Inc., NYC, who had at least a couple dozen styles, with glazed & decorated china pots, Pyrex™ pots, and metal upper parts. 1933 brochure.* **$40-$100+**

Coffee roaster, cast iron frame with 3 legs & thin wire bail, side handles that are held clamped together by the slip-on long dog-leg crank, cast iron 2-piece globe-shaped container rests in frame, looks like something from a planetarium, "Woods Patent," mfd. by Roys & Wilcox & Co., Thomas R. Wood (Cincinnati, OH) R&W in Berlin, CT, ball: 6-1/2" diameter with 5-1/4" L handles; frame: 2-3/4" H x 9" diameter, pat'd April 17, 1849. This is one of the most desirable coffee roasters of all. Another very similar one seen is marked "Roys & Wilcox," plus a patent date of May 17, 1859; it was featured in the 1869 Dover Stamping Co. catalog. A handsome example was for sale by a dealer with a very discerning eye and fabulous iron stock. His price was $900 in late 1988. For the Woods: **$500+**

XIV-45. Coffee roaster. *Similar to the Wood's/Harrington Patent in previous picture, except the legs are shorter and the crank has a curve. This one was depicted in F. A. Walker & Co.'s catalog, 1880s. Another one, with a straight handle, was depicted in the 1866 Dover Stamping Co. catalog.* **$500+**

XIV-46. Coffee roaster which avoids inequal torrefaction. *"The gratefulness of the beverage afforded by the coffee bean depends upon many circumstances, which are seldom all combined. The nature of the soil, the climate, seed, mode of culture and cure, influence greatly the quality of the fruit. But when all these particulars concur, and the berry is of the finest sort, it may be ruined in the roasting." So wrote Andrew Ure, in* A Dictionary of Arts, Manufactures & Mines, *1854. The illustrated commercial roaster was developed by William Law of London, who "conquered the difficulties" of roasting evenly in a sheet metal cylinder by inventing "the globular roaster, actuated by a compound motion like that of our earth. This roaster, with its double, rotary motion, is heated not over an open fire but in an atmosphere of hot air, through a cast metal casting. The globe is so mounted as to revolve horizontally, and also from time to time vertically, whereby the included beans are tossed about and intermingled in all directions. Inequality of torrefaction becomes impossible." Afterwards, the coffee is ground between two flat millstones, and is "thereby capable of giving out all its virtues to either boiling or cold water."* **$1000+**

Coffee roaster, for hearth, sheet iron cylinder with sliding "trap" door, long crooked crank handle out of one end, short iron rod out of other, fit into spit holder or other iron frame, Canadian or American, 20" L tip to tip, cylinder itself is 8-3/4" L x 6-1/4" diameter, sliding hatch opens to 2-1/2", c.1840 to 1860. (NOTE that Griswold did similar pieces, much later.) **$275-$350**

Coffee roaster, for hearth, sheet iron, cylindrical, long shaft & wooden handle knob, American (?), 50" L, early 19th C. **$250+**

Dandelion Coffee, sent in by a reader of a British periodical, *Cottage Gardening*. "Dr. Harrison, of Edinburgh, prefers dandelion coffee to that of Mecca; and many persons all over the Continent prefer a mixture of succory* and coffee to coffee alone. Dig up the roots of dandelion, wash them well, but do not scrape them, dry them, cut them into the size of peas, and then roast them in an earthen pot, or coffee roaster of any kind. The great secret of good coffee, is, to have it fresh burnt and fresh ground." (*I don't know if "succory" is the same as "chicory" in this instance. Food writer Waverley Root says that "succory" sounds as if it ought to be a stand-in word for "chicory" but that it actually means suet. Oh, gag me with a spoon . . . in my coffee? I think it's a word for dandelion root, probably unknown to Waverley Root.) *American Agriculturist*, Sept.1846.

XIV-47. Coffee roaster, *saucepan type. Sheet iron with cast iron crank and probably wrought iron long handle. Depicted in* American Home Cook Book, *by an "American lady," 1854. Directions said to add "to each pound of coffee one table-spoonful of water. The coffee will thoroughly roast without being burned." In early 1997, a tinned sheet iron roaster with "illegible names on cover & base", 9-1/8" diameter x 3-1/4" deep, that looks extremely similar to this one except for the hole in the lid, was advertised by a group shop in New Hampshire.* **$150+**

XIV-48. Coffee roaster — cylinder in frame. *"Patent Flue" roaster to use on cookstoves or ranges. Cast & sheet iron, high carrying handle on top, crank at one end. Mfd. by Stuart, Peterson & Co., of Philadelphia, PA, and Burlington, NJ, who made stoves and stove hollowware. They made this roaster in 4 sizes: one is round to fit a 8" or 9" hole; others ovals to fit two 6" holes, two 7" holes, and two 9" holes. 1875 catalog picture. There is a great similarity in this style of roaster to confectioners' roasters used for "burnt" almonds, and other nuts.* **$200-$350**

Coffee roaster, heavy cast iron, straight sides, top crank that moves the 4 stirring "fingers" inside, 2 large upright fixed ring handles, looks like a cross between an ironclad Civil War submarine & a pirate's chest, not marked, American, 11" H x 8-3/4" diameter, mid-19th C. **$250-$450**

Coffee roaster, heavy sheet iron, sauce pan or frying pan style with long handle, fitted lid with small oval trap door, crank in top, American, 8" diameter (another of these is 7-1/2" diameter x 2-1/2" deep, overall length 16" including handle), c.1870s or 1880s. **$75+**

Reproduction alert — This sauce pan roaster has been reproduced in heavy steel, with same long handle.

Coffee roaster, key wound clockwork mechanism, sets over 2 range eyes, cast iron frame, tall housing of works at one end, long horizontal wire mesh cylinder holds beans, hemi-cylindrical pieced tin cover with strap handle fits down over the wire canister, diagonal revolving plates inside to move the beans around, "American Coffee Roaster," pat'd by C. A. Mills, Hazel Green, WI, 9" H x 18-1/2" L, pat'd Nov. 7, 1863 & April 28, 1868. In his specifications, Mr. Mills wrote "The frame and upright plates may be cast iron, the vessel of sheet metal, and the wheels of the clock mechanism may be of cast or wrought metal, the teeth being cut. I do not, however, confine myself to any particular material or mode of manufacture." **$550+**

Coffee roaster, sheet iron & brass, aluminum, alcohol heating lamp in base, clockwork action, corrugated drum inside bounces beans around, snap lid, looks like a percolator inside, detachable crank looks like a Victrola handle, has 2 speeds, "Rapide" & "Lente" plus "Arrette" (stop), French, turn of century. **$150+**

Coffee roaster, sheet iron can & round, flat cast iron frame with oblong, walled "corral" for the cylinder, and a channel for inserting an iron lid-lifter-like handle, fits over range eye, sliding door in top of canister body, bent-rod side crank, Griswold Mfg. Co., Erie, PA, 9" diameter, looks c.1880s, but Dave Smith, a Griswold expert & author, dates it to c.1910. The handle is the clincher for the high value. **$1000-$1500**

XIV-49. Coffee roaster — cylinder in frame, *"American Coffee Roaster," pat'd 4/28/1863 and 11/7/1865, by C. A. Mills, of Hazel Green, WI and then Bristol, CT.* **Clockwork** *mechanism wound by key seen at right. Sets over 2 eyes of range. You load the heavy wire canister with coffee beans, set it into the cast iron frame, slip tin cylindrical cover over it, wind it, and let 'er roll. 9" H x 18-1/2" L. Collection of Meryle Evans.* **$550-$850**

Coffee roaster, sheet iron, lid with hinged trapdoor for beans, brass gear in center operates iron stirrers inside, American, about 2" deep x 10" diameter, mid 19th C. **$350+**

Coffee roaster, sheet iron, pan shape, fitted lid, lower handle is a pointed shaft, as if it once had wooden handle, no mark, American (?), pan is 7-1/4" diameter, 20-1/4" L overall, mid 19th C. **$125+**

Old Repair — When it doesn't qualify as a make-do, or a repaired piece with some quirkiness or idiosyncracy or charm in the repair (which may add value), an "old" repair still takes away less value than a recent repair. As to whether or not it is an old or new repair, you must examine all the elements — method, metal, condition — to decide. Because cast iron is so friable and pieces tend to crack or break off, legs, stanchions, rods, wingnuts, finials and handles all tend to "go missing," as they say in British mysteries. Old repairs are likely to be frankly repairs; modern repairs, by collectors or dealers, are likely to be much less obvious, and may be cast in iron from a matching part, or from another piece, or even from a carved pattern mold. It is not bad form to ask if anything is a replaced part, or at least to examine things for which you are paying a lot with a magnifying glass and to request a full description on your receipt, noting replacements, repairs or refinishing.

XIV-50. Coffee roaster missing its lid. *Cast iron, 3 short peg legs. 5-1/4" H x 8-1/2" diameter. Pat'd 3/13/1866 by K. Humphrey, and mfd. by I. A. Sheppard & Co., Philadelphia. Lid may have been tin, with a slot or hole in middle, or possibly was cast iron. A very similar roaster, based on the N. Linden (Chicago) patent, Nov. 15, 1870, was made with a heavy sort of "doughnut" cast iron lid with the center opening covered with a tin lid with strap handle. The Linden dasher had a pair of blades reticulated like a backbone. Picture courtesy of the Museum of History and Technology, The Smithsonian Institution. Add another $100 for lid.* **$275+**

Coffee roaster, sheet iron pan style, hinged trapdoor opening in fixed lid through which blades inside are visible, cast iron crank has old repair, marked "#22," American, 19th C. **$100+**

XIV-51. Coffee roaster patents. (A) *Pat'd 11/8/1881, by George A. Bridler, Middletown, PA. This patent application had a model — perhaps you'll be lucky enough to find it. Note the resemblance to the Wood's/Harrington patents. This is a "two-part roasting-vessel provided with a [round] door and a cranked stirring rod with double circular flanged base support, which is reversible. I put a question mark at the end of the crank, not knowing how it was supposed to end, and assuming it was longer in the straight shaft where it first comes out of the frame."* **(B)** *Pat'd 8/2/1881, by Henry A. Leher, Cape Girardeau, MO. The claim, for which Leher got his patent, seems very silly — he showed the wooden handle separate from the crank, and said that it had a socket. The sheet metal oblong box has a revolving cylinder within.* **(C)** *Cylinder in frame. Pat'd 12/1/1885, by Matthew J. Clark, Clermontville, OH. A metallic cylinder in 2 separate longitudinal sections, riveted together, each section "provided with an inwardly-projecting flange formed integral with the section." In addition, one end of the cylinder has a "detachable head" or cover. Compare this with the earlier Stuart, Peterson one in XIV-48. All pictures from* Official Gazette.

XIV-52. Coffee roasters — cylinders in frames. *Somewhat similar types made of sheet iron with round cast iron frames to fit over range eye, and cranked cylinders.* **(L)** *"Imperial Family" roaster, by T. B. C. Burpee, Philadelphia. Ad in* Century, *10/1892.* **(R)** *I've been assured that this is the "Griswold Coffee Roaster," although not identified as such in Albert Pick catalog, 1909. Catalog lists 3 sizes, with cylinders: (No. 1) 6" L x 5-1/2" diameter; (No. 2) 8" x 5-1/2"; and (No. 3) 9-1/2" x 7". These correspond with Griswold. Note that the long handle at left is a sort of lid lifter that fits into slots on the round plate of the frame: that's a Griswold feature. But there are two discernable differences: 1. that right-hand short crank. The Griswold has a bent rod crank. But this may be a commercial adaptation; and 2. the opening in the cylinder under the sliding lid is on the wrong end and is the wrong shape for a Griswold. 85 years ago these cost under $2!* (L) **$150-$250+**; (R) if a Griswold: **$1000-$1500**; (R) if another maker: **$250+**

"LUTE — A Matter to Mend Broken Vessel. — Take any quantity of white of eggs, and beat them well to a froth. Add to this soft curd cheese, and quicklime, and begin beating a-new all together. This may be used in mending whatever you will, even glasses, and will stand both fire and water . . . **Another**, for the same purpose, which resists water. — Take quicklime, turpentine, and soft curd cheese. Mix these well together; and, with the point of a knife, put of this on the edges of the broken pieces of your ware, then join them together." James Cutbush, *The American Artists Manual, or Dictionary of Practical Knowledge*. (Philadelphia, 1814).

Mending With Brads — The most common (or at least visible) repair found on any ceramic wares utilizes the brad, a metal staple-like object made of a fairly soft metal. At a recent auction I saw a lovely Willow Ware soup tureen on stand, with a high domed lid which had a very old brad repair that held the two halves together. The brads, about 10 of them, were set fairly close together, just under an inch apart, and were about 5/8" wide, straddling the break line. The technique is probably very ancient, and probably found in every country where ceramics exist. In the Oct. 1946 *National Geographic Magazine*, on p. 540, there's an interesting picture of an Afghanistan workman sitting on a pad on the floor, holding a broken cup with the toes of one foot while he uses a beautiful bow drill to "bore small cavities into either side of the crack. Brads of soft copper are hammered in, binding the pieces. From Iran to Tientsin [85 miles S.E. of Beijing, China], this is a common repair." The article, "Back to Afghanistan," is by Maynard Owen Williams.

Coffee roaster, stove top, sheet iron oblong box, shallow, with longish handle with ring at end. Hinged lid has pierced holes in it, American, about 20" L including handle, 19th C. The pierced lid gave Mary Earle Gould pause, in *Antique Tin and Tole Ware*, and she thought this might have been a "fire carrier" or "coal carrier" but certain stains inside led her to believe it might have served a double duty. She also had heard it might be a corn popper. Although she didn't mention any names, she wrote that some of these had been found with manufacturers' names stamped in the metal. **$100+**

Coffee urn, chrome plated, orange Bakelite™ (or other molded phenolic resin) handles & spigot handle, "Champion," looks c.1930s but can't find in directories between 1932 & 1944. **$40+**

XIV-53. Portable coffee roaster, *all-in-one stove with revolving cylinder "suspended on a crane over fire, and can be swung outward for filling or discharging," as shown here. Made for hand-cranking or power-hookup. "Hyde's Patent" — July 1, 1862, and Feb. 2, 1864. Came in four sizes, for roasting No. 1 : 20-30 lbs.; No. 2: 30-60 lbs.; No. 3: 75-135 lbs.; and No. 4: 150-270 lbs. Wow! This picture from Duparquet, Huot & Moneuse hotel supply wholesale catalog, c.1904-1910.* **$350+**

XIV-54. Coffee roaster. *Pit bottom style, meant to sit down into eye of range. Heavy cast iron, with crank in lid that stirred beans with four "fingers." Hinged lid, upright lifting rings. 11" H x 8-3/4" diameter, looks English, but may be American, mid 19th C. Collection of Meryle Evans.* **$250-$450**

XIV-56. Tea or hot water boiler, *of early type that was originally made to hang inside fireplace, although it would work on a range top too. The bail with eye on this 20th C. one meant it could be hung on a hook somewhere convenient. Copper, with tinned iron heavy-weight bail, long spigot. Henry Rogers Sons & Co., Wolverhampton, England, 1914 catalog.* **$150-$250+**

XIV-55. Coffee roaster. *Sheet iron with holding handle and crank handle. The crank turned the bevel gears in the center of the top, turning the stirrer "fingers" inside. Note trapdoor. 9" diameter, 20" L overall. Picture contributed by The Primitive Man, Bob Cahn. I believe this may incorporate the Rufus J. Morton (Big Lick, N.C.) patent of 3/23/1880 for a "stirrer for coffee-roaster."* **$175-$250+**

XIV-57. Tea or hot water boiler, *also sometimes called a* **hot water urn.** *Copper, slightly tapered body with long tapered spigot. Flat lid with bracket handle, forged iron bail handle with swivel ring in center. Smithsonian dates between 1854 and 1894, but we see from XIV-56 that it could be much later. 11-1/8" H exclusive of bail x 21-1/4" L overall with faucet. Picture courtesy of the National Museum of American History, John Paul Remensnyder estate.* **$150-$250+**

Coffee urn — called an "**argyle**" in England, copper body, tinned inside, with slender vertical open top cylinder into which fits a heated cast iron slug (looks like a sash weight) that would keep the coffee hot. Cast brass handles & spigot, side handles have opalescent knobby white glass grips, spigot has more opaque white knob, square base, 4 small feet, high decorative rather churchy dome lid with high copper finial, King Manufactory, Hull, England, 16" H, c. mid 19th C. **$275-$350**

Coffee urn, copper, brass spigot, wooden handles, on stand with solid fuel burner underneath, mfd. by Sternau, NYC, turn of century. **$255+**

Coffee urn, electric, chrome plated brass & copper ball, on fluted base, white plastic handles, knob on top, spigot handle, and ring base with 4 small ball feet, looks like a little robot baby, but would "put poise in your parties." "Table Electric" by Chase Brass & Copper Co., Inc., division of Kennecott Copper Corp., 25-cup capacity, c.1937. Crossover interest from Art Deco, Art Moderne, & Chase name brand collectors. **$65-$85**

Coffee urn, electric, nickel-plated, very ornate, with matching creamer & sugar, "Universal," mfd. by Landers, Frary & Clark, only 11" H, patents from 1910 to 1920s. **$35-$45**

Coffee urn, for restaurant or hotel use, copper with brass trim & handles & spout, very lovely graceful form, American, 21" H, turn of century. **$200-$225**

Coffee urn, heavy polished aluminum, electric heating unit concealed in slightly flared perforated base, tall with 2 body sections, each with black plastic side handles, domed lid with black plastic knob, glass viewing tube above spigot, West Bend Aluminum Co., West Bend, WI, made 48 cups, late 1940s. **$15-$20**

Coffee urns — See also tea urn

Conjurer kettle, or **camp kettle**, heavy tin tea kettle in odd shape — a very very short cylinder with flat bottom, flat top with small "biscuit cutter" lid, curved spout comes out of top, with normally sized & placed forged iron handle. This was supposed to set down into a tall cylindrical portable sheet iron stove, with

very short strap iron feet, in the base of which was built a small fire over a draft hole. Conjurers, or conjurors, were meant for cooking in non-kitchen settings, and were said to require but 3 sheets of paper to cook a steak. English (?), 8" diameter, mid 19th C. Price range for kettle, which in a pure sense, is incomplete — not being with its conjurer. **$30-$40**

"The Conjuror, or Camp Kettle. — Some years ago, an apparatus of this name was very generally sold in London, where some may yet be found at the ironmongers, and is remarkable for the expedition with which a small piece of meat may be dressed in it; sufficient for one person may be done in less than five minutes; and a pint of water can be boiled in the same time, the only fuel being half a sheet of thick brown paper. In the interior of a cylinder of sheet iron, an iron cone . . ., perforated, is placed over a hole in the bottom. A shallow dish of tin, with its [flat] cover, holds the meat, suppose a beefsteak, and fits exactly into the top of the cyllinder. There is a little door on the side, through which the paper wrapped round the cone is set fire to; the door is then shut. The heat of the flame being confined altogether within the cylinder, very soon cooks the meat, an effect which is assisted by the steam being confined by the cover of the dish. The smoke passes off by a pipe. . . . This little machine has been found extremely useful, not only in fishing or shooting parties, and other occasions where a dinner might be required at a distance from home, but likewise in numberless instances in the house where cooked meat or hot water may be wanted quickly, and when it is inconvenient to light a fire, particularly in summer. It is, perhaps, impossible to carry economy, convenience, and expedition farther than by this apparatus; but it must be admitted that by this process the meat is neither roasted, fried, baked, nor stewed; but it is completely done, and, with proper management, very palatable for those who have a good appetite." Webster & Parkes, *An Encyclopædia of Domestic Economy.* 1848 NY edition of English book of 1845. Sounds for all the world like a microwave oven!

XIV-58. "Tea & Coffee Urns in Batteries," *meaning in a connected group. Copper & brass with nickel plating overall. Made in 4 set sizes: 3-gallon urns, 5-, 8- and 10-gallons. S. B. Sexton Stove & Mfg. Co., Baltimore, c.1930s. It's not much of a leap of imagination to think of them as The Ladies Come To Tea (and eat a lot of cookies). Value is hard to give; they would probably be worth most as second-hand restaurant supplies, bought to put into use. Required house-room (the "real-estate-factor") has to be calculated when pricing large items of no particular use.* **$100-$400**

XIV-59. "Canteen" urn. *Nickeled copper, shaped like barrel on stand. Two-gallon capacity, so just the right size for a big house-party. From Albert Pick 1909 catalog.* **$150-$350**

Funnel for percolators, enamelware, looks like long cone divided so the top half is like a coffee cup with handle, then a wide flange or lip almost like a saucer, then long conical neck with very small opening at bottom. The flange allowed the percolator funnel to rest on rim of various size coffee pots, to turn them into percolators. Unmarked Matthai-Ingram, about 6-1/2" or 7" L x 4-1/2" diameter, c.1890s. **$35-$50**

Hot beverage urn, for restaurant or hotel, copper with brass fittings, brass spigots, domed covers with knobs, American, 20" H x 18" W, turn of century. **$400+**

Hot drink urn, for restaurant. Nickeled copper & brass, ornamented with "jewels, surmounted with ruby glass 'Hot Drinks' sign with jeweled metal mounted frame." "The Princeton." (They also had "The Harvard," and "The Cornell," but no "The Yale.") Seen in Albert Pick catalog, 1909. Very flashy and neat. **$400+**

Hot water kettle — See tea or hot water kettle. Technically speaking, all tea kettles are actually hot water kettles because you heat water in them, then pour the hot water over the tea into a teapot to steep.

Percolator urn, alcohol burner below, plated metal, antique style body with rounded belly, cabriole legs, side handles, glass percolator top, "Universal Percolator Co.," Landers, Frary & Clark, 12" H, pat'd 1907-1910. **$135+**

Percolator urn, electric, chromium-plated paneled Georgian style urn, ebonized wood handles & spigot handle, on 3-legged base, Royal Rochester Co., No. E639, mfd. by Robeson Rochester Corp., Rochester, NY, 15" H, c.1930s. **$30-$45**

Percolator urn, electric, copper, tinned inside, with straight-sided "milk can" style urn, glass dome, black Bakelite™ (or other phenolic resin plastic) side handles & spigot handle, on rather heavy brass tripod stand, "Universal," mfd. by Landers, Frary & Clark, New Britain, CT, pat'd May 22, 1899. This almost looks Arts & Crafts, and the period is right, so possibly it has some extra value now to the avid A&C collector. **$75-$110**

Percolator urn, electric, nickel-plated, on 3 long cabriole (so-called "Queen Anne") legs, glass percolating top with high domed metal lid & finial, plug screws into bulb socket, Simplex Electric Heating Co., Cambridge, MA, 1906. **$45-$55**

Percolator urn, electric, silver-plated, octagonal base, octagonal paneled urn, Georgian style (of late 18th or early 19th C.), "Automatic Percolator," Hotpoint, Edison Electric Appliance Co., 12" H, c.1930s. **$50-$65**

Percolator urn, electric, nickeled brass and iron, glass, turned wood, very handsome metal urn with spigot, surmounted by sugar-bowl-shaped glass percolating bowl, lion's paw feet, side handles, "Type ECP," mfd. by General Electric, c.1918-1919. **$60-$80**

Percolators — See also coffee percolators

Tea ball, perforated spun aluminum acorn with chain, 1920s or 1930s. **$5-$7**

Tea ball, sterling silver, in shape of tiny fancy teapot, hexagonal body with canted sides, classical handle, high domed lid lifts off for tea leaves, the whole body perforated with fine holes, The Watson Co., Attleboro, MA, about 1-1/2" H, c.1930. **$25+**

Tea bowl, for drinking tea, mocha decoration in blue on white band, yellowware, small foot, English, 7-7/8" diameter, mid 19th C. **$275-$300**

Tea caddy, chromolith decorated tin with image of a flag and a man, American, 1880s-1890s. **$35-$45**

Tea caddy, enameled copper, very Oriental-looking, with birds, butterflies & flowers on white & turquoise background, 4-1/2" H x 5" D, late 19th C. **$85-$100**

Tea kettles, aluminum:

Tea kettle, cast aluminum, high bail handle with wooden grip, "Colonial," Wagner Ware, Sidney, OH, 5 qts., c.1902 to 1920. **$25-$50+**

Tea kettle, cast aluminum, lid swivels sideways, neat little filling hole & lid at top of spout, falling wire bail handle with turned wooden grip, flat bottom, "Colonial Design, Safety Fill #8," Griswold Mfg. Co., Erie, PA, 9-3/4" diameter, 6 qt. capacity, pat'd Sept. 9, 1913. **$65+**

Tea kettle, cast aluminum, rounded body with small flat part under spout, hinged lid, short fat gooseneck spout, coiled wire bail, "No. 330," Wear-Ever, T. A. C. U. Co. (Aluminum Cooking Utensil Co., sales division of Pittsburg Reduction Co.), 8-1/4" diameter, 1903-1915. **$45+**

Tea kettle, cast aluminum with highly polished finish on rounded body, lovely iron wire falling bail handle in "chef's hat" profile characteristic of kettles from the early 19th C, coiled grip, long inquisitive gooseneck spout, "Wear-Ever," T. A. C. U. Co. (The Aluminum Cooking Utensil Co.), 9" diameter, c.1920. **$35+**

Tea kettle, cast aluminum, side-swiveling lid, wire bail handle with wood grip, "Colonial Tea Kettle," Wagner Ware, 6 qts., pat'd 1902. **$55+**

Tea kettle, cast aluminum, sliding lid, turned wood handle with wooden knob, oblong shaped kettle, very dramatic, "Wagner Ware Grand Prize Tea Kettle," 12-5/8" L x 8-7/8" W, pat'd Sept. 28, 1916. **$80+**

Tea kettle, cast aluminum, smooth sides, slightly domed swivel or swingaway lid, flat bottom, wire bail with turned wood grip, "Griswold #6," 8-7/8" diameter at bottom, c.1920. **$100+**

Tea kettle, cast aluminum, very modern style, low arched handle, large hole in molded spout, for filling & pouring, "Magnalite #4135," mfd. by Wagner Ware, 10" diameter, c.1930s. **$55+**

Tea kettle, or hot water kettle, cast aluminum, side-swiveling lid, short coffee-boiler style V-neck lip or spout, wire handle with wooden grip, very simple slanted straight sides, looks thick & it is, Wagner Mfg. Co., 10" diameter at base, c.1910. **$50+**

Tea kettles, cast aluminum, various styles, mfd. by Griswold, Wagner or Wear-Ever T.A.C.U. Co. (The Aluminum Cooking Utensil Co.), about 8-1/4" to 10" diameter, 1903 to about 1915. When I wrote my first book, I only knew one person who collected them: Paul Persoff, my photographer. He used to buy them at Englishtown (NJ) flea market for under $5. General ball-park value range for this type of kettle: **$35-$75**

Tea kettle, cheap, thin aluminum with nifty molded black plastic chef's head whistle-stopper, copper bottom, cane-wrapped handle, "Raineland" with 3 stars, 7-3/4" H, 20th C. **$15-$18**

XIV-60. Tea kettle. *Cast aluminum, wood. Note small filling hole with its own lid, and larger swiveling lid, good for cleaning lime deposits out of interior. 8-1/2" diameter, 4 quart size. "Colonial Design, Safety Fill," mfd. by Griswold, Erie, PA. Pat'd 9/9/1913. Collection of Paul Persoff.*

XIV-61. Tea kettle. *Cast aluminum, wood, bail handle. 10" diameter, c.1910. Wagner Mfg. Co., Sidney, OH. Collection of Paul Persoff, who photographed my first book so long ago.* **$45+**

Contenders for First Aluminum Casting — A 1917 article on Griswold in *House Furnishing Review* states "During the period 1890 to 1894, the **Griswold Manufacturing Company** in conjunction with the original **Pittsburgh Aluminum Company** — now the Aluminum Company of America — first made, in an experimental way, aluminum ware. This aluminum ware was cast in sand molds, and was the first cast aluminum ware known to have been made in the world. A few of these first pieces of cast aluminum ware were offered to the trade during those years, and after long years of service, they have still been found to be in perfect condition.

"A process of hardening the surface of aluminum ware was later discovered. After casting, by a secret electrical treatment, the surface is tempered, hardening and closing all the pores of the metal. This 'tempered surface,' as it is called, is positive proof against discoloration or absorption, and the ware remains for all time a silvery gray." The article adds "the first big trade on Griswold cast aluminum tempered ware came through their London office" and only later became known all through the world! **Auburn Hollow Ware Co.**, of Auburn, NY, made at least one exhibition piece of cast aluminum — a tea kettle, and it may have actually been the first cast aluminum kitchen piece made. This was reported in *The Metal Worker*, April 30, 1892.

Tea kettles, Chromium:

Tea kettle, chrome body, copper bottom, strap handle painted red, plastic bird's head whistle, "Revere," 20th C. **$25+**

Tea kettle, chromium-plated solid copper, red strap handle, copper bottom, very Art Deco design, cast white metal bird whistle, "Made in U. S. A.," 20th C. — similar to the Revere one above. **$25+**

Tea kettles, Copper:

Tea kettle, brass & copper, possibly stripped of original nickel plating, forged iron bail with turned wood grip, white porcelain knob on lid, 5-1/2" H including knob, late 19th C. **$40-$55**

Cleaning Copper With Love Apples — While waiting for dishes to be served in a restaurant in NYC's Chinatown, we used to amuse ourselves cleaning pennies with the Louisiana Hot Sauce™ that was a standard condiment on the table. The darkest penny will turn bright and pink (and unshiny) in seconds. Earl Proulx, in his *Yankee* column, "Plain Talk," Dec. 1987, gives a tip on cleaning a very darkened copper bath tub: "For the inside of the tub, scour it with ketchup."

Tea kettle, copper, beautiful slender gooseneck spout, fixed handle, domed & ridged lid with high acorn finial, mid 19th C. **$140-$160**

Tea kettle, copper, dovetail seam, gooseneck spout, signed "J M W E," English (?), 19th C. A **dovetail seam** is just what it sounds like — small "fingers" of the copper alternating from either side of the seam. The reason for it is that it increases the total area of brazing, thus strengthening the seam. See also Chapter IV. **$175+**

Tea kettle, copper, dovetail seam, high dome lid, pit bottom, little hinged cover for spout, no marks, but hinged lid on spout prob. means English, 8-1/4" H, 2nd quarter 19th C. **$165+**

Tea kettle, copper, dovetail seams, forward thrust gooseneck spout, extremely well-formed falling strap handle of copper, more in profile of a bowler hat than a chef's hat, a few dings, marked "G. Ebert," PA, 6-1/2" H exclusive of handle, 19th C. **$400+**

Tea kettle, copper, gooseneck spout, "Finnemore, Granbrook" (might be Cranbrook), 5 qt. capacity, early 19th C. **$225+**

Tea kettle, copper, gooseneck, with brass finial, unsigned (look on flat of handle usually for stamped maker's name), prob. PA, marked "5," 1830s-1840s. Marked wares bring highest prices. **$275+**

Tea kettle, copper, highly polished, turned wooden grip on wire bail handle, porcelain knob on lid, "Majestic," turn of century. **$65+**

Tea kettle, copper, on stand, with alcohol burner, meant for sideboard or tea table, Swedish, turn of century. **$95-$125**

Tea kettle, copper, pieced, with horizontal seam at "equator" or widest part, cast brass handle frame & handle, no marks, 2 qt. size, 9" diameter, mid 19th C or earlier. **$75+**

Tea kettle, copper, ringed around & shaped like a woven strawgrass bee skip, with bird's head whistle in spout, early 20th C. **$35+**

Tea kettle, copper, tin inside, shaped like a squatty bell, with a very wide (impossible to tip over) base & a narrow opening, strap handle with grip, very large coffee boiler V-neck type spout, close fitting flat lid. I've never seen a real one or even seen a picture of an old one of which this is supposed to be a replica. An ad featuring this **reproduction** has explanatory notes. "A replica of those [the copper captain's kettles] used aboard Nantucket Whalers during the 1800's. Used in the Captain's private pantry for warming his tea or grog." Landfall Collection, S.

XIV-62. Tea kettle. *Copper, tinned inside, brass mushroom finial on domed lid, falling handle of flat copper forming chef's hat shape. This one rakish by being bent — whether that was the intention of the maker or early user or an accident we don't know, but it did make it easier to pour from; I know, I went through the motions of pouring from it. Marked in relief on top of handle "John W. Schlosser." This exact type of small brass finial is also found on early- to mid-19th C. cabinet-work, such as spice chests, and were used as pulls for the small drawers. They were probably bought by the gross from a brass foundry in Connecticut. When handle is up — 11-3/4" H , early 19th C. Photograph by Jennifer Oka. Picture courtesy of the National Museum of American History, Smithsonian Institution, John Paul Remensnyder estate. Value guide is very general — marked copperwares highly collectible, but to a small select market. This "value" is not meant to set a price on a John Schlosser tea kettle, nor on a piece in the Smithsonian's collection, nor on any other particular marked American kettle.* **$300+**

Norwalk, CT, Feb. 1975, *Early American Life* magazine. American-made (?), 10" H including handle, 10" diameter at base, c.1975. A ship's decanter has a squatty, wide-bottomed body so that the center of gravity is as low as possible. I believe this ad is legitimate & that old kettles like this, dating to the early to mid 19th C., probably exist. Price range is for repro, which sold for $47.75 ppd in 1975. **$30-$55**

Tea kettle, copper with brass finial, gooseneck spout, pit bottom, American (?), 6 qt. size, 19th C. **$200-$250**

Tea kettle, copper with brass trim, bail handle with black finished turned wood grip, wooden knob on lid, marked "Rome" where handle is attached, Rome, NY, 1898. Possibly originally nickeled, as many are found that way, or maybe they were offered both ways. **$55+**

Tea kettle, copper with gooseneck spout, falling handle, "J. Gable, Lancaster, PA," 14-3/8" H with handle upright, 1843. Marked, dated & good form = high price. **$450-$600**

Tea kettle, copper, with hollow copper handle, acorn finial on lid, gooseneck spout, English, late 19th C. **$95-$125**

Tea kettle, copper with iron bail handle, wood grip, lid with strap handle, short duckneck spout, marked "Old Colony," sounds like a Colonial Revival reproduction (possibly Old Colony Foundry, in which case it'd be Bridgewater, MA), 7-1/2" H x 9-1/4" diameter, c.1920s. **$35-$50**

Tea kettle, copper with iron whistling bird in spout, late 19th C. **$65-$80**

Tea kettle, copper with simple scrolly handle, gooseneck spout, acorn finial, PA, prob. Philadelphia, 2-cup size, late 18th or early 19th C. **$125-$150**

XIV-65. Tea kettle. *Copper, tinned inside, tapered body, crooked neck spout, falling strap handle in good chef's toque profile, domed lid, brass mushroom finial. Marked on handle "C. Kiefer, Lancaster, PA, 1848." 12-11/16" H with handle up x 13-3/8" overall length. Photograph by Jennifer Oka. Picture courtesy of the National Museum of American History, Smithsonian Institution, John Paul Remensnyder estate.* **$300+**

XIV-63. Tea kettles. *Both copper with barrel handles.* **(L)** *"New Shape Round" kettle, made in capacities from 2 to 10 pints.* **(R)** *"Range" kettle "with well," (ie. a pit bottom kettle.) Made to hold from 6 to 12 pints (skipping 11). Henry Rogers Sons, Wolverhampton, England, 1914 catalog.* **$85-$150+**

XIV-64. Tea kettles. *Square ones, seamless copper with gooseneck spouts, meant for gas stoves.* **(L)** *To be had with barrel or ebonized wood handle.* **(R)** *To be had with amber or "opal" (opalescent glass) handle. Made in several sizes, from 4 to 12 pints. Also Henry Rogers, 1914.* **$95-$150+**

XIV-66. Tea kettle. *Copper, oval cylinder with flat bottom & top, gooseneck spout, fixed handle with barrel grip flanked by small spurs. Small lid with turned wooden knob plus an opening on opposite side which is the top of an inverted funnel. It's a sort of double-boiler vessel within the outer pot. 10-1/4" H overall x 10" L. Embossed medallion fixed on top says "The Cyprus No. 341. 1879. Patented Jan. 28." Probably English. Photograph by Jennifer Oka. Picture courtesy of the National Museum of American History, Smithsonian Institution, John Paul Remensnyder estate.* **$350+**

Tea kettle, copper, with unusual (probably replacement) green & white enameled lid, gooseneck spout, "Majestic," American, 5 qt. capacity, turn of century. **$95-$125**

Arsenic & old copper — "As arsenic frequently enters metallic compositions, especially those of copper and tin, it were much to be wished, that such compound metals could for ever be banished, at least from our Kitchens." Anthony Florian Madinzer Willich, *The Domestic Encyclopedia; or A Dictionary of Facts & Useful Knowledge. . .,* 1st American edition, Philadelphia: W. Y. Birch & A. Small, 1803-04.

• • • •

Finial Shapes — The "Silver" chapter of *The Complete Encyclopedia of Antiques,* compiled by *The Connoisseur,* edited by L. G. G. Ramsey, Hawthorn Books 1962, has a short entry on finials, applicable to silver wares, but — after factoring in a time lag for decorative elements being adopted for other metals, and an even longer lag to reach America — we can use the facts when we study other metals. The timetable for silver finial shapes, according to Ramsey: Early 18th C. = **acorn**; Rococo Period (Mid to Late 18th C.) = **flame and pineapple**; Classic Period (Late 18th to Early 19th C.) = **urn, pine cone**. For application to American copper tea kettles, you would probably be safe adding 50 to 100 or so years to the widespread use of acorns; then a much shorter time, say 30 to 50 years for the flame and pineapple; by the time you get to urns and pine cones, the period is only about 15 to 25 years behind in America compared to Great Britain or the Continent. As with all such "rules" of thumb, it's not true in every case.

• • • •

Reproduction alert — A London company, John Hancock Reproductions Ltd., advertises that they are the "leading specialist wholesaler of reproduction antiques," with "more than 6,000 separate lines," of repros of "brass & copperware, pots, jardiniers, novelties," among many other lines. A brass schoolmarm's bell and brass twisted-shaft candlesticks are the only things in the picture which might apply to our subjects here, but I suspect that much of what is coming from England in containers now is reproduction. Unfortunately this is a signal that the end of a collecting cycle is coming, because it's too dangerous to enter the field. So far, not enough of our "territory" has been encroached upon to make it hard to collect kitchen & housewares, but if you step outside, just a few figurative inches, *caveat emptor.* Study Study Study. And if you buy mail order, insist on return privileges for any reason. This will be hard to get because many mail sellers just want to move stuff out, and generally are priced lower than in-person outlets.

Tea or water kettle, copper, tinned inside, dovetail seams, lid with brass acorn finial, gooseneck spout, marked "J. C. & 'W. Lord," Birmingham, England, 7" H x 5-3/4" diameter, late 19th C. **$100-$145**

Tea or hot water kettle, copper with brass handle, gooseneck, "Majestic," American, 20th C. **$65-$85**

Tea or water kettle, nickeled brass & copper, gooseneck style, "Gilchrist," large size, 1903. **$25-$40**

Tea or water kettle, nickel-plated copper, crescent shaped so that it can be placed on top of stove, against the stovepipe. 7" H x 14" diameter. Maker unknown; seen in Albert Pick wholesale catalog, 1909. **$75+**

Tea kettles, electric:

Tea kettle, electric, chrome-plated metal, very modern in appearance. Electrical element is in back end of handle, & the kettle could also be used stovetop like any other tea kettle. "Speedmaster," (Waters-Genter?, hence Minneapolis?), 1930s. **$35-$45**

Tea kettle, electric, silver-plated copper in hammered finish, 8 sided & footed, with plain fat gooseneck spout, high rattanwrapped handle, acorn finial made of oak, designed by Peter Behrens, German, 1909. **$450-$600**

Tea kettles, enamelware:

Tea kettle, blue & white swirl agateware, white lining, swivel lid, "Wrought Iron Range Co.," St. Louis, MO, 4 qt. capacity, late 19th C. **$175+**

Tea kettle, cobalt blue enamelware, marked only "Iron Range Company," probably same as "Wrought Iron Range Co.," (St. Louis, MO), late 19th C. **$135+**

Tea kettle, cobalt enamelware, in small size sometimes called a <u>Five-O'clock</u>, American, late 19th, early 20th C. **$50+**

Tea kettle, cobalt & white swirl agateware, 19th C. **$130+**

Tea kettle, deep green agateware, white enameled interior, gooseneck spout, high domed hinged lid, "Made in Yugoslavia," early 20th C. **$50-$75**

Tea kettle, gray granite, bell-bottomed, gooseneck, bail handle, 19th C. This particular one is a "shelf," or should I say "hob" piece, as the bottom has holes all over it. **$12-$15**

Tea kettle, green & tan enamelware, gooseneck spout, 1930s. **$25-$45**

Tea kettle, whistling type, steel body decoratively enameled as worried setting hen, handle arches over lid, spout has cast phenolic resin chicken head, the comb attached with a rachet device thumb-activated to pull back for pouring, wings delineated in black lines on white body, "TeaBird™," M. Kamenstein (NYC), but made in Taiwan, 2-1/2 qts. capacity, 1986. **$20-$30**

Futurewatch — Anything with figural detail, whether it's useful or useless, will probably have collector value sometime in the future. Original price of this is $30. Discounted to $23 in 1989. By the mid 1990s there were many figurals — various cats, birds, fruits, etc., for new retail under $50. Secondhand market in perfect condition, possibly close to that. But wait 50 years, and never use it, and it may gain 200% on your investment. But maybe not.

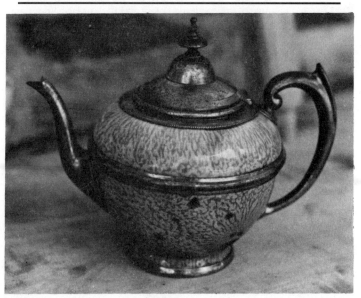

XIV-67. Teapot. *Gray graniteware with white metal (probably Britannia) spout, handle, lid, breast-band and base rim. Late 19th C. From the collection of Susan Kistler, Lenhartsville, PA.* **$75-$125**

Tea kettle, mottled green agateware, tiny flakes chipped off, early 20th C. Condition lowers value. **$35-$55**

Tea kettle, tan with green trim enamelware, probably Vollrath, 1930s. **$30-$45**

Tea kettle, very architectural looking, beige enamelware with black trim & black interior, chrome handle with Art Deco Bakelite™ (or other molded phenolic resin) knob, canted back handle with plastic grip, strainer holes in spout, no mark, 8-1/2" H exclusive of handle, c.1930s. **$45-$60**

Tea kettle & teapot, matched pair, shaded blue ombré enamelware, American, 6" H & 6-1/2" H, early 20th or late 19th C. **$175-$265**

Tea kettle, teapot & coffee pot set, sky blue enamelware, cobalt knobs, coffee pot's glass lid made by H. C. Fry Co., Rochester, PA, 20th C. **$165-$250**

Tea kettles, iron: cast, enameled, sheet, stainless steel:

Tea kettle, white enameled iron, cobalt handle & knob, on bottom in black is a transfer print of a dreaming woman in a corset, with title "Dream of Comfort," adv'g "The 'Specialité' Corset," and on bottom in cobalt is mark "20 C III," 7-5/8" diameter, early 20th C. For a similar motif, see the "Mademoiselle Worth" pitcher in the Container chapter. I think that if corset collectors (they do exist, don't they?) discovered these pieces the prices would go up. **$75-$150**

Tea kettle, blue & white enameled heavy cast iron, late 19th C. A lot of these big kettles are actually <u>water kettles</u>, meant to heat water for tea (or anything else). **$75-$125**

Tea kettle, deep blue & white enamelware over cast iron, low & squat, "Wrought Iron Range Co.," St. Louis, MO, 7" diameter, 4th quarter 19th C. **$85-$140**

Tea kettle, brown & white enameled cast iron, European or American, 2 qt. size, turn of century. **$125-$155**

Tea kettle, deep midnight blue enameled cast iron, low & squat of the type sometimes called a <u>bachelor kettle</u>, fixed handle with wooden grip, very short pouring lip or spout, American, 8" diameter base, late 19th C. **$50-$75**

Tea kettle, red enameled thin metal, little aluminum snap-on whistle with turned wood knob, you have to take whistle off to pour, no mark, 6-7/8" diameter across bottom, c.1930s or 1940s. **$12-$15**

Tea kettle, cast iron, odd square shape with 1" wide flange angled from back to front down sides and top, meant to fit into a specific base burner, forged iron bail handle hooks to end of spout and to hinge of lid, "Spoor's Patent #5114," mfd. by Spoor, and by license by A. Ingraham & Co., Troy, NY, 7" H x 6" W x 10" L including spout, c.1850. **Classic** — This is a spectacular must-have for tea kettle collectors. Spoor also designed and patented a sort of flanged inserted niche that went into the stove, and could then be used as a shelf with a tea steeper or a flat iron or a square frying pan. Oooo whee! **$150+**

Tea kettle, of a size and shape that make it look like a teapot, cast iron, black, very pebbly surface like a warty toad, fine polished surface, small round lift-off lid with cast knob, the round smooth forged bail handle is somewhat bigger around than might be expected (at least from a Western point of view) and is thickest in the center and tapers slightly to ends. Body round with faintly squashed shape, short, almost vestigal, gooseneck spout. Japanese, small, maybe 2 pt. capacity, 19th or 20th C. Such iron wares are considered among the finest of Japanese crafts, and are the so-called <u>Nambu ironware</u>, made from a peculiarly ferrous sand (probably part volcanic material) in the northernmost part of the main island. Nambu iron is also used for cooking wares, including holloware & griddles. The kettles, at least, are beginning to show up regularly at antique shows. The iron sometimes has a very dark brown color. The tea kettles are finely made, and there is little that would alert the first time viewer of some examples that they are Japanese. There is an almost bell-like ringing sound when you put the lid back on that differs from the clunk or dull ring of most Western cast iron. I don't know if the Japanese iron workers add(ed) something to the metal. Sometimes the lids are made of brass, bronze or (rarely) copper, in addition to iron. I have never seen one without a pebbly or hobnailed surface (known as "hailstone" finish, according to Joel Schiff). The craft continues, and newly made "hailstone" Japanese tea kettles are sold in import food and housewares shops. For export to the U. S., they should have country of origin marked somewhere. In addition, modern ones may have an enameled color finish on outside, or a white-enameled; or tinned interior; sometimes an aluminum strainer insert; and the casting gate has been ground off, as opposed to snapped off. (A very charming **miniature** of this already small tea kettle is actually a water vessel, perhaps an inch or so in height, used by sumi painters and calligraphers to moisten the ink blocks. They have a tiny regulating hole, which the user covers with forefinger, while holding lid on too. By removing the finger briefly, the pressure inside is relieved and the water comes out the tiny spout. These antique miniatures (a teapot is only one form the little water vessel may take, some are figural animals or birds or mythological beings) are sold for upwards of $400. I saw one for $800. In Japanese metal work, as in so much else of their artisanry, the master whose name is signed in a teensy mark makes up much of the value.) This is a very sophisticated market. Most of the 1, 2 or 3 pt. sizes are priced in the upper range, although brand new ones might be much less: **$125+**

XIV-68. Teapot. *"Patent decorated pearl agateware," mfd. by Manning, Bowman & Co., in their 1892 catalog. Pat'd in 1883. This style was one of several occasion-related pieces. People could pay extra and really personalize them — this one says "Grandma's Birthday."* **$150-$200+**

XIV-69. Tea kettle. *Cast iron, globular body with wonderful spout. Fitted tin lid, wire bail, 3 short legs. Photograph courtesy Pat Guthman Antiques, Southport, CT. Maybe not "classic," but even better because it's so exuberant and idiosyncratic.* **$250+**

Tea or hot water kettle, cast iron, pit bottom, magnificent & beautiful round body, short gooseneck spout, falling forged iron bail, hinged lid lifts up, hinge opposite spout, the flattish lid has name, plus a beaded design in a circle, "Abbott & Noble," Philadelphia, 10-3/4" H x about 9-1/2" diameter, late 19th C. **$325+**

Tea kettle, bulbous cast iron body, 3 short feet, gooseneck, forged iron handle, no maker's mark, American, late 18th, early 19th C. **$150+**

Tea kettle, cast iron, swiveled or pivoted copper cover, gooseneck spout, American, 9" H, 19th C. **$80-$90**

Tea kettle, cast iron with tin cover, heavy bail handle, long gooseneck spout, American, 5-1/2" H, late 19th C. **$55-$70**

Tea kettle & kettle tilter combined, called a **tipping kettle**, cast iron, nearly straight sides, simple slightly domed lid with ring finial; the curved lever on top, right above spout, is the attached kettle tilter. Forged iron bail handle with ring top, at right angles to the spout, allows it to be hung from trammel or pot hook. Prob. New England, about 15" H x 12" diameter, late 1700s-early 1800s. Signed ones bring more. See X-53. **$600+**

Tea or water kettle, cast iron, bail handle marked with place and date, Vermont, 3 qt. size, "1875." **$90+**

Tea kettle, cast iron, "Rhine Mfg. Co.," 19th C. **$45+**

Tea kettle, cast iron, 3 very short peg feet, long casting gate on bottom, very pronounced angular gooseneck, forged bail, vertical casting seams on both sides, circumferential casting seam around middle, and including lower part of spout, domed lid with riveted cast brass knob (not necessarily original), no mark, American, 7" H, 2nd quarter 19th C. The value here is in the age, the nice form, & especially the spout. **$200-$250+**

Tea kettle, cast iron, "Foxell, Jones & Millard, Troy, NY," 1870s. **$75+**

Tea kettle, cast iron, "bowler hat" profile wire bail handle, domed lid with spoked ridges out from squared finial, pit bottom, "Higgins, Foxell & Martin," Troy, NY, c.1860. **$95+**

Tea kettle, cast iron, brass cover, fixed handle, poss. English because of the brass lid, 19th C. **$95+**

Tea kettle, cast iron, bulbous with gooseneck spout, small feet, iron handle, prob. American, mid 19th C. **$175+**

Tea kettle, cast iron, enameled, swirled cobalt blue & white, bail handle, short "duckneck" spout, marked "St. Louis Stove Works," MO, early 20th C., poss. late 19th. **$75+**

Tea kettle, cast iron, flat bottom, duckneck (short fat gooseneck) spout, casting line curves down & around close to bottom at back, falling bail of nickeled wire with heat-dissipating coil for hand grip, swivel lid covers entire top, and pivots at back where handle is attached, with knob at opposite edge. The center part of the lid, like a mesa, rises up & has sizeable flat top — touted as being a place where you could set something else to keep it hot, "Favorite," Favorite Stove & Range Co., Piqua, OH, advertised July 1890. This line was available in pit bottom style & in various finishes: plain cast iron, "milled" iron, galvanized, nickel-plated, & nickel-plated with white porcelain enamel inside. **Wagner Too?** — In Jan. 1892, an editorial notice in *The Metal Worker* told about a new compa-

XIV-71. Tea kettles. *"Ripley's New" kettles, from 1860 announcement that patent was being extended to March 14, 1867. "The objection for many years existing to the use of the old fashion Cast Iron Tea Kettle, owing to the difficulty in moulding the spout, its liability to clog or fill, especially when use of lime water is made, were fully removed by the production of the Kettle in the above, which was the invention of Mr. Ezra Ripley, to whom letters patent were granted on the 14th of March, 1846. The breast of the Kettle may be so shaped as to prevent any possibility of filling with sediment, and ensuring the greatest rapidity of pouring. The cost of moulding is reduced at least six cents per Kettle, a very material difference from former prices. The pattern may be made in any shape desired, but will be composed of two parts, the spout being connected with the body of the Kettle. Each part of the pattern can be removed from the green sand core separately, elaving the cores of the spout and body of the Kettle together in one entire core, which prevents the old necessity of setting a dry sand core for the spout. The pattern may be made to part vertically or longitudinally at the option of the manufacturer. The spouts being spacious admit of being enameled with the inner surface of the body if desired. ... We are prepared to dispose of foundry rights; patterns and Flasks can be furnished on reasonable terms." Signed Ezra Ripley, Fuller, Warren & Co., Troy, NY, March 15, 1860. A circular sent to "stove and hollow ware manufacturers."* **$150+**

XIV-70. Tea kettle. *Cast iron, oblong, with Mickey Mouse ears. These fins actually form, along with the rib down the sides, a partial heat seal. The kettle was made for a specific type of stove, and was stuck partway into its heat box. The collector was told, when he bought it, that it "came off a barge on the Erie Canal." Such stoves may have been used on canal boats. This was patented as a* **boiling kettle**, *2/23/1869, by S. Spoor, Phelps, NY. Photograph courtesy of David Smith. (See his article following Chapter IV, on cast iron muffin pans, etc.)* **$150+**

ny's new line of "high grade hollow ware, high polish or nickeled finish, including a tea kettle available flat bottom or pit bottom, in seven sizes from 8 to 30 gallons." The linecut used to illustrate the kettle is as close to identical as possible to the linecut showing the Favorite Piqua kettle 18 months before, considering that two differerent firms of cut engravers made the pictures. In addition, a low kettle with bail, round tipping handle and 3 peg feet is shown; it is also the same as an earlier Favorite, though engraved by a different firm. The use of the same linecuts was widespread in retail catalogs, but one wonders what's the case here? Did Wagner copy Favorite's kettles themselves, detail for detail? Did they only make a similar one and require of their engraver to furnish them with "an engraving like this one here" . . . tossing the Favorite one on the artist's desk? No mention is made in *Metal Worker* about the similarity; but this is no surprise as many trade magazines then, as now, were a mix of advertising, editorial puffery, editorial posturing, and serious facts. **$65-$95**

Tea kettle, cast iron, flat bottom, hexagonal dome on flat flanged lid, forged bail, marked "B" on bottom & a large "4" on side, American, 5-1/2" H exclusive of lid, mid 19th C. **$75+**

XIV-72. Kettle tilter. *Wrought iron, swivel ring at top, S-curved handle with ball tip, approx. 14" L. Late 18th or early 19th C. Ex-Keillor Collection.* **$375-$450**

Tea kettle, cast iron, forged bail with turned wood grip, swiveling or pivoting hinged lid, pit bottom, heavily incrusted on outside, marked on lid "John A. Goewey, #8," Albany, NY, 19th C. **$75-$95**

Tea kettle, cast iron, forged iron handle, swiveling lid with no knob, 3 short peg legs, long straight casting gate on bottom is filed down, on side is a sort of palm leaf decoration cast in, marked only "S. C." which may be Spencer Cole, poss. CT, poss. late 18th C or early 19th. **$300-$400**

Tea kettle, cast iron, gooseneck spout, forged iron bail handle unusual in that it's fixed in place — that is, it's not a "**falling bail**." American, 7-1/2" H overall, very small 1-1/2 pt. capacity, early 19th C. **$175+**

Tea kettle, cast iron, gooseneck spout, marked only "Bromwich," Bromwich (or West Bromwich), England, where at least 2 iron foundries were: Siddons, and Kenrick. This one has 2 qt. capacity, mid 19th C. **$80+**

Tea kettle, cast iron, gooseneck spout, forged bail, "J. J. Siddons West Bromwich," England, 2 qt. capacity, 19th C. **$75-$100**

Using a Gazetteer — Many years ago when I first saw the kettle listed above there was some question in my mind (because of the form) if it was American or English. I checked a very useful reference book I bought called *The Centennial Gazetteer of the United States,* by A. von Steinwehr, published by J. C. McCurdy & Co. in 1875. It contains "a geographical and statistical encyclopædia of the states, territories, counties, townships, villages, post-offices, mountains, rivers, lakes, etc., in the American Union," and can be checked for place names from the eighteenth century through 1875. Bromwich seems such a John Updike/Connecticut-type name, but as of 1875 there was no Bromwich or West Bromwich anywhere in the "Union."

• • • •

Pit bottoms & flat bottoms — The "pit" referred to is a hole in the top of a range or cookstove, which is covered with a lid that can be lifted out to gain direct access to the fire's heat. A piece of "pit bottom" hollowware has, in effect, two bottoms: the lower bottom, which has a smaller circumference, to fit down into the hole, fire hole, or range eye; and the flanged part that rests on the flat area around the hole or range eye. Another way of making the hole smaller so that flat bottom hollowware won't fall through is to use an <u>adapter ring</u> (See adapter ring picture, X-3 in Chapter X). A **flat bottom** pot or kettle is flat all the way across the bottom, and is generally a little newer than a pit bottom pot or kettle.

XIV-73. Tea or water kettle. *Cast iron, pit bottom, hinged lid, coiled heat-dissipating bail handle. Nice squat bulbous body. Squared gooseneck ("swan" as in England) spout. Marked "M'Dowell, Phila. PA." 8" H overall to slightly domed lid x 12" diameter. Part that fits down into range eye is 9" diameter x 1-1/2" H. Courtesy of dealer Jean Hatt, Hatt's Hutt, Denver, PA.* **$95-$130**

XIV-74. Closeup of spout of XIV-73. *Note marks of filing to smooth out casting lines; also the small knurled knob to lid.*

Tea kettle, cast iron, pit bottom, chubby body with short duckneck spout, flat falling bail handle connected to the levered lid with small thumb piece, "S. W. Ransom & Co. # 8," pat'd by A. Ransom & R. D. Granger, Albany, NY, Mar. 19, 1861. **$75+**

Tea kettle, cast iron, pit bottom, swivel lid with finely embossed scrolls on it, "A. Bradley & Co., Pittsburg, PA," 1866. **$75+**

Tea kettle, cast iron, pit bottom, hinged lid, flat <u>forged</u> bail, "I. A. Sheppard & Co., Baltimore, MD" (another Sheppard foundry was in Philadelphia), mid 19th C. According to Leander Bishop's book on early manufacturing, Baltimore had, in 1860, ten iron foundries (including stove makers), five brass founders, and 37 tin, copper, and sheet iron wares manufacturers. This is an interesting piece because of the combination of attractive elements: it's cast iron, with a pit bottom, and instead of a heavy iron wire bail handle, it's got a wrought or forged iron handle. **$100+**

Tea kettle, cast iron, pit bottom, ornate scrolled casting on top of sides, 3 tiny peg feet, forged bail, slightly domed lid with tab handle, no mark, American, 7" H exclusive of lid, 2nd to 3rd quarter 19th C. **$75+**

Tea kettle, cast iron, pit bottom, swingaway lid, flat bail handle, neat shape with a sort of decoy-like swooping line, no number or mfr's mark, American, 11" diameter including spout, late 19th C. **$85+**

Tea kettle, cast iron, straight sides, high gooseneck spout, almost serpentine in its curves, with fabulous very wide flat "tu-tu" flange partway down sides — making the kettle a variety of pit bottom for range top, falling bail forged strap handle, American, very early 19th C., transition from hearth to range. **$225+**

Tea kettle, cast iron, pit bottom, swingaway pivoting lid, short stubby spout, small separate washer-like disc fits in depression at back end of lid where forged bail hooks on to lug, "Joseph Bell & Co. #9, Wheeling, WV," pat'd (prob. by B. H. Menke, Cincinnati), June 23, 1863. **$125+**

Tea kettle, cast iron, shallow pit bottom, swivel lid, fat spout, falling forged iron bail, "Bussey & McLeod," stove makers, Troy, NY, 8" H, pat'd Jan. 1, 1861. **$85+**

Tea kettle, cast iron, swivel lid, forged handle, casting gate on bottom, "Wisher & Co.," Philadelphia, PA, 1 gal. size, 6-5/8" H, number "50" on bottom, pat'd 1861. **$75+**

Tea kettle, cast iron, pit bottom, swivel lid, short spout, wire falling bail handle, "Hardwick Stove Co.," Cleveland, TN, late 1800s. **$65+**

Tea kettle, cast iron, pit bottom, swivel top, forged falling bail handle, long casting gate on bottom, "Ohio Stove Co.," Portsmouth, OH, 19th C. **$65+**

XIV-75. Tea kettle. *Enameled cast iron, deep midnight blue, barrel handle. American, late 19th C. Courtesy Darwin Urffer.* **$55+**

Tea kettle, cast iron, tapered sides, half circle hinged lid on top, forged bail, short duckneck spout with flat beveled underside, 4 qt. capacity, "Leibrandt-M'Dowell" (stove company) on lid, Philadelphia, PA, late 19th C. **$75+**

"To remove rust from Iron Ware and Stoves. — New stove or range furniture is sometimes so much rusted as to make the use of it very inconvenient. Put into a rusty kettle as much hay as it will hold, fill it with water and boil many hours. At night set it aside, and the next day boil it again. Rub the rusty spots on a stove with sandpaper and then with sweet oil." Mary Hooker Cornelius, *The Young Housekeepers Friend,* Boston & NY: 1871, a later edition of the 1846 book.

Seasoning New Ironwares. — By 1884, the hay tip had become a recipe for *seasoning* a new cast iron utensil: "Boil Ashes or a bunch of hay or grass in a new iron pot before cooking in it; scour well with soap and sand, then fill with clean water, and boil one or two hours." *Practical Housekeeping,* 1884.

Another recipe for seasoning: "The best way to prepare a new iron kettle for use is to fill it with clean potato-peelings, boil them an hour or more, then wash the kettle with hot water, wipe it dry and rub it with a little lard; repeat the rubbing for six times after using. In this way you will prevent rust, and all the little annoyances liable to occur in the use of a new kettle." Emma Whitcomb Babcock, *Household Hints,* NY: Appleton, 1881. See more on this subject in Chapter IV, especially the section on cast iron baking pans.

● ● ● ●

"Among the . . . colonists of New England many domestic utensils of Iron, with which the humblest dwellings are now [1868] supplied, were quite unknown. Others were comparatively rare, and were prized accordingly. The inventories of property, and the wills of many persons of good estate, particularly enumerate such articles as Iron pots, of which one or two appear frequently to have comprised the whole stock. These were often bequeathed to some member of the household as a mark of esteem. The exclusive use of wrought-iron tea-kettles, and the extreme rarity of iron vessels a century ago [1768], are evidences of the limited product of cast-iron ware, even in the parent country, whence the colonists were supplied with such things as were then in common use. The profusion of such wares in every department of culinary service at this time is the result of comparatively recent improvements in this branch of metallurgy, and is due to the substitution of coke, and still more of anthracite, for charcoal in the reduction of ores." pp 488-89, Vol. I, Leander J. Bishop, *A History of American Manufactures from 1608-1860.* (Philadelphia, 1868).

XIV-76. Tea kettle. *Depicted without caption in* American Home Cook Book, *1854. Probably brass. A charming plump shape, and interesting handle grip.*

Tea or hot water kettle, cast iron, hinged top, coiled wire heat-dissipating handle, squared gooseneck spout, pit bottom, "M'Dowell," Philadelphia, 8" H to slightly domed lid x 12" diameter, pit bottom is 1-1/2" H x 9" diameter, 19th C. **$75-$130**

Tea or hot water kettle, cast iron with brass handle & lid, marked "Cannon Deepfields," English, "No. 2, 5 pints" on bottom, mid 19th C. **$100+**

Tea kettle, galvanized cast iron, pit bottom, swoopy curved pouring spout with outthrust lower lip, falling bail handle with heat-dissipating "Alaska" coil grip, Matthai-Ingram, came in No's 6, 7, 8 and 9, c.1890s. **$35-$50**

Seeger & Guernsey's Cyclopaedia of the Manufactures and Products of the United States, published in **1890**, gives a very long list of stove & range founders; then a long list of **makers of cast iron hollowware**, some of whom also made stoves. It is probably by no means complete, but might be interesting to see here, and to check against your own collections. Abendroth Brothers; Albany Stove; Belleville Stove; Samuel Booth; Bouton Foundry; Bramhall Deane; Broadway Machine Co.; Budke Mfg. Co.; Chamberlain Stove Co.; Cleveland Co-op Stove Co.; Clipper Mfg. Co.; Columbus Iron Works; Cribben, Sexton; Culter & Proctor Stove Co.; Defiance Machine Works; Great Western Stove Co.; Griswold Mfg. Co.; Highland Foundry; Hill, Whitney & Co.; Hoy & Co.; F. & L. Kahn & Bros.; Keokuk Stove Works; Lithgow Mfg. Co.; Magee Furnace; Manning, Bowman & Co.; Marietta Casting Co.; Marietta Hollow Ware & Enamelling Co.; Mount Penn Stove Works; Ohio Stove Co.; Patton Mfg. Co.; J. S. & M. Peckham; Rathbone, Sard & Co.; John Savery's Son; I. A. Sheppard & Co.; Standard Mfg. Co. (Add Sidney Hollowware Co., Sidney, OH, which sold to Wagner in 1898.) A few years later, in *The Buyers' Guide [of] Thomas' Register of American Manufacturers,* NYC: **1905**, the only listings are Atlanta Stove Works, Georgia; Blacklock Foundry Co., South Pittsburg, TN; Marietta Casting Co., and Marietta Holloware & Enamelling Co., both of Marietta, PA; Mobile Stove & Pulley Mfg. Co., Alabama; Phillips & Buttorff Mfg. Co., Nashville; and Wagner Mfg. Co., Sidney, OH. (To which we must add the most obvious omissions: Griswold Mfg. Co., Erie, PA; Wapak, Wapakoneta, OH, which had begun just two years before; The W. C. Davisa Favorite Stove & Range Co., Piqua, OH.)

Tea kettle, sheet iron, unusual inner & outer bodies, pipe vent connects hole in bottom center of outer body & passes through inner body at angle, with exit & entry holes brazed to seal; pipe vent ends up at one of holes around rim near the lid. It draws heat up through the water in the inner kettle, working something like a percolator. Kettle has straight spout in 2 sections, with holes around lower section (part of outer pot) evidently to increase air draft & efficiency in heating the water. Nicely shaped fixed bail handle, like handles from American 1820s kettles, turned wooden grip & hanging ring of wire, lift out lid in center of top of pot, like an ironclad battleship with its airholes & heavy sheet iron. "R. Wall, #568," Grove City, PA, about 6-1/2" H including lid x 10" diameter, c.1880s or poss. a little earlier? **$150-$175**

The Journal of the Franklin Institute of Philadelphia, Aug. 1828, reported on an **"Improvement in the Tea Kettle**, and other vessels for culinary purposes"** as follows: "A Mr. Gordon, of London [England], is manufacturing tea-kettles, and other culinary vessels, which are said to be very economical; the improvement consists simply in enclosing vessels of the ordinary kind, such as tea-kettles, stew-pans, &c., with an outer casing surrounding their sides, but open at the bottom, for the flame of a lamp [alcohol or spirit] to act upon it. When heat is applied to vessels so constructed, the plate of air between the cases becomes highly rarified, and the heat, having no tendency to descend, accumulates in the upper part to such an intense degree, as to be capable of melting a rod of glass if passed up the cavity. In vessels of the usual construction, the greater part of the heated air escapes without producing any useful effect; in these, however, it is detained, and the water may in consequence be boiled in a very short space of time. The chief advantages of the new construction are, therefore, economy of heat, or of the inflammable matter employed in producing it, economy of time, and convenience; the value of these may be variously estimated by different individuals, but all will acknowledge that they are important."

XIV-77. Tea kettle. *Cast iron with forged iron handle, bronze lid. 5-1/4" H x 6" diameter. Early 19th C. Japanese. • "The Accomplished & Lucky Tea-Kettle," a Japanese folk tale about an old tea kettle living at the Morinji temple in Jöshin provine. "One day, when the priest was about to hang it over the hearth to boil the water for his tea, to his amazement, the kettle all of a sudden put forth the head and tail of a badger. What a wonderful kettle, to come out all over fur!" The priest called in the novices to see it, and whilst they were staring, the kettle jumped up into the air and began flying about the room. The priest and his pupils chased it, and finally knocked it down and forced it into a box, "intending to carry it off and throw it away in some distant place, so that they might be no more plagued by the goblin." Unfortunately, a tinker who did work at the temple came by, and the priest thought he might as well make a little money for the kettle by selling it to the tinker. When he took it out of the box, it looked like an ordinary kettle; the tinker paid 20 copper coins for it and left for home. During the night, the tinker was disturbed many times by noises, and was frightened by the sight of the kettle covered with fur, but it always resumed its kettle shape. The tinker decided to set up an exhibition at a traveling show, along with musicians and other performers, and he became rich when all the great nobles of the court came to see the dancing kettle. "At last the tinker grew so rich that he took the kettle back to the temple, where it was laid up as a precious treasure, and worshiped as a saint." Published in Scribner's Monthly, 10/1873, and taken by them from Mitford's Tales of Old Japan.*

XIV-78. Tipping kettle. *Cast iron, bail is flat forged iron. American, early 19th C. Photograph courtesy Pat Guthman Antiques, Southport, CT.* **$550+**

Tea kettle, stainless steel body & spout in round-topped wide-bottomed cone shape, with ring of embossed dots just up from bottom, high straight spout terminated by red plastic bird whistle, high 3/4 round handle, part of which has Wedgwood-blue plastic handgrip with finger holds on underside, & red balls at each end, designed by American architect Michael Graves for Alessi, 2 qt. capacity, ©1985. An editorial note in 1986 said that 25,000+ of these $100 to $125 kettles had been sold in the first three or so months since its introduction late August 1985. **$100-$150**

Tea kettles, tin:

Tea kettle, heavy pieced tin, gooseneck, has "chef's hat" or pop-over-shaped outline to the fixed upright handle, typically American. 5-1/2" D at bottom, sides cant slightly outward as they go upward. 9-3/8" H including handle, prob. 1st quarter of 19th C. **$135+**

Tea kettle, pieced tin, long straight high angle spout, hinged lid, strapwork falling bail handle, strapwork ring finial on lid, American, 6-1/4" H x 3-3/4" diameter, mid 19th C. **$65-$80**

Early Tin — "The Dutch or Irish emigrant far away in his tent on the boundless prairies of the West, the boatman barging down his cotton over the bosom of the Mississippi, the Father of Waters, the rough miners of Nevada fighting with nature to extract the virgin silver from the heart of the Rocky Mountains, all require tin-ware in its rudest form, a tea-pot, a kettle, a pannikin, a wash-bowl, and requiring them are well aware that they will find them ready when desired at the nearest country store. . . . There is no doubt that the immense modern increase in the manufacturing and consumption of tin plates has resulted from the rapid increase of population in the U.S.A." P. W. Flower, *A History of the Trade in Tin,* 1880. [The "plates" are flat sheets of tin plated iron, not dinner plates.]

Tea kettle, tin, painted black, "Kreamer," American, 2 cup capacity, 20th C. **$25-$32**

Tea kettle, tin, with range eye pit bottom made of copper, strap handle, domed lid, American, late 19th C. **$65-$75**

Tea kettle, very low & broad, gooseneck spout, wide falling strap handle, stamped & pieced tin, "for oil stoves," Matthai-Ingram, 8-1/2" diameter, 3 qt. capacity, c.1890s. **$35-$45**

Tea & coffee pot, shiny tin plate, black wooden handle and knob, marked only "Extra Tin Plate," American, 2 qt. capacity, turn of century. **$25-$35**

Tea set, with teapot with brave straight spout & long gently arched ribbed plastic handle, sugar bowl with round lid, creamer, designed by Russell Wright for Chase Copper & Brass, Waterbury, CT, c.1930s. Designer's name is the $$-maker here; there are many collectors of his table settings. **$225-$300**

Tea steeper, cobalt blue enamelware, early 20th C (?). **$35-$65**

Tea steeper, dark green enamelware with white loopy streaks or swirls, white inside, "Chrysolite," American, turn of century. **$85-$135**

Tea steeper, white enamelware with blue trim, turn of century. **$12-$22**

Tea strainer, gray graniteware, turn of century. **$20-$30**

Tea strainer, tin with red wooden handle, depicts teapot & cups on the strainer cup, 1930s-1940s. **$15-$18**

Tea strainer spoon, silverplate, adv'g "Tetley Tea," 20th C. **$20-$25**

Tea strainer & stand, nickeled metal, Main Tool & Mfg. Co., (Brooklyn, NY?), 20th C. **$4-$6**

Tea urn, a sort of English samovar, brass urn is round, tinned inside, set up on 4 pillars, square base, alcohol burner below bolted to base, English, 14" H x 7-1/2" diameter, c.1840s. In silver this form might be as much as 40 years older. **$175+**

Tea urn, brass plated globe on straight legs, sort of Art Deco or Arts & Crafts space station, strips of bamboo wrapped around spigot, heating alcohol lamp below, Austrian, early 20th C. **$175-$200**

Tea urn, copper with brass handles, spigot & trim, on 4 legs, English, 21" H, late 19th C. **$165+**

Tea urn, tin, grape cluster molding, cast iron handles, brass spigot, American (?), 15" H, c.1870s (?). **$100-$125+**

Teapot, 3 metals — tin, brass and copper. Brass finial on lid, footed & very graceful, 19th C. **$85-$100**

Teapot, black & white speckly enamelware, with Britannia collar & lid, strainer inside gooseneck spout, 8-1/2" H, 19th C. **$150-$180**

Teapot, blue glazed earthenware, lid chipped & repaired, double wire bail handle with black painted turned wood grip, no marks, 5-1/2" H to final top, 19th C. **$350-$385**

Teapot, blue & white swirl agateware, hinged lid, 7" H, late 19th or early 20th C. **$165-$225**

Teapot, Britannia, wonderful melon-ribbed shape, small curved feet, marked "James Dixon," early to mid 19th C. **$85-$110**

In **1836**, the *Journal of the Franklin Institute* published a short report of interest to people trying to date Britannia (and other metal) teapots. **"Tea-pots made by steam**. Britannia metal tea-pots are now made by steam; the round bodies are spun, and the wooden handles and knobs are cut up by powerful steam engines. A good workman can spin twenty dozen of pot-bodies in a day." A complex melon shape like this might possibly have been made using a spun blank.

XIV-79. Tea kettle. *Cast iron, small globular body with 3 short feet. Cast in 3 sections, see vertical & horizontal seams. Crookneck spout, flat forged falling bail, stepped dome lid — intriguingly chained to handle. "A. T." cast on side. 6-1/8" H x 12-1/4" L. Photograph by Jennifer Oka. Picture courtesy of the National Museum of American History, Smithsonian Institution, John Paul Remensnyder estate.* **$450+**

XIV-81. Electric tea kettle, *on Art Nouveau-styled stand, mfd. by "Simplex." From Maud Lancaster's* Electric Cooking, *1914.* **$45-$75**

XIV-80. "Toddy kettle" & gas lamp heater. *The "Union Attachment" bracket fits to the gas fixture and provides a place for a smallish (and definitely light weight) tea kettle. Mfd. by Standard Co., NYC. The Metal Worker, 7/8/1882.*

XIV-82. Electric tea kettle. *"Speedmaster," with "independent electric heating element, but is so constructed that it may also be used on any stove the same as the ordinary type of kettle." From* The Electric Home, *E. S. Lincoln, 1936. The styling is so "thirties" and hence collectible.* **$75+**

Czechoslovakian Enamelware — It took a while, but American collectors of enamelware seem to finally have wholeheartedly welcomed European wares made from the mid nineteenth century up through the early 1930s to their collections. These are wares imported in the waning years of the nineteenth century and up to WWI, wares imported during a short resumption of trade, and finally wares only recently imported by containerload, specifically for the collector market. This latest wave of importing will probably include old marked pieces once made for possible export (viz., after 1891, bearing name of country of origin), as well as more truly antique pieces dating back as far as the mid nineteenth century. While there were probably hundreds of European enamelware manufacturers in the late nineteenth century, there were only a handful in all of the United States, and none that I know of in Canada. For today's collectors (perhaps enamored of other "gaudy" wares), **Czechoslovakian pieces** are especially interesting, having been made in really spectacular patterns & bold colors, with skilled, confident painting, peasant or "country look" designs. Sometimes sets are found, recently imported to the U.S. Plaids in cobalt blue & white, or red & white, colorful polkadots, flowers, leaves, stripes, geometric border patterns, often with contrasting colors for spout, handle and finial, are very desirable. Trade journal ads, c.1900, showed imported German, Austrian & Swedish imported wares. A provision of the 1890 McKinley Tariff Act raised an already stiff <u>tariff on imported enamelware</u>. Although American enamelware brought in $4 million yearly, *The New York Times* wrote "It is not very durable, the base being of iron, and the profit is very heavy." Of "Bohemian" enamelware they wrote, "nearly all . . . foreign ware is . . . blue & white. . .more attractive than the mottled [American] graniteware." Steel-based imports were considered three times as durable. McKinley's tariff raised the 45% rate already in effect. In 1890, stores stockpiled foreign enamelware to sell at prices lower than would be seen again for a long time. In 1890, St. Louis Stamping Co.'s **Imperial Decorated Iron Ware** was touted as "closely approximating French china in weight and grace of form. . .The. . .original color decorations in flowers, &c., are in pleasing contrast with the pure white enamel surface." [See Chapter VII for more on Tariff Act.]

Teapot, canal boat or <u>barge china</u>, with dark brown glaze and thickly decorated blue flowers and birds, and pink & white flowers, very small teapot finial on lid, medallion or scroll on front reads "A Present From A Friend 1790," English, 12-3/8" H, 1790. **Barge china.** — This colorful pot is an example of many decorative, exuberant "folk" pottery wares used by the thousands of people who lived on the barges and flat-bottomed boats that plied up and down the vast inner canal system in England. The pieces date well into the 19th C. **$475+**

Teapot, cinnamon colored enamelware, white inside, turned wood handle with black finish, nickeled brass lid & base with wood knob, Manning-Bowman, 6-1/2" H to top of finial, pat'd May 21, 1889. **$250+**

Teapot, cobalt enamelware, white flower decorations, gold trim, hinged lid, European, 7" H, turn of century. **$175-$250**

Teapot, decorated china, hinged metal lid with large finial knob with hole in it, odd spout turns down like a faucet, "Royle's Patent Self Pouring Teapot," mfd. by Doulton Potteries, Manchester, England, 7-1/2" H, pat'd 1886 in England by A. J. Royle. **Classic** — This fabulous piece was advertised as "a boon for mothers of large families" (as most families of the time were). You didn't have to pick up the teapot to pour the tea; instead, you merely lifted the lid, put your finger over the hole in the finial knob, then closed the lid and the tea came out the downturned spout. Woe to the M.o.l.f. if she'd forgotten the cup. An article in *Spinning Wheel* in Oct. 1969 showed examples made of Britannia by Meriden Britannia and told about a teapot marked "Asbury-Paine Mfg Co., Phila. PA" with a patent date of April 3, 1888. This patent date is the American one, and was used on self-pouring teapots made of various materials. **$250-$400**

"End of Day" — The popular, but not necessarily accurate, term for swirled multicolored enamelwares (as well as blown glass wares) is "End of Day" pieces. I have not seen documentary contemporary evidence that would back up a somewhat romantic notion that the dog-tired artisan, at the end of a 10- or 12-hour workday, would be lively enough, and adequately enough supplied with "leftovers," or even allowed, to work past quitting time to make a whimsical end of day piece for a loved one. I am speculating here, just as everyone else does, but it is possible that the first few of this type of thing became so much the rage that artisans everywhere wanted to make or were asked to make such things during regular working hours. Diaries, documents, worksheets, inventories — all would help answer our questions. Do you keep a diary? More subtle color mixtures don't bring the high prices that brighter ones do.

XIV-83. "The Clock That Makes Tea." *"Most people seem to think that America has cornered the world market on Yankee inventive genius, but it remains for our British cousins to cap the climax of inventions intended to permit the weary sojourner on this terrestial ball to roll over and take another nap again" by means of the clock teapot. "Johnny Bull likes his cup of tea upon rising, {and with this] the clock wakes him up, lights a lamp, boils a pint of water, pours the water into handy teapot, puts out the lamp, and rings a gong announcing that tea is ready." This was in* House Furnishing Review, *2/1908, and whether it's true or a ruse, I don't know. But they've got 'em now!*

XIV-84. "Bird tea kettle." *An old idea in a new design — the whistling plastic (or metal in older ones) bird in the spout who whistles when the water is boiling. This stainless steel one with colored plastic handle & bird designed by architect Michael Graves, copyrighted 1985.* **$100-$150**

Teapot, enamelware, white background with gorgeous raspberries, blackberries & leaves in brilliant colors, pewter lid, copper bottom rim to protect from chipping, Manning-Bowman, 9-1/4" H to finial top, pat'd May 21, 1889, in late 1890s catalog as are others. **$325+**

Teapot, "end of day" enamelware with swirls of several bright colors, predominately cobalt & red, with orange & yellow, American (?), small, 19th C. **$250+**

Teapot, globe-shaped, blown-molded glass, with engraved floral spray on sides, press-molded lid with knob, "Pyrex," English, 5-1/2" D; 1-1/2 pt. capacity, c. 1930. This earliest Pyrex teapot is the only one with engraved flowers. **$60-$75**

Teapot, gray graniteware with pewter cover, spout, breast band & handle, copper bottom, footed, handle is scrolled, domed lid with nice finial, body is a beautiful, nearly round form, American, late 19th C. **$150-$200**

Teapot, gray graniteware with tin spout, handle, lid, breast-band & base rim, American, 19th C. **$155-$225**

Teapot, japanned tin, big foot, stamped inside lid with mark — probably maker's not owner's — carpenter's dividers straddling a rising sun, also initials "W & S," American (?), 14" H, c.1840s. **$400-$500**

Teapot, nickeled copper, double walled, wood handle, decorative nickeled cast pot-metal finial on lid, "Sweeney Mfg. Co.," Brooklyn, NY, 3 pt. size, early 20th or late 19th C. **$20-$28**

Teapot, olive drab green enamelware, white inside, pewter handle, nickled brass base, wooden "heat sink" where handle joins lid, "Quality # 5," mfd. by Manning-Bowman, Meriden, CT, 8-3/4" H, late 19th C. **$175-$265**

Teapot, pale green & white marbleized enamelware, gooseneck spout, "Elite," marked Austria, turn of century. **$170-$250**

Teapot, pewter, 8-1/2" H, 20th C. **$35-$45**

Teapot, spun aluminum with wooden handle, chain that feeds through finial of lid is attached to small domed tea ball perforated with circles of holes, looks like "The Little King" of comic strip fame, "Merit," American, 7-1/4" H x 8-1/2" W including spout and handle, c.1920s. **$16-$22**

Teapot, very bulbous shape, bright blue agateware, with Britannia trim — lid, spout, part of handle, Manning-Bowman, 1889. **$125-$150**

Teapot, white & blue speckled enamelware, also called speckleware, possibly United States Stamping Co., Moundsville, WV, 1st quarter 20th C. **$155-$185**

Teapot, yellow enamelware with red poppies & green trim, gooseneck spout, prob. European, 20th C. **$50-$70**

Trivet, for teapot at table, ornate cast iron, with name around edge, "Midget," American, 3-3/4" D, turn of century. **$35-$45**

Trivet for coffee or teapot, cast iron, lacy doily design, 5 little feet, "Griswold Trivet," mid 20th C. **$100+**

Water kettles — See tea kettles

Whistle for tea kettle, stamped & pieced brass, bird has a "stem" to fit into spout, American, 3-1/2" H, pat'd 1923. **$20-$35**

PRESERVING

XV. CHILL & FREEZE

A very early way to preserve food was by lowering its temperature (in ice or cold water) to stop decomposition; some anthropologists even believe that those early humans who followed the Ice Age "harvested" mastodon and other animals preserved (perhaps even for thousands of years) in glacial ice.

Prior to about 150 years ago, people built spring houses and/or ice houses. **Spring houses** utilize a natural year-round spring — lively rather than sluggish — which either courses underground or aboveground. A spring house might be a small 6 x 8 foot outbuilding made of stone, brick, logs, and built into a hillside; or it might be a much larger space, with room for benches, even a work table, built sometimes in a cellar under the house. For the convenience of the housewife, spring houses best had *raised* troughs through which the water flowed, but sometimes a channel was cut at floor level. Stoneware crocks, jugs and stoneware pans were set into the troughs so that the water would flow past and keep the contents fairly cold.

Ice houses are belowground ice "wells" lined in brick or stone, with a drain at the bottom running downgrade for some distance, or percolating down into a sort of tank. They had a built-up thatched wooden roof and — if well-made — a vestibule with a north-facing door to the outside and a door into the well to act as an air lock. Inside, huge chunks of sawn or chopped lake or pond ice, or even "dry" snow, were rammed compactly into place on a bed of clean, dry straw. Then the top of the ice was insulated with straw or marsh grasses or whatever relatively clean vegetable matter could be used to protect the ice from the air, overlaid with boards. Ice stored in the winter could be expected to last well into the summer. Some of these wells or pits had thick stone or brick dome roofs, insulated on top with thick layers of earth and sod. A ladder was kept inside. Stored ice was used to cool drinks and make desserts, as well as to preserve food, especially meat. Somewhat more common methods of preserving food for long spells were smoking, salting, sugaring and drying. (See next chapter.)

The most popular collectibles within this chapter are small **ice chippers, shredders** and **shavers**, and **ice tongs**. Prices haven't moved very much in these categories since the mid 1980s, except for eighteenth- or early nineteenth-century forged-iron ice tools, which have become much more expensive (as have their cousins, the hearth tools). I have placed a **Futurewatch** on **ice cube trays** — aluminum, rubber and any other material I'm not aware of.

The least popular category is still ice boxes and refrigerators — which implies nothing about their artistic or historic merit, merely (and it ain't so mere) their size. For most people, one or two ice boxes is the limit; and most people seek decorative oak ones that go with Arts & Crafts or Mission furniture or Art Moderne decor. They use them as bars or storage cabinets in their living or dining rooms.

You may have expected to find ice cream molds and dishers or scoops here, but they're in Chapter IV with other molds and shapers.

Freezer, fabulous streamlined design with 2 round deep cylinders flanking a finned motor, all in white enameled steel, colored top lids on both compartments, "no food more than 9 inches away from all-surrounding source of cold," 1945 ad states. "You store two units with food. You use the food out of one unit. When this is consumed, you turn it off and start using the food in the second unit." "Deepfreeze," mfd. by Deepfreeze Division of Motor Products Corp., North Chicago, IL, interior of compartments 30" H x 18" diameter, overall 41-1/4" H x 65-5/8" L x 26-11/16" diameter, began making c.1938. **$125+**

"Ice boxes" is what I always assumed ice boxes were called until gas or electric "refrigerators" came in. But many advertisements for and catalogs of "ice boxes" used the word "refrigerator" way back in the nineteenth century. In fact, I wouldn't be surprised to learn that the term "ice box" didn't come in until we needed something to differentiate a refrigerator that was loaded with ice to make it cool, and a refrigerator with coolants. As for the patent record (from the beginning up to 1873), there is one "ice box" patent, in 1867, and one "Ice and coal box" in 1866. On the other hand, there are over 190 "refrigerators," beginning I think in 1837, plus one "ice refrigerator," one "ice-box refrigerator," plus a score of "refrigerating devices," ". . . chambers," ". . .cupboards," etc. The term "fridge," still in wide usage in parts of the country, actually is a shortened version of the brand-name Frigidaire and probably originated in the 1920s. The company that became Frigidaire began in 1916 as the Guardian Frigerator Co.

Ice ball "cubes," large "Aggie"-marble-sized steel balls, filled with a liquid that holds cold. c.1950s (?) Set of 6: **$5+**

Ice box — See refrigerator (ice box) and refrigerator (electric)

Ice breakers — See ice crushers

Ice bucket, metal, shaped like a medieval knight's helmet, top opens to reveal ice, mid 20th C. **$40-$55**

XV-1. Freezer. *The trade name for it became a generic term for home freezers: "Deepfreeze." Two cylinders, each 18" diameter x 30" deep. You used all food in one unit & turned it off, then switched over to food in 2nd unit. Deepfreeze Division, Motor Products Corp., North Chicago, IL.* Country Gentleman *ad, 1945.* **$125+**

Ice chipper, cast iron, "Gilchrist #50," Newark, NJ, 20th C. **$20-$25**

Ice chipper, cast iron, brass ferrule, wood handle, "Briddell #60," Charles D. Briddell, Inc., Crisfield, MD, late 19th or early 20th C. **$12+**

Ice chipper, steel with wood handle, wicked looking, "Crown," mfd. by North Brothers, Philadelphia, PA, c.1900. **$15+**

Ice chipper & bottle opener combined, iron, wooden handle, "Coolerator," Duluth Refrigerator Corp., Duluth, MN, early 20th C. **$15+**

Ice chisel, steel, turned wood handle, downturned chisel head fitted on back with a much shorter head with 4 very broad sharp teeth, "Crown Ice Chipper," mfd. by American Machine Co., Philadelphia, PA, pat'd April 8, 1884. **$15+**

Ice chisel, polished steel blade, turned wooden handle with iron band to keep it from splitting when hit with mallet, 4 wicked sharp beveled teeth, Matthai-Ingram Co., c.1890s. **$15+**

Ice chopper & container — heavy clear glass tumbler with 3 red bands & 2 black bands indicating ounce measurements, chromed lid, fitted with heavily weighted nickeled metal cross bladed chopper with knob handle, blades have teeth, American, 20 oz. capacity, 9" H, c.1930s to 1940s. **$18+**

Ice cracker, long springy chromed steel handle with plastic grip and with heavy round head, used with ice in palm of hand or on towel, "Tap-Icer," Williamsport, PA, c.1960. **$3+**

Ice cream can, gray graniteware, container for ingredients which could be put into some kinds of ice cream freezers. 1 qt. size, late 19th C. **$70-$90**

Ice cream carrier, for picnics, oak box, zinc lining, side door swings open to put in block of ice cream, then you lift off top & pack in ice, "The Bradley Ice Cream Cabinet, Patented," mfd. by the Bradley Mfg. Co., New Haven, CT, 8-1/2" H x 11" x 9", late 19th C. Ice cream is a high ticket area of specialization in kitchen collections. For a collector club, see ice cream molds in Chapter IV. **$225-$275**

Ice cream freezer, "North Pole," Alaska Freezer Co., Winchendon, MA, 20th C. **$45+**

Ice cream freezer, "Champion," Arlington, NJ, early 1900s. **$50+**

Patents for Ice Cream Freezers — Between 1790 and 1873 there were only about 60 patentees for ice cream freezers, beginning with W. G. Young, Baltimore, on May 30, 1848. (**NOTE:** I have a note in my files that E. M. Manigle of Philadelphia also got one on May 30, 1848, but have no idea where that came from — the name is not in the *Subject Index of Patents*.) Young was followed by A. H. Austin, Baltimore, on September 19; then H. B. Masser, Sunbury, PA, on December 12; and two in 1849 — one an Ohioan, the other a Marylander. The next one came in 1854, another Baltimorean. There must be a reason why the city known for canned peaches and oysters, and not a few other kitchen-related inventions, was so into ice cream!

Makers of Ice Cream Freezers — In the *Thomas' Register of American Manufacturers,* for 1905-06, there are but 14 makers of ice cream freezers listed: White Mountain, Nashua, NH; Treman, King & Co., Ithaca, NY; Cordley & Hayes, NYC, who made them of Indurated Fibre ware; Crandall & Godley, and Slotkin & Praglin, both also of NYC; E. C. Stearns & Co., Syracuse, NY; Dana Mfg., H. Day & Co., Kingery Mfg. Co., and The Samuel C. Tatum Co., all of Cincinnati, OH; and J. P. Anderson & Co., Thomas Mills & Brother, North Brothers Mfg. Co., and Charles W. Packer, all four of Philadelphia.

XV-3. Ice chisels. *Most are versions of 4-toothed style. Those with flat-ended handles were used by hitting with mallet.* (T-L) to (T-R): **(1)** *Polished steel blade, iron band around handle kept it from splitting when hit. Matthai-Ingram, c.1890.* **(2)** *Steel blade, tinned "cap" to wood handle, 10-1/2" L. Sexton catalog, 1930s (may be LF&C).* **(3)** *Steel blade, wood handle, choice of 6", 8" or 10" blades, with 8", 10" or 12" handles, 12" handle. Landers, Frary & Clark. Sexton catalog, 1930s.* **(4)** *Steel, iron ferrule, C. W. Dunlap & Co., NYC. c.1904-1910.* **(5)** *Steel & wood. Heinz & Munschauer, 1882.* (B-L) to (B-R) **(6)** *Galvanized iron, hardwood handle, steel points "securely fastened & interchangeable." 9", 11-1/2" or 48" L. Sold by Albert Pick, 1909.* **(7)** *"Gilchrist's Needle Point Ice Chipper No.50," also for "caked salt, sugar, etc." Sexton catalog, 1930s.* **(8)** *"Ice Pick Chipper," tinned steel, 9-1/2" L x 3" W. Pick, 1909.* **(9)** *"Four-Point Ice Shaver," tempered steel, nickeled iron band & ferrule to wood handle. On cap: "N. White City & Co." (?) Pick, 1909.* **(10)** *Combo shave & pick, nickeled malleable iron. 6-1/2" L blade; 12" L overall. Pick, 1909.* **$5-$25**

XV-2. Ice chippers. (B-L) & (B-R) *"Lightning" and* **(T)** *"Crown." Both mfd. by North Brothers Mfg. Co., Philadelphia. "They take the place of the old-time bag and hatchet, and quickly reduce the ice to uniformly small pieces, about the size of a peanut." Lightning was made in No.1, for families; and No.2, with 48" L handle, for confectioners, hotels, restaurants. North's promo-cookbook* Dainty Dishes For All the Year Round, *by Mrs. S. T. Rorer.* **$15-$22**

Ice cream freezer, all metal, galvanized iron outer box, "re-inforced cover," heavy tin round "paint can" cylinder inside with a "friction cover which is absolutely water tight," tinned iron dasher and crank with wooden knob, the crank being outside the box's side, "The Snow Flake Freezer" stenciled on side, mfd. by Snow Flake Mfg Co., came in 1, 2, 3 and 4 qt. sizes, c.1907-1908. With tin ones, condition must be very very good, especially of stencils or paper labels. **$50+**

Ice cream freezer, clamps to table, "Liberty Can Co.," Lancaster, PA, 2 qt. size, pat'd 1920 and 1921. **$50+**

Doughboys Love Ice Cream — "Ice cream has played a great part in this war [WWII] and is recognized as a morale builder, unsurpassed. The importance of ice cream has been testified to by the enormous amounts of prepared mix and portable equipment for freezing provided by the army and used so close to combat lines that battle weary men just back of the front have been able to have a dish of ice cream in the protection of the nearest foxhole." Dr. H. A. Ruehe, American Butter Institute, *The Sealtest Food Adviser,* Fall 1945.

XV-4. Ice cream freezers. (L) *Cedar tub with can and stirrer. Note bung hole. Dubois,* Patisserie d'Aujourd'hui, *1860s-70s.* **(R)** *"Patent Ice Cream Freezer & Mould.— By which Creams, Ices &c., can be frozen fit for table use in a very few minutes. The forms are easily managed and now coming into general family use."* American Home Cook Book, *1854. This freezer also has bung hole at bottom for draining off melted ice. Bail handle, interesting double-ended, knobbed horizontal twisting stirrer for can. In 1854, when this cookbook was published, there were only five pat'd American ice cream freezers; another was pat'd in September of 1854.* **$65+**; *(R)* **$150+**

XV-5. Ice cream or sorbétière freezer, freezer patent. (L) *Cedar tub, large cranked wheel with bevel gears. It is called a <u>turbine</u> in the book it's in — Dubois,* Patisserie d'Aujourd'hui, *c.1860s-70s.* **(R)** *Pat'd 6/10/1856, by Joseph Parisette, Indianapolis, IN. Features spiral scraper which revolves & scrapes sides of can, as well as forcing to the bottom the frozen cream so that the unfrozen will "rise to the top to be mixed and equally frozen."* Official Gazette. *(L)* **$125+**; *(R) if it exists:* **$65+**

Ice cream freezer, galvanized metal canister, snug-fitting lid, vertical crank with wooden knob, wire bail handle, "Glacier Freezer Triple Action," mfd. by Sunburst Alcohol Stove Co., T. W. Houchin, NYC, NY, c.1912. **$55+**

Ice cream freezer, galvanized tin, blue painted lid, outer body, crank, paper label says "Kwik Freeze," 20th C. **$45+**

Ice cream freezer, horizontal heavy tin "duplex" cylinder with stationary dasher blade inside each half, cylinder (which fits into malleable cast iron screw clamp frame) turns freely when cranked, while the dashers remain stationary, oblong hinged hatch in middle for putting in salt & ice, close-fitting caps at each end for adding ingredients for 2 flavors of ice cream, "Acme," mfd. by Palmer Hardware Mfg. Co., Troy, NY, c.1892. **$100+**

Ice cream freezer, japanned & stenciled tin canister, with imitation graining & bronze decorations and label. Heavy porcelain knob with gilding on close-fitting lid, galvanized interior, long cone-shaped insert to hold ingredients with salt packed around, cast iron side handles, "Automatic Ice Cream Freezer," mfd. by Treman King & Co, "System Dr. Meidinger" (refers to a foreign patent?), Ithaca, NY, 13-1/2" H x 6" diameter, c.1880s; still in business 1905. **$165-$225**

Ice cream freezer, pail shaped, crank on top, frame of malleable cast iron, pail is tinned wrought sheet iron, Isaac S. Williams & Co., Philadelphia, pat'd June 21, 1881. **$75+**

"Directions for Freezing Ice-Creams and Custards — Ice-creams, custards and water are so delightful and refreshing for summer desserts and tea, it is to me a matter of astonishment that every family is not supplied with a patent ice-cream freezer, of which there are many in the market. By the use of one of these, the process of freezing is rendered so much more expeditious and satisfactory as to more than compensate for the trifling expense involved in its purpose. If not provided with this convenience, a small quantity of ice-cream can be frozen in a tin bucket, taking care that there are no holes in it to let in the water, and spoil the cream. Set this bucket in a wooden tub or bucket several inches larger. On the bottom of this place a layer of pounded ice and salt; set in the bucket containing the cream, or custard, and pack closely around its sides a mixture of pounded ice and salt (mixed in the proportion of six pounds of ice to one of salt), extending to within two inches of the top of the freezer. Cover the freezer, and keep it in constant motion, removing the cover frequently to scrape the congealed cream from the sides with a silver spoon or wooden paddle, taking care to keep the sides clear, and stirring it well to the bottom. Keep the tub well filled with salt and ice outside the freezer, and take great care that none of the salt water gets in to spoil the cream. The outside tub or bucket should have a hole in or near the bottom, from which the bung can be removed to allow the water to pass out as the ice melts. After the cream is well frozen, it may be packed in moulds, and set in salt and pounded ice. When you wish to serve it, wrap the mould with a hot cloth, turn out the cream and serve immediately.

"For making ice-cream, genuine cream is, of course, preferable. But in the absence of this, equal parts of milk and cream may be used; or, the milk may be heated, and, while hot, perfectly fresh sweet butter added to it in sufficient quantity to give it the richness of cream. Boiled milk or custards must be allowed to become perfectly cold before putting them in the freezer. Sour cream or buttermilk may be used by stirring into them enough soda to correct their acid before sweetening and flavoring. Custards and creams for freezing should be sweetened and flavored more highly than when not frozen." Mrs. A. P. Hill, *Mrs. Hill's New Family Receipt Book.* NY: 1870.

Ice cream freezer, looks like horizontal barrel churn with straight cylindrical sides, on A-frame, all wood but for iron bands on freezer, iron crank in end. A small size one is tabletop & mounted to board. "Tingley's Patent Horizontal," mfd. by the churn maker Charles G. Blatchley as "Blatchley's Horizontal," Philadelphia, PA, sizes from 3 to 40 qts. Pat'd by J. Tingley of Philadelphia Feb. 11, 1868 & June 6, 1871. Advertised by Blatchley in 1874, and as late as 1911. **$125-$150**

Ice cream freezer, staved wooden bucket with wire bail handle, tinned cast iron works, crank turns numerous horizontally fixed beater blades, "Rapid," Clement & Dunbar, Philadelphia, 4 gal. capacity, c.1880s. **$55+**

Ice cream freezer, tin, "Kress," poss. Philadelphia, pat'd July 23, 1912. **$30-$45**

Ice cream freezer, tin cylinder, wooden crank top, "Acme," mfd. by Ritter, Philadelphia, 2 gal. capacity, pat'd Feb. 15, 1910. Later patent shown on other Acmes is July 3, 1912. **$35-$45**

Ice cream freezer, wood bucket with cast iron works, "Arctic," mfd. by White Mountain Freezer Co., Nashua, NH, pat'd 1889. They were still in business 1905. **$35-$45**

Ice cream freezer, wood & galvanized metal, "Frost King," Richmond Cedar Works, Richmond, VA, 20th C. (Still making them in 1930s.) **$45-$55**

"**A Freezing Tub** must be made oblong or oval, the sides to be as upright as possible; may be made to hold two or three sabbatiers, or freezing pots, in length, leaving a sufficient space for the ice; it must have a false bottom with some holes in it; in the side of the tub, near the bottom, make a hole for a peg, by which means you may constantly draw off the water, a precaution highly necessary when freezing, to prevent the water from ever getting into the sabbatier. Sabbatiers, ice moulds, and ice spoons, may be supplied by any experienced pewterer." Joseph Bell, *A Treatise on Confectionary* Newcastle, England, 1817.

"**To freeze Ices.** — If only one sort of ice, set the freezing pot in a small upright pail, made as above, with two bottoms, &c.; if two or three sorts, set your pots at a proper distance in the long pail; fill up the space with ice well beat, mix in three or four handfuls of salt, and press both well down; then take a clean cloth and make the tops of the pots clear of ice and salt; take off the tops; and put into each the creams or waters previously mixed for them; please to observe, that pots must not be more than half full; then replace the top to each; draw the tub a little to one side, and turn each pot as quickly, as possible; if you have two pots in, turn one with each hand; if three, let one stand alternately; when you have turned the pots ten minutes, take off the tops, and scrape the frozen cream down from each with an ice spoon; if the cream appears hard and flinty, you may conclude it is not rich enough mixed; if, on the other hand, it does not freeze, it is over rich, and in either case must be rectified; if right, proceed as before directed, and every ten minutes, scrape it down; when the cream in the pots appears nearly frozen, keep off the covers, and work well with the ice spoon, making the pots turn round in the ice, this will make the cream both smooth and light; as soon as it appears pretty stiff, put on the tops, and cover the pots well up with more ice and salt, until you prepare your moulds to receive it. N.B. It may be necessary here to note, that you must have an ice spoon for each pot; or must be careful to wash it every time, to prevent a mixture of tastes." Joseph Bell, *A Treatise on Confectionary*. Newcastle, England, 1817. For Bell's tips on molding ice cream, see an ice cream mold entry in Chapter IV.

Ice cream freezer, wood, metal, "Auto Vacuum," Auto Vacuum Freezer Co., NYC, pat'd Jan. 2, 1912. **$35-$50**

Ice cream freezer, wood with cast iron crank & frame, 2 gal. size, dated 1858 — probably one pat'd by H. B. Masser of Sunbury, PA, on Jan. 19, 1858. As we see, this is an early patent. **$125-$150**

Ice cream freezer, wooden tub/bucket, bail handle, iron crank & frame, "American," American Machine Co., Philadelphia, c.1880s. **$45+**

Ice cream holder, tin, bail handle, insulated inside, "Thermopak," Joe Lowe Co., Inc., Brooklyn, NY, 1st third 20th C. **$15-$20**

Ice cream jar, glass, "Ice Cream in Glass," 1 pt. capacity, American, early 20th C. **$25+**

Ice cream maker, glass canister with feet, wire frame, with original recipe & instruction folder inside, "Sanitary Crystal Glass Ice Cream Freezer," mfd. by "Consolidated Mfg. Co.," American (poss. Dayton, OH; poss. Quincy, IL), early 20th C. **$50+**

Ice cream mixer, cast aluminum, used with CO_2 cartridges, that came in boxes of 5, then put in freezer tray after mixing, "One Smoothie Whip is required for making. . . . When the Whip has been discharged and removed from the holder it can be thrown out, as it cannot be used again." Marked with decal of name "Smoothie" superimposed over a green sundae dish with ice cream in it, "The Smoothie. The Instant Home Mixer of 'Satin Smooth' Ice Cream," mfd. by Ralmac Corp., Grand Rapids, MI, no date, c. 1950s. **$45-$55**

XV-6. Ice cream freezer. *"Automatic Ice Cream Freezer, Treman King & Co., System Dr. Meidinger, Ithica, NY 1 & 3 East State Street." Japanned tin, imitation graining, galvanized inside, gold & bronze decorations & label. Heavy porcelain knob with gilding on close-fitting lid. Conical insert that holds ingredients lifts out, with a "bayonet" twist — to pack salt & ice in. 13-1/2" H x 6" diameter. 1870s? Collection of Meryle Evans.* **$165-$225**

XV-7. Ice cream freezer. *"Jack Frost," 2 quart size. Wood & cast iron. With litho'd depiction of winter play scene inside lid. "It takes very little ice and salt, being constructed on an entirely new principle. Instead of having the ice and salt on the outside of the can, the can is on the outside, and the ice and salt inside." The Housewife, 7/1891.* **$100-$150**

Ice cream molds & ice cream dishers — See Chapter IV

Ice cream packing tins, set of 4, tin, American, 4 qt., 1 pt., 1/2 pt. & 1/4 pt. capacity, early 20th C. **$35-$50**

Ice crusher, also called **ice cube breaker** or **ice grinder,** mechanical, cream-colored painted cast metal, wood handle crank, on a stand with place for a tumbler, "National Ice-Crusher," 9" H, pat'd 1936. **$20+**

Ice crusher, all cast iron, oblong jaws with "waffled" treads inside, "Stover Ice Cube Kracker," Stover, Freeport, IL, 7-3/4" L, early 1900s. **$18-$25**

Ice crusher, mechanical, malleable cast iron, "Alaska #1," Alaska Freezer Co., Winchendon, MA, 19th C. into 1930s. **$35+**

Ice crusher, mechanical, malleable iron hopper & housing on decorative cast iron double "A" base, side crank, 12" H, marked "Chandler's Ice Cutting Machine," on handle: "pat'd Nov. 16, 1880." **$150+**

Ice crusher or breaker, mechanical, sheet metal hopper above 4-legged cast iron stand on plinth, with lion-head knees to each leg, large wheel crank turns two gears in side. Four sizes, the first two available with a receiver drawer. Size No. 3 "will take a piece of ice about 5" by 8", breaking it into pieces about the size of chestnuts." Advertised in Mrs. Marshall's cookbooks as a "household machine for crushing ice," but in a catalog as for "hotel keepers, ships' cabins, Butlers' pantries," etc. Marked on hopper "Mrs. A. B. Marshall, London." **$375+**

Ice crusher, mechanical, cast iron base , with green glass ice hopper, "Lightning," North Brothers Mfg. Co., Philadelphia, PA, 1932 design patent #86599. Green glass adds some value. **$75+**

Ice crusher, mechanical, enameled steel frame and platform, fitted with square green Depression glass container, hopper above with crank, "Lightning," North Brothers, 1933 patent #1980952. **$65+**

Ice crusher, mechanical, nickel-plated brass, "Coolerator," Duluth Refrigerators, Duluth, MN, 20th C. **$25-$35**

Ice crusher, mechanical, cast metal alloy, Dazey, the churn people, St. Louis, MO, 1940s. **$20-$30**

Ice cube tray, aluminum, dividers so niftily jointed it looks like a millipede, no maker mark, 12-1/8" L, 1938 patents #214795, #2265705, #2212424, and #2212425. **$5-$8**

Ice cube tray, green rubber with metal wire puller or grip, "Flex-oTray," mfd. by Inland Mfg. Co., Dayton, OH, 10-1/2" L, 1929 reissue patent #17273. According to a 1931 ad, the "Flex-oTray" was made for Westinghouse, Kelvinator, Leonard, Electrolux, Servel, Copeland, Universal & other refrigerators. Inland also made the "Quickube Tray" for Frigidaire (c.1937), and the "DuFlex" for General Electric. These various flexible rubber trays were "supplied by all leading automatic refrigerator makers." **$6+**

Ice cube tray, natural colored brownish rubber, very flexible, makes 21 cubes, each cup has interconnecting hole in inner walls, "FlexoTray," mfd. by The Inland Mfg. Co., Dayton, OH, 1-3/4" deep x 12-1/4" L x 3-3/4" W, 1929 reissue patent #s 17278 and 17279. **$8+**

Ice pick, also called an _ice awl_, long pointed steel with rounded knobby turned wooden handle, deep ferrule, made by many companies, one being C. W. Dunlap Mfg. Co., NYC, NY, turn of century & later. **$6-$10**

Ice pick, all metal, steel pick, cast heavy metal handle, adv'g "Coca-Cola," 20th C. **$6+**

Ice pick, iron & steel, "Arcade," Freeport, IL, early 20th C. **$10-$15**

Ice pick, iron with turned wood knob handle, spring action, punch it down & shaft telescopes to increase pounds-per-square-inch force, in F. A. Walker catalog, c.1870s. **$25+**

Ice pick, steel prickers, nicely shaped turned wood handle, cup-like aluminum housing for prickers when not in use, push up & lock aluminum cup with bayonet lock, not marked, 8" L, late 19th or early 20th C. **$30-$40**

Ice pick, steel with cast iron drop weight that slides down shank & hits bottom piece to add power to your punch, American, 11-5/8" L, late 19th C. **$35+**

Ice pick, wood handle has motto, "Use Ice Year Around," early 20th C. **$4-$8**

Ice pick, cast aluminum & steel, handle is shapely woman's leg, 11" L, c.1920s-1930s. (See a stove lid lifter in Chapter XI.) **$75+**

Ice pick & bottle opener combined, cast iron, steel, "Watertown Ice Co.," turn of century. **$8+**

Ice pick or chipper, 4 steel points in fork shape, brass ferrule, turned wooden handle, "Crawford," Newark, NJ, 7-1/2" L, late 19th C. **$28-$40**

XV-8. Ice cream freezer. *"Horizontal Ice-Cream Freezer," cedar, oak frame, has perforated metal "bucket" inside the churn-like body, cast iron crank. "Tingley's Patent," mfd. by Chas. G. Blatchley, Philadelphia. Picture from ad in* Harpers, *April 6, 1872.* **$125-$150**

XV-9. Ice-breaking knives. *Iron or steel. Two types from A. Bertuch catalog of specialties mainly for ice cream makers & confectioners. Berlin, Germany, c.1904.* **$15-$30**

XV-10. Ice crusher or breaker. *No.1 of 4 sizes. This one "for hotel keepers, confectioners, wine merchants, refreshment rooms, ships' cabins, butlers' pantries, &c." Cast iron, cast iron legs with lion's head knees. Circular ring underneath is for pan to catch the ice. Largest styles had drawers underneath. No.3 "will take a piece of ice about 5" x 6" x 8", breaking it into pieces about the size of a chestnut." Ad in* Mrs. A. B. Marshall's Cookery Book, *London, c.1900.* **$375+**

XV-11. Ice picks. **(T)** *Needle point, wood handle with scalloped cap of metal which is a crusher head. 7-5/8" L. Probably Androck, c.1930s.* **(B)** *Mechanical one, with protective housing when not in use. Wood handle with flat top for mallet, steel prickers & shank, aluminum housing. To reveal pick points, you push aluminum cup up shaft, and twist it. Bayonet locking device. 8" L. Located by Primitive Man, Bob Cahn, Carmel, NY. (A similar but newer one to B is a fixed-position one with 5 points, square wood handle, marked "Chip Chop," "Pat Pend, Apex Products Corp, N.Y.C.")* **$7-$15; $30-$40**

XV-14. Ice planes. **(T-R)** *Nickeled iron legs, steel top & blade, wood base. 7-1/2" H x 14-1/2" L x 6-1/4" W. Albert Pick. 1909 catalog.* **(B-L)** *"Keith's Registered Plane," English. "The ice plane is as simple in its construction as its application, being merely rubbing the ice to and fro rapidly upon the surface, when the snowlike flakes will descend into the vessel below. Sherry Cobblers, Mint Juleps, &c.— It will be found of great utility wherever ice is used (more especially the Wenham Lake ice), as it is rendered into a more elegant, aggreeable, and useful form at table than the irregular masses which are less sightly . It will be found indispensable for the preparation of the American beverages, sherry cobblers, mint juleps, &c. Mr. Keith is decidedly at the head of the ice department in this country, and has been so spirited in his enterpises as to keep completely at bay his numerous imitators." The Lady's Newspaper, 6/15/1850. Ice from "Wenham Lake" (on which I could find no information) presumably was very fine, as it was contrasted with "common rough ice."* **$35-$50; $75-$125+**

XV-12. Ice picks. *(L) to (R):* **(1)** *"Unique," steel needle point, malleable cast iron handle slides up & down, serves as a hammer. 8-1/2" L. Albert Pick catalog of kitchen supplies, mainly for hotels, 1909.* **(2)** *Patented, iron bound wood handle, pick with slight "arrowhead" or spear point — the other type of pick point. John Van Range Co., 1914.* **(3)** *5" L pick. Sexton, c.1930.* **(4)** *"Perfection," all iron handle. Mfd. by W. G. Browne Mfg. Co. 1910.* **(5)** *"Ice Pick — Steel Awl," 8-3/4" L, tinned cap. Sexton, c.1930.* **(6 & 7)** *connected by arrows, "Ice mallet with pick that slides into the handle" of the mallet. Most valuable one here. American Home Cook Book, 1854.* **(8)** *Steel point, wood handle. Without iron band. Matthai-Ingram, c.1890.* **(9)** *"Steak pounder & ice mallet No4." Steel pick in head of hammer. Heinz & Munschauer, 1882.* **(10)** *Ice hammer & pick, rosewood handle, tempered steel point, silver-plated hammer & shank. 2nd most valuable. 8-1/2" L x 2-7/8" W.* **(11)** *"Spear point" steel pick, nickeled iron band & ferrule. 8-1/2" L. Has "N. White City & Co." cap mark.* **(12)** *Needle pick, steel, hardwood knob handle, 9-1/4" L. Last 3 all Albert Pick catalog 1909.* **$5-$65**

XV-15. Ice scoop. *Galvanized crimped tin, wood handle, 9" L, c.1890-1920. Other prettier ones of the period, with turned wood handles, were made of nickeled copper and cast aluminum.* **$8-$15**

XV-13. Ice shaver or shredder. *Tinned or nickeled cast iron cup-like saucepan, hinged lid. Cutaway view shows adjustable (& removable) blade inside. Enterprise Mfg. Co., Philadelphia. It is "only necessary to draw the blade upon the ice, the pressure applied producing fine or coarse pieces, as desired. To remove the finely cut ice from the cup the shredder is grasped firmly in the right hand, striking it inverted upon the left, being careful to keep the lid closed. The ice is then scraped into some convenient receptacle. It is not necessary to take the ice out of the refrigerator, as the cup may be filled from the side or top of the cake."* **$25-$45**

Ice pick or hammer, brass, long rod handle with ruffled cuff ferrule and small cast fist holding large tack-shaped thing with point and flat top, English or Continental, about 10" L overall, with fist about 3"L, prob. mid 19th C. **$125-$150**

Ice pick & scraper, nickeled iron with wooden handle, looks like a sort of fork with a frame over top of tines, has a small maw to catch shavings, mfd. by & advertising "Coolerator. The Air Conditioned Refrigerator," Coolerator Co., Duluth, MN, 12"L, 20th C. **$15-$20**

Ice scoop, corrugated galvanized tin with wooden handle, long bowl with high slightly rounded sides, flat heel, American, 9" L, c.1890s. **$8-$15**

Ice scraper & chipper, cast iron with wooden handle, "White Mountain," Nashua, NH, late 19th or early 20th C. **$10-$15**

Ice shaver, cast iron, "Arctic Ice Shave #33," Grey Iron Casting Co., Mount Joy, PA, late 19th C. **$15-$20**

Ice shaver, cast iron, steel, Griswold, Erie, PA, late 19th or early 20th C. **$35-$45**

Ice shaver, cast iron & steel, hand-cranked rotary type, Clawson Machine Co., Flagtown, NJ, early 20th C. **$75-$150**

Ice shaver, heavy cast iron, tinned, lid has a monogram, "ACW" for A. C. Williams Co., Ravenna, OH, 7-5/8" L, turn of century. **$15-$20**

Ice shaver, nickeled cast iron, hinged hopper, removeable blade, "Gem," mfd. by North Brothers Mfg. Co., Philadelphia, patent applied for. **$15-$20**

Ice shaver, cast metal, big cup with adjustable and sharpenable steel blade, "Logan-Strowbridge Iron Co. #12," New Brighton, PA, pat'd Dec. 21, 1897 by John H. Logan as a "self emptying ice shredder." **$20+**

Ice shaver, cast iron base with steel shaving table, stands high on four beautiful scrolled cabriole legs, mid 19th C. **$150-$225+**

Ice shaver, wood with four turned "piano" legs, steel shaver set into top, used with a tumbler or other vessel to catch shavings underneath, called an **Ice Plane** by maker, mfd. by a Mr. Keith, London, England, c.1850. **$75-$125**

Ice shaver or plane, galvanized cast iron (they also made one of cast aluminum) with double-edged tool steel blade, hinged angled top that encloses compartment that catches the shavings, looks almost identical to one made by Stover, "No. 77," Gilchrist Co., Newark, NJ, c.1906. **$7-$10**

Ice shaver, tongs & hammer combined, cast iron, American, 13-1/4" L, pat'd June 1878. **$75+**

Ice shaver — See meat tenderizer combo tool, Chapter I

Ice shredder, tinned cast iron, cone-shaped with lid, shaving blade is in lid so held cone tip up to work, slightly curved double handles hinged at end, one attached to cone, one to lid, held together while scraping, "after the Shredder is scraped full of ice, tap the small end of cone so as to make contents solid," after which you release handle to reveal snow cone, which fits then into paper holder, "especially adapted for the use of vendors selling 'Snow Balls,' as by hole in the small end of cone the ball can be readily flavored and easily ejected." "Enterprise Hardware Co. #43," Philadelphia, c.1890s, sold into 20th C. **$30+**

Ice shredder or shaver, tinned cast iron cup with curved handle, looks like little saucepan with hinged lid, steel shaver teeth inside, makes snow balls for snow cones, or ice for icing oysters on the half shell, or celery, fruits, drinks, marked "Enterprise Mfg. Co. #33" on lid, 7-3/4" L overall, cup is 3-1/2" diameter x 2-1/2" deep, sold at least by July 1892; pat'd July 4, 1893, lucky patent date for ice cold treat! The same size #34 was nickeled, & cost 3 times as much when new, but not now. **$35+**

Ice tongs — All depend on the weight of the ice block itself to pull the two scissor-action, upward-curving hooks inward toward each other to grip the ice when it's lifted. The handles, which are spread apart while positioning around the block, are brought back to starting position for carrying, and the act of lifting seats the hooks' points on opposite sides of the block of ice. Depending on the type, handles may have a starting position that's either very close together, or a hand's breadth apart. A block of ice might weigh 50 pounds or more. A strong man could hold closed the two rubber or wooden grips found on many late nineteenth- and early twentieth-century tongs with one hand. Likewise for those with simple loop handles. But the best and most valuable tongs have a kind of bail handle connecting the two upper ends of the pivoting hooks, so that the ice can be carried as easily as a suitcase. The bail may be a curve of iron rod, or may be a shapely grip of forged iron.

Ice tongs, cast handles & forged iron hooks, American, 21"L, c. 1880s-1900. **$20-$25**

Ice tongs, iron, "Butler Ice Co.," 14" L, c.1900. **$15-$20**

Ice tongs, iron with wooden grips, adv'g "Dixie Gem Coal, Ice & Fuel Co.," 14" L, early 20th C. There were many dealers who sold both ice and coal. **$20-$25**

Ice tongs, all forged iron, including 2 looped handle grips, 12" L, late 19th C. **$15-$25**

Ice tongs, forged iron, pointed tips are bifurcated to seize the ice better, 12" L, probably mid-1800s. **$40-$60**

Ice tongs, forged iron, with simple rod bail handle connecting 2 handles, 14" L, look like calipers more than most, mid 19th C. **$50-$65**

Ice tongs, forged iron with decorative twisting for tensile strength, American, 14-1/2" L, 19th C. **$45+**

XV-16. Ice tongs. *Forged iron, handles have what cataloguer called "pigtail ends." 19" L. Photo courtesy Litchfield Auction Gallery, Litchfield, CT. Ex-Harold Corbin Collection, auctioned 1/1/1989.* **$45-$60**

XV-17. Ice tongs. *"Wrought iron," but not blacksmith-made like previous pair. Medium & large size, from catalogs c.1900-1910.* **$10-$30**

Ice water bottle, green glass, oblong with big rounded top, embossed pebbly surface except for depiction of Monitor Top refrigerator, & words "WATER . . . for use with the GENERAL ELECTRIC REFRIGERATOR" on the front, measures from 1 cup (1/2 pt.) to 3 cups (1/2 pts.) on back, GE, 8-1/2" H x 5" W, 1927. **$75-$95**

Refrigerator for nursery, japanned sheet steel chest with lifting handles at each end, looks like oak graining with pin striping, hasped lid lifts to reveal one compartment of porcelainized steel for ice water or other cold liquid, another compartment for food, insulated with mineral wool (asbestos), mfd. by James R. Wotherspoon, Philadelphia, PA, very early 20th C. Fries & McAleer made these too, almost identical in appearance. **$15-$22**

XV-18. "Closet or Upright Refrigerator." (L) *"The door on the side insures ventilation, and the closet form is most convenient to arrange dishes." American Home Cook Book, 1854. The form of this looks as if ice were in it, but there is no textual evidence of ice. (R) "Glacier Refrigerator," mfd. by Northern Refrigerator Co., Grand Rapids, MI. Their motto: "As far ahead of all others as the electric light excels the candle." Work had probably begun to make an electric refrigerator. Century, 5/1892.*

XV-19. Refrigerator — Ice box. *"White Frost Sanitary," mfd. by C. A. Carey, Home Products Corp., Jackson, MI. Ladies' Home Journal ad, 5/1920: "Our iceman says, 'This is the only refrigerator in town. People could afford to throw their ice boxes away and save the price of a White Frost in ice.' A doctor says, 'From a sanitary standpoint, it cannot be beaten.'" Steel, granulated cork insulation, nickel trim, white glass water cooler, removable top.* **$250-$450**

Refrigerator (ice box), ash, enameled metal interior, 2 door, 57" H, turn of century. **$175+**

Refrigerator (ice box), oak, 4 doors, "Northey Duplex," 6 feet 2-1/2" H x 4 feet 1-1/2" W x 2-1/2 feet deep, turn of century. **$350+**

Refrigerator (ice box), oak, porcelainized interior, lift top lid with zinc-lined box, one door, wire shelves, 47" H x 27-1/2" wide, c.1900. **$175+**

Refrigerator (ice box), unusual tall cupboard type, door over door, oak with paneled sides, bracket feet, M. M. Whitman & Co., Worcester, MA, 60" H x 28-1/2" W x 23-1/2" deep, turn of century. Oak: $$$; pine: $. **$400+**

Refrigerator (ice box), which could be converted to electricity with a compressor, motor & gas coils, large boxy enameled (ivory, grey, blue or green) steel cabinet on casters, 4 hinged doors, lined with white "quarried" stone, "White Mountain," Maine Mfg. Co., Nashua, NH, c.1927. **$100+**

Refrigerator (ice box), white enamel-painted steel inside and out, insulated with cork, 4 stumpy bathtub-like legs with casters, lid lifts off top part where ice goes, hinged door in side reveals 2 (1916 one seems to have 3) round revolving nickel-plated shelves inside, later ones had a spigot on side of top part to draw off ice cold water for drinking (you'd

XV-20. Refrigerator classic. *A General Electric "Monitor Top." 1927 Ladies' Home Journal ad reads: "Here is a new development in electric refrigerators for the home. ... It marks an entirely new conception. ... an entirely new type of icing unit — unlike any other you have ever seen. The entire mechanism of the GE Icing Unit is housed on top of the cabinet in one hermetically sealed casing. That is all the mechanism — none below the box. None in the basement. There are no pipes, no drains, no attachments. All bulky machinery is eliminated — virtually no servicing. The result of fifteen years of intensive research." Electric Refrigeration Dept., GE Co., Cleveland, OH. It lasted forever too — a lesson for today. In 1929 there were six Monitor-top styles, including doublewide ones.* **$175+**

have to trust your ice man!), in 1920 ad, glass water cooler with removable top shown adjacent to the ice compartment, "White Frost," mfd. by Metal Stamping Co., Jackson, MI, 43" H x 23" diameter, pat'd Sept. 11, 1906; Nov. 6, 1906; and June 23, 1908. Advertisements claimed that the White Frost was used by the government during work on the Panama Canal. By 1916 the company was called White Frost Refrigerator Co., and by 1920 it was the Home Products Corporation. It was still selling in 1920, in nearly the same form. Condition of original baked-on enamel paint, and condition of inside affects value. **$55-$100**

Refrigerator (ice box), zinc alloy, nickeled brass hardware, 2 doors with wire shelves, 4 legs, turn of century. **$150+**

Refrigerator (ice box), "side board & china closet" combined. "Antique" ash, with decorative carving, china closet with 4 shelves, glass front, decorative molding on top; drawers for silverware and linen — raised above top of refrigerator, affording a small sideboard serving area. Included a water cooler. About 68" H x 28" W. "Old Maid Refrigerator," "for people desiring the comforts of life in small rooms." "Leonard Cleanable Refrigerators," mfd.. by Grand Rapids Refrigerator Co., Grand Rapids, MI, c.1892. **$350+**

Refrigerator (ice box), in sideboard style, carved ash "finished in antique oak," with beveled mirror above, fancy hardware, meant for dining room. Included water cooler with faucet. "The Siberia," Simmons Hardware Co., St. Louis, MO, 83" H x 45-1/2" W x 23" deep, c.1900. **$400+**

Refrigerator (electric), box on short cabriole legs, motor housing on top is shaped like the Capitol dome in Washington, DC, white enameled steel, "Ice-O-Matic" in Capitol Model, mfd. by Williams Oil-O-Matic Heating Corp., Bloomington, IL, small, c.1930. **$75-$100**

It's What's On Top That Counts — The most famed refrigerator with motor housing on top is the GE Monitor Top, but it is also the most commonly found. According to a 1930 ad, you can have the motor "unit on top of its good-looking cabinet; in the lower compressor compartment or in the basement."

XV-21. Refrigerators. (L) *From 1935 ad comes this "New G-E Model X-4" designed for small homes and apartments.* **(R)** *"Ice-O-Matic Capitol Model," mfd. by Williams Oil-O-Matic Heating Corp., Bloomington, IL. You could have the motor "on top" as illustrated; "in the lower compressor compartment or in the basement."* Country Life, *1930. It's a toss-up which you'd want the most. The only problem is, you lose a horizontal storage space on top! I need every surface I can find.* **$175+**

Refrigerator (electric), but looks just like large icebox, white enameled steel, tall box with nickeled-steel binding around each of 6 doors, plated hinges & handles, louvered motor compartment underneath, upper right door reveals ice cube tray, glass in all doors makes this look like professional restaurant refrigerators sold today to upscale housewives, Servel Corp. (soon to be Electrolux Servel), factories in Evansville, IN, Carteret, NJ, Newburgh, NY, c.1925. **$55-$75**

Refrigerator (electric), white enameled steel, stepped streamline shape, black base, bin compartment with pull-down door at bottom, main door reveals small central freezer compartment, several shelves, many nickeled wire shelves built into drawer, amazing part is the radio built into the top front of the refrigerator, WOW !!! "Crosley Shelvador," Crosley Radio Corp., Cincinnati, OH , c.1938. Because of the radio this has great crossover collector value, even if the radio needs tubes. **$350-$425**

Refrigerator bottle, green glass, pat'd Sept. 15, 1931. **$25+**

Refrigerator container, pale blue "crystal" glass, with lid, "Fire-King," Anchor Hocking Glass Corp., 4-1/2" x 5", 1940s-1950s. **$30+**

Refrigerator container, glass, "Westinghouse," 1930s. **$10-$15**

Refrigerator defroster attachment, electric, enameled steel housing to a timing device which could be set almost like a thermostat, you'd plug the refrigerator into it, and it into the outlet. "Magic Defroster," "makes old refrigerators into modern automatic defrosters." Mfd. by Maxilume Co., Chicago, c.1950. **$5**

Refrigerator ice water dispenser, glass with fired-on opaque pastel green finish, chrome spigot with red rubber gasket, clear glass (called "crystal") lid molded with concentric rings, sort of a glass shoebox that lies on its side with spigot at one end, for getting cold water. In old refrigerators this might fit under the tiny freezer compartment, mfd. by Hall, 12" L, c.1930s. **$65-$80**

Refrigerator ice water dispenser, pebbly textured clear or "crystal," glass body, plain "crystal" lid, white rubber gasket, c.1930s. **$30-$45**

XV-22. Refrigerator with radio. *"Shelvado ... just open the door. There, at your finger-tips, are your most-often-needed foods. No reaching. No searching." This model with "built-in radio." Crosley Electric Refrigerators, mfd. by Crosley Radio Corp., Cincinnati, OH.* McCall's, *6/1938. (Shelvadors introduced c.1936.)* **$250+**

"Jadite" generally refers to a color, most usually a pale green that can be opaque "milk" glass or painted on the inside (as is this refrigerator container), but it is also a trade name for an opaque green that Jeannette Glass Co. (Jeannette, PA) made, and the name "Jade-ite" was used by Anchor Hocking. Other pieces in opaque green were made by Fenton Glass Co., called simply "Jade"; and McKee Glass Co., called "Jade Green." Collectors tend to use the term for a wide range of very pale to rather richly green opaque but translucent glass. When used in ads it often doesn't mean the Jeannette brand name.

Refrigerator jar, saltglazed stoneware, small size, Red Wing, MN, 20th C. **$100-$110**

Refrigerator jar, saltglazed stoneware with 2 blue bands, bail handle, "Red Wing Refrigerator Jar, Compliments of Semon's Fair Store, Athens, Wisc.," mfd. in MN, 5-3/4" H, early 20th C. **$85-$95**

Refrigerator pan, galvanized steel, looks like dog feeding dish for a St. Bernard, round with bowl bottom set in side, 2 side ear handles, catches drips from melting ice, New England Enameling Co., Middletown, CT, turn of century. "A strictly modern newspaper item tells of a bride who declined an invitation to a picnic because she could never be away from the apartment for more than five hours and twenty minutes at a stretch. Her inquisitive friends asked why. 'Well,' she explained reluctantly, 'you see, every five hours and twenty-one minutes, the refrigerator-pan overflows.'" Frances Lester Warner, "When Equipment Overflows," *House Beautiful*, Feb. 1927. **$7-$10**

XV-23. Water cooler. *Stoneware with cobalt flower decoration, rare exagerated ovoid shape, 2 handles. Made by I. Seymour, Troy, NY, 18" H, 19th C. A perfectly beautiful form, sensual & almost figural. Photo courtesy Litchfield Auction Gallery, Litchfield, CT. Ex-Harold Corbin Collection. Auctioned 1/1/1990 for:* **$6000**

Refrigerator water bottle, rich green Depression glass, embossed design of old-fashioned well, American, 1930s. **$25-$30**

Refrigerator water jug, swirled cobalt blue Depression glass, with spigot, 20th C. **$145-$175**

XV-24. Water filter & water coolers. (T-L) *Stoneware filter, for "purifying cistern water for cooking or table use." (T-R) "Water cooler, filled in with charcoal, preserves the ice and keeps water icy cold.— The water is kept cooler than the atmosphere without ice." The cooler looks like japanned sheet metal, but may be stoneware. Both pictures from* American Home Cook Book, *1854. Often coolers and filters were combined. (B-L) "Improved Sanitary," gray stoneware, blue bands, mfd. by Fulper Pottery Co., Flemington, NJ.* House Furnishing Review, *4/1908. [Fulper was established in 1805.] (B-R) Stoneware with leaf decoration, nickeled faucet. 12 sizes, from 2 gallons to 50 gallons. Albert Pick catalog, 1909.* **$75+**

XV-25. "Lady Franklin Family Ice Urns." *"Perfection" granite ironware & "Pearl Agateware" with quadruple silver-plate fittings, mfd. by Manning, Bowman & Co., 1892 catalog. (L) & (M) show detached parts — including "shell" which fit down over handled reservoir, and footed stand. Two sizes, for 6 pints or 8, and had matching footed goblets. (R) "Assorted decorations in winter scenes," 9-pint size with goblets to match, you could order "plain silver band just above the faucet" engraved however you liked.* **$400-$1000**

Water cooler, japanned tin urn, stenciled "Ice Water," with cast iron finial to ridged, domed tin lid & cast iron spigot, in F. A. Walker catalog, came in 8 sizes: 2, 3, 6, 8, 10, 15 & 20 gal., c.1870s. This also came with porcelain liner, in 2, 3, 4, 6, 8 & 10 gallon sizes. **$45+**

Water cooler, saltglazed stoneware jug, ear handles, on wonderful turned stoneware pedestal base, metal spigot, gray with cobalt blue birds on branches, incised & colored, capacity "4" (gallons), PA, 21-1/2" H, mid 19th C. **$750-$1200**

Water cooler, saltglazed stoneware with cobalt blue flower design, pewter spigot, no lid, 4 gal. size, 19th C. **$200-$300**

Water cooler, white & blue spongeware, "Avery & Winter Pottery Co. #6," NYC, NY, 19th C. **$300-$400**

Water filter & cooler, blue & white glazed pottery with relief floral and scroll designs, shapely breasted container with spigot hole near bottom, "The Allen Germ-Proof Filter," Toledo, OH, 13-1/2" H x 10-1/4" diameter, late 19th C. When I lived in Toledo I saw only one of these, the lidless one I bought. Since then, at flea markets all over, I've seen a number of them, all without lids, most chipped. **$125-$300**

PRESERVING

XVI. CAN & DRY

The collectible objects in this chapter were for home use. It seems a bit funny, etymologically, that practically everything in this category has to do with glass *jars,* not tin *cans.* But that is only because the so-called **fruit jars** (also called canning jars) are the most widely collected food-preserving items, and old food cans don't have the potential to become that. Occasionally you see a very old **can,** contents intact if not edible, and there are some collectors for them — mainly identifying themselves with country store and/or advertising collectors. It is true that people could buy ready-to-fill tin cans directly from the can manufacturers, to put up produce in their own kitchens. The cans had different features and selling points, but those with lids already in place, with openings in the center of the lids, were probably favored. The holes, generally speaking, were about 2-1/4" diameter, and were closed by a cap soldered in place, using a "capping steel" and a "tipping copper." To open those cans, people did not melt the solder and take the cap off: a can opener was necessary. See Chapter VIII.

For decades, bottle and glass collectors have been digging up **glass fruit jars** and also glass **jellies,** then cataloguing them and trading and selling them. Both are always in evidence at local and regional bottle shows, some of which convene almost every month, and sometimes fruit jars make headlines in generalist collector newspapers. Fruit jars constitute a very specialized field with a strong resale market and ever-changing market prices as rarities are discovered and as other rarities are found not to be so rare after all. The introduction to this chapter is almost as long as some chapters — a reflection of how ardent and active collectors of glass food containers are.

Knowledge is widely shared about the jars themselves, their closures, seals, marks and colors, and mysterious sightings and reportings of hitherto unknown jars. But unless you are prepared to study them, buy only for decorative or useful value. Obviously, very very large ones, or very early ones, or those with odd closures, or those in unusual-colored glass, or with figural embossing, or just those known to be extremely rare, will usually be worth the most, but you have to get into the "loop" of other collectors and dealers so that information on repros will get to you in time to prevent an expensive mistake. See the bibliography for addresses for the books that follow.

Books — The "**Red Book of Fruit Jars**" series are the six exhaustive illustrated catalogings of many hundreds of jars, with prices, done by Alice M. Creswick. New editions are being done by Douglas M. Leybourne, Jr. A younger, but just as impressive, offering is the **Fruit Jar Annual,** begun in 1996 by Jerry McCann. It's one-fifth illustrated price guide and jar listings, and four-fifths in-depth articles by various experts. See the bibliography.

Clubs — There are many clubs. One club with members from all over the country and Canada, and a monthly newsletter, is **Northwest Fruit Jar Collectors Club**. Contact its founder, Missey Spencer, 12713 142nd Ave. — Court East, Puyallup, WA 98374 (253-770-1658). Another is **Midwest Antique Fruit Jar & Bottle Club,** which has shows twice a year and a newsletter. Contact the Barnetts, POB 38, Flat Rock, IN 47234. A long-established group is **Southeastern Antique Bottle Club,** with an annual show and monthly newsletter. Their shows, like most others, welcome the inclusion of bottle "go-withs" — including bottle openers and jar wrenches — and also jellies. Contact Jack Hewitt, 1765 Potomac Ct., Lawrenceville, GA 30243. A national umbrella organization is the **Federation of Historic Bottle Collectors**. Bottle clubs and individuals are invited to join — for $20 you get membership and 12 issues of "Bottles & Extras." Contact J. Carl Sturm, 88 Sweetbriar Branch, Longwood, FL 32750-2783. Always use an SASE.

My personal favorites in this chapter are the Kerr "Angel & Crown" **jelly glasses**. As a collector of twentieth-century folk art, I find the simple, embossed line "drawings" of angels irresistible; I wish I could have a leaded "window" made from them. (And another made from the opalescent lid inserts for some canning jars.) For information about a jelly club and book see the section on jellies in this chapter.

Can openers is so large a category that it has its own chapter (Chapter VIII), which also contains a few pictures of old cans. The mechanical go-withs for fruit jars *are* included in this chapter: see **fruit jar wrenches** and lifters and **tipping coppers**. A man in Illinois has over 600 different tipping coppers or soldering irons: the variety is endless, and they are handsome. (And not all of them are copper, or copper-plated: some are brass.) He's a man after my own heart, concentrating now on one-of-a-kind homemade examples.

Can openers — See Chapter VIII (Open and Close)

Canner, tin & cold-rolled copper, 2 canisters (they came in other sizes & numbers of canisters) of tin set down into rectangular water reservoir, glass canning jars were set, lidless, into the metal cans for heating. Expensive models had copper bottoms, came with wood, iron & leather strap jar wrench, also booklet of recipes & instructions, "Mudge Patent Processor," mfd. by John L. Gaumer Co., Philadelphia, PA, 14-3/4" H x 13-1/4" L x 8" W, box is 4" H, pat'd July 27, 1886.   **$175-$300**

Using the Mudge — Self-proclaimed as a "household necessity. . . . The cheapest, most efficacious, most economical system of putting up high standard goods." It came in several models, which ranged in price from $3 to $12 before the turn of the century, and differed in size, number of canners, quality and quantity of the "tin plate, cold-rolled copper bottoms, copper tops and steam whistles." You put the processor box on the range, added water, then put the carefully filled cans into the water with the covers placed over them. "Have water boiling to generate steam before using. Keep well boiling vigorously while using the canner as you must have sufficient steam to do good work. Put fruit or vegetables in the jar raw. Place jar on a dry folded towel while pouring in the hot syrup or water to prevent breakage. Pour in slowly. In cooking or canning dry, be careful to temper glass jars before subjecting to the action of the steam. Place wooden blocks on the canner under the jars to prevent breaking. Do not put the lids on the jars while processing. . . . Be careful to sterilize lids and rubbers before sealing. Never allow water to boil away. If steam escapes through the whistle, it is time to refill [the well] to keep the bottom from burning. . . . Be sure to wipe the canner dry after using before putting away. Read Mrs.

Rorer's directions carefully." Finally, to catch every possible purchaser, **the booklet claimed** "While this apparatus is called a cannery, it is an admirable contrivance for cooking vegetables, meats and making tea and coffee. It saves time and fuel and preserves flavor and color." The jar holder (original cost 25¢) that came with the canner claimed "Our adjustable jar holder will be appreciated by those who have burnt their fingers in lifting hot jars. They are leather lined, strongly bound by tin with wooden handles. The adjustment is made so they will fit any size jar. Handy for sealing and removing jar lids too."

Canning jar — See fruit jar; also preserve jar

Canning rack, wire, rectangular & meant for use in a 2-hole boiler, late 19th or early 20th C. **$10-$15**

Corn dryer, all twisted wire, the sharp points were made by clipping the wire at an angle. Hanging ring at top, American, c.1910. **$8-$15**

Corn dryer, or <u>seed corn tree</u>, wooden rod with short iron pins stuck crosswise through it to hold 28 ears of corn, iron T-handle, American, about 20" L, pat'd Feb. 4, 1908 by James C. Blackford. **$25-$35**

XVI-1. Canner. *"Mudge Patent Processor, for Canning and Cooking Fruit & Vegetables," John L. Gaumer Co., Philadelphia, PA. A two-vessel style with iron wire bail handles. Cold-rolled copper bodies and tin lids, 14-3/4" H overall x 13-1/4" L x 8" W. Included here is the all wood jar wrench, 9" L, and Mrs. Sara T. Rorer's instruction & recipe booklet. Note steam whistle lower left corner of box's top. Original prices ranged from $3 to $12, depending on number of cans, size, and the amount of copper. Collection of Meryle Evans. Collector Dolores Thomas sent me pictures of her 4-can completely tinned set, including recipe booklet. Her cans have no bails, but the lids have bracket strap handles. Value for either about evens out:* **$175-$300**

XVI-3. Pressure cooker for canning. *Heavy aluminum, with lid fastened on with wingnuts. Note pressure gauge. Picture originally provided by The Pressure Cooker Co., to* Science & Invention *magazine, 5/1930.* **$15-$25**

XVI-2. Fruit preserving apparatus. *"Payne's 'Common Sense' Fruit Preserver," sold through Williams & Chase, NYC. The "approved apparatus for preserving by steam, an arrangement regarded by scientific judges as the most complete ever offered to the public. Its construction is perfectly simple and easy to manage. Six or more jars can in as many minutes be preserved, with one-fourth the labor and fuel. The fruits retain all their Solidity, Flavor & Beauty, requiring no sugar, unless preferred. When perfect jars are used (those represented in the cut, also Mason's Union and Standard, are regarded by the inventor as among the best." Came in 1-pipe, 2-pipe, 4-pipe and 6-pipe sizes. Pat'd 9/3/1867; and 10/26/1860.* Peterson's Ladies' Magazine, *1870 ad.* **$50-$75**

XVI-4. Canner. *"Iron Horse Cold Pack" canner, mfd. by Rochester Can Co., Rochester, NY, c.1930. "With this the uncooked fruit can be placed directly in the jars, the syrup added and the cooking done directly in the jars, practically eliminating the labor formerly required." Made of charcoal (blackened) tin, bottom double-seamed, wood handle grips at side. Rack for seven quart jars, and a wire jar lifter. 9" H x 13-3/4" diameter. They also made them of copper or galvanized steel. I believe the picture is probably a printed paper label — most desirable to have and key to value.* **$30-$60**

Corn dryer, forged iron with 10 long sharp chiseled hooks, eye hole at top, hangs from ceiling hook, looks like a fish backbone, American, 20" L with 4" L hooks at a 40 angle from vertical, very early 19th C. **$100-$125**

Reproduction alert — Hard to tell age of corn dryers. Late nineteenth- and twentieth-century examples may also be wrought iron, but they look machine-made perfect. There are modern reproductions being made and sold today. I won't spend my money to write off for one, so I can't describe it minutely. Value of late nineteenth- and twentieth-century examples of forged iron, with some aesthetic merit, would be up to $35. Wire ones shouldn't be more than $15.

XVI-5. Cup for jellies or jams. *"The Wedgwood Kleen Kup,"* *mfd. by Mono Service Co., Newark, NJ. Decorated wood fibre with classical Greco-Roman lady. "The jelly may be heated to almost any degree Fahrenheit, and during the filling process it is unnecessary to immerse the kup in cold water, or wrap it in cold, wet cloths. It is suggested, however, that the filled kups be allowed to stand over night, or until thoroughly cold, before the lids are inserted. The use of paraffine wax on top of the cooled jelly is optional." House Furnishing Review ads, 1918.* Per cup: **$3-$7**

XVI-6. Fruit dryer. *Wood with galvanized tin base and wire mesh screening in each of eight drawers. Used on top of range to dry sliced fruit or pitted, halved apricots, etc. 26" H, early 20th C.* **$65-$85+**

Cup, for jellies & jams, pressed wood fiber with impressed design of Classical Greco-Roman woman next to tall stand, lid, & "although the Kleen Kup is made of wood fibre, it may be filled with heated jam, marmalade, jelly, or the like as any glass tumbler may be filled, and under the same conditions. The jelly may be heated to almost any degree Fahrenheit, and during the filling process it is unnecessary to immerse the kup in cold water, or wrap it in cold, wet cloths. . . . The use of paraffine wax on top of the cooled jelly is optional." Called the "Wedgewood [sic] Kleen Kup," mfd. by Mono-Service Co., Newark, NJ, 1918. Came originally in a cardboard box of one dozen. See also jelly glasses. For one: **$3-$7** Set in box: **$10-$15**

Fruit dryer, galvanized tin base to set over stove top, wooden frame with 8 wood drawers with wire screening for bottoms. Used to dry sliced fruit or pitted, halved apricots, pears, etc. paper label mostly gone, American, 25-1/4" H x 18-1/2" L x 14" W, c.1900. **$65-$85**

Fruit dryer, tin frame with wire screen, 3 shelves, removeable trays, for drying sliced apples & other fruits, "Arlington Oven Dryer" on brass ID plate, Arlington, MA, 9" H x 14" x 10-1/2". 19th C. **$120-$150**

FRUIT JARS

Colors — Fruit jars, or canning jars of blow-molded glass, were made in many colors, by far the most common of which are light aqua and clear (or "crystal"). Colors I've seen on price tags or in articles and books also include opaque white; opalescent; smoke; light and dark amber; reddish amber; streaked amber; citron; straw yellow; yellow green; emerald green; light and dark olive green; apple green; amethyst (like the color sunned glass becomes); dark aqua; "Ball blue"; cornflower blue; light, medium and dark cobalt blue; dark greenish blue; brown; even black. Creswick mentions a "dark puce," but I get confused between mauve and puce. I've never read of a red or a pink or dark purple jar, but I feel that somewhere they may exist! **Fake color** — In case you are new to the hobby, you may not know about the fruit jars on the market since 1994 that have had their color artificially induced by irradiation. Several thousand otherwise common clear jars were done by a man in Indiana in amber and in purple and sold cheaply by the man who figured out how to do it. When he quit, a person in Florida began doing it. There are two clues, which are not sure-fire, and one of which wouldn't help you anyway if you had already bought something: (1) the color seems a bit cloudy or smoky, maybe like looking through glasses that haven't been cleaned in a while; (2) the color seems to fade under normal room-temperature conditions — sometimes within two months or so. (Makes you wonder if the faker is keeping them refrigerated before seeding them into the market. And one trouble with the Florida origin is that seeding is easy from there because there are so many generalist dealers from all over the country who include Florida on their show circuit. It's easy for them to innocently acquire a jar or two and take them back to their home communities, like roaches take poison back to their nests.)

Lids and closures — Fruit jar lids may be clear glass or opalescent glass or vitreous pottery or metal. A few nineteenth-century patents are behind most of the jars and lids that were made well into the twentieth century (some still being made). Maybe the most famous patent is John Mason's of Nov. 30, 1858; his lids are threaded bands or full caps, and utilize a rubber gasket. Many lids have a threaded metal band that holds the insert in place: typically made of zinc and most recently those "brass"-plated tin bands used today. There are also full caps with glass liners — zinc, plated steel threaded cap, aluminum, etc. To secure them, some have spring wire attachments — like the 1875 "Lightning" patent — that worked to clamp and lock the lid in place, or spring steel clamps, or iron yokes, that make the fit of the lid snugger. Some lids, of glass or metal, worked like stoppers in the mouth of the jar. An unusual lid is one of the "Squire's Patent" lids, which utilized small knobs on lid and jar to anchor an elastic band that acted sort of like a bungee cord to lace jar and lid together. Another extremely unusual jar and lid is the "New Windsor," which has a cylindrical body but a square mouth and lid!

Lid straighteners and reformers — Another sort of tool came into use to fix metal jar lids that had been bent or distorted during opening of the jar. These worked best with relatively soft zinc lids, and some of them could actually re-tool the screw threads to some extent. The reformers may look like jar wrenches, with a band that can be tightened around the lid and then pulled around (like a clock hand) the circumference to press the metal against the jar's neck or lip. Others look something like biscuit cutters, with a wooden grip raised above a circle of iron. This type fitted down around the band or threaded side of the lid and was firmly rotated. Another type was a cranked machine, screw-clamped to table. The jar lid was fitted onto the threaded chuck, and held firmly while the user cranked the chuck around.

Lid openers or "jar wrenches" became necessary with screw caps or screw bands, and were used to screw the caps on as well as off. If properly and tightly sealed, the jars were hard to open. Many wrenches utilized wood, leather or rubber to cushion the tool.

XVI-7. Fruit jar patent, *framing examples of two Mason jars. In this collage of pictures, the outer drawing is John L. Mason's patent drawing for #102,913, issued to him on May 10, 1870 for an improvement in his earlier fruit jar closure. He sold the patent to Consolidated Fruit-Jar Co., who sued another maker, Wright, for using the patent. The case went to the U.S. Supreme Court, who decided the merits of the suit on the basis of the patentee [Mason] forfeiting his "right to the invention if he constructs it and vends it to others to use, or if he uses it publicly himself in the ordinary way" up to two years before applying for a patent. Poor Mr. Mason had "completed his invention in June 1859, at which time he had at least two dozen jars made. Some of the jars he gave away; others he sold to get the money they yielded and to test salability in the market. Mason failed to file a patent application until January 15, 1868," almost 10 years later! The case was decided against Consolidated and Mason in favor of Wright. Information & patent drawing adapted from a 1947 book by C. D. Tuska,* Patent Notes for Engineers, *from Official Gazette records.*

Turn-of-the-century jar makers — According to *Thomas' Register of American Manufacturers,* 1905-1906, quite a number of companies made glass fruit jars. As listed, they are:

Ball Brothers Glass Mfg. Co., Muncie, IN
Consolidated Fruit Jar Co., New Brunswick, NJ
Co-operative Flint Glass Co., Ltd., Beaver Falls, PA
Crystal Glass Co., Bridgeport, OH
Cumberland Glass Mfg. Co., Bridgeton, NJ
D. Cunningham Glass Co., Pittsburg, PA
S. George Co., Wellsburg, WV
Gilchrist Improved Jar Co., Philadelphia, PA & Elmer, NJ
W. Glenny Glass Co., Cincinnati, OH
Greenfield Fruit Jar & Bottle Co., Greenfield, IN
Hazel-Atlas Glass Co., Wheeling, WV, & Washington, PA
Hemingway Glass Co., Covington, KY
Hero Fruit Jar Co., Philadelphia, PA
Hermetical Closure Co., San Francisco, CA
Louis Hollweg, Indianapolis, IN
Illinois Glass Co., Alton, IL
Kearns-Gorsuch Bottle Co., Zanesville, OH
J. A. Landsberger Co., San Francisco, CA
Marion Fruit Jar & Bottle Co., Marion, IN
Moore Brothers Glass Co., Clayton, NJ
National Glass Co., Pittsburg, PA
F. H. Palmer, Brooklyn, NY
Penna Glass Co., Anderson, IN
Port Glass Works, Bellville, IL
Poughkeepsie Glass Works, Poughkeepsie, NY
Red Key Glass Co., Red Key, IN
Safe Glass Co., Upland, IN, & Chicago, IL
Skillin-Goodin Glass Co., Yorktown, IN
A. G. Smalley & Co., Boston
Sneath Glass Co., Hartford City, IN
Swayzee Glass Co., Swayzee, IN
Terre Haute Glass Mfg. Co., Terre Haute, IN
Upland Co-Operative Glass Co. [which may have included Safe Glass Co.], Upland, IN
Vacuum Jar & Fruit Package Co., San Francisco, CA
Victor Jar Co., Detroit, MI
Weightman Glass Co., Pittsburg, PA
Western Flint Glass Co., Eaton, IN
Weston Glass Co., Weston, WV
Woodbury Bottle Works, Woodbury, NJ
Wormser Glass Co., Pittsburg, PA
R. G. Wright & Co., Buffalo, NY

NOTE: Many of the same companies were still making jars in the early 1930s. The name "Hemingway" may confuse. By the 1930s, there was a company in Muncie, IN, Hemingray, that made insulators and also jars. And a Hemingway Glass Co. in Syracuse, NY.

Fruit jar, also called a <u>canning jar</u>, yellow amber glass, wax sealer, no lid, "Putnam Glass Works," Zanesville, OH, 1 qt. size. According to Alice Creswick, there are two different ambers for this jar: a "deep olive amber" and a "deep yellow amber." This one is a rich color, but not what I'd call "deep." **$350+**

Fruit jar, amber glass, square base & sides with arched shoulders & screw-on metal lid has milky, almost opalescent, insert, jar marked with large monogram of intertwined "A, G & S" and "Full Measure," mfd. by A. G. Smalley & Co., Boston, MA, 1 qt. size, also has 2 patent dates: Dec. 13, 1892, and April 7, 1896. **$30-$50**

Fruit jar, aqua glass, cylindrical body goes in at abruptly rounded shoulder, then goes out again at mouth, wax sealer type with rather deep moat for melted wax, glass stopper lid, missing the iron yoke clamp with hooked-under arms, that was tightened by wingnut to hold lid in place, marked "Millville Atmospheric," also "Whitall's Patent," with date. Inventor J. M. Whitall was from Philadelphia. 1 qt. size, "Preserve-jar" patent granted June 18, 1861. Whitall got a patent for a "Fruit-jar Stopper" on April 11, 1865. A cobalt blue example of this sold for $10,000 in 1982. Wow! **$35-$50**

Fruit jar, aqua glass, cylindrical with abruptly rounded shoulder, glass & metal stopper, best thing about this is its stopper. A much more valuable "Lafayette" has an embossed portrait profile bust of the French hero of the American War of Independence. "Lafayette" in signature script, 1 qt. size. 1880s. **$110-$140**

Fruit jar, aqua glass, iron yoke clamp & glass lid. The yoke clamp, with 2 curved arms that hook under flange just below rim of jar, acts as a press to hold lid against rim, and is tightened by a thumbscrew rather than a wingnut like on the Millville Atmospheric. It doesn't have a spring like the Earle patent, but looks somewhat similar. Jar marked "Eagle" in nice serif cap letters, along with dates, "patd Dec. 28th, 1858. Reisd [reissued] June 16, 1868." I guess this is the J. K. Jenkins patent for "preserving fruit." I can't find anything else that fits the date & the classification. **$90-$125+**

Fruit jar, aqua glass, shaped like a Mason, embossed "Swayzee's Improved Mason," Swayzee Glass Co. , Swayzee, IN, turn of century. **$10-$15**

Fruit jar, aqua glass, slowly sloping shoulder, screw-on cap, the top rim is slightly beveled out, there is no wider flange or ring below the screw threads on the glass, marked "Mason's Patent," 1 qt. size, pat'd Nov. 30, 1858, but made for a long time. This is only one of hundreds of various "Mason" jars made by all kinds of glassmakers. Mason himself was a metalworker, and his patent was for the hermetic lid and ground lip. Through li-

XVI-8. Fruit jar. *"Squire's Patent," mfd. by John B. Bartlett, NYC. Undated flyer from 1860s. The jars shown are quite interesting to a collector, and very valuable. There are three tiny knob "feet" on the bottom, which allowed water to circulate entirely around the jar. Creswick lists five Squire jars: (1) has 3 feet, pat'd Oct. 18, 1864, "two metal crossbars, fitting over the center hub of the lid." (2) Same date & closure, but has 4 feet. (3) Additional patent of March 7, 1865, 3 feet, and has an "opening on lip." New patent calls for a single "locking bar, turning on a central hub on the lid." (4) Like (3) except has two side openings in lip. And (5), jar has 3 feet, and 4 knobs on lip, and has a glass lid that also has 4 knobs around the circumference, with a vent hole in the middle. The woman in the picture is "lacing" on the elastic bands. According to Creswick, these Squire jars were all made in aqua, and are worth a lot of money:* **$750+**

censing, scores of manufacturers made the jars. And the very name "Mason" is sometimes used as a generic term for fruit jar, so well is it known. The best of these, although they are all well-formed and simply functional, are the biggest, the smallest, those in unusual colors (various blues, citron, even black), and those with rare embossed marks. You will have to study, study, study and go to every show and talk to dealers and other collectors if you want to get into this field. I don't know how many collectors still depend on bottle digs for great finds, but they are about the closest thing to old-fashioned archaeology that we find in the collecting world. **$8 on up.**

Fruit jar, aqua glass, wire bail clip handle, "Trademark Lightning Putnam #31." Pat'd by Henry W. Putnam, April 25, 1882. (Earlier patents 1875 & 1877.) **$45+**

Fruit jar, aqua glass, zinc screw-on lid, embossed "Mason's Patent," so-called "midget" 1 pint, Nov. 30, 1858. Please investigate this field carefully before assuming you've got the $$$ jar. This might be worth **$500+**

One of the earliest uses for **rolled zinc**, a sheet form of this rust-proof metal, was canning jar lids. After long exposure to corrosives, a white powdery film develops that's peculiarly unpleasant to the touch.

Fruit jar, bluish-aqua glass (color called "Ball Blue" by Creswick), uses the "Lightning" wire bail lid clip, glass lid, "McDonald New Perfect Seal," pat'd July 14, 1908. **$8-$15**

Fruit jar, clear, embossed "American Improved Preserve Can," on one side, and lo and behold a favorite eggbeater inventor's name and patent date on the other side, arched over & under a star: "Earle's Patent Feb 2d 1864." Timothy Earle, Valley Falls, RI. His patent was actually for the C-shaped curved iron clamp: "This device consists of a yoke, the ends of which are curved so as to fit under a lip or projection on the neck. The yoke turns upon a spindle, and the latter is provided with a coiled spring, which serves to press the cover upon the jar; the object being to dispense with the inclined lips on the lip or projection of the neck of the jar." **$850+**

Fruit jar, clear or "crystal" glass with wax seal groove in lip, "Rau's Improved Groove," American, turn of century. **$35-$45**

Fruit jar, glass, rubber, dried clay, American, c.1880. **Hypothetical entry** — I assume this was made; has anyone seen one? It was described in the pages of the Oct. 1880 *Scribner's Monthly* magazine as, "A new device for preserving fruit in its natural condition [that] consists of a glass jar or tumbler, having a cover with a rubber packing-ring, secured to the jar by a screw clamp. At the bottom of the jar is a hole, designed to be closed air-tight by a suitable stopper, and inside the jar is placed a layer of dried clay, to absorb the moisture that may escape from the fruit. The grapes or other fruits are hung up inside the jar, the cover is put on, and air is withdrawn by means of an air-pump, when the opening in the bottom is closed and sealed." If it exists: **$65-$85+**

Fruit jar, medium cobalt blue glass, glass lid has little notch in its high thick dorsal "fin," wire bail clip, "The Canton Electric Fruit Jar," 1880s. You probably won't see one of these, they're so extremely rare, but it's nice to dream that you might find one at a yard sale! Of course, cobalt blue is a choice color for wretched fakes. So far as I know, the "Canton Electric" hasn't been replicated. **$2500-$4000**

Fruit jar holder, wire, looks like a doll stand, only the arms come around neck of jar, not waist of doll, 6" H, turn of century. **$10-$12**

Fruit jar holder & wrench, 2 tools of steel. Holder is a band of steel with a number of holes (like a belt) to clamp around jar for perfect sizing; the wrench has a shallow cap, divided in 2 unequal parts to make gross adjustments to fit different size lids. "The T. & B.," Tarbox & Bogart Mfg. Co., Cleveland, OH, pat'd Dec. 3, 1901 by Henry W. Bogart. Ad copy: "Don't be balked by the cap, serve <u>plums</u> when you want <u>plums</u>, no matter whether Jack's at home or not." The pair: **$30-$45**

Fruit jar lifter, iron, "E-Z Lift." **$3-$5**

Fruit jar lifter, little one-jar basket, with loop-de-loop sides that form feet for carrier, twisted side pieces with wire bail handle, wooden grip, American, about 5" H, 19th C. **Reproduction alert** — An exact copy is made by Mathews Wire, of Frankfort, IN. Only the turned wooden handle looks too new, and there are no dings, sags, shrugs or banged-up bends in the wire. **$12-$20**

Fruit jar lifter, metal, "Simplex," Gorman Mfg. Co., Boston, MA, late 19th C. **$10-$15**

Fruit jar opener, works like pliers, metal with rubber grips, "The Gunnard Co.," Minneapolis, MN, pat'd 1936. (I've seen this called a "Gunnard Reliner," in which case it means it's a lid re-ligner or straightener.) **$7-$15**

Fruit jar opener," rubber, "Cupples Presto Wrench" is not really a wrench, it's a cap-shaped rubber gripper put over the cap to make it easier to grip with the hand and turn the cap. A similar rubber one is the "Swenson Jar Opener." **$5-$10**

Fruit jar opener, red rubber over heavy wire, "Daisy Jar Opener," 20th C. **$5-$8**

XVI-9. Fruit jars. *Facing pages from an 1860s book:* Philadelphia and Its Manufactures. *See the "Willoughby," the "Kline," the "Franklin," the "Mason" and the "Haller" in A. E. Samuel's ad; and the "Heroine," and "Excelsior," jars of Boorse, Burrows & Co. As well as Bodine patent "pickle and preserve jars."* **(1)** *"H. & S.* **Willoughby's Patent**,*" pat'd Jan. 1, 1859, has metal stopper which was set into mouth, with some "gum," and then tightened to become air-tight by screwing the wingnut. "To open the Jar, apply warm water around the gum ring, partially unscrew, and draw out the stopper." Three sizes: 1 pt., 1 qt., and 1 half-gallon.* **(2)** *"**Kline's Patent**," pat'd Oct. 27,1863. Directions were to "Place the gum over the small end of the stopper, insert it into the mouth of the jar, the gum resting on the shoulder (if the mouth of the Jar is wet the Stopper should also be wet); then by screw action force the Stopper down. Immediately after closing the jar, force a pin in between the Stopper and the gum, for the escape of the air compressed, occasioned in putting in the Stopper. Withdraw the pin in a few seconds. Examine the Jar an hour after closing. If the Stopper has sunk in the Jar is air tight." To open it, you forced a pin in, to admit air, then applied warm water around the gum.* **(3)** *"**Franklin's Patent**," pat'd Aug. 8, 1865. Had a very modern lid: with a threaded rim and a threaded metal band which held on the glass lid.* **(4)** *"**Haller's Patent**," pat'd Aug. 7, 1860. Has a metal stopper & rim, tightened with the wingnut visible in picture.* **(5)** *"**Mason's Patent**," pat'd Nov. 30, 1858. Beyond that, I can't tell from picture how this one distinguishes itself from the hundreds of Mason jars of that patent. Did A. R. Samuel really manufacture this Mason? Various glass companies did.* **(6)** *"**The HERO ine**," pat'd Nov. 26, 1867, with 8 patents on the glass lid insert from 1856 to 1869. The first of these were "The HERO," but obviously something interesting happened to make them add, on a line below "HERO" a smaller "INE".* **(7)** *"**Excelsior**," about which I can tell nothing. The ad states that the advertiser, Boorse, Burrows & Co., Philadelphia, have "the exclusive right of manufacturing the Excelsior and Heroine Fruit Jars, (conceded by all fruit men to be the best Self-sealing Fruit Jars in the market.) Values for quart jars — big ones may be worth 20 times as much; little ones 4 or 5 times as much. (1)* **$50+** *; (2)* **$30+**;*(3)* **$50-$70**; *(4)* **$950+**; *(5)* **$15+**; *(6)* **$25+**; *(7) prob.* **$20+**

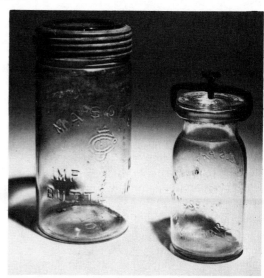

XVI-10. Fruit jars. (L) *"Mason's Improved Butter Jar,"* and **(R)** *the highly desirable "Millville Atmospheric Fruit Jar." The Mason's has a metal screw-band seal and glass lid, and probably dates to the turn of the century. The Millville, with a glass lid held by yoke and thumbscrew, was made with the J. M. Whitall patent of June 18, 1861. Picture courtesy of the National Museum of American History, Smithsonian Institution.* (L) **$45+**; (R) **$95+**

XVI-11. Preserved foods in original jars. (L) *Hermetically sealed glass jar for "soft, rich" cheese. "American Club House Cheese," Chandler & Rudd Co., Cleveland, OH. "A full size jar will be sent to any point in the United States, charges prepaid, on receipt of 50¢." Picture and words probably printed on paper label.* **(M)** & **(R)** *"Preserved Strawberries" in the nifty jar, and "Red Currant Jelly" in the jelly glass. Curtice Brothers Co., Rochester, NY. Both are ads from* Century *magazine, Dec. 1891.* **$5-$18**

XVI-12. Jar holder patent, *actually called by inventor a "dish holder," but obviously with fruit jars sketched in. Pat'd 4/26/1870, by W. P. Walter. Spring wire bails of different types to fit different shapes of fruit jars.*

XVI-15. Jar wrenches. (L) *Wood with heavy wire handles.* **(T-R)** *Wire with leather. A double gripper that grips the jar with the bigger wrench and the lid with the pivoting upper wrench. 9-1/2" L.* **(B-R)** *With 3 bands is copper. The band can be selected to fit the circumference of the jar to be opened. 9-1/2" L. All located by The Primitive Man, Bob Cahn, Carmel, NY.* **$25-$65**

XVI-13. Jar holders. *These were used for handling hot jars — the one at left, for lifting from canner, were left in the kettle while canning.* **(L)** *All wire, like a doll stand, 9" H.* **(R)** *Other one like blanket pin is mostly wood and grips really tight. SEE Mudge canner XVI-1.* **$5-$15**

XVI-16. Mason Jar Sealer & Can Opener combined. *Made of "New Process White Metal," which is "strong, will not break, takes a high polish, and will last a lifetime." Leather strap and malleable cast iron frame. I believe it really was called "The Mason," but don't know who had the license to use the Mason name. From F. W. Seastrand drummers' catalog, c.1912.* **$20-$35**

XVI-14. Jar rack & lifter. (L) *Wire, rack holds 4 jars for sterilizing. Basket part is 3-1/4" H x 10-1/4" diameter.* **(R)** *The lifter works with one hand; your thumb goes through hole at top while fingers pull up on wooden grip. 10" H, early 20th C.* **$18-$35**

XVI-17. Fruit jar wrenches. (T) *Unmarked one of nickeled metal. Note bottle crown cap opener at top.* **(M)** *Looks like a lariat — wire & malleable cast iron. Best & Co., pat'd 1917.* **(B)** *Nickeled steel, mfd. by A. C. Williams, New Jersey, c.1900. They specialized in corkscrews and bottle openers.* **$8-$25**

Fruit jar reformer, plated iron, adjustable, using screw driver, small wheel set at angle runs around edge of glass jar, American, 7-3/8" L, pat'd Mar. 5, 1907.   **$10-$15**

Fruit jar sealer & wrench, nickeled malleable cast iron, plier handle, looks like a short-handled snake catcher with wire hoop that adjusts to fit, one side marked "Up for wrench," mfd. by Stockland, Minneapolis, MN, 6-5/8" L, no date, but early 20th C. This is similar to the one by the Best Co., seen in Chapter XVI, illustration XVI-16, except it has 2 handles. **$15-$20**

Fruit jar wrench, cast iron, "Wilson's," Wilson Mfg. Co., Niles, OH, early 20th C (?).   **$12-$15**

Fruit jar wrench, green painted iron, 2 sets of arms, the lower pair has white rubber sleeves to hold jar safely, upper metal arms swivel or pivot and turn the lid without the lower arms moving. Very ingenious, 8-1/4" L, 20th C.   **$15-$25**

Fruit jar wrench, plier-like, tinned iron, in original box, "Presto," mfd. by Cupples, (possibly Cupples Co., St. Louis, MO), 20th C.   **$5-$10**

Fruit jar wrench, iron, "C. A. Powell, Cleveland, OH," "pat appl for," c. 1910s.   **$10-$15**

Fruit jar wrench, iron & wire, cast iron grip & edge frame, with lasso-like spring steel wire that tightens when grip is cocked. Marked with "on" and "off" position, "Best S. Co.," Lancaster, PA, 7-3/4" L, pat'd May 8, 1917.   **$10-$18**

Fruit jar wrench, metal, "Triumph Fruit Can Wrench," mfd. by Benjamin P. Forbes [Chocolate] Co., Cleveland, OH, 6-1/2" L x 2-1/4" W, "patent pending." Some are seen with the patent date Nov. 3, 1903. And it's in 1932-33 *Thomas' Register*. **NOTE:** When patented, the manufacturer was given as "Benj. P. Forbes, Cleveland, O." I don't know when "Chocolate" came into the name. Forbes also made, c.1903, the "Perfection Fruit Jar Wrench" and the "Perfection Fruit Jar Holder," meant to fit "any Mason jar made." Wrench is flat steel, with handle used to adjust size of flat ring that goes on lid; holder has a band of metal that holds the jar, and cast iron plier handles.   **$15-$25+**

Fruit jar wrench, nickeled steel, adjustable, "Winchester's of Carthage," Carthage, MO.   **$10-$15**

Fruit jar wrench, tinned iron, flat metal, adjustable diameter loop, mfd. by A. C. Williams, Ravenna, OH, 8" L, c.1910. **$7-$10**

Fruit jar wrench & can opener combined, cast iron frame, steel blade, adjustable leather strap, "Mason Jar Sealer and Opener," c. 1912.   **$15-$18**

Fruit jar wrench & can opener combined, steel, has flat loop that fits over lid, tightened by "cocking" the handle. The handle has a sharp point on tip (to start hole for opener), and a sliding adjustable blade. J. C. Forster (or Forester?) & Son, Pittsburgh, PA, Pat'd 9/13/1910. Note spelling of Pittsburgh with an "h". An earlier spelling had no "h."   **$20-$30**

Funnel or fruit jar filler — See Chapter V

Herb drying rack, wood with original old blue paint, 28" L, 19th C. Auction notices are always mentioning "Shaker herb drying rack," but probably very few (if any) are Shaker. The price on this is determined more than anything else by the blue paint.   **$350-$500**

Jars — See also Chapter VII.

Jelly cup — See cup, for jellies & jams

XVI-18. "Angel & crown" Kerr jelly glass bottoms. *Also known as "Bee & crown." Pure folk art. These are only five of an estimated 58 different patterns molded in bottom (inside of the glasses, outside of the tumblers) of the "jellies." Tumblers are 3-3/4" H x 2-7/8" diameter at top. The smaller glasses, with fluted sides, range from about 2-1/4" H x 3-1/4" diameter to 2-3/8" H x 3-1/2" diameter. The mold-makers at Kerr interpreted the crown and angel, seemingly a different way each time. I am deeply indepted to the Jelly Jammers club and to Betty Landis for giving me my first one and setting me off. Special thanks go to Barbara Bowditch, author of a remarkable book,* American Jelly Glasses, *which includes rubbings done by Dennis Smith, of 58 of the angel and crown, as well as much more. (SEE bibliography.) I couldn't do rubbings. Bottoms shown here were done on photocopy machine with a disk of black paper inside tumbler, and a white piece of paper with circle cut out, laid on top of copier's glass. I've collected folk art for 30 years, and this is the first time I've ever seen anything like these angels on a mass-produced object. The various treatments of hair, wings, face-shape, gown, star and crown are remarkable. See XVI-19 for some parallel angels.* **$2-$8**

XVI-19. Other folk art angels & crowns. *These greatly reduced drawings are done from a fraktur-like drawing (top) of the Pennsylvania Germans, and from four gravestone carvings from the mid-to-late 18th C., in Connecticut. There are many other New England gravestone carvings of similar subjects. The A. H. Kerr glass company, of Oklahoma, supposedly took the angel & crown motif from the family coat of arms, but I have no confirmation of that. Interesting how almost Mayan or Aztec the angels look here! For further reading, see Allan I. Ludwig's* Graven Images: New England Stonecarving and its Symbols, 1650-1815. *Middletown, CT: Wesleyan University Press. Also see Scott T. Swank, et al,* Arts of the Pennsylvania Germans, *Wilmington, DE, Winterthur, 1983.*

Jelly glasses, also called **jellies**, **jelly jars**, **jam jars** and **jelly tumblers**, blown or press-molded glass, mostly in clear ("crystal"), but also medium blue, light and dark green, and "Ball Blue," to borrow from fruit jar-collecting. They are usually the size and shape of small tumblers, with slightly slanted sides. But others are bell-shaped, some like cups, some are footed and have stems like goblets. Some are half-size, like low-walled custard cups. The most collectible have a design of some sort — from flutes or "thumb-prints" to very detailed fruit, berries, flowers or patriotic patterns. Although some old jelly glasses were used as molds, and the jelly turned out onto a serving dish in all its quivery beauty, often as not the design is not on the inside (where it would impress the gelatin), but on the outside. There are also jelly glasses known as **table jellies**, which are among the oldest types (late eighteenth century in this country) and were individual dessert glasses. Lids are not often present, and for some jellies (as the collectors call them) it is not known what kind of lid was original — metal or glass — or even if there were a lid at one time, because some were just sealed with wax or parafin, then protected with a circle of cloth tied tightly on. For such an ubiquitous household object, it amazes me how few I see at even the largest of flea markets. I feel even less qualified to write about jellies than I do about fruit jars, although they both are related to kitchen collectibles. Bottle shows almost always include not only fruit jars but at least a few jellies. For the most information about American jellies, I highly recommend a charming and reliable self-published looseleaf book by Barbara Bowditch. ***American Jelly Glasses: A Collector's Notebook*** may be obtained from Mrs. Bowditch at 1173 Peck Road, Hilton, NY 14468. Please send SASE when enquiring about cost and availability. Very clear, enticing line drawings by the late George Bowditch, as well as color pictures, show us side views as well as patterns on the bottom or lid. For me, the most delightful and desirable of all the jellies are the Kerr "Angel & Crown" (sometimes nicknamed "Bee & Crown"), names referring to a figural trademark embossed on the outside bottom of what would otherwise be rather plain glasses. There are many variations, as each mold-carver made his own version of the angel and crown element in the Kerr family coat-of-arms. I have at least 12 different ones — the first was a gift from Betty Landis. Mark-rubbings by Dennis Smith, for Barbara Bowditch's book, show many more. The collectors' group is the **Jelly Jammers**, with a quarterly newsletter. Please use SASE when enquiring of Margaret Shaw, 6086 W. Boggstown Rd., Boggstown, IN 46110. Old, rare jellies may bring much more, but values for **most jellies** are in low end of this range: **$3-$50**

Fig. 1.   Fig. 2.   Fig. 3.   Fig. 4.   Fig. 5.   Fig. 6.   Fig. 7.   Fig. 8.

XVI-20. "Uses for Old Fruit Cans." Make-dos, *mostly from article in* American Agriculturist, *1/1875.* **(T-L)** *Cup at top left was from AA, 1880. "Take round fruit, or vegetable, cans and melt off the top; bend a hickory withe for a handle, as shown in the engraving, and fasten it with wire or rivets. This makes a useful dipper, pitcher, measure, or vessel for many purposes about the barn or house; one may be made for the flour barrel; another for sugar; others for feed, grain, etc." Others:* **(1)** *Emptied can, showing old-type hole in top which was soldered on after canning. You would melt other solder and flatten the tin, which is useful for "covering mouse and rat-holes," etc. If you lived in an old apartment in NYC, you'd find tin can lids nailed down over holes in the floor and wall.* **(2)** *"Little bucket or paint pot."* **(3)** *Scoop.* **(4)** *Saucepan "for small messes."* **(5)** *A fruit-picker.* **(6)** *Coarse grater "for crackers, dry bread, horseradish, and the like." The tin is tacked to board.* **(7)** *"Muffin and cake-rings." Strips cut and held by rivets.* **(8)** *Lantern, with a piece of "stove mica" set into side.*

XVI-21. Tipping copper, *for soldering can lids in home canning, or for mending tinwares. The sharp long tip was copper, which conducted heat very well; held in iron cleft, wood handle. The "pointed portion is to be 'tinned,' as the workmen say, which means that it is to be coated with solder. To tin the point, file it smooth, heat the tool hot enough to melt solder, then quickly file the surface bright, and rub it on a small lump of solder that has been placed on a board for the purpose, using rosin, or a few drops of a zinc solution."* American Agriculturist, *2/1870.* **$15-$20**

XVI-22. Soldering tool patent. *Pat'd 1/13/1880, by William Painter, Baltimore, MD, assignor of 1/2 of right to Louis B. Keizer. A "hand soldering device for capping cans, the combination of a soldering tool whose edge is curved to conform to the groove in the can-top, and is the sole guide of the tool, with a handle." I don't know if it was ever made.*

XVI-23. Fruit can soldering machine, *sometimes described as a <u>cylinder-scraper</u> for automobiles, which for all I know it may have been used for. "Allens'," mfd. by Hull Brothers, Webster & Co., Cleveland, OH. "The only machine ever made which will finish the can completely with one handling. By the use of it the can only requires one handling to finish soldering. Adjusts to size of both top and bottom; they will not spring off while being soldered." I've seen one — it's about 9" or 10" L, nice wooden handle, and it rattles when turned quickly back and forth, so it may also be mistaken for some kind of noisemaker.* The Metal Worker, *7/8/1882.* **$40-$65+**

Meat curing pump, metal, in original cardboard tube with instructions, "Morton Salt," American, 20th C. **$20-$25**

Preserve can — See fruit jar. I've put all glass canning jars under "Fruit jar," and ceramic canning jars here under "Preserve jar."

Preserve jar, brown saltglazed stoneware, wax seal type with ridged flat rim into which wax or paraffin was melted; then the lid was pushed down before wax solidified, "Minnesota Stoneware," MN, 1-1/2 quart size, late 19th C. **Brown saltglaze** was made like gray or buff stoneware, with one extra step. Instead of firing the plain clay vessel, and throwing salt in to vaporize as a glaze, a brown slip was brushed on or the vessel was dipped in it, allowed to dry, then fired just like other pieces, and at the right time the salt was thrown in. **$35-$55+**

Preserve jar, redware, "Galena," Illinois (?), 9" H, late 19th C. **$100-$150**

Preserve jar, saltglazed stoneware, with double rim with recess for wax, called a "wax sealer," with original lid, some nicking where sharp tool has been used over years of use to dig out hardened wax, American (?), 1 qt. size, late 19th C. **Several companies made earthenware** or stoneware canning jars at the turn of the century. The only two listed in *Thomas' Register of American Manufacturers,* 1905-06, are Chicago Pottery Co., Chicago, IL; and Weir Pottery Co., Monmouth, IL. The 1932-33 *Thomas's* includes: Robinson Clay Product Co., of NY, NJ, CT, OH; Western Stoneware Co., Monmouth, IL; White Hall Pottery Works, White Hall, IL; Louisville Pottery Co., Louisville, KY; Dorchester Pottery Works, Boston, MA; Red Wing Union Stoneware Co., Red Wing, MN; United States Stoneware Co., Akron, OH; Logan Pottery Co., Logan, OH; Hyssong Pottery Co., Bloomsburg, PA; and Sherwood Brothers Co., New Brighton, CT. **$40-$50**

Preserve jar, saltglazed stoneware with blue flowers, and stenciled blue capacity number "1," "Hamilton & Jones," Greensboro, PA, one gal. capacity, c.1870s. **$150+**

Preserve jar, saltglazed stoneware, stoneware lid, wire clamp-on lever to hold lid on, top of jar, like a jug, slants up, to only about 1/3 diameter of jar itself, "The Weir Stone Fruit Jar," mfd. by Weir Pottery Co., Monmouth, IL, 1 qt. size, (sizes: 1 pint, 1, 2, 4 & 8 qts. up to 10 gal.), pat'd Mar. 21,1892; made into early 20th C. **$25+**

Preserve jar, stoneware, saltglazed in shades of brown, 12 paneled sides, Peoria Pottery Co., Peoria, IL, 7" H x 4-1/2" diameter, last quarter 19th C. **$45-$55**

Tin cans — See Chapter VIII

Tipping coppers, or **soldering irons** — copper bullet-like or wedge-shaped pointed head, sometimes with hexagonal sides like a large copper crystal, usually have heavy iron wire shaft or handle, sometimes with wooden grip at end, used to solder closed the vent hole left in the top of the early cans. About 8" to 10" L, 19th & 20th C. Such tools are still made. The tin cans were boiled, filled with hot food, and the top soldered on (or a cap in center of top was soldered into place). Then a steam hole was punched in the lid and the can boiled again, and steam escaped from the hole, after which it was immediately soldered closed, using a heated tipping copper and solder. If a can was found with 2 small holes, both soldered up, it indicated that someone had taken a spoiled batch of food, re-heated and re-sealed the can. **$5-$15**

FURNISHING

XVII. CHAIRS, TABLES, CUPBOARDS & CABINETS

You may doubt that there are "collectors" of furniture. But, like a surprising number of people, I happen to collect chairs (mostly not kitchen chairs, however), and I have good friends in Massachusetts who collect wall-hung wooden cupboards, most of which are a couple of centuries old. Most people are constrained by money and room, and find it hard to visualize a collection of tables, for example, arranged anywhere in the house. (Some of my chairs are hung on the wall; some are in storage against the time when one of my dreams — a Chair Room — can be made real.)

A good percentage of collectors of kitchen implements of the twentieth century own, or would like to own, at least one period piece of furniture, which helps set the smaller pieces in a natural context. The most popular item is a **"Hoosier"-type cabinet**, made by Hoosier Mfg. Co. of Indiana, or one of many other companies, frequently located in Indiana.

For collectors of nineteenth-century implements and hollowware, a scrubbed-top table, a **pie safe**, or some Windsor-style kitchen chairs are goals. Hutch tables and wall cupboards with forged iron hardware are favored by collectors of eighteenth- and early nineteenth-century wares. These pieces help set the scene.

What makes up a collection of furniture? Some people say you have to have at least two pieces; others say three or more are needed. I tend to agree with the latter. A pair of something, even an unmatched pair, isn't really a collection. Various assembled pieces of furniture, all in original green paint, or all made of bird's-eye maple, or all with turned legs, or all made in North Carolina — that's a collection.

Baker's cupboard, very like a pie safe, pine with one large door, slatted shelves & screened sides, for cooling fresh-baked bread loaves, turn of century. **$400-$550**

Baker's rack, iron, sides look like intertwined grapevines, 5 shelves, European or poss. American, 6-1/2 feet H x 5 feet W, early 20th C. **$425+**

Butcher block, deep, solid maple on strong thick turned legs, worn & scarred, 20" square, 19th C. **$300-$400**

Cabinet, also called a kitchen piano by the Hoosier Mfg. Co. because it put "everything at her fingers' ends," varnished wood, porcelainized iron counter top, original sifter and bin, revolving spice rack for 7 containers with shaker tops, flour & sugar containers, perfect condition, "Hoosier," New Castle, IN, very early 20th C. Ads in a 1901 and 1902 *Ladies Home Journal* said that it "Does away with tiresome walking around a hot kitchen" and that, "Household Economy is as much a matter of saving your steps as of thrifty living. There is more time and strength left for these things if you have a Hoosier Kitchen Cabinet. Convenient, compact, orderly . . . can be put where you wish." Another ad, in *House Furnishing Review,* Jan. 1908, said that the "Hoosier kitchen cabinet saves as many steps as a bicycle. It is as necessary a convenience as a sewing machine." • NOTE: The term "Kitchen piano" was also applied to the range — a cook's finest instrument. **$800+**

Cabinet, all original finish, double doors above, flanking flour bin with oval glass window, slightly arched top, bins below, 4 drawers, sifter, spice rack, etc., "Hoosier Mfg. Co.," early 20th C. **$600+**

Cabinet, oak in original finish, flour bin & sifter, roll front that works very well, "Hoosier," early 20th C. **$550+**

Cabinet, painted wood, doors above, bins, pull out pastry board, "Sellers," early 20th C. **$475+**

Cabinet, stepback hutch top, 2 doors above, 2 utility drawers over bin, nice legs, Larkin, early 20th C. **$575+**

XVII-1. "A Method of Arranging a Kitchen," *from the* American Agriculturist, 4/1876. A farmhouse kitchen designed by L. D. Snook to suit the farmer's wife — as a complement to city kitchens "arranged with great care to facilitate the work of servants." (**E**) is a wood or iron sink, and if wood, treated with linseed oil inside. "An iron pump is placed in at the end near the wall and connects with the cistern. The outlet pipe is at the opposite end near the window." Below the sink is a "closet" with two doors, and to the right of that is a china closet (**H**) and a lower "closet" for kettles, tinware, and the various cooking utensils. The oiled wooden rack (**B**) below the window is slatted, and for draining dishes. (**F**) is a pass-through to the pantry seen through the door. On the lowest shelf in the pantry appears to be a bread dough raiser. What about the stove? "For convenience the stove should be placed upon the side of the room occupied by the closets [cupboards], or near where the table stands in the illustration." The next picture in the article showed how a pantry should be arranged. We think of a pantry as a place for storing food, but remember the root word: pan. "In houses of old style there was either no pantry at all, the kitchen being furnished with a dresser and shelves, or it was merely a small closet to hold the articles in less common use. In modern houses the pantry is next in importance to the kitchen, and it should be so arranged as to accommodate all the appliances used in cookery, as well as the china, glass-ware, cutlery, and other articles for the table."

Cabinet, maple, bottom has 2 bins, 2 drawers & 2 molding boards for rolling out dough, top section has 8 drawers flanking small cupboard with door, American, 48" W, late 19th C. **$750+**

Cabinet, painted green with green & black marbleized enameled-iron work surface, casters on legs, arched doors, clock set in frame at top, wonderful looking, "Keystone Cabinet Co." with truncated arrowhead-like keystone logo, Littlestown, PA, 39-3/4" W, pat'd Feb. 2, 1922. A spectacular greenie piece for a Depression glass kitchen. Or for any other room; this is a beauty. **$1500-$2500+**

XVII-2. "Plate dresser" & work table, *as depicted in a wood engraving from an 1833 edition of a chapbook,* Mother Goose's Melodies, *published in England. The caption reads "Sing, Sing! — What shall I sing? The Cat's run away with the Pudding-Bag String."*

XVII-3. "A Corner Cupboard." *You've seen in illustrations XVII-1 and -2 precursors of multi-purpose cabinets — the cupboard for utensils, the pantry, and the combination dresser & table. This one shows how an awkward corner between doors leading to a dining room and to a pantry, was made to "be comprehensive, compact, capacious, and convenient."* **(A)** *covers a flour barrel and is a swing-out curved door.* **(B)** *is the hinged cover.* **(C)** *is the top of a "case of drawers"* **(G)**, *but just under it, in* **(E)**, *is "a space for the bread pan and the molding-board, which slides in on cleats; these are reached by the door* **(D)**, *which lifts, and is provided with a spring-catch.*

Cabinets, sometimes called <u>cabinet tables</u>, or <u>baker's cupboards</u>, of the "Hoosier" type, with shelves, drawers, bins, dough-boards, sifters, and work counter, are a mass-produced elaboration of a much earlier free-standing cupboard or dresser dating back hundreds of years ago, especially in Europe. Some from the early nineteenth century, with drawers, bins, and shelves for staples, are obvious predecessors — especially Shaker cupboards.

The late nineteenth-century cabinet-cupboards, to which we've given the generic "Hoosier" name, were marketed aggressively as aids to the "science" of cookery, and helped housewives see themselves as efficient professionals, with their own offices or places of business that were as important as the offices to which their husbands went every day. An article by Mary Jane Hill ("The Changing Kitchen Cabinet," *Antique Trader*, 1/10/1979) tells of an efficiency survey of women's kitchen work done by expert Harrington Emerson in the 1920s. He concluded that "The housewife was taking 2113 steps to prepare three meals a day," but that "only 520 steps were actually necessary" if a cabinet such as the "Napanee Dutch Kitchenet" were used.

By the 1920s there were porcelainized metal cabinets, which were more sanitary than wood, but most of the ones collected now are wood, either varnished natural finish or painted white, some with enameled or porcelainized iron work surface. They have varying numbers of built-in accessories — from spice containers & flour sifters & coffee

XVII-4. Butcher blocks. (T-L) *"Made from 1-1/2 strips of best grade white maple, glued & bolted together," turned legs. Seven sizes: from 15" square to 30" x 40". S. D. Sexton catalog, Baltimore, c.1930s.* **(T-R)** *Not so described, but looks like section of tree trunk. Five diameters, from 18" to 30"; and* **(M-L)** *"Butcher Bench," thick plank 24" W x any length. Braced with iron rods, on heavy turned trestle legs.* **(M-R)** *"Square sectional" block in 3 sizes, from 20" x 25" to 25" x 30", bolted through, on turned legs. Last three all from Duparquet, Huot & Moneuse suppliers' catalog, c.1904-1910.* **(B)** *A high sectional maple block, called a* **chef block.** *18" x 18" x 10" deep; 34" H overall. Also Sexton, c.1930s. Most surface distress from use & age don't devalue.* **$90-$500+**

grinders to clocks, shopping aids and a filing compartment for household bills — and were made by many companies besides Hoosier, in various states, but mostly Indiana, from the turn of the century on for about three decades. (Hoosier closed down in 1942.) A 1902 ad for a large "#20 Hoosier," with drawers on the side, the front, and in the upper half, as well as loads of shelves, said it was "often used instead of a 'built-in' cupboard." But most of these factory-made movable cabinets date after 1910s but before built-in cabinets in 1940s. Value ranges widely; those at the low end are plain or in poor condition. Rather expensive manufactured ones are "possum bellies" — large, with rounded bins, built-in sifters, racks and extra details.

Avoid the overly refinished, and remember than originally many cabinets were painted and all cabinets made of several different woods were painted. Oak was considered the superior wood because it is hard and wouldn't tend to "absorb odors" and get musty-smelling. You will sometimes find cabinets with their original grain-painted finish. Ariel's cabinets were unusual because they used colored stains through which the grain would show. Green was the most popular color. Wide value range of all cabinets due to condition, features, appearance. **$250-$2000+**

• • • •

Work Perch — One offspring of the new style of kitchen work was the **kitchen stool**, with or without a back, but always with a rung or footrest, which could be pulled up to the desk-like cabinet table, affording the housewife a comfortable seat while she worked. It was claimed, of course, that from one spot the housewife could reach everything she needed without the *trudgery* of walking all over the kitchen to do something like make an apple pie! Some cabinet companies also made stools, and some were combo step-ladders & stools. **$15-$65**

• • • •

Makers of kitchen cabinets and/or kitchen safes in the **early 1900s** are listed below. Only a few advertised nationally. The generic name often applied to all kitchen cabinets comes from Hoosier Mfg. Co., New Castle, IN. Others include: Acme, Wilkinson, IN; Acme Kitchen Furn.

Co., Chattanooga, TN; Alles Bros. (made kitchen safes), Henderson, KY; Andrews, in Andrews, IN; Ariel** Cabinet Co., Peru, IN; Aude Furn. Co., St. Louis, MO; Bagby Furn. Co. (safes), Baltimore; Bisk Corp., Brockton, MA; Bryant Furn. Co., Truxton, NY; Campbell, Smith & Ritchie's "Boone," Lebanon, IN; Cardinal's "Mother Hubbard's," Wabash, IN; Coppes, Zook & Mutschler's "Napanee," and "Napanee Dutch Kitchenet," Nappanee, IN; A. D. Deemer Furn. Co., Brookville, PA; Dubuque Cabinet Makers' Assoc., Dubuque, IA; Evansville Furn. Co. (safes), Evansville, IN; Fitts-Crabtree Mfg. Co. (safes), Sanford, NC; Ft. Smith Folding Bed & Table Co., T. Smith, AR; Globe Furn. Co., Evansville, IN; Goshen Pump Co. (latter also made safes), Goshen, IN; Greencastle Cabinet Co., Greencastle, IN; Helmers Mfg. Co., Leavenworth, KS; High Point Mantel & Table Co. (safes), High Point, NC; House & Herrmann, Wheeling, WV; C. A. Hubbard, Martinsville, IN; Ideal Cabinet Co., Evansville, In.; Indiana Furn. Co., Evansville, IN; I-X-L, Goshen, IN; L. A. Jennings, New Castle, IN; Kesslers & Sons (safes), Logan, OH; Klanke, —?—*; Koenig Furn. Co. (safes), St. Louis, MO; Kompass & Stoll, Niles, MI; Jonathan Koontz Sons, Union City, IN; Larkin, —?—*; R. E. Lasher & Co. (safes), St. Louis, MO; Lebanon Mfg. Co., Lebanon, IN; Marysville Cabinet Co., Marysville, OH; McCure Mfg. Co., Marion, IN; G. P. McDougall, Indianapolis & Frankfort, IN, who made "Plainview" for Montgomery Ward; McLoud & Sparks (also safes), Ft. Smith, AR; McNown Mfg. Co., Columbia, IN; A. H. Meyer, Lebanon, IN; Minnesota Furn. Co.'s "Elwell Kitchen Cabinet," Minneapolis, MN; Mound City Furniture Co. (safes), Mound, IL; Parker-Battle-Talbot Mfg. Co. (safes), Tullohoma, TN; Paul Mfg. Co., Ft. Wayne, IN; Queen Cabinet Co., Chicago, IL; G. I. Sellers & Sons Co., Elwood, IN; Charles Sueme (safes), St. Louis, MO; Tillman Bros. (safes), La Crosse, WI; Tipp Bldg. & Mfg. Co., Tippecanoe City, OH; Union Cabinet Co., Marion, IN; Ware Mfg. Co. (safes), Atlanta, GA; Wasmuth-Endicott Co.'s "Kitchen Maid," Andrews, IN; Wilson Co., Grand Rapids, MI; Winter Lumber Co., Sheboygan, WI.
NOTE: *I couldn't find addresses for Larkin or Klanke. I do wonder if maybe Larkin Mfg. Co., Buffalo, NY, who made soap and had a premium program, might not have had cabinets made by another company.
** The name "Ariel" was chosen, reportedly, by the company president, Charles Morrice, who said he was once an aerialist in the circus

XVII-5. "Possum-belly" cabinet tables. *With their original prices!* (**T-L**) *"Princess," made mostly of ash, with sanded top — what became known as a scrub-top. Base finished "antique oak." 27" x 47" L. Two "sliding extension boards; two partitioned sliding bins which may be used for potatoes, etc." $5.65.* (**T-R**) *"Domestic new-style Combination Kitchen Cabinet," made of ash, 18" x 45" with drop leaf shown up; sliding bins and extension carving boards. $6.90.* (**B-L**) *"Convenient," ash, plain top, "antique color" base, 27" x 42" top, two 50-lb bin drawers, $5.90.* (**B-R**) *"Kitchen Queen," seasoned white wood. One large drawer above sliding flour bin. Top unfinished; rest "golden oak." $2.95. All from Albert Pick mail order catalog, 1909.* **$150-$350+**

XVII-6. Combination table & cabinet. *Upper part is an open dresser mainly for china,. There is a drop-down cover for what appears to be the spices on the top shelf. Lower table part was called a* **cabinet table,** *with bin drawers. Unidentified English illustration, c.1900-1910.* **$250-$500+**

Cabinet Restoration — Philip D. Kennedy, 9256 Holyoke Ct., Indianapolis, IN 46268, wrote the only book on Hoosier-type cabinets. He also restores them and makes and sells replacement parts. Phyllis Kennedy Hardware, Inc., has a $3 catalog of flour bins, hinges, sifters and sugar and sifter bowls made from the old dies. Always use SASE when writing for information about these parts.

Cabinet table, elm with maple top, cast iron handles, zinc bin drawer at bottom, 3 drawers at left, door on right half reveals 2 shelves, paneled sides, McDougal's "Plainview," from Montgomery Ward catalog, 2 feet 8" H x 4 feet 4" L x 2 feet 4" deep, c.1895. When the bins' curved fronts show, a popular name for these tables is <u>possum belly</u> tables; the name also applies to bin tables with cabinets above. **$250-$350**

Cabinets or chests for spice — See Chapter VII

Cupboard, also called a <u>pantry cupboard</u>, wall hung, primitive pine, stripped, alas, of original paint, hence much lower in value. It is possibly English — countless (except by U.S. Customs) container loads of stripped pine "country" pieces are being brought over each year. American, Scandinavian or English, 19th C. **$150-$475**

XVII-7. Combination cabinet tables. *All from a 1909 supplier's catalog. (L) to (R) from top:* **(1)** *"Ever Ready Table and Shelf." Overall it's 66" H; table 28-1/2" H x 42" x 26" deep. Bass or cottonwood, light or dark finish. Close to identical to one in previous picture, although that one is supposed to be English.* **(2)** *"Locker," of oak, with base consisting of one tin-lined tilting bin, 2 drawers, 2 pull-out molding boards, 2 compartments. 83" H overall, "golden oak" finish.* **(3)** *"Triumph," with more drawers than the others, glass-fronted cupboard, 81" H overall. Bass or cottonwood, light or dark finish.* **(4)** *"Winner," of oak, sanded table top, tilting 100-lb flour bin with tin lining, glass & wood-panelled cupboard doors, 83" H x 48" W.* **(5)** *"Handy," for china, glass, cutlery, linens, but with no work surface. 79" H.* **(6)** *"Utility," with all sizes of drawers, many features not in any others, including drawers on side, and removable extension boards "for many purposes." Oak, in "golden oak" finish. 75-1/2" H x 42" W. Originally this was the most expensive at $17.25; others ranged from $6.95 to $16.80. Albert Pick catalog, 1909.* **$200-$800+**

Cupboard, brown painted wood, top has crested back & side board and a pair of drawers with turned wood knobs, overhanging lower part by a little over an inch, scalloped apron, very short feet, 2 doors with 2 tins each in punctured star-in-circle design, West VA, 19th C. **$1500+**

Cupboard, cherry in original finish, stepback consisting of a blanket chest or bin with hinged board lid on bottom, 2-shelf cupboard above with molded cornice, 2 doors with 3 punctured tins each door, footed basket with droopy flowers design, PA (?), 19th C. **$3500+**

XVII-8. "Hoosier cabinet," *this one really mfd. by Hoosier. Called by them their "Thirty-Six-Inch Hoosier." 71-1/2" H x 37" W, finished in white enamel, or available in "light golden oak." "Equipment includes white <u>Porceliron</u> top; mouse-proof construction; ant-proof casters; shaker flour sifter; 9-piece glassware set; package rack on lower door; shallow utensil tray suspended from work-table." Has a meat grinder clamped to work surface, and you can see the spice rack on upper right door. Hoosier Mfg. Co., Newcastle, IN, 1922 catalog. Value range is for unrefinished white original finish, which is not as highly prized as the wood.* **$250-$500+**

XVII-9. Cabinet. *"I-XL" Co., Goshen, IN. All white enameled, nickeled hardware, "drop roll curtain" in middle right section. Glass jar equipment includes "swinging sugar bin with metal cap and cut-off, one coffee, one tea, and five spice jars." Tilting metal sifter flour bin with glass front. Sliding top of "polished metal or white porcelain." "Special bracket and block for food grinder." Sliding bread board, metal-lined drawers. 70" H x 40" W. Also available in golden oak finish. From c.1916 catalog. NOTE classy leaded glass panels, resembling house fenestration of the time.* **$450-$650**

Cupboard, red painted walnut (?) with molded cornice, 2 top doors glazed with 6 panes each, 2 drawers in middle with wooden knobs, scalloped apron & bracket feet, 2 lower doors with punctured tins painted green, American, 94" H x 60" W, 19th C. **$3200+**

Cupboard, red painted wood, tall, scalloped apron in front and sides almost to floor, 2 tall doors with 4 punctured tins each door, plus 4 tins on each side, flat board top, punctured design is X with 2 hearts and 2 diamonds filling in spaces between the crossed lines, Ohio (?), 60" H x 42" W x 17" D, 19th C. Dealers Robb and Alice Guss, Youngsville, NY, sold this in 1984. Price range mine. **$3000+**

Cupboard, stepback, of curly cherry — highly figured wood, bottom has scalloped apron, 2 doors, long drawer below counter top, above has molded cornice, 2 doors with 3 punctured tins each, simple concentric curved lines of quarter circles, made by John Richey, Hammersville, OH, 19th C. Sold at Garth's, Nov. 1983, at the Ron Klapmeir Sale, for $2300. Now? **$3000+**

Cupboard, walnut, 2 pieces, 12 small glass windows & 3 spice drawers of tiger maple in top, 3 tiger maple drawers for cutlery in 2-door base, Pennsylvania Dutch, 19th C. **$2000+**

Cupboard or meat safe, hung from beam, tan painted wood frame has short feet, but at top the sides extend like upside down legs, each having a hole for bolting to a beam, 2 shelves, 4 tins with slits in 10 concentric circles, corners with odd X marks, Ohio, mid 19th C. to 3rd quarter. **$800+**

Dry sink, child-size but well-made, wood with cupboard underneath with 2 doors with knobs, sea green paint inside sink, counter & splash board, brown & ochre grain-painted outside, American, 20" H x 22" W, c.1860s. **$450+**

Dry sink, painted pine, zinc lining, one drawer, cupboard below with 2 doors, prob. American, 19th C. Value ranges widely due to paint color & appearance, style, details such as drainboard and drawer, origin and size. Even a gnawed rathole may add value for some collectors. (Such as moi.) **$250-$1500**

XVII-10. Barrel chair. *"Homemade easy chair," reads heading in American Agriculturist, 3/1865. Quite possibly not for the kitchen, but it's made from "a good flour barrel," with a few staves cut away. "A small opening or door can be made under the seat, which will furnish a convenient work box." The article advises nailing the hoops to each stave before commencing the making of such a chair! Value would depend on age of original barrel, its patina or finish, skill of making, and possibly the upholstered cushion.* **$90-$250**

XVII-12. Hutch table. *Trestle-footed (with a foot variation shown next to it), with 3-board round top. Pin goes all the way across (shown in black here). Other hutch tables have other types of legs or feet, including, most rarely, four turned legs. They also have square, oblong or oval tops, though most are round. Some have storage in the seat, accessible through drawer or lifting lid. Many have two much shorter pivoting pins that don't go all the way across. The rarest, and oldest, were made from such huge trees that a single board, or at most two, was wide enough to make even a 50" top. Late 18th or very early 19th C.* **$2000-$10,000+**

XVII-11. Rocking chair patents. (L) *"Fly Fan and Rocking Chair" pat'd in 1899, by James T. Cowan, Boston, MA. Patent #622,123.* **(R)** *"Ventilating Rocking Chair," pat'd 11/24/1857, by D. Kahnweiler, Wilmington, DE. #18,696. Official Gazette. A new combination rocking chair & fan was patented about every seven years. Other combos included rocking chairs with churns, cradles and even one that was also a trunk, and one that played music. The one on the left was actually made — I don't know how many were made, but it's safe to say they're scarce.* **$300+**

XVII-13. "A Useful Piece of Furniture." *"In many rural households, the space allotted to the kitchen is often cramped and narrowed too much. A piece of kitchen furniture that will answer three distinct purposes is a great convenience. Here is one that is at once a settee, trunk, and an ironing table or bake board. There is a box or trunk, in which one may stow away many things that usually lie about, having no special place otherwise. The lid of this trunk forms the seat of the settee. The ends are raised up, forming the arms. The back of it is pivoted upon one side of the ends, and when it is turned down it forms a table. When it is turned down, it is held in place by two small hooks." American Agriculturist, 11/1874.* **$250-$1000**

XVII-14. Kitchen lamps. (L) *The designation "kitchen lamp" is not commonly found in old ads, but the lamp at left, of an old type, was so named. The ad read "Tin kitchen lamps. Strong, neat, well made, durable. Made by Geuder & Paeschke Mfg. Co. Tin Wares, Milwaukee, Wis." The Metal Worker, 1/9/1892. Note horizontal cylindrical reservoir for fuel, with star on end, and the reflector that would put more light where it was needed. It could be set down on a work surface, even a shelf or windowsill, or hung on wall where needed.* **(R)** *"Jaxon" reflector lamp, "made from one piece of 7-gauge steel wire very strong and springy, complete with 7-inch bright tin reflector and 4-1/2-inch front, made for No. 2 burner. New and a ready seller." In mail order catalog of Butler Brothers, 1899.* **$40-$135**

XVII-17. "Wooden Meat Screen, *lined with tin." Trestle feet with what appear to be casters. Note iron handle on right side for pulling it. The measurement is given as 3' 9", but whether that is height or length I don't know. London dealers William S. Adams & Son, "Outfitters for Kitchens," advertised this in small booklet called Francatelli's Cook's Guide Advertiser, c.1860-61.*

XVII-15. Suspension lamps, *suitable for many locations, including a kitchen.* **(L)** *"'Pittsburgh' store or hall lamp, absolutely non-explosive. Burns over 10 hours without refilling." 20" diameter tin shade.* **(R)** *"'Banner' store lamp, with extra feeder wick and oil drip cup on inside of tube to carry any overflow back to the wick. 20" tin shade, No. 3 burner, font wick and chimney." The second would have been nice for a kitchen, but probably only very rarely used for one, at least in a private home. Both also in Butler Brothers catalog, 1899.* **$85-$150**

XVII-18. "Milk Shelves for the Kitchen." *"In many farm-houses the kitchen is obliged to ... serve as the dairy, in which the milk is set, and the cream is kept, especially in the winter, when it is the warmest spot in the house. There is nothing objectionable in this, if the kitchen is kept scrupulously clean, and well ventilated. But a well-contrived cupboard, kept specially for the milk and cream, where they may be safe from dust and drafts, and yet have proper ventilation, will be a great advantage." This one is six-sided, and "wide enough to hold two ten-quart pans across it, or four upon each shelf. This will be nearly or quite 3 feet outside measure. This will be ample for winter use, where ten cows are kept." There's a center post that turns, having a pointed bottom that fits into a small socket in which is put some "fine chips of soap, or a little powdered black lead." Five round shelves are fixed to it. Under the shelves, which are rather close together, is space for two "cream crocks," of stoneware. American Agriculturist, 12/1875.*

XVII-16. Meat safe. *Wood and wire, "to protect food from mice, insects, &c." Wood with wire gauze screens. No. 79 in list of kitchen requisites given in* American Home Cook Book, *by an American Lady. NYC: Dick & Fitzgerald, 1854. This would probably have almost no value unless something interesting had been done to the surface (carving or painting), or unless the iron wire gauze had rusted out and been replaced by homemade punctured tins, which may or may not have predated metal screening.*

XVII-19. Meat safe. *Wood with wire screening. L. H. Mace catalog, 1880s. Value would depend on appearance & finish.* **$100-$300**

Dry sink, pine with cast iron well liner, traces of old gray paint, very plain & handsome, 19th C. The iron liner is unusual; most are zinc or tin or painted wood. **$700+**

Dry sink, wood painted olive drab underneath, sink painted white inside, original tacked-on sink lining, probably metal, probably zinc, now missing, small drawer to right for scouring materials, square drawer knob replaced, American, prob. PA, 43-3/4" W, c.1860s or 1870s. **$1000+**

Dry sink & cupboard, beautiful glowing old red paint, zinc sink, compartment with lid at left of sink for cleaning materials, cupboard was built-in & upper shelves have no back, taken out of an old Easton, PA home, 9 feet high, 19 th or very early 20th C. Dealers Jack and Vicky Pilarski had this superb piece. Wish I'd bought it! **$3500+**

Flour bins — See Chapter VII (Storage and Containers)

Hutch — The "hutch" in hutch cupboard is probably from words in Middle English and Latin that mean "care, keeping, guard" and would therefore be related to a hutch in the sense of a storage chest or coffer, or a "box or box-like pen or 'house' in which an animal is confined." *Oxford English Dictionary,* or a hutch as a kneading trough for dough *op cit.* "Hutch" in hutch table is probably from other words, and is related to what the *OED* calls an "obsolete phonetic variant of **hulch** . . . meaning hunched or humped, as in 'hutch back.' " When the tabletop of a hutch table is in its vertical position, the already anthromorphic shape of the bench or chair underneath takes on a round-shouldered, even "hunch-backed" appearance.

Huck — Mountain or Piedmont Virginians say to this day "huck," as in "huck table" or "huck chair."

Hanging cupboard, old green paint over pine, 3 shelves, one door, simple iron latch, about 37" H x 26" W x 8" deep, Maine, 19th C. **$550+**

Hanging cupboard, pine with grayish blue old paint, one simple paneled door, no molding, brass keyhole probably adapted from another piece of furniture, simple door latch, American c.1830s to 1850s. **$575+**

Hanging cupboard, simple pine butt joints, blue milk paint, 2 door, 2 shelves, prob. PA, European heritage, 1870s or 1880s. **$450+**

XVII-20. "Insect-proof Closet & Safe" patent. *Pat'd 8/30/1881, by Charles H. Larrabee, Napa City, CA, assignor to Hamilton W. Crabb, same place. Bottom drawer serves as a "water-containing tank." Holes served to circulate air from shelf to shelf.* Official Gazette. **$100-$200**

Hutch table, 2-plank top, red over old blue paint, rosehead nails and turned pegs, butterfly cleats on underside hold planks together. Tabletop made to be lifted into upright position to provide a seat when not serving as a table. Really convertible furniture! American, 37-1/2" diameter, this one c.1830s, but the form is much older. **$5500+**

XVII-21. Sideboard & provision safe. *Wood (probably poplar) with punctured tin panels for decoration & ventilation. Sideboard is 54" H x 37" W x 14" deep. "Tin provision safe" is 57" H x 30" W x 14-1/2" deep. Bagby & Rivers, Baltimore, 1882 catalog. Baltimore, by the way, is still famous for painted window & door house screens, usually a form of rural landscape. These paintings do not obstruct the vision from the inside looking out, but serve both to decorate the outside, and to a small extent, make less visible the interior. I have never seen a pie safe with painted screening in its doors or sides. However, the hardware company, John Duer & Sons of Baltimore, offered two interesting things in their 1878 catalog: (1) "wire cloth" with a printed design of a stylized 4-petal flower surrounded by an abstract pattern resembling a basketweave. Offered in "green, or plain colors," and (2) "punched tin," 10" x 14", in the "Baltimore pattern," similar to #7 shown in picture XVII-24, except that it has 3 lobes on each side. Duer was the "Sole Manufacturers of this pattern." The pattern shown in these Bagby & Rivers cabinets looks quite similar also, except the diamond is more accentuated.* **$400-$1000**

XVII-22. Pie safe. *It is not upside down; it's meant to be bolted or hung from rafters. Painted wood case with punctured tins on all four sides, larger than most. Three shelves inside. Front door has flower-stars in the corners to match the center; the sides have fan-shaped, rayed spandrels in the corners. 34" H x 36" W x 22" deep. Ex-collection of Earl F. & Ada F. Robacker, auctioned by T. Glenn Horst, Horst Auctions, Farmersville, Lancaster County, PA, on 6/23-24/1989. Price realized was very low — $475, but apparently other examples of this safe exist.* **$450-$650**

Hutch table, pine & maple in original red stain, circular top above bench base, New England, 27" H x 45-1/4" diameter top, late 18th C. **$5000+**

Jam cupboard, bootjack ends, 5 shelves with 2 doors, stripped exterior, alas, but possibly original light blue inside, American, 50" H, turn of century. **$700+**

Kitchen cabinet — See Hoosier-type cabinets, above

Kitchen tables — See cupboard table; also table

Lamp, tin & glass, wall mounted reflector oil lamp, American, 1860s-1870s. We tend to overlook lamps for the kitchen; ones like this were mounted above work tables, sink, and cook stove. Some have mirrored reflectors. **$45-$70**

Lamps, nickeled brass, double light, reflectors painted white inside, outside enameled dark green, reflector angled light down onto stove, and could be set on the hob shelves, Boston, MA (?), 18" H, c.1840s. **$200-$250+**

Meat safe, "a back porch piece" according to dealer, green painted wood, tall legs, 18 punctured tins in geometric design with rough side out, bottom of legs dipped in tar for setting in pans of water to keep ants out, brass catch on door, once had keyhole, iron catch inside, from New Berne, Craven County, NC, 71-1/2" H x 36-1/2" W x 26-1/2" deep, c.1830s to 1860. **$3000-$3500**

Meat safe hook, cast iron, long screw for beam or ceiling with curvy hook at bottom & cup in middle for bug-deterring water (ever see a roach that couldn't swim an inch?), patented by Joseph C. Moulton as a "suspension hook & insect insulator," Fitchburg, MA, pat'd Oct. 28, 1859. You know what a cup hook looks like? That little piece that fits against the wood with the hook coming out of it? That's what this looks like, only much larger, and it's iron. **$15-$35**

Milk cupboard, also called a milk or cheese safe, tall wooden case, square top, louvred sides and door, lined with thin muslin, central shaft or axle, around which revolve the 8 round shelves, for holding milk pans, meat or other food needing a safe, pat'd by E. H. Nash, Westport, CT, about 50" H x 22" square, pat'd July 27, 1858. **$250-$450**

Milk cupboard, wood with original mustard color paint, 6 shelves, open back & front for air circulation, prob. PA-European heritage, 70" H, 19th C. **$1700-$2500**

Milking stool, cast iron, 3 sproingy insect-like legs, doughnut seat with big hole in center, "E. A. Kaestner Co.," Baltimore, MD, 12" H, 19th or early 20th C. **$40-$60**

Pie safe, almost Biedermeier or Empire in form, with paneled pilasters flanking the 2 doors, 2 drawers above, with keyholes, very short round feet, poss. cut down, 4 tins with punctured pattern of sort of fattened & straightened-out fylfot (pinwheels) & triangular corner spandrels, Southwest VA or East TN, mid 19th C. **$1400-$2200**

Pie safe, black painted wood, 2 drawers, 2 three tin doors with punctured 8-point stars & quarter-round spandrels in corners, latches on both doors, stenciled inside one drawer "J. Zitzer & Son, Furniture Dealer & Undertaker," West Alexandria, OH, late 19th C. **$1000-$1500**

Pie safe, folding, oak with wire screening, sides fold in half, patented but no legible mark, American, late 19th C. Aaron Osborne, of Georgetown, CT, patented this July 5, 1881, "as a new article of manufacture, a provision-safe having its sides hinged, and adapted to fold together without being detached one from the other . . . in combination with a collapsible body . . . a board or stretcher adapted to fit within the body and to hold the same in an expanded condition. . . ." An 1891 *Ladies Home Journal* ad reads: "Mother wants it. Wright's Kitchen Safe, Refrigerator and dumb Waiter combined or separate. Can be instantly lowered into cellar from any part of room floor. — Cochran Safe Co., Cochran, IN." **$650-$900**

Pie safe, green painted wood, 12 tins, 3 on each side, 3 on both doors, punctured holes & slits, depicting footed bowls with tulips, from MD (?), 42-3/4" W, c.1860s. **$1500-$2000**

Pie safe, low counter height cupboard, short bracket feet, one shelf, 2 doors with single oblong punctured tin in each door, double repeat pattern of 6-point flower in circle with 6 bull's eyes in each door, PA, 40" H x 54" W, mid to late 19th C. **$1200-$1500**

Pie safe, painted wood, 8 tins, 2 on each side, 2 in each door, long drawer at bottom, long straight legs, simple punctured geometric design, marked "John M. Smythe Co.," Chicago, IL, turn of century. **$600-$950**

Pie safe, painted wood case in dark greenish black, scalloped apron, interesting long legs with 2 turned bands slightly thicker than legs, flat top, one central door with odd old hardware, screen & mesh panel openings framed with molding — 6 in door, 3 flanking each side of door, almost looks like some kind of hutch or bird cage, but no place for feeding the animals, American, 52" H x 39-1/2" W x 17-1/2" D, mid 19th C. NYC's Ricco-Johnson Gallery, which often comes up with interesting folk art pieces, had this for sale in early 1984. Value range is mine, and it's based on the strong folk art appeal of this piece. **$4500-$5500**

Pie safe, painted wood frame, hangs from beams — the corner pieces project above the top about 5", and have fairly large holes so that they'd be easy to lift up onto nails driven in the beams, sides & front with slit pierced tin panels, single door, 5-point stars or 6-point petals within circles, very free & graphic, perhaps Lancaster, PA, mid 19th C. **$900-$1400**

Pie safe, pine, 12 panels of punctured tin in front & sides, unexceptional concentric circles, etc., geometric pattern, 2 doors, American, 58" H x 37" W, late 19th C or early 20th C. **$475-$750**

Wythe or wythout — "American" pie safes can often be identified by region thanks to recent research. (For example: Roddy Moore's well-illustrated "Wythe County, Virginia, punched tin: its influence and imitators," *The Magazine ANTIQUES,* Sept. 1984). I can't make a more complete study myself, and urge you to read everything you can before plunking down big money. Fine Wythe County safes deserve praise, and Moore's article gave them added cachet, translating to much increased prices. An **urn** of the type frequently seen in Wythe County pieces has a nice rounded bowl body, flared stem, pedestal base and two vertical handles, and is sometimes called a chalice. I recently saw a graphite drawing of what I would have thought was a cast iron or stone urn, with several doves drinking from it or flying about it, and the dealer described it as "doves and chalice," which somehow seems to have a much more religious context than a simple garden scene with an "urn" would have.

Pie safe, pine, 12 panels of punctured tins, front & sides, stars & crescent moons, 2 door, American, 55" H, late 19th C. **$800-$1200**

Pie safe, pine, 3 punctured tin panels on each side & 3 panels on both front doors, whirligig design with quarter-circle spandrels (designs filling each corner of tins), 3 shelves, clean & not refinished, 4 legs all in good condition at bottom, not rat-chewed or water-rotted, American, 47" H, mid to late 19th C. **$1000-$1500+**

Pie safe, pine, 6 punctured tins, star designs on doors only, wood on sides, 4 very long legs, 2 shelves, American, 50" H, mid to late 19th C. **$650-$850**

Pie safe, red painted wood, 12 tins, 3 on each side, 3 on both doors, punctured petaled-flower design adapted to fit rectangular shape (sometimes called a butterfly pattern), white porcelain knobs (could be original or not), southern IL, mid 19th C. **$1200-$1800**

To Get Rid of Ants — Wash the shelves with salt and water; sprinkle salt in their paths. To keep them out of safes: Set the legs of the safe on tin cups; keep the cups filled with water." Mrs. A. P. Hill, *Mrs. Hill's New Family Receipt Book,* NY: 1867, 1870. "If ants are troublesome, set legs in cups of water." Catherine Beecher & Harriet Beecher Stowe, *American Woman's Home,* 1869. (See the meat safe hook above.)

Pie safe, red-stained sycamore & maple, straight case with medium-length legs, long single drawer at bottom, overhanging board top, 2 interesting doors, each with 3 punctured tins in design of clock face with Arabic numerals & curved horn, the time reading 12 minutes to 12 on each one, crescent moons in corners, dealers have called such designs **"New Year" tins**, maybe OH, late 19th or early 20th C. Dealers Tim & Barb Martien, Western Reserve Antiques, Burton, OH, had this for sale in 1984. Price range mine.   **$2500-$3200**

Pie safe, red stained wood, turned feet but straight case and board top, 2 large doors with single tin panel each, punctured with characteristic urn with ear handles & tall multi-stemmed tulip design, star spandrels in corners, side panels punctured too, southwestern VA, classic Wythe County design, mid 19th C.   **$1700-$2500+**

Pie safe, refinished wood, alas, straight-sided case with turned feet, flat board top, 2 large doors with single large tin on each, punctured as if with 4 panels each, centered pinwheels (fylfot), round spandrels in corners, keyhole in door, Wythe County, VA, 54" W, late 19th C. Refinished wood reduces value of pie safes.   **$800-$1200+**

Pie safe, simple wooden case with straight medium-length legs, molded top, fancy scalloped apron or skirt, 2 doors, each with 2 punctured tins, design an 8-petaled flower within circle, 2 shelves, 2 drawers at top with wooden knobs, PA (?), early to mid 19th C.   **$1250-$1500**

Pie safe, tall elegant piece, dark varnish, with molded cornice, 2 doors, each with one square tin in center with punctured rectangular tins above & below, bull's eye (one in square, 2 in rectangles) framed with quarter- & half-round spandrels, plus 6 narrow oblong punctured tins in panels flanking doors, in ad of Georgia dealer, perhaps GA provenance, about 80" to 90" H, late 19th C.   **$1600-$2000**

Reproduction or Fake Tins — Beware the faked country-look tins. An old pine safe can be stripped of its old tins, then be gussied up with distressed tin pierced with valuable eagle, animal, flag, human forms. I saw such a one the summer of 1987 in Charlottesville. The body was old, nice long legs and small 2-shelf box, with 4 front panels and 2 on each side. The tins had coffee cups, forks, spoons, dogs, birds, flowers . . . just too too TOO. Over it all was a layer of what looked like old blue milk paint, scratched and distressed. The price of $1800 was high enough to almost seem OK, but too low if this were for real. You must develop a sixth sense about the look of the tins. Newly made punctured tins have been used to make an old all-wood cupboard into a more desirable pie safe; they have also been used to replace very simple designs with designs that seem folk arty and unique. Beware especially of any pie safe with figural, zoomorphic or pictorial tins, such as men in stovepipe hats, forks and spoons, cows, pigs, dogs and eagles. Know your dealer, ask about provenance, inspect tins carefully on both sides with magnifying glass. For people who want to make

their modern kitchen cupboards into mini pie safes, new punctured tin panels may save some trouble. See ads in "Miscellaneous Specialty Items" section of *Antique Trader Weekly.*

Pie safe, tall simple wood case, flat board top, straight legs, long drawer across top, 2 doors, each with 3 tins, punctured design of a footed sugar bowl with ear handles & domed lid with large round finial & footed cream jug, both with concentric rings forming body, the decoration making you think this might be a cupboard for dairy products, a cheese or butter safe, found in Arkansas, late 19th or early 20th C. Dealer Joan Gould, Summer Kitchen Antiques of Little Rock, said another in this pattern was found in Arkansas. At $595 in 1984, it seemed way under the money.   **$1200-$1750**

Butter cupboards — According to Carl W. Drepperd's *A Dictionary of American Antiques,* the "butter cupboard," dating to fifteenth-century England or the Continent, was for storing butter or cheese. Made entirely of oak (or other woods), they had pierced doors for air circulation. In *Primer of American Antiques,* Drepperd said that pie safes or butter cupboards were known in seventeenth-century America, and probably were first offered as a "commercial product" in the 1880s. Related are the **meat safe** or **meat keep**, and the **gard-manger**. An antique store in NYC advertised in 1993 a nineteenth-century **"Chinese Provincial"** kitchen **cabinet** of "pine." Just over 6 feet high, it stands on 4 long legs, and has an airy compartment with carved fretwork doors; three drawers above that; and another compartment with fretwork doors. It's strange to see "our" pie safes in another guise!

"A closet, called a safe, for keeping food in the cellar, is an important convenience for keeping meat, milk, bread and various articles in daily use." Mrs. Cornelius, *The Young Housekeepers Friend, or, A Guide to Domestic Economy & Comfort,* Boston & NY: 1846.

Pie safe, varnished pine, straight board top, straight simple case & medium length legs, single drawer below cupboard, 2 doors with 3 punctured tins, design of each is a 5-point star within circle, plus 4 smaller stars around circle, smallest star within big star, with 3 straight rows of holes for border, Colorado, 55-1/8" H, c.1875. Described from picture of one in collection of the State Historical Society of Colorado. The value range is mine, not the Society's.   **$1200-$1500**

Pie safe, walnut, 12 tins with tulip & vase (or basket) design, 2 shelves, 2 drawers, short turned wooden legs, not refinished but cleaned up, simple iron latch, American, poss. PA (?), 54" H, mid 19th C. Walnut is a cachet wood.   **$1750-$2500+**

Pie safe, walnut & poplar, straight case with flat board top, shortish straight legs, long dovetailed drawer across top, 2 three tin doors, punctured design of many petaled flower or butterfly, in horizontal rectangles, poss. from the South, or IL, mid 19th C.   **$1500-$2200**

Pie safe, wood with traces of green paint, 2 shelves above double drawers, 2 doors with 3 punctured tin panels, base constructed of cutout boards instead of legs, American, 53" H x 40" W, mid to late 19th C.   **$800+**

"Punched" & "Punctured" — The adjective "punched" is slightly misleading. Pie safes have punctured holes in their "punched tins"; that is, the holes were punched [verb] all the way through. I feel there is a need to differentiate between punched and punctured because the word punched is used specifically to describe a certain kind of tinsmith's decorative work, usually on coffee pots, where a punch [the tool] has been used to make a raised or pimply mark that could be used to make a textured design. A grater (of tin or brass, for example) can have both punctured holes and pierced holes or perforations. The latter two do not have the rough, ragged edge of a punctured hole. The tools used to punch and to puncture are different in that the former are used to make a mark and have a flattened or rounded tip, perhaps even one cast with a letter or symbol or other mark, and the latter must have a point sharp enough to go through the metal. Dealers and authors of auction catalogs and articles describe the tins in pie safes as "punched." They also use "punched" when describing a kind of tin ware decoration where a punch is used to make a dimple or tiny bump. I will fly in the face of common and widely accepted usage and use the slightly clumsy "punctured" in this book. I'm not really being stubborn about this, though I expect to get some pooh-pooh reaction. Part of my reason is based on the ease of retrieving exact information when searching the computer; part of it is to make clear what I mean, with no further explanation needed. I do not expect to change common usage, nor do I want you to think that only an ignoramus would say "punched tins."

NOTE: For more on the tins, see short article below.

PIE SAFE TIN DESIGNS
Filling Empty Rectangles With Patterns

The following pictures show four common design categories used for punctured pie safe tins, including simple geometrics, stars, petaled-flower-like shapes and fylfot (pinwheels). These four form a large proportion of tin designs, but this short overview describes only a couple dozen examples.

I have also included a single category of figurals — urn-and-flower designs (XVII-36) — although many more figurals are to be found, including horsemen, chickens, and cups and saucers. The urn-and-flowers are included because of Wytheville-area safes, which are at the time of writing the only ones to have been written about in a scholarly way (Roddy Moore, "Wythe County, Virginia, punched tin: its influence and imitators," *The Magazine ANTIQUES*, 9/1984), and they are advertised rather frequently.

Before I began collecting and arranging pictures by pattern type, I theorized that the obvious similarities to other repeating geometric patterns were meaningful rather than coincidental, even to the extent that comparison would prove that pie safe tin punchers copied their designs from something previously existing. I assumed that such post hoc likenesses would become especially evident when pie safe designs were compared with quilts and jacquard coverlets. I thought that I would

be able therefore to offer names for the designs, based on established quilt design names.

This turned out to be impossible, except in the most simplistic way, matching a star to a star, for example. I was surprised and pleased to find close similarities between stitch-like slits and holes and quilting stitches (which subtly overlay more easily visible pieces, patches or appliqués, and hold batting or lining in place) — especially in fan and petal motifs.

Although both quilters and tin-punchers were concerned with filling up squares or rectangles with pattern, the methods involved in ventilating a sheet of tin and making a quilt are very different. Tin-punchers break up the surface of a square or oblong blank with rounded or angular shapes defined by holes or slits. Quilters assemble a whole by fitting cut shapes, most of which are straight-edged and angular, together.

The elements of geometric designs include circles, diamonds, triangles, squares and lines, which may be connected or not (i.e., may be parallel or divergent/convergent, such as rays). Petals and pie wedges are formed by combining triangles and circles. All geometric designs, and parts of figural ones, can be laid out with tools no more complex than a pair of dividers, probably found in nearly every nineteenth-century homeowner's toolbox, a straight-edge of some kind, and a scribe or pencil. Fan-shaped spandrels filling the corners of so many tins are easy to do with a compass or dividers. One point is placed at the corner, the other leg is adjusted, and a curve is lightly scratched onto the tin, to be traced with holes.

The several tins of one pie safe may be so alike that you know a tracing of some kind was done. One way would be with a set of cutout tin templates like those for making identical multiple quilt pieces. Another way would be to use heavy paper, rubbed with powdered graphite on the side against the tin, with the design on top traced again and again. With some pie safes, although each tin has the same overall design, all were executed individually, and have obvious differences in measurement or placement.

Probably a majority of geometric designs are a consequence of the tools used and the given shape of the tins, as well as the need to make the tin function as a ventilated screen. For corroborating evidence, look at wood-frame footwarmers with tin sides punctured for ventilation. A motif vocabulary of 5-, 6- or 8-point stars, hearts and stylized geometric flowers was available to most people, no matter whether they were making blanket chests, fraktur, candlewick spreads, pie safes or quilts, but each motif may or may not have any special meaning for its user. In other words, it may be subjective and hence figural, or it may be a pleasing gap-filler. A star may be patriotic or heavenly, or it may be there because it could be made to fit an empty space, or simply because it was easy to do by means of a tool. Not every artisan is an "artist" also.

Generally speaking, most pie safe tin designs, like patterns filling any empty rectangles or squares, are not culture-specific, but are found on ancient tiles, pattern glass, Amerindian as well as Persian rugs, and architectural friezes from Abyssinia to China.

XVII-23. "Perforated plate for kitchen-safes" patent. *Pat'd 11/11/1884, by George W. Knapp, Baltimore, MD. No. 307,959. Knapp's claim was for "The method of ornamenting perforated plates for safes, consisting in first applying a colored design to a surface of the plate, and then making the ventilating-perforations with respect to the features of the said colored design, and producing on the same surface a burr projecting about each perforation, so located as to avoid marring the said colored design."* Official Gazette. *(I've seen only one pie safe with the punctured tins painted in other than the same or contrasting color to the case — not that the idea is odd. That was Pl. VIII, a pie safe from Tennessee, in the 1984 article by Roderick Moore,* ANTIQUES *magazine.) If it were ever made, value dependent on patina and original polychromed tins.* **$500-$900+**

It is arguable that some pie safe tin designs are expanded doodles! Flipping through my old high school notebooks, I see page corners and blank spaces filled with pattern-making dots, lines, triangles, circles, fans, tendrils and even fylfot-like squiggles.

The more figural designs *are* in a way culture-specific, although more than one culture may claim such figures as hearts, tulips, lilies, grapes, urns, horses, etc., and probably would assign different symbolic meaning to them (just as they do to the simpler geometrics).

By conducting this small survey and studying quilt books throughout, I've learned that when comparing different classes of objects, similarity of final appearance does not prove similitude of intent or technique. Patterns of some pie safe tins and some quilts may be strikingly similar when the two are viewed together, but it's sophistry to therefore assume that one was a model and the other a copy. In-

stead, it seems more nearly true to say that all decorative arts draw on a large but nevertheless finite "dictionary" of design elements.

NOTE: All drawings here are of pie safe tins, and were done by me as photo-tracings or from actual safes. The former are generally more accurate, although often the perspective is very slightly skewed off from a perfect rectangle, and occasionally the photo may have misled me with small shadows or scratches. I've used dashes (- ===) for slits or slots, and dots, big or little (• :::::) for nail holes or other basically round holes. An X represents crossed slits in the original. All dealer or collector sources are noted in individual captions.

Portable pantries — See Chapter VII

XVII-24. Pie Safe Tins: Simple Geometrics. *Four of these are square diamonds with circle or fan spandrels in the corner. Two have a petaled or rayed round center medallion, one with fan spandrels, one inside a diamond with half-rounds forming a sort of lovers' knot. One has a large X with hearts & diamonds. The last shows two tins, the one above is completely drawn, the lower tin is only half-drawn, to show how 2 adjacent tins may make corner quarter-rounds into half-rounds. Each tin is credited to its dealer or owner with number of tins the particular safe has in front in parentheses; then there's a note about construction feature, and where the ad appeared. From (L) to (R), top row then bottom.* **(A)** *Calico Cat Antiques, Ann & Dick Wardrop, Wexford, PA, (8), shaped apron, [Ohio]* Antique Review, *5/1990.* **(B)** *Loy's Auction Sales, Kernersville, NC, Jean Craddock photo, (4), 2 drawers above doors,* AntiqueWeek, *3/27/1989.* **(C)** *Vicki & Bruce Waasdorp, Clarence, NY, (6), long drawer below doors, long legs,* New York-Pennsylvania Collector, *11/1989.* **(D)** *Robb & Alice Guss, Youngsville, NY, (8), cupboard has shaped apron, very short legs,* Antiques & Arts Weekly, *7/20/1984.* **(E)** *In "Antiques in Dutchland," by Earl & Ada Robacker,* Pennsylvania Folklife, *Fall 1961. (6), shallow drawer beneath doors, long legs.* **(F)** *Made by John Richey of Hammersville, OH, Garth's Auctions, Inc., Delaware, OH, Ron Klapmeir Sale Plus Additions, 11/25-26/1988, (6), step back cupboard with tins for upper doors,* Ohio Antique Review, *1/1984.* **(G)** *Sheppheards, Schellsburg, PA, (6), drawer below doors, [Ohio]* Antique Review, *10/1990.* **(H)** *Collection of John Little Jr., Fig. 23 in article by Roddy Moore, from Sullivan County, TN, (8), Empire style 1840-60 cupboard with four tins on both of two doors in lower part of cupboard. A full circle is formed in the center of each door by the conjunction of four spandrels. The tins are not divided by wood molding or framework. The elongated hexagonal design in the center of each of the 8 tins are marked in the sort of diapered, or diamond, pattern formed with parallel lines of holes. This was a very popular filler pattern for cut glass and later pressed glass. The magazine* ANTIQUES, *9/1984.*

XVII-25. Pie Safe Tins: Stars. *Three of these feature 5-point stars; two are 6-point stars; one has 8 points. In all but one, the star is encircled, and in the other the spandrels are quartered circles and the interior pattern of small slits was apparently done in a circular fashion. The strangest design is the one with a rayed sunburst in the center of the big star, which is surrounded by kite-like shapes with crosses. (L) to (R) from top:* **(A)** *Tim Martien, Burton, OH, (4), Odd cupboard/safe with top half having 2 doors with the tins, divided from lower half by drawer. Lower half has wood paneled doors. Each side has 4 stacked tins over single wood panel. Thought to be from Tennessee. [Ohio]* Antique Review, *clipping not dated.* **(B)** *Antique Associates, at West Townsend & Joslin Tavern (group shop), (8), 70" H cupboard, 4 over 4, with long drawer in middle, between 2 sets of doors.* New York-Pennsylvania Collector, *5/1990.* **(C)** *Muleskinner, Clarence, NY, (6), long drawer under 2 doors.* Maine Antique Digest, *8/1989.* **(D)** *Collection State Historical Society of Colorado, (6), very shallow drawer below 2 doors. Sides not tinned. Unidentified clipping, probably from the magazine* ANTIQUES. **(E)** *Labeled inside "J. Zitzer & Son, Furniture Dealer and Undertaker, West Alexandria, Ohio." Ohio collector's consignment to Garth's Auctions, Inc., Delaware, OH, 1/6/1984 sale. (6), long drawer under 2 doors.* Ohio Antique Review, *2/1984.* **(F)** *The Blue Door, Mudge Saver, Sunbury, OH, (6), drawer above 2 doors. [Ohio]* Antique Review, *10/1990. NOTE: Charles A. Muller, the editor of the [Ohio]* Antique Review *(name was changed to* Antique Review *in the mid-1980s), is knowledgable about pie safes himself, and his collector paper has the most pie safe ads of any. Perhaps this is because the majority of pie safes seem to come from the Midwest.*

XVII-26. Pie Safe Tins: Pinwheels or Fylfots. *All five designs include the goodluck fylfot design, known in another variation as a swastika (not the Nazi kind). It is an ancient design, found in Egypt and Amerindian arts, and was very popular in late Victorian times. Because of the method of making these drawings, the direction of the pinwheels in A, B, C and E are all reversed; two (A, C) that now go clockwise go counterclockwise on the originals, and two (B, E) that now go counterclockwise, go clockwise on original tins. (A) Thomas C. Queen, (3), this is actually a sideboard with 3 doors side by side. From Lee County, VA, c.1850. Maine Antique Digest, undated clip. (B) Wiltshire Antiques, Milford, OH, (8), two drawers above 2 doors, shallow shaped apron, tapered legs. [Ohio] Antique Review, 4/1986. (C) Kenneth W. Farmer auction, Radford, VA, 2/2-3/1985. (8), low sideboard style with 2 doors, each with 4 tins not divided by molding or framework. [Ohio] Antique Review, 4/1985. (D) Mary Mac & Robert Franklin, VA, (6), short turned legs, found in central Virginia. (E) Muleskinner, Ronald Korman, prop., Clarence, NY, (4), long drawer under 2 doors, tall turned legs, believed to be of Southern origin. Maine Antique Digest, 4/1987.*

XVII-27. Pie Safe Tins: Petals, Flowers, Butterfly. *The 6-petal flower design is sometimes referred to as a star, but because of the rounded edges, I identify them as flowers. All are encircled. Lower left is a design sometimes referred to as a "butterfly," which is a sort of stretched flower & tendril design. It reminds me of the folded-paper blot pictures done by psychologists with ink and by kindergartners with paint. (L) to (R) from top: (A) Belmont Antiques, Belmont, VT, (4), low, bracket-foot cupboard with 2 almost square tins on both of 2 doors, the tins not divided by molding or framework. Pennsylvania origin. Unidentified clipping, probably from New York-Pennsylvania Collector. (B) Private collector, Long Beach, CA, (6), short legged cupboard with exceptionally oblong tins, 3 on each door. Wonderful use of doubled design to fill otherwise awkward space. Safe found in Michigan. (C) Ex-Collection Earl F. & Ada F. Robacker. (1), single large panel on front of wall or rafter-hung safe, which probably has tins on other 3 sides also. Two oblong sheets of tin are joined along the horizontal axis to form one outside tin about 3-1/2 feet wide. From Pennsylvania Folklife, Spring 1961. Next is a design very similar to (A) and (C) is in the Bybee Collection, in the von Rosenberg kitchen, at Round Top, TX. (D) Charles Gerhardt Antiques, Lebanon, OH, (10), but arranged in what may be a unique fashion — with 4-1/2 panels on each of 2 doors. See the larger drawing at the right that shows how the parts are assembled. [Ohio] Antique Review, 1/1990. (E) Dogwood Antiques, Sparta, TN, (6), shallow drawer above 2 doors. Unidentified clipping, possibly* Mid-Atlantic Antiques, *or* Antiques Gazette. *(F) Gus Knapp, Hudson, OH, (3), large hanging safe with large tin on door and a narrower panel (with a star in the center) on either side. Undated* [Ohio] Antique Review *clipping.*

XVII-28. Pie Safe Tins: Urns, Flowers, Columns. *Virginia, Pennsylvania, and possibly Ohio safes. The first three drawings are of beautiful examples of classic Wythe County area urn & flower or urn & grape designs, with stars (or starflowers). Here the stars are separate from the stems; in some similar examples, pinwheels or stars make take the place of some of the grapes or flowers. Sometimes hearts take the place of or are used along with, stars, grapes or flowers. In the lower, and sometimes upper corners, one finds stars, pinwheels, flowers or columns resembling candles, and which may relate to the Fraternal Order of Masons. One constant, in all the examples I saw but one, is that the vertical stalk/stem is made with three lines, possibly signifying the Trinity.* **(A)** *From article about Roddy Moore's research into Southwest VA and East TN safes, prior to the ANTIQUES article. Antique Gazette, 3/1984.* **(B)** *Just Us, J. & S. Schneider, Tucson, AZ, (4), 2 doors with 2 short drawers above, short turned legs. Wythe County area. The 2 tins on each door are joined (and obviously not lined up) horizontally across center, with no molding or framework. Note diapered checker design inside urn. Maine Antique Digest, 10/1984.* **(C)** *Kenneth Farmer auctioneer, Radford, VA, 2/2/1985 sale. (4 tins joined to make 2), with side panels. Wythe County area. This is a drawing of the side tin, showing the star flowers. The front tins have stars instead of flowers; interior decoration of the urn is the same. Note how the "kite"-like shapes attached to the lower part of the flowers resemble those in the upper part of the urn/vase in (A). Maine Antique Digest, 4/1985.* **(D)** *Don & Janie Noyes, Glenford, OH. (6), a stepback cupboard, extremely severe case design, lower part being a lift-top chest. Tins set into 2 upper doorst. Probably Pennsylvania. Maine Antique Digest, 3/1986.* **(E)** *Leland Schmidt, Rockford, IL, number of tins not shown, possibly (6), unidentified clipping, New York-Pennsylvania Collector, or [Ohio] Antique Review.* **(F)** *Carol Ann & Ed Mathias, Bexley, OH, (6), [Ohio] Antique Review, 6/1988.* **(G)** *Collection of Carl & DeEtta Pace, fig. 16 in Moore's ANTIQUES article. (2), long drawer above 2 doors. Depiction of footed compote, possibly meant to represent one in pressed glass. Garlands, lovebirds, hearts, a diamond, 2 candles and 2 trees resembling Cedars of Lebanon complete the striking design. The magazine ANTIQUES, 9/1984.* **(H)** *K & K Antiques, Springfield, OH. (8), 4 tins joined without molding or framework to create effect of one large tin for each door. Short turned legs, sideboard type of safe with low gallery backplate on sides & back of the top. Siever County, TN origin. Maine Antique Digest, 4/1989.*

XVII-29. Pie Safe Case Types. *Showing fronts only; many, even most, pie safes also have tins on the sides. (L) to (R) from top:* **(A)** *Four tins in 2 doors, tins separated by framework (or molding), with 2 drawers above doors, short legs.* **(B)** *Six tins in 2 doors, bracket feet, shaped apron.* **(C)** *Hanging safe with large tin (or joined tins) on single door. Other tins usually on other vertical sides. Hung from rafters.* **(D)** *Six tins in 2 doors, above long drawer, long tapered legs.* **(E)** *Twelve tins joined without framework or molding to form 2 large tins in 2 doors, turned feet.* **(F)** *Wythe County (and neighboring counties), Virginia-type case with 2 drawers above 2 doors, and distinctive urn & grapes (urn & flowers, urn & stars) pattern. Turned feet not always found on type. Single drawer sometimes found. All drawings of composite type not taken from any single model.*

Shelf paper, various patterns & colors, also shelf edge papers — printed, scalloped, pleated or lace. All these are collectible, if unnoticed to this time, and nothing adds a more authentic touch to a shelf with a collection of 1920s or 1930s or 1940s gadgets and implements than authentic shelf paper, or at least edge papers, thumbtacked neatly in place with colored tacks. 1910s to 1950s. (Another thing to do, which I did for my 1870s cupboard, is to cut fancy-edge shelf border strips from a colorful comic strip newspaper section.) **$2-$8**

Shopping list aid, also called a <u>daily reminder</u> or <u>household reminder</u>, tin, lithographed in blue & white with flowers, flat oblong device, with tabs along left & right sides that are pulled out to mark those things on the printed lists to be bought, such as Rice & Sago, Lemons, Blacking, Oatmeal or Wash Blue, named "The Housekeeper's Friend," this one prob. European, c.1908. **$12-$25**

Yo, Bounty! — "The uses of paper in the home are not so many. Shelving in the pantry or kitchen can be kept in renewed health with paper laces. The bungalow, motor trip or picnic can well be supplied with paper or fibre plates. Rather would we warn you against paper uses; such as wrapping up your ice to preserve it, for it doesn't; wrapping up your food stuff in paper in refrigerator; greasing muffin pan with paper, for which you should use a brush. Sometimes, however, a piece of paper will clean off the top of the stove very efficiently, yet even here a brush would be far better. Clean brown paper to absorb French fried potatoes is quite indispensible. The paper napkin has made its place even in the homes of wealth. Wax paper is a delight to wrap up sandwiches and keep breadstuffs and cakes fresh for touring or picnics. Paper lining for drawers is necessary. The pretty paper lace doily for under finger bowls, cake and bread is delightfully pretty and saves the linen, the laundress and the laundry list." Ethel R. Peyser, "Tinware, Rubber and Paper for the Kitchen," *House & Garden,* June 1922.

Shopping list aid, lithographed cardboard, adv'g "Doe-Wah-Jack" stoves, turn of century. **$25-$35**

Shopping list aid, paper, meant for a Hoosier cabinet & marked "Hoosier," early 20th C. **$22-$32**

Shopping list aid, plastic disc with tiny blue plastic knobs to indicate which of the many things printed around the circumference are needed, adv'g "Watkins Awning & Sign Co., Farmville, VA," maker name not shown, 3-3/8" diameter not counting little knobs, c.1948. **$8+**

Step stool or folding stool, painted wood, 3 steps, slightly cutout step shape, very attractive, American, about 1910-1920. **$12-$15**

Celebrity Silliness — In the middle 1980s, a For Sale ad appeared in a collector newspaper for a "Folding kitchen stool used by James Dean before his movie fame; from Fairmount, IN. personal friend. Offers considered, collectors only." I don't know what eventually happened, but this is an example of the <u>Absurd Rub-Off Theory of Collectible Objects</u> which is behind the very high prices of things once belonging to a famous person. Andy Warhol's cookie jars went for 10 times market price, and it's quite possible he never even touched them, merely pointed to them before buying. When James Beard's cookbooks were auctioned, the auction house glued in cheapo copies of his bookplate, despite the fact that Beard himself had chosen to put bookplates in very few books. (At that sale, a box of tatty old dirty bowties sold for hundreds of smackeroos.) While fabulous prices are being paid for Van Gogh's and Picasso's and Frank Stella's paintings, works that were actually created by and intimately "touched" by the masters, objects supposed to have been touched by, or known to have been owned by, famous people who had nothing to do with the objects' creation, are selling for outrageous prices. Auras don't rub off.

Table and 4 chairs, enamelware top, drop leaf & extension, nice geometric or abstract floral design on top in red or black, American, c.1910-1940s. These have gone up greatly in popularity. Sets, with four kitchen chairs and a table (often without extension leaves), varnished or painted in snowy white, show up at every big antique show and sell for many hundreds of dollars. They are in with the modern and Deco stuff at the big shows in NYC. **$400-$1000+**

Table, birch with single wide birch plank top, 2 side drawers, turned legs, late 19th C., Memphis, TN, 28-7/8" H x 59-1/2" L x 30" W, turn of century. My Franklin grandfather worked for a lumber mill in Memphis, and had this table made with an extraordinarily wide single plank top just shy of 1" thick. Unfortunately refinished — with colored stain over what was a wonderful scrubbed finish. **$300-$400**

Table, wide plank pine drop-leaf top, turned sturdy legs, pull-out bread boards each end, with utility drawers for implements at each end. At each end of this tea-cake-for-two working table is a big possum belly flour or meal bin. All drawers, including bins, have single cast iron dog's head pull, American, c.1880 to 1900. The <u>dog's head pulls</u> are what give this table that extra punch & value. **$850+**

Table, child's, wood with blue & white graniteware top, American, early 20th C. **$100-$150**

Table, drop leaf, green paint, very deep overhang at ends, American, 36" L, mid 19th C. **$400-$550**

XVII-30. Shopping list aid or reminder. *"The Housekeeper's Friend." Probably printed celluloid. Advertised by wholesale importer G. M. Thurnauer & Brother who supplied kitchenwares to the trade. The NYC firm imported from Germany and France. Ad in* House Furnishing Review, *11/1909.* **$15-$30**

XVII-31. Convertible step ladders. (T-L &-R) *Folding step ladder chair, shown in both positions, were manufactured by Tucker & Dorsey Mfg. Co., Indianapolis, who made all kinds of woodenwares including ironing boards and pastry boards. Advertised in* The Metal Worker, *6/21/1890. Same linecuts used in 1909 Albert Pick wholesale catalog, advertised as "solid and substantial; it is a good hall chair. As a step ladder it is heavy enough to be used wihtout danger of upsetting. Finished in oak."* **(B)** *Called "utility steps" in F. A. Walker wholesale catalog, Boston, 1870s. Instead of folding, the steps slid under the stool. Finish and condition account for value.* **$40-$125**

XVII-32. Cooks' Table. *Meant for hotel or restaurant kitchen, but could have been used in large household kitchen. "Securely and neatly constructed of natural wood, resting on heavy turned legs, with dish shelf below. Tops are of three strips, tongued and grooved, leaded and securely bolted together. Tables up to 8' in length have one drawer and four legs; those 10' to 16' have two drawers and three sets of legs. Came in choice of 3 widths — 30", 36", and 42", and in 8 lengths — 5', 6', 7', 8', 10', 12', 14', and 16' L." Catalog of S. B. Sexton Stove & Mfg. Co., Baltimore, c.1930s.* **$100-$500**

ELECTRIFYING WORK

XVIII. GADGETS & APPLIANCES

What is most interesting to me about this category of collecting is the social history behind it. First, there were the marketing efforts of power companies who could see the future and knew it had to be electric for their own survival. So power companies in the first quarter of a century drummed up business by actively selling that Electric Future. It's amusing to read articles written for their own trade journals (one is transcribed in this chapter). Such articles offer background to our understanding of public ad campaigns in the first third of the twentieth century.

For example, an article in the *Edison Electric Institute Bulletin* of September 1934 tells about the development of a "distinctive and appealing character" — "Reddy Kilowatt, the Electrical Servant." Reddy, also spelled "Ready" by some companies, formed the basis for a "program . . . to humanize the utility approach to the public by translating . . . the complicated business of serving electricty to all types of customers." Reddy's appeal holds strong today, although it is the rare customer who has a choice about whether or not to use electricity.

Nowadays, power companies issue occasional brochures on "saving energy," and then spend the rest of their time lobbying before state assemblies asking for rate increases because of decreased usage, or fighting people who want to sell them excess power generated by privately-owned windmills. They are otherwise mired in a bureaucracy of meter-reading and kilowatt hours. Obviously they neither have the time nor do they need to fund their own test kitchens as in the old days, or pay well-known cookbook authors to prepare promotional cookbooks. And thankfully they have not used old Reddy to try to humanize nuclear power plants and high tension electric lines. Talk about zap.

The second aspect of the social history of household electricity is the utopian view that it would replace what was a dwindling supply of cheap servants and that it would make the housewives' lives easier. For the majority of plugged-in households in the teens and early 1920s, life in general was pretty trig, and electricity only made it more so. It is to laugh to see the retouched, vignette photographs in old power-company booklets, showing cute young things, in pre-Flapper outfits, sitting at their dressing tables curling their hair, or standing at a tea table, ogled by admiring friends while making waffles, or posing beside tabletop washing machines in which you can be sure there are some dainty silk stockings.

Once electricity was available in a community, probably the biggest problem with electrical appliances in the earliest days was that there was virtually no one to do repairs. And undoubtedly many people were afraid of shocks and electrocution. Find a copy of James Thurber's story "The Car We Had to Push," which appears in a collection of stories published in 1933 called *My Life and Hard Times.* In the story, Thurber tells about one of "the victims and martyrs of the wild-eyed Edison's dangerous experiments" — his mother's mother, who "lived the latter years of her life in the horrible suspicion that electricity was dripping invisibly all over the house. It leaked, she contended, out of empty sockets if the wall switch had been left on." In fact, if you want to be charmed completely, get copies of all of Thurber's wonderful stories and read them again.

Toasters are the big thing here, as you are well aware from booths at shows and ads in trade papers. I use an old (c.1941) toaster myself, with perfect satisfaction. It's not very outré to look at, but it's easy to use, easy to fix and easy to clean. In selecting the couple dozen toasters listed here, I just made notes on the ones I saw at flea markets or antique shows — trying to pick out aesthetic or techno-historical winners; there are also a number that aren't rare but add breadth (and perhaps a bit of cheapth) to a collection. For more information, you can write James Barker, Toaster Master, POB 592, Hawley, PA, 18428. Please use an SASE when writing anyone for information. **Fans** are also very collectible, but are not strictly kitchen collectibles.

In the last few years, other small electrical appliances, many dating well into the 1940s, have become increasingly collectible. There's still time to scout them out at fleas and thrift shops.

There is a club covering all kinds of electric labor-savers: The **Old Appliance Club**, offering a newsletter "The Old Road Home," old ad reprints, help in locating parts, etc. Contact Jack Santoro, J.E.S. Enterprises, POB 65, Ventura, CA 93002. (805) 643-3532 — fax or phone. Santoro, who calls himself the American Antique Appliance Archaeologist, has helped people fix up old ranges for years, and also searches for odd and unusual examples of small and large appliances — from toasters and mixers to dryers and vacuum cleaners.

Baby food warmer, small pitcher-like vessel set on electric base, gray & white enamelware that looks like moss agate, 4 wood button feet screwed on to base, odd plug with flat prongs, many marks, "AGL, #2510," "Triangle Lektrik Baby Food Warmer," American Electrical Heater Co., Detroit, MI, 4-1/2" H, early 20th C. **$30-$50**

Baker, round-cornered oblong chromium box like a big shoe box, with slide-out baking tray drawer, black plastic handle on drawer, 4 little feet, temperature dial on top, "Redi-Baker," mfd. by Knapp Monarch NESCO, St. Louis, MO, c.1963. **$12-$18**

Barber mug, white enamelware with cobalt trim, pat'd 1905. Patent prob. refers to heating element, not mug's design. **$65-$75**

Beater, single stainless steel blade, white glass beater jar, cast with rocket-like 4 strut bottom for stability, red wood knob handle, "K-M," Knapp-Monarch Co., St. Louis, MO, 9-1/2" H, 20th C. **$15-$25**

Beater, heavy metal motor housing with black wood knob on top, sets down in Akro Agate glass bowl with green & rusty pumpkin swirls, original wiring, no mark, bowl is 4-1/2" H, overall height including knob is 7-5/8" H, 20th C. **$35-$55**

Beater, paneled custard slag container, with ivory-painted metal motor housing with shaped knob, simple beater blades, "Vidrio," Vidrio Products Corp. (the glass parts), Cicero, IL, 1920s-1930s. The only time I've seen the name Vidrio it's been on small electric appliances with glass. According to *Thomas' Directory*, 1932-33, glass products were Vidrio's beat. So who made the electrical parts? **$35-$55**

Beater or mixer, cobalt blue panelled glass container fitted with single squiggly beater blade attached to housed motor, strap handle, lid has hole for pouring ingredients in with funnel, "Vidrio Products Corp.," Catalog #E30, Chicago, IL, 2 cup capacity, 1933 patent #1935857. This also came with a Depression green glass jar with green-painted metal lid and motor housing. That one is valued at about a 1/3 or 1/2 of the value of one with a blue jar. **$65-$85**

Bottle warmer, chromed metal, plastic knobs, temperature gauge on top, "Sunbeam," Chicago Flexible Shaft, 12-15/16" H, developed 1951; this one early 1950s. **$20-$35**

Casserole, tan, brown & black enameled body with chrome & red Art Deco design of woman serving steaming casserole dish on front, 2 Bakelite Deco black handles & lid knob, inner bowl, electric cord, high & low settings for heat, "NESCO Thrifty Cook Casserole #B40," National Enamel & Stamping Co., Milwaukee, WI, c.1940s. **$60-$70**

Casserole or chafing dish, chromed metal, white plastic handles, Pyrex™ glass liner, Chase Brass & Copper, with centaur logo, Waterbury, CT, 12" D, 1940s. **Yeah — But Does It Work?** If you don't know a lot about electrical appliances, don't just go plugging things in. Often old electrical things *are* fully restored to working order, with new old-fashioned cloth-wrapped cords, etc. Anything is worth more when it works. **$45-$65**

Chafing dish, nickeled brass & iron, turned wood handle, well-shaped frame & pan, lion's paw feet, domed lid, "Type ECD," mfd. by General Electric, c.1918 or 1919. **$40-$50**

Corn popper, aluminum with wood handles, glass cover, "Knapp-Monarch Co.," St. Louis, MO, c.1930s. **$12-$20**

XVIII-1. Illustration, *by Eric Nitsche, for article in* House Beautiful, *5/1937.*

XVIII-2. Reddy Kilowatt, *with added avoirdupois. This version is a painted cutout plywood sign, probably unique, and used to be propped in window. "Meet Reddy Kilowatt. You will like him — he is a genius of accomplishment — capable, infinitely willing, infinitely powerful. ... He is YOUR servant." About 28" H. 1930s-40s.* **$100-$200**

A FEW THINGS A CENT'S WORTH OF ELECTRICITY WILL DO

It will bring to a boil two quarts of water.
It will run the electric boiler for six minutes.
It will operate a twelve-inch fan for ninety minutes.
It will operate an electric griddle for eight minutes.
It will operate a luminous radiator for eight minutes.
It will make a Welsh rarebit in an electric chafing dish.
It will operate a sewing machine motor for three hours.
It will keep an eight-inch disc stove hot for seven minutes, or long enough to cook a steak.
It will operate a seven-inch frying pan for twelve minutes.
It will make four cups of coffee in an electric coffee percolator.
It will keep a foot-warmer hot for a quarter of an hour.
It will keep a six-pound electric flatiron hot for fifteen minutes.
It will heat an electric curling iron once a day for two weeks.
It will clean seven pairs of boots on a boot polisher.
It will clean five hundred knives on a knife cleaner.
It will carry a passenger up and down about three times in an eighty-foot house elevator.
It will run an electric clock one year.
It will run a small office ventilating fan about two hours.
It will warm sufficient water for shaving three mornings.
It will light three hundred cigars.
It will iron three silk hats.
It will fill and cork twenty-five dozen pint bottles.
It will pump ten gallons of water to a height of twenty-five feet.
It will run or operate an electric piano for one hour.

XVIII-3. One cent of electricity— *what it would do in 1914. You can see from the list that much was done by electricity, at what may seem a very early date. I love the juxtoposition of old & new fangles — silk top hats to ventilating fans! From* Electric Cooking, Heating & Cleaning. A Manual of Electricity in the Service of the Home, *by Maud Lancaster, 1914. This book will be referred to in succeeding captions as* Electric Cooking, *1914.*

XVIII-4. Chafing dishes. *Styled exactly like traditional ones using alcohol lamps, these were touted for making "dainty dishes" right on the table.* (**L**) *General Electric Co., Schenectady;* (**R**) *Landers, Frary & Clark "Universal." Both have ebonized wooden handles and finials, and are somewhat in the Georgian mode of the 1830s. Pictures from* Electric Cooking, *1914.* **$35-$55**

"Wire Your Home Time' and Electrical Housewares. — From April 1 to May 15, 1917, will be known as 'Wire Your Home Time' throughout the country, and the Society of Electrical Development tell us that there are fifteen million homes in America yet to be wired for electric service.

"Here are some facts that are interesting to dealers having Electrical Houseware Departments or who have facilities for handling wiring contracts or sell electrically heated or operated devices: 20,500,000 homes in U.S. 5,500,000 wired for electric service. 15,000,000 yet to be wired, now lighted by other means than electricity. 5,000,000 sockets empty. 1075 per cent. more electric light obtainable for the same money than 20 years ago. 110,000,000 incandescent lamps now sold yearly. Only one in three of the homes on the existing distribution lines of electric companies are wired. Far less than one per cent. of the homes of the country are wired for complete electric service.

"Of course, not all these homes will be wired, but a number of them will, which means that thousands will be able to enjoy the pleasures of electric lighting, cooking, cleaning, sewing, ironing, washing, and the many other forms of electric service.

"The development of the servant question in this modern home is very important to the dealer selling Electrical Housewares. Years ago when all families boasted and enjoyed an entire house for themselves, servants were a necessity. In later years when the apartment or 'flat' came into vogue and the servant in the house was changed to the 'living-out girl' or the one who 'worked by the day,' electricity first received the attention that it deserved. As the family's living quarters became smaller, the necessity of having outside help became less, and the advantages of electrically operated devices became more prominent.

"Then the servant, seeing that eventually she would be supplanted by the 'housekeeping by wire' method, demanded increased wages all out of proportion to the services performed, with the result that electricity again received additional impetus until today it is a recognized factor in the operation of the modern home.

"When munition plants offered to women, even those unskilled in mechanics, large salaries which daily oftentimes equaled their weekly wages, the domestic forsook her pots and pans, the broom and the wash tub, to take her place among the ranks of those employed in making explosives and other necessities for the continuing of the war.

"In despair, the housewife turned a hopeless face toward carrying on the home duties by herself or with less help; and when the alert merchant called her attention to the modern way of washing clothes with the Electric Washer instead of the 'elbow-grease' way of the laundress, she listened carefully, tested thoroughly — and bought. Now many thousands of housewives all over the country sing the praises of the Electric Washing Machine.

"It was the same way with the Electric Vacuum Cleaner. When its efficiency in removing — not merely scattering — the dust and dirt was demonstrated to her, she immediately became a convert to the dustless method, the Vacuum Cleaner way. Now she does not have to spend many weary hours dusting, as the Vacuum Cleaner catches and holds the dust.

"Then when the beauty, convenience and usefulness of electrically operated cooking utensils were shown her, she appreciated their many points of advantage. The Electric Percolator, the Electric Stove, the Electric Egg Boiler, the Electric Chafing Dish, the Electric Toaster, etc., etc. — all of these she bought and found useful.

"In the kitchen she placed an Electric Dish Washer, which eliminated all the dreary drudgery of dish washing. Three times a day, year in and year out, the dishes must be washed. The clothes may be washed once a week, but the dishes cannot wait. The hands of the housewife were saved from this disagreeable task and the electric machine eagerly took up the work, which it performed automatically, efficiently as well as thoroughly and cleanly. Again, the chinaware or glassware does not suffer when the Electric Dish Washer is employed like it does when 'Mamie' does the work.

"The handy 'power unit' was another large factor in cutting down the kitchen labor. It polished the silver, it ground the coffee, turned the ice cream freezer, the egg beater and the grindstone in a business-like way and at a small cost for current.

"The laundry next received attention, and with the Electric Washing Machine safely installed the Electric Iron was added and the Electric Mangle, perhaps.

"For the rooms of the house there were suitable Electric Lamps in a multitude of styles and sizes, while for Milady's room the Electric Curling Iron, Electric Heating Pad, etc., were found of more than ordinary use.

"Today more than ever before the Electric Fan is gaining a foothold in the home and rightly so. For years it was found only in the business office, the store or the factory, but now it is a recognized necessity even in the winter months.

"Although the writer has not touched deeply on the many and different uses of Electrical Housewares, the average alert merchant has already seen the light and has contemplated stocking and selling Electrical Housewares. As the days get longer and the days warmer, these labor and time saving devices should be brought to the attention of the buying public, as the summer time is the season when all of these conveniences are more than ever appreciated." "Electrical Housewares" section, *House Furnishing Review,* March 1917.

Corn popper, heavy tinned short cylindrical steel body, crank in top with a bent blade of heavy wire, like a dough mixer, green wood handles, mark stamped on bottom but illegible, American, 8" diameter, c.1928 to 1935. **$25-$35**

Corn popper, metal straight-sided body on short legs, 2 handles, lid, heating element inside at bottom, perforated with band of holes, "Dominion Electric Co.," Minneapolis, MN, 1930s. **$35-$45**

Corn popper, nickeled steel with perforations, straight-sided basket pan on heating stand with 3 legs, wooden side handle, lid through which top crank comes, green wood & green cord, "Betsy Ross," mfd. by Central Flatiron Mfg. Co., Johnson City, NY, 6-1/2" H x 8-1/2" diameter, introduced June 1930. **$35-$45**

Doughnut maker, electric, oval black sheet metal base, 2 round lids, sort of works like waffle maker, only it makes 7 "donuts," the base & upper molds having the 7 rings with convex centers that touch when closed to create the hole, Wallace Ray Co., Waseca, MN, 1968 ad in *McCall's Needlework & Crafts* magazine. Just 30+ years ago, but the ad copy seems so dated & funny today. The screaming headlines, above the smiling bob-haired woman gazing upon the maker, is **MAKE MONEY MAKING DO-NUTS. - New! - Greaseless! - Different! No experience needed! New electric machine bakes 14 dozen per hour, all kinds: Plain, Iced, Raisin, etc. Costs you only 16¢ per doz. YOU earn up to $125 a month SPARE TIME . . . MUCH MORE FULL TIME! Start in own kitchen. Sell to restaurants, grocers, drugstores, cafeterias, plants, etc. No bookkeeping! Collect cash profits daily! Machine guaranteed. Add more as needed. Write today for Free Recipes, details. No obligation."** **$35-$55**

Drink mixer, electric, various metals, some enameled, "Drinkmaster," Hamilton Beach, Racine, WI, 1926. **$30-$60**

Egg boiler, electric, metal, "El Eggo," mfd. by Pacific Electric Heating Co., Ontario (?), CA, late 1890s. **$15-$25**

Egg cooker, red ceramic, chrome lid, metal poaching rack inside and ceramic insert, includes instruction booklet, Fiesta Ware ceramic; cooker itself "#599," Hankscraft Co., Good Housekeeping Institute Seal of Approval, Madison, WI, c.1930s. The same cooker, in orange or light blue, about the same price; in yellow, slightly less; in pale seafoam green, about $10 less. **$20-$30**

Eggbeater — See beater

Fan, cast iron base, brass blades & cage, Victor Electric Products, Cincinnati, OH, 12" D, early 20th C. **$65-$75**

Fan, cast iron base with black finish, oscillating table fan which could be wall mounted by loosening wing nut at pivot point, cage is Art Deco design, Westinghouse, Style #699785, 14-3/4" H, last patent was 1923 patent #1444923. **$20-$35**

Fan, cast iron base with felt underneath, 4 brass blades in black wire cage that has wavy rayed lines, hinged so it can be tabletop or wall hung, on/off switch, brass disk in middle of cage's rays with banner & letters "R M Airflow," Robbins & Myers, Inc., Springfield, OH, cage 13" diameter, blades 9" diameter, c.1930s. **$25-$35**

Fan, kerosene burner in base to power fan with hot air, floor model, 4 large brass blades, wiggly cage wires, almost as large as its 'plant stand' wrought iron base that has 4 twisted legs. "Lake Breeze #16," Chicago, IL, c.1914-1920 (?). (There was also a Lake Breeze alcohol-powered table fan.) Although it isn't electric, I included it here for comparison with much commoner electric fans, from the same period. **$2000+**

XVIII-6. Egg cooker. *Ceramic bottom by "Fiesta Ware," chromed metal parts including lid and poaching rack mfd. by Hankscraft Co., Madison, WI. Ceramic came in variety of colors; cream or pastel green is most common, bright Fiesta red most desirable. A small "casserole dish" came with this unit, for making coddled eggs or custards, but I've never seen one for sale with that. They do work, but they're a nuisance to clean and maintain.* Electric Home, *1936. Hankscraft also made a bottle warmer along the same lines.* **$20-$30**

XVIII-7. Table fans. (L) *White Cross Breezer Fan No. 60, "especially adapted for use in small rooms, offices, state rooms, telephone booths, by the bed-side, on the desk and enclosed motor boats and automobiles. It is equipped with starting and speed-regulating device and is particularly adapted as a portable electric fan, from the fact of it being lighter in weight than the average eight inch fan. Angle adjustable. Nickeled or oxidized copper cast iron & tool steel.* **(R)** *White Cross Table Fan No. 289, "for use on table as a center piece." AC or DC, any cycle, and was furnished for any voltage from 100 to 220. Three speeds. Nickeled cast iron, brass blades, removable pressed glass bowl on top. 10 1/2" H x 9 1/2" diameter. Both mfd. by Lindstrom-Smith Co., Chicago. Editorial note in* House Furnishing Review, *5/1915.* **$25-$35 and $150-$200**

XVIII-5. Dining room set, *consisting of chafing dish (ECD), a type of hot plate called a "stove" (ES), and a coffee percolator urn (ECP). General Electric, 1918-1919. ES under $20; ECD & ECP $50-$80*

XVIII-8. Hot air, kerosene lamp fan. *The famous "Lake Breeze" floor-standing fan with wrought iron base. This looks like many items of the same period for use on the porch — plant stands and furniture, and its independence of electricity or water meant that it could be used outdoors. The kerosene lamp below caused rising hot air, which eventually caused the blades to turn. It is considered a very desirable collectors' fan, and brings thousands of dollars at auction. Lake Breeze Motor, Chicago, IL. Mfd. between about 1914 and 1920.* **$2000+**

Fan, marbleized glass base, metal blades, maker unknown, (could it be Vidrio?), American (?), 20th C.   **$85-$100**

Fan, nickel-plated table fan to be used as a centerpiece, with the brass blades set horizontally, & a removable cut or pressed glass bowl fitted on the top. The bowl did not revolve, but I'd hate to reach carelessly for a summer peach & miss the bowl. "White Cross No. 289," mfd. by Lindstrom-Smith Co., Chicago, IL, 10-1/2" H x 9-1/2" diameter, 1915.   **$150-$200**

Fan, tabletop, all brass, "Emerson-Trojan," St. Louis, MO. The Fan Man, Inc., Mr. Kurt House, 4606 Travis, Dallas, TX 75205, has a catalog of antique fan parts for sale, a book on mechanical fans, & information on a club. Please use SASE when writing. **$100-$125**

Food warmer, copper with black molded phenolic resin (one famous tradename is Bakelite) handles, 3 compartments, Chase Brass & Copper, with centaur logo, 1940s.   **$30-$45**

Griddle, chromed metal, small rectangle on short legs, "Electrahot" Style 512, Electrahot Mfg. Co., Minneapolis, MN, c.1930s. **$15-$20**

Hot dog cooker, black metal base, green pottery insert with side cup handle & 4 brass feet that fit into holes in metal base, probably something to do with the electrical connection, black plastic handle, "The Lightning Wiener Cooker," mfd. by Lightning Cooker Co., Cleveland, OH, holds 3 hot dogs, c.1920s or 1930s. No patent numbers.   **$25-$40**

Hot dog steamer, white enameled metal house with heavy-duty molded plastic red plastic peaked roof with steam vent chimneys, marked "Dog House"on front, "Sunbeam," Chicago Flexible Shaft Co., 7" H x 7-3/4" L, 1980s. This is a perfect example of an almost instant collectible. It is not a "Snoopy" item, but plays only on word "Dog." Faddish and figural and extremely well-made.   **$20-$30**

Insect killer, chromed metal canister, hangs from ceiling, with removable base (for taking out dead insects), alternating current only. "Vaporizer," mfd. by Manning-Bowman, 1930s. The description of this peculiar item in E.S. Lincoln's 1936 book, *The Electric Home*, it says it "looks like an ordinary birdcage, but

XVIII-9. Frypan & "frittering pan." *"Eclipse" deep frying pan, made by the Electric & Ordnance Accessories Co., Birmingham, England, & unidentified frittering (deep frying) pan, heating elements in their bases. Pictures from a book which combines American and English appliances, cooking techniques and vocabulary — Maud Lancaster's Electric Cooking, Heating & Cleaning, 1914. The indistinct picture of the frittering pan appears to show glass marbles forming the feet. Lancaster gives a list of electrical appliance makers:* <u>English.</u> *— Amorduct Mfg. Co.; Benham & Sons; A. F. Berry, "Tricity"; British Prometheus Co. [founded in 1892]; The Carron Co.; Dowsing Radiant Heat Co. & Mssrs. Crompton & Co. [pioneer mfr. exhibited at Crystal Palace in 1891]; Eastman & Warne; The Electric & Ordnance Accessories Co.; The Electrical Co.; The Falkirk Iron co.; Ferranti; Jackson Electric Stove Co.; Phoenix Electric Heating Co. [founded 1894]; Purcell & Nobbs; Simplex Conduits; Spagnoletti; The British Thomson-Houston Co.* <u>American.</u> *— The Automatic Electric Cook Co.; The Berkeley Electric Cooker Co.; The Cook Stove Co.; The General Electric Co. [there was also G-E of Great Britain]; The Hot-point Electric Heating co.; The Hughes Electric Heating Co.; The Prometheus Electric Co.; The Simplex Electric Heating Co.; The Vulcan Electric Heating Co.; The Western Electric Co.; The Westinghouse Electric Co. She does not mention Edison Electric, probably because most of her list was of companies entering the business "within the last five years" [ie. about 1907].* **$30-$50**

XVIII-10. Hotdog or wiener cooker. *"Here we have the use of electricity in its simplest form where the 'hot dogs' are cooked by running the electricity through them. Alternating current should be used. The electricity boils the water contained in the food and causes it to do its own cooking. Such a cooker has another automatic feature inasmuch as the carrying handle also controls the switch. When the handle is in its vertical position the current is on, and when the wieners are cooked the handle is put to one side or the other of the device, automatically shutting off the current and leaving free space for handling the wieners. These devices are furnished in different sizes and colors to suit one's fancy."* Electric Home, 1936. *This is uncomfortably like a description of electrocution, which had been in use to execute criminals since 1889, when current generated by a Westinghouse alternating-current power plant in New York state provided the electricity. One of the brouhahas at the time of the first electrocution was over whether alternating or direct current would be most efficient. Thomas Edison and others felt that direct current would not work as well as alternating; George Westinghouse, who had developed the first alternating current power plant, protested on general grounds because electricity was already regarded as dangerous, and on specific grounds, because of the "bad press" his kind of electricity would receive.* **$30-$50**

603

instead of containing a canary it contains an ordinary light bulb. The small vertical wires that surround the bulb are charged with electricity and when any insect comes in contact with these wires it is instantly killed." The caption is even weirder: "Electrically heated vaporizor for exterminating moths and other flying insects." **$20-$35**

The Good Die Young — This vaporizer killed flies in the house; but the electric bug zappers that sound so annoying and frenetic on summer evenings, when your neighbors leave them on 24 hours a day, are killing useful insects. Few mosquitoes are killed, and flies sleep at night. Night birds compete with the zappers, and many people have found rare & beautiful moths (not clothes-eating varieties) dead in their killing machines. Kindly turn yours off; you will do Nature a favor.

Juicer, A. F. Dormeyer Co., Chicago, IL, 1930s. **$20-$25**

Juicer, green Jadite glass, dark green enameled motor housing with chrome trim, cream ceramic reamer, alternating current only, "Sunkist Juicit," mfd. by Chicago Electric Mfg. Co., a "Handy Hot" Product, Chicago, IL, 8-3/4" H, 1934 patents #1943270 and #1962856. **$35-$45**

Liquid mixer, enameled iron base for motor, glass top, base looks like a streamlined locomotive front, Hollywood Liquefier Co., South Pasadena, CA, 1930s. **$40-$50**

Malted milk mixer, also called a malt mixer, "Hamilton Beach #51," 20th C. **$50-$60**

Malted milk mixer, metal & glass, "Arnold #15," Arnold Electric Co., subsidiary of Hamilton Beach, 1930s. **$45-$60**

Malted milk machine, green porcelainized cast iron, 2 containers, Hamilton Beach Mfg. Co., Racine, WI, early 1930s-1940s. **$70-$100**

Marshmallow toaster, sheet metal "campstove" like thing on 4 wire legs, red rubber feet on legs, 2 little wire forks to hold marshmallows, 150 volts, 345 watts, "Angelus-Campfire Bar-B-Q Marshmallow Toaster," early 20th C. **$55-$70**

Milk shake mixer, triple head & 3 speed, green or cream enameled steel, glass, this triple head type was for a soda fountain not the home, Hamilton Beach, 1930s. **$150-$185**

Milk shake mixer, white porcelain base, glass, metal, Arnold Mfg. Co., adv'g "Horlicks, The Original Malted Milk," 20th C. **$100-$125**

Milk shaker mixer, various metals, glass, Gilchrist, Newark, NJ, 1922. **$100-$125**

Mixer, cast metal base with detachable mixer, juicer attachment, set of ceramic, heat-proof mixing bowls & lids that could be put directly in oven, Sears' "Powermaster DeLuxe," late (?) 1930s. **$45-$65**

Mixer, cast & sheet metal, nickel-plated, with turned wood spade handle; a portable food mixer in its own heavy wire stand (rather like a doll stand), that allowed it to be used in vertical position with a tumbler or other fairly low container. They advertised "Used on stand or in the hand." To be plugged into lamp socket. "Whip-All," mfd. by Air-O-Mix, Wilmington, DE, 1923 to about 1926-27. Very short-lived, hence very rare. **$95-$120**

Mixer, countertop, cast metal base with mixer that, when first introduced, came with 2 stainless steel mixing bowls, and one attachment: a juicer. That was soon to be joined by other attachments: a food chopper, grater, potato peeler, knife sharpener, polisher, can opener, drink mixer & coffee grinder. "Mixmaster," mfd. by the Chicago Flexible Shaft Co. (later Sunbeam), Chicago, IL, 1930-31. (By 1936, all the other attachments were available.) According to Earl Lifshey, author of *The Housewares Story* (see Bibliography), "By 1936 'Mixmaster' sales reached to more than 300,000 units." So there are plenty of old ones out there for collectors; the trick is finding the attachments. **$125-$150**

XVIII-12. Electric kitchen, *sketched from one in operation in a private home in 1894.* The Womans' Book: Dealing Practically with the Modern Conditions of Home Life.... *NY: Charles Scribner's Sons, 1894. No electric stove is shown; all the appliances are, in effect, tabletop. This picture reminds me of a makeshift kitchen I made in an apartment I had in NYC. I had no kitchen to begin with, only three (!) bathrooms. So I took the toilets and tub out of the first, made a 42" H counter the length of the room, drilled a hole in the wall (and made big plaster lips around the hole) and threaded a heavy cord through from the next room, which had outlets. A power strip plugged in to the heavy cord allowed me to plug in a refrigerator, an electric frying pan, and my Hankscraft egg boiler, and — by not turning them on at the same time — a 1941 toaster which I still use, and a hotplate with two burners.*

XVIII-11. Juicer. *"Sunkist Juicit" deluxe model No. BM-21, in the "Handyhot" line, by Chicago Electric Mfg. Co. "Included in its construction is a Magic Automatic Strainer that oscillates rapidly back and forth, whipping the juice cells of the pulp against sharpened edges of strainer holes, first releasing every drop of juice, and, secondly, cutting the health-giving pulp into tiny particles." Chrome with "French Ivory" glass juice collector bowl and reamer. "Powerful induction type motor does not interfere with radio reception and operates only on 110-120 volts, 50-60 cycle alternating current. Toggle switch. Cord and plug cap attached." Handyhot catalog AA, 1940.* **$30-$55**

XVIII-13. Combination tabletop appliance. *For grilling, making pancakes, poaching eggs, heating liquids. Nickeled steel with black-painted wooden handles. 3 feet pads of nonconducting "fibre." Three heat levels with "snap switch," a removable rack with 4 separate pans for egg poaching. Shape and size (8" diameter) of stove plate permits use of round aluminum vessels. Depths of the 3 utensils are 1/4" (the griddle); 1-1/4", and 2". D. J. Barry jobber catalog, 1924. Manufacturer not given, but probably "Universal" (Landers, Frary & Clark).*

XVIII-14. Electric kitchen, *of Mr. H. J. Dowsing, England, 1894. Instead of a large outlet board serving various small electrical appliances, this kitchen actually has an electric "cooker" or stove, and even a wall oven! Also note the electric fryer on the table at right. "In 1891 Mr. H. J. Dowsing, one of the pioneers of heating and cooking, and founder of the Dowsing Radiant Heat Co., had a stand at the Crystal Palace Electrical Exhibition at which were shown Electric cookers and heaters. He certainly had far-seeing ideas. ... Certainly Messrs. Crompton, who were responsible for the manufacturer of these articles, fully grasped the possibilities of Electricity being applied for perfect cooking in the future...." Lancaster, Electric Cooking, 1914. Dowsing placed these electrical wares on the English market in 1894.*

XVIII-15. Mixer & juicer attachment, *on stand. Enameled metal. Note hinged stantion. General Electric, 1919. Picture courtesy General Electric.* **$75-$120**

XVIII-16. Mixer & food preparer. *The "KitchenAid" for home use — showing the whipping blades. Notice the extra mixing bowl at far right, and the detachable funnel lying on the right of the work stand. "The kitchen is too often a drab kind of place. Yet surely, considering the hours spent there, ... it ought to be the cheerfullest room in the house. In KitchenAid homes, the kitchen has come into its own. It is Mother's workshop — a place where drudgery has given way to self expression — where cooking and baking has become a joy — new recipes a real sport. It is no longer a lonely place. Dad, who admires mechanical ingenuity, likes to watch KitchenAid's deft, steel hands at work — or to 'run' it himself, especially in freezing ice cream. You will find 'Junior' and 'sister' there, too, and very often a guest." Hobart Corp., Troy, OH, "KitchenAid" catalog, 1928. This mixer for home use followed by three years the first commercial electric mixer, for restaurants and hotels. Hobart Corp., founded in 1897, was innovative from the beginning. To quote from a short company history, "During the period from 1905 to 1910, peanut butter and hamburger were becoming popular items in the American diet, and Hobart introduced an electric meat chopepr and a peanut butter machine. To build sales for these products, Hobart pioneered time-payment selling."* **$100-$175**

XVIII-17. Mixer in many roles. *Page decorations for the G-E "Hotpoint Portable Mixer." 1935-36 catalog. Sunbeam and Kitch-enAid mixers also had multiple uses.*

Mixer, enameled cast metal, opaque green custard glass reamer & mixing bowl, Manning Bowman & Co., Meriden, CT, 1930s-1940s. **$55-$75**

Mixer, green cast iron frame, green Jadite bowl, green wooden handle, like a small KitchenAid, "Mixette," mfd. by F. A. Smith Mfg. Co., Rochester, NY, c.1930s. **$60-$80+**

Mixer, plated metal stand has tall post to which multispeed beater motor clamped at any height, revolving metal mixing bowl, "Star-Rite Magic Maid," Fitzgerald Mfg. Co., Torrington, CT, c.1931. **$35-$50**

Mixer, with instruction booklet and many attachments, including ricer, meat grinder, mixing bowls of creamy green glass, "Sunbeam Model FC4," Chicago Flexible Shaft Co., 1934 patent #1926910 is latest patent number. Their first "Mixmaster" was 1930. **$80-$130**

Mixer & food processor, enameled cast iron base and motor housing, holder for mixing bowls, 3 speeds & attachments to beat eggs or mix batters, whip cream, mix dough, strain fruits, sieve & puree vegetables, slice potatoes, chop meats or nuts, make ice cream, grind coffee, shred or grate, extract citrus fruit juice, make applesauce . . . yep, sounds like a you-know-what, KitchenAid division of Hobart Mfg. Co., Troy, OH, early model introduced c.1920; this large one c.1930. **$75-$130**

Women & Machines — In a 1919 speech, Raymond Marsh, Secretary of the American Washing Machine Manufacturers' Association, said "A wonderful story could be told about how women went into factories and recovered entirely from their awe and fear of machinery. Experience has shown that women are and can be efficient at running machinery. . . . During the war, women rendered efficient service working hydraulic presses, heating and charging furnaces, welding brass, forging chains, molding bricks, constructing compasses . . . and a thousand and one other important and necessary tasks." Marsh's point was that WWI encouraged the use of labor-saving devices in the kitchen because women lost their fear of machines (and they had no household servants) when every able-bodied woman in the U.S., England and France (and probably Germany too) went to work in war-industry factories.

XVIII-20. Mixer beater whipper. *"Handyhot" deluxe combination mixer, clear glass beater jar with graduated markings for 3 cups. White motor housing with nickeled handle. 110-120 volts, 50-60 cycle AC current. Chicago Electric Manufacturing Co., 1938 catalog.* **$25-$45**

XVIII-18. Mixer. *General Electric's "DeLuxe Hotpoint Mixer" — a "complete Kitchen Power Unit, designed for thorough mixing, beating, juice-extracting, and numerous other duties." Baked-on Glyptal enamel in 3 color combinations: green with black trim, cream with green trim, green with cream trim. Three speed motor in base, AC or DC, rubber cord, Pyrex™ bowls. G-E catalog, 1935-36.* **$95-$165**

XVIII-19. Mixer beater. *"Quick-Mix" with one speed & one beater. The eye at left of motor housing is for hanging it on a hook when not in use. Manufacturer's name not in* Thomas' Register of American Manufacturers *of the 1930s. Pictured in* Electric Home, *1936.* **$30-$40**

XVIII-21. Mixer. *Single stainless steel blade, red wooden knob, white glass beater jar was press-molded with rocket-fin designs — for stability and style. 9-1/2" H. "K-M," Knapp-Monarch Co., St. Louis, MO, c.1940s.* **$35-$45**

Mixer or beater, iron housing lid with strap handle, looks like part of an old hair dryer, activates 2-wing blade, glass jar, works perfectly, hums quietly, "Challenge," mfd. by CEM Co., "Tyre Avub." (Whur's this? Sounds like a Biblical land of gluttony & sloth.) "CEM" is Chicago Electrical Manufacturing Co., Chicago, IL, 8-1/2" H, with 3-cup capacity, 1930s? (CEM est. c.1903.). "Use Electric Mixer to WAX, POLISH, SAND" — so advertised Towle Mfg. Co., Walnut Creek, CA, in Sept. 1960. Their device, a "slip-on TOOLZON," was fitted on the shaft of "any mixer" so that you could "let your kitchen mixer wax furniture, floors, auto; polish silver, glass, brass; sand wood, metal, ceramics." (I can just see the product liability disclaimers.) In theory it's a great idea. **$15-$35**

Outlet, cast iron, figural with 3 outlets & 2 lions' heads, American or English, 3" L, late 19th C. (?) **$65-$100**

Outlet, twin outlet porcelain plug for appliances, in original box depicting woman demonstrating the plug hanging from a ceiling fixture (shades of George Booth cartoons). "Permits the Use of Two Electrical Conveniences at the Same Time." "GE," Schenectady, NY, 4" L, 1916. **$35-$45**

The best information on the **development of electrical plugs** is found in the July 1986 issue of *Technology and Culture* quarterly of the Society for the History of Technology, in an article by Dr. Fred E. H. Schroeder of the University of Minnesota, entitled "More 'Small Things Forgotten': Domestic Electrical Plugs and Receptacles, 1881-1931." Reprints may be ordered for $5 or so, from The University of Chicago Press, 5801 South Ellis Avenue, Chicago, IL 60637. For anyone interested in electrical appliances, I would highly recommend this.

Ovenette, stand with 3 cabriole legs, rack inside over holes to let heat rise, high cover, wooden knob, plated metal, temperature gauge on side, between 2 legs, "Stanley Ovenette," mfd. by Stanley Savage Mfg Co., Chicago, IL, about 8" diameter, 1930s. **$25-$35**

Potato baker, insulated oven in casserole or chafing dish shape, on 3 sheet metal legs, molded phenolic resin side handles & lid knob, heating element in bottom part, "Knapp-Monarch," St. Louis, MO, 1930s. **$35-$45**

Sandwich grill, oblong streamlined body, thick, heavy lid is removable (for washing) grill surface, inside is smooth, of course, 4 legs, "tassel-like" molded phenolic resin "Bakelite" lid handle, also has accessory broiling and frying grids, "Edicraft," Edison Electric, NJ, 1930s. With all grids & grills: **$45-$55**

Teapots, coffee pots, electric — See Chapter XIV (Coffee, Tea & Chocolate)

Toaster, boxy body, almost as long as high (came with choice of nickel or chrome finish), on wide base with 4 small button feet, embossed on sides with decorative border & medallion that looks for all the world like a Georgian wall mirror, toast holder for one slice pulls out of end, holds bread vertically, clockwork timer, adjustable for brownness; a gussied up & automatic version of the simpler E942. "Universal E9422," Landers, Frary & Clark, New Britain, CT, late 1920s to 1930. This style looks so neo-Georgian/Victorian, it is hard to believe that it was being made at the same time as much more streamlined electric toasters. **$25-$45**

Toaster, brightly chromed, Art Deco, side loading, "Son-Chief," Winsted, CT, 1920s-1930s. In 1983, Charles P. Fisher, an engineer with a special understanding of and fondness for toasters, wrote me that he was beginning work on a book devoted to electric toasters. The book is *Hazlecorn's Price Guide to Old Electric Toasters* (see bibliography), on which Mr. Fisher's name appears in tiny type & abbreviated, only on the title page. But Fisher is the expert. I have referred to his work a few times in the following toaster entries. **$35-$55**

Toaster, chrome, black Bakelite handles, leaping deer Art Deco decoration on door, does only one piece of toast at a time, toast holder controlled by lever handle, tilt down to insert bread, push up to insert holder in toaster, dial on side for degree of toastedness, using letters of alphabet from A to K instead of numbers, GE Appliances Co., 6-3/4" H, late 1920s. **$40-$55**

Toaster, chrome & black Bakelite, high round top body with flat sides and flat bottom, shapely black base, one slice, handles on both ends, Merit-Made Co., Buffalo, NY, early 1940s. **$25-$35**

Toaster, chrome & black-painted sheet metal, tray base, flip down doors, does 4 slices, "Victorian, Model A65," Bersted Mfg. Co., Chicago, IL, 12" L x 6-3/4" W, looks c.1940s, may be a bit earlier. **$20-$35**

XVIII-22. "Preparing dinner with Electric Cooker." *These are called "electric cookers" in England, but they function like stoves. For other stoves, see Chapter XI. General Electric Co. of Great Britain photo, in* Electric Cooking, *1914.*

XVIII-23. "First electric toaster" — *at least according to the Cologne, Germany auction house Auction Team Breker, which sold this "Eclipse" toaster from 1893 at auction, April 28, 1990. The estimated price was $900 to $1200. "Eclipse" was trade name used by the Electric & Ordnance Accessories Co., Birmingham, England, but according to the Lancaster book of 1914, E&O didn't get into the business of electrical appliances until after about 1905. See drawings of various heating elements used in toasters & some other small appliances in XVIII-24. The "Eclipse" element, fifth down, has crimped "high resistance ribbon ... wound over mica strips." (Note: there should be only 11 turned rings in all on the handle.) 1990 auction price:* **$2165**

XVIII-24. Electric heating elements in 1890. *From* Electric Cooking and Heating, *1914. "Early electric heating elements ... for self-contained utensils [were made of] fine German silver wire embedded in enamel in the form in sketch."* **Prometheus:** *Three forms introduced by the Prometheus Co. (American). (1) Strip "consisting of a deposit of gold and platinum on strips of mica"; (2) ribbon in the "key pattern form used for flat irons, hot-plates, etc."; (3) finally, "oven elements took the form of special high resistance wire or tape wound over mica, varnished and encased with thin steel."* **Eclipse:** *"High resistance ribbon crimped to give greater length and free-air space, wound over mica strips with the ends connected to heavy eyelet terminals as in sketch."* **Calor:** *"A base of fireclay with grooves into which spirals of fine high resistance wire are placed."* **Phoenix:** *"Spiral wire coils held lightly at short intervals by porcelain insulators mounted on a suitable base."* **Hot-point:** *"Nichrome wire or ribbon, wound lightly around thin strips of mica; further covered with a thin mica covering and inserted very tightly into grooves or slots made in the hot-plate or iron base to receive the finished strips."* **Belling:** *"Fireclay strip with spirals of nichrome wire stretched across width of base, notches being provided in the base for receiving ends of the spiral and holding them tightly in position."* **Jackson:** *"Has a different class of fireclay base with quite a smooth surface, the section of the strips, being a flat oval, wire or ribbon of nichrome, is wound tightly over strip in one continuous length and clamped between heavy terminals at each end."* **Tricity:** *"Nichrome ribbon wound over thin mica and clamped between thin sheets of mica and metal."* **Bastian** *or* **Quartzalite:** *"Spiral of nichrome wire or ribbon coated with film of oxide insulation & held in or on a quartz tube ... to give it a 'hot-rod' appearance."*

XVIII-25. Toasters & other appliances. *From bottom left:* (1) *Early toaster with high sided basket (like the "Eclipse"), flower-decorated white porcelain base. General Electric. According to engineer Charles P. Fisher (who wrote, with his wife,* Hazelcorn's Price Guide to Old Electric Toasters, 1908-1940*), this is the second version of the G-E D-12, dating to "about 1910." Note the high "railing" of the toast-holding basket. The third version, says Fisher, looks almost the same but has considerably lower sides. It probably dates to about 1912. By the way, an even rarer decorated porcelain toaster would be the one in Blue Willow pattern made by Pan Electrical Mfg. Co., Cleveland, OH, c.1925.* (2) *Above, seemingly floating in air [but on Plexiglas] is a "Universal E947" made by Landers, Frary & Clark. Fisher describes this toaster as "the loveliest and most durable of swingers," and I agree. The base alone is beautiful; it's worth buying the toaster for those angled non-conductive disks forming the feet. This dates to between 1922-29.* (3) *Center is an "Angelus Campfire Bar-B-Q Marshmallow Toaster," with red rubber feet on wire legs. "Pat. Appl. For,"*

c.1920s - 1930s. Angelus Campfire Co., Inc., Chicago. (4) *The pedestal base waffle iron is heavily chromed and has a decorative porcelain insert in the lid. It is undated, but is probably about 1930. Collector Susan Lewis wrote me about hers, similar but with lovebird design, made by "SuperLectric." Hers is also undated. The electric iron is not described by G-E, who provided the photograph. Three value ranges are for the 2 toasters and the waffle iron.* **$250-$350; $45-$75; $85-$150**

XVIII-26. Toaster, *with flat bed. Bread held in horizontal basket, rather than vertical. Not a very efficient toaster for the time, but rather stylish in appearance. Picture from Louise J. Peet & Lenore E. Sater's* Household Equipment, *1934, 1940.* **$15-$25**

XVIII-29. Toaster. *"Universal" E9419, by Landers, Frary & Clark with perforated top plate for keeping toast warm. This is a primitive "flipdown" door type for two slices. Note the angled feet disks — terrific styling. This 340 watt toaster could be had nickel plated or "silver plated," but I don't know if the many toasters offered in silver plate were "german silver" or sterling silver. Came with 6-foot "mercerized silk finish flexible cord, triple contact terminal plug." 1914 catalog. LF&C also offered a "twin" style, with two identical E941 toasters mounted to a single oblong flat base!* **$225-$350**

XVIII-27. Toaster. *General Electric, Model X-2, pat'd 11/9/1915 (not 1905 as stated in 2nd edition). I thank Charles P. Fisher, again, for correcting this error, which resulted because G-E itself gave me a 1905 date. According to Fisher, it may never have been marketed, although obviously the toaster itself exists or G-E couldn't have sent me a picture! If it exists, the value would be very high.* **$350+**

XVIII-28. Toaster. *General Electric, 2nd version of D-12, c.1910. Detachable wire warming rack in place. Painted porcelain base. Picture courtesy G-E shows plug and cord which I am not sure are original because I don't think they had the black cloth-wrapped cords with white dots, as shown here, at the time.* **$250-$350**

XVIII-30. Toaster. *"Thermax" No. E1942, by Landers, Frary & Clark. Although it could be ordered through LFC's "Universal" catalog of 1914, this toaster was in their not-so-well-known "Thermax" line. Available like the previous one in nickel or silver plate, but with 6-foot "flexible cord." Triple contact terminal plug. Note slotted warming rack above and the nifty sleek slotted doors.* **$85-$100**

Toaster, chrome body, black plastic base, does only one piece at a time, bread is inserted in one end & comes out other end of narrow body (which is an elongated oval seen from above), after a rather jerky trip through the length of the toaster . . . a trip you can observe through a very small porthole in the side. Adjustable light & dark lever. Has a fan inside that cools the works (but not the toast). "Toast-O-Lator, Model J," pat'd by Alfredo DeMatteis, and mfd. by Toast-O-Lator Corp., Long Island City, NY, about 11" H, c.1940. **$200-$250**

Toaster, chrome body, brown Bakelite handles, "Faultless Appliances, Model #1249," St. Louis, MO, 1930s-1940s. **$30-$35**

Toaster, chrome half-round body, flat sides, black Bakelite base and handles, red signal light on one side, near base, hinged crumb tray, could be set for "pops toast up" or "keeps toast warm," 2 slices, styling by George Scharfenberg, "Sunbeam", Chicago Flexible Shaft Co., Chicago, IL, 1940. **$30-$45**

Toaster, chrome, makes 2 pieces of toast, has 6 toasting darkness degrees, "Edicraft Automatic," mfd. by Thomas A. Edison Inc., Orange, NJ, 7-1/8" H x 10-1/4" L, early 20th C. **$80-$130**

Toaster, chrome oblong boxy body with control end slightly truncated at top corner, one slice capacity (they also made a 2-slice model), 5 fluted vertical panels on both sides, "Toastmaster Model 185," mfd. by Waters-Genter Co., division of McGraw Electric Co., Minneapolis, MN, 1931. **$35-$55**

XVIII-31. Toaster. *Nickel-plated, blue wooden knobs, 7" H x 8" L x 4-1/4" W, 1920 & 1927 patents. "Electrix" by United Drug Co.* **$55-$65**

XVIII-33. Toaster. *The maker of this "economical, thoroughly dependable" toaster was not given in the general merchandise catalog in which I found the picture, but it is to my eye very attractive. It resembles, in some respects, the products of a wide range of manufacturers', but I couldn't find it in Fisher's book, nor in any of my other catalogs. "Sparkling nickel plate," 7-1/2" x 7-1/2" x 4-1/4", 6-foot cord, 2-piece plug. "All complicated and fragile moving parts are eliminated. Being standard size, it takes a full slice of bread without trimming. Women appreciate its artistic design and quiet elegance." Possibly Lindemann & Hoverson, of Milwaukee, or possibly Russell Electric, Chicago. From Slack Mfg. Co., Chicago, c.1925 catalog. I don't think they actually made electric appliances.* **$35-$45**

XVIII-32. Toaster. *"Marion Giant Flipflop #66," mfd. by Rutenber Electric Co., Marion, IN. According to Charles Fisher, many versions of this were made, with vertical cutouts in the door, cutouts in the bases, different flat tops. Nickel-plated, c.1925-31. From unidentified catalog page. What a name for the marketing director to fuss with!* **$25-$45**

XVIII-34. Toaster, *for one slice; automatic. Toastmaster 1A1, 1926. This was* <u>McGraw-Edison's first domestic toaster,</u> *and was the result of McGraw-Edison mechanic Charles Strite's inventiveness. In 1918, Mr. Strite built the first automatic pop-up toaster, and the principle of its operation, using a spring motor and switch, was patented in 1919. Commercial toasters were made soon after, for restaurants and lunch counters, and sold under the Strite name. There were models for lunchrooms & hotels, such as the "Eight Slice Strite Automatic," which actually could do 12 small slices, or 360 per hour! There was also a "Three Slice Strite," 3 slices every 1-1/4 minutes! But it was not until 1926 that this first home model automatic pop-up appear in housewares departments. It sold in 1926 for the then-whopping $12.50.* **$75-$125**

Toaster, chromed brass pedestal base with ball feet not at corners, embossed fancy decoration on sides, pendant handles at each end, toasting frame is like an abstract slice of toast turned diamond-wise, with point facing down, arched top, basket-flipping operated with pushbutton, "Universal E-9419," mfd. by Landers, Frary & Clark, New Britain, CT, c.1928-29. It is probably safe to say that collectibles utilizing metal made just before a war, or fancy items made just before a financial crash, have rarity added by events that almost certainly halt production. **$225-$350**

Toaster, chromed sheet metal, peaked tent shape with pull down doors decorated with 2 vertical bands with sort of wheat berry design, the dished tray on top — for buttering prepared toast or keeping it warm — lifts off for cleaning, dial control for light, brown or medium sticks out under one side, "Serv-Hot Toast Tray" & "Queen Mary" pattern, "Royal-Rochester" toaster, mfd. by Robeson-Rochester Corp, Rochester, NY, c.1937. **$30-$45**

Toaster, cylindrical shape, revolves on its base and was probably used in center of breakfast table, black plastic knob on top and 3 oblong feet, chrome plated, 4 swingout "car" doors with slot for toast (where car window would be), heating element in central core, "Elem," German, 1958. **$40-$55**

Toaster, enameled black metal base and top, very boxy, chromium body has 2 sets of 4 vertical stamped lines or stripes on both sides (design is "Beaumonde Pattern"), Bakelite (or other

molded phenolic resin) knob on end door, end-loading for 2 slices, "Double-Quick," Universal Electric, mfd. by Landers, Frary & Clark, c.1935. **$25-$35**

Toaster, fabulous 3 slicer, black baked enameled steel 3-sided box frame and base, 3 decorated chrome doors, triangular top of chrome with knob, mica heating element, "Delta," mfd. by Kamco Inc., Unionville, CT, c.1935. Mica is a silicate crystal, built up by nature in thin, somewhat flexible leaves or sheets. It was early used for translucent panels in oven doors, heating stoves & lanterns as well as later for heating elements in electric toasters. **$75-$100**

Toaster, gorgeously simple open-sided metal box on base with curled strap metal legs, black baked enamel finish, toasting elements visible like a modern art sculpture, "Cookenette," no mfr's name, 1920s or 1930s, but not in 1930 *House Furnishing Review Buyer's Guide*. **$60-$80**

Toaster, green painted sheet metal, "The Handy Hot," Chicago Mfg. Co., (or Chicago Electric Mfg. Co.), Chicago, IL, c.1930s. **$20-$25**

Toaster, high & skinny, porcelain base, chromed openwork metal with 6 small cutout stars on top, 2 toast doors are loaded, then you turn to other side, turning knobs on top are molded plastic, "Star-Rite, the Star Electric Toaster," mfd. by Fitzgerald Mfg Co., Torrington, CT, 9" H, c.1929 (?). **$80-$125**

Toaster, moderately interesting Art Deco design, in original box, "Speed Master," mfd. by Son Chief Electric Co., Winsted, CT, 1930s. **$25-$40**

XVIII-35. Toaster. *The "new and improved" pop-up Toastmaster, from 1930. "It comes in 1 and 2-slice sizes and is a revelation in simplicity and smartness. Of the hundreds of thousands who saw the remarkable first model which revolutionized toastmaking in America, not one would have believed it could ever have been improved on. Yet — that has been done! With the new model, all you do is drop in the bread and press but a single lever. And forget about it!" Waters-Genter Co., Division of McGraw Electric Co., Minneapolis, MN. 10/1930 ad in* Good Housekeeping. **$45-$55**

XVIII-37. Toaster. *"Delta," mfd. by Kamco Inc., Unionville, CT, c.1935. Chrome doors in black-enameled frame. Originally only $2.39.* House Furnishing Review, *7/1935.* **$75-$100+**

XVIII-36. Toy toaster. *Note the feet like the Universal. This was described in the 6/1930* House Furnishing Review, *shortly after they began covering the toy market. "The Excel Electric Co., Muncie, IN, makes the Excel Toastoy, a toy electric toaster, for toasting half slices of bread. Nickeled throughout, with "nichrome" heating element, 150-watt capacity. complete with plug and silk cord. Retails at $1." Nickel finish; 5" H x 6" L x 3" W. The "Toastoy" had apparently been for sale in 1929 also, and they continued making them for several years, at least until 1933.* **$70-$115**

XVIII-38. Toaster. *"Hotpoint General Electric," mfd. by Edison General Electric Appliance Co., Chicago, IL, 1931. Chromed steel. Note Art Deco leaping stag design in center of side. Ad from La-dies' Home Journal, 3/1931.* **$45-$65**

Toaster, nearly square chromed box with slightly sloped sides, 4 corner columns rising from little black rolling feet, what the manufacturer called "artistic" pendent handles on 2 sides, lever to cause toast to pop up, 2 slices, automatic switch-off with bell, adjustable for doneness, "Auto-Toastmaker," Bersted Mfg. Co., Chicago, IL, new in 1930. **$35-$55**

Toaster, nickel-plated, 2 openwork flip-down doors, openwork warming shelf above, mica & wire elements, 4 knurled Bakelite knobs at bottom corners of doors, "Westinghouse Turnover Toaster, Model S372788B," mfd. by Westinghouse Electric Mfg. Co., Mansfield, OH. This model dates to c.1925. Westinghouse made several "Turnover" toasters, earlier ones with wire doors, the very earliest with ceramic heating elements, the slightly later ones have doors with less openwork. **$35-$45**

Toaster, nickel-plated, single slice, boxy end-loading oven type, with pull out rack, "Universal E942," Landers, Frary & Clark, pat'd in 1925. **$28-$35**

XVIII-39. Toaster. *"The Hotpointer" No. 129T41, automatic, 2 slices, General Electric. "The thermostat, placed right against one slice of the bread, regulates the color of the toast as determined by the setting of the Control Knob. ... Hotpointer signal light, on top, glows a ruddy red when the current is on, and fades out when the current turns off. Tiny bell concealed in base of toaster chimes gently when toast is done. The Hotpointer is absolutely silent in operation, except for this soft musical chime note." Chromed finish, black Calmold™ plastic knob and handle, nichrome wire with mica, 6-foot detachable cord set with G-E moulded rubber attachment plug and miniature Calmold appliance plug. 850 watts, 115, 125 volts. 1935-36.* **$45-$65**

XVIII-40. Toaster. *"Hotpointer" semi-automatic, similar exterior styling to preceding one. Permanently attached cord set. Came with recipe booklet. It does one side of toast at a time, and when the thermostat shuts off the current, you "lower the doors, which turns the toast, and the current immediately comes on again, to toast the other side." Here they call the thermostat a "Taste Control." General Electric, 1935-36 catalog.* **$35-$55**

Limp versus Crisp — An interesting sidenote: Mr. C. Fisher, who wrote what is now called *Hazelcorn's Price Guide to Old Electric Toasters, 1908-1940,* says that because of the greater air intake through toaster doors with a lot of openwork, toast was crisper when made in them, although it took longer. Toaster doors without openwork, or with very little, were in aid of faster, less crispy toasting. In England, people are accustomed to, and prefer, crisp toast. Perhaps early in the twentieth century, Americans preferred it the English way, whereas later in the century maybe they were looking for ways to save electricity, and persuaded themselves to prefer limper toast!

Toaster, nickel-plated, blue wooden knobs, swing-out baskets with pivoting hinges so that toast could be "turned over" by pushing the baskets back in the opposite way. This pivoting action is interesting relative to pivoting toe toasters of hearth cooking times. "Electrex," United Drug Co.; or "Torrid Pushomatic," by Frank E. Wolcott Mfg. Co.; or Beardsley-Wolcott, so Boston, MA or Waterbury, CT, 7" H x 8" L x 4-1/4" W, 1920 & 1927 patents, Fisher says "Pushomatic" used 1928 to c.1930. **Classic** — Pleasing to know that one of only two old toasters I ever bought is considered by the undisputed expert, Charles Fisher (whose list provided the various markings above), to be "an interesting and important toaster." I love it. **$55-$65**

XVIII-41. Toasters. (**L**) *Unidentified maker. Styling similar to many other non-automatic toasters requiring the doors to be lowered.* (**R**) *"Toastmaster " automatic. Both pictures from* Electric Home, *by E. S. Lincoln, 1936.* **$35-$65**

XVIII-42. Toaster. *Neat tipping action. Safe retrieval of non-pop-up toast was a concern of consumers and manufacturers. Probably a "Universal" model by Landers, Frary & Clark, c.1935. Picture from Peet's book* Household Equipment, *1940.* **$60-$75**

XVIII-43. Toaster. *Two views. Note spider web design — a desirable thing for collectors. General Electric, 1940.* **$50-$65**

XVIII-45. Toaster. *"Toastwell," manufactured by Utility Electric Co., St. Louis. It's completely automatic and "super silent — no 'ticking' annoyance found in the ordinary toasters." I bet he got a bad burn on his cheek! Pop-up, chrome plated with Bakelite handles & base. 7" H x 11-1/2" L. 725 watts; 110-125 volts AC or DC, detachable cord & plug. It also came in a 4-slice style, which was simply elongated to 13-3/8" L, and 7-1/4" H. Pictures from Dearborn catalog, 1942. The 4-slice style would bring more.* **$55-$70**

XVIII-44. Toaster. *"Universal Turn-Easy" model E1321 in the Coronet pattern. "Second to none in styling. Its design follows the modern trend with artistic chasing." Came with matching percolator, waffle iron, etc. Chrome plated, "smart black handles & feet" [they don't mention Bakelite, used in describing others on same page], 6-foot cord and plug. Lowering doors turns toast over. From Ft. Dearborn Mercantile catalog, 1942.* **$45-$55**

XVIII-46. Toaster & toast server-top. *Westinghouse "Pop-Up," automatic "crisper for regular or Melba toast." Streamline design, chrome finish, Bakelite base & handles, curved end for easy parking. Bakelite cover-server is seen protecting innards (**L**), and being used upside down as toast server at (**R**) — a really excellent idea. In Dearborn catalog, 1940.* **$65-$85**

Toaster Go-With — At a thrift shop I recently bought a tee shirt advertising a computer screen saver: "After Dark. The Flying Toaster Squadron — On a mission to save your screen." 10 boxy flying toasters from c. 1945. Adv'g Berkeley Systems, "Heroes of technology."

Toaster, nickeled metal, flip-down doors perforated with 7 long popsicle stick vertical slots, warming platform on top, "patented attachment turns the toast automatically" is activated by touching door handles, "Electric Flipflop Model 65" (by 1922 called the "Marion Flipflop"), mfd. by Rutenber Electric Co., Marion, IN, 1917. **$35-$45**

Toaster, plain white porcelain base, high sided wire basket rack with 11 upright wires on both sides, with heating elements in center, "General Electric D-12," Oct. 20, 1908 patent is for heating element. **$250-$350**

Toaster, plump but sleek, black bottom, chrome upper, 2-slicer pop-up, with brown plastic handles each end, one is also the pushdown, tiny dial at bottom, this is the toaster I use every day since buying it at a thrift shop in the 1970s. And I can fix it myself if something goes wrong. "Toaster with the Tester," Manning-Bowman, about 7-1/2" H, prior to WWII, suspended, then in production again. **$10-$15**

After the War — A 1944 ad in *House & Garden* is interesting because of its insight into the effect of war on domestic appliance production. "Watch for the return of the famous 'Toaster with the Tester' and other top-quality Manning-Bowman appliances. They'll be back (soon we hope) when our production facilities are no longer needed by the armed forces. . . . Manning-Bowman — Means Best. Keep on buying war bonds!"

Toaster, pop-up, nickeled or chromed, interesting one slice top-loader with 6 horizontal louvers on each side, one end squared neatly, the other end rounded off at top, 2 lever control — to set timer and to lower basket inside, "Toastmaster Automatic, Model 1A1," mfd. by Waters-Genter, Minneapolis, MN, pat'd 1926 by Charles Strite. A "2" slice model was also made. **$45-$55**

XVIII-48. Hot water urns. (L) *Edison Electric Co. hot water urn, of nickeled heavy spun copper. Heating disk is in base above little legs. 19" H x 9" W.* **(R)** *"Instantaneous" hot water heater, mfr. unknown. Copper, capacity of 4 pints, 15" H x 7" W. Note the claw & ball feet, which may be glass marbles, although it doesn't say so. 1906. Note the "lamp socket plug" that screws into lightbulb socket. Both from Albert Pick hotel supplies catalog, 1909.* **$50-$120**

XVIII-49. Portable hot water heater. *Unit for heating a pail of water. The "Premier" by the National Ideal Co., Toledo, OH. Ad from* Farm Journal, *11/1947.* **$15-$25**

XVIII-47. Toaster. *"Sunbeam," by Chicago Flexible Shaft Co. "The lovely oval design [is] the last word in modern styling by George Scharfenberg." [Imagine a 1990s toaster ad giving the designer's name, unless it was a famous architect and the toaster was $250.] Ad claimed "every slice of toast the identical shade of every other slice, whether it's first or last." That was useful when making party canapes, I guess. Could be had also as part of a "stunning buffet set including four new intaglio crystal lap trays, 3-compartment appetizer dish and large, roomy walnut tray." The really nifty feature was you could set this one to pop-up or to keep the toast inside until wanted. Saturday Evening Post, 1940.* **$65-$90**

Toaster, pyramid, aluminum, 2 slices, black painted base, black handles, "Riverside Mfg. Co.," Ypsilanti, MI, 20th C. **$15-$25**

Toaster, shapely ceramic body, with resemblance to Oriental temple, 4 feet, mica elements, outstanding underglaze decoration in version of "Blue Willow" pattern, with the typical arched footbridge, 2 figures on bridge, temples & trees, Pan Electrical Mfg. Co., Cleveland, OH, c.1920s. **$200-$250**

Toaster, sheet metal base — black baked enamel over copper, fancy floral embossed doors, openwork top, wooden knobs,"Universal," mfd. by Landers, Frary & Clark, 1930s. **$30-$35**

A children's book that you toaster & electric appliance collectors should try to add to your collection is the delightful *The Brave Little Toaster,* by Thomas M. Disch, illustrated by Karen Lee Schmidt (Doubleday l986). It's about the exploits of an indomitable two-slice toaster and its four friends — all obsolete household appliances.

Toaster, simple heavy wire frame with finer wires criss-crossing inside, "General Electric X-2," pat'd Nov. 9, 1915. Mr. Charles P. Fisher corrects GE's own misinformation that this one was patented in 1905; the patent date is actually 1915. This is the value of specialization in research. Fisher asks, in the caption to this toaster in his book, "Rare? nonexistent?" **$350+**

Toaster, toast warmer rack above for 6 slices, put toast in wire frame of door, it comes down on a spring, you flip it and push it back up to the heating elements, "The Reversible Toaster," Manning -Bowman Co., Meriden, CT, pat'd Dec. 28, 1920, & Dec. 4, 1923. **$55-$75+**

Toaster, very Art Deco, black metal base and top, chrome sides with leaping deer decoration, loads one slice on end, adjusts for brownness, "Hotpoint," mfd. by GE, Edison General Electric Appliance Co., Inc., Chicago, 1931. **$40-$50**

Toaster, very art deco, chrome and black painted tin, very odd angled truncated pyramid shape, red Bakelite (or other molded phenolic resin) double knobs on the 2 doors, engraved with wheet design, 4 little button feet, Nelson Machine & Mfg. Co., Cleveland, OH, c.1930s. **$45-$60**

Toaster, white porcelain base, high frame wire basket with 6 vertical wires on both sides, heating elements in center, does 2 slices of toast, "General Electric D-12," c.1910 according to C. Fisher. This was, he says, 2nd version of "D-12." Add $75+ for detachable wire warming rack; add $100+ for floral decorated porcelain base. **$250-$350+**

Toaster, white porcelain base, wire basket with low sides and 6 vertical wires, with detachable wire warming rack above, "General Electric D-12" (3rd version, according to Fisher), 2 patent dates, for heating elements, 1908 & 1909. Toaster c.1912 until -?- Take off $75 or so for missing toast rack; add $100 or more for floral-decorated porcelain. Price range for "D-12": **$250-$350+**

Toaster, with possible other functions, handsome chrome body in shape of 2 near-halves of ball spread apart with vertical "valley," zigzag wire toast-warming shelf above, long black handle on one side, short handle for other hand on other side, at least 3 insert trays, one with wire arches to hold a piece of toast, one a shallow oblong tray or cradle with arched sides, one a perforated metal box that would fit sideways into the "valley," all with long black handles, the 2 halves "look like 2 reflectors opposite each other with a shelf in between with holes." Label reads "A. Mecky Co.," Philadelphia, PA, pat'd Aug. 1921. **$95-$125**

Toaster, egg cooker & bacon cooker combined, metal, 3-tiered appliance, cooks 4 eggs on the bottom, toast in the middle, bacon on the top, stamped "Hotpoint," mfd. by Edison Electric Appliance Co., Catalog "#116G10W660V110," pat'd Nov. 4, 1913. Collector Pat Castagnola brought this to my attention and sought information about it. I told her I didn't know anything; do any of you? **$55-$65**

Toaster, hot plate & warming oven combined, cast iron base, white enameled metal with black trim, black Bakelite handles, "darker" and "lighter" switch, push down lever for toast, nickeled plate on oven door says "LASKO Toaster Combination," mfd. by Lasko Toaster Co., 7-1/2" H x 9-3/8" x 13" W, c.1930s. **$85-$100**

Toaster stove, little rectangular cooker on cabriole legs, tray and comfit mesh screen, Westinghouse Electric & Mfg. Co., East Pittsburg, PA, early 20th C. **$45-$65**

Toasters, non-electric — See Chapter X and Chapter XI

Waffle irons, electric — See Chapter IV

RESEARCHING

XIX. RESEARCHING PATENTS FOR KITCHEN COLLECTIBLES

FINDING THE GENIUSES BEHIND IT ALL

Thomas Alva Edison defined genius as "1% inspiration and 99% perspiration." It's also the secret of successful invention, but just when we collectors begin a litany of thanks for the ingenious gadgets we love, we notice that Edison also wrote "there is no substitute for hard work." Oh, but praise be, there is, if you think hard is fun! Tracing inventions from the U.S. Patent Office's first century is profitable fun, although the search needs inspiration and perspiration in the same ratio as genius. As a break from the "hard work," we love serendipitous finds of funny-looking inventions found by browsing *Gazettes*. Lucky Don Thornton lives near a patent library where he searches a year's index, sees how interesting the drawing looks in the *Gazette*, puts a microfilm reel on a machine, spins the crank to his target patent, and makes a photocopy right then. Instant gratification! He may have started with eggbeater patents for his book, but was soon on to any subject that appealed. Fortunately, kitchen inventions are numerous throughout the over 200 years the United States has been granting patents!

An early Patron Saint of Kitchen Substitutes for Hard Work (i.e. Labor-Saving) was Moses Coates, a mechanic from Chester County, PA, who — on Feb. 4, 1803 — got the first apple parer patent. No exact Coates are known, but early handmade wooden parers of that type bring $175 and up. Apple parer collectors also celebrate, among others, Horatio Keyes, David H. Whittemore, J. D. Seagrave and E. L. Pratt, Worcester, MA, whose Oct. 4, 1853 parer was probably the first practical parer with a mechanically guided blade. Mass production (and interchangeability) of cast iron gears by 1850 set off a "furious battle to perfect the paring machine," says John Lambert, founder of Apple Parer Enthusiasts. (See Chapter XXIII for a transcription of a report on patents granted during 1849 in the "household furniture" class.)

Many parer patents were granted in 1857 with no corresponding leap in pie pan or pie trimmer patents. You have to wonder if all-American apple pies maybe came of age in 1857, although a new recipe was needed in 1867 when nutmeg graters had *their* great year! In 1857 baseball was already the all-American sport and the country was in turmoil over slavery, the "Mormon War,"and a financial panic. Lambert suspects that 1855-56's crop of really "great designs" (including the turntable parer) spurred others to "top that" if they could. By 1890, when there were over 100 parer patents, the market had a "shake-out" and the few — including the Reading '78, Little Star, and White Mountain — that were left were featured for many decades in hardware stores and mail order catalogs. A newish variation of the "White Mountain" — Model #300 — is manufactured today by the White Mountain Freezer Co.

Patent records hint at a booming canning industry causing a decline of apple parer patents. Peeled apple segments were ready in a jiffy with a can opener; hundreds of *those* were patented, beginning with one in 1858, then skipping past most of the Civil War to 1864. The canning industry itself, which began circa 1840, was the biggest labor-saving "device" between the wheel and 1930, when Clarence Birdseye began to freeze food in little boxes. Instead of having a parer clamped to the kitchen counter all fall — not to mention mechanical pineapple eyesnips, tomato corers, corn shellers, raisin seeders, wheat berry grinders, peach parers, meat tenderizers, cabbage cutters, pea shellers, and the like — you could bypass picking, sorting, washing and parboiling with boxes or tins of food ready to cook or serve straight out of the can. You could even buy extremely large cans of berries or fruit or vegetables, and then re-can them in your own meal-sized fruit jars.

Patented Progress — Established by act of Congress on April 10, 1790 "to promote the progress of useful arts" the Patent Office granted only three patents the first year because almost no inventions met the test of being "sufficiently useful and important." In fact, until a new act of February 24, 1793 took away the power of rejection, or judging of worthiness, there were only seven patents granted. The first one under the new law was Eli Whitney's first patent for a cotton gin. In fact, Whitney got all three of the patents granted in 1794; and in 1795 and 1796 only three patents were granted each year. After that, the pace picked up, so that eventually many thousands of unnumbered patents were granted through 1836. We have only sketchy information on many of them, and Patent Office records cite different numbers of patents for that first 46-year period: from 11,445 or 11,348 on down to 9,957 patents. We laugh to read that in 1833 Patent Office Commissioner John D. Craig wanted to resign because he believed that everything "seems to have been done." Within two years he was succeeded by the more optimistic Henry Ellsworth, under whom, starting in 1836, the burgeoning flood of worthwhile and worthless patents were numbered as granted, sometimes on Tuesday, often another day.

During the next 46 years, from 1836 to 1882, the Patent Office granted 269,819 numbered patents, 13,507 design patents, 10,264 reissues and 9,919 trademarks (reflecting the burgeoning of brand marketing). W.P.N. Fitzgerald was the Patent Examiner in charge of inventions of mills, land conveyances, lumber machinery, hydraulics, pneumatics and textiles. He wrote in his 1849 report to Thomas Ewbanks, the Commissioner of Patents, "The field of invention in many of its departments is limited; and every year must necessarily circumscribe it still more narrowly, leaving little to be invented except what has been invented previously."

Worse Than Useless — For at least six decades, many, shall we say, undeserving inventions were granted patents. Even if well-intentioned, many neither claimed something truly new, nor even described something that would work, let alone save labor. Those silly if imaginative inventions, which patent collectors love to find and photocopy, didn't satisfy what Judge Learned Hand called a requisite for a valid subject for patent: "a new display of ingenuity." In an 1838 *Franklin Institute Journal*, the editor chastised one patentee thusly: "We cannot well conceive of a less promising affair than the foregoing, but things are not stopped in the Patent Office merely because they are trifling." It was cheap and easy to get a patent, and inventors rarely did any kind of patent search such as is done by expensive patent lawyers today, so many self-styled inventors entered what they saw as a get-rich-quick stream by applying for patents for just about anything.

The problem was not a new one. According to an article on the history of the Patent Office, in the *Official Gazette,* Oct. 9, 1877, "From 1790 to the re-organization of the Patent Office in 1836 there were granted 11,348 patents, a large number of which, on account of lack of novelty or usefulness, were valueless. The abuses which grew out of the promiscuous granting of patents without further inquiry than as to the payment of the fee and the form of the application attracted public attention in the early part of the present century," but it wasn't until July 4, 1836, that Congress passed a bill to improve the system of awarding patents. Apparently, the main fraud was by patent pirates, who would go into the model room, draw a patent drawing and copy the specs, make a few little changes, and automatically, upon payment of the required fee of about 50¢, get a patent, for which they would then sell the rights to unsuspecting individuals and companies who wanted to manufacture these inventions.

Women Inventors — The *New York Times* reported on Dec. 14, 1890, that "2,400 women have secured patents but very few have made much money with them with the exception of the lady who was so fortunate as to hit upon the fluting iron. . . . The women who have secured patents have been mostly thrifty housewives, and their inventions have been generally in the nature of kitchen utensils and domestic articles."

The *Times* article was based on a Patent Office publication: an 1809-1888 chronological listing of "Women Inventors," giving names, patent numbers, inventions and dates. Among women's patents we find cookstoves, ice-cream freezers, butter-workers, washing-machines, a combination of sofa and bathing tub, vegetable-graters, culinary boilers, and — beginning in the 1840s — a lot of "improvements on" mincing-knives, sieves, pie-tubes, bathroom racks, pastry-rollers, dish-washers, strawberry-hullers, flour-sifters, cake-stirrers, &c. The 1870s brought a spate of housekeeping helpers including a canning funnel, an egg-poaching pan, a fruit-fork, and an ever-useful "pantaloon tree," for drying those voluminous unmentionables. Sarah Sewell, Mark Centre, OH, patented a combined washing-machine and teeter or seesaw (#330,626), Nov. 17, 1885. A lot of today's day-care centers could use one of those. Predominant in most years were inventions relating to sewing, clothing, corsetry and — as an indication of the hard work involved — laundering and ironing. Many women besides famous Mrs. Potts (the probable "fortunate" lady cited by the *New York Times*) got patents on sad irons and fluting irons.

Hundreds of women's patents, including domestic-science ones, were little machines. Sarah Cooper, Morrisonville, PA, patented (#196,743) an "Improvement in apple quartering and coring machines" on Nov. 6, 1877; Emma Orendorff, Delavan, IL, patented (#199,704) an "Improvement in apple-corers" on Jan. 8, 1878. Another collecting specialty — eggbeaters — is represented by Sarah A. Ulmer, Portland, ME, whose tin churn-like eggbeater (#224,117) was patented Feb. 3, 1880. Ulmer's beater was manufactured, and is in at least one collection. Scores of them may be out there. Others patentees include Katherine Livingood, Womelsdorf, PA, eggbeater (#282,738) on Aug. 7, 1883; Hannah Zephyrene Gibson, Oberlin, OH, eggbeater (#293,648), Feb. 19, 1884; Eugenia Kilborn, Cedar Rapids, IA, eggbeater (#303,022), Aug. 5, 1884; and Edith A. Marsh, New Albany, IN, eggbeater (#345,709), July 20, 1886. All are possible finds, especially in or near patentees' hometowns.

An article in *House Furnishing Review* of January 1903 noted some inventions recently viewed at the Woman's Department of the Mechanics' Fair in Boston. Described as "the most original and unique invention" was Philadelphian Lydia C. Sharpless' bread-making machine. It was already being manufactured by The Scientific Bread Machine Co., Philadelphia. It took her three years, but Sharples made her own working patent model, of cardboard, tin and wood, and I bet her dyspeptic husband, for whom she wished to make digestible bread, was a happy man!

Publication of Patents — Brief note was made of some out-of-the-ordinary inventions in some scientific journals (such as the one from the Franklin Institute in Philadelphia), agricultural newspapers from the 1840s on, *Scientific American* and some English gentlemen's magazines published in American editions from the late 1700s on, but pictures were rare. The Patent Office had to supply a drawing of a patent if someone wrote to ask for one, and by 1861, photographic reproduction of patent drawings was being experimented with. The Civil War intervened, but starting July 1, 1869, twelve copies of each patent was being made. A year later, photolithographic copies were being made — 300 of each patent, but they decided that was in excess of the demand, so the number was cut to 150 for many years. Specifications and drawings were sent to the 50 depository libraries around the country from 1871 to —?—. The weekly *Official Gazette* was begun in 1873 (although one source I've seen says 1872), and at first was bound three or four months per volume. Many American inventors didn't live in or near a city with a depository library of patent records, and few lived in Washington, D.C., where anyone could go to the Patent Office and look at file copies of the patents or at the thousands of meticulous working models that were submitted as required with most primary patents until about 1881.

Patent Models Galore — The galleries at the Patent Office, with huge glass cases full of wonderful models, were a popular tourist site in the nineteenth century — and would be today, if the powers that be had thought enough of our inventive history to keep the models that survived two devastating fires.

The editor of the "Mechanics' Register" section of the *Journal of the Franklin Institute* wrote after the December 15, 1836 fire: "Our readers need not be informed of the great national loss consequent upon the burning of the Patent Office." A precis of the losses included "the records, originals, drawings, models, &c., ... [that] embraced the whole history of American invention for nearly half a century," "168 large folio volumes of records, and 26 large portfolios, containing 9000 drawings," "230 volumes of books ... of scientific subjects," "about seven thousand models [that] displayed great talent, ingenuity, and mechanical science." A new, so-called "fire-proof" building was erected in 1840, and in just nine years 200 patent models had been rebuilt, and 14, 997 new models, half for patents granted, half for rejects, were stored. Most, if not all, patent models that didn't perish in the 1836 fire in the Office's first building, succumbed to the September 24, 1877 fire. A blow-by-blow account of the progress of the fire through the third floor, wooden-raftered and perfect tinder, was published in the *Official Gazette* of October 9, 1877. Firemen from the District were aided by four engine companies rushed from Baltimore to Washington on railroad flatcars, and soldiers and police studded the Mall to guard the treasures that could be rescued. The third floor display galleries, "visited yearly by thousands of people, both for profit and pleasure . . . contained about 200,000 models of American invention." The fire destroyed "about 12,000 rejected models," and another 75,000 models . . . among them were several thousand known as "pending" and "issue" cases. The rejects were not considered a loss, and in fact "the propriety of breaking them up and selling them for old metal had recently been seriously discussed." If the rejects and the other pending and issue patent models were for sale today, we could practically retire the national debt, so greatly are all patent models valued by collectors.

As if the lessons of fire had never been taught, in 1888 Congress decided to sell the models, and inventors were notified. They claimed about 2000 models, and the rest were packed up higgledy-piggledy in crates. Around 1907, the Smithsonian curators were asked if they wanted any — and they unpacked crates and took about 4000 models. Curators at the Henry Ford Museum in Dearborn, Michigan, also acquired several thousand. According to an article by R. James Aber, in the Early American Industries Association magazine, *The Chronicle,* of April 1974, an English business man, Sir Henry Wellcome, bought the remainder of the collection (an estimated 175,000 models packed in about 3500 crates) in 1925 — for under $10,000. He wanted to build a museum, but died before it could be done. Crosby Gaige bought them next, and sold them to a business consortium. They sat in storage for years, and in 1941 or 1942, O. Rundle Gilbert, a well-known auctioneer of Garrison, NY, bought the collection, which was in uncatalogued crates, for an undisclosed amount. Fire destroyed about 20,000 models in one of Gilbert's barns. Extremely important models of every description were unpacked in dribs and drabs over the next three decades and individual models were sold to collectors — usually for a couple of hundred dollars or less. Models still show up on the market — usually for many hundreds or even thousands of dollars.

In the 1980s, an organization called the Patent Model Foundation was formed to attempt to establish a museum and research facility near Baltimore. On July 23, 1995 (which wasn't a "patent Tuesday"), **Inventure Place, Inc.** — home of the National Inventors Hall of Fame — opened. The address is 80 W. Bowery St., Suite 201, Akron, OH 44308-1170.

Probably the most inexpensive, tantalizing pursuit for collectors of cooking or housekeeping tools is patent research. It's so absorbing that more time can be spent researching the genius behind one tool than in finding it (or earning the money to buy it). One devoted patent collector is Don Thornton, whose remarkable eggbeaters compelled him to search out their inventors' thought processes — as revealed in application specifications. Thornton says that "The *Official Gazette* is the history of America in the form of millions of illustrated short stories!" He recommends hanging out at a patent depository library, preferably one with patents on microfilm and also hardbound copies of indices and *Official Gazettes*, which have pictures and short descriptions of every patent, including design patents and trademarks. The good ones don't stop at 1900, either; Don has made great finds in 1940s and 1950s *Gazettes*.

Pictures and claims help determine what if any parts are missing from a piece, or how something is supposed to work. And monetary value is affected by patent knowledge in other ways. About ten years ago I bought a humorously waggly sheet brass and iron wire eggbeater that screw-clamped to a shelf edge. I paid more than I'd ever paid before, but the dealer said it would have been more *if it had been a patented piece.* A few years later the patent drawing for it was found. Now the somewhat rough sawn edges of heavy sheet brass seemed a sign that it that it might be a production prototype, not a one-off piece. The value went up 300% and I sold it. Us patent junkies get hooked by suspenseful searches for patents for things we have — or think we have. At an auction I bought a cast iron gadget billed as a "pea sheller." The only mark was "Dec. 4, 1855"; it had felt-covered wringer-like rollers and a trough. Pop them ol' peapods, thought I. A year later, by chance, I was browsing the *Gazette*'s precursor, the patent report for 1855, and there was a picture of my gadget! It's a knife scourer. The felt pads held scouring powder or pumice, and the trough caught the pasty mess of pumice and water. I don't know if the value went up or down — depends on which class of gadget is most sought-after.

A cast embossed "patent" date on a gear may actually be the date an impatient inventor sent an application to Washington; or it may have been made up so that a gadget already in production would seem patent-protected. For patents after about 1846, you can check our perpetual calendar, (page 621) to confirm that a date found on an object fell on Tuesday. A patent number, permanently marked on a manufactured item, was required by law as of April 1, 1927, but many older patents also included the number.

You can also be a P.I. [Patent Investigator] by (A) using your own three-volume *Subject-Matter Index of Patents, 1790-1873;* (B) consulting the *Official Gazette* of the Patent and Trademark Office (P.T.O.), at regional patent depository libraries; and (C) ordering photocopies of specific patents (typically you'll get a full-page drawing, plus one to four pages of inventor's claims). Order photocopies from the P.T.O. for a few dollars each. For latest cost, query PS Center, CPK-1, Washington, DC 20231, or Rapid Patent Service, which provides libraries with sets of microfilmed patents. For years I got patent copies from the P.T.O. by sending an object's name and date, and sometimes the inventor. Now this germane information is called "narrative comment" by P.T.O, which will only fill an order by patent number. Your local library can advise you on the closest of over 50 depository libraries around the U.S. that have bound (or microfilmed) issues of the weekly *Official Gazette* from 1873 on, or others that have at least some years on microfilm.

Tracking down the thoughts and hopes of inventors, no matter how deluded they were, is a hobby in itself. It's a form of virtual reality for the browser — what might have been, what could be out there. If you are feeling jaded about finding a rare apple parer, an idiosyncratic eggbeater, or a brilliantly efficient can opener to add to your collection, consider taking an *Official Gazette* sabbatical!

RESEARCH PUBLICATIONS & RESOURCES
U.S. PATENTS:
Patent and Trademark Office. For copies of patents query the PS Center, CPK-1, Washington, DC 20231. You will need a patent number.

Subject-Matter Index of Patents for Inventions Issued by the United States Patent Office from 1790 to 1873, Inclusive. **Ayer Co. Pubns, POB 958, Salem, NH 03079, ISBN 0405077378, $158.**

Early Unnumbered U. S. Patents 1790-1836 . Research Publications, 1980. Order from **Rapid Patent Service**, 1921 Jefferson Davis Hwy, Ste#1821-D, Arlington, VA 22202. 1-800 336-5010. For inventors, RPS does patent searches, patent drawings, etc. For collectors, if your depository library doesn't have the years you need, RPS does individual photocopies made off microfilm. They have other books and microfilm on patents, including design patents — pertinent if it was only the design of something (for example a fancy muffin pan or ice-cream mold) that was patentable. Before writing or calling, try to make your query concise. They're friendly, but also very busy.

Journal of the Franklin Institute, Franklin Institute, Philadelphia, 1820s to 1850s. A large section entitled "Mechanics' Register" disseminated details of American patents, often with pithy remarks. Editor Thomas P. Jones became Commissioner of Patents in 1828/29. Some large libraries have copies; occasionally an antiquarian book dealer offers some.

Report of the Commissioner of Patents for the Year _____ : Arts and Manufacturers. Published as a report to the House of Representatives, about 40,000 copies were printed each year — most for the use of the Congressmen. I believe these bound, 2- and 3-volume reports started in the 1840s (and continued until the Patent Office's *Official Gazette* began in 1873). One volume each year has illustrations; another has claim precises.

Official Gazette of the U.S. Patent & Trademark Office, Washington, DC. Began 1873, continues today. Contains brief patent claims and pictures, plus indices of inventor, object and assignor. Individual volumes occasionally show up for sale at antiquarian booksellers.

BRITISH PATENTS:
British patents dating back to 1617 A.D. are represented by specifications and abstracts from the Science Reference & Information Service of the Patent Office Library. From antiquarian booksellers I've bought several 115 pp -150 pp illustrated tri-annual "Abridgments" for Class 28, Cooking and Kitchen Appliances, Bread-making, and Confectionery patents. In 1900, the British Patent Office was preparing illustrated abridgements for some 146 classes, covering the period 1617 to 1854. I've never seen them. Reference materials at the Library are open to the public, but our kind of historical research cannot be undertaken for you by SRIS staff. For services available from the B.P.O., write Head of Marketing & Publicity, **The Patent Office**, State House, 66-71 High Holborn, London WC1R 4TP, England. By the way, it's frustrating to work with British patents because in their system, it's the *application* that gets the number!

Copies of some British and other foreign patents can be ordered through **Rapid Patent Service's Scientific Library**, Foreign Patents Division, 2021 Jefferson Davis Hgwy, Arlington, VA 22202.

NOTE: The foregoing was adapted and enlarged from an article first appearing in *Antique Trader Books 1995 Antiques & Collectibles Price Guide,* ed. by Kyle Husfloen, and is reproduced with permission.

REPORT OF 1849 ON HOUSEHOLD INVENTIONS
The following is taken from the 1849 report by L. D. Gale, the patent examiner for the class of inventions known as "Household Furniture," made to the Commissioner of Patents, Thomas Ewbank, and printed as Ex. Doc. No. 20, for the 31st Congress, by the Office of Printers to House of Representatives, in 1850. Only two patents concern us here, and I have added in brackets the patentee's name, date and number of the patent, as discovered in the *Subject Index to Patents 1836-1873.*

HOUSEHOLD FURNITURE.
"In this class there have been granted fifty-five patents, arranged in the following groups:

Washing machines	6
Cutters of meats and vegetables	7
Bedsteads and fastenings	19
Tables	6
Chairs	7
Brushes, &c.	4
Cream freezers	3
Bottle cleaners	1
Portable water-closet	1
Mosquito bar	1

"Washing Machines.— In relation to this group of patents it is necessary only to say that the subject is so nearly exhausted that, so far as new devices for agitating the materials are concerned, there seems little room for invention. Every contrivance for creating friction seems to have been applied to these machines; the principles adapted to churning, fire engines, water wheels, fulling mills, rolling and smoothing grounds, rolling and smoothing shot, have been made to contribute to this necessary household operation. It is believed, however, that there is no striking feature in this group requiring special notice.

"Cutters of Meat, & c. — This group embraces the different machines for preparing and stuffing sausages, paring, quartering and slicing apples, and cutting vegetables for feeding domestic animals.

"A patent was granted for a small and very simple apparatus to grind the meat and simultaneously press it into the cases prepared to receive it, at a single operation. [Sausage-machine. T. Lockett, Warren County, GA, May 8, 1849, #6,422.]

"The machine consists of a small conoid mill or vessel somewhat resembling a coffee mill, but lying on its side. It has a solid conoid piece or runner within, having a spirally-fluted surface, and corresponding projections on the concave portion, each designed for cutting and pushing forward to the apex of the cone the comminuted material. The hopper placed on the upper side of the cone receives the pieces of meat of suitable size. A crank is fitted to the extremity of the runner at the large end of the cone, and the body of the machine is made fast to a table and worked like a coffee mill. The case is slipped upon the tube of the small end of the cone, and as the crank is turned the meat is comminuted and pushed forward, and the case is slipped off from the tube as it is filled.

"A machine has been patented for paring, coring, and slicing apples, at three several steps of the machine. [Paring, coring, and slicing apples. J. Weed, Painesville, OH, July 31, 1849, 6, 619. This was one of three apple parers patented in 1849.] The machine is in the main constructed like an ordinary paring machine; the apple is placed by hand upon a tridental fork, and against it rests the knife, which, as the machine is turned, moves forward from the stem towards the apex, without any external aid. At this end of the first step of the operation, in order that the knife may move back to the stem to take its place anew for another operation, a weight on this side of the knife haft, which had been carried up a quadrant of a circle by a segment wheel meshing into a bevel wheel, (which last is on the driving wheel,) the said bevel wheel having a space bare of cogs, and as soon as the cogs of the segment wheel reach the bare space in the bevel wheel, the weight rotates through the quarter of the circle, and the knife is thus carried back to the base or stem of the apple. At this stage of the operation, a slide block, working in horizontal guides, carrying a tube of thin sheet metal, and which was placed opposite to and pointing towards the apex of the apple, is now pushed forward by a motion of the hand, and pierces the apple from the apex to the stem, thus taking out the core, and as the block returns to its first position, take sthe apple from the fork; but before it reaches its position the apple strikes against a projection which releases it from the coring tube and allows it to fall upon the hopper-formed base of the machine, where it meets with a series of rotary horizontal knives, moved by gearing from the driving wheel, which knives cut the apple into pieces of uniform thickness suitable for drying."

RESEARCHING

XX. U. S. "PATENT TUESDAYS" OR ...?

I, and other patent devoteés, have at a late date come to a rude awakening concerning the so-called "patent Tuesdays," referred to throughout this book. Unfortunately, my bottom-line dogmatic statement that "If your embossed or printed date is *not* a Tuesday then it's not an American patent date," is dead wrong. And even after the onset of Tuesday grants, some American objects bear dates which weren't Tuesdays, but may have been application dates or some other date put on for the appearance of protection by the maker. (NOTE: The two listings most affected by this subject are the "Union" apple parer in Chapter I, and a cracker pricker & cutter in Chapter IV.)

Pessimism, or perhaps an excess of optimism, in the Patent Office — from 1790 on — contributed to 46+ years of a cavalier, careless attitude toward the worth of inventions, prevention of fire, protection of patents, and even the institution of a numbering system!

Numbers weren't assigned until *after* the big fire in December 1836. And even then, patents were not, as I had thought from spot checks, given out on Tuesdays in a regular way for quite a while.

We have printed perpetual "Tuesday-only" calendars, to check dates that appear in old ads, or marked on utensils. But remember that before about 1846, even though patents had been numbered for a decade, a Tuesday grant was, seemingly, no more likely than a Monday, Thursday or Saturday grant.

The Index below covers 1836 to 1976. The roman numeral next to each year refers you to the specific calendar table you need out of the fourteen. **Leap Years** have their own seven tables: VIII, IX, X, XI, XII, XIII, XIV.) The first year of *numbered* U.S. patents shows up as <u>1836-XIII</u>; refer to <u>Table XIII</u> (a leap year) to see 1836's Tuesdays, from January 5 to December 27.

INDEX	1836 - XIII	1837 - I	1838 - II	1839 - III
1840 - XI	1841 - VI	1842 - VII	1843 - I	1844 - IX
1845 - IV	1846 - V	1847 - VI	1848 - XIV	1849 - II
1850 - III	1851 - IV	1852 - XII	1853 - VII	1854 - I
1855 - II	1856 - X	1857 - V	1858 - VI	1859 - VII
1860 - VIII	1861 - III	1862 - IV	1863 - V	1864 - XIII
1865 - I	1866 - II	1867 - III	1868 - XI	1869 - VI
1870 - VII	1871 - I	1872 - IX	1873 - IV	1874 - V
1875 - VI	1876 - XIV	1877 - II	1878 - III	1879 - IV
1880 - XII	1881 - VII	1882 - I	1883 - II	1884 - X
1885 - V	1886 - VI	1887 - VII	1888 - VIII	1889 - III
1890 - IV	1891 - V	1892 - XIII	1893 - I	1894 - II
1895 - III	1896 - XI	1897 - VI	1898 - VII	1899 - I
1900 - II	1901 - III	1902 - IV	1903 - V	1904 - XIII
1905 - I	1906 - II	1907 - III	1908 - XI	1909 - VI
1910 - VII	1911 - I	1912 - IX	1913 - IV	1914 - V
1915 - VI	1916 - XIV	1917 - II	1918 - III	1919 - IV
1920 - XII	1921 - VII	1922 - I	1923 - II	1924 - X
1925 - V	1926 - VI	1927 - VII	1928 - VIII	1929 - III
1930 - IV	1931 - V	1932 - XIII	1933 - I	1934 - II
1935 - III	1936 - XI	1937 - VI	1938 - VII	1939 - I
1940 - IX	1941 - IV	1942 - V	1943 - VI	1944 - XIV
1945 - II	1946 - III	1947 - IV	1948 - XII	1949 - VII
1950 - I	1951 - II	1952 - X	1953 - V	1954 - VI
1955 - VII	1956 - VIII	1957 - III	1958 - IV	1959 - V
1960 - XIII	1961 - I	1962 - II	1963 - III	1964 - XI
1965 - VI	1966 - VII	1967 - I	1968 - IX	1969 - IV
1970 - V	1971 - VI	1972 - XIV	1973 - II	1974 - III
1975 - IV	1976 - XII			

TABLE I.
JAN 3, 10, 17, 24, 31
FEB 7, 14, 21, 28
MAR·7, 14, 21, 28
APR 4, 11, 18, 25
MAY 2, 9, 16, 23, 30
JUN 6, 13, 20, 27
JUL 4, 11, 18, 25
AUG 1, 8, 15, 22, 29
SEP 5, 12, 19, 26
OCT 3, 10, 17, 24, 31
NOV 7, 14, 21, 28
DEC 5, 12, 19, 26

TABLE II.
JAN 2, 9, 16, 23, 30
FEB 6, 13, 20, 27
MAR 6, 13, 20, 27
APR 3, 10, 17, 24
MAY 1, 8, 15, 22, 29
JUN 5, 12, 19, 26
JUL 3, 20, 27, 24, 31
AUG 7, 14, 21, 28
SEP 4, 11, 18, 25
OCT 2, 9, 16, 23, 30
NOV 6, 13, 20, 27
DEC 4, 11, 18, 25

TABLE III.
JAN 1, 8, 15, 22, 29
FEB 5, 12, 19, 26
MAR 5, 12, 19, 26
APR 2, 9, 16, 23, 30
MAY 7, 14, 21, 28
JUN 4, 11, 18, 25
JUL 2, 9, 16, 23, 30
AUG 6, 13, 20, 27
SEP 3, 10, 17, 24
OCT 1, 8, 15, 22, 29
NOV 5, 12, 19, 26
DEC 3, 10, 17, 24, 31

TABLE IV.
JAN 7, 14, 21, 28
FEB 4, 11, 18, 25
MAR 4, 11, 18, 25
APR 1, 8, 15, 22, 30
MAY 6, 13, 20, 27
JUN 3, 10, 17, 24
JUL 1, 8, 15, 22, 29
AUG 5, 12, 19, 26
SEP 2, 9, 16, 23, 30
OCT 7, 14, 21, 28
NOV 4, 11, 18, 25
DEC 2, 9, 16, 23, 30

TABLE V.
JAN 6, 13, 20, 27
FEB 3, 10, 17, 24
MAR 3, 10, 17, 24, 31
APR 7, 14, 21, 28
MAY 5, 12, 19, 26
JUN 2, 9, 16, 23, 30
JUL 7, 14, 21, 28
AUG 4, 11, 18, 25
SEP 1, 8, 15, 22, 29
OCT 6, 13, 20, 27
NOV 3, 10, 17, 24
DEC 1, 8, 15, 22, 29

TABLE VI.
JAN 5, 12, 19, 26
FEB 2, 9, 16, 23
MAR 2, 9, 16, 23, 30
APR 6, 13, 20, 27
MAY 4, 11, 18, 25
JUN 1, 8, 15, 22, 29
JUL 6, 13, 20, 27
AUG 3, 10, 17, 24, 31
SEP 7, 14, 21, 28
OCT. 5, 12, 19, 26
NOV 2, 9, 16, 23, 30
DEC 7, 14, 21, 28

TABLE VII.
JAN 4, 11, 18, 25
FEB 1, 8, 15, 22
MAR 1, 8, 15, 22, 29
APR 5, 12, 19, 26
MAY 3, 10, 17, 24, 31
JUN 7, 14, 21, 28
JUL 5, 12, 19, 26
AUG 2, 9, 16, 23, 30
SEP 6, 13, 20, 27
OCT 4, 11, 18, 25
NOV 1, 8, 15, 22, 29
DEC 6, 13, 20, 27

TABLE VIII.
JAN 3, 10, 17, 24, 31
FEB 7, 14, 21, 28
MAR 6, 13, 20, 27
APR 3, 10, 17, 24
MAY 1, 8, 15, 22, 29
JUN 5, 12, 19, 26
JUL 3, 10, 17,. 24, 31
AUG 7, 14, 21, 28
SEP 4, 11, 18, 25
OCT 2, 9, 16, 23, 30
NOV 6, 13, 20, 27
DEC 4, 11, 18, 25

TABLE IX.
JAN 2, 9, 16, 23, 30
FEB 6, 13, 20, 27
MAR 5, 12, 19, 26
APR 2, 9, 16, 23, 30
MAY 7, 14, 21, 28
JUN 4, 11, 18, 25
JUL 2, 9, 16, 23, 30
AUG 6, 13, 20, 27
SEP 3, 10, 17, 24
OCT 1, 8, 15, 22, 29
NOV 5, 12, 19, 26
DEC 3, 10, 17, 24, 31

TABLE X.
JAN 1, 8, 15, 22, 29
FEB 5, 12, 19, 26
MAR 4, 11, 18, 25
APR 1, 8, 15, 22, 29
MAY 6, 13, 20, 27
JUN 3, 10, 17, 24
JUL 1, 8, 15, 22, 29
AUG 5, 12, 19, 26
SEP 2, 9, 16, 23, 30
OCT 7, 14, 21, 28
NOV 4, 11, 18, 25
DEC 2, 9, 16, 23, 30

TABLE XI.
JAN 7, 14, 21, 28
FEB 4, 11, 18, 25
MAR 3, 10, 17, 24, 31
APR 7, 14, 21, 28
MAY 5, 12, 19, 26
JUN 2, 9, 16, 23, 30
JUL 7, 14, 21, 28
AUG 4, 11, 18, 25
SEP 1, 8, 15, 22, 29
OCT 6, 13, 20, 27
NOV 3, 10, 17, 24
DEC 1, 8, 15, 22, 29

TABLE XII.
JAN 6, 13, 20, 27
FEB 3, 10, 17, 24
MAR 2, 9, 16, 23, 30
APR 6, 13, 20, 27
MAY 4, 11, 18, 25
JUN 1, 8, 15, 22, 29
JUL 6, 13, 20, 27
AUG 3, 10, 17, 24, 31
SEP 7, 14, 21, 28
OCT 5, 12, 19, 26
NOV 2, 9, 16, 23, 30
DEC 7, 14, 21, 28

TABLE XIII.
JAN 5, 12, 19, 26
FEB 2, 9, 16, 23
MAR 1, 8, 15, 22, 29
APR 5, 12, 19, 26
MAY 3, 10, 17, 24, 31
JUN 7, 14, 21, 28
JUL 5, 12, 19, 26
AUG 2, 9, 16, 23, 30
SEP 6, 13, 20, 27
OCT 4, 11, 18, 25
NOV 1, 8, 15, 22, 29
DEC 6, 13, 20, 27

TABLE XIV.
JAN 4, 11, 18, 25
FEB 1, 8, 15, 22, 29
MAR 7, 14, 21, 28
APR 4, 11, 18, 25
MAY 2, 9, 16, 23, 30
JUN 6, 13, 20, 27
JUL 4, 11, 18, 25
AUG 1, 8, 15, 22, 29
SEP 5, 12, 19, 26
OCT 3, 10, 17, 24, 31
NOV 7, 14, 21, 28
DEC 5, 12, 19, 26

RESEARCHING

XXI. UNITED STATES PATENT NUMBERS

This table shows <u>numbered patents</u> only (there were over 7000 unnumbered patents and design patents issued between 1790 and 1836). I've given the number of the first patent issued each year for four different kinds of patents from 1836 through 1945. Listed are numbered Patents, Design Patents (given for the look of something, not its mechanics), Reissued Patents and Trademark Patents. A reissue patent is meant to correct a "defective" patent that — by inadvertence, accident, or mistake — either claimed too much as new, or for which the specifications were incorrect or insufficient. According to patent law, <u>no new matter could be introduced</u> into the patent except to correct omissions; however, drawings could be remade to conform to the specifications, or the specifications might be rewritten to conform to the drawings. If granted by the Patent Office, a reissue patent is only for the unexpired term of the original patent and doesn't extend it.

If a patent number is marked on your mystery gadget, you can at least find out what year it was patented (assuming the number is correct). Sometimes a number will appear that is not designated as a design or reissue patent. Then you must decide for yourself, from the appearance of the object, what the approximate age is. For example, let's say the item is marked "Pat. # 10,365." That number could be a patent of the year 1854, a design patent of 1878, or a reissue patent of 1883. This is where you must bring into play any and all knowledge and "feel" you have for the thing itself, including the method of manufacture, the purpose of the gadget, the shape of the handle, the material from which it's made, how it relates to objects of known date. This can be confusing, especially for things made in the third or fourth quarter of the nineteenth century, but at least you've narrowed it down — in this case, to three years: 1854, 1878, or 1883. (Most objects or tools would not bear a trademark patent number, although advertising for it might.)

UNITED STATES PATENT NUMBERS

Table showing the First Patent,
Design Patent, Reissue and Trademark Numbers
Issued in Each Year from 1836 to 1945, inclusive.

DATE	PATENT	DESIGN	REISSUE	TRADEMARK
1836	1			
1837	110			
1838	546		1	
1839	1,061		7	
1840	1,465		20	
1841	1,923		30	
1842	2,413		36	
1843	2,901	1	49	
1844	3,395	15	60	
1845	3,873	27	67	
1846	4,348	44	78	
1847	4,914	103	91	
1848	5,409	163	105	
1849	5,993	209	128	
1850	6,981	258	158	
1851	7,865	341	184	
1852	8,622	431	209	
1853	9,512	540	229	
1854	10,358	626	258	
1855	12,117	683	286	
1856	14,009	753	337	
1857	16,324	860	420	
1858	19,010	973	517	
1859	22,477	1,075	643	
1860	26,642	1,183	674	
1861	31,005	1,366	1,106	
1862	34,045	1,508	1,253	
1863	37,266	1,703	1,369	
1864	41,047	1,879	1,596	
1865	45,685	2,018	1,844	
1866	51,784	2,239	2,140	
1867	60,658	2,533	2,430	
1868	72,959	2,858	2,830	
1869	85,503	3,304	3,250	
1870	98,460	3,810	3,784	1
1871	110,617	4,547	4,223	122
1872	122,304	5,452	4,687	608
1873	134,504	6,336	5,216	1,099
1874	146,120	7,083	5,717	1,591
1875	158,350	7,969	6,200	2,150
1876	171,641	8,884	6,831	3,288
1877	185,813	9,686	7,452	4,247
1878	198,733	10,385	8,020	5,463
1879	211,078	10,975	8,529	6,918
1880	223,211	11,567	9,017	7,790
1881	236,137	12,082	9,523	8,139
1882	251,685	12,647	9,994	8,973
1883	269,820	13,508	10,265	9,920
1884	291,016	14,528	10,432	10,822
1885	310,163	15,678	10,548	11,843
1886	333,494	16,451	10,677	12,910
1887	355,291	17,046	10,793	13,939
1888	375,720	17,995	10,892	15,072
1889	395,305	18,830	10,978	16,131
1890	418,665	19,553	11,053	17,360

DATE	PATENT	DESIGN	REISSUE	TRADEMARK
1891	443,987	20,439	11,137	18,775
1892	466,315	21,275	11,217	20,537
1893	486,976	22,092	11,298	22,274
1894	511,744	22,994	11,397	23,951
1895	531,619	23,922	11,461	25,757
1896	552,502	25,037	11,520	27,586
1897	574,369	26,482	11,581	29,399
1898	596,467	28,113	11,646	31,070
1899	616,871	29,916	11,706	32,308
1900	640,167	32,055	11,798	33,957
1901	664,827	33,813	11,879	35,678
1902	690,385	35,547	11,960	37,606
1903	717,521	36,187	12,070	39,612
1904	748,567	36,723	12,189	41,798
1905	778,834	37,280	12,299	43,956
1906	808,618	37,766	12,428	48,446
1907	839,799	38,391	12,587	59,014
1908	875,679	38,980	12,738	66,892
1909	908,436	39,737	12,906	72,083
1910	945,010	40,424	13,066	76,267
1911	980,178	41,063	13,189	80,506
1912	1,013,095	42,073	13,346	84,711
1913	1,049,326	43,425	13,504	89,731
1914	1,083,267	45,098	13,668	94,796
1915	1,123,212	46,813	13,858	101,613
1916	1,166,419	48,358	14,040	107,875
1917	1,210,389	50,177	14,238	114,666
1918	1,251,458	51,629	14,417	120,005
1919	1,290,027	52,836	14,582	124,066
1920	1,326,899	54,359	14,785	128,274
1921	1,364,063	56,844	15,018	138,556
1922	1,401,948	60,121	15,257	150,210
1923	1,440,362	61,478	15,513	163,003
1924	1,478,996	63,675	15,739	177,848
1925	1,521,590	66,346	15,974	193,596
1926	1,568,040	69,170	16,240	207,437
1927	1,612,790	71,772	16,515	222,401
1928	1,654,521	74,159	16,841	236,987
1929	1,696,897	77,347	17,176	251,129
1930	1,742,181	80,254	17,550	265,655
1931	1,787,424	82,966	17,917	278,906
1932	1,839,190	85,903	18,312	290,313
1933	1,892,663	88,847	18,705	299,926
1934	1,941,449	91,258	19,038	309,066
1935	1,985,878	94,179	19,409	320,441
1936	2,026,516	98,045	19,804	331,338
1937	2,066,309	102,601	20,226	342,070
1938	2,104,004	107,738	20,610	353,324
1939	2,142,080	112,765	20,959	363,536
1940	2,185,170	118,358	21,311	374,062
1941	2,227,418	124,503	21,683	384,047
1942	2,268,510	130,989	21,992	392,581
1943	2,307,007	134,717	22,242	399,378
1944	2,338,081	136,916	22,415	404,974
1945	2,366,154	139,862	22,585	411,001
	(to 2,391,855)	(to 143,385)	(to 22,795)	(to 418,493)

RESEARCHING

XXII. BIBLIOGRAPHY OF BOOKS RECOMMENDED AND/OR CONSULTED

This is a very extensive bibliography, meant to allow you to do research in primary and secondary sources — just as I have done. Many of the books include valuable bibliographies of their own. I trust an author who lists sources, and urge you to "collect" bibliographies on your own special subjects.

Many of the listed books are outstanding works — readable, informative, obsessive in detail, well-illustrated. I can't recommend all, except as picture sources. Some books contain information that is incorrect or romanced from thin air. Many valuable secondary research sources are articles published in periodicals. They have been credited throughout the text and are listed in alphabetical order here. Newsletters for particular subjects are found in their particular chapters — often in the introductory paragraphs. Trade catalogs are invaluable and irrefutable. The few hundred I have collected since 1970 are my treasure trove. The ones I have used most are here in this listing.

Unfortunately, many of the books listed are out of print and difficult to get. The search for them is worth the effort, though, and there are now a number of specialized dealers in new, out of print, and antiquarian books on the decorative arts, practical arts, antiques and collectibles. (A few titles — probably foreign or self-published — have incomplete listings because I cannot find any more information about author, publisher or date of publication.)

A & J Mfg. Co. *Colorful Kitchen Tools.* Catalog. Binghampton, NY & Chicago: Edward Katzinger Co., A & J Division, 1930.

Abridgements of Specifications Relating to Cooking, Bread-Making, and ... Confectionery, A.D. 1634-1866. London: Office of the Commissioner of Patents, 1873.

Adams & Son, William S. *Francatelli's Cook's Guide Advertiser.* London, England: Richard Bentley, 1861.

Adamson, Gareth. *Machines At Home.* London: Lutterworth, 1969.

Agricola, Georgius. *De Re Metallica.* Tr. by Herbert Hoover. Ancient classic on metals. Reprint by Dover Books, NYC, of the 1912 edition, 1990.

Aikins, Larry. *Pictorial Price Guide to Metal Lunch Boxes & Thermoses.* Gas City, IN: L-W Book Sales, 1992, 1994.

Alcott, William Alexander. *The Young House-Keeper, or Thoughts on Food and Cookery.* Boston: G. W. Light, 1838; 1842.

Allen, Colonel Bob. *Cook Book Gossip Over the Back Fence.* St. James, MO: Cookbook Collectors Club of America, POB 56, 65559. 1997. 650 pp, columns, 1990-1996, from club newsletter, on authors, etc.

Allen, Col. Bob. *A Guide to Collecting Cookbooks.* Paducah, KY: Collector Books, 1990; rev. 1993; rev. 1995.

Allen, Col. Bob. *A Guide to Collecting 'Jell-O' Cookbooklets.* St. James, MO: 1997.

American Agriculturist. Monthly. NYC: Orange Judd & Co., 1840s-1880s.

American Artisan and Patent Record. NYC: 1864-1875. Volumes 1-17 were weekly; Volumes 18, 19, monthly.

American Heritage Cookbook and Illustrated History of American Eating and Drinking. NYC: American Heritage Pub'g Co., 1964. Incomparable illustrations and invaluable biographies. Reprinted, c.1980s.

American Home Cook Book, by an American lady. NYC: Dick & Fitzgerald, 1854.

Ames, Alex. *Collecting Cast Iron.* England: Moorland Pub., 1980.

Andrews, Edward Deming. *The Community Industries of the Shakers.* Handbook No. 15. Albany, NY: NY State Museum, 1932.

Anthoine, A. *Moules à Glaces en Étain.* Catalog. Paris: c.1900. May have been jobbers, not manufacturers.

Antiquarian Bookman's Weekly (AB Weekly). Box AB, Clifton, NJ 07015. AB has special interest issues throughout year, including one for cookbooks, one for technology & science, and one for "books on books."

Antique & Collectors Reproduction News (ACRN). Monthly. Des Moines, IA: ACRN, POB 71174. 50325. 1-800-227-5531.

Antique Label Collecting: A Primer. Tampa, FL: Society of Antique Label Collectors, POB 24811, Tampa 33623. 1992. Including baking soda, citrus, other fruits & vegetables.

Antique Metalware. Brass, Bronze, Copper, Tin, Wrought & Cast Iron. Edited by James R. Mitchell. NYC: Universe Books, c.1976. Anthology of metal-related articles from *The Magazine ANTIQUES,* 1922-1976.

Antiques & the Arts Weekly. Newtown, CT: Bee Pub'g Co., 5 Church Hill Rd., 06470.

Antique Trader Weekly. POB 1050, Dubuque IA 52004-1050. 1-800-334-7165. Also publishes *Collector Magazine & Price Guide.*

AntiqueWeek tabloid newspaper; several regional offices & editions. POB 90, Knightstown, IN 46148-9900, or 525-K East Market St., Leesburg, VA 22075. For info: 1-800-876-5133.

Arnold, Eleanor, ed. *Voices of American Homemakers.* Oral History Project of the National Extension Homemakers Council. Bloomington, IN: Indiana University Press, 1993.

Arnold, Ken. *Australian Preserving & Storage Jars pre-1920.* © Australia, 1983. Available from Phoenix Press, 5003 W. Berwyn Ave., Chicago IL 60631-1501.

Arthur, Eric & Thomas Ritchie. *Iron. Cast & Wrought Iron in Canada from the Seventeenth Century to the Present.* Toronto: University of Toronto Press, 1982.

Artman, E. Townsend. *Toasters, 1909-1960: A Look at the Ingenuity and Design of Toaster Makers.* Atglen, PA: Schiffer, 1996.

"Arts & Culture." Box 1333, Gracie Square Station, NYC, 10028.

Atwater, Helen. *Selection of Household Equipment.* Washington, DC: U.S. Government Printing Office, 1915.

Auction Team Köln. various catalogs from 1980s and 1990s. A subscription to their auction catalogs of "old technology" sometimes include flat irons, toasters, electrical kitchen gadgets, etc. It costs about 80 to 100 deutsche marks (depending on the exchange rate). Write: POB 50.1119, D-50971, Köln, Germany.

Babcock, Emma Whitcomb. *Household Hints.* Vol. II, Appleton's Home Books. NYC: Appleton, 1881.

Bacchus Corkscrew Collection, The. n.p., 1981, 1987.

Baird, James S. *Hoard's Dairyman Dairy Collectibles.* Ft. Atkinson, WI: W. D. Hoard & Sons co., 28 Milwaukee Ave. W., 53538-0801. 1994.

Baker, Elizabeth F. *Technology and Women's Work.* NYC: Columbia University Press, 1964.

Baker, Eric, & Jane Martin. *Great Inventions/Good Intentions. An Illustrated History of American Design Patents.* San Francisco: Chronicle Books, 1990. Great fun!

Barile, Mary. *Cookbooks Worth Collecting.* Radnor, PA: Chilton Books, 1993.

Barlow, Ron. *Victorian Houseware: Hardware and Kitchenware.* El Cajon, CA: Windmill Pub. Co., 1992. Well-reproduced old catalog linecuts of hundreds of objects used in the 19th C. home.

Barlow, Ron, & Ray Reynolds. *The Insider's Guide to Old Books, Magazines, Newspapers and Trade Catalogs.* El Cajon, CA: Windmill Pub. Co., 2147 Windmill View Dr., 92020. 1995. Straight alphabetical listings include cookbooks; catalogs in separate section.

Barnes, Frank T. *Hooks, Rings & Other Things. ... N.E. Iron, 1660-1860.* Hanover, MA: Christopher Pub., 1988. Some identifications to be taken with a grain of salt.

Barry, D. J., & Co. *Hotel Supplies.* Catalog. NYC: 1924. Manufacturers, jobbers, importers of house furnishings.

Beard, James, Milton Glaser, et al., ed. *The Cook's Catalogue.* NYC: Harper & Row, 1975.

Beard, James, intro. *The International Cooks' Catalogue.* NYC: Random House, 1977. Perhaps even more useful than the other, because it shows today's exotic utensils we might think are much older.

Beckmann, Johann. *Concise History of Ancient Institutions, Inventions and Discoveries in Science and Mechanic Art.* Tr. from German. 3 vol. London: J. Bell, 1797, et al.

Beitz, Les. *Treasury of Frontier Relics.* NYC: Edwin House, 1966.

Bertuch, A. *Katalog A.* Berlin, Germany, 1904. Molds for cake, ice cream, pudding, candy, nougat.

Besterman, Theodore. *Technology, Including Patents. A Bibliography of Bibliographies.* 2 vol. © 1939. Totowa, NJ: Rowman & Littlefield, 1971.

Biblio. Bimonthly magazine for collectors of books, mss, and ephemera. Aster Pub'g Corp., 845 Williamette St., Eugene, OR 97401.

Biringuccio, Vannoccio. *The Pirotechnia.* (The Classic Sixteenth-Century *Treatise on Metals and Metallurgy,* first published 1540.) With introd., forewords, & bibliography. Reprint NYC: Dover Books, 1990.

Bishop, Christina. *Collecting Kitchenware.* Wappingers Falls, NY: Antique Collectors Club, 1995. Mainly English.

Bishop, John Leander. *A History of American Manufacturers from 1608-1860.* Philadelphia: E. Young & Co., 1861.

Bitting, A. W. *Appertizing, or the Art of Canning: Its History and Development.* San Francisco: priv. pub., 1937.

Bivins, John, Jr. *The Moravian Potters in North Carolina.* Chapel Hill: University of N.C. Press, 1972.

Blankenship, Victor A., Sr. *Frigidaire Memorabilia and Advertising Collectibles.* Dayton, OH: Victor Pub'ns, POB 417, 45449. 1991. No pictures, just listing.

Bolton, J. W., comp. *Bibliography on Cast Iron ... for the Use of the Committee On Cast Iron of the A.F.A.* [Chicago]: American Foundrymen's Association, 1927.

Bond, Ralph. *Fruit Jar Patents Vol. I, early 1800s-1869.* n.p.: n.d. Long out of print, but plans are to expand and publish this in late 1990s, as part of Dick Roller's series for Phoenix Press.

Booher, Fred. *Graniteware: Identification & Value Guide.* Paducah, KY: Collector Books, 1977.

Boram, Clifford. *How to Get Parts Cast for Your Antique Stove: Dealing with a Foundry Is Easier than You Think.* Monticello, IN: Autonomy House, 417 N. Main, 47960. 1982.

Bosker, Gideon. *Great Shakes: Salt & Pepper for All Tastes.* NYC: Abbeville, 1986.

Bosker, Gideon, & Lena Lencek. *Salt and Pepper Shakers: Identification and Price Guide.* NY: Avon Paperbacks, 1994.

Bowditch, Barbara. *American Jelly Glasses: A Collector's Notebook.* Drawings by George Bowditch. Hilton, NY: Author, 1173 Peck Rd., 14468. © 1986. A must-have for jelly & glass collectors.

Bradley, Rose. *The English Housewife in the Seventeenth and Eighteenth Centuries.* London: Edward Arnold, 1912.

Brantley, William F. *A Collector's Guide to Ball Jars.* Muncie, IN: Ball Corporation, 1975.

Brazer, Esther Stevens. *Early American Decoration.* Springfield, MA: Pond-Ekberg, 1940.

Breazeale, James F. *Economy in the Kitchen.* NYC: Frye Pub'g Co., 1918.

Breck, Joseph & Sons. *Agricultural Hardware, Implements, Woodenware.* Catalog. Boston: 1903; 1905.

Bridge, Fred, & Jean F. Tibbetts. *The Well-Tooled Kitchen.* NYC: William Morrow & Co., 1991.

Brooke, Sheena. *Hearth and Home: A Short History of Domestic Equipment.* London: Mills & Boon, 1973.

Brown, Henry T. *Manual of Mechanical Movements.* © 1868; renewed 1896. Reprinted: South Orange, NJ: W. M. Clark, 1933.

Brown, J. J. *Ideas In Exile: A History of Canadian Invention.* Toronto: McClelland & Stewart, 1967.

Bull, Donald. *A Price Guide to Beer Advertising Openers & Corkscrews.* Trumbull, CT: Author, 1981.

Bullock, Helen. *A National Treasury of Cooking. Recipes of: Ante Bellum America; Early America; Victorian America; The Young Republic; The Westward Empire.* 5 vol. NYC: Heirloom Pub'g, 1967.

Bunn, Eleanor. *Metal Molds, Ice Cream, Chocolate, Barley Sugar, Cake.* Paducah, KY: Collector Books, 1981.

Burgess, Fred. W. *Chats on Household Curios.* NYC: F. A. Stokes Co.,1914.

Burgess, F. W. *Chats on Old Copper & Brass.* NYC: F. A. Stokes, 1914.

Butler Brothers. *Christmas Catalog.* Chicago: 1899. Thousands of mail order household items.

Butter, Robin, & Gillian Walking. *Book of Wine Antiques.* Wappingers Falls, NY: Antique Collectors Club, Market St., Industrial Park, 12590. 1994.

Byers, Anthony. *Centinary of Service: A History of Electricity In the Home.* London: Electricity Council, 1981.

Campbell, Bonita J. *Depression Silver: Machine Age Craft and Design in Aluminum.* Granada Hills, CA: Author, POB 3151, 91394.

Campbell, Susan. *Cooks' Tools. Complete Manual of Kitchen Implements & How to Use Them.* NYC: William Morrow, 1980. Modern tools; old uses.

Caniff, Tom. *Label Space, The Book.* Chicago, IL: Phoenix Press, 1996. 96 columns from "Bottles & Extras." All about labeled product or packer jars. See McCann, J.

Carey, Larry, & Sylvia Tompkins.*1,001 Salt & Pepper Shakers.* Atglen, PA: Schiffer Pub'g Co. Also *1,002 Salt & Pepper Shakers; 1,003 Salt & Pepper Shakers, 1996.*

Carson, Jane. *Colonial Virginia Cookery.* Williamsburg, VA: Williamsburg Research Studies, 1968. Good on colonial kitchens & early cookbooks.

Carter, Ernest Frank. *Dictionary of Inventions and Discoveries.* London: F. Muller, 1966.

Cast Iron: Architecture and Ornament, Function and Fantasy. London: John Murray, 1987.

Catalogue of the Machines, Models, etc., in the Patent Museum, South Kensington. London: HMSO, 1863.

Celehar, Jane. *Kitchens & Gadgets. 1920 to 1950.* Des Moines, IA: Wallace-Homestead, 1982. Handle shapes, dates, company histories good.

Celehar, J. *Kitchens & Kitchenware.* Lombard, IL: Wallace-Homestead, 1985.

Central Stamping Co. *Catalog No. 43.* NYC: 1920.

Cherry-Bassett Co. *Complete Catalog of Equipment for Milk Plants, Ice Cream Plants . . . No. 53.* Baltimore, Philadelphia: 1921.

Chiurazzi, J. & Fils / S. De Angelis & Fils. *Artistic Founding.* Catalog. Naples, Italy: 1910-11. Reproductions of ancient metalwares found at Pompeii & Herculaneum.

Christensen, E. O. *The Index of American Design.* NYC: Macmillan, 1950.

Chronicle, The. Quarterly journal of Early American Industries Association (EAIA). Organization & publication date back to 1933, dedicated to studying & preserving all tools, including household & kitchen tools. Contact E. W. Hall, EAIA, 167 Bakerville Rd., So. Dartmouth, MA 02748.

Clad, V. & Sons, Inc. *Clad's Advertising Pamphlet.* Philadelphia: c. 1890-1900.

Clark, Hyla. *The Tin Can Book.* NYC: New American Library, 1977.

Coffin, Margaret. *The History & Folklore of American Country Tinware, 1700-1900.* Camden, NJ: Thomas Nelson & Sons, 1968.

Congdon-Martin, Douglas. *Figurative Cast Iron, A Collector's Guide.* Atglen, PA: Schiffer Pub. Co., 1995. Good pix, but *very* short on info.

Consentino, Geraldine, & Regina Stewart. *Kitchenware: A Guide for the Beginning Collector.* NYC: Golden Press, 1977.

Cook, Mary Alexander. *The Cape Kitchen; a Description of Its Position, Lay-out, Fittings and Utensils.* Stellenbosch, South Africa: Stellenbosch Museum, [1973?]. Lots of beautiful metalwares.

Cooley, Anna Maria, & Wilhelmina H. Spohr. *Household Arts for Home and School.* 2 vol. NYC: The Macmillan Co., 1920.

Cooper, Carolyn C. *"The Ghost in the Kitchen: Household Technology at the Brattleboro Museum, Vermont."* Article in *Technology and Culture,* Vol. 28, No. 2. Chicago: University of Chicago Press, 1991.

Corley, Thomas Anthony Buchanan. *Domestic Electrical Appliances.* London: Jonathan Cape, 1966.

Country Accents Collectibles. Flea Market Finds. Quarterly. GCR Pub'g Group, 1700 Broadway, NYC 10019. The editor of this neat magazine likes kitchen things, so you can almost always count on a well-illustrated article on the subject. Some back issues are available. 1-800-955-3870.

Cowan, Ruth Schwartz. *More Work For Mother. The Ironies of Household Technology From the Open Hearth to the Microwave.* NY: Basic Books, 1983.

Creswick, Alice. *The Collector's Guide to Old Fruit Jars.* (Also called the "Red Book of Fruit Jars.") Grand Rapids, MI: Author, 1st, 2nd, 3rd, 4th, 5th, & 6th editions, through 1991. Any edition is desirable. Drawings by Howard Creswick are exquisitely done. See also Leybourne.

Crom, Theodore R. *Trade Catalogues — 1542 to 1842.* Hawthorne, FL: Author, Rte 2, Box 212, 32640. n.d.

Curtis, Tony. *Copper & Brass.* Galashiels, Scotland: Lyle Publications, 1982.

Curtis, Tony. *Kitchen Equipment.* Galashiels, Scotland: Lyle Publications, 1978, rev. 1982. Mostly illus. Price guide to antiques.

Curtis, Will, & Jane Curtis. *Antique Woodstoves.* Ashville, ME: Cobblesmith, 1975.

Davern, Melva. *The Collectors Encyclopedia of Salt and Pepper Shakers, Figural and Novelty.* Paducah, KY: Collector Books, 1991. Author: Box 81914, Pittsburgh, PA 15217. She's also done a "second series."

Davidson, Caroline. *A Woman's Work is Never Done: A Social History of Housework, 1630-1950.* London: Chatto & Windus, 1982.

de Haan, David. *Antique Household Gadgets and Appliances.* Poole, England: Blandford, 1977.

DeMore, Dana, & Darlene DeMore. *Kitchen Antiques & Collectibles News,* bimonthly that began Sept/Oct 1992. 4645 Laurel Ridge Dr., Harrisburg, PA 17110.

DePasquale, Dan, & Gail DePasquale, & Larry Peterson. *Red Wing Collectibles.* Paducah, KY: Collector Books, 1986.

DePasquale, Dan, & Gail DePasquale, & Larry Peterson. *Red Wing Stoneware.* Paducah, KY: Collector Books, 1983, prices updated 1990.

DeVoe, Shirley Spaulding. *The Art of the Tinsmith, English and American.* Exton, PA: Schiffer Publishing, 1981.

DeVoe, Shirley Spaulding. *The Tinsmiths of Connecticut.* Middletown, CT: Wesleyan University Press, 1968.

Dickson, Paul. *The Great American Ice Cream Book.* NYC: Atheneum, 1972.

DiNoto, Andrea. *Art Plastic.* NYC: Abbeville Press, 1984. Glorious colorful things for everywhere in the house.

Divone, Judene. *Chocolate Moulds. A History & Encyclopedia.* Oakton, VA: Oakton Hills Pubns., 1987. Profusely illustrated. Divone also compiled & reprinted an Anton Reiche catalog of schokoladenformen.

Dorchy, Henry. *Le Moule a Chocolat. Un nouvel objet de collection.* Paris: Les Editions de l'Amateur, n.d. (1980s). Copious illustrations from catalogs, factory scenes, and chocolate molds themselves.

Dover Stamping Co. Catalog, 1869. Facsimile. Princeton, NJ: American Historical Catalog Collection, The Pyne Press, 1971.

Dover Stamping Co. *Cook Book.* Boston: 1899.

Dow, George Francis. *The Arts & Crafts in New England, 1704-1775. Gleanings from Boston Newspapers.* Topsfield, MA: Wayside Pr., 1927.

Dragowick, Marilyn, ed. *Metalwares Price Guide.* Dubuque, IA: Antique Trader Books, 1997.

Dubois, Urbain. *La Patisserie D'Aujourd'hui.* 7th ed. Paris: c.1890-93. Most illustrations date to c.1860s-1870s.

Duparquet & Huot. *Catalog of . . . the Imperial French Cooking Range and Broiler: Also, Coffee and Tea Urns, Oyster and Cast-iron Steam Kettles, Cast-iron, Tin, and Copper Cooking Utensils.* NYC: 1885.

Duparquet, Huot & Moneuse. *Catalog.* Housefurnishings mainly for hotels & restaurants. NYC: c.1904-1910.

DuSablon, Mary A. *America's Collectible Cookbooks: The History, the Politics, the Recipes.* Athens, OH: Ohio Univ. Press, 1994.

Dwight, Timothy. *Travels In New England and New York — 1796-1815.* 4 vol. London: W. Baynes & Son, 1823.

Earle, Alice Morse. *Home Life In Colonial Days.* NYC: Macmillan, 1899.

Early American Industries Association — See *Chronicle, The.*

Early American Life. Bi-monthly magazine. Harrisburg, PA: Cowles Magazines, Inc., POB 8200, 17105-8200. Subs: 1-800-435-9610.

Early Unnumbered Patent Index. Woodbridge, CT: Research Publications, 1980. Now available from Rapid Patent Service, 1921 Jefferson Davis Hwy, Ste #1821-D, Arlington, VA 22202.

Eaton, Allen Hendershott. *Handicrafts of New England.* NYC: Harper, 1949. Also one on the *Southern Highlands.* NYC: Russell Sage Fdtn, 1937.

Eikelberner, George, & Serge Agadjanian. *The Compleat American Candy Containers Handbook.* Mentor, OH: Bowden Pub'g, 6252 Cedarwood Rd., 44060. Rev'd ed. 1986.

Electrical Dealer. Monthly. Chicago, IL: Haywood Pub'g, 1928- .

Enchantment of Enameled "Cook Ware." Kermit, TX: Collectors Weekly Books, 1974.

Enterprise Mfg. Co. *Catalog.* Philadelphia: c.1900-1910. Another, 1881.

Fairbairn, Sir William. *Iron; Its History, Properties and Process of Manufacture.* Edinburgh: A. & C. Black, 1865.

Fakes & Reproductions of 1996. Des Moines, IA: Antique & Collectors Reproduction News, POB 12130, 50325. You can also get the 1992-96 books, with 3229 illustrations, and subscription to the monthly *ACRN.*

Fantoni, Maurizio. *Nutcrackers.* Milano, Italy: BE-MA, c. 1990.

Fantoni, Maurizio, & _____ de Sanctis. *Corkscrews. . . I Cavatappi.* Milano, Italy: BE-MA, 1988. 138 pp, color illus.

Faulkner, Wendy, & Erik Arnold, eds. *Smothered By Invention: Technology In Women's Lives.* London: Pluto Press, 1985.

Fearn, Jacqueline. *Domestic Bygones.* Aylesbury, England: Shire, 1977.

Feild, Rachel. *Irons In the Fire. A History of Cooking Equipment.* London: Crowood Press, 1984.

Festliches Backwerk. Holzmodel, Formen aus Zinn, Kupfer und Keramik, Waffel- und Oblateneisen. Nurnberg, Germany: Germanisches National Museum, 1981. Baking molds in tin, copper, ceramic, cast iron.

Fine Tool Journal. Quarterly focusing on carpenters' tools, with some info at times on household tools. Vernon U. Ward, founder and editor. Clarence Blanchard, managing editor. 27 Fickett Road, Pownal, ME 04069.

Fisher, Charles. *Early American Electric Toasters. 1906-1940.* Teaneck, NJ: HJH Publications, c.1980s. Now known as "Hazelcorn's Price Guide to Old Electric Toasters."

Florence, Gene. *Kitchen Glassware of the Depression Years.* 1st, 2nd, 3rd, 4th, 5th editions. Paducah, KY: Collector Books, 1981; 1983; 1987; 1990; 1997. Florence has done many incomparable books on Depression glass of all kinds.

Flower, Philip William. *A History of the Trade in Tin; . . . Tin Mining and Metallurgy; . . . the Tin-plate Trade. . . . Ancient and Modern Processes of Manufacturing tin-Plates.* London, Eng: George Bell & Son, 1880.

For Openers: Illust'd Catalogue of American Patented Corkscrews and Can-openers . . . Exhibition at CHS Oct. 10, 1980 to Jan. 5, 1981. [Hartford, CT]: CT Historical Society, 1980. Text by "Philos Blake," pseud.

Forty, Anne. *Treen & Earthenware.* Midas Books, 1979.

Franklin, Linda Campbell. *Bibliography of Antiques & Collectibles. Books in the English Langauge, 1570-1976.* Metuchen, NJ: Scarecrow Books, 1978.

Franklin, L. C. *From Hearth to Cookstove: An American Domestic History of Gadgets & Utensils . . . 1700-1930.* Florence, AL: House of Collectibles, 1976, 1978. There's a so-called "3rd edition" — with my name removed & the publisher's son's name, "Mark Hudgeons," as author.

Franklin, L. C., ed. *Kitchen Collectibles News.* NYC: 1984-1986. 18 issues.

Franklin, L. C., *300 Years of Housekeeping Collectibles.* Florence, AL: Books Americana, 1992.

Franklin, L. C., *300 Years of Kitchen Collectibles.* Florence, AL: Books Americana, 1st, 2nd, 3rd editions, 1981, 1984, 1991.

Fredericksen, Paul. *Corkscrews That Work.* San Francisco, CA: The Wine Institute, 1946. Typescript of report done by Wine Advisory Board & Wine Institute.

Fredgant, Don. *Electrical Collectibles.* San Luis Obispo, CA: Padre Productions, 1981.

Freeman, Larry. *Collecting Old Granite-ware; Porcelain on Steel, a Forerunner of Aluminum Kitchenware.* Watkins Glen, NY: Century House, 1978.

Fuller, Edmund. *Tinkers and Geniuses, The Story of the Yankee Inventors.* NYC: Hastings House, 1955.

Fuller, John, Sr. *Art of Coppersmithing: A Practical Treatise on Working Sheet Copper Into All Forms.* NYC: David Williams Co., 1894, then 1911. First published serially, 1889-90. Reprinted: Mendham, NJ: Astragal Press, 1993.

Fumagalli, Ambrogio. *Coffeemakers. Macchine da Caffe, 1800-1950, American & European.* San Francisco: Chronicle Books, Bella Cosa Series, 1995. Vintage instruments from tin pots to fancy machines.

Gallo, John. *Nineteenth & Twentieth Century Yellow Ware.* Oneonta, NY 13820. Author, 1985.

Gaston, Mary Frank. *Antique Brass.* Paducah, KY: Collector Books, 1985.

Gentle, Rupert, & Rachael Feild. *English Domestic Brass, 1680-1810.* NYC: E. P. Dutton, 1975. Revised by Belinda Gentle, for Antique Collector's Club, 1994. New one expands date range: 1640-1920, and includes some continental European, some iron, steel and copper.

Geuder, Paeschke & Frey Co. *Cream City Ware.* Catalog. Milwaukee, WI: 1925.

Giarde, Jeffrey L. *Glass Milk Bottles: Their Makers and Marks.* Bryn Mawr, CA: Time Travelers Press, 1980.

Giblin, James C. *From Hand to Mouth: Or, How We Invented Knives, Forks, Spoons, & Chopsticks, & the Table Manners To Go with Them.* NYC: Harper Collins Children's Books, 1987.

Giedion, Siegfried. *Mechanization Takes Command, A Contribution to Anonymous History.* NYC: Oxford University, 1948. One section of great interest is "Mechanization Encounters the Household."

Gilbreath, Lilian. *The Home-Maker and Her Job.* NYC: D. Appleton, 1927.

Gilman, Charlotte Perkins. *The Home: Its Work and Influence.* NYC: McClure Phillips, 1903. Reprint: Urbana, IL: University of Illinois Press, 1972.

Giulian, Bertrand B. *Corkscrews of the Eighteenth Century; Artistry in Iron and Steel.* Yardley, PA: WhiteSpace Pub'g, 769 Sumter Dr., 19067. 1995.

Gobright, John Christopher. *The New York Sketchbook and Merchants Guide, A Directory.* NYC: J. C. Gobright, 1859.

Goldberg, Michael J. *Collectible Plastic Kitchenware & Dinnerware, 1935-1965.* Atglen, PA: Schiffer Pub'g Co., 1995. Mostly post-WWII wares.

Goldberg, Michael J. *Groovy Kitchen Designs for Collectors, 1935-1965: With Value Guide.* Atglen, PA: Schiffer Pub'g, 1996.

Goodholme, Todd S. *Domestic Cyclopedia of Practical Information.* NYC: Henry Holt & Co., 1877.

Gordon, Bob. *Early Electrical Appliances.* Aylesbury, England: Shire, 1984.

Gottesman, Rita Susswein. *The Arts & Crafts in New York, 1726-1776.* NYC: New-York Historical Society, 1938. Also, *1777-1799.* 1954.

Gould, Mary Earle. *Antique Tin & Tole Ware.* Rutland, VT: Charles E. Tuttle, 1962.

Gould, M. E.. *Early American Wooden Ware & Other Kitchen Utensils.* Rutland, VT: Tuttle, 1962.

Graham, J. T. *Scales & Balances. A Guide to Collecting.* Aylesbury, England: Shire, 1981.

Gray, Dorothy. *Gone With the Hearth.* Millbrae, CA: Celestial Arts/Les Femmes, 1976. Utensils, cookbooks, food.

Greaser, Arlene & Paul H. *Cookie Cutters & Molds.* Allentown, PA: 1969.

Green, Harvey, with assistance of Mary-Ellen Perry. *The Light of the Home: An Intimate View of the Lives of Victorian Women in America.* NYC: Pantheon, 1983. Ill'd with artifacts from Margaret Strong Museum.

Green, T. G. *Cornish Ware. Kitchen & Domestic Pottery.* Wappingers Falls, NY: Antique Collectors Club, 1996.

Griswold Mfg. Co. *1928 Catalog Reprint.* Chuck Wafford, 1936 "H" St., Springfield, OR 97477. 1985.

Griswold Cast Iron. A Price Guide. Neil Wood, ed. Gas City, IN: L-W Book Sales, 1993.

Groft, Tammis Kane. *Cast with Style. Nineteenth Century Cast-Iron Stoves from the Albany Area.* Rev. ed. Albany, NY: Albany Institute of History, 1984.

Greguire, Helen. *The Collector's Encyclopedia of Granite Ware.* Paducah, KY: Collector Books, 1990. Full color.

Grigson, Geoffrey, & Charles H. Gibbs-Smith, eds. *Things. A Volume About the Origin and Early History of Many Things, Common and Less Common, Essential and Inessential.* London: Waverley Book Co., 1954. (Vol. 3 of 4 books: *People; Places; Ideas.*)

Grist, Everett. *Collectible Aluminum. Hammered, Wrought, Forged & Cast.* Paducah, KY: Collector Books, 1993.

Guappone, Carmen A. *United States Decorated Stoneware.* McClellandtown, PA: Guappones Publications, RD#1, Box 10, 15458. 1993.

Guarnaccia, Helene. *Salt and Pepper Shakers, Volumes I, II, III, IV.* Paducah, KY: Collector Books, 1985, 1989, 1991, 1995.

Guilland, Harold F. *Early American Folk Pottery.* Radnor, PA: Chilton Books, 1971.

Haines, Leland M. *Round Oak Stoves, Ranges and Furnaces.* 272 pp, many illustrations. Houston: Macy's Texas Stove Works, 5515 Almeda Rd, 77004, c.1994.

Handbook of U.S. Beer Advertising Openers & Corkscrews, 1997. Chapel Hill, NC: Just For Openers, POB 64, 27514-0064.

Handwrought Object, 1776-1976, The. Exhibit catalog, curated by Nancy Neumann Press. Ithaca, NY: Herbert F. Johnson Museum, Cornell, 1976.

Hankenson, Dick. *Trivets.* Bound with Supplement of later date. Maple Plain, MN: Author, 1963.

Hankenson, Dick. *Trivets, Book 1.* Des Moines, IA: Wallace-Homestead, 1972.

Hankenson, Dick. *Trivets. Old and Re-Pro.* (Or *Trivets, Old and New Reproductions.*) Maple Plain, MN: 1972.

Hardyment, Christina. *From Mangle to Microwave. The Mechanization of Household Work.* Oxford, England: Polity Press, 1988.

Harland, Marion *[pseud.].* Mary Virginia Hawes Terhune. *House and Home, A Complete Housewife's Guide.* Philadelphia: Franklin News Co., 1889.

Harned, Bill & Denise. *Griswold Cast Collectibles.* POB 340, Edinboro, PA 18412. 1985.

Harrison, Molly. *The Kitchen in History.* NYC: Charles Scribner's, 1972.

Hayden, Dolores. *The Grand Domestic Revolution: A History of Feminist Designs for American Homes, Neighborhoods, and Cities.* Cambridge, MA, & London: The MIT Press, 1981.

Hazelcorn — See Fisher, Charles.

Heckmann, Manfred. *Corkscrews: An Introduction to Their Appreciation.* San Francisco, CA: The Wine Appreciation Guild, 155 Connecticut St., 94107. 1996.

Henry, Rosemary — See Wetherill, Phyllis.

Herman, Judith, & Marguerite Shallett Herman. *The Cornucopia: Being a Kitchen Entertainment and Cook Book ... 1390-1899.* NYC: Harper & Row, 1973. A salmagundy of recipes, folklore & tidbits.

Heuring, Jerry & Elaine. *Keen Kutter. Illustrated Price Guide.* Paducah, KY: Collector Books, 1984.

Hill, Ozella, & D. L. Hill. *Sleepy Eye Update.* Tulsa, OK: POB 50415, 74150. 1979. Stoneware bottles. See Meugniot, E.

Hine, Thomas. *The Total Package. The Evolution and Secret Meanings of Boxes, Bottles, Cans, and Tubes.* NY: Little Brown, 1994. From the advertising psych viewpoint.

Hofmann, Andrés Alfaro. *Mecanització. Una Historia de L'Electrodomestic.* Valenciana, Spain: Generalitat Valenciana, Conselleria de Cultura, Educacio I Ciencia, 1995. Tri-lingual (Spanish, Catalan, English) exhibit catalog on mechanization of the home & history of electrical appliances, curated by Mr. Hofmann.

Holloway, Laura C. *The Hearthstone; or, Life At Home, a Household Manual.* n.p., 1883.

Hooker, Richard J. *Food & Drink in America, a History.* Indianapolis & NY: Bobbs-Merrill, 1981.

Hoover, Doris. *Too Hot to Handle? Potholders & How to Make Them.* Radnor, PA: Chilton Books, 1993.

Hosley, William. *The Japan Idea: Art and Life in Victorian America.* Catalog of exhibit in 1990 at Wadsworth Atheneum, Hartford, CT.

Hough, Walter. *Collection of Heating and Lighting Utensils in the U.S. National Museum* [Smithsonian]. Washington, DC: GPO, 1928.

House & Garden. NYC: Conde Nast Pubns, 1901-1921+ Monthly. See *These Simple Things.*

House, Kurt D. *Antique Mechanical Fans.* San Antonio, TX: Trade Routes Antiques/The Fan Man, Inc., 218 Country Wood Dr., 78216-1607. 2nd rev. ed. 199-.

House Furnishing Review. NYC: c.1890-1930. Trade journal for buyers in hardware stores & house furnishings departments.

Hueg, Henry & Co. *Book of Designs for Bakers & Confectioners.* Catalog. NYC: 1896.

Hueg, Henry & Co. *The Little Confectioner.* NYC: 1921.

Hughes, Therle. *Sweetmeat & Jelly Glasses.* Guildford, England: Lutterworth Press, 1981.

Hume, Ivor Noël. *Historical Archaeology.* NYC: Alfred A. Knopf, 1968.

Husfloen, Kyle, ed. *Black Americana Price Guide.* Dubuque, IA: Antique Trader Books, 1996.

Hutchinson, Elsie Lillian. *The Housefurnishings Department — Department Store Merchandise Manual.* NYC: NYU, The Ronald Press Co., 1918, 1922.

Hutson, N. Joan. *Heirlooms from the Kitchen.* Huntsville, AL: Dajan Enterprises, 1908 Waxleaf Garden S.E., 35803-1232. 1985.

In Praise of Hot Liquors: The Study of Chocolate, Coffee and Tea-drinking 1600-1850. Catalog of an exhibition. York, England: York Civic Trust, Fairfax House, Castlegate, YO1 1RN, 1995.

International Cooks' Catalogue. See Beard, James, intro.

Irons, Dave. *Irons by Irons. 1600 Pressing Irons.* Northampton, PA: Irons, 223 Covered Bridge Rd., 1996.

Ito, Teiji. *Wabi, Sabi, Suki: The Essence of Japanese Beauty.* Hiroshima, Japan: Mazda Motor Co., 1993.

Jaburg Brothers. *Best of Everything for Bakers.* Catalog. NYC: 1908.

Jacobs, Sharon Ray. *String along With Me: A Collector's Guide to Stringholders With Prices.* Gas City, IN: L-W Book Sales, 1996.

James, P., & N. Thorpe, *Ancient Inventions.* NY: Ballantine.

Jarrett, John. *A Treatise Upon Tin Plate Manufacture in the United States.* [U.S.]: American Tinned Plate Association, 1884.

Jenkins, J. Geraint. *Traditional Country Craftsmen.* London: Routledge & Kegan Paul, 1965. Insight into the Great Britain connection.

Jenkins, Paul. *Twenty By Fourteen: A History of the South Wales Tinplate Industry, 1700-1961.* Llandysul, Wales: Gomer, 1995.

John, W. D., & Anne Simcox. *Pontypool and Usk Japanned Wares, with The Early History of the Iron and Tinplate Industries at Pontypool.* Newport, England: Ceramic Book Co., 1953; 1966.

Johnson, Frances. *Aluminum Giftware.* Atglen, PA: Schiffer Pub'g, 1996.

Johnson, Lawrence A. *Over the Counter and On the Shelf.* Rutland, VT: Charles C. Tuttle Co., 1961.

Jones, Joseph C., Jr. *American Ice Boxes.* Humble, TX: Jobeco Books, 1981.

Joseph, S. Co. *Hotel, Bakery & Restaurant Supplies ... Catalog.* NYC: c.1927.

Journal of Early Southern Decorative Arts, The. Biannual publication of MESDA. Winston-Salem, NC: MESDA, POB 10310, 27108.

Kate-von Eicken, Brigitte ten. *Kuchengerate um 1900.* Stuttgart: Walter Hadecke Verlag, [1979?] 7252 Weil der Stadt, Stuttgart, Germany.

Katzinger Co., Edward. *Katzinger Co. Price List 53.* Chicago: 1940.

Kauffman, Henry J. *American Copper & Brass.* NYC: Thomas Nelson & Sons, 1968. Reprint. NYC: Crown, 1979.

Kauffman, Henry J. *Early American Ironware, Cast & Wrought.* Rutland, VT: Charles E. Tuttle, 1966.

Kauffman, Henry J. *The American Fireplace: Chimneys, Mantelpieces, Fireplaces & Accessories.* NYC: Galahad Books, 1972.

Kauffman, Henry J., & Quentin H. Bowers. *Early American Andirons and Other Fireplace Accessories.* NYC: Thomas Nelson, 1974.

Kaye, Edward R. *The Handbook of Beer Advertising Openers and Corkscrews.* Sanibel Island, FL: Kaye, 968 Greenwood Ct., 33957. 1984.

Kellogg, Ella Ervilla Eaton. *Science in the Kitchen.* Battle Creek, MI: Good Health Pub'g Co., 1910. 1st published in 1893.

Kelly, Rob Roy, and James Ellwood, in conjunction with Shelburne Museum, Vt. *Trivets & Stands.* Lima, OH: Golden Era Publications, POB 934, 45802, 1990. 263 pages, thousands of trivets pictured.

Kennedy, Phillip D. *Hoosier Cabinets.* Indianapolis, IN: 9256 Holyoke Court, 46268.

Kevill-Davies, Sally. *Jelly Moulds.* Guildford, England: Lutterworth Press, 1983.

Kilbride, Richard J. *Art Deco Chrome, The Chase Era, Vol. I.* Stamford, CT: Jo-D Books, 1988.

Kilbride, Richard J. *Art Deco Chrome Book #2, Collectors Guide: Industrial Design in the Chase Era.* Stamford, CT: Jo-D Books, 1992. (Chase Brass & Copper.)

Kindig, Paul E. *Butter Prints & Molds.* West Chester, PA: Schiffer, 1986. Near perfect — well illus., gobs of great info, opinions & history.

Kitchen Collectibles News — See Franklin, L. C.

Kitchen Antiques & Collectibles News — See DeMore, Dana

Klever, Ulrich. *Alte Kuchengerate, Backen und Kochen.* Munich: Wilhelm Heyne Verlag, 1979. Cooking & baking utensils & molds.

Knight, Edward H. *American Mechanical Dictionary.* 2 vol. NYC: J. B. Ford & Co., 1874; NYC: Riverside Press, 1876. Terrific!

Knight, Edward H. *The Practical Dictionary of Mechanics, 1874-1877. Supplement.* Boston: Houghton, Mifflin, 1884.

KOOKS — Kollectors of Old Kitchen Stuff. Contact with SASE: Carol Bohn, 501 Market St., Mifflinburg, PA 17844.

Koren, Leonard. *Wabi-sabi for Artists, Designers, Poets & Philosophers.* Berkeley, CA: Stone Bridge Press, 1994.

Kruger, Laura. *Vom Zauber Alten Hausgerats.* Freiburg im Breisgau: Rombach & Co., 1981.

Ladies' Home Journal. Monthly. Philadelphia: Curtis Pub. Co., 1887-1920 consulted.

Lalance & Grosjean Mfg. Co. Catalog. NYC: 1890. 360 pp of assorted utensils.

Lamprecht Collection of Cast Iron Art, The. Small catalog. Birmingham, AL: American Cast Iron Pipe Co., 1941. Famous collection that needs a better book.

Lancaster, Maud. *Electric Cooking, Heating & Cleaning.* NYC: D. Van Nostrand, 1914.

Landis, Henry Kinzer. *Early Kitchens of the Pennsylvania Germans. A Paper Read in 1935.* Norristown, PA: Pennsylvania German Society, 1939.

Lantz, Louise K. *Old American Kitchenware, 1725-1925.* NYC: Thomas Nelson, 1970. This is accompanied by a price guide booklet that has been updated periodically & published by the author, Hydes, MD.

Larkin, Jack. *The Reshaping of Everyday Life, 1790-1840.* NYC: Harper & Row, 1988. By the historian at Old Sturbridge Village in Mass.

Lasansky, Jeannette. *Central Pennsylvania Redware Pottery 1780-1904.* Lewisburg, PA: Union County Oral Traditions Project, 1979; reprint 1989.

Lasansky, J. *Made of Mud. Stoneware Potteries in Central Pennsylvania, 1831-1929.* Lewisburg, PA: Oral Traditions, 1979. All Lasansky's books are extremely informative & attractive; copious duotone illus.

Lasansky, J. *To Cut, Piece, & Solder. Work of the Rural Pennsylvania Tinsmith 1778-1908.* Lewisburg, PA: Oral Traditions, 1982.

Lasansky, J. *To Draw, Upset, & Weld. Work of the Pennsylvania Rural Blacksmith 1742-1935.* Lewisburg, PA: Oral Traditions, 1980.

Lasansky, J. *Willow, Oak & Rye. Basket Traditions in Pennsylvania.* Lewisburg, PA: Oral Traditions, 1979.

Lechler, Doris Anderson. *Children's Glass Dishes, China, and Furniture. Vol. II.* Paducah, KY: Collector Books, 1986.

Lechner, Mildred, & Ralph Lechner. *The World of Salt Shakers.* Paducah, KY: Collector Books, 1992. Not the kitsch figurals.

Leibowitz, Joan. *Yellow Ware. The Transitional Ceramic.* Exton, PA: Schiffer, 1985.

Lesser, Charles. *Guidebook to Figural Bottle Openers.* Harrington, DE: 1953 Sugar Stick Rd., 19952. © c. 1990s.

Leybourne, Douglas M., Jr. *The Collector's Guide to Old Fruit Jars,* 7th ed.; 8th ed. North Muskegon, MI: Author, POB 5417, 49445.

1994; 1997. Mr. Leybourne is carrying on the compilation and publishing of the six amazing editions done by Alice Creswick.

Leybourne, Doug. *The Fruit Jar Works, Vol. I; Vol. II.* North Muskegon, MI: Author, Box 5417, 49445. Back in print 1996.

Lifshey, Earl. *The Housewares Story: A History of the American Housewares Industry.* Chicago, IL: Nat'l Housewares Mfrs. Assoc., 1973. An incredibly useful trade-sponsored history with copious illustrations. See Matranga, V.K.

Lincoln, E. S. & Paul Smith. *The Electric Home. A Standard Ready Reference Book.* NYC: Electric Home Pub'g, 1936.

Lindenberger, Jan. *Black Memorabilia for the Kitchen, A Handbook & Price Guide.* Atglen, PA: Schiffer Pub'g, 1993.

Lindenberger, Jan. *The 50s & 60s Kitchen: A Collector's Handbook & Price Guide.* Atglen, PA: Schiffer Pub'g, 1994.

Lindenberger, Jan. *Fun Kitchen Collectibles. A Handbook & Price Guide.* Atglen, PA: Schiffer Pub'g, 1996.

Lindsay, J. Seymour. *Iron & Brass Implements of the English & American House* . Boston: Medici Society, 1927. New edition. Bass River, MA: C. Jacobs, 1964.

Lord, Priscilla Sawyer, & Daniel J. Foley. *The Folk Arts and Crafts of New England.* NYC: Chilton, 1965.

Lupton, E. & J. A. Miller. *The Bathroom, the Kitchen, and the Aesthetics of Waste.* New expanded edition. Princeton Architectural Press, 1996.

L. H. Mace & Co. 1883 Catalog. Facsimile. Princeton, NJ: American Historical Catalog Collection, Pyne Press, 1971. Woodenware; Meat Safes.

NOTE: Mc- names, see in strict letter-by-letter alphabetical order

Macdonald, Anne L. *Feminine Ingenuity: Women and Invention in America.* NYC: Ballantine books, 1992. Author is a patent-holder herself.

MacLean, Ron. *Common Corkscrews V. Star Brown Mfg Co.* Mississauga, Ontario, Canada: Ron MacLean, 4201 Sunflower Drive, L5L 2L4. 1994. (Also #I, 198-; #II, 1989; #III, 1990; #IV, 199-.)

MacLean, Ron. *Corkscrews, Canadian Patents.* Mississauga, Ontario: R. MacLean, 1985.

MacMillan, Joseph E. *The MacMillan Index of Antique Coffee Mills.* Marietta, GA: Author, 657 Old Mountain Rd., 30064, 1995. Definitive, 1,322 pp book primarily of patent history, with biographies and copious illustrations & photographs.

Made of Iron. Catalog of an exhibition, Sept.-Dec., 1966. Dominique de Menil, Curator; Stephen V. Grancsay, Introduction. Houston, TX: University of St. Thomas Art Department, 1966. I've treasured this profusely illustrated, impeccably written catalog for over 30 years.

Maine Antique Digest. POB 1429, Waldoboro, ME 04572-1429. 1-800-752-8521.

Manning, Bowman & Co. *Perfection Granite Ironware. Decorated Pearl Agateware.* Catalog. Meriden, CT: c.1892.

Marque C.C. *Fabrique Spéciale de Moules en Etain.* Catalog. Paris: 1900.

Marshall, Jo. *Kitchenware. Collecting for Tomorrow.* London: BPC Publishers, 1976.

Marshall, Mrs. A. B. *Cookery Book.* 45th-thousandth. London: c.1900. Most of it dates to c.1887.

Marshall, Mrs. A. B. *Larger Cookery Book of Extra Recipes.* 10th-thousandth printing. London: c.1902.

Marshall, Mrs. A. B. *The Book of Ices. Including Cream & Water Ices, Sorbets, Mousses, Iced Soufflés.* 14th Ed. London: c.1900-1902.

Mason, Charlotte. *The Ladies' Assistant for Regulating & Supplying the Table.* London: Printed for J. Walter, 1787.

Masters, Thomas. *A Short Treatise Concerning Some Patent Inventions for the Production of Ice, Artificial Cold, etc. Also the Newly Improved Culinary Utensils.* London: 1850.

Martin, Jane — See Baker, Eric

Matranga, Victoria K. *America at Home: A Celebration of Twentieth-Century Housewares.* Chicago, IL: National Housewares Manufacturers Association, 1997. 1-800-843-6462. 6400 Schafer Court, Suite 650, Rosemont, IL 60018. See Lifshey.

Matthai-Ingram Co. *Illustrated Catalogue of Sheet Metal Goods. Catalog 41*. Baltimore: c.1890.

Matthews, Mary Lou. *American Kitchen Collectibles*. Gas City, IN: L-W Promotions, 1973. Some good catalog pix, negligible text.

McAllister, Lisa S., & John L. Michel. *Collecting Yellowware, An Identification & Value Guide*. Paducah, KY: Collector Books, 1993.

McCann, Jerry, comp. & ed. *Fruit Jar Annual, 1996*. Chicago, IL: Phoenix Press, 5003 W. Berwyn Ave., 60630-1501. ©1996. *Fruit Jar Annual, 1997; Fruit Jar Annual, 1998*. (We hope lib infinitum!) These are unique among collector publications; 100s of descriptive, priced entries for jars, 100s of clear drawings; some scholarly, readable articles; collector directory; & ad space for collectors & dealers.

McNerney, Kathryn. *Antique Iron. Identification & Values*. Paducah, KY: Collector Books, 1984.

Mendelson, Anne. *Stand Facing the Stove: The Story of the Women Who Gave America "The Joy of Cooking."* NYC: Henry Holt & Co., 1996. Author of this yummy book on the Rombauers claims America is a "society where cookbooks are replacing cooking."

Mercer, Henry C. *The Bible in Iron*. Doylestown, PA: Bucks County Historical soc., 1914. Third edition with additions by Joseph E. Sandford, 1961. Cast iron 5-, 6- and 10-plate stoves, also firebacks.

Metalwork in Early America — Copper & Its Alloys; Selections from the Winterthur Collection. Wappingers Falls, NY: Antique Collectors Club, 1996.

Metal Worker, Plumber & Steam Fitter, The. NYC: 1882. Trade journal. Assorted dates consulted.

Meugniot, Elinor. *Old Sleepy Eye*. Tulsa, OK: POB 50415, 71450. 1973. Stoneware bottles. See also Hill, Ozella.

MidAtlantic Antiques Magazine, The. P.O. Box 908, Henderson, NC: 27536-0908. 1-800-326-3894.

Miller, Gary, & K. M. Scotty Mitchell. *Price Guide to Collectible Kitchen Appliances*. Des Moines, IA: Wallace-Homestead, 1991.

Miller, Robert William. *American Primitives*. Des Moines, IA: Wallace-Homestead, 1972. Collection of Museum of Appalachia, Norris, TN.

Mills, Thomas & Bro. *Ice Cream Manufacturers' Equipment. Catalog 31*. Philadelphia: c.1915. A larger one dates to 1930.

Mitchell, James R., ed. — See *Antique Metalware*.

Moffet, Jim. *American Corn Huskers. A Patent History*. Sunnyvale, CA: Off Beat Books, 1345 Poplar Ave., 94087. ©1996. 88 pages, 262 patent drawings, inventor index.

Montgomery Ward 1895 Catalogue reprint. NYC: Dover Publications, c.1970s.

Moore, Jan. *Antique Enameled Ware*. Paducah, KY: Collector Books, 1975.

Moore, N. Hudson. *Old Pewter, Brass, Copper & Sheffield Plate*. Garden City, NY: Garden City Pub. Co., 1933.

Morse, Sidney. *Household Discoveries: An Encyclopedia of Practical Recipes and Processes*. Petersburg, NY: The Success Co., c.1909.

Mumford, Lewis. *The Myth of the Machine*. NYC: Harcourt Brace, 1966.

Mundey, Alfred Holley. *Tin and the Tin Industry*. London: I. Pitman, 1926.

Museum fur Volkerkunde und Schweizerisches Museum fur Volkskunde Basel. *Catalog*. Basel, Switzerland: Das Museum, 1963. 32 pp, illus.

Mussey, Barrows, ed. *Yankee Life By Those Who Lived It*. NYC: Alfred Knopf, 1947. Excerpts from journals, autobiographies, letters, etc.

Myerson, Jeremy and Sylvia Katz. *Kitchenware: Conran Design Guides*. NYC: Van Nostrand Reinhold, 1990. The last 50+ years of kitchen collectibles from the industrial design view. Includes designer bios.

Nagler, Bernard. *Patent Pending*. London & Los Angeles, CA: Price Stern, 1968.

New York-Pennsylvania Collector, The. Monthly newspaper. P.O.B. C, Fishers, NY 14453.1-800-836-1868.

Nichols, Harold. *McCoy Cookie Jars from the First to the Last*. Ames, IA: Nichols Wrestling Products, Inc., POB 1067, 50010. 1992. (For those wrestling with the important question: To eat a cookie, or not to eat.)

Nishida, Masayoshi. *Rikyu to Basho: "Wabi" to "Sabi" No Genryu*. Tokyo, Japan: Ofusha, 1975.

North Bros. Mfg. Co. *Dainty Dishes For All the Year Round*, by Mrs. S. T. Rorer. Philadelphia: 1912. Cookbooklet with catalog pages.

Oakley, Ann. *The Sociology of Housework*. London: Martin Robertson, 1974.

Objects for Preparing Food. Exhibit catalog, with intros by Curator Sandra Zimmerman & Mimi Shorr (Sheraton). Washington, DC: Renwick Gallery, 1972. Done in conjunction with the Museum of Contemporary Crafts of the American Crafts Council, NYC.

O'Connor, Hyla. *The Early American Cookbook*. NYC: Rutledge Press, 1974. Includes utensils and food.

Official Gazette. Washington, DC: U.S. Patent Office, 1873.

O'Leary, Fred. *Corkscrews: 1000 Patented Ways to Open a Bottle*. Atglen, PA: Schiffer Pub'g Co., 1996. Many photos.

Osgood, Cornelius. *The Jug and Related Stoneware of Bennington*. Rutland, VT: Charles Tuttle, 1971.

Palmer, Phyllis. *Domesticity & Dirt. Housewives & Domestic Servants in the U.S., 1920-1945*. Philadelphia, PA: Temple University Press, 1989.

Paper and Advertising Collector, The. (P.A.C.). POB 50, Mt. Joy, PA, 17552.

Parloa, Miss Maria. *Kitchen Companion. A Guide For All Who Would Be Good Housekeepers*. Boston: Estes & Lauriat, 1887. By founder of the Original Cooking School in Boston.

Paustenbach, Dennis, & Louise Paustenbach. *Pie Safes*. The Paustenbachs wrote in-depth articles on pie safes for *Antique Review*, an Ohio monthly. They have planned a book for a long time; as of this writing (1997), it has not been published, but I hope it will be soon.

Pearsall, Ronald. *Collecting Mechanical Antiques*. (1830-1880.) Newton Abbot: David & Charles; NYC: Arco, 1973.

Pearse, John Barnard. *A Concise History of the Iron Manufacture of the American Colonists Up To the Revolution*. Philadelphia: Allen, Lane & Scott, 1876.

Pearson, Stanley E. *Just Jarring Around*. Strafford, NH: Author, 1971.

Pearson-Page Co., Ltd. *New Catalogue*. Birmingham & London, England: 1925. Cast brass reproductions of 1000s of household items & decorations.

Peet, Louise Jenison, & Lenore E. Sater. *Household Equipment*. NYC: John Wiley & Sons, 1934; 1940.

Peirce, Josephine H. *Fire On the Hearth. Evolution . . . of the Heating-Stove*. Springfield, MA: Pond-Ekberg, 1951.

Perry, Evan. *Collecting Antique Metalware*. NYC: Doubleday, 1974.

Perry, Evan. *Corkscrews & Bottle Openers*. Aylesbury, England: Shire Pubns, 1980; 2nd rev. ed., 1995.

Phipps, Frances. *Colonial Kitchens, Their Furnishings, and Their Gardens*. NYC: Hawthorne Books, 1972. Still one of the best.

Pick, Albert & Co. *E-6 General Catalog. Hotel, Restaurant, Bar, Fountain Furnishings & Kitchen Utensils*. Chicago: 1905; 1909. Jobber & wholesaler with 1000s of items.

Pick-Barth Co. *General Catalog E-32*. Chicago: 1929.

Pinto, Edward H. *Treen & Other Wooden Bygones*. London: Bell & Hyman, 1969. Reprinted in 1979. Huge & informative, although mostly British & European wares, and many of them now 200-300 years old and not available to collectors.

Player, John. *The Origins and Craft of Antique Tin & Tôle*. Available as of 1997 from Christie & Christie Associates, POB 392, Cookstown, Ontario L0L 1L0, Canada.

Porter, Enid M. *The Hearth and the Kitchen.* 19 pp guidebook. Cambridge, England: Cambridge & County Folk Museum, 1971.

Porter Co., C. B. *Catalogue Illustrating & Describing Plain Enameled Tinware, . . . Water Coolers.* Philadelphia: 1920.

Powers, Beatrice F., & Olive Floyd. *Early American Decorated Tinware.* NYC: Hastings House, 1957.

Prime, Alfred Coxe. *The Arts & Crafts in Philadelphia, Maryland, and South Carolina, 1720-1785.* Topsfield, MA: Walpole Society, 1929. Also — *1786-1800.* 1932.

Punchard, Lorraine May. *Playtime Kitchen Items & Table Accessories.* Bloomington, MN: Author, 8201 Pleasant Ave. So., 55420, 1993.

Punchard, Lorraine May. *Playtime Pottery & Porcelain from the United Kingdom and the United States.* Atglen, PA: Schiffer Pub'g, 1996.

Putnam, J. Pickering. *The Open Fireplace in All Ages.* Boston: J. R. Osgood, 1881; Boston: Ticknor & Co., 1886.

Quennell, M., & C.H.B. Quennell. *A History of Everyday Things in England. Part 3: The Rise of Industrialism, 1733-1851.* London: Batsford, 3rd ed., 1945.

Rawson, Marion Nicholl. *Handwrought Ancestors.* NYC: E. P. Dutton, 1936.

Ray, William, & Marlys Ray. *The Art of Invention; Patent Models and Their Makers.* Princeton, NJ: Pyne Press, 1974.

Reed Mfg. Co. *Matchless Metalware. Catalog 27.* Newark, NY & Canandaigua, NY: 1927.

Reinelt, Sabine. *Puppenküche und Puppenherd in drei Jahrhunderten.* Ludwigsburg, Germany: Kunstverlag Weingarten, 1985. Copious illustrations of kitchen toys of 300 years.

Revi, Albert Christian, ed. *Spinning Wheel's Collectible Iron, Tin, Copper & Brass.* Castle Books, 1974. Anthologized articles from lamented defunct magazine. Mr. Revi, bless you for starting so many of us on our collecting path!

Rickard, T. A. *Man and Metals.* NYC: McGraw-Hill Book Co., 1932.

Ricketts, Linda. *Citrus Juice Reamers.* Laurel, MD: 1970, 1979.

Rittenhouse, Judith A. *Ornamental & Figural Nutcrackers.* Paducah, KY: Collector Books, 1993.

Ritzinger & Grasgreen. *Catalog of Household Goods & Novelties.* NYC: c.1906-1907. Importers & jobbers for door-to-door salesmen.

Robacker, Earl F. *Pennsylvania Dutch Stuff, A Guide to Country Antiques.* NYC: A. S. Barnes, 1944.

Robacker, Earl F. *Pennsylvania German Cooky Cutters & Cookies, Home Craft Course.* Plymouth Meeting, PA: 1946. 20 pp booklet.

Robacker, Earl F. *Touch of the Dutchland.* NY: A. S. Barnes, 194-.

Roerig, Fred, & Joyce Roerig. *Collector's Encyclopedia of Cookie Jars., Vol. I.* Paducah, KY: Collector Books, 1991. *Vol. II,* 1993. Copious illus.

Rogers, Henry, Sons & Co. *Book No. E5528.* Wolverhampton, England: 1914.

Rogove, Susan T., & Marcia B. Steinhauer. *Pyrex by Corning: A Collectors Guide.* Marietta, OH: Antique Publications, POB 553, 45750. 1993.

Rollband, James. *American Nutcrackers: A Patent History and Value Guide.* Sunnyvale, CA: Off Beat Books, 1345 Poplar Ave., 94087. 1996. 180 pp, 537 patent illustrations, inventor index only.

Roller, Dick. *Fruit Jar Patents, Vol. II, 1870-1899.* Chicago: Phoenix Press, 5003 W. Berwyn Ave., 60630-1501. © c.1980s. Due to be reprinted sometime in late 1990s. (See also Bond, Ralph.)

Roller, Dick. *Fruit Jar Patents, Vol. III, 1900-1942.* Chicago: Phoenix Press, 1996. 500 pp, 4 cross-reference indices for foolproof identification.

Roller, Dick. Indiana Glass Factories Notes. Paris, IL: Acorn Press, 607 Driskell St., Paris, IL 61944. ©1994.

Roller, Dick. *The Standard Fruit Jar Reference.* Paris, IL: Acorn Press, 1983.

Romaine, Lawrence B. *Guide to American Trade Catalogs 1744-1900.* NYC: R.R. Bowker, 1960. Reprinted by Dover Books, NYC, 1990. Each of 60+ categories has many listings of trade catalogs, with locator guide.

Runkewich, Fred. *Fred's Price Guide to Modern Bottles.* Cheyenne, WY: Author, POB 1423, 82003.

Russell & Erwin Mfg. Co. *Illustrated Catalog of American Hardware.* New Britain, CT: 1865. A facsimile reprint was published by Assoc. for Preservation Technology, 1980.

Russell, Loris S. *Handy Things to Have Around the House. Oldtime Domestic Appliances of Canada and the U.S.* NY: McGraw-Hill Ryerson Ltd., 1979.

Rybczynski, Witold. *Home.* NYC: Viking Press, 1986. One of the best.

Scammell, Henry B., comp. *Treasure House of Useful Knowledge; An Encyclopedia of Valuable Receipts in the Principal Arts of Life.* St. Louis, MO: Buckland Pub'g co., 1885, 1891. Fascinating stuff, drawn uncredited directly from books by authorities "whose name is legion."

Schiffer, Peter, Nancy, & Herbert. *Antique Iron. Survey of American & English Forms, Fifteenth Through Nineteenth Centuries.* Exton, PA: Schiffer, 1979. Excellent pictures as usual but scant information.

Schiffer, Peter, Nancy, & Herbert. *The Brass Book, American, English & Eurpoean, 15th Century to 1850.* Exton, PA: Schiffer, 1978.

Schneider, Mike. *The Complete Cookie Jar Book.* Atglen, PA: Schiffer, 1991.

Schneider, Mike. *The Complete Salt & Pepper Shaker Book.* Atglen, PA: Schiffer Pub'g, 1993.

Schroeder, Bill. *One Thousand Fruit Jars Priced.* Paducah, KY: Collector Books, 1983.

Scientific American. Weekly. NYC: Munn & Co., 1845-1859. These 19th C. issues almost always contain something on a household improvement.

Scientific Artisan; A Journal of Patents, Science, Art, Discovery, Inventions, Etc. Cincinnati, OH: American Patent co., Nov. 1858-April 1860. Weekly treasure for the curious — then and now.

Sears, Roebuck & Co., 1902 Catalog. Facsimile edition by: NYC: Crown Publishers, 1969. Badly printed — See Montgomery Ward.

Seymour, John. *The National Trust Book of Forgotten Household Crafts.* London: Dorling Kindersley, 1987.

Sferrazza, Julie. *Farber Bros. Krome-Kraft: A Guide for Collectors.* Marietta, OH: Antique Publications, POB 553, 45750. 1988.

Sferrazza, Julie. *Farber Bros. 1941 Catalog reprint.* Marietta, OH: Antique Publications, POB 553, 45750. 1988.

Silver & Co. *Silver's House Furnishings. Catalog No. 18.* Brooklyn, NY: c.1910.

Simpson, Bruce L. *Development of the Metal Castings Industry.* Chicago, IL: American Foundrymen's Association, 1948. From prehistorical use through the mechanization of foundries, from jewelry to cannons. Profusely illustrated. If you love iron, you've got to track this down.

Sipe, Brian M. *Coppersmithing in Nineteenth Century Philadelphia — the Bentley Shop.* Thesis. University of Delaware, 1987.

Slesin, Suzanne. *Kitchen Ceramics.* NYC: Abbeville Press, 1997.

Slesin, Suzanne, & Daniel Rozensztroch. *Wire.* NYC: Abbeville Press, 1994. Fabulous pictures & objects, hardly any info.

Smith, Darrell A. *Black Americana, A Personal Collection.* Tempe, AZ: Black Relics, Inc., POB 24954, zip 85282. 1989.

Smith, David G., & Chuck Wafford. *The Book of Griswold & Wagner. Favorite Piqua, Sidney Hollow Ware, Wapak.* Atglen, PA: Schiffer Pub'd, 1995.

Smith, Elmer Lewis, ed. *Early American Butter Prints.* Witmer, PA: Applied Arts, 1971.

Smith, Elmer, & Mel Horst. *Early Iron Ware.* Lebanon, PA: Applied Arts, 1971. Other books: *Household Tools & Tasks*; and *Tinware, Yesterday & Today.*

Smith, Richard Flanders. *Pennsylvania Butter Prints.* Ephrata, PA: Science Press, 1970.

Smith, Wayne. *Ice Cream Dippers. An Illustrated History & COllector's Guide.* Box 418, Walkersville, MD 21793. Author. 1986. Beautifully photographed & well-researched. *Price Guide* available too.

Sonn, Albert H. *Early American Wrought Iron.* 3 vol. NYC: Charles Scribner's, 1928. Reprinted in 1979. Vol. 3 is *Andirons, Broilers, Trammels, Etc.*

Soyer, Alexis. *The Pantropheon; or, History of Food, and Its Preparation . . .* London: Simpkin, Marshall, 1853. Has 3000 references to various authors.

Sparke, Penny. *Electrical Appliances. Twentieth Century Design.* London: Unwin Hyman, 1987.

Spielman, George B. *Masonic Collectables.* Knoxville, MD: Author, 1604 Rohrersville Rd., 21758.

Spinning Wheel. Albert Christian Revi, ed. Hanover, PA: Everybodys Press, 1950s-1970s. Wonderful source of information on many subjects of interest to kitchen collectors.

Sprackling, Helen. *Customs On the Table Top. How New England Housewives Set Out Their Tables.* Sturbridge, MA: Old Sturbridge Village, 1958, 1966.

Stanley, John R. *The 1994 Handbook of Beer Advertising Openers and Corkscrews.* Durham, NC: Stanley, 1994. 2nd ed.

Stille, Eva. *Doll Kitchens, 1800-1980.* Tr. by Edward Force. English edition: West Chester, PA: Schiffer Pub'g, 1988. Fabulous source, with great pictures by Severin Stille. Eva has done it — how could anyone improve this book?

Stoneback, Diane. *Kitchen Collectibles: The Essential Buyer's Guide.* Radnor, PA: Chilton Book Co., 1993.

Stoudt, John Joseph. *Early Pennsylvania Arts & Crafts.* NYC: A. S. Barnes, 1964.

Stoudt, John Joseph. *Sunbonnets and Shoofly Pies. A Pennsylvania Dutch Cultural History.* Cranbury, NJ: A. S. Barnes, 1973.

Street, Julian. *Wines, Their Selection, Care and Service . . . and on Wineglasses, Cradles, Corkscrews, and Kindred Matters.* NYC: Knopf, 3rd ed., 19—.

Stuart, Peterson & Co. *Celebrated Tinned, Enameled, Turned & Plain Hollow Ware.* NYC: 1975. Also 1866; 1876 & 1888.

Subject-Matter Index of Patents for Inventions. Issued by the U.S. Patent Office, 1790 to 1873, Inclusive. 3 volumes. NYC: Arno Press, 1976. Now available from Ayer Co. Publications, POB 958, Salem, NH, 03079.

Supnick, Mark, & Ellen Supnick. *The Wonderful World of Cookie Jars.* Revised ed. Gas City, IN: L-W Book Sales, 1997.

Swank, James M. *History of the Manufacture of Iron in All Ages . . . Particularly in the U.S. for Three Hundred Years. From 1585-1885.* Philadelphia, PA: for the Author, 1882. I guess I could call my book *400 Years of Kitchen Collectibles!*

"Technology and Culture." Quarterly journal of the Society for the History of Technology. Chicago, IL: Univ. of Chicago Press. Started c.1960.

Tefft, Gary, & Bonnie Tefft. *Red Wing Potters & Their Wares.* Locust Enterprises, first published 1981. New edition & also a price guide. Tefft, W174 N9422 Devonwood Rd., Menomonee Falls, WI 53051.

These Simple Things. Some Appreciation of the Small Joys in Daily Life from House & Garden. Totally charming essays by such as Elizabeth Bowen, Marianne Moore, and Rumer Godden, that first appeared in the magazine. NYC: Simon & Schuster, 1962, 1963, 1965.

Thomas' Register of American Manufacturers and First Hands In All Lines. The Buyers' Guide 1905-1906. Reprint of 1905-06 edition, probably by Thomas Pub'g Co., NY, whose registers are now many volumes per edition. Any old ones you find at library book sales or whatever will reward you in fascinating business history.

Thompson, Sir Benjamin (Count Rumford). *Complete Works.* 4 vol. Boston, MA: American Academy of Arts & Sciences, 1870-1875.

Reprint: Cambridge, MA: Belknap Press, 1968-1970. Inventor and social engineer Count Rumford designed and wrote about many things — notably for us, coffee pots and chimneys.

Thompson, Frances. *Antiques from the Country Kitchen.* Des Moines, IA: Wallace-Homestead, 1985.

Thompson, Frances. *Mountain Relics.* Cranbury, NJ: A. A. Barnes, 1976.

Thornburg, Irene. *Salt & Pepper Shakers in Series.* Battle Creek, MI: Author, 581 Joy Rd., 49014-8450. 1997?

Thornton, Don. *Apple Parers.* Sunnyvale, CA: Off Beat Books, 1997. Copious illustrations, including patents, fully indexed.

Thornton, Don. *Can Openers.* Sunnyvale, CA: 1998.

Thornton, Don. *Nutmeg Graters.* Sunnyvale, CA: Off Beat Books, 1998/99. Will be fully illustrated, including patents, and fully indexed.

Thornton, Don. *The Eggbeater Book. The First and Last Word About Man's Greatest Invention.* NYC: Arbor House, 1983.

Thornton, Don. *Beat This. The Eggbeater Chronicles. The Stirring Story of America's Greatest Invention.* Sunnyvale, CA: Off Beat Books, 1345 Poplar Ave., 94087. 1994. Copious illustrations, including patents, fully indexed, and the end all to beat all.

Thuro, Catherine M. V. *Oil Lamps Vol. I. Kerosene Era in North America.* © c. 1993. *Vol. II,* © c. 1995.

Tice, Patricia M. *Ice Cream For All. Social History & Recipes.* Rochester, NY: Strong Museum, 1990.

Today's Collector: The Marketplace for Antiques and Collectibles. Monthly. Iola, WI: Krause Publications, 700 E. State St., 54990-0001. 1-800-258-0929.

Toller, Jane. *Turned Woodware for Collectors. Treen & Other Objects.* Cranbury, NJ: A. S. Barnes, 1975.

Toulouse, Julian Harrison. *A Collectors' Manual: Fruit Jars.* Hanover, PA: Everybody's Press, 1969. A pioneer in the field.

Trice, James E. *Butter Molds; An Identification & Value Guide.* 2nd edition. Paducah, KY: Collector Books, 1980. Great variety pictured; little information.

Turner, Jean W. *Collectable Aunt Jemima.* Atglen, PA: Schiffer Pub'g, 1994.

Tryon, Rolla Milton. *Household Manufacturers in the U.S., 1640-1860.* Chicago: University of Chicago Press, 1917; reprint. NYC: Johnson Reprint, 1966.

Ure, Andrew. *A Dictionary of Arts, Manufactures & Mines.* 2 vol. England: 1839. NYC: D. Appleton, 1854. A fascinating work.

Usher, Abbott Payson. *A History of Mechanical Inventions.* NYC: McGraw Hill, 1929. Rev. ed. Cambridge, MA: Harvard University Press, 1954.

Van Wieren, Dale. *American Breweries II.* © 1996. Order from John Stanley, POB 64, Chapel Hill, NC 27514-0064. For ID'g beer can openers.

Viel, Lyndon C. *The Clay Giants. The Stoneware of Red Wing, Goodhue County, Minnesota.* Book 2. Des Moines, IA: Wallace-Homestead, 1980.

Vogelzang, Vernagene, & Evelyn Welch. *Graniteware. Collectors' Guide with Prices.* Wallace-Homestead, 1981. *Book II,* 1986. Great pictures and storehouse of in-depth information.

Vosburgh, H. K. *The Tinsmith's Helper and Pattern Book.* Unionville, CT: Union Printing Co., 1879; 1911. Reprint: Mendham, NJ: Astragal Press, 1994.

Wafford, Chuck. See Smith, David G. & Chuck Wafford.

Wagner Ware, Catalog No. 20, 1915, Reprint. Originally published Sidney, OH: Wagner Mfg. Co.; reprint Corvallis, OR: Gary Franzen, 1995. Cast aluminum, polished iron, and nickel-plated cooking utensils.

Wagner Ware 1931 Catalog reprint. Sacramento, CA: Cast Iron Connection, 3084 Yellowstone Lane, 95821-2360.

Walker, F. A. Various catalogs & flyers. Boston: c.1870s-1890s. Large undated catalog of housewares, many imported from France & England; some mfd. by Walker.

Wallance, Don. *Shaping America's Products.* NYC: Reinhold, 1956.

Wapak c.1910 Catalog reprint. Ohio: Combs Pub. Co., 1991.

Warne's Model Cookery & Housekeeping Book, compiled & edited by Mary Jewry. People's Edition. London: Frederick Warne & Co., 1868.

Warren, Geoffrey. *Kitchen Bygones.* London: Souvenir Press, 1984.

Washburn Co. *Sno-Cap. The New Androck Line of Kitchen Equipment.* Worcester, MA & Rockford, IL: 1927.

Washburn Co. *The Androck Line. Balanced Kitchenware. No.225.* 1936.

Watney, Bernard M., & Homer D. Babbidge. Corkscrews for Collectors. London, Eng: Sotheby's, 1981. Revised by B. Watney, 1993.

Weaver, William Woys. *America Eats. Forms of Edible Folk Art.* NYC: Harper & Row, 1989. Cookbook profusely & beautifully illustrated with utensils & decorated, molded food.

Weaver, W. W. *The Christmas Cook. Three Centuries of American Yuletide Sweets.* NYC: Harper & Row, 1990. Molded & painted cookies.

Weeks, Joseph Dame. *Tin and Tin Plate. Their History, Production and Statistics.* Pittsburgh, PA: American Manufacturer and Iron World, 1892. 44 pp supplement to the trade periodical.

Weiner, Piroska. *Carved Honeycake Moulds.* Budapest, Hungary: Corvina Kiado, 1964; 2nd enlarged 1981. London: Collet, 1964. Hungarian "folk arts and crafts" books are excellent, with wonderful pictures.

Welch, Evelyn — See Vogelsang.

Westfall, Ermagene. *Cookie Jars.* Paducah, KY: Collector Books, 1983; *Book II,* 1993.

Wetherill, Phyllis Steiss. *Cookie Cutters & Cookie Molds.* Exton, PA: Schiffer, 1985. Encyclopedic for more modern cutters; much detail.

Wetherill, Phyllis S., & Rosemary Henry. *A Cookie Shapers' Bible.* 1998. For ordering information: SASE to Mrs. Henry, 9610 Greenview Lane, Manassas, VA 20109. Alphabetical encyclopedia of American & foreign cutter & mold makers, emphasis on 20th C., profusely illus.

Wetherill, Phyllis S. *Encyclopedia of Cookie Shaping.* Washington, DC: Author, 1981.

White, Michael L., & Derek S. White. *Early American Coffee Mills. Patent History & Guide for Collectors.* Yardley, PA: WhiteSpace Publishing, 769 Sumter Dr., 19067. 1994.

Wildhaber, Robert. *"Küchengeräte. Wechselausstellung im Schweizerischen Museum fur Volkskund Basel, Dezember 1962 bis Mai 1963."* In *Schweizer Volkskunde Korrespondenzblatt der Schweizerischen. Gesselschaft fur Volkskunde,* No. 5/6, pp. 65-92, 1962.

Willich, Antony Florian M. *The Domestic Encyclopedia . . . Inventions, and Improvements Chiefly Applicable to Rural and Domestic Economy.* 5 vol. Philadelphia: W. Y. Birch & A. Small, 1803-04 (1st American edition); 3 vol., with additions by Dr. Thomas Cooper: Philadelphia, PA: A. Small, 1821. Try to get a set — or even just one volume!

Wills, Geoffrey. *Collecting Copper & Brass.* NYC: Bell Pub'g Co., 1962.

Wire Goods Co. *"Sherwood" Wire Hardware. Wire Kitchen Ware. Catalog 7.* Worcester, MA: 1915. Also a supplement, 1915.

Woman's Book, The. Dealing Practically With the Modern Conditions of Home Life. . . NYC: Charles Scribner's Sons, 1894.

Woman's Home Companion. NYC & Springfield, OH: Crowell & Collier Co., 1897-1902. Monthly, formerly *Ladies' Home Companion.*

Woodall, Allen & Sean Brickell. *Illustrated Encyclopedia of Metal Lunch Boxes.* Atglen, PA: Schiffer Pub'g, 1992.

Woodforde, John. *The Observer's Book of Kitchen Antiques.* London: Warne Books, Observer's Pocket Series, 1982.

Wright, Lawrence. *Home Fires Burning. History of Domestic Heating & Cooking.* London: Routledge & Kegan Paul, 1964.

Wright, Richardson. *Hawkers & Walkers in Early America, Strolling Pedlers, Preachers, Lawyers . . . and Others; From the Beginning to the Civil War.* Philadelphia, PA: J. B. Lippincott, 1927.

Wrinkles & Recipes, Compiled from Scientific American. NYC: Scientific American Publishing co., 1875. Many household tool tips.

Wuhr, Hans. *Alte Kuchen und Küchengeräte.* Darmstadt, Germany: F. Schneekluth, 1955, 1978. 32pp, illus.

Yarwood, Doreen. *500 Years of Technology in the Home.* London: Batsford, 1983.

Yarwood, Doreen. *The British Kitchen. Housewifery Since Roman Times.* London: Batsford, 1981.

Yena, Louise. *The Handbook of Antique Coffee and Tea Collectibles; a Price Guide.* Vol. I. San Antonio, TX: Author, 1971.

Young, Jackie. *Black Collectables. Mammy and Her Friends.* West Chester, PA: Schiffer Pub'g, 1988; Atglen, PA: rev. ed., 1991.

Young, Norman S. *Fabulous But Fake. Vol. I. The Professional's Guide to Fake Antiques.* Albany, NY: Fake Publications, Inc. POB 887, 12201. 199-. For dealers and collectors of tin, ironware, toys, lighting devices, folk art and weathervanes.

RESEARCHING

XXIII. GERMAN KITCHEN UTENSIL GLOSSARY

I've provided this glossary for three reasons: (1) many kitchen things were imported from Germany to the U.S. in the late 1800s and early 1900s; (2) because most of the foreign-language books on kitchen antiques now available are in German; and because (3) German can be so hard (although fun) to translate. Often the words are compounds made up to describe the function: for example, the word for colander actually translates "to slip through" — <u>Durchschlag</u>; or the compound may describe the material from which the gadget or utensil is made. Furthermore, different dictionaries and different authors give different ways of compounding many words — sometimes all run together, sometimes hyphenated, and, even more confusing, sometimes in different order! Some words are capitalized, some aren't, and plurals have different endings. Words listed here are mostly singular nouns, with a few useful adjectives.

For the casual browser, one of the most disconcerting things in a German-language book is a character that looks like a capital "B" that stands for a double *ess* (although not all instances where a double *ess* appears). One of our favorite words as kitchen collectors is **<u>Gusseisen</u> or** (<u>Gußeisen</u>): **cast iron!**

English to German listing:
All-in-one baking tool — <u>Alle Hilfsgeräte beim Backen in einem</u>
Angelfood cake pan —<u>Biskuitkuchenform</u> or <u>Biskuitform</u>
Apple corer — <u>Apfelbohre or Apfelausstechen</u>
Apple parer — <u>Apfelschälmaschine</u>
Appliance — <u>Vorrichtung</u> or <u>Gerät</u>
Apron — <u>Schürze</u>
Asparagus cooker — <u>Spargelkocher</u>
Aspic mold — <u>Aspikform</u> or <u>Geleeform</u>
Aspic mold in fish shape — <u>Sülzform für Fischsülze</u>
Baking mold — <u>Backform</u>
Baking pan (such as a clay muffin pan) — <u>Muldenpfanne für</u> <u>Gebäck</u>
Baking tin — <u>Backblech</u> or <u>Plätzchenblech</u>
Basket spit — <u>Korbförmiger Bratspieß</u>
Bean cutter — <u>Bohnenschneidemaschine</u>
Beetle or pestle — <u>Gemüsestampfe</u> or <u>Stampfer</u>
Biscuit breaker — <u>Teigklopfer</u>
Blender — <u>Mixer</u>
Bottle — <u>Flasche</u>
Brass — <u>Messing</u>
Brazier — <u>Kohlenfeuer</u>
Bread box — <u>Brotbüchse</u> or <u>Brotkasten</u>
Bread cutter — <u>Brotschneider</u>
Bread knife — <u>Brotmesser</u>
Bread peel — <u>Teigspaten</u>
Bread pudding mold — <u>Brotpuddingform</u>
Bread stamp — <u>Brotstempel</u>
Broiler — <u>Bratrost</u>
Bronze — <u>Bronzeguß</u> or <u>Bronze</u>
Butter hands — <u>Butterformer</u>
Butter machine — <u>Buttermaschine</u>
Butter mold — <u>Buttermodel</u> or <u>Butterform</u>
Butter stamp — <u>Butterstempel</u>
Butter stamp, wood with relief design — <u>Butterstempel aus Holz</u> <u>mit Reliefmuster</u>
Butter-shaping ladle — <u>Butterformlöffel</u>
Cabbage cutter — <u>Kräutschneider</u> or <u>Kohlschneider</u>
Cabbage cutter or plane — <u>Kräuterhackmesser mit Brett</u>
Cabbage cutting machine — <u>Kohlschneidemaschine</u>
Cabbage plane — <u>Krauthobel</u>
Cake mold — <u>Kuchenform</u>
Cake tin or pan — <u>Kastenkuchenform</u> or <u>Napfkuchenform</u>
Cake turner — <u>Pfannenwender</u>
Can or tin — <u>Dose</u> or <u>Kanister</u>
Can opener — <u>Konservendosenöffner</u> or <u>Dosenöffner</u>
Can opener (tin box opener) — <u>Büchsenöffner</u>
Candy droppers, or pouring pans — <u>Gießpfannen</u>
Candy droppers with spouts — <u>Gießpfannen feststehenden Rohren</u>
Candy mold — <u>Konditorförmchen</u>

Canning jar — <u>Konfitürengläser</u> or <u>Einweckglas</u> or <u>Weckglas</u>
Caraway seed mill — <u>Kümmelmühle</u>
Carved wood — <u>Holzgeschnitzter</u>
Carving board — <u>Schneidebrett</u>
Carving knife — <u>Vorlegemesser</u> or <u>Tranchiermesser</u>
Cast iron — <u>Gußeisen</u>
Cast iron pot — <u>Gußeisen Töpf</u>
Ceramic — <u>Keramik</u> (n.); <u>keramisch</u> (adj.)
Cheese board — <u>Käsebrett</u>
Cheese press — <u>Käsepresse</u>
Cheese slicer or cheese plane — <u>Käsehobel</u>
Cherry pitter — <u>Kirschenentkerner</u>
Cherry pitter, mechanical — <u>mechanischer Kirschenentkerner</u>
Chocolate or cocoa mill — <u>Kakaomühle</u>
Chocolate mold — <u>Form für Schokolade</u> or <u>Schokoladeform</u>
Chocolate mold, Easter bunny — <u>Osterhase Form für Schokolade</u>
Chopper for vegetables — <u>Hackbeil für Gemüse</u>
Chopper or cleaver — <u>Hackbeil</u>
Chopping bowl for vegetables — <u>Gemüsespülschüssel</u>
Choppping knife — <u>Hackmesser</u>
Chopping knife with curved blade — <u>Wiegemesser</u>
Churn — <u>Butterfaß</u> or <u>Butterstampfer</u>
Cider press — <u>Apfelpresse</u>
Cleaver — <u>Hackbeil</u>
Clock for Kitchen — <u>Küchenuhr</u>
Coffee filter — <u>Kaffeefilter</u>
Coffee mill or grinder — <u>Kaffeemühle</u>
Coffee mill, wall-mounted — <u>Wandkaffeemühle</u>
Coffee pot — <u>Kaffeekanne</u>
Coffee roaster — <u>Kaffeerostmaschine</u> or <u>Kaffeebrenner</u> or <u>Kaffeeröster</u>
Coffee roaster, globe-shaped — <u>kugelförmiger Kaffeeröster</u>
Colander — <u>Durchschlag</u> (literally to slip through) or <u>Seiher</u> or <u>Sieb</u>
Combination knife tool — <u>Kombinationsmesser</u>
Combination baking tool — <u>Alle Hilfsgeräte beim Backen</u> <u>in einem</u> (in einem means "in one")
Combination or all purpose tool — <u>Allzweckgerät</u>
Cookbook — <u>Kochbüch</u>
Cookie or cake cutter — <u>Ausstechform</u>
Cookie cutter, Christmas Eve — <u>Ausstechform für</u> <u>Weihnachtsgebackerie</u>
Cookie sheet — <u>Kuchenblech</u>
Cooking pot — <u>Kochtopf</u>
Cooking spoon — <u>Küchenlöffel</u>
Cooking stove or cooker — <u>Kochmaschine</u> or <u>Küchenmaschine</u>
Copper — <u>Kupfer</u>
Copper mold — <u>Kupferform</u>
Cork drawer — <u>Korkzieher</u> or <u>Korkenzieher</u> and <u>mechanischer</u> <u>Korkenzieher</u>

Cork press — Korkenverkleinerungsappart or Kork-Handpresse
Corking machine or cork driver — Korkmaschine
Corkscrew — Korkenzieher
Cream whip or eggbeater, mechanical — mechanischer Schneebesen
Crock — Krug or Topf
Crockery — Töpferware or Geschirr
Crumb grater — Reibe für Brösel or Reibe für Krümel
Cucumber slicer — Gurkenhobel
Cup spoon (ladle) — Schöpflöffel or Suppenkelle
Cupboard — Schrank
Cutlery — Besteck
Cutlery cleaner — Besteckputzmaschine
Decorating stencils (for cake tops) — Schablonen
Dish cover, wire — Drahtglocken
Dishwashing pan — Spülschüssel
Dough or pastry knife — Teigmesser
Dough or pastry wheel — Teigrad or Teigrädchen
Dough scraper — Teigschaber
Dough tray — Bachmulde
Dough trough — Backtrog
Draining basket for deepfry — Drahteinsatz
Earthenware — Töpferware or Tongeschirr
Egg pan — Eierpfanne or Eierkuchleinpfanne; also (probably dialectical) Poffertjes-Pfanne
Egg slicer — Eierteiler
Egg timer — Eieruhr
Eggbeater or whisk — Schneebesen or Schläger or Schneeschläger
Electric — elektrisch (adj.)
Enameled — emaillierte (adj.)
Enamelware — Emailwaren
Figural — plastischen Figur
Fireless cooker (hay box) — Kochkiste
Fireplace, for the — für die Herdplatte or für den Herd or für die Feuerstelle
Fish lifter — Fischheber or Fischvorlegemesser
Flour dredger or shaker — Mehlstreuer
Flour scoop — Mehlschaufel
Flour sifter — Mehlsieb
Food cupboard or meat safe — Speiseschrank
Food mill — Passiermaschine
Footed base — Standring
Form or shape cutter — Ausstechform
Frosting tube — Zuckergußspritzen
Fruit parer — Obstschälmaschine or mechanische Obstschälmaschine
Fruit press — Fruchtpresse
Fruit scraper — Obstschaber
Fruit stoner — Obstentkerner
Frying pan — Bratpfanne or Frittierpfanne
Funnel — Trichter
Gingerbread mold — Ingwerkuchenmodel
Glass (the material) — Glas
Graniteware — Granitemaille
Grater — Reibe or Raspel
Grater, tinned iron — Reibeisen
Grating machine — Reibmaschine
Griddle — Backblech or Bratpfanne
Gridiron, enameled white inside — Bratrost innen weiss emailliert
Grill — Grill or Bratrost
Handle — Henkel or Stiel or Griff
Hash machine or chopping machine — Hackmaschine
Hearth — Herd (See also Fireplace)
Hearth tools — Herdbesteck
Hearth-hanging saucepan — Kaminhangetopf or Stielkasserolle
Hot plate — Backhaube or Heizplatte or Kochplatte
Ice box — Eisfach or Eisschrank or Kühltasche
Ice-breaking knife — Eisdressiermess
Ice cream "bomb" mold — Eisbombeform or Eisförmchen
Ice cream mold — Eisförmchen
Ice cube tray — Eiswürfelschale or Eiswürfellade
Ice machine or ice cream freezer — Eismaschine
Ice pick — Eispickel
Iron pot or saucepan — eisene Häfen

Jagger — Teigrad
Jar lid wrench — Schraubdeckelöffner
Jelly glass — Geleeglas or Glas
Jelly mold — Geleeform
Jug — Krug or Kanne
Kettle — Kessel
Kettle, brass — Messinger Kessel
Kettle, iron — Eisener Kessel
Kitchen cupboard — Küchenschrank
Kitchen utensils — Küchengeschirr or Küchengeräte
Kitchen scale — Küchenwaage
Kneading machine — Knetmaschine
Knife — Messer
Knife scouring board with sand box — Schmirgelbrett mit Sandkasten
Knife-cleaner — Messerputzmaschine
Knife sharpener — Messerschärfer
Ladle — Schöpflöffel or Suppenkelle
Larding needle — Spicknadel
Lemon press or squeezer — Zitronenpresse
Lemon zester or grater — Zitronenreibe
Lenten dough baby mold — Form für Fatschenkind (or Wickelkind)
Lid — Deckel or Topfdeckel
Marchpane — Marzipan
Marzipan mold — Marzipanform
Mayonnaise maker — Mayonnaiseschläger
Meal sifter — Mehlsieb
Measuring beaker or cup — Meßbecher
Meat chopper — Fleischhacker
Meat grinder — Fleischwolf
Meat press — Fleischpresse
Meat tenderizer — Fleischklopfer
Melon baller — Melonenstech
Metal — Metall (n.); metallen or metallish (adj.)
Milk cooker (a sort of double boiler) — Milchkocher
Mill — Mühle
Mincing knife — Wiegemesser
Mixing appliance or Mixer — Rührapparat or Mischer or Mixer
Mixing bowls for eggs — Schneekessel
Mixing spoon — Rührlöffel
Mold (mould) — Form or Gußform
Mold, clay or ceramic — Tonform
Mold, iron — Eisenguß or Gußeisen
Mortar, brass — Messingmer
Mortar and pestle — Mörser und Stößel
Mortar with pestle — Mörser mit Pistill
Mortar, wooden — Holzmörser
Noodle roller, wooden — Nudelrolle aus Holz or simply Nudelholz
Nutcracker — Tannenhher or Nußknacker
Nutmeg grater — Muskatreibe
Oatmeal cooker — Haferflockenkocher or Hafermehlkocher
Opener — Öffner
Oven — Bakröhre or Backofen
Pan — Pfanne
Pan or pot trivet — Pfannenhalter
Pancake pan — Plett kaker or gußeiserne Platte zum Pfannkuchenbacken
Pancake turner — Pfannenwender
Paring machine — Schälmaschine
Pastry cutter — Ausstechform or Ausstechförmchen
Pastry jagger or wheel — Teigrädchen
Pastry knife — Teigmesser
Pastry or pie rimmer — Rändel
Pastry tube — Teigspritzen
Peppermill — Pfeffermühle
Pestle — Stößel or Gemüsestampfe or Mörserkeule
Pewter marzipan lily mold — Zinnform für Marzipanblume zur Tortendekoration Lilie
Pie funnel — Pastetenschornsteine
Pie jagger — Teigrad
Plum pudding mold — Pflaumepuddingform or Plumpuddingform
Popover pan — Poffertjes-pfanne
Poppyseed mill — Mohnmühle

Pot — Topf or Kochtopf
Pot with three legs — Dreibeinigtopf
Potato beetle — Kartoffelkäfer or Kartoffelstampfe
Potato ricer — Kartoffelpresse
Potato steamer or boiler — Kartoffeldampftopf
Potholder — Topflappen
Poultry shears — Geflügelschere
Poundcake mold — Napfkuchen
Pounder — Stampfer
Pressure cooker — Dampfkochtopf or Umbachschen Dampftopf
    or Schnellkochtopf
Pressure cooker (Papin's Digester) — Papinscher Topf
Pudding mold — Puddingform or Kochpuddingform
Pudding steamer, or steamed-pudding mold — Dampfpuddingform
Refrigerator — Kühlschrank
Revolving grill — Drehgrill
Rice ball — Reisball
Rice cooker (a double boiler steamer) — Reiskocher
Rice mold, ring-shaped — Reisrandform
Rocking mincer or chopper — Wiegemesser
Rolling pin — Wellholz or Rollholz or Teigrolle or
    Plätzchentrommel
Rolling pin, with longitudinal ribbing — Nudelholz or Nudelwalze
Rusk cutter or divider (for a rusk biscuit) — Zwiebackschneider
Salad dryer — Salatschwinge
Salt — Salz
Salt box — Wandsalzfässer
Saucepan — Topf or Tiegel or Stielkasserolle or Kochtopf
Sausage grinding and stuffing machine — Würstfullmaschine
Scale — Waage
Scale (literally quick scale) — Schnellwaage
Scaler for fish — Schupper
Sieve (or colander) — Sieb
Skewer — Bratspieß
Soup strainer — Bouillonsieb
Spatula — Backshaufel or Spatel or Spachtel
Speculas mold (a carved board) — Spekulatiusbrett
Spice box — Gewürzdose
Spice box or chest — Gewürzkasten
Spice grater — Gewürzreibe
Spice mill — Gewürzmühle
Spice rack — Gewürzregal
Spit — Bratspieß or Drehspieß or Spieß or Grillspieß
Spoon — Löffel
Spoons, set of wooden — Kochlöffelgarnitur
Spring balance scale — Federwaage
Spring form baking pan — Springform
Springerle mold — Holzmodel zum Backen von Springerle
Stainless steel — rostfreier Stahl
Stamper (like a beetle or pestle) — Stampfe
Steamer — Dampfkessel or Dampfkochtopf
Steel — Stahl
Steelyard — Schnellwaage or Handwaage
Stew pan — Tiegel or Kasserolle or Bratentopf
Stove or range — Küchenherd or Kochmaschine or Ofen or Herd
Stove plate — Ofenplatte
Strainer — Filtriertrichter
Strainer (also colander) — Seihe or Seiher or Sieb
Sugar loaf cutter — Zange zum Zerkleinern von Hutzucker
Sugar nippers — Zuckerzangen or Zuckerknieper
Sugar shaker or castor — Zuckerstreuer
Syllabub churn — Eiweißschläger
Tea ball — Tee-Eier
Tea kettle — Teekessel; also Wasserkessel
Teapot — Teekanne
Tea strainer — Teesieb
Tin — Blech or Zinn (which is also pewter)
Tin can — Blechdose or Blechbüchse
Tin kettle — Weißblechkessel
Tin opener or can opener — Büchsenöffner or Dosenöffner
Tinned copper — verzinntes Kupfer
Tinware — blechen Geschirr or Blechwaren
Toaster — Toaster or Brotröster
Tongs — Zange

Trammel, sawtooth — Kesselhake in Sägeform
Trivet or stand — Dreifuß or Untersetzer
Tub — Zuber or Bottich (for coopered ware)
Tub, small — kleine Zuber
Turning spit — Bratenwender
Vegetable chopper — Wiegemesser (although word for
    vegetable is Gemüse)
Vegetable chopping machine — Gemüse-Zerkleinerungsmaschine
    or Hackmaschine
Wafer iron (literally wafer bake tongs) — Oblaten-Backzange
Wafer iron or waffle iron — Waffeleisen
Waffle iron electric — Waffelautomat
Waffle iron for stove top — Waffeleisen für die Herdplatte
Water kettle — Wasserkessel
Whisk or eggbeater — Schneebesen or Schläger or Schneeschläger
    or Schlägbesen or prefix holz
Wooden — hölzern (adj.)
Wrought iron — Schmiedeeisen (n. or adj.) or Schmiedeeisern (adj.)

German to English listing:

Alle Hilfsgeräte beim Backen in einem — All-in-one combination
    baking tool
Allzweckgerät — Combination tool or all purpose tool
Apfelbohre or Apfelausstechen — Apple corer
Apfelschälmaschine — Apple parer
Aspikform — Aspic mold
Ausstechform — Cookie or cake or form or shape or pastry cutter
Backform — Baking mold
Backhaube — Hot plate
Backblech — Baking tin or Griddle
Backmulde — Dough tray
Backshaufel — Spatula (literally bake shovel)
Backtrog — Dough trough or kneading tray
Besteckputzmaschine — Cutlery- or knife-cleaning machine
Biskuitform — Cake mold
Blech — Sheet metal (thus, usually, tinned sheet iron)
blechen Geschirr or Blechwaren — Tinware or metal pots and pans
Bohnenhobel — Bean slicer
Bohnenschneidemaschine — Bean cutter
Bouillonsieb — Soup strainer
Bratenwender — Turning spit (but also fish slice!?!)
Bratpfanne — Frying pan
Bratrost — Broiler or Grill
Bratrost innen weiss emailliert — Gridiron, enameled white inside
Bratrost über offenem Feuer auch — Gridiron for hearth
Bratspieß — Spit or Skewer
Bronzeguß — Bronze
Brotbüch or Brotkasten — Bread box
Brotmesser — Bread knife
Brotpuddingform — Bread pudding mold
Brotröster — Toaster for bread
Brotschneider — Bread cutter
Brotstempel — Bread stamp
Büchsenöffner — Tin opener or can opener
Butterfaß — Churn
Butterformer — Butter hands
Butterformlöffel — Butter-shaping ladle
Buttermaschine — Butter machine
Buttermodel or Butterform — Butter mold
Butterstampfer — Churn
Butterstempel — Butter stamp
Dampfkessel — Steamer
Dampfkochtopf — Pressure cooker
Dampfpuddingform — Pudding steamer
Deckel — Lid
Drahteinsatz — Draining basket for deep fry
Drahtglocken — Dish cover of wire gauze
Drahtsieb — Wire sieve
Drehgrill — Revolving grill
Dreibeinigtopf — Pot with three legs
Dreifuß — Trivet
Durchschlag — Colander, sieve or strainer
Eierkuchleinpfanne or Eierpfanne — Egg-cooking pan
Eierschneebese — Eggbeater

Eierteiler — Egg slicer
Eieruhr — Egg timer
Einweckglas — Preserving jar
Eisbombeform — Ice cream "bomb" mold
Eisdressiermess — Ice-breaking knife
eisene Häfen — Iron pots
Eisenerkessel — Kettle, iron
Eisenguß — Mold, iron
eisern — Iron (adj.)
Eisfach — Ice box or freezer compartment
Eisförmchen — Ice cream mold
Eismaschine — Ice machine or ice cream freezer
Eiswaffeleisen — Ice cream cornet or waffle iron
Eiswürfelschale or Eiswürfellade — Ice cube tray
Eiweißschläger —Syllabub churn
elektrisch — Electric (adj.)
emaillierte — Enameled
Fatschenkind or Wickelkind — Lenten dough baby
Federwaage — Spring balance scale
Filtriertrichter — Strainer
Fischheber — Fish lifter
Flasche — Bottle
Flaschengestell — Bottle rack
Fleischklopfer — Meat tenderizer
Fleischpresse — Meat press
Fleischwolf — Meat grinder or mincer
Form — Mold
Förmchen — Small mold
Form für Schokolade — Chocolate mold
Frittierpfanne — Frying pan
Fruchtpresse — Fruit press
Gang — Gear
Geflügelschere — Poultry shears
Geleeform — Jelly mold
Geleegläs — Jelly glass
Gemüsesieb — Colander
Gemüsespülschüssel — Chopping bowl for vegetables
Gemüsestampfe — Beetle or pestle
Gewürz — Spice grater
Gerät — Device or gadget
geschmiedetem Eisen — forged iron (adj.)
Gewugreibe — Spice grater
Gewürzdose — Spice box
Gewürzkasten — Spice box or chest
Gewürzmühle — Spice mill
Gießpfannen — Candy droppers or pouring pans
Griff — Grip or handle
Grillrost — Grill
Gugelhupfform —A mold for gugelhupf or Kugelhupf, a lobed
    ball. Gugel is a varient of Kugel, sphere; hupf is hop or bounce.
Gurkenhobel — Cucumber slicer
Gußeisen — Cast iron
Gußeisen mit reichem Dekor — Cast iron with raised decoration
Gußeisentopf — Cast iron pot
Gußform — Mold
Hackbeil — Chopper or cleaver
Hackbeil für Gemüse — Chopper for vegetables
Hackbrette — Chopping or cutting board
Hackmaschine — Hash machine or chopping machine
Hackmesser — Chopping knife
Haferflockenkocher — Oatmeal (flake) cooker
Hebelkorkenzieher — Corkscrew with levers
Henkel — Handle
Henkeltopf — Pot or pan with handle(s)
Herd — Hearth or stove
Herdbesteck — Hearth tools
Herdplatte, für die — for the Fireplace
Hobel — Plane slicer
hölzern — Wooden
Holzgeschnitzter — Carved wood
Holzmodel zum Backen von Springerle — Wooden Springerle mold
Holzmorser — Mortar, wooden
Ingwerkuchenmodel — Gingerbread mold
Kaffeefilter — Coffee filter

Kaffeekanne — Coffee pot
Kaffeemühle — Coffee mill or grinder
Kafeewärmer — Cosy for coffee pot
Kakaomühle — Cocoa or chocolate mill
Kaffeerostmaschine or Kaffeebrenner or Kaffeeröster) —
    Coffee roaster
Kamin — Fireplace
Kaminhangetopf — Hearth-hanging saucepan
Kanne — Can or pot
Kännchen — Jug or pot
Kartoffeldampftopf — Potato steamer or boiler
Kartoffelkäfer or Kartoffelstampfe — Potato beetle
Kartoffelpresse — Potato ricer
Kartoffelschäler — Potato peeler
Kartoffelstampfer — Potato masher
Käsebrett — Cheese board
Käsehobel — Cheese slicer or cheese plane
Käsepresse — Cheese press
keramisch — Ceramic (adj.)
Kessel — Kettle
Kesselhake in Sägeform — Trammel, sawtooth
Kirschenentkerner — Cherry pitter
kleine Zuber — Small tub
Kleinküchenmaschine — Mixer
Knetmaschine — Kneading machine
Kochkiste — Fireless cooker (hay box)
Kochmaschine — Cooking stove
Kochbüch — Cookbook
Kochpuddingform — Pudding mold
Kochtopf — Cook pot
Kohlenfeuer — Brazier
Kohlschneidemaschine — Cabbage cutting machine
Kombinationsmesser — Combination knife tool
Konditorförmchen — Candy mold
Konfitürengläser — Canning jar or Jam jar
Konservendose — Tin can
Konservendosenöffner — Can opener
Korbförmiger Bratspieß — Basket spit
Korkenverkleinerungsappart or Korkhandpresse — Cork press
Korkenzieher — Corkscrew
Korkmaschine — Corking machine or cork driver
Korkzieher or Korkenzieher or mechanischer Korkenzieher —
    Cork drawer
Kräuterhackmesser mit Brett or Krauthobel — Cabbage cutter
    or plane
Kräutschneider — Cabbage cutter
Krug — Jug or crock
Kuchenblech — Cookie sheet
Kuchenform — Cake mold or Bake mold
Küchengabel — Pastry fork
Küchengeschirr or Küchengeräte — Kitchen utensils or kitchenware
Küchenherd — Stove or range
Küchenhobel — Kitchen plane (slicer)
Küchenlöffel — Cooking spoon
Küchenschrank — Kitchen cupboard
Küchentisch — Kitchen table
Küchenwaage — Kitchen scales
Kugelform — Round mold
Kugelformiger Kaffeeröster — Globe-shaped coffee roaster
Kühlschrank — Refrigerator (literally cold cupboard)
Kümmelmühle — Caraway seed mill
Kupfer — Copper
Kupferform — Copper mold
Löffel — Spoon
Marzipanform — Marzipan mold
Mayonnaiseschläger — Mayonnaise beater or maker
mechanischer Schneebesen — Cream whip or eggbeater,
    mechanical
mechanischer Kirschenentkerner — Cherry pitter, mechanical
Mehlschaufel — Flour scoop
Mehlsiebe — Flour or meal sifter
Melonenstech — Melon baller
Messer — Knife
Messerputzmaschine — Knife-cleaner

Messing — Brass
messinger Kessel — Kettle, brass
Messingmer — Mortar, brass
Messingschild — Brass plate (the metal)
Meßbecher — Measuring beaker or cup
Metall — Metal
mit Glaskörper — with glass jar
Model — Wooden mold (such as for Springerle or Speculas)
Mohnmühle — Poppyseed mill
Mörser mit Pistill — Mortar with pestle
Mörser und Stößel — Mortar and pestle
Mühle — Mill
Muldenpfanne für Gebäck — Baking pan (such as a clay muffin pan)
Muskatreibe — Nutmeg grater
Napfkuchenmold — Poundcake mold in ring-shape
Nudelbrett — Pastryboard or doughboard
Nudelrolle aus Holz or Nudelholz or Nudelwalze — Rolling pin, with longitudinal ribbing — a wooden Noodle roller
Nußknacker — Nutcracker
Oblaten-Backzange — Wafer iron (literally wafer bake tongs)
Obstentkerner — Fruit stoner
Obstschälmaschine or mechanische Obstschälmaschine — Fruit parer
Ofen — Cooking Stove
Ofenplatte — Stove plate
Öffner — Opener
Osterhasen Form für Schokolade — Chocolate mold, Easter bunny
Papinscher Topf — Pressure cooker (Papin's Digester)
Passiermaschine — Food mill
Passiersieb — Strainer
Pastetenschornsteine or Pastetchen — Pie funnel or chimney
Pfanne — Pan
Pfannenhalter — Pan or pot trivet
Pfannenwender — Pancake or cake turner
Pfeffermühle — Peppermill
plastischen Figur — Figural
Plätzchentrommel — Rolling pin
Plätzchenblech — Baking sheet or tin
Plettkakerpfanne — Pancake pan
Pflaumepuddingform — Plum pudding mold
Poffertjes-pfanne — Popover pan or egg pan
Puddingform — Pudding mold
Rändel — Pastry or pie rimmer
Reibe — Grater
Reibe für Brösel — Crumb grater
Reibeisen — Grater, tinned iron
Reibmaschine — Grating machine
Reisbäll — Rice ball
Reiskocher — Rice cooker (a double boiler steamer)
Reisrandform — Rice mold or ring mold for rice
Rollholz — Rolling pin
Rostfreies Besteck — Stainless steel cutlery
Rührapparat or Mixer — Mixing appliance or Mixer
Rührlöffel — Mixing spoon
Salatschleuder — Salad drainer
Salatschwinge — Salad dryer (swinging)
Salz — Salt
Salzfäßchen — Salt cellar
Schablonen — Decorating stencils (for cake tops)
Schälmaschine — Paring machine
Schmiedeeisen — Wrought iron
Schmirgelbrett mit Sandkasten — Knife scouring board with sand box
Schneebesen or Schläger — Whisk or eggbeater
Schneekessel — Mixing bowls for eggs
Schneidebrett — Carving board
Schnellkochtopf — Pressure cooker
Schnellwaage — Steelyard
Schokoladeform — Chocolate mold
Schöpflöffel — Ladle or cup spoon
Schrank — Cupboard
Schraubdeckelöffner — Jar lid wrench (for screw-on lid)
Schupper — Fish scaler

Schürze — Apron
Seiher or Sieher — Strainer or colander
Sieb — Sieve or colander
Spargelkocher — Asparagus cooker
Spatel — Spatula
Speiseschrank — Food cupboard or meat safe
Spekulatiusbrett — Speculas mold (a carved board)
Spicknadeln — Larding needle
Spieß — Spit
Springform — Spring form baking pan
Spülschüssel — Dishwashing pan
Stahl — Steel
Stampfer — Stamper or pounder (a beetle or pestle)
Standring — Footed base
Stiel — Handle
Stielpfanne — Frying pan with long handle
Stößel or Morserkeule — Pestle
Sülzform für Fischsülze — Aspic mold in fish shape
Tannenhher or Nußknacker — Nutcracker
Tee kessel — Tea kettle
Tee-Eier — Tea ball
Teesieb — Tea strainer
Teigklopfer — Biscuit breaker
Teigmesser — Dough or pastry knife
Teigräd or Teigrädchen — Dough or pastry wheel or pie jagger
Teigrolle — Rolling pin
Teigschaber — Dough scraper
Teigspaten — Bread peel
Teigspritzen — Pastry tube
Tiegel — Stew pan or saucepan
Toaster or Brotröster — Toaster
Tonform — Clay or ceramic mold
Topf — Pot or Saucepan
Töpfchen — Small pot
Töpferware — Earthenware or crockery
Trichter — Funnel
Umbachschen Dampftopf — Pressure cooker
Untersetzer — Trivet or stand
verzinntes Kupfer — Tinned copper
Vorlegemesser — Carving knife
Vorrichtung — Appliance Gadget or Device
Waage — Scales for weighing
Waffeleisen — Wafer iron or waffle iron
Wandkaffeemühle — Coffee mill, wall-mounted
Wandsalzfässer — Salt box (to hand on wall)
Wasserkessel — Water kettle (word also used for Tea kettle)
Weckglas — Preserving jar
Weißblechkessel — Tin kettle (weiß is white; Weißmetal is white metal)
Wellholz — Rolling pin with corrugated ribs
Wiegemesser — Vegetable mincing knife, also a rocking chopper with curved blades
Zange zum Zerkleinern von Hutzucker — Sugar loaf cutter (Zange is Pliers)
Zinnform — Pewter mold
Zitronenpresse — Lemon press
Zitronenreibe — Lemon zester or grater
Zuber — Washtub
Zuckergußspritzen — Frosting tube
Zuckerknieper or Zuckerzangen — Sugar nippers
Zuckerstreuer — Sugar shaker
Zwiebackschneider — Rusk cutter or divider (rusks are a sort of biscuit)

Sources: Ulrich Klever's *Alte Küchengeräte;* Laura Krüger's *Vom Zauber alten Hausgeräts;* and Brigitte Kate-von Eicken's *Küchengeräte Um 1900.* Also the following German/English dictionaries; *Langenscheidt's Standard Germany Dictionary* (1970); K. Wichmann's *German-English...Dictionary* (1971); *The Oxford-Duden German Dictionary* (1997); *The Oxford-Duden Pictorial German and English Dictionary* (1994); *Langenscheidt's New College German Dictionary* (1995); and, one of the easiest and most helpful dictionaries I've used, the unabridged *Harper-Collins German Dictionary* (1997). Additional words came from 19th and early 20th century trade catalogs.

INDEX

Subjects & Recipes

If it's really obvious, you may not find it in this index, because you *can* find it in the Table of Contents. But if you wonder about some strange old term used by cooks or tinsmiths, or a metal or material, or an historical kitchen-related event, I hope we've listed it here. I suggest that you personalize the index yourself, while you read. I do it with many books that just don't list what I tend to look up. Note that all recipes are alphabetized under the heading Recipes; and the same for Clubs for Collectors, and Museums.